Fully Revised Edition

Understanding Physics

JEE Main & Advanced

Waves and Thermodynamics

Fully Revised **Edition**

Understanding Physics

JEE Main & Advanced

Waves and Thermodynamics

DC Pandey
[B.Tech, M.Tech, Pantnagar, ID 15722]

arihant
SUCCESS AND NOTHING LESS

arihant
SUCCESS AND NOTHING LESS

ARIHANT PRAKASHAN (Series), MEERUT

Administrative & Production Offices

Regd. Office

'Ramchhaya' 4577/15, Agarwal Road, Darya Ganj, New Delhi -110002
Tele: 011- 47630600, 43518550

Head Office

Kalindi, TP Nagar, Meerut (UP) - 250002
Tel: 0121-7156203, 7156204

Sales & Support Offices

Agra, Ahmedabad, Bengaluru, Bareilly, Chennai, Delhi, Guwahati, Hyderabad, Jaipur, Jhansi, Kolkata, Lucknow, Nagpur & Pune.

PRICE ₹425.00

PO No : TXT-XX-XXXXXXX-X-XX

Published by Arihant Publications (India) Ltd.

For further information about the books published by Arihant, log on to www.arihantbooks.com or e-mail at info@arihantbooks.com

Follow us on

Preface

"The overwhelming response to the previous editions of this book gives me an immense feeling of satisfaction, and I take this as an opportunity to introduce you to the new version of the book, "Waves and Thermodynamics."

"Waves and Thermodynamics" has undergone meticulous revision to ensure accuracy and relevance. We take pride in affirming that this book serves as a standalone resource, encompassing all essential topics without any extraneous content.

This book is designed with a singular focus on providing concise yet complete theory, coupled with an ample number of practice questions covering all pertinent concepts essential for success in JEE Mains & Advanced.

With each chapter, or as we call them, units, subdivided into modular formats, "Waves and Thermodynamics" ensures an organized and structured approach to learning. Each module within a unit is self-contained, comprising theory, illustrative examples, and exercises aimed at reinforcing understanding.

At the end of every unit, readers will find unit exercises presented in two levels, offering ample opportunities for practice and self-assessment. Furthermore, to aid in problem-solving, most exercises are accompanied by helpful hints.

Our commitment to excellence extends to the inclusion of logical problems sourced from reputable resources like **Irodov** and **previous years' question papers.** The level of questions spans from foundational to 1.25 times the highest difficulty level of the JEE Advanced examination, ensuring comprehensive preparation.

In conclusion, I am confident that "Waves and Thermodynamics" will prove to be an indispensable companion for aspirants aiming for success in JEE. It is my belief that with dedication and diligent practice using this book, students will be well-equipped to excel in both JEE Mains and Advanced examinations.

I take this opportunity to express my gratitude to **Prof. Lalit Kumar,** who gave me valuable advice and was kind enough to find time for fruitful discussions. I would also like to thank my student Dheeraj Yadav for managing this project as per my expectations. I am also thankful to Mr. Anoop Dhyani and Mr. Ashish, due to their tireless efforts this book could be transformed into the present form.

To err is human, hence despite such tireless efforts, there may still be scope for improvement in this book. So, comments and criticism from readers will be highly appreciated and incorporated in subsequent editions." I also request the readers to drop me a mail at **arihantcorrections@gmail.com,** if you find any corrections in the book. Your feedback is greatly appreciated and will help to improve the quality of the book.

Thankyou for your support and contribution in making this book the **Best it can be.**

DC Pandey

[B.Tech, M.Tech, Pantnagar, ID 15722]

Contents

This book

is dedicated to

my Honourable Grandfather

(Late) Sh. Pitamber Pandey

a Kumaoni poet and a resident of Village

Dhaura (Almora), Uttarakhand

UNIT-17

WAVE MOTION

Learning Modules

1. Wave Equation
2. Sine Wave
3. Two Graphs in Sine Wave
4. Wave Speed
5. Energy in Wave Motion

MODULE 1

Wave Equation

Introduction

In every wave, a physical quantity y is made to oscillate at one point and gradually these oscillations of y propagate to other points also without transport of matter. In general, a wave also transports energy and momentum (in addition to oscillations of y).

Thus, in a wave, the following three physical quantities transfer from one point to another point:

(i) oscillations of y

(ii) energy and

(iii) momentum

In different situations, the physical quantity y may be different. For example:

y is displacement of medium particles (between $+A$ and $-A$) from the mean position in case of string wave, where A is the amplitude of oscillations. Similarly, y is electric and magnetic fields in electromagnetic waves and it is displacement, pressure and density (which oscillate) in longitudinal (or sound) wave. A wave is said to be **travelling** or **progressive** if it travels from one point to another.

Example 1 In a wave motion $y = a\sin(kx - \omega t)$, y can represent: **(1999 JEE)**

(a) electric field

(b) magnetic field

(c) displacement

(d) pressure

Sol. (a,b,c,d) In case of sound wave, y can represent pressure and displacement, while in the case of electromagnetic wave, it represents electric and magnetic fields.

Example 2 What do you understand by a travelling or a progressive wave?

Sol. A travelling or progressive wave is a wave that moves or propagates through a medium, transferring energy (or momentum) from one point to another. It is a disturbance that travels through a medium, such as water or air, without causing the medium itself to move. Instead, the energy is transferred through the medium in the form of oscillations or vibrations. Some common examples of travelling waves include:

(i) Water waves (ocean waves, ripples on a pond)

(ii) Sound waves (music, voice, echoes)

(iii) Seismic waves (earthquakes)

(iv) Electromagnetic waves (light waves, radio waves, microwaves, infrared radiation).

The key characteristics of travelling waves are:

(i) They move or propagate through a medium.

(ii) They transfer energy from one point to another.

(iii) The medium itself does not move, only the energy (or momentum) is transferred.

(iv) They have a frequency (number of oscillations per second) and a wavelength (distance between two consecutive oscillations).

Note *Later we will see that electromagnetic (EM) waves are special type of wave that can propagate through a vacuum, means they don't require a medium to travel through. This is unlike mechanical waves, such as sound waves or water waves which require a physical medium to propagate. This is why we can see radio signals from space and see light from distant stars, even though there is no physical medium in between.*

Example 3 Which quantities are propagated from one point to another by a wave?

Sol. Waves propagate the following quantities from one point to another:

(i) **Energy** Waves transfer energy from one point to another without transferring matter.

(ii) **Momentum** Waves can also transfer momentum, depending on the type of wave.

(iii) **Information** Waves can carry information, such as sound waves carrying audio signals or light waves carrying visual data.

(iv) **Disturbance** Waves propagate a disturbance or oscillation from one point to another, such as a water wave propagates a disturbance in the water surface. The specific quantity being propagated depends on the type of wave, such as :

Mechanical waves (e.g. sound, water) : energy, momentum and disturbance.

Electromagnetic waves (e.g. light, radio): energy, momentum and information.

Note that matter itself is not propagated by waves, only the energy, momentum and information associated with the disturbance are transferred from one point to another.

Classification of a Wave

Waves can be classified in various ways, depending on their characteristics. Here are some common classifications:

1. **Mechanical *versus* Non-Mechanical Waves** Mechanical waves (e.g. sound, water, seismic): require a physical medium to propagate. Non-mechanical waves (e.g. electromagnetic, light): do not require any physical medium (can propagate through a vacuum).
2. **Transverse *versus* Longitudinal Waves** Transverse waves (e.g. light, water) : particles oscillate perpendicular to the direction of propagation of wave. Longitudinal waves (e.g. sound, seismic) : particles oscillate parallel to the direction of propagation of wave.

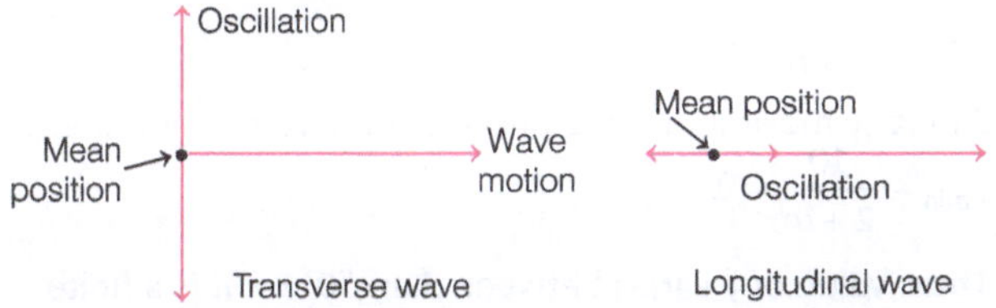

3. **Periodic *versus* Non-Periodic Waves** Periodic waves (e.g. sine wave, square wave) : have a repeating pattern. Non-periodic waves (e.g. pulse, irregular wave) : do not have a repeating pattern.
4. **One-Dimensional *versus* Two-Dimensional *versus* Three-Dimensional Waves**

   One-dimensional waves (e.g. sound in a pipe) : propagate in one direction.

   Two-dimensional waves (e.g. water ripples) : propagate in two directions.

   Three-dimensional waves (e.g. light, seismic): propagate in three directions.
5. **Electromagnetic Waves** Radio waves, microwaves, infrared radiation, visible light, ultraviolet radiation, X-rays, gamma rays.

   Note that these classifications are not mutually exclusive and a wave can belong to multiple categories.

Important POINTS

- Apart from mechanical and non-mechanical waves, there is also another kind of waves called **"matter waves"**.
- Sound wave is basically a part of longitudinal waves with frequency varying from 20 Hz to 20,000 Hz. Similarly, light wave is a part of electromagnetic waves with wavelength varying from approximately 4000 Å to 7000 Å.
- In the propagation of mechanical waves, elasticity and inertia of the medium play an important role.
- Waves travelling through a solid medium can be either transverse or longitudinal waves. But waves travelling through a fluid (such as a liquid or a gas) are always longitudinal waves.
- **Transverse waves require shear strength** Transverse waves are shear waves, means they require a medium that can withstand shearing forces and maintain its shape. Solids can do this, but liquids and gases don't have enough shear strength, causing them to change shape instead of transmitting the wave.
- **Liquids and gases lack rigidity** Transverse waves need a medium that's rigid enough to propagate, which liquids and gases are not. They cannot maintain the perpendicular motion of particles required for transverse waves.
- **Longitudinal waves use compressive strength** Longitudinal waves rely on the compressive strength of the material, which liquids and gases have. They can transmit longitudinal waves by compressing and expanding in the direction of the wave.
- While waves that travel within the depths of the ocean are longitudinal waves, the waves that travel along the surface of the oceans are referred to as surface waves. A **surface wave** is a wave in which particles of the medium undergo a circular motion. Surface waves are neither longitudinal nor transverse. The radius of the circles decreases as the depth into the water increases.
- Earthquakes are capable of producing both types of waves, transverse as well as longitudinal. The **P-waves (Primary waves)** in an earthquake are examples of longitudinal waves. The **S-waves (Secondary waves)** in an earthquake are examples of transverse waves. S-waves propagates with a velocity slower than P-waves, arriving several seconds later.

Wave Equation

As we have already read, in a wave motion a physical quantity y is made to oscillate at one point and these oscillations of y propagate to other places also.

Therefore, in a wave, several particles oscillate (unlike SHM in which normally a single oscillates).

So, to determine the value of y (from its mean position between $+A$ and $-A$) we will have to tell position of the particle and time. Thus,

$$y = f \text{ (position of particle, time)}$$

In three dimensional space, position of the particle can be represented by three variable co-ordinates. Thus, in general, y is a function of four variables, three in co-ordinates and the fourth one is time.

But in physics, we normally keep least number of variables. If the wave is one-dimensional, then position of the particle can be represented by a single variable co-ordinate (say x).

Thus, in a one-dimensional wave, y is a function of two variables x and t. Here, x is used for position of the particle and t for time or

$$y = f(x,t)$$

Note *Since, there are two variables in y, therefore whenever required, y is always differentiated partially. For example,*

$$\frac{\partial y}{\partial x}, \frac{\partial y}{\partial t}, \frac{\partial^2 y}{\partial x^2} \text{ etc.}$$

Now, the question is, there may be infinite number of functions of x and t, like

$$y = x + t$$
$$y = xt + t^3x^2 \text{ etc.}$$

Obviously, all functions will not represent a wave function. Only those functions of x and t will represent a wave function which satisfies the following two conditions :

Condition 1 The given function must satisfy the following differential equation :

$$\left(\frac{\partial^2 y}{\partial t^2}\right) = k\left(\frac{\partial^2 y}{\partial x^2}\right) \quad \text{...(i)}$$

Here, k is a constant which is equal to square of the wave velocity or

$$k = v^2$$

Condition 2 The value of y must be finite for any value of x and t. Or, we can say $y(x, t)$ must be a finite function. Let us take some examples.

Example 4 $y = A \sin (\omega t \pm kx)$ or $y = A \cos (\omega t \pm kx)$ is a finite function. Because value of $\sin \theta$ or $\cos \theta$ lies between ± 1. So, in the above two functions, value of y varies between $\pm A$.

Example 5 $y = A \tan (\omega t \pm kx)$ is not a finite function. Because y is not defined (or y is infinite) at $(\omega t \pm kx) = \frac{\pi}{2}$.

Example 6 $y = \frac{10}{2 + (6x - 2t)^2}$ is a finite function. Reason is :

the variable on right hand side $(6x - 2t)^2$ is a square term. Minimum value of this square term is zero. So,

$$y_{max} = \frac{10}{2 + 0} = 5.$$

Similarly maximum value of this square term is infinite. So,

$$y_{min} = \frac{10}{2 + \infty} = 0.$$

Thus, value of y varies between 5 and 0. So, it is a finite function.

Note (i) *There are actually three conditions for a function to represent a wave function. But at this stage it's difficult for the students to understand them. So, we have simplified them into two conditions.*

(ii) *Any function of the type,*

$$y(x, t) = f(ax \pm bt)$$

definitely satisfies condition 1. So, we have to check only condition 2 whether it is a finite function or not.

Further, in the above type of function if second condition is satisfied, then speed of wave (v) is given by

$$v = \frac{\text{coefficient of } t}{\text{coefficient of } x} = \frac{b}{a}$$

If ax and bt are of same sign (both positive or both negative), then wave will be travelling along negative x-direction. If one is positive and other is negative, then wave travels in positive x-direction.

Here speed of a wave (v) means the speed by which oscillations (of y), energy, momentum or information transfer from one point to another point.

Example 7 Show that the equation, $y = a \sin (\omega t - kx)$ satisfies the wave equation $\frac{\partial^2 y}{\partial t^2} = v^2 \frac{\partial^2 y}{\partial x^2}$. Find speed of wave and the direction in which it is travelling.

Sol. $\frac{\partial^2 y}{\partial t^2} = -\omega^2 a \sin (\omega t - kx)$

and $$\frac{\partial^2 y}{\partial x^2} = -k^2 a \sin(\omega t - kx)$$

We can write these two equations as

$$\frac{\partial^2 y}{\partial t^2} = \frac{\omega^2}{k^2} \cdot \frac{\partial^2 y}{\partial x^2}$$

Comparing this with, $\frac{\partial^2 y}{\partial t^2} = v^2 \frac{\partial^2 y}{\partial x^2}$

We can see that wave speed $v = \frac{\omega}{k}$ **Ans.**

The negative sign between ωt and kx implies that wave is travelling along positive x-direction.

Key Points

In $y(x, t)$ equation if we substitute (or fix) the value of x (let at $x = x_0$) then the equation left is $y(t)$. So, we can draw a graph between y and t. This equation (between y and t) or graph will tell us value of y at different time t for the particle at $x = x_0$.

Similarly if we substitute (or fix) the value of t (let $t = t_0$) then the equation left is $y(x)$. So, we can draw a graph between y and x). This equation (between y and x) or graph will give us value of y for different particles (represented by different x-coordinates) at time t_0.

Typed Problems

Type 1. *Following example will illustrate this type.*

Ex. 1 Which of the following functions will represent a wave function? Find wave speed and direction of wave velocity in each case.

(a) $y = 4 \text{ mm} \cos[200\pi t + 10\pi x]$

Here t is in seconds and x is in metres.

(b) $y = 6 \text{ mm} \tan[20\pi t - \pi x]$

Here t is in seconds and x is in metres.

(c) $y = \frac{20}{4 + (6x - 18t)^2}$

Here x is in metres and t is in seconds.

(d) $y = 8 \text{ mm } e^{(4x - 2t)^2}$

Here x is in metres and t is in seconds.

Sol. All four functions are of type $f(ax \pm bt)$. So, first condition is satisfied by all of them. We have to check only second condition whether the given function of y has finite range or not.

In the theory part we have discussed that (a) and (c) functions have finite range. Therefore (a) and (c) functions represent a wave function.

Part (b) does not have a finite range. So, it does not represent a wave function.

As far as (d) part is concerned, the maximum value of variable square term is infinite. Therefore as,

$$(4x - 2t)^2 \to \infty$$

y also tends to infinity.

So, (d) does not represent a wave function.

Wave Speed and Direction :

Part (a)

(i) Wave speed $= \frac{\text{Coefficient of } t}{\text{Coefficient of } x} = \frac{200\pi}{10\pi} = 20 \text{ m/s}$

(ii) $(200\pi t)$ and $(10\pi x)$ are of same sign.

So, the wave is travelling towards negative x-direction.

Part (c)

(i) Wave speed $= \frac{\text{Coefficient of } t}{\text{Coefficient of } x} = \frac{18}{6} = 3 \text{ m/s}$

(ii) $(6x)$ and $(18t)$ are of opposite signs. So, the wave is travelling towards positive x-direction.

Type 2. *Based on symmetry of wave pulse.*

Concept

To check symmetry of a wave pulse or wave velocity, always concentrate on maximum or minimum value of y. For example,

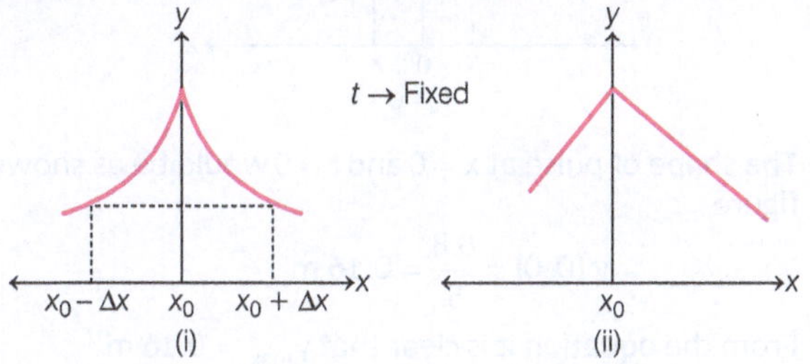

Wave pulse shown in Fig. (i) is symmetric but the wave pulse shown in Fig. (ii) is asymmetric. Now, the question is how will you check whether the pulse is symmetric or not.

The answer is :

In both cases maximum value of y at the given time (say t_0) is at $x = x_0$.

Now, if $y(t = t_0, x = x_0 + \Delta x) = y(t = t_0, x = x_0 - \Delta x)$, then the pulse is symmetric otherwise not. So, at a given time (or any other time of your choice) first of all you have to find that x coordinate where you are getting the maximum value of y. Then you have to check the above condition.

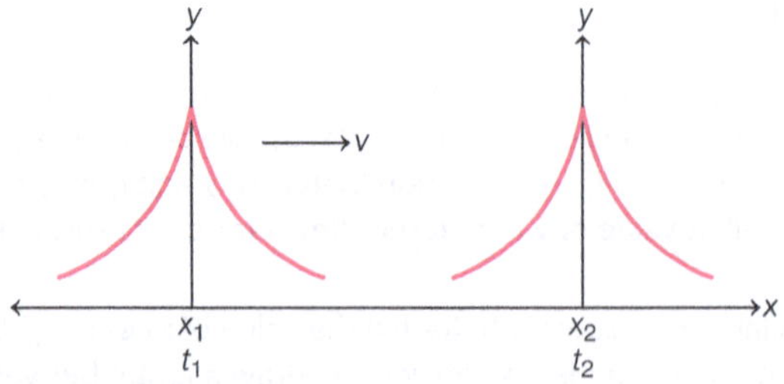

Further, suppose that maximum value of y is at x_1 at time t_1 and at x_2 at time $t_2 (> t_1)$. Then, from the figure we can see that peak of the wave pulse is travelling towards positive x-direction. In time $(t_2 - t_1)$, it has travelled a distance $(x_2 - x_1)$ along positive x-direction. Hence, the wave velocity is

$$v = +\frac{(x_2 - x_1)}{(t_2 - t_1)}$$

Ex. 2 $y(x, t) = \dfrac{0.8}{[(4x + 5t)^2 + 5]}$ represents a moving pulse where x and y are in metre and t in second. Then, choose the correct alternative(s): **(1999 JEE)**

(a) pulse is moving in positive x-direction
(b) in 2 s it will travel a distance of 2.5 m
(c) its maximum displacement is 0.16 m
(d) it is a symmetric pulse

Sol. (b), (c) and (d) are correct options.

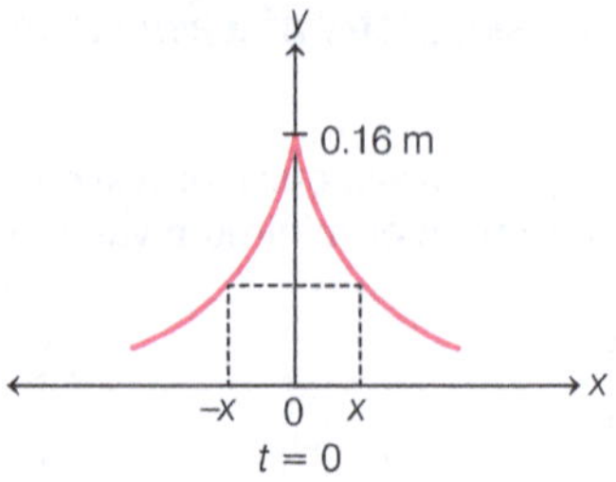

The shape of pulse at $x = 0$ and $t = 0$ would be as shown in figure

$$y(0, 0) = \frac{0.8}{5} = 0.16 \text{ m}$$

From the equation it is clear that $y_{max} = 0.16$ m

Pulse will be symmetric (symmetry is checked about y_{max}) if

At $t = 0$; $\quad y(x) = y(-x)$

From the given equation

$$\left.\begin{aligned} y(x) &= \frac{0.8}{16x^2 + 5} \\ \text{and} \quad y(-x) &= \frac{0.8}{16x^2 + 5} \end{aligned}\right\} \text{at } t = 0$$

or $\quad y(x) = y(-x)$

Therefore, pulse is symmetric.

Speed of pulse

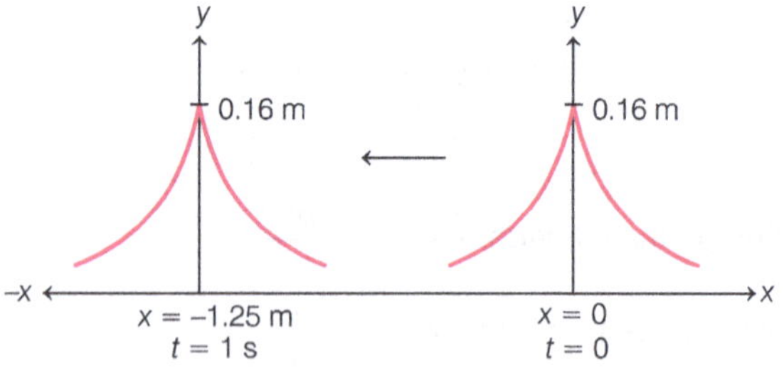

At $t = 1$ s and $x = -1.25$ m, value of y is again 0.16 m, i.e. pulse has travelled a distance of 1.25 m in 1 second in negative x-direction or we can say that the speed of pulse is 1.25 m/s and it is travelling in negative x-direction. Therefore, it will travel a distance of 2.5 m in 2 seconds.

Alternate method :

(i) $v = \dfrac{\text{Coefficient of } t}{\text{Coefficient of } x} = \dfrac{5}{4} = 1.25$ m/s

(ii) $4x$ and $5t$ both are positive. Therefore the wave is travelling in negative x-direction.

Type 3. *To find wave velocity from two $y(x)$ equations given at two different times.*

Concept

In $y(x,t)$ equation, if value of t is substituted then the equation left is $y(x)$ equation.

In this type of problem, $y(x)$ equation will be given at two different times and we have to find the wave velocity.

How to Solve?

At the given times find two x-coordinates where you are getting the maximum (or minimum) value of y. From these two x-coordinates and two times we can calculate the wave velocity by the method discussed in Type 2.

Ex. 3 At time $t = 0$, $y(x)$ equation of a wave pulse is

$$y = \frac{10}{2 + (x - 2)^2}$$

and at $t = 2$s, $y(x)$ equation of the same wave pulse is

$$y = \frac{10}{2 + (x + 4)^2}$$

Here, y is in mm and x in metres. Find the wave velocity.

Sol. From the given $y(x)$ equations at two different times we can see that value of y is maximum $\left(= \dfrac{10}{2} \text{ or } 5 \text{ mm}\right)$ at $x = 2$ m at time $t = 0$ and at $x = -4$ m at time $t = 2$s.

So, peak of the wave pulse has travelled a distance of 6 m (from $x = 2$ m to $x = -4$ m) in 2 s along negative x-direction.

Hence, the wave velocity is $v = -\dfrac{6}{2} = -3$ m/s **Ans.**

Type 4. *To make complete $y(x,t)$ function if $y(x)$ function at some given time and wave velocity are given.*

Concept

(i) Wave speed, $v = \dfrac{\text{coefficient of } t}{\text{coefficient of } x}$

$\therefore$ Coefficient of $t = (v)$(coefficient of x)

(ii) Sign of coefficient of t will be opposite to the sign of coefficient of x if wave travels along positive x-direction and they are of same sign if the wave travels along negative x-direction.

Ex. 4 A wave is travelling along positive x-direction with velocity 2 m/s. Further, $y(x)$ equation of the wave pulse at $t = 0$ is

$$y = \frac{10}{2 + (2x + 4)^2}$$

(a) From the given information make complete $y(x, t)$ equation.

(b) Find $y(x)$ equation at $t = 1$ s

Sol. (a) Here, coefficient to x is 2.

Wave speed is 2 m/s. Therefore, coefficient of $t = v$ (coefficient of x) $= 2 \times 2 = 4$ units.

Further, coefficient of x is positive and the wave is travelling along positive x-direction.

Hence, coefficient of t must be negative.

Now, suppose the $y(x, t)$ function is

$$y = \frac{10}{2 + (2x - 4t + \alpha)^2} \quad \text{...(i)}$$

Here, α is a constant.

At time $t = 0$, Eq. (i) becomes

$$y = \frac{10}{2 + (2x + \alpha)^2}$$ **Ans.**

and the given function is $y = \dfrac{10}{2 + (2x + 4)^2}$

Therefore, the value of α is 4.

Substituting in Eq. (i), we have

$$y = \frac{10}{2 + (2x - 4t + 4)^2}$$ **Ans.**

(b) At $t = 1$ s

$$y = \frac{10}{2 + (2x - 4 \times 1 + 4)^2}$$

or $$y = \frac{10}{2 + 4x^2}$$ **Ans.**

MODULE 1 Exercise

Fill in the Blank

1. The amplitude of a wave disturbance propagating in the positive x-direction is given by $y = \dfrac{1}{(1 + x)^2}$ at time $t = 0$ and by $y = \dfrac{1}{[1 + (x - 1)^2]}$ at $t = 2$ s, where x and y are in meters. The shape of the wave disturbance does not change during the propagation. The velocity of the wave is .... m/s. **(1990 JEE)**

Multiple Correct Options

2. The displacement of particles in a string stretched in the x-direction is represented by y. Among the following expressions for y, those describing wave motion are **(1997 JEE)**

(a) $\cos kx \sin \omega t$ (b) $k^2x^2 - \omega^2t^2$

(c) $\cos^2(kx + \omega t)$ (d) $\cos(k^2x^2 - \omega^2t^2)$

Subjective Questions

3. Prove that the equation $y = a \sin \omega t$ does not satisfy the wave equation and hence it does not represent a wave.

4. A wave pulse is described by $y(x, t) = ae^{-(bx - ct)^2}$, where a, b and c are positive constants. What is the speed of this wave?

5. The equation of a wave travelling on a string stretched along the x-axis is given by

$$y = Ae^{-\left(\frac{x}{a} + \frac{t}{T}\right)^2}$$

(a) Write the dimensions of A, a and T.

(b) Find the wave speed.

(c) In which direction is the wave travelling?

(d) Where is the maximum of the pulse located at $t = T$ and at $t = 2T$?

Answers

1. (0.5) **2.** (a, c) **4.** $\dfrac{c}{b}$ **5.** (a) [L], [L], [T] (b) $\dfrac{a}{T}$ (c) Negative x-direction (d) $x = -a$ and $x = -2a$

See hints on page 36.

MODULE 2

Sine Wave

Oscillations of y in a wave may or may not be simple harmonic in nature.

If oscillations of y are simple harmonic in nature, then $y(x,t)$ function is sine or cosine function. Such type of wave is called **sine wave** or **sinusoidal wave.** For better understanding, we can visualize a sine wave travelling on a string.

The general expression of a sine wave is

$$y = A\sin(\omega t \pm kx \pm \phi)$$

and

$$y = A\cos(\omega t \pm kx \pm \phi)$$

In the above equations,

(i) A is the amplitude of oscillations of y.

(ii) ω is called the angular frequency. Here,

$$\omega = 2\pi f = \frac{2\pi}{T} \quad \text{and} \quad f = \frac{1}{T}$$

where, f is normal frequency of oscillations and T is the time period of oscillations. SI unit of ω is radian/sec while that of f is Hz or s^{-1}.

(iii) k is called the angular wave number, where

$$k = \frac{2\pi}{\lambda}$$

Here, λ is the wavelength of wave.

Wavelength (λ)

In a **transverse wave motion,** the particles of the medium oscillate about their mean or equilibrium position at right angles to the direction of propagation of wave motion itself.

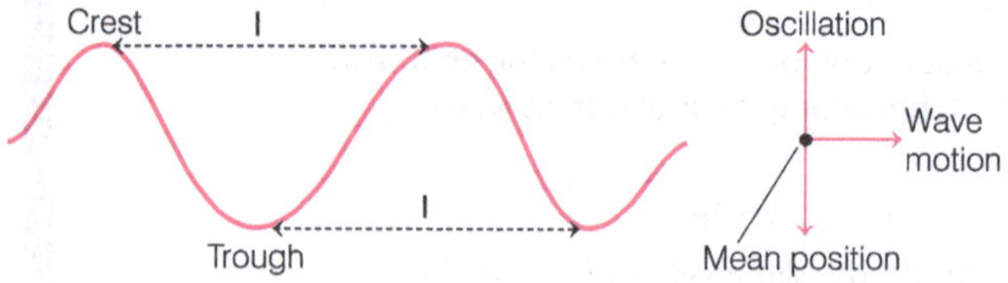

This form of wave motion travels in the form of **crests and troughs**, for example, waves travelling along a stretched string. The distance between two successive crests or troughs is known as **wavelength** (λ) of the wave. In a **longitudinal wave motion,** particles of the medium oscillate about their mean or equilibrium position along the direction of propagation of the wave motion itself. This type of wave motion travels in the form of **compressions** and **rarefactions.**

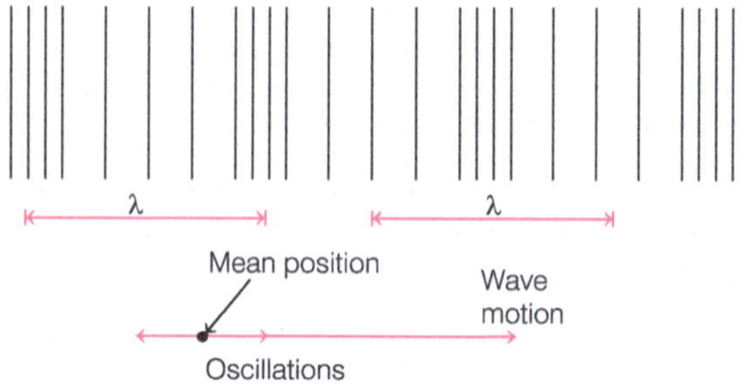

The distance between two successive compressions or rarefactions constitute one wavelength.

Note *Numerically,* $k = \frac{2\pi}{\lambda}$ *or angular wave number is defined as the number of waves in* 2π *length. Similarly, there is one another word called wave number. This is equal to* $\frac{1}{\lambda}$ *and numerically this is equal to number of waves in unit length.*

(iv) Wave speed,

$$v = \frac{\text{Coefficient of } t}{\text{Coefficient of } x}$$

$$\therefore \quad v = \frac{\omega}{k}$$

But $\quad \omega = 2\pi f$

and $\quad k = \frac{2\pi}{\lambda}$

Substituting these values in the above equation, we also get

$$v = f\lambda$$

(v) $\frac{\partial y}{\partial t}$ is SHM velocity of the particle executing oscillations (lying between $+\omega A$ and $-\omega A$).

Similarly, $\frac{\partial^2 y}{\partial t^2}$ is SHM acceleration (lying between $+\omega^2 A$ and $-\omega^2 A$).

Let us take an example: suppose a sine wave travelling on a string is

$$y = A\sin(\omega t - kx + \phi) \qquad \text{...(i)}$$

Then, $$\frac{\partial y}{\partial t} = \omega A\cos(\omega t - kx + \phi) \qquad \text{...(ii)}$$

and $$\frac{\partial^2 y}{\partial \tau^2} = -\omega^2 A \sin(\omega t - kx + \phi) \quad \ldots\text{(iii)}$$

From Eq. (i), we can determine y-displacement of SHM of any particle at position x and at time t. Value of y lies between $+A$ and $-A$.

From Eq. (ii), we can determine $\frac{\partial y}{\partial t}$ or SHM velocity and from Eq. (iii), we can find $\frac{\partial^2 y}{\partial t^2}$ or SHM acceleration of any particle at position x at time t.

Angle $(\omega t - kx + \phi)$ is same in all three equations which is also called phase angle of three functions. With the help of this phase angle, we can determine values of y, $\frac{\partial y}{\partial t}$ and $\frac{\partial^2 y}{\partial t^2}$ at any position x at time t. If we put $x = 0$ and $t = 0$, then this angle is only ϕ. This is called initial phase angle of the particle at co-ordinate $x = 0$. With the help of this angle, we can find the initial values of y, $\frac{\partial y}{\partial t}$ and $\frac{\partial^2 y}{\partial t^2}$ of the string particle (which is executing SHM at position $x = 0$).

Important POINTS

- Alternate expressions of a sine wave travelling along positive x-direction are

$$y = A \sin k(x - vt) = A \sin (kx - \omega t)$$
$$= A \sin \frac{2\pi}{\lambda}(x - vt) = A \sin 2\pi\left(\frac{x}{\lambda} - \frac{t}{T}\right)$$

Similarly, the expression,

$$y = A \sin k(x + vt) = A \sin (kx + \omega t)$$
$$= A \sin 2\pi\left(\frac{x}{\lambda} + \frac{t}{T}\right) \text{etc.}$$

represent a sine wave travelling along negative x-direction.

- **Difference between two equations**

$$\boxed{y = A \sin (\omega t - kx) \quad \text{and} \quad y = A \sin (kx - \omega t)}$$

Both the equations represent a wave travelling in positive x-direction with speed $v = \frac{\omega}{k}$. The difference between them is that they are out of phase, i.e. phase difference between them is π. It means, if a particle in position $x = 0$ at time $t = 0$ is in its mean position and moving upwards (represented by first wave) then the same particle will be in its mean position but moving downwards (represented by the second wave). Similarly, the waves $y = A \sin (kx - \omega t)$ and $y = -A \sin (kx - \omega t)$ are also out of phase.

- Let us now see with an example of sine wave that how it travels along x-axis.

$$\boxed{y = A \sin (\omega t - kx)}$$

is a sine wave travelling along positive x-axis with time period $T = \frac{2\pi}{\omega}$ and wave speed $v = \frac{\omega}{k}$.

In the Chapter of SHM we have seen that in time interval from 0 to $\frac{T}{12}$, particle moves from 0 to $\pm\frac{A}{2}$ and from 0 to $\frac{T}{4}$, it moves from 0 to $\pm A$. So, for better understanding we are taking only these two intervals.

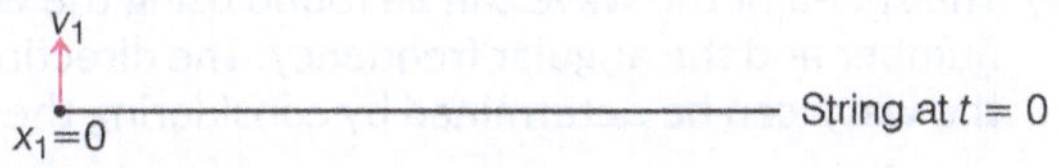

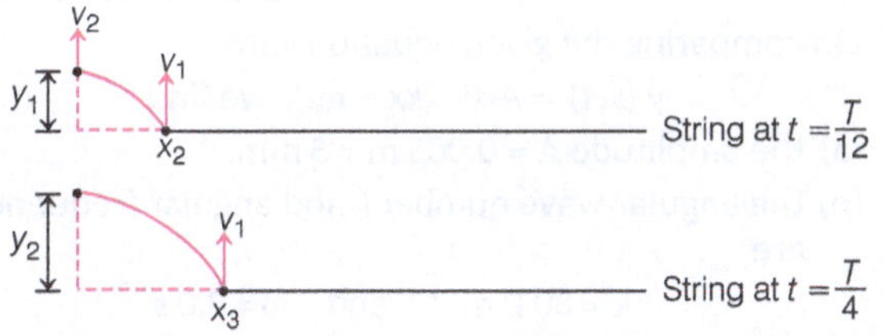

In the figure :

$$y_1 = \frac{A}{2}$$
$$y_2 = A$$
$$v_1 = \omega A$$
$$v_2 = \omega\sqrt{A^2 - y_1^2} = \omega\sqrt{A^2 - \left(\frac{A}{2}\right)^2} = \frac{\sqrt{3}\,\omega A}{2}$$
$$x_2 = v\left(\frac{T}{12}\right) = \left(\frac{\omega}{k}\right)\left(\frac{2\pi/\omega}{12}\right) = \frac{\pi}{6k}$$
$$x_3 = v\left(\frac{T}{4}\right) = \left(\frac{\omega}{k}\right)\left(\frac{2\pi/\omega}{4}\right) = \frac{\pi}{2k}$$

Further if we put $x = 0$ in the given equation then $y(x, t)$ equation becomes $y = A \sin \omega t$. This equation represents that at time $t = 0$, particle (at $x = 0$) is at $y = 0$ and travelling along positive y-direction with simple harmonic motion velocity $v_1 = \omega A$.

At $t = \frac{T}{12}$, particle at $x = 0$ will reach at $y_1 = \frac{A}{2}$. Its simple harmonic motion velocity is v_2 (given above) and the wave will travel a distance $x_2 = v\left(\frac{T}{12}\right)$ along positive direction. Here v is the wave velocity not the SHM velocity. Similarly, we can see the values at $t = \frac{T}{4}$.

- **Summary of a sine wave**

General equation of this wave is

$$y = A \sin(\omega t \pm kx \pm \phi)$$

or $$y = A \cos(\omega t \pm kx \pm \phi)$$

In these equations,

(i) A is amplitude of oscillation,

(ii) ω is angular frequency,

$$T=\frac{2\pi}{\omega}$$

$$\Rightarrow \quad \omega=2\pi f \quad \text{and} \quad f=\frac{1}{T}=\frac{\omega}{2\pi}$$

(iii) k is angular wave number,

$$k=\frac{2\pi}{\lambda} \quad (\lambda=\text{wavelength})$$

(iv) Wave speed, $v=\frac{\omega}{k}=f\lambda$

(v) ϕ is initial phase angle of the particle at $x=0$.

(vi) $(\omega t \pm kx \pm \phi)$ is phase angle at time t at coordinate x.

Example 1 A wave travelling along a string is described by

$$y(x,t)=0.005\sin(80.0\,x-3.0\,t).$$

in which the numerical constants are in SI units. Calculate (a) the amplitude. (b) the wavelength (c) the period and frequency of the wave. Also, calculate the displacement y of the wave at a distance $x=30.0$ cm and time $t=20$ s?

(NCERT Solved Example)

Sol. On comparing the given equation with

$y(x,t)=A\sin(kx-\omega t)$, we find

(a) the amplitude $A=0.005\text{ m}=5\text{ mm}$.

(b) the angular wave number k and angular frequency ω are

$$k=80.0\text{ m}^{-1} \quad \text{and} \quad \omega=3.0\text{ s}^{-1}$$

$$\therefore \quad \lambda=2\pi/k=\frac{2\pi}{80.0}=0.0785\text{ m}$$

$$=7.85\text{ cm}$$ **Ans.**

(c) $T=2\pi/\omega=\frac{2\pi}{3.0}=2.09\text{ s}$ **Ans.**

and frequency, $f=1/T=0.48$ Hz **Ans.**

The displacement y at $x=30.0$ cm and time $t=20$ s is given by

$$y=(0.005\text{ m})\sin(80.0\times0.3-3.0\times20)$$
$$=(0.005\text{ m})\sin(-36)$$
$$=(0.005\text{ m})\sin(-36+12\pi)$$
$$=(0.005\text{ m})\sin(1.714)$$
$$=(0.005\text{ m})\sin(98.27^\circ)=4.94\text{ mm}$$ **Ans.**

Example 2 The equation of a wave is

$$y(x,t)=0.05\sin\left[\frac{\pi}{2}(10\,x-40\,t)-\frac{\pi}{4}\right]\text{m}$$

Find :

(a) the wavelength, the frequency and the wave velocity

(b) the particle velocity and acceleration at $x=0.5$ m and $t=0.05$ s.

Sol. (a) The equation may be rewritten as

$$y(x,t)=0.05\sin\left(5\pi x-20\pi t-\frac{\pi}{4}\right)\text{m}$$

Comparing this with equation of plane progressive harmonic wave,

$y(x,t)=A\sin(kx-\omega t+\phi)$ we have,

Wave number, $k=\frac{2\pi}{\lambda}=5\pi$ rad/m

$$\therefore \quad \lambda=0.4\text{ m}$$ **Ans.**

The angular frequency is

$$\omega=2\pi f=20\pi\text{ rad/s}$$

$$\therefore \quad f=10\text{ Hz}$$ **Ans.**

The wave velocity is,

$$v=f\lambda=\frac{\omega}{k}=4\text{ m/s in }+x\text{-direction}$$ **Ans.**

(b) The particle velocity and particle acceleration at the given values of x and t are

$$\frac{\partial y}{\partial t}=-(20\pi)(0.05)\cos\left(\frac{5\pi}{2}-\pi-\frac{\pi}{4}\right)$$

$$=2.22\text{ m/s}$$ **Ans.**

$$\frac{\partial^2 y}{\partial t^2}=-(20\pi)^2(0.05)\sin\left(\frac{5\pi}{2}-\pi-\frac{\pi}{4}\right)$$

$$=140\text{ m/s}^2$$ **Ans.**

Example 3 A transverse wave on a taut string is given by,

$$y(x,t)=A\sin(kx-\omega t)$$
$$=(0.2\text{ m})\sin(6.28\text{ m}^{-1}x-1.57\text{ s}^{-1}t)$$

Find the amplitude, wavelength, period and speed of the wave.

Sol. (i) The amplitude, wave number and angular frequency can be read directly from the wave equation:

$$y(x,t)=A\sin(kx-\omega t)$$
$$=0.2\text{ m}\sin(6.28\text{m}^{-1}x-1.57\text{ s}^{-1}t)$$

(Given $A=0.2$ m, $k=6.28\text{ m}^{-1}$, $\omega=1.57\text{ s}^{-1}$)

(ii) The wave number can be used to find the wavelength:

$$k=\frac{2\pi}{\lambda}$$

$$\Rightarrow \quad \lambda=\frac{2\pi}{k}=\frac{2\pi}{6.28\text{ m}^{-1}}=1.0\text{ m} \quad \text{...(i)}$$

(iii) The period of the wave can be found using the angular frequency :

$$\omega=\frac{2\pi}{T}$$

$$\Rightarrow \quad T=\frac{2\pi}{\omega}=\frac{2\pi}{1.57\text{ s}^{-1}}=4\text{s} \quad \text{...(ii)}$$

(iv) The speed of the wave can be found using the wave number and the angular frequency. The direction of the wave can be determined by considering the sign of $kx \pm \omega t$: A negative sign suggests that the wave is moving in the positive x-direction :

$$|v| = \frac{\omega}{k} = \frac{1.57\ s^{-1}}{6.28\ m^{-1}} = 0.25\ m/s$$

Significance

Plotting the height of the medium y *versus* the position x for two times $t = 0$ s and $t = \frac{T}{4} = 1$ s can provide a graphical visualization of the wave as shown in the figure.

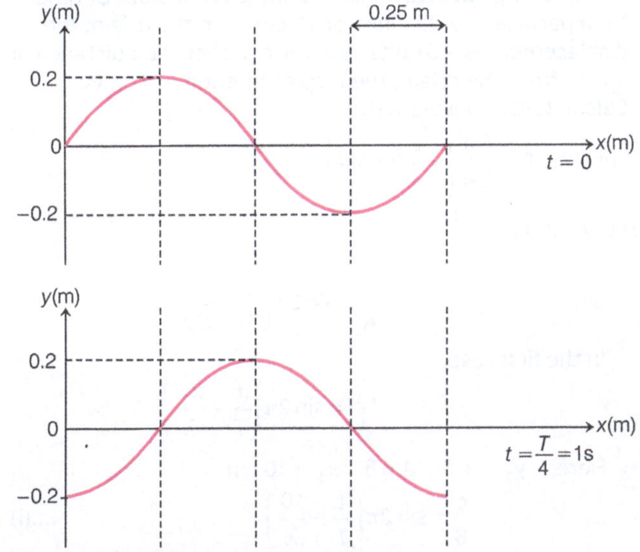

Above figure shows a graph of height of the wave y as a function of position x for snapshots of the wave at two times. One at time $t = 0$ s and the other at $t = \frac{T}{4} = 1$ s.

Putting $x = 0, t = 0$, we get

$$y = 0$$

Again by putting $x = 0$ and $t = \frac{T}{4} = 1$ s, we get

$$y = -0.2\ m$$

INTRODUCTORY Exercise

1. Consider the wave $y = (5\ mm)\sin[1\ cm^{-1}x - (60\ s^{-1})t]$. Find (a) the amplitude, (b) the angular wave number, (c) the wavelength, (d) the frequency, (e) the time period and (f) the wave velocity.
2. A wave is described by the equation $y = (1.0\ mm)\sin\pi\left(\frac{x}{2.0\ cm} - \frac{t}{0.01\ s}\right)$.
   (a) Find time period and wavelength.
   (b) Find the speed of particle at $x = 1.0$ cm and time $t = 0.01$ s.
   (c) What are the speeds of the particles at $x = 3.0$ cm, 5.0 cm and 7.0 cm at $t = 0.01$ s?
   (d) What are the speeds of the particles at $x = 1.0$ cm at $t = 0.011, 0.012$ and 0.013 s?

Answers

1. (a) 5 mm (b) $1\ cm^{-1}$ (c) 2π cm (d) $\frac{30}{\pi}$ Hz (e) $\left(\frac{\pi}{30}\right)$ sec, (f) 60 cm/s
2. (a) 20 ms, 4.0 cm (b) zero (c) zero (d) $9.7\ cms^{-1}$, $18\ cms^{-1}$, $25\ cms^{-1}$

See hints on page 36.

Miscellaneous Examples

Ex. 1 For a wave described by $y = A\sin(\omega t - kx)$, consider the following points

(a) $x = 0$ (b) $x = \frac{\pi}{4k}$ (c) $x = \frac{\pi}{2k}$ and (d) $x = \frac{3\pi}{4k}$

For a particle at each of these points at $t = 0$, describe whether the particle is moving or not and in what direction and describe whether the particle is speeding up, slowing down or instantaneously not accelerating?

Sol. $y = A\sin(\omega t - kx)$

Particle velocity $v_P(x, t) = \frac{\partial y}{\partial t} = \omega A\cos(\omega t - kx)$ and

particle acceleration

$$a_P(x, t) = \frac{\partial^2 y}{\partial t^2} = -\omega^2 A\sin(\omega t - kx)$$

(a) $\mathbf{t = 0,\ x = 0:}$ $\quad v_P = +\omega A$ and $a_P = 0$

i.e. particle is moving **upwards** but its **acceleration is zero.**

(b) $\mathbf{t = 0,\ x = \frac{\pi}{4k}}$

$$x = \frac{\pi}{4k}$$

$$\therefore \quad kx = \frac{\pi}{4}$$

$$v_P = \omega A\cos\left(-\frac{\pi}{4}\right) = +\frac{\omega A}{\sqrt{2}}$$

and $$a_P = -\omega^2 A\sin\left(-\frac{\pi}{4}\right) = +\frac{\omega^2 A}{\sqrt{2}}$$

Velocity of particle is positive, i.e. the particle is moving **upwards** (along positive y-direction). Further v_P and a_P are in the same direction (both are positive). Hence, the particle is **speeding up.**

(c) $t = 0$, $x = \dfrac{\pi}{2k}$

$$x = \frac{\pi}{2k}$$

$$\therefore \quad kx = \frac{\pi}{2}$$

$$v_P = \omega A \cos(-\pi/2) = 0$$

$$a_P = -\omega^2 A \sin(-\pi/2) = \omega^2 A$$

i.e. particle is **stationary** or at its extreme position ($y = -A$). So, it is **speeding up** at this instant.

(d) $t = 0$, $x = \dfrac{3\pi}{4k}$

$$x = \frac{3\pi}{4k}$$

$$\therefore \quad kx = \frac{3\pi}{4}$$

$$v_P = \omega A \cos\left(-\frac{3\pi}{4}\right) = -\frac{\omega A}{\sqrt{2}}$$

$$a_P = -\omega^2 A \sin\left(-\frac{3\pi}{4}\right) = +\frac{\omega^2 A}{\sqrt{2}}$$

Velocity of particle is negative, i.e. the particle is moving **downwards**. Further v_P and a_P are in opposite directions, i.e. the particle is **slowing down**.

Ex. 2 Consider a wave propagating in the negative x-direction whose frequency is 100 Hz. At $t = 5$ s, the displacement associated with the wave is given by

$$y = 0.5 \cos(0.1\, x)$$

where x and y are measured in centimetres and t in seconds. Obtain the displacement (as a function of x) at $t = 10$ s. What is the wavelength and velocity associated with the wave?

Sol. A wave travelling in negative x-direction can be represented as

$$y(x, t) = A \cos(kx + \omega t + \phi)$$

At $t = 5$ s,

$$y(x, t = 5) = A \cos(kx + 5\omega + \phi)$$

Comparing this with the given equation,

We have,

$$A = 0.5 \text{ cm}, k = 0.1 \text{ cm}^{-1}$$

and $\quad 5\omega + \phi = 0 \quad$ ...(i)

Now, $\quad \lambda = \dfrac{2\pi}{k} = \dfrac{2\pi}{0.1} = (20\pi)$ cm **Ans.**

$$\omega = 2\pi f = (200\pi) \text{ rad/s}$$

$\therefore \quad v = \dfrac{\omega}{k} = \dfrac{200\pi}{0.1} = (2000\,\pi)$ cm/s **Ans.**

From Eq. (i), $\phi = -5\omega$

At $t = 10$ s,

$$y(x, t = 10) = 0.5 \cos(0.1\, x + 10\,\omega - 5\omega)$$
$$= 0.5 \cos(0.1\, x + 5\,\omega)$$

Substituting $\quad \omega = 200\,\pi$,

$$y(x, t = 10) = 0.5 \cos(0.1x + 1000\,\pi)$$
$$= 0.5 \cos(0.1\, x)$$ **Ans.**

Ex. 3 A simple harmonic wave of amplitude 8 units travels along positive x-axis. At any given instant of time, for a particle at a distance of 10 cm from the origin, the displacement is + 6 units, and for a particle at a distance of 25 cm from the origin, the displacement is + 4 units. Calculate the wavelength.

$\left[\text{Given } \sin^{-1}\left(\dfrac{3}{4}\right) = 0.85 \text{ rad}\right]$

Sol. $y = A \sin 2\pi\left(\dfrac{t}{T} - \dfrac{x}{\lambda}\right)$

or $$\frac{y}{A} = \sin 2\pi\left(\frac{t}{T} - \frac{x}{\lambda}\right)$$

In the first case,

$$\frac{y_1}{A} = \sin 2\pi\left(\frac{t}{T} - \frac{x_1}{\lambda}\right)$$

Here, $\quad y_1 = +6, \quad A = 8, \quad x_1 = 10$ cm

$\therefore \quad \dfrac{6}{8} = \sin 2\pi\left(\dfrac{t}{T} - \dfrac{10}{\lambda}\right) \quad$ ...(i)

Similarly in the second case,

$\dfrac{4}{8} = \sin 2\pi\left(\dfrac{t}{T} - \dfrac{25}{\lambda}\right) \quad$ ...(ii)

From Eq. (i),

$$2\pi\left(\frac{t}{T} - \frac{10}{\lambda}\right) = \sin^{-1}\left(\frac{6}{8}\right) = \sin^{-1}\left(\frac{3}{4}\right) = 0.85 \text{ rad}$$

or $\quad \dfrac{t}{T} - \dfrac{10}{\lambda} = 0.14 \quad$ ...(iii)

Similarly from Eq. (ii),

$$2\pi\left(\frac{t}{T} - \frac{25}{\lambda}\right) = \sin^{-1}\left(\frac{4}{8}\right) = \frac{\pi}{6} \text{ rad}$$

or $\quad \dfrac{t}{T} - \dfrac{25}{\lambda} = 0.08 \quad$ ...(iv)

Subtracting Eq. (iv) from Eq. (iii), we get

$$\frac{15}{\lambda} = 0.06$$

$\therefore \quad \lambda = 250$ cm **Ans.**

Ex. 4 A sinusoidal wave travelling in the positive direction on a stretched string has amplitude 2.0 cm, wavelength 1.0 m and wave velocity 5.0 m/s. At $x = 0$ and $t = 0$, it is given that $y = 0$ and $\dfrac{\partial y}{\partial t} < 0$. Find the wave function $y(x, t)$.

Sol. We start with a general equation for a wave travelling in positive x-direction.

$$y(x,t) = A \sin(kx - \omega t + \phi)$$

The amplitude given is

$$A = 2.0 \text{ cm} = 0.02 \text{ m}$$

The wavelength is given as

$$\lambda = 1.0 \text{ m}$$

$\therefore$ Angular wave number,

$$k = \frac{2\pi}{\lambda} = (2\pi)\text{m}^{-1}$$

Angular frequency,

$$\omega = vk = (10\pi) \text{ rad/s}$$

$\therefore$ $$y(x,t) = (0.02) \sin[2\pi(x - 5.0t) + \phi]$$

We are given that for $x = 0, t = 0$,

$$y = 0$$

and $$\frac{\partial y}{\partial t} < 0$$

i.e. $\quad 0.02 \sin\phi = 0 \quad$ (as $y = 0$)

and $\quad -0.2\pi \cos\phi < 0$

From these conditions, we may conclude that

$$\phi = 2n\pi \qquad (\text{where } n = 0, 2, 4, 6 \ldots)$$

Therefore,

$y(x,t) = (0.02 \text{ m}) \sin[(2\pi \text{ m}^{-1})x - (10\pi \text{ rads}^{-1})t] \text{ m}$ **Ans.**

Typed Problems

Type 1. *To write the equation corresponding to given y - x graph (or a snapshot) at a given time.*

Concept

From the given y - x graph, we can easily determine A, ω and k. Secondly, we have to check whether the wave is travelling along positive x-direction or negative x-direction. Because this factor will decide whether, ωt and kx should be of same sign or opposite sign.

Ex. 5

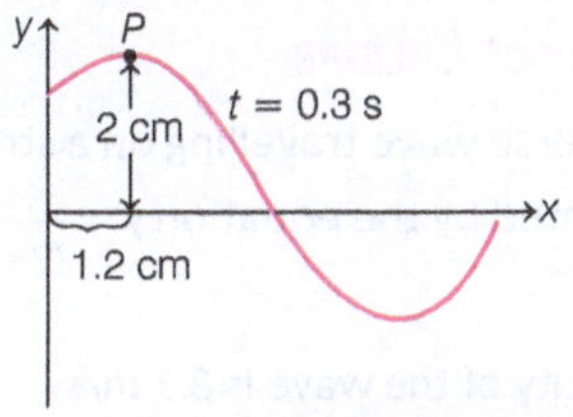

Figure shows a snapshot of a sinusoidal travelling wave taken at $t = 0.3$ s. The wavelength is 7.5 cm and the amplitude is 2 cm. If the crest P was at $x = 0$ at $t = 0$, write the equation of travelling wave.

Sol. Given, $A = 2$ cm, $\lambda = 7.5$ cm

$\therefore$ $$k = \frac{2\pi}{\lambda} = 0.84 \text{ cm}^{-1}$$

The wave has travelled a distance of 1.2 cm in 0.3 s. Hence, speed of the wave,

$$v = \frac{1.2}{0.3} = 4 \text{ cm/s}$$

$\therefore$ Angular frequency $(\omega) = (v)(k) = 3.36$ rad/s

Since the wave is travelling along positive x-direction and crest (maximum displacement) is at $x = 0$ at $t = 0$, we can write the wave equation as

$$y(x,t) = A\cos(kx - \omega t)$$

or $$y(x,t) = A\cos(\omega t - kx)$$

Crest was at $x = 0$ at $t = 0$. So just after few seconds the SHM velocity $\left(\text{or } \frac{\partial y}{\partial t}\right)$ of the particle at $x = 0$ should be in negative direction. Because from the crest it will now come down. Now as, $\cos(-\theta) = \cos(\theta)$. So, we can write either of the two equations.

Therefore, the desired equation is

$y(x,t) = (2\text{cm})\cos[(0.84\text{cm}^{-1})x - (3.36 \text{ rad/s})t]$ **Ans.**

or, $y(x,t) = (2\text{cm})\cos[(3.36 \text{ rad/s})t - (0.84 \text{ cm}^{-1})x]$ **Ans.**

Ex. 6 For the wave shown in figure, write the equation of this wave if its position is shown at $t = 0$. Speed of wave is $v = 300$ m/s.

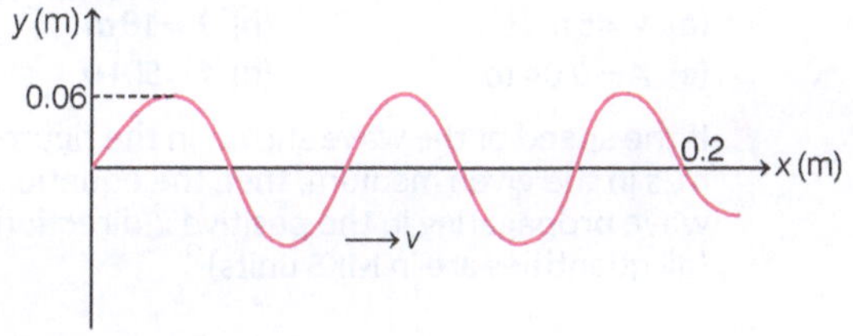

Sol. The amplitude $A = 0.06$ m

$$\frac{5}{2}\lambda = 0.2 \text{ m}$$

$\therefore$ $$\lambda = 0.08 \text{ m}$$

$$f = \frac{v}{\lambda} = \frac{300}{0.08} = 3750 \text{ Hz}$$

$$k = \frac{2\pi}{\lambda} = 78.5 \text{ m}^{-1}$$

and $$\omega = 2\pi f = 23562 \text{ rad/s}$$

At $t = 0$, $x = 0$, $\frac{\partial y}{\partial x}$ = slope of y - x graph = positive

and the given curve is a sine curve.

Hence, equation of wave travelling in positive x-direction should have the form,

$$y(x,t) = A\sin(kx - \omega t)$$

Substituting the values, we have

$y(x,t) = (0.06 \text{ m})\sin[(78.5 \text{ m}^{-1})x - (23562 \text{ s}^{-1})t] \text{ m}$ **Ans.**

MODULE 2 Exercise

Assertion and Reason

Directions : Choose the correct option

*(a) If both **Assertion** and **Reason** are true and the **Reason** is correct explanation of the **Assertion**.*

*(b) If both **Assertion** and **Reason** are true but **Reason** is not the correct explanation of **Assertion**.*

*(c) If **Assertion** is true, but the **Reason** is false.*

*(d) If **Assertion** is false but the **Reason** is true.*

*(e) If both **Assertion** and **Reason** are false.*

1. **Assertion :** Two equations of wave are $y_1 = A\sin(\omega t - kx)$ and $y_2 = A\sin(kx - \omega t)$. These two waves have a phase difference of π.

   Reason : They are travelling in opposite directions.

2. **Assertion :** Wave number is the number of waves per unit length.

   Reason : Wave number $= \frac{1}{\lambda}$.

Single Correct Option

3. Equation of progressive wave is given by

   $y = 4\sin\left[\pi\left(\frac{t}{5} - \frac{x}{9}\right) + \frac{\pi}{6}\right]$, where x and y are in metre.

   Then,

   (a) $v = 5\,m/s$ (b) $\lambda = 18\,m$

   (c) $A = 0.04\,m$ (d) $f = 50\,Hz$

4. If the speed of the wave shown in the figure is 330 m/s in the given medium, then the equation of the wave propagating in the positive x-direction will be (all quantities are in MKS units)

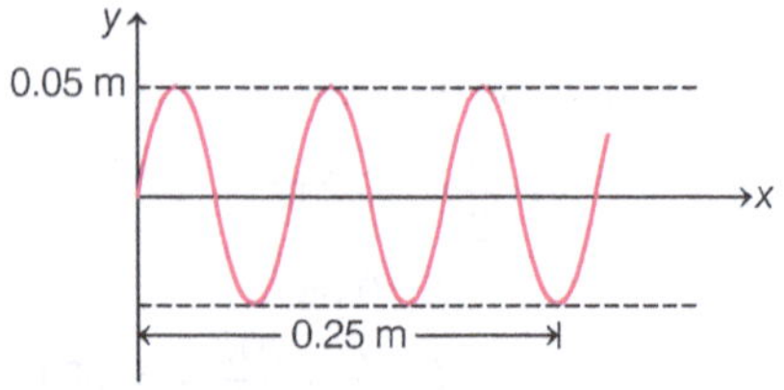

   (a) $y = 0.05\sin 2\pi(4000t - 12.5x)$

   (b) $y = 0.05\sin 2\pi(4000t - 122.5x)$

   (c) $y = 0.05\sin 2\pi(3300t - 10x)$

   (d) $y = 0.05\sin 2\pi(1650x - 5t)$

5. In the wave equation

   $$y = 0.5\sin\frac{2\pi}{\lambda}(400t - x)\ m$$

   the velocity of the wave will be **(2022 Main)**

   (a) 200 m/s (b) $200\sqrt{2}$ m/s

   (c) 400 m/s (d) $400\sqrt{2}$ m/s

6. Which of the following equations correctly represents a travelling wave having wavelength $\lambda = 4.0$ cm, frequency $\nu = 100$ Hz and travelling in positive X-axis direction? **(2022 Main)**

   (a) $y = A\sin[(0.50\,\pi\,cm^{-1})x - (100\,\pi\,s^{-1})t]$

   (b) $y = A\sin 2\pi[(0.25\,cm^{-1})x - (50\,s^{-1})t]$

   (c) $y = A\sin\left[\left(\frac{2\pi}{4}\,cm^{-1}\right)x - \left(\frac{2\pi}{100}\,s^{-1}\right)t\right]$

   (d) $y = A\sin\pi[(0.5\,cm^{-1})x - (200\,s^{-1})\,t]$

7. A travelling harmonic wave is represented by the equation $y(x, t) = 10^{-3}\sin(50t + 2x)$, where x and y are in metre and t is in second. Which of the following is a correct statement about the wave? **(2019 Main)**

   (a) The wave is propagating along the negative X-axis with speed 25 ms^{-1}.

   (b) The wave is propagating along the positive X-axis with speed 25 ms^{-1}.

   (c) The wave is propagating along the positive X-axis with speed 100 ms^{-1}

   (d) The wave is propagating along the negative X-axis with speed 100 ms^{-1}.

Multiple Correct Options

8. A transverse wave travelling on a stretched string is represented by the equation $y = \frac{2}{(2x - 6.2t)^2 + 20}$.

   Then,

   (a) velocity of the wave is 3.1 m/s

   (b) amplitude of the wave is 0.1 m

   (c) frequency of the wave is 20 Hz

   (d) wavelength of the wave is 1 m

9. In the wave equation, $y = A\sin\frac{2\pi}{a}(x - bt)$

   (a) speed of wave is a

   (b) speed of wave is b

   (c) wavelength of wave is a/b

   (d) wavelength of wave is a

Subjective Questions

10. Transverse wave on a string has wave speed 12.0 m/s, amplitude 0.05 m and wavelength 0.4 m. The wave travels in the $+x$-direction and at $t = 0$ the $x = 0$ end of the string has zero displacement and is moving upwards.

    (a) Write a wave function describing the wave.

    (b) Find the transverse displacement of a point at $x = 0.25$ m at time $t = 0.15$ s.

    (c) How much time must elapse from the instant in part (b) until the point at $x = 0.25$ m has zero displacement?

11. A sinusoidal wave travelling in the positive x-direction has an amplitude of 15.0 cm, a wavelength of 40.0 cm and a frequency of 8.00 Hz. The vertical displacement of the medium at $t = 0$ and $x = 0$ is also 15.0 cm as shown in figure.

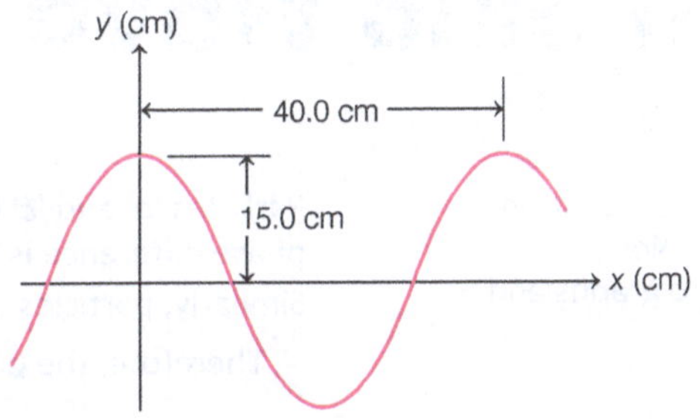

(a) Find the angular wave number k, period T, angular frequency ω and speed v of the wave.
(b) Write a general expression for the wave function.

Answers

1. (c) **2.** (a) **3.** (b) **4.** (c) **5.** (c) **6.** (d) **7.** (a) **8.** (a, b) **9.** (b, d)

10. (a) $y(x, t) = (0.05\text{ m}) \sin [(60\pi\text{ s}^{-1})t - (5\pi\text{m}^{-1})x]$ (b) -3.54 cm (c) 4.2 ms

11. (a) 0.157 rad/cm, 0.125 s, 50.24 rad/s, 320 cm/s (b) $y = (15.0\text{ cm}) \cos (0.157x - 50.24\,t)$ or $(15.0\text{ cm}) \cos (50.24t - 0.157\,x)$

See hints on pages 36-37.

MODULE 3

Two Graphs in Sine Wave

As we have learned in the above article that $y(x,t)$ equation of a sine wave is either sine or cosine equation. Now, corresponding to this equation we can have two graphs and two sinusoidal equations.

First Graph

In $y(x,t)$ equation, if value of t is fixed (or substituted), then the equation left is $y(x)$ equation.So, we can plot y -x graph corresponding to this equation. And obviously the graph (or the equation) will be a sine or cosine graph.

For example Suppose a sine wave is travelling along positive x -direction on a string. At a given time (say at 9 AM), the y -x graph may be as shown in the figure given below.

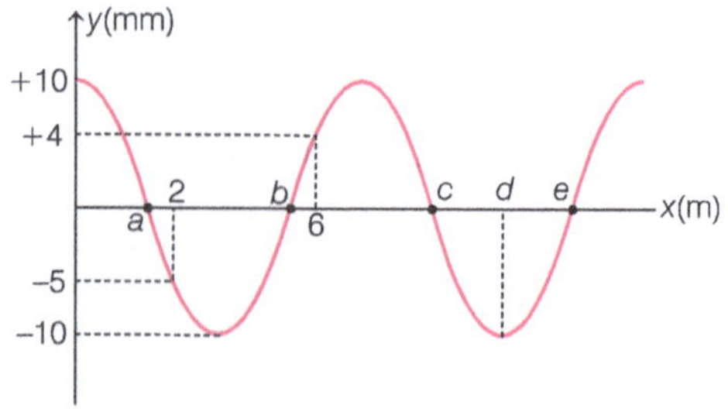

The important points in the above graph are :

(i) Amplitude of oscillation is 10 mm.

(ii) At 9 AM, y -displacement of the string particle at $x = 2$ m is –5mm and of the particle at $x = 6$ m is +4mm. Or, we can say that this graph represents SHM y-displacements of different string particles (at different x -coordinates) at 9 AM. Hence, this is a photograph (or snapshot) of the string at 9 AM.

(iii) Slope of this graph at any point is $\frac{\partial y}{\partial x}\left(\text{not } \frac{dy}{dx}\right)$, as y has two variables x and t.

(iv) Two string particles at different locations are in different phases. The phase difference between them is given by

$$\Delta\phi = \left(\frac{2\pi}{\lambda}\right)(\Delta x)$$

Here, Δx is the path difference between them.

For example

Particles 'a' and 'b' have a path difference of $\frac{\lambda}{2}$. So, phase difference between them is π.

Particles 'a' and 'c' have a path difference of λ. So, phase difference is 2π.

Similarly, particles 'c' and 'd' have a path difference of $\frac{\lambda}{4}$. Therefore, the phase difference is $\frac{\pi}{2}$.

(v) From the above graph, we cannot determine the direction of wave velocity. For that, wave equation will be required.

Second Graph

In $y(x,t)$ equation, if the value of x is fixed (or substituted) then the equation left is $y(t)$ equation.

So, we can plot y -t graph corresponding to this equation. Again, the graph (or the equation) will be a sine or cosine graph.

For example Suppose a sine wave is travelling along positive x -direction on a string. At a given position (say $x = 4$ m), the y -t graph may be as shown in the figure given below.

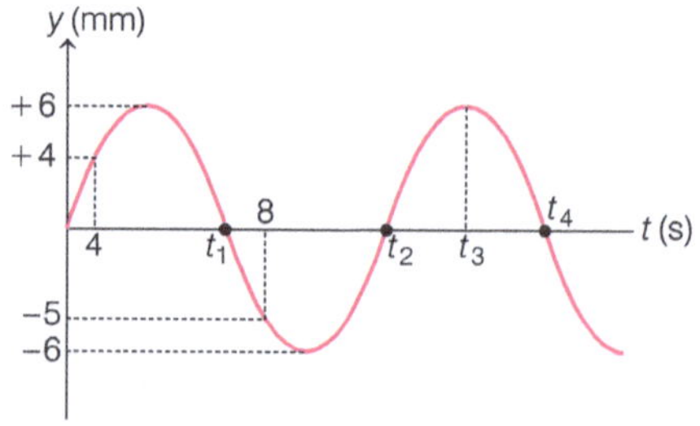

The important points in this graph are :

(i) Amplitude of oscillations is 6 mm.

(ii) y-displacement of the particle at $x = 4$ m is 4 mm at 4 s. Similarly, y-displacement of the particle at $x = 4$ m is – 5 mm at 8 s or we can say that this graph is basically SHM y -t graph of the string particle at $x = 4$ m, which shows different SHM y-displacements of this particle at different times or it is recording of SHM oscillations of this particle.

(iii) Slope of this particle at any time is $\frac{\partial y}{\partial t}$ and this is SHM velocity $(= \pm\omega\sqrt{A^2 - y^2})$ of the particle at $x = 4$ m at that time.

(iv) The same particle at two different times will have different phase angles.

The phase difference in a time interval of Δt is given by

$$\Delta\phi = \left(\frac{2\pi}{T}\right)\Delta t$$

For example,

t_1 and t_2 have a time interval of $\frac{T}{2}$. So, phase difference is π.

t_2 and t_3 have a time interval of $\frac{T}{4}$. So, the phase difference is $\frac{\pi}{2}$.

Similarly, t_1 and t_4 have a time interval of T. Therefore, phase difference is 2π.

Wave Velocity (v), Particle Velocity (v_p) and Particle Acceleration (a_p) in a Sinusoidal Wave

Wave velocity (v) is the velocity by which oscillations of y (or energy) transfer from one point to another point. Later, we will see that this velocity depends on characteristics of medium.

Particle velocity (v_P) and particle acceleration (a_P) are different.

In a sinusoidal wave, particles of the medium oscillate simple harmonically about their mean position. Therefore, all the formulae we have read in SHM can also be applied to the particles.

For example, maximum particle velocity is $\pm A\omega$ at mean position and it is zero at extreme positions. Similarly, maximum particle acceleration is $\pm\omega^2 A$ at extreme positions and zero at mean position. However, the wave velocity is different from the particle velocity. This depends upon certain characteristics of the medium. Unlike the particle velocity which oscillates simple harmonically (between $+A\omega$ and $-A\omega$) the wave velocity is constant for given characteristics of the medium.

Suppose, a sine wave travelling along positive x-axis is

$$y(x,t) = A\sin(kx - \omega t) \quad \text{...(i)}$$

Let us differentiate this function partially with respect to t and x.

$$\frac{\partial y(x,t)}{\partial t} = -A\omega\cos(kx-\omega t) \quad \text{...(ii)}$$

$$\frac{\partial y(x,t)}{\partial x} = Ak\cos(kx-\omega t) \quad \text{...(iii)}$$

From Eqs. (ii) and (iii), we can write

$$\frac{\partial y(x,t)}{\partial t} = -\left(\frac{\omega}{k}\right)\frac{\partial y(x,t)}{\partial x}$$

Here, $\frac{\partial y(x,t)}{\partial t}$ = particle velocity v_P

$\frac{\omega}{k}$ = wave velocity v

and $\frac{\partial y(x,t)}{\partial x}$ = slope of y - x graph when t is fixed

Thus,

$$v_P = -v\,(\text{slope}) \quad \text{...(iv)}$$

i.e. particle velocity at a given position and time is equal to the negative of the product of wave velocity and slope of the y - x graph at a fixed time.

Acceleration of the particle is the second partial derivative of $y(x,t)$ with respect to t,

$$\therefore \quad a_P = \frac{\partial^2 y(x,t)}{\partial t^2} = -\omega^2 A\sin(kx-\omega t) = -\omega^2 y(x,t)$$

i.e. acceleration of the particle equals $-\omega^2$ times its displacement, which is the same result we obtained in SHM. Thus,

$$a_P = -\omega^2\,(\text{displacement}) \quad \text{...(v)}$$

We can also show that,

$$\frac{\partial^2 y(x,t)}{\partial t^2} = \left(\frac{\omega^2}{k^2}\right)\cdot\frac{\partial^2 y(x,t)}{\partial x^2}$$

or

$$\frac{\partial^2 y(x,t)}{\partial t^2} = v^2\frac{\partial^2 y(x,t)}{\partial x^2} \quad \text{...(vi)}$$

which is also the necessary condition for a $y(x,t)$ function to represent a wave function.

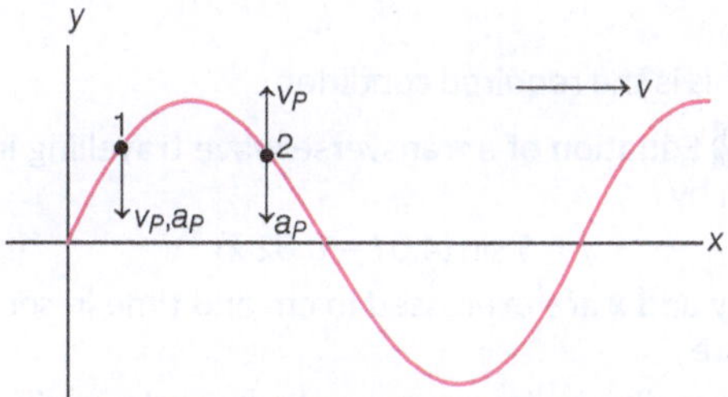

Given figure shows velocity (v_P) and acceleration (a_P) given by Eqs. (iv) and (v) for two points 1 and 2 on a string. The sinusoidal wave is travelling along positive x-direction.

At 1 Slope of the y - x graph is positive. Hence, from Eq. (iv) particle velocity (v_P) is negative or downwards. Because wave velocity v is positive. Similarly, displacement of the particle is positive, so from Eq. (v) acceleration will also be negative or downwards.

At 2 Slope is negative while displacement is positive. Hence, v_P will be positive (upwards) and a_P is negative (downwards).

Note *Direction of v_P will change if the wave travels along negative x-direction. Because v in that case will be negative.*

Important POINTS

1. **Particle velocity (v_P) and wave velocity (v) in sine wave**
   (i) $y = f(x, t)$
   Then, $v_P = \dfrac{\partial y}{\partial t}$
   (ii) In sine wave, particles are executing SHM. Therefore, all equations of SHM can be applied for particles also.
   (iii) Relation between v_P and v
   $$v_P = -v \cdot \frac{\partial y}{\partial x}$$
   Here, $\partial y / \partial x$ is the slope of y-x graph when t is kept constant.

2. **Phase Difference ($\Delta\phi$)**
   Case I $\quad \Delta\phi = \omega(t_1 - t_2)$
   or $\quad \Delta\phi = \dfrac{2\pi}{T} \cdot \Delta t$
   = phase difference of one particle at a time interval of Δt.
   Case II $\quad \Delta\phi = k(x_1 \sim x_2)$
   $= \dfrac{2\pi}{\lambda} \cdot \Delta x$
   = phase difference at one time between two particles at a path difference of Δx.

Example 1 Under what condition, maximum particle velocity is four times the wave velocity corresponding to the equation, $y = A\sin(\omega t - kx)$

Sol. Maximum particle velocity is ωA and wave velocity is $\dfrac{\omega}{k}$.

Now, given that

maximum particle velocity = 4 (wave velocity)

or $$\omega A = 4\left(\frac{\omega}{k}\right)$$

$\therefore$ $$A = \frac{4}{k}$$

So, this is the required condition.

Example 2 Equation of a transverse wave travelling in a rope is given by

$$y = 5\sin(4.0t - 0.02x)$$

where y and x are expressed in cm and time in seconds. Calculate

(a) the amplitude, frequency, velocity and wavelength of the wave.

(b) the maximum transverse speed and acceleration of a particle in the rope.

Sol. (a) Comparing this with the standard equation of wave motion,

$$y = A\sin(\omega t - kx) = A\sin\left(2\pi ft - \frac{2\pi}{\lambda}x\right)$$

where A, f and λ are amplitude, frequency and wavelength respectively.

Amplitude $\quad A = 5$ cm

$\omega = 4$ rad/s, $k = 0.02$ cm^{-1}

$\Rightarrow \quad 2\pi f = \omega = 4$

$\Rightarrow \quad$ Frequency, $f = \dfrac{4}{2\pi} = 0.637$ Hz

Again $k = \dfrac{2\pi}{\lambda} = 0.02$

or $\quad$ Wavelength, $\lambda = \dfrac{2\pi}{0.02} = (100\pi)$ cm

Velocity of the wave, $v = \dfrac{\omega}{k} = \dfrac{4}{0.02} = 200$ cm/s **Ans.**

(b) Maximum velocity of the particle $= \omega A = 20$ cm/s

Maximum particle acceleration $= \omega^2 A = 80$ cm/s^2

Example 3 In the above example, find phase difference $\Delta\phi$

(a) of same particle at two different times with a time interval of 1 s

(b) of two different particles located at a distance of 10 cm at same time

Sol. (a) $\Delta\phi = \left(\dfrac{2\pi}{T}\right)\Delta t$, $\quad$ but $\dfrac{2\pi}{T} = \omega = 4.0$ rad/s

$\therefore \quad \Delta\phi = \omega\Delta t = (4.0)(1.0)$

$= 4$ rad **Ans.**

(b) $\Delta\phi = \left(\dfrac{2\pi}{\lambda}\right)\Delta x$, but $\dfrac{2\pi}{\lambda} = k = 0.02$ cm^{-1}

$\therefore \quad \Delta\phi = (0.02)(10)$

$= 0.2$ rad **Ans.**

MODULE 3 Exercise

Assertion and Reason

See directions on page 14.

1. **Assertion :** y-x graph of a transverse wave on a string is as shown in figure. At the given instant point P is moving downwards. Hence, we can say that wave is moving towards positive y-direction.

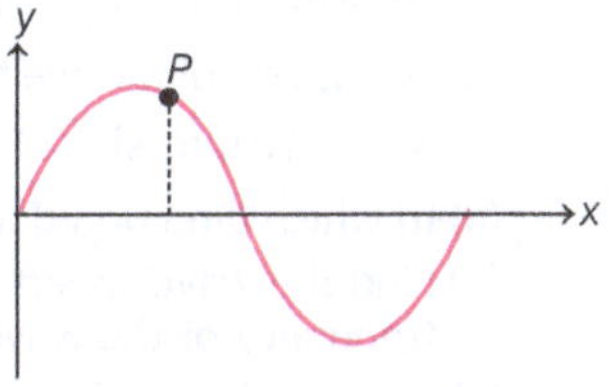

Reason : Particle velocity is given by

$$v_P = -v\frac{\partial y}{\partial x}$$

Single Correct Option

2. The angle between wave velocity and particle velocity in a travelling wave may be

(a) zero (b) $\frac{\pi}{2}$
(c) π (d) All of these

3. A source oscillates with a frequency of 25 Hz and the wave propagates with 300 m/s. Two points A and B are located at distances 10 m and 16 m away from the source. The phase difference between A and B is

(a) $\frac{\pi}{4}$ (b) $\frac{\pi}{2}$ (c) π (d) 2π

4. The rope shown at an instant is carrying a wave travelling towards right, created by a source vibrating at a frequency n.

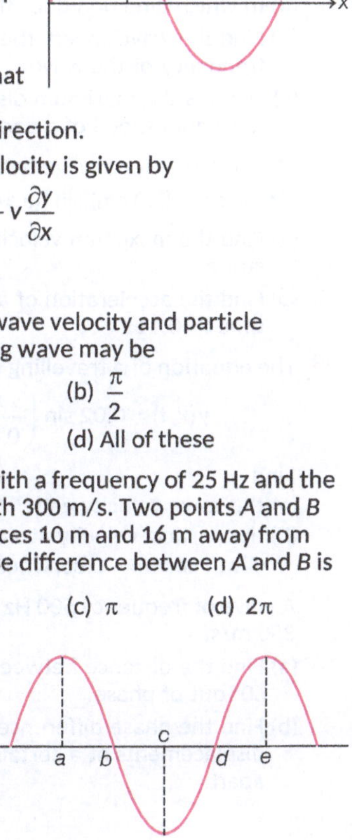

Consider the following statements.
(a) The speed of the wave is $4n \times ab$
(b) The phase difference between b and e is $\frac{3\pi}{2}$
(c) Both (a) and (b) are correct
(d) Both (a) and (b) are wrong

5. Figure shows the wave $y = A\sin(\omega t - kx)$. What is the magnitude of slope of the curve at B ?

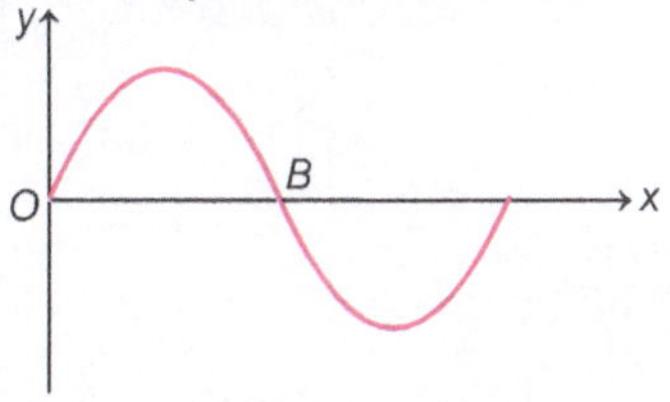

(a) $\frac{\omega}{A}$ (b) $\frac{k}{A}$ (c) kA (d) ωA

6. A transverse wave is represented by $y = 2\sin(\omega t - kx)$ cm. The value of wavelength (in cm) for which the wave velocity becomes equal to the maximum particle velocity, will be **(2022 Main)**

(a) 4π (b) 2π (c) π (d) 2

7. A travelling wave in a stretched string is described by the equation ; $y = A\sin(kx - \omega t)$
The maximum particle velocity is **(1997 JEE)**

(a) $A\omega$ (b) ω/k (c) $d\omega/dk$ (d) x/ω

Multiple Correct Options

8. A wave is travelling along a string. At an instant, shape of the string is as shown in figure. At this instant, point A is moving upwards. Which of the following statement(s) is/are correct?

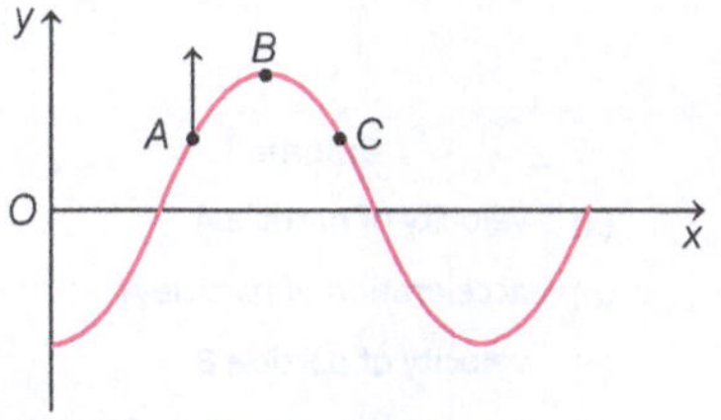

(a) The wave is travelling to the right
(b) Displacement amplitude of the wave is equal to displacement of B at this instant
(c) At this instant velocity of C is also directed upwards
(d) Phase difference between A and C may be equal to $\frac{\pi}{2}$

9. A transverse sinusoidal wave of amplitude a, wavelength λ and frequency f is travelling on a stretched string. The maximum speed of any point on the string is $v/10$, where v is the speed of propagation of the wave. If $a = 10^{-3}$ m and $v = 10\ \text{ms}^{-1}$, then λ and f are given by **(1998 JEE)**

(a) $\lambda = 2\pi \times 10^{-2}$ m (b) $\lambda = 10^{-3}$ m
(c) $f = 10^3\ \text{Hz}/(2\pi)$ (d) $f = 10^4$ Hz

Match the Columns

10. Match the following two columns.

	Column I		Column II
(a)	$y = A\sin(\omega t - kx)$	(p)	travelling in positive x-direction
(b)	$y = A\sin(kx - \omega t)$	(q)	travelling in negative x-direction
(c)	$y = -A\cos(\omega t + kx)$	(r)	at $t = 0$, velocity of particle is positive at $x = 0$
(d)	$y = -A\cos(kx - \omega t)$	(s)	at $t = 0$ acceleration of particle is positive at $x = 0$

11. For the wave equation, $y = (4 \text{ cm}) \sin[\pi t + 2\pi x]$
Here, t is in second and x in metres.

	Column I		Column II
(a)	at $x = 0$, particle velocity is maximum at $t =$	(p)	0.5 s
(b)	at $x = 0$, particle acceleration is maximum at $t =$	(q)	1.0 s
(c)	at $x = 0.5$ m, particle velocity is maximum at $t =$	(r)	zero
(d)	at $x = 0.5$ m, particle acceleration is maximum at $t =$	(s)	1.5 s

12. y-x graph of a transverse wave at a given instant is shown in figure. Match the following two columns.

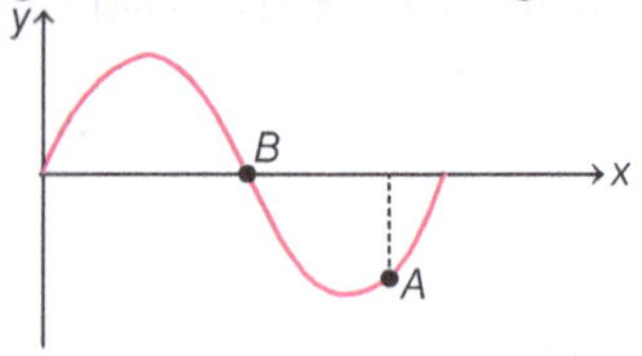

	Column I		Column II
(a)	velocity of particle A	(p)	positive
(b)	acceleration of particle A	(q)	negative
(c)	velocity of particle B	(r)	zero
(d)	acceleration of particle B	(s)	can't tell

Subjective Questions

13. Consider a sinusoidal travelling wave shown in figure. The wave velocity is $+40$ cm/s.

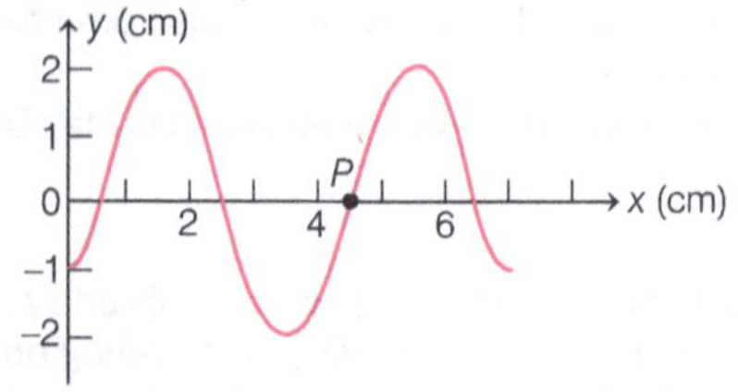

Find
(a) the frequency
(b) the phase difference between two points 2.5 cm apart
(c) how long it takes for the phase at a given position to change by 60°
(d) the velocity of a particle at point P at the instant shown.

14. The equation of a wave travelling on a string is
$$y = (0.10 \text{ mm}) \sin[(31.4 \text{ m}^{-1})x + (314 \text{ s}^{-1})t]$$
(a) In which direction does the wave travel?
(b) Find the wave speed, the wavelength and the frequency of the wave.
(c) What is the maximum displacement and the maximum speed of a particle on the string?

15. The equation for a wave travelling in x-direction on a string is $y = (3.0 \text{ cm}) \sin[(3.14 \text{ cm}^{-1})\, x - (314 \text{ s}^{-1})\, t]$.
(a) Find the maximum velocity of a particle on the string.
(b) Find the acceleration of a particle at $x = 6.0$ cm at time $t = 0.11$ s

16. The equation of a travelling wave is
$$y(x, t) = 0.02 \sin\left(\frac{x}{0.05} + \frac{t}{0.01}\right) \text{m}$$
Find
(a) the wave velocity and
(b) the particle velocity at $x = 0.2$ m and $t = 0.3$ s.
Given $\cos\theta = -0.85$, where $\theta = 34$ rad

17. A wave of frequency 500 Hz has a wave velocity of 350 m/s.
(a) Find the distance between two points which are 60° out of phase.
(b) Find the phase difference between two displacements at a certain point at time 10^{-3} s apart.

Answers

1. (d) **2.** (d) **3.** (c) **4.** (c) **5.** (c) **6.** (a) **7.** (a) **8.** (b, d) **9.** (a, c)
10. (a) $\rightarrow$ p, r ; (b) $\rightarrow$ p ; (c) $\rightarrow$ q, s ; (d) $\rightarrow$ p, s **11.** (a) $\rightarrow$ q, r ; (b) $\rightarrow$ p, s ; (c) $\rightarrow$ q, r ; (d) $\rightarrow$ p, s
12. (a) $\rightarrow$ s ; (b) $\rightarrow$ p ; (c) $\rightarrow$ s ; (d) $\rightarrow$ r **13.** (a) 10 Hz (b) $\frac{5\pi}{4}$ rad (c) $\frac{1}{60}$ s (d) -1.26 m/s
14. (a) Negative x-direction (b) 10 ms^{-1}, 20 cm, 50 Hz (c) 0.10 mm, 3.14 cms^{-1} **15.** (a) 9.4 m/s (b) Zero
16. (a) -5 m/s (b) -1.7 m/s **17.** (a) 0.116 m (b) π

See hints on pages 37-39.

MODULE 4

Wave Speed

Wave speed (v) depends upon the medium or characteristics of the medium. Waves of all frequencies or all wavelengths travel in a given medium with same speed. For examples, all electromagnetic waves travel in vacuum with same speed ($\approx 3 \times 10^8$ m/s).

In water, this speed will be different. Similarly, all longitudinal waves (including the sound wave) travel in air with the same speed (≈ 330 m/s).

Now, frequency of a wave depends on source and wavelength is self adjusted in a value,

$$\lambda = \frac{v}{f}$$

In the above expression, v is same (obviously in a given medium) for all sources (or frequencies). So, with increase in value of f, wavelength λ automatically decreases.

For example : normally frequency of female voice is more than frequency of male voice. So, wavelength of female voice will be less.

Example 1 Speed of sound in air is 330 m/s. Find maximum and minimum wavelength of audible sound in air.

Sol. Frequency of audible sound varies from 20 Hz to 20000 Hz.

Speed of all frequencies in air will be same ($= 330$ m/s).

$$\therefore \quad \lambda_{min} = \frac{v}{f_{max}} = \frac{330}{20000} = 0.0165 \text{ m} \qquad \textbf{Ans.}$$

Similarly,

$$\lambda_{max} = \frac{v}{f_{min}} = \frac{330}{20} = 16.5 \text{ m} \qquad \textbf{Ans.}$$

INTRODUCTORY Exercise 1

1. Speed of light in vacuum is 3×10^8 m/s. Range of wavelength of visible light is 4000 Å - 7000 Å. Find the range of frequency of visible light.
2. Speed of sound in air is 330 m/s. Frequency of Anoop's voice is 1000 Hz and of Shubham's voice is 2000 Hz. Find the wavelength corresponding to their voice.

Answers

1. 7.5×10^{14} Hz - 4.3×10^{14} Hz **2.** 0.33 m, 0.165 m

See hints on page 39.

Transverse Wave Speed on a String

Speed of transverse wave on a string is given by

$$v = \sqrt{\frac{T}{\mu}}$$

Here, μ = mass per unit length of the string

$$= \frac{m}{l} = \frac{mS}{lS} \qquad (S = \text{area of cross-section of the string})$$

$$\therefore \quad \mu = \left(\frac{m}{V}\right) S \qquad (V = \text{volume of string})$$

$$= \rho S \qquad (\rho = \text{density of string})$$

Hence, the above expression can also be written as

$$v = \sqrt{\frac{T}{\rho S}}$$

Proof

To see how the speed of a wave on a string depends on the tension and the linear density, consider a pulse sent down a taut string [Fig.(a)]. When the taut string is at rest at the equilibrium position, the tension in the string T is constant. Consider a small element of the string with a mass equal to $\Delta m = \mu \Delta x$. The mass element is at rest and in equilibrium and the force of tension of either side of the mass element is equal and opposite.

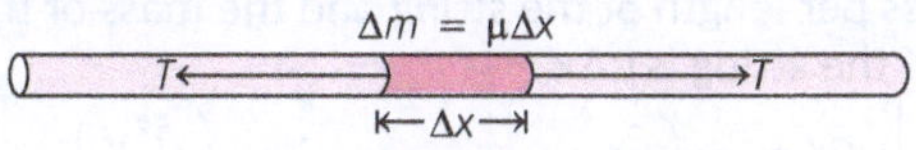

Fig. (a)

If you pluck a string under tension, a transverse wave moves in the positive x-direction as shown in Fig. (b). The mass element is small but is enlarged in the figure to make it visible.

The small mass element oscillates perpendicular to the wave motion as a result of the restoring forces (F_1 and F_2) provided by the string and does not move in the x-direction. The tension T in the string, which acts in the positive and negative x-direction, is approximately constant and is independent of position and time.

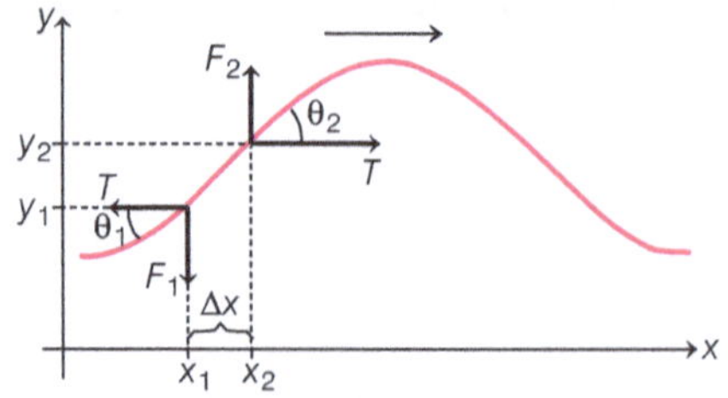

Fig. (b)

Assume that the inclination of the displaced string with respect to the horizontal axis is small. The net force on the element of the string, is the sum of the tension in the string and the restoring forces (F_1 and F_2).

The x-components of the force of tension is cancelled, so the net force is equal to the sum of the y-components of the force. The magnitude of the x-component of the force is equal to the horizontal force of tension of the string T as shown in Fig. (b).

To obtain the y-components of the force, note that $\tan\theta_1 = -\frac{F_1}{T}$ and $\tan\theta_2 = \frac{F_2}{T}$. The $\tan\theta$ is equal to the slope of a function at a point, which is equal to the partial derivative of y with respect to x at that point. Therefore, $\frac{F_1}{T}$ is equal to the negative slope of the string at x_1 and $\frac{F_2}{T}$ is equal to the slope of the string at x_2.

$$\frac{F_1}{T} = -\left(\frac{\partial y}{\partial x}\right)_{x_1} \qquad \text{...(i)}$$

and

$$\frac{F_2}{T} = \left(\frac{\partial y}{\partial x}\right)_{x_2} \qquad \text{...(ii)}$$

The net force on the small mass element can be written as

$$F_{net} = F_1 + F_2 = T\left[\left(\frac{\partial y}{\partial x}\right)_{x_2} - \left(\frac{\partial y}{\partial x}\right)_{x_1}\right] \qquad \text{...(iii)}$$

Using Newton's second law, the net force is equal to the mass times the acceleration. The linear density of the string μ is the mass per length of the string and the mass of the portion of the string is $\mu\Delta x$,

$$\therefore \quad T\left[\left(\frac{\partial y}{\partial x}\right)_{x_2} - \left(\frac{\partial y}{\partial x}\right)_{x_1}\right] = \Delta ma = \mu\Delta x\left(\frac{\partial^2 y}{\partial t^2}\right) \qquad \text{...(iv)}$$

Dividing by $T\Delta x$ and taking the limit as Δx approaches zero,

$$\lim_{\Delta x \to 0} \frac{\left[\left(\frac{\partial y}{\partial x}\right)_{x_2} - \left(\frac{\partial y}{\partial x}\right)_{x_1}\right]}{\Delta x} = \frac{\mu}{T}\frac{\partial^2 y}{\partial t^2}$$

$$\frac{\partial^2 y}{\partial x^2} = \frac{\mu}{T}\frac{\partial^2 y}{\partial t^2} \quad \text{or} \quad \left(\frac{\partial^2 y}{\partial t^2}\right) = \left(\frac{T}{\mu}\right)\left(\frac{\partial^2 y}{\partial x^2}\right)$$

Note *You will learn the above mathematical part in Mathematics.*

Now, comparing this equation will the standard wave equation,

$$\left(\frac{\partial^2 y}{\partial t^2}\right) = v^2\left(\frac{\partial^2 y}{\partial x^2}\right), \text{ we get } v = \sqrt{\frac{T}{\mu}}$$

Longitudinal Wave Speed in Three States

Speed of longitudinal wave through a gas (or a liquid) is given by

$$v = \sqrt{\frac{B}{\rho}}$$

Here, B = Bulk modulus of the gas (or liquid)

and ρ = density of the gas (or liquid)

Now Newton, who first deduced this relation for v, assumed that during the passage of a sound wave through a gas (or air), the temperature of the gas remains constant, i.e. sound wave travels under isothermal conditions and hence took B to be the isothermal elasticity of the gas and which is equal to its pressure p. So, **Newton's** formula for the velocity of a sound wave (or a longitudinal wave) in a gaseous medium becomes

$$v = \sqrt{\frac{p}{\rho}}$$

If, however, we calculate the velocity of sound in air at NTP with the help of this formula by substituting.

$$p = 1.01 \times 10^5 \text{ N/m}^2 \quad \text{and} \quad \rho = 1.29 \text{ kg/m}^3$$

then v comes out to be nearly 280 m/s. Actually, the velocity of sound in air at NTP as measured by Newton himself, is found to be 332 m/s. Newton could not explain this large discrepancy between his theoretical and experimental results.

Laplace after 140 years correctly argued that a sound wave passes through a gas (or air) very rapidly. So, adiabatic conditions are developed. So, he took B to be the adiabatic elasticity of the gas, which is equal to γp where γ is the ratio of C_p (molar heat capacity at constant pressure) and C_V (molar heat capacity at constant volume). Thus, Newton's formula as corrected by Laplace becomes

$$v = \sqrt{\frac{\gamma p}{\rho}}$$

For air, $\gamma = 1.41$, so that in air, $v = \sqrt{\frac{1.41\,p}{\rho}}$

which gives 331.6 m/s as the velocity of sound (in air) at NTP which is in agreement with Newton's experimental result.

Speed of longitudinal wave in a thin rod or wire is given by

$$v = \sqrt{\frac{Y}{\rho}}$$

Here, Y is the Young's modulus of elasticity.

Note *In the chapter of sound wave, we will discuss longitudinal wave speed in detail (with proof and examples). In the present chapter, we are taking examples of only transverse wave speed on a string.*

Summary

Wave Speed

(i) Speed of transverse wave on a stretched wire

$$v = \sqrt{\frac{T}{\mu}} = \sqrt{\frac{T}{\rho S}}$$

(ii) Speed of longitudinal wave

$$v = \sqrt{\frac{E}{\rho}}$$

$E =$ modulus of elasticity

(a) In solids, $E = Y =$ Young's modulus of elasticity

$$\therefore \quad v = \sqrt{\frac{Y}{\rho}}$$

$E =$ modulus of elasticity

(b) In liquids, $E = B =$ Bulk modulus of elasticity

$$\therefore \quad v = \sqrt{\frac{B}{\rho}}$$

(c) In gases, $E =$ adiabatic bulk modulus $= \gamma p$

$$\therefore \quad v = \sqrt{\frac{\gamma p}{\rho}}$$

Example 2 One end of 12.0 m long rod with a total mass of 0.9 kg is fastened to a fixed support. A cord attached to the other end passes over a pulley and supports an object with a mass of 5.0 kg. The rod is struck a transverse blow at one end. Find the time required for the pulse to reach the other end. ($g = 9.8\ \text{m/s}^2$)

Assume that tension in the rod is constant.

Sol. Tension in the rod $AB, T = mg$

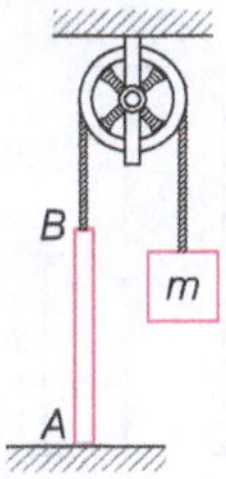

or $\quad T = (5.0)(9.8) = 49\ \text{N}$

Mass per unit length of rod,

$$\mu = \frac{0.9}{12} = 0.075\ \text{kg/m}$$

$\therefore$ Speed of transverse wave on rod,

$$v = \sqrt{\frac{T}{\mu}} = \sqrt{\frac{49}{0.075}} = 25.56\ \text{m/s}$$

$\therefore$ The required time is, $t = \frac{AB}{v} = \frac{12}{25.56} = 0.47\ \text{s}$ **Ans.**

Example 3 A wire of uniform cross-section is stretched between two points 100 cm apart. The wire is fixed at one end and a weight is hung over a pulley at the other end. A weight of 9 kg produces a fundamental frequency of 750 Hz.

(a) What is the velocity of the wave in wire?

(b) If the weight is reduced to 4 kg, what is the velocity of wave?

Note *Fundamental frequency is given by*

$$f = \frac{v}{2L}$$

Sol. (a) $L = 100\ \text{cm}$, $f_1 = 750\ \text{Hz}$

$$v_1 = 2Lf_1 = 2 \times 100 \times 750$$
$$= 150000\ \text{cms}^{-1} = 1500\ \text{ms}^{-1}$$ **Ans.**

(b) $v_1 = \sqrt{\frac{T_1}{\mu}}$ and $v_2 = \sqrt{\frac{T_2}{\mu}}$

$$\frac{v_2}{v_1} = \sqrt{\frac{T_2}{T_1}} = \sqrt{\frac{m_2 g}{m_1 g}} = \sqrt{\frac{m_2}{m_1}}$$

$$\therefore \quad \frac{v_2}{1500} = \sqrt{\frac{4}{9}}$$

$$\therefore \quad v_2 = 1000\ \text{ms}^{-1}$$ **Ans.**

INTRODUCTORY Exercise 2

1. Figure shows a string of linear mass density $1.0\ \text{g cm}^{-1}$ on which a wave pulse is travelling. Find the time taken by the pulse in travelling through a distance of 50 cm on the string. Take $g = 10\ \text{ms}^{-2}$.

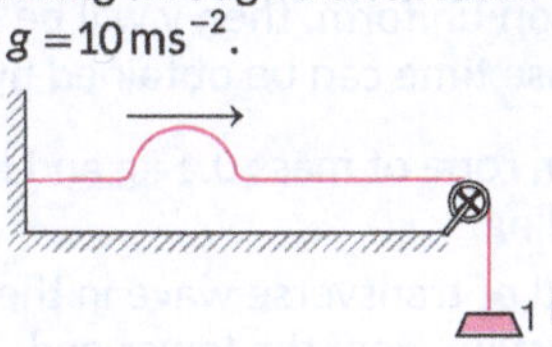

2. A steel wire of length 64 cm weighs 5 g. If it is stretched by a force of 8 N, what would be the speed of a transverse wave passing on it?

3. Two blocks each having a mass of 3.2 kg are connected by a wire CD and the system is suspended from the ceiling by another wire AB. The linear mass density of the wire AB is $10\ \text{gm}^{-1}$ and that of CD is $8\ \text{gm}^{-1}$. Find the speed of a transverse wave pulse produced in AB and in CD.

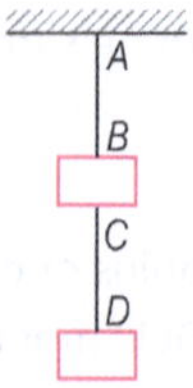

4. In the arrangement shown in figure, the string has a mass of 4.5 g. How much time will it take for a transverse disturbance produced at the floor to reach the pulley? Take $g = 10\ \text{ms}^{-2}$.

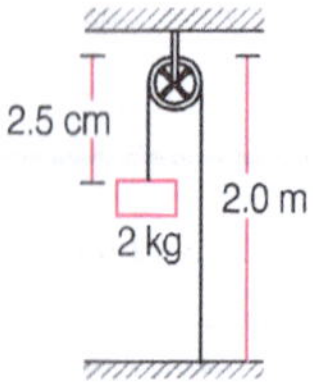

5. A copper wire 2.4 mm in diameter is 3 m long and is used to suspend a 2 kg mass from a beam. If a transverse disturbance is sent along the wire by striking it lightly with a pencil, how fast will the disturbance travel? The density of copper is $8920\ \text{kg/m}^3$.

6. One end of a horizontal rope is attached to a prong of an electrically driven tuning fork that vibrates at 120 Hz. The other end passes over a pulley and supports a 1.50 kg mass. The linear mass density of the rope is 0.0550 kg/m.
(a) What is the speed of a transverse wave on the rope?
(b) What is the wavelength?
(c) How would your answers to parts (a) and (b) change if the mass were increased to 3.00 kg?

Answers

1. 0.05 s **2.** $32\ \text{ms}^{-1}$
3. $79\ \text{ms}^{-1}$ and $63\ \text{ms}^{-1}$
4. 0.02 s approximately
5. 22 m/s
6. (a) 16.3 m/s (b) 0.136 m (c) both increase by $\sqrt{2}$ times

See hints on page 39.

Typed Problems

Type 1. *Based on transverse wave speed on a string.*

Concept

(i) We know that transverse wave speed is given by

$$v = \sqrt{\frac{T}{\mu}} \quad \text{or} \quad \sqrt{\frac{T}{\rho S}}$$

(ii) If tension is uniform, then v is also uniform and we can calculate the time taken by the wave pulse in travelling from one point to another point by the direct relation

$$t = \frac{\text{distance}}{\text{speed}}$$

If tension is non-uniform, then v will be non-uniform and in that case time can be obtained by integration.

Ex. 1 A uniform rope of mass 0.1 kg and length 2.45 m hangs from a ceiling.
(a) Find the speed of transverse wave in the rope at a point 0.5 m distant from the lower end.
(b) Calculate the time taken by a transverse wave to travel the full length of the rope.

Sol. (a) As the string has mass and it is suspended vertically, tension in it will be different at different points. For a point at a distance x from the free end, tension will be due to the weight of the string below it. So, if m is the mass of string of length l, the mass of length x of the string will be $\left(\frac{m}{l}\right)x$.

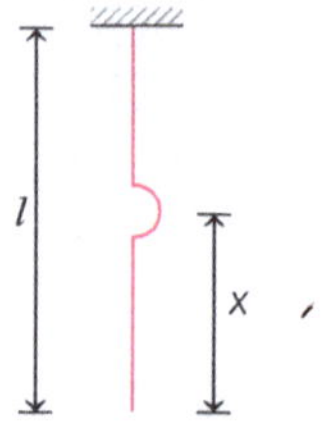

$$\therefore \quad T = \left(\frac{m}{l}\right)xg = \mu xg \qquad \left(\because \frac{m}{l} = \mu\right)$$

$$\therefore \quad \frac{T}{\mu} = xg$$

$$\text{or} \quad v = \sqrt{\frac{T}{\mu}} = \sqrt{xg} \qquad \text{...(i)}$$

At $x = 0.5$ m, $v = \sqrt{0.5 \times 9.8} = 2.21$ m/s

(b) From Eq. (i), we can see that velocity of the wave is different at different points. So, if at point x the wave travels a distance dx in time dt, then

$$dt = \frac{dx}{v} = \frac{dx}{\sqrt{gx}}$$

$$\therefore \quad \int_0^t dt = \int_0^l \frac{dx}{\sqrt{gx}}$$

$$\text{or} \quad t = 2\sqrt{\frac{l}{g}} = 2\sqrt{\frac{2.45}{9.8}}$$

$$= 1.0\ \text{s}$$

Ans.

Miscellaneous Examples

Ex. 2 A block of mass $M = 2$ kg is suspended from a string AB of mass 6 kg as shown in figure. A transverse wave pulse of wavelength $\lambda_0 (= 6 \text{ cm})$ is produced at point A. Find its wavelength while reaching at point B. **(2022 Main)**

Concept

While moving from B to A, tension will increase. So, wave speed will also increase (as $v = \sqrt{T/\mu}$). Frequency will remain unchanged because it depends on source. Therefore, wavelength will also increase (as $\lambda = \frac{v}{f}$ or $\lambda \propto v$).

Sol. $\lambda = \frac{v}{f} = \frac{\sqrt{T/\mu}}{f}$

or $\lambda \propto \sqrt{T}$ (as μ and f are constants)

$\therefore \quad \frac{\lambda_B}{\lambda_A} = \sqrt{\frac{T_B}{T_A}}$

$\therefore \quad \lambda_B = \left(\sqrt{\frac{T_B}{T_A}}\right)\lambda_A$

$= \left[\sqrt{\frac{(2+6)g}{2g}}\right]$

$= 2\lambda_0$

$= (2)(6) = 12 \text{ cm}$ **Ans.**

Ex. 3 A wave moves with speed 300 m/s on a wire which is under a tension of 500 N. Find how much tension must be changed to increase the speed to 312 m/s?

Sol. Speed of a transverse wave on a wire is,

$$v = \sqrt{\frac{T}{\mu}} \quad \text{...(i)}$$

Differentiating with respect to tension, we have

$$\frac{dv}{dT} = \frac{1}{2\sqrt{\mu T}} \quad \text{...(ii)}$$

Dividing Eq. (ii) by Eq. (i), we have

$$\frac{dv}{v} = \frac{1}{2}\frac{dT}{T} \quad \text{or} \quad dT = (2T)\frac{dv}{v}$$

Substituting the proper values, we have

$$dT \text{ or } \Delta T = \frac{(2)(500)(312 - 300)}{300}$$

$= 40$ N **Ans.**

i.e. tension should be increased by 40 N.

MODULE 4 Exercise

Assertion and Reason

See directions on page 14.

1. **Assertion :** Wave speed is given by $v = f\lambda$. If frequency f is doubled, v will become two times.

   Reason : For given conditions of medium wave speed remains constant.

2. **Assertion :** Two strings shown in figure have the same tension. Speed of transverse waves in string-1 will be more.

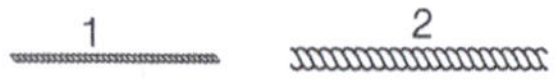

   Reason : $v \propto \dfrac{1}{\sqrt{\mu}}$, Here μ is mass per unit length of string.

Single Correct Option

3. The equation of a transverse wave propagating in a string is given by

$$y = 0.02 \sin (x + 30t)$$

   where, x and y are in metre and t is in second.

   If linear density of the string is 1.3×10^{-4} kg/m, then the tension in the string is

   (a) 0.12 N (b) 1.2 N (c) 12 N (d) 120 N

4. A rope of length L and mass M hangs freely from the ceiling. If the time taken by a tranverse wave to travel from the bottom to the top of the rope is T, then time to cover first half length is

   (a) T (b) $T\left(\dfrac{\sqrt{2}-1}{\sqrt{2}}\right)$

   (c) $\dfrac{T}{\sqrt{2}}$ (d) $\dfrac{T}{2}$

5. Both the strings, shown in figure are made of same material and have same cross-section. The pulleys are light. The wave speed in the string AB is v_1 and in CD, it is v_2. Then v_1/v_2 is

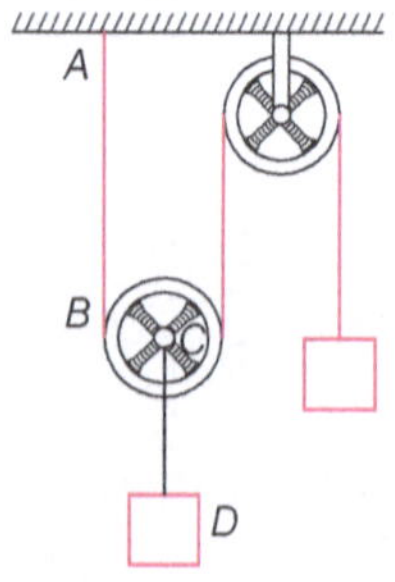

   (a) 1 (b) 2 (c) $\sqrt{2}$ (d) $\dfrac{1}{\sqrt{2}}$

6. A uniform string of length 20 m is suspended from a rigid support. A short wave pulse is introduced at its lowest end. It starts moving up the string. The time taken to reach the support is (Take, $g = 10\ \text{ms}^{-2}$) **(2016 Main)**

   (a) $2\pi\sqrt{2}$ s (b) 2 s (c) $2\sqrt{2}$ s (d) $\sqrt{2}$ s

Multiple Correct Options

7. A block M hangs vertically at the bottom end of a uniform rope of constant mass per unit length. The top end of the rope is attached to a fixed rigid support at O. A transverse wave pulse (Pulse I) of wavelength λ_0 is produced at point O on the rope. The pulse takes time T_{OA} to reach point A. If the wave pulse of wavelength λ_0 is produced at point A (Pulse 2) without disturbing the position of M it takes time T_{AO} to reach point O. **(2017 Adv.)**

   Which of the following options is/are correct?

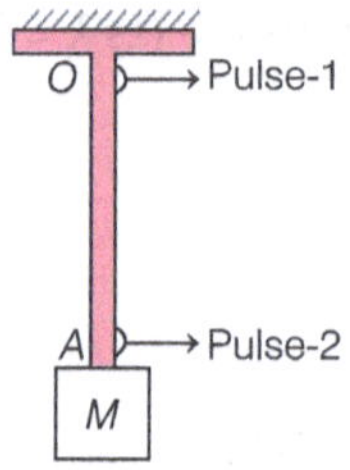

   (a) The time $T_{AO} = T_{OA}$

   (b) The velocities of the two pulses (Pulse 1 and Pulse 2) are the same at the midpoint of rope

   (c) The wavelength of Pulse 1 becomes longer when it reaches point A

   (d) The velocity of any pulse along the rope is independent of its frequency and wavelength

Subjective Questions

8. A non-uniform wire of length L and mass M has a variable linear mass density given by $\mu = kx$, where x is distance from one end of wire and k is a constant. Find the time taken by a pulse starting at one end to reach the other end when the tension in the wire is T.

9. A loop of rope is whirled at a high angular velocity ω, so that it becomes a taut circle of radius R. A kink develops in the whirling rope.

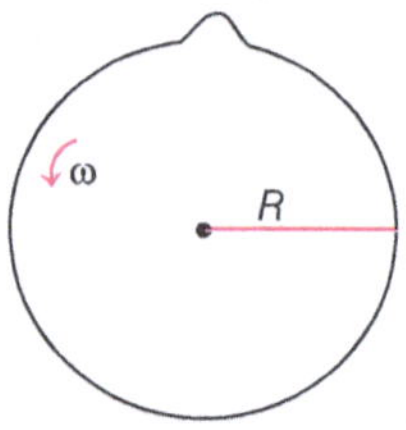

(a) Show that the speed of the kink in the rope is $v = \omega R$.
(b) Under what conditions does the kink remain stationary relative to an observer on the ground?

10. A flexible steel cable of total length L and mass per unit length μ hangs vertically from a support at one end. (a) Show that the speed of a transverse wave down the cable is $v = \sqrt{g\,(L - x)}$, where x is measured from the support.
(b) How long will it take for a wave to travel down the cable?

11. Calculate the speed of a transverse wave in a wire of 1.0 mm^2 cross-section under a tension of 0.98 N. Density of the material of wire is 9.8×10^3 kg/m^3.

12. A copper wire is held at the two ends by rigid supports. At 30°C, the wire is just taut, with negligible tension. Find the speed of transverse waves in this wire at 10°C. Given, Young's modulus of copper $= 1.3 \times 10^{11}$ N/m^2. Coefficient of linear expansion of copper $= 1.7 \times 10^{-5}$ $°C^{-1}$.
Density of copper $= 9 \times 10^3$ kg/m^3. **(1979 JEE)**

Answers

1. (d) **2.** (d) **3.** (a) **4.** (c) **5.** (d) **6.** (c) **7.** (a, d) **8.** $\frac{2}{3}\sqrt{\frac{2ML}{T}}$

9. (b) The kink will be stationary with respect to the ground if it moves clockwise with respect to the rope.

10. (b) $t = 2\sqrt{\frac{L}{g}}$ **11.** 10 m/s **12.** 70.1 m/s

See hints on pages 39-40.

MODULE 5

Energy in Wave Motion

In a wave, many particles oscillate. In a sinusoidal wave, these oscillations are simple harmonic in nature. Each particle has some energy of oscillation. At the same time, energy transfer also takes place. Related to energy of oscillation and energy transfer, there are three terms, namely, energy density (u), power (P) and intensity (I).

Energy Density (u)

Energy of oscillation per unit volume is called energy density (u). Its SI unit is J/m^3. In case of SHM, energy of oscillation (of a single particle) is $E = \frac{1}{2} m\omega^2 A^2$. In a sinusoidal wave, each particle of the string oscillates simple harmonically. Therefore,

$$\text{Energy density} = \frac{\text{energy of oscillation}}{\text{volume}}$$

or $$u = \frac{E}{V} = \frac{\frac{1}{2} m\omega^2 A^2}{V}$$

But, $$\frac{m}{V} = \text{density or } \rho$$

$\therefore$ $$\boxed{u = \frac{1}{2}\rho\omega^2 A^2}$$

Power (P)

Energy transferred per unit time is called power. The expression of power is

$$\boxed{P = \frac{1}{2}\rho\omega^2 A^2 Sv}$$

Here, S is area of cross-section of the medium in which wave is travelling and v is the wave speed. SI unit of power is J/s or Watt. Now, let us derive the above expression for a sinusoidal travelling wave on a string. Area of cross-section of string is S and the wave speed is v.

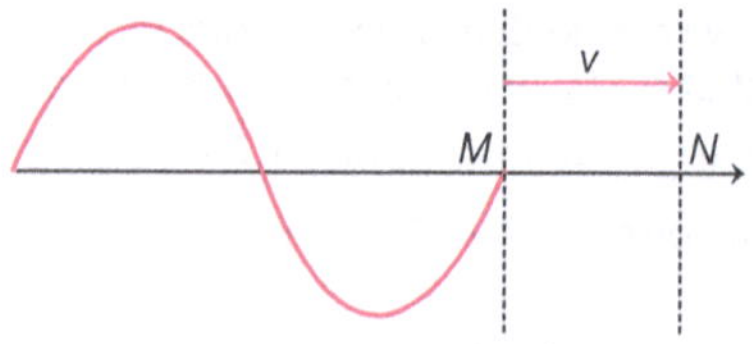

Suppose at time $t = 0$, wave is at point M. In 1 s, it will travel a distance v and it will reach at point N. Or, we can say that v new length of string will start oscillating. Area of cross-section of string is S. Therefore, in 1 s, Sv new volume of string will start oscillating. Energy of oscillation per unit volume is called energy density (u). So, (uSv) new energy will be added in 1 s. Or (uSv) energy will be transferred from the source per second. Energy transferred in one second is called power.

$\therefore$ $$P = uSv = \frac{1}{2}\rho\omega^2 A^2 Sv \qquad \left(\text{as } u = \frac{1}{2}\rho\omega^2 A^2\right)$$

or $$P = \frac{1}{2}\rho\omega^2 A^2 Sv$$

This is the desired expression of power.

Intensity (I)

Energy transferred per unit cross-sectional area per unit time is called intensity.

Thus,

$$I = \frac{\text{Energy transferred}}{(\text{time})(\text{cross-sectional area})} = \frac{\text{Power}}{\text{cross-sectional area}} = \frac{P}{S}$$

$$= \frac{\frac{1}{2}\rho\omega^2 A^2 Sv}{S}$$

or $$\boxed{I = \frac{1}{2}\rho\omega^2 A^2 v}$$

The SI unit of intensity is $J/s\text{-}m^2$ or $Watt/m^2$.

Important POINTS

- Although the above relations for power and intensity have been discussed for a transverse wave on a string, they hold good for other waves also.
- In SHM, potential energy is maximum (and kinetic energy is zero) at the extreme positions.
- For a string segment, the potential energy depends on the slope of the string and is maximum when the slope is maximum, which is at the equilibrium position of the segment. At the same position the kinetic energy is also maximum.

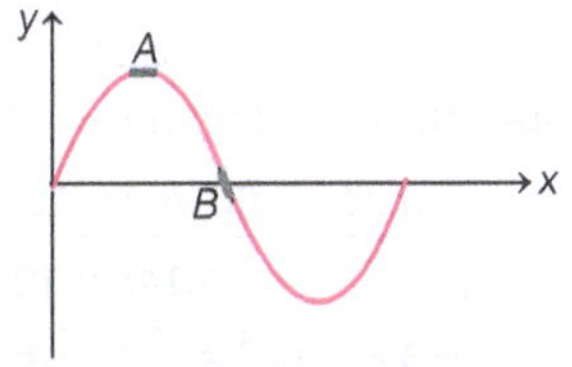

At A : Kinetic energy and potential energy both are zero.
At B : Kinetic energy and potential energy both are maximum.

- **Intensity due to a point source** If a point source emits wave uniformly in all directions, the energy at a distance r from the source is distributed uniformly on a spherical surface of radius r and area $S = 4\pi r^2$. If P is the power emitted by the source, the power per unit area at a distance r from the source is $\frac{P}{4\pi r^2}$. The average power per unit area that is incident perpendicular to the direction of propagation is called the intensity. Therefore,

$$I = \frac{P}{4\pi r^2}$$

or

$$\boxed{I \propto \frac{1}{r^2}}$$

- **Summary of Energy Density (u), Power (P) and Intensity (I) in Sine Wave**

(i) Energy density, $u = \frac{1}{2}\rho\omega^2 A^2$ = energy of oscillation per unit volume

(ii) Power, $P = \frac{1}{2}\rho\omega^2 A^2 S v$ = energy transferred per unit time

(iii) Intensity, $I = \frac{1}{2}\rho\omega^2 A^2 v$ = energy transferred per unit time per unit area

Example 1 A stretched string is forced to transmit transverse waves towards positive direction by means of an oscillator coupled to one end. The string has a diameter of 4 mm. The amplitude of the oscillation is 10^{-4} m and the frequency is 10 Hz. Tension in the string is 100 N and mass density of wire is 4.2×10^3 kg/m^3. Find

(a) the equation of the waves along the string

(b) the energy per unit volume of the wave

(c) the average energy flow per unit time across any section of the string and

(d) power required to drive the oscillator.

Sol. (a) Speed of transverse wave on the string is

$$v = \sqrt{\frac{T}{\rho S}} \qquad (\text{as } \mu = \rho S)$$

Substituting the values, we have

$$v = \sqrt{\frac{100}{(4.2 \times 10^3)\left(\frac{\pi}{4}\right)(4.0 \times 10^{-3})^2}}$$

$$= 43.53 \text{ m/s}$$

$$\omega = 2\pi f = 20\pi = 62.83 \text{ rad/s}$$

$$k = \frac{\omega}{v} = 1.44 \text{ m}^{-1}$$

$\therefore$ Equation of the waves along the string,

$$y(x, t) = A \sin(kx - \omega t)$$

$$= (10^{-4} \text{ m}) \sin[(1.44 \text{ m}^{-1})\, x - (62.83 \text{ rad/s})\, t]$$

Ans.

(b) Energy per unit volume of the string,

$$u = \text{energy density} = \frac{1}{2}\rho\omega^2 A^2$$

Substituting the values, we have

$$u = \left(\frac{1}{2}\right)(4.2 \times 10^3)(62.83)^2(10^{-4})^2$$

$$= 8.29 \times 10^{-2} \text{ J/m}^3$$

Ans.

(c) Average energy flow per unit time, P = power

$$= \left(\frac{1}{2}\rho\omega^2 A^2\right)(Sv) = (u)(Sv)$$

Substituting the values, we have

$$P = (8.29 \times 10^{-2})\left(\frac{\pi}{4}\right)(4.0 \times 10^{-3})^2(43.53)$$

$$= 4.53 \times 10^{-5} \text{ J/s}$$

Ans.

(d) Therefore, power required to drive the oscillator is 4.53×10^{-5} W. **Ans.**

Example 2 A thin string is held at one end and oscillates vertically so that,

$$y(x = 0, t) = 8 \sin 4t \text{ (cm)}$$

Neglect the gravitational force. The string's linear mass density is 0.2 kg/m and its tension is 1 N. The string passes through a bath filled with 1 kg water. Due to friction heat is transferred to the bath. The heat transfer efficiency is 50%. Calculate how much time passes before the temperature of the bath rises one degree kelvin?

Sol. Comparing the given equation with equation of a travelling wave,

$$y = A \sin(kx \pm \omega t) \quad \text{at} \quad x = 0 \quad \text{we find,}$$

$$y = A \sin \omega t$$

$$\therefore \quad A = 8 \text{ cm} = 8 \times 10^{-2} \text{ m}$$

$$\omega = 4 \text{ rad/s}$$

Speed of travelling wave, $v = \sqrt{\frac{T}{\mu}} = \sqrt{\frac{1}{0.2}} = 2.236$ m/s

Further, $\rho S = \mu = 0.2$ kg/m

The average power over a period is

$$P = \frac{1}{2}(\rho S)\,\omega^2 A^2 v$$

Substituting the values, we have

$$P = \frac{1}{2}(0.2)(4)^2(8 \times 10^{-2})^2(2.236)$$

$$= 2.29 \times 10^{-2} \text{ J/s}$$

The power transferred to the bath is,

$$P' = 0.5P = 1.145 \times 10^{-2} \text{ J/s}$$

Now let, it takes t second to raise the temperature of 1 kg water by 1 degree kelvin. Then

$$P't = ms\Delta t$$

Here, s = specific heat of water $= 4.2 \times 10^3$ J/kg-°K

$$\therefore \quad t = \frac{ms\Delta t}{P'} = \frac{(1)(4.2 \times 10^3)(1)}{1.145 \times 10^{-2}}$$

$$= 3.6 \times 10^5 \text{ s}$$

$$\approx 4.2 \text{ day}$$

Ans.

MODULE 5 Exercise

Single Correct Option

1. Two waves represented by the following equations are travelling in the same medium.

$$y_1 = 5 \sin 2\pi(75t - 0.25x),$$
$$y_2 = 10 \sin 2\pi(150t - 0.50x)$$

The intensity ratio $\frac{I_1}{I_2}$ of the two waves is

(a) 1 : 2
(b) 1 : 4
(c) 1 : 8
(d) 1 : 16

Multiple Correct Options

2. For energy density, power and intensity of any wave choose the correct options.

(a) u = energy density $= \frac{1}{2}\rho\omega^2A^2$

(b) P = power $= \frac{1}{2}\rho\,\omega^2A^2v$

(c) I = intensity $= \frac{1}{2}\rho\,\omega^2A^2Sv$

(d) $I = \frac{P}{S}$

Match the Columns

3. For a travelling wave, match the following two columns.

	Column I		Column II
(a)	energy density	(p)	$[ML^2T^{-3}]$
(b)	power	(q)	$\frac{1}{2}\rho\omega^2A^2Sv$
(c)	intensity	(r)	$[M^0L^{-1}T]$
(d)	wave number	(s)	None

Subjective Questions

4. Spherical waves are emitted from a 1.0 W source in an isotropic non-absorbing medium. What is the wave intensity 1.0 m from the source?

5. A line source emits a cylindrical expanding wave. Assuming the medium absorbs no energy, find how the amplitude and intensity of the wave depend on the distance from the source?

6. A certain 120 Hz wave on a string has an amplitude of 0.160 mm. How much energy exists in an 80 g length of the string?

7. A taut string for which $\mu = 5.00 \times 10^{-2}$ kg/m is under a tension of 80.0 N. How much power must be supplied to the string to generate sinusoidal waves at a frequency of 60.0 Hz and an amplitude of 6.00 cm?

8. A 200 Hz wave with amplitude 1 mm travels on a long string of linear mass density 6 g/m kept under a tension of 60 N.
(a) Find the average power transmitted across a given point on the string.
(b) Find the total energy associated with the wave in a 2.0 m long portion of the string.

9. A transverse wave of amplitude 0.50 mm and frequency 100 Hz is produced on a wire stretched to a tension of 100 N . If the wave speed is 100 m/s. What average power is the source transmitting to the wire?

Answers

1. (d) **2.** (a,d)

3. (a) → s; (b) → p,q; (c) → s; (d) → s

4. $\frac{1}{4\pi}$ W/m^2 **5.** $A \propto \frac{1}{\sqrt{r}}, I \propto \frac{1}{r}$

6. 0.58 mJ **7.** 512 W

8. (a) 0.47 W (b) 9.4 mJ **9.** 49 mW

See hints on pages 40-41.

Unit Exercise (Cumulative)

Level 1

Fill in the Blanks

1. A plane progressive wave of frequency 25 Hz, amplitude 2.5×10^{-5} m and initial phase zero propagates along the negative x-direction with a velocity of 300 m/s. At any instant, the phase difference between the oscillations at two points 6 m apart along the line of propagation is ...... and the corresponding amplitude difference is ...... m. **(1997 JEE)**

2. A point source emits sound equally in all directions in a non-absorbing medium. Two points P and Q are at a distance 9 m and 25 m respectively from the source. The ratio of amplitudes of the waves at P and Q is .... **(1989 JEE)**

3. A travelling wave has the frequency ν and the particle displacement amplitude A. For the wave the particle velocity amplitude is .... and the particle acceleration amplitude is .... **(1983 JEE)**

True/False

4. A sound wave travelling in air is incident upon a plane water surface. The angle of incidence is 60°. Assuming Snell's law to be valid for sound waves, it follows that the sound wave will be refracted into water away from the normal. **(1984 JEE)**

Assertion and Reason

See directions on page 14.

5. **Assertion :** Mechanical transverse waves cannot travel in gaseous medium.
Reason : They do not possess modulus of rigidity.

6. **Assertion :** y-x graph of a transverse wave on a string is as shown in figure. At point A potential energy and kinetic energy both are minimum.

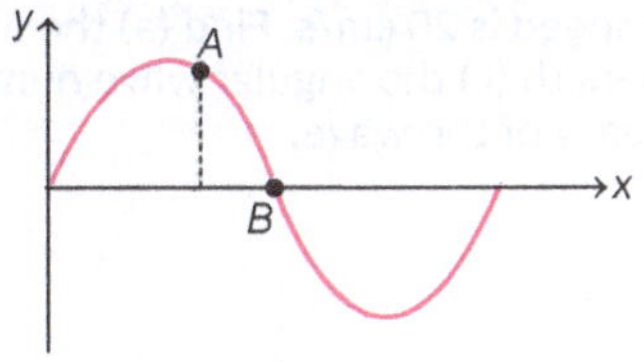

Reason : At point B kinetic energy and potential energy both are maximum.

Single Correct Option

7. A wave motion has the function $y = a_0 \sin(\omega t - kx)$. The graph in figure shows how the displacement y at a fixed point varies with time t. Which one of the labelled points shows a displacement equal to that at the position $x = \frac{\pi}{2k}$ at time $t = 0$?

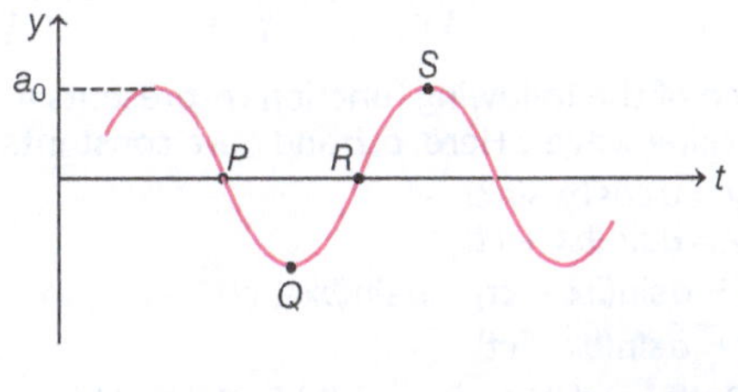

(a) P (b) Q (c) R (d) S

8. The speed of propagation of a wave in a medium is 300 m/s. The equation of motion of a point at $x = 0$ is given by $y = 0.04 \sin 600\pi t$ (metre). The displacement of a point $x = 75$ cm at $t = 0.01$ s is
(a) 0.02 m (b) 0.04 m (c) zero (d) 0.028 m

9. Transverse waves are generated in two uniform steel wires A and B by attaching their free ends to a fork of frequency 500 Hz. The diameter of wire A is half that of B and tension in wire A is half the tension in wire B. What is the ratio of velocities of waves in A and B?
(a) $1:2$ (b) $\sqrt{2}:1$ (c) $2:1$ (d) $1:\sqrt{2}$

10. The extension in a string, obeying Hooke's law is x. The speed of transverse wave in the stretched string is v. If the extension in the string is increased to $1.5x$, the speed of transverse wave will be
(a) 1.22 v (b) 0.61 v (c) 1.50 v (d) 0.75 v

11. Identify the figure, which correctly represents the given wave function

$$y = 2\sqrt{3} \sin \pi \left(x - 2t + \frac{1}{6} \right)$$

(a)

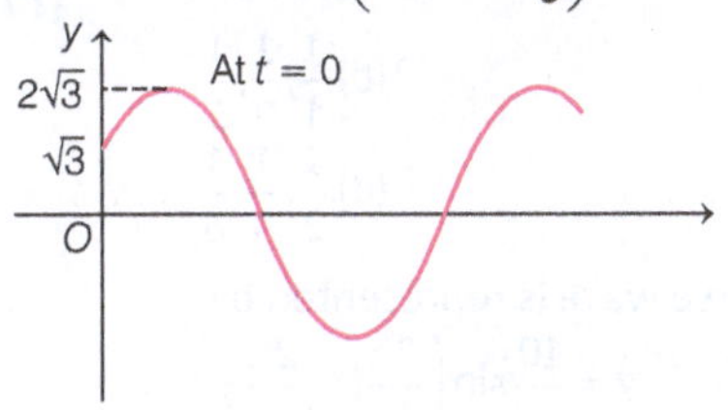

(b) 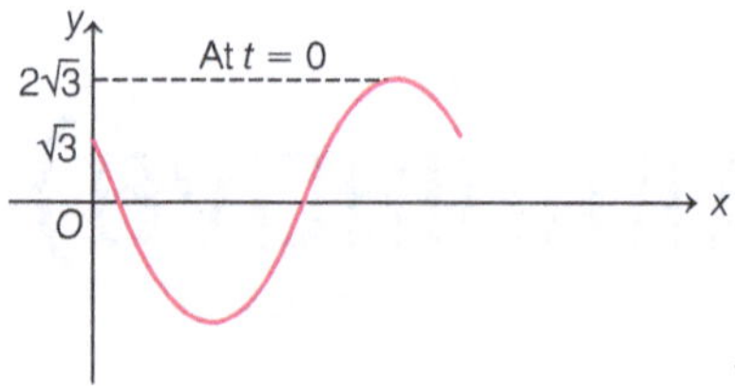

(c) Both graphs are possible
(d) None of the two graphs are possible

12. A metal string is fixed between two rigid supports. It is initially at negligible tension. Its Young's modulus is Y. Density is ρ and coefficient of thermal expansion is α. If it is now cooled through a temperature $= t$, transverse waves will move along it with speed

(a) $Y\sqrt{\frac{\alpha t}{\rho}}$ (b) $\alpha t\sqrt{\frac{Y}{\rho}}$ (c) $\sqrt{\frac{Y\alpha t}{\rho}}$ (d) $t\sqrt{\frac{Y\alpha}{\rho}}$

13. Which of the following functions represents a travelling wave ? Here, a, b and c are constants.
I. $y = a\cos bx \sin ct$
II. $y = a\sin(bx + ct)$
III. $y = a\sin(bx + ct) + a\sin(bx - ct)$
IV. $y = a\sin(bx - ct)$

(a) Both I and IV (b) Both I and III
(c) Both II and IV (d) Both II and III

14. A string has a mass 10 g and a length $L = 3$ m. Its two ends are tied to two walls a distance $d = 2$ m apart. Two blocks, each of mass $m = 2$ kg, are suspended from the string as shown in the figure. In what time will a wave pulse sent from a point P_1 reach point P_2?

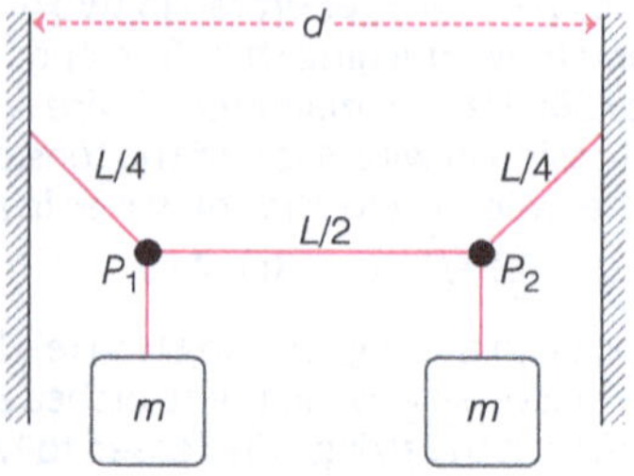

(a) 52.9 ms (b) 42.9 ms (c) 32.9 ms (d) 22.9 ms

15. For a transverse wave travelling along a straight line, the distance between two peaks (crests) is 5 m, while the distance between one crest and one trough is 1.5 m. The possible wavelengths (in m) of the waves are **(2020 Main)**

(a) 1, 3, 5, ... (b) $\frac{1}{1}, \frac{1}{3}, \frac{1}{5}, \ldots$
(c) 1, 2, 3, ... (d) $\frac{1}{2}, \frac{1}{4}, \frac{1}{6}, \ldots$

16. A transverse wave is represented by

$$y = \frac{10}{\pi}\sin\left(\frac{2\pi}{T}t - \frac{2\pi}{\lambda}x\right)\text{cm}$$

For what value of the wavelength the wave velocity is twice the maximum particle velocity? **(2014 Main)**

(a) 40 cm (b) 20 cm (c) 10 cm (d) 60 cm

Multiple Correct Options

17. For the transverse wave equation $y = A\sin(\pi x + \pi t)$, choose the correct options at $t = 0$
(a) points at $x = 0$ and $x = 1$ are at mean positions
(b) points at $x = 0.5$ and $x = 1.5$ have maximum accelerations
(c) points at $x = 0.5$ and $x = 1.5$ are at rest
(d) the given wave is travelling in negative x-direction

18. As a wave propagates **(1999 JEE)**
(a) the wave intensity remains constant for a plane wave
(b) the wave intensity decreases as the inverse of the distance due to a line source
(c) the wave intensity decreases as the inverse square of the distance from the source for a spherical wave
(d) intensity due to a line source is constant at all points

Subjective Questions

19. A harmonically moving transverse wave on a string has a maximum particle velocity and acceleration of 3m/s and 90 m/s^2 respectively. Velocity of the wave is 20 m/s. Find the waveform. **(2005 JEE)**

20. The equation of a travelling plane sound wave has the form $y = 60\cos(1800t - 5.3x)$, where y is expressed in micrometres, t in seconds, and x in metres. Find:
(a) the ratio of the displacement amplitude, with which the particles of medium oscillate, to the wavelength;
(b) the velocity oscillation amplitude of particles of the medium and its ratio to the wave propagation velocity. **(4.155 Irodov)**

21. A wave pulse is travelling on a string with a speed v towards the positive x-axis. The shape of the string at $t = 0$ is given by $y(x) = A\sin(x/a)$, where A and a are constants.
(a) What are the dimensions of A and a?
(b) Write the equation of the wave for a general time t, if the wave speed is v.

22. Figure shows a plot of the transverse displacement of the particle of a string at $t = 0$ through which a travelling wave is passing in the positive x-direction. The wave speed is 20 cm/s. Find (a) the amplitude (b) the wavelength (c) the angular wave number and (d) the frequency of the wave.

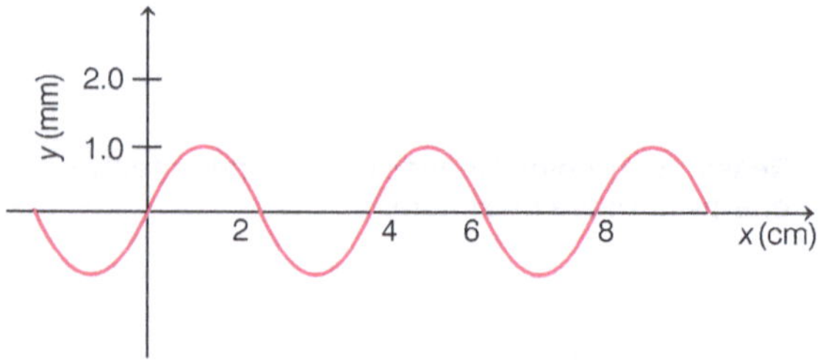

23. Two wires of different densities but same area of cross-section are soldered together at one end and are stretched to a tension T. The velocity of a transverse wave in the first wire is double of that in the second wire. Find the ratio of the density of the first wire to that of the second wire.

24. Two long strings A and B, each having linear mass density 1.2×10^{-2} kg/m are stretched by different tensions 4.8 N and 7.5 N respectively and are kept parallel to each other with their left ends at $x = 0$. Wave pulses are produced on the strings at the left ends at $t = 0$ on string A and at $t = 20$ ms on string B. When and where will the pulse on B overtake that on A?

25. A sinusoidal transverse wave travels on a string. The string has length 8.00 m and mass 6.00 g. The wave speed is 30.0 m/s and the wavelength is 0.200 m. (a) If the wave is to have an average power of 50.0 W, what must be the amplitude of the wave? (b) For this same string, if the amplitude and wavelength are the same as in part (a) what is the average power for the wave if the tension is increased such that the wave speed is doubled?

26. Three pieces of string, each of length L, are joined together end-to-end, to make a combined string of length $3L$. The first piece of string has mass per unit length μ_1, the second piece has mass per unit length $\mu_2 = 4\mu_1$ and the third piece has mass per unit length $\mu_3 = \mu_1/4$.
   (a) If the combined string is under tension F, how much time does it take a transverse wave to travel the entire length $3L$? Give your answer in terms of L, F and μ_1.
   (b) Does your answer to part (a) depend on the order in which the three piece are joined together? Explain.

Integer Type Question

27. A certain 120 Hz wave on a string has an amplitude of 0.16 mm. The energy that exists in an 80 g length of the string is $(0.29)\beta$ mJ. Find the value of β.

Level 2

Single Correct Option

28. A 100 Hz sinusoidal wave is travelling in the positive x-direction along a string with a linear mass density of 3.5×10^{-3} kg/m and a tension of 35 N. At time $t = 0$, the point $x = 0$, has maximum displacement in the positive y-direction. Next when this point has zero displacement, the slope of the string is $\pi/20$. Which of the following expression represent(s) the displacement of string as a function of x (in metre) and t (in second)?
   (a) $y = 0.025 \cos(200\pi t - 2\pi x)$
   (b) $y = 0.5 \cos(200\pi t - 2\pi x)$
   (c) $y = 0.025 \cos(100\pi t - 10\pi x)$
   (d) $y = 0.5 \cos(100\pi t - 10\pi x)$

29. Vibrations of period 0.25 s propagate along a straight line at a velocity of 48 cm/s. One second after the emergence of vibrations at the initial point, displacement of the point, 47 cm from it, is found to be 3 cm. [Assume that at initial point particle is in its mean position at $t = 0$ and moving upwards]. Then,
   (a) amplitude of vibrations is 6 cm
   (b) amplitude of vibrations is $3\sqrt{2}$ cm
   (c) amplitude of vibrations is 3 cm
   (d) None of the above

30. A man generates a symmetrical pulse in a string by moving his hand up and down. At $t = 0$, the point in his hand moves downwards from mean position. The pulse travels with speed 3 m/s on the string and his hand passes 6 times in each second from the mean position. Then, the point on the string at a distance 3 m will reach its upper extreme first time at $t =$
   (a) 1.25 s
   (b) 1 s
   (c) $\frac{11}{12}$ s
   (d) $\frac{23}{24}$ s

Passage Based Questions

Passage 1 (Q.31 to Q.34)

Figure shows two snapshots of a travelling wave on a string of mass per unit length $\mu = 0.25$ kg m^{-1}. The first snap is taken at $t = 0$ s and the second is taken at $t = 0.05$ s.

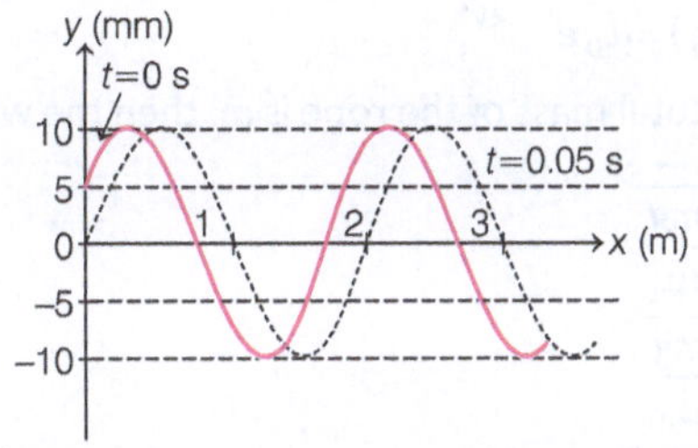

31. The speed of the wave is
   (a) 5 ms^{-1} (b) $\frac{20}{3}$ ms^{-1}
   (c) $\frac{5}{3}$ ms^{-1} (d) $\frac{10}{3}$ ms^{-1}

32. The wavelength and frequency are respectively
   (a) 1m, $\frac{10}{3}$ Hz (b) 2 m, $\frac{10}{3}$ Hz
   (c) 2 m, $\frac{5}{3}$ Hz (d) 1 m, $\frac{5}{3}$ Hz

33. The maximum speed of the particle is
   (a) $\frac{\pi}{20}$ms^{-1} (b) $\frac{\pi}{30}$ms^{-1}
   (c) $\frac{\pi}{10}$ms^{-1} (d) $\frac{\pi}{5}$ms^{-1}

34. The equation of the wave is

(a) $y = 10 \times 10^{-3} \sin\left(\frac{10\pi}{3}t - \pi x + \frac{5\pi}{6}\right)$

(b) $y = 10 \times 10^{-3} \sin\left(\frac{10\pi}{3}t + \pi x - \frac{5\pi}{6}\right)$

(c) $y = 10 \times 10^{-3} \sin\left(\frac{10\pi}{3}t - \pi x\right)$

(d) $y = 10 \times 10^{-3} \cos\left(\frac{10\pi}{3}t - \pi x\right)$

Passage 2 (Q.35 to Q.38)

The wave speed (v) in a uniform freely hanging rope varies with the distance y from the top. The tension T varies while the mass per unit length μ remains same. We want to design a rope in which v is independent of y. For such a rope μ cannot be constant.

35. Let μ_0 is the mass per unit length at the top of the rope ($y = 0$). If the rope is infinitely long and the velocity of wave is constant throughout it, then

(a) $\mu(y) = \mu_0 e^{\left(-\frac{g}{v^2} \cdot y\right)}$

(b) $\mu(y) = \frac{\mu_0}{2} e^{\left(-\frac{g}{v^2} \cdot y\right)}$

(c) $\mu(y) = \frac{\mu_0}{2} e^{\left(-\frac{2g}{v^2} \cdot y\right)}$

(d) $\mu(y) = \mu_0 e^{\left(-\frac{g}{2v^2} \cdot y\right)}$

36. If the total mass of the rope is m, then the wave speed is

(a) $\sqrt{\frac{mg}{2\mu_0}}$

(b) $\sqrt{\frac{mg}{\mu_0}}$

(c) $\sqrt{\frac{2mg}{\mu_0}}$

(d) $\frac{1}{2}\sqrt{\frac{mg}{\mu_0}}$

37. μ, in terms of μ_0, m and y only, is

(a) $\mu_0 e^{-\mu_0 y/2m}$

(b) $\frac{\mu_0}{2} e^{-\mu_0 y/m}$

(c) $\mu_0 e^{-\mu_0 y/m}$

(d) None of the above

38. Suppose we cut the rope at length L (from the top). We can still have constant wave speed on the finite rope, if we hang a mass m_0 on the end provided

(a) $m_0 = \frac{m}{2} e^{-\mu_0 L/m}$

(b) $m_0 = m e^{-\mu_0 L/2m}$

(c) $m_0 = \frac{m}{2} e^{-\mu_0 L/2m}$

(d) $m_0 = m e^{-\mu_0 L/m}$

Subjective Questions

39. The figure shows a snap photograph of a vibrating string at $t = 0$. The particle P is observed moving up with velocity $20\sqrt{3}$ cm/s. The tangent at P makes an angle $60°$ with x-axis.

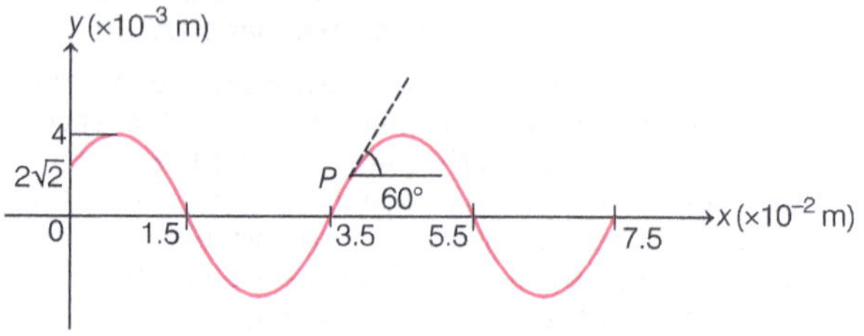

(a) Find the direction in which the wave is moving.

(b) Write the equation of the wave.

(c) The total energy carried by the wave per cycle of the string. Assuming that the mass per unit length of the string is 50 g/m.

40. A long string having a cross-sectional area $0.80\ \text{mm}^2$ and density $12.5\ \text{g/cm}^3$ is subjected to a tension of 64 N along the positive x-axis. One end of this string is attached to a vibrator at $x = 0$ moving in transverse direction at a frequency of 20 Hz. At $t = 0$, the source is at a maximum displacement $y = 1.0$ cm.

(a) Find the speed of the wave travelling on the string.

(b) Write the equation for the wave.

(c) What is the displacement of the particle of the string at $x = 50$ cm at time $t = 0.05$ s?

(d) What is the velocity of this particle at this instant?

41. One end of two identical springs, each of force constant 0.5 N/m are attached on the opposite sides of a wooden block of mass 0.01 kg. The other ends of the springs are connected to separate rigid supports such that the springs are unstretched and are collinear in a horizontal plane. To the wooden piece is fixed a pointer which touches a vertically moving plane paper. The wooden piece kept on a smooth horizontal table is now displaced by 0.02 m along the line of springs and released. If the speed of paper is 0.1 m/s, find the equation of the path traced by the pointer on the paper and the distance between two consecutive maximas on this path.

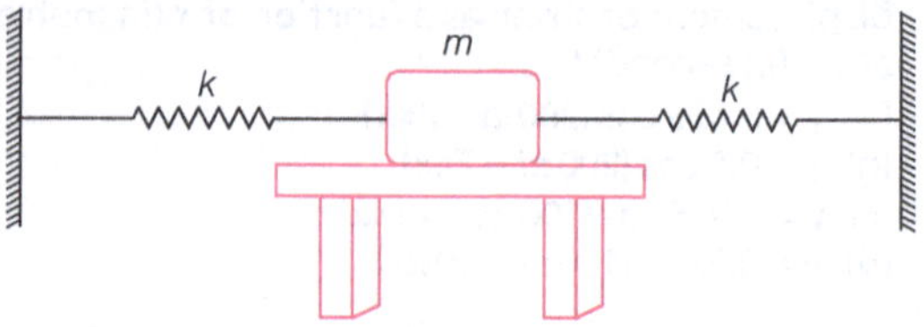

42. A uniform rope with length L and mass m is held at one end and whirled in a horizontal circle with angular velocity ω. You can ignore the force of gravity on the rope. Find the time required for a transverse wave to travel from one end of the rope to the other.

Hint : $\int \frac{dx}{\sqrt{a^2 - x^2}} = \sin^{-1}\left(\frac{x}{a}\right)$

43. A plane wave $y = A\cos(\omega t - kx)$ propagates in a homogeneous elastic medium. For the moment $t = 0$ draw **(4.156 Irodov)**

(a) the plots of $y, \frac{\partial y}{\partial t}, \frac{\partial y}{\partial x}$ versus x;

(b) the velocity direction of the particles of the medium at the points where $y = 0$, for the cases of longitudinal and transverse waves;

(c) the approximate plot of density distribution $\rho(x)$ of the medium for the case of longitudinal waves.

Integer Type Question

44. A string of length 0.3 m and mass 10^{-2} kg is clamped at both its ends. The tension in the string is 1.2 N. When a pulse travels along the string, the shape the string is found to be the same at times t and $t + \Delta t$. The minimum value of Δt is $\frac{1}{2k}$ s. Find the value of k.

Answers

Level 1

1. $(\pi, 0)$ **2.** (25/9) **3.** $(2\pi v A, 4\pi^2 v^2 A)$ **4.** (True) **5.** (a) **6.** (d) **7.** (b) **8.** (b) **9.** (b) **10.** (a) **11.** (a) **12.** (c) **13.** (c) **14.** (c) **15.** (b) **16.** (a) **17.** (a,b,c,d) **18.** (a,b,c)

19. $y = (0.1\text{m})\sin[(30\text{ rad/s})t \pm (1.5\text{m}^{-1})x + \phi]$ **20.** (a) 5.1×10^{-5} (b) 11 cm/s, 3.2×10^{-4}

21. (a) [L], [L] (b) $y(x, t) = A\sin\left(\frac{x - vt}{a}\right)$ **22.** (a) 1.0 mm (b) 4 cm (c) 1.6 cm^{-1} (d) 5 Hz **23.** (0.25)

24. At $t = 0.1$s, at $x = 2.0$ m **25.** (a) 7.07 cm (b) 400.0 W **26.** (a) $\frac{7L}{2}\sqrt{\frac{\mu_1}{F}}$ (b) No **27.** (2)

Level 2

28. (a) **29.** (a) **30.** (c) **31.** (d) **32.** (c) **33.** (b) **34.** (a) **35.** (a) **36.** (b) **37.** (c)

38. (d) **39.** (a) Negative x (b) $y = (0.4\text{ cm})\sin\left(10\pi t + \frac{\pi}{2}x + \frac{\pi}{4}\right)$s (c) 1.6×10^{-5} J

40. (a) 80 m/s (b) $y = (1.0\text{ cm})\cos\left[(40\pi\text{s}^{-1})t - \left(\frac{\pi}{2}\text{ m}^{-1}\right)x\right]$ (c) $\frac{1}{\sqrt{2}}$ cm (d) 89 cm/s

41. $y = 0.02\cos(10t - 100x)$ m, 0.0628 m **42.** $\frac{\pi}{\sqrt{2}\omega}$ **43.** See the hints **44.** (5)

See hints on pages 41-46.

Hints & SOLUTIONS

Module 1.

1. Given, $y = \frac{1}{(1+x)^2}$

   At $t=0$ we get $y=1$ when $x=0$

   Again, $y = \frac{1}{1+(x-1)^2}$, at $t=2$ s

   So, at $t=2$ $y=1$ when $x=1$

   The wave pulse has travelled a distance of 1 m in 2 s.

   ∴ Velocity of wave pulse,

   $$v = \frac{1}{2} = 0.5 \text{ ms}^{-1}$$

2. Options (a) and (c) satisfy the condition ;

   $$\frac{\partial^2 y}{\partial x^2} = (\text{constant}) \frac{\partial^2 y}{\partial t^2}$$

3. $\frac{\partial^2 y}{\partial t^2} = -\omega^2 a \sin \omega t$

   and $\frac{\partial^2 y}{\partial x^2} = 0$

   Since, $\frac{\partial^2 y}{\partial t^2} \neq \frac{\partial^2 y}{\partial x^2}$ (constant)

   Hence, the given equation does not represent a wave equation.

4. Speed of wave $= \frac{\text{Coefficient of } t}{\text{Coefficient of } x} = \frac{c}{b}$

5. (a) A has the dimensions of y.

   $\frac{x}{a}$ and $\frac{t}{T}$ are dimensionless.

   (b) $v = \frac{\text{Coefficient of } t}{\text{Coefficient of } x}$

   (c) $\frac{x}{a}$ and $\frac{t}{T}$ are of same sign

   (d) $y_{max} = A$

Module 2.

Introductory Exercise

1. Comparing the given equation with

   $$y = \sin(kx - \omega t)$$

   we find,

   (a) Amplitude $A = 5$ mm

   (b) Angular wave number $k = 1 \text{ cm}^{-1}$

   (c) Wavelength, $\lambda = \frac{2\pi}{k} = 2\pi$ cm

   (d) Frequency, $\nu = \frac{\omega}{2\pi} = \frac{60}{2\pi} \text{ Hz} = \frac{30}{\pi} \text{ Hz}$

   (e) Time period, $T = \frac{1}{\nu} = \frac{\pi}{30}$ s

   (f) Wave velocity, $v = \nu\lambda = 60 \text{ cm s}^{-1}$

2. (a) $T = \frac{2\pi}{\omega}, \lambda = \frac{2\pi}{k}$

   (b) Find $\frac{\partial y}{\partial t}$ and then substitute the given values of x and t.

   (c) and (d) Procedure is same.

Exercise

1. In both waves ωt and kx are of opposite signs, so both are travelling in positive directions.

3. $\lambda = \frac{2\pi}{k} = \frac{2\pi}{\pi/9} = 18$ m

4. Here, $A = 0.05$ m, $\frac{5\lambda}{2} = 0.25$

   $\Rightarrow \lambda = 0.1$ m

   $K = \frac{2\pi}{\lambda} = (20\pi) \frac{\text{rad}}{\text{m}}$

   Now standard equation of wave is,

   $$y = 0.05 \sin 2\pi (3300t - 10x)$$

5. $v = \frac{\text{Coefficient of } t}{\text{Coefficient of } x} = \frac{400}{1}$

   $= 400 \frac{\text{m}}{\text{s}}$

6. From the question,

   $k = \frac{2\pi}{\lambda} = \frac{2\pi}{4} = 0.5\pi \text{ cm}^{-1}$

   $\Rightarrow \omega = 2\pi f = 2\pi \times 100$

   $= 200\pi \text{s}^{-1}$

7. Velocity of the wave,

   $$v = \frac{\omega}{k} = \frac{50}{2} = 25 \text{ m/s}$$

   As both ωt and kx are of same sign, the wave will be travelling along negative x-direction.

8. $\because v = \frac{\text{Coefficient of } t}{\text{Coefficient of } x} = \frac{6.2}{2} = 3.1$ m/s

   $A = \frac{2}{20} = 0.1$ m

9. Speed of wave

   $= \frac{\text{Coefficient of } t}{\text{Coefficient of } x} = \frac{b}{1} = b$

   $\lambda = \frac{2\pi}{k} = \frac{2\pi}{(2\pi/a)} = a$

10. (a) $\omega = 2\pi f = 2\pi\left(\frac{v}{\lambda}\right) = 2\pi\left(\frac{12}{0.4}\right)$

$= (60\,\pi)\ \text{rad/s}$

$k = \frac{2\pi}{\lambda} = \frac{2\pi}{0.4}$

$= (5\pi)\ \text{m}^{-1}$

Since, wave is travelling along + ve x-direction, ωt and kx should have opposite sign. Further at $t = 0$, $x = 0$ the string has zero displacement and moving upward (in positive direction). Hence at $x = 0$, we should have $A \sin \omega t$ not $-A \sin \omega t$. Therefore, the correct expression is

$$y = A \sin (\omega t - kx)$$

or $$y = 0.05 \sin (60\,\pi t - 5\pi x)$$

(b) Putting $x = 0.25$ m and $t = 0.15$ s in above equation, we have

$y = -0.0354$ m

$= -3.54$ cm

(c) In part (b), $y = A/\sqrt{2}$

From $y = \frac{A}{\sqrt{2}}$ to $y = 0$, time taken is

$t = \frac{T}{8} = \frac{2\pi}{\omega \times 8} = \frac{2\pi}{(60\pi)(8)}$

$= 4.2 \times 10^{-3}$ s

$= 4.2$ ms

11. (a) $k = \frac{2\pi}{\lambda} = \frac{2\pi}{40} = 0.157\ \text{rad/cm}$

$T = \frac{1}{f} = \frac{1}{8} = 0.125$ s

$\omega = 2\pi f = 50.24$ rad/s

$v = f\lambda = 8 \times 40$

$= 320$ cm/s

(b) At $t = 0$, $y = +A$ at $x = 0$

Therefore, y may be $A \cos (\pm\, \omega t)$

Since, wave is travelling towards positive x-axis, maximum y-displacement at $x = 0$, is moving towards positive x-axis. So, particle velocity or $\frac{\partial y}{\partial t}$ of the particles lying between $0 < x < \frac{\lambda}{4}$ is positive or upwards at $t = 0$ as they are moving upwards. Therefore, the correct equation is $A \cos(kx - \omega t)$ or $A \cos (\omega t - kx)$.

Module 3.

1. In $v_P = -v \frac{\partial y}{\partial x}$,

v_P is negative and $\frac{\partial y}{\partial x}$ (the slope) is also negative. Hence, the velocity v should also be negative.

2. In transverse wave angle is $\frac{\pi}{2}$. In longitudinal wave it is either zero or π.

3. $\Delta\phi = \frac{2\pi}{\lambda}(\Delta x) = \frac{2\pi f(\Delta x)}{v}$ $\left(\text{as } \lambda = \frac{v}{f}\right)$

$= \frac{2\pi(25)(16 - 10)}{300} = \pi$

4. Speed $= n\lambda = n(4ab) = 4n \times ab$ $\left(\text{as } ab = \frac{\lambda}{4}\right)$

Path difference between b and e is $\frac{3\lambda}{4}$.

So, the phase difference $= \frac{2\pi}{\lambda} \times$ Path difference

$= \frac{2\pi}{\lambda} \times \frac{3\lambda}{4} = \frac{3\pi}{2}$

5. The particle velocity is maximum at B and is given by

$(v_p)_{max} = \omega A$

Also wave velocity is $v = \frac{\omega}{k}$

So, slope $\frac{\partial y}{\partial x} = \frac{(v_p)_{max}}{v} = kA$

6. $y = 2 \sin (\omega t - kx)$

Maximum particle velocity, $v_m = A\omega$

As we know, wave velocity, $v_p = \frac{\omega}{k}$

$v_p = v_m \Rightarrow \frac{\omega}{k} = A\omega$

$\Rightarrow$ $k = \frac{1}{A} = \frac{2\pi}{\lambda}$

$\lambda = 2\pi A = 2\pi \times 2 = 4\pi$

7. This is an equation of a travelling wave in which particles of the medium are in SHM and maximum particle velocity in SHM is $A\omega$, where A is the amplitude and ω the angular velocity.

8. Since A is moving upwards, therefore after an elemental time interval the wave will be as shown dotted in below figure. It means, the wave is travelling leftward. Therefore, (a) is wrong. Displacement amplitude of the wave means maximum possible displacement of medium particles due to propagation of the wave, which is equal to the displacement at B at the instant shown in figure. Hence, (b) is correct.

From figure, it is clear that C is moving downward at this instant. Hence, (c) is wrong.

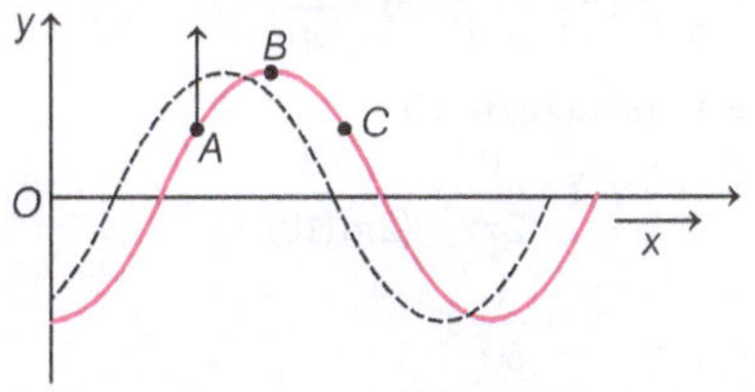

The phase difference between two points will be equal to $\frac{\pi}{2}$, if distance between them is equal to $\frac{\lambda}{4}$. It may be

equal to $\frac{\lambda}{4}$. Hence, phase difference between these two points may be equal to $\frac{\pi}{2}$.

9. The maximum velocity of a transverse sinusoidal wave travelling on a string is $v_{max} = a\omega$.
Given maximum velocity

$$= \frac{v}{10} = \frac{10}{10} = 1 \text{ m/s}$$

$\therefore$ $a\omega = 1$

$\Rightarrow$ $10^{-3} \times 2\pi f = 1$ $[\because \omega = 2\pi f]$

$\Rightarrow$ $f = \frac{1}{2\pi \times 10^{-3}} = \frac{10^3}{2\pi}$ Hz

And $\lambda = \frac{v}{f} = \frac{10}{10^3/2\pi}$

$= (2\pi \times 10^{-2})$ m

10. $v_P = \frac{\partial y}{\partial t}$, $a_P = \frac{\partial^2 y}{\partial t^2}$

If ωt and kx are of same sign, then wave travel in negative x-direction.
If they are of opposite signs, then wave travels in positive direction.

11. $v_P = \frac{\partial y}{\partial t} = (4\pi)$ cm/s $\cos[\pi t + 2\pi x]$

$a_P = \frac{\partial^2 y}{\partial t^2} = (-4\pi^2)$ cm/s^2 $\sin[\pi t + 2\pi x]$

Now, substitute the values of t and x.

12. For velocity, $v_P = -v \frac{\partial y}{\partial x}$

$\frac{\partial y}{\partial x}$ = Slope of y-x graph.

Sign of v is not given in the question.
Hence, direction of v_P cannot be determined.
For particle acceleration, $a_P \propto -y$
i.e. a_P and y are always in opposite directions.
If $y = 0$, then $a_P = 0$

13. (a) $\frac{\lambda}{2} = 2$ cm $\Rightarrow$ $\lambda = 4$ cm

$$f = \frac{v}{\lambda} = \frac{40}{4} = 10 \text{ Hz}$$

(b) $\Delta\phi = \frac{2\pi}{\lambda}\Delta x = \left(\frac{2\pi}{4}\right)(2.5) = \frac{5\pi}{4}$

(c) $\omega t = \theta$ or $(2\pi/t) = \theta$

$\therefore$ $t = \frac{\theta}{2\pi f} = \frac{\pi/3}{(2\pi)(10)}$

$= \frac{1}{60}$ s

(d) At P, particle is at mean position. So,

v = maximum velocity

$= \omega A = 2\pi f A$

$= (2\pi)(10)(2) = (40\pi)$ cm/s

$= 125.7$ cm/s

$= 1.26$ m/s

Further, $v_P = -(v)\left(\frac{\partial y}{\partial x}\right)$ ...(i)

Sign of v_1, the wave velocity is given positive. Sign of $\frac{\partial y}{\partial x}$, slope of y-x graph is also positive. Hence, from Eq. (i) particle velocity is negative.

$\therefore$ $v_P = -1.26$ m/s

14. (a) Coefficient of x and t are of same sign.

(b) $v = \frac{314}{31.4} = 10$ m/s $\Rightarrow$ $\lambda = \frac{2\pi}{k}, f = \frac{\omega}{2\pi}$

(c) $v_{max} = \omega A$

15. (a) The velocity of the particle at x at time t is

$$v = \frac{\partial y}{\partial t} = (3.0 \text{ cm})(-314 \text{ s}^{-1}) \cos[(3.14 \text{ cm}^{-1}) x - (314 \text{ s}^{-1})t]$$

$$= (-9.4 \text{ ms}^{-1})\cos[(3.14 \text{ cm}^{-1})x - (314 \text{ s}^{-1})t]$$

The maximum velocity of a particle will be

$$v = 9.4 \text{ ms}^{-1}$$

(b) The acceleration of the particle at x at time t is

$$a = \frac{\partial v}{\partial t} = -(9.4 \text{ ms}^{-1})(314 \text{ s}^{-1}) \sin[(3.14 \text{ cm}^{-1}) x - (314 \text{ s}^{-1})t]$$

$$= -(2952 \text{ ms}^{-1})\sin[(3.14 \text{ cm}^{-1})x - (314 \text{ s}^{-1})t].$$

The acceleration of the particle at $x = 6.0$ cm at time $t = 0.11$ s is

$$a = -(2952 \text{ ms}^{-2})\sin[6\pi - 11\pi] = 0$$

16. (a) Wave velocity $= \frac{\text{Coefficient of } t}{\text{Coefficient of } x}$

$$= \frac{1/0.01}{1/0.05} = 5 \text{ m/s}$$

Since, coefficient of t and coefficient of x are of same sign. Hence, wave is travelling in negative x-direction.

or $v = -5$ m/s

(b) Velocity of particle,

$$v_P = \frac{\partial y}{\partial t} = 2\cos\left(\frac{x}{0.05} + \frac{t}{0.01}\right)$$

Substituting $x = 0.2$ and $t = 0.3$, we have

$v_P = 2\cos(34)$

$= 2(-0.85)$

$= -1.7$ m/s

17. (a) $\Delta\phi = \frac{2\pi}{\lambda}\Delta x$

$\therefore$ $\Delta x = \frac{\lambda\Delta\phi}{2\pi} = \frac{v(\Delta\phi)}{2\pi f}$

$= \frac{(350)(\pi/3)}{(2\pi)(500)} = 0.116$ m

(b) $\Delta\phi = (\omega)\Delta t$

$= (2\pi f)(\Delta t) = (2\pi)(500)(10^{-3})$

$= \pi$ or $180°$

Module 4.

Introductory Exercise 1

1. $f_{max} = \dfrac{c}{\lambda_{min}} \Rightarrow f_{min} = \dfrac{c}{\lambda_{max}}$

2. $\lambda = \dfrac{v}{f}$ for both

Introductory Exercise 2

1. The tension in the string is $T = mg = 10$ N. The mass per unit length is $\mu = 1.0 \text{ g cm}^{-1} = 0.1 \text{ kg m}^{-1}$. The wave velocity is, therefore, $v = \sqrt{\dfrac{T}{\mu}} = \sqrt{\dfrac{10 \text{ N}}{0.1 \text{ kg m}^{-1}}} = 10 \text{ ms}^{-1}$.

   The time taken by the pulse in travelling through 50 cm is, therefore, 0.05 s.

2. $v = \sqrt{\dfrac{T}{\mu}}$

3. $T_{CD} = 3.2\,g, T_{AB} = 6.4\,g$ and $v = \sqrt{\dfrac{T}{\mu}}$

4. $v = \sqrt{\dfrac{T}{\mu}}, \quad \mu = \dfrac{m}{l}$ and $t = \dfrac{d}{v}$

5. $v = \sqrt{\dfrac{T}{\rho S}} = \sqrt{\dfrac{T}{\rho(\pi d^2/A)}}$

   $= \sqrt{\dfrac{4T}{\rho \pi d^2}}$ $\quad (T = mg)$

   $= \sqrt{\dfrac{4 \times 20}{(8920)(\pi)(2.4 \times 10^{-3})^2}}$

   $= 22$ m/s

6. (a) $v = \sqrt{\dfrac{T}{\mu}} = \sqrt{\dfrac{mg}{\mu}}$ ...(i)

   $= \sqrt{\dfrac{1.5 \times 9.8}{0.055}} = 16.3$ m/s

   (b) $\lambda = \dfrac{v}{f} = \dfrac{16.3}{120} = 0.136$ m

   (c) From Eq. (i), we can see that $v \propto \sqrt{m}$. If m is doubled, then v will become $\sqrt{2}$ times. Hence, from the relation $\lambda = \dfrac{v}{f} \cdot \lambda$ will also become $\sqrt{2}$ times. As f remains unchanged.

Exercise

1. If f is doubled (which is source dependent), then λ will automatically become half, so that speed remains same. Because speed is only medium dependent.

2. Just by observation we cannot say that $\mu_2 > \mu_1$ and hence $v_2 > v_1$.

   If their densities are different, then μ_2 may be less than μ_1 also.

3. $v = \dfrac{\omega}{k} = \sqrt{\dfrac{T}{\mu}}$

   $\therefore \quad T = \mu\left(\dfrac{\omega}{k}\right)^2 = (1.3 \times 10^{-4})\left(\dfrac{30}{1}\right)^2$

   $= 0.12$ N

4. In example we have proved that :

   $t = 2\sqrt{\dfrac{l}{g}}$

   $T = 2\sqrt{\dfrac{L}{g}}$ and $T' = 2\sqrt{\dfrac{L/2}{g}}$

   $\therefore \quad T' = \dfrac{T}{\sqrt{2}}$

5. 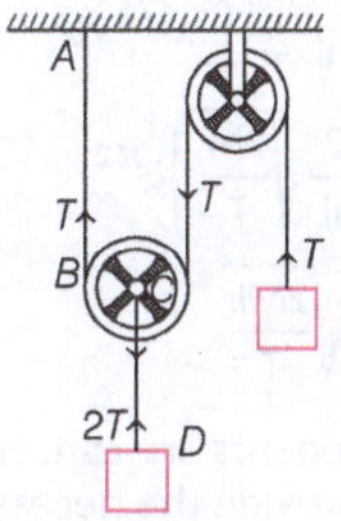

   $v \propto \sqrt{T}$

   $\dfrac{v_1}{v_2} = \sqrt{\dfrac{T_{AB}}{T_{CD}}} = \sqrt{\dfrac{T}{2T}} = \dfrac{1}{\sqrt{2}}$

6. At distance x from the bottom

   $v = \sqrt{\dfrac{T}{\mu}} = \sqrt{\dfrac{\left(\dfrac{mgx}{L}\right)}{\left(\dfrac{m}{L}\right)}} = \sqrt{gx} \qquad \left[\because v = \dfrac{dx}{dt}\right]$

   $\therefore \quad \dfrac{dx}{dt} = \sqrt{x}\sqrt{g}$

   $\Rightarrow \quad \int_0^L x^{-1/2} dx = \sqrt{g}\int_0^t dt$

   $\Rightarrow \quad \left[\dfrac{x^{1/2}}{(1/2)}\right]_0^L = \sqrt{g} \cdot t$

   $\Rightarrow \quad t = \dfrac{2\sqrt{L}}{\sqrt{g}}$

   $\Rightarrow \quad t = 2\sqrt{\dfrac{20}{10}} = 2\sqrt{2}$ s

7. Wavelength of pulse,

   $\lambda = \dfrac{v}{f} = \dfrac{1}{f}\sqrt{\dfrac{T}{\mu}}$ or $T \propto \sqrt{T}$

where, T = tension of string.

Here $T_1 > T_2$, therefore $\lambda_1 > \lambda_2$

Velocity being a vector quantity has both direction and magnitudes. As such the velocities of the two pulses at mid-point cannot be the same.

$v = \sqrt{\frac{T}{\mu}}$, so speed at any position will be same for both pulses, therefore time taken by both pulses will be same, i.e. $T_{AO} = T_{OA}$.

8. $M = \int_0^L kx\,dx = \frac{kL^2}{2}$

$\therefore \quad k = \frac{2M}{L^2}$

$$v_x = \sqrt{\frac{T}{\mu_x}} = \sqrt{\frac{T}{kx}} = \sqrt{\frac{T}{(2M/L^2)\,x}}$$

$$= \left(L\sqrt{\frac{T}{2M}}\right) x^{-1/2} = \frac{dx}{dt}$$

$$\therefore \quad \int_0^t dt = \frac{1}{L}\sqrt{\frac{2M}{T}} \int_0^L x^{1/2}\,dx$$

or
$$t = \left(\frac{2}{3L}\sqrt{\frac{2M}{T}}\right) L^{3/2}$$

$$= \frac{2}{3}\sqrt{\frac{2ML}{T}}$$

9. (a) $T \cos d\theta$ components are cancelled. $T \sin d\theta$ components provide the necessary centripetal force to PQ.

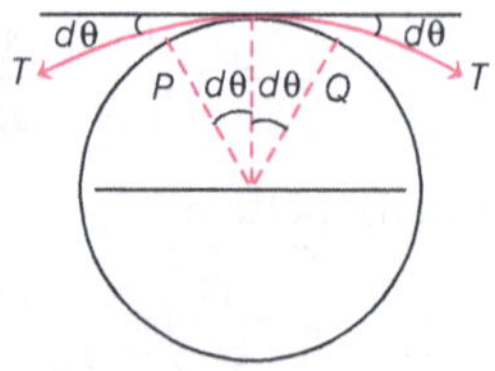

$\therefore \quad 2T \sin d\theta = m_{PQ} R\omega^2$

For small angles $\sin d\theta \approx d\theta$

$\therefore \quad 2T\, d\theta = [\mu\,(2R)\,d\theta]\, R\omega^2$

Solving the equation, we get

$$\sqrt{\frac{T}{\mu}} = v = R\omega$$

(b) Kink remains stationary when rope and kink moves in opposite sence, i.e. if rope is rotating anticlockwise, then kink has to move clockwise.

10. (a) $T_x = (m_{L-x})\, g = \mu\,(L - x)\, g$

where, μ = mass per unit length

$$\therefore \quad v_x = \sqrt{\frac{T_x}{\mu}} = \sqrt{g\,(L-x)}$$

(b) $$v_x = -\frac{dx}{dt} = \sqrt{g\,(L-x)}$$

$$\therefore \quad \int_0^t dt = -\int_{x=L}^{x=0} \sqrt{g\,(L-x)}\,dx$$

Solving we get,

$$t = 2\sqrt{\frac{L}{g}}$$

11. $v = \sqrt{\frac{T}{\rho S}} = \sqrt{\frac{0.98}{9.8 \times 10^3 \times 10^{-6}}} = 10$ m/s

12. Tension due to thermal stresses, using Young's modulus,

$$T = YS\alpha\,.\,\Delta\theta$$

where S = cross-section area

α = coefficient of linear expansion

$\Delta\theta$ = temperature difference

$$\Rightarrow \quad v = \sqrt{\frac{T}{\mu}}$$

Here, μ = mass per unit length $= \rho S$

$$\therefore \quad v = \sqrt{\frac{T}{\rho S}} = \sqrt{\frac{YA\alpha\,.\,\Delta\theta}{\rho S}} = \sqrt{\frac{Y\alpha\,\Delta\theta}{\rho}}$$

Substituting the values, we have

$$v = \sqrt{\frac{1.3 \times 10^{11} \times 1.7 \times 10^{-5} \times 20}{9 \times 10^3}}$$

$= 70.1$ m/s

Module 5.

1. $$\frac{I_1}{I_2} = \frac{A_1^2\omega_1^2}{A_2^2\omega_2^2} = \left(\frac{5}{10}\right)^2 \left(\frac{2\pi \times 75}{2\pi \times 150}\right)^2 = \frac{1}{16}$$

3. Energy density $= \frac{1}{2}\rho\omega^2 A^2$

= Energy per unit volume

Power = energy transfer per unit time

$$= \frac{1}{2}\rho\omega^2 A^2 Sv$$

Intensity = energy transfer per unit time per unit area

$$= \frac{1}{2}\rho\omega^2 A^2 v = \frac{P}{S}$$

Wave number $= \frac{1}{\lambda}$

4. $I = \frac{P}{4\pi r^2} = \frac{1.0}{4\pi (1)^2} = \frac{1}{4\pi}$ W/m^2

5. Suppose power of line source is P. Then, at distance r, surface area is $2\pi rl$.

$$\therefore \quad I = \frac{P}{S} = \frac{P}{2\pi rl} \quad \text{or} \quad I \propto \frac{1}{r}$$

Further, $I \propto A^2$

$\therefore \quad A \propto \frac{1}{\sqrt{r}}$

6. Energy density, $u = \frac{1}{2}\rho\omega^2 A^2$

Total energy $= (u)(V)$

$$= \frac{1}{2}(\rho V)(2\pi f)^2 A^2$$
$$= 2\pi^2 m f^2 A^2$$
$$= (2)(\pi)^2 (0.08)(120)^2 (0.16 \times 10^{-3})^2$$
$$= 581 \times 10^{-3}\ \text{J}$$
$$= 0.58\ \text{mJ}$$

7. Power $= \frac{1}{2}\rho\omega^2 A^2 Sv$

But, $\rho S = \mu$

and $v = \sqrt{\frac{T}{\mu}}$

$\therefore \quad \rho S v = \sqrt{\mu T}$

Hence, power $= \frac{1}{2}(2\pi f)^2 A^2 \sqrt{T\mu}$

$$= 2\pi^2 f^2 A^2 \sqrt{T\mu}$$
$$= (2)(\pi)^2 (60)^2 (0.06)^2 \sqrt{80 \times 5 \times 10^{-2}}$$
$$= 512\ \text{W}$$

8. (a) As derived in above problem, power

$$= 2\pi^2 f^2 A^2 \sqrt{T\mu}$$
$$= (2)(\pi)^2 (200)^2 (10^{-3})^2 \sqrt{60 \times (0.006)}$$
$$= 0.47\ \text{W}$$

(b) Energy density, $u = \frac{1}{2}\rho\omega^2 A^2$

Total energy $= (u)(V)$

$$= \left(\frac{1}{2}\rho\omega^2 A^2\right)(lS)$$

But, $\rho S = \mu$

$\therefore$ Total energy $= \frac{1}{2}\mu l (2\pi f)^2 A^2$

$$= 2\pi^2 f^2 A^2 \mu l$$
$$= (2)(\pi)^2 (200)^2 (10^{-3})^2 (0.006)(2.0)$$
$$= 9.4 \times 10^{-3}\ \text{J} = 9.4\ \text{mJ}$$

9. $P = \frac{1}{2}\rho\omega^2 A^2 Sv \quad \ldots\text{(i)}$

But, $\rho S = \mu$

and $v = \sqrt{\frac{T}{\mu}} = \sqrt{\frac{T}{\rho S}}$

$\therefore \quad \rho S = \frac{T}{v^2}$ or $\rho S v = \frac{T}{v}$

Substituting in Eq. (i), we have

$$P = \frac{1}{2}(2\pi f)^2 A^2 \frac{T}{v}$$
$$= \frac{2\pi^2 f^2 A^2 T}{v}$$
$$= \frac{(2)(\pi)^2 (100)^2 (0.0005)^2 (100)}{100}$$
$$= 0.049\ \text{W} = 49\ \text{mW}$$

Unit Exercise (Cumulative)

Level 1

1. $v = 300$ m/s, $f = 25$Hz

$\therefore$ Wavelength $\lambda = \frac{v}{f} = \frac{300}{25} = 12$ m

(a) Phase difference $\Delta\phi = \frac{2\pi}{\lambda}$ (path difference)

$$= \frac{2\pi}{12} \times 6 = \pi$$

(b) Amplitude remains constant for a plane progressive wave.

2. $I \propto \frac{1}{r^2}$ (in case of point source)

and $I \propto A^2$

$A \propto \frac{1}{r}$ or $\frac{A_1}{A_2} = \frac{r_2}{r_1} = \frac{25}{9}$

3. (a) Particle velocity amplitude is also maximum speed

$$= \omega A = 2\pi\nu A$$

(b) Particle acceleration amplitude

$$= \omega^2 A = 4\pi^2\nu^2 A$$

4. Speed of sound wave in water is greater than in air, so water behaves as rarer medium and hence sound wave will be refracted into water away from the normal. Sound waves travel through a speed v through a medium of density f as $v \propto f$.

As such a wave will get refracted; away from the normal in water.

6. At mean position kinetic energy is maximum and there is a maximum stretch in string. Because one side particles are moving up and the other side particles are moving down. Hence, potential energy is also maximum.

7. At $t = 0$ and $x = \frac{\pi}{2k}$.

The displacement, $y = a_0 \sin\left(-k \times \frac{\pi}{2k}\right)$

$$= -a_0 \sin\frac{\pi}{2} = -a_0$$

Point of maximum displacement (a_0) in negative direction is Q

8. $\because \quad v = \frac{\omega}{k}$

$\therefore \quad k = \dfrac{\omega}{v} = \dfrac{600\pi}{300} = 2\pi\,\text{m}^{-1}$

$\therefore \quad y = 0.04 \sin(600\,\pi t - 2\pi x)$

Now, put $t = 0.01$ s and $x = 0.75$ m

9. $v = \sqrt{\dfrac{T}{\rho S}} = \sqrt{\dfrac{T}{\rho(\pi d^2/4)}}$

$\therefore \quad v \propto \sqrt{\dfrac{T}{d^2}}$

10. From Hooke's law,

Tension in a string $(T) \propto$ extension (x)

and speed of sound in string

$$v = \sqrt{T/\mu} \quad \text{or} \quad v \propto \sqrt{T}$$

Therefore, $v \propto \sqrt{x}$

x is increased to 1.5 times, i.e. speed will increase by $\sqrt{1.5}$ times or 1.22 times. Therefore, speed of sound in new position will be 1.22 v.

11. At $x = 0, t = 0, y = \sqrt{3}$

Further if x is slightly greater than 0, y is slightly greater than $\sqrt{3}$. Therefore, the current graph is (a).

12. $\Delta l = l\,\alpha t$ or $\dfrac{\Delta l}{l} = \alpha t$, stress $= Y \times$ strain $= Y\,\alpha t$

(also called thermal stress)

Force = stress × area

$\therefore$ Tension, $T = Y s\,\alpha t$

Now, $v = \sqrt{\dfrac{T}{\rho s}} = \sqrt{\dfrac{Y\alpha s t}{\rho s}} = \sqrt{\dfrac{Y\alpha t}{\rho}}$

13. The equation should satisfy $\dfrac{\partial^2 y}{\partial t^2} = v^2 \dfrac{\partial^2 y}{\partial x^2}$

This will be satisfied by II and IV. Besides satisfying the equation y should be finite everywhere (i.e. for all values of x) all the time (i.e. for all values of t).

14. In the figure,

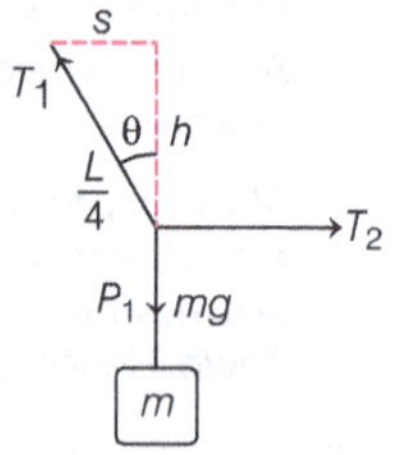

$$s = \frac{0.5}{2} = 0.25 \text{ m}$$

$$\frac{L}{4} = \frac{3}{4} = 0.75 \text{ m}$$

$$h = \sqrt{(0.75)^2 - (0.25)^2}$$

$$= 0.707 \text{ m}$$

From Lami's theorem,

$$\frac{mg}{\sin(90° + \theta)} = \frac{T_2}{\sin(180° - \theta)}$$

$$T_2 = mg\tan\theta = (2)(9.8)\left(\frac{0.25}{0.707}\right)$$

$$= 6.93 \text{ N}$$

Mass per unit length of the string is

$$\mu = \frac{10 \times 10^{-3}}{3}$$

$$= 3.33 \times 10^{-3} \text{ kg m}^{-1}$$

$\therefore$ Speed of pulse, $v = \sqrt{\dfrac{T_2}{\mu}} = \sqrt{\dfrac{6.93}{3.33 \times 10^{-3}}}$

$$= 45.62 \text{ ms}^{-1}$$

$\therefore$ Time taken $= \dfrac{P_1P_2}{v} = \dfrac{L/2}{v} = \dfrac{1.5}{45.62}$

$$= 0.0329 \text{ s} = 32.9 \text{ ms}$$

15. Waves solution distance between triangle and crest

$= (2n_1 + 1)\dfrac{\lambda}{2}$

Distance between two crests $= n_2\lambda$

$$\therefore \quad \frac{15}{5} = \frac{(2n_1 + 1)\frac{\lambda}{2}}{n_2\lambda}$$

$$3n_2 = 10n_1 + 5$$

$$n_1 = 1,\ n_2 = 5 \Rightarrow \lambda = 1$$

$$n_1 = 4,\ n_2 = 15 \Rightarrow \lambda = \frac{1}{3}$$

$$n_1 = 7,\ n_2 = 25 \Rightarrow \lambda = \frac{1}{5}$$

Distance between two crests $= n_2\lambda$

$$\therefore \quad \frac{15}{5} = \frac{(2n_1 + 1)\frac{\lambda}{2}}{n_2\lambda}$$

$$3n_2 = 10n_1 + 5$$

$$n_1 = 1,\ n_2 = 5 \Rightarrow \lambda = 1$$

$$n_1 = 4,\ n_2 = 15 \Rightarrow \lambda = \frac{1}{3}$$

$$n_1 = 7,\ n_2 = 25 \Rightarrow \lambda = \frac{1}{5}$$

Possible wavelengths $= \dfrac{1}{1}, \dfrac{1}{3}, \dfrac{1}{5}$

16. Given, amplitude, $A = 10$ cm

wave velocity $= 2 \times$ maximum particle velocity

i.e. $\dfrac{\omega\lambda}{2\pi} = 2\dfrac{A\omega}{\pi}$

or $\lambda = 4A = 4 \times 10 = 40$ cm

17. $y = A\sin(\pi x + \pi t)$

$$v_P = \frac{\partial y}{\partial t} = \pi A\cos(\pi x + \pi t)$$

$$a_P = \frac{\partial^2 y}{\partial t^2} = -\pi^2 A\sin(\pi x + \pi t)$$

Now, substitute $t = 0$ and given value of x.

Since, ωt and kx are of same sign, hence the wave is travelling in negative x-direction.

18. In the case of a plane wave, intensity at all points is constant.

But for a spherical wave, intensity at a distance r from a point source.

$$I \propto \frac{1}{r^2}$$

For line source $I \propto \frac{1}{r}$ spherical wave is not produced by the line source.

19. Maximum particle velocity,

$$\omega A = 3 \text{ m/s} \quad \text{...(i)}$$

Maximum particle acceleration,

$$\omega^2 A = 90 \text{ m/s}^2 \quad \text{...(ii)}$$

Velocity of wave,

$$\frac{\omega}{k} = 20 \text{ m/s} \quad \text{...(iii)}$$

From Eqs. (i), (ii) and (iii), we get

$$\omega = 30 \text{ rad/s}$$

$\Rightarrow$ $A = 0.1$ m

and $k = 1.5 \text{ m}^{-1}$

$\therefore$ Equation of waveform should be

$$y = A \sin(\omega t \pm kx + \phi)$$

$$\Rightarrow \quad y = (0.1 \text{ m}) \sin[(30 \text{ rad/s})t \pm (1.5 \text{ m}^{-1})x + \phi]$$

20. (a) $A = 60 \times 10^{-6}$ m

$$K = 5.3 \text{ m}^{-1}$$

$$\therefore \quad \lambda = \frac{2\pi}{K} = \frac{2\pi}{5.3} = 1.18 \text{ m}$$

$$\therefore \quad \frac{A}{\lambda} = \frac{60 \times 10^{-6}}{1.18} = 5.1 \times 10^{-5}$$

(b) $(v_P)_{max} = \omega A = 1800 \times 60 \times 10^{-6}$ m/s

$$\approx 11 \times 10^{-2} \text{ m/s or } 11 \text{ cm/s}$$

and $v = \frac{\omega}{K}$

$$\therefore \quad \frac{(v_P)_{max}}{v} = KA = \left(\frac{2\pi}{\lambda}\right)A = 2\pi \times 5.1 \times 10^{-5} = 3.2 \times 10^{-4}$$

21. (a) Dimensions of A and Y are same.
Similarly, dimensions of a and x are same.

(b) As the wave is travelling towards positive x-axis, there should be negative sign between term of x and term of t.

Further, speed of wave $v = \frac{\text{Coefficient of } t}{\text{Coefficient of } x}$

$\therefore$ Coefficient of $t = (v) \times$ coefficient of x

22. From the given figure, we can see that

(a) Amplitude, $A = 1.0$ mm

(b) Wavelength, $\lambda = 4$ cm

(c) Angular wave number,

$$k = \frac{2\pi}{\lambda} = 1.57 \text{ cm}^{-1} \approx 1.6 \text{ cm}^{-1}$$

(d) Frequency, $f = \frac{v}{\lambda} = \frac{20}{4} = 5$ Hz

23. $v = \sqrt{\frac{T}{\rho S}}$ or $v \propto \frac{1}{\sqrt{\rho}}$

$$\therefore \quad \frac{v_1}{v_2} = \sqrt{\frac{\rho_2}{\rho_1}}$$

$$\therefore \quad \frac{\rho_1}{\rho_2} = \left(\frac{v_2}{v_1}\right)^2 = \left(\frac{1}{2}\right)^2 = \frac{1}{4}$$

24. $v_1 = \sqrt{\frac{T_1}{\mu_1}} = \sqrt{\frac{4.8}{1.2 \times 10^{-2}}} = 20$ m/s

$$v_2 = \sqrt{\frac{T_2}{\mu_2}} = \sqrt{\frac{7.5}{1.2 \times 10^{-2}}} = 25 \text{ m/s}$$

Pulses will meet when $x_A = x_B$

or $20t = 25(t - 0.02)$

$\therefore$ $t = 0.1$ s

and x_A or $x_B = 20 \times 0.1 = 2$ m

25. (a) $P = \frac{1}{2}\rho\omega^2 A^2 Sv$

or $$A = \frac{1}{\omega}\sqrt{\frac{2P}{\rho S v}} \quad \text{...(i)}$$

Here, $\rho S = \mu =$ mass per unit length

$$= \frac{6 \times 10^{-3}}{8} \text{ kg/m}$$

$$\omega = 2\pi f = \frac{2\pi v}{\lambda} = \frac{2\pi \times 30}{0.2}$$

Substituting these values in Eq. (i), we have

$$A = \frac{0.2}{2\pi \times 30}\sqrt{\frac{2 \times 50 \times 8}{6 \times 10^{-3} \times 30}}$$

$$= 0.0707 \text{ m} = 7.07 \text{ cm}$$

(b) $P \propto v\omega^2$

or $P \propto v(v^2)$ or $P \propto v^3$

When wave speed is doubled, then power will become eight times.

26. (a) $v_1 = \sqrt{T/\mu_1}$

$$v_2 = \sqrt{F/4\mu_1} = \frac{1}{2}\sqrt{F/\mu_1},$$

$$v_3 = \sqrt{F/(\mu_1/4)} = 2\sqrt{F/\mu_1}$$

$$\therefore \quad t = t_1 + t_2 + t_3 = \frac{L}{v_1} + \frac{L}{v_2} + \frac{L}{v_3}$$

$$= \frac{7L}{2}\sqrt{\frac{\mu_1}{F}} \quad \textbf{Ans.}$$

27. Energy in unit volume (i.e. energy density) is

$$u = \frac{1}{2}\rho\omega^2 A^2 = \frac{1}{2}\frac{m}{sL}\omega^2 A^2$$

(where, s is cross-section area)

Energy in length L is $E = \frac{1}{2}\frac{m}{sL}\omega^2 A^2 (sL)$

$$= \frac{1}{2}m\omega^2 A^2$$

or $$E = \frac{1}{2}(0.08)(2\pi \times 120)^2(0.16 \times 10^{-3})^2$$

$$= 0.58 \text{ mJ} = (0.29) 2 \text{ mJ}$$

$$\Rightarrow \quad \beta = 2$$

Level 2

28. $\because \quad \omega = 2\pi f = (2\pi)(100)$

$$= (200\,\pi) \text{ rad/s}$$

$$v = \frac{\omega}{k}$$

$$\therefore \quad k = \frac{\omega}{v} = \omega\sqrt{\frac{\mu}{T}}$$

$$= (200\pi)\sqrt{\frac{3.5 \times 10^{-3}}{35}}$$

$$= 2\pi \text{ m}^{-1}$$

At zero displacement,

$$v_P = \omega A = -v\frac{\partial y}{\partial x}$$

$$\therefore \quad |A| = \frac{v\left(\frac{\partial y}{\partial x}\right)}{\omega} = \frac{\left(\sqrt{\frac{T}{\mu}}\right)(\text{slope})}{\omega}$$

$$= \frac{\left(\sqrt{\frac{35}{3.5 \times 10^{-3}}}\right)(\pi/20)}{200\pi}$$

$$= 0.025 \text{ m}$$

29. $\because \quad \omega = \frac{2\pi}{T} = \frac{2\pi}{0.25} = 8\pi \text{ rad/s}$

$$v = \frac{\omega}{k}$$

$$\therefore \quad k = \frac{\omega}{v} = \frac{8\pi}{0.48} = \left(\frac{50}{3}\right)\pi \text{m}^{-1}$$

$$y = A\sin(\omega t - kx)$$

$$= A\sin\left(8\pi t - \frac{50}{3}\pi x\right)$$

Put $y = 3$ cm, $t = 1$ s, $x = 0.47$ m

showing we get $A = 6$ cm

30. $f = 3$ Hz

$$\therefore \quad \omega = 2\pi f = (6\pi) \text{ rad/s}$$

$$k = \frac{\omega}{v} = \frac{6\pi}{3} = (2\pi) \text{ rad/m}$$

$$y = A\sin(kx - \omega t)$$

$$= A\sin(2\pi x - 6\pi t)$$

Putting $y = \pm A$

and $x = 3$, we get

$$(2\pi)(3) - 6\pi t = \frac{\pi}{2}$$

$$\therefore \quad 6\pi t = \frac{11}{2}\pi$$

$$\therefore \quad t = \frac{11}{12} \text{ s}$$

Explanations for Q. Nos. (31-34)

The wave is travelling along positive x-axis (from the figure).

So, let $\quad y = A\sin(\omega t - kx + \delta)$

From the figure, $A = 10$ mm and $\lambda = 2$ m

$$\therefore \quad k = \frac{2\pi}{\lambda} = \frac{2\pi}{2} = \pi \text{m}^{-1}$$

At $\quad t = 0, x = 0, y = 5 \times 10^{-3}$ m (from figure)

$$\therefore \quad 5 \times 10^{-3} = 10 \times 10^{-3}\sin(0 + 0 + \delta)$$

$$\Rightarrow \quad \sin\delta = \frac{1}{2}$$

For left end at $x = 0$,

$$v_P = -v\left(\frac{dy}{dx}\right) = -(+\text{ve})(+\text{ ve}) = -\text{ve}$$

$$\therefore \quad \delta = \frac{\pi}{2} + \frac{\pi}{3} = \frac{5\pi}{6}$$

Also, at $t = 0.05$ s, $x = 0$, $y = 0$ (from figure)

$$\therefore \quad 0 = 10 \times 10^{-3}\sin\left(\omega \times 0.05 - 0 + \frac{5\pi}{6}\right)$$

$$\therefore \quad \frac{5\omega}{100} + \frac{5\pi}{6} = \pi$$

$$\Rightarrow \quad \omega = \frac{\pi}{6} \times 20 = \frac{10\pi}{3}$$

$$f = \frac{\omega}{2\pi} = \frac{5}{3} \text{Hz}$$

$$(v_P)_{max} = A\omega = 10 \times 10^{-3}\left(\frac{10\pi}{3}\right) = \frac{\pi}{30} \text{ms}^{-1}$$

$\therefore$ The equation of the wave is

$$y = 10 \times 10^{-3}\sin\left(\frac{10\pi}{3}t - \pi x + \frac{5\pi}{6}\right)$$

Speed of wave is $v = \lambda f = 2 \times \frac{5}{3} = \frac{10}{3} \text{ms}^{-1}$

35. Consider a differential element dy of the rope at a distance y from the top. The element is in equilibrium

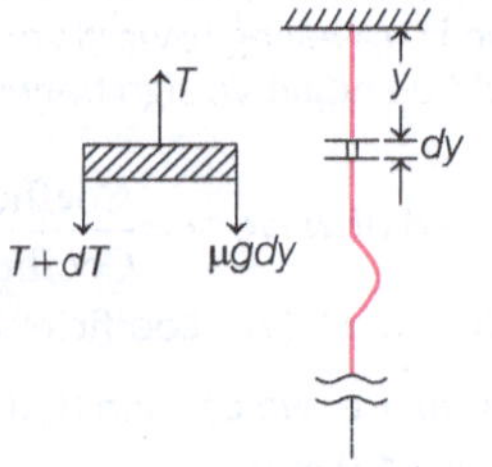

$$\therefore \quad \Sigma F_y = 0$$

$$\text{or} \quad [(T + dT) + \mu g\,dy] - T = 0$$

$$\text{or} \quad dT = -\mu g\,dy \quad \text{...(i)}$$

Wave speed on a string is

$$v = \sqrt{\frac{T}{\mu}}$$

$$\Rightarrow \quad T = \mu v^2$$

Differentiating this equation, we get

$$dT = (d\mu)v^2 + 2v \cdot dv \cdot \mu$$

As, v is independent of y, $dv = 0$

$$\therefore \quad dT = v^2 d\mu \quad \text{...(ii)}$$

From Eqs. (i) and (ii), $v^2 d\mu = -\mu g\, dy$

$$\frac{1}{\mu}\, d\mu = -\frac{g}{v^2}\, dy$$

$$\int_{\mu_0}^{\mu} \frac{1}{\mu}\, d\mu = -\frac{g}{v^2}\int_0^y dy$$

$$\Rightarrow \quad \ln\frac{\mu}{\mu_0} = -\frac{g}{v^2}\cdot y$$

$$\frac{\mu}{\mu_0} = e^{\left(-\frac{g}{v^2}\cdot y\right)}$$

$$\Rightarrow \quad \mu = \mu_0 e^{\left(\frac{-g}{v^2}\cdot y\right)} \quad \text{...(iii)}$$

36. Mass of differential element is $dm = \mu\, dy$

Hence, total mass of the string is $m = \int_0^\infty \mu_0 e^{-\frac{g}{v^2}\cdot y}\, dy$

$$\text{or} \quad m = \mu_0\left(-\frac{v^2}{g}\right)\left[e^{-\frac{g}{v^2}\cdot y}\right]_0^\infty$$

$$\text{or} \quad m = \frac{\mu_0 v^2}{g}$$

$$\Rightarrow \quad v = \sqrt{\frac{mg}{\mu_0}} \quad \text{...(iv)}$$

37. From Eqs. (iii) and (iv),

$$\mu = \mu_0 e^{-\frac{g\mu_0}{mg}\cdot y} = \mu_0 e^{-\frac{\mu_0 y}{m}}$$

38. If we cut the rope at length L, the tension at the free end must equal the weight of string from infinity to free end. Hence, required mass is

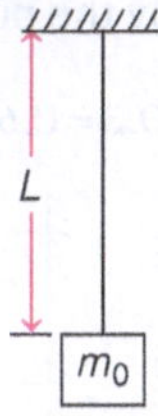

$$m_0 = \int_L^\infty \mu dy = \int_L^\infty \mu_0 e^{-\frac{g}{v^2}\cdot y}\, dy$$

$$m_0 = \mu_0\left(-\frac{v^2}{g}\right)\left[e^{-\frac{g}{v^2}\cdot y}\right]_L^\infty$$

$$= \mu_0 \frac{v^2}{g} e^{-\frac{g}{v^2}\cdot L} = \frac{\mu_0}{g}\cdot\frac{mg}{\mu_0} e^{-\frac{g\mu_0}{mg}\cdot L} \quad \left(\because v = \sqrt{\frac{mg}{\mu_0}}\right)$$

$$= m\, e^{-\mu_0 L/m}$$

39. (a) $v_P = -v\left(\frac{dy}{dx}\right)$

As v_P and (slope)$_P$ are both positive, v must be negative. Hence, the wave is moving in negative x-axis.

(b) $$y = A\sin(\omega t + kx + \phi) \quad \text{...(i)}$$

$$k = \frac{2\pi}{\lambda} = \frac{\pi}{2}\text{ cm}^{-1}$$

$$A = 4\times 10^{-3}\text{ m} = 0.4\text{ cm}$$

At $t = 0$, $x = 0$, slope $\frac{dy}{dx} = +\text{ve}$

$$\therefore \quad v_P = -v(\text{slope}) = +\text{ve}$$

Further at $t = 0, x = 0, y = +\text{ve}$

$$\therefore \quad \phi = \frac{\pi}{4}$$

Further, $20\sqrt{3} = -v\tan 60°$

$$\therefore \quad v = -20\text{ cm/s}$$

$$f = \frac{v}{\lambda} = 5\text{ Hz}$$

$$\therefore \quad \omega = 2\pi f = 10\pi$$

$$\therefore \quad y = (0.4\text{ cm})\sin\left(10\pi t + \frac{\pi}{2}x + \frac{\pi}{4}\right) \quad \textbf{Ans.}$$

(c) $P = 2\pi^2 A^2 f^2 \mu v$

$\therefore$ Energy carried per cycle,

$$E = PT = \frac{P}{f} = 2\pi^2 A^2 f \mu v$$

Substituting the values, we have

$$E = 1.6\times 10^{-5}\text{ J} \quad \textbf{Ans.}$$

40. (a) $v = \sqrt{\frac{T}{\rho S}} = \sqrt{\frac{64}{12.5\times 10^3 \times 0.8\times 10^{-6}}}$

$$= 80\text{ m/s} \quad \textbf{Ans.}$$

(b) $\omega = 2\pi f = 2\pi(20) = 40\pi\text{ rad/s}$

$$k = \frac{\omega}{v} = \frac{40\pi}{80} = \frac{\pi}{2}\text{m}^{-1}$$

$$\therefore \quad y = (1.0\text{ cm})\cos\left[(40\pi s^{-1})t - \left(\frac{\pi}{2}m^{-1}\right)x\right] \quad \textbf{Ans.}$$

(c) Substituting $x = 0.5$ m and $t = 0.05$ s, we get

$$y = \frac{1}{\sqrt{2}}\text{ cm} \quad \textbf{Ans.}$$

(d) Particle velocity at time t,

$$v_P = \frac{\partial y}{\partial t}$$

$$= -(40\pi\text{ cm/s})\sin\left[(40\pi\text{ s}^{-1})t - \left(\frac{\pi}{2}\text{m}^{-1}\right)x\right]$$

Substituting $x = 0.5$ m and $t = 0.05$ s, we get

$$v_P = 89\text{ cm/s} \quad \textbf{Ans.}$$

41. $k_{\text{eff}} = 2k = 1.0$ N/m

$$f = \frac{1}{2\pi}\sqrt{\frac{k_{\text{eff}}}{m}} = \frac{10}{2\pi}\text{ s}^{-1}$$

$$v = 0.1\text{ m/s}, \quad A = 0.02\text{ m}$$

$$\lambda = \frac{v}{f} = \frac{0.1}{\left(\frac{10}{2\pi}\right)} = \frac{2\pi}{100}\,\text{m}$$

$$y = A\cos\left(\frac{2\pi}{\lambda}\right)(vt - x)$$

$$= 0.02\cos 100\,(0.1t - x)$$

$$= 0.02\cos(10t - 100x)\,\text{m}$$ **Ans.**

The distance between two successive maxima

$$= \lambda = \frac{2\pi}{100} = 0.0628\text{ m}$$ **Ans.**

42. $-dT = (dm)x\omega^2 = \left(\frac{m}{L}dx\right)x\omega^2$

or $$-\int_0^T dT = \frac{m}{L}\omega^2\int_{x=L}^{x} x\,dx$$

$\therefore$ $$-T = \frac{m}{L}\omega^2\left(\frac{x^2}{2} - \frac{L^2}{2}\right)$$

or $$T = \frac{m\omega^2}{2L}(L^2 - x^2)$$

$$v = \sqrt{\frac{T}{\mu}} = \sqrt{\frac{\frac{m\omega^2}{2L}(L^2 - x^2)}{m/L}} = \omega\sqrt{\frac{L^2 - x^2}{2}}$$

or $$\frac{dx}{dt} = \frac{\omega}{\sqrt{2}}\sqrt{L^2 - x^2}$$

$\therefore$ $$\int_0^t dt = \frac{\sqrt{2}}{\omega}\int_0^L \frac{dx}{\sqrt{L^2 - x^2}}$$

$\therefore$ $$t = \frac{\sqrt{2}}{\omega}\left[\sin^{-1}\left(\frac{x}{L}\right)\right]_0^L$$

$$= \frac{\sqrt{2}}{\omega}\cdot\frac{\pi}{2} = \frac{\pi}{\sqrt{2}\omega}$$ **Ans.**

43. (a) $y = A\cos(\omega t - kx)$

$$\frac{\partial y}{\partial t} = -\omega A\sin(\omega t - kx)$$

$$\frac{\partial y}{\partial x} = kA\sin(\omega t - kx)$$

At $t = 0$,

$$y = A\cos kx \qquad \text{(cos graph)}$$

$$\frac{\partial y}{\partial t} = \omega A\sin kx \qquad \text{(sine graph)}$$

and $$\frac{\partial y}{\partial x} = -kA\sin kx \qquad \text{(– sine graph)}$$

Corresponding graphs are as shown below,

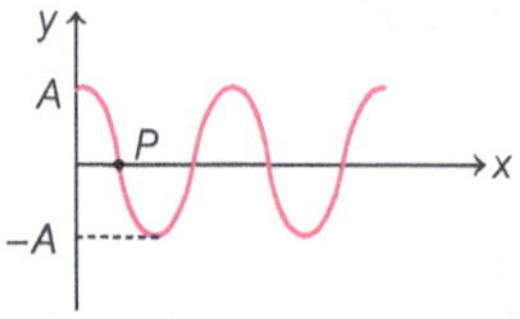

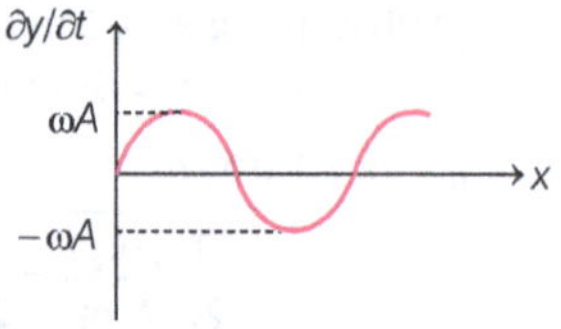

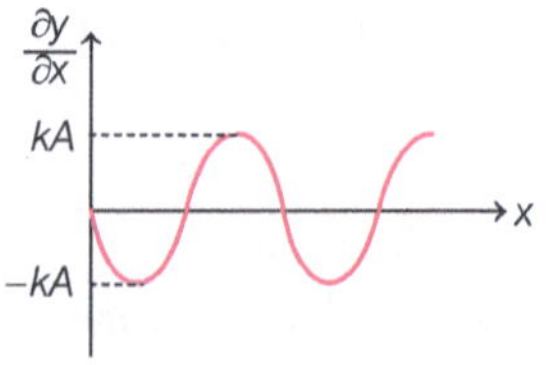

(b) Particle velocity is given by,

$$v_P = -v\frac{\partial y}{\partial x} \qquad \text{...(i)}$$

Here ωt and kx have opposite signs. So wave is travelling in positive x-direction. Therefore sign of v in Eq. (i) is positive.

$\frac{\partial y}{\partial x}$ is slope of y-x graph at a given time. Here, $t = 0$.

At point P in the first graph, $y = 0$ and $\frac{\partial y}{\partial x}$ is negative.

So v_P comes out to be positive.

In case of transverse wave v_P is positive means it is in positive y-direction and in longitudinal wave it's towards positive x-direction.

(c) $$\Delta\rho = -\rho_0\frac{\partial y}{\partial x} \qquad (\rho_0 = \text{mean density})$$

and $\frac{\partial y}{\partial x}$ is $-kA\sin kx$

$\therefore$ $$\Delta\rho_0 = \rho_0 Ak\sin kx$$

$\therefore$ $$\rho = \rho_0 + \Delta\rho$$

$$= \rho_0 + \rho_0 Ak\sin kx \qquad \text{(sine graph)}$$

So, ρ-x graph is as shown below.

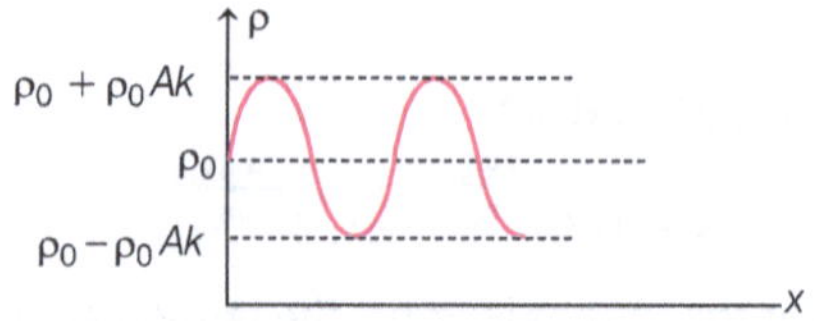

44. The string has same shape in figures first and last.

The distance travelled by the pulse (between these two situations)

$$= 2\times 0.3 = 0.6\text{ m}$$

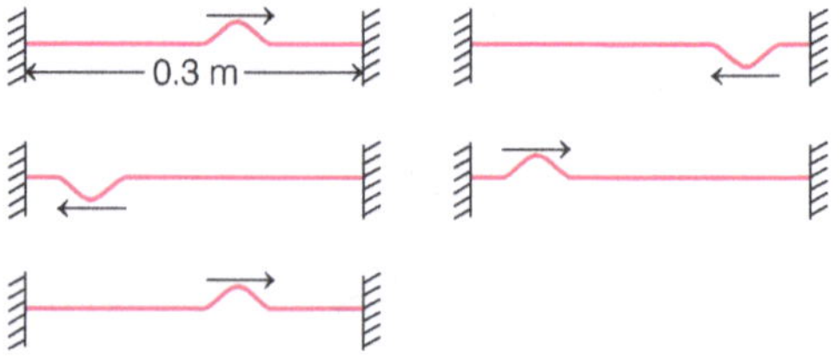

$$v = \sqrt{\frac{T}{\mu}} = \sqrt{\frac{1.2}{10^{-2}/0.3}} = 6\,\text{ms}^{-1}$$

$\therefore$ $$\Delta t = \frac{0.6}{6} = 0.1 = \frac{1}{2\times 5}\text{ s}$$

$\therefore$ $$k = 5$$

UNIT–18

SUPERPOSITION OF WAVES

Learning Modules

1. Resultant Amplitude and Intensity due to Coherent Sources
2. Interference
3. Standing Wave
4. Oscillations of a Stretched Wire (or String)
5. Reflection and Transmission of a Wave

MODULE 1

Resultant Amplitude and Intensity due to Coherent Sources

Principle of Superposition

Suppose there are two sources of waves S_1 and S_2.

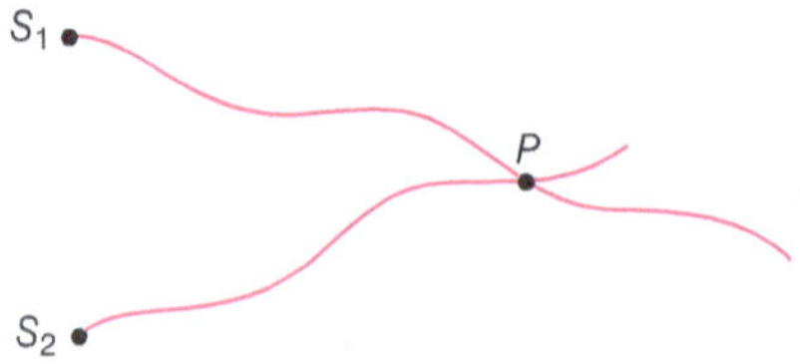

Now, the two waves from S_1 and S_2 meet at some point (say P). Then, according to principle of superposition net displacement at P (from its mean position) at any time is given by

$$\boxed{y = y_1 + y_2}$$

Here, y_1 and y_2 are the displacements of P due to two waves individually.

For example : suppose at 9AM, displacement of P above its mean position should be 6 mm accordingly to wave-1 and at the same time its displacement should be 2 mm below its mean position accordingly to wave-2, then at 9AM net displacement of P will be 4 mm above its mean position.

Now, based upon the principle of superposition we have two phenomena in physics : interference and beats. Stationary waves (or standing waves) and Young's double slit experiment (or YDSE) are two examples of interference.

Based on principle of superposition means two or more than two waves meet at one point or several points and at every point net displacement is $y = y_1 + y_2$ or $y = y_1 + y_2 + y_3$ etc.

Resultant Amplitude and Intensity due to Coherent Sources

In Module 1, we have seen that the two waves from two sources S_1 and S_2 were meeting at point P. Suppose they meet at point P in a phase difference $\Delta\phi$ (or ϕ). If this phase difference remains constant with time, then sources are called coherent, otherwise incoherent.

For sources to be coherent the frequencies (f, ω or T) of the two sources must be same. This can be explained by the following example.

Suppose the phase difference is 0°. It means they are in same phase. Both reach their extremes ($+A$ or $-A$), simultaneously. They cross their mean positions (in the same direction) simultaneously. Now, if we want their phase difference to remain constant or we want that the above situation is maintained all the time, then obviously their time periods (or frequencies) must be same.

Resultant Amplitude

1. Consider the superposition of two sinusoidal waves of same frequency (means sources are coherent) at a point. Let us assume that the two waves are travelling in the same direction with same velocity. The equation of the two waves reaching at a point can be written as

$$y_1 = A_1 \sin (kx - \omega t)$$

and $$y_2 = A_2 \sin (kx - \omega t + \phi)$$

The resultant displacement of the point where the waves meet is

$$\begin{aligned} y &= y_1 + y_2 \\ &= A_1 \sin (kx - \omega t) + A_2 \sin (kx - \omega t + \phi) \\ &= A_1 \sin (kx - \omega t) + A_2 \sin (kx - \omega t) \cos \phi + A_2 \cos (kx - \omega t) \sin \phi \\ &= (A_1 + A_2 \cos \phi) \sin (kx - \omega t) + A_2 \sin \phi \cos (kx - \omega t) \\ &= A \cos\theta \sin (kx - \omega t) + A \sin \theta \cos (kx - \omega t) \end{aligned}$$

or $$y = A \sin (kx - \omega t + \theta)$$

Here, $A_1 + A_2 \cos \phi = A \cos \theta$

and $$A_2 \sin \phi = A \sin \theta$$

or $$A^2 = (A_1 + A_2 \cos \phi)^2 + (A_2 \sin \phi)^2$$

or $$\boxed{A = \sqrt{A_1^2 + A_2^2 + 2A_1A_2 \cos \phi}} \quad \text{...(i)}$$

and $$\tan \theta = \frac{A \sin \theta}{A \cos \theta} = \frac{A_2 \sin \phi}{A_1 + A_2 \cos \phi}$$

or $$\boxed{\tan \theta = \frac{A_2 \sin \phi}{A_1 + A_2 \cos \phi}}$$

2. The above results can be obtained by graphical method as well. Assume a vector $\mathbf{A}_1$ of length A_1 to represent the amplitude of first wave.

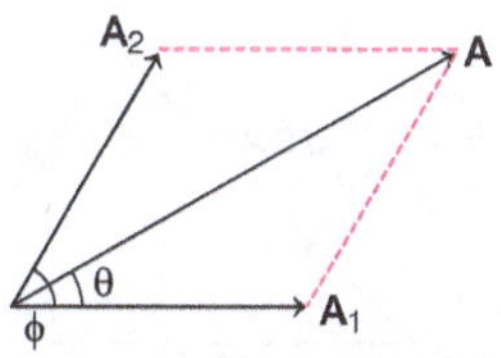

Another vector $\mathbf{A}_2$ of length A_2, making an angle ϕ with $\mathbf{A}_1$ represent the amplitude of second wave. The resultant of $\mathbf{A}_1$ and $\mathbf{A}_2$ represent the amplitude of resulting function y. The angle θ represents the phase difference between the resulting function and the first wave.

From the knowledge of vector addition we know that we will get the same results.

Resultant Intensity

In the previous chapter, we have read that intensity of a wave is given by

$$I = \frac{1}{2}\rho\omega^2 A^2 v$$

or $\quad I \propto A^2$

So, if ρ, ω and v are same for the both the interfering waves, then Eq. (i) can also be written as

$$I = I_1 + I_2 + 2\sqrt{I_1 I_2}\cos\phi \qquad \text{...(ii)}$$

Here, proportionality constant ($I \propto A^2$) cancels out on right hand side and left hand side.

Note *(i) Equations (i) and (ii) are two equations for finding resultant amplitude and resultant intensity at some point due to two coherent sources.*

(ii) In the above equations ϕ is the constant phase difference at that point. As the sources are coherent, value of this constant phase difference will be different at different points.

(iii) The special case of the above two equations is : when the individual amplitudes (or intensities) are equal.

or $\quad A_1 = A_2 = A_0$ *(say)*

$\Rightarrow \quad I_1 = I_2 = I_0$ *(say)*

In this case, Eqs. (i) and (ii) become

$$A = 2A_0 \cos\frac{\phi}{2} \qquad \text{...(iii)}$$

and

$$I = 4I_0 \cos^2\frac{\phi}{2} \qquad \text{...(iv)}$$

(iv) From Eqs. (i) to (iv) we can see that, for given values of A_1, A_2, I_1 and I_2 the resultant amplitude and the resultant intensity are the functions of only ϕ.

(v) If three or more than three waves (due to coherent sources) meet at some point, then there is no direct formula for finding resultant amplitude or resultant intensity. In this case, first of all we will find resultant amplitude by vector method (either by using polygon law of vector addition or component method) and then by the relation $I \propto A^2$, we can also determine the resultant intensity.

For example, if resultant amplitude comes out to be $\sqrt{2}$ times then resultant intensity will become two times.

Example 1 Two coherent sources emit waves of amplitude A_0 each and intensity I_0 each. They meet at some point. Find resultant amplitude A and resultant intensity I if phase difference ϕ between them is

(a) 0° (b) 60° (c) 90° (d) 120°
(e) 180°

Sol. Using the equations :

$$A = 2A_0 \cos\frac{\phi}{2} \quad \text{and}$$

$$I = 4I_0 \cos^2\frac{\phi}{2}$$

We have the result in tabular form as given below.

Part	ϕ	$A = 2A_0 \cos\frac{\phi}{2}$	$I = 4I_0 \cos^2\frac{\phi}{2}$ or, $I \propto A^2$
(a)	0°	$2A_0$	$4I_0$
(b)	60°	$\sqrt{3}A_0$	$3I_0$
(c)	90°	$\sqrt{2}A_0$	$2I_0$
(d)	120°	A_0	I_0
(e)	180°	0	0

Example 2 Find the resultant amplitude and phase of a point at which N sinusoidal waves interfere. All the waves have same amplitude A and their phases increase in arithmetic progression of common difference ϕ.

Sol. The diagram for their sum is shown in figure for $N = 6$.

The resultant amplitude is A_R. The apex angle of every isosceles triangle is ϕ. So, the angle subtended by the resultant is $N\phi$. Since, the heads of the vectors are all at the same distance r from the apex of the diagram.

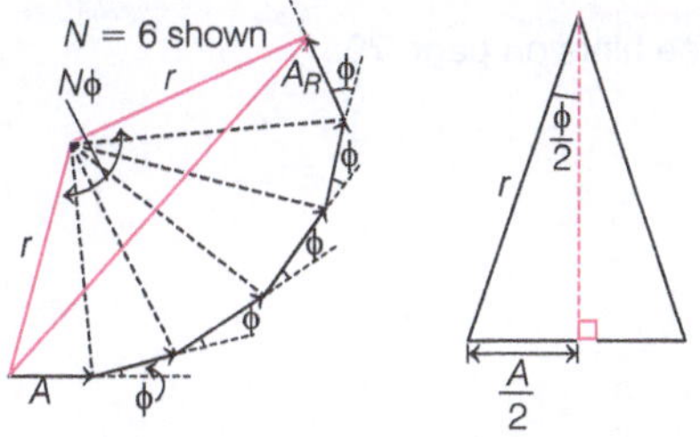

(a) (b)

From Fig. (a),

$$\frac{A_R}{2} = r\sin\frac{N\phi}{2} \qquad \text{...(i)}$$

and from Fig. (b),

$$\frac{A}{2} = r\sin\frac{\phi}{2} \qquad \text{...(ii)}$$

Dividing Eq. (i) by Eq. (ii), we get

$$\frac{A_R}{A} = \frac{\sin\frac{N\phi}{2}}{\sin\frac{\phi}{2}} \quad \text{or} \quad A_R = A\left(\frac{\sin\frac{N\phi}{2}}{\sin\frac{\phi}{2}}\right) \qquad \textbf{Ans.}$$

Note *Suppose $N = 2$ and $\phi = 90°$, then*

$$A_R = \sqrt{2}A$$

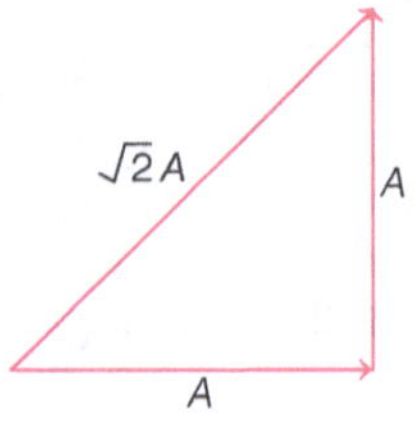

Similarly, we can also check the above result for other special cases.

MODULE 1 Exercise

Single Correct Option

1. Three one-dimensional mechanical waves in an elastic medium are given as :

$y_1 = 3A\sin(\omega t - kx)$, $y_2 = A\sin(\omega t - kx + \pi)$ and $y_3 = 2A\sin(\omega t + kx)$

They are superimposed with each other. The maximum displacement amplitude of the medium particle would be

(a) $4A$ (b) $3A$ (c) $2A$ (d) A

2. Three harmonic waves having equal frequency ν and same intensity I_0 have phase angles 0, $\frac{\pi}{4}$ and $-\frac{\pi}{4}$ respectively. When they are superimposed, the intensity of the resultant wave is close to **(2020 Main)**

(a) $5.8\,I_0$ (b) $0.2\,I_0$
(c) $3\,I_0$ (d) I_0

Integer Type Questions

3. Two waves executing simple harmonic motion travelling in the same direction with same amplitude and frequency are superimposed. The resultant amplitude is equal to the $\sqrt{3}$ times of amplitude of individual motions. The phase difference between the two motions is .... (degree) **(2022 Main)**

4. When two progressive waves $y_1 = 4\sin(2x - 6t)$ and $y_2 = 3\sin\left(2x - 6t - \frac{\pi}{2}\right)$ are superimposed, the amplitude of the resultant wave is .... **(2010 JEE)**

Answers

1. (a) **2.** (a) **3.** (60) **4.** (5)

See hints on page 79.

MODULE 2

Interference

For interference phenomena to take place, sources must be coherent. So, phase difference at some point should remain constant. The value of this constant phase difference will be different at different points. And since the sources are coherent, therefore the following four equations can be applied for finding resultant amplitude and intensity (in case of two sources)

$$A = \sqrt{A_1^2 + A_2^2 + 2A_1A_2 \cos\phi} \quad \text{...(i)}$$

$$I = I_1 + I_2 + 2\sqrt{I_1 I_2}\cos\phi \quad \text{...(ii)}$$

$$A = 2A_0 \cos\frac{\phi}{2} \quad (\text{if } A_1 = A_2 = A_0) \text{...(iii)}$$

$$I = 4I_0 \cos^2\frac{\phi}{2} \quad (\text{if } I_1 = I_2 = I_0) \quad \text{...(iv)}$$

For given values of A_1, A_2, I_1 and I_2 the resultant amplitude and resultant intensity are the functions of only ϕ.

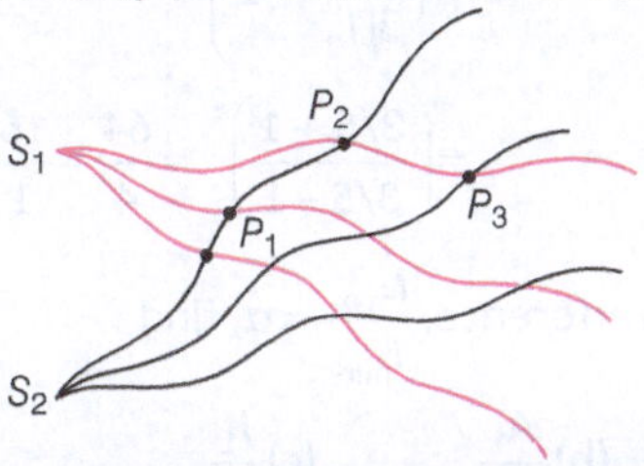

Now, suppose S_1 and S_2 are two coherent sources, then we can see that the two waves are meeting at several points (P_1, P_2, P_3 ... etc.). At different points path difference Δx will be different and therefore phase difference $\Delta\phi$ or ϕ will also be different. Because the phase difference depends on the path difference $\left[\Delta\phi \text{ or } \phi = \left(\frac{2\pi}{\lambda}\right)\Delta x \text{ or } \Delta x = \phi\left(\frac{\lambda}{2\pi}\right)\right]$.

And since phase difference at different points is different, therefore from the above four equations we can see that resultant amplitude and intensity will also be different. But whatever is the intensity at some point, it will remain constant at that point because the sources are coherent and the phase difference is constant at that point.

Constructive Interference

These are the points where resultant amplitude or intensity is maximum or

$$A_{max} = A_1 + A_2 \quad \text{[from Eq. (i)]}$$

or $$A_{max} = \pm 2A_0 \quad \text{[from Eq. (iii)]}$$

and $$I_{max} = (\sqrt{I_1} + \sqrt{I_2})^2 \quad \text{[from Eq. (ii)]}$$

or $$I_{max} = 4I_0 \quad \text{[from Eq. (iv)]}$$

These are the points where,

$$\cos\phi = +1 \quad \text{[from Eqs. (i) or (ii)]}$$

or $$\phi = 0, 2\pi, 4\pi, \ldots, 2n\pi \quad (\text{where, } n = 0, 1, 2)$$

$$\therefore \quad \Delta x = 0, \lambda, 2\lambda, \ldots, n\lambda \quad \left[\text{as } \Delta x = \phi\left(\frac{\lambda}{2\pi}\right)\right]$$

Destructive Interference

These are the points where resultant amplitude or intensity is minimum or

$$A_{min} = A_1 \sim A_2 \quad \text{[from Eq. (i)]}$$

or $$A_{min} = 0 \quad \text{[from Eq. (iii)]}$$

and $$I_{min} = (\sqrt{I_1} - \sqrt{I_2})^2 \quad \text{[from Eq. (ii)]}$$

or $$I_{min} = 0 \quad \text{[from Eq. (iv)]}$$

These are the points where,

$$\cos\phi = -1 \quad \text{[from Eqs. (i) or (ii)]}$$

or $$\phi = \pi, 3\pi .. (2n-1)\pi \quad (\text{where, } n = 1, 2\ldots)$$

$$\therefore \quad \Delta x = \frac{\lambda}{2}, \frac{3\lambda}{2} \ldots (2n-1)\frac{\lambda}{2} \quad \left[\text{as } \Delta x = \phi\left(\frac{\lambda}{2\pi}\right)\right]$$

Important POINTS

- In amplitude, it hardly matters whether it is s $+2A_0$ or $-2A_0$. This is the reason we have taken, $A_{max} = \pm 2A_0$.
- In interference, two or more than two waves from coherent sources meet at several points. At different points Δx, $\Delta\phi$ or ϕ, resultant amplitude and therefore resultant intensity will be different (varying from I_{max} to I_{min}). But whatever is the resultant intensity at some point, it remains constant at that point.
- In interference,

$$\frac{I_{max}}{I_{min}} = \left(\frac{\sqrt{I_1} + \sqrt{I_2}}{\sqrt{I_1} - \sqrt{I_2}}\right)^2 = \left(\frac{\sqrt{I_1/I_2} + 1}{\sqrt{I_1/I_2} - 1}\right)^2$$

$$= \left(\frac{A_1/A_2 + 1}{A_1/A_2 - 1}\right)^2 = \left(\frac{A_1 + A_2}{A_1 - A_2}\right)^2 = \left(\frac{A_{max}}{A_{min}}\right)^2$$

Example 1 In interference, two individual amplitudes are A_0 each and the intensity is I_0 each. Find resultant amplitude and intensity at a point, where

(a) phase difference between two waves is 60°

(b) path difference between two waves is $\frac{\lambda}{3}$.

Sol. (a) Substituting $\phi = 60°$ in the equations,

$$A = 2A_0 \cos\frac{\phi}{2} \qquad \ldots\text{(i)}$$

and $$I = 4I_0 \cos^2\frac{\phi}{2} \qquad \ldots\text{(ii)}$$

We get, $A = \sqrt{3}A_0$ and $I = 3I_0$ **Ans.**

(b) Given, $\Delta x = \dfrac{\lambda}{3}$

$$\therefore \qquad \phi \text{ or } \Delta\phi = \left(\frac{2\pi}{\lambda}\right)\cdot \Delta x$$

$$= \left(\frac{2\pi}{\lambda}\right)\left(\frac{\lambda}{3}\right) = \frac{2\pi}{3} \text{ or } 120°$$

Now, substituting $\phi = 120°$ in the above two equations we get

$A = A_0$ and $I = I_0$ **Ans.**

Example 2 Three waves from three coherent sources meet at some point. Resultant amplitude of each is A_0. Intensity corresponding to A_0 is I_0. Phase difference between first wave and second wave is 60°. Path difference between first wave and third wave is $\dfrac{\lambda}{3}$. The first wave lags behind in phase angle from second and third wave. Find resultant intensity at this point.

Sol. Here, the sources are three. So, we don't have any direct formula for finding the resultant intensity. First we will find the resultant amplitude by vector method and then by the relation $I \propto A^2$, we can also find the resulting intensity.

Further, a path difference of $\dfrac{\lambda}{3}$ is equivalent to a phase difference of 120° ($\Delta\phi$ or $\phi = \dfrac{2\pi}{\lambda}\cdot\Delta x$). Hence, the phase difference between first and second is 60° and between first and third is 120°. So, vector diagram for amplitude is as shown below.

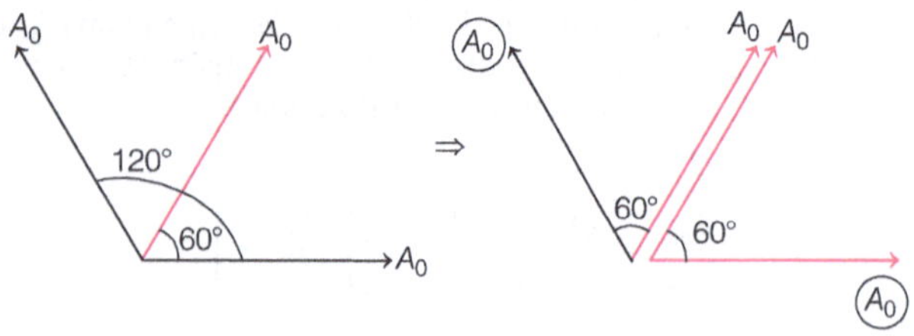

Now, resultant of first and third amplitude vectors acting at 120° is also A_0 (as $A = 2A_0 \cos\dfrac{\phi}{2}$ and $\phi = 120°$) and since the first and third are equal, so this resultant A_0 passes through the bisector line of these two or in the direction of second amplitude vector. Therefore, the resultant amplitude is

$$A = A_0 + A_0 = 2A_0$$

and the resultant intensity is

$$I = 4I_0 \qquad (\text{as } I \propto A^2)$$ **Ans.**

Example 3 Two waves of equal frequencies have their amplitudes in the ratio of 3 : 5. They are superimposed on each other. Calculate the ratio of maximum and minimum intensities of the resultant wave.

Sol. Given, $\dfrac{A_1}{A_2} = \dfrac{3}{5}$

$$\therefore \qquad \sqrt{\frac{I_1}{I_2}} = \frac{3}{5} \qquad (\text{as } I \propto A^2)$$

Hence, $$\frac{I_{max}}{I_{min}} = \left(\frac{\sqrt{\dfrac{I_1}{I_2}} + 1}{\sqrt{\dfrac{I_1}{I_2}} - 1}\right)^2$$

$$= \left(\frac{3/5 + 1}{3/5 - 1}\right)^2 = \frac{64}{4} = \frac{16}{1}$$ **Ans.**

Example 4 In interference, $\dfrac{I_{max}}{I_{min}} = \alpha$, find

(a $\dfrac{A_{max}}{A_{min}}$ (b) $\dfrac{A_1}{A_2}$ (c) $\dfrac{I_1}{I_2}$

Sol. (a) $\dfrac{A_{max}}{A_{min}} = \sqrt{\dfrac{I_{max}}{I_{min}}} = \sqrt{\alpha}$ **Ans.**

(b) $\dfrac{A_{max}}{A_{min}} = \sqrt{\alpha} = \dfrac{A_1 + A_2}{A_1 - A_2} = \dfrac{A_1/A_2 + 1}{A_1/A_2 - 1}$

Solving this equation, we get

$$\frac{A_1}{A_2} = \frac{\sqrt{\alpha}+1}{\sqrt{\alpha}-1}$$ **Ans.**

(c) $\dfrac{I_1}{I_2} = \left(\dfrac{A_1}{A_2}\right)^2 = \left(\dfrac{\sqrt{\alpha}+1}{\sqrt{\alpha}-1}\right)^2$

MODULE 2 Exercise

Assertion and Reason

See directions on page 14.

1. **Assertion :** Three waves of equal amplitudes interfere at a point. Phase difference between two successive waves is $\pi/2$. The resultant intensity will be the same as the intensity due to individual wave.

   Reason : For interference to take place sources must be coherent.

Multiple Correct Options

2. For interference to take place
   (a) sources must be coherent
   (b) sources must have same amplitude
   (c) waves should travel in opposite directions
   (d) sources must have same frequency

Subjective Questions

3. A wave is represented by

$$y_1 = 10\cos(5x + 25t)$$

where, x is measured in metres and t in seconds. A second wave for which

$$y_2 = 20\cos\left(5x + 25t + \frac{\pi}{3}\right)$$

interferes with the first wave. Deduce the amplitude and phase of the resultant wave.

4. The ratio of intensities of two waves is 9:16. If these two waves interfere, then determine the ratio of the maximum and minimum possible intensities.

5. In Interference, two individual amplitudes are 5 units and 3 units. Find
   (a) $\dfrac{A_{max}}{A_{min}}$
   (b) $\dfrac{I_{max}}{I_{min}}$

6. Three waves due to three coherent sources meet at one point. Their amplitudes are $\sqrt{2}A_0$, $3A_0$ and $\sqrt{2}A_0$. Intensity corresponding to A_0 is I_0. Phase difference between first and second is 45°. Path difference between first and third is $\dfrac{\lambda}{4}$. In phase angle, first wave lags behind from the other two waves. Find resultant intensity at this point.

Integer Type Question

7. The displacement equations of two interfering waves are given by $y_1 = 10\sin\left(\omega t + \dfrac{\pi}{3}\right)$ cm,

$y_2 = 5\,[\sin\omega t + \sqrt{3}\cos\omega t]$ cm, respectively.

The amplitude of the resultant wave is ...... cm. **(2023 Main)**

Answers

1. (b) **2.** (a,d) **3.** 26.46 cm, $(5x + 25t + 0.714)$ rad **4.** (49 : 1) **5.** (a) 4 : 1 (b) 16 : 1 **6.** $(25\,I_0)$ **7.** (20)

See hints on pages 79-80.

MODULE 3

Standing Wave

Standing wave is an example of interference. When two **identical** waves travel in opposite directions, then they superimpose almost at every point. Now, since the waves are identical (or their frequencies are same), sources are coherent. So, interference will take place. By their superposition (or interference) standing waves (also called stationary waves) are formed.

By identical waves we mean that all properties (like f, ω, T, λ and k) are same. Only amplitudes may be different but still we prefer equal amplitudes ($A_1 = A_2 = A_0$).

Given below are some of the important points in standing wave.

(i) Here, the constructive interference points are called antinodes (denoted by A) and destructive interference points are called nodes (denoted by N).

(ii) Distance between two successive nodes (or two successive antinodes) is $\frac{\lambda}{2}$ or $\frac{\pi}{k}\left(\text{as } k = \frac{2\pi}{\lambda}\right)$. Similarly, distance between a node and its adjacent antinode is $\frac{\lambda}{4}$ or $\frac{\pi}{2k}$. Here, λ and k are the values corresponding to constituent waves from which stationary waves are formed.

(iii) Amplitude of oscillation in stationary wave varies from a maximum value ($A_1 + A_2$ or $2A_0$ at antinode) to a minimum value ($A_1 \sim A_2$ or zero at node). But now onwards (unless mentioned in the question) we will talk about the equal amplitudes of the constituent waves. So, amplitude at antinode will be $2A_0$ and at node it is zero.

Thus, now we can say that, in stationary wave all particles (except nodes for the case when $A_1 = A_2$) oscillate with same frequency but different amplitudes.

(iv) All points lying between two successive nodes are in same phase. They cross their mean positions (in the same direction) simultaneously and reach their extreme positions also simultaneously. But they are out of phase with the particles lying between adjacent two nodes. This can be shown by the following figure.

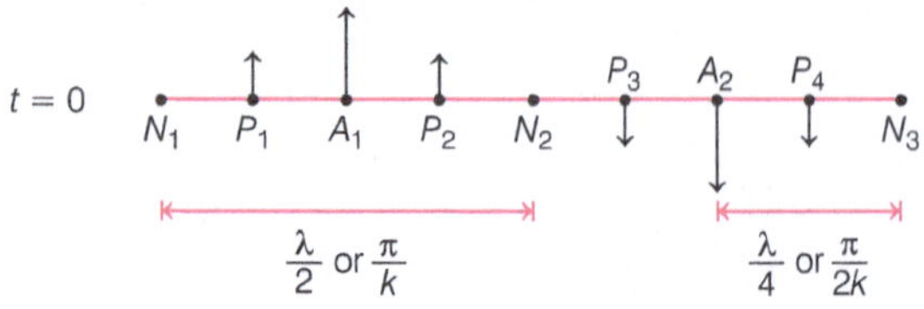

In the above figure N_1, N_2 and N_3 are nodes and A_1, A_2 are antinodes. Amplitude at nodes is zero and amplitude at antinodes is $2A_0$. In between them we have taken four more points P_1, P_2, P_3 and P_4. Suppose amplitude at these points is A_0 (between $2A_0$ and 0). Now, at $t = 0$ all particles are at their mean positions. Particles P_1, A_1 and P_2 are moving upwards (as they are in same phase) and the particles P_3, A_2 and P_4 are moving downwards. At this time, they have maximum speed. For example, in case of sine wave,

$$v_{P_1} = \omega A_0 \qquad (v_{max} = \omega A \text{ in SHM})$$

$$v_{A_1} = \omega(2A_0)$$

Now, in the chapter of SHM we have read that at time $t = \frac{T}{12}$ a particle reaches from its mean position to half its extreme position and in time $t = \frac{T}{4}$ it reaches from mean position to extreme position. So, at different times positions of different particles are as shown below.

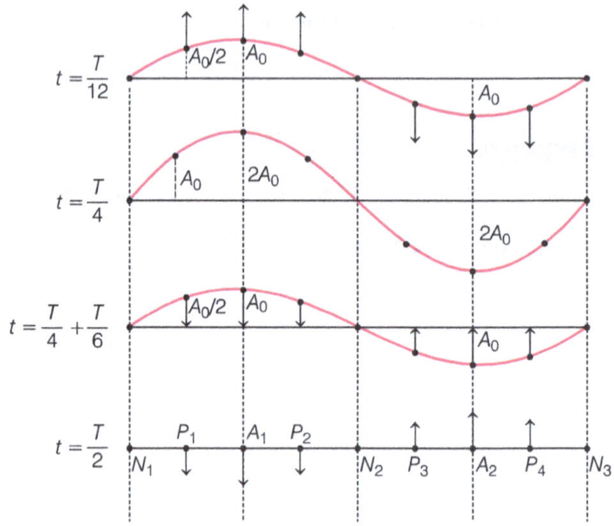

(v) Equation of a stationary wave depends upon the equations of constituent waves by which the stationary wave is formed. Let us take an example.

Suppose two identical waves travelling in opposite directions are

$$y_1 = A \sin (kx - \omega t)$$

and

$$y_2 = A \sin (kx + \omega t)$$

By the principle of superposition, their sum is

$$y = y_1 + y_2$$

or $$y = A[\sin(kx - \omega t) + \sin(kx + \omega t)]$$

By using the identity,

$$\sin A + \sin B = 2\sin\left(\frac{A+B}{2}\right)\cos\left(\frac{A-B}{2}\right),$$ we obtain

$$y = 2A\sin kx \cos \omega t \quad \text{...(i)}$$

This expression is different from wave equations that we have encountered until now. It doesn't have the form $f(x \pm vt)$ or $f(ax \pm bt)$ and therefore, does not describe a travelling wave. Instead Eq. (i) represents what is known as a **standing wave.**

Eq. (i) can also be written as

$$y = A_x \cos \omega t \quad \text{...(ii)}$$

where, $$A_x = 2A\sin kx \quad \text{...(iii)}$$

This equation of a standing wave [Eq. (ii)] is really an equation of simple harmonic motion, whose amplitude [Eq. (iii)] is a function of x.

$$A_x = 0, \text{ where } \sin kx = 0$$

or $$kx = 0, \pi, 2\pi, \ldots, n\pi \quad (n = 0, 1, 2, \ldots)$$

Substituting $k = \frac{2\pi}{\lambda}$, we have

$$A_x = 0 \quad \text{where,} \quad x = 0, \frac{\lambda}{2}, \lambda, \ldots, \frac{n\lambda}{2}$$

These are the points which never oscillate about their mean position. These points are known as the **nodes.** The distance between two adjacent nodes is $\frac{\lambda}{2}$.

Further, from Eq. (iii), we can see that maximum value of $|A_x|$ is $2A$, where

$$\sin kx = \pm 1$$

or $$kx = \frac{\pi}{2}, \frac{3\pi}{2}, \ldots, (2n-1)\frac{\pi}{2} \quad (n = 0, 1, 2, \ldots)$$

or $$x = \frac{\lambda}{4}, \frac{3\lambda}{4}, \ldots, (2n-1)\frac{\lambda}{4} \quad \left(k = \frac{2\pi}{\lambda}\right)$$

These are the points of maximum amplitudes called **antinodes.** The distance between two adjacent antinodes is also $\frac{\lambda}{2}$, while that between a node and an antinode is $\frac{\lambda}{4}$.

Important POINTS

S.No.	Travelling waves	Stationary waves
1.	In these waves, all particles of the medium oscillate with same frequency and amplitude	In these waves, all particles (except nodes) oscillate with same frequency but different amplitudes. Amplitudes is zero at nodes and maximum at antinodes
2.	At any instant phase difference between any two particles can have any value between 0 and 2π.	At any instant phase difference between any two particles can be either zero or π.
3.	In these waves, all the particles of the medium never pass through their mean positions simultaneously.	In these waves, all particles of the medium pass through their mean positions simultaneously twice in each time period.
4.	These waves transmit energy in the medium.	These waves do not transmit energy in the medium unless $A_1 \neq A_2$.

Summary

Until now, we have come across the following three sets of equations :

$$\left.\begin{aligned} y &= A\sin(\omega t \pm \phi) \\ y &= A\cos(\omega t \pm \phi) \end{aligned}\right\} \text{SHM}$$

$$\left.\begin{aligned} y &= A\sin(kx \pm \omega t \pm \phi) \\ y &= A\cos(kx \pm \omega t \pm \phi) \end{aligned}\right\} \text{Travelling wave}$$

$$\left.\begin{aligned} y &= A\sin kx \cos \omega t \quad \text{or} \quad 2A\sin kx \cos \omega t \\ y &= 2A\sin \omega t \cos kx \quad \text{or} \quad A\sin \omega t \cos kx \\ y &= A\sin kx \sin \omega t \quad \text{or} \quad 2A\sin kx \sin \omega t \\ y &= 2A\cos kx \cos \omega t \quad \text{or} \quad A\cos kx \cos \omega t \end{aligned}\right\} \text{Standing wave}$$

Note *In standing waves, we have given four sets of equations. The equation of standing wave basically depends upon the component waves. Further, if the maximum amplitude is 2A, it means amplitude of travelling waves is A and if it is A, then amplitude of travelling waves is* $\frac{A}{2}$.

Example 1 The displacement of a standing wave on a string is given by

$$y(x,t) = 0.4\sin(0.5x)\cos(30t)$$

where x and y are in centimetres and t in seconds.

(a) Find the frequency, amplitude and wave speed of the component waves.

(b) What is the particle velocity at $x = 2.4$ cm at $t = 0.8$ s ?

Sol. (a) According to the given equation,

$\omega = 30$ rad/s and $k = 0.5\ \text{cm}^{-1}$

Frequency, $f = \frac{\omega}{2\pi} = \frac{15}{\pi}$ Hz **Ans.**

Amplitude, $A = \frac{0.4}{2} = 0.2$ cm **Ans.**

and wave speed, $v = \frac{\omega}{k} = \frac{30}{0.5}$

$= 60$ cm/s **Ans.**

(b) Particle velocity,

$$v_P(x,t) = \frac{\partial y}{\partial t}$$

$$= -12 \sin(0.5x) \sin(30t)$$

$\therefore$ $v_P(x = 2.4\ \text{cm}, t = 0.8\ \text{s})$

$$= -12 \sin(1.2) \sin(24)$$

Substituting the values, we get

$v_P = 10.12$ cm/s **Ans.**

Example 2 The vibrations of a string of length 60 cm fixed at both ends are represented by the equation $y = 4\sin\left(\frac{\pi x}{15}\right)\cos(96\pi t)$, where x and y are in cm and t in seconds.

(a) What is the maximum displacement of a point at $x = 5$ cm?

(b) Where are the nodes located along the string?

(c) What is the velocity of the particle at $x = 7.5$ cm and $t = 0.25$ s?

(d) Write down the equations of the component waves whose superposition gives the above wave.

Sol. (a) $A_x = 4\sin\left(\frac{\pi x}{15}\right)$

At $x = 5$ cm,

$$A_x = 4\sin\frac{\pi}{3} = 4 \times \frac{\sqrt{3}}{2}$$

$\therefore$ Maximum displacement $= 2\sqrt{3}$ cm

(b) The nodes are the points of permanent rest. Thus, they are those points for which

$$\sin\left(\frac{\pi x}{15}\right) = 0$$

i.e. $\frac{\pi x}{15} = n\pi$, where $n = 0, 1, 2, 3, 4 \ldots$

$\Rightarrow$ $x = 15n$, i.e. at $x = 0$, 15, 30, 45 and 60 cm.

(c) The particle velocity is equal to

$$\left(\frac{\partial y}{\partial t}\right) = 4\sin\left(\frac{\pi x}{15}\right)(96\pi)(-\sin 96\pi t)$$

$$= -384\,\pi \sin\left(\frac{\pi x}{15}\right)\sin(96\,\pi t)$$

At $x = 7.5$ cm and $t = 0.25$ s, we get

$$\left(\frac{\partial y}{\partial t}\right) = -384\pi \sin\left(\frac{\pi}{2}\right)\sin(24\pi) = 0$$

(d) The equations of the component waves are

$$y_1 = 2\sin\left(\frac{\pi x}{15} + 96\pi t\right)$$

and $$y_2 = 2\sin\left(\frac{\pi x}{15} - 96\pi t\right)$$

as we can see that $y = y_1 + y_2$

MODULE 3 Exercise

True/False

1. In stationary wave, phase difference between two particles can't be $\frac{\pi}{3}$. Is this statement true or false?

Assertion and Reason

See directions on page 14.

2. **Assertion :** Two waves $y_1 = A\sin(\omega t + kx)$ and $y_2 = A\cos(\omega t - kx)$ are superimposed, then $x = 0$ becomes a node.

Reason : At node resultant amplitude due to two waves should be zero or minimum.

Single Correct Option

3. In a standing wave on a string
(a) in one time period all the particles are simultaneously at rest twice
(b) all the particles must be at their positive extremes simultaneously once in a time period
(c) all the particles may be at their positive extremes simultaneously twice in a time period
(d) all the particles are never at rest simultaneously

4. A standing wave is formed by the superposition of two waves travelling in opposite directions. The transverse displacement is given by

$$y(x, t) = 0.5\sin\left(\frac{5\pi}{4}x\right)\cos(200\,\pi t)$$

What is the speed of the travelling wave moving in the positive x direction?
(x and t are in meter and second, respectively) **(2017 Main)**

(a) 160 m/s (b) 90 m/s (c) 180 m/s (d) 120 m/s

5. A wave disturbance in a medium is described by $y(x, t) = 0.02\cos\left(50\pi t + \frac{\pi}{2}\right)\cos(10\pi x)$ where x and y are in metre and t is in second. **(1995 JEE)**
Choose the **incorrect** option
(a) A node occurs at $x = 0.15$ m
(b) An antinode occurs at $x = 0.3$ m
(c) The speed of wave is 5 ms^{-1}
(d) The wavelength is 0.3 m

6. The displacement y of a particle executing periodic motion is given by
$$y = 4\cos^2\left(\frac{1}{2}t\right)\sin(1000t)$$
This expression may be considered to be a result of the superposition of .... independent harmonic motions. **(1992 JEE)**
(a) two (b) three (c) four (d) five

7. A wave represented by the equation $y = a\cos(kx - \omega t)$ is superposed with another wave to form a stationary wave such that the point $x = 0$ is a node. The equation for the other wave is **(1988 JEE)**
(a) $a\sin(kx + \omega t)$ (b) $-a\cos(kx - \omega t)$
(c) $-a\cos(kx + \omega t)$ (d) $-a\sin(kx - \omega t)$

Multiple Correct Options

8. Regarding stationary waves, choose the correct options.
(a) This is an example of interference
(b) Amplitudes of waves may be different
(c) Particles at nodes are always at rest
(d) Energy is conserved

9. Which of the following equations can form stationary waves?
(i) $y = A\sin(\omega t - kx)$ (ii) $y = A\cos(\omega t - kx)$
(iii) $y = A\sin(\omega t + kx)$ (iv) $y = A\cos(\omega t + kx)$
(a) (i) and (ii) (b) (i) and (iii)
(c) (iii) and (iv) (d) (ii) and (iv)

10. Two waves $y_1 = A\sin(\omega t - kx)$ and $y_2 = A\sin(\omega t + kx)$ superimpose to produce a stationary wave, then
(a) $x = 0$ is a node
(b) $x = 0$ is an antinode
(c) $x = \frac{\pi}{k}$ is a node
(d) $\pi = \frac{2\pi}{k}$ is an antinode

Subjective Questions

11. A string vibrates according to the equation
$$y = 5\sin\frac{\pi x}{3}\cos 40\pi t$$
where, x and y are in centimetres and t is in seconds
(a) What is the speed of the component wave?
(b) What is the distance between the adjacent nodes?
(c) What is the velocity of the particle of the string at the position $x = 1.5$ cm when $t = \frac{9}{8}$ s?

12. If two waves differ only in amplitude and are propagated in opposite directions through a medium, will they produce standing waves. Is energy transported?

13. Two sinusoidal waves travelling in opposite directions interfere to produce a standing wave described by the equation
$$y = (1.5\text{ m})\sin(0.400x)\cos(200t)$$
where, x is in metres and t is in seconds. Determine the wavelength, frequency and speed of the interfering waves.

14. A standing wave is formed by the interference of two travelling waves, each of which has an amplitude $A = \pi$ cm, angular wave number $k = (\pi/2)$ per centimetre.
(a) Calculate the distance between two successive antinodes.
(b) What is the amplitude of the standing wave at $x = 0.50$ cm from a node?

Integer Type Question

15. Two travelling waves of equal amplitudes and equal frequencies move in opposite directions along a string. They interfere to produce a stationary wave whose equation is given by $y = \left(10\cos\pi x\sin\frac{2\pi t}{T}\right)$ cm. The amplitude of the particle at $x = \frac{4}{3}$ cm will be .... cm. **(2021 Main)**

Answers

1. (True) **2.** (d) **3.** (a) **4.** (a) **5.** (d) **6.** (b) **7.** (c) **8.** (a,b,d) **9.** (b,d) **10.** (b,d)
11. (a) 120 cm/s (b) 3 cm (c) Zero **12.** Yes, Yes **13.** 15.7 m, 31.8 Hz, 500 m/s **14.** (a) 2 cm, (b) $\sqrt{2}\pi$ cm
15. (5)

See hints on page 80.

MODULE 4

Oscillations of a Stretched Wire (or String)

(i) As shown in figure, *AB* is a stretched wire or wire under tension. We may also refer to wire as a string.

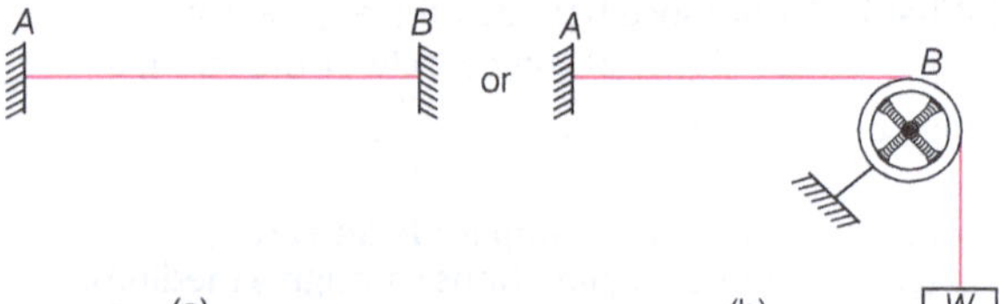

(a) (b)

(ii) Tension in wire *AB* can be produced by following three methods :

Method 1 : Wire *AB* in Fig. (a) is first stretched and then fixed at points *A* and *B*.

Method 2 : Wire *AB* in Fig. (a) is stretched at some higher temperature (than the normal room temperature). When temperature decreases, thermal stresses are produced and the wire comes under tension. Thermal stresses will be discussed in the forthcoming chapters.

Method 3 : By suspending a weight *W* from the wire *AB* as shown in Fig. (b).

(iii) Transverse stationary waves are produced in wire *AB*.

(iv) When we setup a sinusoidal wave on such a string, it gets reflected from the fixed ends. By the superposition of two identical waves travelling in opposite directions standing waves are established on the string.

(v) Stationary waves of certain fixed frequencies can only be produced in the string.

(vi) Those set of frequencies depend upon :

(a) tension in the wire

(b) mass per unit length of the wire and

(c) length of the wire.

Those set of frequencies

Before finding those set of frequencies let us first take an example.

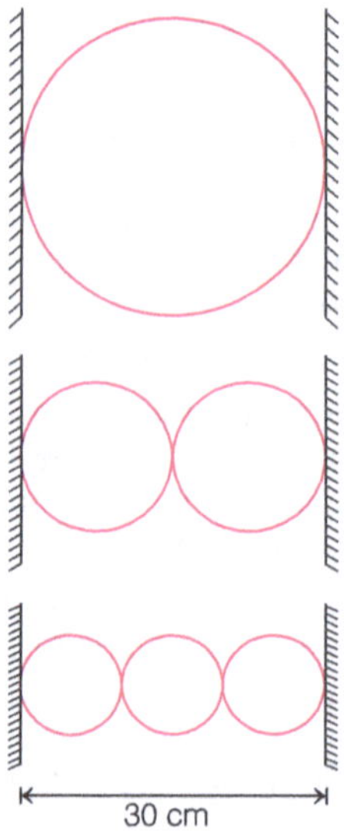

Suppose distance between two fixed walls is 30 cm. Now, we want to fix balls (of same size) between them.

In first figure diameter of ball is 30 cm. In second figure diameter is 15 cm and in third figure 10 cm.

So, we can fix balls of diameters 30 cm, 15 cm, 10 cm.... and so on. We can't fix balls of diameter 13 cm or 14 cm etc.

Same is the case here. Between stretched wire *AB* waves of certain fixed wavelengths can be produced. So, after finding the wavelength we can find frequency corresponding to that wavelength by using the formula $\left(f = \frac{v}{\lambda}\right)$.

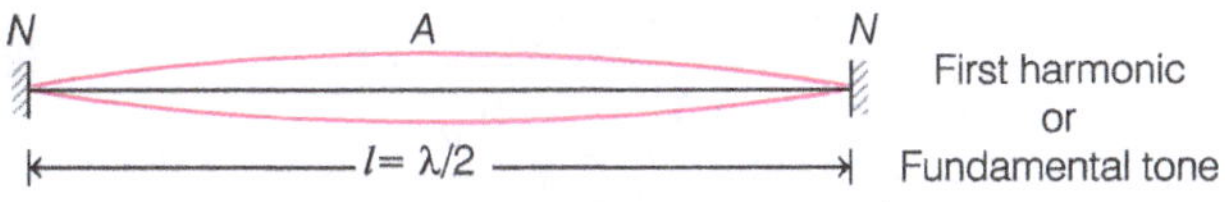

(a) $n = 1$

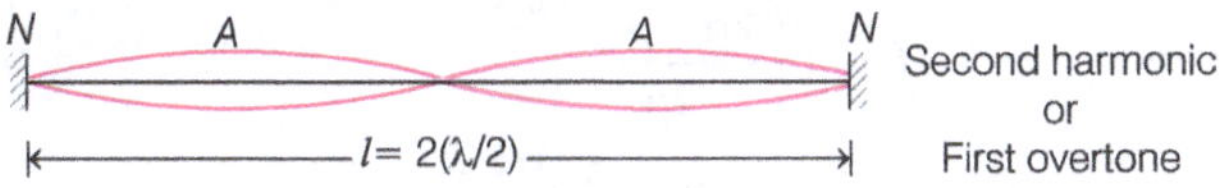

(b) $n = 2$

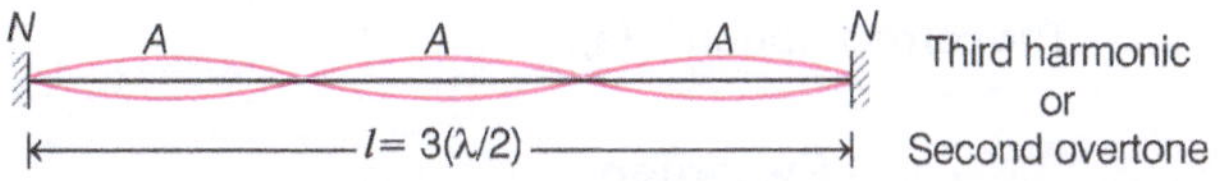

(c) $n = 3$

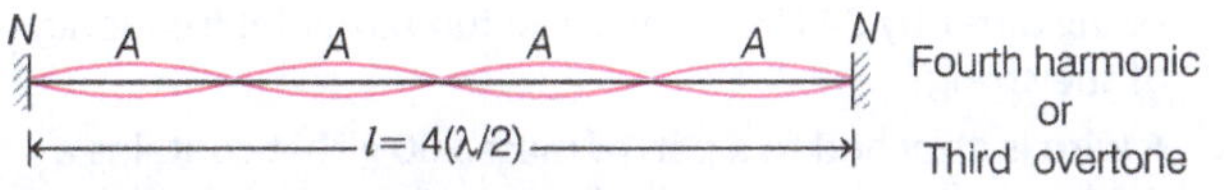

(d) $n = 4$

Fixed points will always become nodes as they can't oscillate. Therefore in the first figure l should be equal to $\frac{\lambda}{2}$.

$$l = \frac{\lambda}{2} \quad \text{or} \quad \lambda = 2l$$

The smallest frequency f_1 corresponds to the largest wavelength $\lambda_1 = 2l$

$$f_1 = \frac{v}{\lambda_1} = \frac{v}{2l}$$

This is called the **fundamental frequency.**

Here, $\quad v = \sqrt{\frac{T}{\mu}}$

In the second figure, l should be equal to $2\left(\frac{\lambda}{2}\right)$.

$$l = 2\left(\frac{\lambda}{2}\right) = \lambda$$

Therefore, the next higher frequency f_2 corresponds to the wavelength, $\lambda_2 = l$. Here, $\lambda_2 < \lambda_1$.

$$\therefore \quad f_2 = \frac{v}{\lambda_2} = \frac{v}{l} = 2\left(\frac{v}{2l}\right) = 2f_1$$

Similarly, f_3, f_4 etc.

These frequencies are called **harmonics**. Musicians sometimes call them **overtones**. Students are advised to remember these frequencies by name.

For example,

f_1 = fundamental tone or first harmonic

$f_2 = 2f_1$ = first overtone or second harmonic

$f_3 = 3f_1$ = second overtone or third harmonic and so on.

Thus, the natural frequencies of oscillation of the stretched wire are :

$$f = n\left(\frac{v}{2l}\right) = \frac{n}{2l}\sqrt{\frac{T}{\mu}} \qquad (n = 1, 2, 3 \ldots)$$

Important POINTS

- If by somehow, tension is decreased (for example: when weight is partially or fully immersed in a liquid), then from the above expression we can see that the set of frequencies will decrease.
- As n increases, T, μ, l and therefore $v\left(=\sqrt{\frac{T}{\mu}}\right)$ remain unchanged. Frequency increases, therefore wavelength $\left(\lambda = \frac{v}{f}\right)$ and the loop size $(= \lambda/2)$ decreases.
- Even and odd both harmonics $(n = 1, 2, 3, \ldots)$ are obtained from the stretched wire fixed at both ends.

Example 1 In terms of T, μ and l, find frequency of

(a) fourth overtone mode

(b) third harmonic

Sol. (a) Fourth overtone mode means

$$n = 5 \qquad (n = 1, 2, 3, 4, 5)$$

Therefore, using the equation

$$f = \frac{n}{2l}\sqrt{\frac{T}{\mu}}$$

We have, $\quad f = \frac{5}{2l}\sqrt{\frac{T}{\mu}}$ **Ans.**

(b) Third harmonic means

$$n = 3$$

$\therefore \quad f = \frac{3}{2l}\sqrt{\frac{T}{\mu}}$ **Ans.**

Example 2 A massless rod BD of length l is suspended by two identical massless strings AB and CD of equal lengths. A block of mass m is suspended from point P such that BP is equal to x. If the fundamental frequency of the left wire is twice the fundamental frequency of right wire, then the value of x is

(2006 JEE)

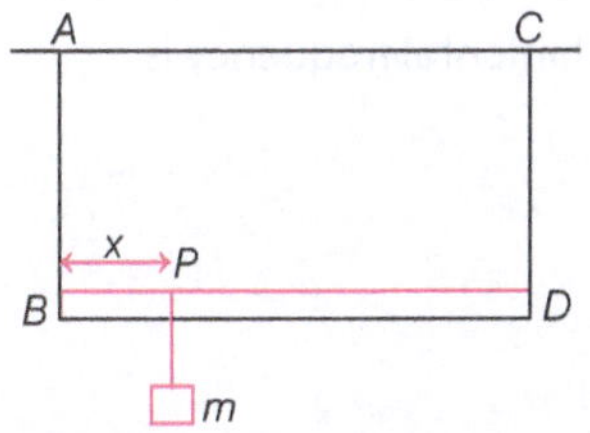

(a) $l/5$ (b) $l/4$ (c) $4l/5$ (d) $3l/4$

Sol. $f \propto v \propto \sqrt{T} \Rightarrow f_{AB} = 2f_{CD}$

$\therefore \quad T_{AB} = 4T_{CD}$ ...(i)

Further $\quad \Sigma\tau_P = 0$

$\therefore \quad T_{AB}(x) = T_{CD}(l - x)$

or $\quad 4x = l - x$ (as $T_{AB} = 4T_{CD}$)

or $\quad x = l/5$

$\therefore$ The correct option is (a).

Example 3 An object of specific gravity ρ is hung from a thin steel wire. The fundamental frequency for transverse standing waves in the wire is 300 Hz. The object is immersed in water, so that one half of its volume is submerged. The new fundamental frequency (in Hz) is **(1995 JEE)**

(a) $300\left(\dfrac{2\rho - 1}{2\rho}\right)^{1/2}$ (b) $300\left(\dfrac{2\rho}{2\rho - 1}\right)^{1/2}$

(c) $300\left(\dfrac{2\rho}{2\rho - 1}\right)$ (d) $300\left(\dfrac{2\rho - 1}{2\rho}\right)$

Sol. The diagrammatic representation of the given problem is shown in figure. The expression of fundamental frequency is

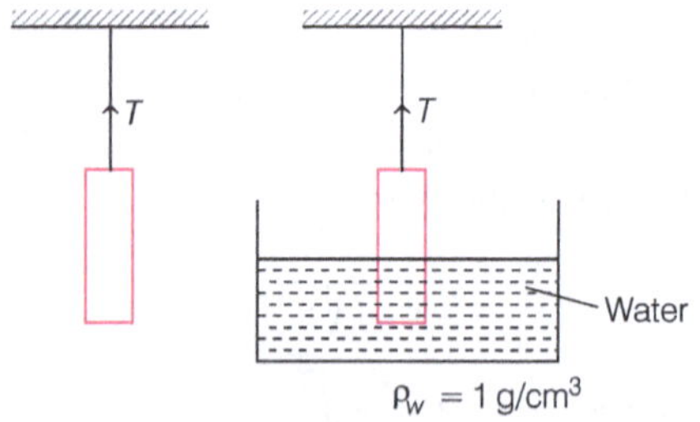

$$f = \frac{1}{2l}\sqrt{\frac{T}{\mu}}$$

In air, $\quad T = mg = (V\rho)\,g$

$$\therefore \quad f = \frac{1}{2l}\sqrt{\frac{V\rho g}{\mu}} \qquad \text{...(i)}$$

When the object is half immersed in water, then

$$T' = mg - \text{upthrust} = V\rho g - \left(\frac{V}{2}\right)\rho_w g$$

$$= \left(\frac{V}{2}\right) g\,(2\rho - \rho_w)$$

The new fundamental frequency is

$$f' = \frac{1}{2l} \times \sqrt{\frac{T'}{\mu}} = \frac{1}{2l}\sqrt{\frac{(Vg/2)(2\rho - \rho_w)}{\mu}} \qquad \text{...(ii)}$$

$$\therefore \quad \frac{f'}{f} = \left(\sqrt{\frac{2\rho - \rho_w}{2\rho}}\right)$$

or $$f' = f\left(\frac{2\rho - \rho_w}{2\rho}\right)^{1/2}$$

$$= 300\left(\frac{2\rho - 1}{2\rho}\right)^{1/2} \text{Hz} \qquad \textbf{Ans.}$$

$\therefore$ The correct option is (a).

INTRODUCTORY Exercise

1. If the frequencies of the second and fifth harmonics of a string differ by 54 Hz. What is the fundamental frequency of the string?
2. A wire is attached to a pan of mass 200 g that contains a 2.0 kg mass as shown in the figure. When plucked, the wire vibrates at a fundamental frequency of 220 Hz. An additional unknown mass M is then added to the pan and a fundamental frequency of 260 Hz is detected. What is the value of M?

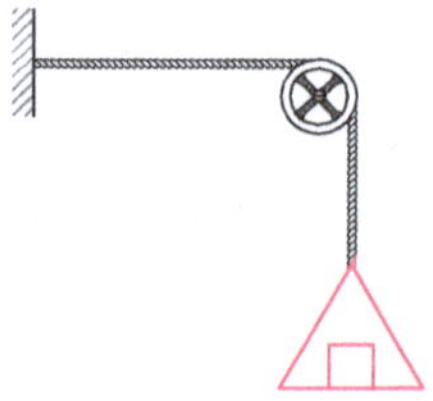

3. A wire fixed at both ends is 1.0 m long and has a mass of 36g. One of its oscillation frequencies is 250 Hz and the next higher one is 300 Hz.
   (a) Which harmonics do these frequencies represent?
   (b) What is the tension in the wire?
4. Two different stretched wires have same tension and mass per unit length. Fifth overtone frequency of the first wire is equal to second harmonic frequency of the second wire. Find the ratio of their lengths.

Answers

1. 18 Hz **2.** 0.873 kg

3. (a) 5th and 6th (b) 360 N **4.** $\dfrac{l_1}{l_2} = 3$

See hints on page 81.

Typed Problems

Type 1. *To find length of oscillating wire from the equation of stationary wave.*

How to Solve?

From the given equation of stationary wave find the value of wave number k and then λ. Now, from the given mode of oscillations we can also find number of loops. Suppose number of loops are n and one loop size is $\frac{\lambda}{2}$. Then, total length of wire will be

$$l = n\left(\frac{\lambda}{2}\right)$$

Ex. 1 A stretched wire is oscillating in third overtone mode. Equation of transverse stationary wave produced in this wire is

$$y = A\sin(6\pi x)\sin(20\pi t)$$

Here, x is in metres. Find the length of the wire.

Sol. From the given equation we can see that

$$k = 6\pi \text{ m}^{-1}$$

$$\therefore \quad \lambda = \frac{2\pi}{k} = \frac{2\pi}{6\pi} = \frac{1}{3}\text{ m}$$

Now, third overtone mode means four loops as shown below

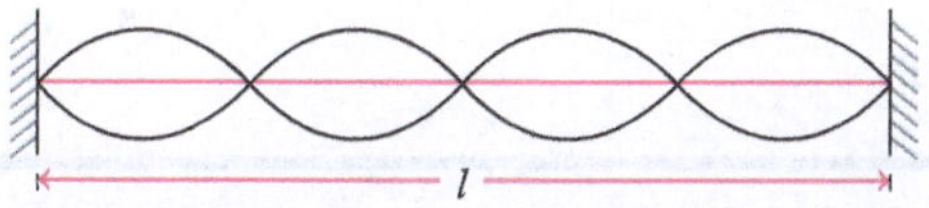

One loop size is $\frac{\lambda}{2}$, therefore total length of wire,

$$l = 4\left(\frac{\lambda}{2}\right) = 2\lambda$$

$$= 2\left(\frac{1}{3}\right)\text{m}$$

$$= \frac{2}{3}\text{ m}$$

Ans.

Type 2. *To find amplitude at some given point in stationary wave.*

Concept

In a stationary wave amplitude at different points varies from 0 at node (when $A_1 = A_2 = A_0$) to maximum $(= 2A_0)$ at antinode. If A_{max}, k and position of node or position of antinode is known to us then we can find amplitude at any general point. For example, if position of node is known, then take this point as $x = 0$. Now, amplitude at any general point x is

$$A_x = A_{max}\sin kx$$

In this expression we can see that $A_x = 0$ at $x = 0$.

Similarly, if position of antinode is known then amplitude at general point x is

$$A_x = A_{max}\cos kx$$

Again we can see that, $A_x = A_{max}$ at $x = 0$.

Ex. 2 Length of a stretched wire is 2 m. It is oscillating in its fourth overtone mode. Maximum amplitude of oscillations is 2 mm. Find amplitude of oscillation at a distance of 0.2 m from one fixed end.

Sol. Fourth overtone mode means five loops.

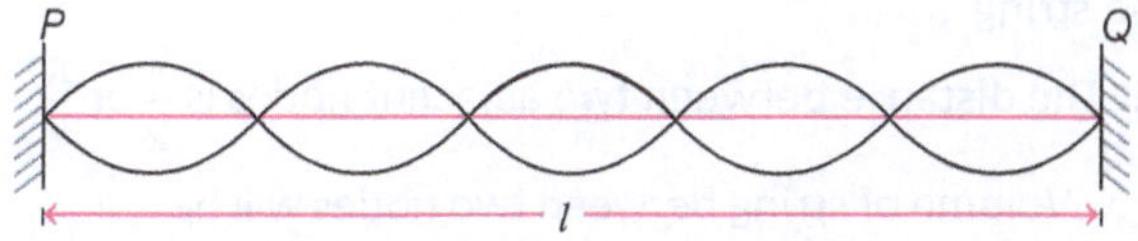

$$\therefore \quad l = 5\left(\frac{\lambda}{2}\right) \quad \text{or} \quad \lambda = \frac{2l}{5}$$

$$= \frac{2\times 2}{5} = 0.8\text{ m}$$

$$k = \frac{2\pi}{\lambda} = \frac{2\pi}{0.8} = (2.5\,\pi)\text{ m}^{-1}$$

Now, P is a node. So, take $x = 0$ at P.

Then, at a distance x from P,

$$A_x = A_{max}\sin kx$$

$$= (2\text{ mm})\sin(2.5\pi)(0.2)$$

$$= (2\text{ mm})\sin\left(\frac{\pi}{2}\right)$$

$$= 2\text{ mm}$$

Ans.

Note *At $x = 0.2$ m, we are getting $A_x = A_{max}$. Hence, $x = 0.2$ m is an antinode.*

Type 3. *To find energy of oscillation in a given portion in stationary wave.*

Concept

In SHM, energy of oscillation of a single particle is given by

$$E = \frac{1}{2}m\omega^2 A^2$$

In a travelling sine wave, all particles oscillate with same amplitude and same frequency. Energy density (or energy per unit volume) is given by

$$u = \frac{1}{2}\rho\omega^2 A^2$$

Since ρ, ω and A are same at all points. Therefore, energy density will be same at all points. So, in each unit volume equal amount of energy will be stored. Therefore, to find total energy of oscillation in a given volume, we just multiply the given volume by this constant energy density.

In stationary wave, amplitude is different at different positions. So, energy density will be non-uniform. Hence, total energy of oscillation in a given volume can be obtained by integration.

There is an alternate method also. By adding two energy densities of the travelling waves (from which standing wave is formed) first of all we find the total energy density. Then, we multiply the given volume with this energy density.

Ex. 3 A standing wave is formed by two harmonic waves, $y_1 = A\sin(kx - \omega t)$ and $y_2 = A\sin(kx + \omega t)$ travelling on a string in opposite directions. Mass density of the string is ρ and area of cross-section is S. Find the total mechanical energy between two adjacent nodes on the string.

Sol. The distance between two adjacent nodes is $\frac{\lambda}{2}$ or $\frac{\pi}{k}$.

$\therefore$ Volume of string between two nodes will be

$V =$ (area of cross-section) $\times$ (distance between two nodes)

$$= (S)\left(\frac{\pi}{k}\right)$$

Energy density (energy per unit volume) of a travelling wave is given by

$$u = \frac{1}{2}\rho A^2\omega^2$$

A standing wave is formed by two identical waves travelling in opposite directions. Therefore, the energy stored between two nodes in a standing wave.

$E = 2$ [energy stored in a distance of $\frac{\pi}{k}$ of a travelling wave]

$$= 2 \text{ (energy density) (volume)}$$

$$= 2\left(\frac{1}{2}\rho A^2\omega^2\right)\left(\frac{\pi S}{k}\right)$$

or $$E = \frac{\rho A^2\omega^2\pi S}{k}$$ **Ans.**

Alternate Method The equation of the standing wave

$$y = y_1 + y_2 = 2A\sin kx \cos\omega t = A_x \cos\omega t$$

Here, $A_x = 2A\sin kx$

i.e. first node is at $x = 0$ and the next node is at $x = \frac{\pi}{k}$. Let us take an element of length dx at a distance x from N_1. Mass of this element is dm $(= \rho S dx)$. This can be treated as a point mass. This element oscillates simple harmonically with angular frequency ω and amplitude $2A\sin kx$.

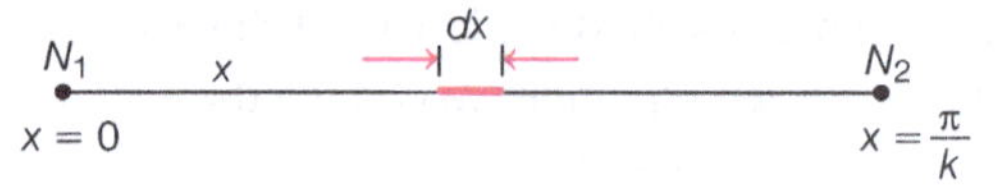

Hence, energy of this element

$$dE = \frac{1}{2}(dm)(2A\sin kx)^2(\omega^2)$$

$$dE = \frac{1}{2}(\rho S dx)(2A\sin kx)^2\,\omega^2$$

Integrating dE with the limits from $x = 0$ to $x = \frac{\pi}{k}$, we get the same result.

Miscellaneous Examples

Ex. 4 A string fixed at both ends has consecutive standing wave modes for which the distances between adjacent nodes are 18 cm and 16 cm, respectively.

(a) What is the minimum possible length of the string?

(b) If the tension is 10 N and the linear mass density is 4 g/m, what is the fundamental frequency?

Sol. (a)

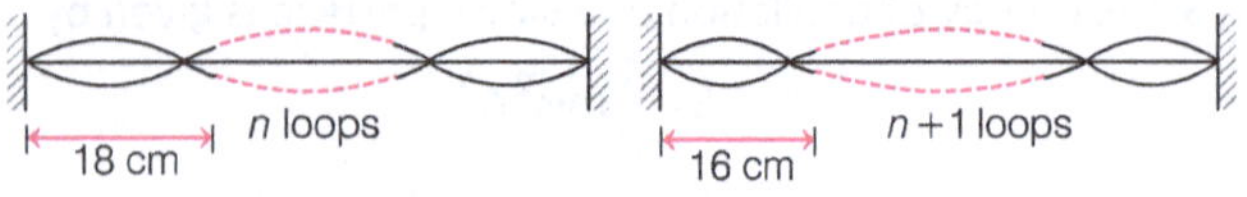

Let l be the length of the string. Then,

$$18n = l \quad \ldots\text{(i)}$$

$$16(n+1) = l \quad \ldots\text{(ii)}$$

From Eqs. (i) and (ii), wet get

$$n = 8$$

and $$l = 144 \text{ cm}$$

Therefore, the minimum possible length of the string can be 144 cm. **Ans.**

(b) For fundamental frequency, $l = \frac{\lambda}{2}$

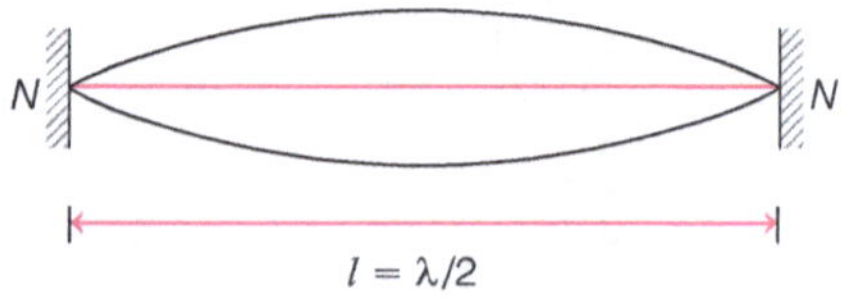

or $$\lambda = 2l = 288 \text{ cm}$$

$$= 2.88 \text{ m}$$

Speed of wave on the string,

$$v = \sqrt{\frac{T}{\mu}}$$

$$= \sqrt{\frac{10}{4 \times 10^{-3}}} = 50 \text{ m/s}$$

$\therefore$ Fundamental frequency,

$$f = \frac{v}{\lambda} = \frac{50}{2.88}$$

$$= 17.36 \text{ Hz}$$ **Ans.**

Ex. 5 Two wires are fixed on a sonometer. Their tensions are in the ratio 8 : 1, their lengths are in the ratio 36 : 35, the diameters are in the ratio 4 : 1 and densities are in the ratio 1:2. Find the value of lower frequency if higher frequency is 360 Hz.

Sol. Given, $\frac{T_1}{T_2} = \frac{8}{1}, \frac{L_1}{L_2} = \frac{36}{35}$

$$\frac{D_1}{D_2} = \frac{4}{1}, \frac{\rho_1}{\rho_2} = \frac{1}{2}$$

Let μ_1 and μ_2 be the linear mass densities, then

$$\therefore \quad \mu_1 = \pi \times \frac{D_1^2}{4} \times \rho_1 \text{ and } \mu_2 = \pi \times \frac{D_2^2}{4} \times \rho_2 \qquad (\mu = \rho S)$$

$$\therefore \quad \frac{\mu_1}{\mu_2} = \left(\frac{D_1}{D_2}\right)^2 \times \frac{\rho_1}{\rho_2} = \left(\frac{4}{1}\right)^2 \times \frac{1}{2} = \frac{8}{1}$$

$$\therefore \quad \frac{f_1}{f_2} = \frac{L_2}{L_1} \times \sqrt{\frac{T_1}{T_2} \times \frac{\mu_2}{\mu_1}} = \frac{35}{36}\sqrt{\frac{8}{1} \times \frac{1}{8}} = \frac{35}{36} \qquad \left(f = \frac{1}{2L}\sqrt{\frac{T}{\mu}}\right)$$

$$f_2 > f_1$$

We have $f_2 = 360$

$\therefore$ $f_1 = 350$ **Ans.**

Ex. 6 A string of linear mass density 5.0×10^{-3} kg/m is stretched under a tension of 65 N between two rigid supports 60 cm apart.

(a) If the string is vibrating in its second overtone so that the amplitude at one of its antinodes is 0.25 cm, what are the maximum transverse speed and acceleration of the string at antinodes?

(b) What are these quantities at a distance 5.0 cm from an node?

Sol. (a) In second overtone,

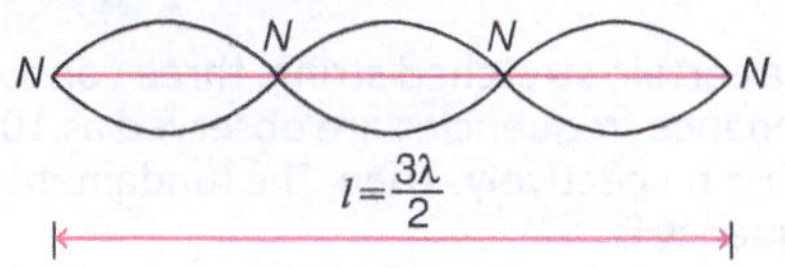

$$l = \frac{3\lambda}{2} \text{ or } \lambda = \frac{2l}{3} = \frac{2 \times 60}{3}$$

$$= 40 \text{ cm} = 0.4 \text{ m}$$

$$k = \frac{2\pi}{\lambda} = \frac{2\pi}{0.4} = 5\pi \text{ m}^{-1}$$

$$v = \sqrt{\frac{T}{\mu}} = \sqrt{\frac{65}{5.0 \times 10^{-3}}}$$

$$= 114 \text{ m/s}$$

$$\therefore \omega = kv = 570\pi \text{ rad/s}$$

Maximum transverse speed at antinode $= A_0\omega$

Here, A_0 = amplitude of antinode = 0.25 cm

$$= 2.5 \times 10^{-3} \text{ m}$$

$\therefore$ Maximum speed $= (2.5 \times 10^{-3})(570\pi)$ m/s

$$= 4.48 \text{ m/s}$$ **Ans.**

Maximum acceleration $= \omega^2 A_0$

$$= (570\pi)^2 (2.5 \times 10^{-3}) \text{ m/s}^2$$

$$= 8.0 \times 10^3 \text{ m/s}^2$$ **Ans.**

(b) At a distance x from the node, the amplitude can be written as

$$A = A_0 \sin kx = (2.5 \times 10^{-3}) \sin(5\pi x) \text{ metre}$$

Here, x is in metres.

Therefore, at $x = 5.0 \text{ cm} = 5.0 \times 10^{-2}$ m

$$A = (2.5 \times 10^{-3}) \sin(5\pi \times 5.0 \times 10^{-2})$$

$$= 1.8 \times 10^{-3} \text{ m}$$

Maximum speed $= A\omega$

$$= (1.8 \times 10^{-3})(570\pi) \text{ m/s}$$

$$= 3.22 \text{ m/s}$$ **Ans.**

and maximum acceleration $= \omega^2 A$

$$= (570\pi)^2 (1.8 \times 10^{-3}) \text{ m/s}^2$$

$$= 5.8 \times 10^3 \text{ m/s}^2$$ **Ans.**

Ex. 7 An aluminium wire of cross-sectional area 10^{-6} m^2 is joined to a steel wire of the same cross-sectional area. This compound wire is stretched on a sonometer pulled by a weight of 10 kg. The total length of the compound wire between the bridges is 1.5 m of which the aluminium wire is 0.6 m and the rest is steel wire. Transverse vibrations are setup in the wire by using an external source of variable frequency. Find the lowest frequency of excitation for which the standing waves are formed such that the joint in the wire is a node. What is the total number of nodes at this frequency? The density of aluminium is 2.6×10^3 kg/m^3 and that of steel is 1.04×10^4 kg/m^3($g = 10$ m/s^2).

Sol. Let n_a loops are formed in aluminium wire and n_s in steel. Then,

$$f_a = f_s$$

or $$n_a\left(\frac{v_a}{2l_a}\right) = n_s\left(\frac{v_s}{2l_s}\right)$$

or $$\frac{n_a}{n_s} = \left(\frac{v_s}{v_a}\right)\left(\frac{l_a}{l_s}\right)$$

But, $$v = \sqrt{\frac{T}{\mu}} = \sqrt{\frac{T}{\rho S}} \propto \frac{1}{\sqrt{\rho}}$$

Therefore, $$\frac{v_s}{v_a} = \sqrt{\frac{\rho_a}{\rho_s}}$$

$$\therefore \quad \frac{n_a}{n_s} = \sqrt{\frac{\rho_a}{\rho_s}} \cdot \frac{l_a}{l_s}$$

Substituting the values, we have

$$\frac{n_a}{n_s} = \sqrt{\frac{2.6 \times 10^3}{1.04 \times 10^4}} \cdot \frac{0.6}{0.9} = \frac{1}{3}$$

i.e. at lowest frequency, one loop is formed in aluminium wire and three loops are formed in steel wire as shown in figure.

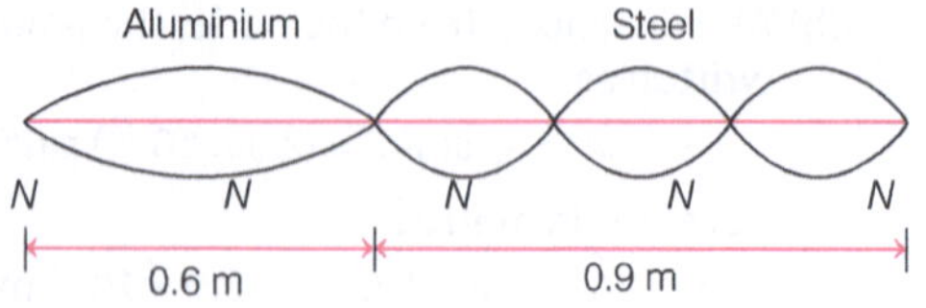

$$f_{min} = n_a \left(\frac{v_a}{2l_a} \right)$$

$$= \frac{1}{2l_a} \sqrt{\frac{T}{\rho_a S}} \qquad (T = mg = 100\, N)$$

$$= \frac{1}{2 \times 0.6} \sqrt{\frac{10 \times 10}{2.6 \times 10^3 \times 10^{-6}}}$$

or $f_{min} = 163.4$ Hz **Ans.**

Total number of nodes are five as shown is figure. **Ans.**

Note *In such type of problems nature of junction will be known to us. Normally it is a node. Then, we have to equate frequencies on the two sides. By equating the frequencies, we find $\frac{n_1}{n_2}$. Suppose this comes out to be 0.4. Write it, $\frac{n_1}{n_2} = \frac{2}{5}$.*

At lowest oscillation frequency 2 loops are formed on side 1 and 5 on side 2. At next higher frequency 4 loops will be formed on side 1 and 10 on side 2 and so on.

MODULE 4 Exercise

Assertion and Reason

See directions on page 14.

1. **Assertion :** A wire is stretched and then fixed at two ends. It oscillates in its second overtone mode. There are total four nodes and three antinodes.

   Reason : In second overtone mode, length of wire should be $l = \frac{3\lambda}{2}$, where λ is wavelength.

2. **Assertion :** In a standing wave $x = 0$ is a node. Then, total mechanical energy lying between $x = 0$ and $x = \frac{\lambda}{8}$ is not equal to the energy lying between $x = \frac{\lambda}{8}$ and $x = \frac{\lambda}{4}$.

   Reason : Energy lying between $x = \frac{\lambda}{8}$ to $x = \frac{\lambda}{4}$ will be more.

3. **Assertion :** A wire is stretched and then fixed at two ends. Wavelength of second overtone mode is $\frac{2}{3}$rd of the wavelength of first overtone mode.

   Reason : Frequency of second overtone mode is 3/2 times the frequency of first overtone mode.

Single Correct Option

4. Two strings A and B have lengths l_A and l_B and carry masses M_A and M_B at their lower ends, the upper ends being supported by rigid supports. If n_A and n_B are their fundamental frequencies of their vibrations, then $n_A : n_B$ is

   (a) $\frac{M_A l_A}{M_B l_B}$ (b) $\frac{l_A}{l_B} \sqrt{\frac{M_A}{M_B}}$

   (c) $\frac{M_A}{M_B} \sqrt{\frac{l_A}{l_B}}$ (d) None of these

5. If λ_1, λ_2 and λ_3 are the wavelength of the waves giving resonance to the fundamental, first and second overtone modes respectively in a string fixed at both ends. The ratio of the wavelengths $\lambda_1 : \lambda_2 : \lambda_3$ is

   (a) 1 : 2 : 3 (b) 1 : 3 : 5 (c) $1 : \frac{1}{2} : \frac{1}{3}$ (d) $1 : \frac{1}{3} : \frac{1}{5}$

6. For a certain stretched string, three consecutive resonance frequencies are observed as 105, 175 and 245 Hz respectively. Then, the fundamental frequency is

   (a) 30 Hz (b) 45 Hz

   (c) 35 Hz (d) None of these

7. A string 1 m long is drawn by a 300 Hz vibrator attached to its end. The string vibrates in three segments. The speed of transverse waves in the string is equal to

   (a) 100 m/s (b) 200 m/s (c) 300 m/s (d) 400 m/s

8. Three resonant frequencies of string with both rigid ends are 90, 150 and 210 Hz. If the length of the string is 80 cm, what is the speed of the transverse wave in the string?

   (a) 45 m/s (b) 75 m/s (c) 48 m/s (d) 80 m/s

9. Four wires of identical length, diameters and of the same material are stretched on a sonometer wire. If the ratio of their tensions is 1 : 4 : 9 : 16, then the ratio of their fundamental frequencies are
(a) 16 : 9 : 4 : 1 (b) 4 : 3 : 2 : 1
(c) 1 : 4 : 2 : 16 (d) 1 : 2 : 3 : 4

10. The correct graph between the frequency n and square root of density (ρ) of a wire, keeping its length, radius and tension constant, is

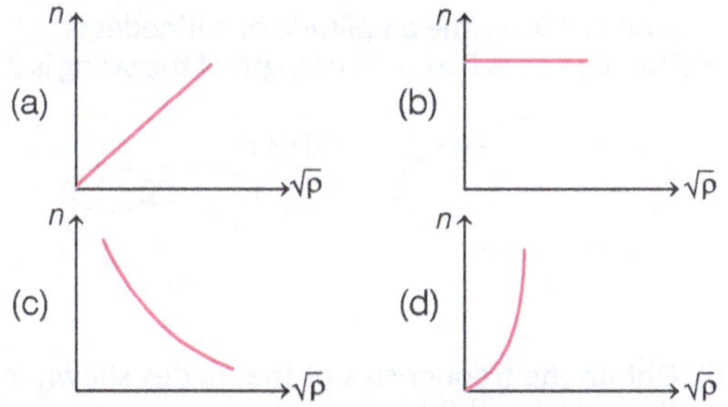

11. When the string of a sonometer of length L between the bridges vibrates in the second overtone mode, the amplitude of vibration is maximum at
(a) $\left(\frac{L}{2}\right)$ (b) $\left(\frac{L}{4}\right)$ and $\left(\frac{3L}{4}\right)$
(c) $\frac{L}{6}$ and $\frac{3L}{6}$ (d) $\frac{L}{8}, \frac{3L}{8}, \frac{5L}{6}$

12. The length of a sonometer wire AB is 110 cm. Where should the two bridges be placed between A and B dividing the wire in 3 segments whose fundamental frequencies are in the ratio of 1 : 2 : 3
(a) 30 cm and 90 cm (b) 40 cm and 80 cm
(c) 60 cm and 90 cm (d) 30 cm and 60 cm

13. When tension of a string is increased by 2.5 N, the initial frequency is altered in the ratio of 3 : 2. The initial tension in the string is
(a) 6 N (b) 5 N (c) 4 N (d) 2 N

14. The lengths of two wires of same material are in the ratio 1 : 2, their tensions are in the ratio 1 : 2 and their diameters are in the ratio 1 : 3. The ratio of the notes they emit when sounded together by the same source is
(a) $\sqrt{2}$ (b) $\sqrt{3}$ (c) $2\sqrt{3}$ (d) $3\sqrt{2}$

15. If f_1, f_2 and f_3 are the fundamental frequencies of three segments into which a string is divided, then the original fundamental frequency f_0 of the whole string is
(a) $f_0 = f_1 + f_2 + f_3$ (b) $\frac{1}{f_0} = \frac{1}{f_1} + \frac{1}{f_2} + \frac{1}{f_3}$
(c) $\frac{1}{\sqrt{f_0}} = \frac{1}{\sqrt{f_1}} + \frac{1}{\sqrt{f_2}} + \frac{1}{\sqrt{f_3}}$ (d) None of these

16. A string is stretched so that its length is increased by $1/\eta$ of its original length. The ratio of fundamental frequency of transverse vibration to that of fundamental frequency of longitudinal vibration will be
(a) $\eta : 1$ (b) $1 : \eta$ (c) $\sqrt{\eta} : 1$ (d) $1 : \sqrt{\eta}$

17. A rod of length 1 m and linear mass density 0.01 kg/m is stretched to a tension of 100 N. When both ends of the rod are fixed, the three lowest frequencies for standing wave are f_1, f_2 and f_3. When only one end of the rod is fixed, the three lowest frequencies for standing wave are n_1, n_2 and n_3. Then,
(a) $n_3 = 5n_1 = f_3 = 125$ Hz (b) $f_3 = 5f_1 = n_2 = 125$ Hz
(c) $f_3 = n_2 = 3f_1 = 150$ Hz (d) $n_2 = \frac{f_1 + f_2}{2} = 75$ Hz

Multiple Correct Options

18. If the tension in a stretched string fixed at both ends is increased by 21%, the fundamental frequency is found to be changed by 15 Hz. Then, the
(a) original frequency is 150 Hz
(b) velocity of propagation of the transverse wave along the string increases by 5%
(c) velocity of propagation of the transverse wave along the string increases by 10%
(d) fundamental wavelength on the string does not change

19. A wire is stretched and fixed at two ends. Transverse stationary waves are formed in it. It oscillates in its third overtone mode. The equation of stationary wave is

$$y = A \sin kx \cos \omega t$$

Choose the correct options.
(a) Amplitude of constituent waves is $\frac{A}{2}$
(b) The wire oscillates in three loops
(c) The length of the wire is $\frac{4\pi}{k}$
(d) Speed of stationary wave is $\frac{\omega}{k}$

Match the Columns

20. Transverse waves are produced in a stretched wire. Both ends of the string are fixed. Let us compare between second overtone mode (in numerator) and fifth harmonic mode (in denominator). Match the following two columns.

	Column I		Column II
(a)	Frequency ratio	(p)	2/3
(b)	Number of nodes ratio	(q)	4/5
(c)	Number of antinodes ratio	(r)	3/5
(d)	Wavelength ratio	(s)	5/3

21. A wire is stretched and fixed at its two ends. Its second overtone frequency is 210 Hz. Then, match the following two columns.

	Column I		Column II
(a)	Fundamental frequency	(p)	210 Hz
(b)	Third harmonic frequency	(q)	350 Hz
(c)	Third overtone frequency	(r)	280 Hz
(d)	Second harmonic frequency	(s)	None of these

Subjective Questions

22. Find the fundamental frequency and the next three frequencies that could cause a standing wave pattern on a string that is 30.0 m long, has a mass per unit length of 9.00×10^{-3} kg/m and is stretched to a tension of 20.0 N.

23. A string vibrates in its first normal mode with a frequency of 220 vibrations/s. The vibrating segment is 70.0 cm long and has a mass of 1.20 g.
(a) Find the tension in the string.
(b) Determine the frequency of vibration when the string vibrates in three segments.

24. A 60.0 cm guitar string under a tension of 50.0 N has a mass per unit length of 0.100 g/cm. What is the highest resonance frequency of the string that can be heard by a person able to hear frequencies upto 20000 Hz?

25. The vibrations from an 800 Hz tuning fork set up standing waves in a string clamped at both ends. The wave speed in the string is known to be 400 m/s for the tension used. The standing wave is observed to have four antinodes. How long is the string?

26. A string vibrates in 4 segments to a frequency of 400 Hz.
(a) What is its fundamental frequency?
(b) What frequency will cause it to vibrate into 7 segments?

27. A guitar string is 90 cm long and has a fundamental frequency of 124 Hz. Where should it be pressed to produce a fundamental frequency of 186 Hz?

28. A 1.50 m long rope is stretched between two supports with a tension that makes the speed of transverse waves 48.0 m/s. What are the wavelength and frequency of (a) the fundamental? (b) the second overtone? (c) the fourth harmonic?

29. A thin taut string tied at both ends and oscillating in its third harmonic has its shape described by the equation $y(x,t) = (5.60 \text{ cm}) \sin [(0.0340 \text{ rad/cm})x] \sin[(50.0 \text{ rad/s})t]$, where the origin is at the left end of the string, the x-axis is along the string and the y-axis is perpendicular to the string.
(a) Draw a sketch that shows the standing wave pattern.
(b) Find the amplitude of the two travelling waves that make up this standing wave.
(c) What is the length of the string?
(d) Find the wavelength, frequency, period and speed of the travelling wave.
(e) Find the maximum transverse speed of a point on the string.
(f) What would be the equation $y(x,t)$ for this string, if it were vibrating in its eighth harmonic?

30. A wire with mass 40.0 g is stretched so that its ends are tied down at points 80.0 cm apart. The wire vibrates in its fundamental mode with frequency 60.0 Hz and with an amplitude at the antinodes of 0.300 cm.
(a) What is the speed of propagation of transverse wave in the wire?
(b) Compute the tension in the wire.
(c) Find the maximum transverse velocity and acceleration of particles in the wire.

31. Figure shows different standing wave patterns on a string of linear mass density 4.0×10^{-2} kg/m under a tension of 100 N. The amplitude of antinodes is indicated in each figure. The length of the string is 2.0 m.

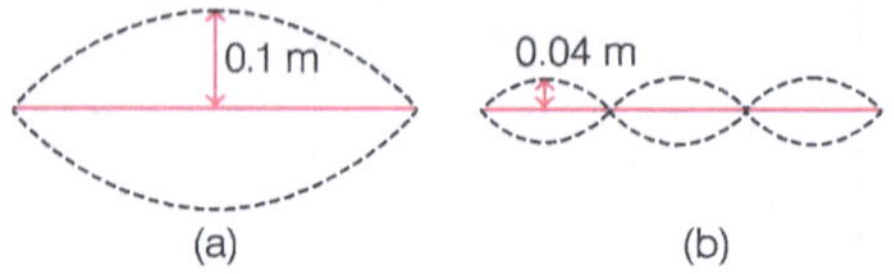

(i) Obtain the frequencies of the modes shown in figures (a) and (b).
(ii) Write down the transverse displacement y as a function of x and t for each mode. (Take the initial configuration of the wire in each mode to be as shown by the dark lines in the figure).

32. A string fastened at both ends has successive resonances with wavelengths of 0.54 m for the nth harmonic and 0.48 m for the $(n+1)$th harmonic.
(a) Which harmonics are these?
(b) What is the length of the string?
(c) What is the wavelength of the fundamental frequency?

Answers

1. (b)	**2.** (a)	**3.** (a)	**4.** (d)	**5.** (c)
6. (c)	**7.** (b)	**8.** (c)	**9.** (d)	**10.** (c)
11. (c)	**12.** (c)	**13.** (d)	**14.** (d)	**15.** (b)
16. (d)	**17.** (d)	**18.** (a,c,d)	**19.** (a,c)	

20. (a) $\to$ r; (b) $\to$ p; (c) $\to$ r; (d) $\to$ s

21. (a) $\to$ s; (b) $\to$ p; (c) $\to$ r; (d) $\to$ s

22. 0.786 Hz, 1.57 Hz, 2.36 Hz, 3.14 Hz

23. (a) 163 N (b) 660 Hz **24.** 19977 Hz **25.** 1 m

26. (a) 100 Hz (b) 700 Hz

27. The string should be pressed at 60 cm from one end.

28. (a) 3 m, 16 Hz (b) 1 m, 48 Hz (c) 0.75 m, 64 Hz

29. (b) 2.8 cm (c) 277 cm (d) 185 cm, 7.96 Hz, 0.126 s, 1470 cm/s (e) 280 cm/s (f) $y(x, t) = (5.6 \text{ cm}) \sin [(0.0907 \text{ rad/cm})x] \sin [(133 \text{ rad/s})t]$

30. (a) 96.0 m/s (b) 461 N (c) 1.13 m/s, 426.4 m/s^2

31. (i) Fundamental 12.5 Hz, third harmonic 37.5 Hz (ii) (a) $y = 0.1 \sin \frac{\pi x}{2} \sin 25\pi t$ (b) $y = 0.04 \sin \frac{3\pi x}{2} \sin 75\pi t$

32. (a) 8th and 9th (b) 2.16 m (c) 4.32 m

See hints on pages 81-84.

MODULE 5

Reflection and Transmission of a Wave

Following points are important in reflection and transmission of a wave :

(i) **Speed** From wave point of view that medium is called a denser medium in which speed of wave is less.

For example : for a sound wave (or longitudinal wave) air is denser medium compared to water because speed of sound in air is less. On the other hand, air is rarer medium for an electromagnetic wave, as speed of electromagnetic wave in air is more. When a wave strikes the boundary separating two different media, part of it is reflected and part is transmitted.

Since, wave speed depends upon the medium, in reflection wave speed does not change because medium does not change. In transmission, medium changes, therefore wave speed also changes. In denser medium it decreases.

(ii) **Frequency** Frequency (ω and T also) depends upon source. In reflection as well as transmission, source does not change. Therefore, frequency does not change.

(iii) **Wavelength** Wavelength (and therefore wave number $k = \frac{2\pi}{\lambda}$ also) is self adjusted in a value, $\lambda = \frac{v}{f}$. In reflection both v and f do not change, therefore λ and k do not change. In transmission, f remains unchanged but v changes. Therefore, λ and k both change. In a denser medium, v decreases, therefore λ also decreases but k increases.

(iv) **Phase change** A phase change of π or 180° occurs only during the reflection from a denser medium. In any other case (in transmission or reflection from a rarer medium) phase change is zero.

(v) **Amplitude** In reflection as well as transmission, amplitude changes.

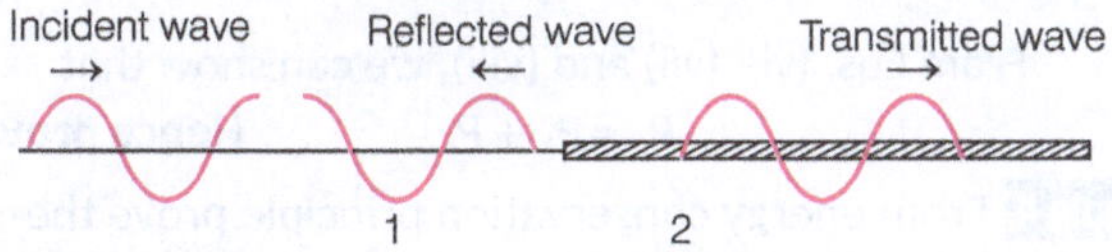

If amplitude of incident wave in medium-1 is A_i, it is partly reflected and partly transmitted at the boundary of two media-1 and 2. Wave speeds in two media are v_1 and v_2. If amplitudes of reflected and transmitted waves are A_r and A_t, then

$$A_r = \left(\frac{v_2 - v_1}{v_2 + v_1}\right) A_i \quad \text{and} \quad A_t = \left(\frac{2v_2}{v_1 + v_2}\right) A_i$$

From the above two expressions, we can make the following conclusions :

Conclusion 1 If $v_1 = v_2$, then $A_r = 0$ and $A_t = A_i$

Basically $v_1 = v_2$ means both media are same from wave point of view. So, in this case there is no reflection ($A_r = 0$), only transmission ($A_t = A_i$) is there.

Conclusion 2 If $v_2 < v_1$, then A_r comes out to be negative. Now, $v_2 < v_1$ means the second medium is denser. A_r in this case is negative means, there is a phase change of π.

Conclusion 3 If $v_2 > v_1$, then $A_t > A_i$. This implies that amplitude always increases as the wave travels from a denser medium to a rarer medium (as $v_2 > v_1$, so second medium is rarer).

(vi) **Power** At the boundary of two media,

energy incident per second = energy reflected per second + energy transmitted per second.

or

Power incident = power reflected + power transmitted

or $$P_i = P_r + P_t$$

Let us summarise the above points in tabular form as below.

Table 1.

Wave property	Reflection	Transmission (Refraction)
v	does not change	changes
f, T, ω	do not change	do not change
λ, k	do not change	change
A	change	change
ϕ	$\Delta\phi = 0$, from a rarer medium $\Delta\phi = \pi$, from a denser medium	$\Delta\phi = 0$

Example 1 Two strings 1 and 2 are taut between two fixed supports (as shown in figure) such that the tension in both strings is same. Mass per unit length of 2 is more than that of 1. Explain which string is denser for a transverse travelling wave.

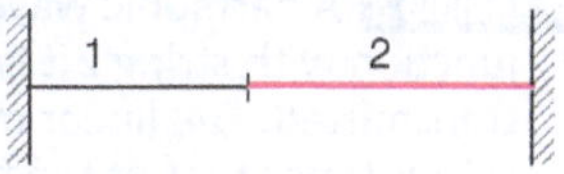

Sol. Speed of a transverse wave on a string,

$$v = \sqrt{\frac{T}{\mu}} \quad \text{or} \quad v \propto \frac{1}{\sqrt{\mu}}$$

Now, $\mu_2 > \mu_1$ (given)

$\therefore$ $v_2 < v_1$

i.e. medium 2 is denser and medium 1 is rarer.

Example 2 A sound wave and a light wave are reflected and refracted (or transmitted) from water surface. Show the changes in different physical quantities associated with a wave.

Sol. **Sound wave** We have seen, that water is a rarer medium for sound. When a wave travels from a denser to rarer medium, it bends away from normal. Its speed, wavelength and amplitude increase but angular wave number decreases. Further, in reflection from a rarer medium and in transmission there is no change in phase angle.

In the figure shown, 1 is incident wave 2 is reflected wave and 3 is transmitted wave.

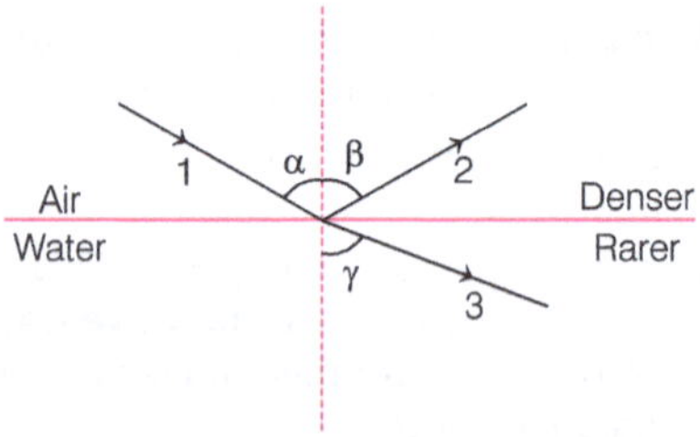

$\alpha = \beta, \gamma > \alpha, f_1 = f_2 = f_3, v_1 = v_2, \lambda_1 = \lambda_2, k_1 = k_2,$
$v_1 < v_3, \lambda_3 > \lambda_1 = \lambda_2, k_3 < k_1, \Delta\phi_{12} = \Delta\phi_{13} = 0°.$

Electromagnetic Wave For electromagnetic wave, water is denser medium. So, in water, ray of light will bend towards normal.

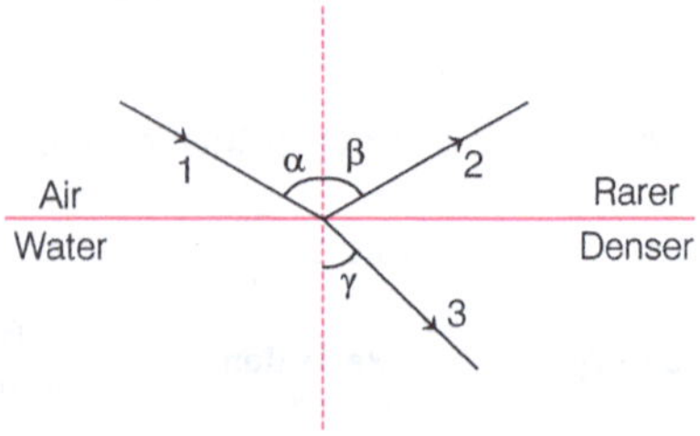

Further, speed and wavelength in this medium will decrease. But value of k will increase.

$\alpha = \beta, \gamma < \alpha, f_1 = f_2 = f_3, v_1 = v_2, \lambda_1 = \lambda_2, k_1 = k_2,$
$v_3 < v_1, \lambda_3 < \lambda_1, k_3 > k_1, \Delta\phi_{12} = \pi$ and $\Delta\phi_{13} = 0°$

Example 3 A harmonic wave is travelling on string 1. At a junction with string 2 it is partly reflected and partly transmitted. The linear mass density of the second string is four times that of the first string, and that the boundary between the two strings is at $x = 0$. If the expression for the incident wave is $y_i = A_i \cos(k_1 x - \omega_1 t)$

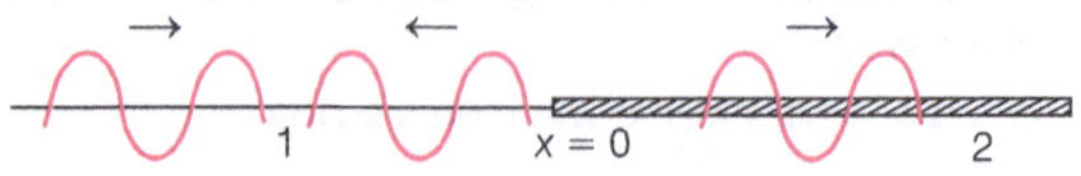

(a) What are the expressions for the transmitted and the reflected waves in terms of A_i, k_1 and ω_1?

(b) Show that the average power carried by the incident wave is equal to the sum of the average power carried by the transmitted and reflected waves.

Sol. (a) Since, $v = \sqrt{T/\mu}$, $T_2 = T_1$ and $\mu_2 = 4\mu_1$

We have, $$v_2 = \frac{v_1}{2} \quad \text{...(i)}$$

From Table 1, we can see that the frequency does not change, that is

$$\omega_1 = \omega_2 \quad \text{...(ii)}$$

Also, because $k = \dfrac{\omega}{v}$, the wave numbers of the harmonic waves in the two strings are related by

$$k_2 = \frac{\omega_2}{v_2} = \frac{\omega_1}{v_1/2} = 2\frac{\omega_1}{v_1} = 2k_1 \quad \text{...(iii)}$$

The amplitudes are

$$A_t = \left(\frac{2v_2}{v_1 + v_2}\right)A_i = \left[\frac{2(v_1/2)}{v_1 + (v_1/2)}\right] = \frac{2}{3}A_i \quad \text{...(iv)}$$

and $$A_r = \left(\frac{v_2 - v_1}{v_1 + v_2}\right)A_i = \left[\frac{(v_1/2) - v_1}{v_1 + (v_1/2)}\right]A_i = -\frac{A_i}{3} \quad \text{...(v)}$$

Now with Eqs. (ii), (iii) and (iv), the transmitted wave can be written as

$$y_t = \frac{2}{3}A_i \cos(2k_1 x - \omega_1 t)$$ **Ans.**

Similarly the reflected wave can be expressed as

$$y_r = -\frac{A_i}{3}\cos(k_1 x + \omega_1 t) = \frac{A_i}{3}\cos(k_1 x + \omega_1 t + \pi)$$ **Ans.**

(b) The average power of a harmonic wave on a string is given by

$$P = \frac{1}{2}\rho A^2\omega^2 Sv = \frac{1}{2}A^2\omega^2\mu v \quad (\text{as } \rho S = \mu)$$

Now, $$P_i = \frac{1}{2}\omega_1^2 A_i^2 \mu_1 v_1 \quad \text{...(vi)}$$

$$P_t = \frac{1}{2}\omega_1^2\left(\frac{2}{3}A_i\right)^2(4\mu_1)\left(\frac{v_1}{2}\right) = \frac{4}{9}\omega_1^2 A_i^2 \mu_1 v_1 \quad \text{...(vii)}$$

and $$P_r = \frac{1}{2}\omega_2^2\left(-\frac{A_i}{3}\right)^2(\mu_1)(v_1) = \frac{1}{18}\omega_1^2 A_i^2 \mu_1 v_1 \quad \text{...(viii)}$$

From Eqs. (vi), (vii) and (viii), we can show that

$$P_i = P_t + P_r$$ **Hence proved.**

Example 4 From energy conservation principle prove the relations,

$$A_r = \left(\frac{v_2 - v_1}{v_1 + v_2}\right)A_i \quad \text{and} \quad A_t = \left(\frac{2v_2}{v_1 + v_2}\right)A_i$$

Here, symbols have their usual meanings.

Sol. By conservation of energy, the average incident power equals the average reflected power plus the average transmitted power

or $$P_i = P_r + P_t$$

$$\therefore \quad \frac{1}{2}\mu_1\omega^2 A_i^2 v_1 = \frac{1}{2}\mu_1\omega^2 A_r^2 v_1 + \frac{1}{2}\mu_2\omega^2 A_t^2 v_2$$

or $$\left(\frac{T}{v_1^2}\right)\omega^2 A_i^2 v_1 = \left(\frac{T}{v_1^2}\right)\omega^2 A_r^2 v_1 + \left(\frac{T}{v_2^2}\right)\omega^2 A_t^2 v_2$$

or $$\frac{A_i^2}{v_1} = \frac{A_r^2}{v_1} + \frac{A_t^2}{v_2} \qquad \text{...(i)}$$

Further $A_i + A_r = A_t$ ...(ii)

Solving these two equations for A_r and A_t, we get

$$A_r = \left(\frac{v_2 - v_1}{v_1 + v_2}\right)A_i$$

and $$A_t = \left(\frac{2v_2}{v_1 + v_2}\right)A_i$$

Hence proved.

Example 5 In a stationary wave pattern that forms as a result of reflection of waves from an obstacle the ratio of the amplitude at an antinode and a node is $\beta = 1.5$. What percentage of the energy passes across the obstacle?

Sol. $$\frac{A_{max}}{A_{min}} = \frac{A_i + A_r}{A_i - A_r}$$

This ratio is given as 1.5 or $\frac{3}{2}$.

$$\therefore \quad \frac{A_i + A_r}{A_i - A_r} = \frac{3}{2} \quad \text{or} \quad \frac{1 + \frac{A_r}{A_i}}{1 - \frac{A_r}{A_i}} = \frac{3}{2}$$

Solving this equation, we get

$$\frac{A_r}{A_i} = \frac{1}{5}$$

$$\Rightarrow \quad \frac{I_r}{I_i} = \left(\frac{A_r}{A_i}\right)^2 = \frac{1}{25}$$

or $$I_r = 0.04\, I_i$$

i.e. 4% of the incident energy is reflected or 96% energy passes across the obstacle. **Ans.**

INTRODUCTORY Exercise

1. Two pulses of identical shape overlap such that the displacement of the rope is momentarily zero at all points, what happens to the energy at this time?
2. The pulse shown in figure has a speed of 10 cm/s.

(a) If the linear mass density of the right string is 0.25 that of the left string. At what speed does the transmitted pulse travel?

(b) Compare the heights of the transmitted pulse and the reflected pulse to that of the incident pulse.

3. The harmonic wave $y_i = (2.0 \times 10^{-3})\cos \pi(2.0\,x - 50t)$ travels along a string toward a boundary at $x = 0$ with a second string. The wave speed on the second string is 50 m/s. Write expressions for reflected and transmitted waves. Assume SI units.

Answers

1. Energy is in the form of kinetic energy
2. (a) 20 cms^{-1} (b) $\frac{A_r}{A_i} = \frac{1}{3}, \frac{A_t}{A_i} = \frac{4}{3}$
3. $y_r = \frac{2}{3} \times 10^{-3} \cos \pi(2.0x + 50t)$, $y_t = \frac{8}{3} \times 10^{-3} \cos \pi(x - 50t)$

See hints on page 84.

Important POINTS

- **Reason of phase change of π in reflection from a denser medium** When a transverse wave is reflected at the rigid support, a phase change of π takes place in the displacement.

  Suppose a transverse pulse is produced along a string PQ whose end Q is attached to a rigid support. If the pulse travels in the form of a crest, then on reaching the rigid support, the pulse would exert an upward force.

  Since the support is rigid, it remains unaffected but a reaction force act in the downward direction on the string which reverses the sign of the displacement of the particle at Q. As a result, an inverted pulse in the form of a trough travels back as shown.

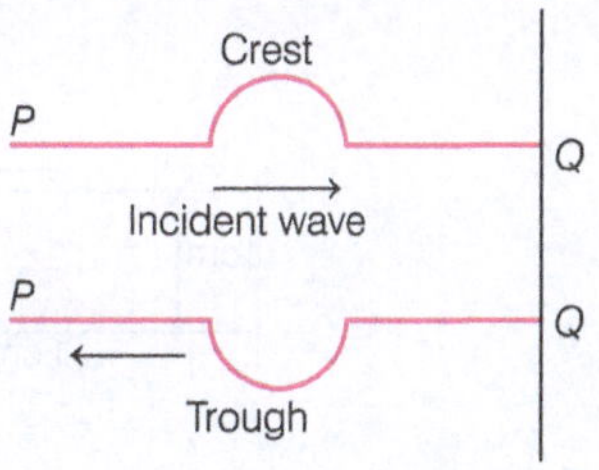

This concept can also be understood by a second thought process. Incident wave and reflected wave are two identical waves travelling in opposite directions.

So, they should produce a stationary wave. Point Q is a fixed point, which cannot oscillate at all. So, Q should become a node.

This is possible only when the two displacements (one due to incident wave y_1 and the other due to reflected wave y_2) are always equal and opposite ($y = y_1 + y_2 = 0$ or $y_1 = -y_2$). Or, they have a phase difference of π.

Typed Problems

Type 1. *Based on the formation of the reflected pulse, either from a rigid boundary or from a free boundary.*

Concept

The formation of the reflected pulse can be obtained by overlapping two pulses travelling in opposite directions. The net displacement at any point is given by the principle of superposition.

(a) Rigid boundary (b) Free boundary

Ex. 1 A triangular wave pulse moving at 2 cm/s on a rope approached an end at which it is free to slide on a vertical pole. Draw the pulse at $\frac{1}{2}$ s interval until it is completely reflected.

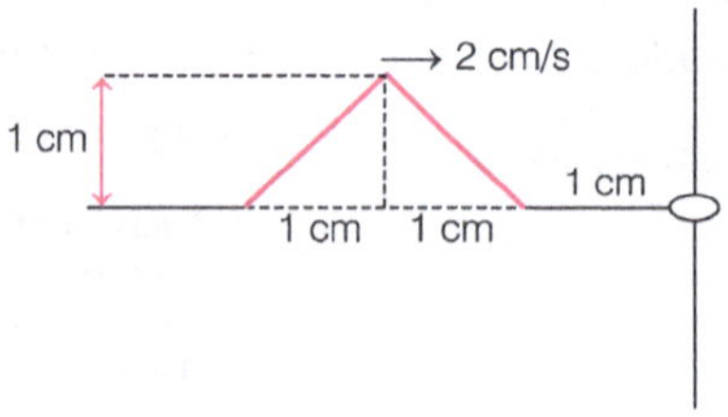

Sol. (a) Reflection of pulse from a free boundary is really the superposition of two identical waves travelling in opposite directions. This can be shown as under.

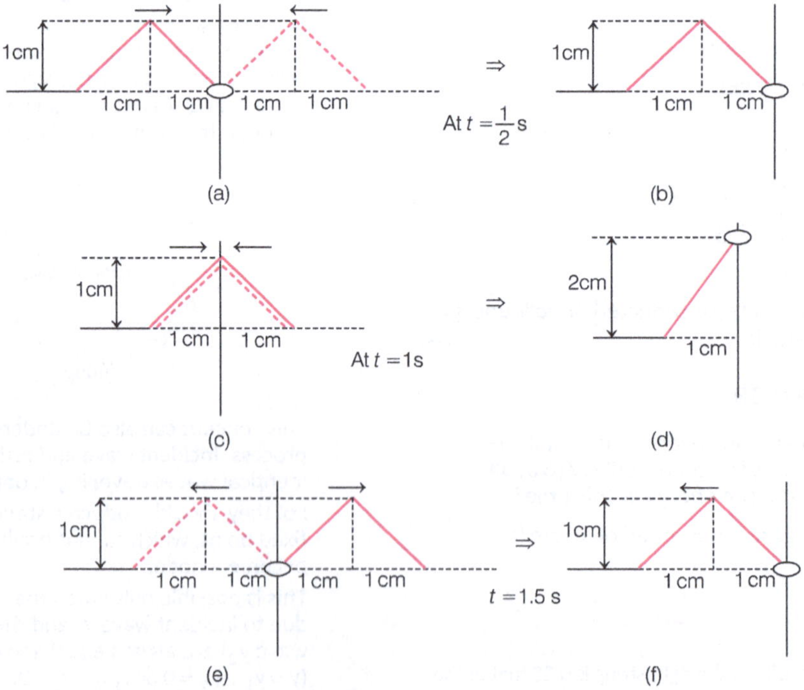

In every $\frac{1}{2}$ s, each pulse (one real moving towards right and one imaginary moving towards left) travels a distance of 1 cm as the wave speed is 2 cm/s.

MODULE 5 Exercise

Single Correct Option

1. Two identical harmonic pulses travelling in opposite directions in a taut string approach each other. At the instant when they completely overlap, the total energy of the string will be **(2001 JEE)**

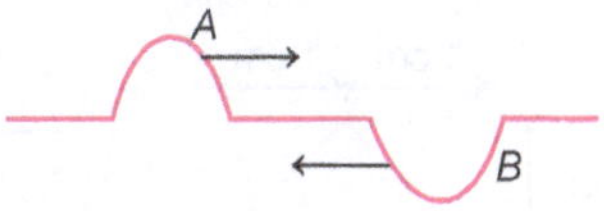

(a) zero
(b) partly kinetic and partly potential
(c) purely kinetic
(d) purely potential

2. Figure shows an incident pulse P reflected from a rigid support. Which one represents the reflected pulse correctly?

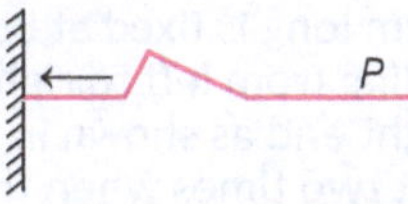

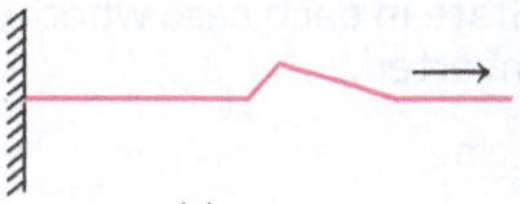

(a)

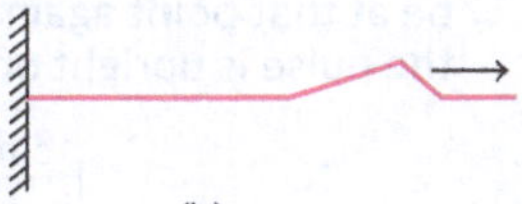

(b)

(c)

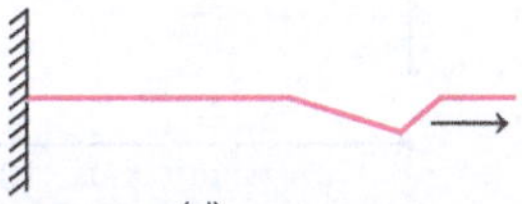

(d)

3. Two wires with different densities, are joined at $x = 0$. An incident wave $y_i = a_i \sin(\omega t - k_1 x)$, travelling from left to right is partly reflected and partly transmitted at $x = 0$. $y_t = a_t \sin(\omega t - k_2 x)$. If the amplitude of reflected and transmitted waves be a_r and a_t respectively, then $\frac{a_r}{a_t}$ is

(a) $\frac{2k_1}{k_1 + k_2}$
(b) $\frac{2k_2}{k_1 + k_2}$
(c) $\frac{k_1 - k_2}{2k_1}$
(d) $\frac{\sqrt{k_1} - \sqrt{k_2}}{\sqrt{k_1} + \sqrt{k_2}}$

4. In the above question, $\frac{a_t}{a_i}$ is

(a) $\frac{2k_1}{k_1 + k_2}$
(b) $\frac{2k_2}{k_1 + k_2}$
(c) $\frac{k_1 - k_2}{k_1 + k_2}$
(d) $\frac{\sqrt{k_1} - \sqrt{k_2}}{\sqrt{k_1} + \sqrt{k_2}}$

5. A wave $y_i = 0.3 \cos(2x - 40t)$ is travelling along a string towards a boundary at $x = 0$. If at $x = 0$, the string has fixed end, the expression for reflected wave is (Assume SI units)

(a) $y_r = 0.3 \cos(2x + 40t)$
(b) $y_r = 0.3 \cos\left(2x + 40t + \frac{\pi}{2}\right)$
(c) $y_r = 0.3 \cos(2x + 40t + \pi)$
(d) $y_r = 0.3 \cos(2x - 40t + \pi)$

6. A harmonic wave $y_i = 0.002 \cos(2\pi x - 50\pi t)$ travels along a string towards a boundary at $x = 0$, with a second string. The wave speed on the second string is 50 ms^{-1}. The expression for reflected wave is (Assume SI units)

(a) $y_r = (6.67 \times 10^{-3}) \cos(2\pi x + 50\pi t)$
(b) $y_r = (6.67 \times 10^{-4}) \cos(2\pi x + 50\pi t)$
(c) $y_r = (6.67 \times 10^{-5}) \cos(2\pi x + 50\pi t)$
(d) $y_r = -6.67 \times 10^{-5} \cos(2\pi x + 50\pi t)$

7. In the above question, the expression for transmitted wave is (Assume SI units)

(a) $y_t = (2.67 \times 10^{-4}) \cos(2\pi x - 50\pi t)$
(b) $y_t = (2.67 \times 10^{-4}) \cos(\pi x - 50\pi t)$
(c) $y_t = (2.67 \times 10^{-3}) \cos(2\pi x - 50\pi t)$
(d) $y_t = (2.67 \times 10^{-3}) \cos(\pi x - 50\pi t)$

Match the Columns

8. In the figure shown, mass per unit length of string-2 is nine times that of string-1. Tension in both the strings is same. A transverse wave is incident at the boundary as shown. Part of wave is reflected in medium-1 and part is transmitted to medium-2. Match the following two columns.

	Column I		Column II
(a)	$\lvert A_1/A_2 \rvert$	(p)	9
(b)	v_1/v_2	(q)	1
(c)	I_1/I_2	(r)	3
(d)	P_2/P_1	(s)	data insufficient

Here A is amplitude, v the speed of wave, I the intensity and P the power. Abbreviation 1 is used for reflected wave and 2 for transmitted wave.

9. A wave travels from a denser medium to a rarer medium, then match the following two columns.

	Column I		Column II
(a)	speed of wave	(p)	will increase
(b)	wavelength of wave	(q)	will decrease
(c)	amplitude of wave	(r)	will remain unchanged
(d)	frequency of wave	(s)	may increase or decrease

Subjective Questions

10. Two pulses travelling in opposite directions along a string are shown for $t = 0$ in the figure. Plot the shape of the string at $t = 1.0, 2.0, 3.0, 4.0$ and 5.0 s respectively.

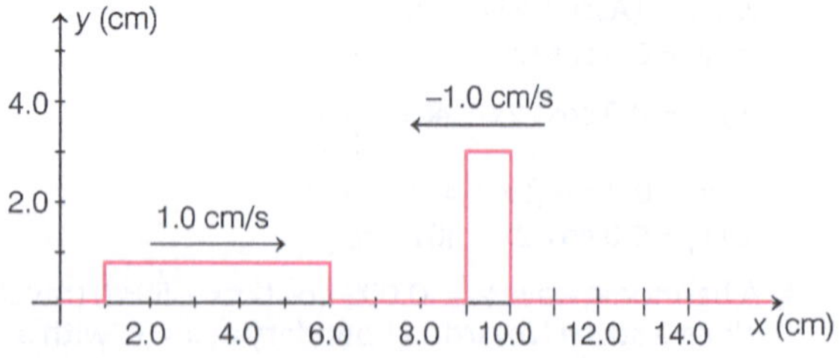

11. Two wires of different densities are soldered together end to end then stretched under tension T. The wave speed in the first wire is twice that in the second wire.
   (a) If the amplitude of incident wave is A, what are amplitudes of reflected and transmitted waves?
   (b) Assuming no energy loss in the wire, find the fraction of the incident power that is reflected at the junction and fraction of the same that is transmitted.

12. A string of length 20 cm and linear mass density 0.4 g/cm is fixed at both ends and is kept under a tension of 16 N. A wave pulse is produced at $t = 0$ near an end as shown in figure which travels towards the other end.
   (a) When will the string have the shape shown in the figure again?
   (b) Sketch the shape of the string at a time half of that found in part (a).

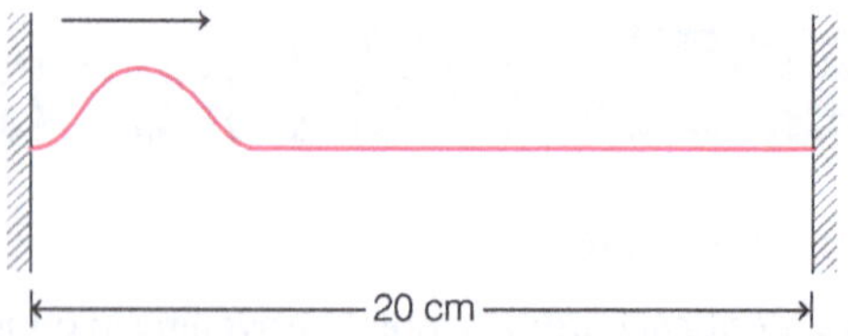

13. A wave pulse on a string has the dimensions shown in figure. The wave speed is $v = 1$ cm/s.

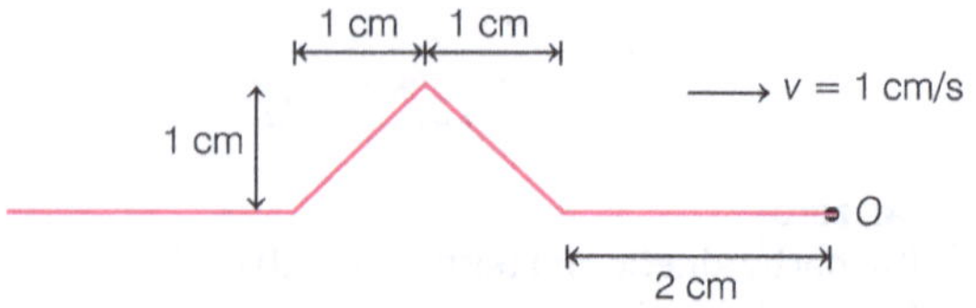

   (a) If point O is a fixed end, draw the resultant wave on the string at $t = 3$ s and $t = 4$ s.
   (b) Repeat part (a) for the case in which O is a free end.

14. A string that is 10 cm long is fixed at both ends. At $t = 0$, a pulse travelling from left to right at 1 cm/s is 4.0 cm from the right end as shown in figure. Determine the next two times when the pulse will be at that point again. State in each case whether the pulse is upright or inverted.

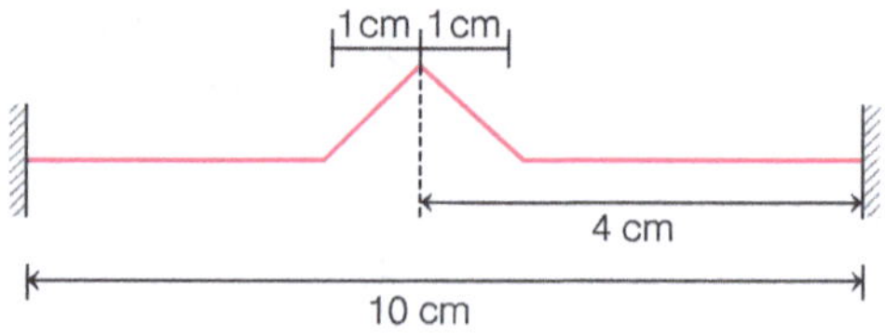

Answers

1. (c) **2.** (d) **3.** (c) **4.** (a) **5.** (c) **6.** (b) **7.** (d)

8. (a) → q; (b) → r; (c) → s; (d) → r **9.** (a) → p; (b) → p; (c) → p; (d) → r **10.** See the hints

11. (a) $-\frac{A}{3}, \frac{2}{3}A$ (b) $\frac{1}{9}, \frac{8}{9}$ **12.** (a) 0.02 s

13. (a) (i)  (ii)  (b) (i)  (ii) 

14. 8 s, inverted, 20 s upright

See hints on pages 84-86.

Unit Exercise (Cumulative)

Level 1

Single Correct Option

1. In a standing wave, node is a point of
(a) maximum strain (b) maximum pressure
(c) maximum density (d) All of these

2. The ends of a stretched wire of length L are fixed at $x = 0$ and $x = L$. In one experiment the displacement of the wire is $y_1 = A\sin(\pi x / L)\sin\omega t$ and energy is E_1 and in another experiment its displacement is $y_2 = A\sin(2\pi x / L)\sin 2\omega t$ and energy is E_2. Then **(2001 JEE)**
(a) $E_2 = E_1$ (b) $E_2 = 2E_1$ (c) $E_2 = 4E_1$ (d) $E_2 = 16E_1$

3. A string is clamped at both the ends and it is vibrating in its 4th harmonic. The equation of the stationary wave is $Y = 0.3\sin(0.157\,x)\cos(200\,\pi t)$. The length of the string is (All quantities are in SI units) **(2019 Main)**
(a) 20 m (b) 80 m (c) 40 m (d) 60 m

4. Two vibrating strings of the same material but lengths L and $2L$ have radii $2r$ and r respectively. They are stretched under the same tension. Both the strings vibrate in their fundamental nodes, the one of length L with frequency n_1 and the other with frequency n_2. The ratio n_1 / n_2 is given by **(2000 JEE)**
(a) 2 (b) 4 (c) 8 (d) 1

5. A wire having a linear density 0.1 kg/m is kept under a tension of 490 N. It is observed that it resonates at a frequency of 400 Hz. The next higher frequency is 450 Hz. Find the length of the wire.
(a) 0.4 m (b) 0.7 m (c) 0.6 m (d) 0.49 m

6. A string vibrates in 5 segments to a frequency of 480 Hz. The frequency that will cause it to vibrate in 2 segments will be
(a) 96 Hz (b) 192 Hz (c) 1200 Hz (d) 2400 Hz

7. The tension, length, diameter and density of a string B are double than that of another string A. Which of the following overtones of B is same as the fundamental frequency of A?
(a) 1st (b) 2nd
(c) 3rd (d) 4th

8. A sonometer wire when vibrated in full length has frequency n. Now, it is divided by the help of bridges into a number of segments of lengths $l_1, l_2, l_3, \ldots$. When vibrated, these segments have frequencies $n_1, n_2, n_3, \ldots$. Then, the correct relation is
(a) $n = n_1 + n_2 + n_3 + \ldots$
(b) $n^2 = n_1^2 + n_2^2 + n_3^2 + \ldots$
(c) $\dfrac{1}{n} = \dfrac{1}{n_1} + \dfrac{1}{n_2} + \dfrac{1}{n_3} + \ldots$
(d) $\dfrac{1}{\sqrt{n}} = \dfrac{1}{\sqrt{n_1}} + \dfrac{1}{\sqrt{n_2}} + \dfrac{1}{\sqrt{n_3}} + \ldots$

Multiple Correct Options

9. One end of a taut string of length 3 m along the X-axis is fixed at $x = 0$.The speed of the waves or the string is 100 ms^{-1}. The other end of the string is vibrating in the y-direction so that stationary waves are set up in the string. The possible waveform (s) of these stationary waves is/are **(2014 Adv.)**
(a) $y(t) = A\sin\dfrac{\pi x}{6}\cos\dfrac{50\pi t}{3}$
(b) $y(t) = A\sin\dfrac{\pi x}{3}\cos\dfrac{100\pi t}{3}$
(c) $y(t) = A\sin\dfrac{5\pi x}{6}\cos\dfrac{250\pi t}{3}$
(d) $y(t) = A\sin\dfrac{5\pi x}{2}\cos 250\pi t$

10. A horizontal stretched string, fixed at two ends, is vibrating in its 5th harmonic according to the equation, $y(x, t) = (0.01\text{ m})\sin[(62.8\text{ m}^{-1})x]\cos[(628\text{ s}^{-1})t]$. Assuming $\pi = 3.14$, the correct statement(s) is (are) **(2013 Adv.)**
(a) The number of nodes is 5
(b) The length of the string is 0.25 m
(c) The maximum displacement of the mid point of the string, from its equilibrium position is 0.01m
(d) The fundamental frequency is 100 Hz.

Subjective Questions

11. Two waves passing through a region are represented by
$$y_1 = (1.0\text{ cm})\sin[(3.14\text{ cm}^{-1})x - (157\text{ s}^{-1})t]$$
and $$y_2 = (1.5\text{ cm})\sin[(1.57\text{ cm}^{-1})x - (314\text{ s}^{-1})t]$$
Find the displacement of the particle at $x = 4.5$ cm at time $t = 5.0$ ms.

12. Two sinusoidal waves combining in a medium are described by the equations
$$y_1 = (3.0\text{ cm})\sin\pi(x + 0.60\,t)$$
and $$y_2 = (3.0\text{ cm})\sin\pi(x - 0.60\,t)$$
where, x is in centimetres and t is in seconds. Determine the maximum displacement of the medium at

(a) $x = 0.250$ cm,
(b) $x = 0.500$ cm and
(c) $x = 1.50$ cm.
(d) Find the three smallest values of x corresponding to antinodes.

13. Adjacent antinodes of a standing wave on a string are 15.0 cm apart. A particle at an antinode oscillates in simple harmonic motion with amplitude 0.850 cm and period 0.0750 s. The string lies along the $+x$-axis and is fixed at $x = 0$.
(a) Find the displacement of a point on the string as a function of position and time.
(b) Find the speed of propagation of a transverse wave in the string.
(c) Find the amplitude at a point 3.0 cm to the right of an antinode.

14. Two harmonic waves are represented in SI units by
$$y_1(x, t) = 0.2 \sin(x - 3.0\,t) \quad \text{and}$$
$$y_2(x, t) = 0.2 \sin(x - 3.0t + \phi)$$
(a) Write the expression for the sum $y = y_1 + y_2$ for $\phi = \frac{\pi}{2}$ rad.
(b) Suppose the phase difference ϕ between the waves is unknown and the amplitude of their sum is 0.32 m what is ϕ?

15. A 160 g rope 4 m long is fixed at one end and tied to a light string of the same length at the other end. Its tension is 400 N.
(a) What are the wavelengths of the fundamental and the first two overtones?
(b) What are the frequencies of these standing waves?

[**Hint :** In this case, fixed end is a node and the end tied with the light string is antinode.]

16. Find the ratio of the fundamental tone frequencies of two identical strings after one of them was stretched by $\eta_1 = 2.0\,\%$ and the other by $\eta_2 = 4.0\%$. The tension is assumed to be proportional to the elongation. **(Irodov 4.167)**

17. Determine in what way and how many times will the fundamental tone frequency of a stretched wire change if its length is shortened by 35% and the tension increased by 70%. **(Irodov 4.168)**

18. A standing wave $y = a \sin kx \cdot \cos \omega t$ is maintained in a homogeneous rod with cross-sectional area S and density ρ. Find the total mechanical energy confined between the sections corresponding to the adjacent displacement nodes. **(Irodov 4.173)**

19. Three component sinusoidal waves progressing in the same direction along the same path have the same period but their amplitudes are A, $\frac{A}{2}$ and $\frac{A}{3}$. The phases of the variation at any position x on their path at time $t = 0$ are 0, $-\frac{\pi}{2}$ and $-\pi$ respectively. Find the amplitude and phase of the resultant wave.

Integer Type Questions

20. A guitar string of length 90 cm vibrates with a fundamental frequency of 120 Hz. The length of the string producing a fundamental frequency of 180 Hz will be .... cm. **(2023 Main)**

21. The fundamental frequency of vibration of a string stretched between two rigid support is 50 Hz. The mass of the string is 18 g and its linear mass density is 20 g/m. The speed of the transverse waves produced in the string is .... ms^{-1}. **(2023 Main)**

22. A string of length 1 m and mass 2×10^{-5} kg is under tension T. When the string vibrates, two successive harmonics are found to occur at frequencies 750 Hz and 1000 Hz. The value of tension T is ...... Newton. **(2023 Adv.)**

23. A wire of length 30 cm, stretched between rigid supports, has it's nth and $(n + 1)$ th harmonics at 400 Hz and 450 Hz, respectively. If tension in the string is 2700 N, it's linear mass density is .... kg/m. **(2022 Main)**

24. A wire having a linear mass density 9.0×10^{-4} kg/m is stretched between two rigid supports with a tension of 900 N. The wire resonates at a frequency of 500 Hz. The next higher frequency at which the same wire resonates is 550 Hz. The length of the wire is .... m. **(2021 Main)**

Level 2

Single Correct Option

25. A string of length 1.5 m with its two ends clamped is vibrating in fundamental mode. Amplitude at the centre of the string is 4 mm. Distance between the two points having amplitude 2 mm is
(a) 1 m (b) 75 cm (c) 60 cm (d) 50 cm

26. Among two interfering sources, let S_1 be ahead of the phase by 90° relative to S_2. If an observation point P is such that $PS_1 - PS_2 = 1.5\,\lambda$, the phase difference between the waves from S_1 and S_2 reaching P is
(a) 3π (b) $\frac{5\pi}{2}$ (c) $\frac{7\pi}{2}$ (d) 4π

27. One end of a 2.4 m long string is held fixed and the other end is attached to a weightless ring that can slide along a frictionless rod as shown in the figure. The three longest possible wavelengths for standing waves in this string respectively are

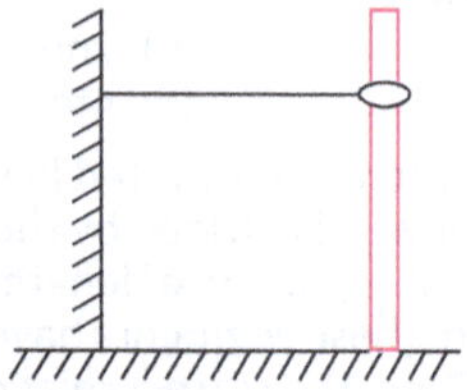

(a) 9.6 m, 3.2 m, 1.92 m (b) 4.8 m, 1.6 m, 0.96 m
(c) 2.4 m, 0.8 m, 0.48 m (d) 1.2 m, 0.4 m, 0.24 m

28. A uniform horizontal rod of length 0.4 m and mass 1.2 kg is supported by two identical wires as shown in the figure. Where should a mass of 4.8 kg be placed on the rod, so that the same tuning fork may excite the wire on the left into its fundamental vibrations and that on right into its first overtone? (Take, $g = 10\ ms^{-2}$)

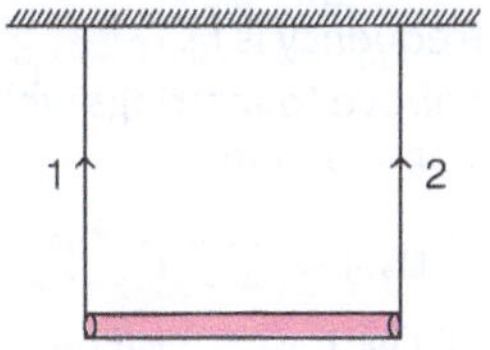

(a) 15 cm from left end
(b) 20 cm from left end
(c) 10 cm from left end
(d) 5 cm from left end

29. One end of a horizontal string is attached to a vibrating blade and the other end passes over a pulley as shown in the figure. A sphere of mass 2 kg hangs at the end of the string. The string is vibrating in its second harmonic. A container of water is raised under the sphere so that the sphere is completely submerged. In this configuration, the string vibrates in its fifth harmonic. What is the radius of the sphere?

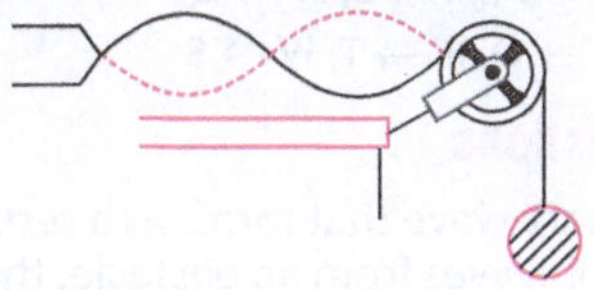

(a) 5.38 cm (b) 6.38 cm
(c) 7.38 cm (d) 4.38 cm

30. A wire of length $2L$, is made by joining two wires A and B of same length but different radii r and $2r$ and made of the same material. It is vibrating at a frequency such that the joint of the two wires forms a node. If the number of antinodes in wire A is p and that in B is q, then the ratio $p : q$ is **(2019 Main)**

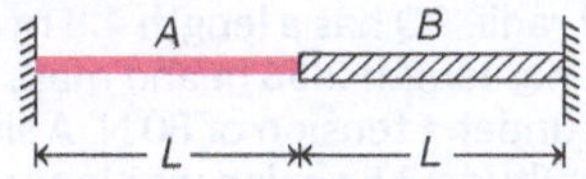

(a) 3 : 5 (b) 4 : 9
(c) 1 : 2 (d) 1 : 4

31. Two wires W_1 and W_2 have the same radius r and respective densities ρ_1 and ρ_2 such that $\rho_2 = 4\rho_1$. They are joined together at the point O, as shown in the figure. The combination is used as a sonometer wire and kept under tension T. The point O is midway between the two bridges. When a stationary wave is set up in the composite wire, the joint is found to be a node. The ratio of the number of antinodes formed in W_1 to W_2 is **(2017 Main)**

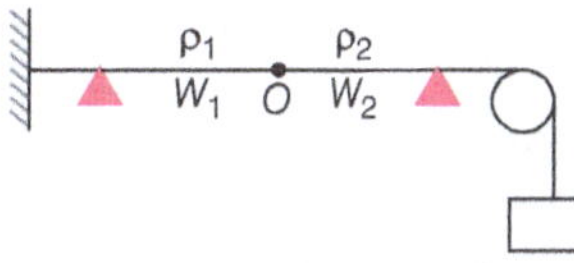

(a) 1 : 1 (b) 1 : 2 (c) 1 : 3 (d) 4 : 1

32. The total length of a sonometer wire between fixed ends is 110 cm. Two bridges are placed to divide the length of wire in ratio 6 : 3 : 2. The tension in the wire is 400 N and the mass per unit length is 0.01 kg/m. What is the minimum common frequency with which three parts can vibrate? **(2014 Main)**

(a) 1100 Hz (b) 1000 Hz (c) 166 Hz (d) 100 Hz

33. A sonometer wire of length 1.5 m is made of steel. The tension in it produces an elastic strain of 1%. What is the fundamental frequency of steel if density and elasticity of steel are $7.7 \times 10^3\ kg/m^3$ and $2.2 \times 10^{11}\ N/m^2$ respectively? **(2013 Main)**

(a) 188.5 Hz (b) 178.2 Hz (c) 200.5 Hz (d) 770 Hz

34. A sonometer wire resonates with a given tuning fork forming standing waves with five antinodes between the two bridges when a mass of 9 kg is suspended from the wire. When this mass is replaced by a mass M, the wire resonates with the same tuning fork forming three antinodes for the same positions of the bridges. The value of M is **(2002 JEE)**

(a) 25 kg (b) 5 kg (c) 12.5 kg (d) 1/25 kg

Passage Based Questions

Passage 1 (Q. 35 to Q. 37)

Incident wave $y = A \sin\left(ax + bt + \frac{\pi}{2}\right)$ *is reflected by an obstacle at* $x = 0$ *which reduces intensity of reflected wave by 36%. Due to superposition, the resulting wave consists of a standing wave and a travelling wave given by*

$$y = -1.6 \sin ax \sin bt + cA \cos (bt + ax)$$

where A, a, b and c are positive constants.

35. Amplitude of reflected wave is

(a) 0.6 A (b) 0.8 A (c) 0.4 A (d) 0.2 A

36. Value of c is

(a) 0.2 (b) 0.4 (c) 0.6 (d) 0.3

37. Position of second antinode is

(a) $x = \frac{\pi}{3a}$ (b) $x = \frac{3\pi}{a}$ (c) $x = \frac{3\pi}{2a}$ (d) $x = \frac{2\pi}{3a}$

Passage 2 (Q. 38 to Q.40)

A sinusoidal pulse is generated at $x = 0$ *and* $t = 0$ *on a string lying along X-axis. The pulse is travelling with a speed* $1\ ms^{-1}$*. A rectangular pulse is generated at* $t = 0$ *and is travelling in opposite direction with speed* $1\ ms^{-1}$ *as shown in the figure.*

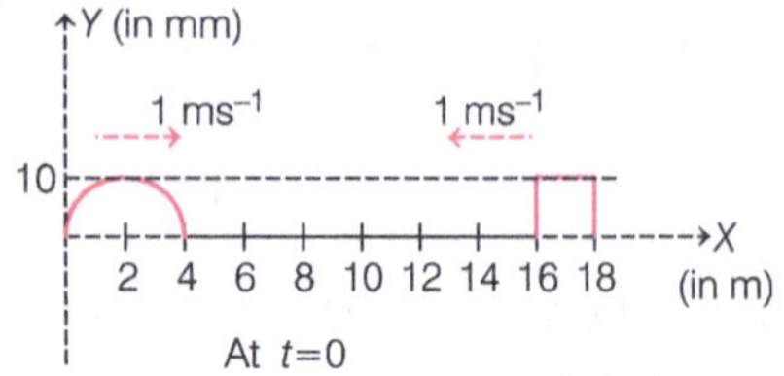

38. The velocity of particle at $x = 4$ m and $t = 0$ s is

(a) zero (b) $\frac{\pi}{6}$ cms^{-1} (c) $\frac{\pi}{2}$ cms^{-1} (d) $\frac{\pi}{4}$ cms^{-1}

39. The displacement of the particle at $x = 9$ m and $t = 8$ s is

(a) $\sqrt{2}$ cm (b) $\frac{3}{2}$ cm

(c) $(\sqrt{2}+1)$ cm (d) $\left(\frac{\sqrt{2}+1}{\sqrt{2}}\right)$ cm

40. The velocity of particle at $x = 9$ m and $t = 8$ s is

(a) $\frac{\pi}{2\sqrt{2}}$ cms^{-1} in $-y$-direction

(b) $\frac{\pi}{4\sqrt{2}}$ cms^{-1} in $-y$-direction

(c) $\frac{\pi}{4}$ cms^{-1} in $+y$-direction

(d) $\frac{\pi}{4}$ cms^{-1} in $-y$-direction

Passage 3 (Q.41 to Q.43)

In the arrangement shown, a mass can be hung from a string with a linear mass density of 2×10^{-3} *kg m*$^{-1}$, *that passes over a light pulley. The string is connected to a vibrator of frequency 700 Hz and the length of the string between the vibrator and the pulley is 1 m.*

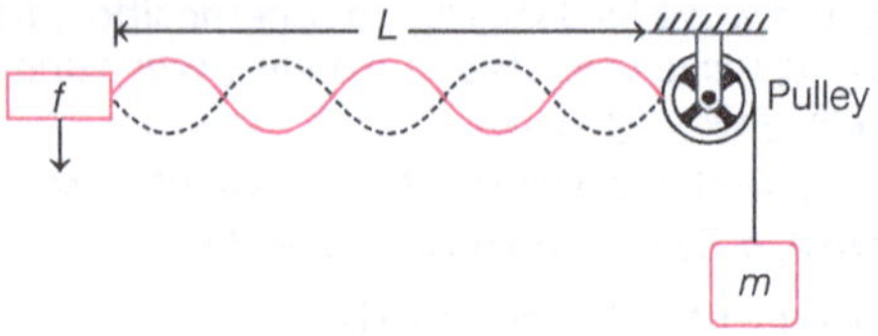

41. If the standing waves are observed, the largest mass to be hung is

(a) 32 kg (b) 25 kg
(c) 16 kg (d) 400 kg

42. If the mass suspended is 16 kg, then the number of loops formed in the string is

(a) 8 (b) 5
(c) 3 (d) 1

43. The string is set into vibrations and represented by the equation $y = 6\sin\left(\frac{\pi x}{10}\right)\cos(14000\,\pi t)$, where x and y are in cm and t in second. The maximum displacement at $x = 5$ m from the vibrator (in cm) is :

(a) 2 cm (b) 3 cm
(c) 6 cm (d) 5 cm

Match the Columns

44. A musical instrument is made using four different metal strings 1, 2, 3 and 4 with mass per unit length μ, 2μ, 3μ and 4μ respectively. The instrument is played by vibrating the strings by varying the free length in between the range L_0 and $2L_0$. It is found that in string-I at free length L_0 and tension T_0 the fundamental frequency is f_0.

List-I gives the above four strings while list-II the magnitude of some quantity. **(2019 Adv.)**

	List-I		List-II
(I)	String-1	(P)	1
(II)	String-2	(Q)	1/2
(III)	String-3	(R)	$1/\sqrt{2}$
(IV)	String-4	(S)	$1/\sqrt{3}$
		(T)	3/16
		(U)	1/16

If the tension in each string is T_0, the correct match for the highest fundamental frequency in f_0 units will be,

(a) I $\rightarrow$ Q, II $\rightarrow$ P, III $\rightarrow$ R, IV $\rightarrow$ T
(b) I $\rightarrow$ Q, II $\rightarrow$ S, III $\rightarrow$ R, IV $\rightarrow$ P
(c) I $\rightarrow$ P, II $\rightarrow$ R, III $\rightarrow$ S, IV $\rightarrow$ Q
(d) I $\rightarrow$ P, II $\rightarrow$ Q, III $\rightarrow$ T, IV $\rightarrow$ S

Subjective Questions

45. In a stationary wave that forms as a result of reflection of waves from an obstacle, the ratio of the amplitude at an antinode to the amplitude at node is 6. What percentage of energy is transmitted?

46. A string of mass per unit length μ is clamped at both ends such that one end of the string is at $x = 0$ and the other is at $x = l$. When string vibrates in fundamental mode, amplitude of the mid-point of the string is a and tension in the string is T. Find the total oscillation energy stored in the string.

47. A long wire PQR is made by joining two wires PQ and QR of equal radii. PQ has a length 4.8 m and mass 0.06 kg. QR has length 2.56 m and mass 0.2 kg. The wire PQR is under a tension of 80 N. A sinusoidal wave pulse of amplitude 3.5 cm is sent along the wire PQ from the end P. No power is dissipated during the propagation of the wave pulse. Calculate

(a) The time taken by the wave pulse to reach the other end R.

(b) The amplitude of the reflected and transmitted wave pulse after the incident wave pulse crosses the joint Q.

48. A light string is tied at one end to fixed support and to a heavy string of equal length L at the other end as shown in figure. Mass per unit length of the strings are μ and 9μ and the tension is T. Find the possible values of frequencies such that point A is a node/antinode.

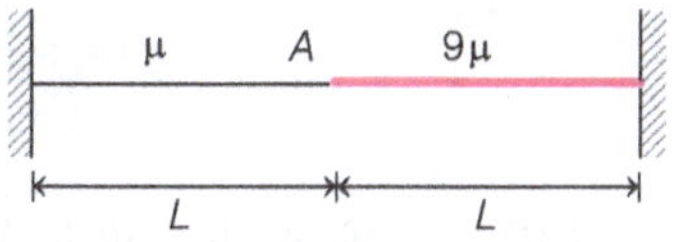

49. A string fixed at both ends is vibrating in the lowest possible mode of vibration for which a point at quarter of its length from one end is a point of maximum displacement. The frequency of vibration in this mode is 100 Hz. What will be the frequency emitted when it vibrates in the next mode such that this point is again a point of maximum displacement?

50. Sources separated by 20 m vibrate according to the equation $y_1 = 0.06 \sin \pi t$ and $y_2 = 0.02 \sin \pi t$. They send out waves along a rod with speed 3 m/s. What is the equation of motion of a particle 12 m from the first source and 8 m from the second, y_1, y_2 are in metre?

51. $y_1 = 8 \sin(\omega t - kx)$ and $y_2 = 6 \sin(\omega t + kx)$ are two waves travelling in a string of area of cross-section s and density ρ. These two waves are superimposed to produce a standing wave.

(a) Find the energy of the standing wave between two consecutive nodes.

(b) Find the total amount of energy crossing through a node per second.

52. The following equations represent transverse waves;

$z_1 = A \cos(kx - \omega t)$; $z_2 = A \cos(kx + \omega t)$:

$z_3 = A \cos(ky - \omega t)$

Identify the combination (s) of the waves which will produce

(a) standing wave (s)

(b) a wave travelling in the direction making an angle of 45 degrees with the positive X and positive Y-axes.

In each case, find the position at which the resultant intensity is always zero. **(1987 JEE)**

53. The displacement of the medium in a sound wave is given by the equation $y_1 = A\cos(ax + bt)$ where A, a and b are positive constants. The wave is reflected by an obstacle situated at $x = 0$. The intensity of the reflected wave is 0.64 times that of the incident wave. **(1991 JEE)**

(a) What are the wavelength and frequency of incident wave?

(b) Write the equation for the reflected wave.

(c) In the resultant wave formed after reflection, find the maximum and minimum values of the particle speeds in the medium.

(d) Express the resultant wave as a superposition of a standing wave and a travelling wave. What are the positions of the antinodes of the standing wave? What is the direction of propagation of travelling wave?

54. A string 120 cm in length sustains a standing wave, with the points of the string at which the displacement amplitude is equal to 3.5 mm being separated by 15.0 cm. Find the maximum displacement amplitude. To which overtone do these oscillations correspond? **(Irodov 4.166)**

55. A copper rod of length $l = 50$ cm is clamped at its mid-point. Find the number of natural longitudinal oscillations of the rod in the frequency range from 20 to 50 kHz. What are those frequencies equal to? **(Irodov 4.171)**

56. A string of mass m is fixed at both ends. The fundamental tone oscillations are excited with angular frequency ω and maximum displacement amplitude a_{max}. Find :

(a) the maximum kinetic energy of the string;

(b) the mean kinetic energy of the string averaged over one oscillation period. **(Irodov 4.172)**

Integer Type Question

57. An aluminium wire of length $L = 60$ cm and of cross-sectional area 0.01 cm^2 is connected to a steel wire of the same cross-sectional area. The compound wire is loaded with a block of mass 10 kg as shown in the figure. The distance L_2 from the joint to the supporting pulley is 86.6 cm. Transverse waves are set up in the composite wire at its lowest frequency, such that the joint in the wire is a node. What is the total number of nodes observed at this frequency excluding the two at the ends of the wire ? Density of aluminium is 2.6 g cm^{-3} and that of steel is 7.8 g cm^{-3}.

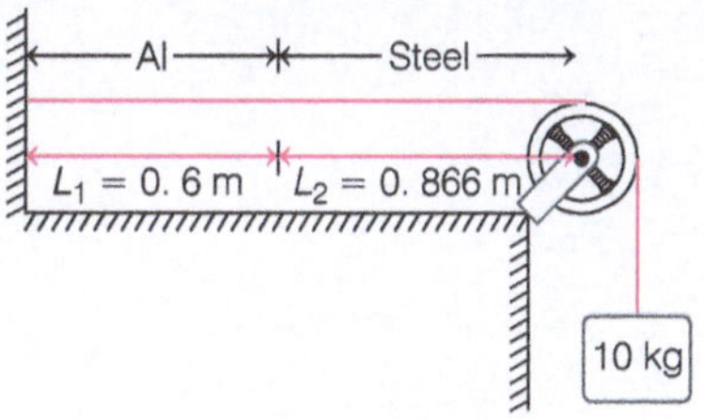

Answers

Level 1

1. (d) **2.** (c) **3.** (b) **4.** (d) **5.** (b) **6.** (b) **7.** (c) **8.** (c) **9.** (a,c,d) **10.** (b,c)

11. $-\dfrac{1}{2\sqrt{2}}$ cm **12.** (a) 4.24 cm (b) 6.00 cm (c) 6.00 cm (d) 0.5 cm, 1.5 cm, 2.5 cm

13. (a) $y(x, t) = (0.85 \text{ cm}) \sin\left[\dfrac{\pi x}{15 \text{ cm}}\right] \sin\left[\dfrac{2\pi t}{0.075 \text{ s}}\right]$ (b) 4.00 m/s (c) 0.688 cm

14. (a) $y = 0.28 \sin\left(x - 3.0t + \dfrac{\pi}{4}\right)$ (b) $\phi = \cos^{-1}(0.28)$ **15.** (a) 16 m, 5.33 m, 3.2 m (b) 6.25 Hz, 18.75 Hz, 31.25 Hz

16. 1.4 **17.** Two times **18.** $E = \dfrac{1}{4}\dfrac{\pi S \rho \omega^2 a^2}{k}$ **19.** $\dfrac{5}{6}A, -\tan^{-1}\left(\dfrac{3}{4}\right)$ **20.** (60) **21.** (90) **22.** (5)

23. (3) **24.** (10)

Level 2

25. (a) **26.** (b) **27.** (a) **28.** (d) **29.** (c) **30.** (c) **31.** (b) **32.** (b) **33.** (b) **34.** (a)
35. (b) **36.** (a) **37.** (c) **38.** (d) **39.** (d) **40.** (b) **41.** (d) **42.** (b) **43.** (c) **44.** (c)
45. (49%) **46.** $\pi^2 a^2 T / 4l$ **47.** (a) 0.14 s (b) – 1.5 cm, 2.0 cm

48. $\dfrac{f}{2}, f, \dfrac{3f}{2} \ldots$ etc. when A is a node, $\dfrac{3}{4}f, \dfrac{5}{4}f, \dfrac{7}{4}f \ldots$ etc. when A is an antinode. Here, $f = \dfrac{1}{L}\sqrt{\dfrac{T}{\mu}}$ **49.** 300 Hz

50. $0.05 \sin \pi t - 0.0173 \cos \pi t$ **51.** (a) $\dfrac{50\pi}{k} \rho \omega^2 S$ (b) $\dfrac{2\rho\omega^3 S}{k}$

52. (a) z_1 and z_2, $x = (2n + 1)\dfrac{\pi}{2k}$ where $n = 0, \pm 1, \pm 2 \ldots$ (b) z_1 and z_3, $(x - y) = (2n + 1)\dfrac{\pi}{k}$, where $n = 0, \pm 1, \pm 2 \ldots$

53. (a) $\lambda = \dfrac{2\pi}{a}, f = \dfrac{b}{2\pi}$ (b) $y_r = -0.8A \cos(ax - bt)$ (c) $v_{max} = 1.8 Ab, v_{min} = 0$ (d) See the hints

54. 5 mm, third overtone **55.** Four, 26.7 kHz, 34.4 kHz, 42 kHz, 49.6 kHz

56. (a) $K_m = \dfrac{1}{4} m\omega^2 a_{max}^2$ (b) $< K > = \dfrac{1}{8} m\omega^2 a_{max}^2$ **57.** (6)

See hints on pages 86-96.

Hints & SOLUTIONS

Module 1.

1. $y_1 + y_2 = 2A\sin(\omega t - kx) = y_4$ (say)

Now, y_4 and y_3 produce standing waves where,

$$A_{max} = 2 \quad \text{(Amplitude of constituent wave)}$$
$$= 2(2A) = 4A$$

2. $A_{res} = \sqrt{2}\,A + A$

$$= (\sqrt{2} + 1)A$$

As $I \propto A^2$

$$I_{res} = (\sqrt{2} + 1)^2 I_0 = 5.8 I_0$$

Option (a)

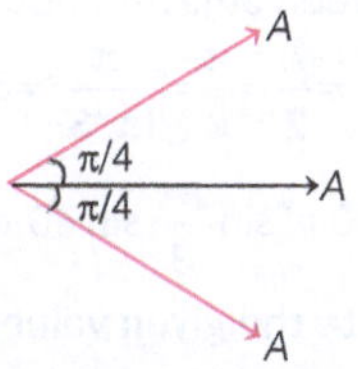

3. The resultant amplitude is given as,

$$A_{res} = \sqrt{A_1^2 + A_2^2 + 2A_1A_2\cos\phi}$$
$$\Rightarrow \quad \sqrt{3}A = \sqrt{A^2 + A^2 + 2A^2\cos\phi}$$
$$\Rightarrow \quad 3A^2 = 2A^2 + 2A^2\cos\phi$$
$$\Rightarrow \quad \cos\phi = \frac{1}{2}$$
$$\therefore \quad \phi = 60°$$

4. Phase difference between the two waves is 90°. Amplitudes are added by vector method.

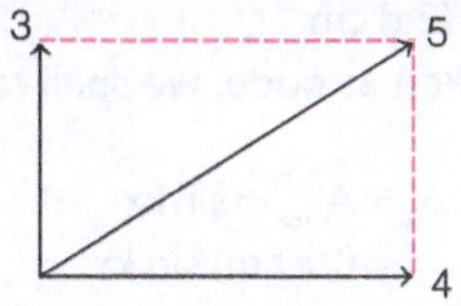

$$A = \sqrt{3^2 + 4^2} = 5$$

Module 2.

1.

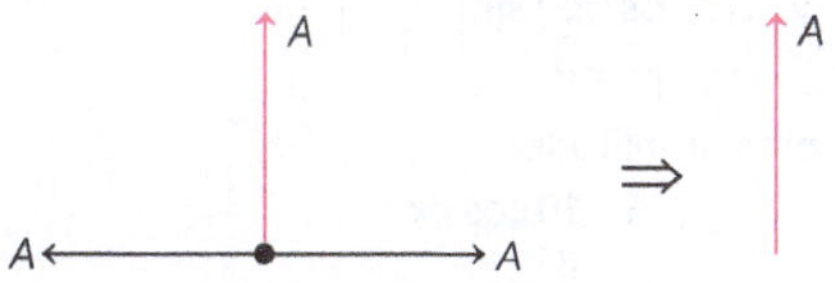

Resultant amplitude is A.
So, intensity will remain same.

3. $A = \sqrt{(10)^2 + (20)^2 + 2(10)(20)\cos 60°}$

$$= 26.46 \text{ cm}$$

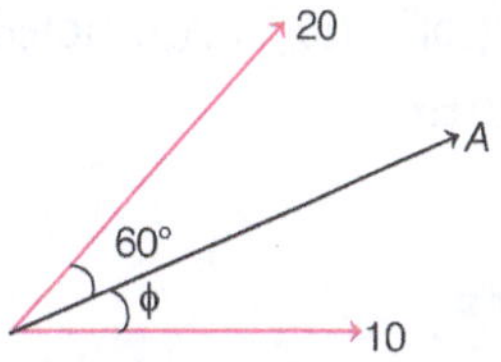

$$\tan\phi = \frac{20\sin 60°}{10 + 20\cos 60°} = 0.866$$
$$\therefore \quad \phi = 40.89° = 0.714 \text{ rad}$$

4. $\dfrac{I_{max}}{I_{min}} = \left(\dfrac{\sqrt{I_1/I_2} + 1}{\sqrt{I_1/I_2} - 1}\right)^2$

5. (a) $\dfrac{A_{max}}{A_{min}} = \dfrac{A_1 + A_2}{A_1 - A_2}$

(b) $\dfrac{I_{max}}{I_{min}} = \left(\dfrac{A_{max}}{A_{min}}\right)^2$

6. Path difference of $\dfrac{\lambda}{4}$ is equivalent to a phase difference of $\dfrac{\pi}{2}$.

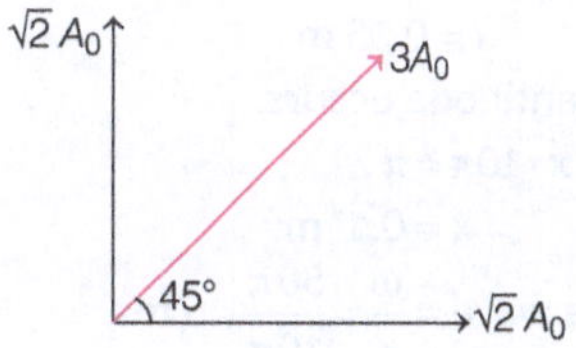

$$A_{net} = 5A_0$$
$$I \propto A^2$$
$$\Rightarrow \quad I_{net} = 25\, I_0$$

7. Given, $y_1 = 10\sin\left(\omega t + \dfrac{\pi}{3}\right)$ cm

$$y_2 = 5[\sin\omega t + \sqrt{3}\cos\omega t]$$
$$y_2 = 5[\sin\omega t + \sqrt{3}\cos\omega t] \times \frac{2}{2}$$
$$y_2 = 10\left[\sin\omega t \times \frac{1}{2} + \cos\omega t \times \frac{\sqrt{3}}{2}\right]$$
$$y_2 = 10\left[\sin\omega t\cos\frac{\pi}{3} + \cos\omega t\sin\frac{\pi}{3}\right]$$
$$y_2 = 10\sin\left(\omega t + \frac{\pi}{3}\right) \text{cm}$$

From given equation,

$$A_1 = 10 \text{ cm}, A_2 = 10 \text{ cm},$$

$$\phi = \frac{\pi}{3} - \frac{\pi}{3} = 0$$

Amplitude of resultant wave,

$$R = \sqrt{A_1^2 + A_2^2 + 2A_1A_2 \cos\phi}$$
$$= \sqrt{(10)^2 + (10)^2 + 2(10)(10)\cos 0°}$$
$$R = 20 \text{ cm}$$

Module 3.

1. It is either 0 or π.
2. At $x = 0$, $y = y_1 + y_2 = A \sin \omega t + A \cos \omega t$. So, it is neither a node nor an antinode.
4. Given, $y(x,t) = 0.5 \sin\left(\frac{5\pi}{4}x\right)\cos(200\,\pi t)$, comparing with equation $- y(x,t) = 2a \sin kx \cos \omega t$

$$\omega = 200\,\pi, k = \frac{5\pi}{4}$$

As speed of wave is given by

$$v = \frac{\omega}{k} = \frac{200\pi}{5\pi/4} = 160 \text{ m/s}$$

5. The given equation

$$y(x,t) = 0.02\cos(50\,\pi t + \pi/2)\cos 10\pi x$$

When compared with

$$y(x,t) = A\cos(\omega t + \pi/2)\cos kx$$

If $kx = \pi/2$, a node occurs.

$\therefore$ $x \cdot 10\pi = \pi/2$

$\Rightarrow$ $x = 0.05$ m

If $kx = \pi$, an antinode occurs.

$\therefore$ $x \cdot 10\pi = \pi$

$x = 0.1$ m

Speed of the wave $= \frac{\omega}{k} = \frac{50\pi}{10\pi} = 5 \text{ ms}^{-1}$

$$\lambda = 2\pi/k = 2\pi/10\pi = 0.2 \text{ m}$$

Node will also occur at $0.05 \text{ m} + \frac{\lambda}{2}$ or 0.15 m.

Similarly antinode will also occur at $0.1 + \lambda$ or 0.3 m.

6. From the question,

$$y = 4\cos^2(t/2)\sin(1000t)$$
$$= 2(2\cos^2(t/2)\sin(1000t)$$
$$= 2(\cos t + 1)\sin(1000t)$$
$$= 2\cos t \sin 1000t + 2\sin 1000t$$
$$= \sin(1001t) + \sin(999t) + 2\sin(1000t)$$

For the given periodic motion, three independent harmonic motions are superposed.

7. When two identical waves travel in opposite directions and superpose they form stationary wave.

Now, $y = a\cos(kx - \omega t) - a\cos(kx + \omega t)$

$\therefore y = 2a \sin kx \sin \omega t$ is equation of stationary wave which gives a node at $x = 0$.

$y = -a\cos(kx - \omega t)$ cannot be as their directions are not opposite.

9. Two identical waves should travel in opposite directions.
10. $y = y_1 + y_2 = (2A\cos kx)\sin \omega t$

$$= A_x \sin \omega t$$

Here, $A_x = 2A\cos kx$

At $x = 0$, A_x is maximum or $2A$.

So, it is an antinode. Next antinode will occur at

$$x = \frac{\lambda}{2}, \lambda \ldots\text{etc.}$$

or $$x = \frac{\pi}{k}, \frac{2\pi}{k} \ldots \text{ etc.}$$

11. (a) $v = \frac{\omega}{k} = \frac{40\pi}{\pi/3} = 120 \text{ cm/s}$

(b) Distance between adjacent nodes

$$= \frac{\lambda}{2} = \frac{\pi}{k} = \frac{\pi}{(\pi/3)} = 3 \text{ cm}$$

(c) $v_P = \frac{\partial y}{\partial t} = (-200\,\pi)\sin\frac{\pi x}{3}\sin 40\pi t$

Now, substitute the given values of x and t.

12. In this case, node points will also oscillate, but standing waves are formed.
13. $\lambda = \frac{2\pi}{k} = \frac{2\pi}{0.4} = 15.7$ m

$$f = \frac{\omega}{2\pi} = \frac{200}{2\pi} = 31.8 \text{ Hz}$$
$$v = f\lambda = 500 \text{ m/s}$$

14. (a) Distance between successive antinodes

$$= \frac{\lambda}{2} = \frac{\pi}{k} = \frac{\pi}{(\pi/2)} = 2 \text{ cm}$$

(b) $A_{max} = 2A = (2\pi)$ cm

If $x = 0$ is taken as node, we shall taken sin equation for A_x

$\therefore$ $A_x = A_{max} = \sin kx$

$= (2\pi \text{ cm})\sin kx$

Put $k = \frac{\pi}{2}$ and $x = 0.5$

15. The standing wave equation is

$$y = \underbrace{10\cos(\pi x)}_{\text{Denotes amplitude}}\sin\left(\frac{2\pi t}{T}\right)$$

$\therefore$ $A = 10\cos \pi x$

$$x = \frac{4}{3} \text{ cm}$$

$\therefore$ $A = 10\cos\left(\frac{4\pi}{3}\right)$

Clearly, $|A| = \left|10\cos\frac{4\pi}{3}\right| = 5$ cm

Module 4.

Introductory Exercise

1. $5f - 2f = 54$

$$3f = 54$$

$$\therefore \quad f = 18\,\text{Hz}$$

2. $f \propto \sqrt{T}$

$$\therefore \quad \frac{f_1}{f_2} = \sqrt{\frac{T_1}{T_2}}$$

or
$$\frac{220}{260} = \sqrt{\frac{2.2\,g}{(2.2 + M)\,g}}$$

Solving we get,

$$M = 0.873\,\text{kg}$$

3. (a) $\frac{f_1}{f_2} = \frac{250}{300} = \frac{5}{6}$

So, f_1 is 5th harmonic and f_2 is 6th harmonic.

(b) $f_1 = (5) = \frac{v}{2l} = \frac{2.5\sqrt{T/\mu}}{l}$

$$\therefore \quad T = \frac{\mu f_1^2 l^2}{(2.5)^2} = \frac{(0.036)(250)^2(1)^2}{(2.5)^2}$$

$$= 360\,\text{N}$$

4. $6\left[\frac{T/\mu}{2l_1}\right] = 2\left[\frac{T/\mu}{2l_2}\right]$

$$\therefore \quad \frac{l_1}{l_2} = 3$$

Exercise

1.

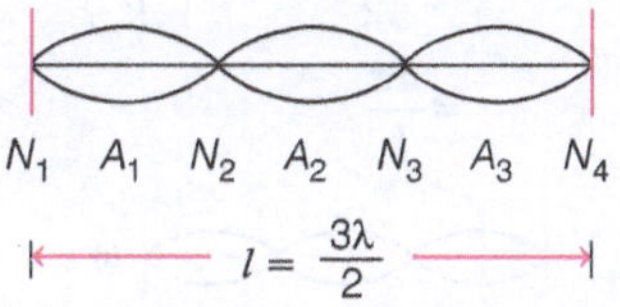

2.

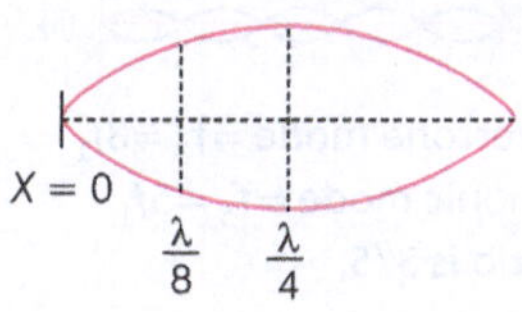

Energy lying between $\frac{\lambda}{8}$ and $\frac{\lambda}{4}$ will be more.

3. Frequency of first overtone mode,

$$f_2 = 2\left(\frac{v}{2l}\right)$$

and frequency of second overtone mode,

$$f_3 = \frac{3}{2} f_2$$

$$\therefore \quad \lambda_3 = \frac{2}{3}\lambda_2$$

As v = constant

4. $n \propto \frac{\sqrt{T}}{l}$ or $n \propto \frac{\sqrt{M}}{l}$

$$\therefore \quad \frac{n_A}{n_B} = \sqrt{\frac{M_A}{M_B}}\,\frac{l_B}{l_A}$$

5. $f_1 : f_2 : f_3 = 1 : 2 : 3$

$$\lambda = \frac{v}{f} \quad \text{or} \quad \lambda \propto \frac{1}{f}$$

$$\therefore \quad \lambda_1 : \lambda_2 : \lambda_3 = 1 : \frac{1}{2} : \frac{1}{3}$$

6. All frequencies are integral multiples of 35 Hz.

7. $3\left(\frac{v}{2l}\right) = 300$

$$\therefore \quad v = 200\,l = (200)(1)$$

$$= 200\,\text{m/s}$$

8. These are multiples of 30 Hz. Hence, fundamental frequency

$$f_0 = 30\,\text{Hz}$$

Now,
$$f_0 = \frac{v}{2l}$$

$$\therefore \quad v = 2f_0 l$$

$$= 2 \times 30 \times 0.8$$

$$= 48\,\text{m/s}$$

9. Fundamental frequency $= \frac{v}{2l} = \frac{\sqrt{T/\mu}}{2l}$ or $f \propto \sqrt{T}$

10. We know that, frequency, $n = \frac{p}{2l}\sqrt{\frac{T}{\pi r^2 \rho}}$

$$\Rightarrow \quad n \propto \frac{1}{\sqrt{\rho}}$$

i.e. graph between n and $\sqrt{\rho}$ will be rectangular hyperbola.

11. Second overtone means three loops.

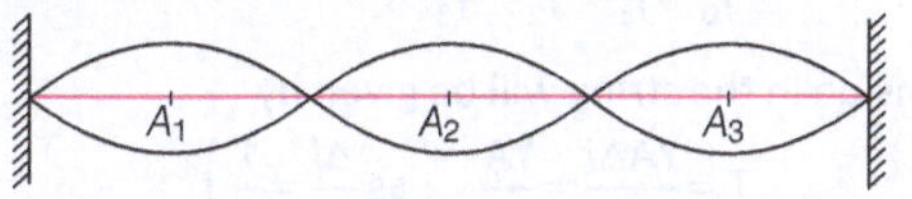

$$\therefore \quad 3\frac{\lambda}{2} = L \quad \text{or} \quad \lambda = \frac{2L}{3}$$

Anitnodes will be obtained at $\frac{\lambda}{4}, \frac{3\lambda}{4}, \frac{5\lambda}{4}$

or
$$\frac{L}{6}, \frac{3L}{6} \quad \text{and} \quad \frac{5L}{6}$$

12. Fundamental frequency, $f \propto \frac{1}{l}$

Given, $f_1 : f_2 : f_3 = 1 : 2 : 3$

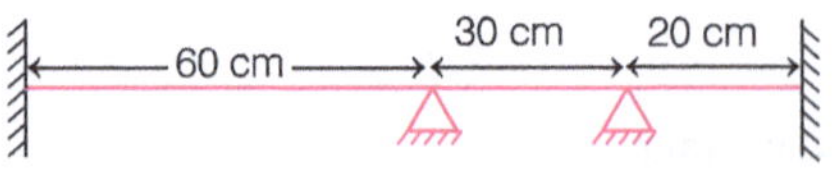

or $\frac{1}{l_1}:\frac{1}{l_2}:\frac{1}{l_3}=1:2:3$

or $l_1:l_2:l_3=\frac{1}{1}:\frac{1}{2}:\frac{1}{3}$

or $l_1:l_2:l_3=6:3:2$

$l_1=\frac{6}{11}\times 110=60$ m

$l_2=\frac{3}{11}\times 110=30$ cm

and $l_3=\frac{2}{11}\times 110=20$ cm

13. $\because \quad f\propto\sqrt{T}$

$\therefore \quad \frac{f_1}{f_2}=\sqrt{\frac{T_1}{T_2}}$

$\therefore \quad \frac{3}{2}=\sqrt{\frac{T+2.5}{T}}$

Solving, we get $T=2$ N

14. $f=\frac{v}{2l}=\frac{\sqrt{T/\mu}}{2l}=\frac{\sqrt{T/\rho S}}{l}$

$=\frac{\sqrt{T/\rho(\pi d^2/4)}}{l}$ or $f\propto\frac{\sqrt{T}}{dl}$

$\therefore \quad \frac{f_1}{f_2}=\left(\sqrt{\frac{T_1}{T_2}}\right)\left(\frac{d_2}{d_1}\right)\left(\frac{l_2}{l_1}\right)$

$=\sqrt{\frac{1}{2}}\left(\frac{3}{1}\right)\left(\frac{2}{1}\right)=3\sqrt{2}$

15. $f\propto\frac{1}{l} \Rightarrow \quad l=\frac{k}{f}$

Now, $l=l_1+l_2+l_3$

$\therefore \quad \frac{k}{f_0}=\frac{k}{f_1}+\frac{k}{f_2}+\frac{k}{f_3}$

$\therefore \quad \frac{1}{f_0}=\frac{1}{f_1}+\frac{1}{f_2}+\frac{1}{f_3}$

16. Tension in the string will be given by

$T=\frac{YA\Delta l}{l}=\frac{YA}{\eta} \quad \left(\text{as } \frac{\Delta l}{l}=\frac{1}{\eta}\right)$

Now, $f\propto v$

$\frac{f_1}{f_2}=\frac{v_1}{v_2}=\frac{\sqrt{T/\rho A}}{\sqrt{Y/\rho}}$

$=\sqrt{\frac{T}{YA}}=\frac{1}{\sqrt{\eta}}$

17. $f_1=\frac{v}{2l}=\frac{\sqrt{T/\mu}}{2l}=\frac{\sqrt{100/0.01}}{2}=50$ Hz

$f_2=2f_1=100$ Hz

$f_3=3f_1=150$ Hz

$n_1=\frac{v}{4l}=25$ Hz

$n_2=3n_1=75$ Hz

$n_3=5n_1=125$ Hz

18. $f\propto\sqrt{T}$

$\frac{f_2}{f_1}=\sqrt{\frac{T_2}{T_1}}$

$\therefore \quad \frac{f_1+15}{f_1}=\sqrt{\frac{1.21T_1}{T_1}}$

$=1.1$

Solving we get $f_1=150$ Hz

$v\propto\sqrt{T}$

$\therefore \quad \frac{v_2}{v_1}=\sqrt{\frac{T_2}{T_1}}$

or $v_2=\left(\sqrt{\frac{1.21T_1}{T_1}}\right)v_1$

$=1.1\,v_1$

Hence, increase in v is 10%

$\frac{\lambda}{2}=l$

$\therefore \quad \lambda=2l$

$\therefore$ Fundamental wavelength $=2\lambda$ is unchanged.

19.

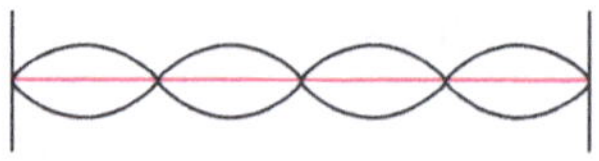

$l=4\frac{\lambda}{2}=2\lambda=2\left(\frac{2\pi}{k}\right)$

$=\frac{4\pi}{k}$

20.

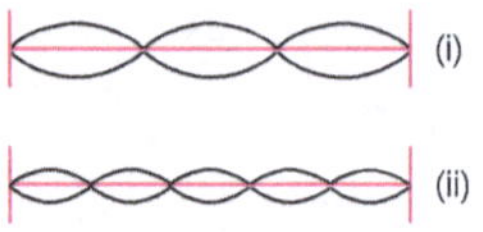

(a) Second overtone mode $=f_3=3f_1$

Fifth harmonic mode $=f_5=5f_1$

So, the ratio is 3/5,

(d) $\lambda=\frac{v}{f}$

or $\lambda\propto\frac{1}{f}$

$\therefore \quad \frac{\lambda_3}{\lambda_5}=\frac{f_5}{f_3}=\frac{5}{3}$

21. Second overtone frequency means

$f_3=3f_1=210$ Hz

$\therefore \quad f_1=70$ Hz $=$ fundamental frequency

Third overtone frequency $= f_4 = 4f_1$

Second harmonic frequency $= f_2 = 2f_1$

22. $v = \sqrt{\frac{T}{\mu}} = \sqrt{\frac{20}{9\times10^{-3}}} = 47.14\ \text{m/s}$

$$f_1 = \frac{v}{2l} = \frac{47.14}{2\times30}$$

$$= 0.786\ \text{Hz}$$

Next three frequencies are $2f_1, 3f_1$ and $4f_1$

23. (a) $f = \frac{v}{2l} = \frac{\sqrt{T/\mu}}{2l}$

$\therefore\ T = 4l^2f^2\mu$

$$= (4)(0.7)^2(220)^2\left(\frac{1.2\times10^{-3}}{0.7}\right)$$

$$= 163\ \text{N}$$

(b) $f_3 = 3f_1 = 3\times220 = 660\ \text{Hz}$

24. Fundamental frequency,

$$f = \frac{v}{2l} = \frac{\sqrt{T/\mu}}{2l}$$

$$= \frac{\sqrt{(50)/(0.1\times10^{-3}/10^{-2})}}{2\times0.6}$$

$$= 58.93\ \text{Hz}$$

Let, n th harmonic is the highest frequency, then

$$(58.93)\,n = 20000$$

$\therefore\ n = 339.38$

Hence, 339 is the highest frequency.

$\therefore\ f_{max} = (339)(58.93)\ \text{Hz} = 19977\ \text{Hz}$

25. $\lambda = \frac{v}{f} = 0.5\ \text{m}$

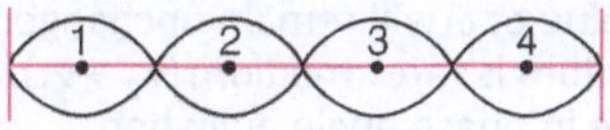

$$l = 4\left(\frac{\lambda}{2}\right) = 1\ \text{m}$$

26. (a) $f_4 = 4f_0$

$\therefore\ f_0 = \frac{f_4}{4} = \frac{400}{4} = 100\ \text{Hz}$

(b) $f_7 = 7f_0 = 700\ \text{Hz}$

27. $f \propto \frac{1}{l}$

$\therefore\ \frac{f_1}{f_2} = \frac{l_2}{l_1}$

or $l_2 = \left(\frac{f_1}{f_2}\right)l_1$

$$= \left(\frac{124}{186}\right)(90\ \text{cm})$$

$$= 60\ \text{cm}$$

28. (a) $f_1 = \frac{v}{2l} = \frac{48}{3} = 16\ \text{Hz}$

$$\lambda_1 = \frac{v}{f_1} = 3\ \text{m}$$

(b) Second overtone means f_3.

$$f_3 = 3f_1 \text{ and hence } \lambda_3 = \frac{\lambda_1}{3}$$

(c) Fourth harmonic means f_4.

$$f_4 = 4f_1 \quad\text{and}\quad \lambda_4 = \frac{\lambda_1}{4}$$

29. (a)

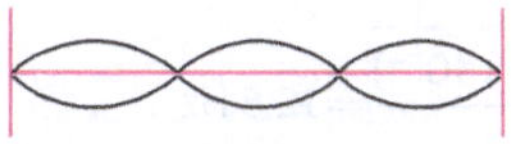

Third harmonic

(b) $A = \frac{5.6}{2} = 2.8\ \text{cm}$

(c) $k = 0.034\ \text{cm}^{-1}$

$$\lambda = \frac{2\pi}{k} = 184.7\ \text{cm} \approx 185\ \text{cm}$$

$$l = \frac{3\lambda}{2} = 277\ \text{cm}$$

(d) $\lambda = 184.7\ \text{cm} \approx 185\ \text{cm}$

$$f = \frac{\omega}{2\pi} = \frac{50}{2\pi} = 7.96\ \text{Hz}$$

$$T = \frac{1}{f} = 0.126\ \text{s}$$

$$v = f\lambda = 1470\ \text{cm/s}$$

(e) $v_{max} = \omega A_{max}$

$$= (50)(5.60)$$

$$= 280\ \text{cm/s}$$

(f) Frequency and hence ω will become $\frac{8}{3}$ times.

$\therefore\ \omega' = 50\times\frac{8}{3} = 133\ \text{rad/s}$

$$k = \frac{\omega}{v} \quad\text{or}\quad k \propto \omega$$

Hence, k will become $\frac{8}{3}$ times.

$$k' = \left(\frac{8}{3}\right)(0.034)$$

$$= 0.0907\ \text{rad/cm}$$

30. (a) $\frac{\lambda}{2} = l$ or $\lambda = 2l = 1.6\ \text{m}$

$$v = f\lambda = 60\times1.6$$

$$= 96\ \text{m/s}$$

(b) $v = \sqrt{\frac{T}{\mu}}$

$\therefore\ T = \mu v^2 = \left(\frac{0.04}{0.8}\right)(96)^2$

$$= 461\ \text{N}$$

(c) $v_{max} = \omega A_{max}$
$= (2\pi f) A_{max}$
$= (2\pi)(60)(0.003)$
$= 1.13 \text{ m/s}$

$a_{max} = \omega^2 A_{max} = (2\pi f)^2 A_{max}$
$= (2\pi \times 60)^2 (0.003)$
$= 426.4 \text{ m/s}^2$

31. (i) $f_a = \frac{v}{2l} = \frac{\sqrt{T/\mu}}{2l}$

$$= \frac{\sqrt{(100/4\times 10^{-2})}}{2\times 2} = 12.5 \text{ Hz}$$

$$f_b = 3\left(\frac{v}{2l}\right) = 3fa$$

$$= 37.5 \text{ Hz}$$

(ii) $\omega = 2\pi f$

$\therefore$ $\omega_a = 2\pi f_a = 25\pi$

$\omega_b = 2\pi f_b = 75\pi$

$$v = \sqrt{\frac{T}{\mu}} = \sqrt{\frac{100}{4\times 10^{-2}}} = 50 \text{ m/s}$$

$$k = \frac{\omega}{v}$$

$\therefore$ $k_a = \frac{\omega a}{v} = \frac{25\pi}{50} = \frac{\pi}{2}$

$$k_b = \frac{\omega_b}{v} = \frac{75\pi}{50} = \frac{3\pi}{2}$$

32. (a) $\frac{n\lambda_1}{2} = l$

$\therefore$ $\frac{n(0.54)}{2} = l$

or $n = \frac{l}{0.27}$ ...(i)

Similarly, $\frac{(n+1)\lambda_2}{2} = l$

or $\frac{(n+1)(0.48)}{2} = l$

or $(n+1) = \frac{l}{0.24}$ ...(ii)

From Eqs. (i) and (ii) we have,

$$\frac{n}{n+1} = \frac{8}{9}$$

(b) From Eq. (i),

$l = (0.27)n$
$= 0.27 \times 8$
$= 2.16 \text{ m}$

(c) $\frac{\lambda}{2} = l$ (Fundamental)

$\therefore$ $\lambda = 2l = 4.32 \text{ m}$

Module 5.

Introductory Exercise

1. At mean position, energy is in the form of kinetic energy.

2. (a) Assuming tension to be same

$$v \propto \frac{1}{\sqrt{\mu}}$$

$$\mu_{RHS} = \frac{\mu_{RHS}}{4}$$

$\therefore$ $v_{RHSD} = 2v_{LHS} = 20 \text{ cm/s}$

(b) $A_r = \left(\frac{v_2 - v_1}{v_2 + v_1}\right) A_i$

$\therefore$ $\frac{A_r}{A_i} = \frac{20-10}{20+10} = \frac{1}{3}$

$$\frac{A_t}{A_i} = \left(\frac{2v_2}{v_1 + v_2}\right) = \frac{2\times 20}{20+10} = \frac{4}{3}$$

3. Speed of wave in first medium is,

$$v_1 = \frac{\text{Coefficient of } t}{\text{Coefficient of } x}$$

$$= \frac{50}{2} = 25 \text{ m/s}$$

$v_2 = 50 \text{ m/s}$

$A_i = 2\times 10^{-3} \text{ m}$

$$A_r = \left(\frac{v_2 - v_1}{v_2 + v_1}\right) A_i = \frac{2}{3}\times 10^{-3} \text{ m}$$

$$A_t = \left(\frac{2v_2}{v_1 + v_2}\right) A_i = \frac{8}{3}\times 10^{-3} \text{ m}$$

In second medium, speed becomes two times. Therefore, λ also becomes two times. So, k remains one-half, value of ω will remain unchanged. Further, second medium is rarer medium ($v_2 > v_1$). Hence, there is no change in phase angle anywhere.

$\therefore$ $y_r = \frac{2}{3}\times 10^{-3} \cos \pi(2.0x + 50t)$

and $y_t = \frac{8}{3}\times 10^{-3} \cos \pi(x - 50t)$

Exercise

1. All particles are at mean position. So energy is in the form of kinetic energy.

2. When pulse is reflected from a rigid support, the pulse is inverted both length and side wise.

3. $v_1 = \frac{\omega}{k_1}$ and $v_2 = \frac{\omega}{k_2}$

$$a_r = \left(\frac{v_2 - v_1}{v_2 + v_1}\right) a_i$$

$$a_t = \left(\frac{2v_2}{v_2 + v_1}\right) a_i$$

$$\therefore \quad \frac{a_r}{a_t} = \frac{v_2 - v_1}{2v_2} = \frac{1}{2}\left(1 - \frac{v_1}{v_2}\right)$$

$$= \frac{1}{2}\left(1 - \frac{k_2}{k_1}\right) = \frac{k_1 - k_2}{2k_1}$$

4. $\dfrac{a_t}{a_i} = \dfrac{2v_2}{v_1 + v_2} = \dfrac{2(\omega/k_2)}{(\omega/k_1) + (\omega/k_2)} = \dfrac{2k_1}{k_1 + k_2}$

5. The direction of velocity of the pulse reverses after reflection. So, positive sign has to be there between $2x$ and $40t$. And the crest becomes trough after reflection, so $+\pi$ has to be added.

So, $y_r = 0.3 \cos(2x + 40t + \pi)$.

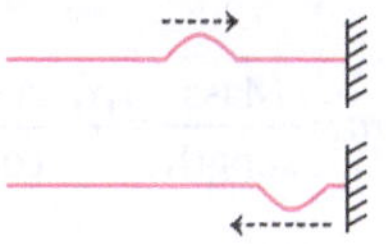

6. $v_1 = \dfrac{\omega_1}{k_1} = \dfrac{50\pi}{2\pi} = 25\ \text{ms}^{-1}$

$v_2 = 50\ \text{ms}^{-1}$ (given)

$$\therefore \quad A_r = \left(\frac{v_2 - v_1}{v_1 + v_2}\right) A_i = \frac{50 - 25}{25 + 50}(0.002)$$

$$= \frac{0.002}{3} = 0.000667$$

$$\therefore \quad y_r = (0.000667) \cos(2\pi x + 50\pi t)$$

7. $v_1 = \dfrac{\omega_1}{k_1} = \dfrac{50\pi}{2\pi} = 25\ \text{ms}^{-1}$ and $v_2 = 50\ \text{ms}^{-1}$ (given)

$$A_t = \left(\frac{2v_2}{v_1 + v_2}\right) A_i = \frac{2 \times 50}{25 + 50}(0.002) = 2.67 \times 10^{-3}$$

$\omega_1 = \omega_2$ ($\because$ frequency depends on source)

$$\therefore \quad k_2 = \frac{\omega_2}{v_2} = \frac{\omega_1}{v_2} = \frac{50\pi}{50} = \pi$$

$$\therefore \quad y_t = (2.67 \times 10^{-3}) \cos(\pi x - 50\pi t)$$

8. $v \propto \dfrac{1}{\sqrt{\mu}}$

$$\mu_2 = 9\mu_1$$

Hence, $\quad v_2 = \dfrac{v_1}{3}$

So let $v_1 = 3$ units, then $v_2 = 1$ unit

(a) $\quad A_1 = \left(\dfrac{v_2 - v_1}{v_1 + v_2}\right) A_i$

and $\quad A_2 = \left(\dfrac{2v_2}{v_1 + v_2}\right) A_i$

$$\therefore \quad \left|\frac{A_1}{A_2}\right| = \left|\frac{v_2 - v_1}{2v_2}\right| = \left|\frac{1 - 3}{2}\right| = 1$$

(b) $\dfrac{v_1}{v_2} = 3$

(c) $I = \dfrac{1}{2}\rho\omega^2 A^2 v$

ρ is not given, so we cannot find I_1/I_2.

(d) $P = \dfrac{1}{2}\rho\omega^2 A^2 Sv$

But, $\quad S\rho = \mu$

$$\therefore \quad P = \frac{1}{2}\omega^2 A^2 \mu v$$

or $\quad P \propto A^2 \mu v \quad$ (as $\omega \rightarrow$ same)

$$\frac{P_1}{P_2} = \left(\frac{A_1}{A_2}\right)^2 \left(\frac{\mu_1}{\mu_2}\right)\left(\frac{v_1}{v_2}\right)$$

$$= (1)^2 \left(\frac{1}{9}\right)(3) = \frac{1}{3}$$

or $\quad \dfrac{P_2}{P_1} = 3$

9. (d) $A_t = \left(\dfrac{2v_2}{v_1 + v_2}\right) A_i$

If $v_2 > v_1$, i.e. 2 is rarer then $A_t > A_i$.

10. Let us plot at $t = 3$ s

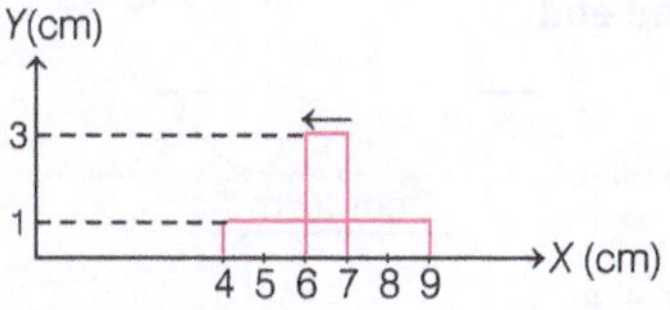

Net $\quad y = y_1 + y_2$

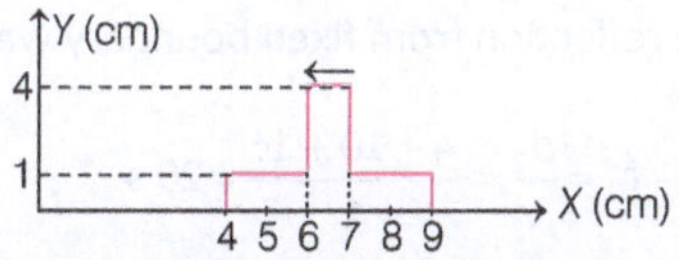

Similarly, we can draw at other times.

11. $v_2 = \dfrac{v_1}{2}$

(a) $A_r = \left(\dfrac{v_2 - v_1}{v_1 + v_2}\right) A$

$$= \left[\frac{(v_1/2) - v_1}{v_1 + v_1/2}\right] A = -\frac{A}{3}$$

$$A_t = \left(\frac{2v_2}{v_1 + v_2}\right) A = \left[\frac{2 \times v_1/2}{v_1 + v_1/2}\right] A$$

$$= \frac{2}{3} A$$

(b) Since, reflected waves come in the same medium, we can say that

$$P \propto A^2$$

$$\frac{P_r}{P_i} = \left(\frac{A_r}{A_i}\right)^2 = \left(\frac{-A/3}{A}\right)^2 = \frac{1}{9}$$

$\therefore$ Fraction of power transmitted

$$= 1 - \frac{1}{9} = \frac{8}{9}$$

12. $v=\sqrt{\frac{T}{\mu}}=\sqrt{\frac{16}{(0.4\times10^{-3})/(10^{-2})}}$

$=20\,\text{m/s}$

(a) $t=\frac{d}{v}=\frac{2l}{v}=\frac{0.4\,\text{m}}{20}$

$=0.02\,\text{s}$

(b) At half the time pulse is at other end and it gets a phase difference of π. Hence, the shape is as shown below.

13. (a) **For fixed end**

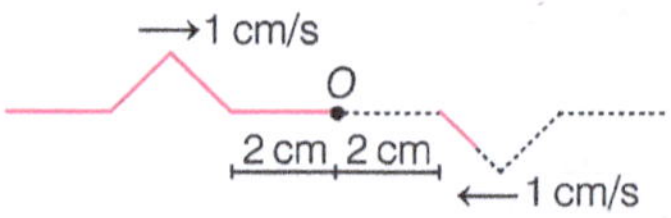

By the superposition of these two pulses we will get the resultant. But only to the left of point O, where string is actually present.

(b) **For free end**

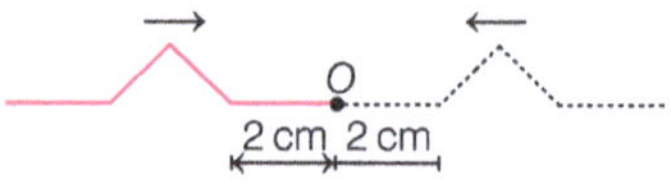

14. $t_1=\frac{d_1}{v}=\frac{4+4}{1}=8\,\text{s}$

After one reflection from fixed boundary wave is inverted.

$$t_2=\frac{d_2}{v}=\frac{4+10+16}{1}=20\,\text{s}$$

After two times reflection from fixed boundaries wave pulse will again become upright.

Unit Exercise (Cumulative)

Level 1

2. Energy, $E\propto A^2\nu^2$ where

$A=$ amplitude and $\nu=$ frequency.

Also $\omega=2\pi\nu$

$\Rightarrow$ $\omega\propto\nu$

Experiment = 1 : Amplitude $=A$ and $\nu_1=\nu$

Experiment = 2 : Amplitude $=A$ and $\nu_2=2\nu$

$$\frac{E_2}{E_1}=\frac{A^2\nu_2^2}{A^2\nu_1^2}=4$$

$\therefore$ $E_2=4E_1$

3. Given, $y=0.3\sin(0.157x)\cos(200\pi t)$

$k=0.157\,\text{m}^{-1}$

$\therefore$ $\lambda=\frac{2\pi}{k}=\frac{(2)(3.14)}{0.157}=40\,\text{m}$

$l=4\left(\frac{\lambda}{2}\right)=2\lambda=80\,\text{m}$

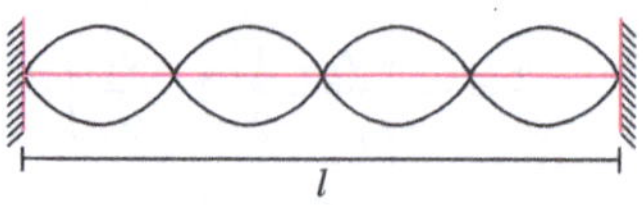

4. $n_1=\frac{1}{2l}\sqrt{\left(\frac{T}{4\pi r^2\rho}\right)}$

and $n_2=\frac{1}{4l}\sqrt{\left(\frac{T}{\pi r^2\rho}\right)}$; $n=\frac{v}{\lambda}=\frac{1}{\lambda}\sqrt{\frac{T}{m}}$

[where $\frac{\lambda}{2}=$ length of string]

$\therefore$ $\frac{n_1}{n_2}=2\times\frac{1}{2}=1$

$\left[\because m=\frac{\text{Mass}}{\text{Length}}=\frac{\rho\times A\times\text{Length}}{\text{Length}}=\rho A=\frac{v_1}{v_2}\right]$

5. Fundamental frequency,

$f_0=450-400=50\,\text{Hz}$

$f_0=\frac{v}{2l}=\frac{\sqrt{T/\mu}}{2l}$

$\therefore$ $l=\frac{\sqrt{T/\mu}}{2f_0}=\frac{\sqrt{490/0.1}}{2\times50}$

$=0.7\,\text{m}$

6. $\frac{f_5}{f_2}=\frac{5f_1}{2f_1}=\frac{5}{2}$

$\therefore$ $f_2=\frac{2}{5}f_5$

$=\frac{2}{5}\times480$

$=192\,\text{Hz}$

7. $\eta\left(\frac{v}{2l}\right)_B=\left(\frac{v}{2l}\right)_A$

$\eta=\left(\frac{\sqrt{T/\rho S}}{2l}\right)_B=\left(\frac{v}{2l}\right)_A$

or $\eta\left(\frac{\sqrt{4T/\rho\pi}}{2ld}\right)_B=\left(\frac{\sqrt{4T/\rho\pi}}{2ld}\right)_A$ ...(i)

Given, $T_B=2T_A, l_B=2l_A$

$d_B=2d_A$

and $\rho_B=2\rho_A$

Putting in Eq. (i), we get

$\eta=4$

$\eta=4$ means 4th harmonic or 3rd overtone.

8. $n\propto\frac{1}{l}$ or $nl=k$ (constant)

$\therefore$ $l=l_1+l_2+l_3+\dots$

or $\frac{k}{n}=\frac{k}{n_1}+\frac{k}{n_2}+\frac{k}{n_3}+\dots$

or $\frac{1}{n}=\frac{1}{n_1}+\frac{1}{n_2}+\frac{1}{n_3}+\dots$

9. The fixed end is a node while the free end is an antinode.

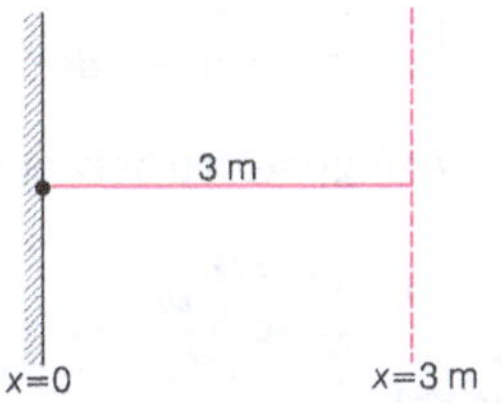

Therefore, at $x=0$ is a node and at $x=3$ m is an antinode. Possible modes of vibration are

$$L=(2n+1)\frac{\lambda}{4}, \text{ where } n=0,1,2,3,\ldots$$

or $\lambda=\frac{4L}{2n+1}=\frac{12}{2n+1}$ $\quad [\because L=3 \text{ m (Given)}]$

$$k=\frac{2\pi}{\lambda}=\frac{2\pi}{12/(2n+1)}=\frac{(2n+1)\pi}{6} \quad \ldots\text{(i)}$$

$v=\frac{\omega}{k}=100$ m/s is true in all four options.

For $n=0,\ k=\frac{\pi}{6}$

For $n=2,\ k=\frac{5\pi}{6}$

For $n=7,\ k=\frac{5\pi}{2}$

$\therefore$ Options (a), (c) and (d) are correct.

10. $y=[0.01\sin(62.8x)]\cos(628t)$. [Given]

From the given equation, $k=\frac{2\pi}{\lambda}=62.8$

$\therefore \quad \lambda=\frac{2\pi}{62.8}=0.1$ m

Length of string,

$$l=5\times\frac{\lambda}{2}=5\times\frac{1}{20}=0.25 \text{ m}$$

An antinode is formed at mid-point M. Thus maximum displacement is also found at M.

The fundamental frequency,

$$f=\frac{v}{2l}=\frac{\omega/k}{2l}=\frac{628}{2\times 0.25\times 62.8}=20 \text{ Hz}$$

11. Find y_1 and y_2 at given values of x and t and then simply add them to get net value of y.

12. $y=y_1+y_2=(6.0 \text{ cm})\sin(\pi x)\cos(0.6\pi t)$

$\therefore \quad A_x=6.0 \text{ cm}\sin(\pi x) \quad \ldots\text{(i)}$

In parts (a), (b) and (c) substitute the given values of x and find the displacement amplitude at these locations.

(d) At antinodes

$$A_x=\text{ maximum }=\pm 6.0 \text{ cm}$$

$\therefore \quad \pi x=\frac{\pi}{2},\frac{3\pi}{2},\frac{5\pi}{2}$

or $\quad x=0.5$ cm, 1.5 cm, 2.5 cm

13. (a) $\frac{\lambda}{2}=15$ cm

$\therefore \quad \lambda=30$ cm

$$k=\frac{2\pi}{\lambda}=\left(\frac{\pi}{15}\right)\text{cm}^{-1}$$

$$\omega=\frac{2\pi}{T}=\frac{2\pi}{0.075}\text{ s}^{-1}$$

Since, $x=0$ is a node we will write sin equation.

$\therefore \quad A_x=A_{max}\sin kx \quad \ldots\text{(i)}$

and $\quad y=A_x\sin\omega t$

(b) $v=\frac{\omega}{k}=\frac{(2\pi/0.075)}{(\pi/15)}=400 \text{ cm/s}=4 \text{ m/s}$

(c) $x=0$

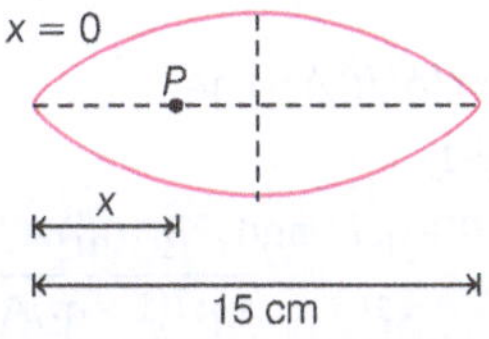

$$x=7.5-3=4.5 \text{ cm}$$

From Eq. (i),

$$A_x=(0.85 \text{ cm})\sin\left(\frac{\pi}{15}\times 4.5\right)$$

$$=0.688 \text{ cm}$$

14. (a) $y=y_1+y_2$

$$=0.2\sin(x-3.0t)+0.2\sin\left(x-3.0t+\frac{\pi}{2}\right)$$

$$=A\sin(x-3.0t+\theta)$$

Here, $A=\sqrt{(0.2)^2+(0.2)^2}$

and $\theta=\frac{\pi}{4}$

$\therefore \quad y=0.28\sin\left(x-3.0t+\frac{\pi}{4}\right)$ **Ans.**

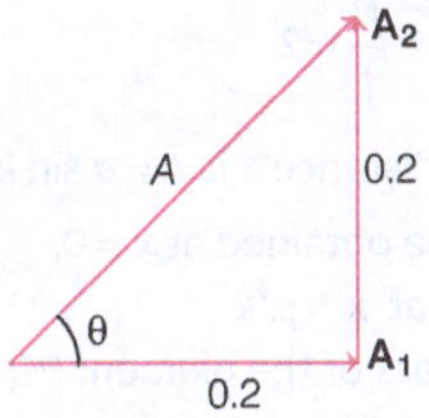

(b) Since, the amplitude of the resulting wave is 0.32 m and $A=0.2$ m, we have

$$0.32=\sqrt{(0.2)^2+(0.2)^2+(2)(0.2)(0.2)\cos\phi}$$

Solving this, we get

$$\phi=\cos^{-1}(0.28)$$ **Ans.**

15. (a) $l=\lambda_1/4$

$\therefore \quad \lambda_1=4l=16$ m, $l=3\lambda_2/4$

$\therefore \quad \lambda_2=\frac{4l}{3}=5.33$ m

$$l = 5\lambda_3/4$$

$$\therefore \quad \lambda_3 = \frac{4l}{5} = 3.2 \text{ m}$$

(b) $$v = \sqrt{\frac{T}{\mu}} = \sqrt{\frac{400}{(0.16/4)}} = 100 \text{ m/s}$$

Now, $$f_1 = \frac{v}{\lambda_1} = \frac{100}{16} = 6.25 \text{ Hz}$$

Similarly, f_2 and f_3.

16. Fundamental frequency

$$f = \frac{v}{2l} = \frac{\sqrt{T/\mu}}{2l} = \frac{1}{2l}\sqrt{\frac{Tl}{m}}$$

Further, $\frac{T/A}{\Delta l/l} = Y$

or $$T = Y(\Delta l/l)A = Y\eta A$$

Now, for string-1,

$$l_1 = l + \eta_1 l \quad \text{and} \quad T_1 = \eta_1 YA$$

$$\therefore \quad f_1 = \frac{1}{2l(1+\eta_1)}\sqrt{\frac{\eta_1 Yl(1+\eta_1)A}{m}}$$

Similarly, $$f_2 = \frac{1}{2l(1+\eta_2)}\sqrt{\frac{\eta_2 Yl(1+\eta_2)A}{m}}$$

So, $$\frac{f_1}{f_2} = \sqrt{\frac{\eta_2(1+\eta_1)}{\eta_1(1+\eta_2)}}$$

Substituting the values, we get

$$\frac{f_1}{f_2} = 1.4 \qquad (\eta_1 = 0.02 \text{ and } \eta_2 = 0.04)$$

17. Fundamental frequency,

$$f = \frac{1}{2l}\sqrt{\frac{T}{\mu}}$$

$$\Rightarrow \quad f' = \frac{1}{2(0.65l)}\sqrt{\frac{1.7T}{\mu}}$$

$$\therefore \quad \frac{f'}{f} = 2$$

18. Amplitude at a distance x is $A = a \sin kx$

First node can be obtained at $x = 0$,

and the second at $x = \pi/k$

At position x, mass of the element PQ is

$$dm = (\rho S)dx$$

Its amplitude is $A = a \sin kx$

Hence, mechanical energy stored in this element is

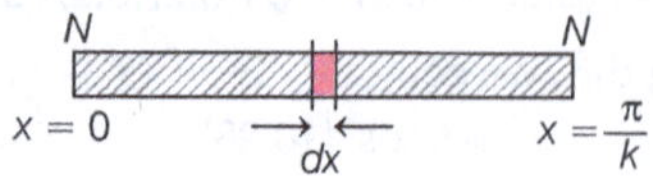

$$dE = \frac{1}{2}(dm)A^2\omega^2 \qquad \text{(energy of particle in SHM)}$$

or $$dE = \frac{1}{2}(\rho SA^2\omega^2)\,dx$$

$$= \frac{1}{2}(\rho Sa^2\omega^2 \sin^2 kx)\,dx$$

Therefore, total energy stored between two adjacent nodes will be

$$E = \int_{x=0}^{x=\pi/k} dE$$

Solving this, we get

$$E = \frac{\pi S\rho\omega^2 a^2}{4k} \qquad \textbf{Ans.}$$

19. Resultant amplitude

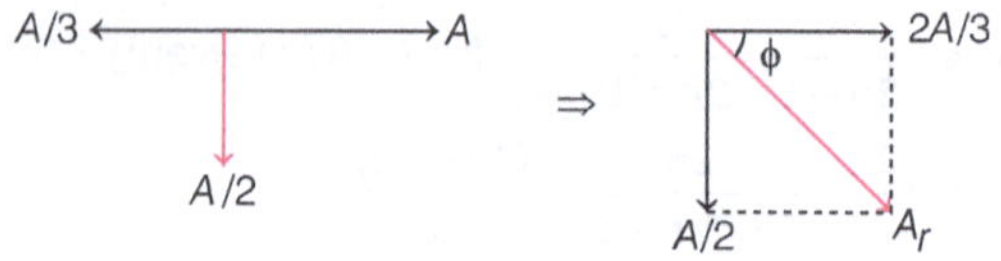

$$A_r = \sqrt{\left(\frac{2A}{3}\right)^2 + \left(\frac{A}{2}\right)^2}$$

$$= \frac{5}{6}A \qquad \textbf{Ans.}$$

$$\tan\phi = -\frac{A/2}{2A/3} = -\frac{3}{4}$$

or $$\phi = -\tan^{-1}(3/4) \qquad \textbf{Ans.}$$

20. Using $f = \frac{v}{2L}$, we get

$$120 = \frac{v}{2L_1} \qquad \text{...(i)}$$

and $$180 = \frac{v}{2L'} \qquad \text{...(ii)}$$

Dividing Eq. (ii) from Eq. (i), we get

$$\frac{L'}{L} = \frac{120}{180} = \frac{2}{3}$$

$$\Rightarrow \quad L' = 90 \times \frac{2}{3} = 60 \text{ cm}$$

21. Given, mass of the string,

$$m = 18 \text{ g} = 0.018 \text{ kg}$$

Linear mass density,

$$\mu = 20 \text{ g/m} = 0.02 \text{ kg/m}$$

If l be the length of the string, then

$$\mu = \frac{m}{l} \Rightarrow l = \frac{m}{\mu} = \frac{0.018}{0.02} = 0.9 \text{ m}$$

Speed of transverse wave in the string,

$$v = f_0\lambda = f_0\left(\frac{2l}{n}\right) \qquad \left(\because \lambda = \frac{2l}{n}\right)$$

$$= f_0\,\frac{2l}{1} \qquad \text{(for fundamental node, } n = 1)$$

$$= 50 \times 2 \times 0.9 \qquad (\because f_0 = 50 \text{ Hz})$$

$$= 90 \text{ m/s}$$

22. $\frac{nv}{2l} = 750 \text{ Hz}$

$$\frac{(n+1)v}{2l} = 1000 \text{ Hz}$$

$$\therefore \quad \frac{v}{2l} = 1000 - 750 = 250 \text{ Hz}$$

$$\Rightarrow \quad v = 2 \times 250 \times 1$$

$$\Rightarrow \quad \sqrt{\frac{T}{\mu}} = 500$$

$$\Rightarrow \quad T = 5 \text{ N}$$

23. For nth harmonic,

Frequency, $f_1 = \frac{nv}{0.6} = 400$

For $(n+1)$ th harmonic,

$$f_2 = \frac{(n+1)v}{0.6} = 450$$

$$\Rightarrow \left[\frac{0.6 \times 400}{v} + 1\right]\frac{v}{0.6} = 450$$

$$\Rightarrow \quad v = 30$$

$\Rightarrow$ Speed of wave on a string

$$v = \sqrt{\frac{T}{\mu}} = 30$$

$$\Rightarrow \quad \frac{2700}{\mu} = 900 \text{ or } \mu = 3 \text{ kg/m}$$

24. Linear mass density

$$\mu = 9.0 \times 10^{-4} \frac{\text{kg}}{\text{m}}$$

Tension, $T = 900$ N

$\therefore$ For velocity of wire,

$$v = \sqrt{\frac{T}{\mu}} = \sqrt{\frac{900}{9 \times 10^{-4}}}$$

$$= 10^3 \text{ m/s}$$

$$f_n = \frac{nv}{2l} = 500 \quad \text{...(i)}$$

And $\quad (n+1)v = 550 \quad$ ...(ii)

From Eqs. (i) and (ii),

$$f_{n+1} - f_n = \frac{v}{2l} = 50$$

$$\therefore \quad l = \frac{10^3}{2 \times 50} = 10 \text{ m}$$

Level 2

25. $\frac{\lambda}{2} = 1.5$ m

$$\therefore \quad \lambda = 3.0 \text{ m}$$

$$= k = \frac{2\pi}{\lambda} = \left(\frac{2\pi}{3}\right)\text{m}^{-1}$$

Let us take antinode at $x = 0$, then

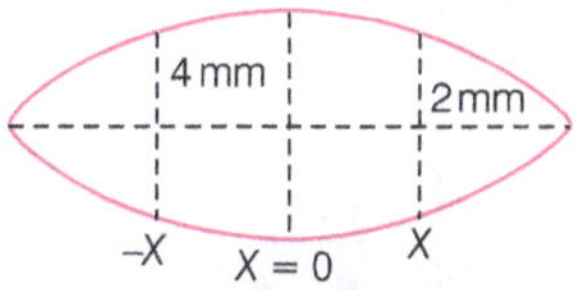

$$A_x = A_{max} \cos kx$$

$$\therefore \quad (2 \text{ mm}) = (4 \text{ mm}) \cos\left(\frac{2\pi}{3}\right)x$$

$$\therefore \quad \left(\frac{2\pi}{3}\right)x = \frac{\pi}{3}$$

or $\quad x = 0.5$ m

The asked distance is $2x$ or 1.0 m.

26. $\Delta\phi_1 = \pi/2$

$$\Delta\phi_2 = \left(\frac{2\pi}{\lambda}\right)(\Delta x)$$

$$= \left(\frac{2\pi}{\lambda}\right)(1.5\,\lambda)$$

$$= 3\pi$$

$$\therefore \quad \Delta\phi_{net} = \Delta\phi_2 - \Delta\phi_1 = \frac{5\pi}{2}$$

27. This is a string fixed at one end and free at the other.

$\therefore$ The three first modes are as shown.

$L = \frac{\lambda_1}{4}$ $\qquad$ $L = \frac{3\lambda_2}{4}$

$$\therefore \quad \lambda_1 = 4 \times 2.4 = 9.6 \text{ m}$$

$$\lambda_2 = \frac{4 \times 2.4}{3} = 3.2 \text{ m}$$

$$\lambda_3 = \frac{4 \times 2.4}{5} = 1.92 \text{ m}$$

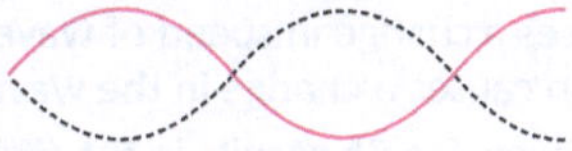

$L = \frac{5\lambda_3}{4}$

28. $f_1 = f_2$

$$f_1 = \frac{1}{2L}\sqrt{\frac{F_1}{\mu}}$$

$$f_2 = \frac{2}{2L}\sqrt{\frac{F_2}{\mu}}$$

$$\therefore \quad \sqrt{F_1} = 2\sqrt{F_2} \Rightarrow F_1 = 4F_2$$

For vertical equilibrium,

$$F_1 + F_2 = (4.8 + 1.2)\,g = 60 \text{ N}$$

$$\therefore \quad 4F_2 + F_2 = 60 \Rightarrow F_2 = 12 \text{ N}$$

$$\therefore \quad F_1 = 48 \text{ N}$$

Taking moments about O,

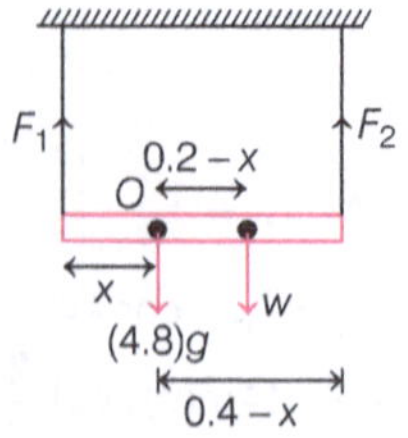

$$F_1x + W(0.2 - x) = F_2(0.4 - x)$$
$$48x + 12(0.2 - x) = 12(0.4 - x)$$
$$48x = 4.8 - 2.4 = 2.4$$
$$x = \frac{2.4}{48} = 0.05 \text{ m}$$
$$= 5 \text{ cm}$$

29.

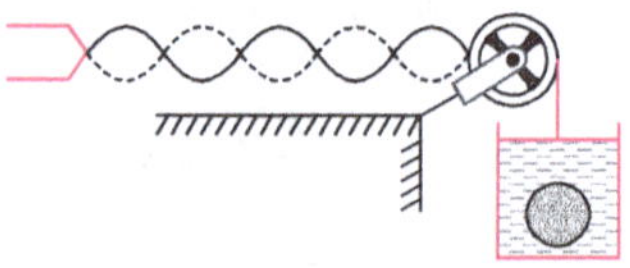

Initially FBD of sphere is

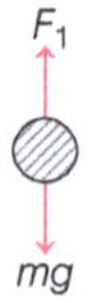

After immersion into water, FBD of sphere is

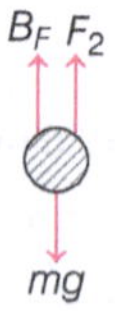

When sphere is immersed in water, buoyant force (B_F) acts upwards and reduces tension (F). The change in tension causes a change in speed of waves on the string, which in turn causes a change in the wavelength.

This altered wavelength results in the fifth harmonic. As vibrating element is same, frequency is same in both the cases.

From figures, $F_1 = mg$ ...(i)

and $B_F + F_2 = mg$

or $B_F = mg - F_2$ ...(ii)

$$f = \frac{n_1}{2L}\sqrt{\frac{F_1}{\mu}}, f = \frac{n_2}{2L}\sqrt{\frac{F_2}{\mu}}$$

$$\therefore \quad 1 = \frac{n_1}{n_2}\sqrt{\frac{F_1}{F_2}}$$

$$\Rightarrow \quad F_2 = \left(\frac{n_1}{n_2}\right)^2 F_1 = \left(\frac{2}{5}\right)^2 (2 \times 9.8) = 3.14 \text{ N}$$

Using this in Eq. (ii),

$$B_F = 19.6 - 3.14 = 16.46 \text{ N}$$

Also, $B_F = V_{sphere}\, \rho_{water}\, g = \frac{4}{3}\pi r^3 (1000)(9.8)$

$$\therefore \quad r^3 = \frac{16.46 \times 3}{4 \times 3.14 \times 1000 \times 9.8}$$

$$\Rightarrow \quad r = 0.0738 \text{ m}$$
$$= 7.38 \text{ cm}$$

Note *Only certain radii of the sphere will result in the string vibrating in a normal mode. The speed of waves on the string must be changed to a value such that the length of the string is integer multiple of half wavelengths.*

30.

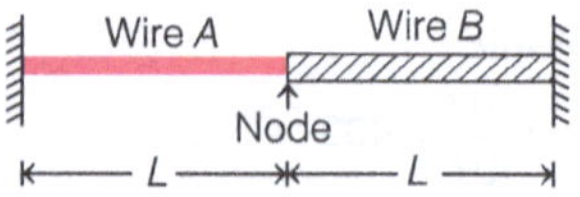

$$f_A = f_B$$

$$\Rightarrow \quad p\frac{v_A}{2L} = q\frac{v_B}{2L}$$

$$\Rightarrow \quad \frac{p}{q} = \frac{v_B}{v_A} = (\sqrt{T/\rho S})_B / (\sqrt{T/\rho S})_A$$

$$= \sqrt{\frac{S_A}{S_B}} = \frac{r_A}{r_B} = \frac{1}{2}$$

31. $\because n_1 : n_2$

$$\Rightarrow \quad \frac{p_1}{2l_1}\sqrt{\frac{T_1}{\pi r_1^2 l_1 d_1}} = \frac{p_2}{2l_2}\sqrt{\frac{T_2}{\pi r_2^2 l_2 d_2}}$$

$[\because l_1 = l_2 = l, T_1 = T_2 = T, r_1 = r_2 = r]$

$$\frac{p_1}{2l_1}\sqrt{\frac{T}{\pi r^2 l d_1}} = \frac{p_2}{2l}\sqrt{\frac{T}{\pi r^2 l d_2}}$$

$$\frac{p_1}{p_2} = \sqrt{\frac{d_1}{d_2}}$$

$$\because \quad d_2 = 4d_1$$

$$\frac{p_1}{p_2} = \sqrt{\frac{d_1}{4d_1}} = \frac{1}{2}$$

32. Total length of sonometer wire, $l = 110 \text{ cm} = 1.1 \text{ m}$

Length of wire is in ratio, 6 : 3 : 2 i.e.

60 cm, 30 cm, 20 cm. [As $l = 1.1$ m]

Tension in the wire, $T = 400$ N

Mass per unit length, $m = 0.01$ kg

Minimum common frequency = ?

Frequency, $\nu = \frac{1}{2l}\sqrt{\frac{T}{m}} = \frac{1000}{11}$ Hz

Similarly, $\nu_1 = \frac{1000}{6}$ Hz

$$\nu_2 = \frac{1000}{3} \text{ Hz}$$

and $\nu_3 = \frac{1000}{2}$ Hz

Hence common frequency= 1000 Hz.

33. Fundamental frequency of sonometer wire

$$f = \frac{v}{2l} = \frac{1}{2l}\sqrt{\frac{T}{\mu}} = \frac{1}{2l}\sqrt{\frac{T}{Ad}}$$

$$Y = \frac{Tl}{A\Delta l} \Rightarrow \frac{T}{A} = \frac{Y\Delta L}{L}$$

$$f = \frac{1}{2L}\sqrt{\frac{Y\Delta L}{Ld}}$$

$L = 1.5 \text{ m } \Delta L / L = 0.01$

$d = 7.7 \times 10^3 \text{ kg m}^{-3}$

$Y = 2.2 \times 10^{11} \text{ N/m}^2$

$$f = \frac{1}{2(1.5)}\sqrt{\frac{2.2 \times 10^{11} \times 0.01}{7.7 \times 10^3}}$$

$$= \frac{1}{3} \times \sqrt{285714.28}$$

$$f = \frac{534.5}{3}$$

$\Rightarrow \quad f = 178.2 \text{ Hz}$

34. Fundamental frequency, $f_0 = \frac{P}{2l}\sqrt{\frac{T}{\mu}}$

$$= \frac{5}{2l}\sqrt{\frac{9g}{\mu}} = \frac{3}{2l}\sqrt{\frac{Mg}{\mu}}$$

$\Rightarrow \quad M = 25 \text{ kg}$

As frequency is corresponds to 5th and 3rd harmonic $P = 5$ and $P = 3$ respectively.

35. Reflected and incident rays are in the same medium. Hence,

$$I \propto A^2$$

I_r has become 64% or 0.64 times of I_i

$\therefore \quad A_r = 0.8 A_i = 0.8 A$

36. $y = y_i + y_r$

$= A \sin(ax + bt + \pi/2) + 0.8 A \sin(ax - bt + \pi/2)$

$$= \left[0.8 A \sin\left(ax + bt + \frac{\pi}{2}\right) + 0.8 A \sin\left(ax - bt + \frac{\pi}{2}\right)\right] + 0.2A \sin\left(ax + bt + \frac{\pi}{2}\right)$$

$= -1.6 \sin ax \sin bt + 0.2 A \cos(bt + ax)$

$\therefore \quad c = 0.2$

37. $A_x = -1.6 \sin ax$

$\therefore \quad x = 0$ is a node

Second antinode is at a distance.

$$x = \frac{\lambda}{4} + \frac{\lambda}{2}$$

$$= \frac{3\lambda}{4} = \frac{3}{4}\left(\frac{2\pi}{k}\right)$$

But, $k = a$

$$\therefore \quad x = \frac{3\pi}{2a}$$

38. $y = -A \sin(\omega t - kx)$ [At $t = 0$, $x = 0$ is moving down]

From the figure, $\lambda = 8$ m and $A = 10$ mm

$$\therefore \quad k = \frac{2\pi}{k} = \frac{\pi}{4}\text{m}^{-1}, \ \omega = kv = \frac{\pi}{4} \times 1 = \frac{\pi}{4}\text{s}^{-1}$$

$$\therefore \quad y = -10 \times 10^{-3} \sin\left[\frac{\pi}{4}t - \frac{\pi}{4}x\right]$$

$$\frac{\partial y}{\partial t} = v_P = -10 \times 10^{-3}\left(\frac{\pi}{4}\right)\cos\left[\frac{\pi}{4}t - \frac{\pi}{4}x\right]$$

$$= \frac{\pi}{4}\text{ cm s}^{-1}$$

39. Distance moved by each pulse in $t = 8$ s is

$$s = 8 \times 1 = 8 \text{ m}$$

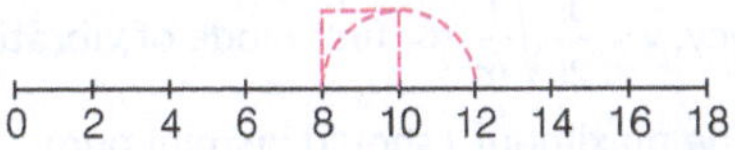

Due to sinusoidal pulse

$$(y_1)_{\text{at } x = 9\text{m } t = 8\text{s}} = -10 \times 10^{-3} \sin\left[\frac{\pi}{4} \times 8 - \frac{\pi}{4} \times 9\right]$$

or $\quad y_1 = -10^{-2} \sin\left(-\frac{\pi}{4}\right)$

$$= \frac{10^{-2}}{\sqrt{2}}\text{m} = \frac{1}{\sqrt{2}}\text{cm}$$

$(y_2)_{\text{at } x = 9\text{ m}, t = 8\text{ s}} = 1 \text{ cm}$

$$\therefore \quad y = y_1 + y_2 = \frac{1}{\sqrt{2}} + 1$$

$$= \frac{\sqrt{2} + 1}{\sqrt{2}}\text{ cm}$$

40. $(v_P)_1 = -10^{-2}\left(\frac{\pi}{4}\right)\cos\left[\frac{\pi}{4} \times 8 - \frac{\pi}{4} \times 9\right]$

$$= -10^{-2}\frac{\pi}{4}\left(\frac{1}{\sqrt{2}}\right)\text{ms}^{-1}$$

$$= -\frac{\pi}{4\sqrt{2}}\text{ cm s}^{-1}$$

Due to square pulse $(v_P)_2$ at $x = 9$ m, $t = 1$ s in y-direction is zero.

$$\therefore \quad v_P = (v_P)_1 + 0 = -\frac{\pi}{4\sqrt{2}}\text{ cm s}^{-1}$$

41. For largest mass, $n = 1$

$$\therefore \quad f = \frac{n}{2L}\sqrt{\frac{F}{\mu}}$$

$$\Rightarrow \quad 700 = \frac{1}{2 \times 1}\sqrt{\frac{F}{2 \times 10^{-3}}}$$

or $\quad F = 3920 \text{ N}$

$$\therefore \quad M_{\max} = \frac{F}{g} = \frac{3920}{9.8}$$

$$= 400 \text{ kg}$$

42. Here, $F = 16 \times 9.8 = 156.8$ N

$$f = \frac{n}{2L}\sqrt{\frac{F}{\mu}}$$

$$\Rightarrow \quad 700 = \frac{n}{2 \times 1}\sqrt{\frac{156.8}{2 \times 10^{-3}}}$$

$$\Rightarrow \quad n = 5$$

43. $A(x) = 6 \sin\left(\frac{\pi x}{10}\right)$

At $x = 5$ cm,

$A(x) = 6 \sin\left(\frac{\pi \times 5}{10}\right) = 6$ cm

44. Frequency, $v = \frac{1}{2l}\sqrt{\frac{T}{m}}$ for first mode of vibration

For v to be maximum, l should be minimum.

String 1 $f_0 = \frac{1}{2L_0}\sqrt{\frac{T_0}{\mu}}$

String 2 $f_2 = \frac{1}{2L_0}\sqrt{\frac{T_0}{2\mu}} = \frac{f_0}{\sqrt{2}}$

String 3 $f_3 = \frac{1}{2L_0}\sqrt{\frac{T_0}{4\mu}} = \frac{f_0}{\sqrt{3}}$

String 4 $f_4 = \frac{1}{2L_0}\cdot\sqrt{\frac{T_0}{4\mu}} = \frac{f_0}{2}$

45. Let a_i and a_r be the amplitudes of incident and reflected waves.

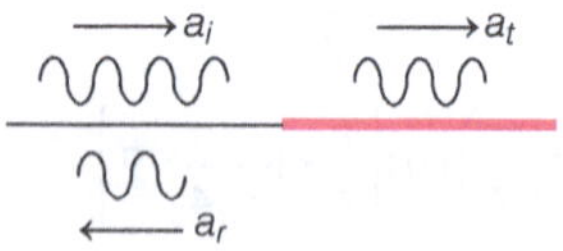

Then,

$$\frac{a_i + a_r}{a_i - a_r} = 6 \qquad \text{(given)}$$

Hence, $$\frac{a_r}{a_i} = \frac{5}{7}$$

Now, $$\frac{E_r}{E_i} = \left(\frac{a_r}{a_i}\right)^2 = \left(\frac{5}{7}\right)^2$$

$$= 0.51$$

or percentage of energy reflected is

$$100 \times \frac{E_r}{E_i} = 51\%.$$

So, percentage of energy transmitted will be

$$(100 - 51)\% \text{ or } 49\%.$$ **Ans.**

46. $l = \frac{\lambda}{2}$

or $$\lambda = 2l, k = \frac{2\pi}{\lambda} = \frac{\pi}{l}$$

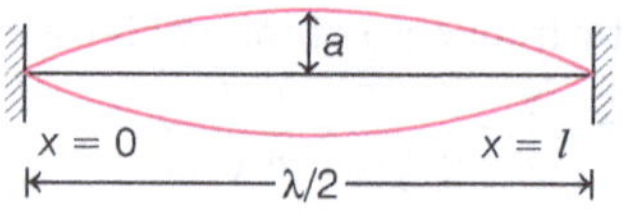

The amplitude at a distance x from $x = 0$ is given by

$$A = a \sin kx$$

Total mechanical energy at x of length dx is

$$dE = \frac{1}{2}(dm)A^2\omega^2$$

$$= \frac{1}{2}(\mu dx)(a \sin kx)^2(2\pi f)^2$$

or $$dE = 2\pi^2 \mu f^2 a^2 \sin^2 kx \, dx \qquad \text{...(i)}$$

Here, $$f = \frac{v^2}{\lambda^2} = \frac{\left(\frac{T}{\mu}\right)}{(4l^2)} \text{ and } k = \frac{\pi}{l}$$

Substituting these values in Eq. (i) and integrating it from $x = 0$ to $x = l$, we get total energy of string.

$$E = \frac{\pi^2 a^2 T}{4l}$$ **Ans.**

47. Tension, $T = 80$ N

Amplitude of incident wave, $A_i = 3.5$ cm

Mass per unit length of wire PQ is

$$m_1 = \frac{0.06}{4.8} = \frac{1}{80} \text{ kg/m}$$

and mass per unit length of wire QR is

$$m_2 = \frac{0.2}{2.56} = \frac{1}{12.8} \text{ kg/m}$$

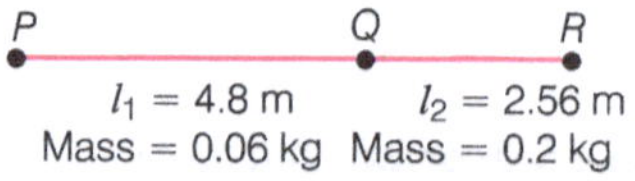

(a) Speed of wave in wire PQ is

$$v_1 = \sqrt{T/m_1} = \sqrt{\frac{80}{1/80}}$$

$$= 80 \text{ m/s}$$

and speed of wave in wire QR is

$$v_2 = \sqrt{T/m_2}$$

$$= \sqrt{\frac{80}{1/12.8}} = 32 \text{ m/s}$$

$\therefore$ Time taken by the wave pulse to reach from P to R is

$$t = \frac{4.8}{v_1} + \frac{2.56}{v_2} = \left(\frac{4.8}{80} + \frac{2.56}{32}\right) \text{s}$$

$$= 0.14 \text{ s}$$ **Ans.**

(b) The expressions for reflected and transmitted amplitudes (A_r and A_t) in terms of v_1, v_2 and A_i are as follows :

$$A_r = \frac{v_2 - v_1}{v_2 + v_1} A_i$$

and $$A_t = \frac{2v_2}{v_1+v_2}A_i$$

Substituting the values, we get

$$A_r = \left(\frac{32-80}{32+80}\right)(3.5)$$

$$= -1.5 \text{ cm}$$

i.e. the amplitude of reflected wave will be 1.5 cm. Negative sign of A_r indicates that there will be a phase change of π in reflected wave.

Similarly, $A_t = \left(\frac{2\times 32}{32+80}\right)(3.5)$

$$= 2.0 \text{ cm}$$

i.e. the amplitude of transmitted wave will be 2.0 cm.

48. **When A is a node** Suppose n_1 and n_2 are the complete loops formed on left and right side of point A. Then,

$$f_1 = f_2$$

or $$n_1\left(\frac{v_1}{2L}\right) = n_2\left(\frac{v_2}{2L}\right)$$

or $$\frac{n_1}{n_2} = \left(\frac{v_2}{v_1}\right) = \sqrt{\frac{\mu_1}{\mu_2}} = \frac{1}{3}, \frac{2}{6}, \frac{3}{9}, \ldots, \text{ etc}$$

$$\left(\text{as } v \propto \frac{1}{\sqrt{\mu}}\right)$$

$\therefore$ Possible frequencies are

$$\frac{v_1}{2L}, 2\left(\frac{v_1}{2L}\right), \frac{3v_1}{2L}, \ldots, \text{etc.} \qquad \left(v_1 = \sqrt{\frac{T}{\mu}}\right)$$

or $$\frac{1}{2L}\sqrt{\frac{T}{\mu}}, \frac{1}{L}\sqrt{\frac{T}{\mu}}, \frac{3}{2L}\sqrt{\frac{T}{2\mu}}, \ldots, \text{etc.}$$

When A is an antinode Suppose n_1 and n_2 are complete loops on left and right side of point A,

$$n_1\frac{\lambda_1}{2} + \frac{\lambda_1}{4} = L$$

or $$f_1 = \frac{v_1}{L}\left(\frac{n_1}{2} + \frac{1}{4}\right)$$

$$n_2\frac{\lambda_2}{2} + \frac{\lambda_2}{4} = L$$

or $$f_2 = \frac{v_2}{L}\left(\frac{n_2}{2} + \frac{1}{4}\right)$$

Substituting $f_1 = f_2$, we get

$$\frac{2n_1+1}{2n_2+1} = \frac{1}{3}$$

For $$n_1 = 1, \quad n_2 = 4$$
$$n_1 = 2, \quad n_2 = 7$$
$$n_1 = 3, \quad n_2 = 10, \text{ etc.}$$
$$\ldots \quad \ldots \quad \ldots$$

Therefore, the possible frequencies are

$$\frac{v_1}{L}\left(\frac{1}{2}+\frac{1}{4}\right), \frac{v_1}{L}\left(\frac{2}{2}+\frac{1}{4}\right), \frac{v_1}{L}\left(\frac{3}{2}+\frac{1}{4}\right), \ldots, \text{etc.}$$

or $$\frac{3}{4L}\sqrt{\frac{T}{\mu}}, \frac{5}{4L}\sqrt{\frac{T}{\mu}}, \frac{7}{4L}\sqrt{\frac{T}{\mu}}, \ldots, \text{etc.}$$

49. $\frac{L}{4} = \frac{\lambda}{4}$

$\therefore$ $$L = \lambda$$

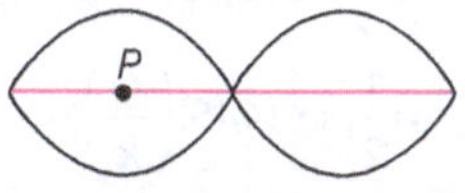

In the next higher mode, there will be total 6 loops and the desired frequency is

$$\left(\frac{6}{2}\right)(100) = 300 \text{ Hz}$$ **Ans.**

50. $\because$ $k = \frac{\omega}{v} = \frac{\pi}{3}$

$$y_1 = 0.06\,(\pi t - kx)$$
$$= 0.06 \sin\left(\pi t - \frac{\pi}{3}\times 1.2\right)$$
$$= 0.06 \sin(\pi t - 4\pi)$$

Similarly,

$$y_2 = 0.02 \sin(\pi t - kx')$$
$$= 0.02 \sin\left(\pi t - \frac{\pi}{3}\times 8\right)$$
$$= 0.02 \sin\left(\pi t - \frac{8\pi}{3}\right)$$

$$y = y_1 + y_2$$
$$= 0.06 \sin \pi t \cos 4\pi - 0.06 \cos \pi t \sin 4\pi$$
$$+ 0.02 \sin \pi t \cos\frac{8\pi}{3} - 0.02 \cos \pi t \sin\frac{8\pi}{3}$$
$$= 0.05 \sin \pi t - 0.0173 \cos \pi t$$ **Ans.**

51. (a) Distance between two nodes is $\lambda/2$ or π/k. The volume of string between two nodes is

$$V = \frac{\pi}{k}s \quad \ldots\text{(i)}$$

Energy density (energy per unit volume) of each wave will be

$$u_1 = \frac{1}{2}\rho\omega^2(8)^2$$
$$= 32\,\rho\omega^2$$

and $$u_2 = \frac{1}{2}\rho\omega^2(6)^2$$
$$= 18\,\rho\omega^2$$

$\therefore$ Total mechanical energy between two consecutive nodes will be

$$E = (u_1 + u_2)V$$
$$= 50\frac{\pi}{k}\rho\omega^2 s$$

(b) $y = y_1 + y_2$
$$= 8\sin(\omega t - kx) + 6\sin(\omega t + kx)$$
$$= 2\sin(\omega t - kx) + \{6\sin(\omega t + kx) + 6\sin(\omega t + kx)\}$$

$$=2\sin(\omega t - kx) + 12\cos kx \sin \omega t$$

Thus, the resultant wave will be a sum of standing wave and a travelling wave.

Energy crossing through a node per second = power or travelling wave

$$\therefore \quad P = \frac{1}{2}\rho\omega^2(2)^2 Sv$$

$$= \frac{1}{2}\rho\omega^2(4)(S)\left(\frac{\omega}{k}\right)$$

$$= \frac{2\rho\omega^3 S}{k}$$

52. (a) Standing waves can only be produced by the interference of two identical waves. Therefore, z_1 and z_2 will produce a standing wave. The equation of standing wave in this case would be,

$$z = z_1 + z_2 = 2A\cos kx \cos \omega t$$

$$= A_x \cos \omega t$$

Here, $A_x = 2A\cos kx$

Resultant intensity will be zero, at the positions

where, $A_x = 0$

or $kx = (2n+1)\frac{\pi}{2}$

where $n = 0, \pm 1, \pm 2......$ etc.

or $x = (2n+1)\frac{\pi}{2k}$

where $n = 0, \pm 1, \pm 2 ...$ etc.

(b) Since z_3 and z_1 travel in Y-axis and X-axis respectively, the wave formed by their superposition will also travel in positive x and positive Y-axis. The equation of wave would be

$$z = z_1 + z_3 = 2A\cos\left[\frac{kx+ky}{2} - \omega t\right]\cos\left(\frac{kx-ky}{2}\right)$$

The resultant intensity is zero, where

$$\cos k\left(\frac{x-y}{2}\right) = 0$$

or $\frac{k(x-y)}{2} = (2n+1)\frac{\pi}{2}$

or $(x-y) = (2n+1)\frac{\pi}{k}$

where $n = 0, \pm 1, \pm 2, \ldots$ etc.

53. (a) Compare the given equation $y_1 = A\cos(ax+bt)$ with the standard equation of a plane progressive wave

$$y = A\cos\left(\frac{2\pi}{\lambda}x + 2\pi vt\right)$$

$$\Rightarrow \quad \frac{2\pi}{\lambda} = a \Rightarrow \lambda = \frac{2\pi}{a}$$

Also, $2\pi f = b$

$\therefore$ Frequency of incident wave, $f = \frac{b}{2\pi}$

(b) The wave is reflected by an obstacle, it will suffer a phase difference of π. The intensity of the reflected wave is 0.64 times of the incident wave.

Intensity of original wave $I \propto A^2$

Intensity of reflected wave $I' = 0.64 I$

$$\Rightarrow \quad I' \propto A'^2$$

$$\Rightarrow \quad 0.64 I \propto A'^2$$

$$\Rightarrow \quad 0.64 A^2 \propto A'^2$$

$$\Rightarrow \quad A' \propto 0.8A$$

So the equation of reflected wave

$$y_r = 0.8A\cos(ax - bt + \pi)$$

$$= -0.8A\cos(ax - bt)$$

(c) The resultant wave equation

$$y = y_i + y_r = A\cos(ax+bt) + [-0.8A\cos(ax-bt)]$$

Particle velocity

$$v = \frac{dy}{dt} = -Ab\sin(ax+bt) - 0.8Ab\sin(ax-bt)$$

$$= -Ab[\sin(ax+bt) + 0.8\sin(ax-bt)]$$

$$= -Ab[\sin ax\cos bt + \cos ax \sin bt + 0.8\sin ax\cos bt - 0.8\cos ax\sin bt]$$

$$v = -Ab[1.8\sin ax\cos bt + 0.2\cos ax\sin bt]$$

The maximum velocity will occur when $\sin ax = 1$ and $\cos bt = 1$ under these condition $\cos ax = 0$ and $\sin bt = 0$

$\therefore$ $|v_{max}| = 1.8\,Ab$ Also, $|v_{min}| = 0$

(d) $y = [A\cos(ax+bt)] - [0.8A\cos(ax-bt)]$

$$= [0.8A\cos(ax+bt) + 0.2A\cos(ax+bt)] - [0.8A\cos(Ax-bt)]$$

$$= [0.8A\cos(ax+bt) - 0.8A\cos(ax-bt)] + [0.2A\cos(ax+bt)]$$

$$= 0.8A\left[-2\sin\left\{\frac{(ax+bt)-(ax-bt)}{2}\right\}\right] 0.2A\cos(ax+bt)]$$

$$\frac{\sin\{(ax+bt)-(ax-bt)\}}{2}$$

$$\Rightarrow \quad y = -1.6A\sin ax\sin bt + 0.2A\cos(ax+bt)$$

where $(-1.6A\sin ax\sin bt)$ is the equation of a standing wave and $0.2A\cos(ax+bt)$ is the equation of travelling wave.

The wave is travelling in $-x$-direction.

Antinodes are the points where the amplitude is maximum,

i.e. $\sin ax = 1 = \sin\left[n\pi + (-1)^n\frac{\pi}{2}\right]$

or $ax = \left[n\pi + (-1)^n\frac{\pi}{2}\right]$

or $x = \left[n + \frac{(-1)^n}{2}\right]\frac{\pi}{a}$

Similarly, nodes are points of minimum amplitude.

54. Distance between two dotted lines is given 15 cm.

$$\therefore \quad AB = CD = \frac{15}{2}$$

$$= 7.5 \text{ cm}$$

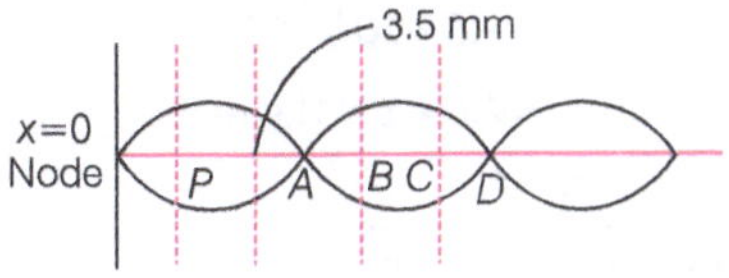

$\therefore$ One loop length or $\dfrac{\lambda}{2} = AB + BC + CD = 30$ cm

String is 120 cm long. So, there will be four loops as shown below.

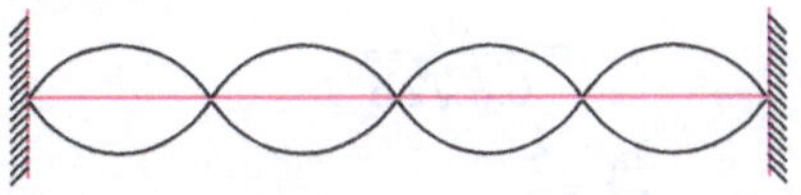

So this corresponds to 4th harmonic or third overtone.

In the first figure, x = 0 is a node. So, we can write

$$A_x = A_{max} \sin Kx$$

$$\Rightarrow \quad A_x = A_{max} \sin\left(\frac{2\pi}{\lambda}x\right) = A_{max} \sin\left[\frac{\pi}{\lambda/2} \times x_P\right]$$

At x_P, amplitude $A_x = 3.5$ mm.

Substituting the proper values, we get

$$3.5 = A_{max} \sin\left[\frac{\pi}{30} \times 7.5\right]$$

Solving this equation, we get

$$A_{max} = 5 \text{ mm}$$

55.

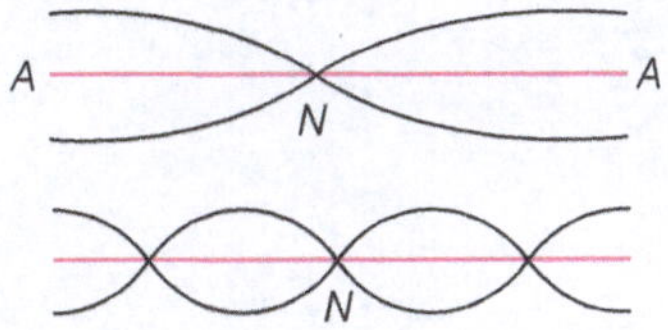

In first figure, $\dfrac{\lambda_1}{2} = l$

$$\Rightarrow \quad \lambda_1 = 2l$$

$$f = \frac{v}{\lambda_1} = \frac{v}{2l} = f_1 \quad \text{(say)}$$

In second figure,

$$\frac{3\lambda_2}{2} = l$$

$$\Rightarrow \quad \lambda_2 = \frac{2l}{3}$$

$$\text{or} \quad f = \frac{v}{\lambda_2} = 3\left(\frac{v}{2l}\right) = 3f_1 = f_3 \quad \text{(say)}$$

Thus, general expression of frequency is $(2n-1)\dfrac{v}{2l}$, where $n = 1, 2, 3$ .....

Here, $v = \sqrt{\dfrac{Y_{Cu}}{\rho_{Cu}}} = \sqrt{\dfrac{130 \times 10^9}{8900}}$

≈ 3822 m/s

So, now

$$20000 < (2n-1)\frac{v}{2l} < 5000$$

Substituting the values, we get

$$3.11 < n < 7.04$$

Thus four frequencies are possible corresponding to $n = 4, 5, 6$ and 7.

$$f_1 = \frac{(2 \times 4 - 1) \times 3822}{2 \times 0.5}$$

$$= 26754 \text{ Hz or } 26.7 \text{ kHz}$$

$$f_2 = \frac{(2 \times 5 - 1) \times 3822}{2 \times 0.5} = 34398 \text{ Hz or } 34.4 \text{ kHz}$$

$$f_3 = \frac{(2 \times 6 - 1) \times 3822}{2 \times 0.5} = 42042 \text{ Hz or } 42 \text{ kHz}$$

$$f_4 = \frac{(2 \times 7 - 1) \times 3822}{2 \times 0.5} = 49686 \text{ Hz or } 49.6 \text{ kHz}$$

56. (a) Equation of stationary wave in the given stretched wire can be written as,

$$y = A_x \cos \omega t$$

x=0 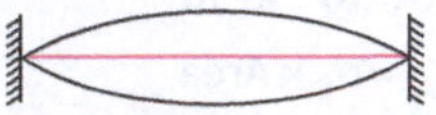

Here, $A_x = a_{max} \sin kx$ as $x = 0$ is a node.

Here $\dfrac{\lambda}{2} = l$

$$\text{or} \quad \lambda = 2l$$

$$\therefore \quad k = \frac{2\pi}{\lambda} = \frac{\pi}{l}$$

$$\therefore \quad A_x = a_{max} \sin \frac{\pi}{l} x$$

At a distance x, if we take a small length dx, then its mass would be,

$$dm = \left(\frac{m}{l}\right) dx$$

Its maximum kinetic energy

$$dK_m = \frac{1}{2}(dm)(\omega A_x)^2$$

$$= \frac{1}{2}\left(\frac{m}{l}dx\right)(\omega)^2\left[a_{max} \sin\left(\frac{\pi}{l}x\right)\right]^2$$

Integrating it from $x = 0$ to $x = l$, we get maximum kinetic energy which comes out to be,

$$K_m = \frac{1}{4} m\omega^2 a_{max}^2$$

Note *Maximum velocity at mean position is* ωA

(b) $y = A_x \cos \omega t$

$$v_P = \frac{\partial y}{\partial t} = -\omega A_x \sin \omega t$$

Small kinetic energy of the element taken in part (a) at time t will be,

$$dK = \frac{1}{2}(dm)(v_P^2)$$

$$= \frac{1}{2}\left(\frac{m}{l}dx\right)(\omega^2 A_x^2)\sin^2 \omega t$$

Now average value of $\sin^2 \omega t$ in one complete cycle is $\frac{1}{2}$. Hence,

$$< dK > = \frac{1}{4}\left(\frac{m}{l}dx\right)(\omega^2)\left[a_{max}\sin\left(\frac{\pi}{l}x\right)\right]^2$$

Integrating it from $x = 0$ to $x = l$, we get the average value of kinetic energy, which comes out to be,

$$< K > = \frac{1}{8}m\omega^2 a_{max}^2$$

57. Velocities on Al and steel wires are different because μ is different for both of them. So, λ is also different as f is same for both.

$$\mu_1 = \mu_{steel} = \rho_1 \times \text{Area} = 7.8 \times 10^3 \times 10^{-6}$$

$$= 7.8 \times 10^{-3}\ \text{kg m}^{-1}$$

$$\mu_2 = \mu_{Al} = \rho_2 \times \text{Area}$$

$$= 2.6 \times 10^3 \times 10^{-6}$$

$$= 2.6 \times 10^{-3}\ \text{kg m}^{-1}$$

$$f_1 = f_2$$

$$\Rightarrow \quad \frac{n_1}{2L_1}\sqrt{\frac{F}{\mu_1}} = \frac{n_2}{2L_2}\sqrt{\frac{F}{\mu_2}}$$

$$= \frac{n_1}{0.866 \times \sqrt{7.8}}$$

$$= \frac{n_2}{0.6\sqrt{2.6}}$$

$$\Rightarrow \quad \frac{n_1}{n_2} = \frac{5}{2}$$

Therefore, lowest frequency oscillation causes 2 loops in Al and 5 loops in steel.

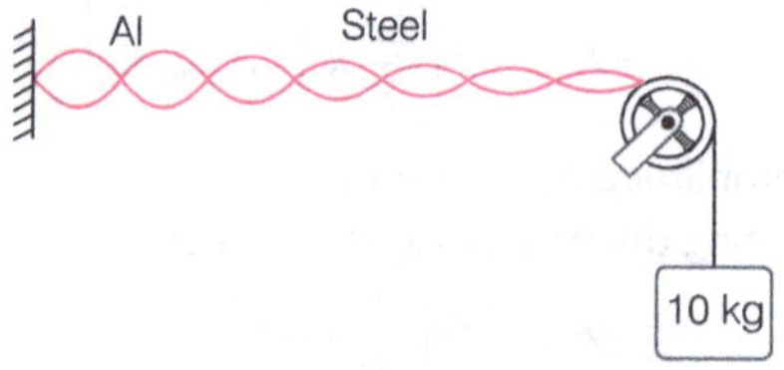

So, total no. of nodes = 8, required no. of nodes = 6

UNIT–19

SOUND WAVES

Learning Modules

1. Displacement, Pressure and Density Waves
2. Speed of Longitudinal (or Sound) Wave
3. Sound Intensity
4. Interference in Sound Wave and Stationary Wave
5. Standing Longitudinal Waves in Organ Pipes
6. Beats
7. The Doppler Effect

MODULE 1

Displacement, Pressure and Density Waves

Introduction

Of all the mechanical waves that occur in nature, the most important in our everyday life are longitudinal waves in a medium, usually air, called **sound waves.**

The reason is that the human ear is tremendously sensitive and can detect sound waves even of very low intensity.

The human ear is sensitive to waves in the frequency range from about 20 to 20000 Hz called the **audible range**, but we also use the term sound for similar waves with frequencies above **(ultrasonic)** and below **(infrasonic)** the range of human hearing.

Our main concern in this chapter is with sound waves in air, but sound can travel through any gas, liquid or solid.

In this unit, we will discuss several important properties of sound waves, including **pressure wave** and **density wave.**

We will find that superposition of two sound waves differing slightly in frequency causes a phenomenon called **beats.** When a source of sound or a listener moves through the air, the listener may hear a different frequency than the one emitted by the source. This is the **Doppler's effect.**

Note *Sound wave (rather we can call audible sound wave) is a part of longitudinal wave with frequency range varying from 20 Hz to 20,000 Hz.*

Up to this point we have described mechanical waves primarily in terms of displacement. As we have discussed in Unit 17, a sinusoidal wave equation $y(x, t)$ travelling in positive x-direction can be written as

$$y(x, t) = A\sin(kx - \omega t)$$

which gives the instantaneous displacement y of a particle in the medium at position x at time t.

Note *In a longitudinal wave the displacements are parallel to the direction of motion of the wave. So, x and y are measured parallel to each other, not perpendicular as in a transverse wave.*

If value of y is suppose $+4$ mm, it means displacement of particle from mean position is 4 mm in positive x-direction (or towards right). Similarly if y is -2 mm. It means displacement from mean position is 2 mm towards negative direction (or towards left).

The amplitude A is the maximum displacement of a particle in a medium from its equilibrium position.

These displacements are along the direction of the motion of the wave and lead to **variations in the density and pressure** of air. Hence, a sound wave can also be described in terms of variations of pressure or density at various points. The pressure fluctuations are of the order of 1 Pa $(= 1\ \text{N/m}^2)$, whereas atmospheric pressure is about 10^5 Pa. In a sinusoidal sound wave in air, the pressure fluctuates above and below atmospheric pressure p_0 with the same frequency as the motions of the air particles. Similarly, the density of air also vibrates sinusoidally above and below its normal level. So, we can express a sound wave either in terms of $y(x, t)$ or $\Delta p(x, t)$ or $\Delta\rho(x, t)$. All the three equations are related to one another. For example, amplitude of pressure variation $(\Delta p)_m$ is related to amplitude of displacement A by the equation,

$$\Delta p_m = BAk$$

where B is the bulk modulus of the medium. Moreover, pressure or density wave is 90° out of phase with the displacement wave, i.e. when the displacement is zero, the pressure and density changes are maximum and when the displacement is a maximum, the pressure and density changes are zero. Now, let us find the relation between them.

Relation between Displacement Wave and Pressure Wave

Figure shows a harmonic displacement wave moving through air contained in a long tube of cross-sectional area S.

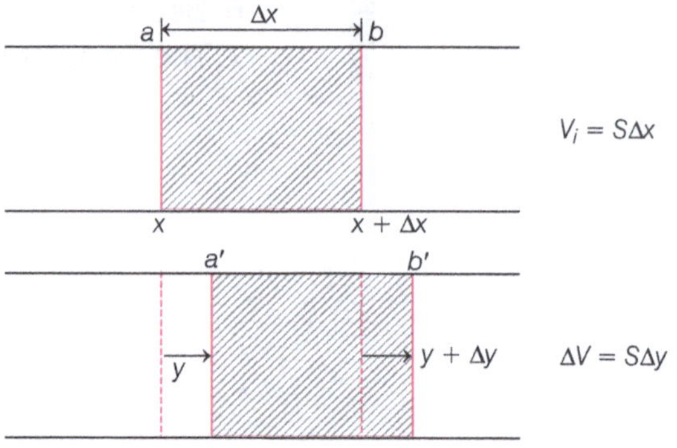

The volume of gas that has a thickness Δx in the horizontal direction is $V_i = S\Delta x$. The change in volume ΔV is $S\Delta y$, where Δy is the difference between the value of y at $x + \Delta x$ and the value of y at x. From the definition of bulk modulus, the pressure variation in the gas is

$$\Delta p = -B\frac{\Delta V}{V_i} = -B\left(\frac{S\Delta y}{S\Delta x}\right) = -B\left(\frac{\Delta y}{\Delta x}\right)$$

As Δx approaches zero, the ratio $\frac{\Delta y}{\Delta x}$ becomes $\frac{\partial y}{\partial x}$. (The partial derivative indicates that we are interested in the variation of y with position at a fixed time).

Therefore, $$\Delta p = -B\frac{\partial y}{\partial x} \quad \text{...(i)}$$

So, this is the equation which relates the displacement equation with the pressure equation. Suppose the displacement equation is

$$y = A\cos(kx - \omega t) \quad \text{...(ii)}$$

Then, $$\frac{\partial y}{\partial x} = -kA\sin(kx - \omega t) \quad \text{...(iii)}$$

and from Eqs. (i) and (iii), we find that

$$\Delta p = BAk\sin(kx - \omega t) = (\Delta p)_m \sin(kx - \omega t) \quad \text{...(iv)}$$

Here, $$(\Delta p)_m = BAk$$

where Δp_m is the amplitude of pressure variation. From Eqs. (ii) and (iv), we see that pressure equation is 90° out of phase with displacement equation. When the displacement is zero, the pressure variation is maximum and when pressure variation is zero, displacement is maximum. Fig. (a) shows displacement from equilibrium position of air molecules in a harmonic sound wave *versus* position at some instants. Points x_2 and x_1 are points of zero displacement. Now, refer Fig. (b) : Just to the left of x_2, the displacement is negative indicating that the gas molecules are displaced to left away from point x_2 at this instant. Just to the right of x_2, the displacement is positive indicating that the molecules are displaced to the right, which is again away from point x_2. So, at point x_2 the pressure of the gas is minimum. So, if p_0 is the atmospheric pressure (normal pressure), the pressure at x_2 will be

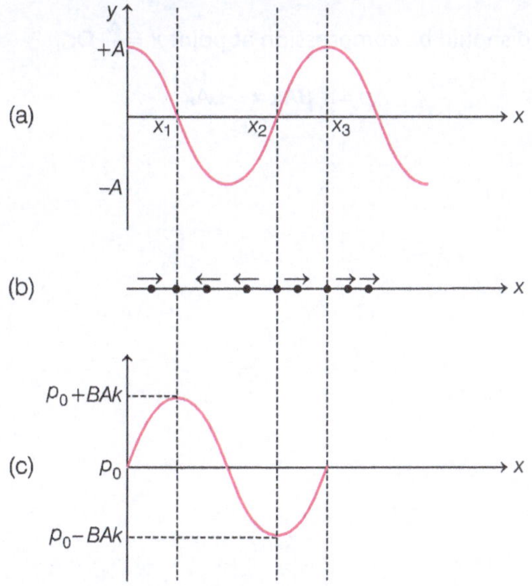

$$p(x_2) = p_0 - (\Delta p)_m = p_0 - BAk$$

At point x_1, the pressure (and hence the density also) is maximum because the molecules on both sides of that point are displaced toward point x_1. Hence,

$$p(x_1) = p_0 + (\Delta p)_m = p_0 + BAk$$

At point x_3, the pressure (and hence the density) does not change because the gas molecules on both sides of that point have equal displacements in the same direction or

$$p(x_3) = p_0$$

From Fig. (a) and (c), we see that pressure change and displacement are 90° out of phase.

Relation between Pressure Wave and Density Wave

In this section, we will find the relation between pressure wave and density wave.

According to the definition of bulk modulus (B),

$$B = \left(-\frac{dp}{dV/V}\right) \quad \text{...(i)}$$

Further, $$\text{volume} = \frac{\text{mass}}{\text{density}}$$

or $$V = \frac{m}{\rho} \quad \text{or} \quad dV = -\frac{m}{\rho^2}\cdot d\rho = -\frac{V}{\rho}\cdot d\rho$$

or $$\frac{dV}{V} = -\frac{d\rho}{\rho}$$

Substituting in Eq. (i), we get

$$d\rho = \frac{\rho\,(dp)}{B} = \frac{dp}{v^2} \qquad \left(v = \sqrt{\frac{B}{\rho}} \Rightarrow \frac{\rho}{B} = \frac{1}{v^2}\right)$$

Or, this can be written as

$$\Delta\rho = \frac{\rho}{B}\cdot\Delta p = \frac{1}{v^2}\cdot\Delta p$$

So, this relation relates the pressure equation with the density equation. For example, if

$$\Delta p = (\Delta p)_m \sin(kx - \omega t)$$

then $$\Delta\rho = (\Delta\rho)_m \sin(kx - \omega t)$$

where, $$(\Delta\rho)_m = \frac{\rho}{B}(\Delta p)_m = \frac{(\Delta p)_m}{v^2}$$

Thus, density equation is in phase with the pressure equation and this is 90° out of phase with the displacement equation.

Example 1 Corresponding to displacement equation,

$$y = A\sin(kx + \omega t)$$

of a longitudinal wave make its pressure and density wave. Bulk modulus of the medium is B and density is ρ.

Sol. Given, $y(x, t) = A\sin(kx + \omega t)$

$$\frac{\partial y}{\partial x} = kA\cos(kx + \omega t) \quad \text{...(i)}$$

Now, pressure equation is given by

$$\Delta p = -B\left(\frac{\partial y}{\partial x}\right)$$

Substituting the value of $\frac{\partial y}{\partial x}$ from Eq. (i), we have

$$\Delta p = -BAk\cos(kx + \omega t) \quad \textbf{Ans.}$$

Similarly, density equation is given by

$$(\Delta \rho) = \frac{\rho}{B}(\Delta p)$$

$$= \frac{\rho}{B}\left(-B\frac{\partial y}{\partial x}\right)$$

$$= -\rho\left(\frac{\partial y}{\partial x}\right)$$

Substituting the values of $\frac{\partial y}{\partial x}$ from Eq. (i), we have

$$\Delta \rho = -\rho Ak\cos(kx + \omega t) \quad \textbf{Ans.}$$

Note *We have seen above that*

$y = A\sin(kx + \omega t)$ *and*

$\Delta p = -BAk\cos(kx + \omega t)$

Now let us examine the above equations at $t = 0$,

These two equations are (at $t = 0$*) :*

$y = A\sin kx$

and $\Delta p = -BAk\cos kx$

Now let us draw y-x, Δp-x *and* p-x *graphs as shown below at time* $t = 0$.

Let us now discuss a point at $x = \frac{\lambda}{2}$. In y - x graph we can see that $y = 0$ at this point.

Further y - x and Δp - x equations have a phase difference of $\frac{\pi}{2}$.

So, Δp should have $\pm BAk$. In the second graph we can see that it is $+BAk$ at $x = \frac{\lambda}{2}$. Or, $p = p_0 + BAk$ at $x = \frac{\lambda}{2}$.

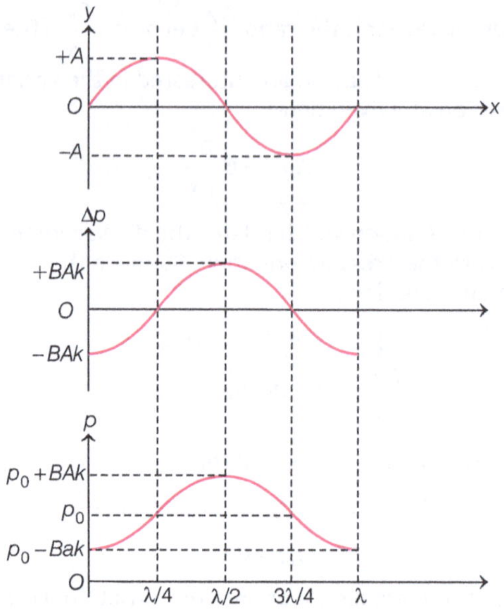

From the y - x graph we can see that value of y is positive for a particle situated to the left of the particle at $x = \frac{\lambda}{2}$. But this is a longitudinal wave. So, positive displacement means displacement towards right. Similarly, displacement of the particle situated to right of particle at $x = \frac{\lambda}{2}$ is towards left.

So there should be compression at point $x = \frac{\lambda}{2}$. Or,

$$\Delta p = +BAk \neq -BAk$$

MODULE 1 Exercise

Single Correct Option

1. Longitudinal waves are possible in
   (a) solids
   (b) liquids
   (c) gases
   (d) All of the above

2. The pressure variation in a sound wave in air is given by

$$\Delta p = 12\sin\left(8.18x - 2700t + \frac{\pi}{4}\right)\text{Nm}^{-2}.$$

If density of air is 1.29 kg m^{-3}, the displacement amplitude is
   (a) 0.089×10^{-5} m
   (b) 1.044×10^{-5} m
   (c) 2.011×10^{-5} m
   (d) 2.732×10^{-5} m

Multiple Correct Options

3. Choose the correct options for longitudinal wave
   (a) maximum pressure variation is BAk
   (b) maximum density variation is ρAk
   (c) pressure equation and density equation are in phase
   (d) pressure equation and displacement equation are out of phase

Subjective Questions

4. Calculate the bulk modulus of air from the following data for a sound wave of wavelength 35 cm travelling in air. The pressure at a point varies between $(10^5 \pm 14)$ Pa and the particles of the air vibrate in SHM of amplitude 5.5×10^{-6} m.

5. Find the minimum and maximum wavelengths of sound in water that is in the audible range for an average human ear. Speed of sound in water is 1450 m/s.

6. A typical loud sound wave with a frequency of 1 kHz has a pressure amplitude of about 10 Pa
   (a) At $t = 0$, the pressure is a maximum at some point. What is the displacement at that point at $t = 0$?
   (b) What is the maximum value of the displacement at any time and place? Take the density of air to be 1.29 kg/m^3 and speed of sound in air is 340 m/s.

Answers

1. (d) **2.** (b) **3.** (a,b,c) **4.** 1.4×10^5 N/m^2 **5.** 7.25 cm, 72.5 m **6.** (a) Zero (b) 3.63×10^{-6}m

See hints on page 146.

MODULE 2

Speed of Longitudinal (or Sound) Wave

First of all we calculate the speed at which a longitudinal pulse propagates through a fluid. We will apply Newton's second law to the motion of an element of the fluid and from this we derive the wave **equatiopn.**

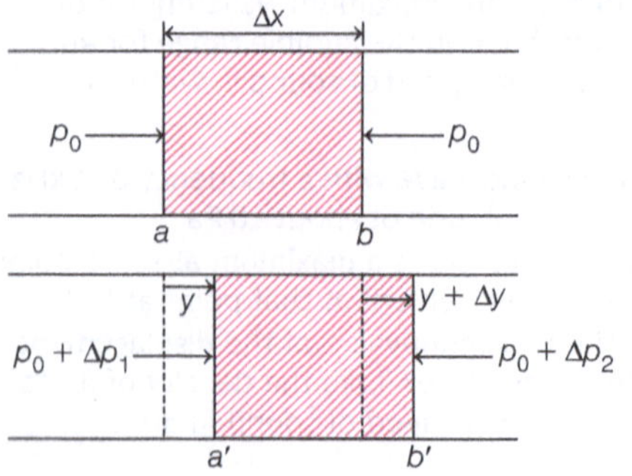

Consider a fluid element ab confined to a tube of cross-sectional area S as shown in figure. The element has a thickness Δx. We assume that the equilibrium pressure of the fluid is p_0. Because of the disturbance, the section 'a' of the element moves a distance y from its mean position to a new mean position a' and section 'b' moves a distance $y + \Delta y$ to a new position b'. The pressure on the left side of the element becomes $p_0 + \Delta p_1$ and on the right side it becomes $p_0 + \Delta p_2$. If ρ is the equilibrium density, the mass of the element is $\rho S \Delta x$. (When the element moves its mass does not change, even though its volume and density do change).

The net force acting on the element is

$$F = (\Delta p_1 - \Delta p_2)\, S$$

and its acceleration is

$$a = \frac{\partial^2 y}{\partial t^2}$$

Thus, Newton's second law applied to the motion of the element is

$$(\Delta p_1 - \Delta p_2)\, S = ma = \rho S \Delta x \frac{\partial^2 y}{\partial t^2} \qquad \text{...(i)}$$

Divide both sides by Δx and note that in the limit as $\Delta x \to 0$, we have $(\Delta p_1 - \Delta p_2)/\Delta x \to \partial p/\partial x$, Eq. (i) then take the form

$$-\frac{\partial p}{\partial x} = \rho \frac{\partial^2 y}{\partial t^2} \qquad \text{...(ii)}$$

The excess pressure Δp may be written as

$$\Delta p = -B\frac{\partial y}{\partial x} \Rightarrow \frac{\partial p}{\partial x} = -B\frac{\partial^2 y}{\partial x^2}$$

When this is used in Eq. (ii), we obtain the wave equation.

$$\frac{\partial^2 y}{\partial x^2} = \frac{\rho}{B} \cdot \frac{\partial^2 y}{\partial t^2} \quad \text{or} \quad \frac{\partial^2 y}{\partial t^2} = \frac{B}{\rho}\frac{\partial^2 y}{\partial x^2}$$

Comparing this equation with the wave equation,

$$\frac{\partial^2 y}{\partial t^2} = v^2 \frac{\partial^2 y}{\partial x^2}$$

We have $v = \sqrt{\frac{B}{\rho}}$ (speed of longitudinal wave in a fluid)

This is the speed of longitudinal waves within a **gas** or a **liquid.**

When a longitudinal wave propagates in a solid rod or bar, the rod expands sideways slightly when it is compressed longitudinally and the speed of a longitudinal wave in a rod is given by

$v = \sqrt{\frac{Y}{\rho}}$ (speed of a longitudinal wave in a solid rod)

Sound Waves in Gases

In the preceding section, we derived the equation

$$v = \sqrt{B/\rho}$$

for the speed of longitudinal waves in a fluid of bulk modulus B and density ρ. We use this to find the speed of sound in an ideal gas. The bulk modulus of the gas, however depends on the process. When a wave travels through a gas, are the compressions and expansions adiabatic, or isothermal?

Because thermal conductivities of gases are very small, it turns out that for ordinary sound frequencies (20 Hz to 20,000 Hz) propagation of sound is very nearly adiabatic. Thus, in the above equation, we use the **adiabatic bulk modulus (B_s)**, which is given by

$$B_s = \gamma p$$

Here, γ is the ratio of molar heat capacity C_p/C_V. Thus,

$$v = \sqrt{\frac{\gamma p}{\rho}}$$

We can get a useful alternative form of the above equation by substituting density ρ of an ideal gas

$$\rho = \frac{pM}{RT}$$

where, R is the gas constant, M the molecular mass and T is the absolute temperature. Combining all these equations, we can write

$$v = \sqrt{\frac{\gamma RT}{M}} \quad \text{(speed of sound in an ideal gas)}$$

Effect of Temperature, Pressure and Humidity on the Speed of Sound in Air

(i) **Effect of temperature** From the equation,

$$v = \sqrt{\frac{\gamma RT}{M}}$$

We can see that,

$$v \propto \sqrt{T} \quad \text{or} \quad \frac{v_1}{v_2} = \sqrt{\frac{T_1}{T_2}}$$

At STP, the temperature is 0°C or 273 K. If the speed of sound at 0°C is v_0, its value at t°C will satisfy

$$\frac{v_t}{v_0} = \sqrt{\frac{273+t}{273}} = \left(1 + \frac{t}{273}\right)^{\frac{1}{2}} = 1 + \frac{t}{546}$$

$$\therefore \quad v_t = v_0\left(1 + \frac{t}{546}\right)$$

If the speed of sound in air at 0°C (v_0) be taken 332 m/s, then

$$v_t = 332\left(1 + \frac{t}{546}\right) \quad \text{or} \quad v_t = 332 + 0.61t$$

Thus, the speed of sound in air increases roughly by 0.61 m/s per degree centigrade rise in temperature.

(ii) **Effect of pressure** From the formula for the speed of sound in a gas $v = \sqrt{\frac{\gamma p}{\rho}}$, it appears that $v \propto \sqrt{p}$. But actually it is not so. Because :

$$\frac{p}{\rho} = \frac{RT}{M} = \text{constant at constant temperature.}$$

That is, at constant temperature if p changes then ρ also changes in such a way that p/ρ remains constant.

Hence, in the formula $v = \sqrt{\frac{\gamma p}{\rho}}$, the value of p/ρ does not change when p changes. From this it is clear that if the temperature of the gas remains constant, then there is no effect of the pressure change on the speed of sound.

(iii) **Effect of humidity** The density of moist air (i.e. air mixed with water-vapour) is less than the density of dry air. This is because, in moist air heavy dust particles settle down due to condensation. Hence, density of air gets decreased, thus increasing the speed of sound. Therefore, assuming the value of γ for moist air same as for dry air (which is actually slightly less than that for dry air) it is clear from the formula $v = \sqrt{\frac{\gamma p}{\rho}}$ that the speed of sound in moist air is slightly greater than in dry air.

Example 1 Calculate the speed of longitudinal waves in the following gases at 0°C and 1 atm (= 10^5 Pa) :

(a) oxygen for which the bulk modulus is 1.41×10^5 Pa and density is 1.43 kg/m^3.

(b) helium for which the bulk modulus is 1.7×10^5 Pa and the density is 0.18 kg/m^3.

Sol. (a) $v_{O_2} = \sqrt{\frac{B}{\rho}} = \sqrt{\frac{1.41 \times 10^5}{1.43}} = 314 \text{ m/s}$ **Ans.**

(b) $v_{He} = \sqrt{\frac{B}{\rho}} = \sqrt{\frac{1.7 \times 10^5}{0.18}} = 972 \text{ m/s}$ **Ans.**

Example 2 Find speed of sound in hydrogen gas at 27°C. Ratio C_p/C_V for H_2 is 1.4. Gas constant $R = 8.31$ J/ mol -K.

Sol. $\because \quad v = \sqrt{\frac{\gamma RT}{M}}$

Here, $T = 27 + 273 = 300$ K, $\gamma = 1.4$, $R = 8.31$ J/mol-K, $M = 2 \times 10^{-3}$ kg/mol

$$\therefore \quad v = \sqrt{\frac{1.4 \times 8.31 \times 300}{2 \times 10^{-3}}}$$

$$= 1321 \text{ m/s}$$ **Ans.**

Note *In the above formula, put $M = 2 \times 10^{-3}$ kg/mol. Don't put it 2 kg.*

Example 3 At what temperature will the speed of sound in hydrogen be the same as in oxygen at 100°C? Molar masses of oxygen and hydrogen are in the ratio 16 : 1.

Sol. $v = \sqrt{\frac{\gamma RT}{M}}$

$$v_{H_2} = v_{O_2}$$

$$\therefore \quad \sqrt{\frac{\gamma_{H_2} RT_{H_2}}{M_{H_2}}} = \sqrt{\frac{\gamma_{O_2} RT_{O_2}}{M_{O_2}}}$$

$$\gamma_{H_2} = \gamma_{O_2} \quad \text{(as both are diatomic)}$$

$$\therefore \quad T_{H_2} = \left(\frac{M_{H_2}}{M_{O_2}}\right)(T_{O_2}) = \left(\frac{1}{16}\right)(100 + 273)$$

$$= 23.31 \text{ K}$$

$$\approx -249.7\text{°C}$$ **Ans.**

MODULE 2 Exercise

Assertion and Reason

See directions on page 14.

1. **Assertion :** A balloon filled with CO_2 gas acts as a converging lens for a sound wave.

   Reason : Sound waves travel faster in air than in CO_2.

2. **Assertion :** Vacuum is densest for sound and rarerest for light.

   Reason : A medium is said to be denser, when velocity of wave in this medium is less.

Single Correct Option

3. Velocity of sound in vacuum is
   (a) equal to 330 m/s
   (b) greater than 330 m/s
   (c) less than 330 m/s
   (d) None of the above

4. Oxygen is 16 times heavier than hydrogen. At NTP equal volumes of hydrogen and oxygen are mixed. The ratio of speed of sound in the mixture to that in hydrogen is

   (a) $\sqrt{8}$ (b) $\sqrt{\frac{1}{8}}$ (c) $\sqrt{\frac{2}{17}}$ (d) $\sqrt{\frac{32}{17}}$

Subjective Questions

5. Calculate the temperature at which the velocity of sound in air is double its velocity at 0°C.

6. Calculate the difference in the speeds of sound in air at −3°C, 60 cm pressure of mercury and 30°C, 75 cm pressure of mercury. The speed of sound in air at 0°C is 332 m/s.

7. In a liquid with density 900 kg/m^3, longitudinal waves with frequency 250 Hz are found to have wavelength 8.0 m. Calculate the bulk modulus of the liquid.

8. Calculate the speed of sound in oxygen at 273 K.

9. Helium is a monoatomic gas that has a density of 0.179 kg/m^3 at a pressure of 76 cm of mercury and a temperature of 0°C. Find the speed of compressional waves (sound) in helium at this temperature and pressure.

10. What must be the stress (F/A) in a stretched wire of a material whose Young's modulus is Y for the speed of longitudinal waves equal to 30 times the speed of transverse waves?

11. A gas is a mixture of two parts by volume of hydrogen and one part by volume of nitrogen at STP. If the velocity of sound in hydrogen at 0°C is 1300 m/s. Find the velocity of sound in the gaseous mixture at 27°C.

Answers

1. (a) **2.** (a or b) **3.** (d) **4.** (c) **5.** 819°C **6.** 19.6 m/s **7.** 3.6×10^9 N/m^2

8. 315 m/s **9.** 972 m/s **10.** $\frac{Y}{900}$ **11.** 590 m/s

See hints on pages 146-147.

MODULE 3

Sound Intensity

Travelling sound waves, like all other travelling waves, transfer energy from one region of space to another. We define the **intensity** of a wave (denoted by I) to be the time average rate at which energy is transported by the wave, per unit area across a surface perpendicular to the direction of propagation. We have already derived an expression for the intensity of a mechanical wave

$$I=\frac{1}{2}\rho A^2\omega^2 v \quad \text{...(i)}$$

For a sound wave,

$$(\Delta p)_m = BAk = BA\left(\frac{\omega}{v}\right)$$

or

$$\omega=\frac{(\Delta p)_m v}{BA}$$

Substituting this value in Eq. (i), we have

$$I=\frac{1}{2}\rho A^2\frac{(\Delta p)_m^2 v^2}{B^2A^2}v \qquad (\rho v^2 = B)$$

or

$$I=\frac{v(\Delta p)_m^2}{2B} \quad \text{...(ii)}$$

Thus, intensity of a sound wave can be calculated by either of the Eqs. (i) or (ii).

Sound Intensity in Decibels

The physiological sensation of loudness is closely related to the intensity of wave producing the sound. At a frequency of 1 kHz people are able to detect sounds with intensities as low as 10^{-12} W/m^2. On the other hand, an intensity of 1 W/m^2 can cause pain and prolonged exposure to sound at this level will damage a person's ears. Because the range in intensities over which people hear is so large, it is convenient to use a logarithmic scale to specify intensities. This scale is defined as follows.

If the intensity of sound in watts per square metre is I, then the intensity level β in decibels (dB) is given by

$$\beta=10\log\frac{I}{I_0} \quad \text{...(iii)}$$

where the base of the logarithm is 10, and $I_0=10^{-12}$ W/m^2 (roughly the minimum intensity that can be heard).

On the decibel scale, the pain threshold of 1 W/m^2 is then

$$\beta=10\log\frac{1}{10^{-12}}=120 \text{ dB}$$

Note *For the comparison of two different sounds in dB ; we can modify Eq. (iii) as*

$$\beta_2-\beta_1=10\log_{10}\frac{I_2}{I_1} \quad \text{...(iv)}$$

Table 1 gives typical values for the intensity levels of some of the common sounds.

Table 1. Sound intensity levels in decibels

(Threshold of hearing = 0 dB; threshold of pain = 120 dB)

Source of sound	dB
Rusting leaves	10
Whisper	20
Quiet room	30
Normal level of speech (inside)	65
Street traffic (inside car)	80
Riveting tool	100
Thunder	110
Indoor rock concert	120

Note *Sound intensity (in dB) is also sometimes called loudness and denoted by L.*

Example 1 For a person with normal hearing, the faintest sound that can be heard at a frequency of 400 Hz has a pressure amplitude of about 6.0×10^{-5} Pa. Calculate the corresponding intensity in W/m^2. Take speed of sound in air as 344 m/s and density of air 1.2 kg/m^3.

Sol. $\because \quad I=\dfrac{v(\Delta p)_m^2}{2B}$

Substituting $B=\rho v^2$, the above equation reduces to

$$I=\frac{(\Delta p)_m^2}{2\rho v}=\frac{(6.0\times10^{-5})^2}{2\times1.2\times344}$$

$$=4.4\times10^{-12} \text{ W/m}^2$$ **Ans.**

Example 2 Find intensity of sound in dB if its intensity in Watt/m^2 is 10^{-10}.

Sol. Using the equation,

$\beta=10\log_{10}\dfrac{I}{I_0}$, we have

$$\beta=10\log_{10}\left(\frac{10^{-10}}{10^{-12}}\right)=10\log_{10}(10^2)$$

$$=20 \text{ dB}$$ **Ans.**

Example 3 A point source of sound emits a constant power with intensity inversely proportional to the square of the distance from the source. By how many decibels does the sound intensity level change when you move from point P_1 to P_2? Distance of P_2 from the source is two times the distance of source from P_1.

Sol. $\beta_2 - \beta_1 = 10 \log_{10} \frac{I_2}{I_1}$

Further, $I \propto \frac{1}{r^2}$

$$\therefore \quad \frac{I_2}{I_1} = \left(\frac{r_1}{r_2}\right)^2 = \frac{1}{4} \quad \text{as} \quad r_2 = 2r_1$$

$$\therefore \quad \beta_2 - \beta_1 = (10 \text{ dB}) \log\left(\frac{1}{4}\right)$$

$$= -6.0 \text{ dB}$$ **Ans.**

Example 4 At a distance 20 m from a point source of sound the loudness level is 30 dB. Neglecting the damping, find

(a) the loudness at 10 m from the source

(b) the distance from the source at which sound is not heard. **(Irodov 4.183)**

Sol. (a) Intensity due to a point source varies with distance r from it as

$$I \propto \frac{1}{r^2}$$

or $$\frac{I_1}{I_2} = \left(\frac{r_2}{r_1^2}\right)^2$$

Now, $$L_1 = 10 \log \frac{I_1}{I_0}$$

and $$L_2 = 10 \log \frac{I_2}{I_0}$$

$$\therefore \quad L_1 - L_2 = 10\left[\log \frac{I_1}{I_0} - \log \frac{I_2}{I_0}\right]$$

$$= 10 \log \frac{I_1}{I_2} = 10 \log\left(\frac{r_2}{r_1}\right)^2$$

Substituting, $L_1 = 30$ dB, $r_1 = 20$ m and $r_2 = 10$ m

we have $$30 - L_2 = 10 \log\left(\frac{10}{20}\right)^2 = -6.0$$

or $$L_2 = 36 \text{ dB}$$ **Ans.**

(b) $$L_1 - L_2 = 10 \log\left(\frac{r_2}{r_1}\right)^2$$

Sound is not heard at a point where $L_2 = 0$

or $$30 = 10 \log\left(\frac{r_2}{r_1}\right)^2$$

$$\therefore \quad \left(\frac{r_2}{r_1}\right)^2 = 1000$$

or $$\frac{r_2}{r_1} = 31.62$$

$$\therefore \quad r_2 = (31.62)(20) \approx 632 \text{ m}$$ **Ans.**

MODULE 3 Exercise

Single Correct Option

1. How many times more intense is 90 dB sound than 40 dB sound?

   (a) 5 (b) 50 (c) 500 (d) 10^5

2. The intensity level of a sound wave is 4 dB. If the intensity of the wave is doubled, then the intensity level of the sound, as expressed in dB, would be

   (a) 8 (b) 16
   (c) 7 (d) 14

3. A person speaking normally produces a sound intensity of 40 dB at a distance of 1 m. If the threshold intensity for reasonable audibility is 20 dB, the maximum distance at which person can be heard clearly is

   (a) 4 m (b) 5 m
   (c) 10 m (d) 20 m

4. A small speaker delivers 2 W of audio output. At what distance from the speaker will one detect 120 dB intensity sound? [Given, reference intensity of sound as 10^{-12} W/m^2] **(2019 Main)**

   (a) 40 cm (b) 20 cm
   (c) 10 cm (d) 30 cm

Subjective Questions

5. A sound wave in air has a frequency of 300 Hz and a displacement amplitude of 6.0×10^{-3} mm. For this sound wave calculate the

   (a) pressure amplitude
   (b) intensity
   (c) sound intensity level (in dB)

   Speed of sound $= 344$ m/s and density of air $= 1.2$ kg/m^3.

6. A baby's mouth is 30 cm from her father's ear and 3.0 m from her mother's ear. What is the difference between the sound intensity levels heard by the father and by the mother.

7. The faintest sound that can be heard has a pressure amplitude of about 2×10^{-5} N/m^2 and the loudest that can be heard without pain has a pressure amplitude of about 28 N/m^2. Determine in each case (a) the intensity of the sound both in W/m^2 and in dB and (b) the amplitude of the oscillations if the frequency is 500 Hz. Assume an air density of 1.29 kg/m^3 and a velocity of sound is 345 m/s.

8. The explosion of a fire cracker in the air at a height of 40 m produces a 100 dB sound level at ground below. What is the instantaneous total radiated power? Assuming that it radiates as a point source.

9. (a) What is the intensity of a 60 dB sound?
   (b) If the sound level is 60 dB close to a speaker that has an area of 120 cm^2. What is the acoustic power output of the speaker?

10. What is the amplitude of motion for the air in the path of a 60 dB, 800 Hz sound wave? Assume that $\rho_{air} = 1.29$ kg/m^3 and $v = 330$ m/s.

11. If it were possible to generate a sinusoidal 300 Hz sound wave in air that has a displacement amplitude of 0.200mm. What would be the sound level of the wave? (Assume $v = 330$ m/s and $\rho_{air} = 1.29$ kg/m^3)

Answers

1. (d) **2.** (c) **3.** (c) **4.** (a) **5.** (a) 4.67 Pa (b) 2.64×10^{-2} W/m^2 (c) 104 dB **6.** 20 dB

7. Faintest (a) 4.49×10^{-13} W/m^2, -3.48 dB (b) 1.43×10^{-11} m Loudest (a) 0.881 W/m^2, 119 dB (b) 2.01×10^{-5} m

8. 201 W **9.** (a) 10^{-6} W/m^2 (b) 1.2×10^{-8} W **10.** 13.6 nm **11.** 134.4 dB

See hints on pages 147-148.

MODULE 4

Interference in Sound Wave and Stationary Wave

In unit 18, we have already discussed about the principle of superposition, interference and stationary wave. In the similar manner, we can make stationary waves with longitudinal (or sound) waves also.

When two identical sound waves travel in opposite directions, then by their superposition (and hence interference) longitudinal stationary waves are formed.

But, as we know that, with every longitudinal travelling wave three equations are associated : $y(x,t)$, $\Delta P(x,t)$ and $\Delta\rho(x,t)$. So, with every longitudinal stationary wave three equations are associated, $y(x,t)$, $\Delta P(x,t)$ and $\Delta\rho(x,t)$.

Following three points are important with longitudinal stationary wave :

(i) If individual displacement amplitudes of constituent travelling waves are A_0 each, then displacement amplitude in stationary wave varies from 0 to $2A_0$.

(ii) If two identical (same frequency) longitudinal waves travel in opposite directions, standing waves are produced by their superposition. If the pressure equations of the two waves are written as

$$\Delta p_1 = (\Delta p)_m \sin(kx - \omega t)$$

and $$\Delta p_2 = (\Delta p)_m \sin(kx + \omega t)$$

then from the principle of superposition, the resultant wave is

$$\Delta p = \Delta p_1 + \Delta p_2 = 2(\Delta p)_m \sin kx \cos \omega t \quad \text{...(i)}$$

This equation is similar to the equation obtained in unit 18 for standing waves on a string.

From Eq. (i), we can see that

$\Delta p = 0$ at $x = 0, \lambda/2, \lambda, \ldots$, etc. (pressure nodes)

and $\Delta p =$ maximum $= 2(\Delta p)_m$ at $x = \lambda/4, 3\lambda/4, \ldots$, etc. (pressure antinodes)

The distance between two adjacent nodes or between two adjacent antinodes is $\lambda/2$. Longitudinal standing waves can be produced in air columns trapped in tubes of cylindrical shape. Organ pipes are such vibrating air columns.

Note *In module 2, we have seen that* $(\Delta p)_m = BAk$.
Therefore, in standing wave $(\Delta p)_{max} = 2(\Delta p)_m = 2BAk$.

(iii) Because the pressure wave is 90° out of phase with the displacement wave. Consequently, the displacement node behaves as a pressure antinode and *vice-versa*.

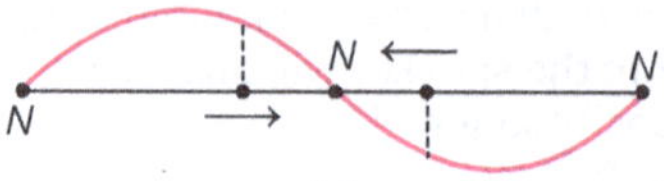

(a)

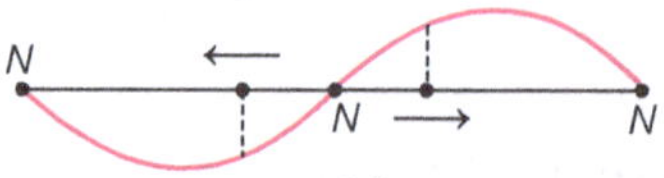

(b)

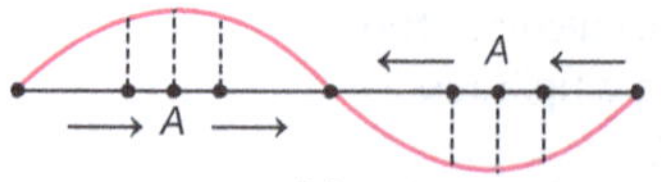

(c)

This can be explained by realizing that two small volume elements of fluid on opposite sides of a displacement node are vibrating in opposite phase. Hence, when they approach each other [see Fig. (a)] the pressure at this node is a maximum, and when they recede from each other, [see Fig. (b)] the pressure at this node is a minimum. Similarly, two small elements of fluid which are on opposite sides of a displacement antinode vibrate in phase and therefore give rise to no pressure variations at the antinode [see Fig. (c)].

Important POINTS

- Most of the problems of interference can be solved by calculating the path difference Δx and then by putting

$$\Delta x = 0, \lambda, 2\lambda, \ldots \quad \text{(constructive interference)}$$

$$\Delta x = \frac{\lambda}{2}, \frac{3\lambda}{2} \ldots \quad \text{(destructive interference)}$$

provided the waves emitted from S_1 and S_2 are in phase.

- If the two waves emitted from S_1 and S_2 have already a phase difference of π, the conditions of maximas and minimas are interchanged, i.e. path difference

$$\Delta x = \frac{\lambda}{2}, \frac{3\lambda}{2} \ldots \quad \text{(for constructive interference)}$$

and $\quad \Delta x = \lambda, 2\lambda, \ldots \quad$ (for destructive interference)

- In stationary longitudinal wave, displacement node is pressure antinode. Therefore at this point,

$$\Delta p = (\Delta p)_{max} = 2(\Delta p)_m = 2\,BAk$$

$$\therefore \quad p_{max} = p_0 + 2\,BAk$$

and $\quad p_{min} = p_0 - 2\,BAk$

So the pressure oscillates between p_{max} and p_{min}.

Similarly, displacement antinode is pressure node. Therefore, $\Delta p = 0$. Or, pressure at these points is always p_0.

Example 1 Two sound sources S_1 and S_2 emit pure sinusoidal waves in phase. If the speed of sound is 350 m/s, then

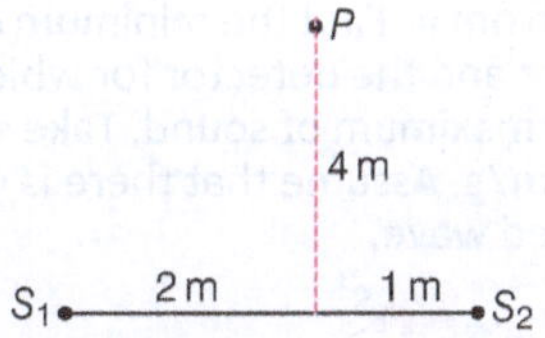

(a) for what frequencies does constructive interference occur at P?

(b) for what frequencies does destructive interference occur at point P?

Sol. Path difference, $\Delta x = S_1P - S_2P$

$$= \sqrt{(2)^2 + (4)^2} - \sqrt{(1)^2 + (4)^2}$$

$$= 4.47 - 4.12 = 0.35 \text{ m}$$

(a) Constructive interference occurs when the path difference is an integer multiple of wavelength.

or $\quad \Delta x = n\lambda = \dfrac{nv}{f}$

or $\quad f = \dfrac{nv}{\Delta x} \quad$ where, $n = 1, 2, 3, \ldots$

$$\therefore \quad f = \frac{350}{0.35}, \frac{2 \times 350}{0.35}, \frac{3 \times 350}{0.35}, \ldots$$

$f = 1000$ Hz, 2000 Hz, 3000 Hz,.., etc. **Ans.**

(b) Destructive interference occurs when the path difference is a half-integer multiple of wavelengths

or $\quad \Delta x = (2n+1)\dfrac{\lambda}{2} \quad n = 0, 1, 2, \ldots$

or $\quad \Delta x = (2n+1)\dfrac{v}{2f}$

$$\therefore \quad f = \frac{(2n+1)\,v}{2\,\Delta x}$$

$$= \frac{350}{2 \times 0.35}, \frac{3 \times 350}{2 \times 0.35}, \frac{5 \times 350}{2 \times 0.35}, \ldots$$

$= 500$ Hz, 1500 Hz, 2500 Hz, ... **Ans.**

MODULE 4 Exercise

Single Correct Option

1. Two sources of sound A and B produce the wave of frequency 350 Hz, in the same phase. A particle P is vibrating under the influence of these two waves. If the amplitudes at the point P produced by the two waves are 0.3 mm and 0.4 mm, then the resultant amplitude of the point P will be (when $AP - BP = 25$ cm. Velocity of sound is 350 m/s)
   (a) 0.7 mm (b) 0.1 mm
   (c) 0.2 mm (d) 0.5 mm

2. Two loudspeakers L_1 and L_2 driven by a common oscillator and amplifier, are arranged as shown. The frequency of the oscillator is gradually increased from zero and the detector at D records a series of maxima and minima. If the speed of sound is 330 ms^{-1}, then the frequency at which the first maximum is observed is

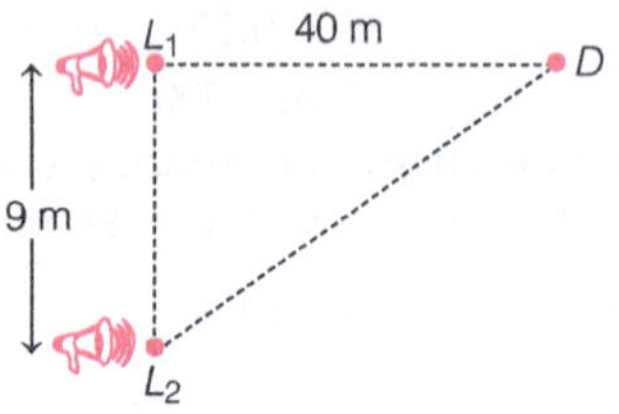

   (a) 165 Hz (b) 330 Hz
   (c) 496 Hz (d) 660 Hz

3. S_1 and S_2 are two coherent sources of sound having no initial phase difference. The velocity of sound is 330 m/s. No maxima will be formed on the line passing through S_2 and perpendicular to the line joining S_1 and S_2. If the frequency of both the sources is

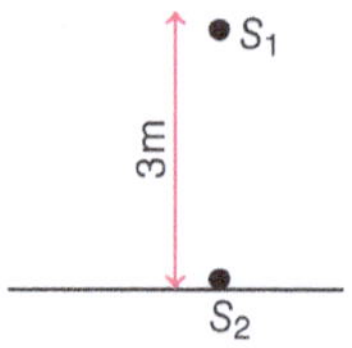

   (a) 330 Hz (b) 120 Hz
   (c) 100 Hz (d) 220 Hz

4. Four sources of sound each of sound level 10 dB are sounded together in phase, the resultant intensity level will be ($\log_{10} 2 = 0.3$)
   (a) 40 dB (b) 26 dB (c) 22 dB (d) 13 dB

Subjective Questions

5. Two sound waves emerging from a source reach a point simultaneously along two paths. When the path difference is 12 cm or 36 cm, then there is a silence at that point. If the speed of sound in air be 330 m/s, then calculate maximum possible frequency of the source.

6. A source of sound emitting waves at 360 Hz is placed in front of a vertical wall, at a distance 2 m from it. A detector is also placed in front of the wall at the same distance from it. Find the minimum distance between the source and the detector for which the detector detects a maximum of sound. Take speed of sound in air $= 360$ m/s. Assume that there is no phase change in reflected wave.

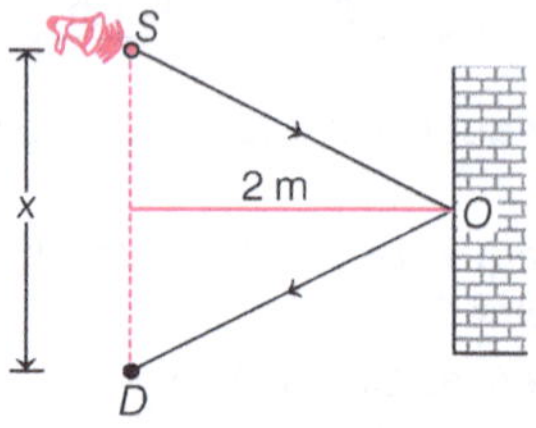

7. Two loudspeakers S_1 and S_2 each emit sounds of frequency 220 Hz uniformly in all directions. S_1 has an acoustic output of 1.2×10^{-3} W and S_2 has 1.8×10^{-3} W.
   S_1 and S_2 vibrate in phase. Consider a point P such that $S_1P = 0.75$ m and $S_2P = 3$ m. How are the phases arriving at P related? What is the intensity at P when both S_1 and S_2 are on? Speed of sound in air is 330 m/s.

8. Sound waves from a tuning fork A reach a point P by two separate paths ABP and ACP. When ACP is greater than ABP by 11.5 cm there is silence at P. When the difference is 23 cm the sound becomes loudest at P and when 34.5 cm there is silence again and so on. Calculate the minimum frequency of the fork if the velocity of sound is taken to be 331.2 m/s.

Answers

1. (d) **2.** (b) **3.** (c) **4.** (c) **5.** 1375 Hz **6.** 7.5 m
7. $\Delta\phi_1 = \pi$, $\Delta\phi_2 = 4\pi$, Resultant intensity $= 8.2 \times 10^{-5}$ Wm^{-2} **8.** 1440 Hz

See hints on pages 148-149.

Standing Longitudinal Waves in Organ Pipes

As we have discussed in Unit 18, Module 5, transverse stationary waves of certain fixed frequencies are formed in a stretched wire. Similarly longitudinal stationary (or standing) waves of certain fixed frequencies are formed in organ pipes. Organ pipes are of two types as shown below.

Closed organ pipe (a) Open organ pipe (b)

Those set of frequencies depend upon :

(i) Nature of pipe (open or closed)
(ii) Length of pipe
(iii) Nature of gas in the pipe and
(iv) Temperature of the gas

Note *In most of the cases there will be air in the pipe.*

When longitudinal waves propagate in a fluid in a pipe with finite length, the waves are reflected from the ends in a same way the transverse waves on a string are reflected at its ends. The superposition of the waves travelling in opposite directions forms a longitudinal standing wave.

Transverse waves on a string, including standing waves, are usually described only in terms of the displacement of the string. But longitudinal standing waves in a fluid may be described either in terms of the displacement of the fluid or in terms of the pressure variation in the fluid.

To avoid confusion we will use the terms **displacement node** and **displacement antinode** to refer to points where particles of the fluid have zero displacement and maximum displacement respectively. Similarly, **pressure node** and **pressure antinode** to refer the points where pressure and density variation in the fluid is zero or maximum, respectively.

Conditions at the Boundary of an Organ Pipe

Let us take an example of a closed organ pipe. In a closed pipe one end is closed and the other is open. When a longitudinal wave encounters the closed end of the pipe it gets reflected from this end. But the reflected wave is 180° out of phase with the incident wave, i.e. a compression is reflected as a compression and a rarefaction is reflected as a rarefaction. This is a necessary condition because the displacement of the small volume elements at the closed end must always be zero. Hence, a closed end is a displacement node.

A sound wave is also reflected from an open end. You may wonder how a sound wave can reflect from an open end, since there may not appear to be a change in the medium at this point. At the open end pressure is the same as atmospheric pressure and does not vary.

Thus, there is a pressure node (or displacement antinode) at this end. A compression is therefore reflected as a rarefaction and rarefaction as a compression. Now let us see how this reflection takes place.

When a rarefaction reaches an open end, the surrounding air rushes towards this region and creates a compression that travels back along the pipe. Similarly, when a compression reaches an open end, the air expands to form a rarefaction.

This can be said in a different way as : **at the open end of the tube, fluid elements are free to move, so there is a displacement antinode**. Thus, in a nutshell we can say that closed end of an organ pipe is a displacement node or pressure antinode and open end of the pipe is displacement antinode or pressure node.

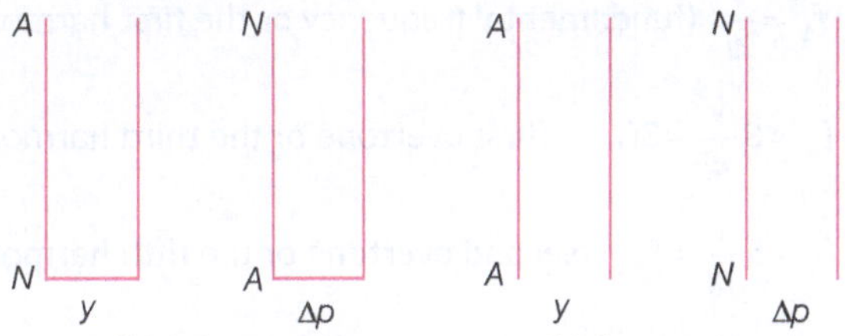

(a) Closed organ pipe (b) Open organ pipe

Similarly, both ends of an open organ pipe (open at both ends) are displacement antinodes or pressure nodes.

Set of Frequencies of a Closed Organ Pipe

To get resonance in a closed organ pipe sound waves are sent in by a source (normally a tuning fork) near the open end. Resonance corresponds to a pressure antinode at the closed end and a pressure node at the open end. The standing wave patterns for the three lowest harmonics in this situation are shown in figure. Since the node-antinode separation is $\frac{\lambda}{4}$, the resonance condition for the first harmonic is, $l = \frac{\lambda_1}{4}$ or $\lambda_1 = 4l$.

$$\therefore \quad f_1 = \frac{v}{\lambda_1} = \frac{v}{4l}$$

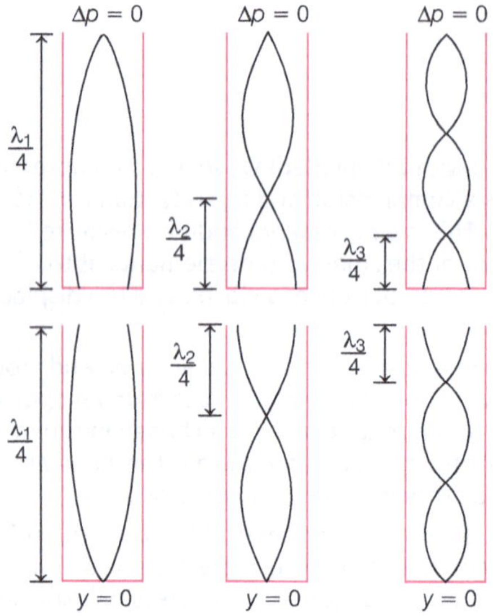

Similarly, the resonance conditions for the higher harmonics are $l = \frac{3\lambda_2}{4}, \frac{5\lambda_3}{4}, \ldots$, etc. or, $\lambda_n = \frac{4l}{n}$ (where $n = 1, 3, 5\ldots$).

The natural frequencies of oscillation of the air in the tube closed at one end and open at the other are therefore

$$f_n = \frac{v}{\lambda_n} = n\frac{v}{4l} = nf_1 \quad (n = 1, 3, 5, \ldots)$$

Here, v = speed of sound in the tube

$$f_1 = \frac{v}{4l} \text{ (fundamental frequency or the first harmonic)}$$

$$f_3 = 3\frac{v}{4l} = 3f_1 \quad \text{(first overtone or the third harmonic)}$$

and $$f_5 = 5\frac{v}{4l} = 5f_1 \text{ (second overtone or the fifth harmonic)}$$

and so on.

Thus, in a pipe closed at one end and open at the other, the natural frequencies of oscillation form a harmonic series that includes only odd integer multiples of the fundamental frequency.

Set of Frequencies of an Open Organ Pipe

Since both ends of the tube are open, there are pressure nodes (or displacement antinodes) at both ends. Figure shows the resulting standing waves for the three lowest resonant frequencies. Since the distance between successive pressure nodes is $\lambda/2$, the resonance condition is $l = n\left(\frac{\lambda_n}{2}\right)$ where $n = 1, 2, 3, \ldots$ and l is the length of the tube.

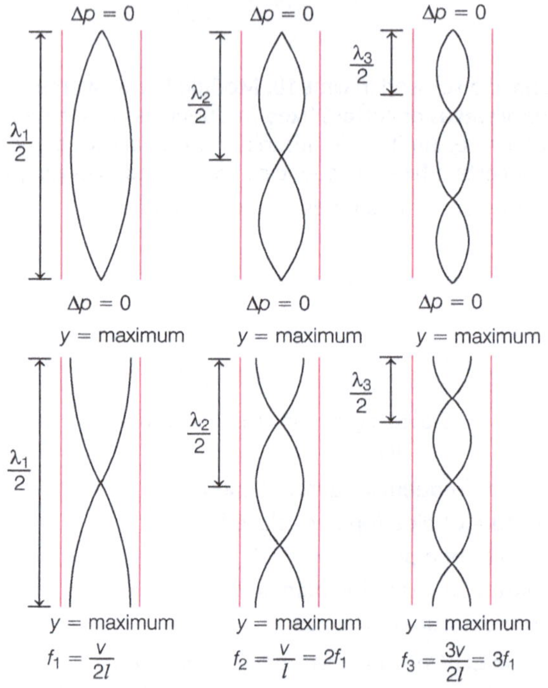

The resonant frequencies for a tube open at both ends are then :

$$f_n = \frac{v}{\lambda_n} = n\frac{v}{2l} = nf_1 \quad (n = 1, 2, 3, \ldots)$$

Here, $$f_1 = \frac{v}{2l} \quad \text{(fundamental frequency or first harmonic)}$$

$$f_2 = \frac{v}{l} = 2f_1 \quad \text{(first overtone or second harmonic)}$$

$$f_3 = 3\left(\frac{v}{2l}\right) = 3f_1 \quad \text{(second overtone or third harmonic)}$$

and so on.

Thus, in a pipe open at both ends, the natural frequencies of oscillation form a harmonic series that includes all integral multiples of the fundamental frequency.

Important POINTS

- $f_n = n\left(\frac{v}{4l}\right)$ for closed pipe $(n = 1, 3, 5 \ldots)$

  $= n\left(\frac{v}{2l}\right)$ for open pipe $(n = 1, 2, 3 \ldots.)$

- **Laplace end correction** In practice, the pressure nodes lie slightly beyond the ends of the tube. A compression reaching an open end does not reflect until it passes beyond the end. For a thin walled tube of circular cross-section, this **end correction** is approximately $0.6\,r$ where r is the tube's radius. Hence, the effective length of the tube is longer than the true length l.

  Therefore, Laplace correction $e = 0.6\,r$ (in closed pipe) and $2e = 1.2\,r$ (in open pipe)

  Hence, $$f = n\left[\frac{v}{2(l + 1.2\,r)}\right] \quad \text{(in open pipe)}$$

  and $$f = n\left[\frac{v}{4(l + 0.6\,r)}\right] \quad \text{(in closed pipe)}$$

  However, we neglect this small correction if the length of the tube is much larger than its diameter.

- This e $(= 0.6\,r$ or $1.2\,r)$ is called the end correction.

- If an open pipe and a closed pipe are of same lengths, then fundamental frequency of open pipe $\left(= \frac{v}{2l}\right)$ is two times the fundamental frequency of closed pipe $\left(= \frac{v}{4l}\right)$.

- In the above equations v is the speed of constituent longitudinal waves by which stationary wave is formed. This speed in air is given by

  $$v = \sqrt{\frac{\gamma RT}{M}}$$

  So, we can see that f_n depends upon nature of pipe (closed or open), l, M, γ (nature of gas) and T.

  If temperature is increased or some light gas is filled in the pipe, then v will increase. So, the set of frequencies will also increase.

- As n increases, v remains unchanged, f increases. Therefore, $\lambda(= v/f)$ and the loop size $\left(= \frac{\lambda}{2}\right)$ decrease.

- In closed pipe only odd harmonics are obtained. Whereas in an open pipe both even and odd harmonics are obtained.

Example 1 Third overtone of a closed organ pipe is in unison with fourth harmonic of an open organ pipe. Find the ratio of the lengths of the pipes.

Sol. Third overtone of closed organ pipe means seventh harmonic.

Given, $$(f_7)_{\text{closed}} = (f_4)_{\text{open}}$$

$$7\left(\frac{v}{4l_c}\right) = 4\left(\frac{v}{2l_o}\right)$$

$$\therefore \quad \frac{l_c}{l_o} = \frac{7}{8} \qquad \textbf{Ans.}$$

Example 2 An open organ pipe has a fundamental frequency of 300 Hz. The first overtone of a closed organ pipe has the same frequency as the first overtone of this open pipe. How long is each pipe? (Speed of sound in air $= 330$ m/s)

Sol. Fundamental frequency of an open organ pipe,

$$f_1 = \frac{v}{2l_o} \Rightarrow l_o = \frac{v}{2f_1} = \frac{330}{2 \times 300}$$

$$= 0.55 \text{ m} \quad = 55 \text{ cm} \qquad \textbf{Ans.}$$

Given, first overtone of closed organ pipe = first overtone of open organ pipe

Hence, $$3\left(\frac{v}{4l_c}\right) = 2\left(\frac{v}{2l_o}\right)$$

$$\therefore \quad l_c = \frac{3}{4}l_o = \left(\frac{3}{4}\right)(0.55)$$

$$= 0.4125 \text{ m} = 41.25 \text{ cm} \qquad \textbf{Ans.}$$

Example 3 A cylindrical tube, open at both ends, has a fundamental frequency f in air. The tube is dipped vertically in water so that half of its length is in water. The fundamental frequency of the air column is now **(1981 JEE)**

(a) $f/2$ (b) $3f/4$ (c) f (d) $2f$

Sol. Initially, the tube was open at both ends and then it is closed.

$$f_o = \frac{v}{2l_o} \quad \text{and} \quad f_c = \frac{v}{4l_c}$$

Since, tube is half dipped in water, $l_c = \frac{l_o}{2}$

$$\therefore \quad f_c = \frac{v}{4\left(\frac{l_o}{2}\right)} = \frac{v}{2l_o} = f_o = f$$

Hence, the correct option is (c).

Example 4 A closed organ pipe of length L and an open organ pipe contain gases of densities ρ_1 and ρ_2, respectively. The compressibility of gases are equal in both the pipes. Both the pipes are vibrating in their first overtone with same frequency. The length of the open organ pipe is **(2004 JEE)**

(a) $\frac{L}{3}$ (b) $\frac{4L}{3}$ (c) $\frac{4L}{3}\sqrt{\frac{\rho_1}{\rho_2}}$ (d) $\frac{4L}{3}\sqrt{\frac{\rho_2}{\rho_1}}$

Sol. $f_c = f_o$ (both first overtone)

or $3\left(\frac{v_c}{4L}\right)=2\left(\frac{v_o}{2l_o}\right)$

$\therefore \quad l_o=\frac{4}{3}\left(\frac{v_o}{v_c}\right)L=\frac{4}{3}\frac{\sqrt{B/\rho_2}}{\sqrt{B/\rho_1}}L$

$=\frac{4}{3}\sqrt{\frac{\rho_1}{\rho_2}}L$

Hence, the correct option is (c).

Note *Compressibility* $=\frac{1}{\text{Bulk modulus}}$. *Compressibility is same.*
Therefore, bulk modulus is also same.

INTRODUCTORY Exercise

1. An open pipe is suddenly closed at one end with the result that the frequency of third harmonic of the closed pipe is found to be higher by 100 Hz than the fundamental frequency of the open pipe. The fundamental frequency of the open pipe is **(1996 JEE)**
   (a) 200 Hz (b) 300 Hz (c) 240 Hz (d) 480 Hz
2. An organ pipe P_1 closed at one end vibrating in its first harmonic and another pipe P_2 open at both ends vibrating in its third harmonic are in resonance with a given tuning fork. The ratio of the length of P_1 and P_2 is **(1988 JEE)**
   (a) 8/3 (b) 3/8 (c) 1/6 (d) 1/3
3. A tube closed at one end and containing air produces, when excited the fundamental note of frequency 512 Hz. If the tube is now opened at both ends, the fundamental frequency that can be excited is (in Hz) **(1986 JEE)**
   (a) 1024 (b) 512
   (c) 256 (d) 128
4. The fundamental frequency of a closed organ pipe is 220 Hz.
   (a) Find the length of this pipe.
   (b) The second overtone of this pipe has the same frequency as the third harmonic of an open pipe. Find the length of this open pipe. Take speed of sound in air 345 m/s.
5. Standing sound waves are produced in a pipe that is 0.8 m long, open at one end, and closed at the other. For the fundamental and first two overtones, where along the pipe (measured from the closed end) are
   (a) the displacement antinodes
   (b) the pressure antinodes.
6. An organ pipe has two successive harmonics with frequencies 400 and 560 Hz. The speed of sound in air is 344 m/s.
   (a) Is this an open or a closed pipe?
   (b) What two harmonics are there?
   (c) What is the length of the pipe?
7. Sound waves of frequency 660 Hz fall normally on a perfectly reflecting wall. The shortest distance from the wall at which the air particles have maximum amplitude of vibration is ...... m. Speed of sound = 330 m/s. **(JEE 1984)**

Answers

1. (a) **2.** (c) **3.** (a)
4. (a) 0.392 m (b) 0.47 m
5. (a) Fundamental 0.8 m, first overtone 0.267 m, 0.8 m, second overtone 0.16 m, 0.48 m, 0.8 m
(b) Fundamental 0, first overtone 0, 0.533 m. Second overtone 0, 0.32 m, 0.64 m
6. (a) Closed (b) 5, 7 (c) 1.075 m
7. 0.125

See hints on pages 149 -150.

Typed Problems

Type 1. *Based on the experiment of finding speed of sound using resonance tube.*

Concept

(i) If a vibrating tuning fork (of known frequency) is held over the open end of a resonance tube, then resonance is obtained at some position as the level of water is lowered.

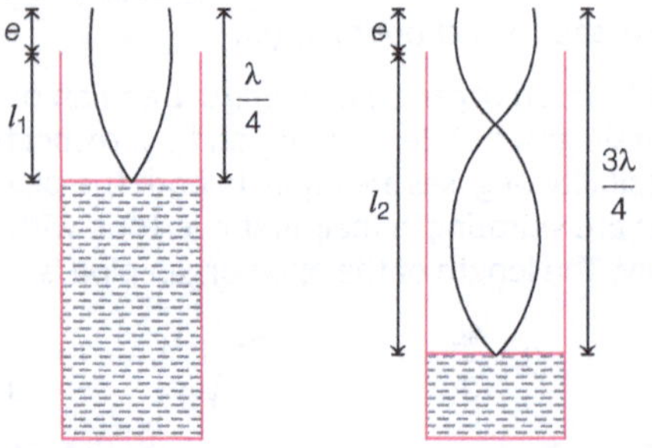

(i) (ii)

If e is the end correction of the tube and l_1 is the length from the water level to the top of the tube, then

$$l_1+e=\frac{\lambda}{4} \quad \text{...(i)}$$

Now, the water level is further lowered until a resonance is again obtained. If l_2 is new length of the air column, then

$$l_2+e=\frac{3\lambda}{4} \quad \text{...(ii)}$$

Subtracting Eq. (i) from Eq. (ii), we get

$$l_2-l_1=\frac{\lambda}{2}$$

or $$\lambda=2(l_2-l_1)=\frac{v}{f} \qquad \left(\lambda=\frac{v}{f}\right)$$

$\therefore$ $$\boxed{v=2f(l_2-l_1)}$$

(ii) The above result is independent of the end correction e.

(iii) In the above two figures v, λ, f and loop size $\left(=\frac{\lambda}{2}\right)$ are same in both figures. Length of closed organ pipe is different. In the second figure, length is more. So, the fundamental frequency $\left(f=\frac{v}{4l}\right)$ will be less.

Suppose frequency of given tuning fork is 300 Hz. Then, fundamental frequency of first pipe is also 300 Hz. But fundamental frequency of the second pipe should be 100 Hz. So, that its next higher frequency (or first overtone frequency) which is three times the fundamental ($=3\times 100=300$Hz) should also be in resonance with the given tuning fork.

Thus in different figures length of pipe is different. So, set of frequencies will be different. From this experiment we find wavelength $\lambda\,[=2(l_2-l_1)]$ corresponding to the frequency of tuning fork by matching any one frequency of the pipe with the frequency of tuning fork.

For example fundamental frequency of first pipe is matched with frequency of tuning fork. Similarly first overtone frequency of second pipe is matched with the frequency of tuning fork.

$\therefore$ Frequency of tuning fork

= fundamental frequency of first pipe

= first overtone frequency of second pipe.

After finding wavelength corresponding to frequency of tuning fork we can find speed of sound by the relation,

$$v=f\lambda \qquad (f = \text{frequency of tuning fork})$$
$$=2f(l_2-l_1)$$

Ex. 1 A tuning fork of 512 Hz is used to produce resonance in a resonance tube experiment. The level of water at first resonance is 30.7 cm and at second resonance is 63.2 cm. The error in calculating velocity of sound is **(2005 JEE)**

(a) 204.1 cm/s (b) 110 cm/s
(c) 58 cm/s (d) 280 cm/s

Sol. Actual speed of sound in air is 330 m/s

$$\frac{\lambda}{2}=(l_2-l_1)=(63.2-30.7)\text{ cm}=32.5\text{ cm}=0.325\text{ m}$$

or $\lambda=0.65$ m

$\therefore$ Speed of sound observed,

$$v_0=f\lambda=512\times 0.65=332.8\text{ m/s}$$

$\therefore$ Error in calculating velocity of sound $=2.8$ m/s $=280$ cm/s

$\therefore$ The correct option is (d).

Ex. 2 In the experiment for the determination of the speed of sound in air using the resonance column method, the length of the air column that resonates in the fundamental mode, with a tuning fork is 0.1 m. When this length is changed to 0.35 m, the same tuning fork resonates with the first overtone. Calculate the end correction. **(2003 JEE)**

(a) 0.012 m (b) 0.025 m (c) 0.05 m (d) 0.024 m

Sol. Let e be the end correction.

Given that, fundamental tone for a length 0.1m = first overtone for the length 0.35 m.

$$\frac{v}{4(0.1+e)}=\frac{3v}{4(0.35+e)}$$

Solving this equation, we get $e=0.025$ m

$\therefore$ The correct option is (b).

Alternate method

$$l_2+e=3\lambda/4$$

and $$l_1+e=\lambda/4$$

Solving these two equations, we get

$$e=\frac{l_2-3l_1}{2}$$
$$=\frac{0.35-3\times 0.1}{2}=0.025\text{ m}$$

Ex. 3 A student is performing the experiment of resonance column. The diameter of the column tube is 4 cm. The frequency of the tuning fork is 512 Hz. The air temperature is 38° C in which the speed of sound is 336 m/s. The zero of the meter scale coincides with the top end of the resonance column tube. When the first resonance occurs, the reading of the water level in the column is **(2012 JEE)**

(a) 14.0 cm (b) 15.2 cm
(c) 16.4 cm (d) 17.6 cm

Sol. With end correction,

$$f=n\left[\frac{v}{4(l+e)}\right], \qquad \text{(where, } n=1,3,\ldots)$$
$$=n\left[\frac{v}{4(l+0.6r)}\right] \qquad (e=0.6\,r)$$

For first resonance, $n=1$

$$\therefore \quad f=\frac{v}{4(l+0.6r)} \quad \text{or} \quad l=\frac{v}{4f}-0.6r$$
$$=\left[\left(\frac{336\times 100}{4\times 512}\right)-0.6\times 2\right]\text{cm}$$
$$=15.2\text{ cm}$$

$\therefore$ The correct option is (b).

Miscellaneous Examples

Ex. 4 The water level in a vertical glass tube 1.0 m long can be adjusted to any position in the tube. A tuning fork vibrating at 660 Hz is held just over the open top end of the tube. At what positions of the water level will there be resonance? Speed of sound is 330 m/s.

Sol. Length of air column

$$l = n\frac{\lambda}{4} = n\left(\frac{v}{4f}\right)$$

Here, $n = 1, 3, 5, \ldots$

$$l_1 = (1)\left(\frac{330}{4 \times 660}\right) = 0.125 \text{ m}$$

$$l_2 = 3l_1 = 0.375 \text{ m}$$
$$l_3 = 5l_1 = 0.625 \text{ m}$$
$$l_4 = 7l_1 = 0.875 \text{ m}$$
$$l_5 = 9l_1 = 1.125 \text{ m}$$

Since, $l_5 > 1$ m (the length of tube), the length of air columns can have the values from l_1 to l_4 only.

Therefore, level of water at resonance will be

$(1.0 - 0.125)$ m $= 0.875$ m

$(1.0 - 0.375)$ m $= 0.625$ m

$(1.0 - 0.625)$ m $= 0.375$ m

and $(1.0 - 0.875)$ m $= 0.125$ m **Ans.**

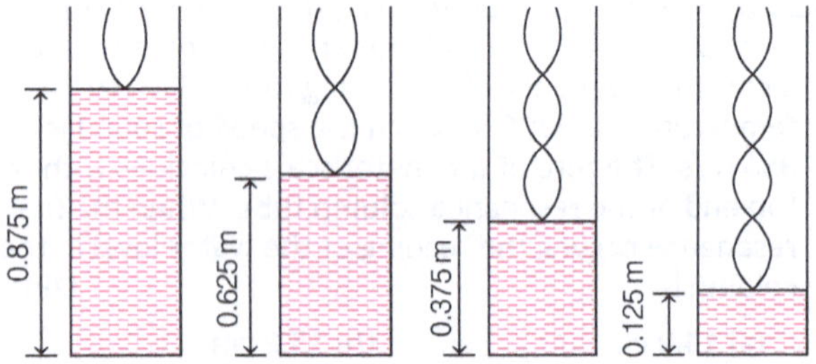

In all the four cases shown in figure, the resonance frequency is 660 Hz but first one is the fundamental tone or first harmonic. Second is first overtone or third harmonic and so on.

Ex. 5 A tube 1.0 m long is closed at one end. A stretched wire is placed near the open end. The wire is 0.3 m long and has a mass of 0.01 kg. It is held fixed at both ends and vibrates in its fundamental mode. It sets the air column in the tube into vibration at its fundamental frequency by resonance. Find

(a) the frequency of oscillation of the air column and

(b) the tension in the wire.

Speed of sound in air $= 330$ m/s.

Sol. (a) Fundamental frequency of closed pipe $= \dfrac{v}{4L}$

$$= \frac{330}{4 \times 1} = 82.5 \text{ Hz}$$ **Ans.**

(b) Given that :

Fundamental frequency of stretched wire (at both ends) = fundamental frequency of air column

$$\therefore \quad \frac{v}{2l} = 82.5 \text{ Hz}$$

$$\therefore \quad \frac{\sqrt{T/\mu}}{2l} = 82.5$$

or $$T = \mu\,(2 \times 0.3 \times 82.5)^2$$

$$= \left(\frac{0.01}{0.3}\right)(2 \times 0.3 \times 82.5)^2$$

$$= 81.675 \text{ N}$$ **Ans.**

Ex. 6 The air column in a pipe closed at one end is made to vibrate in its second overtone by a tuning fork of frequency 440 Hz. The speed of sound in air is 330 m/s. End corrections may be neglected. Let p_0 denotes the mean pressure at any point in the pipe, and Δp_0 the maximum amplitude of pressure variation.

(a) Find the length L of the air column.

(b) What is the amplitude of pressure variation at the middle of the column?

(c) What are the maximum and minimum pressures at the open end of the pipe?

(d) What are the maximum and minimum pressures at the closed end of the pipe?

Sol. (a) Frequency of second overtone of the closed pipe

$$= 5\left(\frac{v}{4L}\right) = 440 \text{ Hz} \qquad \text{(Given)}$$

$$\therefore \quad L = \frac{5v}{4 \times 440} \text{ m}$$

$$v = 330 \text{ m/s}$$

$$\therefore \quad L = \frac{5 \times 330}{4 \times 440} = \frac{15}{16} \text{ m}$$

(b) $$L = 5\left(\frac{\lambda}{4}\right)$$

$$\therefore \quad \lambda = \frac{4L}{5} = \frac{4\,(15/16)}{5} = \frac{3}{4} \text{ m}$$

Open end is displacement antinode. Therefore, it would be a pressure node

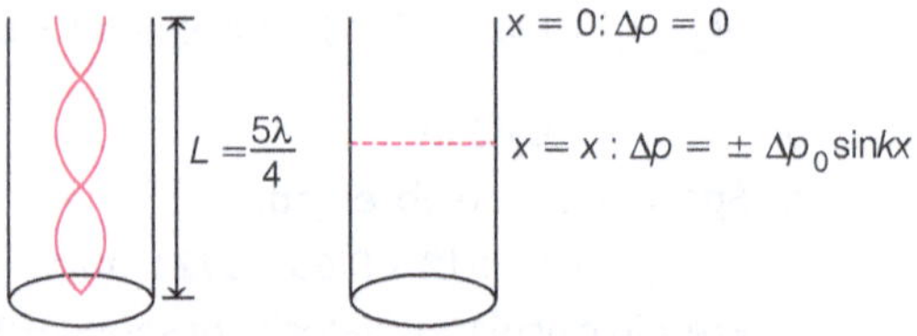

or at $x = 0$; $\Delta p = 0$

$\therefore$ Pressure amplitude at $x = x$ can be written as

$$\Delta p = \pm\, \Delta p \sin kx$$

where, $k = \frac{2\pi}{\lambda} = \frac{2\pi}{3/4} = \frac{8\pi}{3}\ \text{m}^{-1}$

Therefore, pressure amplitude at

$x = \frac{L}{2} = \frac{15/16}{2}$ m or (15/32) m will be

$$\Delta p = \pm\, \Delta p_0 \sin\left(\frac{8\pi}{3}\right)\left(\frac{15}{32}\right)$$

$$= \pm\, \Delta p_0 \sin\left(\frac{5\pi}{4}\right)$$

$$\Delta p = \pm \frac{\Delta p_0}{\sqrt{2}}$$ **Ans.**

(c) Open end is a pressure node, i.e. $\Delta p = 0$

Hence, $p_{max} = p_{min}$ = Mean pressure (p_0)

(d) Closed end is a displacement node or pressure antinode.

Therefore, $p_{max} = p_0 + \Delta p_0$

and $p_{min} = p_0 - \Delta p_0$

MODULE 5 Exercise

Assertion and Reason

See directions on page 14.

1. **Assertion :** A closed pipe and an open organ pipe are of same length. Then, neither of their frequencies can be same.

   Reason : In the above case fundamental frequency of closed organ pipe will be two times the fundamental frequency of open organ pipe.

2. **Assertion :** In the experiment of finding speed of sound by resonance tube method, as the level of water is lowered, wavelength increases.

   Reason : By lowering the water level number of loops increases.

3. **Assertion :** In the experiment of finding speed of sound, $l_2 > 3l_1$, (l_1 and l_2 are the first and second resonating lengths).

   Reason : $e = \frac{l_2 - 3l_1}{2}$ (e = end correction) and e remains always positive.

Single Correct Option

4. A closed organ pipe is excited to vibrate in the third overtone. It is observed that there are
   (a) three nodes and three antinodes
   (b) three nodes and four antinodes
   (c) four nodes and three antinodes
   (d) four nodes and four antinodes

5. A closed organ pipe and an open organ pipe are tuned to the same fundamental frequency. The ratio of their lengths is
   (a) 1 : 2 (b) 2 : 1
   (c) 1 : 4 (d) 4 : 1

6. A tuning fork of frequency 500 Hz is sounded on a resonance tube. The first and second resonances are obtained at 17 cm and 52 cm. The velocity of sound is
   (a) 170 m/s (b) 350 m/s (c) 520 m/s (d) 850 m/s

7. How many frequencies below 1 kHz of natural oscillations of air column will be produced if a pipe of length 1 m is closed at one end? [velocity of sound in air is 340 m/s]
   (a) 3 (b) 6
   (c) 4 (d) 8

8. The first resonance length of a resonance tube is 40 cm and the second resonance length is 122 cm. The third resonance length of the tube will be
   (a) 200 cm (b) 202 cm
   (c) 203 cm (d) 204 cm

9. A tuning fork of frequency 340 Hz is sounded above an organ pipe of length 120 cm. Water is now slowly poured in it. The minimum height of water column required for resonance is (speed of sound in air = 340 m/s)
   (a) 25 cm (b) 95 cm (c) 75 cm (d) 45 cm

10. In a closed end pipe of length 105 cm, standing waves are set up corresponding to the third overtone. What distance from the closed end, amongst the following is a pressure node?
    (a) 20 cm (b) 60 cm
    (c) 85 cm (d) 45 cm

11. Speed of sound in air is 320 m/s. A pipe closed at one end has a length of 1 m and there is another pipe open at both ends having a length of 1.6 m. Neglecting end corrections, both the air columns in the pipes can resonate for sound of frequency
    (a) 80 Hz (b) 240 Hz
    (c) 320 Hz (d) 400 Hz

12. A longitudinal sound wave given by $p = 2.5 \sin \frac{\pi}{2}(x - 600t)$ (p is in N/m^2, x is in metre and t is in second) is sent down a closed organ pipe. If the pipe vibrates in its second overtone, the length of the pipe is
    (a) 6 m (b) 8 m
    (c) 5 m (d) 10 m

13. Sound waves of frequency 600 Hz fall normally on perfectly reflecting wall. The distance from the wall at which the air particles have the maximum amplitude of vibration is
(speed of sound in air $= 330$ m/s)
(a) 13.75 cm (b) 40.25 cm
(c) 70.5 cm (d) 60.75 cm

14. In case of closed pipe which harmonic the pth overtone will be
(a) $2p+1$ (b) $2p-1$ (c) $p+1$ (d) $p-1$

15. In a resonance column experiment the first resonance is obtained when the level of the water in tube is 20 cm from the open end. Resonance will also be obtained when the water level is at a distance of
(a) 40 cm from the open end
(b) 60 cm from the open end
(c) 80 cm from the open end
(d) 90 cm from the open end

16. First overtone frequency of a closed organ pipe is equal to the first overtone frequency of an open organ pipe. Further nth harmonic of closed organ pipe is also equal to the mth harmonic of open pipe, where n and m are
(a) 5, 4 (b) 7, 5
(c) 9, 6 (d) 7, 3

17. For a certain organ pipe, three successive resonance frequencies are observed at 425, 595 and 765 Hz. The speed of sound in air is 340 ms^{-1}. The pipe is a
(a) closed pipe of length 1 m
(b) closed pipe of length 2 m
(c) open pipe of length 1 m
(d) open pipe of length 2 m

18. A glass tube of 1.0 m length is filled with water. The water can be drained out slowly at the bottom of the tube. If a vibrating tuning fork of frequency 500 c/s is brought at the upper end of the tube and the velocity of sound is 330 m/s, then the total number of resonances obtained will be
(a) 4 (b) 3
(c) 2 (d) 1

19. The vibrations of four air columns are represented in the figure given below. The ratio of frequencies $n_p : n_q : n_r : n_s$ is

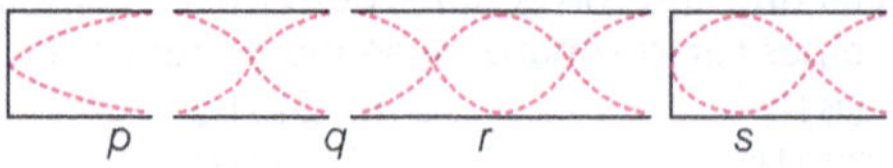

(a) 12 : 6 : 3 : 4 (b) 4 : 2 : 3 : 1
(c) 1 : 2 : 4 : 3 (d) 1 : 2 : 3 : 4

20. In a resonance tube, closed at one end by a smooth moving piston and the other end open, exhibits the first three resonance lengths of air column, L_1, L_2 and L_3 for the same tuning fork. Then they are related by
(a) $L_3 = 2L_2 = 4L_1$
(b) $L_3 = \frac{5}{3}L_2 = 5L_1$
(c) $(L_3 - L_2) = \left(\frac{L_2 - L_1}{2}\right)$
(d) $(L_3 - L_2) = 2(L_2 - L_1)$

21. n_1 is the fundamental frequency of the pipe closed at one end and n_2 is the fundamental frequency of the pipe open at both ends. If both are joined end to end, find the fundamental frequency of closed pipe so formed.
(a) $\frac{n_1 n_2}{n_2 + 2n_1}$ (b) $\frac{n_1 n_2}{2n_2 + n_1}$
(c) $\frac{n_1 + 2n_2}{n_2 n_1}$ (d) $\frac{2n_1 + n_2}{n_2 n_1}$

Multiple Correct Options

22. An air column in a pipe, which is closed at one end, is in resonance with a vibrating tuning fork of frequency 264 Hz. If $v = 330$ m/s, the length of the air column in cm is (are)
(a) 31.25 (b) 62.50
(c) 93.75 (d) 125

23. Which of the following is/are correct?

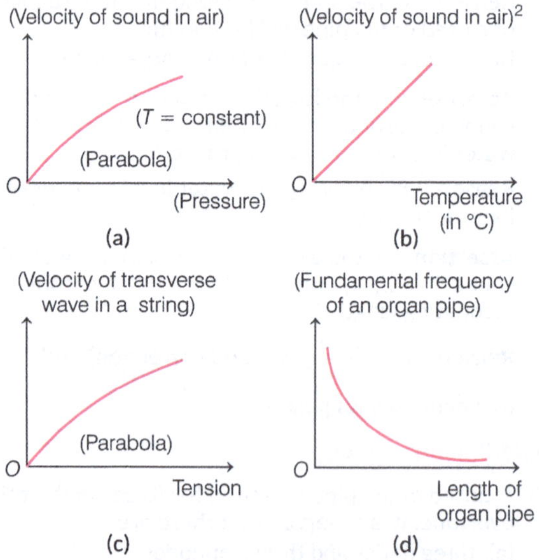

24. Second overtone frequency of a closed pipe and fourth harmonic frequency of an open pipe are same. Then, choose the correct options.
(a) Fundamental frequency of closed pipe is more than the fundamental frequency of open pipe
(b) First overtone frequency of closed pipe is more than the first overtone frequency of open pipe
(c) Fifteenth harmonic frequency of closed pipe is equal to twelfth harmonic frequency of open pipe
(d) Tenth harmonic frequency of closed pipe is equal to eighth harmonic frequency of open pipe

25. For fundamental frequency f of a closed pipe, choose the correct options.
(a) If radius of pipe is increased, f will decrease
(b) If temperature is increased, f will increase
(c) If molecular mass of the gas filled in the pipe is increased, f will decrease.
(d) If pressure of gas (filled in the pipe) is increased without change in temperature, f will remain unchanged

Match the Columns

26. Fundamental frequency of an open organ pipe is f. Match the following two columns for a closed pipe of double the length.

	Column I		Column II
(a)	Fundamental frequency	(p)	$1.25f$
(b)	Second overtone frequency	(q)	f
(c)	Third harmonic frequency	(r)	$0.75f$
(d)	First overtone frequency	(s)	None of these

27. The equation of longitudinal stationary wave in second overtone mode in a closed organ pipe is

$$y = (4\text{ mm})\sin \pi x \cos \pi t$$

Here, x is in metre and t in second. Then, match the following two columns.

	Column I		Column II
(a)	Length of pipe	(p)	1 m
(b)	Wavelength	(q)	1.5 m
(c)	Distance of displacement node from the closed end	(r)	2.0 m
(d)	Distance of pressure node from the closed end	(s)	None of these

Subjective Questions

28. In a resonance tube experiment to determine the speed of sound in air, a pipe of diameter 5 cm is used. The column in pipe resonates with a tuning fork of frequency 480 Hz when the minimum length of the air column is 16 cm. Find the speed of sound in air column at room temperature.

29. A wire of length 40 cm which has a mass of 4 g oscillates in its second harmonic and sets the air column in the tube to vibrations in its fundamental mode as shown in figure. Assuming the speed of sound in air as 340 m/s, find the tension in the wire.

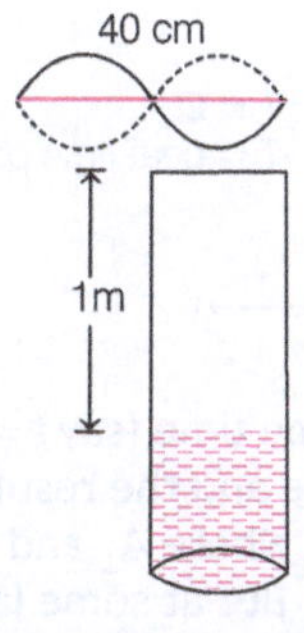

30. On a day when the speed of sound is 345 m/s the fundamental frequency of a closed organ pipe is 220 Hz (a) How long is this closed pipe? (b) The second overtone of this pipe has the same wavelength as the third harmonic of an open pipe. How long is the open pipe?

Answers

1. (c) **2.** (d) **3.** (a) **4.** (d) **5.** (a) **6.** (b) **7.** (b) **8.** (d) **9.** (d) **10.** (d)
11. (d) **12.** (c) **13.** (a) **14.** (a) **15.** (b) **16.** (c) **17.** (a) **18.** (b) **19.** (c) **20.** (b)
21. (a) **22.** (a, c) **23.** (c, d) **24.** (b,c) **25.** (a,b,c,d) **26.** (a) → s; (b) → p; (c) → r; (d) → r
27. (a) → s; (b) → r; (c) → p, r; (d) → q **28.** 336 m/s **29.** 11.56 N **30.** (a) 0.392 m (b) 0.470 m

See hints on pages 150-152.

MODULE 6

Beats

When two waves of the same frequency travel along the same line in opposite directions, standing waves are formed in accordance with the principle of superposition. In standing waves, amplitude is a function of position. This illustrates a type of interference that we can call **interference in space.**

The same principle of superposition leads us to another type of interference, which we can call **interference in time.** It occurs when two waves of slightly different frequency travel through the same region.

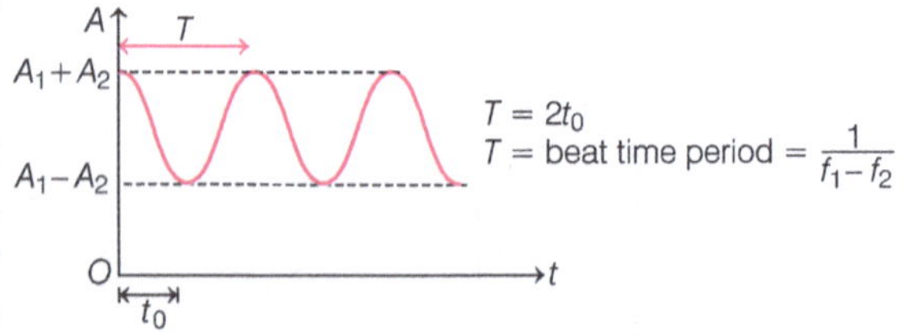

If the waves are in phase at some time (say $t=0$) the interference will be constructive and the resultant amplitude at this moment will be A_1+A_2, where A_1 and A_2 are the amplitudes of individual waves. But at some later time (say $t=t_0$), because the frequencies are different, the waves will be out of phase or the interference will be destructive and the resultant amplitude will be A_1-A_2 (if $A_1>A_2$). We can prove that the time t_0 is $\frac{1}{2(f_1-f_2)}$.

Thus, the resultant amplitude oscillates between A_1+A_2 and A_1-A_2 with a time period $T=2t_0=\frac{1}{f_1-f_2}$ or with a frequency $f=f_1-f_2$ known as **beat frequency.** Thus,

$$\boxed{\text{Beat frequency, } f=f_1-f_2} \qquad (f_1>f_2)$$

Calculation of Beat Frequency

Suppose two waves of frequencies f_1 and f_2 ($<f_1$) are meeting at some point in space. The corresponding periods are T_1 and T_2 ($>T_1$).

If the two waves are in phase at $t=0$, they will again be in phase when the first wave has gone through exactly one more cycle than the second. This will happen at a time $t=T$, the beat time period. Let n be the number of cycles of the first wave in time T, then the number of cycles of the second wave in the same time is $(n-1)$. Hence,

$$T=nT_1 \qquad \text{...(i)}$$

and

$$T=(n-1)T_2 \qquad \text{...(ii)}$$

Eliminating n from these two equations, we have

$$T=\frac{T_1T_2}{T_2-T_1}=\frac{1}{\frac{1}{T_1}-\frac{1}{T_2}}=\frac{1}{f_1-f_2}$$

The reciprocal of the beat time period is the beat frequency

$$f=\frac{1}{T}=f_1-f_2$$

Alternate Method

Let the oscillations at some point in space (say $x=0$) due to two waves be

$$y_1=A_1\sin 2\pi f_1 t$$

and

$$y_2=A_2\sin 2\pi f_2 t \qquad (\omega=2\pi f)$$

If they are in phase at some time t, then

$$2\pi f_1 t=2\pi f_2 t$$

or

$$f_1 t=f_2 t \qquad \text{...(i)}$$

They will be again in phase at time $(t+T)$ if,

$$2\pi f_1(t+T)=2\pi f_2(t+T)+2\pi$$

or

$$f_1(t+T)=f_2(t+T)+1 \qquad \text{...(ii)}$$

Solving Eqs. (i) and (ii), we get

$$T=\frac{1}{f_1-f_2}$$

Note *If a tuning fork is loaded with wax, its frequency decreases. On the other hand, when tuning fork is filed, its frequency increases.*

Example 1 Two tuning forks A and B produce 6 beats per second. Frequency of A is 300 Hz. When B is slightly loaded with wax, beat frequency decreases. Find original frequency of B.

Sol. Since, A and B produce 6 beats per second. Therefore, original frequency of B may be 306 Hz or 294 Hz.

When B is loaded with wax, its frequency will decrease (suppose it decreases by 1Hz). So, if it is 306 Hz, it will become 305 Hz. If it is 294 Hz, it will become 293 Hz.

Frequency of A is unchanged (=300 Hz). If f_B becomes 305 Hz, then beat frequency will become 5 Hz. If f_B becomes 293 Hz, then it will become 7 Hz. But in the question it is given that beat frequency has decreased. So, the correct answer is 306 Hz.

Example 2 The string of a violin emits a note of 400 Hz at its correct tension. The string is bit taut and produces 5 beats per second with a tuning fork of frequency 400 Hz. Find frequency of the note emitted by this taut string.

Sol. The frequency of vibration of a string increases with increase in the tension. Thus, the note emitted by the string will be a little more than 400 Hz. As it produces 5 beats per second with the 400 Hz tuning fork, the frequency will be 405 Hz.

Example 3 Two tuning forks P and Q when set vibrating, give 4 beats per second. If a prong of the fork P is filed, the beats are reduced to 2 per second. Determine the original frequency of P, if that of Q is 250 Hz.

Sol. There are four beats between P and Q, therefore the possible frequencies of P are 246 or 254 (that is 250 ± 4) Hz.

When the prong of P is filed, its frequency becomes greater than the original frequency.

If we assume that the original frequency of P is 254, then on filing its frequency will be greater than 254. The beats between P and Q will be more than 4. But it is given that the beats are reduced to 2, therefore, 254 is not possible.

Therefore, the required frequency must be 246 Hz.

(This is true, because on filing the frequency may increase to 248, giving 2 beats with Q of frequency 250 Hz) **Ans.**

Example 4 Three sound sources A, B and C have frequencies 400, 401 and 402 Hz, respectively. Calculate the number of beats noted per second.

Sol. Let us make the following table.

Group	Beat frequency $(f_1 - f_2)$ Hz	Beat time period $\left(\frac{1}{f_1 - f_2}\right)$ second
A and B	1	1
B and C	1	1
A and C	2	0.5

Beat time period for A and B is 1 s. It implies that if A and B are in phase at time $t = 0$, they are again in phase after 1 s. Same is the case with B and C. But beat time period for A and C is 0.5 s.

Therefore, beat time period for all together A, B and C will be 1 s. Because if, at $t = 0$, A, B and C all are in phase then after 1 s. (A and B) and (B and C) will again be in phase for the first time while (A and C) will be in phase for the second time. Or we can say that all A, B and C are again in phase after 1 s.

$\therefore$ Beat time period, $T_b = 1$ s

or Beat frequency, $f_b = \dfrac{1}{T_b} = 1$ Hz **Ans.**

Example 5 Frequencies of two tuning forks are f_1 and f_2 with $f_1 > f_2$. They produce some beats. Now wax is loaded in first tuning fork. Then beat frequency :

(a) may decrease
(b) may increase
(c) may remain same
(d) may become zero.

Sol. In this problem all given options are correct. Let us prove this with some values.

Suppose, $f_1 = 15$ Hz and $f_2 = 10$ Hz. Then beat frequency $f_b = 15 - 10 = 5$ Hz.

By loading wax on first tuning fork, f_1 will decrease. Now depending upon the decrease in the value of f_1 all options may be correct as shown below.

(a) If f_1 becomes 14 Hz. Then, $f_b = 4$ Hz
or, beat frequency will decrease

(b) If f_1 becomes 4 Hz. Then, $f_b = 6$ Hz
or, beat frequency will increase.

(c) If f_1 becomes 5 Hz. Then, $f_b = 5$ Hz
or, beat frequecy will remain same.

(d) If f_1 becomes 10 Hz. Then, $f_b = 0$

Typed Problems

Type 1. *Two oscillating systems are producing some beats.*

If some changes are made in one of the system, then frequency of this system changes. Therefore beat frequency changes.

Following example will illustrate this type.

Ex. 1 System -1 is a stretched wire and system -2 is a closed organ pipe. Second harmonic of system -1 and third overtone of system -2 produce 10 beats per second. When tension in the wire is slightly increased, beat frequency decreases. Make the correct equation.

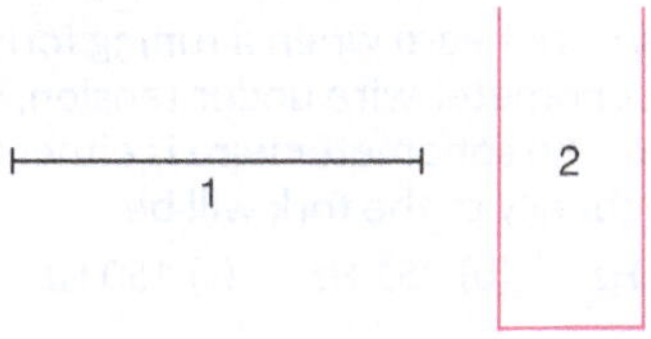

Sol. Second harmonic frequency of system -1

$$= 2\left(\frac{v}{2l_1}\right) = \frac{v_1}{l_1} = \frac{\sqrt{T_1/\mu_1}}{l_1} = F_1 \quad \text{(Say)} \qquad \text{...(i)}$$

Third overtone frequency of system -2

$$= 7\left(\frac{v_2}{4l_2}\right) = \frac{7}{4}\left[\frac{\sqrt{\gamma_2 RT_2/M_2}}{l_2}\right] = F_2 \quad \text{(Say)} \qquad \text{...(ii)}$$

Now F_1 and F_2 are producing 10 beats per second. So, either

$$F_1 - F_2 = 10 \qquad \text{...(iii)}$$

or

$$F_2 - F_1 = 10 \qquad \text{...(iv)}$$

When tension T_1 is increased then from Eq. (i) we can see that F_1 will increase.

Beat frequency is decreasing (with increase in the value of F_1). So, Eq. (iv) is correct. Or,

$$F_2 - F_1 = 10$$

In the above expressions, T_1 represents tension and T_2 the temperature.

Type 2. *In this type, problems of two simple pendulums can be compared with beats.*

Following example will illustrate this concept.

Ex. 2 Two pendulums have time periods $\frac{1}{4}$ s and $\frac{1}{6}$ s. At time $t = 0$, they are at their extreme points on same side and released from rest. At what time, both of them are again in same position simultaneously?

Sol. Frequency of first pendulum, $f_1 = \frac{1}{T_1} = 4$ Hz

Frequency of second pendulum,

$$f_2 = \frac{1}{T_2} = 6 \text{ Hz}$$

$$\Rightarrow \quad f_2 > f_1$$

$\therefore$ Beat frequency $f_b = f_2 - f_1 = 2$ Hz

$\Rightarrow$ Beat time period,

$$T_b = \frac{1}{f_b} = \frac{1}{2} \text{ s}$$

So, the pendulums will repeat the same situation after one beat time period.

$$\therefore \quad t = T_b = \frac{1}{2} \text{ s}$$ **Ans.**

MODULE 6 Exercise

Single Correct Option

1. A, B and C are three tuning forks. Frequency of A is 350 Hz. Beats produced by A and B are 5/s and by B and C are 4/s. When a wax is put on A beat frequency between A and B is 2 Hz and between A and C is 6 Hz. Then, frequency of B and C respectively, are
   (a) 355 Hz, 349 Hz
   (b) 345 Hz, 341 Hz
   (c) 355 Hz, 341 Hz
   (d) 345 Hz, 349 Hz

2. Two identical wires are stretched by the same tension of 100 N and each emits a note of frequency 200 Hz. If the tension in one wire is increased by 1 N, then the beat frequency is
   (a) 2 Hz (b) $\frac{1}{2}$ Hz
   (c) 1 Hz (d) None of these

3. The wavelength of two sound waves are 49 cm and 50 cm, respectively. If the room temperature is 30°C, then the number of beats produced by them is approximately (velocity of sound in air at 30°C = 332 m/s)
   (a) 6 (b) 10
   (c) 13 (d) 18

4. Two closed pipes produce 10 beats per second when emitting their fundamental nodes. If their lengths are in ratio of 25 : 26. Then, their fundamental frequencies in Hz, are
   (a) 270, 280 (b) 260, 270
   (c) 260, 250 (d) 260, 280

5. A closed organ pipe and an open organ pipe of same length produce 2 beats when they are set into vibrations simultaneously in their fundamental mode. The length of open organ pipe is now halved and of closed organ pipe is doubled. The number of beats produced will be
   (a) 8 (b) 7 (c) 4 (d) 2

6. The frequency of tuning forks A and B are respectively 3% more and 2% less than the frequency of tuning fork C. When A and B are simultaneously excited, 5 beats per second are produced. Then, the frequency of the tuning fork A (in Hz) is
   (a) 98 (b) 100
   (c) 103 (d) 105

7. The velocity of sound in a gas in which two wavelengths 4.08 m and 4.16 m produce 40 beats in 12 s, will be **(2022 Main)**
   (a) 2.828 ms^{-1} (b) 175.5 ms^{-1}
   (c) 353.6 ms^{-1} (d) 707.2 ms^{-1}

8. A tuning fork A of unknown frequency produces 5 beats/s with a fork of known frequency 340 Hz. When fork A is filed, the beat frequency decreases to 2 beats/s What is the frequency of fork A? **(2021 Main)**
   (a) 335 Hz (b) 338 Hz
   (c) 345 Hz (d) 342 Hz

9. A tuning fork vibrates with frequency 256 Hz and gives one beat per second with the third normal mode of vibration of an open pipe. What is the length of the pipe? (Speed of sound of air is 340 ms^{-1}) **(2018 Main)**
   (a) 190 cm (b) 180 cm
   (c) 220 cm (d) 200 cm

10. 5 beats/s are heard when a tuning fork is sounded with a sonometer wire under tension, when the length of the sonometer wire is either 0.95 m or 1 m. The frequency of the fork will be **(2018 Main)**
    (a) 195 Hz (b) 251 Hz (c) 150 Hz (d) 300 Hz

Match the Columns

11. A tuning fork is placed near a vibrating stretched wire. A boy standing near the two hears a beat frequency f. It is known that frequency of tuning fork is greater than frequency of stretched wire. Match the following two columns.

	Column I		Column II
(a)	If tuning fork is loaded with wax,	(p)	beat frequency must increase.
(b)	If prongs of tuning fork are filed,	(q)	beat frequency must decrease.
(c)	If tension in stretched wire is increased,	(r)	beat frequency may increase.
(d)	If tension in stretched wire is decreased,	(s)	beat frequency may decrease.

Subjective Questions

12. A tuning fork produces 4 beats per second with another tuning fork of frequency 256 Hz. The first one is now loaded with a little wax and the beat frequency is found to increase to 6 per second. What was the original frequency of the first tuning fork?

13. A tuning fork of unknown frequency makes three beats per second with a standard fork of frequency 384 Hz. The beat frequency decreases when a small piece of wax is put on a prong of the first fork. What is the frequency of this fork?

14. Two tuning forks A and B sounded together give 8 beats per second. With an air resonance tube closed at one end, the two forks give resonances when the two air columns are 32 cm and 33 cm respectively. Calculate the frequencies of forks.

Integer Type Question

15. A set of 20 tuning forks is arranged in a series of increasing frequencies. If each fork gives 4 beats with respect to the preceding fork and the frequency of the last fork is twice the frequency of the first, then the frequency of last fork is .... Hz. **(2022 Main)**

Answers

1. (b) **2.** (c) **3.** (c) **4.** (c) **5.** (b) **6.** (c) **7.** (d) **8.** (a) **9.** (d) **10.** (a)

11. (a) → r,s; (b) → p; (c) → r,s; (d) → p **12.** 252 Hz **13.** 387 Hz **14.** $f_1 = 264$ Hz and $f_2 = 256$ Hz **15.** (152)

See hints on pages 152-154.

MODULE 7

The Doppler Effect

If a source of sound and an observer are moving relative to each other, the frequency observed by the observer (f') is different from the actual source frequency (f). This phenomenon is called the **Doppler's effect**, named after the Austrian physicist Christian Johann Doppler (1803–1853), who discovered it in light waves.

Perhaps you might have noticed how the sound of a vehicle's horn changes as the vehicle moves past you. The frequency (pitch) of the sound you hear as the vehicle approaches you is higher than the frequency you hear as it moves away from you. The Doppler's effect applies to waves in general. Let us apply it to sound waves. We consider the special case in which the source and observer move along the line joining them. We will use the following symbols,

v = speed of sound, v_s = speed of source and

v_o = speed of observer

and v_m = speed of medium in which sound travels.

For example, if Doppler's effect is observed in air, it is wind speed. If Doppler's effect is observed inside a river, then it is river speed.

The general formula of the changed frequency is

$$f' = \left(\frac{v \pm v_m \pm v_o}{v \pm v_m \pm v_s}\right) f$$

Sign Convention

v_m : We are talking about that sound which is travelling from source to observer (S to O). If the medium is also travelling in the same direction, then it means medium is supporting the sound. So, take positive sign both in numerator and denominator. If the medium travels in opposite direction, then take negative sign. If nothing is given in the question, then take it zero.

v_o and v_s : The concept is : **approaching nature always increases the frequency**. So, take positive sign with v_o (because it is in numerator) and negative sign with v_s (as it is in denominator). On the other hand, receding nature decreases the frequency. So, take negative sign with v_o and positive sign with v_s. Now, let us discuss some different cases.

Case 1

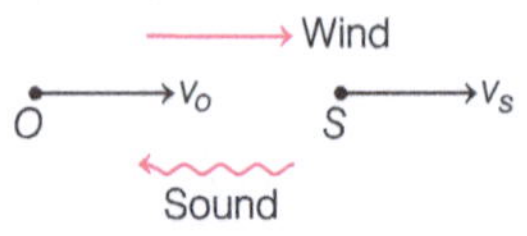

In the given figure, sound is travelling from right to left but wind is blowing from left to right, so we will have to take negative sign with wind velocity. Observer is approaching towards source, so take positive sign with v_o because this will increase the frequency. Source is receding from the observer, so take positive sign with v_s because this will decrease the frequency. The correct formula is given below :

$$f' = \left(\frac{v - v_{wind} + v_o}{v - v_{wind} + v_s}\right) f$$

Case 2

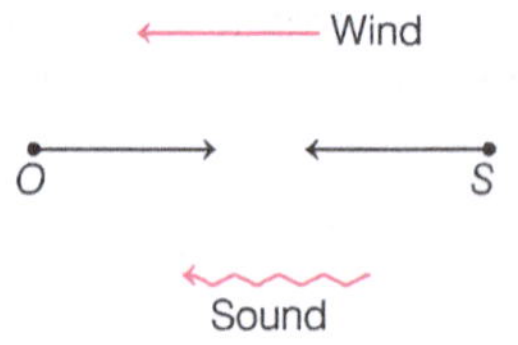

Sound and wind both are travelling in the same direction (from S to O). So take positive sign with wind velocity. Source and observer both are approaching towards each other. So, take positive sign with v_o and negative sign with v_s as both will increase the frequency. Therefore, the correct formula is

$$f' = \left(\frac{v + v_{wind} + v_o}{v + v_{wind} - v_s}\right) f$$

Now, let us derive two special cases when medium velocity is zero.

Source at Rest, Observer Moves

Suppose that the observer O moves towards the source S at speed v_o. The speed of the sound waves relative to O is $v_r = v + v_o$, but wavelength has its normal value $\lambda = \frac{v}{f}$. Thus, the frequency heard by O is

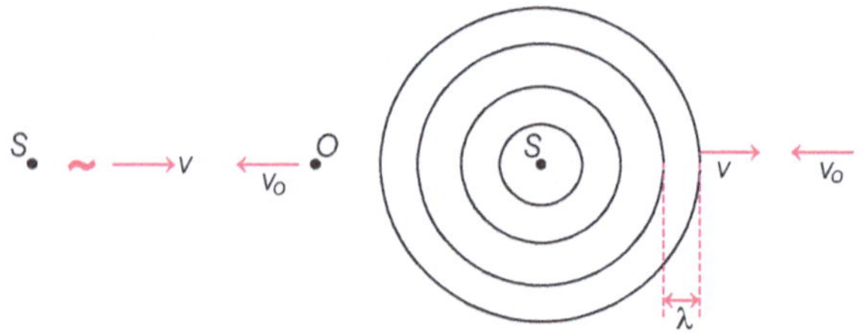

$$f' = \frac{v_r}{\lambda} = \left(\frac{v + v_o}{v}\right) f$$

If O were moving away from S, the frequency heard by O would be

$$f' = \left(\frac{v - v_o}{v}\right) f$$

Combining these two expressions, we can write

$$f' = \left(\frac{v \pm v_o}{v}\right) f \qquad \text{...(i)}$$

Source Moves, Observer at Rest

Suppose that the source S moves towards O as shown in figure.

If S were at rest, the distance between two consecutive wave pulses emitted by sound would be $\lambda = \frac{v}{f} = vT$. However, in one time period S moves a distance $v_s T$ before it emits the next pulse. As a result the wavelength is modified. Directly ahead of S the effective wavelength (for both S and O) is

$$\lambda' = vT - v_s T = (v - v_s)T = \left(\frac{v - v_s}{f}\right)$$

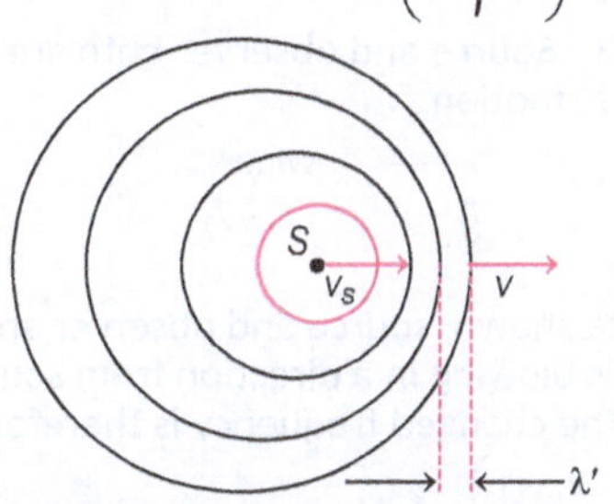

The wavelength in front of the source is less than the normal

The speed of sound waves relative to O is simply v. Thus, the frequency observed by O is

$$f' = \frac{v}{\lambda'} = \left(\frac{v}{v - v_s}\right) f$$

If S were moving away from O, the effective wavelength would be $\lambda' = \left(\frac{v + v_s}{f}\right)$ and the apparent frequency would be

$$f' = \left(\frac{v}{v + v_s}\right) f$$

Combining these two results, we have

$$f' = \left(\frac{v}{v \pm v_s}\right) f \qquad \text{...(ii)}$$

Alternate Method

The above formulae can be derived alternately as discussed below.

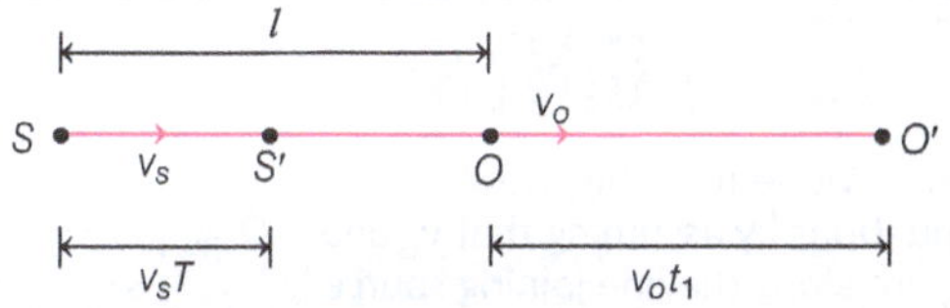

Assume that the source and observer are moving along the same line and that the observer O is to the right of the source S. Suppose that at time $t = 0$, when the source and the observer are separated by a distance $SO = l$, the source emits a wave pulse (say p_1) that reaches the observer at a later time t_1. In that time the observer has moved a distance $v_o t_1$ and the total distance travelled by p_1 in the time t_1 has been $l + v_o t_1$. If v is the speed of sound, this distance is also vt_1. Then,

$$vt_1 = l + v_o t_1$$

or

$$t_1 = \frac{l}{v - v_o}$$

Next wave pulse (say P_2) is emitted after one time period $T\left(=\frac{1}{f}\right)$. At time $t = T$, the source is at S' and the wave pulse P_2 emitted at this time will reach the observer at a time say t_2, measured from the same time $t = 0$, as before.

The total distance travelled by P_2 till it is received by the observer (measured from S') is $(l - v_s T) + v_o t_2$. The actual travel time for p_2 is $(t_2 - T)$ and the distance travelled is $v(t_2 - T)$. Therefore,

$$v(t_2 - T) = (l - v_s T) + v_o t_2$$

or

$$t_2 = \frac{l + (v - v_s)T}{v - v_o}$$

The changed time period observed by the observer between the two pulses emitted by the source at S and at S' is

$$T' = t_2 - t_1 = \left(\frac{v - v_s}{v - v_o}\right) T$$

Hence, the new frequency is

$$f' = \frac{1}{T'} = \left(\frac{v - v_o}{v - v_s}\right) \frac{1}{T}$$

or

$$f' = \left(\frac{v - v_o}{v - v_s}\right) f$$

This is a result which we can expect by using the general equation of f' in the case when source is moving towards observer and observer is moving away from the source with medium velocity = 0.

Important POINTS

- We have derived the above equations by assuming that v_o and v_s are along the line joining source and observer. If the motion is not along the line. So, the components of velocities along the line joining source and observer are considered.

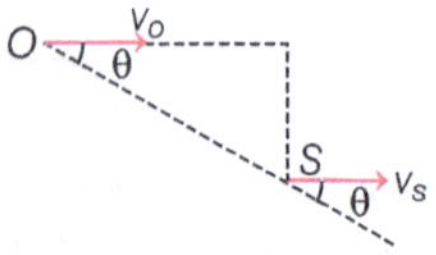

For example in the figure shown, $f' = \left(\dfrac{v + v_o \cos\theta}{v + v_s \cos\theta}\right) f$

- Change in frequency depends on the fact that whether the source is moving towards the observer or the observer is moving towards the source. But when the speed of source and observer are much lesser than that of sound, the change in frequency becomes independent of the fact whether the source is moving or the observer. This can be shown as under.

  Suppose a source is moving towards a stationary observer, with speed u and the speed of sound is v, then

$$f' = \left(\frac{v}{v-u}\right) f = \left(\frac{1}{1-\dfrac{u}{v}}\right) f = \left(1-\frac{u}{v}\right)^{-1} f$$

  Using the binomial expansion, we have

$$\left(1-\frac{u}{v}\right)^{-1} \approx 1+\frac{u}{v} \quad \text{if } u << v$$

$$\therefore \qquad f' \approx \left(1+\frac{u}{v}\right) f \quad \text{if } \quad u << v$$

  On the other hand, if an observer moves towards a stationary source with same speed u, then

$$f' = \left(\frac{v+u}{v}\right) f = \left(1+\frac{u}{v}\right) f$$

  which is same as above.

- As long as v_s and v_o are along the line joining S and O, Doppler's effect (or change in frequency) does not depend on the distance between S and O. For example, in the given figure,

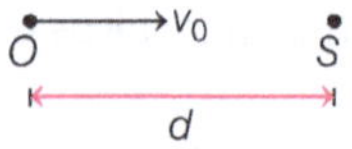

$$f' = f\left(\frac{v+v_o}{v}\right)$$

  $f' > f$ but it is constant and independent of d.

- Frequency is given by $f = \dfrac{v}{\lambda}$

  By the motion of source, λ changes, therefore frequency changes. But, from the motion of observer, relative velocity between sound and observer changes, therefore frequency changes.

- Despite the motion of source or observer (or both), Doppler's effect is not observed (or $f' = f$) under the following four conditions.

  Condition 1 $\mathbf{v}_s$ or $\mathbf{v}_o$ is making an angle of 90° with the line joining S and O. This is illustrated in the following figure.

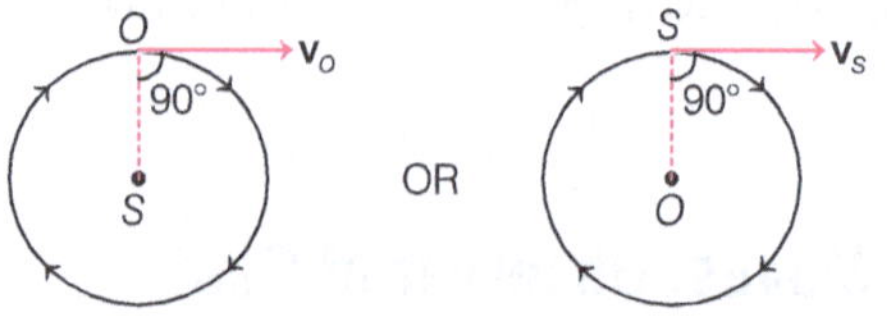

Condition 2 Source and observer both are in motion but their velocities are equal or relative motion between them is zero.

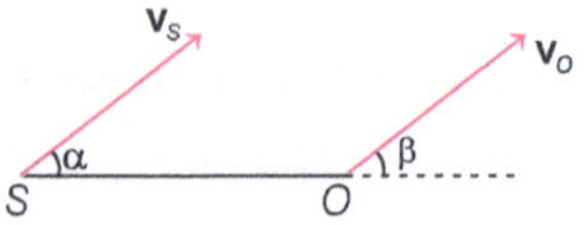

In the figure shown, $\mathbf{v}_s = \mathbf{v}_o$ if $v_s = v_o$ and $\alpha = \beta$

Taking the components along SO, we have

$$f' = f\left(\frac{v - v_o \cos\beta}{v - v_s \cos\alpha}\right) \Rightarrow \quad f' = f \text{ because } v_s = v_o \text{ and } \alpha = \beta$$

Condition 3 Source and observer both are at rest. Only medium is in motion.

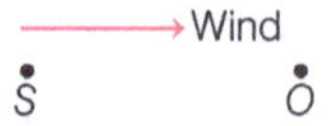

In the figure shown, source and observer are at rest. Only wind is blowing in a direction from source to observer. The changed frequency is therefore,

$$f' = f\left(\frac{v + v_{wind}}{v + v_{wind}}\right) = f$$

Condition 4

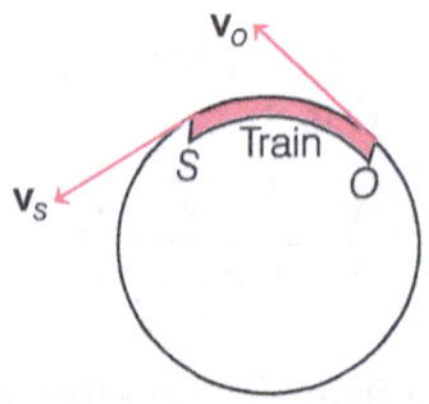

A train is travelling on a circular track. Engine is the source of sound and guard is the observer. Although,

$$\mathbf{v}_s \neq \mathbf{v}_o$$

yet f' comes out to be f.

Exercise Derive the above result.

- **Doppler's Effect in Light**

  Light waves also show Doppler's effect.

  If the light source or the observer is moving with a velocity v such that the distance between them is decreasing, then the apparent frequency of the source will be given by

$$f' = f\sqrt{\frac{1+\dfrac{v}{c}}{1-\dfrac{v}{c}}}$$

It means frequency is increasing. So, the wavelength will be decreasing. If the distance between the light source and the observer is increasing, then the apparent frequency of the source is given by

$$f' = f\sqrt{\frac{1-\frac{v}{c}}{1+\frac{v}{c}}}$$

So, the frequency will decrease and the wavelength will increase.

The change in wavelength can be determined by

$$\Delta\lambda = \frac{v}{c}\cdot\lambda$$

If the light source is moving away from the observer, the shift in the spectrum is towards red and if it is moving towards the observer the shift is towards the violet.

Note *The Doppler's effect in light depends only on the relative motion between the source and the observer while the Doppler's effect in sound also depends upon whether the source is moving or the observer is moving.*

Example 1 A car approaching a crossing C at a speed of 20 m/s sounds a horn of frequency 500 Hz when 80 m from the crossing. Speed of sound in air is 330 m/s. What frequency is heard by an observer (at rest) 60 m from the crossing on the straight road which crosses car road at right angles?

Sol. The situation is as shown in figure.

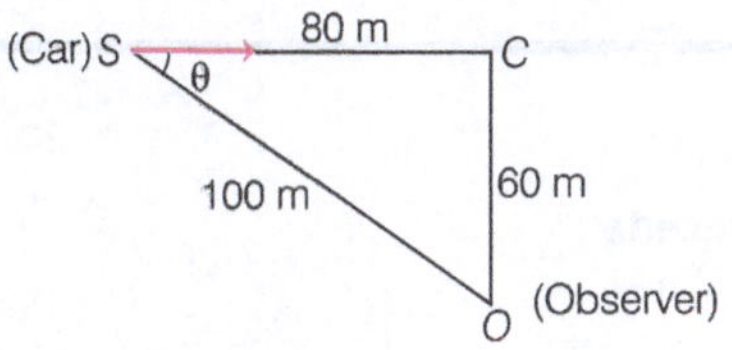

$$\cos\theta = \frac{80}{100} = \frac{4}{5}$$

$\therefore$ Apparent frequency,

$$f_{app} = \left(\frac{v}{v - v_s\cos\theta}\right)f = \left(\frac{330}{330 - 20\times\frac{4}{5}}\right)(500)$$

$$= 525.5 \text{ Hz}$$ **Ans.**

Example 2 A whistle of frequency 540 Hz rotates in a circle of radius 2 m at a linear speed of 30 m/s. What is the lowest and highest frequency heard by an observer a long distance away at rest with respect to the centre of circle? Take speed of sound in air as 330 m/s. Can the apparent frequency be ever equal to actual?

Sol. Apparent frequency will be minimum when the source is at N and moving away from the observer.

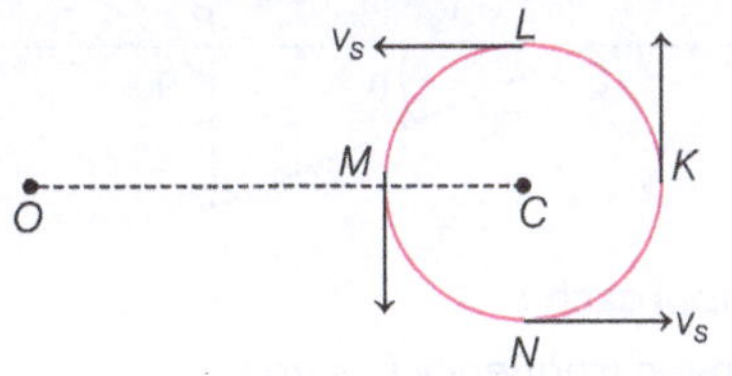

$$f_{min} = \left(\frac{v}{v+v_s}\right)f = \left(\frac{330}{330+30}\right)(540)$$

$$= 495 \text{ Hz}$$ **Ans.**

Frequency will be maximum when source is at L and approaching the observer.

$$f_{max} = \left(\frac{v}{v-v_s}\right)f$$

$$= \left(\frac{330}{330-30}\right)(540) = 594 \text{ Hz}$$ **Ans.**

Further, when the source is at M and K, angle between velocity of source and line joining source and observer is $90°$ or $v_s\cos\theta = v_s\cos 90° = 0$. So, there will be no change in the apparent frequency.

Note *Although the source velocity v_s is not along the line joining S and O but at a long distance we can assume that it is along SO. Or, $\theta \to 0$.*

Example 3 Two tuning forks with natural frequencies 340 Hz each move relative to a stationary observer. One fork moves away from the observer while the other moves towards him at the same speed. The observer hears beats of frequency 3 Hz. Find the speed of the tuning fork (velocity of sound in air is 340 m/s). **(1986 JEE)**

Note *The difference in apparent frequencies is very small (3 Hz). So, we may conclude that the speed of source $(v_s) <<$ speed of sound (v). Therefore, we can neglect the higher terms of $\frac{v_s}{v}$.*

Sol. Given, $f_1 - f_2 = 3$

or $\left(\frac{v}{v-v_s}\right)f - \left(\frac{v}{v+v_s}\right)f = 3$

or $\left[\frac{1}{\left(1-\frac{v_s}{v}\right)} - \frac{1}{\left(1+\frac{v_s}{v}\right)}\right]f = 3$

or $\left[\left(1-\frac{v_s}{v}\right)^{-1} - \left(1+\frac{v_s}{v}\right)^{-1}\right]f = 3$

or $\left[\left(1+\frac{v_s}{v}\right) - \left(1-\frac{v_s}{v}\right)\right]f = 3$

or $\frac{2v_s f}{v} = 3$

or Speed of tuning fork, $v_s = \frac{3v}{2f}$

Substituting the values, we get

$$v_s = \frac{(3)(340)}{(2)(340)} = 1.5 \text{ m/s}$$ **Ans.**

INTRODUCTORY Exercise

1. A whistle giving out 450 Hz approaches a stationary observer at a speed of 33 m/s. The frequency heard by the observer (in Hz) is (Speed of sound = 330 m/s) **(2000 JEE)**
   (a) 409 (b) 429 (c) 517 (d) 500
2. A train moves towards a stationary observer with speed 34m/s. The train sounds a whistle and its frequency registered by the observer is f_1. If the train's speed is reduced to 17 m/s, the frequency registered is f_2. If the speed of sound is 340 m/s, then the ratio f_1/f_2 is **(1997 JEE)**
   (a) 18/19 (b) 1/2
   (c) 2 (d) 19/18
3. A siren placed at a railway platform is emitting sound of frequency 5 kHz. A passenger sitting in a moving train *A* records a frequency of 5.5 kHz, while the train approaches the siren. During his return journey in a different train *B* he records a frequency of 6.0 kHz while approaching the same siren. The ratio of the velocity of train *B* to that of train *A* is **(2002 JEE)**
   (a) 242/252 (b) 2 (c) 5/6 (d) 11/6
4. A train is moving on a straight track with speed 20 ms^{-1}. It is blowing its whistle at the frequency of 1000 Hz. The percentage change in the frequency heard by a person standing near the track as the train passes him is close to (speed of sound $= 320 \text{ ms}^{-1}$) **(2015 Main)**
   (a) 12% (b) 6% (c) 18% (d) 24%

Answers

1. (d) 2. (d) 3. (b) 4. (a)

See hints on page 154.

Typed Problems

Type 1. *When $\mathbf{v}_s$ or $\mathbf{v}_o$ are not along the line joining S and O but they are very far from each other.*

Concept

In this case, we take components of $\mathbf{v}_s$ and $\mathbf{v}_o$ along the line *SO*. For example in the figure shown below,

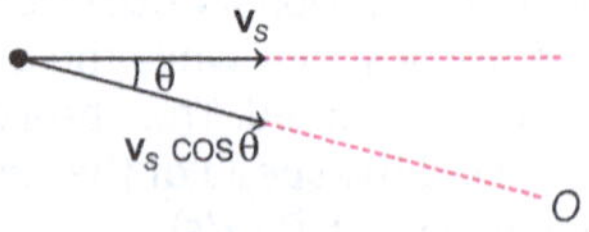

$$f' = f\left(\frac{v}{v - v_s\cos\theta}\right)$$

If source is very far from observer, then

$$\theta \to 0° \quad \text{or} \quad \cos\theta \to 1$$

$$\therefore \qquad f' = f\left(\frac{v}{v - v_s}\right)$$

Ex. 1 A source of frequency *f* is moving towards the observer along the line *SO* with a constant velocity v_s as shown in figure. Plot *f′ versus t* graph. Where *f′* is the changed frequency observed by the observer.

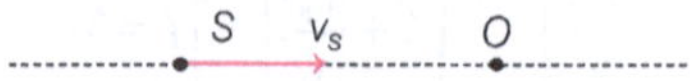

Sol. During approach :

$$f' = f\left(\frac{v}{v - v_s}\right) = f_1 \text{ (say)}$$

$$f_1 > f$$

but f_1 is constant with time.

During recede

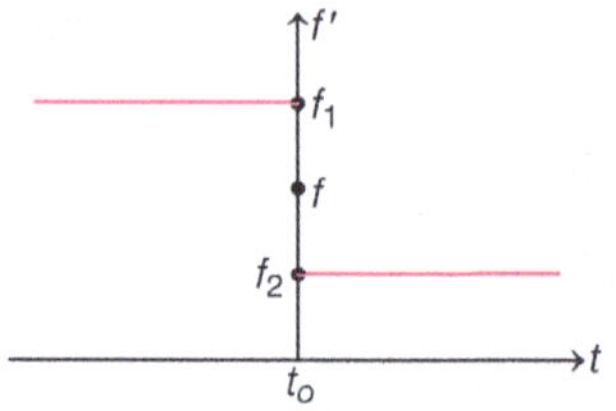

$$f' = f\left(\frac{v}{v + v_s}\right) = f_2 \qquad \text{(say)}$$

$$f_2 < f$$

But f_2 is constant with time. The correct *f′ versus t* graph is as shown.

In the figure, t_o is the time when source is crossing the observer.

Ex. 2 Repeat Ex. 1 if source does not move along the line *SO*.

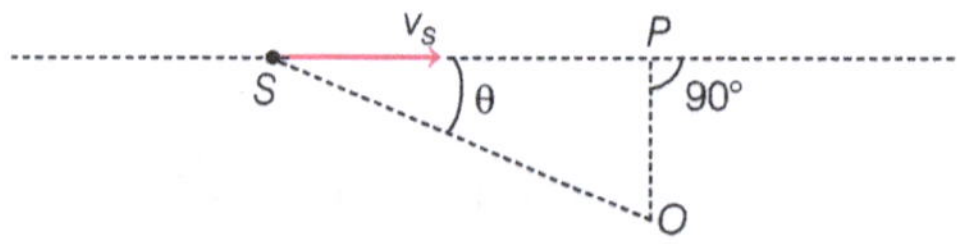

Sol. During approach :

The changed frequency *f′* is now,

$$f' = f\left(\frac{v}{v - v_s\cos\theta}\right)$$

This time *f′* is not constant but it is a function of θ, which is variable. But, at a far distance,

$\theta \to 0°$ or $\cos\theta \to 1$

$$\therefore \quad f' = f\left(\frac{v}{v - v_s}\right)$$

and this is the maximum value of f' (say f_{max})

At point P, $\theta = 90°$

$$\therefore \quad f' = f$$

During receding (to the right of P)

$$f' = f\left(\frac{v}{v + v_s\cos\theta}\right)$$

Again, at large distance from P,

$\theta \to 0°$ or $\cos\theta \to 1$

$$\therefore \quad f' = f\left(\frac{v}{v + v_s}\right)$$

This time, this is the minimum value of f' (say f_{min}).

Hence, f' varies from f_{max} to f_{min}, with $f' = f$ at the time of crossing P.

The correct f' *versus* t graph is as shown below.

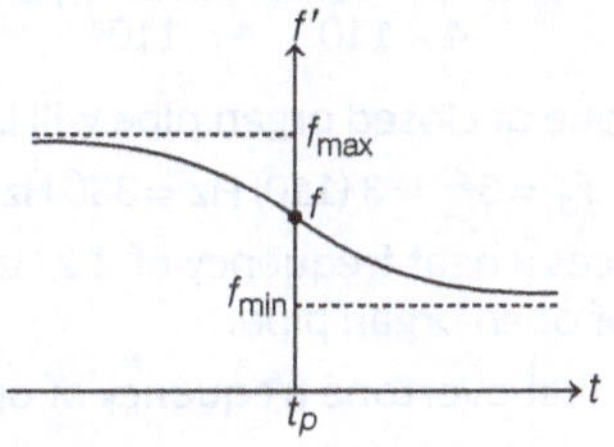

Ex. 3 A whistle emitting a sound of frequency 440 Hz is tied to a string of 1.5 m length and rotated with an angular velocity of 20 rad/s in the horizontal plane. Calculate the range of frequencies heard by an observer stationed at a large distance from the whistle. (Speed of sound = 330 m/s). **(1996 JEE)**

Sol. v_s = Speed of source (whistle) $= R\omega = (1.5)(20)$ m/s

$$\therefore \quad v_s = 30 \text{ m/s}$$

Maximum frequency will be heard by the observer in position P and minimum in position Q.

Now,

$$f_{max} = f\left(\frac{v}{v - v_s}\right)$$

where, v = speed of sound in air = 330 m/s

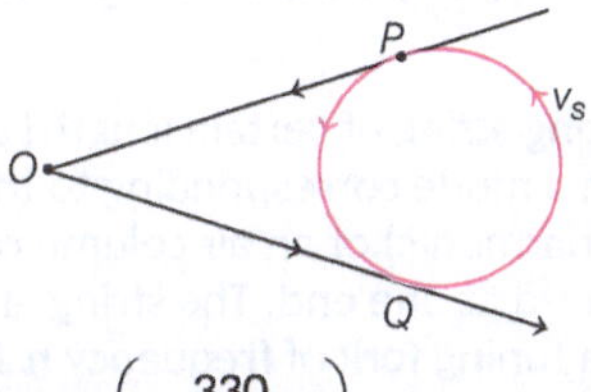

$$\therefore \quad f_{max} = (440)\left(\frac{330}{330 - 30}\right) \text{Hz} \quad \text{or} \quad f_{max} = 484 \text{ Hz}$$

and $\quad f_{min} = f\left(\frac{v}{v + v_s}\right) = (440)\left(\frac{330}{330 + 30}\right)$

$$f_{min} = 403.33 \text{ Hz}$$

Therefore, range of frequencies heard by observer is from 484 Hz to 403.33 Hz.

Type 2. *Based on a situation which is similar to Doppler's effect.*

Concept

Let us take an example.

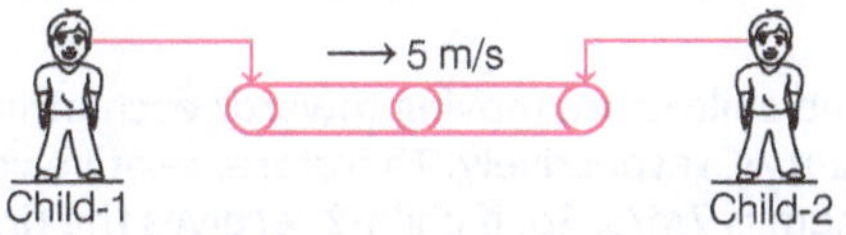

A belt shown in figure is moving with velocity 5 m/s. Child-1 is placing some coins over the belt at a regular interval of 1sec. Child -2 is receiving the coins on the other hand. Now, let us compare this situation with Doppler's effect.

Child-1 is source, child-2 is observer, velocity of belt is net velocity of sound $(= v \pm v_m)$ by which sound travels from source to observer. Actually, in this case

v = velocity of coin (similar to velocity of sound) $= 0$

v_m = velocity of medium (or velocity of belt) $= 5$ m/s

T = time interval of placing two successive coins $= 1$ sec

$\therefore \quad f = \frac{1}{T} = 1$ Hz = number of coins placed per second

λ = distance between two coins $= v_m T = 5$ m.

Now, let us consider the different cases.

Case 1 When source (child-1) and observer (child-2) both are at rest and only belt (or medium) is in motion. In this case, distance between two coins moving towards child-2 with 5 m/s is 5m. If child-2 receives first coin at time $t_1 = 0$, then he will receive the second coin at $t_2 = \frac{5 \text{ m}}{5 \text{ m/s}} = 1$ sec.

$\therefore \quad T'$ = time interval of receival of two successive coins $= t_2 - t_1 = 1$ sec

$$\therefore \quad f' = \frac{1}{T'} = 1 \text{ Hz}$$

Result By the motion of only medium, there is no change in frequency.

Case 2 If child-1 (or source) starts moving towards child-2 with 2 m/s. Then, in $T = 1$sec, belt will move a distance of 5m towards child-2 and child-1 will also travel a distance of 2m towards child-2 at the time of placing the second coin. Hence,

λ = new distance between two successive coins $= (5 - 2)$m $= 3$ m

Now, if child-2 receives the first coin at time $t_1 = 0$, then he will receive the second coin (at a distance of 3m from first coin) moving towards him with 5 m/s at time $t_2 = \frac{3}{5}$ sec.

$$\therefore \quad T' = t_2 - t_1 = \frac{3}{5}\text{sec} \quad \text{or} \quad f' = \frac{1}{T'} = \frac{5}{3}\text{Hz} \quad \text{or} \quad f' > f$$

Result By the motion of source only wavelength changes therefore frequency changes.

Case 3 Child-1 (or source) is stationary and child-2 starts moving towards child-1 with 2 m/s. This time,

λ = distance between two successive coins is unchanged or 5 m.

But coins and child-2 are moving towards each other with 5 m/s and 2 m/s, respectively. Therefore, relative velocity between them is 7m/s. So, if child-2 receives the first coin at time $t_1 = 0$, then he will receive the second coin at time

$$t_2 = \frac{5}{7}\text{sec}$$

$$\therefore \quad T' = t_2 - t_1 = \frac{5}{7}\text{sec} \quad \text{or} \quad f' = \frac{1}{T'} = \frac{7}{5}\text{Hz}$$

or $\quad f' > f$

Result By the motion of observer, relative velocity between sound and observer changes. Therefore, frequency changes.

Note *In case-2, $f' = \frac{5}{3}$Hz and in case-3, $f' = \frac{7}{5}$Hz. These two are not same, although speeds (of source and observer) are same in both cases but change in frequency is different. This is because in first case,*

$$f_1 = \left(\frac{v}{v - v_s}\right) f \text{ is used}$$

and in second case,

$$f_2 = \left(\frac{v + v_o}{v}\right) f \text{ is used. So, even if } v_s = v_o$$

$$f_1 \neq f_2.$$

Type 3. *Based on Doppler's effect and Beats.*

Concept

(i) If there is a relative motion between source and observer, frequency changes.

(ii) Natural frequencies of a stretched wire are

$$f_n = n\left(\frac{v}{2l}\right) = n\left[\frac{\sqrt{T/\mu}}{2l}\right] \qquad \text{(where } n = 1, 2, \ldots)$$

If tension in the wire is changed, then frequency changes.

(iii) Natural frequencies of a closed pipe are

$$f_n = n\left(\frac{v}{4l}\right) \qquad \text{(where } n = 1, 3, \ldots)$$

and natural frequencies of an open pipe are

$$f_n = n\left(\frac{v}{2l}\right) \qquad \text{(where } n = 1, 2, \ldots)$$

Here, $\quad v = \sqrt{\frac{\gamma RT}{M}}$

When temperature changes, these sets of frequencies also change.

(iv) Beat frequency is given by

$$f_b = f_1 - f_2 \qquad (\text{if } f_1 > f_2)$$

Ex. 4 The first overtone of an open organ pipe beats with the first overtone of a closed organ pipe with a beat frequency of 2.2 Hz. The fundamental frequency of the closed organ pipe is 110 Hz. Find the lengths of the pipes. Speed of sound in air $v = 330$ m/s.

Sol. Let l_1 and l_2 be the lengths of closed and open pipes respectively.

Fundamental frequency of closed organ pipe is given by

$$f_1 = \frac{v}{4l}$$

$$\therefore \quad \frac{v}{4l_1} = 110 \text{ Hz}$$

$$\therefore \quad l_1 = \frac{v}{4 \times 110} = \frac{330}{4 \times 110} \text{ m} = 0.75 \text{ m}$$

First overtone of closed organ pipe will be

$$f_3 = 3f_1 = 3\,(110) \text{ Hz} = 330 \text{ Hz}$$

This produces a beat frequency of 2.2 Hz with first overtone of open organ pipe.

Therefore, first overtone frequency of open organ pipe is either

$$(330 + 2.2) \text{ Hz} = 332.2 \text{ Hz}$$

or $\quad (330 - 2.2) \text{ Hz} = 327.8 \text{ Hz}$

If it is 332.2 Hz, then

$$2\left(\frac{v}{2l_2}\right) = 332.2 \text{ Hz}$$

or $\quad l_2 = \frac{v}{332.2} = \frac{330}{332.2} \text{ m} = 0.99 \text{ m}$

and if it is 327.8 Hz, then

$$2\left(\frac{v}{2l_2}\right) = 327.8 \text{ Hz}$$

or $\quad l_2 = \frac{v}{327.8} \text{ m} = \frac{330}{327.8} \text{ m} = 1.0067 \text{ m}$

Therefore, length of the closed organ pipe is $l_1 = 0.75$ m while length of open pipe is either $l_2 = 0.99$ m or 1.0067 m. **Ans.**

Ex. 5 A vibrating string of certain length l under a tension T resonates with a mode corresponding to the first overtone (third harmonic) of an air column of length 75 cm inside a tube closed at one end. The string also generates 4 beats/s with a tuning fork of frequency n. Now when the tension of the string is slightly increased the number of beats reduces to 2 per second. Assuming the velocity of sound in air to be 340 m/s, the frequency n of the tuning fork in Hz is **(2008 JEE)**

(a) 344 (b) 336

(c) 117.3 (d) 109.3

Sol. With increase in tension, frequency of vibrating string will increase. Since, number of beats are decreasing. Therefore, frequency of vibrating string or third harmonic frequency of closed pipe should be less than the frequency of tuning fork by 4.

$\therefore$ Frequency of tuning fork = third harmonic frequency of closed pipe + 4

$$= 3\left(\frac{v}{4l}\right) + 4 = 3\left(\frac{340}{4 \times 0.75}\right) + 4$$

$$= 344 \text{ Hz}$$

$\therefore$ Correct option is (a).

Ex. 6 Two identical straight wires are stretched so as to produce 6 beats/s when vibrating simultaneously. On changing the tension slightly in one of them, the beat frequency remains unchanged. Denoting by T_1, T_2 the higher and the lower initial tension in the strings, then it could be said that while making the above changes in tension **(1991 JEE)**

(a) T_2 was decreased (b) T_2 was increased

(c) T_1 was decreased (d) T_1 was increased

Sol. $T_1 > T_2$

$\therefore$ $v_1 > v_2$

or $f_1 > f_2$

and $f_1 - f_2 = 6 \text{ Hz}$

Now, if T_1 is increased, f_1 will increase or $f_1 - f_2$ will increase. Therefore, (d) option is wrong.

If T_1 is decreased, f_1 will decrease and it may be possible that now $f_2 - f_1$ become 6 Hz. Therefore, (c) option is correct.

Similarly, when T_2 is increased, f_2 will increase and again $f_2 - f_1$ may become equal to 6 Hz. So, (b) is also correct. But (a) is wrong.

$\therefore$ The correct options are (b) and (c).

Ex. 7 A sonometer wire under tension of 64 N vibrating in its fundamental mode is in resonance with a vibrating tuning fork. The vibrating portion of the sonometer wire has a length of 10 cm and mass of 1 g. The vibrating tuning fork is now moved away from the vibrating wire with a constant speed and an observer standing near the sonometer hears one beat per second. Calculate the speed with which the tuning fork is moved, if the speed of sound in air is 300 m/s. **(1983 JEE)**

Sol. Fundamental frequency of sonometer wire,

$$f = \frac{v}{2l} = \frac{1}{2l}\sqrt{\frac{T}{\mu}}$$

$$= \frac{1}{2 \times 0.1}\sqrt{\frac{64 \times 0.1}{10^{-3}}}$$

$$= 400 \text{ Hz}$$

Given beat frequency, $f_b = f - f' = 1 \text{ Hz}$

$\therefore$ $f' = 399 \text{ Hz}$

Using $f' = f\left(\frac{v}{v + v_s}\right)$

or $399 = 400\left(\frac{300}{300 + v_s}\right)$

Solving we get, $v_s = 0.75 \text{ m/s}$ **Ans.**

Type 4. *Reflection of a sound from a wall and beats.*

Concept

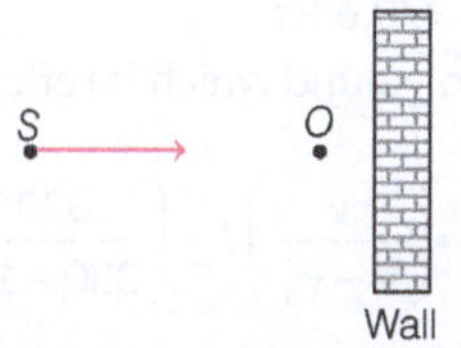

A source of sound is approaching towards a wall. An observer hears two sounds. One is direct from the source and the other reflected from the wall. If both frequencies are same, then the observer will hear no beats and if there is a frequency difference then beats are heard to the observer. This all depends on the position of observer. For finding the frequency of reflected sound we can use the following two approaches.

Approach 1 Take the wall as a plane mirror. Image of S on this plane mirror will behave like another source S' for the reflected sound.

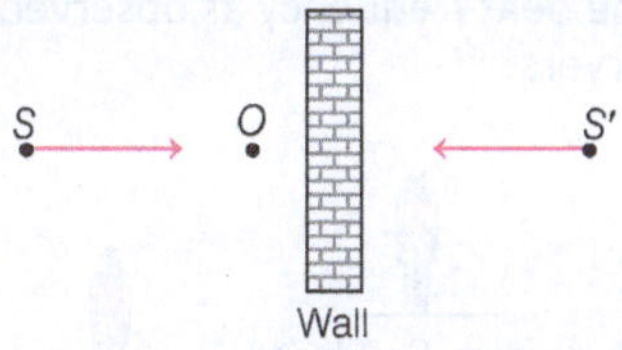

For example, in the shown figure both direct sound source S and reflected sound source S' are approaching towards the observer.

Approach 2 First consider wall as an observer for the sound received to it from the source S. Now, consider this wall as a source for reflected sound.

Ex. 8 A siren emitting a sound of frequency 1000 Hz moves away from you towards a cliff at a speed of 10 m/s.

(a) What is the frequency of the sound you hear coming directly from the siren?

(b) What is the frequency of the sound you hear reflected off the cliff?

(c) What beat frequency would you hear? Take the speed of sound in air as 330 m/s.

Sol. The situation is as shown in figure.

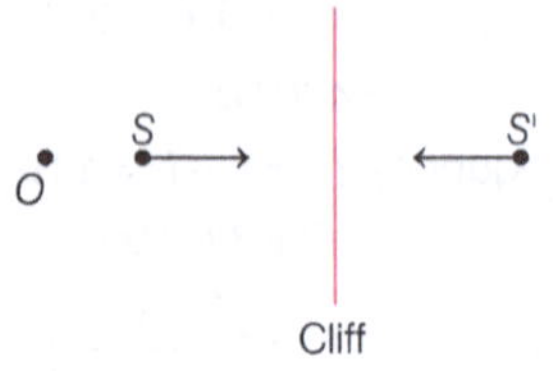

(a) Frequency of sound reaching directly to us (by S)

$$f_1 = \left(\frac{v}{v+v_s}\right)$$

$$f = \left(\frac{330}{330+10}\right)(1000)$$

$$= 970.6 \text{ Hz}$$ **Ans.**

(b) Frequency of sound which is reflected from the cliff (from S')

$$f_2 = \left(\frac{v}{v-v_s}\right) f = \left(\frac{330}{330-10}\right)(1000)$$

$$= 1031.3 \text{ Hz}$$ **Ans.**

(c) Beat frequency $= f_2 - f_1$

$$= 60.7 \text{ Hz}$$ **Ans.**

Note *Numerically the beat frequency comes out to be 60.7 Hz. But, beats between two tones can be detected by ear upto a frequency of about 7 per second. At higher frequencies beats cannot be distinguished in the sound produced. Hence, the correct answer of part (c) should be zero.*

Ex. 9 A source of sound of frequency f is approaching towards a wall with speed v_s. Speed of sound is v. Three observers O_1, O_2 and O_3 are at different locations as shown. Find the beat frequency as observed by three different observers.

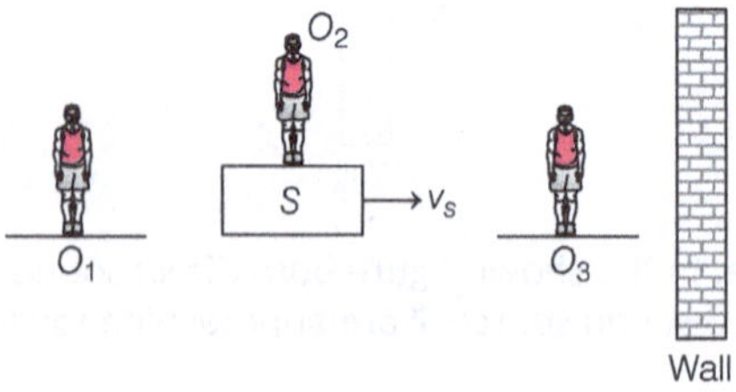

Sol. For reflected sound we can take wall as a plane mirror.

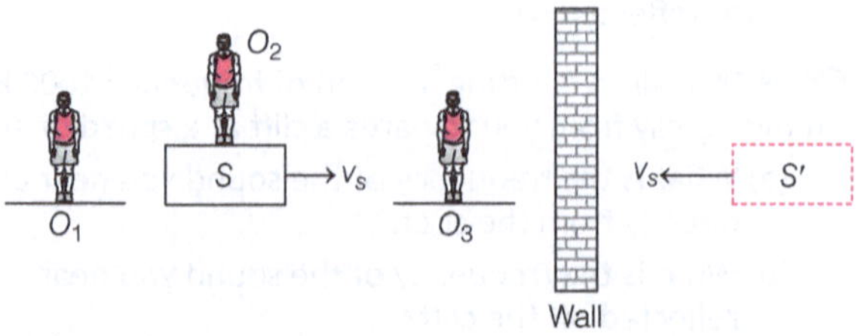

Observer O_1 S is receding from O_1 and S' is approaching towards him. So,

$$f_{s'} > f_s$$

$$f_b = f_{s'} - f_s$$

$$= f\left(\frac{v}{v-v_s}\right) - f\left(\frac{v}{v+v_s}\right)$$

$$= \left(\frac{2vv_s}{v^2 - v_s^2}\right) f$$ **Ans.**

Observer O_2 O_2 has no relative motion with S. Therefore, there will be no change in the frequency of direct sound from S. Further, O_2 and S' are approaching towards each other. Therefore, the frequency of reflected sound will increase.

$$f_b = f_{s'} - f_s$$

$$= f\left(\frac{v+v_{O_2}}{v-v_s}\right) - f$$

But $v_{O_2} = v_s$

$$\therefore \quad f_b = f\left(\frac{v+v_s}{v-v_s}\right) - f$$

$$= \left(\frac{2v_s}{v-v_s}\right) f$$ **Ans.**

Observer O_3 S and S' both are approaching towards O_3. So, both frequencies will increase. But after the increase they are equal. So, beat frequency will be zero.

$$f_s = f_{s'} = f\left(\frac{v}{v-v_s}\right)$$

$$\therefore \quad f_b = f_s - f_{s'} = 0$$

Ex. 10 A sound wave of frequency f travels horizontally to the right. It is reflected from a large vertical plane surface moving to left with a speed v. The speed of sound in medium is c **(1995 JEE)**

(a) The number of waves striking the surface per second is $f\dfrac{(c+v)}{c}$

(b) The wavelength of reflected wave is $\dfrac{c(c-v)}{f(c+v)}$

(c) The frequency of the reflected wave is $f\dfrac{(c+v)}{(c-v)}$

(d) The number of beats heard by a stationary listener to the left of the reflecting surface is $\dfrac{vf}{c-v}$

Sol. Moving plane is like a moving observer. Therefore, number of waves encountered by moving plane,

$$f_1 = f\left(\frac{v_{\text{sound}} + v_{\text{observer}}}{v_{\text{sound}}}\right) = f\left(\frac{c+v}{c}\right)$$

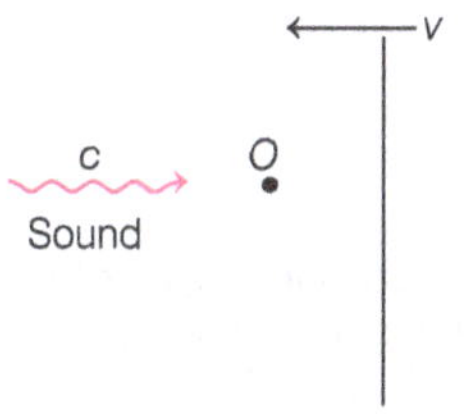

Frequency of reflected wave,

$$f_2 = f_1 \left(\frac{v_{sound}}{v_{sound} - v_{source}} \right) = f \left(\frac{c + v}{c - v} \right)$$

Wavelength of reflected wave, $\lambda_2 = \frac{c}{f_2} = \frac{c}{f} \left(\frac{c - v}{c + v} \right)$

Beat frequency, $f_b = f_2 - f = f \left(\frac{c + v}{c - v} \right) - f = \frac{2fv}{c - v}$

Therefore, the correct options are (a), (b) and (c).

Miscellaneous Examples

Ex. 11 A fighter plane moving in a vertical loop with constant speed of radius R. The centre of the loop is at a height h directly overhead of an observer standing on the ground. The observer receives maximum frequency of the sound produced by the plane when it is nearest to him. Find the speed of the plane. Velocity of sound in air is v.

Sol. Let the speed of the plane (source) be v_s. Maximum frequency will be observed by the observer when v_s is along SO. The observer receives maximum frequency when the plane is nearest to him. That is as soon as the wave pulse reaches from S to O with speed v the plane reaches from S to S' with speed v_s. Hence,

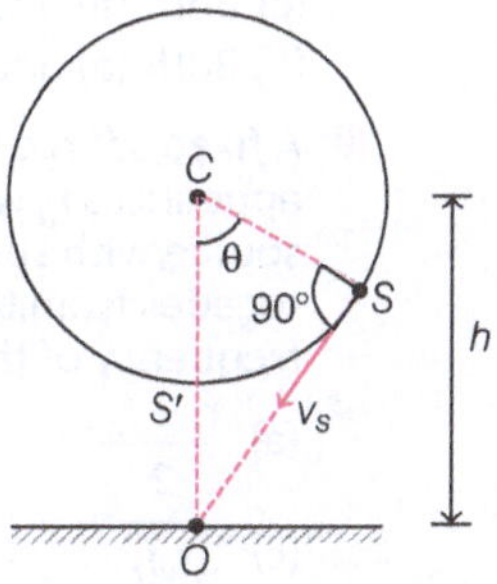

$$t = \frac{SO}{v} = \frac{SS'}{v_s}$$

or $$v_s = \left(\frac{SS'}{SO} \right) v = \frac{R\theta}{\sqrt{h^2 - R^2}} v$$ **Ans.**

Here, $\cos \theta = \frac{R}{h}$ or $\theta = \cos^{-1} \left(\frac{R}{h} \right)$

Ex. 12 A boat is travelling in a river with a speed 10 m/s along the stream flowing with a speed 2 m/s. From this boat, a sound transmitter is lowered into the river through a rigid support. The wavelength of the sound emitted from the transmitter inside the water is 14.45 mm. Assume that attenuation of sound in water and air is negligible.

(a) What will be the frequency detected by a receiver kept inside the river downstream?

(b) The transmitter and the receiver are now pulled up into air. The air is blowing with a speed 5 m/s in the direction opposite the river stream. Determine the frequency of the sound detected by the receiver.

(Temperature of the air and water = 20°C; Density of river water = 10^3 kg/m^3; Bulk modulus of the water = 2.088×10^9 Pa; Gas constant, $R = 8.31$ J/mol-K; Mean molecular mass of air = 28.8×10^{-3} kg/mol; C_p/C_V for air = 1.4) **(2001 JEE)**

Sol. Velocity of sound in water is

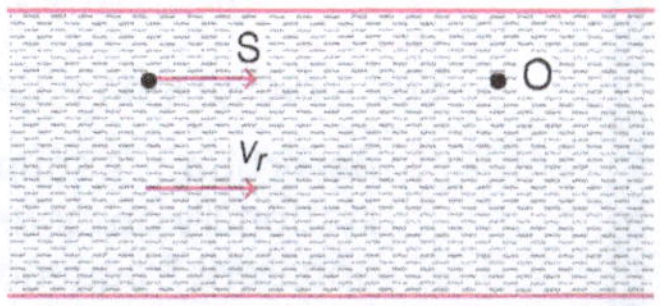

$$v_w = \sqrt{\frac{B}{\rho}} = \sqrt{\frac{2.088 \times 10^9}{10^3}} = 1445 \text{ m/s}$$

Frequency of sound in water will be

$$f = \frac{v_w}{\lambda_w} = \frac{1445}{14.45 \times 10^{-3}} \text{ Hz}$$

$$f = 10^5 \text{ Hz}$$

(a) Frequency of sound detected by receiver (observer) at rest in water would be

$$f_1 = f \left(\frac{v_w + v_r}{v_w + v_r - v_s} \right) = (10^5) \left(\frac{1445 + 2}{1445 + 2 - 10} \right) \text{Hz}$$

$$f_1 = 1.0069 \times 10^5 \text{ Hz}$$ **Ans.**

(b) Velocity of sound in air is

$$v_a = \sqrt{\frac{\gamma RT}{M}} = \sqrt{\frac{(1.4)(8.31)(20 + 273)}{28.8 \times 10^{-3}}}$$

$$= 344 \text{ m/s}$$

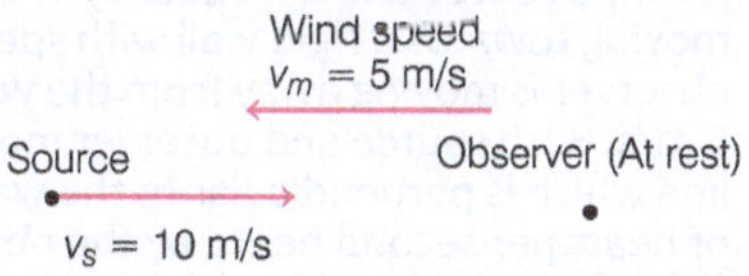

Frequency does not depend on the medium. Therefore, frequency in air is also $f = 10^5$ Hz.

∴ Frequency of sound detected by receiver (observer) in air would be

$$f_2 = f \left(\frac{v_a - v_w}{v_a - v_w - v_s} \right) = 10^5 \left[\frac{344 - 5}{344 - 5 - 10} \right] \text{Hz}$$

$$f_2 = 1.0304 \times 10^5 \text{ Hz}$$ **Ans.**

MODULE 7 Exercise

Fill in the Blank

1. A bus is moving towards a huge wall with a velocity of $5\ ms^{-1}$. The driver sounds a horn of frequency 200 Hz. The frequency of the beats heard by a passenger of the bus will be .... Hz (Speed of sound in air $= 342\ ms^{-1}$) **(1994 JEE)**

True/False

2. A source of sound with frequency 256 Hz is moving with a velocity v towards a wall and an observer is stationary between the source and he will hear beats. **(1985 JEE)**

Assertion and Reason

See directions on page 14.

3. **Assertion :** A sound source is approaching towards a stationary observer along the line joining them. Then, apparent frequency to the observer will go on increasing.

   Reason : If there is no relative motion between source and observer, apparent frequency is equal to the actual frequency.

Single Correct Option

4. When a source is going away from a stationary observer with the velocity equal to that of sound in air, then the frequency heard by observer is n times the original frequency. The value of n is

   (a) 0.5 (b) 0.25
   (c) 1.0 (d) No sound is heard

5. A vehicle, with a horn of frequency n is moving with a velocity of 30 m/s in a direction perpendicular to the straight line joining the observer and the vehicle. The observer perceives the sound to have a frequency $(n + n_1)$. If the sound velocity in air is 300 m/s, then

   (a) $n_1 = 10n$ (b) $n_1 = 0$
   (c) $n_1 = 0.1n$ (d) $n_1 = -0.1n$

6. A sound source emits frequency of 180 Hz when moving towards a rigid wall with speed 5 m/s and an observer is moving away from the wall with speed 5 m/s. Both source and observer moves on a straight line which is perpendicular to the wall. The number of beats per second heard by the observer will be [speed of sound = 355 m/s]

   (a) 5 Hz (b) 10 Hz
   (c) 6 Hz (d) 8 Hz

7. Two sound waves of wavelengths λ_1 and λ_2 $(\lambda_2 > \lambda_1)$ produce n beats/s, the speed of sound is

   (a) $\dfrac{n\lambda_1\lambda_2}{\lambda_2 - \lambda_1}$ (b) $n\left(\dfrac{1}{\lambda_1} - \dfrac{1}{\lambda_2}\right)$
   (c) $n(\lambda_2 - \lambda_1)$ (d) $n(\lambda_2 + \lambda_1)$

8. One train is approaching an observer at rest and another train is receding from him with the same velocity 4 m/s. Both trains blow whistles of same frequency of 243 Hz. The beat frequency in Hz as heard by the observer is (speed of sound in air = 320 m/s)

   (a) 10 (b) 6
   (c) 4 (d) 1

9. Two persons A and B, each carrying a source of frequency 300 Hz, are standing a few metre apart. A starts moving towards B with velocity 30 m/s. If the speed of sound is 300 m/s, which of the following is true?

   (a) Number of beats heard by A is higher than the beats heard by B
   (b) The number of beats heard by B are 30 Hz
   (c) Both (a) and (b) are correct
   (d) Both (a) and (b) are wrong

10. A fixed source of sound emitting a certain frequency appears as f_a when the observer is approaching the source with speed v_0 and f_r when the observer recedes from the source with the same speed. The frequency of the source is

   (a) $\dfrac{f_r + f_a}{2}$ (b) $\dfrac{f_r - f_a}{2}$
   (c) $\sqrt{f_a f_r}$ (d) $\dfrac{2f_r f_a}{f_r + f_a}$

11. A small source of sound moves in a circle as shown in the figure and an observer is standing as shown. Let n_1, n_2 and n_3 be the frequencies heard when the source is at A, B and C respectively. Then,

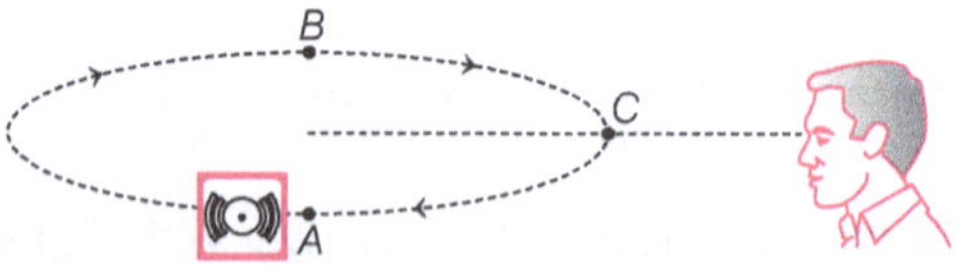

   (a) $n_1 > n_2 > n_3$
   (b) $n_2 > n_3 > n_1$
   (c) $n_1 = n_2 > n_3$
   (d) $n_2 > n_1 > n_3$

12. When an observer moves towards a stationary source with a certain velocity, he observes an apparent frequency f. When it moves away from the source with same velocity, the observed frequency is $0.8f$. If the velocity of sound is v, then the speed of the observer is

   (a) $\dfrac{v}{4}$ (b) $\dfrac{v}{8}$
   (c) $\dfrac{v}{9}$ (d) None of these

13. A locomotive engine approaches a railway station and whistles at a frequency of 400 Hz. A stationary observer on the platform observes a change of 40 Hz as the engine passes across him. If the velocity of sound is 340 m/s, the speed of the engine is
(a) 34 m/s (b) 40 m/s (c) 17 m/s (d) 20 m/s

14. Two cars are moving on two perpendicular roads towards a crossing with uniform speeds of 72 km/h and 36 km/h. If first car blows horn of frequency 280 Hz, then the frequency of horn heard by the driver of second car when line joining the cars make 45° angle with the roads, will be
(a) 321 Hz (b) 298 Hz (c) 289 Hz (d) 280 Hz

15. The engine of a train moving with speed $10\ ms^{-1}$ towards a platform sounds a whistle at frequency 400 Hz. The frequency heard by a passenger inside the train is (Speed of sound in air $= 330\ ms^{-1}$) **(2023 Main)**
(a) 400 Hz (b) 388 Hz
(c) 412 Hz (d) 200 Hz

16. A car P travelling at $20\ ms^{-1}$ sounds its horn at a frequency of 400 Hz. Another car Q is travelling behind the first car in the same direction with a velocity $40\ ms^{-1}$. The frequency heard by the passenger of the car Q is approximately
(Take, velocity of sound $= 360\ ms^{-1}$) **(2023 Main)**
(a) 471 Hz (b) 421 Hz
(c) 485 Hz (d) 514 Hz

17. A person observes two moving trains, A reaching the station and B leaving the station with equal speed of 30 m/s. If both trains emit sounds with frequency 300 Hz, (Speed of sound: 330 m/s) approximate difference of frequencies heard by the person will be **(2023 Main)**
(a) 55 Hz (b) 10 Hz
(c) 80 Hz (d) 33 Hz

18. For a specific wavelength 670 nm of light coming from a galaxy moving with velocity v, the observed wavelength is 670.7 nm. the value of v is **(2022 Main)**
(a) $3 \times 10^8\ ms^{-1}$ (b) $3 \times 10^{10}\ ms^{-1}$
(c) $3.13 \times 10^5\ ms^{-1}$ (d) $4.48 \times 10^5\ ms^{-1}$

19. A stationary observer receives sound from two identical tuning forks, one of which approaches and the other one recedes with the same speed (much less than the speed of sound). The observer hears 2 beats/s. The oscillation frequency of each tuning fork is $f_0 = 1400$ Hz Hz and the velocity of sound in air is 350 m/s. The speed of each tuning fork is close to **(2020 Main)**
(a) $\frac{1}{2}$ m/s (b) 1 m/s (c) $\frac{1}{4}$ m/s (d) $\frac{1}{8}$ m/s

20. Two sources of sound S_1 and S_2 produce sound waves of same frequency 660 Hz. A listener is moving from source S_1 towards S_2 with a constant speed u m/s and he hears 10 beats/s. The velocity of sound is 330 m/s. Then u equals **(2019 Main)**
(a) 5.5 m/s (b) 15.0 m/s (c) 2.5 m/s (d) 10.0 m/s

21. Two engines pass each other moving in opposite directions with uniform speed of 30 m/s. One of them is blowing a whistle of frequency 540 Hz. Calculate the frequency heard by driver of second engine before they pass each other. Speed of sound is 330 m/s. **(2016 Main)**
(a) 450 Hz (b) 540 Hz (c) 270 Hz (d) 648 Hz

Subjective Questions

22. A railroad train is travelling at 30 m/s in still air. The frequency of the note emitted by the locomotive whistle is 500 Hz. What is the wavelength of the sound waves :
(a) in front of the locomotive?
(b) behind the locomotive?
What is the frequency of the sound heard by a stationary listener
(c) in front of the locomotive?
(d) behind the locomotive?
(Speed of sound in air is 344 m/s.)

23. A sound source moves with a speed of 80 m/s relative to still air toward a stationary listener. The frequency of sound is 200 Hz and speed of sound in air is 340 m/s.
(a) Find the wavelength of the sound between the source and the listener.
(b) Find the frequency heard by the listener.

24. A 300 Hz source, an observer and a wind are moving as shown in the figure with respect to the ground. What frequency is heard by the observer? Take speed of sound in air = 340 m/s.

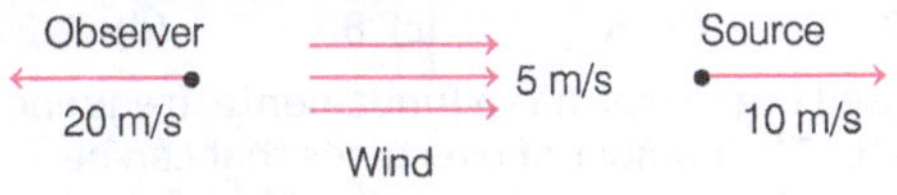

Answers

1. (6)	**2.** (False)	**3.** (d)	**4.** (a)	**5.** (b)	**6.** (a)	**7.** (a)	**8.** (b)	**9.** (d)	**10.** (a)
11. (b)	**12.** (c)	**13.** (c)	**14.** (b)	**15.** (a)	**16.** (b)	**17.** (a)	**18.** (c)	**19.** (c)	**20.** (c)

21. (d) **22.** (a) 0.628 m (b) 0.748 m (c) 548 Hz (d) 460 Hz **23.** (a) 1.3 m (b) 262 Hz **24.** 274 Hz

See hints on pages 154-156.

Unit Exercise (Cumulative)

Level 1

Fill in the Blank

1. Sound waves of frequency 660 Hz fall normally on a perfectly reflecting wall. The shortest distance from the wall at which the air particles have maximum amplitude of vibration is .... metres. **(1984 JEE)**
   (Velocity of sound in air is 330 m/s)

Single Correct Option

2. A progressive wave of frequency 500 Hz is travelling with a speed of 350 m/s. A compressional maximum appears at a place at a given instant. The minimum time interval after which a rarefaction maximum occurs at the same point is
   (a) $\frac{1}{150}$ s (b) $\frac{1}{500}$ s (c) $\frac{1}{1000}$ s (d) $\frac{1}{350}$ s
3. When interference is produced by two progressive waves of equal frequencies and amplitudes, then the maximum intensity of the resulting sound are N times the intensity of each of the component waves. The value of N is
   (a) 1 (b) 2 (c) 4 (d) 8
4. The fundamental frequency of a closed pipe is 220 Hz. If $\frac{1}{4}$ of the pipe is filled with water, the frequency of the first overtone of the pipe now is
   (a) 220 Hz (b) 440 Hz (c) 880 Hz (d) 1760 Hz
5. A closed organ pipe and an open organ pipe of same length produce 2 beats/s while vibrating in their fundamental modes. The length of the open organ pipe is halved and that of closed pipe is doubled. Then, the number of beats produced per second while vibrating in the fundamental mode is
   (a) 2 (b) 6 (c) 8 (d) 7
6. A closed organ pipe has a fundamental frequency of 1.5 kHz. The number of overtones that can be distinctly heard by a person with this organ pipe will be (assume that the highest frequency a person can hear is 20,000 Hz) **(2019 Main)**
   (a) 6 (b) 4
   (c) 7 (d) 5
7. The end correction of a resonance column is 1 cm. If the shortest length resonating with the tuning fork is 10 cm, the next resonating length should be **(2018 Main)**
   (a) 32 cm (b) 40 cm
   (c) 28 cm (d) 36 cm
8. If λ_1, λ_2 and λ_3 are the wavelengths of the waves giving resonance with the fundamental, first and second overtones respectively of a closed organ pipe. Then, the ratio of wavelengths $\lambda_1 : \lambda_2 : \lambda_3$ is
   (a) $1:3:5$ (b) $1:2:3$ (c) $5:3:1$ (d) $1:\frac{1}{3}:\frac{1}{5}$
9. A pipe of length 85 cm is closed from one end. Find the number of possible natural oscillations of air column in the pipe whose frequencies lie below 1250 Hz. The velocity of sound in air is 340 m/s. **(2014 Main)**
   (a) 12 (b) 8 (c) 6 (d) 4
10. The end correction of a resonance column is 1.0 cm. If the shortest length resonating with the tuning fork is 15.0 cm, the next resonating length will be
    (a) 31 cm (b) 45 cm (c) 46 cm (d) 47 cm
11. A hollow pipe of length 0.8 m is closed at one end. At its open end a 0.5 m long uniform string is vibrating in its second harmonic and it resonates with the fundamental frequency of the pipe. If the tension in the wire is 50 N and the speed of sound is 320 ms^{-1}, the mass of the string is **(2010 JEE)**
    (a) 5 g (b) 10 g (c) 20 g (d) 40 g
12. A bat moving at 10 ms^{-1} towards a wall sends a sound signal of 8000 Hz towards it. On reflection it hears a sound of frequency f. The value of f in Hz is close to (speed of sound = 320 ms^{-1}) **(2015 Main)**
    (a) 8516 (b) 8258 (c) 8424 (d) 8000
13. Two factories are sounding their sirens at 800 Hz. A man goes from one factory to other at a speed of 2m/s. The velocity of sound is 320 m/s. The number of beats heard by the person in one second will be **(2014 Main)**
    (a) 2 (b) 4 (c) 8 (d) 10
14. A police car moving at 22 m/s, chases a motorcyclist. The police man sounds his horn at 176 Hz, while both of them move towards a stationary siren of frequency 165 Hz. Calculate the speed of the motorcycle, if it is given that he does not observe any beats. **(2003 JEE)**

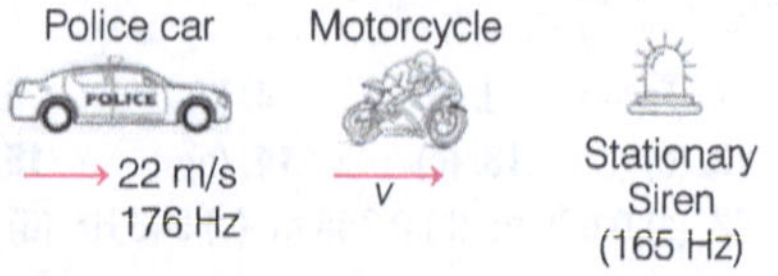

    (a) 33 m/s (b) 22 m/s (c) zero (d) 11 m/s

Multiple Correct Options

15. In an experiment to measure the speed of sound by a resonating air column, a tuning fork of frequency 500 Hz is used. The length of the air column is varied by changing the level of water in the resonance tube. Two successive resonances are heard at air columns of length 50.7 cm and 83.9 cm. Which of the following statements is (are) true? **(2017 Adv.)**
(a) The speed of sound determined from this experiment is 332 ms^{-1}
(b) The magnitude of end correction in this experiment is 0.9 cm
(c) The wavelength of the sound wave is 66.4 cm
(d) The resonance at 50.7 cm corresponds to the fundamental harmonic

Match the Columns

16. I represents intensity of sound wave, A the amplitude and r the distance from the source. Then, match the following two columns.

	Column I		Column II
(a)	Intensity due to a point source.	(p)	proportional to $r^{-1/2}$
(b)	Amplitude due to a point source.	(q)	proportional to r^{-1}
(c)	Intensity due to a line source.	(r)	proportional to r^{-2}
(d)	Amplitude due to a line source.	(s)	proportional to r^{-4}

Subjective Questions

17. A tuning fork of frequency 256 Hz produces 4 beats per second with a wire of length 25 cm vibrating in its fundamental mode. The beat frequency decreases when the length is slightly shortened. What could be the minimum length by which the wire be shortened so that it produces no beats with the tuning fork?

18. The speed of a certain compressional wave in air at standard temperature and pressure is 330 m/s. A point source of frequency 300 Hz radiates energy uniformly in all directions at the rate of 5 Watt.
(a) What is the intensity of the wave at a distance of 20 m from the source?
(b) What is the amplitude of the wave there?
[Density of air at STP $= 1.29\ kg/m^3$]

19. (a) A longitudinal wave propagating in a water-filled pipe has intensity $3.00 \times 10^{-6}\ W/m^2$ and frequency 3400 Hz. Find the amplitude A and wavelength λ of the wave. Water has density 1000 kg/m^3 and bulk modulus 2.18×10^9 Pa.
(b) If the pipe is filled with air at pressure 1.00×10^5 Pa and density 1.20 kg/m^3, what will be the amplitude A and wavelength λ of a longitudinal wave with the same intensity and frequency as in part (a)?
(c) In which fluid is the amplitude larger, water or air? What is the ratio of the two amplitudes? Why is this ratio so different from one? Consider air as diatomic.

20. The atomic mass of iodine is 127 g/mol. A standing wave in iodine vapour at 400 K has nodes that are 6.77 cm apart when the frequency is 1000 Hz. At this temperature, is iodine vapour monoatomic or diatomic.

21. A uniform tube of length 60 cm stands vertically with its lower end dipping into water. First two air column lengths above water are 15 cm and 45 cm, when the tube responds to a vibrating fork of frequency 500 Hz. Find the lowest frequency to which the tube will respond when it is open at both ends.

22. Write the equation for the fundamental standing sound waves in a tube that is open at both ends. If the tube is 80 cm long and speed of the wave is 330 m/s. Represent the amplitude of the wave at an antinode by A.

23. A long glass tube is held vertically, dipping into water, while a tuning fork of frequency 512 Hz is repeatedly struck and held over the open end. Strong resonance is obtained, when the length of the tube above the surface of water is 50 cm and again 84 cm, but not at any intermediate point. Find the speed of sound in air and next length of the air column for resonance.

24. A closed organ pipe is sounded near a guitar, causing one of the strings to vibrate with large amplitude. We vary the tension of the string until we find the maximum amplitude. The string is 80% as long as the closed pipe. If both the pipe and the string vibrate at their fundamental frequency, calculate the ratio of the wave speed on the string to the speed of sound in air.

25. Two identical violin strings, when in tune and stretched with the same tension, have a fundamental frequency of 440.0 Hz. One of the string is retuned by adjusting its tension. When this is done, 1.5 beats per second are heard when both strings are plucked simultaneously. (a) What are the possible fundamental frequencies of the retuned string? (b) By what fractional amount was the string tension changed if it was (i) increased (ii) decreased?

26. A railroad train is travelling at 30.0 m/s in still air. The frequency of the note emitted by the train whistle is 262 Hz. What frequency is heard by a passenger on a train moving in the opposite direction to the first at 18.0 m/s and (a) approaching the first? (b) receding from the first? Speed of sound in air $= 340$ m/s.

27. A boy is walking away from a wall at a speed of 1.0 m/s in a direction at right angles to the wall. As he walks, he blows a whistle steadily. An observer towards whom the boy is walking hears 4.0 beats per second. If the speed of sound is 340 m/s, what is the frequency of the whistle?

28. A tuning fork P of unknown frequency gives 7 beats in 2 seconds with another tuning fork Q. When Q runs towards a wall with a speed of 5 m/s it gives 5 beats per second with its echo. On loading P with wax, it gives 5 beats per second with Q. What is the frequency of P ? Assume speed of sound $= 332$ m/s.

29. A train approaching a hill at a speed of 40 km/h sounds a whistle of frequency 580 Hz when it is at a distance of 1 km from a hill. A wind with a speed of 40 km/h is blowing in the direction of motion of the train. Find **(1998 JEE)**
   (a) the frequency of the whistle as heard by an observer on the hill,
   (b) the distance from the hill at which the echo from the hill is heard by the driver and its frequency.
   (Velocity of sound in air = 1200 km/h)

30. A band playing music at a frequency f is moving towards a wall at a speed v_b. A motorist is following the band with a speed v_m. If v is the speed of sound, obtain an expression for the beat frequency heard by the motorist. **(1997 JEE)**

31. How long will it take for the sound waves to travel the distance l between two points A and B if the air temperature between them varies linearly from T_1 to T_2? The velocity of sound propagation in air is equal to $v = \alpha\sqrt{T}$, where α is a constant. **(4.150 Irodov)**

32. To determine the sound velocity in air by acoustic resonance technique one can use a pipe with a piston and a sonic membrane closing one of its ends. Find the velocity of sound if the distance between the adjacent positions of the piston at which resonance is observed at a frequency $f = 2000$ Hz is equal to $l = 8.5$ cm. **(Irodov 4.169)**

33. Find the number of possible natural oscillations of air column in a pipe whose frequencies lie below $f_0 = 1250$ Hz. The length of the pipe is $l = 85$ cm. The velocity of sound is $v = 340$ m/s. Consider the two cases:
   (a) the pipe is closed from one end;
   (b) the pipe is opened from both ends. **(Irodov 4.170)**
   The open ends of the pipe are assumed to be the antinodes of displacement.

34. A source of sonic oscillations with frequency $f_0 = 1700$ Hz and a receiver are located on the same normal to a wall. Both the source and the receiver are stationary, and the wall recedes from the source with velocity $u = 6.0$ cm/s. Find the beat frequency registered by the receiver. The velocity of sound is equal to $v = 340$ m/s. **(Irodov 4.180)**

Integer Type or Numerical Value Based Questions

35. A person driving car at a constant speed of 15 m/s is approaching a vertical wall. The person notices a change of 40 Hz in the frequency of his car's horn upon reflection from the wall. The frequency of horn is .... Hz. (Given, speed of sound = 330 m/s) **(2023 Main)**

36. A train blowing a whistle of frequency 320 Hz approaches an observer standing on the platform at a speed of 66 m/s. The frequency observed by the observer will be .... Hz.
   (Given, speed of sound = 330 ms^{-1}) **(2023 Main)**

37. The frequency of echo will be .... Hz if the train blowing a whistle of frequency 320 Hz is moving with a velocity of 36 km/h towards a hill from which an echo is heard by the train driver. Velocity of sound in air is 330 m/s. **(2022 Main)**

38. An employee of a factory moving away from his workplace by a car listens to the siren of the factory, He drives the car at the speed of 72 kmh^{-1} in the direction of wind which is blowing at 72 kmh^{-1} speed. Frequency of siren is 720 Hz. The employee hears an apparent frequency of .... Hz. (Assume speed of sound to be 340 ms^{-1}) **(2022 Main)**

39. An observer is riding on a bicyle and moving towards a hill at 18 kmh^{-1}. He hears a sound from a source at some distance behind him directly as well as after its reflection from the hill. If the original frequency of the sound as emitted by source is 640 Hz and velocity of the sound in air is 320 m/s, the beat frequency between the two sounds heard by observer will be .... Hz. **(2022 Main)**

40. Two cars X and Y are approaching each other with velocities 36 km/h and 72 km/h respectively. The frequency of a whistle sound as emitted by a passenger in car X, heard by the passenger in car Y is 1320 Hz. If the velocity of sound in air is 340 m/s, the actual frequency of the whistle sound produced is .... Hz. **(2021 Main)**

41. A stationary tuning fork is in resonance with an air column in a pipe. If the tuning fork is moved with a speed of 2 ms^{-1} in front of the open end of the pipe and parallel to it, the length of the pipe should be changed for the resonance to occur with the moving tuning fork. If the speed of sound in air is 320 ms^{-1}, the smallest value of the percentage change required in the length of the pipe is .... **(2020 Adv.)**

Level 2

Single Correct Option

42. A plane wave of sound travelling in air is incident upon a plane water surface. The angle of incidence is 60°. If velocity of sound in air and water are 330 m/s and 1400 m/s then the wave undergoes
   (a) refraction only
   (b) reflection only
   (c) Both reflection and refraction
   (d) neither reflection nor refraction

43. An open pipe is in resonance in 2nd harmonic with frequency f_1. Now one end of the tube is closed and frequency is increased to f_2 such that the resonance again occurs in nth harmonic. Choose the correct option **(2005 JEE)**
   (a) $n = 3, f_2 = \frac{3}{4} f_1$
   (b) $n = 3, f_2 = \frac{5}{4} f_1$
   (c) $n = 5, f_2 = \frac{3}{4} f_1$
   (d) $n = 5, f_2 = \frac{5}{4} f_1$

44. Two sources of sound are moving in opposite directions with velocities v_1 and v_2 $(v_1 > v_2)$. Both are moving away from a stationary observer. The frequency of both the sources is 1700 Hz. What is the value of $(v_1 - v_2)$ so that the beat frequency observed by the observer is 10 Hz? $v_{sound} = 340$ m/s and assume that v_1 and v_2 both are very much less than v_{sound}.

(a) 1 m/s (b) 2 m/s (c) 3 m/s (d) 4 m/s

45. A sounding body emitting a frequency of 150 Hz is dropped from a height. During its fall under gravity it crosses a balloon moving upwards with a constant velocity of 2 m/s one second after it started to fall. The difference in the frequency observed by the man in balloon just before and just after crossing the body will be (velocity of sound = 300 m/s, $g = 10$ m/s^2)

(a) 12 (b) 6 (c) 8 (d) 4

46. A closed organ pipe has length L. The air in it is vibrating in third overtone with maximum amplitude a. The amplitude at distance $\frac{L}{7}$ from closed end of the pipe is

(a) 0 (b) a

(c) $\frac{a}{2}$ (d) Data insufficient

47. A source is moving with constant speed $v_s = 20$ m/s towards a stationary observer due east of the source. Wind is blowing at the speed of 20 m/s at 60° north of east. The source has frequency 500 Hz. Speed of sound = 300 m/s. The frequency registered by the observer is approximately

(a) 541 Hz (b) 552 Hz (c) 534 Hz (d) 517 Hz

48. A car travelling towards a hill at 10 m/s sounds its horn which has a frequency 500 Hz. This is heard in a second car travelling behind the first car in the same direction with speed 20 m/s. The sound can also be heard in the second car by reflection of sound from the hill. The beat frequency heard by the driver of the second car will be (speed of sound in air = 340 m/s)

(a) 31 Hz (b) 24 Hz (c) 21 Hz (d) 34 Hz

49. Two sounding bodies are producing progressive waves given by $y_1 = 2 \sin(400\pi t)$ and $y_2 = \sin(404\pi t)$ where t is in second, which superpose near the ears of a person. The person will hear

(a) 2 beats/s with intensity ratio 9/4 between maxima and minima

(b) 2 beats/s with intensity ratio 9 between maxima and minima

(c) 4 beats/s with intensity ratio 16 between maxima and minima

(d) 4 beats/s with intensity ratio 16/9 between maxima and minima

50. The air in a closed tube 34 cm long is vibrating with two nodes and two antinodes and its temperature is 51°C. What is the wavelength of the waves produced in air outside the tube, when the temperature of air is 16°C?

(a) 42.8 cm (b) 68 cm (c) 17 cm (d) 102 cm

51. A vibrating string of certain length l under a tension T resonates with a mode corresponding to the first overtone (third harmonic) of an air column of length 75 cm inside a tube closed at one end. The string also generates 4 beats/s, when excited along with a tuning fork of frequency n. Now the tension of the string is slightly increased and the number of beats reduces to 2 per second. Assuming the velocity of sound in air to be 340 m/s, the frequency n of the tuning fork (in Hz) is

(a) 344 (b) 336

(c) 117.3 (d) 109.3

52. A closed organ pipe resonates in its fundamental mode at a frequency of 200 Hz with O_2 in the pipe at a certain temperature. If the pipe now contains 2 moles of O_2 and 3 moles of ozone, then what will be the fundamental frequency of same pipe at same temperature?

(a) 268.23 Hz (b) 184.6 Hz

(c) 149.45 Hz (d) None of these

53. A detector is released from rest over a source of sound of frequency $f_0 = 10^3$ Hz. The frequency observed by the detector at time t is plotted in the graph. The speed of sound in air is ($g = 10$ m/s^2)

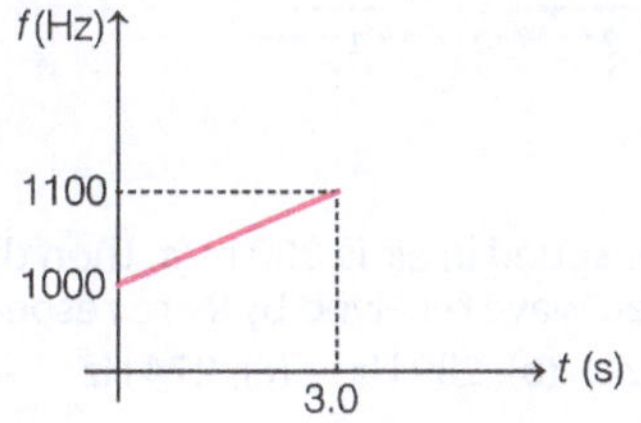

(a) 330 m/s (b) 350 m/s

(c) 300 m/s (d) 310 m/s

54. Sound waves are travelling along positive x-direction. Displacement of particle at any time t is as shown in figure. Select the correct statement.

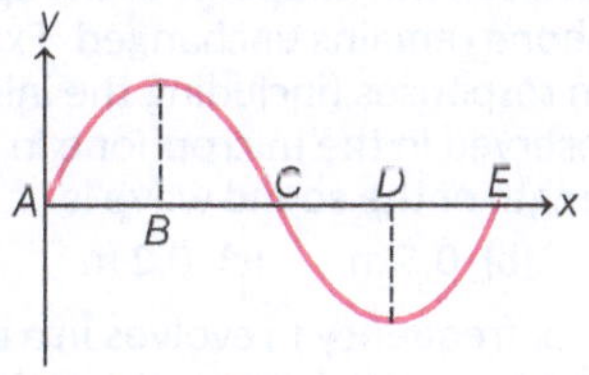

(a) Particle located at E has its velocity in negative x-direction

(b) Particle located at D has zero velocity

(c) Both (a) and (b) are correct

(d) Both (a) and (b) are wrong

55. In a large room, a person receives direct sound waves from a source 120 m away from him. He also receives waves from the same source which reaches him after being reflected from the 25 m high ceiling at a point mid-way between them. The two waves interfere constructively for wavelength (in m) of

(a) 20, 20/3, 20/5, etc. (b) 10, 5, 2.5 , etc.

(c) 10, 20, 30, etc. (d) 15, 25, 35, etc.

56. Two tuning forks P and Q are vibrated together. The number of beats produced are represented by the straight line OA in the following graph.

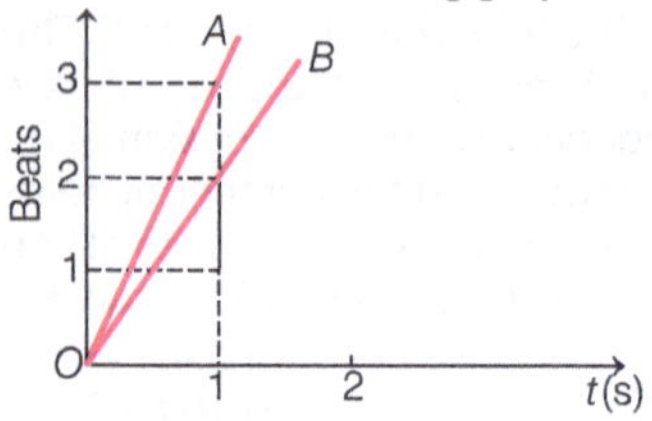

After loading Q with wax again these are vibrated together and the beats produced are represented by the line OB. If the frequency of P is 341 Hz, the frequency of Q will be

(a) 341 Hz (b) 338 Hz
(c) 344 Hz (d) None of these

57. A point source of sound S of natural frequency 256 Hz and a receiver R are moving along same line with speed $u = 10$ m/s, towards a reflecting surface which is approaching them with speed u as shown in figure.

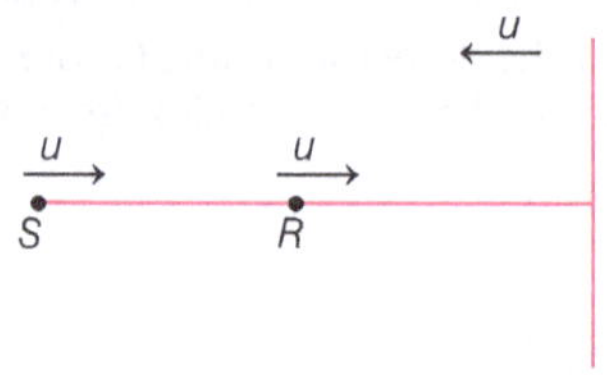

If speed of sound in air is 330 m/s, then the frequency of reflected wave received by R are respectively

(a) 270 Hz (b) 289 Hz (c) 274 Hz (d) 254 Hz

58. Two speakers connected to the same source of fixed frequency are placed 2 m apart in a box. A sensitive microphone placed at a distance of 4 m from the mid-point along the perpendicular bisector shows maximum response. The box is slowly rotated until the speakers are in line with the microphone. The distance between the midpoint of the speakers and the microphone remains unchanged. Exactly, 5 maximum responses (including the initial and last one) are observed in the microphone in doing this. The wavelength of the sound wave is

(a) 0.8 m (b) 0.5 m (c) 0.2 m (d) 1.6 m

59. A whistle S of frequency f revolves in a circle of radius R at a constant speed v. What is the ratio of maximum and minimum frequency detected by a detector D at rest at a distance $2R$ from the centre of circle as shown in figure? (Take c as speed of sound)

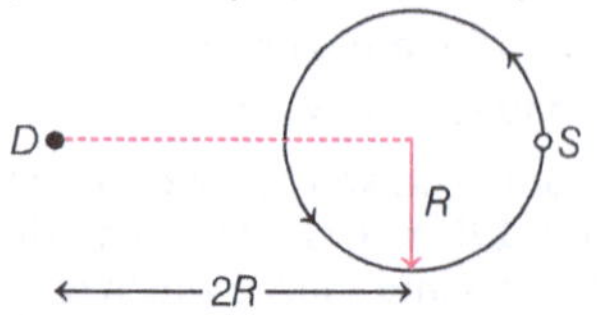

(a) $\left(\frac{c+v}{c-v}\right)$ (b) $\sqrt{2}\left(\frac{c+v}{c-v}\right)$

(c) $\sqrt{2}$ (d) $\frac{(c+v)}{c\sqrt{2}}$

60. A source of sound is travelling at $\frac{100}{3}$ ms^{-1} along a road, towards a point A. When the source is 3m away from A, a person standing at a point O on a road perpendicular to velocity of source observes a frequency f'. The distance of O from A at that time is 4 m. If the original frequency is 640 Hz, then the value of f' is (Given that velocity of sound = 340 ms^{-1})

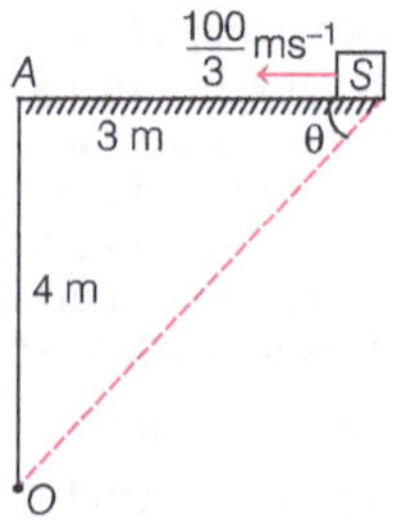

(a) 620 Hz (b) 680 Hz
(c) 720 Hz (d) 840 Hz

61. A source of sound emits sound waves at frequency f_0. It is moving towards an observer with fixed speed v_s ($v_s < v$, where v is the speed of sound in air). If the observer were to move towards the source with speed v_0, one of the following two graphs (A and B) will give the correct variation of the frequency f heard by the observe as v_0 is changed. **(2015 Main)**

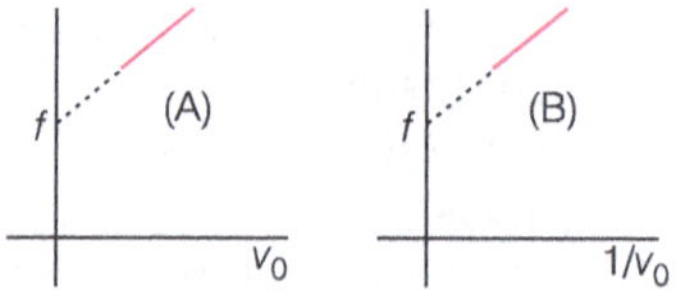

The variation of f with v_0 is given correctly by

(a) graph A with slope $= \frac{f_0}{(v+v_s)}$

(b) graph B with slope $= \frac{f_0}{(v-v_s)}$

(c) graph A with slope $= \frac{f_0}{(v-v_s)}$

(d) graph B with slope $= \frac{f_0}{(v+v_s)}$

Multiple Correct Options

62. A source, approaching with speed u towards the open end of a stationary pipe of length L, is emitting a sound of frequency f_s. The farther end of the pipe is closed. The speed of sound in air is v and f_0 is the fundamental frequency of the pipe. For which of the following combination(s) of u and f_s, will the sound reaching the pipe lead to a resonance? **(2021 Adv.)**

(a) $u = 0.8v$ and $f_s = f_0$
(b) $u = 0.8\,v$ and $f_s = 2f_0$
(c) $u = 0.8\,v$ and $f_s = 0.5\,f_0$
(d) $u = 0.5\,v$ and $f_s = 1.5\,f_0$

Passage Type Questions

Passage 1 (Q.63 to Q.65)

A man of mass 50 kg is running on a plank of mass 150 kg with speed of 8 m/s relative to plank as shown in the figure (both were initially at rest and the velocity of man with respect to ground any how remains constant). Plank is placed on smooth horizontal surface. The man, while running, whistles with frequency f_0. A detector (D) placed on plank detects frequency. The man jumps off with same velocity (w.r.t. to ground) from point D and slides on the smooth horizontal surface [Assume coefficient of friction between man and horizontal is zero]. The speed of sound in still medium is 330 m/s. Answer the following questions on the basis of above situations.

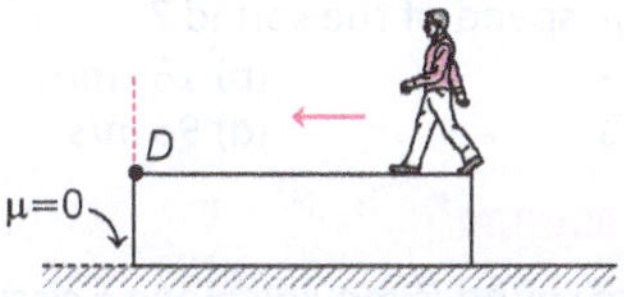

63. The frequency of sound detected by detector D, before man jumps off the plank is

(a) $\frac{332}{324} f_0$ (b) $\frac{330}{322} f_0$ (c) $\frac{328}{336} f_0$ (d) $\frac{330}{338} f_0$

64. The frequency of sound detected by detector D, after man jumps off the plank is

(a) $\frac{332}{324} f_0$ (b) $\frac{330}{322} f_0$ (c) $\frac{328}{336} f_0$ (d) $\frac{330}{338} f_0$

65. Choose the correct plot between the frequency detected by detector *versus* position of the man relative to detector.

(a)
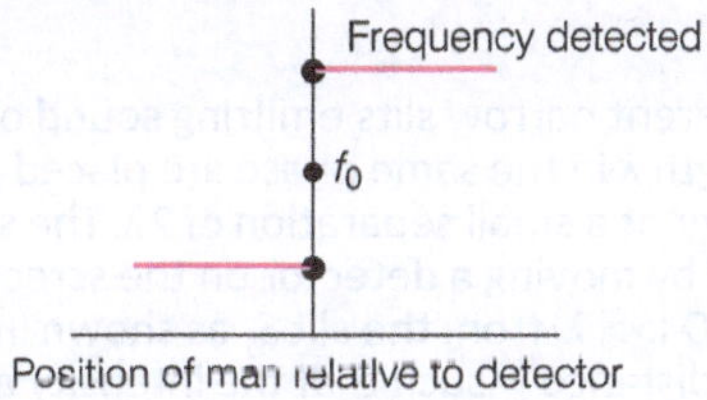

(b)
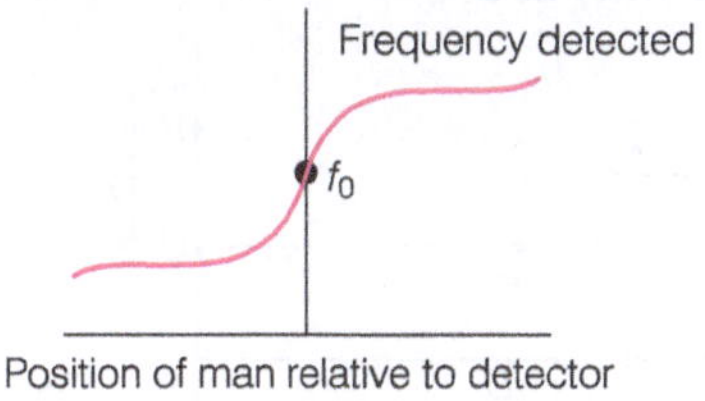

(c)
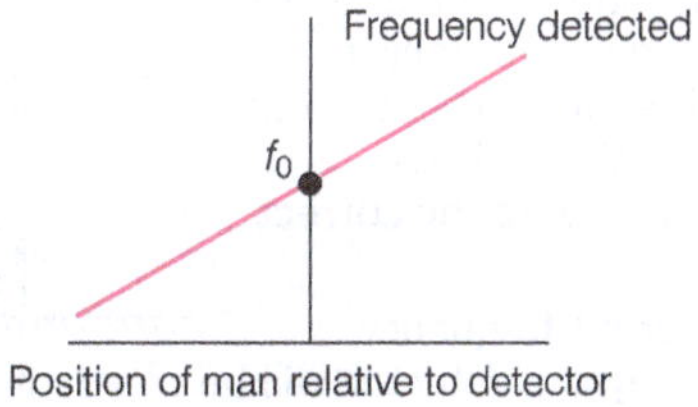

(d)
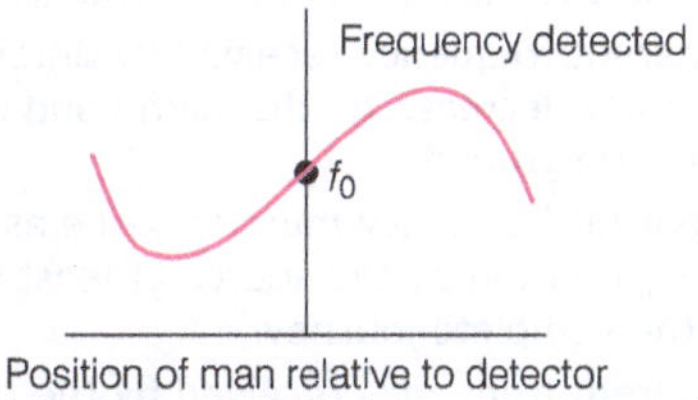

Passage 2 (Q.66 to Q.68)

A source S emitting sound of frequency $f_0 = 960$ Hz is projected with velocity $10\sqrt{2}$ ms^{-1} at an angle $\theta = 45°$ with the horizontal. Simultaneously, a detector O is projected vertically upwards with a speed 10 ms^{-1}. There is no wind and speed of sound in air is 310 ms^{-1}. After the source and detector fall to the ground, they come to rest. (Take, $g = 10$ ms^{-2})

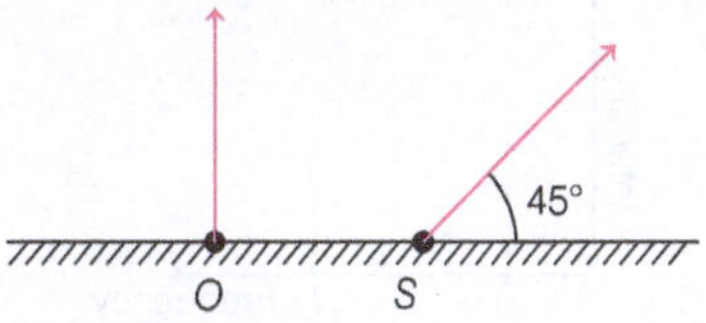

66. The maximum apparent frequency received by the detector is equal to

(a) 992 Hz (b) 952 Hz (c) 682 Hz (d) 930 Hz

67. The graph of apparent frequency f' *versus* time t is best represented by (for time $0 \le t \le 2$ s)

(a)
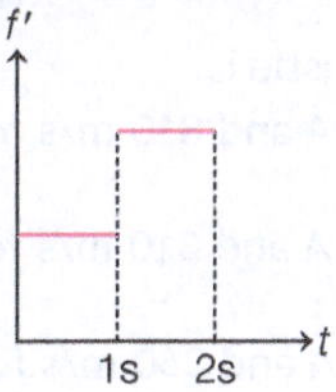

(b)
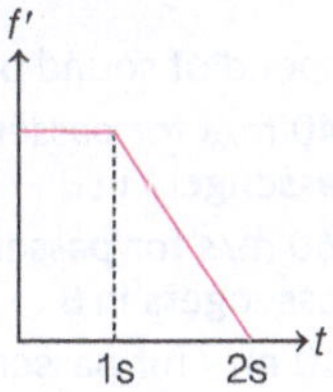

(c)
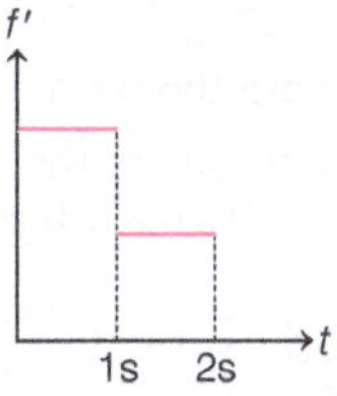

(d)
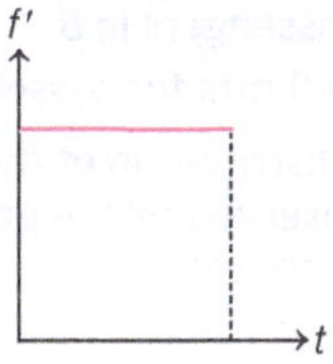

68. Suppose the source and detector are projected horizontally in opposite directions from the top of a tower as shown in the figure. Then, choose the correct options.

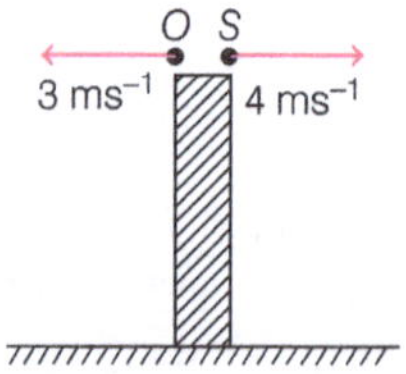

(a) The apparent frequency received by the detector will be constant till the source and the detector fall on to the ground
(b) The apparent frequency received by detector will continuously decrease till the sound and detector fall on to the ground
(c) The apparent frequency must be same as the frequency emitted by the source at least once during the complete journey
(d) The apparent frequency received by the detector will continuously increase till the source and detector fall on to the ground

Passage 3 (Q.69 to Q.71)

Two trains A and B moving with speeds 20 m/s and 30 m/s respectively in the same direction on the same straight track, with B ahead of A. The engines are at the front ends. The engine of train A blows a long whistle.

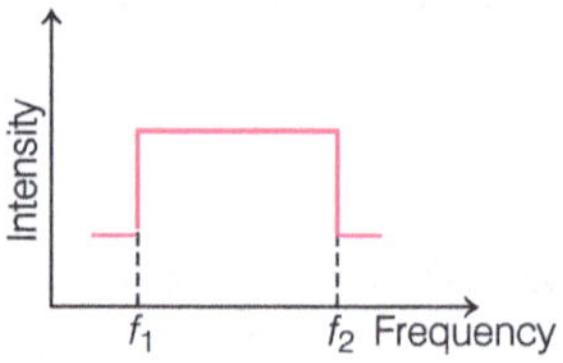

Assume that the sound of the whistle is composed of components varying in frequency from $f_1 = 800$ Hz to $f_2 = 1120$ Hz, as shown in the figure. The spread in the frequency (highest frequency–lowest frequency) is thus 320 Hz. The speed of sound in still air is 340 m/s. **(2007 JEE)**

69. The speed of sound of the whistle is
(a) 340 m/s for passengers in A and 310 m/s for passengers in B
(b) 360 m/s for passengers in A and 310 m/s for passengers in B
(c) 310 m/s for passengers in A and 360 m/s for passengers in B
(d) 340 m/s for passengers in both the trains

70. The distribution of the sound intensity of the whistle as observed by the passengers in train A is best represented by

(a) 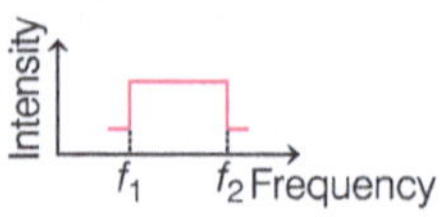

(b) 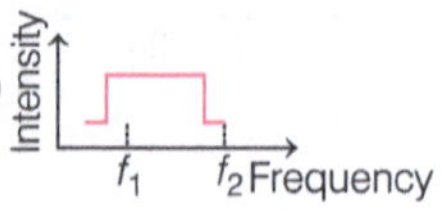

(c) 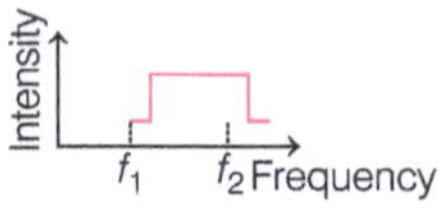

(d) 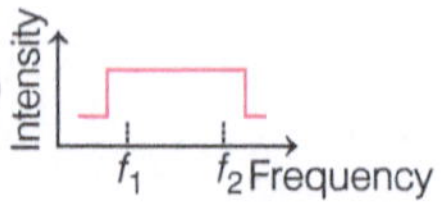

71. The spread of frequency as observed by the passengers in train B is
(a) 310 Hz (b) 330 Hz
(c) 350 Hz (d) 290 Hz

Passage 4 (Q.72 to Q.73)

Two plane harmonic sound waves are expressed by the equations.

$$y_1(x, t) = A\cos(0.5\pi x - 100\pi t)$$
$$y_2(x, t) = A\cos(0.46\pi x - 92\pi t)$$

(All parameters are in MKS) **(2006 JEE)**

72. How many times does an observer hear maximum intensity in one second ?
(a) 4 (b) 10
(c) 6 (d) 8

73. What is the speed of the sound ?
(a) 200 m/s (b) 180 m/s
(c) 192 m/s (d) 96 m/s

Subjective Questions

74. A source of sound is moving along a circular orbit of radius 3 metres with an angular velocity of 10 rad/s. A sound detector located far away from the source is executing linear simple harmonic motion along the line BD with an amplitude $BC = BD = 6$ metres. The frequency of oscillation of the detector is $\frac{5}{\pi}$ per second. The source is at the point A when the detector is at the point B. If the source emits a continous sound wave of frequency 340 Hz, find the maximum and the minimum frequencies recorded by the detector. **(1990 JEE)**

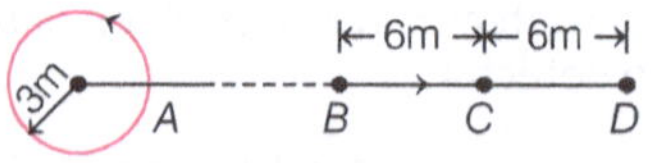

75. Two coherent narrow slits emitting sound of wavelength λ in the same phase are placed parallel to each other at a small separation of 2λ. The sound is detected by moving a detector on the screen at a distance D (>> λ) from the slit S_1 as shown in figure. Find the distance y such that the intensity at P is equal to intensity at O.

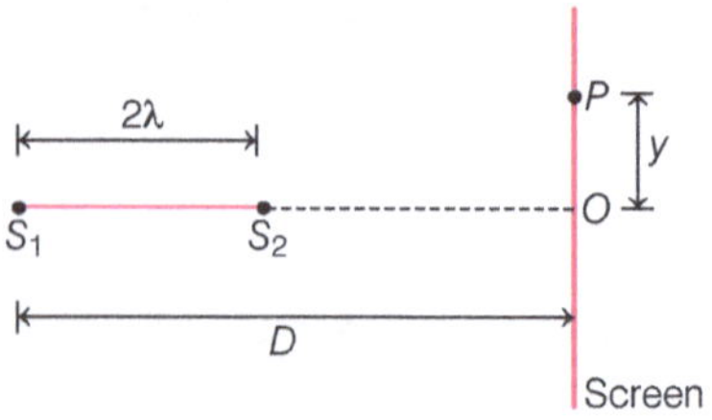

76. A window whose area is $2\ m^2$ opens on a street where the street noise results at the window an intensity level of 60 dB. How much acoustic power enters the window through sound waves? Now, if a sound absorber is fitted at the window, how much energy from the street will it collect in a day?

77. A point A is located at a distance $r = 1.5$ m from a point source of sound of frequency 600 Hz. The power of the source is 0.8 W. Speed of sound in air is 340 m/s and density of air is 1.29 kg/m^3. Find at the point A,

(a) the pressure oscillation amplitude $(\Delta p)_m$

(b) the displacement oscillation amplitude A.

78. A flute which we treat as a pipe open at both ends is 60 cm long.

(a) What is the fundamental frequency when all the holes of the flute are covered?

(b) How far from the mouthpiece should a hole be uncovered for the fundamental frequency to be 330 Hz? Take speed of sound in air as 340 m/s.

79. A source S and a detector D of high frequency waves are a distance d apart on the ground. The direct wave from S is found to be in phase at D with the wave from S that is reflected from a horizontal layer at an altitude H. The incident and reflected rays make the same angle with the reflecting layer. When the layer rises a distance h, no signal is detected at D. Neglect absorption in the atmosphere and find the relation between d, h, H and the wavelength λ of the waves.

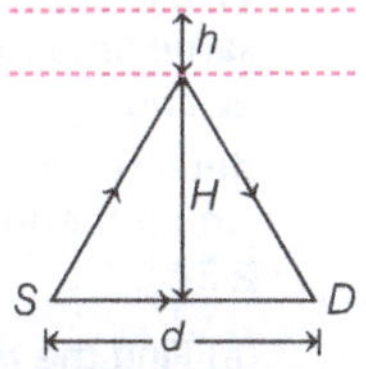

80. Two sound speakers are driven in phase by an audio amplifier at frequency 600 Hz. The speed of sound is 340 m/s. The speakers are on the y-axis, one at $y = +1.0$ m and the other at $y = -1.0$ m. A listener begins at $y = 0$ and walks along a line parallel to the y-axis at a very large distance x away.

(a) At what angle θ (between the line from the origin to the listener at the x-axis) will she first hear a minimum sound intensity?

(b) At what angle will she first hear a maximum (after $\theta = 0°$) sound intensity?

(c) How many maximas can she possibly hear if she keeps walking in the same direction?

81. Two speakers separated by some distance emit sound of the same frequency. At some point P the intensity due to each speaker separately is I_0. The path difference from P to one of the speakers is $\frac{1}{2}\lambda$ greater than that from P to the other speaker. What is the intensity at P if

(a) the speakers are coherent and in phase;

(b) the speakers are incoherent; and

(c) the speakers are coherent but have a phase difference of 180°?

82. Two loudspeakers radiate waves in phase at 170 Hz. An observer sits at 8 m from one speaker and 11m from the other. The intensity level at that point from either speaker is 60 dB. The speed of sound is 340 m/s.

(a) Find the observed intensity when both speakers are ON together.

(b) Find the observed intensity level when both speakers are ON together but one has its leads reversed so that the speakers are 180° out of phase.

(c) Find the observed intensity level when both speakers are ON and in phase but the frequency is 85 Hz.

83. Two identical speakers emit sound waves of frequency 680 Hz uniformly in all directions with a total audio output of 1 mW each. The speed of sound in air is 340 m/s. A point P is a distance 2.00 m from one speaker and 3.00 m from the other.

(a) Find the intensities I_1 and I_2 from each speaker at point P separately.

(b) If the speakers are driven coherently and in phase, what is the intensity at point P ?

(c) If they are driven coherently but out of phase by 180°, what is the intensity at point P ?

(d) If the speakers are incoherent, what is the intensity at point P ?

84. A 3 m long organ pipe open at both ends is driven to third harmonic standing wave. If the amplitude of pressure oscillations is 1 per cent of mean atmospheric pressure ($p_0 = 10^5$ Nm^2). Find the amplitude of particle displacement and density oscillations. Speed of sound $v = 332$ m/s and density of air $\rho = 1.03$ kg/m^3.

85. A siren creates a sound level of 60 dB at a location 500 m from the speaker. The siren is powered by a battery that delivers a total energy of 1.0 kJ. Assuming that the efficiency of siren is 30%, determine the total time the siren can sound.

86. A cylinder of length 1 m is divided by a thin perfectly flexible diaphragm in the middle. It is closed by similar flexible diaphragms at the ends. The two chambers into which it is divided contain hydrogen and oxygen. The two diaphragms are set in vibrations of same frequency. What is the minimum frequency of these diaphragms for which the middle diaphragm will be motionless? Velocity of sound in hydrogen is 1100 m/s and that in oxygen is 300 m/s.

87. A boy is moving along a circular track in anticlockwise sense. A toy train moves along a square path with centres of circular track and square both coinciding, as shown in the figure. The train as well as the boy start from points P_2 and P_1 such that points O, P_1 and P_2 always lie on the same radial line. The speed of listener (i.e. the boy) is 11 ms^{-1}. The train continuously whistles at frequency 330 Hz. Speed of sound is 330 ms^{-1}. During one complete rotation, determine the maximum frequency and minimum frequency heard by the boy. Given $R = \frac{L}{4}$.

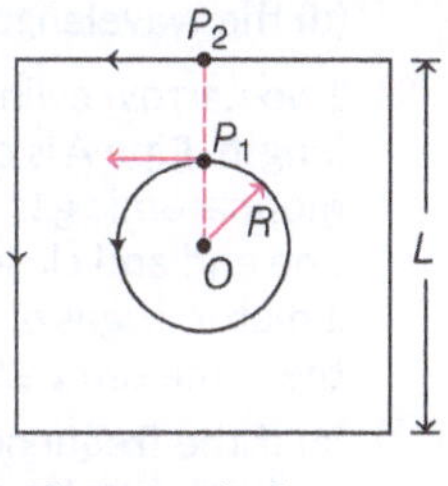

88. A point sound source is situated in a medium of bulk modulus 1.6×10^5 N/m^2. An observer standing at a distance 10 m from the source writes down the equation for the wave as $y = A \sin(15\pi x - 6000\pi t)$. Here y and x are in metres and t is in second. The maximum pressure amplitude received to the observer's ear is (24π) Pa, then find

(a) the density of the medium,

(b) the displacement amplitude A of the waves received by the observer and

(c) the power of the sound source.

89. The figure shows the location of a source and detector at time $t = 0$. The source and detector are moving with velocities $\bar{v}_S = 5\hat{i}$ ms^{-1} and $\bar{v}_O = 10\hat{j}$ ms^{-1} respectively. Frequency of the source is 100 Hz. Determine the frequency of signals received by the detector (O) at the moment, when the source crosses origin. Speed of sound is 330 ms^{-1}.

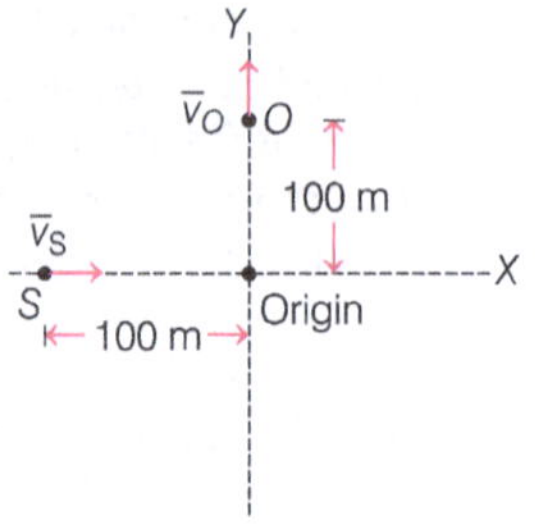

90. A string 25 cm long and having a mass of 2.5 g is under tension. A pipe closed at one end is 40 cm long. When the string is set vibrating in its first overtone and the air in the pipe in its fundamental frequency, 8 beats per second are heard. It is observed that decreasing the tension in the string decrease the beat frequency. If the speed of sound in air is 320 m/s, find the tension in the string.

91. A source emits sound waves of frequency 1000 Hz. The source moves to the right with a speed of 32 m/s relative to ground. On the right a reflecting surface moves towards left with a speed of 64 m/s relative to the ground. The speed of sound in air is 332 m/s. Find

(a) the wavelength of sound in front of the source,

(b) the number of waves arriving per second which meets the reflecting surface,

(c) the speed of reflected waves and

(d) the wavelength of reflected waves.

92. Two narrow cylindrical pipes A and B have the same length. Pipe A is open at both ends and is filled with a monoatomic gas of molar mass M_A. Pipe B is open at one end and closed at the other end, and is filled with a diatomic gas of molar mass M_B. Both gases are at the same temperature. **(2002 JEE)**

(a) If the frequency of the second harmonic of the fundamental mode in pipe A is equal to the frequency of the third harmonic of the fundamental mode in pipe B, determine the value of M_A / M_B.

(b) Now the open end of pipe B is also closed (so that the pipe is closed at both ends). Find the ratio of the fundamental frequency in pipe A to that in pipe B.

93. A 3.6 m long vertical pipe resonates with a source of frequency 212.5 Hz when water level is at certain heights in the pipe. Find the height of water level (from the bottom of the pipe) at which resonance occurs. Neglect end correction. Now, the pipe is filled to a height $H(\approx 3.6$ m). A small hole is drilled very close to its bottom and water is allowed to leak. Obtain an expression for the rate of fall of water level in the pipe as a function of H. If the radii of the pipe and the hole are 2×10^{-2} m and 1×10^{-3} m respectively, calculate the time interval between the occurance of first two resonances. Speed of sound in air is 340 m/s and $g = 10$ m/s^2. **(2000 JEE)**

94. Two radio stations broadcast their programmes at the same amplitude A and at slightly different frequencies ω_1 and ω_2 respectively; where $\omega_1 - \omega_2 = 10^3$ Hz. A detector receives the signals from the two stations simultaneously. It can only detect signals of intensity $\geq 2A^2$. **(1993 JEE)**

(a) Find the time interval between successive maxima of the intensity of the signal received by the detector.

(b) Find the time for which the detector remains idle in each-cycle of the intensity of the signal.

95. Two sources of sound S_1 and S_2 vibrate at the same frequency and are in phase. The intensity of sound detected at a point P (as shown in figure) is I_0.

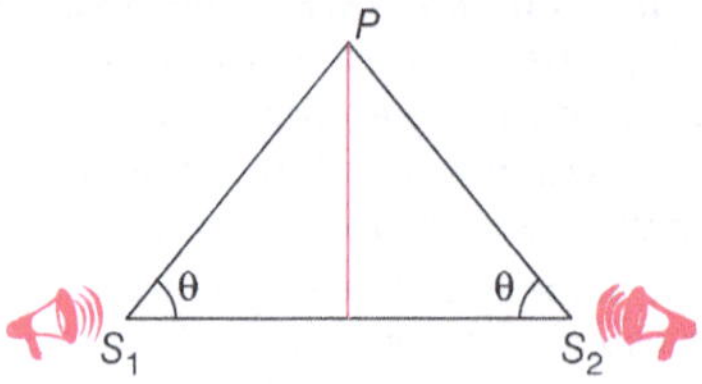

(a) If $\theta = 45°$ what will be the intensity of sound detected at this point if one of the sources is switched off ?

(b) What will be the intensity of sound detected at P if $\theta = 60°$ and both the sources are now switched on?

96. A source of sonic oscillations with frequency $f_0 = 1700$ Hz and a receiver are located at the same point. At the moment $t = 0$ the source starts receding from the receiver with constant acceleration $a = 10.0$ m/s^2. Assuming the velocity of sound to be equal to $v = 340$ m/s, find the oscillation frequency registered by the stationary receiver $t = 10.0$ s after the start of motion. **(Irodov 4.177)**

97. A stationary source sends forth monochromatic sound. A wall approaches it with velocity $u = 33$ cm/s. The propagation velocity of sound in the medium is $v = 330$ m/s. In what way and how much, in per cent, does the wavelength of sound change on reflection from the wall? **(Irodov 4.179)**

98. A metal rod of length 1 m is clamped at two points as shown in the figure. Distance of the clamp from the

two ends are 5 cm and 15 cm, respectively. Find the minimum and next higher frequency of natural longitudinal oscillation of the rod. Given that Young's modulus of elasticity and density of aluminium are $Y = 1.6 \times 10^{11}\ \text{Nm}^{-2}$ and $\rho = 2500\ \text{kgm}^{-3}$, respectively.

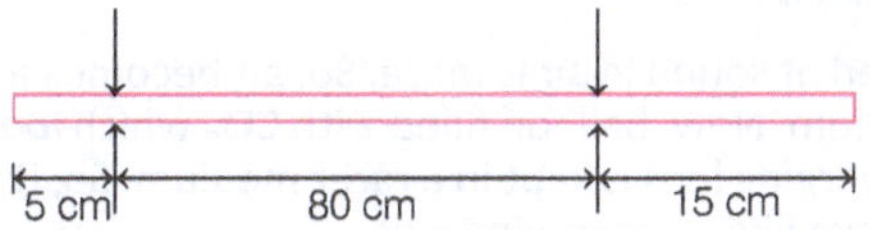

99. A source of sonic oscillations with frequency $f_0 = 1000$ Hz moves at right angles to the wall with a velocity $u = 0.17$ m/s. Two stationary receivers R_1 and R_2 are located on a straight line, coinciding with the trajectory of the source, in the following succession : R_1-source-R_2-wall. Which receiver registers the beatings and what is the beat frequency? The velocity of sound is equal to $v = 340$ m/s. **(Irodov 4.174)**

100. A receiver and a source of sonic oscillations of frequency $f_0 = 2000$ Hz are located on the x-axis. The source swings harmonically along that axis with an angular frequency ω and an amplitude $A = 50$ cm. At what value of ω will the frequency bandwidth registered by the stationary receiver be equal to $\Delta f = 200$ Hz? The velocity of sound is equal to $v = 340$ m/s. **(Irodov 4.176)**

Integer Type or Numerical Based Questions

101. A plane sound wave passes from medium 1 to medium 2. The speed of sound in medium 1 is $200\ \text{ms}^{-1}$ and in medium 2 is $100\ \text{ms}^{-1}$. If the ratio of amplitude of the transmitted wave to that of incident wave is $\frac{2}{k}$, then find the value of k.

102. The speed of sound in hydrogen at 0°C is $1200\ \text{ms}^{-1}$. When some amount of oxygen is mixed with hydrogen, the speed decreases to $500\ \text{ms}^{-1}$. If density of oxygen is 16 times that of hydrogen, the ratio of hydrogen to oxygen by volume in this mixture is $\frac{11}{10}\alpha$. Find the value of α.

103. A train S_1, moving with a uniform velocity of 108 km/h approaches another train S_2 standing on a platform. An observer O moves with a uniform velocity of 36 km/h towards S_2 as shown in figure. Both the trains are blowing whistles of same frequency 120 Hz. When O is 600 m away from S_2 and distance between S_1 and S_2 is 800 m, the number of beats heard by O is .... [Speed of the sound = 330 m/s] **(2019 Adv.)**

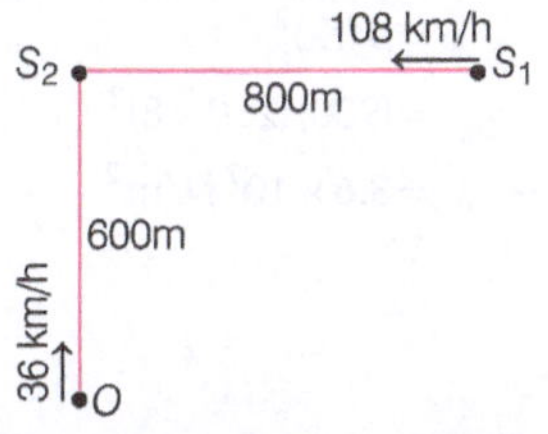

Answers

Level 1

1. (0.125) **2.** (c) **3.** (c) **4.** (c) **5.** (d)
6. (a) **7.** (a) **8.** (d) **9.** (c) **10.** (d)
11. (b) **12.** (a) **13.** (d) **14.** (b) **15.** (a,b,c)
16. (a) → r; (b) → q; (c) → q; (d) → p **17.** 0.4 cm
18. (a) $9.95 \times 10^{-4}\ \text{W/m}^2$ (b) 1.15×10^{-6} m
19. (a) 9.44×10^{-11} m, 0.43 m (b) 5.66×10^{-9} m, 0.1 m (c) Air, $\frac{A_{air}}{A_{water}} = 60$ **20.** Diatomic **21.** 250 Hz
22. $y = A\cos(3.93x)\sin(1297t)$ **23.** 348.16 m/s, 118 cm
24. 0.40 **25.** (a) 441.5 Hz, 438.5 Hz (b) (i) + 0.68% (ii) – 0.68%
26. (a) 302 Hz (b) 228 Hz **27.** 680 Hz **28.** 160 Hz
29. (a) 599 Hz (b) 0.935 km, 621 Hz **30.** $\Delta f = \frac{2v_b(v + v_m)}{(v^2 - v_b^2)} f$
31. $t = \frac{2l}{\alpha(\sqrt{T_1} + \sqrt{T_2})}$ **32.** 340 m/s **33.** (a) Six (b) Six
34. 0.60 Hz **35.** (420) **36.** (400) **37.** (340) **38.** (680)
39. (20) **40.** (1210) **41.** (0.62 to 0.63)

Level 2

42. (b) **43.** (d) **44.** (b) **45.** (a) **46.** (b)
47. (c) **48.** (a) **49.** (b) **50.** (a) **51.** (a)
52. (d) **53.** (c) **54.** (c) **55.** (a) **56.** (c)
57. (b) **58.** (b) **59.** (a) **60.** (b) **61.** (c)
62. (a,d) **63.** (a) **64.** (c) **65.** (a) **66.** (d)
67. (d) **68.** (a) **69.** (b) **70.** (a) **71.** (a)
72. (a) **73.** (a) **74.** 438.7 Hz and 257.3 Hz
75. $y = \sqrt{3}D$ **76.** 2 μW, 0.173 J
77. (a) $4.98\ \text{N/m}^2$ (b) 3.0×10^{-6} m
78. (a) 283.33 Hz (b) 51.5 cm
79. $\lambda = 2\sqrt{4(H + h)^2 + d^2} - 2\sqrt{4H^2 + d^2}$
80. (a) 8.19° (b) 16.5° (c) Three maxima beyond the maximum corresponding to $\theta = 0°$ **81.** (a) 0 (b) $2I_0$ (c) $4I_0$
82. (a) 0 (b) 66 dB (c) 63 dB
83. (a) $I_1 = 19.9\ \mu\text{W/m}^2$, $I_2 = 8.84\ \mu\text{W/m}^2$ (b) $54.2\ \mu\text{W/m}^2$ (c) $2.2\ \mu\text{W/m}^2$ (d) $28.7\ \mu\text{W/m}^2$
84. 0.28 cm, $9.0 \times 10^{-3}\ \text{kg/m}^3$ **85.** 95.5 s **86.** 1650 Hz
87. 364.4 Hz and 301.6 Hz **88.** (a) 1 kg/m^3 (b) 10 μm (c) $288\pi^3$ W
89. 97 Hz **90.** 27.04 N
91. (a) 0.3 m (b) 1320 (c) 332 m/s (d) 0.2 m
92. (a) $\frac{400}{189}$ (b) $\frac{3}{4}$ **93.** 43 s
94. (a) $2\pi \times 10^{-3}$ s (b) $\frac{\pi}{2} \times 10^{-3}$ s **95.** (a) $\frac{I_0}{4}$ (b) I_0
96. 1.34 kHz **97.** – 0.2% **98.** 40 kHz, 120 kHz
99. R_1, $f_b = 1.0$ Hz **100.** 34 rad/s **101.** (3)
102. (2) **103.** (8.13)

See hints on pages 157-173.

Hints & SOLUTIONS

Module 1.

2. From the given equation,

$$(\Delta p)_m = 12\text{ Pa}$$
$$k = 8.18\text{ m}^{-1}$$

and $\omega = 2700\text{ s}^{-1}$

$$\therefore \quad \lambda = \frac{2\pi}{k} = \frac{2\pi}{8.18}$$

and $f = \frac{\omega}{2\pi} = \frac{2700}{2\pi}\text{ s}^{-1}$

So, speed of wave is

$$v = f\lambda = \frac{2700}{2\pi} \times \frac{2\pi}{8.18} = 330\text{ ms}^{-1}$$
$$v = \sqrt{\frac{B}{\rho}}$$
$$B = \rho v^2 = 1.29 \times (330)^2$$
$$= 140.5 \times 10^3\text{ Nm}^{-2}$$

We know

$$(\Delta p)_m = BAk$$
$$\therefore \quad A = \frac{(\Delta p)_m}{Bk} = \frac{12}{140.5 \times 10^3 \times 8.18}$$
$$= 1.044 \times 10^{-5}\text{ m}$$

4. $\Delta p_{max} = BAk$

$$B = \frac{\Delta p_{max}}{Ak} = \frac{\Delta p_{max}}{A(2\pi/\lambda)}$$
$$= \frac{(\Delta p_{max})\lambda}{2\pi A}$$
$$= \frac{(14)(0.35)}{(2\pi)(5.5 \times 10^{-6})}$$
$$= 1.4 \times 10^5\text{ N/m}^2$$

5. $\lambda_{min} = \frac{v}{f_{max}} = \frac{1450}{20000}$

$$= 0.0725\text{ m} = 7.25\text{ cm}$$
$$\lambda_{max} = \frac{v}{f_{min}} = \frac{1450}{20}$$
$$= 72.5\text{ m}$$

6. (a) Displacement is zero when pressure is maximum.

(b) $\Delta p_{max} = BAk$

$$= (\rho v^2)A\left(\frac{\omega}{v}\right) = 2\pi f A \rho v$$
$$\therefore \quad A = \frac{\Delta p_{max}}{2\pi f \rho v} = \frac{10}{(2\pi)(10^3)(1.29)(340)}$$
$$= 3.63 \times 10^{-6}\text{ m}$$

Module 2.

1. Speed of sound in air is more. So, air becomes a rarer medium. Now, balloon filled with CO_2 which looks like a converging lens is kept in a rarer medium. So, it will behave like a converging lens.

2. Sound waves cannot travel in vacuum and light wave has maximum velocity in vacuum.

3. Sound waves cannot travel in vacuum.

4. Number of moles $\propto$ Volume

$$M = \frac{n_1 M_{O_2} + n_2 M_{H_2}}{n_1 + n_2}$$
$$= \frac{(1)(32) + (1)(2)}{2} = 17$$

Now, $v = \sqrt{\frac{\gamma RT}{M}} \propto \frac{1}{\sqrt{M}}$

$$\frac{v_1}{v_2} = \sqrt{\frac{M_2}{M_1}} = \sqrt{\frac{2}{17}}$$

5. $v \propto \sqrt{T}$

$$\therefore \quad \frac{v_2}{v_1} = \sqrt{\frac{T_2}{T_1}} \text{ or } T_2 = \left(\frac{v_2}{v_1}\right)^2 T_1 = (2)^2(273)$$
$$= 1092\text{ K}$$
$$= 819°\text{C}$$

6. $\because \quad v \propto \sqrt{T}$

$$\therefore \quad v_2 = \left(\sqrt{\frac{T_2}{T_1}}\right)v_1$$
$$v_{-3°C} = \left(\sqrt{\frac{270}{273}}\right)(332)$$
$$= 330.17\text{ m/s}$$
$$v_{30°C} = \left(\sqrt{\frac{273+30}{273}}\right)(332)$$
$$= 349.77\text{ m/s}$$

The difference in these two speeds is approximately 19.6 m/s.

7. $\because \quad v = f\lambda = \sqrt{\frac{B}{\rho}}$

$$\therefore \quad B = \rho(f\lambda)^2$$
$$= (900)(250 \times 8)^2$$
$$= 3.6 \times 10^9\text{ N/m}^2$$

8. $v = \sqrt{\frac{\gamma RT}{M}}$

$$= \sqrt{\frac{(7/5)(8.31)(273)}{(32 \times 10^{-3})}}$$

$$= 315 \text{ m/s}$$

9. $v = \sqrt{\frac{\gamma p}{\rho}} = \sqrt{\frac{(5/3) \times 0.76 \times 13.6 \times 10^3 \times 9.8}{0.179}}$

where, $p = h\rho g$

$\therefore \quad v \approx 972 \text{ m/s}$

10. $\sqrt{\frac{Y}{\rho}} = 30\sqrt{\frac{T}{\mu}} = 30\sqrt{\frac{F}{\rho A}}$ (as $T = F$ and $\mu = \rho A$)

$\therefore \quad \frac{F}{A} = \frac{Y}{900}$

11. Equal volume of different gases contains equal number of moles at STP.

$\therefore \quad n \propto V$

$$M = \frac{n_1 M_1 + n_2 M_2}{n_1 + n_2}$$

$$= \frac{(2)(2) + (1)(28)}{2 + 1} = 10.67$$

$$v = \sqrt{\frac{\gamma RT}{M}}$$

$\therefore \quad \frac{v_2}{v_1} = \sqrt{\frac{T_2}{T_1} \cdot \frac{M_1}{M_2}}$

or $\quad v_2 = \left(\sqrt{\frac{T_2}{T_1} \cdot \frac{M_1}{M_2}}\right) v_1$

$$= \left(\sqrt{\frac{300}{273} \times \frac{2}{10.67}}\right)(1300)$$

$$\approx 590 \text{ m/s}$$

Module 3.

1. $90 - 40 = 10 \log \frac{I_2}{I_0} - 10 \log \frac{I_1}{I_0}$

or $\quad 50 = 10 \log \left(\frac{I_2}{I_1}\right)$

$\therefore \quad \frac{I_2}{I_1} = 10^5$

2. $L_2 - L_1 = 10 \log \frac{I_2}{I_0} - 10 \log \frac{I_1}{I_0} = 10 \log \left(\frac{I_2}{I_1}\right)$

$$L_2 - 4 = 10 \log (2)$$

Given, $\quad \frac{I_2}{I_1} = 2$

$\therefore \quad L_2 = 7 \text{ dB}$

3. $L = 10 \log_{10} \left(\frac{I}{I_0}\right)$, where $I_0 = 10^{-12} \text{ Wm}^{-2}$

Since, $\quad 40 = 10 \log_{10} \left(\frac{I_1}{I_0}\right)$

$\Rightarrow \quad \frac{I_1}{I_0} = 10^4 \quad$ ...(i)

Also, $\quad 20 = 10 \log_{10} \left(\frac{I_2}{I_0}\right)$

$\Rightarrow \quad \frac{I_2}{I_0} = 10^2 \quad$ ...(ii)

$\therefore \quad \frac{I_2}{I_1} = 10^{-2} = \frac{r_1^2}{r_2^2}$

$\Rightarrow \quad r_2^2 = 100\, r_1^2$

$\Rightarrow \quad r_2 = 10 \text{ m} \quad (\because r_1 = 1 \text{ m})$

4. Loudness of sound in decibel is given by

$$B = 10 \log_{10} \left(\frac{I}{I_0}\right)$$

$\Rightarrow \quad 120 = 10 \log_{10} \left(\frac{I}{10^{-12}}\right)$

$\Rightarrow \quad 12 = \log_{10} \left(\frac{I}{10^{-12}}\right)$

Taking antilog,

$$10^{12} = \frac{I}{10^{-12}} \Rightarrow I = 1 \text{ W/m}^2$$

This is the intensity of sound reaching the observer.

Now, intensity, $I = \frac{P}{A} = \frac{P}{4\pi r^2}$

$\Rightarrow \quad 1 = \frac{2}{4\pi r^2}$

$\Rightarrow \quad r = \sqrt{\frac{1}{2\pi}}$

$\Rightarrow \quad r = 0.398 \text{ m}$

$$\approx 0.4 \text{ m} = 40 \text{ cm}$$

5. (a) $\Delta p_{max} = BAk$

$$= (\rho v^2)(A)\left(\frac{\omega}{v}\right)$$

$$= (2\pi f A \rho v)$$

$$= (2\pi)(300)(6.0 \times 10^{-3})(1.2)(344)$$

$$= 4.67 \text{ Pa}$$

(b) $I = \frac{v(\Delta p)^2_{max}}{2B} = \frac{(\Delta p)^2_{max}}{2\rho v}$ (as $B = \rho v^2$)

$$= \frac{(4.67)^2}{(2)(1.2)(344)}$$

$$= 0.0264 \text{ W/m}^2$$

$$= 2.64 \times 10^{-2} \text{ W/m}^2$$

(c) $L = \log_{10} \left(\frac{I}{I_0}\right)$

$$= 10 \log_{10} \left(\frac{2.64 \times 10^{-2}}{10^{-12}}\right)$$

$$= 104 \text{ dB}$$

6. $I \propto \frac{1}{r^2}$

$\therefore \quad \frac{I_1}{I_2} = \left(\frac{r_2}{r_1}\right)^2 = \left(\frac{300}{30}\right)^2 = 100$

Now, $L_1 - L_2 = 10 \log_{10}\left(\frac{I_1}{I_2}\right)$

Substituting $\frac{I_1}{I_2} = 100$

We get, $L_1 - L_2 = 20$ dB

7. (a) $I = \frac{v(\Delta p)^2_{max}}{2B} = \frac{(\Delta p)^2_{max}}{2\rho v}$

For faintest sound,

$$I = \frac{(2\times 10^{-5})^2}{2\times 1.29\times 345}$$
$$= 4.49\times 10^{-13}\ \text{W/m}^2$$
$$L = 10\log_{10}\left(\frac{I}{I_0}\right)$$
$$= 10\log_{10}\left(\frac{4.49\times 10^{-13}}{10^{-12}}\right)$$
$$= -3.48\ \text{dB}$$

Same formulae can be applied for loudest sound.

(b) $(\Delta p)_{max} = BAk$

$$= (\rho v^2)(A)\left(\frac{\omega}{v}\right) = 2\pi f\rho v$$

$\therefore \quad A = \frac{(\Delta p)_{max}}{2\pi f\rho v}$

For faintest sound,

$$A = \frac{2\times 10^{-5}}{(2\pi)(500)(1.29)(345)}$$
$$= 1.43\times 10^{-11}\ \text{m}$$

8. $L_1 = 10\log_{10}\left(\frac{I}{I_0}\right)$

$$100 = 10\log_{10}\left(\frac{I}{10^{-12}}\right)$$

Solving we get, $I = 10^{-2}$ W/m^2

Now, $I = \frac{P}{4\pi r^2}$

$\therefore \quad P = I(4\pi r^2) = (10^{-2})(4\pi)(40)^2$

$$= 201\ \text{W}$$

9. (a) $L = 10\log_{10}\left(\frac{I}{I_0}\right)$

$$60 = 10\log_{10}\left(\frac{I}{10^{-12}}\right)$$

Solving we get,

$$I = 10^{-6}\ \text{W/m}^2$$

(b) $I = \frac{P}{S}$

$\therefore \quad P = (I)(S)$

$$= (10^{-6})(120\times 10^{-4})$$
$$= 1.2\times 10^{-8}\ \text{W}$$

10. $L = 10\log_{10}\left(\frac{I}{I_0}\right)$

$$60 = 10\log_{10}(I/10^{-12})$$

Solving, we get $I = 10^{-6}$ W/m^2

Now, using the result derived in above problem,

$$A = \sqrt{\frac{2I}{\rho(2\pi f)^2 v}}$$
$$= \sqrt{\frac{2\times 10^{-6}}{1.29(2\pi\times 800)^2(330)}}$$
$$= 1.36\times 10^{-8}\ \text{m}$$
$$= 13.6\ \text{nm}$$

11. $I = \frac{1}{2}\rho\omega^2 A^2 v$

$$= 2\rho\pi^2 f^2 A^2 v \qquad (\text{as } \omega = 2\pi f)$$
$$= (2)(1.29)(\pi)^2(300)^2(0.2\times 10^{-3})^2(330)$$
$$= 30.27\ \text{W/m}^2$$
$$L = 10\log_{10}(I/I_0)$$

where, $I_0 = 10^{-12}$ W/m^2

Substituting the values, we get

$$L = 134.4\ \text{dB}$$

Module 4.

1. $\lambda = \frac{v}{n} = \frac{350}{350} = 1\ \text{m} = 100\ \text{cm}$

Also, path difference (Δx) between the waves at the point of observation is $AP - BP = 25$ cm.

Hence, $\Delta\phi = \frac{2\pi}{\lambda}(\Delta x)$

$$= \frac{2\pi}{1}\times\left(\frac{25}{100}\right) = \frac{\pi}{2}$$

$\Rightarrow \quad A = \sqrt{(a_1)^2 + (a_2)^2}$

$$= \sqrt{(0.3)^2 + (0.4)^2}$$
$$= 0.5\ \text{mm}$$

2. $\Delta x = L_2D - L_1D = \sqrt{(9)^2 + (40)^2} - 40$

$$= 41 - 40 = 1\ \text{m}$$

For maximum intensity,

$$\Delta x = n\lambda = n\frac{v}{f}$$
$$f = \frac{nv}{\Delta x} = \frac{n\times 330}{1} = 330\,n$$
$$n = 1, f = 330\ \text{Hz}$$

3. $\Delta x_{max} = 3\text{m} = \lambda$

$\therefore \quad f = \frac{v}{\lambda} = \frac{330}{3} = 110\text{ Hz}$. For frequencies less than 100 Hz, λ will be more than 3m and no maximum will be obtained.

4. Resultant amplitude will become 4 times. Therefore, resultant intensity is 16 times.

$$\therefore \quad L_2 - L_1 = 10\log_{10}\frac{I_2}{I_1}$$

or $\quad L_2 - 10 = 10\log_{10}(16)$

or $\quad L_2 = 22\text{ dB}$

5. $\Delta x = \lambda/2 = \frac{v}{2f}$

$$\therefore \quad f = \frac{v}{2\Delta x} = \frac{330}{2(0.12)} = 1375\text{ Hz}$$

6. $SOD - SD = \lambda$

where, $\quad \lambda = \frac{v}{f} = \frac{360}{360} = 1\text{ m}$

$$\therefore \quad 2\sqrt{\frac{x^2}{4} + (2)^2} - x = \lambda = 1$$

Solving this equation, we get

$$x = 7.5\text{ m}$$

7. $\lambda = \frac{v}{f} = \frac{330}{220} = 1.5\text{ m}$

$$\Delta\phi_1 = \left(\frac{2\pi}{\lambda}\right)(\Delta x_1) = \left(\frac{2\pi}{1.5}\right)(0.75) = \pi$$

$$\Delta\phi_2 = \left(\frac{2\pi}{\lambda}\right)(\Delta x_2) = \left(\frac{2\pi}{1.5}\right)(3) = 4\pi$$

Since, $\quad \phi = \Delta\phi_2 - \Delta\phi_1 = 3\pi$

They will interfere destructively.

$$\therefore \quad I_R = (\sqrt{I_1} - \sqrt{I_2})^2 \quad \text{...(i)}$$

where,

$$I_1 = \frac{P_1}{4\pi r_1^2} = \frac{1.2\times 10^{-3}}{(4\pi)(0.75)^2} = 16.97\times 10^{-5}\text{ W/m}^2$$

$$I_2 = \frac{P_2}{4\pi r_2^2} = \frac{1.8\times 10^{-3}}{(4\pi)(3)^2} = 1.59\times 10^{-5}\text{ W/m}^2$$

Substituting in Eq. (i), we get

$$I_R = 8.2\times 10^{-5}\text{ W/m}^2$$

8. $\frac{\lambda}{2} = 11.5\text{ cm}$ or $\lambda = 23\text{ cm}$ or 0.23 m

$$f = \frac{v}{\lambda} = \frac{331.2}{0.23} = 1440\text{ Hz}$$

Module 5.

Introductory Exercise

1. Fundamental frequency of open pipe is $f_1 = \frac{v}{2l}$ and frequency of third harmonic of closed pipe will be

$$f_2 = 3\left(\frac{v}{4l}\right)$$

Now, $\quad f_2 = f_1 + 100$

or $\quad f_2 - f_1 = 100$

or $\quad \frac{3}{4}\left(\frac{v}{l}\right) - \left(\frac{1}{2}\right)\left(\frac{v}{l}\right) = 100$

$\Rightarrow \quad \frac{v}{4l} = 100$

$\Rightarrow \quad v = 400l$

$$f_1 = \frac{v}{2l} = \frac{400l}{2l} = 200\text{ Hz}$$

2. First harmonic of closed pipe = Third harmonic of open pipe

$$\therefore \quad \frac{v}{4l_1} = 3\left(\frac{v}{2l_2}\right) \Rightarrow \frac{l_1}{l_2} = \frac{1}{6}$$

3. $f_c = \frac{v}{4l} = 512\text{ Hz}$

$$f_o = \frac{v}{2l} = 2f_c = 1024\text{Hz}$$

4. (a) $f_1 = \frac{v}{4l}$

$$\therefore \quad l = \frac{v}{4f_1} = \frac{345}{4\times 220} = 0.392\text{ m}$$

(b) $5\left(\frac{v}{4l_c}\right) = 3\left(\frac{v}{2l_0}\right)$

$$\therefore \quad l_0 = \frac{6}{5}l_c = \left(\frac{6}{5}\right)(0.392) = 0.47\text{ m}$$

5.

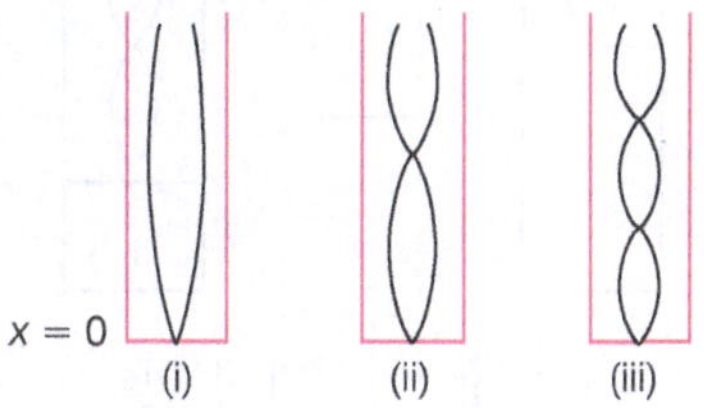

(a) In second figure, $l = \frac{3\lambda}{4}$

$$\therefore \quad \frac{\lambda}{4} = \frac{l}{3} = \frac{0.8}{3} = 0.267\text{ m}$$

Displacement antinode is at

$$x = \frac{\lambda}{4} = 0.267 \text{ m} \quad \text{and} \quad x = 3\frac{\lambda}{4} = 0.8 \text{ m}$$

(b) Pressure antinode is displacement node:

In third figure,

Pressure antinode or displacement node is at

$$x = 0, x = \frac{\lambda}{2} \quad \text{and} \quad x = \lambda$$

6. (a) Ratio of frequencies are $\frac{400}{560} = \frac{5}{7}$

i.e. given two successive frequencies are belongs to odd harmonics. Hence, the given pipe is closed organ pipe.

(b) The frequencies belongs to fifth and seventh harmonics $n_5 = 400$ Hz and $n_7 = 560$ Hz

(c) Given frequencies are integer multiples of 80 Hz. Hence, fundamental frequency is 80 Hz.

$$\frac{v}{4l} = 80$$

$$\therefore \quad l = \frac{v}{320} = \frac{344}{320} = 1.075 \text{ m}$$

7. Wall will be a node (displacement). Therefore, shortest distance from the wall at which air particles have maximum amplitude of vibration (displacement antinode) should be $\lambda/4$.

Here, $\lambda = \frac{v}{f} = \frac{330}{660} = 0.5$ m

$\therefore$ Desired distance $= \frac{\lambda}{4} = \frac{0.5}{4} = 0.125$ m.

Exercise

1. Closed pipe Frequencies are,

$$\frac{v}{4l}, \frac{3v}{4l}, \frac{5v}{4l}$$

Open pipe Frequencies are

$$\frac{v}{2l}, 2\left(\frac{v}{2l}\right), 3\left(\frac{v}{2l}\right)$$

They are never same.

2. Wavelength remains same.

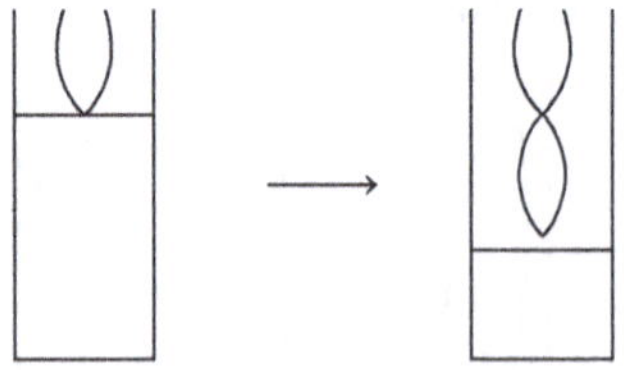

3.

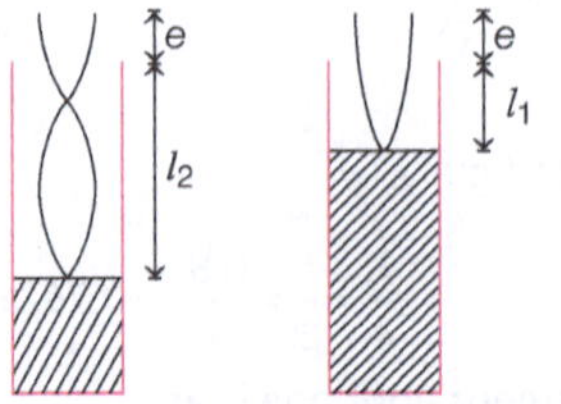

$$l_2 + e = \frac{3\lambda}{4} \quad \text{...(i)}$$

$$l_1 + e = \frac{\lambda}{4} \quad \text{...(ii)}$$

From Eqs. (i) and (ii), we get

$$l_2 + e = 3(l_1 + e)$$

$$\therefore \quad e = \frac{l_2 - 3l_1}{2}$$

or $\quad l_2 = 3l_1 + 2e$

So, $\quad l_2 > 3l_1$

4.

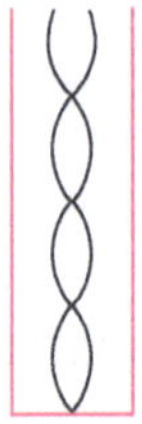

Third overtone

5. $\frac{v}{2l_0} = \frac{v}{4l_c}$

$\Rightarrow \quad l_c : l_0 = 1 : 2$

6. $\frac{\lambda}{2} = 52 - 17 = 35$ cm

$$\therefore \quad \lambda = 70 \text{ cm} = 0.7 \text{ m}$$

$$v = f\lambda = 500 \times 0.7$$

$$= 350 \text{ m/s}$$

7. Fundamental frequency,

$$f_0 = \frac{v}{4l} = \frac{340}{4 \times 1}$$

$$= 85 \text{ Hz}$$

Six frequencies can be produced below 1 kHz. Those six frequencies are, $f_0, 3f_0, 5f_0, 7f_0, 9f_0$ and $11f_0$.

As $13f_0 = 1105$ Hz > 1000 Hz or 1 kHz.

8. $\frac{\lambda}{2} = 122 - 40 = 82$ cm

$\therefore$ Next resonance length $= 122$ cm $+ 82$ cm

$= 204$ cm

9. $\lambda = \frac{v}{f} = \frac{340}{340} = 1$ m $= 100$ cm

$$\frac{\lambda}{4} = 25 \text{ cm}$$

Air column lengths required are,

$$\frac{\lambda}{4}, \frac{3\lambda}{4}, \frac{5\lambda}{4} \text{ etc.}$$

or 25 cm, 75 cm, 125 cm etc.

Maximum we can take 75 cm.

$\therefore$ Minimum water length

$= 120 - 75$

$= 45$ cm

10. Pressure node means displacement antinode

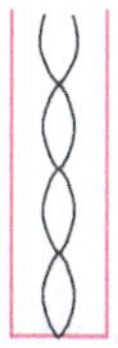

$$\frac{7\lambda}{4} = 105 \text{ cm}$$

$$\frac{\lambda}{4} = 15 \text{ cm}$$

Displacement antinodes are at a distance $\frac{\lambda}{4}, \frac{3\lambda}{4}, \frac{5\lambda}{4}$ and $\frac{7\lambda}{4}$ from closed end or at a distance of 15 cm, 45 cm, 75 cm and 105 cm.

11. **Closed pipe**

Fundamental frequency is

$$f_1 = \frac{v}{4l} = \frac{320}{4 \times 1} = 80 \text{ Hz}$$

Other frequencies are

$3f_1 : 5f_1$ etc. or 240 Hz, 400 Hz etc.

Open pipe Fundamental frequency is

$$f_1 = \frac{v}{2l} = \frac{320}{2 \times 1.6} = 100 \text{ Hz}$$

Other frequencies are $2f_1 : 3f_1 : 4f_1$ etc. or 200 Hz, 300 Hz and 400 Hz etc. So, they resonate at 400 Hz.

12. $\lambda = \frac{2\pi}{k} = \frac{2\pi}{\pi/2} = 4 \text{ m}$

For second overtone in closed organ pipe,

$$l = \frac{5\lambda}{4} = 5 \text{ m}$$

13. $\lambda = \frac{v}{f} = \frac{330}{600} = 0.55 \text{ m} = 55 \text{ cm}$

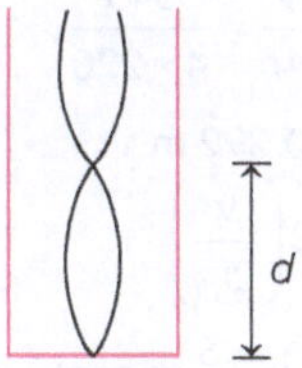

The desired distance, $d = \frac{\lambda}{4} = 13.75 \text{ cm}$

14. First overtone is 3rd harmonic.

Second overtone is 5th harmonic

Hence, pth overtone is $(2p+1)^{th}$ harmonic

15. $\frac{\lambda}{4} = 20 \text{ cm}$

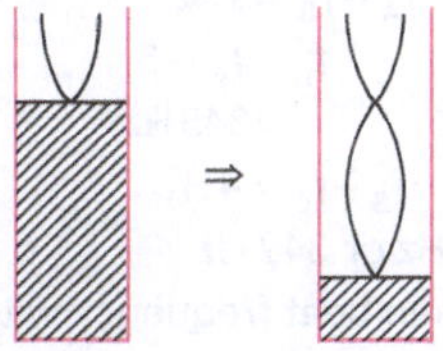

Next is $\frac{3\lambda}{4}$ or 60 cm.

16. Given, $3\left(\frac{v}{4l_c}\right) = 2\left(\frac{v}{2l_o}\right)$ or $\frac{l_c}{l_o} = \frac{3}{4}$

Now, $n\left(\frac{v}{4l_c}\right) = m\left(\frac{v}{2l_o}\right)$

or $$\frac{n}{m} = 2\frac{l_c}{l_o} = \frac{3}{2}$$

Thus, ratio $\frac{n}{m}$ should be $\frac{3}{2}$ but n is only odd, while m may be even or odd.

17. $f_1 : f_2 : f_3 = 425 : 595 : 765 = 5 : 7 : 9$

Since, these are odd harmonics, pipe is closed.

Further, $5\left(\frac{v}{4l}\right) = 425$

$$\therefore \quad l = \frac{5v}{425 \times 4} = \frac{5 \times 340}{425 \times 4} = 1 \text{ m}$$

18. $\lambda = \frac{v}{f} = \frac{330}{500} = 0.66 \text{ m}$

Length of air column at resonance can be

$$\frac{\lambda}{4}, \frac{3\lambda}{4}, \frac{5\lambda}{4}, \frac{7\lambda}{4}, \text{ etc.}$$

or 0.165 m, 0.495 m, 0.825 m, 1.155 m, etc.

But length of tube is only 1 m. Hence, first three resonances will be obtained.

19. $n_p = \frac{v}{4l}, n_q = \frac{v}{2l}, n_r = 2 \cdot \frac{v}{2l}, n_s = 3 \cdot \frac{v}{4l}$

$$n_p : n_q : n_r : n_s = \frac{1}{4} : \frac{1}{2} : 1 : \frac{3}{4} = 1 : 2 : 4 : 3$$

20. $L_1 = \frac{\lambda}{4}, L_2 = \frac{3\lambda}{4}$ and $L_3 = \frac{5\lambda}{4}$

21. Frequency of closed pipe, $n_1 = \frac{v}{4l_1} \Rightarrow l_1 = \frac{v}{4n_1}$

Frequency of open pipe, $n_2 = \frac{v}{2l_1} \Rightarrow l_2 = \frac{v}{2n_2}$.

When both pipes are joined, then length of closed pipe

$$l = l_1 + l_2$$

$$\frac{v}{4n} = \frac{v}{4n_1} + \frac{v}{2n_2}$$

Solving we get, $$n = \frac{n_1 n_2}{n_2 + 2n_1}$$

22. $\because \quad f = n\left(\frac{v}{4l}\right) \qquad (n = 1, 3, 5..)$

$$\therefore \quad l = \frac{nv}{4f} = n\left(\frac{330}{4 \times 264}\right)$$

$$= (0.3125\, n) \text{ m}$$

$$= (31.25\, n) \text{ cm}$$

Now, keep on substituting $n = 1, 3,$ etc.

23. (a) Velocity of sound wave in air independent of pressure if T = constant

(b) $v=\sqrt{\frac{\gamma RT}{M}}=\sqrt{\frac{\gamma R(t+273)}{M}}$

or $v^2 \propto (t+273)$

(c) $v=\sqrt{T/\mu}$

$\therefore$ $v\propto\sqrt{T}$ or $v^2 \propto T$

(d) $f_0=\frac{v}{2l}$ or $\frac{v}{4l}$

$\Rightarrow$ $f_0 \propto \frac{1}{l}$

24. Let f_1 = fundamental frequency of closed pipe and f_2 = fundamental frequency of open pipe.

(a) Given, $5f_1=4f_2$

or $f_2=\frac{5}{4}f_1$

$\therefore$ $f_2>f_1$

(b) First overtone frequency of closed pipe $=3f_1$ and first overtone frequency of open pipe

$$=2f_2=2\left(\frac{5}{4}f_1\right)=2.5\,f_1$$

(c) Fifteenth harmonic of closed pipe $=15f_1$
Twelfth harmonic of open pipe

$$=12f_2=12\left(\frac{5}{4}f_1\right)=15\,f_1$$

(d) Only odd harmonics are obtained in closed pipe.

25. $f=\frac{v}{4(l+0.6\,r)}=\frac{\sqrt{\gamma RT/M}}{4(l+0.6r)}$

(d) v does not depend on pressure if temperature is kept constant.

26. (a) $f=\frac{v}{2l}$

$$f_c=\frac{v}{4(2l)}=\frac{v}{8l}=\frac{f}{4}$$

(b) Second overtone frequency

$$=5f_c=5\,(f/4)=1.25\,f$$

(c) Third harmonic frequency $=3f_c$

$$=3\,(f/4)=0.75\,f$$

(d) First overtone frequency $=3f_c$

$$=3\,(f/4)=0.75\,f$$

27. $\because$ $k=\pi$

$$\lambda=\frac{2\pi}{k}=2\,\text{m}$$

$$l=\frac{5\lambda}{4}=\frac{5}{4}(2)$$

$$=2.5\text{ m}$$

Distance of displacement node from the closed end

$$=\frac{\lambda}{2}\quad\text{or}\quad\lambda$$

$$=1\,\text{m}\quad\text{or}\quad 2\text{m}$$

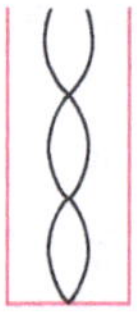

Pressure node means displacement antinode. Its distance from closed end

$$=\frac{\lambda}{4}\quad\text{or}\quad\frac{3\lambda}{4}\quad\text{or}\quad\frac{5\lambda}{4}$$

$$=0.5\text{ m}, 1.5\text{ m and } 2.5\text{ m}$$

28. $f=\frac{v}{4(l+0.6\,r)}$

$\therefore$ $v=4f\,(l+0.6\,r)$

$$=4\times 480\,(0.16+0.6\times 0.025)$$

$$=336\,\text{m/s}$$

29. $2\left(\frac{v}{2l_1}\right)=\left(\frac{v_2}{4l_2}\right)$

or $\frac{\sqrt{T/\mu}}{l_1}=\left(\frac{v_2}{4l_2}\right)$

$\therefore$ $T=\mu\left(\frac{v_2 l_1}{4l_2}\right)^2$

$$=\left(\frac{4\times10^{-3}}{0.4}\right)\left(\frac{340\times 40}{4\times 100}\right)^2$$

$$=11.56\text{ N}$$

30. (a) $f=\frac{v}{4l}$

$\therefore$ $l=\frac{v}{4f}=\frac{345}{4\times 220}$

$$=0.392\text{ m}$$

(b) $5\left(\frac{v}{4l_c}\right)=3\left(\frac{v}{2l_0}\right)$

$\therefore$ $l_0=\frac{6}{5}l_c=\frac{6}{5}(0.392)$

$$=0.470\,\text{m}$$

Module 6.

1. By putting wax on A. Its frequency will decrease. But beat frequency between A and B is also decreasing.

$\therefore$ $f_A>f_B$

or $f_A-f_B=5\,\text{Hz}$ ...(i)

$\therefore$ $f_B=f_A-5$

$$=345\,\text{Hz}$$

Now, $f_B \sim f_C=4\,\text{Hz}$

f_C is either 341 Hz or 349 Hz.

If it is 341 Hz, then beat frequency with A will be 9 Hz.

If it is 349 Hz, then beat frequency will be 1 Hz.

If wax is loaded on A, its frequency will decrease.

To produce 6 beats/s with C it should become either 347 Hz (if $f_C = 341$ Hz) or it should become 343 Hz (if $f_C = 349$ Hz).

If it becomes 347 Hz, then only it produces 2 beats/s with B, which is given in the question.

$\therefore \quad f_C = 341$ Hz **Ans.**

2. $f \propto \sqrt{T}$

$$\frac{f'}{f} = \sqrt{\frac{T'}{T}} = \sqrt{\frac{101}{100}} = 1.0049$$

$$f' = (1.0049)(200) \approx 201 \text{ Hz}$$

$$\therefore \quad f_b = f' - f = 1 \text{ Hz}$$

3. $f_b = f_1 - f_2 = \dfrac{v}{\lambda_1} - \dfrac{v}{\lambda_2}$

$$= \frac{332}{0.49} - \frac{332}{0.5} \approx 13 \text{ Hz}$$

4. $n_1 = n_2 = 10$ ...(i)

Using $\quad n_1 = \dfrac{v}{4l_1}$ and $n_2 = \dfrac{v}{4l_2}$

$$\Rightarrow \quad \frac{n_1}{n_2} = \frac{l_2}{l_1} = \frac{26}{25} \quad \text{...(ii)}$$

After solving these equations,

$$n_1 = 260 \text{ Hz}, n_2 = 250 \text{ Hz}$$

5. $f - \dfrac{f}{2} = 2$ or $f = 4$ Hz

Here, $\quad f = \dfrac{v}{2l}$ = fundamental frequency of open pipe

and $\quad \dfrac{f}{2} = \dfrac{v}{4l}$ = of closed pipe

Now, new beat frequency

$$= 2f - \frac{f}{4} = \frac{7f}{4}$$

$$= \frac{7}{4} \times 4 = 7 \text{ Hz}$$

6. Let n be the frequency of fork C, then

$$n_A = n + \frac{3n}{100} = \frac{103n}{100}$$

and $\quad n_B = n - \dfrac{2n}{100} = \dfrac{98n}{100}$

But $\quad n_A - n_B = 5$

$$\Rightarrow \quad \frac{5n}{100} = 5 \quad \Rightarrow \quad n = 100 \text{ Hz}$$

$$\therefore \quad n_A = \frac{(103)(100)}{100} = 103 \text{ Hz}$$

7. Beat frequency $= f_1 - f_2$

$$\frac{40}{12} = \frac{v}{4.08} - \frac{v}{4.16}$$

$$\Rightarrow \quad \frac{10}{3} = v\left(\frac{0.08}{4.08 \times 4.16}\right)$$

$$\Rightarrow \quad v = 707.2 \text{ m/s}$$

8. $f_A = 340 \pm 5 = 335$ or 340 Hz

When fork A is filled, then beat frequency decreases to 2 beats/s.

It is possible only when

$$f_A = 335 \text{ Hz}$$

9. According to question, tuning fork gives 1 beat/s with (N) 3rd normal mode. Therefore, organ pipe will have frequency (256 ± 1) Hz. In open organ pipe, frequency

$$f = \frac{nv}{2l}$$

$$\Rightarrow \quad 255 = \frac{3 \times 340}{2 \times l}$$

$$\Rightarrow \quad l = 2 \text{ m} = 200 \text{ cm}$$

10. Frequency of a sonometer wire, $f = \dfrac{1}{LD}\sqrt{\dfrac{T}{\pi\rho}}$

$$\therefore \quad f \propto \frac{1}{L}$$

As per question, $\quad \dfrac{f_1}{f_2} = \dfrac{100}{95}$ ...(i)

Also, $\quad f_1 - f_2 = 10$ ...(ii)

Solving Eqs. (i) and (ii)

$$f_1 = 200 \text{ Hz}, f_2 = 190 \text{ Hz}$$

Frequency of tuning fork,

$$f = f_1 - 5 = f_1 + 5 = 195 \text{ Hz}$$

11. Let f_1 = frequency of tuning fork and

f_2 = frequency of streamed wire

Given, $\quad f_1 > f_2$

$\therefore \quad f_b = f_1 - f_2$

(a) By loading wax on turning fork f_1 will decrease. Hence, $f_1 - f_2$ may be less than f_b or $f_2 - f_1$ may be greater than f_b.

(b) If prongs are filed, f_1 will increase. Hence,

$$f_1 - f_2 > f_b$$

(c) If tension in stretched wire is increased, f_2 will increase. Hence, $f_1 - f_2$ may be less than f_b or $f_2 - f_1$ may be greater than f_b.

(d) If tension in stretched wire is decreased, f_2 will decrease. Hence,

$$f_1 - f_2 > f_b$$

12. Frequency of first will decrease by loading wax over it. Beat frequency is increasing. Hence,

$$f_2 > f_1$$

or $\quad f_2 - f_1 = 4$

$$\therefore \quad f_1 = f_2 - 4 = 256 - 4 = 252 \text{ Hz}$$

13. By putting wax on first tuning fork, its frequency will decrease.

Beat frequency is also decreasing. Hence,

$$f_1 > f_2$$

$\therefore$ $f_1 - f_2 = 3$

or $f_1 = 3 + f_2 = 3 + 384 = 387\text{ Hz}$

14. Let the frequency of the first fork be f_1 and that of second be f_2.

We have,

$$f_1 = \frac{v}{4 \times 32} \quad \text{and} \quad f_2 = \frac{v}{4 \times 33}$$

We also see that $f_1 > f_2$

$\therefore$ $f_1 - f_2 = 8$ ...(i)

and $\frac{f_1}{f_2} = \frac{33}{32}$ ...(ii)

Solving Eqs. (i) and (ii), we get

$f_1 = 264\text{ Hz}$

and $f_2 = 256\text{ Hz}$ **Ans.**

15. Let $f_1 = f_0$. Then

$f_2 = f_0 + 4$

$f_3 = f_0 + 2 \times 4$

$f_4 = f_0 + 3 \times 4$

$\vdots \qquad \vdots$

$f_{20} = f_0 + 19 \times 4$

Now, $f_{20} = 2f_1 \Rightarrow f_0 + 19 \times 4 = 2f_0$

$\Rightarrow$ $f_0 = 76\text{ Hz}$

So, $f_{20} = 76 + 19 \times 4 = 152\text{ Hz}$

Module 7.

Introductory Exercise

1. Source is moving towards the observer

$$f' = f\left(\frac{v}{v - v_s}\right) = 450\left(\frac{330}{330 - 33}\right)$$

$f' = 500\text{ Hz}$

2. $f_1 = f\left(\frac{v}{v - v_s}\right)$

$\therefore$ $f_1 = f\left(\frac{340}{340 - 34}\right) = f\left(\frac{340}{306}\right)$

and $f_2 = f\left(\frac{340}{340 - 17}\right) = f\left(\frac{340}{323}\right)$

$\therefore$ $\frac{f_1}{f_2} = \frac{323}{306} = \frac{19}{18}$

3. Using the formula, $f' = f\left(\frac{v + v_0}{v}\right)$

We get, $5.5 = 5\left(\frac{v + v_A}{v}\right)$ ...(i)

and $6.0 = 5\left(\frac{v + v_B}{v}\right)$ ...(ii)

Here, v = speed of sound

v_A = speed of train A

and v_B = speed of train B

Solving Eqs. (i) and (ii), we get $\frac{v_B}{v_A} = 2$

4. Observer is stationary and source is moving.

During approach, $f_1 = f\left(\frac{v}{v - v_s}\right)$

$$= 1000\left(\frac{320}{320 - 20}\right)$$

$$= 1066.67\text{ Hz}$$

During recede, $f_2 = f\left(\frac{v}{v + v_s}\right) = 1000\left(\frac{320}{320 + 20}\right)$

$$= 941.18\text{ Hz}$$

$$|\Delta f| = 125.49\text{ Hz}$$

$\therefore$ % change $= \left(\frac{125.49}{1066.67}\right) \times 100$

$$= 11.7\,\% \approx 12\,\%$$

Exercise

1. The observer and source are moving towards each other. The image of the source serves as source of reflected sound and this is the second source.

The frequency of sound reflected from the wall

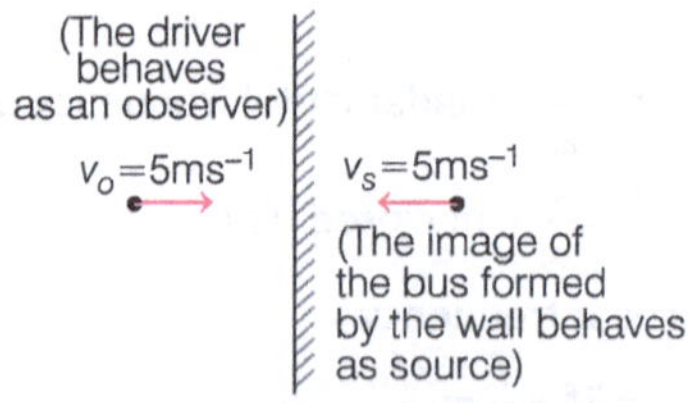

This frequency of sound reflected from the wall

$$v' = v\left[\frac{v + v_0}{v - v_s}\right]$$

$\Rightarrow$ $v' = 200\left[\frac{342 + 5}{342 - 5}\right] \approx 206\text{ Hz}$

$\therefore$ Frequency of beats

$= v' - v = 206 - 200$

$= 6\text{ Hz}$

2. If the sound reaches the observer after being reflected from a stationary surface and the medium is also stationary, the image of the source will become the source of reflected sound.

Thus in both the cases, one sound coming directly from the source and the other coming after reflection will have the same apparent frequency. Hence, no beats will be heard.

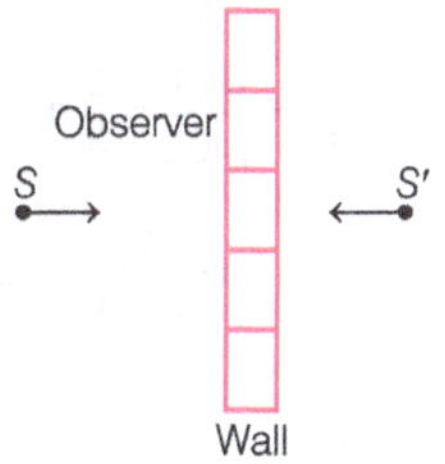

3. $f' = f\left(\dfrac{v}{v - v_s}\right) \Rightarrow f' > f$ but $f' =$ constant.

4. $f' = f\left(\dfrac{v}{v + v_s}\right) = f\left(\dfrac{v}{v + v}\right) = 0.5\, f$

5. $f' = f\left(\dfrac{v}{v \pm v_s \cos\theta}\right)$

At $\theta = 90°; f' = f$

$\therefore \quad n_1 = 0$

6. There is no relative motion between O and S'.

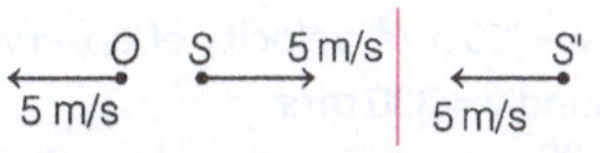

$$\begin{aligned} f_b &= f_{S'} - f_S \\ &= f - f_S \\ &= 180 - 180\left(\frac{355 - 5}{355 + 5}\right) \\ &= 5\text{ Hz} \end{aligned}$$

7. $n = n_1 - n_2 = \dfrac{v}{\lambda_1} - \dfrac{v}{\lambda_2}$

$\therefore \quad v = \dfrac{n\lambda_1\lambda_2}{\lambda_2 - \lambda_1}$

8. $f_b = 243\left(\dfrac{320}{320 - 4}\right) - 243\left(\dfrac{320}{320 + 4}\right) = 6$ Hz

9. $(f_b)_A = f_B - f_A$

$$\begin{aligned} &= 300\left(\frac{300 + 30}{300}\right) - 300 \\ &= 30\text{ Hz} \end{aligned}$$

$$\begin{aligned} (f_b)_B &= f_A - f_B \\ &= 300\left(\frac{300}{300 - 30}\right) - 300 = 33.33\text{ Hz} \end{aligned}$$

10. $f_a = f\left(\dfrac{v + v_0}{v}\right)$

$\therefore \quad \dfrac{v_0}{v} = \dfrac{f_a}{f} - 1 \quad$ ...(i)

$f_r = f\left(\dfrac{v - v_0}{v}\right)$

$\therefore \quad \dfrac{v_0}{v} = 1 - \dfrac{f_r}{f} \quad$ ...(ii)

From Eqs. (i) and (ii), we get

$$f = \frac{f_a + f_r}{2}$$

11. At point A, source is moving away from observer so apparent frequency $n_1 < n$ (actual frequency). At point B source is coming towards observer so apparent frequency $n_2 > n$ and at point C source is moving perpendicular to observer so $n_3 = n$.

Hence, $\quad n_2 > n_3 > n_1$

12. Suppose f_0 be the actual frequency. Then,

$$f = f_0\left(\frac{v + v_0}{v}\right)$$

and $\quad 0.8\, f = f_0\left(\dfrac{v - v_0}{v}\right)$

Solving these two equations, we get, $v_0 = \dfrac{v}{9}$

13. $f_1 - f_2 = 40$

or $\quad f\left(\dfrac{340}{340 - v_s}\right) - f\left(\dfrac{340}{340 + v_s}\right) = 40$

or $\quad 400\left(\dfrac{340}{340 - v_s}\right) - 400\left(\dfrac{340}{340 + v_s}\right) = 40$

Applying Binomial theorem and then solving, we get

$$v_s = 17\text{ m/s}$$

14. Here, $v_A = 72$ km/h $= 20$ m/s

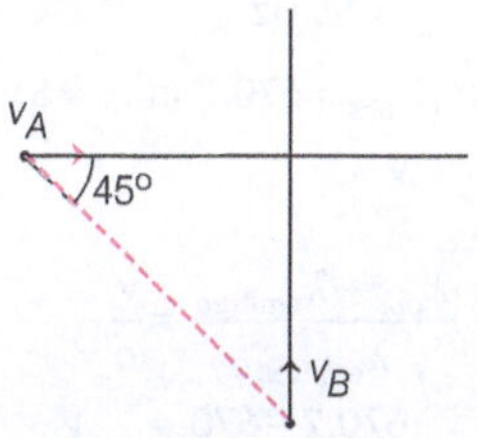

$$v_B = 36\text{ km/h} = 10\text{ m/s}$$

$$n' = n\left(\frac{v + v_B\cos 45°}{v - v_A\cos 45°}\right)$$

$$\Rightarrow \quad n' = 280\left(\frac{340 + 10/\sqrt{2}}{340 - 20/\sqrt{2}}\right) = 298\text{ Hz}$$

15. As passenger inside train has no relative speed relative to engine of train, so frequency heard by passenger is same as that of true frequency.

$\therefore$ Frequency heard by passenger

$= 400$ Hz

16. [Q] $\to$ 40 m/s, [P] $\to$ 20 m/s

Using Doppler's effect,

$$f' = f_0\left(\frac{v_w + v_D}{v_w + v_s}\right)$$

$$f' = 400\left(\frac{360 + 40}{360 + 20}\right) = 421\text{ Hz}$$

17. Given,

Given; Frequency of horn,

$$f_A = 300 \text{ Hz}$$

Speed of sound, $v = 330$ m/s

Speed of trains, $v_s = 30$ m/s

In case of train A, source is moving towards an stationary observer.

So, frequency of sound heard will be

$$f_A' = f_A\left(\frac{v}{v - v_s}\right)$$

$$= 300\left(\frac{330}{330 - 30}\right) = 330 \text{ Hz}$$

For train B, source is moving away from a stationary observer.

So, $f_B' = f_B\left(\dfrac{v}{v + v_s}\right)$

$$= \frac{300 \times 330}{(330 + 30)} = 275 \text{ Hz}$$

Difference of frequencies is

$$f_A' - f_B' = 330 - 275$$

$$= 55 \text{ Hz}$$

18. $\lambda_{\text{emitted}} = 670\,\text{nm}, \lambda_{\text{obs}} = 670.7\,\text{nm}, c = 3 \times 10^8\ \text{m/s},$

$$v = ?$$

If $v << c$

$$\frac{\lambda_{\text{obs}} - \lambda_{\text{emitted}}}{\lambda_{\text{emitted}}} = \frac{v}{c}$$

$$\Rightarrow \quad \frac{670.7 - 670}{670} = \frac{v}{3 \times 10^8}$$

$$\Rightarrow \quad v = 3.13 \times 10^5 \text{ m/s}$$

19. Apparent frequency of sound due to Doppler's effect is

$$f_1 = f_0\left(\frac{c}{c - v}\right)$$

Here, c = velocity of sound

v = velocity of source

Frequency of sound heard (f_2) when source is receding

$$f_2 = f_0\left(\frac{c}{c + v}\right)$$

Beat frequency $= f_1 - f_2$

$$\Rightarrow \quad 2 = f_1 - f_2 = f_0\, c\left[\frac{1}{c - v} - \frac{1}{c + v}\right]$$

$$= f_0 c \frac{2v}{c^2\left[1 - \dfrac{v^2}{c^2}\right]}$$

For $c >> v$

$$\Rightarrow \quad v = \frac{2c}{2f_0} = \frac{c}{f_0} = \frac{350}{1400} = \frac{1}{4} \text{ m/s}$$

20. $f_1 = f_0\left(\dfrac{v - v_0}{v}\right)$ and $f_2 = f_0\left(\dfrac{v + v_0}{v}\right)$

By frequency,

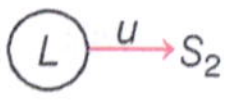

$$f_2 - f_1 = f_0 \times \frac{2v_0}{v}$$

or $$10 = 660 \times \frac{2u}{330}$$

$\therefore$ $$u = 2.5 \text{ m/s}$$

21. Using formula for apparent frequency, Doppler's effect

f = actual frequency

v = speed of sound.

$$f' = \left(\frac{v - v_0}{v - v_s}\right) f$$

where $v_0 = v_s = 30$ m/s, velocity of observer and source

Speed of sound $v = 330$ m/s

$\therefore\ f' = \dfrac{330 + 30}{330 - 30} \times 540$ [$\because$ Frequency of whistle $(f) = 540$ Hz]

$= 648$ Hz

22. In front of locomotive,

$$f' = f\left(\frac{v}{v - v_s}\right)$$

$$= 500\left(\frac{344}{344 - 30}\right) = 548 \text{ Hz}$$

$\therefore$ $$\lambda' = \frac{v}{f'} = \frac{344}{548} = 0.628 \text{ m}$$

Behind the locomotive,

$$f' = f\left(\frac{v}{v + v_s}\right)$$

$$= 500\left(\frac{344}{344 + 30}\right) = 460 \text{ Hz}$$

$\therefore$ $$\lambda' = \frac{v}{f'} = \frac{344}{460} = 0.748 \text{ m}$$

23. $f' = f\left(\dfrac{v}{v - v_s}\right) = 200\left(\dfrac{340}{340 - 80}\right)$

$$= 261.53 \text{ Hz} \approx 262 \text{ Hz}$$

$$\lambda' = \frac{v}{f'} = \frac{340}{261.53} = 1.3 \text{ m}$$

24. $f' = f\left(\dfrac{v - v_w - v_0}{v - v_w + v_s}\right)$

$$= 300\left[\frac{340 - 5 - 20}{340 - 5 + 10}\right]$$

$$= 274 \text{ Hz}$$

Unit Exercise (Cumulative)

Level 1

1. As $c = v\lambda$

$\therefore \quad \lambda = \frac{c}{v} = \frac{330}{660} = 0.5 \text{ m}$

Shortest distance from the wall at which air particles have maximum amplitude of vibration

$= \lambda/4 = \frac{0.5}{4} = 0.125 \text{ m}$

2. $T = \frac{1}{f} = \frac{1}{500} \text{ s}$

$\Rightarrow \quad t = \frac{T}{2} = \frac{1}{1000} \text{ s}$

3. $I_R = I_{max} = (\sqrt{I_1} + \sqrt{I_2})^2$

If $\quad I_1 = I_2 = I_0$, then

$I_R = 4I_0$

4. Fundamental frequency of closed pipe,

$n = \frac{v}{4l} = 220 \text{ Hz}$

$\Rightarrow \quad v = 220 \times 4l$

If $\frac{1}{4}$ of the pipe is filled with water, then remaining length of air column is $\frac{3l}{4}$.

Now, fundamental frequency $= \frac{v}{4\left(\frac{3l}{4}\right)} = \frac{v}{3l}$ and

First overtone $= 3 \times$ fundamental frequency

$= 3 \times \frac{v}{3l} = \frac{3 \times 220 \times 4l}{3l}$

$= 880 \text{ Hz}$

5. Given, $\quad f_o - f_c = 2 \quad$ ...(i)

Frequency of fundamental mode for a closed organ pipe,

$f_c = \frac{v}{4L_c}$

Similarly, frequency of fundamental mode for an open organ pipe,

$f_o = \frac{v}{2L_o}$

Given, $\quad L_c = L_o$

$\Rightarrow \quad f_o = 2f_c \quad$ ...(ii)

From Eqs. (i) and (ii), we get

$f_o = 4 \text{Hz}$ and $f_c = 2 \text{Hz}$

When the length of the open pipe is halved, its frequency of fundamental mode is

$f_o' = \frac{v}{2\left[\frac{L_o}{2}\right]} = 2f_o$

$= 2 \times 4 \text{ Hz} = 8 \text{ Hz}$

When the length of the closed pipe is doubled, its frequency of fundamental mode is

$f_c' = \frac{v}{4(2L_c)} = \frac{1}{2} f_c = \frac{1}{2} \times 2 = 1 \text{ Hz}$

Hence, number of beats produced per second is

$f_o' - f_c' = 8 - 1 = 7$

6. Number of overtones are 6. These frequencies less than 20 kHz are 4.5 kHz, 7.5 kHz, 10.5 kHz, 13.5 kHz, 16.5 kHz and 19.5 kHz.

7. For first resonance,

$\frac{\lambda}{4} = l_1 + e = 11 \text{ cm} \quad (\because \text{end correction, } e = 1 \text{ cm})$

$\Rightarrow \quad \lambda = 4(l_1 + e) = 44 \text{ cm}$

$\Rightarrow \quad \lambda = 44 \text{ cm}$

For second resonance,

$\frac{3\lambda}{4} = l_2 + e$

$\Rightarrow \quad l_2 = \frac{3\lambda}{4} - e$

$= \frac{3(44)}{4} - 1$

$\Rightarrow \quad l_2 = 32 \text{ cm}$

8. According to the question,

$\lambda = \frac{\lambda_1}{2}$

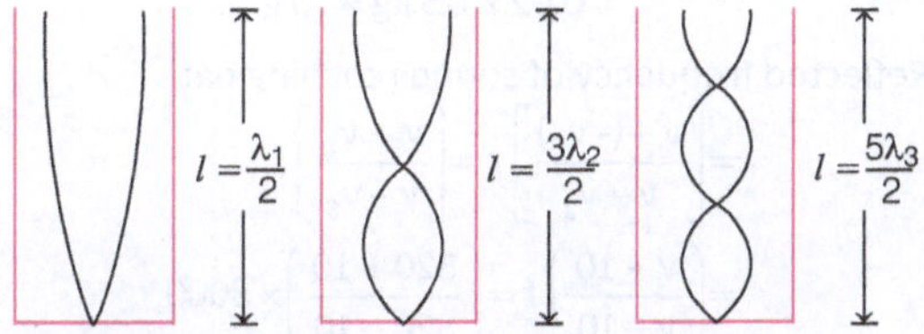

Fundamental tone   First overtone   Second overtone

$l = \frac{\lambda_1}{2} \Rightarrow \lambda_1 = 2l$

$l = \frac{3\lambda_2}{2} \Rightarrow \lambda_2 = \frac{2l}{3}$

$l = \frac{5\lambda_3}{2} \Rightarrow \lambda_3 = \frac{2l}{5}$

$\therefore \quad \lambda_1 : \lambda_2 : \lambda_3 = 2l : \frac{2l}{3} : \frac{2l}{5} = 1 : \frac{1}{3} : \frac{1}{5}$

9. Length of pipe $= 85 \text{ cm} = 0.85 \text{ m}$

For frequency of oscillations of air column in closed organ pipe;

$f = \frac{(2n-1)v}{4L}$

$\Rightarrow \quad f = \frac{(2n-1)v}{4L} \leq 1250$

$\Rightarrow \quad \frac{(2n-1) \times 340}{0.85 \times 4} \leq 1250$

$$\Rightarrow \quad 2n-1 \le 12.5 \approx 6$$

10. $\frac{\lambda}{4} = l_1 + e$ and $\frac{3\lambda}{4} = l_2 + e$

$$\Rightarrow \quad \frac{l_2+e}{l_1+e} = 3$$

$$\Rightarrow \quad l_2 = 3l_1 + 2e = 3\times 15 + 2\times 1.0$$
$$= 47 \text{ cm}$$

11. Frequency of 2nd harmonic of string = fundamental frequency produced in the pipe

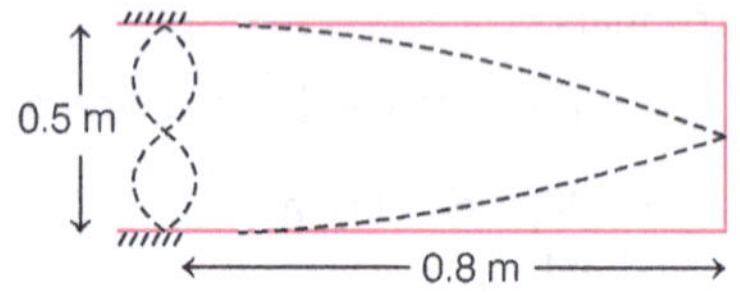

i.e. $$2\left(\frac{v_1}{2l_1}\right) = \frac{v_2}{4l_2}$$

$$\Rightarrow \quad 2\times\left[\frac{1}{2l_1}\sqrt{\frac{T}{\mu}}\right] = \frac{v}{4l_2}$$

$$\Rightarrow \quad \frac{1}{0.5}\sqrt{\frac{50}{\mu}} = \frac{320}{4\times 0.8}$$

$$\Rightarrow \quad \mu = 0.02 \text{ kg m}^{-1}$$

Hence, the mass of the string,

$$m_1 = \mu l_1$$
$$= 0.02\times 0.5 \text{ kg} = 10 \text{ g}$$

12. Reflected frequency of sound reaching bat

$$= \left[\frac{v-(-v_0)}{v-v_s}\right]f = \left[\frac{v+v_0}{v-v_s}\right]f$$
$$= \left(\frac{v+10}{v-10}\right)f = \left(\frac{320+10}{320-10}\right)\times 8000$$
$$\approx 8516 \text{ Hz}$$

13. $$f_b = \left(\frac{320+2}{320}\right)(800) - \left(\frac{320-2}{320}\right)(800)$$
$$= 805 - 795$$
$$= 10 \text{ Hz}$$

14. The motorcyclist observes no beats. So, the apparent frequency observed by him from the two sources must be equal.

$$f_1 = f_2$$

$$\therefore \quad 176\left(\frac{330-v}{330-22}\right) = 165\left(\frac{330+v}{330}\right)$$

Solving this equation, we get

$$v = 22 \text{ m/s}$$

15. According to question, the length of the air column is varied by changing the level of water in the resonance tube, So

$$(2n+1)\frac{\lambda}{4} = 50.7 + e \quad \text{...(i)}$$

and $$(2n+3)\frac{\lambda}{4} = 83.9 + e \quad \text{...(ii)}$$

Dividing Eq. (i) by Eq. (ii), we get

$$\frac{(2n+1)(\lambda/4)}{(2n+3)(\lambda/4)} = \frac{50.7+e}{83.9+e}$$

For $n = 1$,

$$\frac{(2(1)+1)(\lambda/4)}{(2(1)+3)(\lambda/4)} = \frac{50.7+e}{83.9+e}$$

$$\Rightarrow \quad \frac{3}{5} = \frac{50.7+e}{83.9+e}$$

$$\Rightarrow \quad 3(83.9+e) = 5(50.7+e)$$

$$\Rightarrow \quad 2e = 251.7 - 253.5$$

$$\Rightarrow \quad 2e = -1.8$$

$$\Rightarrow \quad e = -0.9 \text{ cm}$$

$$\therefore \quad \frac{3\lambda}{4} = 50.7 - 0.9 = 49.8$$

or $$\lambda = 4\times\frac{49.8}{3}$$

$$\Rightarrow \quad \lambda = 66.4 \text{ cm}$$
$$v = \nu\lambda = 500\times 0.664$$
$$= 332.0 \text{ ms}^{-1}$$

16. $I \propto A^2$ or $A \propto \sqrt{I}$

Due to a point source,

$$I = \frac{P}{4\pi r^2} \quad (P = \text{power of source})$$

or $$I \propto \frac{1}{r^2} \text{ and } A \propto \frac{1}{r}$$

Due to a line source

$$I = \frac{P}{2\pi r l}$$

or $$I \propto \frac{1}{r}$$

$$\therefore \quad A \propto \frac{1}{\sqrt{r}}$$

17. $f \propto \frac{1}{l}$

By decreasing the length, frequency of wire will increase. But beat frequency is decreasing. Hence, its original frequency was (256 − 4) Hz or 252 Hz. Now, we have to make it 256 Hz for no beats.

$$\frac{f_1}{f_2} = \frac{l_2}{l_1}$$

$$\therefore \quad l_2 = \left(\frac{f_1}{f_2}\right)l_1 = \left(\frac{252}{256}\right)(25) = 24.6 \text{ cm}$$

$$\therefore \quad \Delta l = l_1 - l_2 = 0.4 \text{ cm}$$

18. (a) $I = \frac{P}{4\pi r^2} = \frac{5}{4\pi(20)^2}$

$$=9.95\times10^{-4}\ \text{W/m}^2$$

(b) $I=\frac{1}{2}\rho\omega^2A^2v$

$$\therefore\quad A=\sqrt{\frac{2I}{\rho(2\pi f)^2v}}$$

$$=\sqrt{\frac{2\times9.95\times10^{-4}}{1.29(2\pi\times300)^2(330)}}$$

$$=1.15\times10^{-6}\text{m}$$

19. (a) $v=\sqrt{\frac{B}{\rho}}=\sqrt{\frac{2.18\times10^9}{1000}}=1476\ \text{m/s}$

$$\lambda=\frac{v}{f}=\frac{1476}{3400}=0.43\ \text{m}$$

$$I=\frac{1}{2}\rho\omega^2A^2v$$

$$\therefore\quad A=\sqrt{\frac{2I}{\rho(2\pi f)^2v}}$$

$$=\sqrt{\frac{2\times3\times10^{-6}}{(1000)(2\pi\times3400)^2(1476)}}$$

$$=9.44\times10^{-11}\ \text{m}$$

(b) $v=\sqrt{\frac{\gamma p}{\rho}}=\sqrt{\frac{(1.4)(10^5)}{(1.2)}}$

$$=341.56\ \text{m/s}$$

$$\lambda=\frac{v}{f}=\frac{341.56}{3400}=0.1\ \text{m}$$

$$A=\sqrt{\frac{2I}{\rho(2\pi f)^2v}}$$

$$=\sqrt{\frac{2\times3.0\times10^{-6}}{1.2\times(2\pi\times3400)^2(341.56)}}$$

$$=5.66\times10^{-9}\text{m}$$

(c) $\frac{A_{air}}{A_{water}}=\frac{5.66\times10^{-9}}{9.44\times10^{-11}}=60$

$$I=\frac{1}{2}\rho\omega^2A^2v$$

ρ and v are less in air. So, for same intensity A should be large in air.

20. $\therefore\ v=f\lambda=(1000)(2\times6.77\times10^{-2})$

$$=135.4\ \text{m/s}=\sqrt{\frac{\gamma RT}{M}}$$

$$\therefore\quad \gamma=(135.4)^2\left(\frac{M}{RT}\right)$$

$$=\frac{(135.4)^2(0.127)}{(8.31\times400)}=0.7$$

Since, $\gamma<1$

So, we will have to substitute,

$$M=2\times0.127$$

The γ comes out to be 1.4 which is the γ of a diatomic gas.

21. $\frac{\lambda}{2}=(45-15)\ \text{cm}$

$$\therefore\quad \lambda=60\ \text{cm}$$

$$v=f\lambda=(500)(0.6)$$

$$=300\ \text{m/s}$$

Lowest frequency when open from both ends is $\frac{v}{2l}$.

$$=\frac{300}{2\times0.6}=250\ \text{Hz}$$

22. Fundamental frequency $=\frac{v}{2l}$

$$f=\frac{330}{2\times0.8}$$

$$f=206.25\ \text{Hz}$$

$$\omega=2\pi f\approx1297\ \text{rad/s}$$

$$k=\frac{\omega}{v}=\frac{1297}{330}$$

$$=3.93\ \text{rad/s}$$

Now, $x=0$ (the open end) is an antinode. Hence, we can write the equation,

$$y=A\cos kx\sin\omega t$$

23. $\frac{\lambda}{2}=(84-50)\ \text{cm}=34\ \text{cm}$

Next length $=84+\frac{\lambda}{2}=118\ \text{cm}$

$$\lambda=68\ \text{cm}\quad\text{or}\quad0.68\ \text{m}$$

$$v=f\lambda=(512)(0.68)$$

$$=348.16\ \text{m/s}$$

24. $\frac{v_1}{2(0.8l)}=\frac{v_2}{4l}\ \Rightarrow\ \frac{v_1}{v_2}=0.40$

25. (a) Possible fundamental frequencies of retuned string is (440 ± 1.5) Hz.

(b) $f\propto\sqrt{T}$

$$\therefore\quad \frac{f_1}{f_2}=\sqrt{\frac{T_1}{T_2}}$$

$$\therefore\quad T_2=\left(\frac{f_2}{f_1}\right)^2T_1$$

(i) $T_2=\left(\frac{441.5}{440}\right)^2$

$$T_1=1.0068\ T_1$$

$$\%\ \text{change}=\frac{T_2-T_1}{T_1}\times100$$

$$=+0.68\%$$

(ii) $T_2=\left(\frac{438.5}{440}\right)^2T_1$

$$=0.9932\,T_1$$

$$\% \text{ change} = \frac{T_2 - T_1}{T_1} \times 100$$
$$= -0.68\%$$

26. (a) $f' = f\left(\frac{v + v_O}{v - v_s}\right)$

$$= 262\left(\frac{340 + 18}{340 - 30}\right) = 302 \text{ Hz}$$

(b) $f' = f\left(\frac{v - v_O}{v + v_s}\right) = 262\left(\frac{340 - 18}{340 + 30}\right)$

$$= 228 \text{ Hz}$$

27.

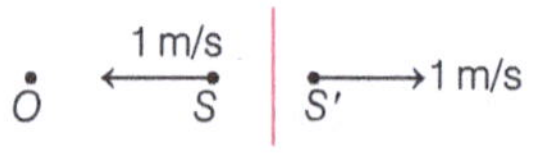

$$f_b = f_S - f_{S'}$$
$$4 = f\left(\frac{340}{340 - 1}\right) - f\left(\frac{340}{340 + 1}\right)$$

or $$4 = f\left(1 - \frac{1}{340}\right)^{-1} - f\left(1 + \frac{1}{340}\right)^{-1}$$

Applying Binomial, we get

$$4 = f\left(1 + \frac{1}{340}\right) - f\left(1 - \frac{1}{340}\right)$$
$$= \frac{f}{170} \quad \text{or} \quad f = 680 \text{ Hz}$$

28. Beat frequency between P and Q is $\frac{7}{2}$ or 3.5 Hz.

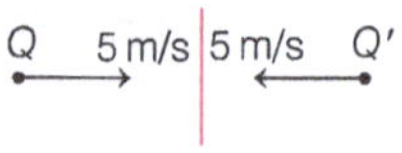

On loading P with wax, its frequency will decrease and beat frequency is increasing.

$\therefore$ $$f_Q > f_P$$

or $$f_Q - f_P = 3.5 \quad \text{...(i)}$$

Given, $f'_Q - f_Q = 5$

or $$f_Q\left(\frac{332 + 5}{332 - 5}\right) - f_Q = 5$$

Solving this equation, we get

$$f_Q = 163.5 \text{ Hz}$$

Now, from Eq. (i), we have

$$f_P = 160 \text{ Hz}$$

29. (a) The frequency of the whistle heard by observer on the hill

$$n' = n\left[\frac{v + v_W}{v + v_W - v_s}\right] = 580\left[\frac{1200 + 40}{1200 + 40 - 40}\right]$$
$$= 599 \text{ Hz}$$

(b) Let echo from the hill is heard by the driver at B which is at a distance x from the hill sound produced by train at a distance 1 km from the hill. The time taken by the driver to reach from A to B

$$t_1 = \frac{1 - x}{40} \quad \text{...(i)}$$

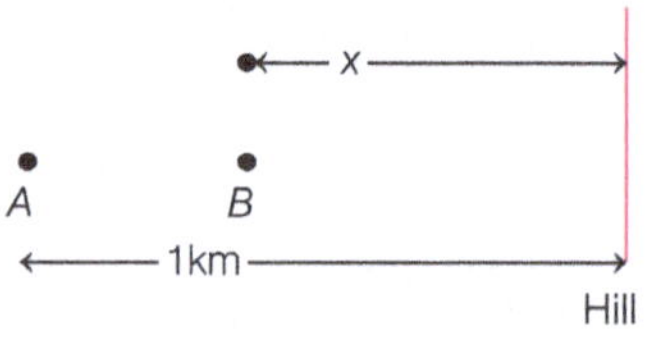

The time taken by echo to reach from hill

$$t_2 = t_{AH} + t_{HB}$$
$$t_2 = \frac{1}{(1200 + 40)} + \frac{x}{(1200 - 40)} \quad \text{...(ii)}$$

where t_{AH} = time taken by sound from A to hill with velocity $(1200 + 40)$

t_{HB} = time taken by sound from hill to B with velocity $1200 - 40$

From Eqs. (i) and (ii),

$$t_1 = t_2$$
$$\Rightarrow \quad \frac{1 - x}{40} = \frac{1}{1200 + 40} + \frac{x}{1200 - 40}$$
$$\Rightarrow \quad x = 0.935 \text{ km}$$

The frequency of echo as heard by the driver

$$n^n = n\left[\frac{(v - v_w) + v_s}{(v - v_w) - v_O}\right]$$
$$= 580\left[\frac{(1200 - 40) + 40}{(1200 - 40) - 40}\right] = 621 \text{ Hz}$$

30. The frequency noticed at the wall

$$f_1 = f\left(\frac{v}{v - v_b}\right) \quad \text{...(i)}$$

This frequency is reflected back and picked by motorist, then

$$f_2 = f_1\left(\frac{v + v_m}{v}\right) \quad \text{...(ii)}$$

From Eqs. (i) and (ii), we have

$$f_2 = f\left(\frac{v + v_m}{v - v_b}\right)$$

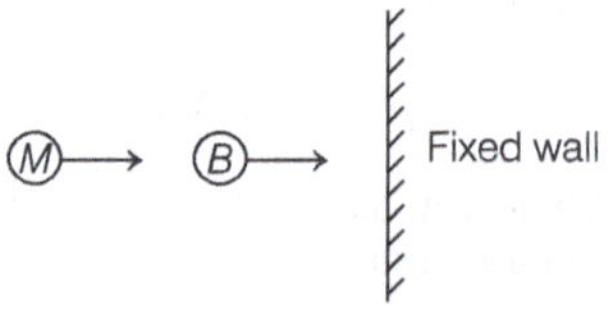

This frequency of sound noticed directly

$$f' = f\left(\frac{v + v_m}{v + v_b}\right) \quad \text{...(iii)}$$

$\therefore$ Beat frequency

$$\Delta f = f_2 - f' = f\left(\frac{2v_b(v + v_m)}{v^2 - v_b^2}\right)$$

31. At a distance x from end A, temperature is,

$$T = T_1 + \left(\frac{T_1 - T_2}{l}\right)x$$

$$v = \alpha\sqrt{T} = \alpha\sqrt{T_1 + \left(\frac{T_1 - T_2}{l}\right)x}$$

or $$\frac{dx}{dt} = \alpha\sqrt{T_1 + \left(\frac{T_1 - T_2}{l}\right)x}$$

$$\Rightarrow \int_0^t dt = \int_0^l \frac{dx}{\alpha\sqrt{T_1 + \left(\frac{T_1 - T_2}{l}\right)x}}$$

Solving this integration, we get

$$t = \frac{2l}{\alpha(\sqrt{T_1} + \sqrt{T_2})}$$

32.

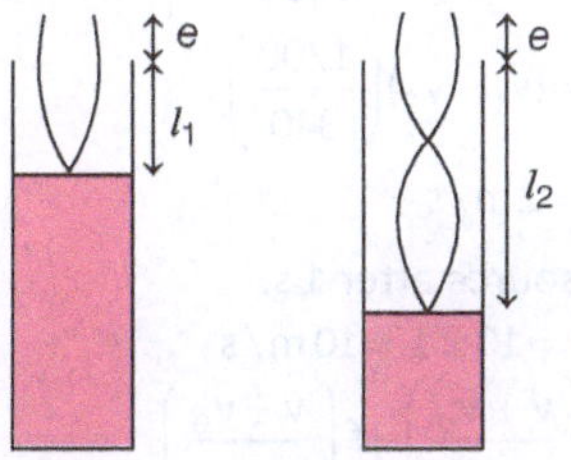

$$l_2 + e = \frac{3\lambda}{4} \quad \text{...(i)}$$

$$l_1 + e = \frac{\lambda}{4} \quad \text{...(ii)}$$

Subtracting Eq. (ii) from Eq. (i), we get

$$(l_2 - l_1) = \frac{\lambda}{2} \quad \text{or} \quad \lambda = 2(\lambda_2 - l_1)$$

$\therefore$ $v = f\lambda = 2f(\lambda_2 - l_1)$

or $v = 2 \times 2000 \times 8.5 \times 10^{-2}$

or $v = 340\,\text{m/s}$

33. (a) $(2n+1)\dfrac{v}{4l} < 1250,\ n = 0, 1, 2\ldots$

$\therefore$ $(2n+1) < \dfrac{4l(1250)}{v}$

or $n < \dfrac{1}{2}\left[\dfrac{4l(1250)}{v} - 1\right]$

or $n < \dfrac{1}{2}\left[\dfrac{4 \times 0.85 \times 1250}{340} - 1\right]$

or $n < 5.75$

$\therefore$ $n = 0, 1, 2, 3, 4$ and 5

Therefore answer is six.

(b) $n\left(\dfrac{v}{2l}\right) < 1250,\ n = 1, 2, 3\ldots$

or $n < \dfrac{(1250)(2l)}{v}$

or $n < \dfrac{1250 \times 2 \times 0.85}{340}$

or $n < 6.25$

or $n = 1, 2, 3, 4, 5, 6$

Hence the answer is again six.

34. Frequency received by wall (assume wall as an observer)

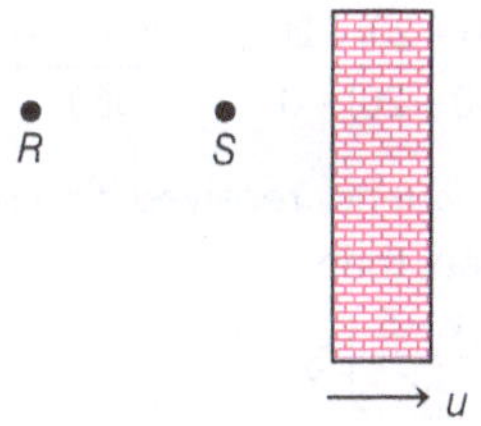

$$f_1 = f_0\left(\frac{v - u}{v}\right) = 1700\left(\frac{340 - 0.06}{340}\right)$$

$= 1699.7$ Hz

Now reflected frequency received by receiver from wall (now assume wall as a source)

$$f_2 = f_1\left(\frac{v}{v + u}\right) = 1699.7\left(\frac{340}{340 + 0.06}\right)$$

$= 1699.4$ Hz

Direct frequency received by receiver from the source will be f_0 or 1700 Hz. Therefore beat frequency,

$$f_b = f_0 - f_2 = (1700 - 1699.4)\,\text{Hz}$$

or $f_b = 0.60$ Hz

35. $f' = f_0 + 40$

$\Rightarrow$ $f_0\left(\dfrac{330 + 15}{330 - 15}\right) = f_0 + 40$

$$f_0 \times \frac{345}{315} = f_0 + 40$$

$$f_0 \times \frac{345}{315} - f_0 = 40$$

$$f_0 \times \frac{30}{315} = 40 = \frac{40 \times 315}{30}$$

$$f_0 = 420\,\text{Hz}$$

36. Frequency of whistle blowing by train, $f = 320$ Hz

Speed of train, $v_s = 66$ m/s

Speed of sound, $v = 330\ \text{ms}^{-1}$

Frequency observed by the observer,

$$f' = f\left(\frac{v}{v - v_s}\right) = 320\left(\frac{330}{330 - 66}\right)$$

$$= 320 \times \frac{330}{264} = 400\,\text{Hz}$$

37. From Doppler's effect, frequency of the train w.r.t. the hill

$$f_1 = \left(\frac{v}{v - v_s}\right)f = \left(\frac{330}{320}\right)320 = 330\,\text{Hz}$$

$\therefore$ Frequency of the sound reflected by hill w.r.t. the train i.e., echoheard by observer.

$$f_2 = \left(\frac{v + v_0}{v}\right)f_1 = \left(\frac{330 + 10}{330}\right) \times 330$$

$= 340$ Hz

38. Here, the apparent frequency is given by $f' = f\left(\frac{v - v_0}{v + v_s}\right)$

$$=720\left(\frac{(340+20)-20}{(340+20)-0}\right)=\frac{720\times 340}{360}=680\text{ Hz}$$

39. Let f_1 be the frequency received directly and f_2 received due to reflection, then

$$f_1 = \left(\frac{v-5}{v}\right)f_0$$

$$f_2 = \left(\frac{v+5}{v}\right)f_0$$

So, $$f_{\text{Beat}} = f_2 - f_1 = \frac{10}{v}f_0$$

$$=\frac{10\times 640}{320}=20\text{ Hz}$$

40. Apparent frequency

$$\nu = \nu_0\left(\frac{v+v_0}{v-v_s}\right) \Rightarrow 1320 = \nu_0\left(\frac{340+20}{340-10}\right)$$

$$\Rightarrow \qquad \nu_0 = 1210\text{ Hz}$$

41. Let l_1 = initial length of pipe

l_2 = new length of pipe

v_T = Speed of tuning fork

In closed organ pipe, $f = \frac{v}{4l_1}$

When tuning fork is moved,

$$f' = f\left(\frac{v}{v - v_T}\right) = \frac{v}{4l_2}$$

$$\Rightarrow \quad \frac{v}{4l_1}\left(\frac{v}{v-v_T}\right)=\frac{v}{4l_2} \Rightarrow \frac{v-v_T}{v}=\frac{l_2}{l_1}$$

$$\Rightarrow \quad \frac{l_2}{l_1}-1=\frac{v-v_T}{v}-1 \Rightarrow \frac{l_2-l_1}{l_1}=\frac{-v_T}{v}$$

Percentage change required in the length of the pipe

$$\frac{l_2-l_1}{l_1}\times 100=\frac{-2}{320}\times 100=-0.625\%$$

The smallest value of percentage change that will be seen is 0.625%.

Level 2

42. $\sin\theta_C = \frac{330}{1400} = 0.2357$

$\therefore \quad \theta_C = 13.6°$

Since, $i > \theta_C$, therefore only reflection will take place.

43. Frequency of 2nd harmonic open pipe,

$$f_1 = \frac{v}{\lambda} = \frac{v}{l} \qquad \text{... (i)}$$

Frequency of nth harmonic of closed pipe,

$$f_2 = \frac{v}{\lambda} = \frac{nv}{4l} \qquad \text{... (ii)}$$

Here n is a odd number. From Eqs. (i) and (ii)

$$f_2 = \frac{n}{4}f_1, \text{ For first resonance, } n = 5$$

$$\therefore \quad f_2 = \frac{5}{4}f_1$$

44. $f_b = f_1 - f_2$

or $$10 = 1700\left(\frac{340}{340+v_2}\right) - 1700\left(\frac{340}{340+v_1}\right)$$

$$=1700\left(1+\frac{v_2}{340}\right)^{-1} - 1700\left(1+\frac{v_1}{340}\right)^{-1}$$

Using Binomial theorem, we get

$$10 = 1700\left(1-\frac{v_2}{340}\right) - 1700\left(1-\frac{v_1}{340}\right)$$

$$=(v_1 - v_2)\left(\frac{1700}{340}\right)$$

$\therefore \quad v_1 - v_2 = 2\text{ m/s}$

45. Velocity of source after 1 s,

$$v_s = gt = 10\times 1 = 10\text{ m/s}$$

$$\Delta f = f\left(\frac{v+v_0}{v-v_s}\right) - f\left(\frac{v-v_0}{v+v_s}\right)$$

$$=150\left(\frac{300+2}{300-10}\right)-150\left(\frac{300-2}{300+10}\right)$$

$$=12\text{ Hz}$$

46. $L = \frac{7\lambda}{4}$

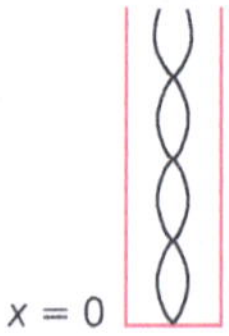

$$\therefore \quad \lambda = \frac{4L}{7}$$

$$k = \frac{2\pi}{\lambda} = \frac{2\pi}{4L/7} = \frac{7\pi}{2L}$$

$x = 0$ is a node

$$\therefore \quad A_x = a\sin kx = a\sin\left(\frac{7\pi}{2L}\right)\left(\frac{L}{7}\right) = a$$

47.

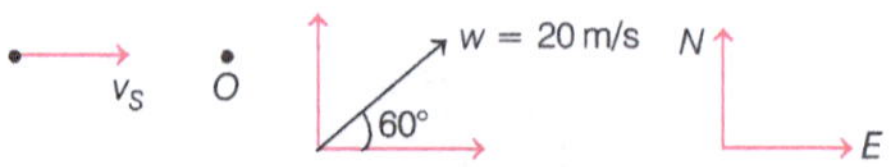

$$f' = f\left(\frac{v + w\cos 60°}{v + w\cos 60° - v_s}\right)$$

$$=500\left(\frac{300+10}{300+10-20}\right)\approx 534\text{ Hz}$$

48.

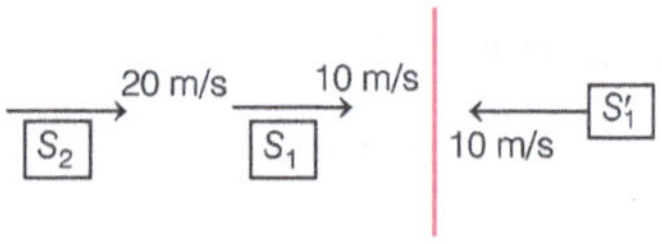

$$f_b = f_{S'} - f_{S_1}$$

$$=500\left[\frac{340+20}{340-10}\right]-500\left[\frac{340+20}{340+10}\right]$$

$$\approx 31\text{ Hz}$$

49. $f_1=\frac{\omega_1}{2\pi}=\frac{(400\pi)}{2\pi}=200\text{ Hz}$

$$f_2=\frac{\omega_2}{2\pi}=\frac{404\pi}{2\pi}=202\text{ Hz}$$

$\therefore$ $f_b=f_2-f_1=2\text{ Hz}$

$A_1=2$

and $A_2=1$

Hence, $\frac{I_{max}}{I_{min}}=\left(\frac{A_1+A_2}{A_1-A_2}\right)^2=\frac{9}{1}$

50. $l=\frac{3\lambda}{4}$

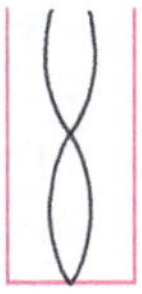

$\therefore$ $\lambda=\frac{4l}{3}=\frac{4(34)}{3}=45.33\text{ cm}$

$\lambda=\frac{v}{f}$

$\lambda\propto v$ (as f = constant)

and $v\propto\sqrt{T}$ (T = temperature)

$\therefore$ $\lambda\propto\sqrt{T}$

$\because$ $\frac{\lambda_2}{\lambda_1}=\sqrt{\frac{T_2}{T_1}}$

$\therefore$ $\lambda_2=\left(\sqrt{\frac{T_2}{T_1}}\right)\lambda_1$

$=\left(\sqrt{\frac{16+273}{51+273}}\right)(45.33)$

$=42.8\text{ cm}$

51. With increase in tension, frequency of vibrating string will increase. Since number of beats are decreasing. Therefore, frequency of vibrating string or third harmonic frequency of closed pipe should be less than the frequency of tuning fork by 4.

$\therefore$ Frequency of tuning fork

= third harmonic frequency of closed pipe + 4

$=3\left(\frac{v}{4l}\right)+4$

$=3\left(\frac{340}{4\times0.75}\right)+4=344\text{ Hz}$

52. $M=\frac{n_1M_1+n_2M_2}{n_1+n_2}$

$=\frac{(2)(32)+(3)(48)}{5}=41.6$

$f=\frac{v}{4l}$ or $f\propto v$

But, $v=\sqrt{\frac{\gamma RT}{M}}$ or $v\propto\frac{1}{\sqrt{M}}$

$\therefore$ $f\propto\frac{1}{\sqrt{M}}$

$\therefore$ $\frac{f_2}{f_1}=\sqrt{\frac{M_1}{M_2}}$ or $f_2=\left(\sqrt{\frac{M_1}{M_2}}\right)f_1$

$=\left(\sqrt{\frac{32}{48}}\right)(200)=163.3\text{ Hz}$

53. $f=f_0\left(\frac{v+v_0}{v}\right)$

$=10^3\left(1+\frac{10t}{v}\right)$ (as $v_0=gt$)

Hence, f *versus* t graph is a straight line of slope $\frac{10^4}{v}$.

$\therefore$ $\frac{10^4}{v}=\text{slope}=\frac{100}{3}$

$\therefore$ $v=300\text{ m/s}$

54. $\because$ $v_p=-v\left(\frac{\partial y}{\partial x}\right)$, where $v=+\text{ve}$.

At E, $\frac{\partial y}{\partial x}$ or slope is positive.

Hence, v_p is negative.

At D, $\frac{\partial y}{\partial x}$ or slope is zero. Hence, v_p is zero.

55. Let S be the source of sound and P the person or listener. The waves from S reach point P directly following the path SMP and being reflected from the ceiling at point A following the path SAP. M is mid-point of SP (i.e. $SM=MP$) and $\angle SMA=90°$.

Path difference between waves

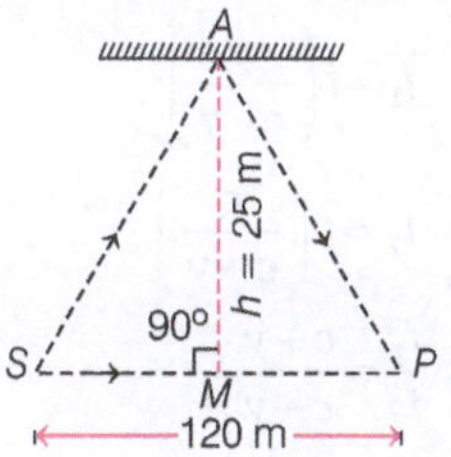

$\Delta x=SAP-SMP$

$SAP=2\sqrt{(60^2+25^2)}=130\text{ m}$

$\therefore$ Path difference

$=SAP-SMP=130-120=10\text{ m}$

Path difference due to reflection from ceiling $=\frac{\lambda}{2}$

If $\Delta x=\frac{\lambda}{2},\frac{3\lambda}{2},\frac{5\lambda}{2}$, etc., interference will be constructive

$\therefore$ $\lambda=20\text{ m},\ \frac{20}{3}\text{ m},\ \frac{20}{5}\text{ m}$, etc.

56. $n_Q=341\pm3=344\text{ Hz}$ or 338 Hz.

On waxing Q, the number of beats decreases hence $n_Q=344\text{ Hz}$.

57. Frequency received by reflecting surface,

$$f_1=256\left[\frac{330+10}{330-10}\right]$$

$=272\text{ Hz}$

Now, frequency of reflected sound as received by the receiver,

$$f_2 = 272\left[\frac{330+10}{330-10}\right] = 289\text{ Hz}$$

58. In the starting $\Delta x = 0$ and maximum intensity is observed.

Next maxima will correspond to $\Delta x = \lambda$, and the last, i.e. 5th maxima will correspond to

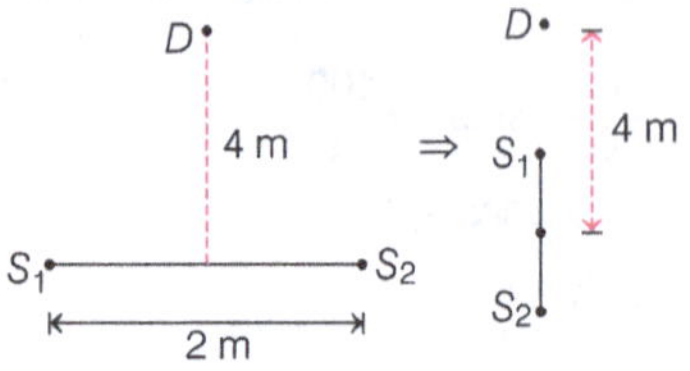

$$\Delta x = 4\lambda.$$

But $\Delta x = S_1S_2 = 2\text{ m}$

$\therefore$ $4\lambda = 2\text{ m}$ or $\lambda = 0.5\text{ m}$

59.

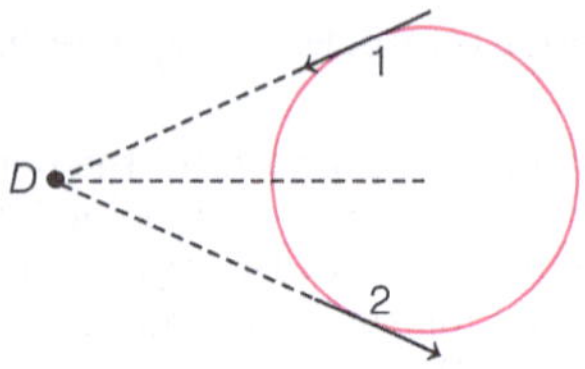

At 1, frequency will be maximum and at 2, frequency is minimum.

$$f_1 = f\left(\frac{c}{c-v}\right)$$

and $$f_2 = f\left(\frac{c}{c+v}\right)$$

$\therefore$ $$\frac{f_1}{f_2} = \frac{c+v}{c-v}$$

60. Effective value of velocity of source,

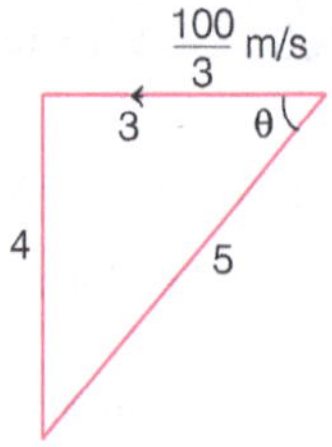

$$v_s = \frac{100}{3}\cos\theta$$

$$= \frac{100}{3} \times \frac{3}{5} = 20\text{ m/s}$$

$$f' = \frac{v}{v - v_s} f$$

$$f' = \frac{340}{340-20} \times 640\text{ Hz}$$

$$= 680\text{ Hz}$$

61. According to Doppler's effect,

Apparent, frequency $f = \left(\dfrac{v + v_0}{v - c_s}\right) f_0$

where, v = Speed of sound

v_0 = Speed of observer

v_s = Speed of source

f_0 = actual frequency

Now, $f = \left(\dfrac{f_0}{v - v_s}\right) v_0 + \dfrac{v f_0}{v - v_s}$

So, Slope $= \dfrac{f_0}{v - v_s}$

62. From Doppler's effect

$$f = f_s\left(\frac{v}{v-u}\right)$$

where, f_s = actual frequency

f = apparent frequency

v = speed of sound

u = speed of source

As the pipe is closed at one end.

$\therefore$ For resonance,

$$f = f_0\left(\frac{v}{v-u}\right) = nf_0$$

where n = odd integer

(a) For $u = 0.8v$ and $f_s = f_0$

$$f = f_0\left(\frac{v}{v - 0.8v}\right) = 5f_0$$

(b) For $u = 0.8v$ and $f_s = 2f_0$

$$\Rightarrow \quad f = 2f_0\left(\frac{v}{v-0.8v}\right) = 10f_0$$

(c) For $u = 0.8v$ and $f_s = 0.5f_0$

$$f = 0.5f_0\left(\frac{v}{v-0.8v}\right) = 2.5f_0$$

(d) For $u = 0.5v$ and $f_s = 1.5f_0$

$$f = 1.5f_0\left(\frac{v}{v-0.5v}\right) = 3f_0$$

63.

From conservation of linear momentum,

$$50(8 - v) = 150v$$

$\therefore$ $$v = 2\text{ m/s}$$

$$8 - v = 6\text{ m/s}$$

$$f_1 = f_0\left(\frac{v + v_0}{v - v_s}\right)$$

$$= f_0\left(\frac{330+2}{330-6}\right) = \frac{332}{324} f_0$$

64. 

$$f_2 = f_0\left(\frac{v - v_O}{v + v_s}\right)$$

$$= f_0\left(\frac{330-2}{330+6}\right) = \left(\frac{328}{336}\right) f_0$$

65. $f_1 > f_0$ but $f_1 =$ constant.

Similarly, $f_2 < f_0$ but $f_2 =$ constant

66. Initial vertical components of velocity for both are same. So, there is no relative motion in the vertical direction (Note that relative acceleration is also zero)

$$f' = \left(\frac{v}{v + v_s}\right) f_0$$

$$= \left(\frac{310}{310 + 10\sqrt{2}\cos 45°}\right) 960$$

$$= 930 \text{ Hz}$$

And this apparent frequency is constant as both of them reach the ground simultaneously at $t = 2$ s.

67. The best option is (d).

68. In the vertical direction, there is no relative motion. And in the horizontal direction, relative velocity is constant. So, apparent frequency heard by the detector will be constant.

69. The speed of sound depends on the frame of reference of the observer.

$$v_{SA} = 340 + 20 = 360 \text{ m/s}$$

and $$v_{SB} = 340 - 30 = 310 \text{ m/s}$$

70. There is no relative motion between source and observer for the passengers in train *A*. Since all the passengers in train *A* are moving with a velocity of 20 m/s therefore the distribution of sound intensity of the whistle by the passengers in train *A* is uniform.

71. For the passengers in train *B*, source is approaching with velocity 20 m/s and observer is receding with velocity 30 m/s

$$f' = f_1\left[\frac{v_1 - v_O}{v - v_s}\right]$$

$$= 800\left[\frac{340-30}{340-20}\right] = 800 \times \frac{31}{32}$$

$$f'' = f_2\left[\frac{v - v_O}{v - v_s}\right] = 1120 \times \frac{31}{32}$$

$$\therefore \quad f'' - f' = (1120 - 800) \times \frac{31}{32}$$

$$= 320 \times \frac{31}{32} = 310 \text{ Hz}$$

72. In one second number of maximas is called the beat frequency. Hence,

$$f_b = f_1 - f_2 = \frac{100\pi}{2\pi} - \frac{92\pi}{2\pi}$$

$$= 4 \text{ Hz}$$

73. Speed of wave, $v = \dfrac{\omega}{k}$

or $$v = \frac{100\pi}{0.5\,\pi}$$

or $$\frac{92\,\pi}{0.46\,\pi} = 200 \text{ m/s}$$

74. The angular frequency of the detector,

$$\omega = 2\pi v = 2\pi \times \frac{5}{\pi} = 10 \text{ rad/s}$$

The angular frequency of the detector and the source of sound are equal.

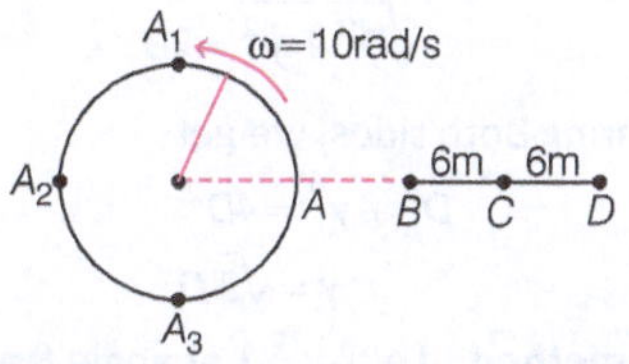

Frequency heard is minimum when movement of detector is from *C* towards *D* and movement of source is from *A* towards A_2.

$$f_{min} = f\left[\frac{v - v_O}{v + v_s}\right]$$

$$= 340 \times \frac{(340-60)}{(340+30)} = 257.3 \text{ Hz}$$

$$(\because v_O = A\omega = 6 \times 10 = 60 \text{ m/s}$$

$$v_s = R\omega = 3 \times 10 = 30 \text{ m/s})$$

Again when the detector is at *C* moving towards *B*, the source is at A_3 moving rightward. It is in this situation that frequency heard is maximum.

$$f_{max} = f\left[\frac{v + v_O}{v - v_s}\right] = 340 \times \frac{(340+60)}{(340-30)}$$

$$= 438.7 \text{ Hz}$$

75. At point *O* on the screen the path difference between the sound waves reaching from S_1 and S_2 is 2λ, i.e. constructive interference is obtained at *O*. At a very large distance from point *O* on the screen the path difference is zero.

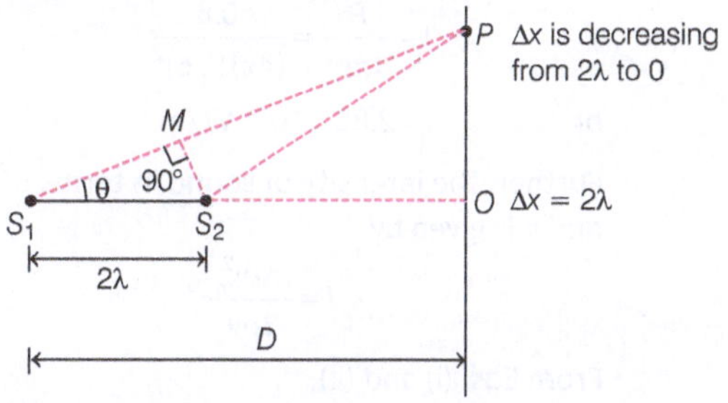

Thus, we can conclude that as we move away from point O on the screen path difference decreases from 2λ to zero. At O constructive interference is obtained (where $\Delta x = 2\lambda$). So, next constructive interference will be obtained where $\Delta x = \lambda$. Hence,

$$S_1P - S_2P = \lambda$$

or $$\sqrt{D^2 + y^2} - \sqrt{y^2 + (D - 2\lambda)^2} = \lambda$$

$\therefore$ $$\sqrt{D^2 + y^2} - \lambda = \sqrt{y^2 + (D - 2\lambda)^2}$$

On squaring both sides, we get

$$D^2 + y^2 + \lambda^2 - 2\lambda\sqrt{D^2 + y^2} = y^2 + D^2 + 4\lambda^2 - 4\lambda D$$

or $$2\sqrt{D^2 + y^2} = 4D - 3\lambda$$

as $$D >> \lambda, 4D - 3\lambda \approx 4D$$

$\therefore$ $$2\sqrt{D^2 + y^2} = 4D$$

or $$\sqrt{D^2 + y^2} = 2D$$

Again squaring both sides, we get

$$D^2 + y^2 = 4D^2$$

or $$y = \sqrt{3}\, D$$ **Ans.**

Alternate method Let $\Delta x = \lambda$ at angle θ as shown. Path difference between the waves is $S_1M = 2\lambda \cos\theta$ because $S_2P \approx MP$

$\therefore$ $$2\lambda\cos\theta = \lambda \qquad (\Delta x = \lambda)$$

or $$\theta = 60°$$

Now, $$PO = S_1O \tan\theta = S_1O \tan 60°$$

or $$y = \sqrt{3}\, D$$ **Ans.**

76. By definition sound level $= 10\log\left(\dfrac{I}{I_0}\right) = 60$

or $$\frac{I}{I_0} = 10^6$$

$\Rightarrow$ $$I = 10^{-12} \times 10^6$$
$$= 1\ \mu\text{W/m}^2$$

Power entering the room $= IA$

$$= 1 \times 10^{-6} \times 2 = 2\ \mu\text{W}$$

Energy collected in a day $= 2 \times 10^{-6} \times 86400$

$$= 0.173\ \text{J}$$ **Ans.**

77 (a) At a distance r from a point source of power P, the intensity of the sound is

$$I = \frac{P}{4\pi r^2} = \frac{0.8}{(4\pi)(1.5)^2}$$

or $$I = 2.83 \times 10^{-2}\ \text{W/m}^2 \qquad \text{...(i)}$$

Further, the intensity of sound in terms of $(\Delta p)_m$, ρ and v is given by

$$I = \frac{(\Delta p)_m^2}{2\rho v} \qquad \text{...(ii)}$$

From Eqs. (i) and (ii),

$$(\Delta p)_m = \sqrt{2 \times 2.83 \times 10^{-2} \times 1.29 \times 340}$$
$$= 4.98\ \text{N/m}^2$$ **Ans.**

(b) Pressure oscillation amplitude $(\Delta p)_m$ and displacement oscillation amplitude A are related by the equation

$$(\Delta p)_m = BAk$$

Substituting $B = \rho v^2$, $k = \dfrac{\omega}{v}$ and $\omega = 2\pi f$

We get, $(\Delta p)_m = 2\pi A\rho v f$

$\therefore$ $$A = \frac{(\Delta p)_m}{2\pi\rho v f}$$
$$= \frac{4.98}{(2\pi)(1.29)(340)(600)}$$
$$= 3.0 \times 10^{-6}\ \text{m}$$ **Ans.**

78. (a) Fundamental frequency when the pipe is open at both ends is

$$f_1 = \frac{v}{2l} = \frac{340}{2 \times 0.6}$$
$$= 283.33\ \text{Hz}$$ **Ans.**

(b) Suppose the hole is uncovered at a length l from the mouthpiece, the fundamental frequency will be

$$f_1 = \frac{v}{2l}$$

$\therefore$ $$l = \frac{v}{2f_1} = \frac{340}{2 \times 330}$$
$$= 0.515\ \text{m}$$
$$= 51.5\ \text{cm}$$ **Ans.**

Note *Opening holes in the side effectively shortens the length of the resonance column, thus increasing the frequency.*

79. $$2\sqrt{H^2 + d^2/4} - d = n\lambda \qquad \text{...(i)}$$

Now, $$2\sqrt{(H + h)^2 + d^2/4} - d = n\lambda + \frac{\lambda}{2} \qquad \text{...(ii)}$$

Solving these two equations, we get

$$\lambda = 2\sqrt{4(H + h)^2 + d^2} - 2\sqrt{4H^2 + d^2}$$

80. (a) $\lambda = \dfrac{v}{f} = \dfrac{340}{600} = 0.57$ m

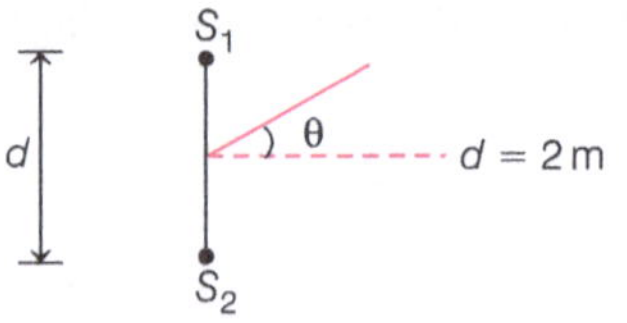

$$d\sin\theta = \frac{\lambda}{2}$$

$\therefore$ $$\theta = \sin^{-1}\left(\frac{\lambda}{2d}\right)$$
$$= \sin^{-1}\left(\frac{0.57}{4}\right)$$
$$= 8.19°$$

(b) $d \sin\theta = \lambda$ or $\theta = \sin^{-1}\left(\frac{\lambda}{d}\right)$

$$= \sin^{-1}\left(\frac{0.57}{2}\right) = 16.5°$$

(c) $d \sin\theta = n\lambda$

$\therefore$ $n_{max} = \frac{d}{\lambda}$ (When $\sin\theta = 1$)

$$= \frac{2}{0.57} = 3.5$$

$\therefore$ Maximum 3 maximas can be heard corresponding to $n = 1, 2$ and 3 (beyond $\theta = 0°$)

81. $\Delta\phi_1 = \left(\frac{2\pi}{\lambda}\right)\Delta x = \left(\frac{2\pi}{\lambda}\right)\frac{\lambda}{2} = \pi$

(a) $\Delta\phi_{net} = \Delta\phi_1 + \Delta\phi_2$

$$= \pi + 0 = \pi$$

So, they will interfere destructively and

$$I_{net} = 0$$

(b) No interference will take place. Hence,

$$I_{net} = I_1 + I_2 = 2I_0$$

(c) $\Delta\phi_{net} = \Delta\phi_1 \pm \Delta\phi_2$

$= 2\pi$ or 0 (as $\Delta\phi_2 = \pi$)

In both conditions, they interfere constructively. Hence,

$$I = I_{max} = 4I_0$$

82. (a) $\Delta\phi = \frac{2\pi}{\lambda}(\Delta x) = \left(\frac{2\pi f}{v}\right)(\Delta x)$

$$= \frac{(2\pi)(170)}{340}(11 - 8)$$

$= 3\pi = \phi$ (say)

$$I = 4I_0 \cos^2\frac{\theta}{2} \quad \text{...(i)}$$

Substituting value of ϕ, we get

$$I = 0$$

(b) Now, $\phi = 3\pi \pm \pi = 4\pi$ or 2π

Hence, from Eq. (i)

$$I = 4I_0$$

Now, $L_1 - L_2 = 10\log_{10}\frac{I_1}{I_2}$

$\therefore$ $L_1 - 60 = 10\log_{10}\left(\frac{4I_0}{I_0}\right) = 6$

$\therefore$ $L_1 = 66$ dB

(c) Sources are incoherent.

Hence,

$$I = I_0 + I_0 = 2I_0$$

$$L_1 - L_2 = 10\log_{10}\frac{I_1}{I_2}$$

$$= 10\log_{10}\frac{2I_0}{I_0}$$

$\therefore$ $L_1 - 60 = 10\log_{10} 2 = 3$

or $L_1 = 63$ dB

83. (a) $I = \frac{P}{4\pi r^2}$

$\therefore$ $I_1 = \frac{1\times10^{-3}}{4\pi(2)^2} = 19.9\times10^{-6}\ \text{W/m}^2$

$$= 19.9\ \mu\text{W/m}^2$$

$$I_2 = \frac{1\times10^{-3}}{4\pi(3)^2} = 8.84\times10^{-6}\ \text{W/m}^2$$

$$= 8.84\ \mu\text{W/m}^2$$

(b) $I_p = I_{max} = (\sqrt{I_1} + \sqrt{I_2})^2$

$$= 54.2\ \mu\text{W/m}^2$$

(c) $I_p = I_{min} = (\sqrt{I_1} - \sqrt{I_2})^2 = 2.2\ \mu\text{W/m}^2$

(d) $I_p = I_1 + I_2 = 28.7\ \mu\text{W/m}^2$

84. Given length of pipe, $l = 3$ m

Third harmonic implies that

$$3\left(\frac{\lambda}{2}\right) = l$$

or $\lambda = \frac{2l}{3} = \frac{2\times3}{3} = 2$ m

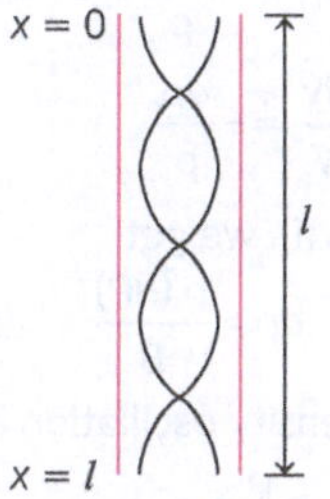

The angular frequency is

$$\omega = 2\pi f = \frac{2\pi v}{\lambda} = \frac{(2\pi)(332)}{2}$$

or $\omega = 332\pi$ rad/s

The particle displacement $y(x, t)$ can be written as

$$y(x, t) = A\cos kx \sin\omega t$$

$$k = \frac{2\pi}{\lambda} = \frac{2\pi}{(2l/3)} = \frac{3\pi}{l}$$

and $\omega = kv = \frac{3\pi v}{l}$ $\left(v = \frac{\omega}{k}\right)$

$\therefore$ $y(x, t) = A\cos\left(\frac{3\pi x}{l}\right)\cdot\sin\left(\frac{3\pi v}{l}\right)t$

The longitudinal oscillations of an air column can be viewed as oscillations of particle displacement or pressure wave or density wave. Pressure variation is related to particle displacement as

$p(x, t) = -B\frac{\partial y}{\partial x}$ (B = Bulk modulus)

$$= \left(\frac{3BA\pi}{l}\right)\sin\left(\frac{3\pi x}{l}\right)\sin\left(\frac{3\pi v}{l}\right)t$$

The amplitude of pressure variation is

$$p_{max} = \frac{3BA\pi}{l} \Rightarrow v = \sqrt{\frac{B}{\rho}} \text{ or } B = \rho v^2$$

$$\therefore \quad p_{max} = \frac{3\rho v^2 A\pi}{l}$$

$$\text{or} \quad A = \frac{p_{max} l}{3\rho v^2 \pi}$$

Here, $p_{max} = 1\%$ or $p_0 = 10^3 \text{ N/m}^2$

Substituting the values,

$$A = \frac{(10^3)(3)}{(3)(1.03)(332)^2 \pi}$$

$$= 0.0028 \text{ m}$$

$$\text{or} \quad A = 0.28 \text{ cm}$$ **Ans.**

According to definition of Bulk modulus (B)

$$B = \frac{-dp}{(dV/V)} \quad \text{...(i)}$$

$$\text{Volume} = \frac{\text{Mass}}{\text{Density}}$$

$$\text{or} \quad V = \frac{m}{\rho}$$

$$\text{or} \quad dV = -\frac{m}{\rho^2} d\rho = -\frac{V d\rho}{\rho}$$

$$\text{or} \quad \frac{dV}{V} = -\frac{d\rho}{\rho}$$

Substituting in Eq. (i), we get

$$d\rho = \frac{\rho\,(dP)}{B}$$

or amplitude of density oscillation is

$$d\rho_{max} = \frac{\rho}{B} p_{max}$$

$$= \frac{p_{max}}{v^2} \quad \left(\because \frac{\rho}{B} = \frac{1}{v^2}\right)$$

$$= \frac{10^3}{(332)^2} = 9 \times 10^{-3} \text{ kg/m}^3$$

85. Sound level (in dB)

$$L = 10 \log_{10}\left(\frac{I}{I_0}\right)$$

where, $I_0 = 10^{-12} \text{ W/m}^2$

$L = 60 \text{ dB}$

Hence, $I = (10^6) I_0 = 10^{-6} \text{ W/m}^2$

$$I = \frac{P}{A} = \frac{E}{tA}$$

$$\therefore \quad t = \frac{E}{IA}$$

$$\therefore \quad \text{Time, } t = \frac{(1.0 \times 10^3)\left(\frac{30}{100}\right)}{3.14}$$

$$t = 95.5 \text{ s}$$

86. Let n_1 harmonic of the chamber containing H_2 is equal to n_2 harmonic of the chamber containing O_2. Then,

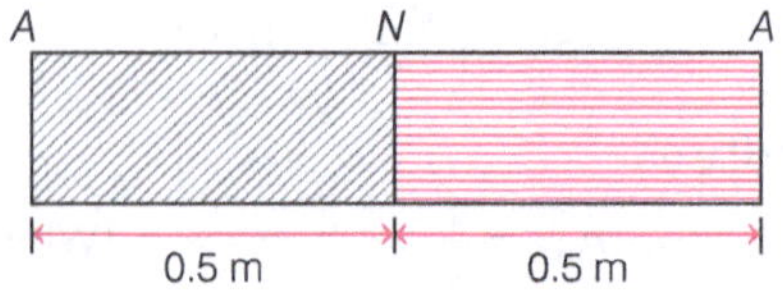

$$n_1\left(\frac{v_{H_2}}{4l}\right) = n_2\left(\frac{v_{O_2}}{4l}\right)$$

$$\therefore \quad \frac{n_1}{n_2} = \frac{v_{O_2}}{v_{H_2}} = \frac{300}{1100} = \frac{3}{11}$$

$$\therefore \quad f_{min} = 3\left(\frac{v_{H_2}}{4l}\right) = 3\left(\frac{1100}{4 \times 0.5}\right)$$

$$= 1650 \text{ Hz}$$ **Ans.**

87. When the boy has displaced by an angle θ (i.e from P_1 to P_1'), then the train has moved from P_2 to P_2'.

Displacement of train, $P_2 P_2' = \frac{L}{2} \tan\theta$

Velocity of train is $v_T = \frac{d}{dt}\left(\frac{L}{2} \tan\theta\right)$

$$\text{or} \quad v_T = \frac{L}{2} \sec^2\theta \left(\frac{d\theta}{dt}\right) = \frac{L}{2} \omega \sec^2\theta$$

Angular velocity of boy is $\omega = \frac{v}{R} = \frac{v}{L/4} \quad \left(\because R = \frac{L}{4}\right)$

$$\text{or} \quad \omega = \frac{4v}{L} = \frac{4 \times 11}{L} = \frac{44}{L}$$

Velocity of toy train at

$$P_2 = \frac{L}{2} \omega \sec^2 0$$

$$= \frac{L}{2} \omega = \frac{L}{2} \times \frac{44}{L} = 22 \text{ ms}^{-1}$$

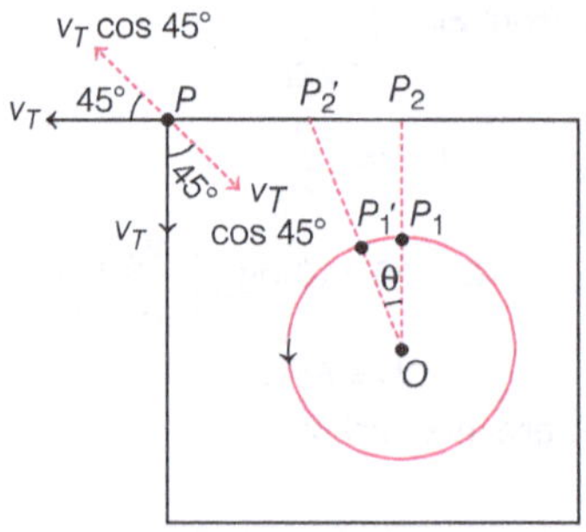

Angular velocity is same for both boy and toy train. As, θ changes from 0 to $\pi/4$, as the train moves from P_2 to P, the velocity of train increases. Just before the turn, the component of velocity of train along the line joining boy and train is away from the boy. Similarly just after the turn, the component of velocity of the train is towards the boy. Thus, in the former case, the frequency heard by the boy is minimum and in the latter case it is maximum.

Velocity of train at P is $v_T = \frac{L}{2}\omega \sec^2 45°$

$$= (22)(2) = 44\ \text{ms}^{-1}$$

$\therefore$ Minimum frequency heard is

$$f_1' = \left(\frac{v}{v + v_T \cos 45°}\right) f_0$$

or $$f_1' = \left[\frac{330}{330 + (44/\sqrt{2})}\right] 330\ \text{Hz} = 301.6\ \text{Hz}$$

and maximum frequency heard is

$$f_2' = \left(\frac{v}{v - v_T \cos 45°}\right) f_0$$

or $$f_2' = \left[\frac{330}{330 - (44/\sqrt{2})}\right] 330\ \text{Hz}$$

$$= 364.4\ \text{Hz}$$

88. (a) Comparing with the equation of a travelling wave

$$y = a \sin (kx - \omega t)$$

$$k = 15\pi \quad \text{and} \quad \omega = 6000\pi$$

$\therefore$ Velocity of the sound, $v = \frac{\omega}{k}$

$$= \frac{6000\pi}{15\pi} = 400\ \text{ms}^{-1}$$

as $$v = \sqrt{\frac{B}{\rho}}$$

Hence, $$\rho = \frac{B}{v^2} = \frac{1.6 \times 10^5}{(400)^2}$$

$$= 1\ \text{kg/m}^3 \qquad \textbf{Ans.}$$

(b) Pressure amplitude, $p_0 = BAk$

Hence, $$A = \frac{p_0}{Bk} = \frac{24\pi}{1.6 \times 10^5 \times 15\pi}$$

$$= 10^{-5}\ \text{m} = 10\ \mu\text{m} \qquad \textbf{Ans.}$$

(c) Intensity received by the person,

$$I = \frac{W}{4\pi R^2} = \frac{W}{4\pi (10)^2}$$

Also, $$I = \frac{p_0^2}{2\rho v}$$

$$\Rightarrow \quad \frac{W}{4\pi(10)^2} = \frac{(24\pi)^2}{2 \times 1 \times 400}$$

$$W = 288\pi^3\ \text{W} \qquad \textbf{Ans.}$$

89. Time taken by the source to cross the origin

$$= \frac{100}{5} = 20\ \text{s}$$

Distance moved by detector (O') in this time

$$= 10 \times 20 = 200\ \text{m}$$

The signals received by detector at $t = 20$ s are not produced, when the source is at the origin but from some previous instant t' (say), shown in the figure. The time in which source travels $S'O$, the signal travels $S'O'$.

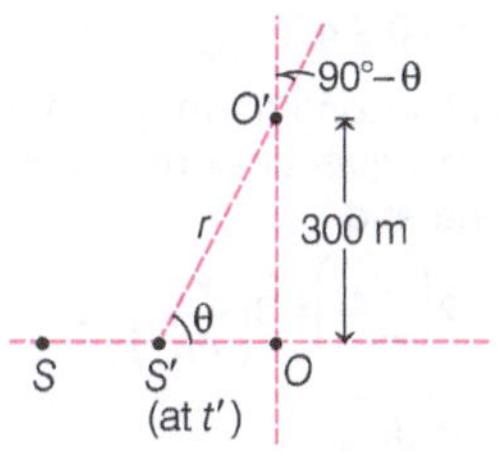

$\therefore$ $$t = \frac{S'O}{v_s} = \frac{S'O'}{v}, \text{ where } v = \text{speed of sound}$$

Now, $$\cos\theta = \frac{S'O}{S'O'}$$

$\therefore$ $$\cos\theta = \frac{v_s}{v} = \frac{5}{330} = \frac{1}{66}$$

$\therefore$ $$\sin\theta = \sqrt{1 - \left(\frac{1}{66}\right)^2} \simeq 1$$

Frequency observed by detector is

$$f' = \left(\frac{v - v_{O'} \cos(90 - \theta)}{v - v_s \cos\theta}\right) f_0$$

or $$f' = \left[\frac{v - v_{O'} \sin\theta}{v - v_s \cos\theta}\right] f_0 = \left[\frac{330 - 10(1)}{330 - 5\left(\frac{1}{66}\right)}\right](100)$$

or $$f' = 97\ \text{Hz}$$

90. Frequency of fundamental mode of closed pipe,

$$f_1 = \frac{v}{4l} = 200\ \text{Hz}$$

Decreasing the tension in the string decrease the beat frequency.

Hence, frequency of string > frequency of pipe

Hence, the first overtone frequency of the string should be 208 Hz (not 192 Hz)

$\therefore$ $$208 = \frac{1}{l}\sqrt{\frac{T}{\mu}}$$

$\therefore$ $$T = \mu \cdot l^2 (208)$$

$$= \left(\frac{2.5 \times 10^{-3}}{0.25}\right)(0.25)^2 (208)^2$$

$$= 27.04\ \text{N} \qquad \textbf{Ans.}$$

91. (a) Wavelength of sound ahead of the source is

$$\lambda' = \frac{v - v_s}{f} = \frac{332 - 32}{1000}$$

$$= 0.3\ \text{m} \qquad \textbf{Ans.}$$

(b) $$f' = f\left(\frac{v + v_0}{v - v_s}\right) = 1000\left(\frac{332 + 64}{332 - 32}\right)$$

$$= 1320\ \text{Hz} \qquad \textbf{Ans.}$$

(c) Speed of reflected wave will remain 332 m/s. **Ans.**

(d) Wavelength of reflected wave

$$\lambda'' = \frac{v - v_0}{f'} = \frac{332 - 64}{1320}$$

$$= 0.2 \text{ m} \qquad \textbf{Ans.}$$

92. (a) Frequency of second harmonic in pipe A open at both ends = frequency of third harmonic in pipe B closed at one end

$$\therefore \quad 2\left(\frac{v_A}{2l_A}\right) = 3\left(\frac{v_B}{4l_B}\right) \quad \text{or} \quad \frac{v_A}{v_B} = \frac{3}{4}$$

$$\text{or} \quad \frac{\sqrt{\frac{\gamma_A R T_A}{4M_A}}}{\sqrt{\frac{\gamma_B R T_B}{M_B}}} = \frac{3}{4} \qquad (\because l_A = l_B)$$

$$\text{or} \quad \sqrt{\frac{\gamma_A}{\gamma_B}}\sqrt{\frac{M_B}{M_A}} = \frac{3}{4} \qquad (\text{as } T_A = T_B)$$

$$\Rightarrow \quad \frac{M_A}{M_B} = \frac{\gamma_A}{\gamma_B}\left(\frac{16}{9}\right)$$

$$= \left(\frac{5/3}{7/5}\right)\left(\frac{16}{9}\right) \qquad \left(\gamma_A = \frac{5}{3} \text{ and } \gamma_B = \frac{7}{5}\right)$$

$$\therefore \quad \frac{M_A}{M_B} = \left(\frac{25}{21}\right)\left(\frac{16}{9}\right) = \frac{400}{189}$$

(b) According to question

$$\frac{f_A}{f_B} = \frac{v_A / 2l_A}{v_B / 2l_B} = \frac{v_A}{v_B} \qquad (\text{as } l_A = l_B)$$

$$\frac{v_A}{v_B} = \frac{\sqrt{\frac{\gamma_A R T_A}{M_A}}}{\sqrt{\frac{\gamma_B R T_B}{M_B}}} = \sqrt{\frac{\gamma_A}{\gamma_B} \cdot \frac{M_B}{M_A}} \qquad (\because T_A = T_B)$$

Substituting $\frac{M_B}{M_A} = \frac{189}{400}, \gamma_A = \frac{5}{3}$

$$\text{and} \quad \gamma_B = \frac{7}{3} \quad \Rightarrow \quad \frac{f_A}{f_B} = \sqrt{\frac{25}{21} \times \frac{189}{400}} = \frac{3}{4}$$

93. Speed of sound, $v = 340$ m/s

Let l_0 be the length of air column corresponding to the fundamental frequency. Then

$$\frac{v}{4l_0} = 212.5$$

$$\Rightarrow \quad l_0 = \frac{v}{4(212.5)} = \frac{340}{4(212.5)}$$

$$= 0.4 \text{ m}$$

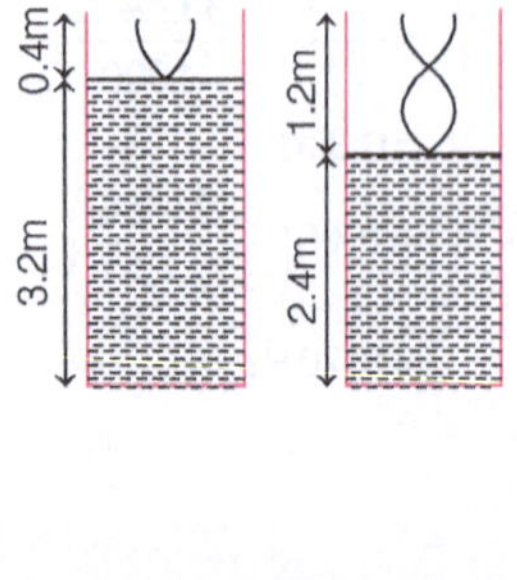

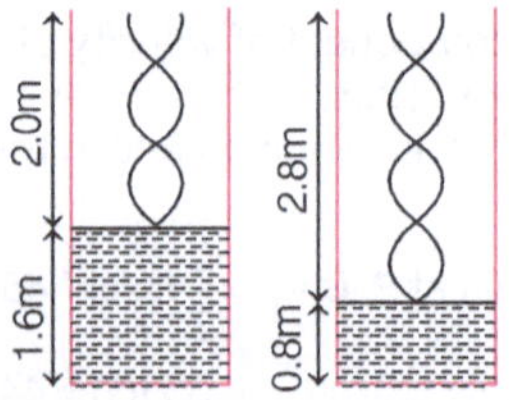

In a closed pipe only odd harmonics are obtained. Now, let l_1, l_2, l_3, l_4, etc. be the lengths corresponding to the 3rd harmonic, 5th harmonic, 7th harmonic etc. Then

$$3\left(\frac{v}{4l_1}\right) = 212.5 \Rightarrow l_1 = 1.2 \text{ m};$$

$$5\left(\frac{v}{4l_2}\right) = 212.5 \Rightarrow l_2 = 2.0 \text{ m}$$

$$7\left(\frac{v}{4l_3}\right) = 212.5 \Rightarrow l_3 = 2.8 \text{ m};$$

$$9\left(\frac{v}{4l_4}\right) = 212.5 \Rightarrow l_4 = 3.6 \text{ m}$$

or heights of water level are $(3.6 - 0.4)$ m, $(3.6 - 1.2)$ m, $(3.6 - 2.0)$ m and $(3.6 - 2.8)$ m.

Hence, heights of water level are 3.2 m, 2.4 m, 1.6 m and 0.8 m. Let A and a be the area of cross-sections of the pipe and hole respectively. Then

$$A = \pi(2 \times 10^{-2})^2 = 1.26 \times 10^{-3} \text{ m}^{-2}$$

$$\text{and} \quad a = \pi(10^{-3})^2 = 3.14 \times 10^{-6} \text{ m}^2$$

Velocity of efflux,

$$v = \sqrt{2gH}$$

Continuity equation at 1 and 2 gives,

$$a\sqrt{2gH} = A\left(\frac{-dH}{dt}\right)$$

So, rate of fall of water level in the pipe,

$$\left(\frac{-dH}{dt}\right) = \frac{a}{A}\sqrt{2gH}$$

Substituting the values, we get

$$\frac{-dH}{dt} = \frac{3.14 \times 10^{-6}}{1.26 \times 10^{-3}}\sqrt{2 \times 10 \times H}$$

$$\Rightarrow \quad \frac{-dH}{dt} = (1.11 \times 10^{-2})\sqrt{H}$$

Between first two resonances, the water level falls from 3.2 m to 2.4 m.

$$\therefore \quad \frac{dH}{\sqrt{H}} = -1.11 \times 10^{-2} dt$$

$$\Rightarrow \quad \int_{3.2}^{2.4} \frac{dH}{\sqrt{H}} = -(1.11 \times 10^{-2}) \int_0^t dt$$

$$\Rightarrow \quad 2[\sqrt{2.4} - \sqrt{3.2}] = -(1.1 \times 10^{-2}).t$$

$$\text{or} \quad t \approx 43 \text{ s}$$

94. (a) Let the two radio waves be represented by the equations

$$y_1 = A\sin 2\pi v_1 t$$

$$y_2 = A\sin 2\pi\nu_2 t$$

Since, $A_1 = A_2 = A$ and detector is at $x = 0$

The equation of resultant wave according to superposition principle

$$y = y_1 + y_2$$
$$= A\sin 2\pi\nu_1 t + A\sin 2\pi\nu_2 t$$
$$= A[\sin 2\pi\nu_1 t + \sin 2\pi\nu_2 t]$$
$$= A \times 2\sin\frac{(2\pi\nu_1 + 2\pi\nu_2)t}{2}\cos\frac{(2\pi\nu_1 - 2\pi\nu_2)t}{2}$$
$$= 2A\sin\pi(\nu_1 + \nu_2)t\cos\pi(\nu_1 - \nu_2)t$$

where the amplitude

$$A' = 2A\cos\pi(\nu_1 - \nu_2)t$$

Now, intensity $\propto$ (Amplitude)^2

$$\Rightarrow \quad I \propto A'^2$$
$$I \propto 4A^2\cos^2\pi(\nu_1 - \nu_2)t$$

Intensity will be maximum when

$$\cos^2\pi(\nu_1 - \nu_2)t = 1$$

or, $\quad \cos\pi(\nu_1 - \nu_2)t = 1$

or, $\quad \pi(\nu_1 - \nu_2)t = n\pi$

$$\Rightarrow \quad \frac{(\omega_1 - \omega_2)}{2}t = n\pi$$

or $\quad t = \dfrac{2n\pi}{\omega_1 - \omega_2}$

$\therefore$ Time interval between two successive maxima

$$t = \frac{2n\pi}{\omega_1 - \omega_2} - \frac{2(n-1)\pi}{\omega_1 - \omega_2}$$

or, $\quad t = \dfrac{2\pi}{\omega_1 - \omega_2} = \dfrac{2\pi}{10^3}$ s

Time interval between two successive maximas is $2\pi \times 10^{-3}$ s

(b) The detector can detect if resultant intensity $\geq 2A^2$

$\therefore$ Resultant amplitude $\geq \sqrt{2}A$

or, $\quad 2A\cos\pi(\nu_1 - \nu_2)t \geq \sqrt{2}A$

or, $\quad \cos\pi(\nu_1 - \nu_2)t \geq \dfrac{1}{\sqrt{2}}$

or, $\quad \cos\left[\dfrac{(\omega_1 - \omega_2)t}{2}\right] \geq \dfrac{1}{\sqrt{2}}$

The detector lies idle when the values of

$\cos\left[\dfrac{(\omega_1 - \omega_2)t}{2}\right]$ is between 0 and $\dfrac{1}{\sqrt{2}}$

$\therefore \quad \dfrac{(\omega_1 - \omega_2)t}{2}$ is between $\dfrac{\pi}{2}$ and $\dfrac{\pi}{4}$

$$\therefore \quad t_1 = \frac{\pi}{\omega_1 - \omega_2}$$

and $\quad t_2 = \dfrac{\pi}{2(\omega_1 - \omega_2)}$

$\therefore$ The time gaps $= t_1 - t_2$

$$= \frac{\pi}{\omega_1 - \omega_2} - \frac{\pi}{2(\omega_1 - \omega_2)}$$
$$= \frac{\pi}{2(\omega_1 - \omega_2)}$$
$$= \frac{\pi}{2} \times 10^{-3}\text{ s}$$

95. (a) Path difference and hence phase difference at P from both the sources is 0°, whether $\theta = 45°$, or $\theta = 60°$. So, both the wave will interfere constructively. Or maximum intensity will be obtained. From

$$I_{max} = (\sqrt{I_1} + \sqrt{I_2})^2 \text{ we have}$$
$$I_0 = (\sqrt{I} + \sqrt{I})^2 = 4I \quad (I_1 = I_2 = I, \text{say})$$
$$\therefore \quad I = I_0/4$$

When one source is switched off, no interference will be obtained. Intensity will be due to a single source or $I_0/4$.

(b) At $\theta = 60°$, also maximum intensity or I_0 will be observed.

96. Let pulse emitted at time t_0 is heard by the observer at time t.

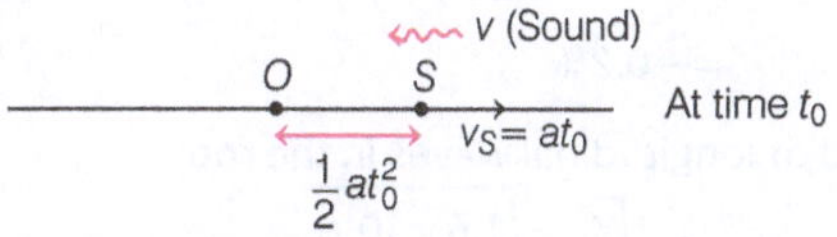

Then, $\quad t = t_0 + \dfrac{\frac{1}{2}at_0^2}{v}$

$$\therefore \quad 10 = t_0 + \frac{\frac{1}{2} \times 10 \times t_0^2}{340}$$

Solving this equation, we get

or $\quad t_0 = 9.3$ s

$$v_S = at_0 = 10 \times 9.3 = 93\text{ m/s}$$

$$\therefore \quad f = f_0\left(\frac{v}{v + v_S}\right) = 1700\left(\frac{340}{340 + 93}\right)$$

or $\quad f = 1335$ Hz

or $\quad f \approx 1.34$ kHz

97. Let the original frequency is f. Then,

$$\lambda_1 = \frac{v}{f} \quad \text{...(i)}$$

Frequency received by wall (let us assume the wall as an observer

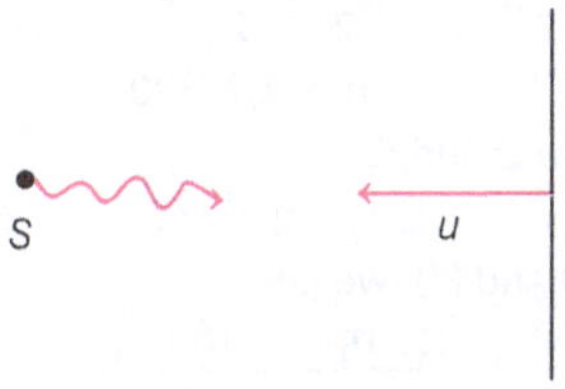

$$f_1 = f\left(\frac{v + u}{v}\right)$$

Now frequency of reflected sound (assume the wall as a source)

$$f_2 = f_1\left(\frac{v}{v-u}\right)$$

Substituting the value of f_1, we get

$$f_2 = f\left(\frac{v+u}{v-u}\right)$$

So, frequency of reflected sound,

$$\lambda_2 = \frac{v}{f_2} = \frac{v}{f}\left(\frac{v-u}{v+u}\right)$$

Percentage change in wavelength

$$= \frac{\lambda_2 - \lambda_1}{\lambda_1} \times 100$$

$$= \left(\frac{\lambda_2}{\lambda_1} - 1\right) \times 100$$

$$= \left(\frac{v-u}{v+u} - 1\right) \times 100$$

$$= \left(\frac{330 - 0.33}{330 + 0.33} - 1\right) \times 100$$

$$= -0.2\%$$

98. Speed of longitudinal waves in the rod,

$$v = \sqrt{\frac{Y}{\rho}} = \sqrt{\frac{1.6 \times 10^{11}}{2500}}$$

$$= 8000 \text{ m/s}$$

At the clamped position nodes will be formed. Between the clamps integer number of loops will be formed. Hence,

$$n_1 \frac{\lambda}{2} = 80$$

or $$n_1 \lambda = 160 \quad \text{...(i)}$$

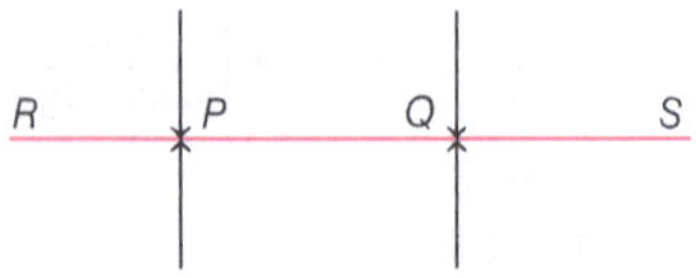

Between P and R, P is a fixed end and R is the free end. It means the number of loops between P and R will be odd multiple of $\frac{\lambda}{4}$. Then,

$$\frac{(2n_2 - 1)}{2}\frac{\lambda}{2} = 5$$

or $$(2n_2 - 1)\lambda = 20 \quad \text{...(ii)}$$

Also between Q and S,

$$(2n_3 - 1)\lambda = 60 \quad \text{...(iii)}$$

From Eqs. (i) and (ii), we get

$$\frac{n_1}{2n_2 - 1} = \frac{160}{20} = 8 \quad \text{...(iv)}$$

and from Eqs. (i) and (iii),

$$\frac{n_1}{2n_3 - 1} = \frac{160}{60} = \frac{8}{3} \quad \text{...(v)}$$

For minimum frequency n_1, n_2 and n_3 should be least from Eqs. (iv) and (v).

We get, $n_1 = 8,\ n_2 = 1,\ n_3 = 2$

$$\lambda = \frac{20}{2n_2 - 1} = 20 \text{ cm} \quad \text{[from Eq. (ii)]}$$

$$= 0.2 \text{ m}$$

$$\therefore \quad f_{min} = \frac{v}{\lambda} = \frac{8000}{0.2}$$

$$= 40 \text{ kHz}$$ **Ans.**

Next higher frequency corresponds to

$$n_1 = 24,\ n_2 = 2 \text{ and } n_3 = 5$$

$$f = 120 \text{ kHz}$$ **Ans.**

99. For reflected sound, we can assume wall as a plane mirror and take an image S' of S moving towards the wall with same speed u.

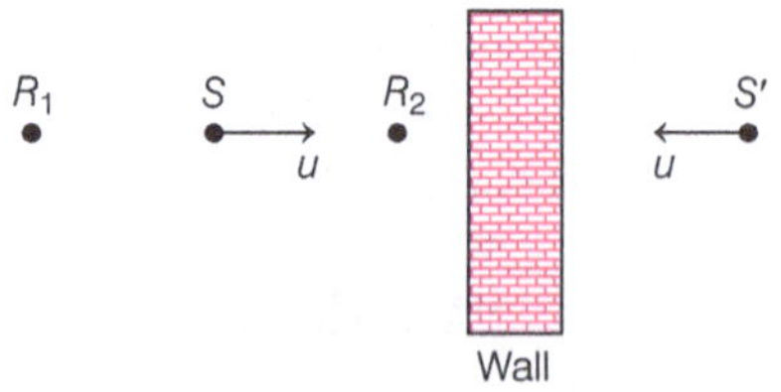

R_2 will not observe any beats as S and S' both are approaching towards him.

R_1 will observe beats as S recedes from R_1 and S' approaches towards him.

$$f_b = f_{S'} - f_S$$

$$= f_0\left(\frac{v}{v - v_S}\right) - f_0\left(\frac{v}{v + v_S}\right) \quad \text{...(i)}$$

Here, v = speed of sound

and $v_S = u$

Substituting the given values in Eq. (i), we get

$$f_b = \frac{2f_0 vu}{v^2 - u^2}$$

We can write $v^2 - u^2 \approx v^2$ as $v >> u$

$$\therefore \quad f_b = \frac{2f_0 u}{v} = \frac{2 \times 1000 \times 0.17}{340}$$

$$= 1.0 \text{ Hz}$$

Thus, $f_b = 1.0$ Hz

Note *We have assumed that S is approaching towards the wall. Even if we assume that v is receding from the wall, answer will be same. Think why?*

100.

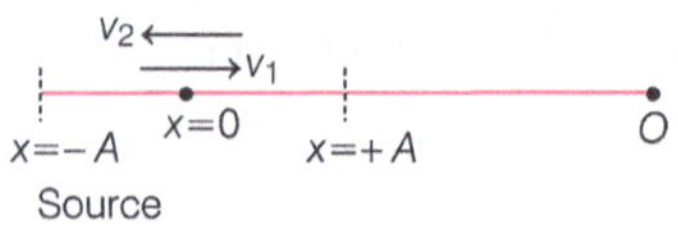

$v_1 = v_2$ = maximum speed of SHM $= \omega A$

$$\Delta f = f_0\left(\frac{v}{v - v_1}\right) - f_0\left(\frac{v}{v + v_2}\right)$$

$$= f_0\left(\frac{v}{v - \omega A}\right) - f_0\left(\frac{v}{v + \omega A}\right)$$

$$\Delta f = \frac{2f_0 v\omega A}{v^2 - \omega^2 A^2}$$

Substituting $\Delta f = 200$ Hz, $v = 340$ m/s, $A = 0.5$ m and $f_0 = 2000$ Hz and then solving, we get

$$\omega = 34 \text{ rad/s}$$

101. Let A_i and A_t are the amplitudes of incident and transmitted waves respectively. Then,

$$\frac{A_t}{A} = \frac{2v_2}{v_1 + v_2}$$

$$= \frac{2(100)}{200+100} = \frac{2}{3}$$

$\Rightarrow \quad k = 3$

102. $1200 = \sqrt{\frac{\gamma p}{\rho_{H_2}}}$ ...(i)

Let x is volume of H_2 and y volume of O_2. Then,

$$(x+y)\rho_{mix} = x\rho_{H_2} + y\rho_{O_2} = x\rho_{H_2} + 16y\rho_{H_2}$$

$\therefore \quad \rho_{mix} = \frac{x+16y}{x+y} \cdot \rho_{H_2}$

$\therefore \quad 500 = \sqrt{\frac{\gamma p(x+y)}{(x+16y)\rho_{H_2}}} = \sqrt{\frac{\gamma p}{\rho_{mix}}}$ ...(ii)

Dividing Eq. (i) by Eq. (ii), we get

$$\frac{12}{5} = \sqrt{\frac{x+16y}{x+y}}$$

or $\quad \frac{x}{y} = \frac{2.2}{1} = \frac{11}{10} \times 2$

$\Rightarrow \quad \alpha = 2$

103. Let v be the apparent frequency heard by observer due to source S_1.

$$f_1 = f\left[\frac{v+v_0}{v}\right] = 120\left[\frac{330+10}{330}\right]$$

$$= 120 \times \frac{34}{33} = 123.636 \text{ Hz}$$

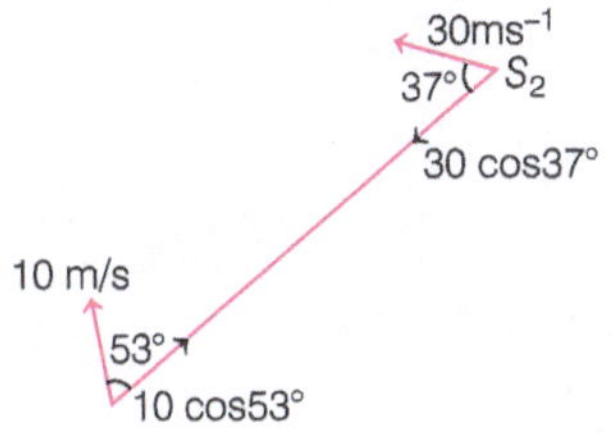

Let f_2 be the apparent frequency heard by observer due to source S_2.

$$f_2 = f\left[\frac{v+v_0}{v-v_s}\right] = 120\left[\frac{330+10\cos 53^\circ}{330-30\cos 37^\circ}\right]$$

$\therefore \quad f_2 = 120\left[\frac{330+10\times 0.6}{330-30\times 0.8}\right]$

$$= 120\left[\frac{336}{306}\right] = 131.764 \text{ Hz}$$

$\therefore$ Beat frequency,

$$f_b = f_2 - f_1 = 131.764 - 123.636$$

$$= 8.125 \text{ Hz}$$

$$\approx 8.13 \text{ Hz}$$

UNIT-20

THERMOMETRY, THERMAL EXPANSION AND KINETIC THEORY OF GASES

Learning Modules

1. Thermometers and Temperature Scale
2. Thermal Expansion
3. Behaviour of Gases
4. Degree of Freedom and Internal Energy of an Ideal Gas
5. Molar Heat Capacity
6. Kinetic Theory of Gases

MODULE 1

Thermometers and Temperature Scale

Thermometers are devices that are used to measure temperatures. All thermometers are based on the principle that some physical properties of a system change as the system's temperature changes. Some physical properties that change with temperature are :

1. The volume of a liquid
2. The length of a solid
3. The pressure of a gas at constant volume
4. The volume of a gas at constant pressure and
5. The electric resistance of a conductor.

A common thermometer in everyday use consists of a mass of liquid, usually mercury or alcohol that expands in a glass capillary tube when heated. In this case, the physical property is the **change in volume of the liquid**. Any temperature change is proportional to the change in length of the liquid column.

The thermometer can be calibrated accordingly. On the temperature celsius scale, a thermometer is usually calibrated between 0°C (called the ice point of water) and 100°C (called the steam point of water). Once the liquid levels in the thermometer have been established at these two points, the distance between the two points is divided into 100 equal segments to create the celsius scale.

Thus, each segment denotes a change in temperature of one degree celsius (1°C). A practical problem in this type of thermometer is that readings may vary for two different liquids. When one thermometer reads a temperature, for example 40°C the other may indicate a slightly different value.

This discrepancies between thermometers are especially large at temperatures far from the calibration points. To surmount this problem we need a universal thermometer whose readings are independent of the substance used in it. The gas thermometer meets this requirement.

The Constant Volume Gas Thermometer and The Absolute Temperature Scale

The physical property used by the constant volume gas thermometer is the **change in pressure of a gas at constant volume.**

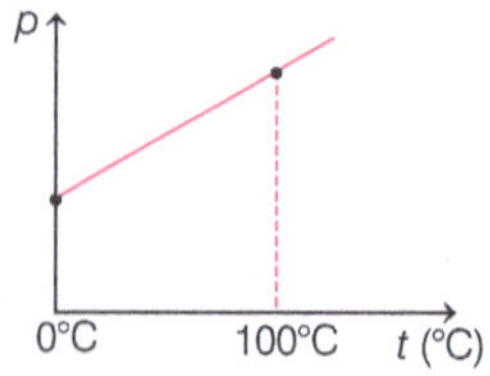

The pressure *versus* temperature graph for a typical gas taken with a constant volume is shown in figure.

The two dots represent the two reference temperatures namely, the ice and steam points of water. The line connecting them serves as a calibration curve for unknown temperatures.

Experiments show that the thermometer readings are nearly independent of the type of gas used as long as the gas pressure is low and the temperature is well above the point at which the gas liquefies.

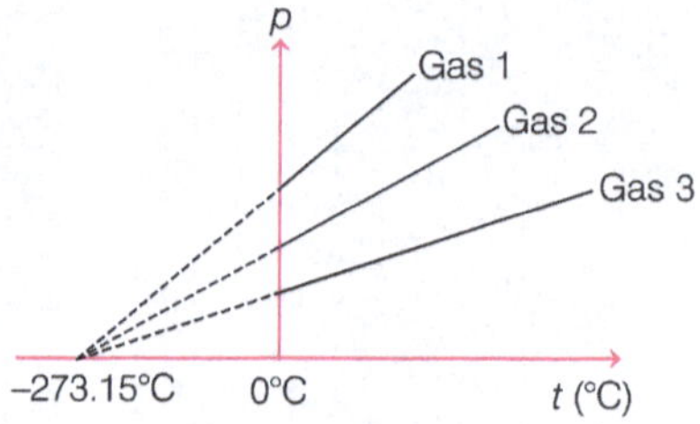

If you extend the curves shown in figure toward negative temperatures, you find, in every case, that the pressure is zero when the temperature is –273.15°C. This significant temperature is used as the basis for the **absolute temperature scale**, which sets –273.15°C as its zero point.

This temperature is often referred to as **absolute zero**. The size of a degree on the absolute temperature scale is identical to the size of a degree on the celsius scale. Thus, the conversion between these temperatures is

$$\boxed{T_C = T - 273.15} \quad \text{...(i)}$$

In 1954, by the International committee on weights and measures, the **triple point of water** was chosen as the reference temperature for this new scale. The triple point of water is the single combination of temperature and pressure at which liquid water, gaseous water and ice (solid water) coexist in equilibrium. This triple point occurs at a temperature of approximately $0.01°C$ and a pressure of 4.58 mm of mercury. On the new scale, which uses the unit **kelvin**, the temperature of water at the triple point was set at 273.16 kelvin, abbreviated as 273.16 K. (No degree sign is used with the unit kelvin).

This new absolute temperature scale (also called the kelvin scale) employs the SI unit of absolute temperature, the kelvin which is defined to be "$\frac{1}{273.16}$ of the difference between absolute zero and the temperature of the triple point of water".

The Celsius, Fahrenheit and Kelvin Temperature Scales

Eq. (i) shows the relation between the temperatures in celsius scales and kelvin scale. Because the size of a degree is the same on the two scales, a temperature difference of 10°C is equal to a temperature difference of 10 K.

The two scales differ only in the choice of the zero point. The ice point temperature on the kelvin scale, 273.15 K, corresponds to 0.00°C and the kelvin steam point 373.15 K, is equivalent to 100.00°C.

A common temperature scale in everyday use in US is the **Fahrenheit scale.** The ice point in this scale is 32°F and the steam point is 212°F. The distance between these two points are divided in 180 equal parts. The relation between celsius scale and Fahrenheit scale is as derived below.

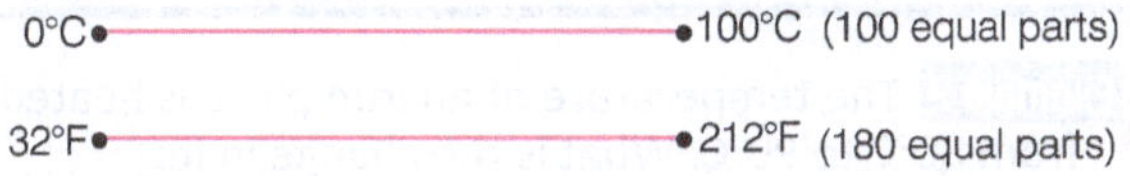

100 parts of celsius scale = 180 parts of Fahrenheit scale

$\therefore$ 1 part of celsius scale $= \frac{9}{5}$ parts of Fahrenheit scale

Hence, $$T_F = 32 + \frac{9}{5} T_C \quad \text{...(ii)}$$

Further, $$\Delta T_C = \Delta T = \frac{5}{9} \Delta T_F \quad \text{...(iii)}$$

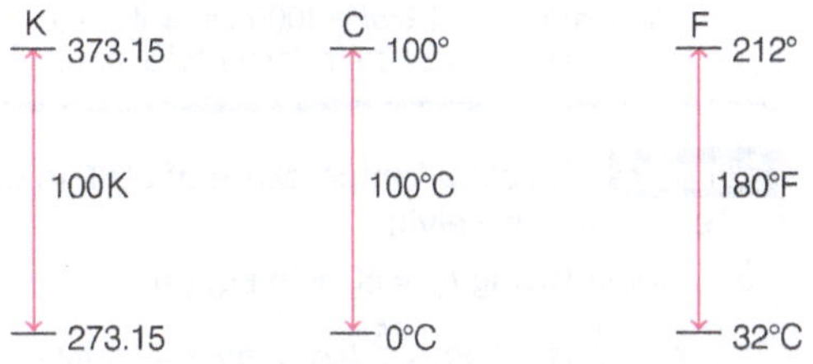

Relation among Kelvin, Celsius and Fahrenheit temperature scales

Important POINTS

- **Different Thermometers**

  Thermometric property It is the property that can be used to measure the temperature. It is represented by any physical quantity such as length, volume, pressure and resistance etc., which varies linearly with a certain range of temperature. Let X denotes the thermometric physical quantity and X_0, X_{100} and X_t be its values at 0°C, 100°C and t °C respectively. Then,

$$t = \left(\frac{X_t - X_0}{X_{100} - X_0} \right) \times 100°C$$

  (i) Constant volume gas thermometer The pressure of a gas at constant volume is the thermometric property. Therefore,

$$t = \left(\frac{p_t - p_0}{p_{100} - p_0} \right) \times 100°C$$

  (ii) Platinum resistance thermometer The resistance of a platinum wire is the thermometric property. Hence,

$$t = \left(\frac{R_t - R_0}{R_{100} - R_0} \right) \times 100°C$$

  (iii) Mercury thermometer In this thermometer, the length of a mercury column from some fixed point is taken as thermometric property. Thus,

$$t = \left(\frac{l_t - l_0}{l_{100} - l_0} \right) \times 100°C$$

- Two other thermometers, commonly used are **thermocouple thermometer** and **total radiation pyrometer.**
- **Total radiation pyrometer** is used to measure very high temperatures. When a body is at a high temperature, it glows brightly and the radiation emitted per second from unit area of the surface of the body is proportional to the fourth power of the absolute temperature of the body.

  If this radiation is measured by some device, the temperature of the body is calculated. This is the principle of a total radiation pyrometer. The main advantage of this thermometer is that the experimental body is not kept in contact with it.

  Hence, there is no definite higher limit of its temperature range. It can measure temperature from 800°C to 3000°C-4000°C. However, it cannot be used to measure temperatures below 800°C because at low temperatures the emission of radiation is so poor that it cannot be measured directly.

- **Ranges of different thermometers**

Thermometer	Lower limit	Upper limit
Mercury thermometer	−30°C	300°C
Gas thermometer	−268°C	1500°C
Platinum resistance thermometer	−200°C	1200°C
Thermocouple thermometer	−200°C	1600°C
Radiation thermometer	800°C	No limit

- **Reaumur's scale** Other than Celsius, Fahrenheit and Kelvin temperature scales **Reaumur's scale** was designed by Reaumur in 1730. The lower fixed point is 0°R representing melting point of ice. The upper fixed point is 80°R, which represents boiling point of water.

  The distance between the two fixed points is divided into 80 equal parts. Each part represents 1°R. If T_C, T_F and T_R are temperature values of a body on Celsius scale, Fahrenheit scale and Reaumur scale respectively, then

$$\frac{T_C - 0}{100} = \frac{T_F - 32}{180} = \frac{T_R - 0}{80}$$

- **Heat and Temperature**

  The word heat is always used during transfer of thermal energy from hot body to cold body (due to temperature difference between them). Following are given some statements. Some of them are right and some are wrong. From those statements, you will be able to find the difference between heat and temperature.

- **Incorrect Statements**

  (i) This body has large quantity of heat.

  (ii) Temperature transfer is taking place from body A to body B.

- **Correct Statements**
  (i) Temperature of body *A* is more than temperature of body *B*.
  (ii) Heat transfer is taking place from body *A* to body *B* because *A* is at higher temperature than body *B*.

Note *One calorie (1 cal) is defined as the amount of heat required to raise the temperature of one gram of water from 14.5°C to 15.5°C.*
Experiments have shown that 1 cal = 4.186 J
Similarly, 1 kcal = 1000 cal = 4186 J
The calorie is not a fundamental SI unit.

Example 1 Express a temperature of 60°F in degrees Celsius and in Kelvin.

Sol. Substituting $T_F = 60°F$ in Eq. (ii),

$$T_C = \frac{5}{9}(T_F - 32) = \frac{5}{9}(60° - 32°) = 15.56°C \quad \textbf{Ans.}$$

From Eq. (i), $T = T_C + 273.15$
$= 15.56°C + 273.15$
$= 288.7$ K **Ans.**

Example 2 The temperature of an iron piece is heated from 30°C to 90°C. What is the change in its temperature on the Fahrenheit scale and on the kelvin scale?

Sol. $\Delta T_C = 90°C - 30°C = 60°C$

Using Eq. (iii), $\Delta T_F = \frac{9}{5}\Delta T_C = \frac{9}{5}(60°C) = 108°F$ **Ans.**

and $\Delta T = \Delta T_C = 60$ K

MODULE 1 Exercise

Single Correct Option

1. On a temperature scale *X*, the boiling point of water is 65°X and the freezing point is – 15°X. Assume that the *X* scale is linear. The equivalent temperature corresponding to – 95°X on the Farenheit scale would be **(2023 Main)**
(a) –148°F (b) –112°F
(c) – 48°F (d) –63°F

2. The graph between two temperature scales *P* and *Q* is shown in the figure. Between upper fixed point and lower fixed point, there are 150 equal divisions of scale *P* and 100 divisions on scale *Q*. The relationship for conversion between the two scales is given by **(2023 Main)**

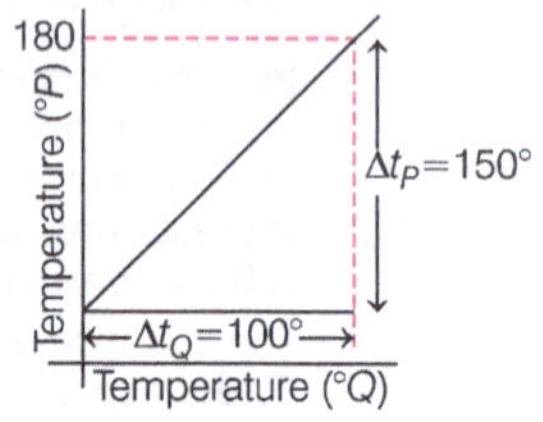

(a) $\frac{t_P}{180} = \frac{t_Q - 40}{100}$ (b) $\frac{t_Q}{100} = \frac{t_P - 30}{150}$
(c) $\frac{t_Q}{150} = \frac{t_P - 180}{100}$ (d) $\frac{t_P}{100} = \frac{t_Q - 180}{150}$

Subjective Questions

3. What is the value of
(a) 0°F in Celsius scale? (b) 0 K on Fahrenheit scale?

4. At what temperature is the Fahrenheit scale reading equal to
(a) twice (b) half of Celsius?

5. A faulty thermometer reads 5°C in melting ice and 99°C in steam. Find the correct temperature in °F when this faulty thermometer reads 52°C.

6. At what temperature the Fahrenheit and Kelvin scales of temperature give the same reading?

7. At what temperature the Fahrenheit and Celsius scales of temperature give the same reading?

8. The steam point and the ice point of a mercury thermometer are marked as 80° and 20°. What will be the temperature in centigrade mercury scale when this thermometer reads 32°?

9. A platinum resistance thermometer reads 0°C when its resistance is 80Ω and 100°C when its resistance is 90Ω. Find the temperature at which the resistance is 86Ω.

Answers

1. (a) **2.** (b) **3.** (a) –17.8°C (b) – 459.4°F **4.** (a) 160°C (b) – 24.6°C **5.** 122°F
6. 574.25°F or 574.25K **7.** – 40° C or – 40° F **8.** 20°C **9.** 60°C

See hints on page 224.

MODULE 2

Thermal Expansion

Most substances expand when they are heated. Thermal expansion is a consequence of the change in average separation between the constituent atoms of an object. Atoms of an object can be imagined to be connected to one another by stiff springs as shown in figure.

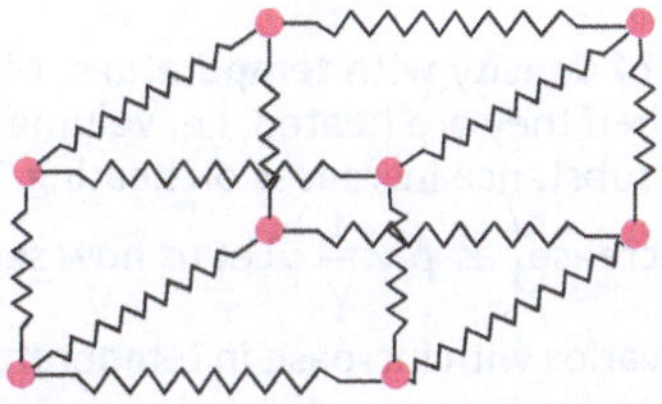

At ordinary temperatures, the atoms in a solid oscillate about their equilibrium positions with an amplitude of approximately 10^{-11} m. The average spacing between the atoms is about 10^{-10} m.

As the temperature of solid increases, the atoms oscillate with greater amplitudes, as a result the average separation between them increases, consequently the object expands.

Linear Expansion

Suppose that the temperature of a thin rod of length l is changed from T to $T + \Delta T$. It is found experimentally that, if ΔT is not too large, the corresponding change in length Δl of the rod is directly proportional to ΔT and l. Thus,

$$\Delta l \propto \Delta T \quad \text{and} \quad \Delta l \propto l$$

Introducing a proportionality constant α (which is different for different materials) we may write Δl as

$$\Delta l = l\alpha\Delta T \qquad \text{...(i)}$$

Here, the constant α is called the **coefficient of linear expansion** of the material of the rod and its units are K^{-1} or $(°C)^{-1}$. Remember that $\Delta T = \Delta T_C$ or $\Delta\theta$.

Actually, α does depend slightly on the temperature, but its variation is usually small enough to be negligible, even over a temperature range of 100°C. We will always assume that α is a constant.

Volume Expansion

Because the linear dimensions of an object change with temperature, it follows that surface area and volume change as well. Just as with linear expansion, experiments show that if the temperature change ΔT is not too great (less than 100°C or so), the increase in volume ΔV is proportional to both, the temperature change ΔT and the initial volume V. Thus,

$$\Delta V \propto \Delta T \quad \text{and} \quad \Delta V \propto V$$

Introducing a proportionality constant γ, we may write ΔV as

$$\boxed{\Delta V = V \times \gamma \times \Delta T} \qquad \text{...(ii)}$$

Here, γ is called the **coefficient of volume expansion**. The units of γ are K^{-1} or $(°C)^{-1}$.

Relation Between γ and α

For an isotropic solid (which has the same value of α in all directions) $\gamma = 3\alpha$. To see that $\gamma = 3\alpha$ for a solid, consider a cube of length l and volume $V = l^3$.

When the temperature of the cube is increased by dT, the side length increases by dl and the volume increases by an amount dV given by

$$dV = \left(\frac{dV}{dl}\right) \cdot dl = 3l^2 \cdot dl$$

Now, $\quad dl = l\alpha dT$

$\therefore \quad dV = 3l^3\alpha dT = (3\alpha)VdT$

This is consistent with Eq. (ii),

$$dV = \gamma VdT, \text{ only if}$$

$$\boxed{\gamma = 3\alpha} \qquad \text{...(iii)}$$

Average values of α and γ for some materials are listed in Table 1. You can check the relation $\gamma = 3\alpha$, for the materials given in the table.

Table 1

Material	α [K^{-1} or $(°C)^{-1}$]	γ [K^{-1} or $(°C)^{-1}$]
Steel	1.2×10^{-5}	3.6×10^{-5}
Copper	1.7×10^{-5}	5.1×10^{-5}
Brass	2.0×10^{-5}	6.0×10^{-5}
Aluminium	2.4×10^{-5}	7.2×10^{-5}

The Anomalous Expansion of Water

Most liquids also expand when their temperatures increase. Their expansion can also be described by Eq. (ii). The volume expansion coefficients for liquids are about 100 times larger than those for solids.Some substances contract when heated over a certain temperature range. The most common example is water.

Figure shows how the volume of 1 g of water varies with temperature at atmospheric pressure.

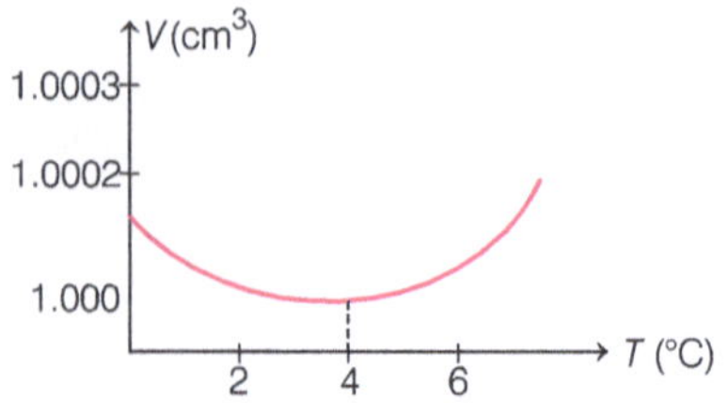

The volume decreases as the temperature is raised from 0°C to about 4°C. At 4°C the volume is a minimum and the density is a maximum (1000 kg/m^3). Above 4°C, water expands with increasing temperature like other substances.

This anomalous behaviour of water causes ice to form first at the surface of a lake in cold weather. As winter approaches, the water temperature decreases initially at the surface.

The water there sinks because of its increased density. Consequently, the surface reaches 0°C first and the lake becomes covered with ice. Now ice is bad conductor of heat so water at the bottom remains at 4°C, the highest density of water. Aquatic life is able to survive the cold winter as the bottom of the lake remains unfrozen at a temperature of about 4°C.

Important POINTS

- If a solid object has a hole in it, what happens to the size of the hole, when the temperature of the object increases? A common misconception is that if the object expands, the hole will shrink because material expands into the hole. But the truth is that if the object expands, the hole will expand too, because every linear dimension of an object changes in the same way when the temperature changes.

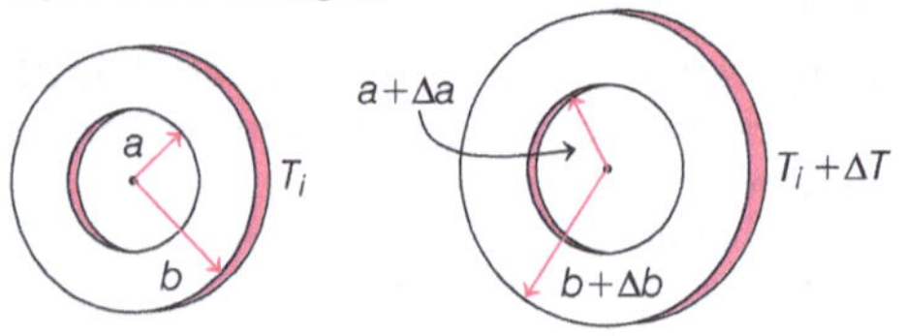

- **Expansion of a bimetallic strip** As Table 1 indicates, each substance has its own value of coefficient of expansion.

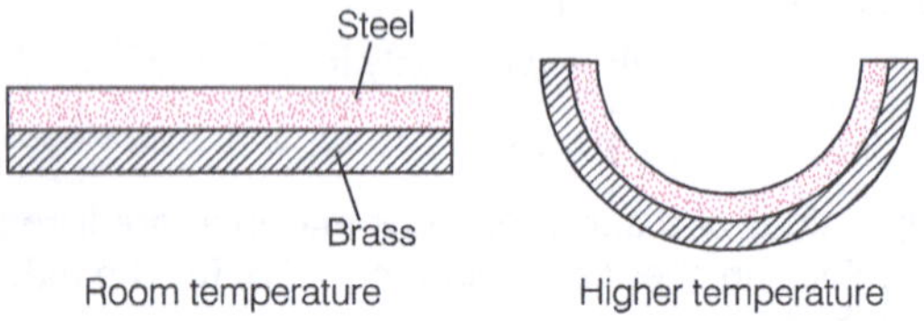

For example, when the temperatures of a brass rod and a steel rod of equal length are raised by the same amount from some common initial value, the brass rod expands more than the steel rod because brass has a greater value of coefficient of expansion than steel. Such type of bimetallic strip is found in practical devices such as **thermostats** to break or make electrical contact.

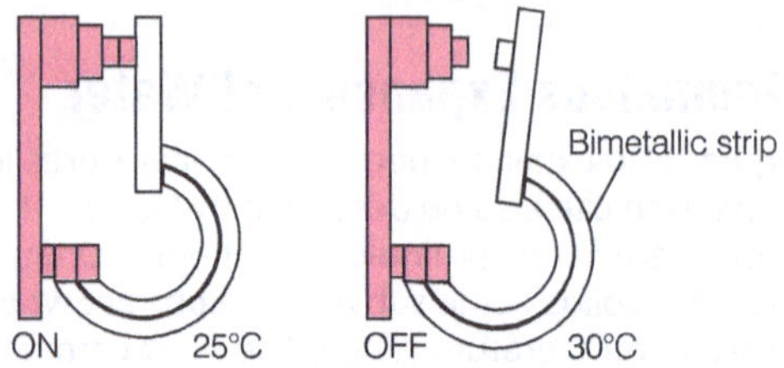

- **Variation of density with temperature** Most substances expand when they are heated, i.e. volume of a given mass of a substance increases on heating, so the density should decrease $\left(\text{as } \rho \propto \frac{1}{V}\right)$. Let us now see how the density ρ varies with increase in temperature.

$$\rho = \frac{m}{V} \quad \text{or} \quad \rho \propto \frac{1}{V} \qquad \text{(for a given mass)}$$

$$\therefore \quad \frac{\rho'}{\rho} = \frac{V}{V'} = \frac{V}{V+\Delta V}$$

$$= \frac{V}{V+\gamma V \Delta T} = \frac{1}{1+\gamma \Delta T}$$

$$\therefore \quad \boxed{\rho' = \frac{\rho}{1+\gamma \Delta T}}$$

This expression can also be written as

$$\rho' = \rho(1+\gamma\Delta T)^{-1}$$

If γ is very small, $(1+\gamma\Delta T)^{-1} \approx 1-\gamma\Delta T$

$$\therefore \quad \boxed{\rho' \approx \rho(1-\gamma\Delta T)}$$

- **Effect of temperature on apparent weight when immersed in a liquid** When a solid body is completely immersed in a liquid, its apparent weight gets decreased due to an upthrust acting on it by the liquid. The apparent weight is given by

$$w_{app} = w - F$$

Here, $F = \text{upthrust} = V_S \rho_L g$

where, V_S = volume of solid and ρ_L = density of liquid

Now, as the temperature is increased V_S increases while ρ_L decreases. So, F may increase or decrease (or may remain constant also) depending upon the condition that which factor dominates on the other. We can write

$$F \propto V_S \rho_L \quad \text{or} \quad \frac{F'}{F} = \frac{V_S'}{V_S} \cdot \frac{\rho_L'}{\rho_L} = \frac{(V_S + \Delta V_S)}{V_S} \cdot \left(\frac{1}{1+\gamma_L \Delta T}\right)$$

$$= \left(\frac{V_S + \gamma_S V_S \Delta T}{V_S}\right)\left(\frac{1}{1+\gamma_L \Delta T}\right)$$

or $$F' = F\left(\frac{1+\gamma_S \Delta T}{1+\gamma_L \Delta T}\right)$$

Now, if $\gamma_S > \gamma_L, F' > F$ or $w'_{app} < w_{app}$

If $\gamma_S = \gamma_L$, $F' = F$ or $w'_{app} = w_{app}$

If $\gamma_S < \gamma_L$

$F' < F$ or $w'_{app} > w_{app}$

- **Effect of temperature on immersed fraction of a solid in floating condition**
  When a solid, whose density is less than the density of liquid is floating in it, then

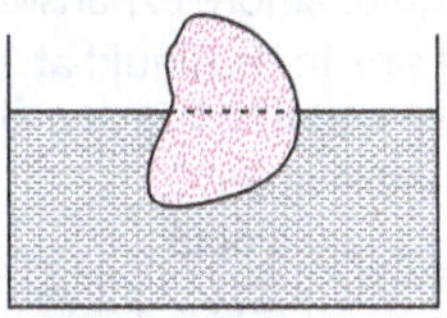

Weight of the solid = Upthrust on solid from liquid

$$\therefore \quad V\rho_s g = V_i \rho_l g \quad \ldots(i)$$

Here, ρ_s = density of solid

ρ_l = density of liquid

V_i = immersed volume of solid and

V = total volume of solid

From Eq. (i),

$$\frac{V_i}{V} = \frac{\rho_s}{\rho_l} = f \quad \ldots(ii)$$

where, f = immersed fraction of solid.

With increase in temperature, ρ_s and ρ_l both will decrease. Therefore, this fraction may increase, decrease or remain constant. At some higher temperature,

$$f' = \frac{\rho_s'}{\rho_l'} \quad \ldots(iii)$$

From Eqs. (ii) and (iii), we have

$$\frac{f'}{f} = \left(\frac{\rho_s'}{\rho_s}\right)\left(\frac{\rho_l}{\rho_l'}\right) = \left(\frac{1}{1+\gamma_s \Delta\theta}\right)(1+\gamma_l \Delta\theta)$$

or $$\frac{f'}{f} = \left(\frac{1+\gamma_l \Delta\theta}{1+\gamma_s \Delta\theta}\right)$$

Now, if $\gamma_l > \gamma_s, f' > f$ or immersed fraction will increase.

If $\gamma_l = \gamma_s$, $f' = f$ or immersed fraction will remain unchanged and if,

$\gamma_l < \gamma_s$, then $f' < f$ or immersed fraction will decrease.

- **Effect of temperature on the time period of a pendulum** The time period of a simple pendulum is given by

$$T = 2\pi\sqrt{\frac{l}{g}} \text{ or } T \propto \sqrt{l}$$

As the temperature is increased, length of the pendulum and hence, time period gets increased or a pendulum clock becomes slow and it loses the time.

$$\frac{T'}{T} = \sqrt{\frac{l'}{l}} = \sqrt{\frac{l+\Delta l}{l}}$$

Here, $\Delta l = l\alpha\Delta\theta$. Thus,

$$\frac{T'}{T} = \sqrt{\frac{l + l\alpha\Delta\theta}{l}} = (1+\alpha\Delta\theta)^{1/2}$$

or $$T' \approx T\left(1+\frac{1}{2}\alpha\Delta\theta\right) \quad (\text{if } \alpha\Delta\theta \ll 1)$$

or $$\Delta T = T' - T = \frac{1}{2}T\alpha\Delta\theta$$

Time lost in time t (by a pendulum clock whose actual time period is T and the changed time period at some higher temperature is T') is

$$\Delta t = \left(\frac{\Delta T}{T'}\right)t$$

- At some higher temperature a scale will expand and scale reading will be lesser than the true value.
  However, at lower temperatures scale reading will be more or true value will be less.
- When a rod whose ends are rigidly fixed such as to prevent from expansion or contraction undergoes a change in temperature, thermal stresses are developed in the rod. This is because, if the temperature is increased, the rod has a tendency to expand but since it is fixed at two ends it is not allowed to expand. So, the rod exerts a force on supports to expand.

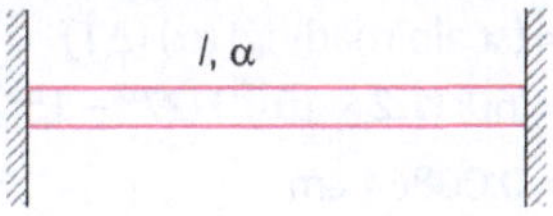

Thermal strain $= \frac{\Delta l}{l} = \alpha\Delta T$. So thermal stress

$= (Y)(\text{thermal strain}) = Y\alpha\Delta T$

or force on supports $F = A(\text{stress}) = YA\alpha\Delta T$

Here, Y = Young's modulus of elasticity of the rod.

$$\therefore \quad F = YA\alpha\Delta T$$

- **Real expansion and apparent expansion of liquids** For heating of a liquid it has to be kept in a container. Obviously when the liquid is heated, the container will also expand.

  Assume that initially container was completely filled with liquid. Now temperature is increased by ΔT.

  Final volume of liquid $V_L = V_O(1+\gamma_L \Delta T)$

  Final volume of container $V_C = V_O(1+\gamma_C \Delta T)$

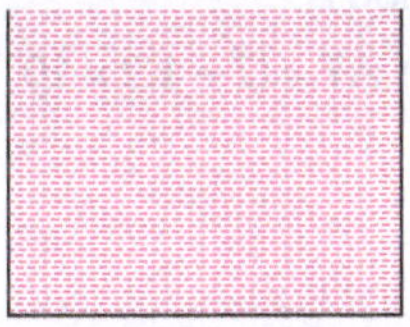

Volume = V_0

So, overflow volume of liquid relative to container

$$\Delta V = V_L - V_C \Rightarrow \Delta V = V_O(\gamma_L - \gamma_C)\Delta T$$

So coefficient of apparent expansion of liquid with respect to container

$$\gamma_{app} = \gamma_L - \gamma_C$$

Example 1 A steel ruler exactly 20 cm long is graduated to give correct measurements at 20°C.

(a) Will it give readings that are too long or too short at lower temperatures?

(b) What will be the actual length of the ruler when it is used in the desert at a temperature of 40°C ?

$\alpha_{steel} = 1.2 \times 10^{-5} (°C)^{-1}$.

Sol. (a) If the temperature decreases, the length of the ruler also decreases. Below 20°C, each centimetre division is actually somewhat shorter than 1.0 cm, so the steel ruler gives readings more than the actual.

(b) At 40°C, the increase in length of the ruler is

$$\Delta l = l\alpha\Delta T$$
$$= (20)\,(1.2 \times 10^{-5})\,(40° - 20°)$$
$$= 0.48 \times 10^{-2}\ \text{cm}$$

∴ The actual length of the ruler is

$$l' = l + \Delta l = 20.0048\ \text{cm}$$ **Ans.**

Example 2 The scale on a steel meter stick is calibrated at 15°C. What is the error in the reading of 60 cm at 27°C? $\alpha_{steel} = 1.2 \times 10^{-5}\ (°C)^{-1}$.

Sol. The error in the reading will be

$$\Delta l = (\text{scale reading})\,(\alpha)\,(\Delta T)$$
$$= (60)\,(1.2 \times 10^{-5})\,(27° - 15°)$$
$$= 0.00864\ \text{cm}$$ **Ans.**

Example 3 A second's pendulum clock has a steel wire. The clock is calibrated at 20°C. How much time does the clock lose or gain in one week when the temperature is increased to 30°C? $\alpha_{steel} = 1.2 \times 10^{-5} (°C)^{-1}$.

Sol. The time period of second's pendulum is 2 second. As the temperature increases length and hence, time period increases. Clock becomes slow and it loses the time. The change in time period is

$$\Delta T = \frac{1}{2} T\alpha\Delta\theta$$
$$= \left(\frac{1}{2}\right)(2)\,(1.2 \times 10^{-5})\,(30° - 20°)$$
$$= 1.2 \times 10^{-4}\ \text{s}$$

∴ New time period is

$$T' = T + \Delta T = (2 + 1.2 \times 10^{-4}) = 2.00012\ \text{s}$$

∴ Time lost in one week

$$\Delta t = \left(\frac{\Delta T}{T'}\right) t$$
$$= \frac{(1.2 \times 10^{-4})}{(2.00012)}(7 \times 24 \times 3600)$$
$$= 36.28\ \text{s}$$ **Ans.**

Example 4 A sphere of diameter 7 cm and mass 266.5 g floats in a bath of liquid. As the temperature is raised, the sphere just sinks at a temperature of 35°C. If the density of the liquid at 0°C is 1.527 g/cm^3, find the coefficient of cubical expansion of the liquid. Ignore expansion of sphere.

Sol. The sphere will sink in the liquid at 35°C, when its density becomes equal to the density of liquid at 35°C.

The density of sphere at 35°C,

$$\rho_{35} = \frac{m}{V} = \frac{266.5}{\frac{4}{3} \times \left(\frac{22}{7}\right) \times \left(\frac{7}{2}\right)^3} = 1.483\ \text{g/cm}^3$$

Using $\frac{\rho'}{\rho} = \frac{1}{1 + \gamma\Delta T}$, we have

$$\rho_0 = \rho_{35}\,[1 + \gamma\Delta T)$$

$$\Rightarrow \quad 1.527 = 1.483\,[1 + \gamma \times 35]$$
$$1.029 = 1 + \gamma \times 35$$
$$\Rightarrow \quad \gamma = \frac{1.029 - 1}{35}$$
$$= 0.00085/°C$$ **Ans.**

Example 5 A glass beaker holds exactly 1 L at 0°C

(a) What is its volume at 50°C?

(b) If the beaker is filled with mercury at 0°C, what volume of mercury overflows when the temperature is 50°C ?

$\alpha_g = 8.3 \times 10^{-6}$ per °C and $\gamma_{Hg} = 1.82 \times 10^{-4}$ per °C.

Sol. (a) The volume of beaker after the temperature change is

$$V_{beaker} = V_0\,(1 + 3\alpha_g\Delta\theta) = (1)\,[1 + 3 \times 8.3 \times 10^{-6} \times 50]$$
$$= 1.001\ \text{L}$$ **Ans.**

(b) Volume of mercury at 50°C is

$$V_{mercury} = V_0\,(1 + \gamma_{Hg}\Delta\theta)$$
$$= (1)\,[1 + 1.82 \times 10^{-4} \times 50]$$
$$= 1.009\ \text{L}$$

The overflow is thus $1.009 - 1.001 = 0.008$ L or 8 mL

MODULE 2 Exercise

Note *Take the value of α and γ from the Table 1 given in the theory unless given in the question.*

Assertion and Reason

See directions on page 14.

1. **Assertion :** A glass of water is filled at 4°C. Water will overflow, if temperature is increased or decreased. (Ignore expansion of glass).

   Reason : Density of water is minimum at 4°C.

Single Correct Option

2. The radius of a ring is R and its coefficient of linear expansion is α. If the temperature of ring increases by θ, then its circumference will increase by

   (a) $\pi R\alpha\,\theta$ (b) $2\pi R\alpha\,\theta$ (c) $\pi R\alpha\frac{\theta}{2}$ (d) $\pi R\alpha\frac{\theta}{4}$

3. A steel rod of length 1 m is heated from 25° to 75°C keeping its length constant. The longitudinal strain developed in the rod is (Given, coefficient of linear expansion of steel $= 12\times10^{-6}/°C$)

   (a) 6×10^{-4} (b) -6×10^{-5} (c) -6×10^{-4} (d) zero

4. The coefficient of linear expansion of steel and brass are $11\times10^{-6}/°C$ and $19\times10^{-6}/°C$, respectively. If their difference in lengths at all temperatures has to kept constant at 30 cm, their lengths at 0°C should be

   (a) 71.25 cm and 41.25 cm (b) 82 cm and 52 cm
   (c) 92 cm and 62 cm (d) 62.25 cm and 32.25 cm

5. On heating a liquid having coefficient of volume expansion γ in a container having coefficient of linear expansion $\gamma/2$, the level of the liquid in the container would

   (a) rise (b) fall
   (c) remains same (d) cannot be predicted

6. In a vertical U-tube containing a liquid, the two arms are maintained at different temperatures t_1 and t_2. The liquid columns in the two arms have heights l_1 and l_2 respectively. The coefficient of volume expansion of the liquid is equal to

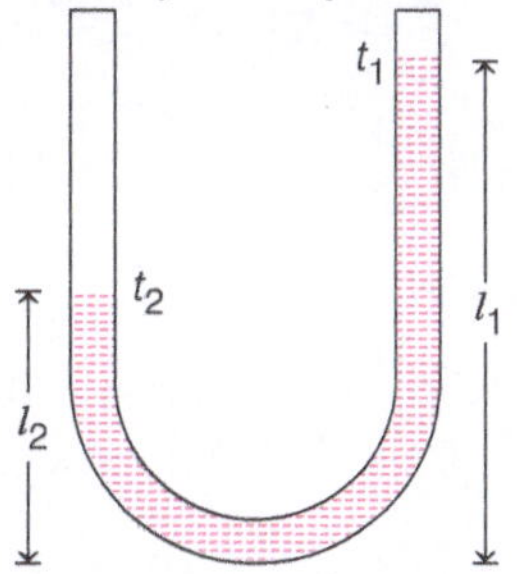

   (a) $\frac{l_1-l_2}{l_2t_1-l_1t_2}$ (b) $\frac{l_1-l_2}{l_1t_1-l_2t_2}$
   (c) $\frac{l_1+l_2}{l_2t_1+l_1t_2}$ (d) $\frac{l_1+l_2}{l_1t_1+l_2t_2}$

7. The figure below shows four isotropic solids having positive coefficient of thermal expansion. A student predicts that on heating the solid, following things can happen. Mark true (T) or False (F) for comments made by the student.

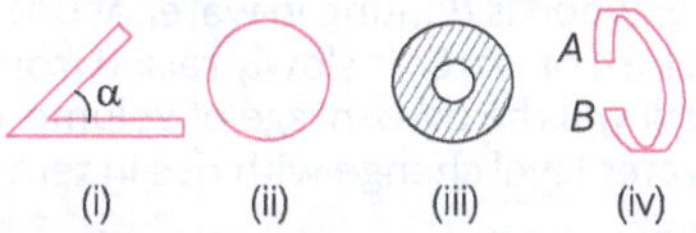

   I. The angle α in figure (i) will not change.
   II. The length of circular line drawn on a metallic plate in figure (ii) will decrease.
   III. The radius of hole in figure (iii) will decrease.
   IV. The distance AB in figure (iv) will increase.

   (a) T F F T (b) F T T F
   (c) T T T T (d) F F T F

8. A liquid with coefficient of volume expansion γ is filled in a container of a material having coefficient of linear expansion α. If the liquid overflows on heating, then

   (a) $\gamma = 3\alpha$ (b) $\gamma > 3\alpha$
   (c) $\gamma < 3\alpha$ (d) $\gamma = \alpha^3$

9. A metal ball immersed in alcohol weighs w_1 at 0°C and w_2 at 50°C. The coefficient of cubical expansion of the metal is less than that of alcohol. Assuming that the density of metal is large compared to that of alcohol, it can be shown that

   (a) $w_1 > w_2$ (b) $w_1 = w_2$
   (c) $w_1 < w_2$ (d) $w_2 = w_1/2$

Multiple Correct Options

10. A bimetallic strip is formed out of two identical strips–one of copper and the other of brass. The coefficients of linear expansion of the two metals are α_C and α_B. On heating, the temperature of the strip goes up by ΔT and the strip bends to form an arc of radius of curvature R. Then, R is

    (a) proportional to ΔT
    (b) inversely proportional to ΔT
    (c) proportional to $|\alpha_B - \alpha_C|$
    (d) inversely proportional to $|\alpha_B - \alpha_C|$

Match the Columns

11. With increase in temperature, match the following two columns.

	Column I		Column II
(a)	Density of water	(p)	will increase
(b)	Fraction of a solid floating in a liquid	(q)	will decrease
(c)	Apparent weight of a solid immersed in water	(r)	will remain unchanged
(d)	Time period of pendulum	(s)	may increase or decrease

Subjective Questions

12. A pendulum clock of time period 2 s gives the correct time at 30°C. The pendulum is made of iron. How many seconds will it lose or gain per day when the temperature falls to 0°C? $\alpha_{Fe} = 1.2 \times 10^{-5}\ (°C)^{-1}$.

13. A block of wood is floating in water at 0°C. The temperature of water is slowly raised from 0°C to 10°C. How will the percentage of volume of block above water level change with rise in temperature?

14. A piece of metal floats on mercury. The coefficient of volume expansion of metal and mercury are γ_1 and γ_2, respectively. If the temperature of both mercury and metal are increased by an amount ΔT, by what factor does the fraction of the volume of the metal submerged in mercury changes?

15. A brass disc fits tightly in a hole in a steel plate. Should you heat or cool the system to losen the disc from the hole? Given that $\alpha_B > \alpha_{Fe}$.

16. An iron ball has a diameter of 6 cm and is 0.010 mm too large to pass through a hole in a brass plate when the ball and plate are at a temperature of 30°C. At what temperature, the same for ball and plate, will the ball just pass through the hole?

17. (a) An aluminium measuring rod which is correct at 5°C, measures a certain distance as 88.42cm at 35°C. Determine the error in measuring the distance due to the expansion of the rod. (b) If this aluminium rod measures a length of steel as 88.42 cm at 35°C, what is the correct length of the steel at 35°C?

    (Take, coefficient of linear expansion of the aluminium $= 2.4 \times 10^{-5}\ °C^{-1}$)

18. A steel tape is calibrated at 20°C. On a cold day when the temperature is -15°C, what will be the percentage error in the tape?

Answers

1. (c) **2.** (b) **3.** (c) **4.** (a) **5.** (b) **6.** (a) **7.** (a) **8.** (b) **9.** (c) **10.** (b,d)

11. (a) $\to$s; (b) $\to$s; (c) $\to$s; (d) $\to$p **12.** Gains, 15.55 s **13.** It will first increase and then decrease

14. $1 + (\gamma_2 - \gamma_1)\,\Delta T$ **15.** Cool the system **16.** 50.83°C **17.** (a) 0.064 cm (b) 88.484 cm **18.** – 0.042%

See hints on pages 224-226.

MODULE 3

Behaviour of Gases

Gases, unlike solids and liquids have indefinite shape and indefinite volume. As a result, they are subjected to pressure changes, volume changes and temperature changes. Real gas behaviour is simpler. By understanding ideal gas behaviour, real gas behaviour becomes more tangible.

Real Gases *versus* Ideal Gases

Real Gas	Ideal Gas
A real gas is a gaseous compound that really exists in the environment.	An ideal gas is a hypothetical gas that does not really exist in the environment.
There are intermolecular attraction forces between real gas particles.	There are no intermolecular attraction forces between ideal gas particles.
The particles have a definite volume and a mass.	The particles do not have a definite volume and a mass.
Collisions between real gas molecules are non-elastic.	Collisions between ideal gas molecules are elastic.
Kinetic energy of real gas particles is changed with collisions.	Kinetic energy of ideal gas particles does not change during collisions.
A real gas may behave as an ideal gas at low pressure and high temperature conditions.	An ideal gas may behave like a real gas at high pressure and low temperature conditions.

Note *Ideal gases always obey* $pV = nRT$. *Real gases obey* $\left(p+\frac{an^2}{V^2}\right)(V-nb) = nRT$, *a modified form of* $pV = nRT$.

Gas Laws

Assuming permanent (or real) gases to be ideal, through experiments, it was established that gases irrespective of their nature obey the following laws :

Boyle's Law

According to this law, for a given mass of a gas, the volume of a gas at constant temperature (called **isothermal process**) is inversely proportional to its pressure, i.e.

$$V \propto \frac{1}{p} \;(T = \text{constant}) \;\text{ or }\; pV = \text{constant} \;\text{ or }\; p_iV_i = p_fV_f$$

Thus, p-V graph in an isothermal process is a rectangular hyperbola. Or pV *versus* p or V graph is a straight line parallel to p or V axis.

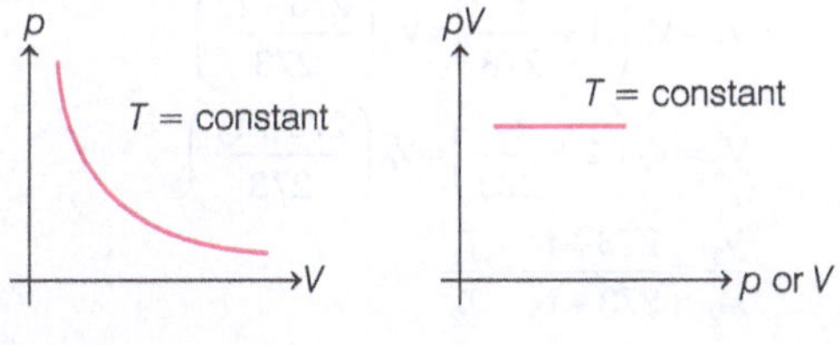

Charles' Law

According to this law, for a given mass of a gas the volume of a gas at constant pressure (called **isobaric** process) is directly proportional to its absolute temperature, i.e.

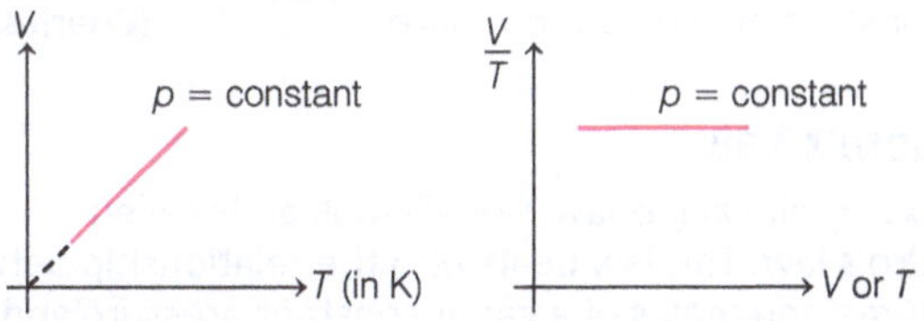

$$V \propto T \qquad (p = \text{constant})$$

or $$\frac{V}{T} = \text{constant} \;\text{ or }\; \frac{V_i}{T_i} = \frac{V_f}{T_f}$$

Thus, V-T graph in an isobaric process is a straight line passing through origin. Or V/T *versus* V or T graph is a straight line parallel to V or T axis.

Gay Lussac's Law or Pressure Law

According to this law, for a given mass of a gas the pressure of a gas at constant volume (called **isochoric process**) is directly proportional to its absolute temperature, i.e.

$$p \propto T \;(V = \text{constant}) \;\text{ or }\; \frac{p}{T} = \text{constant} \;\text{ or }\; \frac{p_i}{T_i} = \frac{p_f}{T_f}$$

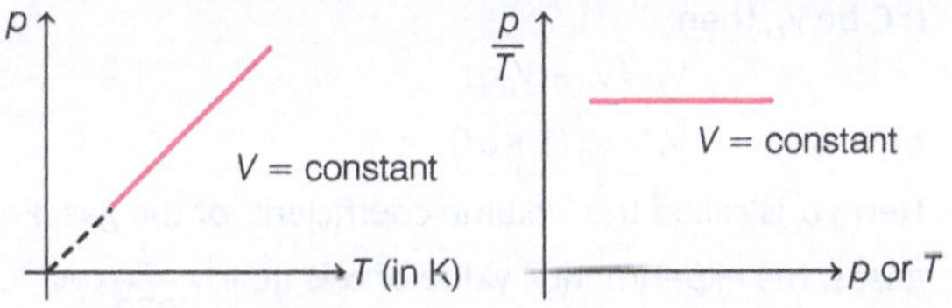

Thus, p-T graph in an isochoric process is a straight line passing through origin or p/T *versus* p or T graph is a straight line parallel to p or T axis.

Ideal Gas Equation

All the above four laws can be written in one single equation known as ideal gas equation. According to this equation.

$$pV = nRT = \frac{m}{M}RT$$

In this equation, n = number of moles of the gas

$$= \frac{m}{M}$$

m = total mass of the gas

M = molecular mass of the gas

and R = universal gas constant

$= 8.31$ J/mol-K

$= 2.0$ cal/mol-K

The above three laws can be derived from this single equation. For example, for a given mass of a gas (m = constant)

pV = constant at constant temperature (Boyle's law)

$\frac{p}{T}$ = constant at constant volume (Pressure law)

$\frac{V}{T}$ = constant at constant pressure (Charles' law)

Avogadro's Law

The next empirical gas law, we will look at, is called Avogadro's law. This law deals with the relationship between the volume and moles of a gas at constant pressure and temperature. According to this law, at same temperature and pressure equal volumes of all gases contain equal number of molecules. Let's derive this law from the ideal gas law.

$$pV_1 = n_1RT$$

and $$pV_2 = n_2RT$$

From these two equations, we have

$$\frac{n_1}{V_1} = \frac{n_2}{V_2} = \frac{p}{RT}$$

Thus, the number of molecules per unit volume is same for all gases at a fixed temperature and pressure. The number in 22.4 litres of any gas is 6.02×10^{23}. This is known as Avogadro number and is denoted by N_A. The mass of 22.4 litres of any gas is equal to its molecular weight in grams at S.T.P. (standard temperature 273 K and pressure 1 atm). This amount of substance is called a mole.

Note $k = \frac{R}{N_A}$ *is called* ***Boltzmann constant****. Its value in SI unit is* 1.38×10^{-23} *J/K.*

Important POINTS

- Until now, we have discussed Charles' law and pressure law in absolute temperature scale. In centigrade scale, these laws are as under :

Charles' law

When a given mass of a gas is heated at constant pressure then for each 1°C rise in temperature the volume of the gas increases by a fraction α of its volume at 0°C. Thus, if the volume of a given mass of a gas at 0°C is V_0, then on heating at constant pressure to t°C its volume will increase by $V_0\alpha t$. Therefore, if its volume at t°C be V_t, then

$$V_t = V_0 + V_0\alpha t$$

or $$V_t = V_0(1 + \alpha t)$$

Here, α is called the 'volume coefficient' of the gas. For all gases, the experimental value of α is nearly $\frac{1}{273}$ per °C.

$$\therefore \quad V_t = V_0\left(1 + \frac{t}{273}\right)$$

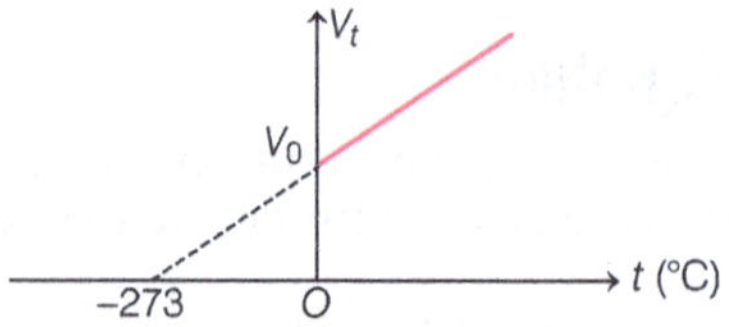

Thus, V_t *versus* t graph is a straight line with slope $\frac{V_0}{273}$ and positive intercept V_0. Further $V_t = 0$ at $t = -273$°C.

Pressure law

According to this law, when a given mass of a gas is heated at constant volume then for each 1°C rise in temperature, the pressure of the gas increases by a fraction β of its pressure at 0°C. Thus, if the pressure of a given mass of a gas at 0°C be p_0, then on heating at constant volume to t°C, its pressure will increase by $p_0\beta t$. Therefore, if its pressure at t°C be p_t, then

$$p_t = p_0 + p_0\beta t$$

or $$p_t = p_0(1 + \beta t)$$

Here, β is called the 'pressure coefficient' of the gas. For all gases the experimental value of β is also $\frac{1}{273}$ per °C

$$\Rightarrow \quad p_t = p_0\left(1 + \frac{t}{273}\right)$$

p_t *versus* t graph is as shown in figure.

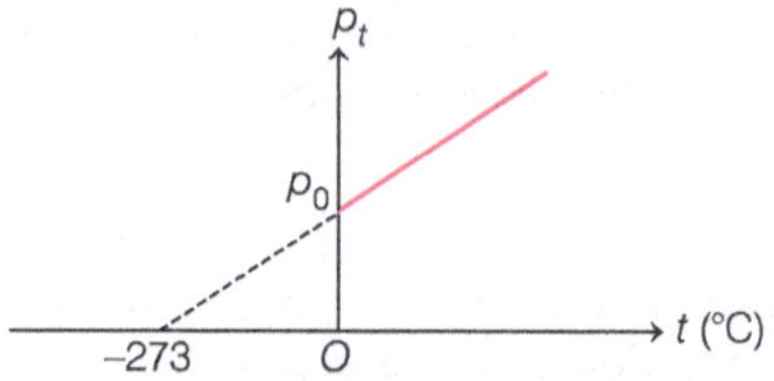

- The above forms of Charles' law and pressure law can be simply expressed in terms of absolute temperature.

Let at constant pressure, the volume of a given mass of a gas at 0°C, t_1°C and t_2°C be V_0, V_1 and V_2 respectively. Then,

$$V_1 = V_0\left(1 + \frac{t_1}{273}\right) = V_0\left(\frac{273 + t_1}{273}\right)$$

$$V_2 = V_0\left(1 + \frac{t_2}{273}\right) = V_0\left(\frac{273 + t_2}{273}\right)$$

$$\therefore \quad \frac{V_1}{V_2} = \frac{273 + t_1}{273 + t_2} = \frac{T_1}{T_2}$$

where, T_1 and T_2 are the absolute temperatures corresponding to t_1°C and t_2°C. Hence,

$$\frac{V_1}{T_1}=\frac{V_2}{T_2}$$

or $$\frac{V}{T}=\text{constant}$$

or $$V \propto T$$

This is the form of Charles' law which we have already studied earlier. In the similar manner, we can prove the pressure law.

- Under isobaric conditions ($p=$ constant), V-T graph is a straight line passing through origin (where, T is in kelvin). The slope of this line is $\left(\frac{nR}{p}\right)$ as $V=\left(\frac{nR}{p}\right)T$ or slope of the line is directly proportional to $\frac{n}{p}$.

$$\text{Slope}=\frac{nR}{p} \quad \text{or} \quad \text{Slope} \propto \frac{n}{p}$$

Similarly, under isochoric conditions ($V=$ constant), p-T graph is a straight line passing through origin whose slope is $\frac{nR}{V}$ or slope is directly proportional to $\frac{n}{V}$.

- **Density of a gas** The ideal gas equation is

$$pV=nRT=\frac{m}{M}RT$$

$$\therefore \quad \frac{m}{V}=\rho=\frac{pM}{RT} \qquad (\rho=\text{density})$$

$$\therefore \quad \boxed{\rho=\frac{pM}{RT}}$$

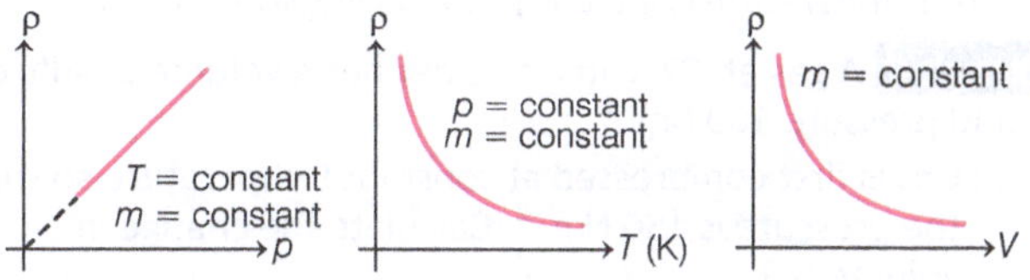

From this equation, we can see that ρ-p graph is straight line passing through origin at constant temperature ($\rho \propto p$) and ρ-T graph is a rectangular hyperbola at constant pressure $\left(\rho \propto \frac{1}{T}\right)$.

Similarly, for a given mass of a gas ρ-V graph is a rectangular hyperbola $\left(\rho \propto \frac{1}{V}\right)$.

Example 1 p-V diagrams of same mass of a gas are drawn at two different constant temperatures T_1 and T_2. Explain whether $T_1 > T_2$ or $T_2 > T_1$.

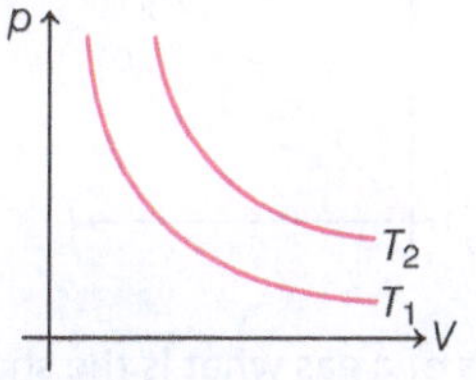

Sol. The ideal gas equation is

$$pV=nRT \quad \text{or} \quad T=\frac{pV}{nR}$$

$T \propto pV$ if number of moles of the gas are kept constant. Here, mass of the gas is constant, which implies that number of moles are constant, i.e. $T \propto pV$. In the given diagram, product of p and V for T_2 is more than T_1 at all points (keeping either p or V same for both graphs). Hence,

$$T_2 > T_1 \qquad \textbf{Ans.}$$

Example 2 The p-V diagram of two different masses m_1 and m_2 are drawn (as shown) at constant temperature T. State whether $m_1 > m_2$ or $m_2 > m_1$.

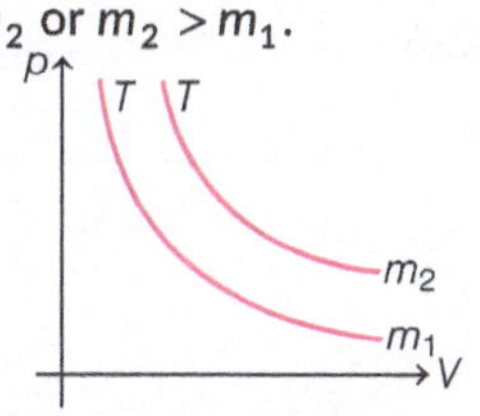

Sol. $$pV=nRT=\frac{m}{M}RT$$

$$\therefore \quad m=(pV)\left(\frac{M}{RT}\right)$$

or $m \propto pV$ if $T=$ constant

From the given graph, we can see that $p_2V_2 > p_1V_1$ (for same p or V). Therefore,

$$m_2 > m_1 \qquad \textbf{Ans.}$$

Example 3 The p-T graph for the given mass of an ideal gas is shown in figure. What inference can be drawn regarding the change in volume (whether it is constant, increasing or decreasing)?

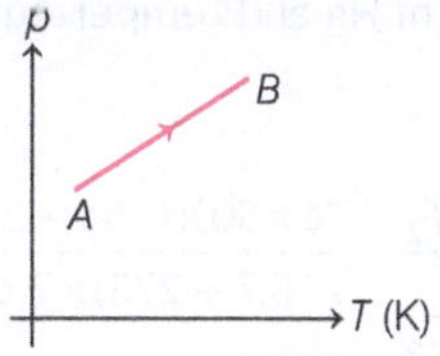

Sol. Definitely, volume is not constant. Because when volume of the gas is constant, p-T graph is a straight line passing through origin. The given line does not pass through origin, hence volume is not constant.

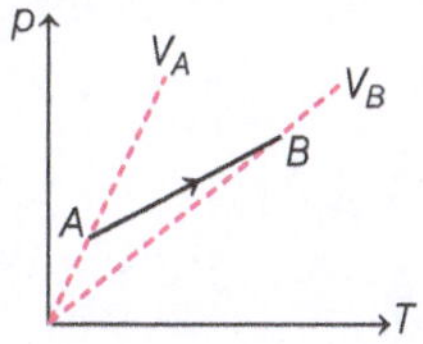

Two dotted lines shown in figure are passing through origin. So, volume along these dotted lines is constant.

V_A = constant along the line passing through A

V_B = constant along the line passing through B

In theory part we have seen that, slope $\propto \frac{1}{V}$

$$\text{Slope}_B < \text{Slope}_A \Rightarrow T_B > T_A$$

or temperature is increasing in moving from A to B.

Example 4 A gas at 27°C in a cylinder has a volume of 4 litre and pressure 100 Nm^{-2}.

(i) Gas is first compressed at constant temperature so that the pressure is 150 Nm^{-2}. Calculate the change in volume.

(ii) It is then heated at constant volume so that temperature becomes 127°C. Calculate the new pressure.

Sol. (i) Using Boyle's law for constant temperature,

$$p_1V_1 = p_2V_2$$

$$\therefore \quad V_2 = \frac{p_1V_1}{p_2} = \frac{100 \times 4}{150}$$

$$= 2.667 \text{ L}$$

$\therefore$ Change in volume

$$= V_2 - V_1 = 2.667 - 4$$

$$= -1.333 \text{ L}$$

(ii) Using Gay Lussac's law for constant volume,

$$\frac{p_2}{p_1} = \frac{T_2}{T_1}$$

or $$p_2 = \frac{T_2}{T_1} \times p_1 = \frac{(127 + 273) \times 150}{(27 + 273)}$$

$$= 200 \text{ Nm}^{-2}$$

Example 5 A balloon partially filled with helium has a volume of 30 m^3, at the earth's surface, where pressure is 76 cm of Hg and temperature is 27°C. What will be the increase in volume of gas if balloon rises to a height, where pressure is 7.6 cm of Hg and temperature is −54°C?

Sol. As $\frac{p_1V_1}{T_1} = \frac{p_2V_2}{T_2}$

$$\therefore \quad V_2 = \frac{p_1V_1T_2}{T_1p_2} = \frac{76 \times 30 \times (-54 + 273)}{(27 + 273) \times 7.6}$$

$$= 219 \text{ m}^3$$

$\therefore$ Increase in volume of gas

$$= V_2 - V_1 = 219 - 30$$

$$= 189 \text{ m}^3$$

INTRODUCTORY Exercise

1. From the graph for an ideal gas, state whether m_1 or m_2 is greater. (m = mass of gas)

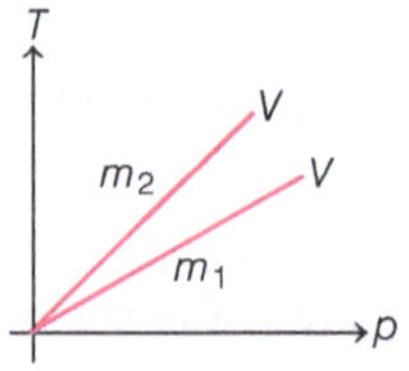

2. A vessel is filled with an ideal gas at a pressure of 20 atm and is at a temperature of 27°C. One-half of the mass is removed from the vessel and the temperature of the remaining gas is increased to 87°C. At this temperature, find the pressure of the gas.
3. A vessel contains a mixture of 7 g of nitrogen and 11 g of carbon dioxide at temperature $T = 290$ K. If pressure of the mixture is 1 atm ($= 1.01 \times 10^5$ N/m^2), calculate its density ($R = 8.31$ J/mol-K).
4. An electric bulb of volume 250 cm^3 was sealed off during manufacture at a pressure of 10^{-3} mm of mercury at 27°C. Compute the number of air molecules contained in the bulb. Given that $R = 8.31$ J/mol-K and $N_A = 6.02 \times 10^{23}$ per mol.
5. State whether $p_1 > p_2$ or $p_2 > p_1$ for given mass of a gas?

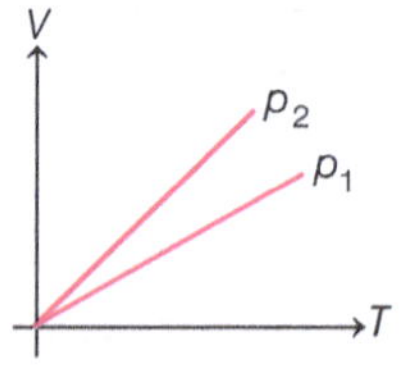

6. For a given mass of a gas what is the shape of p *versus* $\frac{1}{V}$ graph at constant temperature?
7. For a given mass of a gas, what is the shape of pV *versus* T graph in isothermal process?

Answers

1. $m_1 > m_2$	**2.** 12 atm
3. 1.5 kg/m^3	**4.** 8×10^{15}

5. $p_1 > p_2$

6. Straight line passing through origin

7. A dot

See hints on page 226.

Important POINTS

1. Departures from ideal gas behaviour for a real gas

An ideal gas is a simple theoretical model of a gas. No real gas is truly ideal. Figure shows departures from ideal gas behaviour for a real gas at three different temperatures. Notice that all curves approach the ideal gas behaviour for low pressures and high temperatures.

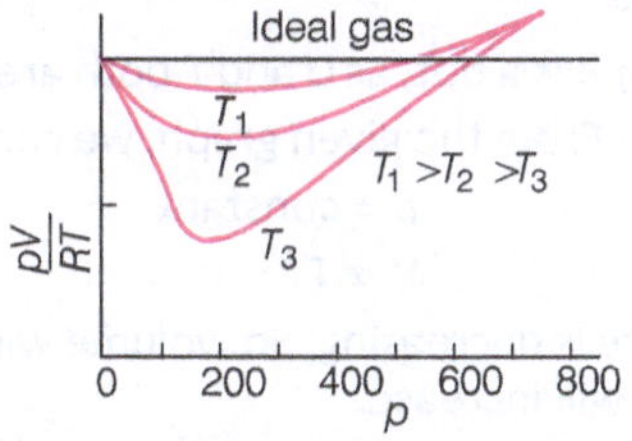

At low pressures or high temperatures the molecules are far apart and molecular interactions are negligible. Without interactions, the gas behaves like an ideal one .

2. van der Waal's Equation

Experiments have proved that real gases deviate largely from ideal behaviour. The reason of this deviation is two wrong assumptions of the ideal gases.

(i) The size of the molecules is much smaller in comparison to the volume of the gas, hence, it may be neglected.

(ii) Molecules do not exert intermolecular force on each other.

van der Waal made corrections for these assumptions and gave a new equation. This equation is known as van der Waal's equation for real gases.

(a) **Correction for the finite size of molecules**

Molecules occupy some volume. Therefore, the volume in which they perform thermal motion is less than the observed volume of the gas. It is represented by $(V - b)$. Here, b is a constant which depends on the effective size and number of molecules of the gas. Therefore, we should use $(V - b)$ in place of V in gas equation.

(b) **Correction for intermolecular attraction**

Due to the intermolecular force between gas molecules the molecules which are very near to the wall experiences a net inward force. Due to this inward force there is a decrease in momentum of the particles of a gas. Thus, the pressure exerted by real gas molecules is less than the pressure exerted by the molecules of an ideal gas. So, we use $\left(p + \frac{a}{V^2}\right)$ in place of p in gas equation. Here, again a is a constant.

van der Waal's equation of state for real gases thus becomes,

$$\left(p + \frac{a}{V^2}\right)(V - b) = RT \qquad (n = 1)$$

3. Critical Temperature, Pressure and Volume

Gases can't be liquified above a temperature called critical temperature (T_C) however large the pressure may be. The pressure required to liquify the gas at critical temperature is called critical pressure (p_C) and the volume of the gas at critical temperature and pressure is called critical volume (V_C). Value of critical constants in terms of van der Waal's constants a and b are as under :

$$V_C = 3b, \quad p_C = \frac{a}{27b^2}$$

and
$$T_C = \frac{8a}{27Rb}$$

Further, $\frac{RT_C}{p_C V_C} = \frac{8}{3}$ is called critical coefficient and is same for all gases.

Typed Problems

Type 1. Conversion of graph.

Concept

(i) In heat, we normally find the following graphs:

S.No	Equation type	Nature of graph
1.	$y \propto x$	Straight line passing through origin
2.	$y \propto \frac{1}{x}$	Rectangular hyperbola
3.	y = constant	Straight line parallel to x -axis
4.	x = constant	Straight line parallel to y -axis
5.	x = constant and y = constant	Dot

(ii) Density of any substance is given by

$$\rho = \frac{m}{V}$$

For given mass of any substance, density only depends on V. It varies with V as

$$\rho \propto \frac{1}{V}$$

If V increases, ρ decreases and *vice-versa*.

(iii) For an ideal gas, density is also given as

$$\rho = \frac{pM}{RT}$$

For a given gas,

$$\rho \propto \frac{p}{T}$$

(iv) For an ideal gas,

$$pV = nRT \quad \text{and} \quad U = \frac{nf}{2}RT$$

For given moles of the gas,

$$U \propto T \quad \text{and} \quad T \propto pV$$

If product of p and V is increasing, it means temperature is increasing. So, U is increasing.

For example, in isothermal process, T is constant. Therefore, U is constant. Hence, U *versus* T graph is a dot.

Ex. 1

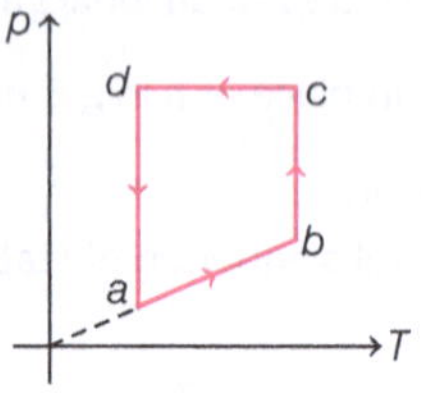

Corresponding to p-T graph as shown in figure, draw

(a) p-V graph (b) V-T graph

(c) ρ-T graph and (d) U-T graph

Sol. ***ab* process** From the given graph, we can see that

$$p \propto T$$

$\Rightarrow$ $V = \text{constant}$ (isochoric)

or $\rho = \text{constant}$ $\left(\text{as } \rho \propto \frac{1}{V}\right)$

p and T both are increasing.

Therefore, U is also increasing (as $U \propto T$)

Now,

(i) p-V graph is straight line parallel to p-axis as V is constant.

(ii) V-T graph is a straight line parallel to T-axis as V is constant.

(iii) ρ-T graph is a straight line parallel to T-axis as ρ is constant.

(iv) U-T graph is a straight line passing through origin as $U \propto T$.

***bc* process** From the given graph, we can see that

$T = \text{constant}$ (isothermal)

$\Rightarrow$ $U = \text{constant}$

$\Rightarrow$ $pV = \text{constant}$

or $p \propto \frac{1}{V}$

p is increasing. Therefore, V will decrease.

Hence, ρ will increase.

Now,

(i) p-V graph is a rectangular hyperbola $\left(\text{as } P \propto \frac{1}{V}\right)$.

(ii) V-T graph is a straight line parallel to V-axis, as T is constant

(iii) ρ-T graph is a straight line parallel to ρ-axis, as T is constant

(iv) U-T graph is a dot, as U and T both are constants.

***cd* process** From the given graph, we can see that

$p = \text{constant}$ (isobaric)

$\Rightarrow$ $V \propto T$

Temperature is decreasing. So, volume will also decrease. But density will increase.

Now,

(i) p-V graph is a straight line parallel to V-axis because p is constant.

(ii) V-T graph is a straight line passing through origin, as $V \propto T$.

(iii) $\rho = \frac{pM}{RT}$

$\Rightarrow$ $\rho \propto \frac{1}{T}$ as p, M and R all are constants.

Hence, ρ-T graph is rectangular hyperbola.

(iv) U-T graph is a straight line passing through origin as $U \propto T$.

***da* process** This process is just inverse of *bc* process. So, this process will complete the cycle following the steps discussed in process *bc*.

The four graphs are as shown below.

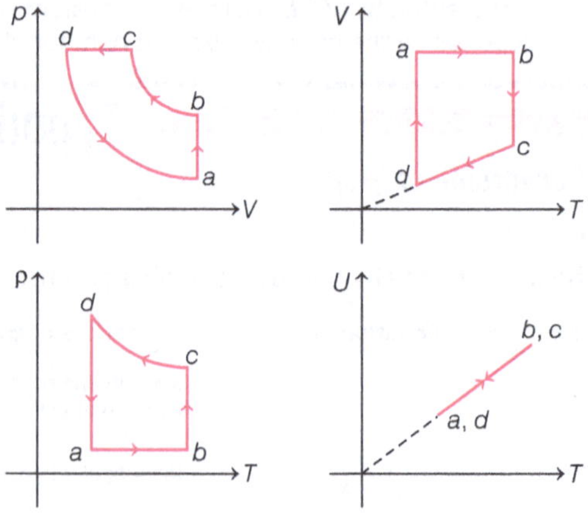

Miscellaneous Examples

Ex. 2 An air bubble starts rising from the bottom of a lake. Its diameter is 3.6 mm at the bottom and 4 mm at the surface. The depth of the lake is 250 cm and the temperature at the surface is 40°C. What is the temperature at the bottom of the lake? Given atmospheric pressure = 76 cm of Hg and $g = 980\ \text{cm/s}^2$.

Sol. At the bottom of the lake, volume of the bubble

$$V_1 = \frac{4}{3}\pi r_1^3 = \frac{4}{3}\pi(0.18)^3\ \text{cm}^3$$

Pressure on the bubble p_1 = Atmospheric pressure + Pressure due to a column of 250 cm of water

$$= 76 \times 13.6 \times 980 + 250 \times 1 \times 980$$
$$= (76 \times 13.6 + 250)\,980\ \text{dyne/cm}^2$$

At the surface of the lake, volume of the bubble

$$V_2 = \frac{4}{3}\pi r_2^3 = \frac{4}{3}\pi(0.2)^3\ \text{cm}^3$$

Pressure on the bubble, p_2 = atmospheric pressure

$$= (76 \times 13.6 \times 980)\ \text{dyne/cm}^2$$

$$T_2 = 273 + 40°\text{C}$$
$$= 313°\ \text{K}$$

Now $\frac{p_1V_1}{T_1} = \frac{p_2V_2}{T_2}$

or $$\frac{(76 \times 13.6 + 250)980 \times \left(\frac{4}{3}\right)\pi(0.18)^3}{T_1} = \frac{(76 \times 13.6) \times 980\left(\frac{4}{3}\right)\pi(0.2)^3}{313}$$

or $T_1 = 283.37\ \text{K}$

$\therefore$ $T_1 = 283.37 - 273.15$

$= 10.22°\text{C}$

Ex. 3 p-V diagram of n moles of an ideal gas is as shown in figure. Find the maximum temperature between A and B.

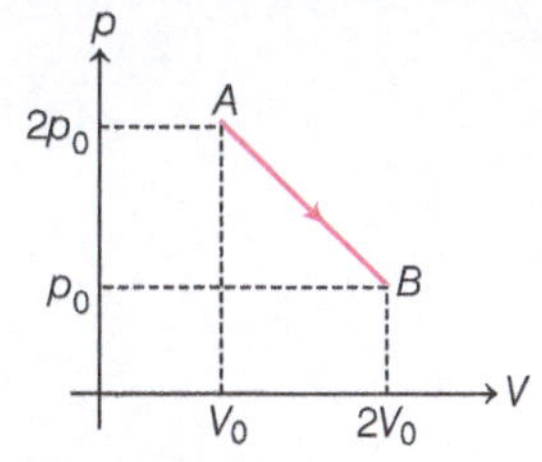

How to Proceed For given number of moles of a gas,

$$T \propto pV \qquad (pV = nRT)$$

Although $(pV)_A = (pV)_B = 2p_0V_0$ or $T_A = T_B$, yet it is not an isothermal process. Because in isothermal process p-V graph is a rectangular hyperbola while it is a straight line. So, to see the behaviour of temperature, first we will find either T-V equation or T-p equation and from that equation we can judge how the temperature varies. From the graph, first we will write p-V equation, then we will convert it either in T-V equation or in T-p equation with the help of equation, $pV = nRT$.

Sol. From the given graph, the p-V equation can be written as

$$p = -\left(\frac{p_0}{V_0}\right)V + 3p_0 \qquad (y = -mx + c)$$

or $$pV = -\left(\frac{p_0}{V_0}\right)V^2 + 3p_0V$$

or $$nRT = 3p_0V - \left(\frac{p_0}{V_0}\right)V^2 \qquad (\text{as } pV = nRT)$$

or $$T = \frac{1}{nR}\left[3p_0V - \left(\frac{p_0}{V_0}\right)V^2\right]$$

This is the required T-V equation. This is quadratic in V. Hence, T-V graph is a parabola. Now, to find maximum or minimum value of T, we can substitute.

$$\frac{dT}{dV} = 0$$

or $$3p_0 - \left(\frac{2p_0}{V_0}\right)V = 0 \quad \text{or} \quad V = \frac{3}{2}V_0$$

Further $\frac{d^2T}{dV^2}$ is negative at $V = \frac{3}{2}V_0$.

Hence, T is maximum at $V = \frac{3}{2}V_0$ and this maximum value is

$$T_{max} = \frac{1}{nR}\left[(3p_0)\left(\frac{3V_0}{2}\right) - \left(\frac{p_0}{V_0}\right)\left(\frac{3V_0}{2}\right)^2\right]$$

or $$T_{max} = \frac{9p_0V_0}{4nR}$$ **Ans.**

Thus, T-V graph is as shown in figure.

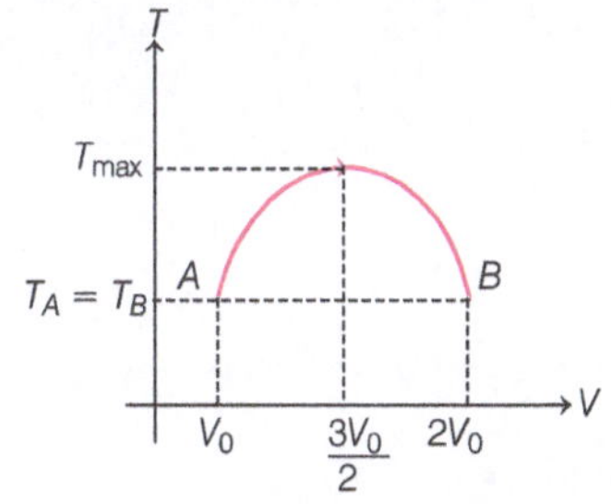

$$T_A = T_B = \frac{2p_0V_0}{nR} \quad \text{and} \quad T_{max} = \frac{9p_0V_0}{4nR}$$
$$= 2.25\frac{p_0V_0}{nR}$$

Note *Most of the problems of T_{max}, p_{max} and V_{max} are solved by differentiation. Sometimes graph will be given and sometimes direct equation will be given. For p_{max} you will require either p-V or p-T equation.*

Ex. 4 Plot p-V, V-T and ρ-T graphs corresponding to the p-T graph for an ideal gas shown in figure.

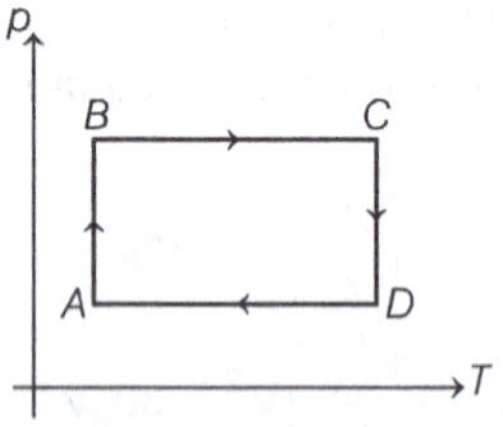

Sol. **Process *AB*** is an isothermal process with $T =$ constant and $p_B > p_A$.

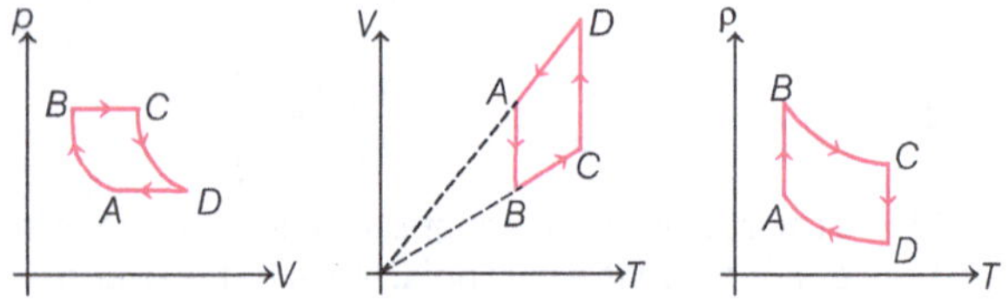

***p*-*V* graph :** $p \propto \frac{1}{V}$ i.e. p-V graph is a rectangular hyperbola with $p_B > p_A$ and $V_B < V_A$.

***V*-*T* graph :** $T =$ constant. Therefore, V-T graph is a straight line parallel to V-axis with $V_B < V_A$.

ρ-*T* graph : $\rho = \frac{pM}{RT}$

or $\rho \propto p$

As T is constant. Therefore, ρ-T graph is a straight line parallel to ρ-axis with $\rho_B > \rho_A$ as $p_B > p_A$.

Process *BC* is an isobaric process with $P =$ constant and $T_C > T_B$.

***p*-*V* graph :** As p is constant. Therefore, p-V graph is a straight line parallel to V-axis with $V_C > V_B$ (because $V \propto T$ in an isobaric process)

***V*-*T* graph :** In isobaric process $V \propto T$, i.e. V-T graph is a straight line passing through origin, with $T_C > T_B$ and $V_C > V_B$.

ρ-*T* graph : $\rho \propto \frac{1}{T}$ (when $P =$ constant), i.e. ρ-T graph is a hyperbola with $T_C > T_B$ and $\rho_C < \rho_B$

There is no need of discussing *C*-*D* and *D*-*A* processes. As they are opposite to *AB* and *BC* respectively. The corresponding three graphs are shown above.

MODULE 3 Exercise

Fill in the Blanks

1. A ring shaped tube contains two ideal gases with equal masses and relative molar masses $M_1 = 32$ and $M_2 = 28$. The gases are separated by one fixed partition P and another movable stopper S which can move freely without friction inside the ring. The angle α as shown in the figure is ...... degrees. **(1997 JEE)**

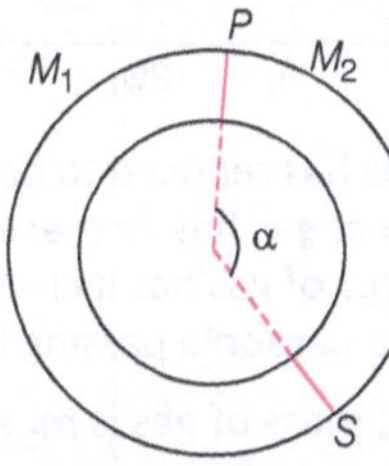

2. During an experiment, an ideal gas is found to obey an additional law $p^2V =$ constant. The gas is initially at a temperature T and volume V. When it expands to a volume $2V$, the temperature becomes .... **(1987 JEE)**

Assertion and Reason

See directions on page 14.

3. **Assertion :** Real gases behave as ideal gases most closely at low pressure and high temperature.

   Reason : Intermolecular force between ideal gas molecules is assumed to be zero.

Single Correct Option

4. Figure shows the isotherms of a fixed mass of an ideal gas at three temperatures T_A, T_B and T_C, then

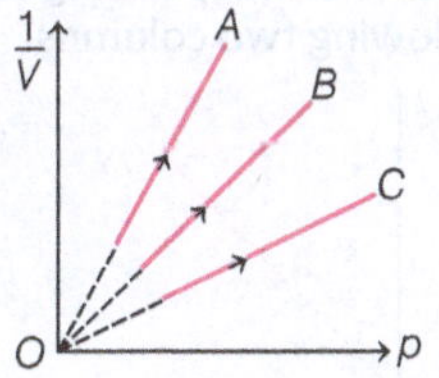

(a) $T_A > T_B > T_C$ (b) $T_A < T_B < T_C$
(c) $T_B < T_A < T_C$ (d) $T_A = T_B = T_C$

5. The temperature at the bottom of a 40 m deep lake is 12°C and that at the surface is 35°C. An air bubble of volume 1.0 cm^3 rises from the bottom to the surface. Its volume becomes (atmospheric pressure = 10 m of water)

(a) 2.0 cm^3
(b) 3.2 cm^3
(c) 5.4 cm^3
(d) 8.0 cm^3

6. In a process, the pressure of a gas remains constant. If the temperature is doubled, then the change in the volume will be

(a) 100% (b) 200% (c) 50% (d) 25%

7. The expansion of an ideal gas of mass m at a constant pressure p is given by the straight line B. Then, the expansion of the same ideal gas of mass $2m$ at a pressure $2p$ is given by the straight line

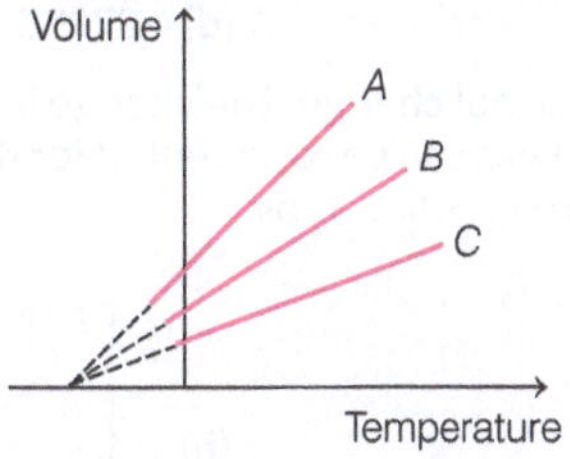

(a) C (b) A
(c) B (d) data insufficient

8. pV *versus* T graph of equal masses of H_2, He and O_2 is shown in figure. Choose the correct alternative.

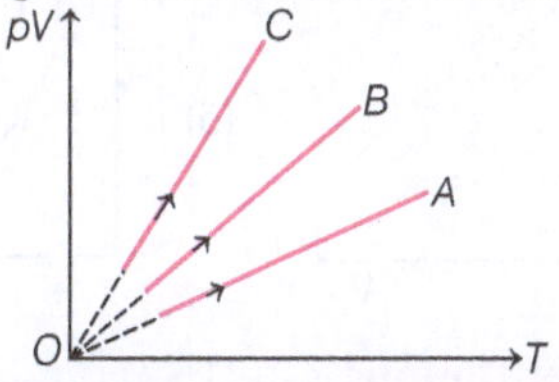

(a) A corresponds to O_2, B to He and C to H_2
(b) A corresponds to He, B to H_2 and C to O_2
(c) A corresponds to He, B to O_2 and C to H_2
(d) A corresponds to O_2, B to H_2 and C to He

9. The gas equation $\frac{pV}{T} =$ constant is true for a constant mass of an ideal gas undergoing

(a) isothermal change (b) adiabatic change
(c) isobaric change (d) any type of change

10. Pressure *versus* temperature graph of an ideal gas is as shown in figure. Density of the gas at point A is ρ_0. Density at B will be

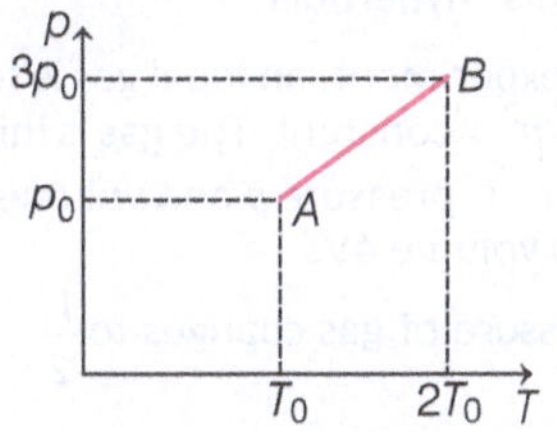

(a) $\frac{3}{4}\rho_0$ (b) $\frac{3}{2}\rho_0$ (c) $\frac{4}{3}\rho_0$ (d) $2\rho_0$

11. For three low density gases A, B, C, pressure *versus* temperature graphs are plotted while keeping them at constant volume, as shown in the figure.

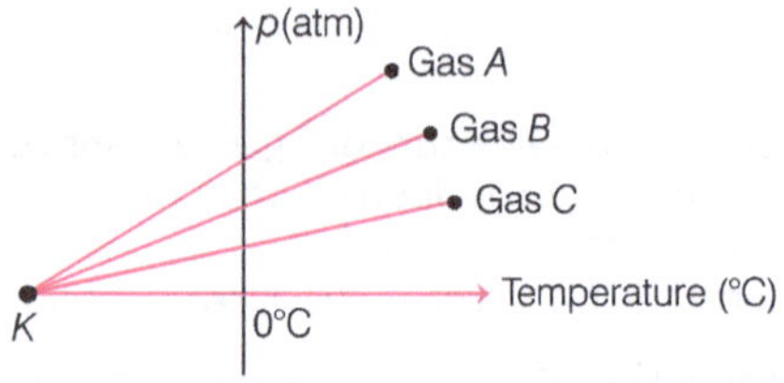

The temperature corresponding to the point K is **(2023 Main)**

(a) $-40°C$ (b) $-100°C$
(c) $-273°C$ (d) $-373°C$

12. In an isothermal change, the change in pressure and volume of a gas can be represented for three different temperature $T_3 > T_2 > T_1$ as **(2023 Main)**

(a)
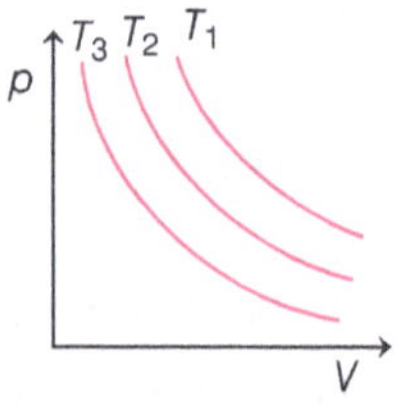

(b)
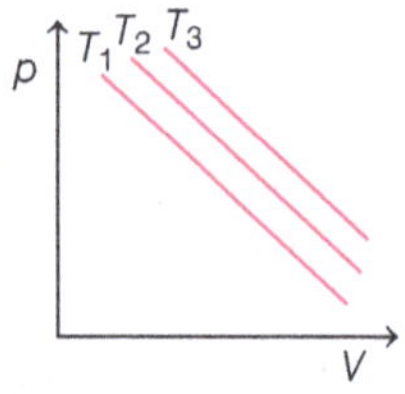

(c)
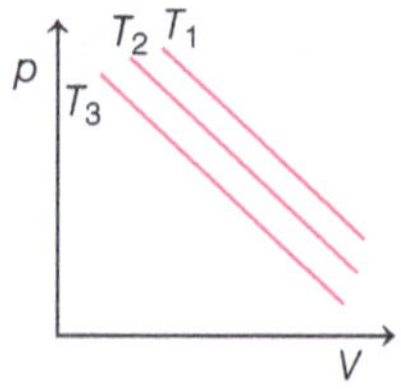

(d)
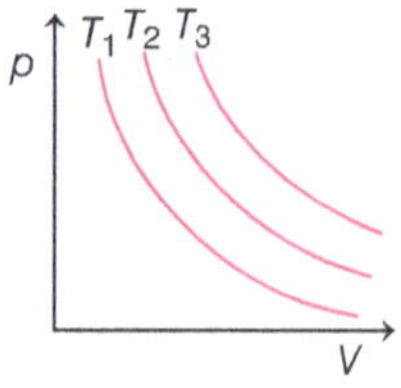

Multiple Correct Options

13. During an experiment, an ideal gas is found to obey a condition $\frac{p^2}{\rho}$ = constant. (ρ = density of the gas). The gas is initially at temperature T, pressure p and density ρ. The gas expands such that density changes to $\rho/2$.
(a) The pressure of the gas changes to $\sqrt{2}\, p$
(b) The temperature of the gas changes to $\sqrt{2}\, T$
(c) The graph of the above process on p-T diagram is parabola
(d) The graph of the above process on p-T diagram is rectangular hyperbola

14. During an experiment, an ideal gas is found to obey a condition Vp^2 = constant. The gas is initially at a temperature T, pressure p and volume V. The gas expands to volume $4V$.
(a) The pressure of gas changes to $\frac{p}{2}$
(b) The temperature of gas changes to $4T$
(c) The graph of the above process on p-T diagram is parabola
(d) The graph of the above process on p-T diagram is rectangular hyperbola

15. In the p-V diagram shown in figure, choose the correct options for the process a-b :

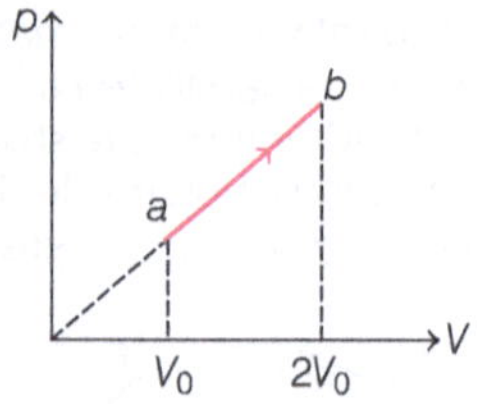

(a) density of gas has reduced to half
(b) temperature of gas has increased to two times
(c) internal energy of gas has increased to four times
(d) T-V graph is a parabola passing through origin

16. Along the line-1, mass of gas is m_1 and pressure is p_1. Along the line-2 mass of same gas is m_2 and pressure is p_2. Choose the correct options.

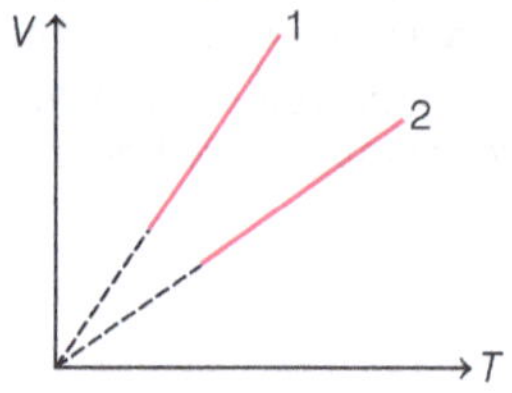

(a) m_1 may be less than m_2
(b) m_2 may be less than m_1
(c) p_1 may be less than p_2
(d) p_2 may be less than p_1

Match the Columns

17. In the graph shown, U is the internal energy of gas and ρ the density. Corresponding to given graph, match the following two columns.

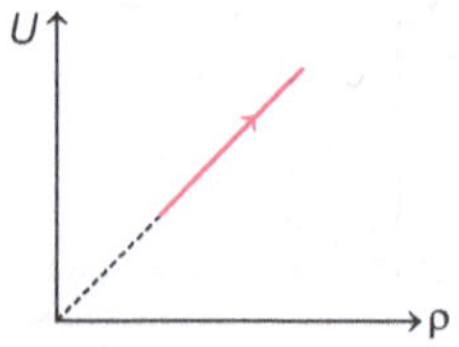

	Column I		Column II
(a)	Pressure	(p)	is constant
(b)	Volume	(q)	is increasing
(c)	Temperature	(r)	is decreasing
(d)	Ratio T/V	(s)	None of these

18. Corresponding to isobaric process, match the following two columns.

	Column I		Column II
(a)	p-T graph	(p)	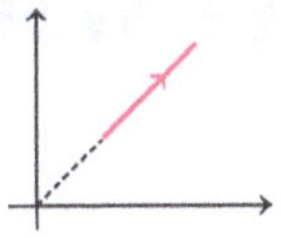
(b)	U-ρ graph	(q)	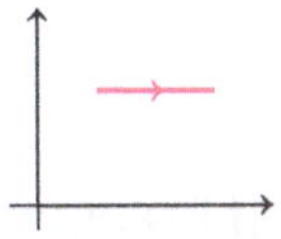
(c)	T-V graph	(r)	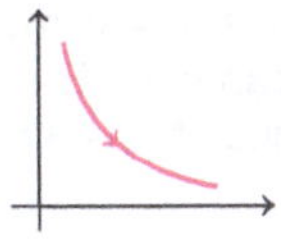
(d)	T-ρ graph	(s)	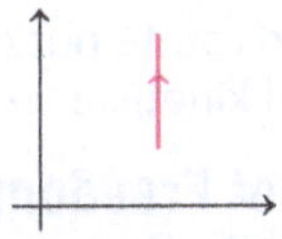

Note *First physical quantity is along y-axis.*

Subjective Questions

19. Find the mass (in kilogram) of an ammonia molecule NH_3.

20. If the water molecules in 1.0 g of water were distributed uniformly over the surface of earth, how many such molecules would there be in 1.0 cm^2 of earth's surface?

21. The pressure of the gas in a constant volume gas thermometer is 80 cm of mercury in melting ice. When the bulb is placed in a liquid, the pressure becomes 160 cm of mercury. Find the temperature of the liquid.

22. An ideal gas exerts a pressure of 1.52 MPa when its temperature is 298.15 K and its volume is $10^{-2} m^3$. (a) How many moles of gas are there? (b) What is the mass density if the gas is molecular hydrogen? (c) What is the mass density if the gas is oxygen?

23. A compressor pumps 70 L of air into a 6 L tank with the temperature remaining unchanged. If all the air is originally at 1 atm. What is the final absolute pressure of the air in the tank?

24. A partially inflated balloon contains 500 m^3 of helium at 27°C and 1 atm pressure. What is the volume of the helium at an altitude of 18000 ft, where the pressure is 0.5 atm and the temperature is −3°C?

25. Two gases occupy two containers A and B. The gas in A of volume 0.11 m^3 exerts a pressure of 1.38 MPa. The gas in B of volume 0.16 m^3 exerts a pressure of 0.69 MPa. Two containers are now joined by a tube of negligible volume and the gases are allowed to intermingle. What is the final pressure in the container if the temperature remains constant ?

26. A glass bulb of volume 400 cm^3 is connected to another of volume 20 cm^3 by means of a tube of negligible volume. The bulbs contain dry air and are both at a common temperature and pressure of 20°C and 1.00 atm. The larger bulb is immersed in steam at 100°C and the smaller in melting ice at 0°C. Find the final common pressure.

Answers

1. (192) **2.** $\sqrt{2}$ times **3.** (b) **4.** (b) **5.** (c) **6.** (a) **7.** (c) **8.** (a) **9.** (d) **10.** (b)
11. (c) **12.** (d) **13.** (b,d) **14.** (a,d) **15.** (a,c,d) **16.** (a,b,c,d) **17.** (a) → q; (b) → r; (c) → q; (d) → q
18. (a) → q; (b) → r; (c) → p; (d) → r **19.** 2.82×10^{-26} kg **20.** 6500 **21.** 546 K
22. (a) 6.135 mol (b) 1.24 kg/m^3 (c) 19.68 kg/m^3 **23.** 11.7 atm (absolute pressure) **24.** 900 m^3 **25.** 0.97 MPa
26. 1.13 atm

See hints on pages 226-229.

MODULE 4

Degree of Freedom and Internal Energy of an Ideal Gas

Degree of Freedom (f)

The minimum number of ways in which motion of a body (or a system) can be described completely is called its degree of freedom.

For example In Fig. (a), block has one degree of freedom, because it is confined to move in a straight line and has only one translational degree of freedom.

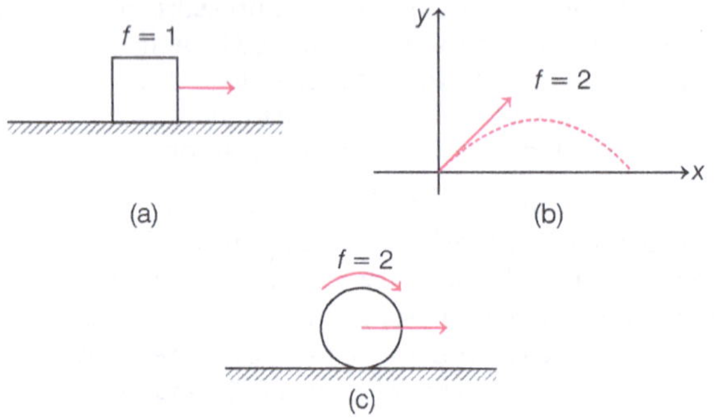

In Fig. (b), the particle has two degrees of freedom because it is confined to move in a plane and so it has two translational degrees of freedom.

In Fig. (c), the sphere has two degrees of freedom one rotational and another translational.

Similarly, a particle free to move in space will have three translational degrees of freedom.

Degree of Freedom of Gas Molecules

A gas molecule can have, the following three types of energies :

(i) translational kinetic energy
(ii) rotational kinetic energy
(iii) vibrational energy (potential + kinetic)

Vibrational Energy

The forces between different atoms of a gas molecule (interatomic force) may be visualized by imagining every atom as being connected to its neighbours by springs. Each atom can vibrate along the line joining the atoms. Energy associated with this is called vibrational energy.

Degree of Freedom of Monoatomic Gas

A monoatomic gas molecule (like He) consists of a single atom. It can have translational motion in any direction in space. Thus, it has 3 translational degrees of freedom.

$$\boxed{f = 3} \quad \text{(all translational)}$$

It can also rotate but due to its small moment of inertia, rotational kinetic energy is neglected.

Degree of Freedom of a Diatomic and Linear Polyatomic Gas

The molecules of a diatomic and linear polyatomic gas (like O_2, CO_2 and H_2) can not only move bodily but also rotate about any one of the three coordinate axes as shown in figure. However, its moment of inertia about the axis joining the two atoms (x-axis) is negligible. Hence, it can have only two rotational degrees of freedom. Thus, a diatomic molecule has 5 degrees of freedom : 3 translational and 2 rotational.

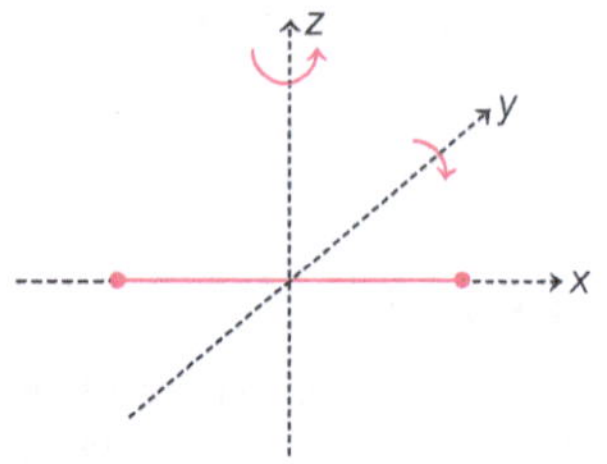

At sufficiently high temperatures, it has vibrational energy as well providing it two more degrees of freedom (one vibrational kinetic energy and another vibrational potential energy). Thus, at high temperatures a diatomic molecule has 7 degrees of freedom, 3 translational, 2 rotational and 2 vibrational. Thus,

> $f = 5$ (3 translational + 2 rotational) at room temperatures and $f = 7$ (3 translational + 2 rotational + 2 vibrational) at high temperatures.

Degree of Freedom of Non-linear Polyatomic Gas

A non-linear polyatomic molecule (such as NH_3) can rotate about any of three coordinate axes. Hence, it has 6 degrees of freedom 3 translational and 3 rotational. At room temperatures, a polyatomic gas molecule has insignificant vibrational energy. But at high enough temperatures it is also significant. So, it has 8 degrees of freedom 3 rotational, 3 translational and 2 vibrational. Thus,

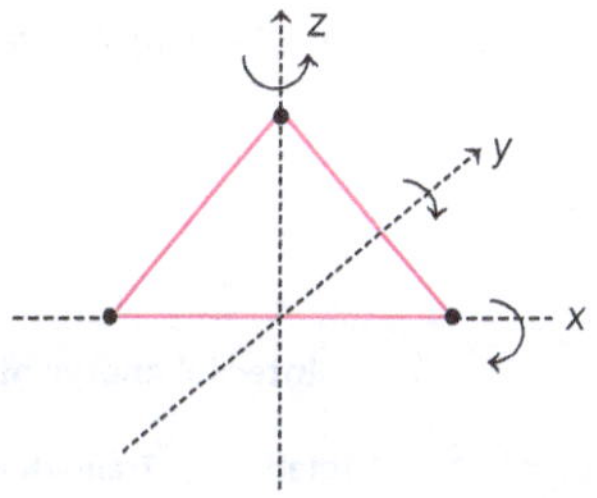

$f = 6$ (3 translational + 3 rotational) at room temperatures and $f = 8$ (3 translational + 3 rotational + 2 vibrational) at high temperatures.

Degree of Freedom of a Solid

An atom in a solid has no degrees of freedom for translational and rotational motion. At high temperatures, due to vibration along 3 axes it has $3 \times 2 = 6$ degrees of freedom.

$f = 6$ (all vibrational) at high temperatures

Note *(i) Degrees of freedom of a diatomic and polyatomic gas depends upon temperature and there is no clear cut demarcation line above which vibrational energy become significant. Moreover, this temperature varies from gas to gas. On the other hand, for a monoatomic gas there is no such confusion. Degree of freedom here is 3 at all temperatures. So, unless stated in the question you can take $f = 3$ for monoatomic gas, $f = 5$ for a diatomic gas and $f = 6$ for a non-linear polyatomic gas.*

(ii) When a diatomic or polyatomic gas dissociates into atoms it behaves as a monoatomic gas. Whose degrees of freedom are changed accordingly.

Internal Energy of an Ideal Gas

Suppose a gas is contained in a closed vessel as shown in figure. If the container as a whole is moving with some speed, then this motion is called the **ordered motion** of the gas. Source of this motion is some external force. The *zig-zag* motion of gas molecules within the vessel is known as the **disordered motion.**

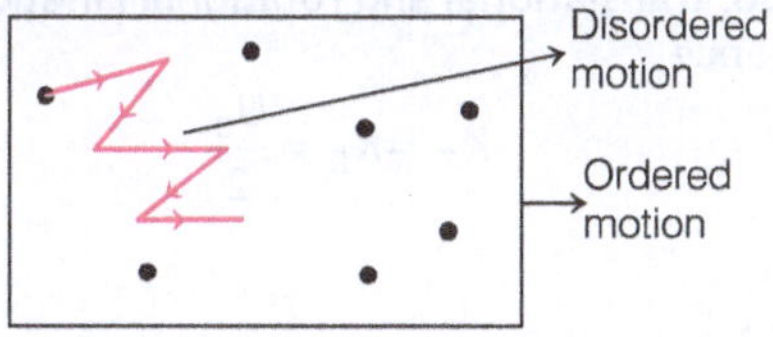

This motion is directly related to the temperature of the gas. As the temperature is increased, the disordered motion of the gas molecules gets fast. The internal energy (U) of the gas is associated only with its disordered motion. It is in no way concerned with its ordered motion. When the temperature of the gas is increased, its disordered motion and hence its internal energy is increased.

Intermolecular forces in an ideal gas is zero. Thus, PE due to intermolecular forces of an ideal gas is zero. A monoatomic gas is having a single atom. Hence, its vibrational energy is zero. For dia and polyatomic gases vibrational energy is significant only at high temperatures. So, they also have only translational and rotational KE. We may thus conclude that at room temperature the internal energy of an ideal gas (whether it is mono, dia or poly) consists of only translational and rotational KE. Thus, U (of an ideal gas) $= K_T + K_R$ at room temperatures.

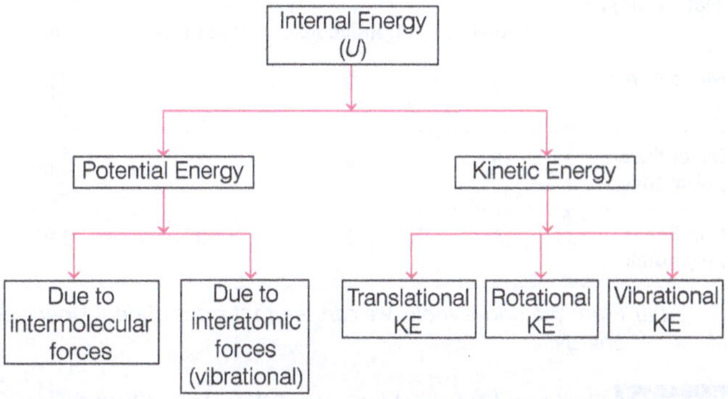

Later in the next article, we will see that K_T (translational KE) and K_R (rotational KE) depends on T only. They are directly proportional to the absolute temperature of the gas. Thus, **internal energy of an ideal gas depends only on its absolute temperature (T) and is directly proportional to T.**

$$U \propto T$$

Law of Equipartition of Energy

An ideal gas is just like an ideal father. An ideal father distributes whole of its properties and assets equally among his children. Same is the case with an ideal gas. It distributes its internal energy equally in all degrees of freedom. In each degree of freedom energy of one mole of an ideal gas is $\frac{1}{2}RT$, where T is the absolute temperature of the gas. Thus, if f be the number of degrees of freedom, the internal energy of 1 mole of the gas will be $\frac{f}{2}RT$ or internal energy of n moles of the gas will be $\frac{n}{2}fRT$. Thus,

$$U = \frac{n}{2}fRT \quad \text{...(i)}$$

For a monoatomic gas, $f = 3$.

Therefore, $U = \frac{3}{2}RT$ (for 1 mole of a monoatomic gas)

For a dia and linear polyatomic gas at low temperatures, $f = 5$, so

$$U = \frac{5}{2}RT \quad \text{(for 1 mole)}$$

and for non-linear polyatomic gas at low temperatures, $f = 6$, so

$$U = \frac{6}{2}RT = 3RT \quad \text{(for 1 mole)}$$

Note *(i) For one molecule, R (the gas constant) is replaced by k (the Boltzmann constant). For example, internal energy of one molecule in one degree of freedom will be* $\frac{1}{2}kT$.

(ii) Ignoring the vibrational effects we can summarise the above results in tabular form as below.

Table 1.

Nature of gas	Degree of freedom			Internal energy of 1 mole			Internal energy of 1 molecule		
	Total	Translational	Rotational	Total	Translational	Rotational	Total	Translational	Rotational
Monoatomic	3	3	0	$\frac{3}{2}RT$	$\frac{3}{2}RT$	0	$\frac{3}{2}kT$	$\frac{3}{2}kT$	0
Dia or linear polyatomic	5	3	2	$\frac{5}{2}RT$	$\frac{3}{2}RT$	RT	$\frac{5}{2}kT$	$\frac{3}{2}kT$	kT
Non-linear polyatomic	6	3	3	$3RT$	$\frac{3}{2}RT$	$\frac{3}{2}RT$	$3kT$	$\frac{3}{2}kT$	$\frac{3}{2}kT$

(iii) From the above table, we can see that translational kinetic energy of all types of gases is same. The difference is in rotational kinetic energy.

Example 1 Find total internal energy of 3 moles of hydrogen gas at temperature T.

Sol. Using the relation, $U = \frac{nf}{2}RT$

we have, $n = 3$, $f = 5$ for diatomic H_2 gas.

$$\therefore \quad U = \frac{3 \times 5}{2} RT = 7.5\, RT \qquad \textbf{Ans.}$$

Example 2 Ten moles of O_2 gas are kept at temperature T. At some higher temperature $2T$, forty percent of molecular oxygen breaks into atomic oxygen. Find change in internal energy of the gas.

Sol. Initial energy Using the relation, $U = \frac{nf}{2}RT$

we have, $n = 10$, $f = 5$ for diatomic O_2 gas

$$U_i = \frac{10 \times 5}{2}(RT) = 25\, RT$$

Final energy Forty percent means 4 moles O_2 breaks into O. So, it will become 8 moles of monoatomic gas O. Remaining 6 moles are of diatomic gas O_2. But now the new temperature is $2T$.

$$\therefore \quad U_f = \frac{8 \times 3}{2}(R)(2T) + \frac{6 \times 5}{2}(R)(2T) = 54\, RT$$

So, change in internal energy,

$$\Delta U = U_f - U_i = 29\, RT \qquad \textbf{Ans.}$$

Example 3 At a given temperature internal energy of a monoatomic, diatomic and non-linear polyatomic gas is U_0 each. Find their translational and rotational kinetic energies separately.

Sol. Monoatomic gas Translational degree of freedom of monoatomic gas is 3 and rotational degree of freedom is zero. Therefore, whole internal energy is in the form of translational kinetic energy.

$$\therefore \quad K_T = U_0 \quad \text{and} \quad K_R = 0$$

Diatomic gas Translational degree of freedom of diatomic gas is 3 and rotational degree of freedom is 2. Hence, ratio of translational and rotational kinetic energy will be 3 : 2

$$\therefore \quad K_T = \frac{3}{5}U_0 \quad \text{and} \quad K_R = \frac{2}{5}U_0$$

Non-linear polyatomic gas In non-linear polyatomic gas translational and rotational both degrees of freedom are 3 each. So, translational and rotational kinetic energy are equal. Hence,

$$K_T = K_R = \frac{U_0}{2}$$

MODULE 4 Exercise

Assertion and Reason

See directions on page 14.

1. **Assertion :** If a gas container is placed in a moving train, the temperature of gas will increase.

   Reason : Kinetic energy of gas molecules will increase.

2. **Assertion :** The total translational kinetic energy of all the molecules of a given mass of an ideal gas is 1.5 times the product of its pressure and its volume.

   Reason : The molecules of a gas collide with each other and the velocities of the molecules change due to the collision. **(2007 JEE)**

Single Correct Option

3. The average kinetic energy of the molecules of an ideal gas at 10°C has the value E. The temperature at which the kinetic energy of the same gas becomes $2E$ is

   (a) 5°C (b) 10°C
   (c) 40°C (d) None of these

4. A polyatomic gas with n degrees of freedom has a mean energy per molecule given by

   (a) $\frac{n}{2}RT$ (b) $\frac{1}{2}RT$
   (c) $\frac{n}{2}kT$ (d) $\frac{1}{2}kT$

5. The graph which represents the variation of mean kinetic energy E of gas molecules with temperature t°C is

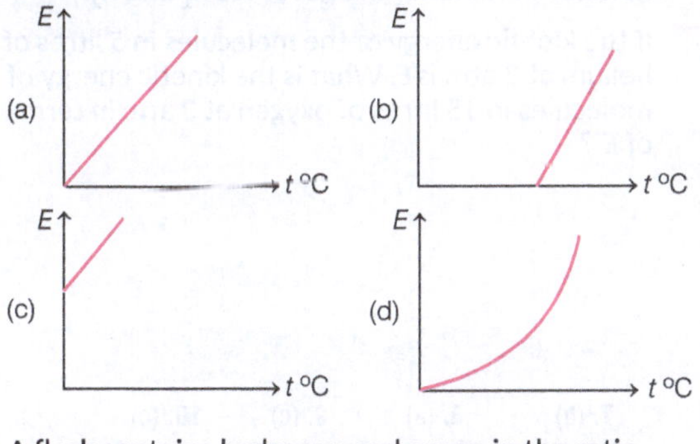

6. A flask contains hydrogen and argon in the ratio 2 : 1 by mass. The temperature of the mixture is 30°C. The ratio of average kinetic energy per molecule of the two gases ($K_{argon}/K_{hydrogen}$) is
   (Given, atomic weight of Ar = 39.9) **(2023 Main)**

   (a) 2 (b) 39.9
   (c) $\frac{39.9}{2}$ (d) 1

7. The temperature at which the kinetic energy of oxygen molecules becomes double than its value at 27°C is **(2023 Main)**

   (a) 927°C (b) 327°C
   (c) 627°C (d) 1227°C

8. Following statements are given

   (A) The average kinetic energy of a gas molecule decreases when the temperature is reduced.
   (B) The average kinetic energy of a gas molecule increases with increase in pressure at constant temperature.
   (C) The average kinetic energy of a gas molecule decreases with increase in volume.
   (D) Pressure of a gas increases with increase in temperature at constant volume.
   (E) The volume of gas decreases with increase in temperature. **(2022 Main)**

   Choose the correct answer from the options given below.

   (a) (A) and (D) only (b) (A), (B) and (D) only
   (c) (B) and (D) only (d) (A), (B) and (E) only

9. What will be the average value of energy for a monoatomic gas in thermal equilibrium at temperature T? **(2021 Main)**

   (a) $\frac{2}{3}k_BT$ (b) k_BT
   (c) $\frac{3}{2}k_BT$ (d) $\frac{1}{2}k_BT$

10. The internal energy (U), pressure (p) and volume (V) of an ideal gas are related as $U = 3pV + 4$. The gas is **(2021 Main)**

    (a) diatomic only
    (b) either monoatomic or diatomic
    (c) polyatomic only
    (d) monoatomic only

11. The number of molecules in one litre of an ideal gas at 300 K and 2 atmospheric pressure with mean kinetic energy 2×10^{-9} J per molecule is **(2021, 2020 Main)**

    (a) 0.75×10^{11} (b) 3×10^{11}
    (c) 1.5×10^{11} (d) 6×10^{11}

12. Consider a gas of triatomic molecules. The molecules are assumed to be triangular and made of massless rigid rods whose vertices are occupied by atoms.

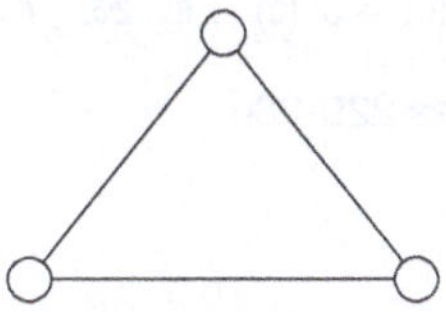

The internal energy of a mole of the gas at temperature T is **(2020 Main)**

(a) $\frac{5}{2}RT$ (b) $\frac{3}{2}RT$

(c) $\frac{9}{2}RT$ (d) $3RT$

13. An ideal gas occupies a volume of $2\ m^3$ at a pressure of 3×10^6 Pa. The energy of the gas is **(2019 Main)**

(a) 6×10^4 J (b) 10^8 J

(c) 9×10^6 J (d) 3×10^2 J

14. 2 kg of a monoatomic gas is at a pressure of 4×10^4 N/m^2. The density of the gas is 8 kg/m^3. What is the order of energy of the gas due to its thermal motion ? **(2019 Main)**

(a) 10^6 J (b) 10^3 J

(c) 10^4 J (d) 10^5 J

15. A vessel contains a mixture of one mole of oxygen and two moles of nitrogen at 300 K. The ratio of the average rotational kinetic energy per O_2 molecule to per N_2 molecule is **(1998 JEE)**

(a) 1 : 1

(b) 1 : 2

(c) 2 : 1

(d) depends on the moment of inertia of the two molecules

16. A gas mixture consists of 2 moles of oxygen and 4 moles of argon at temperature T. Neglecting all vibrational modes, the total internal energy of the system is **(2023 Main, 1999 JEE)**

(a) $4RT$ (b) $15RT$ (c) $9RT$ (d) $11RT$

17. The average translational kinetic energy of O_2 (molar mass 32) molecules at a particular temperature is 0.048 eV. The translational kinetic energy of N_2 (molar mass 28) molecules in eV at the same temperature is **(1997 JEE)**

(a) 0.0015 (b) 0.003

(c) 0.048 (d) 0.768

Multiple Correct Options

18. Choose the **wrong** options

(a) Translational kinetic energy of all ideal gases at same temperature is same

(b) In one degree of freedom all ideal gases has internal energy $=\frac{1}{2}RT$

(c) Translational degree of freedom of all ideal gases is three

(d) Translational kinetic energy of one mole of all ideal gases is $\frac{3}{2}RT$

Match the Columns

19. Match the following two columns for 2 moles of an ideal diatomic gas at room temperature T.

	Column I		Column II
(a)	Translational kinetic energy	(p)	$2RT$
(b)	Rotational kinetic energy	(q)	$4RT$
(c)	Potential energy	(r)	$3RT$
(d)	Total internal energy	(s)	None of these

Subjective Questions

20. At a given temperature, rotational kinetic energy of diatomic gas is K_o. Find its translational and total kinetic energy.

21. One mole of an ideal monoatomic gas is taken at a temperature of 300 K. Its volume is doubled keeping its pressure constant. Find the change in internal energy.

22. Two perfect monoatomic gases at absolute temperatures T_1 and T_2 are mixed. There is no loss of energy. Find the temperature of the mixture if the number of moles in the gases are n_1 and n_2.

23. If the kinetic energy of the molecules in 5 litres of helium at 2 atm is E. What is the kinetic energy of molecules in 15 litres of oxygen at 3 atm in terms of E ?

Answers

1. (d) **2.** (b) **3.** (d) **4.** (c) **5.** (c) **6.** (d) **7.** (b) **8.** (a) **9.** (c) **10.** (c)

11. (c) **12.** (d) **13.** (c) **14.** (c) **15.** (a) **16.** (d) **17.** (c) **18.** (a,b)

19. (a) → r; (b) → p; (c) → s; (d) → s **20.** $\frac{3}{2}K_o, \frac{5}{2}K_o$ **21.** 450 R **22.** $T=\frac{n_1T_1+n_2T_2}{n_1+n_2}$ **23.** 7.5 E

See hints on pages 229-230.

MODULE 5

Molar Heat Capacity

"Molar heat capacity C is the heat required to raise the temperature of 1 mole of a gas by 1°C (or 1 K)." Thus,

$$C = \frac{\Delta Q}{n\Delta T}$$

or

$$\Delta Q = nC\Delta T$$

For a gas, the value of C depends upon the process through which its temperature is raised.

For example, in an isothermal process $\Delta T = 0$ or $C_{iso} = \infty$. In an adiabatic process, (we will discuss it later) $\Delta Q = 0$. Hence, $C_{adi} = 0$. Thus, molar heat capacity of a gas varies from 0 to ∞ depending on the process. In general, experiments are made either at constant volume or at constant pressure.

In case of solids and liquids, due to small thermal expansion, the difference in measured values of molar heat capacities is very small and is usually neglected.

However, in case of gases molar heat capacity at constant volume C_V is quite different from that at constant pressure C_p. Later in the next chapter, we will derive the following relations, (for an ideal gas)

$$C_V = \frac{dU}{dT} = \frac{d}{dT}\left(\frac{f}{2}RT\right) = \frac{f}{2}R = \frac{R}{\gamma - 1}$$

$$C_p = C_V + R = \left(1 + \frac{f}{2}\right)R = \frac{\gamma R}{\gamma - 1}$$

$$\gamma = \frac{C_p}{C_V} = 1 + \frac{2}{f}$$

Here, U is the internal energy of one mole of the gas. The most general expression for C in the process pV^x = constant is

$$C = \frac{R}{\gamma - 1} + \frac{R}{1 - x}$$ (we will derive it later)

For example : For isobaric process p = constant or $x = 0$

$\therefore$ $$C = C_p = \frac{R}{\gamma - 1} + \frac{R}{1 - 0} = C_V + R$$

For an isothermal process, pV = constant or $x = 1$

$\therefore$ $C = \infty$ and

For an adiabatic process pV^γ = constant or $x = \gamma$

$\therefore$ $C = 0$

Values of f, U, C_V, C_p and γ for different gases are given in Table 1.

Table 1.

Nature of gas	f	$U = \frac{f}{2}RT$	$C_V = \frac{dU}{dT} = \frac{f}{2}R$	$C_p = C_V + R$	$\gamma = \frac{C_p}{C_V} = 1 + \frac{2}{f}$
Monoatomic	3	$\frac{3}{2}RT$	$\frac{3}{2}R$	$\frac{5}{2}R$	$\frac{5}{3} = 1.67$
Dia and linear polyatomic	5	$\frac{5}{2}RT$	$\frac{5}{2}R$	$\frac{7}{2}R$	$\frac{7}{5} = 1.4$
Non-linear polyatomic	6	$3RT$	$3R$	$4R$	$\frac{4}{3} = 1.33$

Mixture of non-reactive gases

(a) $n = n_1 + n_2$

(b) $p = p_1 + p_2$

(c) $U = U_1 + U_2$

(d) $\Delta U = \Delta U_1 + \Delta U_2$

(e) $C_V = \dfrac{n_1 C_{V_1} + n_2 C_{V_2}}{n_1 + n_2}$

(f) $C_p = \dfrac{n_1 C_{p_1} + n_2 C_{p_2}}{n_1 + n_2} = C_V + R$

(g) $\gamma = \dfrac{C_p}{C_V}$ or $\dfrac{n}{\gamma - 1} \Rightarrow \dfrac{n_1 + n_2}{\gamma - 1} = \dfrac{n_1}{\gamma_1 - 1} + \dfrac{n_2}{\gamma_2 - 1}$

(h) $M = \dfrac{n_1 M_1 + n_2 M_2}{n_1 + n_2}$

Example 1 Two moles of helium (He) are mixed with four moles of hydrogen (H_2). Find

(a) C_V of the mixture

(b) C_p of the mixture and

(c) γ of the mixture.

Sol. Helium is a monoatomic gas.

$\therefore \quad C_V = \frac{3}{2}R, C_P = \frac{5}{2}R$

and $\quad \gamma = \frac{5}{3}$

Hydrogen is a diatomic gas.

$\therefore \quad C_V = \frac{5}{2}R$

and $\quad C_P = \frac{7}{2}R \quad$ and $\quad \gamma = \frac{7}{5}$

(a) **C_V of the mixture**

$$C_V = \frac{n_1 C_{V_1} + n_2 C_{V_2}}{n_1 + n_2}$$

$$= \frac{(2)\left(\frac{3}{2}R\right) + 4\left(\frac{5}{2}R\right)}{2+4}$$

$$= \frac{13}{6}R \qquad \textbf{Ans.}$$

(b) **C_p of the mixture**

$$C_p = C_V + R = \frac{13}{6}R + R$$

$$= \frac{19}{6}R \qquad \textbf{Ans.}$$

Alternate method

$$C_p = \frac{n_1 C_{p_1} + n_2 C_{p_2}}{n_1 + n_2}$$

$$= \frac{(2)\left(\frac{5}{2}R\right) + (4)\left(\frac{7}{2}R\right)}{2+4}$$

$$= \frac{19}{6}R \qquad \textbf{Ans.}$$

(c) **γ of the mixture**

$$\gamma = \frac{C_p}{C_V} = \frac{(19/6)R}{(13/6)R} = \frac{19}{13} \qquad \textbf{Ans.}$$

Alternate method

$$\frac{n_1 + n_2}{\gamma - 1} = \frac{n_1}{\gamma_1 - 1} + \frac{n_2}{\gamma_2 - 1}$$

$$\therefore \quad \frac{2+4}{\gamma - 1} = \frac{2}{\frac{5}{3} - 1} + \frac{4}{\frac{7}{5} - 1}$$

Solving this equation, we get

$$\gamma = \frac{19}{13}$$

Example 2 Temperature of two moles of a monoatomic gas is increased by 300 K in the process $p \propto V$. Find

(a) molar heat capacity of the gas in the given process

(b) heat required in the given process.

Sol. (a) Molar heat capacity C is given by

$$C = C_V + \frac{R}{1-x} \qquad \text{...(i)}$$

in the process $pV^x =$ constant.

Now, $C_V = \frac{3}{2}R$ for monoatomic gas.

Further, the given process can be written as

$$PV^{-1} = \text{constant}$$

$$\therefore \quad x = -1$$

Substituting the values in Eq. (i), we have

$$C = \frac{3}{2}R + \frac{R}{1+1} = 2R \qquad \textbf{Ans.}$$

(b) Q or $\Delta Q = nC\Delta T$

Substituting the values, we have

$$\Delta Q = (2)(2R)(300)$$

$$= 1200R \qquad \textbf{Ans.}$$

Type 1. *When ordered motion of a gas converts into disordered motion.*

Concept

Earlier, we have seen that if a container filled with a gas is in motion, then the gas molecules have some ordered motion also. When the container is suddenly stopped, this ordered motion of gas molecules converts into disordered motion. Therefore, internal energy (and hence the temperature) of the gas will increase. In such situation, we can apply the equation,

$$\frac{1}{2}mv^2 = \Delta U$$

where, $\quad U = \frac{nf}{2}RT$

$$\therefore \quad \Delta U = \frac{nf}{2}R\Delta T$$

where, $\quad n = \frac{m}{M}$

Example 3 An insulated box containing a monoatomic gas of molar mass M moving with a speed v_0 is suddenly stopped. Find the increment in gas temperature as a result of stopping the box. **(2003 JEE)**

Sol. Decrease in kinetic energy = increase in internal energy of the gas

$$\therefore \quad \frac{1}{2}mv_0^2 = \frac{nf}{2}R\Delta T$$

$$= \left(\frac{m}{M}\right)\left(\frac{3}{2}R\right)\Delta T$$

$$\therefore \quad \Delta T = \frac{Mv_0^2}{3R}$$

Important POINTS

1. Detailed Discussion on Molar Heat Capacity

For monatomic gases value of C_V is $\frac{3}{2}R$. No variation is observed in this. So, value of $C_V, C_p, C_p - C_V$ and γ comes out to be same for different monatomic gases (Table 2).

Table 2.

Gas	C_p	C_V	$C_p - C_V$	$\gamma = \frac{C_p}{C_V}$
Monoatomic Gases				
He	20.8	12.5	8.33	1.67
Ar	20.8	12.5	8.33	1.67
Diatomic Gases				
H_2	28.8	20.4	8.33	1.41
N_2	29.1	20.8	8.33	1.40
O_2	29.4	21.1	8.33	1.40
CO_2	29.3	21.0	8.33	1.40
Cl_2	34.7	25.7	8.96	1.35
Polyatomic Gases				
CO_2	37.0	28.5	8.50	1.30
SO_2	40.4	31.4	9.00	1.29
H_2O	35.4	27.0	8.37	1.30
CH_2	35.5	27.1	8.41	1.31

*All values except that for water were obtained at 300 K. SI units (J/mol-K) are used for C_p and C_V. For dia and polyatomic gases these values are not equal for different gases. These values vary from gas to gas. Even for one gas, values are different at different temperatures.

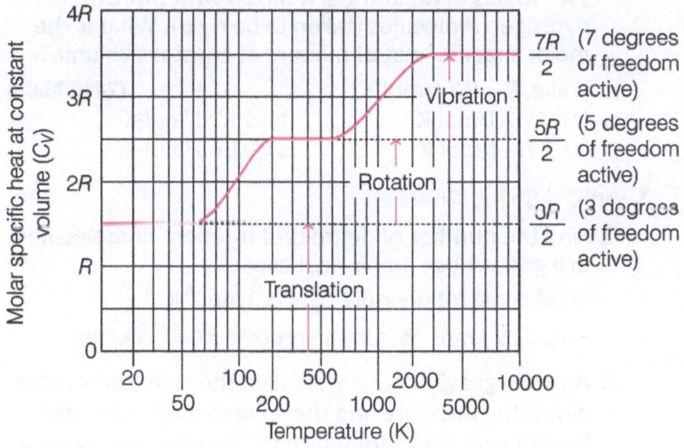

Figure illustrates the variation in the molar specific heat (at constant volume) for H_2 over a wide range in temperatures. (Note that T is drawn on a logarithmic scale). Below about 100 K, C_V is $\frac{3R}{2}$ which is characteristic of three translational degrees of freedom. At room temperature (300 K) it is $\frac{5R}{2}$ which includes the two rotational degrees of freedom. It seems, therefore, that at low temperatures, rotation is not allowed. At high temperatures, C_V starts to rise toward the value $\frac{7R}{2}$. Thus, the vibrational degrees of freedom contribute only at these high temperatures. In Table 2, the large values of C_V for some polyatomic molecules show the contributions of vibrational energy. In addition, a molecule with three or more atoms that are not in a straight line has three, not two, rotational degrees of freedom.

From this discussion, we expect heat capacities to be temperature-dependent, generally increasing with increasing temperature.

2. Solids In crystalline solids (monoatomic), the atoms are arranged in a three dimensional array, called a lattice. Each atom in a lattice can vibrate along three mutually perpendicular directions, each of which has two degrees of freedom. One corresponding to vibrational KE and the other vibrational PE. Thus, each atom has a total of six degrees of freedom.

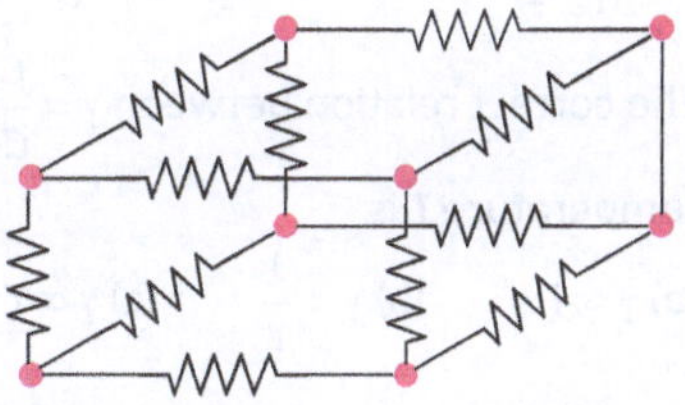

The volume of a solid does not change significantly with temperature, and so there is little difference between C_V and C_p for a solid. The molar heat capacity is expected to be

$$C = \frac{f}{2}R = \frac{6}{2}R$$

or $\quad C = 3R \quad$ (ideal monatomic solid)

Its numerical value is $C \approx 25$ J/mol-K ≈ 6 cal/mol-K.

MODULE 5 Exercise

Fill in the Blank

1. One mole of a monoatomic ideal gas is mixed with one mole of a diatomic ideal gas. The molar specific heat of the mixture at constant volume is .... **(1984 JEE)**

True/False

2. At a given temperature, the specific heat of a gas at a constant pressure is always greater than its specific heat at constant volume. **(1987 JEE)**

Single Correct Option

3. For a gas, if the ratio of specific heats at constant pressure p and constant volume V is γ, then the value of degree of freedom is

   (a) $\frac{\gamma+1}{\gamma-1}$ (b) $\frac{\gamma-1}{\gamma+1}$ (c) $\frac{1}{2}(\gamma-1)$ (d) $\frac{2}{\gamma-1}$

4. Internal energy of two moles of an ideal gas at a temperature of 127°C is 1200 R. Then, the specific heat of the gas at constant pressure is

   (a) 0.5 R (b) 0.1 R (c) 1.5 R (d) 2.5 R

5. If the ratio of specific heat of a gas at constant pressure to that at constant volume is γ, the change in internal energy of a gas, when the volume changes from V to $2V$ at constant pressure p is

   (a) $\frac{R}{(\gamma-1)}$ (b) pV (c) $\frac{pV}{(\gamma-1)}$ (d) $\frac{\gamma pV}{(\gamma-1)}$

6. The correct relation between $\gamma = \frac{C_p}{C_V}$ and temperature T is **(2023 Main)**

   (a) $\gamma \propto T$ (b) $\gamma \propto \frac{1}{T}$ (c) $\gamma \propto T^0$ (d) $\gamma \propto \frac{1}{\sqrt{T}}$

7. Let γ_1 be the ratio of molar specific heat at constant pressure and molar specific heat at constant volume of a monoatomic gas and γ_2 be the similar ratio of diatomic gas. Considering the diatomic gas molecules as a rigid rotator, the ratio, $\frac{\gamma_1}{\gamma_2}$ is **(2023 Main)**

   (a) $\frac{27}{35}$ (b) $\frac{35}{27}$ (c) $\frac{21}{25}$ (d) $\frac{25}{21}$

8. According to the law of equipartition of energy the molar specific heat of a diatomic gas at constant volume where the molecule has one additional vibrational mode is **(2023 Main)**

   (a) $\frac{9}{2}R$ (b) $\frac{7}{2}R$ (c) $\frac{5}{2}R$ (d) $\frac{3}{2}R$

9. The specific heats, C_p and C_V of a gas of diatomic molecules, A are given (in units of J mol^{-1}K^{-1}) by 29 and 22, respectively. Another gas of diatomic molecules B, has the corresponding values 30 and 21. If they are treated as ideal gases, then **(2019 Main)**

   (a) A has a vibrational mode but B has none
   (b) Both A and B have a vibrational mode each
   (c) A has one vibrational mode and B has two
   (d) A is rigid but B has a vibrational mode

10. A vessel contains 16 g of hydrogen and 128 g of oxygen at standard temperature 'and pressure. The volume of the vessel (in cm^3) is **(2022 Main)**

    (a) 72×10^5 (b) 32×10^5 (c) 27×10^4 (d) 54×10^4

11. A cylindrical container of volume 4.0×10^{-3} m^3 contains one mole of hydrogen and two moles of carbon dioxide. Assume the temperature of the mixture is 400 K. The pressure of the mixture of gases is [Take, gas constant as 8.3 J mol^{-1} K^{-1}] **(2021 Main)**

    (a) 249×10^1 Pa (b) 24.9×10^3 Pa
    (c) 24.9×10^5 Pa (d) 24.9 Pa

12. Two ideal polyatomic gases at temperatures T_1 and T_2 are mixed so that there is no loss of energy. If F_1 and F_2, m_1 and m_2, n_1 and n_2 be the degrees of freedom, masses, number of molecules of the first and second gas respectively, the temperature of mixture of these two gases is **(2021 Main)**

    (a) $\frac{n_1F_1T_1 + n_2F_2T_2}{F_1 + F_2}$ (b) $\frac{n_1T_1 + n_2T_2}{n_1 + n_2}$
    (c) $\frac{n_1F_1T_1 + n_2F_2T_2}{n_1 + n_2}$ (d) $\frac{n_1F_1T_1 + n_2F_2T_2}{n_1F_1 + n_2F_2}$

13. Two moles of helium gas is mixed with three moles of hydrogen molecules (taken to be rigid). What is the molar specific heat of mixture at constant volume? [Take, $R = 8.3$ J/mol-K] **(2019 Main)**

    (a) 19.7 J/mol-K (b) 15.7 J/mol-K
    (c) 17.4 J/mol-K (d) 21.6 J/mol-K

Subjective Questions

14. Find the number of degrees of freedom of molecules in a gas. Whose molar heat capacity

    (a) at constant pressure $C_p = 29$ J mol^{-1}K^{-1}
    (b) $C = 29$ J mol^{-1}K^{-1} in the process $pT =$ constant.

15. An ideal gas ($C_p / C_V = \gamma$) is taken through a process in which the pressure and the volume vary as $P = aV^b$. Find the value of b for which the specific heat capacity in the process is zero.

Answers

1. $2R$	**2.** True	**3.** (d)	**4.** (d)	**5.** (c)
6. (c)	**7.** (d)	**8.** (b)	**9.** (a)	**10.** (c)
11. (c)	**12.** (d)	**13.** (c)	**14.** (a) 5 (b) 3	**15.** $-\gamma$

See hints on pages 231-232.

MODULE 6

Kinetic Theory of Gases

We have studied the mechanics of single particles. When we approach the mechanics associated with the many particles in systems such as gases, liquids and solids, we are faced with analyzing the dynamics of a huge number of particles. The dynamics of such many particle systems is called statistical mechanics.

The kinetic theory that we study in this article is a special aspect of the statistical mechanics of large number of particles. We begin with the simplest model for a monatomic ideal gas, a dilute gas whose particles are single atoms rather than molecules.

Macroscopic variables of a gas are pressure, volume and temperature and microscopic properties are speed of gas molecules, momentum of molecules, etc. Kinetic theory of gases relates the microscopic properties to macroscopic properties. Furthermore, the kinetic theory provides us with a physical basis for our understanding of the concept of pressure and temperature.

The Ideal Gas Approximation

We make the following assumptions while describing an ideal gas :

1. The number of particles in the gas is very large.
2. The volume V containing the gas is much larger than the total volume actually occupied by the gas particles themselves.
3. The dynamics of the particles is governed by Newton's laws of motion.
4. The particles are equally likely to be moving in any direction.
5. The gas particles interact with each other and with the walls of the container only *via* elastic collisions.
6. The particles of the gas are identical and indistinguishable.

The Pressure of an Ideal Gas

Consider an ideal gas consisting of N molecules in a container of volume V. The container is a cube with edges of length d. Consider the collision of one molecule moving with a velocity **v** toward the right hand face of the cube. The molecule has velocity components v_x, v_y and v_z.

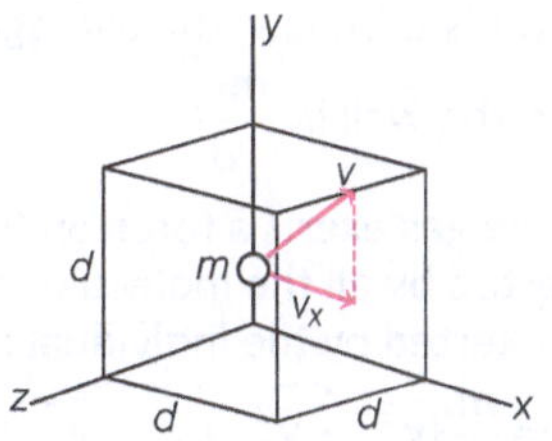

A cubical box with sides of length d containing an ideal gas. The molecule shown moves with velocity v.

Previously, we used m to represent the mass of a sample, but in this article we shall use m to represent the mass of one molecule. As the molecule collides with the wall elastically its x-component of velocity is reversed, while its y and z-components of velocity remain unaltered. Because the x-component of the momentum of the molecule is mv_x before the collision and $-mv_x$ after the collision, the change in momentum of the molecule is

$$\Delta p_x = -mv_x - (mv_x) = -2mv_x$$

Applying impulse = change in momentum to the molecule

$$F\Delta t = \Delta p_x = -2mv_x$$

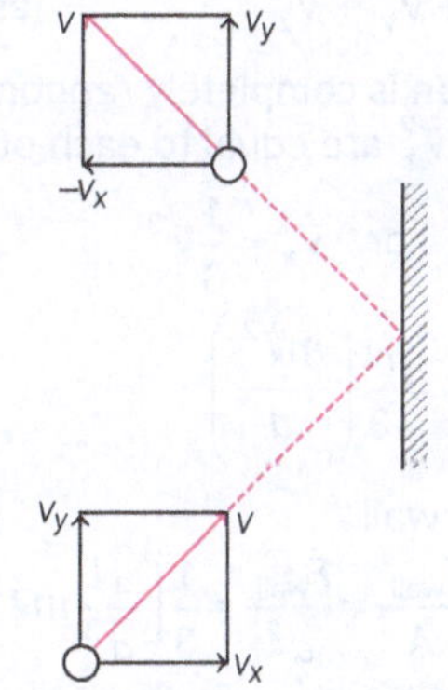

A molecule makes an elastic collision with the wall of the container. Its x-component of momentum is reversed, while its y-component remains unchanged. In this construction, we assume that the molecule moves in the x-y plane.

where, F is the magnitude of the average force exerted by the wall on the molecule in time Δt. For the molecules to collide second time with the same wall, it must travel a distance $2d$ in the x-direction. Therefore, the time interval between two collisions with the same wall is $\Delta t = \frac{2d}{v_x}$. Over a time interval that is long compared with Δt, the average force exerted on the molecules for each collision is

$$F = \frac{-2mv_x}{\Delta t} = \frac{-2mv_x}{2d/v_x} = \frac{-mv_x^2}{d}$$

According to Newton's third law, the average force exerted by the molecule on the wall is, $\frac{mv_x^2}{d}$.

Each molecule of the gas exerts a force on the wall. We find the total force exerted by all the molecules on the wall by adding the forces exerted by the individual molecules.

$$\therefore \quad F_{\text{wall}} = \frac{m}{d}(v_{x_1}^2 + v_{x_2}^2 + \ldots + v_{x_N}^2)$$

$$= \frac{mN}{d}\left(\frac{v_{x_1}^2 + v_{x_2}^2 + \ldots + v_{x_N}^2}{N}\right)$$

N = total number of molecules

This can also be written as

$$F_{\text{wall}} = \frac{Nm}{d}\bar{v}_x^2$$

where,

$$\bar{v}_x^2 = \frac{v_{x_1}^2 + v_{x_2}^2 + \ldots + v_{x_N}^2}{N}$$

Since, the velocity has three components v_x, v_y and v_z, we can have

$$\bar{v}^2 = \bar{v}_x^2 + \bar{v}_y^2 + \bar{v}_z^2 \qquad (\text{as } v^2 = v_x^2 + v_y^2 + v_z^2)$$

Because the motion is completely random, the average values $\bar{v}_x^2, \bar{v}_y^2$ and $\bar{v}_z^2$ are equal to each other. So,

$$\bar{v}^2 = 3\bar{v}_x^2 \quad \text{or} \quad \bar{v}_x^2 = \frac{1}{3}\bar{v}^2$$

Therefore,

$$F_{\text{walll}} = \frac{N}{3}\left(\frac{m\bar{v}^2}{d}\right)$$

$\therefore$ Pressure on the wall

$$p = \frac{F_{\text{wall}}}{A} = \frac{F_{\text{wall}}}{d^2} = \frac{1}{3}\left(\frac{N}{d^3}m\bar{v}^2\right)$$

$$= \frac{1}{3}\left(\frac{N}{V}\right)m\bar{v}^2 = \frac{2}{3}\left(\frac{N}{V}\right)\left(\frac{1}{2}m\bar{v}^2\right)$$

$$\therefore \quad p = \frac{1}{3}\frac{mN}{V}\bar{v}^2 = \frac{2}{3}\left(\frac{N}{V}\right)\left(\frac{1}{2}m\bar{v}^2\right) \qquad \text{...(i)}$$

This result indicates that the pressure is proportional to the number of molecules per unit volume (N/V) and to the average translational kinetic energy of the molecules $\frac{1}{2}m\bar{v}^2$.

This result relates the large scale quantity (macroscopic) of pressure to an atomic quantity (microscopic)—the average value of the square of the molecular speed. The above equation verifies some features of pressure with which you are probably familiar. One way to increase the pressure inside a container is to increase the number of molecules per unit volume in the container.

The Meaning of the Absolute Temperature

Rewriting Eq. (i) in the more familiar form

$$pV = \frac{2}{3}N\left(\frac{1}{2}m\bar{v}^2\right)$$

Let us now compare it with the ideal gas equation

$$pV = nRT$$

$$nRT = \frac{2}{3}N\left(\frac{1}{2}m\bar{v}^2\right)$$

Here, $\quad n = \frac{N}{N_A} \quad$ (N_A = Avogadro number)

$$\therefore \quad T = \frac{2}{3}\left(\frac{N_A}{R}\right)\left(\frac{1}{2}m\bar{v}^2\right)$$

or

$$T = \frac{2}{3k}\left(\frac{1}{2}m\bar{v}^2\right) \qquad \text{...(ii)}$$

where, k is **Boltzmann's constant** which has the value

$$k = \frac{R}{N_A} = 1.38 \times 10^{-23}\ \text{J/K}$$

By rearranging Eq. (ii) we can relate the translational molecular kinetic energy to the temperature

$$\frac{1}{2}mv^2 = \frac{3}{2}kT$$

That is, the average translational kinetic energy per molecule is $\frac{3}{2}kT$. Further,

$$\bar{v}_x^2 = \frac{1}{3}\bar{v}^2, \quad \text{it follows that}$$

$$\frac{1}{2}m\bar{v}_x^2 = \frac{1}{2}kT$$

In the similar manner, it follows that

$$\frac{1}{2}m\bar{v}_y^2 = \frac{1}{2}kT$$

and

$$\frac{1}{2}m\bar{v}_z^2 = \frac{1}{2}kT$$

Thus, in each translational degree of freedom one gas molecule has an energy $\frac{1}{2}kT$. One mole of a gas has N_A number of molecules. Thus, one mole of the gas has an energy $\frac{1}{2}(kN_A)T = \frac{1}{2}RT$ in each degree of freedom. Which is nothing but the law of equipartition of energy. The total translational kinetic energy of one mole of an ideal gas is therefore, $\frac{3}{2}RT$.

$$(\text{KE})_{\text{Trans}} = \frac{3}{2}RT \quad (\text{of one mole})$$

Root Mean Square Speed

The square root of $\overline{v}^2$ is called the root mean square (rms) speed of the molecules. From Eq. (ii), we obtain, for the rms speed

$$v_{rms} = \sqrt{\overline{v}^2} = \sqrt{\frac{3kT}{m}}$$

Using $\quad k = \frac{R}{N_A}, \; mN_A = M$

and $\quad \frac{RT}{M} = \frac{p}{\rho}$

Therefore we can write,

$$v_{rms} = \sqrt{\frac{3kT}{m}} = \sqrt{\frac{3RT}{M}} = \sqrt{\frac{3p}{\rho}}$$

Mean Speed or Average Speed

The particles of a gas have a range of speeds. The average speed is found by taking the average of the speeds of all the particles at a given instant. Remember that the speed is a positive scalar since it is the magnitude of the velocity.

$$v_{av} = \frac{v_1 + v_2 + \ldots + v_N}{N}$$

From Maxwellian speed distribution law (which is not in your syllabus), we can show that

$$v_{av} = \sqrt{\frac{8kT}{\pi m}} = \sqrt{\frac{8RT}{\pi M}} = \sqrt{\frac{8p}{\pi \rho}}$$

Most Probable Speed

This is defined as the speed which is possessed by maximum fraction of total number of molecules of the gas. For example, if speeds of 10 molecules of a gas are, 1, 2, 2, 3, 3, 3, 4, 5, 6, 6 km/s, then the most probable speed is 3 km/s, as maximum fraction of total molecules possess this speed. Again from Maxwellian speed distribution law :

$$v_{mp} = \sqrt{\frac{2kT}{m}} = \sqrt{\frac{2RT}{M}} = \sqrt{\frac{2p}{\rho}}$$

Note 1. *In the above expressions of v_{rms}, v_{av} and v_{mp}, M is the molar mass in kilogram per mole. For example, molar mass of hydrogen is 2×10^{-3} kg/mol.*

2. $v_{rms} > v_{av} > v_{mp}$ *(RAM)*

3. $v_{rms} : v_{av} : v_{mp} = \sqrt{3} : \sqrt{\frac{8}{\pi}} : \sqrt{2}$

and since, $\frac{8}{\pi} \approx 2.5$,

we have $v_{rms} : v_{av} : v_{mp} \approx \sqrt{3} : \sqrt{2.5} : \sqrt{2}$

Important POINTS

- Pressure exerted by an ideal gas is numerically equal to two-third of the mean kinetic energy of translation per unit volume of (E) the gas. Thus,

$$p = \frac{2}{3}E = \frac{1}{3}\frac{mN}{V}v_{rms}^2$$

Here, m = mass of one gas molecule

N = total number of molecules

Note *This equation is identical to equation (i) which we derived earlier.*

- **Mean Free Path** Every gas consists of a very large number of molecules. These molecules are in a state of continuous rapid and random motion. They undergo perfectly elastic collisions against one another. Therefore, path of a single gas molecule consists of a series of short *zig-zag* paths of different lengths.

The mean free path of a gas molecule is the average distance between two successive collisions.

It is represented by λ.

$$\lambda = \frac{kT}{\sqrt{2}\pi\sigma^2 p}$$

Here, σ = diameter of the molecule

k = Boltzmann's constant

- **Avogadro's Hypothesis** At constant temperature and pressure equal volumes of different gases contain equal number of molecules. In 1 g-mole of any gas there are 6.02×10^{23} molecules of that gas. This is called Avogadro's number. Thus,

$$N = 6.02 \times 10^{23} \text{ per g-mole}$$

Therefore, the number of molecules in mass m of the substance

$$\text{Number of molecules} = nN = \frac{m}{M} \times N$$

- **Dalton' Law of Partial Pressure** According to this law if the gases filled in a vessel do not react chemically, then the combined pressure of all the gases is due to the partial pressure of the molecules of the individual gases. If $p_1, p_2, \ldots$ represent the partial pressures of the different gases, then the total pressure is,

$$p = p_1 + p_2 \ldots$$

Example 1 Find the rms speed of hydrogen molecules at room temperature (=300 K).

Sol. Mass of 1 mole of hydrogen gas

$$= 2\text{g} = 2 \times 10^{-3} \text{ kg}$$

$$\Rightarrow \quad v_{rms} = \sqrt{\frac{3RT}{M}}$$

$$= \sqrt{\frac{3 \times 8.31 \times 300}{2 \times 10^{-3}}}$$

$$= 1.93 \times 10^3 \text{m/s}$$ **Ans.**

Example 2 A tank used for filling helium balloons has a volume of 0.3 m^3 and contains 2.0 mol of helium gas at 20.0°C. Assuming that the helium behaves like an ideal gas.

(a) What is the total translational kinetic energy of the molecules of the gas?

(b) What is the average kinetic energy per molecule?

Sol. (a) Using $(\text{KE})_{\text{Trans}} = \frac{3}{2} nRT$

with $n = 2.0$ mol and $T = 273 + 20 = 293$ K, we find that

$$(\text{KE})_{\text{Trans}} = \frac{3}{2}(2.0)(8.31)(293)$$

$$= 7.3 \times 10^3 \text{ J}$$ **Ans.**

(b) The average kinetic energy per molecule is $\frac{3}{2} kT$.

$$\text{or} \quad \frac{1}{2} m\bar{v}^2 = \frac{1}{2} m\bar{v}_{rms}^2 = \frac{3}{2} kT$$

$$= \frac{3}{2}(1.38 \times 10^{-23})(293)$$

$$= 6.07 \times 10^{-21} \text{ J}$$ **Ans.**

Example 3 Consider an 11000 particles gas system with speeds distribution as follows :

1000 particles each with speed 100 m/s

2000 particles each with speed 200 m/s

4000 particles each with speed 300 m/s

3000 particles each with speed 400 m/s and

1000 particles each with speed 500 m/s

Find the average speed, and rms speed.

Sol. The average speed is

$$v_{av} = \frac{(1000)(100) + (2000)(200) + (4000)(300) + (3000)(400) + (1000)(500)}{11000}$$

$$= 309 \text{ m/s}$$ **Ans.**

The rms speed is

$$v_{rms} = \sqrt{\frac{(1000)(100)^2 + (2000)(200)^2 + (4000)(300)^2 + (3000)(400)^2 + (1000)(500)^2}{11000}}$$

$$= 328 \text{ m/s}$$ **Ans.**

Note *Here,* $\frac{v_{rms}}{v_{av}} \neq \sqrt{\frac{3}{8/\pi}}$ *as values and gas molecules are arbitrarily taken.*

Example 4 In a crude model of a rotating diatomic molecule of chlorine (Cl_2), the two Cl atoms are 2.0×10^{-10} m apart and rotate about their centre of mass with angular speed $\omega = 2.0 \times 10^{12}$ rad/s. What is the rotational kinetic energy of one molecule of Cl_2, which has a molar mass of 70.0 g/mol?

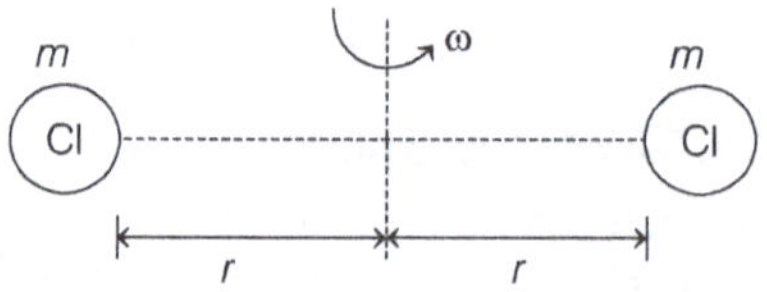

Sol. Moment of inertia,

$$I = 2(mr^2) = 2mr^2$$

$$\text{Here,} \quad m = \frac{1}{2}\left(\frac{M}{N_A}\right) = \frac{70 \times 10^{-3}}{2 \times 6.02 \times 10^{23}}$$

$$= 5.81 \times 10^{-26} \text{kg}$$

$$\text{and} \quad r = \frac{2.0 \times 10^{-10}}{2}$$

$$= 1.0 \times 10^{-100} \text{m}$$

$$\therefore \quad I = 2(5.81 \times 10^{-26})(1.0 \times 10^{-10})^2$$

$$= 1.16 \times 10^{-45} \text{ kg-m}^2$$

$$\therefore \quad K_R = \frac{1}{2} I\omega^2$$

$$= \frac{1}{2} \times (1.16 \times 10^{-45}) \times (2.0 \times 10^{12})^2$$

$$= 2.32 \times 10^{-21} \text{ J}$$

Example 5 Prove that the pressure of an ideal gas is numerically equal to two third of the mean translational kinetic energy per unit volume of the gas.

Sol. Translational KE per unit volume

$$E = \frac{1}{2}(\text{mass per unit volume})(\bar{v}^2)$$

$$= \frac{1}{2}(\rho)\left(\frac{3p}{\rho}\right) = \frac{3}{2} p$$

$$\text{or} \quad p = \frac{2}{3} E$$ **Hence Proved.**

Example 6 An ideal diatomic gas with $C_V = \frac{5R}{2}$ occupies a volume V_i at a pressure p_i. The gas undergoes a process in which the pressure is proportional to the volume. At the end of the process, it is found that the rms speed of the gas molecules has doubled from its initial value. Determine the amount of energy transferred to the gas by heat.

Sol. Given that, $p \propto V$

or $pV^{-1} = \text{constant}$

As we know, molar heat capacity in the process $pV^x = \text{constant}$ is

$$C = \frac{R}{\gamma - 1} + \frac{R}{1-x} = C_V + \frac{R}{1-x}$$

In the given problem,

$$C_V = \frac{5R}{2} \quad \text{and} \quad x = -1$$

$$\therefore \quad C = \frac{5R}{2} + \frac{R}{2} = 3R \quad \text{...(i)}$$

At the end of the process rms speed is doubled, i.e. temperature has become four times ($v_{rms} \propto \sqrt{T}$).

Now,
$$\Delta Q = nC\Delta T$$
$$= nC(T_f - T_i)$$
$$= nC(4T_i - T_i)$$
$$= 3T_i nC$$
$$= (3T_i)(n)(3R)$$
$$= 9(nRT_i)$$

or $\Delta Q = 9p_iV_i$ **Ans.**

INTRODUCTORY Exercise

1. Five gas molecules chosen at random are found to have speed of 500, 600, 700, 800 and 900 m/s. Find the rms speed. Is it the same as the average speed?
2. The average speed of all the molecules in a gas at a given instant is not zero, whereas the average velocity of all the molecules is zero. Explain why?
3. A sample of helium gas is at a temperature of 300 K and a pressure of 0.5 atm. What is the average kinetic energy of a molecule of a gas?
4. A sample of helium and neon gases has a temperature of 300 K and pressure of 1.0 atm. The molar mass of helium is 4.0 g/mol and that of neon is 20.2 g/mol.
   (a) Find the rms speed of the helium atoms and of the neon atoms.
   (b) What is the average kinetic energy per atom of each gas?
5. At what temperature will the particles in a sample of helium gas have an rms speed of 1.0 km/s?
6. For any distribution of speeds $v_{rms} \geq v_{av}$. Is this statement true or false?

Answers

1. $v_{rms} = 714$ m/s, $v_{av} = 700$ m/s, No
2. Speed is a scalar quantity while velocity is a vector quantity.
3. 6.21×10^{-21} J
4. (a) 1368 m/s, 608 m/s (b) 6.21×10^{-21} J
5. 160 K
6. True

See hints on page 232.

Typed Problems

Type 1. *Based on the concept of pressure exerted by gas molecules striking elastically with walls of a container.*

Concept

(i) Gas molecules are assumed to be moving with v_{rms}.

(ii) They strike with the wall elastically. So, in each collision change in linear momentum is $2mv_{rms}$.

(iii) Time interval between two successive collisions is $\frac{2L}{v_{rms}}$, if we have a cubical box of side L and,

(iv) $F = \frac{\Delta p}{\Delta t}$, Pressure $= \frac{F}{A}$

Ex. 1 A cubical box of side 1 m contains helium gas (atomic weight 4) at a pressure of $100\ \text{N/m}^2$. During an observation time of 1 second, an atom travelling with the root-mean-square speed parallel to one of the edges of the cube, was found to make 500 hits with a particular wall, without any collision with other atoms.

Take $R = \frac{25}{3}$ J/mol-K and $k = 1.38 \times 10^{-23}$ J/K. **(2002 JEE)**

(a) Evaluate the temperature of the gas.
(b) Evaluate the average kinetic energy per atom.
(c) Evaluate the total mass of helium gas in the box.

Sol. Volume of the box $= 1\ \text{m}^3$, pressure of the gas $= 100\ \text{N/m}^2$. Let T be the temperature of the gas.

(a) Time between two consecutive collisions with one wall $= \frac{1}{500}$ s.

This time should be equal to $\frac{2l}{v_{rms}}$, where l is the side of the cube.

$$\frac{2l}{v_{rms}} = \frac{1}{500}$$

or $v_{rms} = 1000 \text{ m/s}$ (as $l = 1$ m)

$$\therefore \quad \sqrt{\frac{3RT}{M}} = 1000$$

or $$T = \frac{(1000)^2 M}{3R} = \frac{(10^6)(4 \times 10^{-3})}{3\left(\frac{25}{3}\right)}$$

$$= 160 \text{ K}$$ **Ans.**

(b) Average kinetic energy per atom $= \frac{3}{2} kT$

$$= \frac{3}{2} (1.38 \times 10^{-23})(160) \text{ J}$$

$$= 3.312 \times 10^{-21} \text{ J}$$ **Ans.**

(c) From the relation $pV = nRT = \frac{m}{M} RT$

We get mass of helium gas in the box,

$$m = \frac{pVM}{RT}$$

Substituting the values, we get

$$m = \frac{(100)(1)^3 (4 \times 10^{-3})}{\left(\frac{25}{3}\right)(160)}$$

$$= 3.0 \times 10^{-4} \text{ kg}$$ **Ans.**

Ex. 2 1 g mole of oxygen at 27°C and 1 atmospheric pressure is enclosed in a vessel.

(a) Assuming the molecules to be moving with v_{rms}, find the number of collisions per second which the molecules make with one square metre area of the vessel wall.

(b) The vessel is next thermally insulated and moved with a constant speed v_0. It is then suddenly stopped. The process results in a rise of temperature of the gas by 1°C.

Calculate the speed v_0. [$k = 1.38 \times 10^{-23}$ J/K and $N_A = 6.02 \times 10^{23}$ /mol] **(2002, 1983 JEE)**

Sol. (a) Mass of one oxygen molecule,

$$m = \frac{M}{N_A} = \frac{32}{6.02 \times 10^{23}} \text{ g}$$

$$= 5.316 \times 10^{-23} \text{ g}$$

$$= 5.316 \times 10^{-26} \text{ kg}$$

$$v_{rms} = \sqrt{\frac{3kT}{m}}$$

$$= \sqrt{\frac{3 \times 1.38 \times 10^{-23} \times 300}{5.316 \times 10^{-26}}}$$

$$= 483.35 \text{ m/s}$$

Change in momentum per collision,

$$\Delta p = mv_{rms} - (-mv_{rms}) = 2mv_{rms}$$

$$= (2)(5.316 \times 10^{-26})(483.35)$$

$$= 5.14 \times 10^{-23} \text{ kg-m/s}$$

Now, suppose n particles strike per second

$$F = n\Delta p = (n)(5.14 \times 10^{-23}) \text{ N} \quad \left(\because F_{ext} = \frac{dp}{dt}\right)$$

Now, as $p = \frac{F}{A}$, for unit area $F = p$

$$\therefore \quad (n)(5.14 \times 10^{-23}) = 1.01 \times 10^5$$

or $n = 1.965 \times 10^{27}$ per second **Ans.**

(b) When the vessel is stopped, the ordered motion of the vessel converts into disordered motion and temperature of the gas is increased.

$$\therefore \quad \frac{1}{2} mv_0^2 = \Delta U \quad \text{...(i)}$$

$$U = \frac{5}{2} RT \quad \text{(for 1 g mole of } O_2)$$

$$\therefore \quad \Delta U = \frac{5}{2} R\Delta T$$

Here, m is not the mass of one gas molecule but it is the mass of the whole gas.

$$m = \text{mass of 1 mol} = 32 \times 10^{-3} \text{ kg}$$

Substituting these values in Eq. (i), we get

$$v_0 = \sqrt{\frac{5R\Delta T}{m}}$$

$$= \sqrt{\frac{5 \times 8.31 \times 1}{32 \times 10^{-3}}} = 36 \text{ m/s}$$ **Ans.**

MODULE 6 Exercise

True/False

1. The root mean square (rms) speed of oxygen molecules (O_2) at a certain temperature T (degree absolute) is v. If the temperature is doubled and oxygen gas dissociates into atomic oxygen, the rms speed remains unchanged. **(1987 JEE)**

2. The root mean square speeds of the molecules of different ideal gases, maintained at the same temperature are the same. **(1981 JEE)**

Statements Type Question

3. Given below are two statements.

   Statement I The temperature of a gas is $-73°C$. When the gas is heated to $527°C$, the root mean square speed of the molecules is doubled.

   Statement II The product of pressure and volume of an ideal gas will be equal to translational kinetic energy of the molecules. **(2023 Main)**

   In the light of the above statements, choose the correct answer from the options given below.

   (a) Statement I is false but Statement II is true.
   (b) Both Statement I and Statement II are true.
   (c) Statement I is true but Statement II is false.
   (d) Both Statement I and Statement II are false.

Assertion and Reason

See directions on page 14.

4. **Assertion :** In the equation $p=\frac{1}{3}\alpha v_{rms}^2$, the term α represents density of gas.

   Reason : $v_{rms}=\sqrt{\frac{3RT}{M}}$.

Single Correct Option

5. In a mixture of gases, the average number of degree of freedoms per molecule is 6. The rms speed of the molecule of the gas is c. The velocity of sound in the gas is

   (a) $\frac{c}{\sqrt{3}}$ (b) $\frac{c}{\sqrt{2}}$
   (c) $\frac{2c}{3}$ (d) $\frac{3c}{3}$

6. The temperature of an ideal gas is increased from 200 K to 800 K. If r.m.s. speed of gas at 200 K is v_0. Then, r.m.s. speed of the gas at 800 K will be **(2023 Main)**

   (a) $\frac{v_0}{4}$ (b) v_0
   (c) $4v_0$ (d) $2v_0$

7. The root mean square speed of molecules of nitrogen gas at 27°C is approximately : (Given, mass of a nitrogen molecule $= 4.6\times10^{-26}$ kg and take Boltzmann constant $k_B = 1.4\times10^{-23}$ JK^{-1}) **(2023 Main)**

   (a) 91 m/s (b) 532 m/s
   (c) 27.4 m/s (d) 1260 m/s

8. If the rms speed of chlorine molecule is 490 m/s at 27°C, the rms speed of argon molecules at the same temperature will be (Atomic mass of argon = 39.9 u, molecular mass of chlorine = 70.9 u) **(2023 Main)**

   (a) 751.7 m/s (b) 451.7 m/s
   (c) 651.7 m/s (d) 551.7 m/s

9. The root mean square velocity of molecules of gas is **(2023 Main)**

   (a) inversely proportional to square root of temperature $\left(\sqrt{\frac{1}{T}}\right)$
   (b) proportional to square root of temperature $(\sqrt{T})$
   (c) proportional to temperature (T)
   (d) proportional to square of temperature (T^2)

10. At 300 K, the rms speed of oxygen molecules is $\sqrt{\frac{\alpha+5}{\alpha}}$ times to that of its average speed in the gas. Then, the value of α will be $\left(\text{use } \pi=\frac{22}{7}\right)$ **(2023 Main)**

    (a) 28 (b) 24 (c) 32 (d) 27

11. The rms speed of oxygen molecule in a vessel at particular temperature is $\left(1+\frac{5}{x}\right)^{1/2} v$, where v is the average speed of the molecule. The value of x will be $\left(\text{Take, } \pi=\frac{22}{7}\right)$ **(2023 Main)**

    (a) 28 (b) 8
    (c) 4 (d) 27

12. Three vessels of equal volume contain gases at the same temperature and pressure. The first vessel contains neon (monoatomic), the second contains chlorine (diatomic) and third contains uranium hexafloride (polyatomic). Arrange these on the basis of their root mean square speed (v_{rms}) and choose the correct answer from the options given below **(2023 Main)**

    (a) v_{rms}(mono) = v_{rms} (dia) = v_{rms} (poly)
    (b) v_{rms}(mono) < v_{rms} (dia) < v_{rms} (poly)
    (c) v_{rms}(dia) < v_{rms} (poly) < v_{rms} (mono)
    (d) v_{rms}(mono) > v_{rms} (dia) > v_{rms} (poly)

13. The root mean square speed of smoke particles of mass 5×10^{-17} kg in their Brownian motion in air at NTP is approximately. [Given, $k = 1.38 \times 10^{-23}$ JK^{-1}] **(2022 Main)**

(a) 60 mm s^{-1} (b) 12 mm s^{-1}
(c) 15 mm s^{-1} (d) 36 mm s^{-1}

14. Same gas is filled in two vessels of the same volume at the same temperature. If the ratio of the number of molecules is 1 : 4, then

A. The rms velocity of gas molecules in two vessels will be the same.
B. The ratio of pressure in these vessels will be 1 : 4.
C. The ratio of pressure will be 1 : 1.
D. The rms velocity of gas molecules in two vessels will be in the ratio of 1 : 4. **(2022 Main)**

Choose the correct answer from the options given below :

(a) A and C only (b) B and D only
(c) A and B only (d) C and D only

15. Sound travels in a mixture of two moles of helium and *n* moles of hydrogen. If rms speed of gas molecules in the mixture is $\sqrt{2}$ times the speed of sound, then the value of *n* will be **(2022 Main)**

(a) 1 (b) 2 (c) 3 (d) 4

16. If the rms speed of oxygen molecules at 0° C is 160 m/s, find the rms speed of hydrogen molecules at 0°C. **(2021 Main)**

(a) 640 m/s (b) 40 m/s
(c) 80 m/s (d) 332 m/s

17. The rms speeds of the molecules of hydrogen, oxygen and carbon dioxide at the same temperature are v_H, v_O and v_C respectively then **(2021 Main)**

(a) $v_H > v_O > v_C$ (b) $v_C > v_O > v_H$
(c) $v_H = v_O > v_C$ (d) $v_H = v_O = v_C$

18. Consider a sample of oxygen behaving like an ideal gas. At 300 K, the ratio of root mean square (rms) velocity to the average velocity of gas molecule would be : (Molecular weight of oxygen is 32 g/mol; $R = 8.3\ J\ K^{-1}\ mol^{-1}$) **(2021 Main)**

(a) $\sqrt{\frac{8\pi}{3}}$ (b) $\sqrt{\frac{3}{3}}$
(c) $\sqrt{\frac{8}{3}}$ (d) $\sqrt{\frac{3\pi}{8}}$

19. The temperature, at which the root mean square velocity of hydrogen molecules equals their escape velocity from the earth, is closest to :
[Boltzmann constant $k_B = 1.38 \times 10^{-23}$ J/K, Avogadro number $N_A = 6.02 \times 10^{26}$/kg, Radius of earth $= 6.4 \times 10^6$ m, Gravitational acceleration on earth $= 10\ ms^{-2}$] **(2019 Main)**

(a) 10^4 K (b) 650 K
(c) 3×10^5 K (d) 800K

20. A mixture of 2 moles of helium gas (atomic mass = 4u) and 1 mole of argon gas (atomic mass = 40u) is kept at 300 K in a container. The ratio of their rms speeds $\left[\frac{v_{rms\,(helium)}}{v_{rms\,(argon)}}\right]$ is close to **(2019 Main)**

(a) 0.32 (b) 2.24
(c) 3.16 (d) 0.45

21. The number of air molecules per cm^3 increased from 3×10^{19} to 12×10^{19}. The ratio of collision frequency of air molecules before and after the increase in number respectively is **(2023 Main)**

(a) 0.75 (b) 0.50
(c) 1.25 (d) 0.25

22. The mean free path of molecules of a certain gas at STP is 1500*d*, where *d* is the diameter of the gas molecules. While maintaining the standard pressure, the mean free path of the molecules at 373K is approximately **(2023 Main)**

(a) 2049*d* (b) 1500*d*
(c) 750*d* (d) 1098*d*

23. According to kinetic theory of gases,

A. The motion of the gas molecules freezes at 0°C.
B. The mean free path of gas molecules decreases if the density of molecules is increased.
C. The mean free path of gas molecules increases if temperature is increased keeping pressure constant.
D. Average kinetic energy per molecule per degree of freedom is $\frac{3}{2}k_BT$ (for monoatomic gases).

Choose the most appropriate answer from the options given below. **(2022 Main)**

(a) A and C only (b) B and C only
(c) A and B only (d) C and D only

24. Calculate the value of mean free path (λ) for oxygen molecules at temperature 27°C and pressure 1.01×10^5 Pa. Assume the molecular diameter 0.3 nm and the gas is ideal. ($k = 1.38 \times 10^{-23}\ J\ K^{-1}$) **(2021 Main)**

(a) 86 nm (b) 32 nm
(c) 58 nm (d) 102 nm

25. A $25 \times 10^{-3}\ m^3$ volume cylinder is filled with 1 mol of O_2 gas at room temperature (300 K). The molecular diameter of O_2 and its root mean square speed are found to be 0.3 nm and 200 m/s, respectively. What is the average collision rate (per second) for an O_2 molecule? **(2019 Main)**

(a) $\sim 10^{10}$ (b) $\sim 10^{12}$
(c) $\sim 10^{11}$ (d) $\sim 10^{13}$

26. An ideal gas is enclosed in a cylinder at pressure of 2 atm and temperature, 300 K. The mean time between two successive collisions is 6×10^{-8} s. If the pressure is doubled and temperature is increased to

500 K, the mean time between two successive collisions will be close to **(2019 Main)**

(a) 4×10^{-8} s

(b) 3×10^{-6} s

(c) 2×10^{-7} s

(d) 0.5×10^{-8} s

Multiple Correct Options

27. A container of fixed volume has a mixture of one mole of hydrogen and one mole of helium in equilibrium at temperature T. Assuming the gases are ideal, the correct statements is/are **(2015 Adv.)**

(a) The average energy per mole of the gas mixture is $2RT$

(b) The ratio of speed of sound in the gas mixture to that in helium gas is $\sqrt{\frac{6}{5}}$

(c) The ratio of the rms speed of helium atoms to that of hydrogen molecules is 1/2

(d) The ratio of the rms speed of helium atoms to that of hydrogen molecules is $\frac{1}{\sqrt{2}}$

28. Let $\bar{v}$, v_{rms} and v_p respectively denote the mean speed, root mean square speed and most probable speed of the molecules in an ideal monoatomic gas at absolute temperature T. The mass of a molecule is m. Then, **(1998 JEE)**

(a) no molecule can have a speed greater than $\sqrt{2}v_{rms}$

(b) no molecule can have speed less than $v_p/\sqrt{2}$

(c) $v_p < \bar{v} < v_{rms}$

(d) the average kinetic energy of a molecule is $\frac{3}{4}mv_p^2$

Match the Columns

29. At a given temperature T,

$v_1 = \sqrt{\frac{x_1 RT}{M}}$ = rms speed of gas molecules,

$v_2 = \sqrt{\frac{x_2 RT}{M}}$ = average speed of gas molecules,

$v_3 = \sqrt{\frac{x_3 RT}{M}}$ = most probable speed of gas molecules,

$v_4 = \sqrt{\frac{x_4 RT}{M}}$ = speed of sound,

Column I		Column II	
(a)	x_1	(p)	1.5
(b)	x_2	(q)	2.0
(c)	x_3	(r)	3.0
(d)	x_4	(s)	None of these

Integer Type Question

30. The root mean square speed of molecules of a given mass of a gas at 27°C and 1 atmosphere pressure is 200 ms^{-1}. The root mean square speed of molecules of the gas at 127°C and 2 atmosphere pressure is $\frac{x}{\sqrt{3}}$ ms^{-1}. The value of x will be .... **(2021 Main)**

Answers

1. False	**2.** False	**3.** (c)	**4.** (b)	**5.** (c)	**6.** (d)	**7.** (b)	**8.** (c)	**9.** (b)	**10.** (a)
11. (a)	**12.** (d)	**13.** (c)	**14.** (c)	**15.** (b)	**16.** (a)	**17.** (a)	**18.** (d)	**19.** (a)	**20.** (c)
21. (d)	**22.** (a)	**23.** (b)	**24.** (d)	**25.** (a)	**26.** (a)	**27.** (a,b,d)	**28.** (c,d)		

29. (a) → r; (b) → s; (c) → q; (d) → s **30.** 400

See hints on pages 232-236.

Unit Exercise (Cumulative)

Level 1

Single Correct Option

1. In case of hydrogen and oxygen at NTP, which of the following is the same for both?
(a) Average linear momentum per molecule
(b) Average KE per molecule
(c) KE per unit volume
(d) KE per unit mass

2. 5 L of benzene weighs
(a) more in summer than in winter
(b) more in winter than in summer
(c) equal in winter and summer
(d) None of the above

3. 16 g of oxygen, 14 g of nitrogen and 11 g of carbon dioxide are mixed in an enclosure of volume 5 L and temperature 27°C. The pressure exerted by the mixture is approximately
(a) 4×10^5 Nm^{-2} (b) 5×10^5 Nm^{-2}
(c) 6×10^5 Nm^{-2} (d) 9×10^5 Nm^{-2}

4. A gas at absolute temperature 300 K has pressure $= 4 \times 10^{-10}$ N/m^2. Boltzmann constant $k = 1.38 \times 10^{-23}$ J/K. The number of molecules per cm^3 is of the order of
(a) 100 (b) 10^5 (c) 10^8 (d) 10^{11}

5. The energy density $\frac{U}{V}$ of an ideal diatomic gas is related to its pressure p as
(a) $\frac{U}{V} = 3p$ (b) $\frac{U}{V} = \frac{3}{2}p$ (c) $\frac{U}{V} = \frac{p}{3}$ (d) $\frac{U}{V} = \frac{5}{2}p$

6. A gas is found to obey the law $p^2 V =$ constant. The initial temperature and volume are T_0 and V_0. If the gas expands to a volume $3V_0$, its final temperature becomes
(a) $\frac{T_0}{3}$ (b) $\frac{T_0}{\sqrt{3}}$
(c) $3T_0$ (d) None of these

7. The pressure of the gas in a constant volume gas thermometer is 100 cm of mercury when placed in melting ice at 1 atm. When the bulb is placed in a liquid, the pressure becomes 180 cm of mercury. Temperature of the liquid is
(Given, $0°C = 273$ K) **(2022 Main)**
(a) 300 K (b) 400 K
(c) 600 K (d) 491 K

8. Which of the following graphs represent the behaviour of an ideal gas? Symbols have their usual meaning. **(2021 Main)**

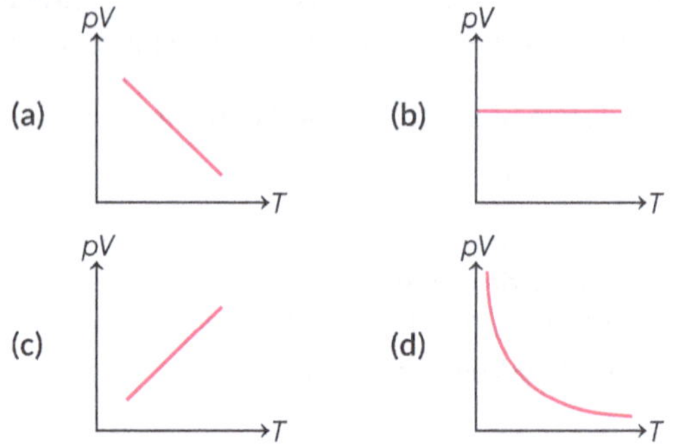

9. A balloon carries a total load of 185 kg at normal pressure and temperature of 27°C. What load will the balloon carry on rising to a height at which the barometric pressure is 45 cm of Hg and the temperature is -7°C?
[Assuming, the volume constant.] **(2021 Main)**
(a) 181.46 kg (b) 214.15 kg (c) 219.07 kg (d) 123.54 kg

10. A vessel contains 1 mole of O_2 gas (molar mass 32) at a temperature T. The pressure of the gas is p. An identical vessel containing one mole of the gas (molar mass 4) at a temperature $2T$ has a pressure of **(1997 JEE)**
(a) $p/8$ (b) p (c) $2p$ (d) $8p$

11. An ideal gas is in thermodynamic equilibrium. The number of degrees of freedom of a molecule of the gas is n. The internal energy of one mole of the gas is U_n and the speed of sound in the gas is v_n. At a fixed temperature and pressure, which of the following is the correct option? **(2023 Adv.)**
(a) $v_3 < v_6$ and $U_3 > U_6$ (b) $v_5 > v_3$ and $U_3 > U_5$
(c) $v_5 > v_7$ and $U_5 < U_7$ (d) $v_6 < v_7$ and $U_6 < U_7$

12. A gas has n degrees of freedom. The ratio of specific heat of gas at constant volume to the specific heat of gas at constant pressure will be **(2022 Main)**
(a) $\frac{n}{n+2}$ (b) $\frac{n+2}{n}$ (c) $\frac{n}{2n+2}$ (d) $\frac{n}{n-2}$

13. An HCl molecule has rotational, translational and vibrational motions. If the rms velocity of HCl molecules in its gaseous phase is $\bar{v}$, m is its mass and k_B is Boltzmann constant, then its temperature will be **(2019 Main)**
(a) $\frac{m\bar{v}^2}{3k_B}$ (b) $\frac{m\bar{v}^2}{7k_B}$ (c) $\frac{m\bar{v}^2}{5k_B}$ (d) $\frac{m\bar{v}^2}{6k_B}$

14. The average translational kinetic energy and the rms speed of molecules in a sample of oxygen gas at 300 K are 6.21×10^{-21} J and 484 m/s respectively. The corresponding values at 600 K are nearly (assuming ideal gas behaviour) **(1997 JEE)**
(a) 12.42×10^{-21} J, 968 m/s
(b) 8.78×10^{-21} J, 684 m/s
(c) 6.21×10^{-21} J, 968 m/s
(d) 12.42×10^{-21} J, 684 m/s

Match the Columns

15. Match List-I with List-II

	List-I		List-II
A.	3 Translational degrees of freedom	I.	Monoatomic gases
B.	3 Translational, 2 rotational degrees of freedoms	II.	Polyatomic gases
C.	3 Translational, 2 rotational and 1 vibrational degrees of freedom	III.	Rigid diatomic gases
D.	3 Translational, 2 rotational and more than one vibrational degrees of freedom	IV.	Non-rigid diatomic gases

Choose the correct answer from the options given below : **(2023 Main)**
(a) (A)-(IV), (B)-(III), (C)-(II), (D)-(I)
(b) (A)-(I), (B)-(III), (C)-(IV), (D)-(II)
(c) (A)-(IV). (B)-(II), (C)-(I), (D)-(III)
(d) (A)-(I), (B)-(IV), (C)-(III), (D)-(II)

Subjective Questions

16. The heat capacity at constant volume of a sample of a monatomic gas is 35 J/K. Find
(a) the number of moles
(b) the internal energy at 0°C
(c) the molar heat capacity at constant pressure.

17. For a certain gas the heat capacity at constant pressure is greater than that at constant volume by 29.1 J/K.
(a) How many moles of the gas are there?
(b) If the gas is monatomic, what are heat capacities at constant volume and pressure?
(c) If the gas molecules are diatomic which rotate but do not vibrate, what are heat capacities at constant volume and at constant pressure.

18. You work in a materials testing lab and your boss tells you to increase the temperature of a sample by 40.0°C. The only thermometer you can find at your workbench reads in °F. If the initial temperature of the sample is 68.2 °F. What is its temperature in °F, when the desired temperature increase has been achieved?

19. The pressure of a gas in a 100 mL container is 200 kPa and the average translational kinetic energy of each gas particle is 6×10^{-21} J. Find the number of gas particles in the container. How many moles are there in the container?

20. At 0°C and 1.0 atm ($=1.01 \times 10^5$ N/m^2) pressure the densities of air, oxygen and nitrogen are 1.284 kg/m^3, 1.429 kg/m^3 and 1.251 kg/m^3 respectively. Calculate the percentage of nitrogen in the air from these data, assuming only these two gases to be present.

21. How many degrees of freedom have the gas molecules, if under standard conditions the gas density is $\rho = 1.3$ kg/m^3 and velocity of sound propagation on it is $v = 330$ m/s? **(Irodov 2.66)**

22. (a) What is the average translational kinetic energy of a molecule of an ideal gas at temperature of 27°C ?
(b) What is the total random translational kinetic energy of the molecules in one mole of this gas?
(c) What is the rms speed of oxygen molecules at this temperature?

23. At what temperature is the "effective" speed of gaseous hydrogen molecules (molecular weight = 2) equal to that of oxygen molecules (molecular weight = 32) at 47°C ?

24. At what temperature is v_{rms} of H_2 molecules equal to the escape speed from earth's surface. What is the corresponding temperature for escape of hydrogen from moon's surface?
Given, $g_m = 1.6$ m/s^2, $R_e = 6367$ km and $R_m = 1750$ km.

25. Call the rms speed of the molecules in an ideal gas v_0 at temperature T_0 and pressure p_0. Find the speed if
(a) the temperature is raised from $T_0 = 293$ K to 573 K
(b) the pressure is doubled and $T = T_0$
(c) the molecular weight of each of the gas molecules is tripled.

26. A 2.00 mL volume container contains 50 mg of gas at a pressure of 100 kPa. The mass of each gas particle is 8.0×10^{-26} kg. Find the average translational kinetic energy of each particle.

27. A steel wire of 2.0 mm^2 cross-section is held straight (but under no tension) by attaching it firmly to two points a distance 1.50 m apart at 30 °C. If the temperature now decreases to −10°C and if the two points remain fixed, what will be the tension in the wire? For steel, $Y = 20{,}0000$ MPa.

28. A metallic bob weighs 50 g in air. If it is immersed in a liquid at a temperature of 25°C, it weighs 45 g. When the temperature of the liquid is raised to 100°C, it weighs 45.1g. Calculate the coefficient of cubical expansion of the liquid. Given that coefficient of cubical expansion of the metal is 12×10^{-6} °C^{-1}.

29. A cylinder whose inside diameter is 4.00 cm contains air compressed by a piston of mass $m = 13.0$ kg which can slide freely in the cylinder. The entire arrangement is immersed in a water bath whose temperature can be controlled. The

system is initially in equilibrium at temperature $t_i = 20°C$. The initial height of the piston above the bottom of the cylinder is $h_i = 4.00$ cm. The temperature of the water bath is gradually increased to a final temperature $t_f = 100°C$. Calculate the final height h_f of the piston.

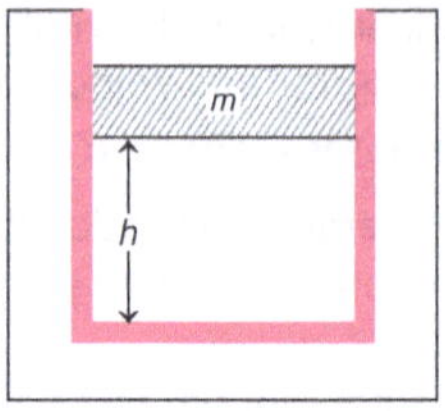

30. The closed cylinder shown in figure has a freely moving piston separating chambers 1 and 2. Chamber 1 contains 25 mg of N_2 gas and chamber 2 contains 40 mg of helium gas. When equilibrium is established what will be the ratio L_1 / L_2? What is the ratio of the number of moles of N_2 to the number of moles of He? (Molecular weights of N_2 and He are 28 and 4).

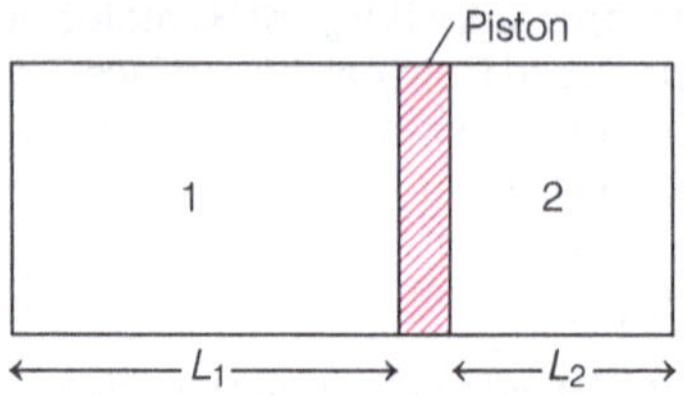

31. The condition called standard temperature and pressure (STP) for a gas is defined as temperature of $0°C = 273.15$ K and a pressure of 1 atm $= 1.013 \times 10^5$ Pa. If you want to keep one mole of an ideal gas in your room at STP, how big a container do you need?

32. A large cylindrical tank contains 0.750 m^3 of nitrogen gas at 27°C and 1.50×10^5 Pa (absolute pressure). The tank has a tight fitting piston that allows the volume to be changed. What will be the pressure if the volume is decreased to 0.480 m^3 and the temperature is increased to 157°C.

33. A vessel of volume 5 litres contains 1.4 g of N_2 and 0.4 g of He at 1500 K. If 30% of the nitrogen molecules are dissociated into atoms then find the gas pressure.

34. Temperature of diatomic gas is 300 K. If moment of inertia of its molecules is 8.28×10^{-38} g-cm^2. Calculate their root mean square angular velocity.

35. In a certain gas $\frac{2}{5}$th of the energy of molecules is associated with the rotation of molecules and the rest of it is associated with the motion of the centre of mass.
(a) What is the average translational energy of one such molecule when the temperature is 27°C?
(b) How much energy must be supplied to one mole of this gas at constant volume to raise the temperature by 1°C?

36. One gram mole NO_2 at 57°C and 2 atm pressure is kept in a vessel. Assuming the molecules to be moving with rms velocity. Find the number of collisions per second which the molecules make with one square metre area of the vessel wall.

37. A vessel contains a mixture of nitrogen ($m_1 = 7.0$ g) and carbon dioxide ($m_2 = 11$ g) at a temperature $T = 290$ K and pressure $p_0 = 1.0$ atm. Find the density of this mixture, assuming the gases to be ideal. **(Irodov 2.4)**

38. A vessel of volume $V = 7.5$ L contains a mixture of ideal gases at a temperature $T = 300$ K: $n_1 = 0.10$ mole of oxygen, $n_2 = 0.20$ mole of nitrogen, and $n_3 = 0.30$ mole of carbon dioxide. Assuming the gases to be ideal, find:
(a) the pressure of the mixture
(b) the mean molar mass M of the given mixture which enters in the equation of state $pV = (m / M)RT$, where m is the mass of the mixture. **(Irodov 2.5)**

39. Under what pressure will carbon dioxide have the density $\rho = 500$ g/L at the temperature $T = 300$ K? Carry out the calculations both for an ideal and for Van der Waals gas. **(Irodov 2.21)**

40. Demonstrate that the internal energy U of the air in a room is independent of temperature provided the outside pressure p is constant. Calculate U, if p is equal to the normal atmospheric pressure and the room's volume is equal to $V = 40 \text{ m}^3$. **(Irodov 2.26)**

41. Calculate the value of $\gamma = C_p/C_V$ for a gaseous mixture consisting of $n_1 = 2.0$ moles of oxygen and $n_2 = 3.0$ moles of carbon dioxide. The gases are assumed to be ideal. **(Irodov 2.33)**

42. Modern vacuum pumps permit the pressures down to $p = 4 \times 10^{-15}$ atm to be reached at room temperatures. Assuming that the gas exhausted is nitrogen, find the number of its molecules per 1 cm^3 and the mean distance between them at this pressure. **(Irodov 2.62)**

43. Determine the ratio of the sonic velocity v in a gas to the root mean square velocity of molecules of this gas, if the molecules are
(a) monoatomic (b) rigid diatomic. **(Irodov 2.67)**

44. Calculate at the temperature $t = 17°C$, the root mean square velocity and the mean kinetic energy of an oxygen molecule in the process of translational motion. **(Irodov 2.75)**

45. Calculate the most probable, the mean, and the root mean square velocities of a molecule of a gas whose density under standard atmospheric pressure is equal to $\rho = 1.00$ g/L **(Irodov 2.83)**

46. Determine the gas temperature at which the root mean square velocity of hydrogen molecules exceeds their most probable velocity by $\Delta v = 400$ m/s. **(Irodov 2.85)**

47. At what temperature of a nitrogen and oxygen mixture do the most probable velocities of nitrogen and oxygen molecules differ by $\Delta v = 30$ m/s? **(Irodov 2.87)**

Level 2

Single Correct Option

48. Two thermally insulated vessels 1 and 2 are filled with air at temperatures (T_1, T_2), volumes (V_1, V_2) and pressures (p_1, p_2) respectively. If the valve joining the two vessels is opened, the temperature inside the vessel at equilibrium will be (p = common pressure)

(a) $T_1 + T_2$ (b) $(T_1 + T_2)/2$

(c) $\dfrac{T_1T_2p(V_1+V_2)}{p_1V_1T_2+p_2V_2T_1}$ (d) $\dfrac{T_1T_2(p_1V_1+p_2V_2)}{p_1V_1T_2+p_2V_2T_1}$

49. Two marks on a glass rod 10 cm apart are found to increase their distance by 0.008 mm when the rod is heated from 0°C to 100°C. A flask made of the same glass as that of rod measures a volume of 100 cc at 0°C. The volume it measures at 100°C in cc is

(a) 100.24 (b) 100.12 (c) 100.36 (d) 100.48

50. The given curve represents the variation of temperature as a function of volume for one mole of an ideal gas. Which of the following curves best represents the variation of pressure as a function of volume?

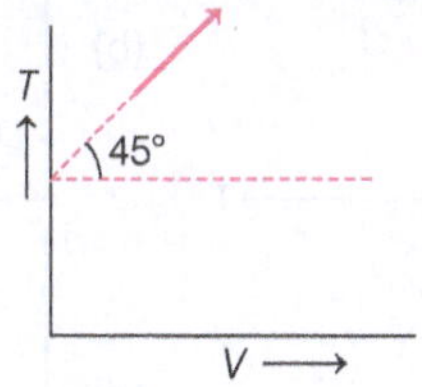

(a)
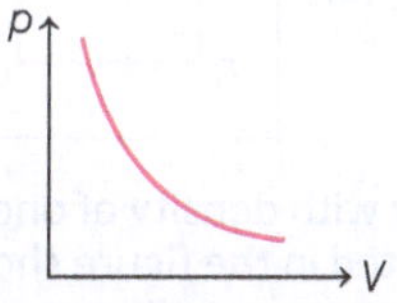

(b)
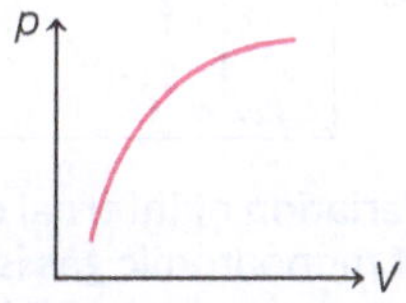

(c)
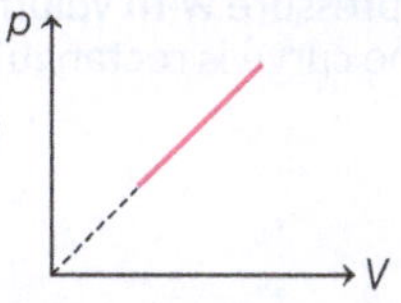

(d)
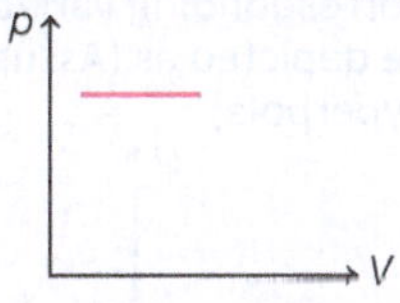

51. An ideal gas undergoes a process whose process equation is $p = \dfrac{a}{\left[1+\left(\dfrac{V}{b}\right)^2\right]}$

where, a and b are constants. When volume of gas $V = b$ the temperature of the gas will be

(a) $\dfrac{ab}{2R}$ (b) $\dfrac{ab}{R}$ (c) ab (d) zero

52. Air fills a room in winter at 7°C and in summer at 37°C. If the pressure is the same in winter and summer, the ratio of the weight of the air filled in winter and that in summer is

(a) 2.2 (b) 1.75
(c) 1.1 (d) 3.3

53. Three closed vessels A, B and C are at the same temperature T and contain gases which obey Maxwell distribution law of velocities. Vessel A contains O_2, B only N_2 and C mixture of equal quantities of O_2 and N_2. If the average speed of the O_2 molecules in vessel A is v_1 that of N_2 molecules in vessel B is v_2, then the average speed of the O_2 molecules in vessel C is **(1992 JEE)**

(a) $\dfrac{(v_1+v_2)}{2}$ (b) v_1

(c) $\sqrt{v_1v_2}$ (d) None of these

54. In a very good vacuum system in the laboratory, the vacuum attained was 10^{-13} atm. If the temperature of the system was 300 K, the number of molecules present in a volume of 1 cm^3 is

(a) 2.4×10^6 (b) 24 (c) 2.4×10^9 (d) zero

55. If nitrogen gas molecule goes straight up with its rms speed at 0°C from the surface of the earth and there are no collisions with other molecules, then it will rise to an approximate height of

(a) 8 km (b) 12 km (c) 12 m (d) 8 m

56. The given p-U graph shows the variation of internal energy of an ideal gas with increase in pressure. Which of the following pressure-volume graph is equivalent to this graph?

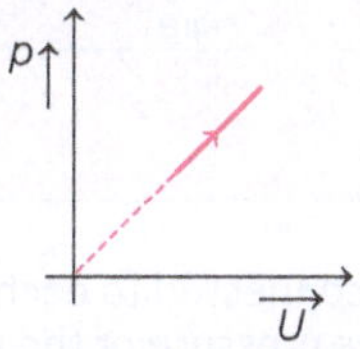

(a)
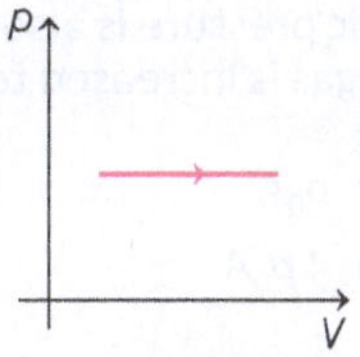

(b)
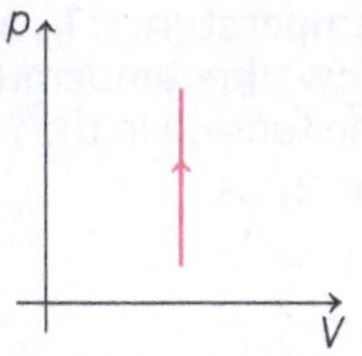

(c)
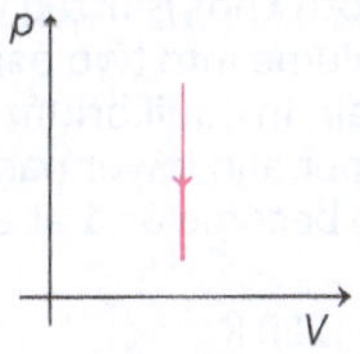

(d)
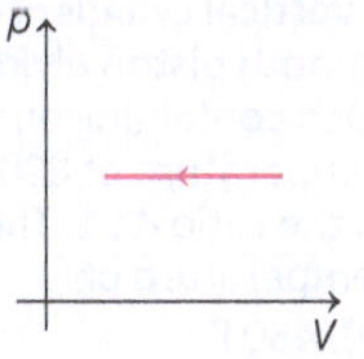

57. 28 g of N_2 gas is contained in a flask at a pressure of 10 atm and at a temperature of 57°C. It is found that due to leakage in the flask, the pressure is reduced to half and the temperature to 27°C. The quantity of N_2 gas that leaked out is

(a) 11/20 g (b) 20/11 g (c) 5/63 g (d) 63/5 g

58. A mixture of 4 g of hydrogen and 8 g of helium at STP has a density about

(a) 0.22 kg/m^3 (b) 0.62 kg/m^3
(c) 1.12 kg/m^3 (d) 0.13 kg/m^3

59. The pressure (p) and the density (ρ) of given mass of a gas expressed by Boyle's law, $p = K\rho$ holds true
(a) for any gas under any condition
(b) for same gas under any condition
(c) only if the temperature is kept constant
(d) None of the above

60. The mass of hydrogen molecule is 3.32×10^{-27} kg. If 10^{23} hydrogen molecules strike per second at 2 cm^2 area of a rigid wall at an angle of 45° from the normal and rebound back with a speed of 1000 m/s, then the pressure exerted on the wall is **(2018 Main)**

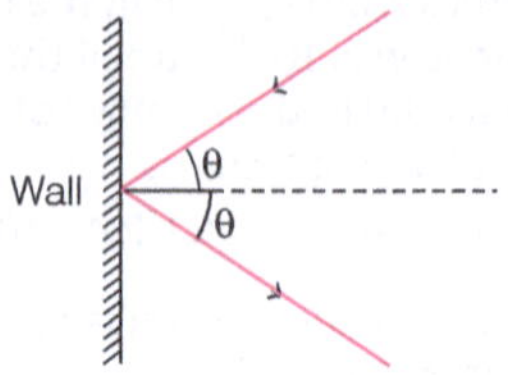

(a) 2.34×10^3 Pa (b) 0.23×10^6 Pa
(c) 0.23×10^3 Pa (d) 23.4×10^3 Pa

61. A cylindrical tube of uniform cross-sectional area A is fitted with two air tight frictionless pistons.

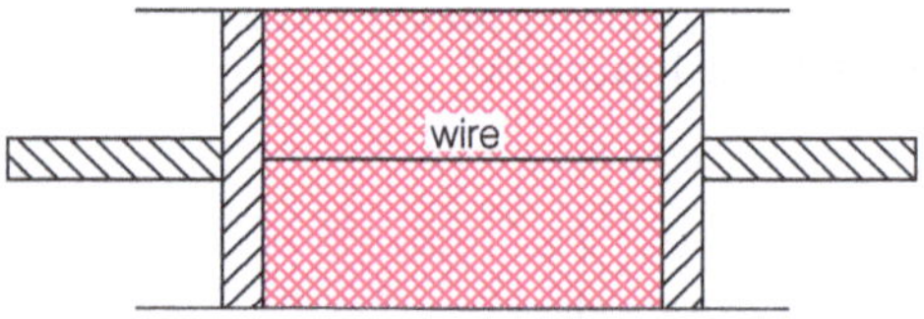

The pistons are connected to each other by a metallic wire. Initially, the pressure of the gas is p_0 and temperature is T_0, atmospheric pressure is also p_0. Now, the temperature of the gas is increased to $2T_0$, the tension in the wire will be
(a) $2p_0A$ (b) p_0A
(c) $\frac{p_0A}{2}$ (d) $4p_0A$

62. A vertical cylinder closed at both ends is fitted with a smooth piston dividing the volume into two parts each containing one mole of air. In equilibrium temperature of 320 K, the upper and lower parts are in the ratio 4 : 1. The ratio will become 3 : 1 at a temperature of
(a) 450 K (b) 228 K
(c) 420 K (d) 570 K

63. A cyclic process 1-2-3-4-1 is depicted on V-T diagram. The p-T diagram and p-V diagrams for this cyclic process are given below. Select the **incorrect** option.

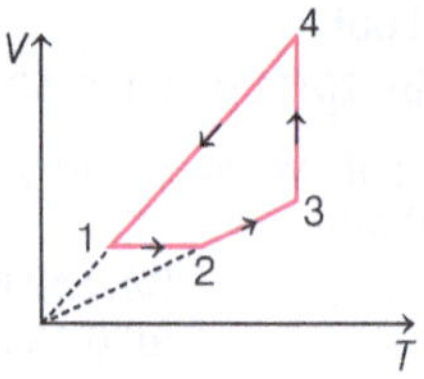

(a)
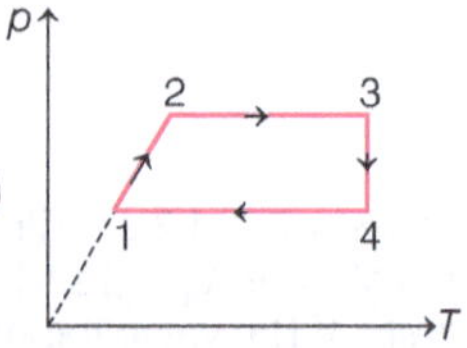

(b)
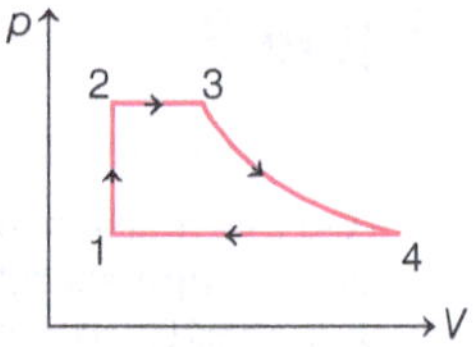

(c)
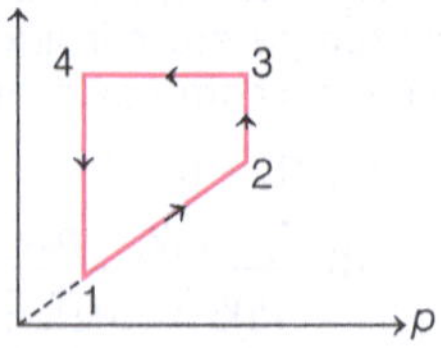

(d) None of these

64. A cyclic process $ABCD$ is shown in the p-V diagram. Which of the following curves represent the same process?

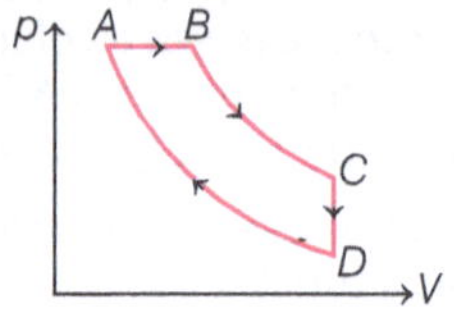

(a)
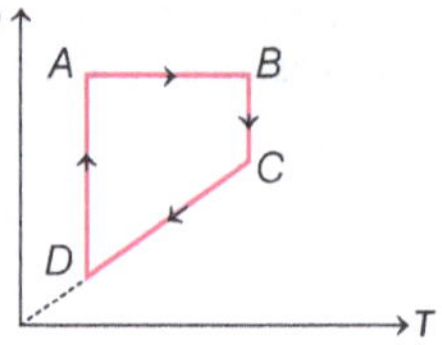

(b)
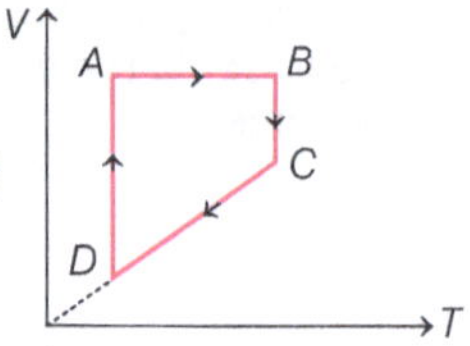

(c)
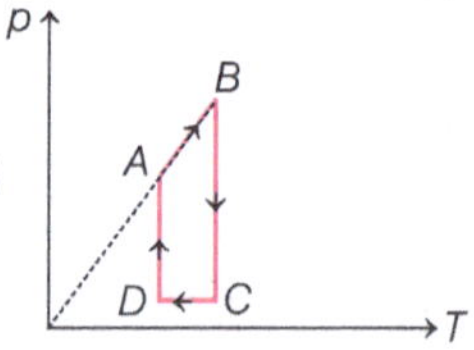

(d)
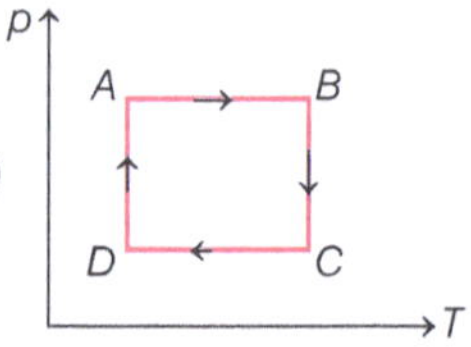

65. Variation of internal energy with density of one mole of monoatomic gas is depicted in the figure shown. Corresponding variation of pressure with volume can be depicted as (Assuming the curve is rectangular hyperbola)

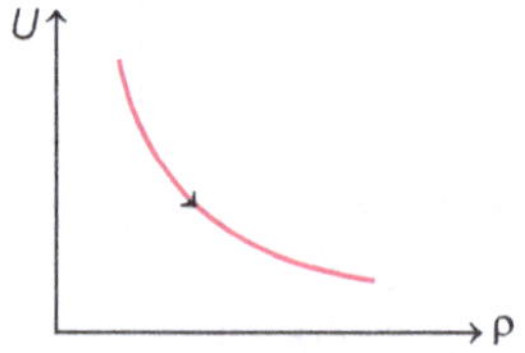

(a)
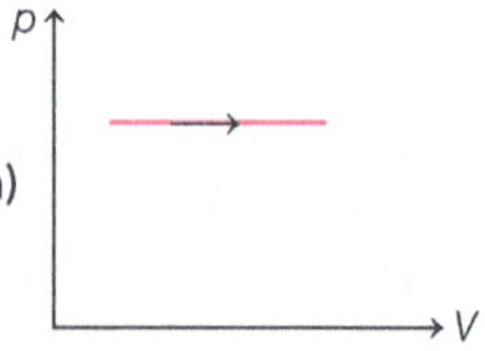

(b)
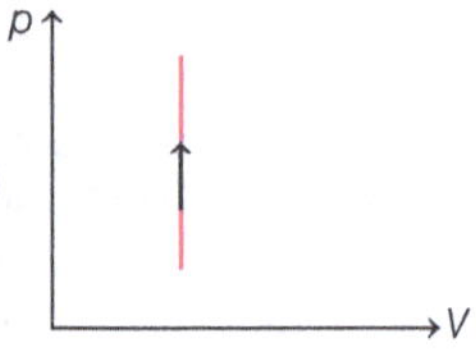

(c)
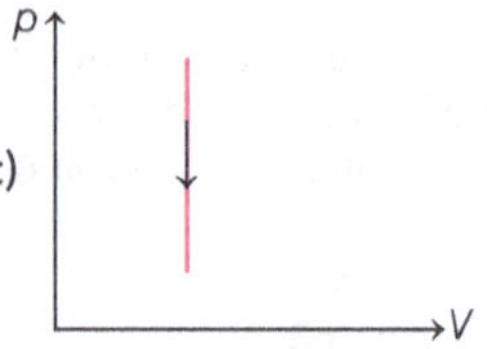

(d)
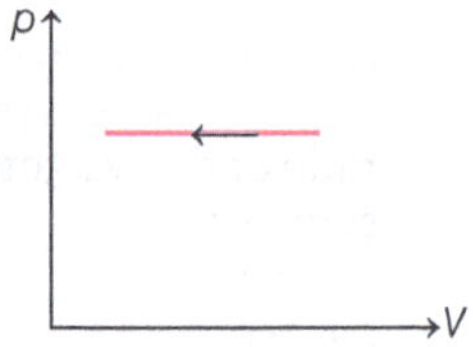

66. The number of molecules in 1 cc of water is closest to

(a) 6×10^{23} (b) 22.4×10^{24}

(c) $\frac{10^{23}}{3}$ (d) 10^{23}

67. The number of molecules per unit volume of a gas is given by

(a) $\frac{p}{kT}$ (b) $\frac{kT}{p}$ (c) $\frac{p}{RT}$ (d) $\frac{RT}{p}$

68. Two identical containers joined by a small pipe initially contain the same gas at pressure p_0 and absolute temperature T_0. One container is now maintained at the same temperature while the other is heated to $2T_0$. The common pressure of the gases will be

(a) $\frac{3}{2}p_0$ (b) $\frac{4}{3}p_0$ (c) $\frac{5}{3}p_0$ (d) $2p_0$

69. A piece of metal weighs 46 g in air. When it is immersed in a liquid of specific gravity 1.24 at 27°C, it weighs 30 g. When the temperature is raised to 42°C, the metal piece weighs 30.5 g. If the specific gravity of the liquid at 42°C is 1.20, the coefficient of linear expansion of the metal is

(a) $1.4 \times 10^{-5}/°C$ (b) $2.3 \times 10^{-5}/°C$

(c) $4.3 \times 10^{-5}/°C$ (d) $3.4 \times 10^{-5}/°C$

70. A sealed cubical container with volume V contains 20 particles with each of mass m and having various speeds. Two particles have speed v, three particles have speed $2v$, five particles have speed $3v$, four particles have speed $4v$, three particles have speed $5v$, two particles have speed $6v$ and one has speed $7v$. Pressure exerted by these particles on the walls of container is p. Then, $p \cdot V$ is

(a) $\frac{319}{3}mv^2$ (b) $\frac{8}{3}mv^2$ (c) $51\,mv^2$ (d) $20\,mv^2$

71. Three rods of equal length l are joined to form an equilateral triangle PQR. O is the mid-point of PQ. Distance OR remains same for small change in temperature. Coefficient of linear expansion for PR is α_2 but that for PQ is α_1. Then,

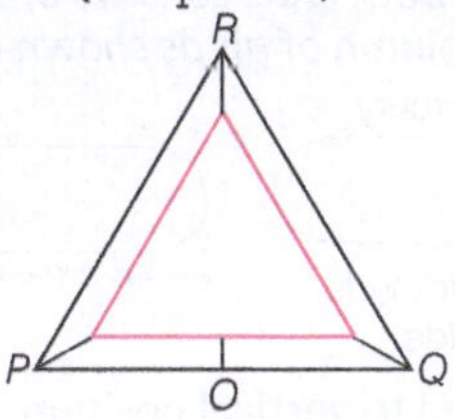

(a) $\alpha_2 = 3\alpha_1$ (b) $\alpha_2 = 4\alpha_1$

(c) $\alpha_1 = 3\alpha_2$ (d) $\alpha_1 = 4\alpha_2$

72. The apparent coefficient of expansion of a liquid when heated in a brass vessel is X and when heated in a tin vessel is Y. If α is the coefficient of linear expansion for brass, the coefficient of linear expansion of tin is

(a) $\frac{X+Y+3\alpha}{3}$ (b) $\frac{X+3\alpha-Y}{3}$

(c) $\frac{X+Y-2\alpha}{3}$ (d) $\frac{(X+Y-2\alpha)}{2}$

73. One mole of an ideal gas goes from an initial state A to final state B *via* two processes. It first undergoes isothermal expansion from volume V to $3V$ and then its volume is reduced from $3V$ to V at constant pressure. The correct p-V diagram representing the two processes is

(a) 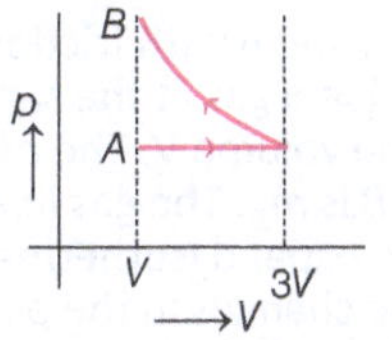

(b) 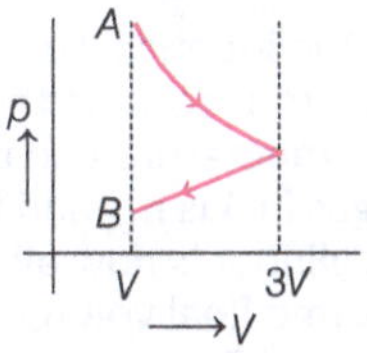

(c) 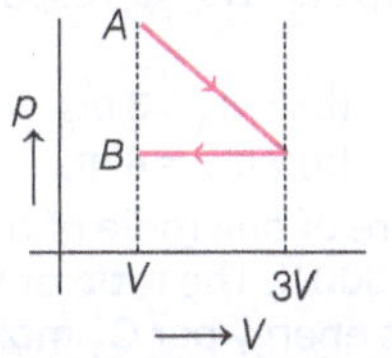

(d) 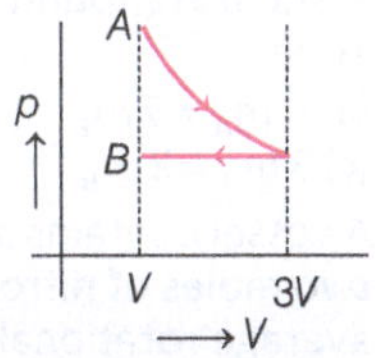

74. An ideal gas is initially at temperature T and volume V. Its volume is increased by ΔV due to an increase in temperature ΔT, pressure remaining constant. The physical quantity $\delta = \frac{\Delta V}{V \Delta T}$ varies with temperature as

(a) 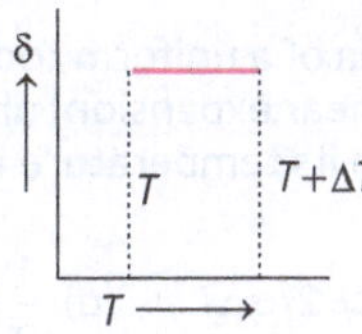

(b) 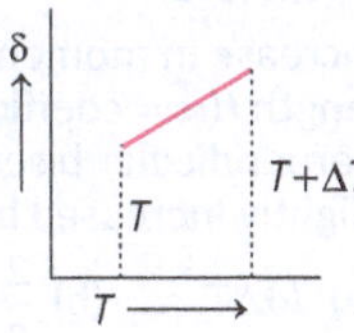

(c) 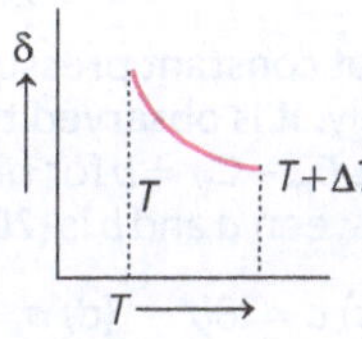

(d) 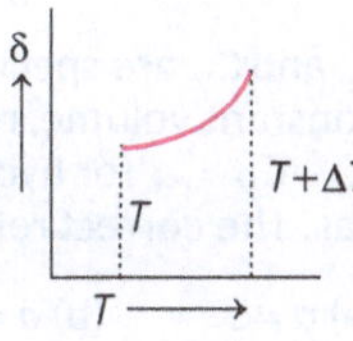

75. Air is filled at 60°C in a vessel of open mouth. The vessel is heated to a temperature T so that $\frac{1}{4}$th part of air escapes. Assuming the volume of the vessel remaining constant, the value of T is

(a) 80° C (b) 444° C

(c) 333° C (d) 171° C

76. Consider a gas with density ρ and c as the root mean square velocity of its molecules contained in a volume. If the system moves as a whole with velocity v, then the pressure exerted by the gas is

(a) $\frac{1}{3}\rho(c)^2$ (b) $\frac{1}{3}\rho(c+v)^2$

(c) $\frac{1}{3}\rho(c-v)^2$ (d) $\frac{1}{3}\rho(c^2+v)^2$

77. A gas is at equilibrium at T kelvin. Its molecular weight is M and its component of velocity in x-direction is v_x. Then, mean value of its v_x^2 is

(a) $\frac{3RT}{M}$ (b) $\frac{2RT}{M}$ (c) $\frac{RT}{M}$ (d) zero

78. Two non-reactive monoatomic ideal gases have their atomic masses in the ratio 2 : 3. The ratio of their partial pressures, when enclosed in a vessel kept at a constant temperature, is 4 : 3. The ratio of their densities is
(a) 1:4 (b) 1:2 (c) 6:9 (d) 8:9

79. Two identical containers A and B with frictionless pistons contain the same ideal gas at the same temperature and the same volume V. The mass of the gas in A is m_A and that in B is m_B. The gas in each cylinder is now allowed to expand isothermally to the same final volume $2V$. The changes in the pressure in A and B are found to be Δp and $1.5\,\Delta p$, respectively. Then,
(a) $4\,m_A = 9\,m_B$ (b) $2\,m_A = 3\,m_B$
(c) $3\,m_A = 2\,m_B$ (d) $9\,m_A = 4\,m_B$

80. A vessel contains a mixture of one mole of oxygen and two moles of nitrogen at 300 K. The ratio of the average rotational kinetic energy per O_2 molecule to per N_2 molecule is
(a) 1 : 1
(b) 1 : 2
(c) 2 : 1
(d) depends on the moment of inertia of the two molecules

81. Increase in moment of inertia of a uniform rod of length l(α = coefficient of linear expansion) about its perpendicular bisector when its temperature is slightly increased by ΔT, is
(a) $l\alpha\Delta T$ (b) $\frac{2}{3}l\alpha\Delta T$ (c) $2l\alpha\Delta T$ (d) $\frac{1}{2}l\alpha\Delta T$

82. C_p and C_V are specific heats at constant pressure and constant volume, respectively. It is observed that $C_p - C_V = a$ for hydrogen gas $C_p - C_V = b$ for nitrogen gas. The correct relation between a and b is **(2017 Main)**
(a) $a = b$ (b) $a = 14b$ (c) $a = 28b$ (d) $a = \frac{1}{14}b$

83. An ideal gas is expanding such that, pT^3 is a constant. The coefficient of volumetric expansion of the gas is
(a) $\frac{4}{T}$ (b) $\frac{2}{T}$ (c) $\frac{3}{T}$ (d) $\frac{1}{T}$

Multiple Correct Options

84. Iron floats over mercury because density of mercury is more than the density of iron. Coefficient of volumetric expansion of iron and mercury are $35 \times 10^{-6}\,°C^{-1}$ and $180 \times 10^{-6}\,°C^{-1}$. Now consider an iron cube floating in a bowl of mercury at 0°C. When temperature is increased up to 25°C, then choose the correct options.
(a) Cube submerged more at 25°C
(b) Cube submerged less at 25°C
(c) Percentage change in the fraction of volume submerged is about 1%
(d) Percentage change in the fraction of volume submerged is about 0.4%

85. Choose the correct options.
(a) In $p = \frac{m}{M}RT$, m is mass of gas per unit volume
(b) In $pV = \frac{m}{M}RT$, m is mass of one molecule of gas
(c) In $p = \frac{1}{3}\frac{mN}{V}v_{rms}^2$, m is total mass of gas.
(d) In $v_{rms} = \sqrt{\frac{3kT}{m}}$, m is mass of one molecule of gas

86. C_V and C_p denote the molar specific heat capacities of a gas at constant volume and constant pressure, respectively. Then, **(2009 JEE)**
(a) $C_p - C_V$ is larger for a diatomic ideal gas than for a monoatomic ideal gas
(b) $C_p + C_V$ is larger for a diatomic ideal gas than for a monoatomic ideal gas
(c) C_p / C_V is larger for a diatomic ideal gas than for a monoatomic ideal gas
(d) $C_p \cdot C_V$ is larger for a diatomic ideal gas than for a monoatomic ideal gas

87. From the following statements concerning ideal gas at any given temperature T, select the correct one (s). **(1995 JEE)**
(a) The coefficient of volume expansion at constant pressure is the same for all ideal gases
(b) The average translational kinetic energy per molecule of oxygen gas is $3\,kT$, k being Boltzmann constant
(c) The mean free path of molecules increases with decrease in the pressure
(d) In a gaseous mixture, the average translational kinetic energy of the molecules of each component is different

Passage Based Questions

Passage (Q.88 to Q.89)

Most of the real gases obey Boyle's law at the room temperature. So, the product $p \times V$ is constant as long as temperature remains constant. Now, consider a tube closed at both ends consists of some mercury trapped in a column of air as shown in the figure.

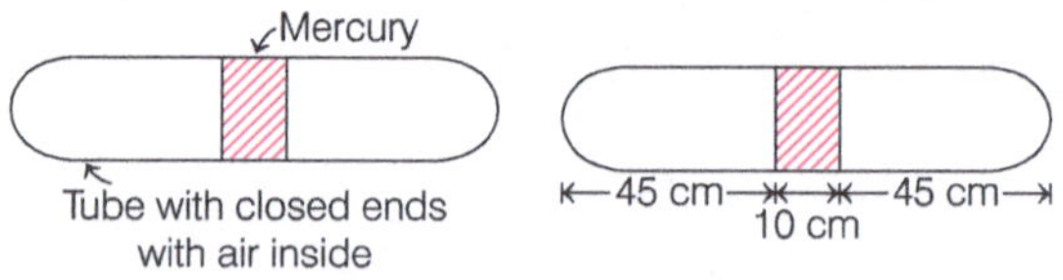

88. If tube is turned to vertical position, what will be the displacement x in level of mercury column?
(a) 10 cm
(b) 5 cm
(c) 4 cm
(d) 3 cm

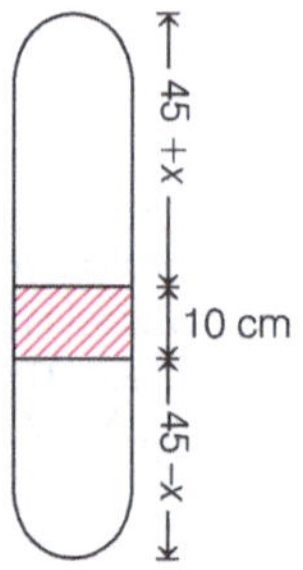

89. If tube is held at an angle of 60° with vertical, the length of air column above and below mercury column are 46 cm and 44 cm respectively. Initial pressure inside the tube is
(a) less than 76 cm of mercury
(b) above 110 cm of mercury
(c) 5 cm of mercury
(d) below 2.5 cm of mercury

Subjective Questions

90. Show that the volume thermal expansion coefficient for an ideal gas at constant pressure is $\frac{1}{T}$.

91. The volume of a diatomic gas ($\gamma = 7/5$) is increased two times in a polytropic process with molar heat capacity $C = R$. How many times will the rate of collision of molecules against the wall of the vessel be reduced as a result of this process?

92. A perfectly conducting vessel of volume $V = 0.4\ m^3$ contains an ideal gas at constant temperature $T = 273$ K. A portion of the gas is let out and the pressure of the gas falls by $\Delta p = 0.24$ atm. (Density of the gas at STP is $\rho = 1.2\ kg/m^3$). Find the mass of the gas which escapes from the vessel.

93. A thin-walled cylinder of mass m, height h and cross-sectional area A is filled with a gas and floats on the surface of water. As a result of leakage from the lower part of the cylinder, the depth of its submergence has increased by Δh. Find the initial pressure p_1 of the gas in the cylinder if the atmospheric pressure is p_0 and the temperature remains constant.

94. Find the minimum attainable pressure of an ideal gas in the process $T = T_0 + \alpha V^2$, where T_0 and α are positive constants and V is the volume of one mole of gas. **(Irodov 2.12)**

95. A solid body floats in a liquid at a temperature $t = 50°C$ being completely submerged in it. What percentage of the volume of the body is submerged in the liquid after it is cooled to $t_0 = 0°C$, if the coefficient of cubic expansion for the solid is $\gamma_s = 0.3 \times 10^{-5}\ °C^{-1}$ and of the liquid $\gamma_l = 8 \times 10^{-5}\ °C^{-1}$.

96. Two vessels connected by a pipe with a sliding plug contain mercury. In one vessel, the height of mercury column is 39.2 cm and its temperature is 0°C, while in the other, the height of mercury column is 40 cm and its temperature is 100°C. Find the coefficient of cubical expansion for mercury. The volume of the connecting pipe should be neglected.

97. Two steel rods and an aluminium rod of equal length l_0 and equal cross-section are joined rigidly at their ends as shown in the figure below. All the rods are in a state of zero tension at 0°C.

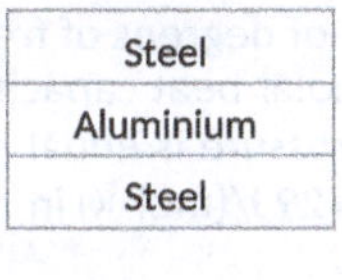

Find the length of the system when the temperature is raised to θ. Coefficient of linear expansion of aluminium and steel are α_a and α_s, respectively. Young's modulus of aluminium is Y_a and of steel is Y_s.

98. A metal rod A of 25 cm length expands by 0.050 cm when its temperature is raised from 0°C to 100°C. Another rod B of a different metal of length 40 cm expands by 0.040 cm for the same rise in temperature. A third rod C of 50 cm length is made up of pieces of rods A and B placed end to end expands by 0.03 cm on heating from 0°C to 50°C. Find the lengths of each portion of the composite rod.

99. A closed container of volume $0.02\ m^3$ contains a mixture of neon and argon gases, at a temperature of 27°C and pressure of $1 \times 10^5\ Nm^{-2}$. The total mass of the mixture is 28 g. If the molar masses of neon and argon are 20 and 40 $g\,mol^{-1}$ respectively, find the masses of the individual gases in the container assuming them to be ideal.
(Universal gas constant $R = 8.314$ J/mol-K). **(1994 JEE)**

100. A vessel of volume $V = 30$ L contains ideal gas at the temperature 0°C. After a portion of the gas has been let out, the pressure in the vessel decreased by $\Delta p = 0.78$ atm (the temperature remaining constant). Find the mass of the released gas. The gas density under the normal conditions $\rho = 1.3$ g/L. **(Irodov 2.1)**

101. Two identical vessels are connected by a tube with a valve letting the gas pass from one vessel into the other if the pressure difference $\Delta p \geq 1.10$ atm. Initially there was a vacuum in one vessel while the other contained ideal gas at a temperature $t_1 = 27°C$ and pressure $p_1 = 1.00$ atm. Then both vessels were heated to a temperature $t_2 = 107°C$. Up to what value will the pressure in the first vessel (which had vacuum initially) increase? **(Irodov 2.2)**

102. A vessel of volume $V = 20$ L contains a mixture of hydrogen and helium at a temperature $t = 20°C$ and pressure $p = 2.0$ atm. The mass of the mixture is equal to $m = 5.0$ g. Find the ratio of the mass of hydrogen to that of helium in the given mixture. **(Irodov 2.3)**

103. A vertical cylinder closed from both ends is equipped with an easily moving piston dividing the volume into two parts, each containing one mole of air. In equilibrium at $T_0 = 300$ K the volume of the upper part is $\eta = 4.0$ times greater than that of the lower part. At what temperature will the ratio of these volumes be equal to $\eta' = 3.0$? **(Irodov 2.6)**

104. A vessel of volume V is evacuated by means of a piston air pump. One piston stroke captures the volume ΔV. How many strokes are needed to reduce the pressure in the vessel η times? The process is assumed to be isothermal, and the gas ideal. **(Irodov 2.7)**

105. Find the pressure of air in a vessel being evacuated as a function of evacuation time t. The vessel volume is V, the initial pressure is p_0. The process is assumed to be isothermal, and the evacuation rate equal to C and independent of pressure. **(Irodov 2.8)**

Note *The evacuation rate is the gas volume being evacuated per unit time, with that volume being measured under the gas pressure attained by that moment.*

106. A chamber of volume $V = 87$ L is evacuated by a pump whose evacuation rate (see Note to the foregoing problem) equals $C = 10$ L/s. How soon will the pressure in the chamber decrease by $\eta = 1000$ times? **(Irodov 2.9)**

107. A smooth vertical tube having two different sections is open from both ends and equipped with two pistons of different areas. Each piston slides within a respective tube section. One mole of ideal gas is enclosed between the pistons tied with a non-stretchable thread. The cross-sectional area of the upper piston is $\Delta S = 10\ \text{cm}^2$ greater than that of the lower one. The combined mass of the two pistons is equal to $m = 5.0$ kg. The outside air pressure is $p_0 = 1.0$ atm. By how many kelvins must the gas between the pistons be heated to shift the pistons through $l = 5.0$ cm? **(Irodov 2.10)**

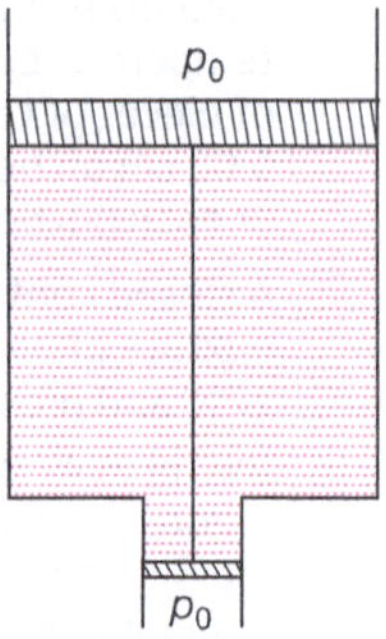

108. Find the maximum attainable temperature of ideal gas in each of the following processes:
(a) $p = p_0 - \alpha V^2$
(b) $p = p_0 e^{-\beta V}$
where p_0, α and β are positive constants, and V is the volume of one mole of gas. **(Irodov 2.11)**

109. A tall cylindrical vessel with gaseous nitrogen is located in a uniform gravitational field in which the free-fall acceleration is equal to g. The temperature of the nitrogen varies along the height h so that its density is the same throughout the volume. Find the temperature gradient dT/dh. **(Irodov 2.13)**

110. Suppose the pressure p and the density ρ of air are related as $p/\rho^n = $ constant regardless of height (n is a constant here). Find the corresponding temperature gradient. **(Irodov 2.14)**

111. Let us assume that air is under standard conditions close to the Earth's surface. Presuming that the temperature and the molar mass of air are independent of height, find the air pressure at the height 5.0 km over the surface and in a mine at the depth 5.0 km below the surface. **(Irodov 2.15)**

112. Assuming the temperature and the molar mass of air, as well as the free-fall acceleration, to be independent of the height, find the difference in heights at which the air densities at the temperature 0°C differ
(a) e times (b) by $\eta = 1.0\%$. **(Irodov 2.16)**

113. An ideal gas of molar mass M is contained in a tall vertical cylindrical vessel whose base area is S and height h. The temperature of the gas is T, its pressure on the bottom of the vessel is p_0. Assuming the temperature and the free-fall acceleration g to be independent of the height, find the mass of gas in the vessel. **(Irodov 2.17)**

114. An ideal gas of molar mass M is contained in a very tall vertical cylindrical vessel in the uniform gravitational field in which the free-fall acceleration equals g. Assuming the gas temperature to be the same and equal to T, find the height at which the centre of gravity of the gas is located. **(Irodov 2.18)**

115. An ideal gas of molar mass M is located in the uniform gravitational field in which the free-fall acceleration is equal to g. Find the gas pressure as a function of height h, if $p = p_0$ at $h = 0$, and the temperature varies with height as
(a) $T = T_0(1 - ah)$ (b) $T = T_0(1 + ah)$
where a is a positive constant. **(Irodov 2.19)**

116. A horizontal cylinder closed from one end is rotated with a constant angular velocity ω about a vertical axis passing through the open end of the cylinder. The outside air pressure is equal to p_0, the temperature T, and the molar mass of air M. Find the air pressure as a function of the distance r from the rotation axis. The molar mass is assumed to be independent of r. **(Irodov 2.20)**

117. Find the specific heat capacities c_V and c_p for a gaseous mixture consisting of 7.0 g of nitrogen and 20 g of argon. The gases are assumed to be ideal. **(Irodov 2.34)**

118. Draw the approximate plots of isochoric, isobaric, isothermal, and adiabatic processes for the case of an ideal gas, using the following variables:
(a) p, T (b) V, T. **(Irodov 2.38)**

119. A vessel of volume $V = 5.0$ L contains $m = 1.4$ g of nitrogen at a temperature $T = 1800$ K. Find the gas pressure, taking into account that $\eta = 30\%$ of molecules are dissociated into atoms at this temperature. **(Irodov 2.63)**

120. Under standard conditions the density of the helium and nitrogen mixture equals $\rho = 0.060$ g/L. Find the concentration of helium atoms in the given mixture. **(Irodov 2.64)**

121. A parallel beam of nitrogen molecules moving with velocity $v = 400$ m/s impinges on a wall at an angle $\theta = 30°$ to its normal. The concentration of molecules in the beam $\eta = 0.9 \times 10^{19}\ \text{cm}^{-3}$. Find the pressure exerted by the beam on the wall assuming the molecules to scatter in accordance with the perfectly elastic collision law. **(Irodov 2.65)**

122. Find the molar mass and the number of degrees of freedom of molecules in a gas if its heat capacities are known: $c_V = 0.65$ J/(g-K) and $c_p = 0.91$ J/(g·K). **(Irodov 2.71)**

123. Find the number of degrees of freedom of molecules in a gas whose molar heat capacity
(a) at constant pressure is equal to $C_p = 29$ J/(mol - K)
(b) is equal to $C = 29$ J/(mol·K) in the process $pT = $ constant. **(Irodov 2.72)**

124. The volume of gas consisting of rigid diatomic molecules was increased $\eta = 2.0$ times in a polytropic process with the molar heat capacity $C = R$. How many times will the rate of collisions of molecules against a vessel's wall be reduced as a result of this process? **(Irodov 2.81)**

125. A gas consisting of rigid diatomic molecules was expanded in a polytropic process so that the rate of collisions of the molecules against the vessel's wall did not change. Find the molar heat capacity of the gas in this process. **(Irodov 2.82)**

Integer Type or Numerical Based Questions

126. One mole of a monoatomic gas is mixed with three moles of a diatomic gas. The molecular specific heat of mixture at constant volume is $\frac{\alpha^2}{4}R$ J/mol-K; then the value of α will be .... (Assume that the given diatomic gas has no vibrational mode). **(2022 Main)**

127. A container is divided into two chambers by a partition. The volume of first chamber is 4.5 L and second chamber is 5.5 L. The first chamber contains 3.0 mol of gas at pressure 2.0 atm and second chamber contains 4.0 mol of gas at pressure 3.0 atm. After the partition is removed and the mixture attains equilibrium, then the common equilibrium pressure existing in the mixture is $x \times 10^{-1}$ atm. Value of x is .... **(2021 Main)**

Answers

Level 1

1. (b) **2.** (b) **3.** (c) **4.** (b) **5.** (d)
6. (d) **7.** (d) **8.** (c) **9.** (d) **10.** (c)
11. (c) **12.** (a) **13.** (a) **14.** (d) **15.** (b)

16. (a) 2.81 mol (b) 9.56 kJ (c) 20.8 J/mol-K

17. (a) 3.5 mol (b) 43.65 J/K, 72.75 J/K (c) 72.75 J/K, 101.86 J/K

18. 140.2°F **19.** 5×10^{21}, 8.3×10^{-3} mol

20. 76.5% by mass **21.** (5)

22. (a) 6.21×10^{-21} J (b) 3740 J (c) 484 m/s **23.** -253°C

24. $T_E = 10063$ K, $T_M = 449$ K

25. (a) $1.40\, v_0$ (b) v_0 (c) $0.58\, v_0$ or $v_0/\sqrt{3}$

26. 4.8×10^{-22} J **27.** 192 N **28.** 3.1×10^{-4} per °C

29. 5.09 cm **30.** 0.089, 0.089 **31.** 22.4 L

32. 3.36×10^5 Pa **33.** 4.1×10^5 N/m^2 **34.** 10^{13} rad/s

35. (a) 6.21×10^{-21} J (b) 20.8 J **36.** 3.1×10^{27} **37.** 1.5 g/L

38. (a) $p \approx 2$ atm (b) $M = 36.7$ g/mol

39. $p = 283 \times 10^5$ Pa ≈ 283 atm **40.** $U \approx 10$ MJ **41.** $\gamma = 1.4$

42. $N = 10^5$ per cm^3, $a \approx 0.2$ mm **43.** (a) 0.75 (b) 0.68

44. $v_{rms} = 0.47$ km/s, 6.0×10^{-21} J

45. 0.45 km/s, 0.51 km/s, 0.55 km/s **46.** $T \approx 380$ K **47.** $T \approx 0.37$ K

Level 2

48. (c) **49.** (a) **50.** (a) **51.** (a) **52.** (c)
53. (b) **54.** (a) **55.** (b) **56.** (b) **57.** (d)
58. (d) **59.** (c) **60.** (a) **61.** (b) **62.** (a)
63. (d) **64.** (a) **65.** (d) **66.** (c) **67.** (a)
68. (b) **69.** (b) **70.** (a) **71.** (d) **72.** (b)
73. (d) **74.** (c) **75.** (d) **76.** (a) **77.** (c)
78. (d) **79.** (c) **80.** (a) **81.** (c) **82.** (b)
83. (a) **84.** (a, d) **85.** (a,d) **86.** (b,d) **87.** (a,c)
88. (d) **89.** (b) **91.** $(2)^{4/3}$ times **92.** 115.2 g

93. $p_1 = \left(p_0 + \frac{mg}{A}\right)\left(1 - \frac{\Delta h}{h}\right)$ **94.** $2R\sqrt{\alpha T_0}$

95. 99.61% **96.** 2.0×10^{-4} per °C **97.** $l_0\left[1 + \left(\frac{\alpha_a Y_a + 2\alpha_s Y_s}{Y_a + 2Y_s}\right)\theta\right]$

98. 10 cm, 40 cm **99.** 4.074 g Neon, 23.926 g Argon

100. 30g **101.** 0.10 atm **102.** 0.50

103. 421 K **104.** $n = \frac{\ln \eta}{\ln(1 + \Delta V/V)}$ **105.** $p = p_0 e^{-\frac{c}{V}t}$

106. $t = 60$ s or 1 min **107.** $\Delta T = 0.9$ K

108. (a) $T_{max} = \frac{2}{3}\left(\frac{p_0}{R}\right)\sqrt{\frac{p_0}{3\alpha}}$ (b) $T_{max} = \frac{p_0}{e\beta R}$

109. -0.033 K/m **110.** $\frac{dT}{dh} = -\frac{(n-1)}{nR}Mg$

111. 0.5 and 2 atm **112.** (a) $h \approx 8$ km (b) $h \approx 0.09$ km

113. $m = \frac{\left(1 - e^{-\frac{Mgh}{RT}}\right)p_0 S}{g}$ **114.** $h_{CG} = \frac{RT}{Mg}$

115. (a) $p = p_0(1 - ah)^{\frac{Mg}{aRT_0}}$ (b) $p = \frac{p_0}{(1 + ah)^{\frac{Mg}{aRT_0}}}$

116. $p = p_0 e^{\frac{M\omega^2 r^2}{2RT}}$ **117.** $c_V = 0.42$ J/g-K, $c_p = 0.65$ J/g-K

118. (See the hints) **119.** 1.9 atm **120.** 1.6×10^{19} per cm^3

121. 1.0 atm **122.** $M = 32$ g/mol, $f = 5$

123. (a) $f \approx 5$ (b) $f \approx 3$

124. Rate of collisions will decrease 2.5 times

125. $C = 3R$ **126.** (3) **127.** (25.5)

See hints on pages 236-254.

Hints & SOLUTIONS

Module 1.

1. $\frac{X_T - X_L}{X_H - X_L} = \frac{T_F - 32}{212 - 32}$

$\Rightarrow \quad \frac{-95-(-15)}{65-(-15)} = \frac{T_F - 32}{180}$

$\Rightarrow \quad \frac{-80}{80} = \frac{T_F - 32}{180}$

$\Rightarrow \quad -180 = T_F - 32$

$\Rightarrow \quad T_F = -180 + 32$

$\Rightarrow \quad T_F = -148°F$

2. In the given graph, for scale P

Lower fixed point $= 30°$

Upper fixed point $= 180°$

and for the scale Q,

Lower fixed point (LFP) $= 0°$

Upper fixed point $= 100°$

∵ The relationship between the two scales P and Q is given by

$$\frac{t_P - (\text{LFP})_P}{\text{Number of divisions on scale } P} = \frac{t_Q - (\text{LFP})_Q}{\text{Number of divisions on scale } Q}$$

$\Rightarrow \quad \frac{t_P - 30}{150} = \frac{t_Q - 0}{100}$

$\Rightarrow \quad \frac{t_P - 30}{150} = \frac{t_Q}{100}$

3. (a) $\frac{T_C - 0}{100} = \frac{T_F - 32}{180}$

Putting $T_F = 0$, we get

$T_C = -17.8°C$

(b) $\frac{T_C - 0}{100} = \frac{T_F - 32}{180}$

or $\quad \frac{T_K - 273}{100} = \frac{T_F - 32}{180}$

Putting $T_K = 0$, we get

$T_F = -459.4°F$

4. (a) $\frac{T_C - 0}{100} = \frac{T_F - 32}{180}$

Putting $T_F = 2T_C$, we get

$T_C = 160°C$

(b) Putting $T_F = \frac{T_C}{2}$, we get

$T_C = -24.6°C$

5. $\frac{T_C}{52-5} = \frac{100}{99-5}$

$\therefore \quad T_C = 50°C$

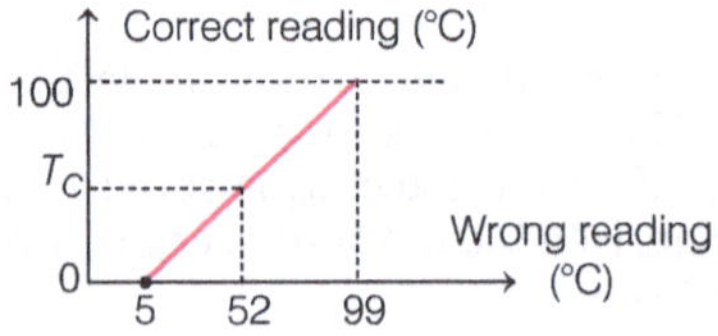

Now, using the equation, $\frac{T_C - 0}{100} = \frac{T_F - 32}{180}$

Putting $T_C = 50°C$, we get

$T_F = 122°F$

6. $\frac{T_C - 0}{100} = \frac{T_F - 32}{180}$

or $\quad \frac{T_K - 273}{100} = \frac{T_F - 32}{180}$

Putting $T_F = T_K$, we get

$T_F = 574.25°F$ or $T_K = 574.25$ K

7. $\frac{T_C - 0}{100} = \frac{T_F - 32}{180}$

Putting $T_C = T_F$, we get

T_C or $T_F = -40°C$ or $-40°F$

8.

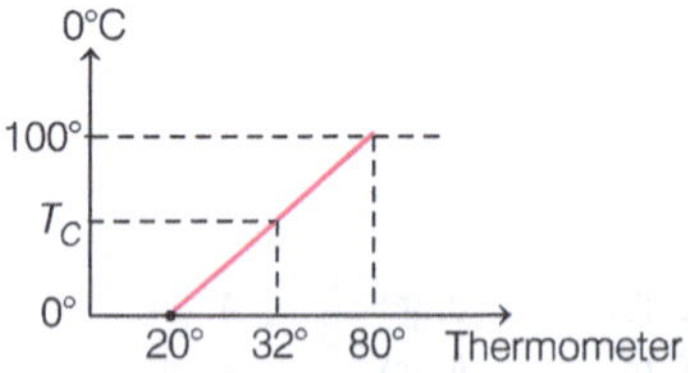

$\frac{T_C}{32-20} = \frac{100}{80-20}$

or $\quad T_C = 20°C$

9. The temperature on the platinum scale is

$$t = \frac{R_t - R_0}{R_{100} - R_0} \times 100°$$

$$= \frac{86-80}{90-80} \times 100°C$$

$$= 60°C$$ **Ans.**

Module 2.

1. Density of water is maximum at 4°C. Hence, volume is minimum at 4°C.

2. Original value of circumference, $l = 2\pi R$

$\therefore \quad \Delta l = l\alpha\theta = (2\pi R)\,\alpha\theta$

3. It means rod is compressed from its natural length by Δl.

$\therefore \quad \text{Strain} = -\frac{\Delta l}{l} = -\frac{l\Delta\alpha\Delta\theta}{l}$

$$= (-\alpha d\theta) = -(12 \times 10^{-6})(50)$$
$$= -6 \times 10^{-4}$$

4. $\Delta l_1 = \Delta l_2$

$\therefore \quad l_1 \alpha_1 \Delta\theta = l_2 \alpha_2 \Delta\theta$

or $\quad \dfrac{l_1}{l_2} = \dfrac{\alpha_2}{\alpha_1} = \dfrac{19}{11}$

In option (a), ratio is $\dfrac{19}{11}$

5. Coefficient of volume expansion of container will become $3\left(\dfrac{\gamma}{2}\right)$, which is greater than coefficient of volume expansion of liquid. Hence, container expands more.

6. $l_2 < l_1$

$\Rightarrow \quad \rho_2 > \rho_1$ or $t_2 < t_1$

Now, $\quad \rho_2 l_2 = \rho_1 l_1$

$\Rightarrow \quad \dfrac{\rho_2}{\rho_1} = \dfrac{l_1}{l_2} = 1 + \gamma(t_1 - t_2)$

Solving, we get

$$\gamma = \frac{l_1 - l_2}{l_2 t_1 - l_2 t_2}$$

7. Thermal expansion is always like a photographic expansion.

8. $(\Delta V)_1 > (\Delta V)_g$

$$V\gamma\Delta\theta > V(3\alpha)\Delta\theta$$
$$\gamma > 3\alpha$$

9. $\gamma_{metal} < \gamma_{liquid}$, neglect expansion of metal ball

$$w_1 = w_0 - \rho_0 Vg$$

w_0 : weight of ball in air

$$w_2 = w_0 - \rho_{50} Vg$$
$$\rho_{50} = \frac{\rho_0}{1 + \gamma_l(50 - 0)}$$

$\Rightarrow \quad \rho_{50} < \rho_0$

$$w_2 > w_1$$

10. Let l_0 be the initial length of each strip before heating. Length after heating will be

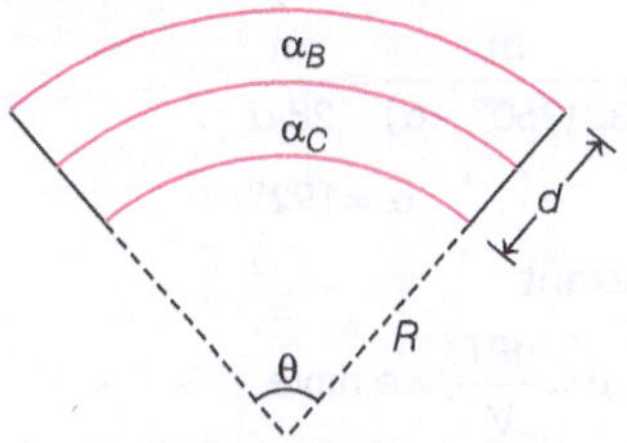

$$l_B = l_0(1 + \alpha_B \Delta T) = (R + d)\theta$$

and $\quad l_C = l_0(1 + \alpha_C \Delta T) = R\theta$

$\therefore \quad \dfrac{R + d}{R} = \left(\dfrac{1 + \alpha_B \Delta T}{1 + \alpha_C \Delta T}\right)$

$\therefore \quad 1 + \dfrac{d}{R} = 1 + (\alpha_B - \alpha_C)\Delta T$

[From binomial expansion]

$\therefore \quad R = \dfrac{d}{(\alpha_B - \alpha_C)\Delta T}$

or $\quad R \propto \dfrac{1}{\Delta T} \propto \dfrac{1}{|\alpha_B - \alpha_C|}$

11. (a) Density of water is maximum at 4°C. From 0°C to 4°C, density will first increase, then decrease.

(b) and (c) : Concept is given in important points

(d) $T = 2\pi\sqrt{\dfrac{l}{g}}$ or $T \propto \sqrt{l}$

As temperature is increased, length will increase. So, time period will also increase.

12. $\Delta T = \dfrac{1}{2} T \alpha \Delta\theta$

Temperature is decreased. Hence, l or T will decrease. So, it will gain time.

Time gained $= \dfrac{\Delta T}{T'} t \approx \dfrac{\Delta T}{T} t \quad$ (as $T' \approx T$)

$$= \frac{1}{2}\alpha\Delta\theta t = \frac{1}{2}(1.2 \times 10^{-5})(30)(24 \times 60 \times 60)$$
$$= 15.55 \text{ s}$$

13. Density of water will increase by increasing the temperature from 0 to 4°C, then it will decrease. Fraction of volume immersed is given by

$$f_i = \frac{\rho_s}{\rho_l}$$

ρ_l is first increased and then decreased. Or percentage of volume above water level will first increase and then decrease.

14. $f_i = \dfrac{\rho_s}{\rho_l} \Rightarrow f_i' = \dfrac{\rho_s'}{\rho_l'}$

$\therefore \quad \dfrac{f_i'}{f_i} = \left(\dfrac{\rho_s'}{\rho_s}\right)\left(\dfrac{\rho_l}{\rho_l'}\right) = \left(\dfrac{1 + \gamma_l \Delta T}{1 + \gamma_s \Delta T}\right) = \left(\dfrac{1 + \gamma_2 \Delta T}{1 + \gamma_1 \Delta T}\right)$

Now, $\quad \dfrac{1}{1 + \gamma_1 \Delta T} \approx (1 - \gamma_1 \Delta T)$

$\therefore \quad \dfrac{f_i'}{f_i} = (1 + \gamma_2 \Delta T)(1 - \gamma_1 \Delta T)$

Neglecting $\gamma_1 \gamma_2 (\Delta T)^2$ term, we get

$$\frac{f_i'}{f_i} \approx 1 + (\gamma_2 - \gamma_1)\Delta T$$

15.

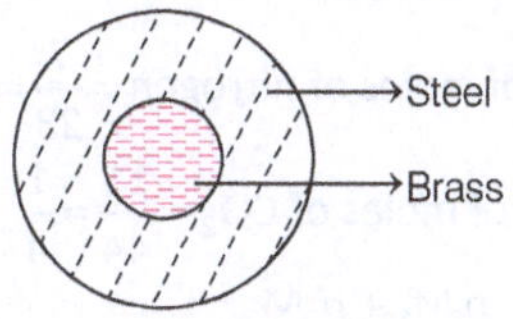

Since, $\alpha_B > \alpha_{Fe}$

On cooling brass will contract more.

16. $\Delta d = d(\alpha_B - \alpha_{Fe})\Delta\theta$

$\therefore \quad \Delta\theta = \dfrac{\Delta d}{d(\alpha_B - \alpha_{Fe})}$

$= \dfrac{0.01}{60 \times 0.8 \times 10^{-5}}$

$= 20.83°C$

$\therefore$ New temperature $= (30 + 20.83)$

$= 50.83°C$

17. (a) $\Delta l = l\,\alpha\Delta\theta$

$= (88.42)(2.4 \times 10^{-5})(35 - 5)$

$= 0.064$ cm

(b) At higher temperature, it measures less. Hence,

$l = l' + \Delta l$

$= (88.42) + (0.064)$

$= 88.484$ cm

18. $\dfrac{\Delta l}{l} \times 100 = \dfrac{-l\,\alpha\,\Delta\theta}{l} \times 100$

$= -(\alpha\Delta\theta) \times 100$

$= -(1.2 \times 10^{-5})(35) \times 100$

$= -0.042\%$

Module 3.

Introductory Exercise

1. $pV = nRT = \left(\dfrac{m}{M}\right)RT$

$\therefore \quad T = \left(\dfrac{VM}{mR}\right)p$

At constant volume T-p graph is a straight line of

slope $= \dfrac{VM}{mR} \propto \dfrac{1}{m}$

Slope of m_1 is less. Hence, m_1 is greater.

2. $p = \dfrac{nRT}{V}$

or $\quad p \propto nT$

$\therefore \quad \dfrac{p_2}{p_1} = \dfrac{n_2T_2}{n_1T_1}$

or $\quad p_2 = \left(\dfrac{n_2}{n_1}\right)\left(\dfrac{T_2}{T_1}\right)p_1$

$= \left(\dfrac{1}{2}\right)\left(\dfrac{87 + 273}{27 + 273}\right)(20\text{ atm})$

$= 12$ atm

3. $n_1 =$ number of moles of nitrogen $= \dfrac{7}{28} = \dfrac{1}{4}$

$n_2 =$ number of moles of $CO_2 = \dfrac{11}{44} = \dfrac{1}{4}$

$M = \dfrac{n_1M_1 + n_2M_2}{n_1 + n_2}$

$= \dfrac{\left(\frac{1}{4}\right)(28) + \left(\frac{1}{4}\right)(44)}{\left(\frac{1}{4}\right) + \left(\frac{1}{4}\right)} = 36$

Now, $\quad \rho = \dfrac{pM}{RT}$

$= \dfrac{(1.01 \times 10^5)(36 \times 10^{-3})}{(8.31)(290)}$

$= 1.5\text{ kg/m}^3$

4. $pV = nRT$

$\therefore \quad n = \dfrac{pV}{RT} = \dfrac{(\rho gh)V}{RT}$

$= \dfrac{(13.6 \times 10^3)(9.8)(10^{-6})(250 \times 10^{-6})}{8.31 \times 300}$

$= 1.33 \times 10^{-8}$

$\therefore$ Number of molecules $= (n)N_A$

$= (1.33 \times 10^{-8})(6.02 \times 10^{23})$

$= 8 \times 10^{15}$

5. $V = \dfrac{nRT}{p} = \left(\dfrac{nR}{p}\right)T$

For given mass, V-T graph is a straight line passing through origin having

slope $= \dfrac{nR}{p} \propto \dfrac{1}{p}$

Slope of p_2 is more.

Hence, $p_2 < p_1$.

6. $p = (nRT)\dfrac{1}{V}$

i.e. p versus $\dfrac{1}{V}$ graph is a straight line passing through origin of slope nRT.

7. pV and T both are constants.

Exercise

1. Pressure on both sides should be same or,

$\dfrac{n_1RT}{V_1} = \dfrac{n_2RT}{V_2}$

or $\quad \dfrac{m}{32(360° - \alpha)} = \dfrac{m}{28\,\alpha}$

or $\quad \alpha = 192°$

2. $Vp^2 =$ constant

Putting $\quad p = \dfrac{nRT}{V}$, we have

$\dfrac{T^2}{V} = \text{constant}$ or $T \propto \sqrt{V}$

So, if V is doubled, T becomes $\sqrt{2}$ times.

4. $pV = nRT \Rightarrow \left(\frac{1}{V}\right) = \left(\frac{1}{nRT}\right)p$

$\frac{1}{V}$ *versus* p graph is a straight line passing through origin with slope $= \frac{1}{nRT}$ or Slope $\propto \frac{1}{T}$

More slope, less temperature.

$\therefore \quad T_A < T_B < T_C$

5.

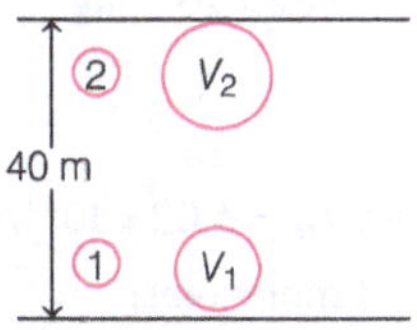

$p_1 = p_{atm} + p_{water} = 10 + 40 = 50$ m of water

$V_1 = 1$ cc, $T_1 = 12 + 273 = 285$ K

$p_2 = p_{atm} = 10$ m of water

$T_2 = 35 + 273 = 308$ K

Since, number of moles in the bubble remains same

$$\frac{p_1 V_1}{RT_1} = \frac{p_2 V_2}{RT_2}$$

$$\frac{50 \times 1}{285} = \frac{10\, V_2}{308}$$

$$\Rightarrow \quad V_2 = 5.4 \text{ cm}^3$$

6. If $p =$ constant, then $V \propto T$

7. $V = \frac{nRT}{p} = \frac{mR(t + 273)}{Mp}$

Here, $\frac{m}{p}$ ratio is same. Therefore, slope and intercept of straight line between V and t should also remain same.

8. $pV = nRT = \frac{m}{M}RT$

$\Rightarrow \quad \frac{pV}{T}$ or slope $\propto \frac{1}{M}$

9. $\frac{pV}{T} = \frac{nRT}{T} = nR =$ constant

So, the given constant is nR. For a given mass (where $n =$ constant) nR is constant for all processes.

10. $\rho = \frac{pM}{RT} \Rightarrow \rho \propto \frac{p}{T}$

From graph,

$$\left(\frac{p}{T}\right)_A = \frac{p_0}{T_0} \text{ and } \left(\frac{p}{T}\right)_B = \frac{3p_0}{2T_0}$$

$$\Rightarrow \quad \rho_B = \frac{3}{2}\rho_A = \frac{3}{2}\rho_0$$

11. From ideal gas equation,

$$pV = \mu RT$$

If volume is constant,

$$p \propto T$$

From the given graph, it is clear that all the gases lines of graphs meet at same value or point. On the horizontal axis (temperature axis) pressure is zero but temperature is negative and it will be equal to 0K or $-273°$C.

12. For an isothermal change,

$$pV = \text{constant or } p \propto \frac{1}{V}.$$

Also, pV value will be more at higher temperature.

$\therefore$ Correct isotherms will be,

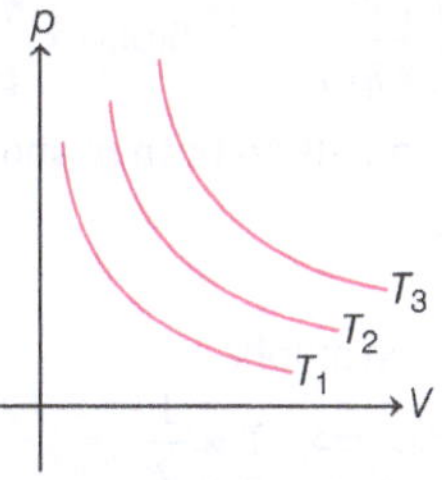

13. $p \propto \sqrt{\rho}$ as per process. If ρ becomes half, then p will becomes $\frac{1}{\sqrt{2}}$ times.

Further, $\quad \rho \propto \frac{1}{V}$

$\therefore \quad \frac{p^2}{(1/V)} = \text{constant}$

or $\quad (pV)\,p = \text{constant}$

Hence, $\quad Tp = \text{constant} \quad$ (as $pV \propto T$)

$\therefore \quad p \propto \frac{1}{T}$

or p-T graph is a rectangular hyperbola.

14. $p \propto \frac{1}{\sqrt{V}}$

If volume becomes 4 times, then p will remain half.

$$V \propto \frac{T}{p}$$

$\therefore \quad Vp^2 = \text{constant}$

$\therefore \quad \left(\frac{T}{p}\right)p^2 = \text{constant}$

or $\quad pT = \text{constant} \quad$ or $\quad p \propto \frac{1}{T}$

i.e. p-T graph is a rectangular hyperbola.

If p is halved, then T will becomes two times.

15. $\rho \propto \frac{1}{V}$

V is doubled so ρ will remain half.

$$U \propto T \propto pV$$

According to given graph, $p \propto V$

$\therefore \quad U \propto T \propto p^2 \text{ or } V^2$

V is doubled, so U and T both will become four times.

$$p \propto V$$

$\therefore \quad \frac{T}{V} \propto V \left(\text{as } p \propto \frac{T}{V} \right)$

$\therefore \quad T \propto V^2$

or T-V graph is a parabola passing through origin.

16. $V = \frac{nRT}{p} = \frac{mRT}{Mp} = \left(\frac{mR}{Mp} \right) T$

i.e. V-T graph is a straight line passing through origin of slope

$$= \left(\frac{mR}{Mp} \right) \Rightarrow \text{Slope} \propto \frac{m}{p}$$

Hence, slope depends on both m and p.

17. $U \propto T$ and $\rho \propto \frac{1}{V}$

According to given graph,

$$U \propto \rho \Rightarrow T \propto \frac{1}{V}$$

$\therefore \quad pV \propto \frac{1}{V}$ or $p \propto \frac{1}{V^2}$

Density is increasing. So, volume is decreasing. Hence, pressure will increase.

U is increasing. So, temperature will also increase.

Now, $\frac{T}{V} \propto \frac{1}{V^2}$

Volume is decreasing. Hence, $\frac{T}{V}$ will increase.

18. (a) p = constant. Hence p-T graph is as shown below.

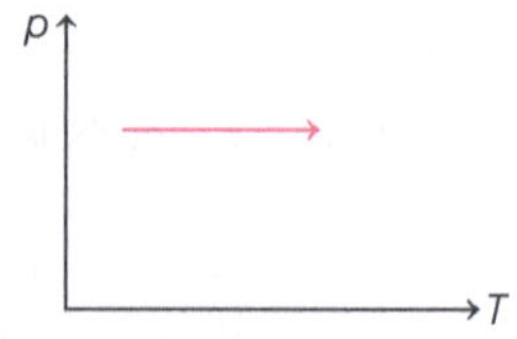

(b) $\rho = \frac{pM}{RT}$

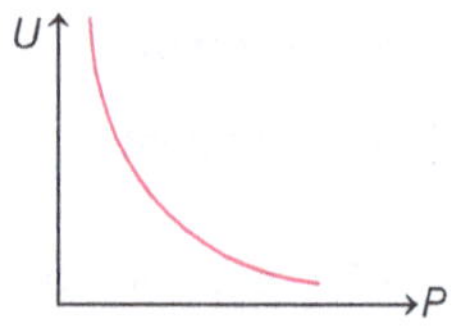

If p = constant, then

$$\rho \propto \frac{1}{T}$$

or $\rho \propto \frac{1}{U}$ (as $U \propto T$)

(c) If p = constant, then

$$T \propto V$$

i.e. T-V graph is a straight line passing through origin.

(d) $\rho = \frac{pM}{RT}$

If p = constant, then $\rho \propto \frac{1}{T}$

i.e. ρ-T graph is rectangular hyperbola.

19. Mass of 6.02×10^{23} molecules is 17 g or 0.017 kg.

$\therefore$ Mass of one NH_3 molecule

$$= \frac{0.017}{6.02 \times 10^{23}} \text{ kg}$$

$$= 2.82 \times 10^{-26} \text{ kg}$$

20. Number of gram moles $= \frac{1}{18} = n$

Avogadro number, $N_A = 6.02 \times 10^{23}$/g-mol

$\therefore$ Total number of molecules,

$$N = nN_A = 3.34 \times 10^{22}$$

$\therefore$ Number of molecules per cm^2

$$= \frac{N}{4\pi R^2} \quad (R \rightarrow \text{in cm})$$

$$= \frac{3.34 \times 10^{22}}{(4\pi)(6400 \times 10^5)^2} = 6500$$

21. At constant volume,

$$p \propto T$$

$\therefore \quad \frac{p_1}{T_1} = \frac{p_2}{T_2}$

$\therefore \quad T_2 = \left(\frac{p_2}{p_1} \right) T_1$

$$= \left(\frac{160}{80} \right)(273)$$

$$= 546 \text{ K}$$

22. (a) $n = \frac{pV}{RT} = \frac{(1.52 \times 10^6)(10^{-2})}{(8.31)(298.15)} = 6.135 \text{ mol}$

(b) $\rho = \frac{pM}{RT} = \frac{(1.52 \times 10^6)(2 \times 10^{-3})}{8.31 \times 298.15}$

$$= 1.24 \text{ kg/m}^3$$

(c) $\rho \propto M$ (if P and T are same)

$\therefore \quad \frac{\rho_{O_2}}{\rho_{H_2}} = \frac{M_{O_2}}{M_{H_2}}$

$\therefore \quad \rho_{O_2} = \left(\frac{M_{O_2}}{M_{H_2}} \right) \rho_{H_2}$

$$= \left(\frac{32}{2} \right)(1.23)$$

$$= 19.68 \text{ kg/m}^3$$

23. If T = constant, then

$$p_1V_1 = p_2V_2$$

$\therefore \quad p_2 = p_1 \left(\frac{V_1}{V_2} \right) = (1 \text{ atm}) \left(\frac{70}{6} \right)$

$$= 11.7 \text{ atm}$$

24. $n_1 = n_2$

$$\therefore \quad \frac{p_1V_1}{RT_1} = \frac{p_2V_2}{RT_2}$$

$$\therefore \quad V_2 = \left(\frac{p_1}{p_2}\right)\left(\frac{T_2}{T_1}\right)V_1$$

$$= \left(\frac{1}{0.5}\right)\left(\frac{270}{300}\right)(500)$$

$$= 900\ \text{m}^3$$

25. $n = n_1 + n_2$

$$\frac{pV}{RT} = \frac{p_1V_1}{RT} + \frac{p_2V_2}{RT}$$

$$\therefore \quad p = \frac{p_1V_1 + p_2V_2}{V}$$

$$= \frac{(0.11)(1.38) + (0.16)(0.69)}{0.11 + 0.16}$$

$$= 0.97\ \text{MPa}$$

26. $(n_1 + n_2)_i = (n_1 + n_2)_f$

$$\therefore \quad \frac{p_iV_1}{RT_i} + \frac{p_iV_2}{RT_i} = \frac{pV_1}{RT_1} + \frac{pV_2}{RT_2}$$

$$\therefore \quad p = \frac{p_i(V_1 + V_2)}{T_i(V_1/T_1 + V_2/T_2)}$$

$$= \frac{(1\ \text{atm})(600)}{(293)\left(\frac{400}{373} + \frac{200}{273}\right)} = 1.13\ \text{atm}$$

Module 4.

1. Temperature of the gas is associated with random or disordered motion of the gas molecules. By the motion of container total kinetic energy of gas molecules will increase. But temperature will not increase.

2. Total translational kinetic energy

$$= \frac{3}{2}nRT = \frac{3}{2}pV = 1.5\,pV$$

3. $E \propto T$

$$\therefore \quad \frac{T_2}{T_1} = \frac{E_2}{E_1} = \frac{2E}{E} = 2$$

$$\therefore \quad T_2 = 2T_1 = 2(273 + 10)$$

$$= 566\ \text{K} = 293°\text{C}$$

4. According to law of equipartition of energy of one molecule in one degree of freedom is $\frac{1}{2}kT$. Therefore energy of n-degrees of freedom would be $\frac{n}{2}kT$.

5. Mean kinetic energy of gas molecules,

$$E = \frac{f}{2}kT = \frac{f}{2}k(t + 273)$$

$$= \left(\frac{f}{2}k\right)t + \frac{f}{2} \times 273\,k$$

Comparing it with standard equation of straight line $y = mx + c$. We get $m = \frac{f}{2}k$ and $c = \frac{f}{2}273\,k$. So, the graph between E and t will be a straight line with positive intercept on E-axis and positive slope with t-axis.

6. The average kinetic energy per molecule of any gas (hydrogen, argon, O_2, N_2 etc.) is always equal to $\frac{3}{2}k_BT$.

It depends only on temperature and is independent of the nature of the gas. Since, hydrogen and argon both have the same temperature as 30° in the flask hence, the ratio of average kinetic energy (per molecule) of the two gases will be 1:1.

7. Kinetic energy K of a gas molecule at absolute temperature T is

$$K = \frac{3}{2}k_BT$$

where, k_B = Boltzmann constant
T = absolute temperature

So, $$\frac{K_2}{K_1} = \frac{T_2}{T_1}$$

or $$T_2 = \frac{K_2}{K_1} \times T_1$$

Here $T_1 = 27°\text{C} = 273 + 27 = 300\ \text{K}$

and $K_2 = 2K_1$

$$\Rightarrow \quad T_2 = 2 \times T_1 = 2 \times 300 = 600\ \text{K} = (600 - 273)°\text{C} = 327°\text{C}$$

8. Average KE of a gas molecule is

$$E_{avg} = \frac{1}{2}k_BT$$

i.e. $E_{avg} \propto T$

So, average energy decrease with decrease of temperature.

$\therefore$ Statement (A) is correct.

Average KE of a gas molecule does not depends on pressure volume or nature of gas.

$\therefore$ Statement (B) is incorrect.

Average KE does not changes with volume.

$\therefore$ Statement (C) is incorrect.

As, $pV = nRT$.

So, $p \propto T$ at constant volume.

$\therefore$ Statement (D) is correct and statement (E) is incorrect.

9. According to Equipartition law, each degree of freedom contributes $\frac{1}{2}k_BT$.

$$\text{Average energy} = f\left(\frac{1}{2}k_BT\right)$$

$$\therefore \text{Average energy} = 3 \times \frac{1}{2}k_BT = \frac{3}{2}k_BT \qquad [\because f_{\text{monoatomic}} = 3]$$

10. Given, $U = 3pV + 4$

$\because \quad U = \frac{f}{2}nRT = \frac{f}{2}pV$

$\therefore \quad \frac{f}{2}pV = 3pV + 4 \quad \text{or} \quad f = 6 + \frac{8}{pV}$

So $f_{min} = 6$

Hence the gas is polyatomic.

11. Total kinetic energy $= \frac{f}{2}pV = \frac{3}{2}pV$

According the question,

$$\frac{3}{2}pV = N \times 2 \times 10^{-9}\ \text{J}$$

$$\frac{3}{2} \times 2 \times 10^5 \times 1000 \times 10^{-6} = N \times 2 \times 10^{-9}$$

$$\Rightarrow \quad N = \frac{3}{4} \times 2 \times \frac{10^5 \times 10^3 \times 10^{-6}}{10^{-9}}$$

$$= \frac{3}{2} \times 10^{11} = 1.5 \times 10^{11}$$

12. Internal energy is given by

$$U = \frac{f}{2}RT = \frac{6}{2}RT = 3RT$$

13. $E = \frac{3}{2}pV = \frac{3}{2}(3 \times 10^6)(2) = 9 \times 10^6$ J

14. $E = \frac{3}{2}pV = \frac{3}{2}\frac{pM}{8} \qquad \left(\because V = \frac{M}{\rho} \text{ and } \rho = 8\ \text{kg/m}^3\right)$

$$= \frac{3}{2} \times \frac{4 \times 10^4 \times 2}{8}$$

$$= 1.5 \times 10^4$$

$\therefore$ Order $= 10^4$ J

15. Average kinetic energy per molecule per degree of freedom $= \frac{1}{2}kT$. Since both the gases are diatomic and at same temperature (300 K), both will have the same number of rotational degree of freedom, i.e. two. Therefore, both the gases will have the same average rotational kinetic energy per molecule

$$= 2 \times \frac{1}{2}kT \text{ or } kT$$

$\Rightarrow$ Thus, ratio will be 1 : 1.

16. Internal energy of n moles of an ideal gas at temperature T is given by

$$U = n\left(\frac{f}{2}RT\right)$$

where, f = degrees of freedom = 5 for O_2 and 3 for Ar

Hence, $U = U_{O_2} + U_{Ar}$

$$= 2\left(\frac{5}{2}RT\right) + 4\left(\frac{3}{2}RT\right)$$

$$= 11\,RT$$

17. Average translational kinetic energy of an ideal gas molecule is $\frac{3}{2}kT$ which depends on temperature only. Therefore, if temperature is same, translational kinetic energy of O_2 and N_2 both will be equal.

19. (a) $K_T = \frac{nf_T}{2}RT = \frac{(2)(3)RT}{2} = 3RT$

(b) $K_R = \frac{nf_R RT}{2} = \frac{(2)(2)RT}{2} = 2RT$

(c) Potential energy = 0

(d) $U = K_R + K_T = 5RT$

20. $\frac{f_T}{f_R} = \frac{3}{2} = \frac{K_T}{K_R} = \frac{K_T}{K_O}$

$\therefore \quad K_T = \frac{3}{2}K_O$

$\therefore \quad K_{Total} = K_T + K_O = \frac{5}{2}K_O$

21. Since, pressure is constant.

$\therefore \quad V \propto T$

$\therefore \quad \frac{V_i}{T_i} = \frac{V_f}{T_f}$

$\therefore \quad T_f = \frac{V_f}{V_i}T_i$

$\Rightarrow \quad T_f = 2T_i = 600\text{K}$

$\therefore \quad \Delta U = \frac{f}{2}nR\Delta T$

$$= \frac{3}{2}R(600 - 300)$$

$$= 450R \qquad \textbf{Ans.}$$

22. From energy conservation principle,

$$E_i = E_f$$

or $\quad E_1 + E_2 = E$

$\therefore \quad n_1\left(\frac{3}{2}RT_1\right) + n_2\left(\frac{3}{2}RT_2\right) = (n_1 + n_2)\left(\frac{3}{2}RT\right)$

$\therefore \quad T = \frac{n_1T_1 + n_2T_2}{n_1 + n_2} \qquad$ **Ans.**

23. $pV = nRT$

$\therefore \quad nRT = pV$

$U = \frac{f}{2}(nRT) \qquad (f = \text{degree of freedom})$

$\therefore \quad U = \frac{f}{2}(pV)$

or $\quad U \propto fpV$

f has become $\frac{5}{3}$ time (3 for He and 5 for O_2). p has become $\frac{3}{2}$ times and V has become 3 times.

$\therefore \quad U$ will become $\frac{5}{3} \times \frac{3}{2} \times 3$ or 7.5 times.

Module 5.

1. $C_V = \dfrac{n_1C_{V_1} + n_2C_{V_2}}{n_1+n_2}$

$$= \frac{(1)\left(\frac{3}{2}R\right) + (1)\left(\frac{5}{2}R\right)}{1+1} = 2R$$

2. $C_p = C_V + R$

$\therefore \quad C_p > C_V$

3. $\because \quad \gamma = 1 + \dfrac{2}{f} \Rightarrow f = \dfrac{2}{\gamma - 1}$

4. $U = \dfrac{f}{2}nRT$. Here, f is degree of freedom and n the number of moles.

$\therefore \quad 1200\,R = \dfrac{f}{2}(2)(R)(400)$

or $\quad f = 3$

i.e. the given gas is monoatomic. For which $C_p = \dfrac{5}{2}R$.

5. $\Delta U = nC_V\,\Delta T = n\dfrac{R}{\gamma-1}(T_f - T_i)$

$$= \frac{p_fV_f - p_iV_i}{\gamma - 1} = \frac{pV}{\gamma - 1}$$

6. Molar specific heat capacity C_p and C_V both do not depend on temperature.

γ is ratio of C_p and C_V which is also independent of temperature.

$$\gamma \propto T^0$$

7. Ratio of molar specific heat at constant pressure and molar specific heat at constant volume is

$$\frac{C_p}{C_V} = 1 + \frac{2}{f}$$

where, f = degree of freedom of gas molecule.

As, $f = 3$ for monoatomic and $f = 5$ for diatomic gas, we have,

$$\gamma_1 = \frac{C_p}{C_V} = 1 + \frac{2}{3} = \frac{5}{3} \quad \text{(monoatomic)}$$

and $\quad \gamma_2 = 1 + \dfrac{2}{5} = \dfrac{7}{5} \quad$ (diatomic)

So, ratio $\dfrac{\gamma_1}{\gamma_2} = \dfrac{5}{3} \times \dfrac{5}{7} = \dfrac{25}{21}$

8. Molecules of diatomic gas have 7 degree of freedom : 3 translational, 2 rotational and 2 vibrational.

i.e. $\quad f = 3 + 2 + 2 = 7$

Thus, total internal energy of one mole of diatomic gas,

$$U = \frac{f}{2}RT = \frac{7}{2}RT$$

$\therefore$ Molar specific heat at constant volume,

$$C_V = \frac{dU}{dT} = \frac{d}{dT}\left(\frac{7}{2}RT\right) = \frac{7}{2}R$$

9. Given,

For gas A,

$$C_p = 29, C_V = 22$$

For gas B,

$$C_p = 30, C_V = 21$$

By $\quad C_p - C_V = R$

$$R_A = 7, R_B = 9$$

Also, $\quad C_{V_A} = \dfrac{7f_A}{2}$

$\Rightarrow \quad f_A = \dfrac{44}{7} \approx 6.3$

$$C_{V_B} = \frac{9f_B}{2}$$

$\Rightarrow \quad f_B = \dfrac{42}{9} \approx 4.6$

As the degree of freedom of A is close to 6, it will have vibrational mode and B will not. So option (a) is correct.

10. Number of mole $(n) = n_h + n_o$

$$= \frac{16}{2} + \frac{128}{32} = 8 + 4 = 12$$

At STP, 1 mole occupy $22.4\,l$

So, 12 moles occupy $(22.4 \times 12)\,l$

i.e. 268.8×10^3 cm^3

i.e. 27×10^4 cm^3

11. Given, volume of cylinder,

$$V = 4 \times 10^{-3}\ \text{m}^3$$

$$n = 1 + 2 = 3 \text{ moles}$$

Temperature of the mixture,

$$T = 400\ \text{K}$$

From ideal gas equation,

$$pV = nRT$$

$\Rightarrow \quad p = \dfrac{nRT}{V}$

$\Rightarrow \quad p = \dfrac{3 \times 8.3 \times 400}{4 \times 10^{-3}}$

$\Rightarrow \quad p = 24.9 \times 10^5$ Pa

12. Here, initial internal energy = Final internal energy

$$\frac{F_1}{2}n_1RT_1 + \frac{F_2}{2}n_2RT_2 = \frac{F_1}{2}n_1RT + \frac{F_2}{2}n_2RT$$

or $\quad T = \dfrac{n_1F_1T_1 + n_2F_2T_2}{n_1F_1 + n_2F_2}$

13. $C_V = \dfrac{n_1C_{V_1} + n_2C_{V_2}}{n_1 + n_2}$

$$= \frac{(2)\left(\frac{3}{2}R\right) + (3)\left(\frac{5}{2}R\right)}{2+3}$$

or $C_V = \frac{21R}{10}$

$= \frac{21 \times 8.3}{10}$ [$\because R = 8.3$ J/mol-K]

$\therefore$ $C_V = 17.4$ J/mol-K

14. (a) $C_p = (1 + f/2)R$

$29 = (1 + f/2)8.31$

Solving, we get

$f = 5$

(b) $pT =$ constant

$\therefore$ $p(pV) =$ constant

or $pV^{1/2} =$ constant

C in the process $pV^x =$ constant is given by

$$C = C_V + \frac{R}{1-x} = \frac{f}{2}R + \frac{R}{1-x}$$

$$\therefore \quad 29 = 8.311\left(\frac{f}{2} + \frac{1}{1-1/2}\right)$$

Solving, we get $f = 3$

15. $pV^{-b} =$ constant

$$C = \frac{R}{\gamma - 1} + \frac{R}{1-(-b)}$$

$C = 0$, if $\gamma - 1 = -(1+b)$

$\therefore$ $b = -\gamma$

Module 6.

Introductory Exercise

1. $v_{av} = \frac{500 + 600 + 700 + 800 + 900}{5} = 700$ m/s

$$v_{rms} = \sqrt{\frac{(500)^2 + (600)^2 + (700)^2 + (800)^2 + (900)^2}{5}}$$

$= 714$ m/s

3. Helium gas is monoatomic. So, its degree of freedom $f = 3$. Average kinetic energy of 1 molecule of gas

$$= \frac{f}{2}kT = \frac{3}{2}kT$$

$$= \frac{3}{2}(1.38 \times 10^{-23})(300)$$

$$= 6.21 \times 10^{-21} \text{ J}$$

4. (a) $v_{rms} = \sqrt{\frac{3RT}{M}}$

For He gas : $v_{rms} = \sqrt{\frac{3 \times 8.31 \times 300}{4 \times 10^{-3}}}$

$= 1368$ m/s

For Ne gas : $v_{rms} = \sqrt{\frac{3 \times 8.31 \times 300}{20.2 \times 10^{-3}}}$

$= 608$ m/s

(b) Each gas is monoatomic for which degree of freedom $f = 3$. Hence, average kinetic energy of one atom

$$= \frac{f}{2}kT = \frac{3}{2}kT$$

$$= \frac{3}{2} \times (1.38 \times 10^{-23}) \times (300)$$

$$= 6.21 \times 10^{-21} \text{ J}$$

5. $v_{rms} = \sqrt{\frac{3RT}{M}}$

$$\therefore \quad T = \frac{Mv_{rms}^2}{3R} = \frac{(4 \times 10^{-3})(10^3)^2}{3 \times 8.31}$$

$= 160$ K

6. Suppose n_1 molecules have v_1 velocity and n_2 molecules have v_2 velocity. Then,

$$v_{av} = \frac{n_1 v_1 + n_2 v_2}{n_1 + n_2}$$

But, $v_{rms} = \sqrt{\frac{n_1 v_1^2 + n_2 v_2^2}{n_1 + n_2}}$

Now, $v_{rms} \geq v_{av}$ because v_1 and v_2 may be in opposite directions also.

Exercise

1. $v_{rms} = \sqrt{\frac{3RT}{M}}$ or $v_{rms} \propto \sqrt{\frac{T}{M}}$ ...(i)

When oxygen gas dissociates into atomic oxygen its atomic mass M will be halved. Temperature is doubled. So, from Eq. (i) v_{rms} will become two times.

2. $v_{rms} = \sqrt{\frac{3RT}{M}}$

It not only depends on T but also on M.

3. **Statement I** As,

$$v_{rms} = \sqrt{\frac{3kT}{m}}$$

So, at $T = -73^\circ$C

$= 273 + (-73) = 200$ K

we get $(v_{rms})_1 = \sqrt{\frac{3k(200)}{m}} = 10\sqrt{\frac{6k}{m}}$

and at $T = 527^\circ\text{C} = (527 + 273)$ K

$= 800$ K

we get $(v_{rms})_2 = \sqrt{\frac{3k(800)}{m}} = 20\sqrt{\frac{6k}{m}}$

So, Statement I is correct, as

$$(v_{rms})_2 = 2(v_{rms})_1$$

Statement II

Translational kinetic energy

$$= \frac{3}{2}nRT$$

As, $pV = nRT$

So, translational KE

$$= \frac{3}{2} pV$$

So, Statement II is false.

4. $p = \frac{1}{3}\left(\frac{mN}{V}\right) v_{rms}^2$

$$\frac{mN}{V} = \frac{\text{Total mass of gas}}{\text{Volume of gas}} = \text{density of gas}$$

5. $v_{rms} = \sqrt{\frac{3RT}{M}}$

and $$v_{sound} = \sqrt{\frac{\gamma RT}{M}}$$

$$\frac{v_{sound}}{v_{rms}} = \sqrt{\frac{\gamma}{3}}$$

Degree of freedom is 6.

$$\therefore \quad \gamma = 1 + \frac{2}{f} = 1 + \frac{2}{6} = \frac{4}{3}$$

$$\therefore \quad v_{sound} = \sqrt{\frac{4/3}{3}}\, v_{rms}$$

$$= \frac{2}{3} v_{rms} = \frac{2c}{3}$$

6. Using $v_{rms} = \sqrt{\frac{3RT}{M}}$

$$v_0 = \sqrt{\frac{3R \times 200}{M}} \quad \text{...(i)}$$

$$v' = \sqrt{\frac{3R \times 800}{M}} \quad \text{...(ii)}$$

On dividing Eq. (ii) by Eq. (i), we get

$$\frac{v'}{v_0} = \sqrt{\frac{800}{200}} = \sqrt{4} = 2$$

$$v' = 2v_0$$

7. $v_{rms} = \sqrt{\frac{3k_BT}{m}}$

$$T = 27°\text{C} = (273 + 27) = 300 \text{ K}$$

$$= \sqrt{\frac{3 \times 1.4 \times 10^{-23} \times 300}{4.6 \times 10^{-26}}}$$

$$= \sqrt{\frac{1302 \times 10^{-23}}{4.6 \times 10^{-26}}}$$

$$= \sqrt{283.043 \times 10^3}$$

$$= \sqrt{283043} = 532 \text{ m/s}$$

8. Given, rms speed of chlorine molecule = 490 m/s

Temperature $(T) = 27°\text{C}$

$$= 273 + 27 = 300 \text{ K}$$

Atomic mass of argon = 39.9 u

Atomic mass of chlorine = 70.9 u

rms speed is given by,

$$v_{rms} = \sqrt{\frac{3RT}{M}}$$

$$\Rightarrow \quad \frac{v_{Ar}}{v_{Cl}} = \sqrt{\frac{M_{Cl}}{M_{Ar}}}$$

$$\Rightarrow \quad v_{Ar} = 490\sqrt{\frac{70.9}{39.9}}$$

$$= 490 \times 1.33$$

$$= 651.7 \text{ m/s}$$

9. The root mean square velocity of molecules of gas is given as

$$v_{rms} = \sqrt{\frac{3RT}{M}}$$

$$\Rightarrow \quad v_{rms} \propto \sqrt{T}$$

10. rms speed of gas molecules,

$$v_{rms} = \sqrt{\frac{3RT}{M}}$$

Average speed of gas molecules,

$$v_{avg} = \sqrt{\frac{8\,RT}{\pi\,M}}$$

$$\text{Given,} \quad \frac{v_{rms}}{v_{avg}} = \sqrt{\frac{\alpha + 5}{\alpha}} \quad \text{at 300 K}$$

$$\Rightarrow \quad \frac{\sqrt{3\frac{RT}{M}}}{\sqrt{\frac{8}{\pi}\frac{RT}{M}}} = \sqrt{\frac{\alpha + 5}{\alpha}}$$

$$\Rightarrow \quad \frac{3\pi}{8} = \frac{\alpha + 5}{\alpha}$$

$$\Rightarrow \quad \frac{3}{8} \times \frac{22}{7} \times \alpha = \alpha + 5$$

$$\alpha = 28$$

11. We know that,

$$v_{rms} = \sqrt{\frac{3RT}{M}} \quad \text{...(i)}$$

and $$v_{avg} = \sqrt{\frac{8RT}{\pi M}} = v$$

$$\Rightarrow \quad v^2 = \frac{8RT}{\pi M}$$

$$\Rightarrow \quad \frac{\pi v^2}{8} = \frac{RT}{M} \quad \text{...(ii)}$$

From Eqs. (i) and (ii), we have

$$v_{rms} = \sqrt{\frac{3\pi v^2}{8}} = \sqrt{\frac{3\pi}{8}}\, v$$

$$= \sqrt{\frac{3 \times 22}{56}}\, v = \sqrt{\frac{33}{28}}\, v$$

$$= \left(1 + \frac{5}{28}\right)^{\frac{1}{2}} v = \left(1 + \frac{5}{x}\right)^{\frac{1}{2}} v \quad \text{[given]}$$

$$\therefore \quad x = 28$$

12. $$v_{rms} = \sqrt{\frac{\gamma RT}{m}} \quad \text{...(i)}$$

$$\gamma = 1 + \frac{2}{f}$$

$$\gamma_{monoatomic} > \gamma_{diatomic} > \gamma_{polyatomic}$$

$$v_{rms} \propto \sqrt{\gamma}$$

$$v_{monoatomic} > v_{diatomic} > v_{poly}$$

13. The root mean square speed of smoke particles will be given by

$$v_{rms} = \sqrt{\frac{3kT}{m}}$$

$$= \sqrt{\frac{3 \times 1.38 \times 10^{-23} \times 293}{5 \times 10^{-17}}}$$

$$\approx 15 \text{ mm/s}$$

14. $v_{rms} = \sqrt{\frac{3RT}{M}}$

$v_{rms} \propto \frac{T}{\sqrt{M}}$. As T and M are same for both gas. So, v_{rms} will be same and point (A) is correct.

$\therefore \quad pV = NkT$

As, V and T are constants.

$$\Rightarrow \quad p \propto N \Rightarrow \frac{p_1}{p_2} = \frac{N_1}{N_2}$$

$$\Rightarrow \quad \frac{p_1}{p_2} = \frac{1}{4}$$

So, point (B) is correct.

As points (A) and (B) are correct. So (C) and (D) must be wrong.

15. Speed of sound is given as

$$v_S = \sqrt{\frac{\gamma RT}{M}} \text{ and } v_{rms} = \sqrt{\frac{3RT}{M}}$$

$$\text{So, } \frac{v_S}{v_{rms}} = \sqrt{\frac{\gamma}{3}} = \frac{1}{\sqrt{2}}$$

$$\Rightarrow \quad \frac{\gamma}{3} = \frac{1}{2} \Rightarrow \gamma = \frac{3}{2}$$

As we know, $\gamma = 1 + \frac{2}{f_{mix}}$

and $$f_{mix} = \frac{2 \times 3 + n \times 5}{n+2} = \frac{6+5n}{(n+2)}$$

$$\gamma = 1 + \frac{2(n+2)}{6+5n} = \frac{6+5n+2n+4}{6+5n}$$

$$\Rightarrow \quad \gamma = \frac{7n+10}{6+5n} = \frac{3}{2}$$

$$\Rightarrow \quad 14n + 20 = 18 + 15n$$

$$\Rightarrow \quad n = 2$$

16. Root mean square speed is given by

$$v_{rms} = \sqrt{\frac{3RT}{M}} \Rightarrow v_{rms} \propto \frac{1}{M}$$

$$\therefore \quad \frac{(v_{rms})_{O_2}}{(v_{rms})_{H_2}} = \sqrt{\frac{M_{H_2}}{M_{O_2}}}$$

$$\Rightarrow \quad \frac{(v_{rms})_{O_2}}{(v_{rms})_{H_2}} = \sqrt{\frac{2}{32}} = \frac{1}{4}$$

$$\Rightarrow \quad (v_{rms})_{H_2} = 4 \times (v_{rms})_{O_2} \quad [\because (v_{rms})_{O_2} = 160 \text{ m/s}]$$

$$= 4 \times 160$$

$$= 640 \text{ m/s}$$

17. Root mean square speed is given by

$$v_{rms} = \sqrt{\frac{3RT}{M}} \Rightarrow v_{rms} \propto \frac{1}{\sqrt{M}}$$

$$\Rightarrow \quad v_H > v_O > v_C$$

18. RMS speed of gas molecule at NTP is given by,

$$v_{rms} = \sqrt{\frac{3RT}{M}}$$

Average speed of gas molecule at NTP

$$v_{avg} = \sqrt{\frac{8RT}{\pi M}}$$

The required ratio will be

$$\frac{v_{rms}}{v_{avg}} = \sqrt{\frac{3\pi}{8}}$$

19. $v_{rms} = v_{escape}$

$$\sqrt{\frac{3RT}{M}} = \sqrt{2gR_e}$$

$$\Rightarrow \quad T = \frac{2gR_eM}{3R}$$

$$= \frac{2 \times 10 \times 6.4 \times 10^6 \times 2}{3 \times 1.38 \times 10^{-23} \times 6.02 \times 10^{26}}$$

$$= 10^4 \text{ K}$$

20. $v_{rms} \propto \frac{1}{\sqrt{M}}$

$$\frac{v_{rms(He)}}{v_{rms(Ar)}} = \sqrt{\frac{M_{Ar}}{M_{He}}} = \sqrt{\frac{40}{4}}$$

$$= \sqrt{10} \approx 3.16$$

21. Collision frequency is given by

$$f = n\pi d^2 v_{avg}$$

where, n is number of molecules per unit volume

$$\frac{f_1}{f_2} = \frac{n_1}{n_2} = \frac{3}{12} = \frac{1}{4}$$

$$= 0.25$$

22. The mean free path

$$(\lambda) = \frac{RT}{\sqrt{2}\pi d^2 N_A P}$$

$$\Rightarrow \quad \lambda \propto T$$

$$\frac{1500d}{\lambda} = \frac{273}{373}$$

$$\Rightarrow \quad \lambda = \frac{1500d \times 373}{273}$$

$$\Rightarrow \quad \lambda = 2049d$$

23. According to kinetic theory of gases :

A. The motion of the gas molecules freezes at 0 K.

B. The mean free path of gas molecules decreases on increasing the number density of gas molecules as

$$\lambda = \text{ mean free path} = \frac{1}{\sqrt{2}\,\pi n d^2}$$

$$\Rightarrow \quad \lambda \propto \frac{1}{n}$$

The mean free path increases with the increasing of volume.

C. If pressure is constant and temperature is increased, then volume should increase, hence mean free path increases.

D. Average KE per molecule per degree of freedom is $\frac{1}{2}k_B T$.

Hence, statements (B) and (C) are correct.

Therefore, option (b) is correct.

24. Given, temperature of oxygen molecules, $T = 27°C$

Pressure of oxygen $= 1.01 \times 10^5$ Pa

$$\lambda_{mean} = \frac{RT}{\sqrt{2}\pi d^2 N_A p}$$

$$= \frac{1.38 \times 300 \times 10^{-23}}{\sqrt{2} \times 3.14 \times (0.3 \times 10^{-9})^2 \times 1.01 \times 10^5}$$

$$= 102 \times 10^{-9} \text{ m} = 102 \text{ nm}$$

25. Collision frequency, $\nu = \frac{v_{av}}{\lambda}$

$$\lambda = \frac{RT}{\sqrt{2}\pi\sigma^2 N_A p}$$

$$\sigma = 2 \times 3 \times 10^{-9}$$

$$p = \frac{RT}{V}$$

$$\Rightarrow \quad \lambda = \frac{V}{\sqrt{2}\pi\sigma^2 N_A}$$

$$v_{av} = \sqrt{\frac{8}{3\pi}} \times v_{rms}$$

$$\therefore \quad \nu = \frac{200 \times \sqrt{2}\pi \times \sigma^2 N_A}{25 \times 10^{-3}} \times \sqrt{\frac{8}{3\pi}}$$

$$= 17.68 \times 10^8 \text{ /sec}$$

$$= 0.1768 \times 10^{10}\text{/sec} \approx 10^{10}$$

26. As we know that,

$$\tau = \frac{\text{mean free path}}{v_{avg}}$$

$$\text{mean free path} \propto V \propto \frac{T}{p}$$

$$v_{av} \propto \sqrt{T}$$

$$\Rightarrow \quad \tau \propto \sqrt{\frac{T}{p}}$$

$$\frac{\tau}{6 \times 10^{-8}} = \sqrt{\frac{500}{300}\left(\frac{p}{2p}\right)}$$

$$\tau = (3 \times 10^{-8})\sqrt{\frac{5}{3}}$$

$$\approx 4 \times 10^{-8} \text{ s}$$

27. (a) Total internal energy

$$U = \frac{f_1}{2}nRT + \frac{f_2}{2}nRT$$

$$(U_{av})_{\text{per mole}} = \frac{U}{2n} = \frac{1}{4}[5RT + 3RT]$$

$$= 2RT$$

(b) $$\gamma_{mix} = \frac{n_1 C_{p_1} + n_2 C_{p_2}}{n_1 C_{V_1} + n_2 C_{V_2}}$$

$$= \frac{(1)\frac{7R}{2} + (1)\frac{5R}{2}}{(1)\frac{5R}{2} + (1)\frac{3R}{2}} = \frac{3}{2}$$

$$M_{mix} = \frac{n_1 M_1 + n_2 M_2}{n_1 + n_2}$$

$$= \frac{M_1 + M_2}{2} = \frac{2+4}{2} = 3$$

Speed of sound

$$v = \sqrt{\frac{\gamma RT}{M}}$$

$$\Rightarrow \quad v \propto \sqrt{\frac{\gamma}{M}}$$

$$\frac{v_{mix}}{v_{He}} = \sqrt{\frac{\gamma_{mix}}{\gamma_{He}} \times \frac{M_{He}}{M_{mix}}}$$

$$= \sqrt{\frac{3/2}{5/3} \times \frac{4}{3}} = \sqrt{\frac{6}{5}}$$

(d) $$v_{rms} = \sqrt{\frac{3RT}{M}}$$

$$\Rightarrow \quad v_{rms} \propto \frac{1}{\sqrt{M}}$$

$$\frac{v_{He}}{v_H} = \sqrt{\frac{M_H}{M_{He}}} = \sqrt{\frac{2}{4}} = \frac{1}{\sqrt{2}}$$

28. $$v_{rms} = \sqrt{\frac{3RT}{M}}$$

$$\bar{v} = \sqrt{\frac{8}{\pi} \cdot \frac{RT}{M}} \approx \sqrt{\frac{2.5RT}{M}}$$

and $$v_p = \sqrt{\frac{2RT}{M}}$$

From these expressions we can see that,

$$v_p < \bar{v} < v_{rms}$$

Secondly, $v_{rms} = \sqrt{\frac{3}{2}} v_p$

and average kinetic energy of a gas molecule

$$= \frac{1}{2} m v_{rms}^2 = \frac{1}{2} m \left(\sqrt{\frac{3}{2}} v_p \right)^2 = \frac{3}{4} m v_p^2$$

29. Speed of sound $= \sqrt{\frac{\gamma RT}{M}}$

$$v_{rms} = \sqrt{\frac{3RT}{M}}$$

$$v_{av} = \sqrt{\frac{8RT}{\pi M}}$$

$$v_{mp} = \sqrt{\frac{2RT}{M}}$$

30. Root mean square speed of molecule is given by

$$v_{rms} = \sqrt{\frac{3RT}{M}}$$

$\therefore$ $v_{rms} \propto \sqrt{T}$

Now, $\frac{(v_{rms})_2}{(v_{rms})_1} = \sqrt{\frac{T_2}{T_1}}$

$T_1 = 300$ K

and $T_2 = 400$ K

$\therefore$ $\frac{(v_{rms})_2}{(v_{rms})_1} = \sqrt{\frac{400}{300}} = \frac{2}{\sqrt{3}}$

$\Rightarrow$ $(v_{rms})_2 = \frac{2}{\sqrt{3}} (v_{rms})_1$

$$= \frac{2}{\sqrt{3}} \times 200 = \frac{400}{\sqrt{3}} \text{ m/s}$$

Unit Exercise (Cumulative)

Level 1

1. Hydrogen and oxygen both are diatomic gases. Therefore, average kinetic energy per molecule is

$\frac{f}{2} kT$ or $\frac{5}{2} kT$ (as $f = 5$)

2. Benzene contracts in winter. So, 5 L of benzene will weigh more in winter than in summer.

3. $p = p_1 + p_2 + p_3$

$$= \left(\frac{nRT}{V} \right)_1 + \left(\frac{nRT}{V} \right)_2 + \left(\frac{nRT}{V} \right)_3$$

$$= (n_1 + n_2 + n_3) \frac{RT}{V} = \frac{(0.5 + 0.5 + 0.25)(8.31)(300)}{5 \times 10^{-3}}$$

$$= 6.23 \times 10^5 \text{ N/m}^2$$

4. $pV = nRT = n \cdot N \cdot \left(\frac{R}{N} \right) \cdot T = nNkT$

$\therefore$ $\left(\frac{nN}{V} \right) = \frac{p}{kT}$

Here, $\frac{nN}{V}$ are the number of molecules per m^3.

Hence, number of molecules per cm^3 will be

$$\frac{p}{kT} \times 10^{-6} = \frac{4 \times 10^{-10} \times 10^{-6}}{1.38 \times 10^{-23} \times 300}$$

$$\approx 1.0 \times 10^5$$

5. Total internal energy of an ideal diatomic gas will be

$$U = 5 \left(\frac{1}{2} nRT \right) = \frac{5}{2} pV$$

$\Rightarrow$ $\frac{U}{V} = \frac{5}{2} p$

6. $p^2 V = \text{constant}$

$p = \frac{nRT}{V}$ or $p = \frac{CT}{V}$ (C = constant)

$\therefore$ $\frac{T^2}{V} = \text{constant}$ or $T \propto \sqrt{V}$

V is increased to 3 times.

Hence, T will increase $\sqrt{3}$ times.

7. At constant volume $p \propto T$

Therefore,

$$T_2 = T_1 \times \frac{p_2}{p_1} = 273 \times \frac{180}{100}$$

$$= 273 \times \frac{9}{5} \approx 491 \text{ K}$$

8. From the ideal gas equation,

$pV = nRT \Rightarrow pV \propto T$

Therefore, pV-T graph is straight line passing through origin.

9. $pV = nRT$

$\Rightarrow$ $pV = \frac{m}{M} RT$

$\because$ $\frac{p_1}{p_2} = \frac{m_1}{m_2} \times \frac{T_1}{T_2}$

$p_1 = \rho g h_1 = \rho g$ (76 cm)

$p_2 = \rho g h_2 = \rho g$ (45 cm)

$m_1 = 185$ kg, $T_1 = 300$ K, $T_2 = 266$ K

$\therefore$ $\frac{76}{45} = \frac{185}{m_2} \times \frac{300}{266}$

$\Rightarrow$ $m_2 = \frac{300 \times 185 \times 45}{266 \times 76}$

$= 123.54$ kg

10. $pV = nRT$ or $p = \frac{nRT}{V}$ or $p \propto T$

if V and n are same. Therefore, if T is doubled, pressure also becomes two times i.e. $2p$.

11. Given, internal energy, $U = \frac{nfRT}{2}$

For one mole gas, $n = 1$

$\therefore \quad U = \frac{fRT}{2}$ ...(i)

where f is degree of freedom.

$\therefore \quad v_n = \sqrt{\frac{\gamma RT}{M}}$

$v_n = \sqrt{\frac{\left(1+\frac{2}{f}\right)RT}{M}}$ ...(ii)

$\left[\because \gamma = 1 + \frac{2}{f}\right]$

From Eqs. (i) and (ii), it is clear that when f increases, then U increases but v_n decreases.

Hence, option (c) is correct.

12. According to law of equipartition of energy, average kinetic energy of each molecule $= \frac{n}{2}k_B T$

where, n = degree of freedom,

k_B = Boltzmann constant and

T = temperature.

$\therefore$ Internal energy of one mole of the gas,

$$U = \frac{n}{2}k_B T \times N_A = \frac{n}{2}RT$$

$$\therefore \quad C_V = \frac{dU}{dT} = \frac{d}{dt}\frac{n}{2}RT = \frac{nR}{2}$$

and $\quad C_p = C_V + R = \frac{nR}{2} + R$

$$= R\left(\frac{n}{2}+1\right)$$

$$\therefore \quad \frac{C_V}{C_p} = \frac{\frac{nR}{2}}{R\left(\frac{n}{2}+1\right)} = \frac{n}{n+2}$$

13. $\frac{1}{2}m\bar{v}^2 = \frac{3}{2}kT \Rightarrow T = \frac{m\bar{v}^2}{3k_B}$

14. The average translational KE $= \frac{3}{2}kT$ which is directly proportional to T, while rms speed of molecules is given by

$$v_{rms} = \sqrt{\frac{3RT}{M}} \text{ i.e. } v_{rms} \propto \sqrt{T}$$

When temperature of gas is increased from 300 K to 600 K (i.e. 2 times), the average translational KE will increase to 2 times and rms speed to $\sqrt{2}$ or 1.414 times.

$\therefore$ Average translational KE

$$= 2 \times 6.21 \times 10^{-21} \text{ J}$$
$$= 12.42 \times 10^{-21} \text{ J}$$

and $\quad v_{rms} = (1.414)(484) \text{ m/s}$

$$\approx 684 \text{ m/s}$$

15. A-I, B-III, C-IV, D-II

A monoatomic gas molecule has 3-translational degree of freedom.

A rigid diatomic molecule has 3-translational and 2-rotational degree of freedom.

A non-rigid diatomic gas molecule has 3-translational, 2-rotational and 1-vibrational degree of freedom.

A polyatomic gas molecule has 3-translational, 2-rotational and more than one vibrational degree of freedom.

16. (a) As discussed in the above problem,

$$C_V = nC_V$$

$$\therefore \quad n = \frac{C_V}{C_V} = \frac{C_V}{(3/2)R}$$

$$= \frac{35}{1.5 \times 8.31} = 2.81 \text{ mol}$$

(b) Internal energy,

$$U = n\left(\frac{f}{2}RT\right)$$

f = degree of freedom = 3

$$\therefore \quad U = (2.81)\left(\frac{3}{2}\right)(8.31)(273)$$

$$= 9562 \text{ J} = 9.56 \text{ kJ}$$

(c) $C_p = \frac{5}{2}R = \left(\frac{5}{2}\right)(8.31)$

$$= 20.8 \text{ J/mol-K}$$

17. (a) Molar heat capacity $C_p = \frac{Q}{n\Delta T}$

and heat capacity $C_p = \frac{Q}{\Delta T}$

$\therefore \quad C_p = nC_p$

Similarly, $\quad C_V = nC_V$

Now, $\quad C_p - C_V = n(C_p - C_V) = nR$

$$\therefore \quad n = \frac{C_p - C_V}{R} = \frac{29.1}{8.31} = 3.5 \text{ mol}$$

(b) $C_p = nC_p = n\left(\frac{5}{2}R\right)$

$$= (3.5)(2.5)(8.31) = 72.75 \text{ J/K}$$

$$C_V = nC_V = n\left(\frac{3}{2}R\right)$$

$$= (3.5)(1.5)(8.31)$$
$$= 43.65 \text{ J/K}$$

(c) $C_p = nC_p = n\left(\frac{7}{2}R\right)$

$$= (3.5)(3.5)(8.31)$$
$$= 101.8 \text{ J/K}$$

$$C_V = nC_V = n\left(\frac{5}{2}R\right)$$

$$= (3.5)(2.5)(8.31)$$
$$= 72.75 \text{ J/K}$$

18. **Initially** $T_C = \left(\frac{T_F - 32}{180}\right)(100)$

$$= \left(\frac{68.2 - 32}{180}\right)(100)$$

$$= 20.11°C$$

Finally $T_C = 20.11 + 40 = 60.11°C$

$$\therefore \quad T_F = 32 + \left(\frac{180}{100}\right)T_C$$

$$= 32 + \left(\frac{180}{100}\right)(60.11)$$

$$= 140.2°F$$

19. $K = \frac{3}{2}kT$

$$\Rightarrow \quad T = \frac{2K}{3k}$$

Now, $n = \frac{pV}{RT} = \frac{3kpV}{2KR}$

$$= \frac{3(200 \times 10^3)(0.1 \times 10^{-3})(1.38 \times 10^{-23})}{2 \times 6 \times 10^{-21} \times 8.31}$$

$$= 8.3 \times 10^{-3} \text{ mol}$$

Now, $N = nN_A$

$$= (8.3 \times 10^{-3})(6.02 \times 10^{23})$$

$$= 5 \times 10^{21}$$

20. Let mass of nitrogen $= (m)$ g. Then, mass of oxygen $= (100 - m)$ g. Number of moles of nitrogen, $n_1 = \frac{m}{28}$ and number of moles of oxygen $n_2 = \left(\frac{100 - m}{32}\right)$

For air

$$\rho = \frac{pM}{RT} = \frac{p}{RT}\left(\frac{m_1 + m_2}{n_1 + n_2}\right)$$

$$\therefore \quad 1.284 = \frac{1.01 \times 10^5}{8.31 \times 273}\left[\frac{100 \times 10^{-3}}{(m/28) + (100 - m)/32}\right]$$

Solving this equation, we get

$$m = 76.5 \text{ g}$$

This is also percentage of N_2 by mass on air as total mass we have taken is 100 g.

21. $v = \sqrt{\frac{\gamma p}{\rho}}$

$$\therefore \quad \gamma = \frac{\rho v^2}{p} = \frac{1.3 \times (330)^2}{1.013 \times 10^5} = 1.4$$

$$\gamma = 1 + \frac{2}{f} \qquad (f = \text{degree of freedom})$$

$$1.4 = 1 + \frac{2}{f}$$

Solving, we get $f = 5$

22. (a) $K_T = \frac{3}{2}kT$

$$= \frac{3}{2}(1.38 \times 10^{-23})(300)$$

$$= 6.21 \times 10^{-21} \text{ J}$$

(b) K_T in one mole $= \frac{3}{2}RT$

$$= \frac{3}{2} \times 8.31 \times 300$$

$$= 3740 \text{ J}$$

(c) $v_{rms} = \sqrt{\frac{3RT}{M}} = \sqrt{\frac{3 \times 8.31 \times 300}{32 \times 10^{-3}}}$

$$= 484 \text{ m/s}$$

23. $v_{rms} = \sqrt{\frac{3RT}{M}} \propto \sqrt{\frac{T}{M}}$

v_{rms} is same. Hence,

$$\left(\frac{T}{M}\right)_{H_2} = \left(\frac{T}{M}\right)_{O_2}$$

or $T_{H_2} = \left(\frac{M_{H_2}}{M_{O_2}}\right)T_{O_2}$

$$= \left(\frac{2}{32}\right)(273 + 47)$$

$$= 20 \text{ K} = -253°C$$

24. (i) $\sqrt{\frac{3RT}{M}} = 11.2 \times 10^3 \text{ m/s}$

$$\therefore \quad T = \frac{(11.2 \times 10^3)^2 M}{3R} \qquad \text{...(i)}$$

$$= \frac{(11.2 \times 10^3)^2 \times 2 \times 10^{-3}}{3 \times 8.31}$$

$$= 10063 \text{ K}$$

(ii) Escape velocity from moon

$$= \sqrt{2g_m R_m}$$

$$= \sqrt{1.6 \times 2 \times 1750 \times 10^3}$$

$$= 2366 \text{ m/s}$$

Substituting in Eq. (i), we have

$$T = \frac{(2366)^2 \times 2 \times 10^{-3}}{3 \times 8.31} = 449 \text{ K}$$

25. (a) $v_{rms} \propto \sqrt{T}$

$$\therefore \quad v_0' = \left(\sqrt{\frac{T'}{T}}\right)v_0$$

$$= \left(\sqrt{\frac{573}{293}}\right)v_0$$

$$= 1.40 \, v_0$$

(b) v_{rms} does not depend on pressure, as long as temperature remains constant.

(c) $v_{rms} = \sqrt{\frac{3RT}{M}}$

or $v_{rms} \propto \frac{1}{\sqrt{M}}$

26. $K_T = \frac{3}{2}kT = \frac{3}{2}k\left(\frac{pV}{nR}\right)$

$= \frac{3}{2}k \frac{pV}{(M/mN_A)R}$

$= \frac{3kpV\, m N_A}{2MR}$

$= \frac{(3 \times 1.38 \times 10^{-23})(100 \times 10^3)(2 \times 10^{-6})(8.0 \times 10^{-23})(6.02 \times 10^{23})}{2 \times (50 \times 10^{-3})(8.31)}$

$= 4.8 \times 10^{-22}$ J

27. Strain $= \frac{\Delta l}{l} = (\alpha\Delta\theta)$

Stress $= Y \times$ strain $= \gamma\alpha\Delta\theta$

$\therefore$ Tension $= (A)$ (stress) $= YA\alpha\Delta\theta$

Substituting the values, we get

$T = YA\alpha\Delta\theta$

$= (2.0 \times 10^{11})(2 \times 10^{-6})(1.2 \times 10^{-5})(40)$

$= 192$ N

28. Change in weight = upthrust on 100% volume

$\therefore \frac{\Delta W'}{\Delta W} = \frac{F'}{F} = \left(\frac{1 + \gamma_s \Delta\theta}{1 + \gamma_l \Delta\theta}\right)$

or $\frac{(50 - 45.1)}{(50 - 45)} = \frac{1 + (12 \times 10^{-6})(75)}{1 + \gamma_l (75)}$

Solving this equation, we get

$\gamma_l = 3.1 \times 10^{-4}$ per°C

29. p = constant

$\therefore V \propto T$ or $h \propto T$

$\therefore \frac{h_f}{T_f} = \frac{h_i}{T_i}$ or $h_f = \left(\frac{T_f}{T_i}\right)h_i$

$= \left(\frac{273 + 100}{273 + 20}\right)(4) = 5.09$ cm

30. $n_1 = \frac{0.025}{28} = 8.93 \times 10^{-4}$

$n_2 = \frac{0.04}{4} = 0.01$

$\therefore \frac{n_1}{n_2} = 0.089$

In equilibrium p and T are same.

$\therefore pV = nRT$

$\because V \propto n$ or $L \propto n$

$\therefore \frac{L_1}{L_2} = \frac{n_1}{n_2} = 0.089$

31. $V = \frac{nRT}{p} = \frac{(1)(8.31)(273.15)}{1.013 \times 10^5}$

$= 0.0224$ m^3

$= 22.4$ L

32. $n_1 = n_2$

$\therefore \frac{p_1V_1}{RT_1} = \frac{p_2V_2}{RT_2}$ or $p_2 = \left(\frac{V_1}{V_2}\right)\left(\frac{T_2}{T_1}\right)p_1$

$= \left(\frac{0.75}{0.48}\right)\left(\frac{273 + 157}{273 + 27}\right)(1.5 \times 10^5)$

$= 3.36 \times 10^5$ Pa

33. n_1 = number of moles of $N_2 = \frac{1.4}{28} = 0.05$

30% of the gas dissociates into atoms.

$\therefore n_1' = 2(0.3)(0.05) + (0.7)(0.05) = 0.065$

n_2 = number of moles of He $= \frac{0.4}{4} = 0.1$

$\therefore n = n_1' + n_2 = 0.165$

Now, $p = \frac{nRT}{V}$

$= \frac{(0.165)(8.31)(1500)}{(5 \times 10^{-3})}$

$= 4.1 \times 10^5$ N/m^2

34. In diatomic gas rotational degree of freedom is two.

$\therefore$ Rotational KE of one molecule

$\frac{1}{2}I\omega^2 = \frac{f}{2}kT = kT$ (as $f = 2$)

$\therefore \omega = \sqrt{\frac{2kT}{I}}$

$= \sqrt{\frac{2 \times 1.38 \times 10^{-23} \times 300}{8.28 \times 10^{-38} \times 10^{-9}}}$

$= 10^{13}$ rad/s

35. (a) Average translational kinetic energy of any type of molecules is

$\frac{3}{2}kT = \frac{3}{2}(1.38 \times 10^{-23})(300)$

$= 6.21 \times 10^{-21}$ J

(b) $\frac{2}{5}$ energy is associated with rotation. Hence, it is diatomic gas.

$Q = nC_V\Delta T = (1)\left(\frac{5}{2}R\right)(1)$

$= \frac{5}{2} \times 8.31 = 20.8$ J

36. $v_{rms} = \sqrt{\frac{3RT}{M}} = \sqrt{\frac{3 \times 8.31 \times (273 + 57)}{46 \times 10^{-3}}}$

$= 423$ m/s

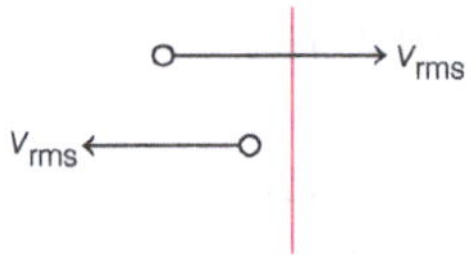

$$\Delta p = 2 m v_{rms}$$

Mass of one gas molecule,

$$m = \frac{46}{6.02 \times 10^{23}} \text{ g}$$

$$= 7.64 \times 10^{-26} \text{ kg}$$

Let n molecules strike per second per unit area. Then,

$$\text{Pressure} = \frac{F}{A} = \frac{\Delta P/\Delta t}{A} = 2 mn\, v_{rms}$$

$$\therefore \quad n = \frac{\text{Pressure}}{(2m)\, v_{rms}}$$

$$= \frac{2 \times 1.013 \times 10^5}{2 \times 7.64 \times 10^{-26} \times 423}$$

$$= 3.1 \times 10^{27}$$

37. n_1 = number of moles of nitrogen $= \frac{7}{28} = \frac{1}{4}$

n_2 = number of moles of carbon dioxide $= \frac{11}{44} = \frac{1}{4}$

Molecular mass of mixture is given by,

$$M = \frac{n_1 M_1 + n_2 M_2}{n_1 + n_2}$$

$$\therefore \quad M = \frac{M_1 + M_2}{2} \quad (\because n_1 = n_2)$$

$$= \frac{28 + 44}{2}$$

$$= 36 \text{ g/mol}$$

Now density is given by

$$\rho = \frac{pM}{RT} = \frac{(1.03 \times 10^5 \text{ N/m}^2)(0.036 \text{ kg/mol})}{(9.314 \text{ J/mol-K})(290 \text{ K})}$$

$$= 1.53 \text{ kg/m}^3$$

$$1 \text{ kg} = 10^3 \text{ g} \quad \text{and} \quad 1 \text{ m}^3 = 10^3 \text{ L}$$

$$\therefore \quad 1 \text{ kg/m}^3 = 1 \text{ g/L}$$

$$\rho \approx 1.5 \text{ g/L}$$

38. (a) $p = \frac{(n_1 + n_2 + n_3)RT}{V}$

$$= \frac{\{(0.1 + 0.2 + 0.3) \text{ mol}\}(8.314 \text{ J/mol-K})(300 \text{ K})}{(7.5 \times 10^{-3} \text{ m}^3)}$$

$$= 1.9 \times 10^5 \text{ N/m}^2 \approx 2 \text{ atm}$$

Thus, $p \approx 2$ atm

(b) Mean molar mass is given by,

$$M = \frac{n_1 M_1 + n_2 M_2 + n_3 M_3}{n_1 + n_2 + n_3}$$

$$= \frac{0.1 \times 32 + 0.2 \times 28 + 0.3 \times 44}{0.1 + 0.2 + 0.3}$$

or $\quad M = 36.7$ g/mol

39. For ideal gas

$$\rho = \frac{pM}{RT} \Rightarrow p = \frac{\rho RT}{M}$$

Substituting the values, we get

$$p = 283 \times 10^5 \text{ Pa} \approx 283 \text{ atm}$$

Note *Students can skip for Van der Waals gas.*

40. Internal energy is given by,

$$U = n\left(\frac{f}{2}\right)RT$$

Here n = number of moles

and f = degree of freedom of gas.

We can write,

$$nRT = pV \quad \text{...(i)}$$

$$\therefore \quad U = \frac{f}{2}(pV) \quad \text{...(ii)}$$

As p and V are constants. Therefore U will be constant.

Note *If temperature in room increases, then number of moles will decrease. So, nRT or pV will remain constant. Or, internal energy will be constant.*

Taking air to be diatomic or degree of freedom $f = 5$.

Substituting proper values in Eq. (ii), we get

$$U = \frac{5}{2} \times 1.03 \times 10^5 \times 40 = 10.3 \times 10^6 \text{ J}$$

or $\quad U \approx 10$ MJ

41. Note Answer in original book is wrong.

γ of a mixture (of non-reactive gases) is given by,

$$\frac{n_1 + n_2}{\gamma - 1} = \frac{n_1}{\gamma_1 - 1} + \frac{n_2}{\gamma_2 - 1} \quad \text{...(i)}$$

For O_2, diatomic, $\gamma_1 = \frac{7}{5}$ and $n_1 = 2$

For CO_2, linear triatomic, $\gamma_2 = \frac{7}{5}$ and $n_2 = 3$

Substituting in Eq. (i), we have

$$\frac{2+3}{\gamma - 1} = \frac{2}{\frac{7}{5} - 1} + \frac{3}{\frac{7}{5} - 1}$$

$$\Rightarrow \quad \frac{5}{\gamma - 1} = \frac{25}{2} \quad \text{or} \quad \gamma = 1.4$$

Note *Derivation of Eq. (i)*

$$U = U_1 + U_2$$

$$n\frac{f}{2}RT = n_1\frac{f_1}{2}RT + n_2\frac{f_2}{2}RT$$

Here n is number of moles and f the degree of freedom.

So, the above equation becomes,

$$nf = n_1 f_1 + n_2 f_2 \quad \text{...(ii)}$$

Now, $\quad \gamma = 1 + \frac{2}{f}$

or $\quad f = \frac{2}{\gamma - 1}$

Substituting in Eq. (ii), we get the expression of Eq. (i).

Note *Since both gases have same value of γ (= 1.4). So, γ of the mixture is also 1.4. If values of γ are different, then we apply the above method.*

42. $pV = nRT = \frac{N}{N_A}RT$

Here, N = number of molecules

and N_A = Avogadro number

$1 \text{ atm} \approx 1.03 \times 10^5 \text{ N/m}^2$

$\therefore \quad N = \frac{pVN_A}{RT}$

Here, $V = 1 \text{ cm}^3 = 10^{-6} \text{ m}^3$ and $T = 300 \text{ K}$

Substituting the values, we get

$$N = \frac{(4 \times 10^{-15})(1.03 \times 10^5)(10^{-6})(6.02 \times 10^{23})}{8.314 \times 300}$$

$$= 10^5$$

$\therefore \quad N = 10^5$ per cm^3

Now, 1 cm^3 volume have 10^5 molecules. So, volume occupied by 1 molecule is 10^{-5} cm^3. So, this volume is like a cube of side say a. Then,

$$a^3 = 10^{-5} \text{ cm}^3$$

Solving this equation, we get

$$a \approx 0.2 \text{ mm}$$

43. $\frac{v}{v_{rms}} = \frac{\sqrt{\frac{\gamma RT}{M}}}{\sqrt{\frac{3RT}{M}}} = \sqrt{\frac{\gamma}{3}}$

(a) For monoatomic gas, $\gamma = \frac{5}{3}$

$$\therefore \quad \frac{v}{v_{rms}} = \frac{\sqrt{5}}{3} \approx 0.75$$

(b) For diatomic gas, $\gamma = \frac{7}{5}$

$$\therefore \quad \frac{v}{v_{rms}} = \sqrt{\frac{7}{15}} \approx 0.68$$

44. $v_{rms} = \sqrt{\frac{3RT}{M}} = \sqrt{\frac{3 \times 8.314 \times 290}{32 \times 10^{-3}}} = 475 \text{ m/s}$

or $\quad v_{rms} \approx 0.47 \text{ km/s}$

Note *Mean translational kinetic energy is a better word.*

Mean translational kinetic energy of any gas molecule

$$= \frac{3}{2}kT \qquad (k = \text{Boltzmann's constant})$$

$$= \frac{3}{2} \times (1.38 \times 10^{-23})(290) = 6.0 \times 10^{-21} \text{ J}$$

45. $v_{mp} = \sqrt{\frac{2p}{\rho}}$ = most probable speed

$v_{mean} = \sqrt{\frac{8p}{\pi\rho}}$ = mean or average speed and

$v_{rms} = \sqrt{\frac{3p}{\rho}}$ = root mean square velocity

Substituting $p = 1.03 \times 10^5 \text{ N/m}^2$ and $\rho = 1.00$ g/L $= 1.00 \text{ kg/m}^3$ in the above expressions, we can find the respective values.

46. Given $v_{rms} - v_{mp} = 400 \text{ m/s}$

$$\Rightarrow \quad \sqrt{\frac{3RT}{M}} - \sqrt{\frac{2RT}{M}} = 400$$

Substituting $R = 8.314$ J/mol-K

and $\quad M = 2 \text{ g/mol} = 2 \times 10^{-3}$ kg/mol, we get

$$T \approx 380 \text{ K}$$

47. Given $(v_{mp})_{N_2} - (v_{mp})_{O_2} = 30 \text{ m/s}$

$$\therefore \quad \sqrt{\frac{2RT}{M_{N_2}}} - \sqrt{\frac{2RT}{M_{O_2}}} = 30 \text{ m/s}$$

Substituting $R = 8.314$ J/mol-K,

$M_{N_2} = 28$ g/mol

$= 28 \times 10^{-3}$ kg/mol,

$M_{O_2} = 32$ g/mol

$= 32 \times 10^{-3}$ kg/mol, we get

$$T \approx 0.37 \text{ K}$$

Level 2

48. $(n_1 + n_2)_i = (n_1 + n_2)_f$

$$\therefore \quad \frac{p_1V_1}{RT_1} + \frac{p_2V_2}{RT_2} = \frac{p(V_1 + V_2)}{RT}$$

Solving, we get

$$T = \frac{T_1T_2p(V_1 + V_2)}{p_1V_1T_2 + p_2V_2T_1}$$

49. $\Delta l = l\alpha\Delta\theta$

$$\therefore \quad \alpha = \frac{\Delta l}{l\,\Delta\theta} = \frac{0.008}{(10)(100)}$$

$$= 8 \times 10^{-6} \text{ per °C}$$

$$\gamma = 3\alpha = 2.4 \times 10^{-5} \text{ per°C}$$

$$\Delta V = V\gamma\,\Delta\theta$$

$$= (100)(2.4 \times 10^{-5})(100)$$

$$= 0.24 \text{ cc}$$

$$\therefore \quad V' = V + \Delta V$$

$$= 100.24 \text{ cc}$$

50. $T = mV + C$

$$\therefore \quad \frac{pV}{nR} = mV + C$$

or $$p = nR\left(m + \frac{C}{V}\right)$$

$\therefore$ p-V graph is as shown in graph (a).

51. $p = \dfrac{a}{1+\left(\dfrac{V}{b}\right)^2} = \dfrac{RT}{V}$

When $V = b$,

$$\frac{a}{1+(1)^2} = \frac{RT}{b}$$

$$\Rightarrow \quad T = \frac{ab}{2R}$$

52. $n = \dfrac{pV}{RT}$

$$\therefore \quad n \propto \frac{1}{T} \text{ or } m \propto \frac{1}{T}$$

$$\frac{m_1}{m_2} = \frac{T_2}{T_1} = \frac{273+37}{273+7}$$

$$= \frac{310}{280} = 1.1$$

53. $v_{av} = \sqrt{\dfrac{8RT}{\pi M}}$

T and M are same. Hence, average speed of O_2 molecules in both vessels will remain same or v_1.

54. $n = \dfrac{pV}{RT}$

$$\therefore \ N = nN_A = \frac{pVN_A}{RT}$$

$$= \frac{(1.013 \times 10^5 \times 10^{-13})(10^{-6})(6.02 \times 10^{23})}{(8.31)(300)}$$

$$= 2.4 \times 10^6$$

55. $v_{rms} = \sqrt{\dfrac{3RT}{M}} = \sqrt{\dfrac{3 \times 8.31 \times 273}{28 \times 10^{-3}}}$

$$= 493 \text{ m/s}$$

Now, increase in gravitation PE

= decrease in kinetic energy

$$\therefore \quad \frac{(mgh)}{1+\dfrac{h}{R}} = \frac{1}{2} m v_{rms}^2$$

or $$\frac{2gh}{1+(h/R)} = v_{rms}^2$$

or $$\frac{2 \times 9.81 \times h}{1+(h/6400 \times 10^3)} = (493)^2$$

Solving this equation, we get

$$h \approx 12000 \text{ m} \quad \text{or} \quad 12 \text{ km}$$

56. $U \propto T$

According to given graph,

$$p \propto U$$

$$\therefore \quad p \propto T$$

Hence, $V =$ constant

57. 28 g of N_2 mean 1 g-mol.

Now, $n = \dfrac{pV}{RT}$ or $n \propto \dfrac{p}{T}$

$$\frac{n_f}{n_i} = \left(\frac{p_f}{p_i}\right)\left(\frac{T_i}{T_f}\right) = \left(\frac{1}{2}\right)\left(\frac{273+57}{273+27}\right)$$

$$= \frac{11}{20}$$

or $$n_f = \left(\frac{11}{20}\right) n_i = \frac{11}{20} \text{ mol}$$

$$\Delta n = n_i - n_f = 1 - \frac{11}{20} = \frac{9}{20} \text{ g-mol}$$

$$\Delta m = \frac{9}{20} \times 28 \text{ g}$$

$$= \frac{63}{5} \text{ g}$$

58. 4g H_2 means 2 g-moles and 8g means 2 g-moles.

Now, $M = \dfrac{n_1 M_1 + n_2 M_2}{n_1 + n_2}$

$$= \frac{(2)(2)+(2)(4)}{2+2} = 3 \text{ g/mol}$$

$$\rho = \frac{PM}{RT} = \frac{(1.013 \times 10^5)(3 \times 10^{-3})}{(8.31)(273)}$$

$$= 0.13 \text{ kg/m}^3$$

59. $\rho = \dfrac{1}{V}$

Given, $p \propto K\rho$

$$\therefore \quad p \propto \frac{1}{V}$$

or $pV =$ constant

$\therefore$ $T =$ constant

60. $F = \dfrac{\Delta p}{\Delta t} = (nm)(2v \cos\theta)$

Pressure, $p = \dfrac{F}{A} = \dfrac{(nm)(2v\cos\theta)}{A}$

$$= \frac{10^{23} \times 3.32 \times 10^{-27} \times 2 \times 1000 \times \cos 45°}{2 \times 10^{-4}}$$

$$= 2.34 \times 10^3 \text{ Pa}$$

61. Volume of the gas is constant. So, $V =$ constant

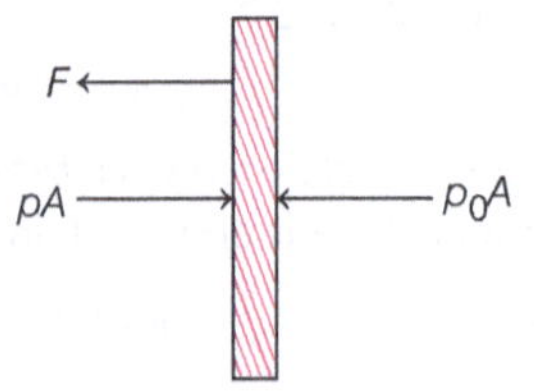

$\therefore$ $p \propto T$ i.e. pressure will be doubled, if temperature is doubled.

$$\therefore \quad p = 2p_0$$

Now, let F be the tension in the wire. Then equilibrium of any one piston gives

$$F = (p - p_0)A$$

$$= (2p_0 - p_0)A = p_0 A$$

62. $(p_2 - p_1)A = mg$

or $$\frac{mg}{A} = \frac{RT_i}{V_1} - \frac{RT_i}{4V_1} = \frac{3RT_i}{4V_1} \quad \text{...(i)}$$

Similarly, in second case

$$\frac{mg}{A} = \frac{RT_f}{V_2} - \frac{RT_f}{3V_2} = \frac{2RT_f}{3V_2} \quad \text{...(ii)}$$

Further $5V_1 = 4V_2$

Equating Eqs. (i) and (ii), we get

$$\frac{3T_i}{4V_1} = \frac{2T_f}{3V_2}$$

or $$T_f = \frac{9}{8} \times \frac{V_2}{V_1} \times T_i = \frac{9}{8} \times \frac{5}{4} \times 320$$

$$= 450\,\text{K}$$

63. Process 1-2 V = constant, $p \propto T$

T is increasing. Therefore, pressure will increase.

Process 2-3 p = constant, $V \propto T$

V and T both are increasing.

Process 3-4 T = constant, $p \propto \frac{1}{V}$

V is increasing. Therefore, p will decrease.

Process 4-1 Inverse of process 2-3.

64. ***AB*** Isobaric process. Both volume and temperature are increasing.

BC Isothermal process. Volume is increasing so pressure should decrease. (T = constant, $p \propto \frac{1}{V}$)

CD Isochoric process. Pressure and temperature both are decreasing. (V = constant, $p \propto T$)

DA Again isothermal process. Volume is decreasing so pressure should decrease (T = constant, $p \propto \frac{1}{V}$)

65. $U \propto \frac{1}{\rho}$ or $T \propto \frac{1}{(1/V)} \Rightarrow T \propto V$

Hence, p = constant

Further ρ is increasing. Therefore, V should decrease.

66. 1.0 cc of water = 1 g of water

$$= \frac{1}{18} \text{ g-moles of water}$$

$$\therefore \quad N = \frac{1}{18} \times 6.02 \times 10^{23}$$

$$\approx \frac{10^{23}}{3}$$

67. $$pV = nRT = \left(\frac{n_1}{N}\right)RT \qquad (n_1 = \text{number of molecules})$$

$$= n_1 kt \qquad \left(\because \frac{R}{N} = k\right)$$

$$\therefore \quad \frac{n_1}{V} = \frac{p}{kT}$$

68. $$(n_1 + n_2)_i = (n_1 + n_2)_f$$

$$\frac{p_0V}{RT_0} + \frac{p_0V}{RT_0} = \frac{pV}{RT_0} + \frac{pV}{2RT_0}$$

$$\therefore \quad p = \frac{4}{3}p_0$$

69. Change in weight = Upthrust (F)

where, $$F = V_s \rho_l g$$

$$F' = V_s' \rho_l' g$$

$$\frac{F'}{F} = \frac{V'_s}{V_s} \cdot \frac{\rho'_l}{\rho_l}$$

or $$\frac{F'}{F} = (1 + \gamma_s \Delta\theta)\frac{\rho'_l}{\rho_l}$$

$$\left(\frac{46 - 30.5}{46 - 30}\right) = (1 + 3 \times \alpha_s \times 15)\left(\frac{1.20}{1.24}\right)$$

or $$\alpha_s = 2.3 \times 10^{-5}/^\circ\text{C}$$

70. $$pV = \frac{1}{3}Nm\,v_{av}^2$$

$$= \frac{1}{3} \times 20 \times m \times \frac{(2 \times v^2 + 3 \times (2v)^2 + \cdots)}{2 + 3 + 5 + 4 + 3 + 2 + 1}$$

$$= \frac{319}{3}mv^2$$

71. $$(OR)^2 = (PR)^2 - (PO)^2 = l^2 - \left(\frac{l}{2}\right)^2$$

$$= [l(1 + \alpha_2 t)]^2 - \left[\frac{l}{2}(1 + \alpha_1 t)\right]^2$$

$$l^2 - \frac{l^2}{4} = l^2(1 + \alpha_2^2 t^2 + 2\alpha_2 t) - \frac{l^2}{4}(1 + \alpha_1^2 t^2 + 2\alpha_1 t)$$

Neglecting $\alpha_2^2 t^2$ and $\alpha_1^2 t^2$

$$0 = l^2(2\alpha_2 t) - \frac{l^2}{4}(2\alpha_1 t)$$

$$\Rightarrow \quad 2\alpha_2 = \frac{2\alpha_1}{4}$$

$$\Rightarrow \quad \alpha_1 = 4\alpha_2$$

72. $$Y_{\text{Red}} = Y_{\text{app}} + Y_{\text{container}}$$

or $$Y_R = Y_a + 3\alpha$$

$$Y_R = X + 3\alpha = Y_R = Y + 3\alpha$$

Equating two equations, we get

$$X + 3\alpha = Y + 3\alpha$$

$$\alpha = \frac{X + 3\alpha - Y}{3}$$

73. According to question, first gas goes from volume V to $3V$ and after this volume is reduced from $3V$ to V at constant pressure.

In isothermal expansion, p-V curve is rectangular hyperbola.

74. From ideal gas equation,

$$pV = RT$$

or $$p\Delta V = R\Delta T$$

$$\Rightarrow \quad \frac{\Delta V}{V} = \frac{\Delta T}{T}$$

$$\Rightarrow \quad \frac{\Delta V}{V\Delta T} = \frac{1}{T} = \delta$$

$$\therefore \quad \delta = \frac{1}{T}$$

So, the graph between δ and T will be rectangular graph.

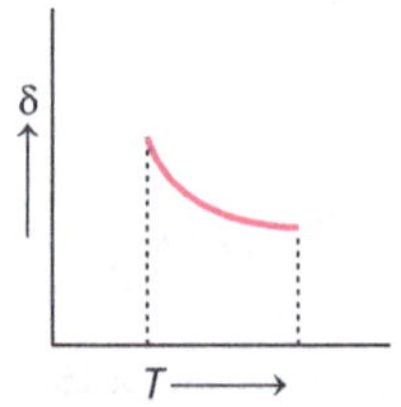

75. For open mouth vessel, pressure is constant.

Volume is also given constant.

Hence, from $\quad pV = \mu RT = \left(\frac{m}{M}\right)RT$

$$\Rightarrow \quad T \propto \frac{1}{m}$$

$$\Rightarrow \quad \frac{T_1}{T_2} = \frac{m_2}{m_1}$$

$\therefore$ $\frac{1}{4}$th part escapes, so remaining mass in the vessel

$$m_2 = \frac{3}{4}m_1 \Rightarrow \frac{(273+60)}{T} = \frac{\left(\frac{3}{4}\right)m_1}{m_1}$$

$$\Rightarrow \quad T = 444\,\text{K} = 171°\text{C}$$

76. $$c = \sqrt{\frac{3p}{\rho}}$$

$$\Rightarrow \quad p = \frac{1}{3}\rho c^2$$

Motion of vessel will not contribute in pressure.

77. $$p = \frac{1}{3}\frac{m_0 n_0}{V} v_{rms}^2$$

m_0 = mass of one gas molecule and

n_0 = total number of molecules.

$\therefore \quad m_0 n_0$ = total mass of gas = m

and $$v_{rms}^2 = 3 < v_r^2 >$$

$$\therefore \quad p = \frac{1}{3}\frac{m}{V}[3 < v_r^2 >]$$

$$\therefore \quad < v_x^2 > = \frac{pV}{m} = \frac{nRT}{m}$$

$$n = \frac{m}{M}$$

$$\Rightarrow \quad \frac{n}{m} = \frac{1}{M}$$

Hence, $$< v_x^2 > = \frac{RT}{M}$$

78. $\rho = \frac{pM}{RT} \quad \Rightarrow \quad \rho \propto pM$

or $$\frac{\rho_1}{\rho_2} = \left(\frac{p_1}{p_2}\right)\left(\frac{M_1}{M_2}\right)$$

$$= \left(\frac{2}{3}\right)\left(\frac{4}{3}\right) = \frac{8}{9}$$

79. Process is isothermal. Therefore, T = constant. $\left(p \propto \frac{1}{V}\right)$ volume is increasing, therefore pressure will decrease.

In chamber A

$$-\Delta p = (p_A)_i - (p_A)_f = \frac{n_A RT}{V} - \frac{n_A RT}{2V} = \frac{n_A RT}{2V} \quad \text{...(i)}$$

In chamber B

$$-1.5\,\Delta p = (p_B)_i - (p_B)_f = \frac{n_B RT}{V} - \frac{n_B RT}{2V}$$

$$= \frac{n_B RT}{2V} \quad \text{...(ii)}$$

From Eqs. (i) and (ii), we get

$$\frac{n_A}{n_B} = \frac{1}{1.5} = \frac{2}{3} \quad \text{or} \quad \frac{m_A/M}{m_B/M} = \frac{2}{3}$$

or $$\frac{m_A}{m_B} = \frac{2}{3} \quad \text{or} \quad 3m_A = 2m_B$$

80. Average kinetic energy per molecule per degree of freedom $= \frac{1}{2}kT$. Since, both the gases are diatomic and at same temperature (300 K), both will have the same number of rotational degree of freedom, i.e. two. Therefore, both the gases will have the same average rotational kinetic energy per molecule

$$= 2 \times \frac{1}{2}kT \quad \text{or} \quad kT$$

$\Rightarrow$ Thus, ratio will be 1: 1.

81. $I = \frac{1}{12}Ml^2$

So, $$I' = \frac{1}{12}M(l + \Delta l)^2$$

$$\Rightarrow \quad I' = \frac{1}{12}(Ml^2 + 2Ml\,\Delta l + M(\Delta l)^2\alpha)$$

$$I' \approx I + \frac{1}{12}Ml^2 2\alpha\Delta T$$

$$\therefore \quad I' - I = 2\alpha I\Delta T$$

82. Let us denote molar heat capacity S and specific heat by C. Then,

$$S = \frac{Q}{n\Delta T} = \frac{Q}{\left(\frac{m}{M}\right)\Delta T} = \left(\frac{Q}{m\Delta T}\right)M = CM$$

Now, for hydrogen

$$S_p - S_V = R = (C_p - C_V)_{H_2} M_{H_2}$$

$$S_p - S_V = R = (a)(2) \quad \text{...(i)}$$

Similarly for N_2,

$$S_p - S_V = R = (b)(28) \quad \text{...(ii)}$$

From Eqs. (i) and (ii),

$$a = 14b$$

83. $pT^3 = \text{constant}$

$$\frac{nRT}{V} \cdot T^3 = \text{constant} \Rightarrow T^4V^{-1} = \text{constant}$$

$$\Rightarrow 4T^3V^{-1} - T^4 \cdot V^{-2}\frac{dV}{dT} = 0$$

$$\Rightarrow \frac{4T^3}{V} = \frac{T^4}{V^2} \cdot \frac{dV}{dT} \Rightarrow \frac{4}{T} = \frac{dV}{V \cdot dT}$$

So, $\gamma = \frac{dV}{V \cdot dT}$ = volumetric expansion coefficient of gas

$= \frac{4}{T}$.

84. As, $\gamma_{Hg} > \gamma_{Fe}$, density of mercury decreases more on heating, so iron cube will sink more on heating.

Also, fraction of volume submerged $= \frac{V_{out}}{V_{cube}}$

Fractional change on heating is given by

$$\frac{(V_0/V_c)_{25°C} - (V_0/V_c)_{0°C}}{(V_0/V_c)_{0°C}} = \frac{(1 + 180 \times 10^{-6}) \times 25}{(1 + 35 \times 10^{-6}) \times 25} - 1$$

$$= 3.6 \times 10^{-3}$$

$\therefore$ % change = 0.36% ≈ 0.40%

85. (a) $p = \frac{nRT}{V} = \frac{(m/V)RT}{M}$

So, given m in the question is mass of gas per unit volume.

(b) m = total mass of gas

(c) m = mass of one molecule of gas.

86. For monoatomic gas,

$$C_p = \frac{5}{2}R \text{ and } C_V = \frac{3}{2}R$$

For diatomic gas,

$$C_p = \frac{7}{2}R \text{ and } C_V = \frac{5}{2}R$$

87. For one mole of an ideal gas

$$pV = RT$$

The coefficient of volume expansion at constant pressure is given by,

$$\left(\frac{\Delta V}{\Delta T}\right)_p = \frac{R}{p} = \text{constant} \quad \text{[option (a)]}$$

The average translational kinetic energy per molecule is $(3/2)kT$ and not $3\,kT$. With decrease of pressure, volume of the gas increases so its mean free path also increases. The average translational kinetic energy of the molecules is independent of their nature, so each component of the gaseous mixture will have the same value of average translational kinetic energy.

88. Let A = cross-sectional area of tube.

Let pressure initially on each side of tube is atmospheric.

When tube is held in vertical position,

let x = displacement of mercury column.

Then, pV = constant is applied to top part and bottom part.

$$p \times 45 \times A = p_1(45 - x)A$$

and

$$p \times 45 \times A = p_2(45 + x)A$$

$$p_1 = \frac{45}{45 - x} \cdot p, \; p_2 = \frac{45}{45 + x} \cdot p$$

Also, $p_1 - p_2 = 10$ cm of mercury column

$$\Rightarrow \left(\frac{45}{45 - x}\right)p - \left(\frac{45}{45 + x}\right)p = 10$$

where, $p = 76$ cm of mercury column

$$\therefore \quad x = 2.95 \text{ cm} \approx 3 \text{ cm}$$

89.

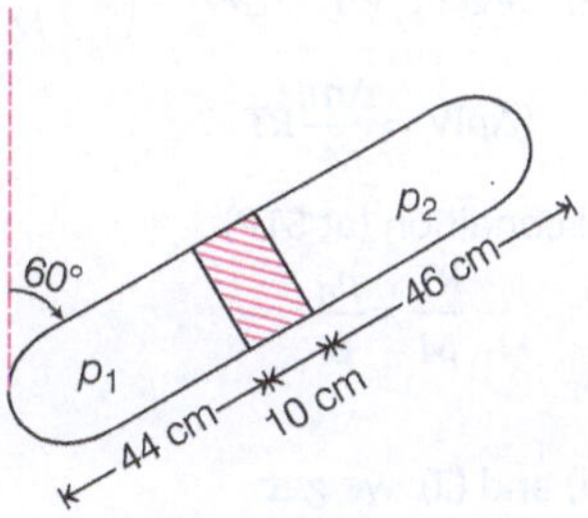

$p_1 - p_2$ = pressure due to 10 cm slanted mercury column

$$= 10\cos 60° = \frac{10}{2} = 5 \text{ cm of mercury column}$$

pV = constant for each side of tube

$$\therefore \quad p \times 45 \times A = p_1 \times 44 \times A$$

and

$$p \times 45 \times A = p_2 \times 46 \times A$$

$$p_1 = \frac{45p}{44}, \; p_2 = \frac{45p}{46}$$

$$p_1 - p_2 = \frac{45p}{44} - \frac{45p}{46} = 5 \text{ cm of Hg column}$$

$$\Rightarrow \quad p = 112.4 \text{ cm of Hg column}$$

90. $pV = nRT$

$$pdV = nRdT$$

$$\frac{dV}{dT} = \frac{nR}{p}, \; dV = V\gamma dT$$

$$\therefore \quad \gamma = \frac{dV/dT}{V} = \frac{nR}{pV} = \frac{1}{T}$$

91. In the process $pV^x =$ constant $C = \frac{R}{\gamma - 1} + \frac{R}{1-x}$

Given, $C = R$ and $\gamma = 7/5$

Substituting these values, we get $x = \frac{5}{3}$

Now, $pV^{5/3} =$ constant or $p \propto \frac{1}{(V)^{5/3}}$

By increasing volume to two times pressure will decrease $(2)^{5/3}$ times.

$$v_{rms} \propto \sqrt{T} \quad \text{or} \quad v_{rms} \propto \sqrt{pV}$$

or v_{rms} will become $\sqrt{\frac{(2)}{(2)^{5/3}}}$ times

or v_{rms} will become $(2)^{-1/3}$ times

or $\frac{1}{(2)^{1/3}}$ times.

Now, $p \propto$ (number of collisions) (v_{rms})

$$\frac{1}{(2)^{5/3}} \propto \text{(number. of collisions)} \frac{1}{(2)^{1/3}}$$

or number of collisions will decrease $(2)^{4/3}$ times. **Ans.**

92. $p_1 V = n_1 RT$

$$p_2 V = n_2 RT \qquad (T = 273\,\text{K})$$

$$\therefore \quad (p_1 - p_2)V = (n_1 - n_2)RT = \left(\frac{m_1 - m_2}{M}\right)RT$$

$$(\Delta p)V = \frac{\Delta m}{M} RT \qquad \text{...(i)}$$

In the initial condition (at STP)

$$\frac{RT}{M} = \frac{p_0}{\rho} \qquad \text{...(ii)}$$

$$(T = 273\,\text{K})$$

From Eqs. (i) and (ii), we get

$$\Delta m = \frac{\rho V \Delta p}{p_0} = \frac{1.2 \times 0.4 \times 0.24}{1.0}$$

$$= 0.1152\ \text{kg} = 115.2\ \text{g}$$ **Ans.**

93. $p_2 =$ pressure at depth x

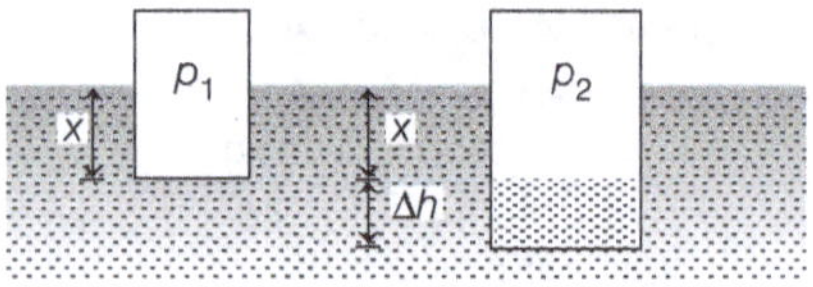

$$p_1 V_1 = p_2 V_2$$

or $$p_1 (Ah) = p_2 (A)(h - \Delta h)$$

$$\therefore \quad p_1 = \frac{p_2 (h - \Delta h)}{h} \qquad \text{...(i)}$$

Initially, $$mg = \rho g x A$$

Now, $$p_2 = p_0 + \rho g x = p_0 + \frac{mg}{A}$$

Substituting in Eq. (i), we have

$$p_1 = \left(p_0 + \frac{mg}{A}\right)\left(1 - \frac{\Delta h}{h}\right)$$ **Ans.**

94. $p = \frac{RT}{V} \qquad (n = 1)$

or $$p = \frac{R}{V}(T_0 + \alpha V^2) \qquad \text{...(i)}$$

For minimum attainable pressure

$$\frac{dp}{dV} = 0$$

or $$\frac{-RT_0}{V^2} + \alpha R = 0$$

or $$V = \sqrt{\frac{T_0}{\alpha}}$$

At this volume we can see that $\frac{d^2 p}{dV^2}$ is positive or p is minimum.

From Eq. (i)

$$p_{min} = \frac{RT_0}{\sqrt{T_0/\alpha}} + \alpha R \sqrt{T_0/\alpha}$$

$$= 2R\sqrt{\alpha T_0}$$ **Ans.**

95. At 50°C, density of solid = density of liquid.

At 0°C, fraction submerged $\left(\frac{\rho_s}{\rho_l}\right)_{0°C} \times 100 \qquad \text{...(i)}$

$$(\rho)_{50} = \frac{\rho_0}{1 + 50\gamma}$$

$$\therefore \quad \rho_0 = \rho_{50}(1 + 50\gamma)$$

Substituting in Eq. (i), we have

% of fraction submerged

$$= \left(\frac{1 + 50\gamma_s}{1 + 50\gamma_l}\right) \times 100 = \left(\frac{1 + 15 \times 10^{-5}}{1 + 400 \times 10^{-5}}\right) \times 100$$

$$= 99.61\ \%$$ **Ans.**

96. Equating pressure at the bottom of the vessel,

$$\rho_{100} g h_{100} = \rho_0 g h_0$$

or $$\frac{\rho_{100}}{\rho_0} = \frac{h_0}{h_{100}}$$

$$\left(\frac{1}{1 + 100\gamma}\right) = \frac{39.2}{40}$$

Solving this equation, we get

$$\gamma = 2.0 \times 10^{-4} \text{ per °C}$$

97. Let Δl be the change in length. (let $\Delta l_s > \Delta l > \Delta l_a$)

$$\text{Strain in steel} = \frac{\Delta l_s - \Delta l}{l_0}$$

and $$\text{strain in aluminium} = \frac{\Delta l - \Delta l_a}{l_0}$$

In equilibrium, $2F_s = F_a$

$$2\left[\frac{\Delta l_s - \Delta l}{l_0}\right] Y_s A = \left[\frac{\Delta l - \Delta l_a}{l_0}\right] Y_a A$$

or $$2\,(l_0 \alpha_s \theta - \Delta l)\, Y_s = (\Delta l - l_0 \alpha_a \theta) Ya$$

Solving this equation, we get

$$\Delta l = \left(\frac{2\alpha_s Y_s + \alpha_a Y_a}{2Ys + Y_a}\right) l_0 \theta$$

$\therefore$ Total length

$$= l_0 + \Delta l = l_0 \left[1 + \left(\frac{\alpha_a Y_a + 2\alpha_s Y_s}{2Y_s + Y_a}\right)\theta\right] \qquad \textbf{Ans.}$$

98. From $\Delta l = l\alpha\Delta\theta$, we have

$$0.05 = 25\,\alpha_A (100)$$

$$\therefore \quad \alpha_A = 0.00002 \text{ per}^\circ\text{C}$$

$$0.04 = 40\,\alpha_B (100)$$

$$\therefore \quad \alpha_B = 0.00001 \text{ per}^\circ\text{C}$$

In third case let l is the length of rod A. Then, length of rod B will be $(50 - l)$ cm.

$$\Delta l = \Delta l_1 + \Delta l_2$$

or $\quad 0.03 = l(0.00002)(50) + (50 - l)(0.00001)(50)$

Solving, we get

$$l = 10 \text{ cm and } 50 - l = 40 \text{ cm} \qquad \textbf{Ans.}$$

99. Given, temperature of the mixture,

$$T = 27^\circ\text{C} = 300\text{ K}$$

Let m be the mass of the neon gas in the mixture. Then, mass of argon would be $(28 - m)$.

Number of gram moles of neon, $n_1 = \dfrac{m}{20}$

Number of gram moles of argon,

$$n_2 = \frac{(28 - m)}{40}$$

From Dalton's law of partial pressures;

Total pressure of the mixture (p)

= Pressure due to neon (p_1) + Pressure due to argon (p_2)

or $\quad p = p_1 + p_2 = \dfrac{n_1 RT}{V} + \dfrac{n_2 RT}{V} = (n_1 + n_2)\dfrac{RT}{V}$

Substituting the values, we get

$$1.0 \times 10^5 = \left(\frac{m}{20} + \frac{28 - m}{40}\right)\frac{(8.314)(300)}{0.02}$$

Solving this equation, we get

$$28 - m = 23.926 \text{ g}$$

$$\Rightarrow \quad m = 4.074 \text{ g}$$

Therefore, in the mixture, 4.074 g neon is present and the rest i.e. 23.926 g argon is present.

100. $\rho = \dfrac{p_0 M}{RT_0}$

$$\Rightarrow \quad M = \frac{\rho R T_0}{p_0} \qquad \text{...(i)}$$

$$pV = nRT = \frac{m}{M} RT$$

$$\Rightarrow \quad m = \frac{pVM}{RT}$$

Substituting value of M from Eq. (i), we get

$$m = \left(\frac{pV}{RT}\right)\left(\frac{\rho R T_0}{p_0}\right) = \left(\frac{\rho T_0 V}{T p_0}\right) p$$

Here, $\dfrac{\rho T_0 V}{T p_0}$ is a constant

$$\therefore \quad \Delta m = \left(\frac{\rho T_0 V}{T p_0}\right)\Delta p \qquad \text{...(ii)}$$

Further, $T_0 = 273\,\text{K}$,

$$\Delta p = 0.78 \text{ atm}$$

and $\quad p_0 = 1 \text{ atm}$

Substituting in Eq. (ii), we get

$$\Delta m = \frac{(1.3) \times (273)(30) \times (0.78)}{(273)(1)} = 30.42 \text{ g}$$

$$\therefore \quad \Delta m \approx 30 \text{ g}$$

101. Initially gas was present only in second container. So,

$$n_i = \frac{p_1 V}{RT_1} \qquad \text{...(i)}$$

Let final pressure in the first container (which had initially vacuum) is p. Then final pressure in the second container will be,

$$p_2 = p + \Delta p$$

Total number of moles after heating the containers,

$$n_f = n_1 + n_2 = \frac{(p + \Delta p)V}{RT_2} + \frac{pV}{RT_2} \qquad \text{...(ii)}$$

Equating Eqs. (i) and (ii) and then simplifying the equation, we get

$$p = \frac{1}{2}\left[\frac{p_1 T_2}{T_1} - \Delta p\right]$$

$$= \frac{1}{2}\left[\frac{1.0 \times 380}{300} - 1.10\right]$$

or $\quad p = 0.08$ atm

or $\quad p \approx 0.10$ atm

102. Let $m_{H_2} = m_1$ and $m_{He} = m_2$

Then, $\quad n_{H_2} = \dfrac{m_1}{2} = n_1$

and $\quad n_{He} = \dfrac{m_2}{4} = n_2$

$$m_1 + m_2 = m \qquad \text{...(i)}$$

$$pV = (n_1 + n_2)RT$$

$$\Rightarrow \quad n_1 + n_2 = \frac{pV}{RT}$$

or $\quad \dfrac{m_1}{2} + \dfrac{m_2}{4} = \dfrac{pV}{RT}$

or $\quad 2m_1 + m_2 = \dfrac{4pV}{RT} \qquad \text{...(ii)}$

On dividing Eq. (ii) by Eq. (i), we get

$$\frac{2m_1 + m_2}{m_1 + m_2} = \frac{4pV}{mRT}$$

or $$\frac{2(m_1/m_2)+1}{(m_1/m_2)+1}=\frac{4pV}{mRT}$$

Substituting the values of p, V, m, R and T in proper SI units, we get

$$\frac{m_1}{m_2}=0.50$$

103.

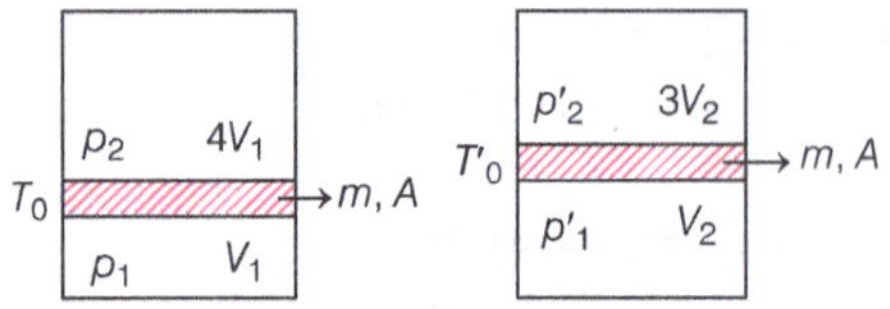

$$5V_1=4V_2$$

or $$\frac{V_2}{V_1}=\frac{5}{4} \quad \text{...(i)}$$

Equilibrium of piston in two cases gives the equation,

$$mg=(p_1-p_2)A=(p_1'-p_2')A$$

or $$p_1-p_2=p_1'-p_2'$$

$\therefore$ $$\frac{RT_0}{V_1}-\frac{RT_0}{4V_1}=\frac{RT_0'}{V_2}-\frac{RT_0'}{3V_2} \quad (\text{as } n=1)$$

or $$\frac{3T_0}{4V_1}=\frac{2T_0'}{3V_2}$$

$\therefore$ $$T_0'=\left(\frac{9}{8}\right)\left(\frac{V_2}{V_1}\right)T_0$$

$$=\frac{9}{8}\times\frac{5}{4}\times 300=421.87\text{ K}$$

$\therefore$ $$T_0'\approx 421\text{ K}$$

104. Process is isothermal, so

$$p_1V_1=p_2V_2$$

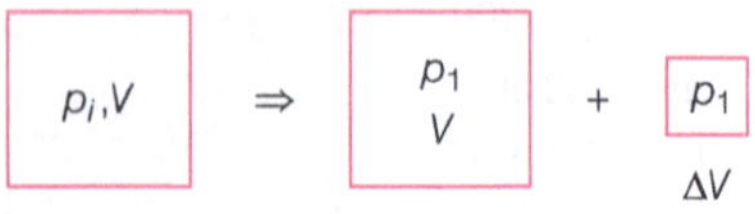

After first stroke let pressure is p_1 and initial pressure is p_i. Then,

$$p_iV=p_1(V+\Delta V) \quad \text{or} \quad p_1=p_i\left(\frac{V}{V+\Delta V}\right)$$

After second stroke let pressure is p_2. Then,

$$p_1V=p_2(V+\Delta V)$$

$\Rightarrow$ $$p_2=p_1\left(\frac{V}{V+\Delta V}\right)$$

$$=p_i\left(\frac{V}{V+\Delta V}\right)^2$$

and so on. Therefore pressure after n^{th} stroke pressure will be,

$$p_n=p_i\left(\frac{V}{V+\Delta V}\right)^n \quad \text{...(i)}$$

Given, $p_n=\dfrac{p_i}{\eta}$

Substituting in Eq. (i), we have

$$\frac{1}{\eta}=\left(\frac{V}{V+\Delta V}\right)^n \quad \text{or} \quad \eta=\left(\frac{V+\Delta V}{V}\right)^n$$

Taking log both sides, we get

$$\ln\eta=n\ln\left(\frac{V+\Delta V}{V}\right)$$

$$n=\frac{\ln\eta}{\ln(1+\Delta V/V)}$$

105. Applying $p_1V_1=p_2V_2$, we have

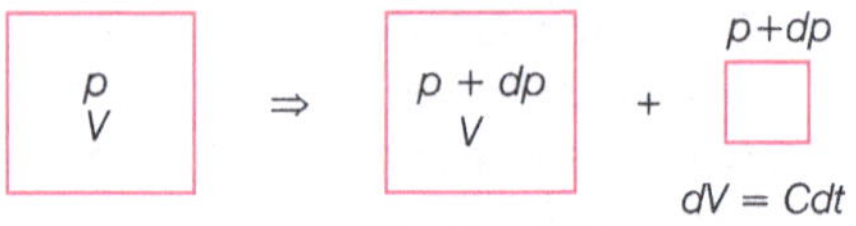

After time 'dt'

After time dt,

$$pV=(p+dp)(V+Cdt)$$
$$=pV+pCdt+Vdp+C(dt)(dp)$$

Neglecting the term $C(dt)(dp)$, we have

$$-\frac{dp}{p}=\frac{C}{V}dt \quad \text{...(i)}$$

or $$\frac{C}{V}\int_0^t dt=-\int_{p_0}^{p}\frac{dp}{p}$$

Solving this equation, we get

$$p=p_0e^{-\frac{C}{V}t}$$

Note *Negative sign in Eq. (i) implies that we are increasing volume, so pressure will decrease with time.*

106. According to previous problem,

$$p=p_0e^{-\frac{C}{V}t} \quad \text{...(i)}$$

In this problem, $V=87\text{ L}$

$C=10\text{ L/s}$

$p/p_0=\dfrac{1}{1000}$

Substituting in Eq. (i) and then solving by taking log, we get

$$t=60\text{ s} \quad \text{or} \quad 1\text{ min}$$

107. Area difference between two pistons is ΔS. Therefore net downward force due to p_0 is $p_0\Delta S$.

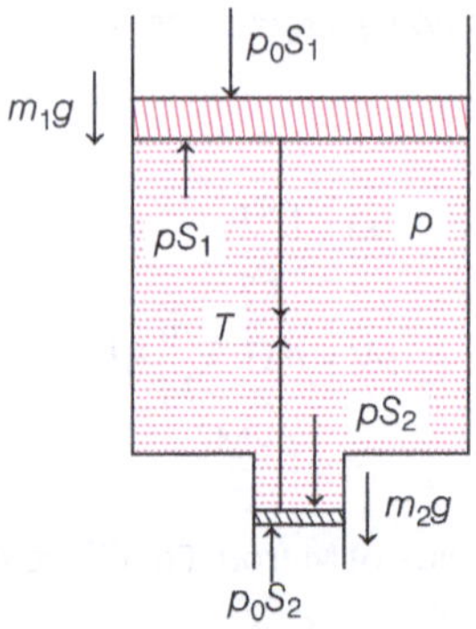

If pressure of gas is p, then net upward force due to p is $p\Delta S$. This difference of force should be equal to total weight.

or $$p\Delta S - p_0\Delta S = mg$$

or $$p = p_0 + \frac{mg}{\Delta S} = \text{constant} \quad \text{(in both conditions)}$$

Change in volume on heating,

$$\Delta V = l(\Delta S)$$

$p = p' \Rightarrow$ pressure is constant. Hence, for 1 mol,

$$pV = RT$$

or $$p\Delta V = R\Delta T$$

$\therefore$ $$\Delta T = \frac{p\Delta V}{R}$$

$$= \frac{\left(p_0 + \frac{mg}{\Delta S}\right)(l\Delta S)}{R}$$

$$\Delta T = (p_0\Delta S + mg)\frac{l}{R}$$

Substituting the values, we get

$$\Delta T = 0.9\text{ K}$$

108. (a) For one mole of gas,

$$T = \frac{pV}{R} = \frac{(p_0 - \alpha V^2)V}{R} \quad \text{...(i)}$$

For maximum temperature,

$$\frac{dT}{dV} = 0$$

or $$p_0 - 3\alpha V^2 = 0$$

or $$V = \sqrt{\frac{p_0}{3\alpha}}$$

At this volume, we can see that $\frac{d^2T}{dV^2}$ comes out to be negative. Therefore at $V = \sqrt{\frac{p_0}{3\alpha}}$, temperature is maximum.

Substituting this value of V in Eq. (i), we get

$$T_{max} = \frac{2}{3}\left(\frac{p_0}{R}\right)\sqrt{\frac{p_0}{3\alpha}}$$

(b) $p = p_0 e^{-\beta V}$

$$T = \frac{pV}{R} = \frac{p_0 V e^{-\beta V}}{R} \quad \text{...(ii)}$$

For maximum temperature,

$$\frac{dT}{dV} = 0$$

$\Rightarrow$ $$\frac{p_0}{R}[e^{-\beta V} - \beta V^2 e^{-\beta V}] = 0$$

or $$V = \frac{1}{\beta}$$

At this V, we can show that $\frac{d^2T}{dV^2}$ is negative. So, T is maximum. Substituting $V = \frac{1}{\beta}$ in Eq. (ii), we get

$$T_{max} = \frac{p_0}{e\beta R}$$

109.

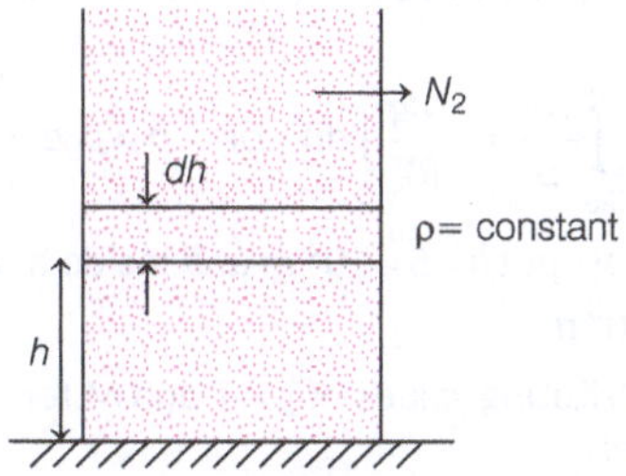

$$\rho = \frac{pM}{RT}$$

$\therefore$ $$pM = \rho RT$$

Only p and T are variables.

$\therefore$ $$M(dp) = \rho R dT \quad \text{...(i)}$$

In fluid mechanics, we know that,

$$\frac{dp}{dh} = -\rho g$$

$\therefore$ $$dp = -\rho g dh$$

Substituting in Eq. (i), we get

$$(-\rho g\, dh)M = \rho\, R dT$$

So, $$\frac{dT}{dh} = -\frac{Mg}{R}$$

Substituting the values of M (for N_2), g and R, we get

$$\frac{dT}{dh} = -0.033\text{ K/m}$$

110. $\frac{p}{\rho^n} = \alpha$ (say) ...(i)

$\therefore$ $$p = \alpha\rho^n$$

$\Rightarrow$ $$\rho = \left(\frac{p}{\alpha}\right)^{1/n} = \frac{pM}{RT}$$

$\therefore$ $$p^{1-\frac{1}{n}}\alpha^{\frac{1}{n}} = \frac{RT}{M}$$

Differentiating, we get

$$\left(1 - \frac{1}{n}\right)p^{-\frac{1}{n}}\alpha^{\frac{1}{n}}(dp) = \frac{R}{M}\cdot dT \quad \text{...(ii)}$$

$$\frac{dp}{dh} = -\rho g$$

or $$dp = -\rho g dh \quad \text{...(iii)}$$

Solving Eqs. (i), (ii) and (iii), we get

$$\frac{dT}{dh} = -\frac{(n-1)}{nR}Mg$$

Note *Students are advised to attempt Q-113 before this.*

111. $\rho = \dfrac{pM}{RT}$

$$\Rightarrow \qquad pM = \rho RT \qquad \text{...(i)}$$

$$\frac{dp}{dh} = -\rho g$$

$$\therefore \qquad \rho = -\frac{dp}{g\,(dh)}$$

Substituting this value in Eq. (i) and then simplifying, we get

$$\int_{p_0}^{p} \frac{dp}{p} = -\frac{Mg}{RT}\int_0^h dh \quad \text{or} \quad p = p_0 e^{-\frac{Mgh}{RT}}$$

For first part put $h = 5 \times 10^3$ m and inside a mine put $h = -5 \times 10^3$ m.

Then substituting values of p_0, T and M for air, we get the answer.

112. In the above question, we have obtained variation of p with height as,

$$p = p_0 e^{-\frac{Mgh}{RT}} \qquad \text{...(i)}$$

Now $\qquad \rho = \dfrac{pM}{RT}$

Substituting value of p from Eq. (i), we get

$$\rho = \frac{p_0 M}{RT} e^{-\frac{Mgh}{RT}} \qquad \text{...(ii)}$$

(a) At $h = 0, \rho_1 = \dfrac{p_0 M}{RT}$

At $h = h, \rho_2 = \dfrac{p_0 M}{RT} e^{-\frac{Mgh}{RT}}$

Given, $\rho_2 = \dfrac{\rho_1}{e}$

Substituting in Eq. (ii), we get

$$h = \frac{RT}{Mg}$$

Putting the values of T, M and g, we get

$$h \approx 8 \text{ km}$$

(b) Eq. (ii) can be re-written as,

$$\rho_2 = \rho_1 e^{-\frac{Mgh}{RT}}$$

or $\qquad \dfrac{\rho_2}{\rho_1} = e^{-\frac{Mgh}{RT}}$

Given $\qquad \dfrac{\rho_2}{\rho_1} = 0.99$

$$\therefore \qquad 0.99 = e^{-\frac{Mgh}{RT}}$$

Taking log both sides, we get

$$\log_e(0.99) = -\frac{Mgh}{RT}\log_e(e)$$

$$\therefore \qquad h = -\frac{RT}{Mg}\log_e(0.99)$$

Substituting the values of T, M and g, we get

$$h \approx 0.09 \text{ km}$$

113. In the above example, we have obtained density at height h,

$$\rho = \frac{p_0 M}{RT} e^{-\frac{Mgh}{RT}}$$

Volume of element shown in figure is,

$$dV = S \cdot dh$$

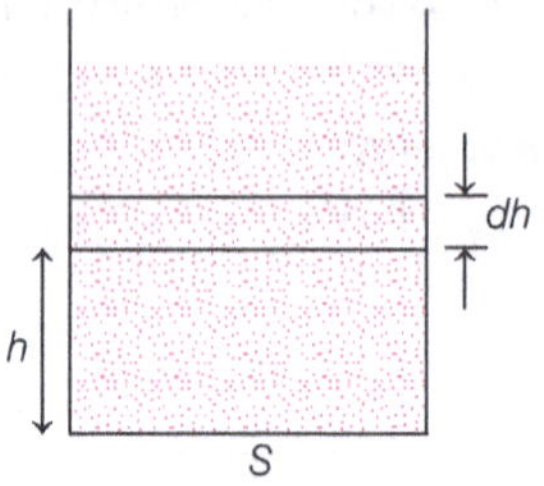

$\therefore$ Mass of gas in the element will be,

$$dm = \rho \cdot dV = \frac{p_0 MS}{RT}\left(e^{-\frac{Mgh}{RT}}\right) dh$$

Integrating dm from $h = 0$ to $h = h$, we get total mass of gas from $h = 0$ to $h = h$, which comes out to be,

$$m = \frac{\left(1 - e^{-\frac{Mgh}{RT}}\right) p_0 S}{g}$$

114. $h_{CG} = \dfrac{\int_0^\infty (dm)\, gh}{\int_0^\infty (dm)\, g}$

Here, $dm = \dfrac{p_0 MS}{RT}\left(e^{-\frac{Mgh}{RT}}\right) dh$

Note *(i) Since cylinder is very tall, so we have taken upper limit infinity.*

(ii) From the above problem, we can take expression of (dm) at height h. So, finally, we get

$$h_{CG} = \frac{\int_0^\infty h\left[e^{-\frac{Mgh}{RT}}\right] dh}{\int_0^\infty \left[e^{-\frac{Mgh}{RT}}\right] dh}$$

After simplifying and solving, we get

$$h_{CG} = \frac{RT}{Mg}$$

115. (a) $\dfrac{dp}{dh} = -\rho g = -\dfrac{pM}{RT} g$

Substituting the value of T, we get

$$\frac{dp}{p} = -\frac{Mg}{RT_0(1 - ah)} dh$$

or $$\int_{p_0}^{p}\frac{dp}{p}=-\frac{Mg}{RT_0}\int_0^h\frac{dh}{(1-ah)}$$

Solving this equation, we get

$$p=p_0(1-ah)^{\frac{Mg}{aRT_0}}$$

Note *Pressure can't be negative. Therefore*

$$ah<1 \quad or \quad h<\frac{1}{a}$$

(b) In this part only change is in the value of T, which is $T_0(1+ah)$. So proceeding in the similar manner the final answer comes out to be,

$$p=\frac{p_0}{(1+ah)^{\frac{Mg}{aRT_0}}}$$

116. $(p+dp)A-pA=$ centripetal force to the small element shown in the figure.

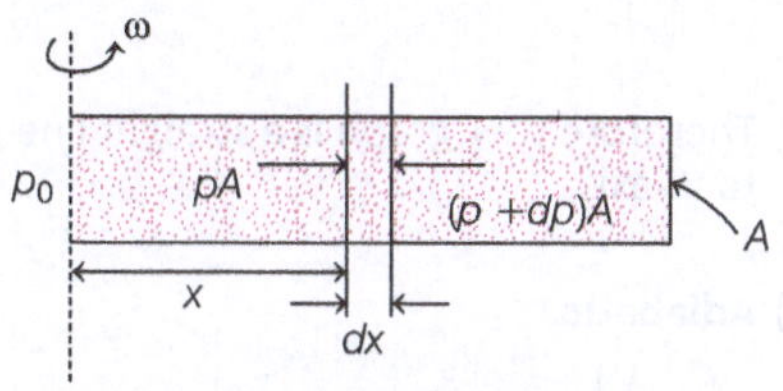

or $$(dp)\,A=(dm)\,x\,\omega^2$$

or $$(dp)A=(\rho A dx)\,x\,\omega^2$$

Here, $$\rho=\frac{pM}{RT}$$

$\therefore$ $$dp=\frac{pM\omega^2}{RT}x\cdot dx$$

or $$\int_{p_0}^{p}\frac{dp}{p}=\frac{M\omega^2}{RT}\int_0^r x\,dx$$

Solving this integration, we get

$$p=p_0\,e^{\frac{M\omega^2r^2}{2RT}}$$

117. 7.0 g of N_2 means 0.25 moles of N_2.

It's diatomic gas, so $C_V=\frac{5}{2}R$.

20 g of Ar means 0.5 moles of Ar.

Its monoatomic, so $C_V=\frac{3}{2}R$

Now, c_V of a mixture is given by,

$$C_V=\frac{n_1C_{V_1}+n_2C_{V_2}}{n_1+n_2} \quad ...(i)$$

Substituting the values in Eq. (i), we have

$$C_V=\frac{0.25\left(\frac{5}{2}R\right)+(0.5)\left(\frac{3}{2}R\right)}{0.25+0.5}$$

$$=1.83R$$

$$C_p=C_V+R=2.83R$$

These are molar heat capacities. If we divide them by molar mass of mixture then only it will become specific heat capacities.

Molar mass of a mixture of gases is given by,

$$M=\frac{n_1M_1+n_2M_2}{n_1+n_2} \quad ...(ii)$$

$$=\frac{0.25\times 28+0.5\times 40}{0.25+0.5}$$

$$=36 \text{ g/mol}$$

Now, $$c_v=\frac{C_V}{M}=\frac{1.83R}{M}=\frac{1.83\times 8.314}{36}$$

$$=0.42 \text{ J/g-K}$$

and $$c_p=\frac{C_p}{M}=\frac{2.83R}{M}=\frac{2.83\times 8.314}{36}$$

$$=0.65 \text{ J/g-K}$$

Thus, $c_v=0.42$ J/g-K

and $c_p=0.65$ J/g - K

118. (a) ***p* - *T* graphs**

(i) **Isochoric**

$$V=\text{constant}$$

$\therefore$ $$p\propto T \quad ...(i)$$

or p *versus* T graph is a straight line passing through origin.

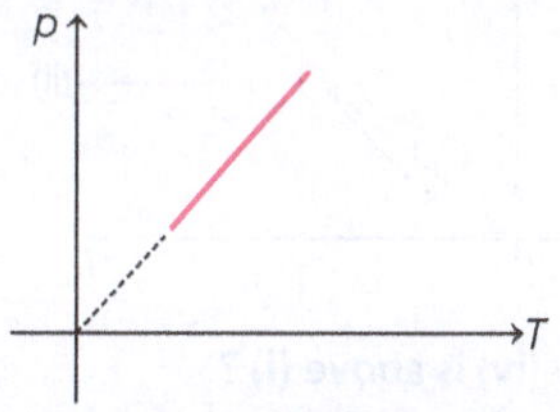

(ii) **Isobaric**

$$p=\text{constant}$$

Therefore p - T graph is a straight line parallel to T - axis.

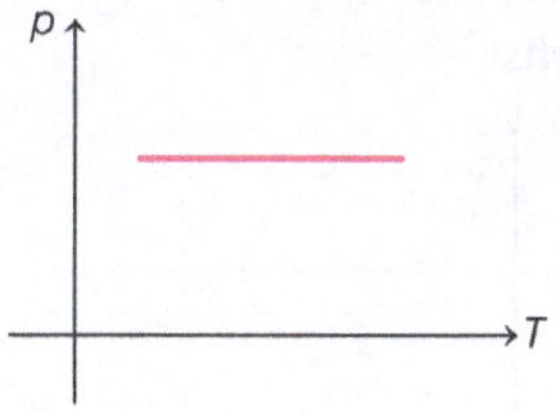

(iii) **Isothermal**

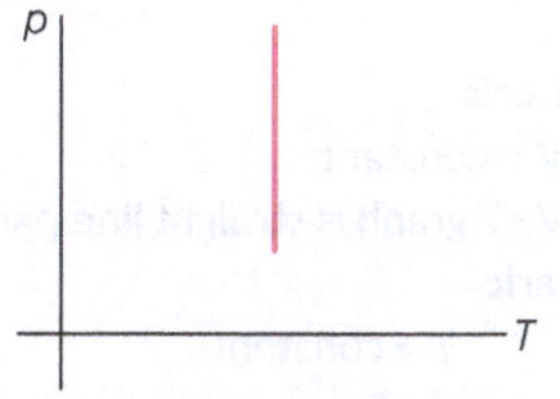

$$T=\text{constant}$$

$\therefore$ p - T graph is a straight line parallel to p - axis.

(iv) **Adiabatic**

$$T^{\gamma} p^{1-\gamma} = \text{constant}$$

$$\Rightarrow \quad p \propto \frac{1}{T^{(\gamma/1-\gamma)}}$$

Let us take an example of ideal diatomic gas for which $\gamma = \frac{7}{5}$.

$$\therefore \quad p \propto \frac{1}{T^{-3.5}}$$

$$\text{or} \quad p \propto T^{3.5} \quad \text{...(ii)}$$

So p - T graph is as shown below

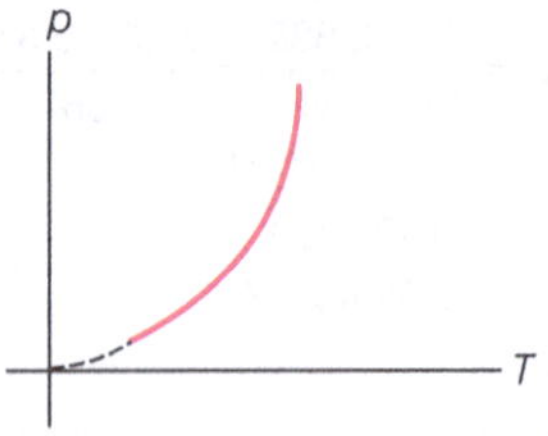

All four graphs in one diagram

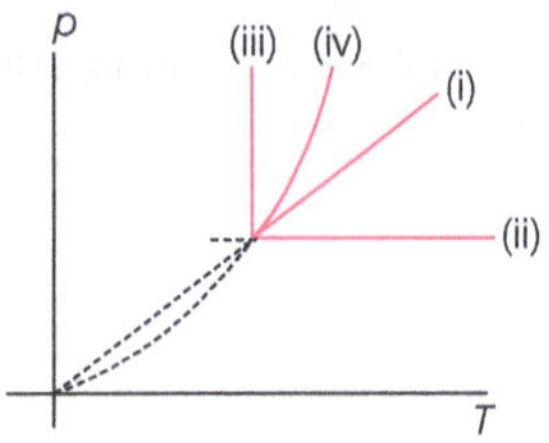

Why (iv) is above (i) ?

In Eq. (i) $p \propto T$

In Eq. (ii) $p \propto T^{3.5}$

If T is doubled then from Eq. (i) p will become two times, while from Eq. (ii) p will become $(2)^{3.5}$ times.

(b) **V - T graphs**

(i) **Isochoric**

$$V = \text{constant}$$

$\therefore$ V - T graph is straight line parallel to T - axis.

(ii) **Isobaric**

$$p = \text{constant}$$

$$\therefore \quad V \propto T$$

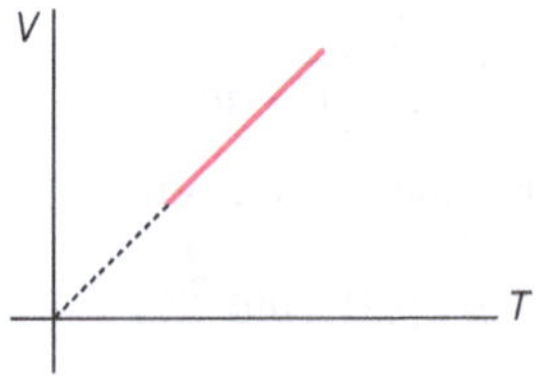

$\Rightarrow$ V - T graph is a straight line passing through origin.

(iii) **Isothermal**

$$T = \text{constant}$$

Therefore V - T graph is a straight line parallel to V - axis.

(iv) **Adiabatic**

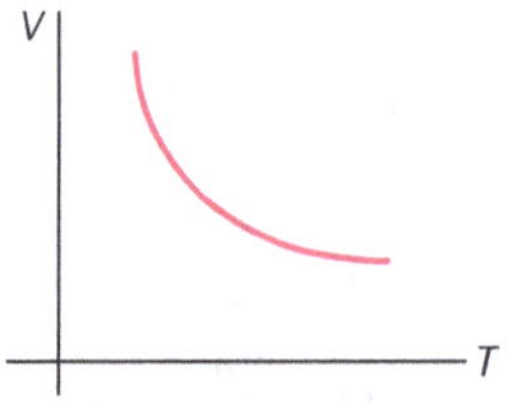

$$TV^{\gamma-1} = \text{constant}$$

$$\therefore \quad V \propto \frac{1}{T^{\gamma-1}}$$

Let us take ideal diatomic gas for which $\gamma = \frac{7}{5}$

$$\therefore \quad V \propto \frac{1}{T^{0.4}}$$

If T increases then V decreases and *vice-versa*.

All four graphs in one diagrams

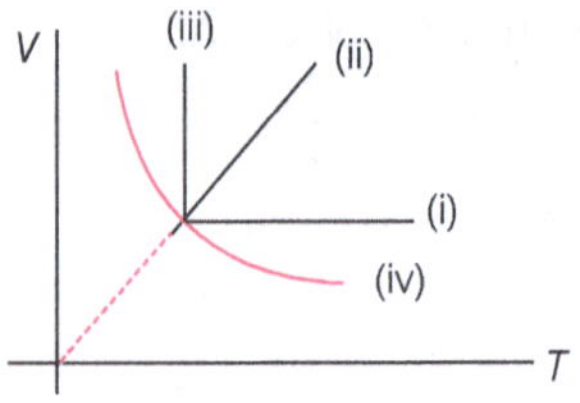

119. Let n be the number of molecules of 1.4 g of N_2.

0.7 n are N_2 molecules and $0.3\,n$ molecules of N_2 are dissociated into N.

So, they will become 0.6 n of N.

Further 1.4 g of N_2 will have number of molecules given by,

$$n = fN_A \qquad (f = \text{number of moles})$$
$$= \frac{1.4}{28} \times 6.02 \times 10^{23}$$
$$= 3.0 \times 10^{22}$$
$$0.7\,n = 2.1 \times 10^{22}$$
$$0.6\,n = 1.8 \times 10^{22}$$

So, let f_1 and f_2 are number of moles of N_2 and N in the mixture, then

$$f_1 = \frac{2.1 \times 10^{22}}{6.02 \times 10^{23}} = 0.035$$

and
$$f_2 = \frac{1.8 \times 10^{23}}{6.02 \times 10^{23}} = 0.03$$

Now,
$$p = p_1 + p_2$$
$$= \frac{f_1 RT}{V} + \frac{f_2 RT}{V} = \frac{(f_1 + f_2)\,RT}{V}$$
$$= \frac{(0.035 + 0.03)(8.314)(1800)}{5 \times 10^{-3}}$$
$$= 1.94 \times 10^5 \text{ N/m}^2$$

or
$$p \approx 1.9 \text{ atm}$$

120. Let number of molecules per unit volume of He is n_1 and that of nitrogen is n_2. Then,

$$\rho = \text{Total mass per unit volume}$$
$$\rho = n_1(M_{He}) + n_2(M_{N_2}) \qquad \text{...(i)}$$

Pressure per unit volume

$$p = fRT \qquad (f = \text{number of moles})$$
$$= f\,(kN_A)T \qquad (R = kN_A)$$
$$= nkT \qquad (fN_A = \text{total molecules } n)$$

or
$$p = (n_1 + n_2)\,kT \qquad \text{...(ii)}$$

Here k = Boltzmann equation

We have two equations and two unknowns n_1 and n_2. Solving them, we can find n_1, which comes out to be,

$$n_1 = 1.6 \times 10^{19} \text{ per cm}^3$$

Note *Under standard conditions, p and T are known to us. Further k, M_{He} and M_{N_2} are also known.*

121. Let m be the mass of one gas molecule. Then,

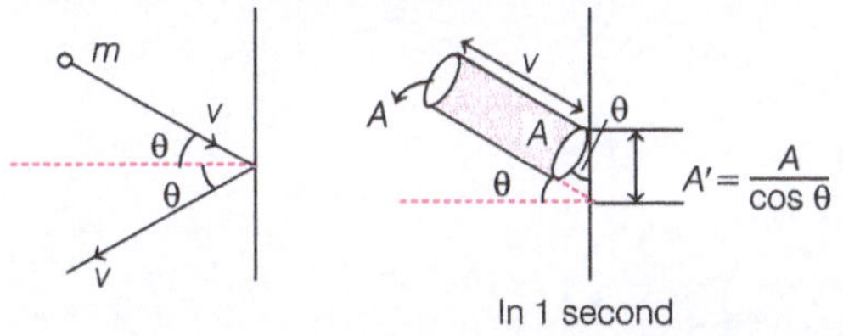

In 1 second

momentum transfer in one collision $= 2mv\cos\theta$

In one second molecules in volume (vA) will collide with wall. So, number of molecules colliding per second will be (ηvA). Thus,

$$F = \frac{dp}{dt} = (\eta vA)(2mv\cos\theta)$$

$$\therefore \quad \text{Pressure} = \frac{F}{A'} = \frac{F}{(A/\cos\theta)} = \left(\frac{F}{A}\right)\cos\theta$$
$$= 2m\eta v^2 \cos^2\theta$$

Substituting the proper values, we get

$$p \approx 1.0 \text{ atm}$$

122. Molar mass

$$c_p = \frac{C_p}{M}$$

or
$$C_p = Mc_p$$

Similarly, $C_V = Mc_V$

$$C_p - C_V = R = M(c_p - c_V)$$
$$\Rightarrow \quad M = \frac{R}{c_p - c_V} = \frac{8.314}{(0.91 - 0.65)} \approx 32 \text{ g/mol}$$

Thus, $\quad M = 32$ g/mol

Degree of freedom

$$\gamma = \frac{C_p}{C_V} = 1 + \frac{2}{f} = \frac{Mc_p}{Mc_V} = \frac{c_p}{c_V}$$
$$\therefore \quad f = \frac{2}{\dfrac{c_p}{c_V} - 1} = \frac{2}{\dfrac{0.91}{0.65} - 1}$$

or
$$f = 5$$

123. (a) $\gamma = \dfrac{C_p}{C_V} = \dfrac{C_p}{C_p - R} = 1 + \dfrac{2}{f}$

or
$$f = \frac{2}{\dfrac{C_p}{C_p - R} - 1} = \frac{2(C_p - R)}{R}$$
$$f = 2\left(\frac{C_p}{R} - 1\right)$$
$$\Rightarrow \quad f = 2\left[\frac{29}{8.314} - 1\right]$$

or
$$f = 4.97 \quad \text{or} \quad f \approx 5$$

(b) $pT = \text{constant}$

$$\Rightarrow \quad p\left(\frac{pV}{nR}\right) = \text{constant}$$

or
$$pV^{\frac{1}{2}} = \text{constant}$$

Comparing with $pV^n = \text{constant}$

We have, $n = \dfrac{1}{2}$

$$\therefore \quad C = C_V + \frac{R}{1 - n}$$
$$C_V = \frac{f}{2}R \qquad (f = \text{degree of freedom})$$
$$\therefore \quad C = \frac{f}{2}R + \frac{R}{1 - \frac{1}{2}} = \frac{f}{2}R + 2R$$

$$\therefore \quad f = \frac{2(C-2R)}{R} = 2\left(\frac{C}{R} - 2\right)$$

$$= 2\left(\frac{29}{8.314} - 2\right)$$

$$= 2.97 \quad \text{or} \quad f \approx 3$$

124. In the process $pV^x =$ constant, molar heat capacity C is given by,

$$C = C_V + \frac{R}{1-x} \quad \text{...(i)}$$

For di-atomic gas, $C_V = \frac{5}{2}R$

and given that $C = R$. Substituting in Eq. (i), we get

$$x = \frac{5}{3}$$

If we replace γ by x or $\frac{5}{3}$ and η by 2. Then, we get

$$N_f = \frac{N_i}{(\eta)^{\frac{\gamma+1}{2}}}$$

or $$N_f = \frac{N_i}{(2)^{4/3}} \approx \frac{N_i}{2.5} \quad \left[\gamma = x = \frac{5}{3} \text{ and } \eta = 2\right]$$

Thus rate of collisions will decrease 2.5 times.

125. In the process $pV^\gamma =$ constant.

$$N_f = \frac{1}{(\eta)^{\frac{\gamma+1}{2}}} N_i$$

In general, we can say that in the process,

$$pV^x = \text{constant}$$

$$N_f = \frac{N_i}{(\eta)^{\frac{x+1}{2}}}$$

Here it is given that,

$$N_f = N_i \Rightarrow \frac{x+1}{2} = 0$$

or $$x = -1$$

Now, in the process $pV^x =$ constant, molar heat capacity is given by,

$$C = C_V + \frac{R}{1-x} \quad \text{...(i)}$$

For diatomic gases, $C_V = \frac{5}{2}R$

Substituting $C_V = \frac{5}{2}R$ and $x = -1$ in Eq. (i), we get

$$C = 3R$$

126. Specific heat capacity $(C_V)_{mix}$ of two mixed gases given as,

$$(C_V)_{mix} = \frac{n_1 C_{V_1} + n_2 C_{V_2}}{n_1 + n_2}$$

$$= \frac{1 \cdot \frac{3R}{2} + 3 \cdot \frac{5R}{2}}{1+3} = \frac{9R}{4} = \frac{\alpha^2}{4}R$$

$$\Rightarrow \quad \alpha = 3$$

127. Given, volume of 1st chamber,

$$V_1 = 4.5 \text{ L}$$

Volume of 2nd chamber,

$$V_2 = 5.5 \text{ L}, n_1 = 3 \text{ mol}$$

$$\Rightarrow \quad p_1 = 2 \text{ atm}, n_2 = 4 \text{ mol}$$

$$\Rightarrow \quad p_2 = 3 \text{ atm}$$

By using ideal gas equation,

$$pV = nRT$$

$$\therefore \quad p_1V_1 + p_2V_2 = p(V_1 + V_2)$$

$$\Rightarrow \quad 2 \times 4.5 + 3 \times 5.5 = p \times 10$$

$$\Rightarrow \quad 9 + 16.5 = 10p$$

$$\Rightarrow \quad \frac{25.5}{10} = p$$

$$\therefore \quad p = 25.5 \times 10^{-1} \text{ atm}$$

Hence, $x = 25.5$ atm.

UNIT-21

LAWS OF THERMODYNAMICS

Learning Modules

1. The First Law of Thermodynamics
2. Further Explanation of Three Terms Used in First Law
3. Heat Engine and Refrigerator
4. Zeroth and Second Law of Thermodynamics

MODULE 1

The First Law of Thermodynamics

The first law of thermodynamics is basically law of conservation of energy. This law can be applied for any type of system like solid, liquid and gas. But, in most of the cases the system will be an ideal gas. A process in which there are changes in the state of a thermodynamic system (like p, V, T, U and ρ etc.) is called a **thermodynamic process.**

We now come to the first law

Suppose Q heat is given to a system, then part of it is used by the system in doing work W against the surroundings (like atmosphere) and part is used by the system in increasing its internal energy ΔU. Thus,

$$Q = W + \Delta U \quad \ldots \text{(i)}$$

Let us take a real life situation similar to first law.

Consider a person X. Suppose his monthly income is Rs. 50,000 (Q). He spends Rs. 30,000 (W) as his monthly expenditure. Then, obviously the remaining Rs. 20,000 goes to his savings (ΔU). In some month it is also possible that he spends more than his income. In that case he will withdraw it from his bank and his savings will get reduced ($\Delta U < 0$). In the similar manner, other combinations can be made.

Sign Convention

(i) **Q** If heat is given to the system, then Q is positive and if heat is taken from the system, then it is negative.

(ii) **W** Work done used in Eq. (i) is the work done by the system (not work done on the system). This work done is positive if volume of the system increases. Sign of work done in different situations is given in tabular form as below :

Table 1.

S.No	Volume of the system	Work done by the system used in Eq. (i)	Work done on the system
1.	is increasing	positive	negative
2.	is decreasing	negative	positive
3.	is constant	zero	zero

(iii) **ΔU** Internal energy of a system is due to disordered motion of its constituent particles. It mainly depends on state (solid, liquid and gas) and temperature.

For example, two different states at same temperature will have different internal energy. Ice at 0°C and water at 0°C have different energies.

Similarly, same state at different temperatures will have different energies. For example water at 50°C and 70°C will have different internal energies. If $U_f > U_i$, then $\Delta U = U_f - U_i$ is positive.

Let us take example of an ideal gas whose internal energy is given by :

$$U = \frac{nf}{2} RT \quad \text{or} \quad U \propto T$$

If temperature increases, internal energy also increases and $\Delta U = U_f - U_i$ will be positive.

Key Point

- If a thermodynamic system of an ideal gas changes from an initial equilibrium state A to final equilibrium state B through three different paths 1, 2 and 3, then Q and W may be different along these three paths. But $Q - W$ or ΔU will be same along all three paths. This is because, Q and W are path functions. But U is a state function. Thus,

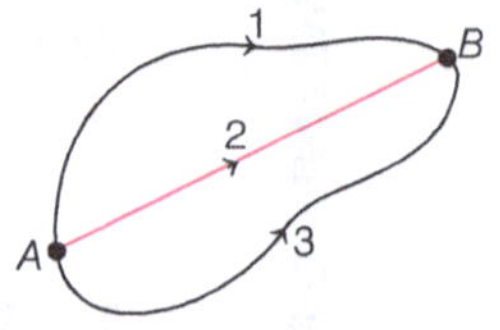

$$Q_1 - W_1 = Q_2 - W_2 = Q_3 - W_3 = \Delta U$$

In a closed path, $\Delta U = 0$

Example 1 When a system of an ideal gas goes from state A to state B, it is supplied with 400 J of heat and it does 100 J of work.

(a) For this transition, what is the system's change in internal energy?

(b) If the system moves from B to A, what is the change in internal energy?

(c) If in moving from A to B along a different path in which $W'_{AB} =$ 400 J of work is done on the system, how much heat does it absorb?

Sol. (a) From the first law,

$$\Delta U_{AB} = Q_{AB} - W_{AB} = (400 - 100) \text{ J}$$
$$= 300 \text{ J}$$

(b) Consider a closed path that passes through the state A and B. Internal energy is a state function so ΔU is zero for a closed path.

Thus, $\Delta U = \Delta U_{AB} + \Delta U_{BA} = 0$

or $\Delta U_{BA} = -\Delta U_{AB} = -300$ J

(c) The change in internal energy is the same for any path, so

$$\Delta U_{AB} = \Delta U'_{AB} = Q'_{AB} - W'_{AB}$$
$$300 \text{ J} = Q'_{AB} - (-400 \text{ J})$$

and the heat exchanged is $Q'_{AB} = -100$ J

The negative sign indicates that the system loses heat in this transition.

INTRODUCTORY Exercise

1. The quantities in the following table represent four different paths for the same initial and final states. Find *a*, *b*, *c*, *d*, *e*, *f* and *g*.

Table 2.

Q(J)	W(J)	ΔU(J)
−80	−120	*d*
90	*c*	*e*
a	40	*f*
b	−40	*g*

2. In a certain chemical process, a lab technician supplies 254 J of heat to a system. At the same time, 73 J of work is done on the system by its surroundings. What is the increase in the internal energy of the system?

Answers

1. $a = 80$ J, $b = 0$, $c = 50$ J, $d = 40$ J, $e = 40$ J, $f = 40$ J, $g = 40$ J
2. 327 J

See hints on page 305.

MODULE 2

Further Explanation of Three Terms Used in First Law

First law of thermodynamics basically revolves round the three terms Q, ΔU and W. If you substitute these three terms correctly with proper signs in the equation $Q = \Delta U + W$, then you are able to solve most of the problems of first law. Let us take each term one by one. Here, an ideal gas is our system.

(i) **Heat Transfer (Q or ΔQ)** There are two methods of finding Q or ΔQ.

Method 1. Q or $\Delta Q = nC\Delta T$

Here, C is the molar heat capacity of the gas, n is the number of moles of the gas and

$$\Delta T = T_f - T_i$$

where, T_f is the final temperature and T_i the initial temperature of the gas. Further, we have discussed earlier, that molar heat capacity of an ideal gas in the process pV^x = constant is

$$C = \frac{R}{\gamma - 1} + \frac{R}{1 - x} = C_V + \frac{R}{1 - x}$$

$$C = C_V = \frac{R}{\gamma - 1} \text{ in isochoric process and}$$

$$C = C_p = C_V + R \text{ in isobaric process}$$

Mostly C_p and C_V are used.

Note *For finding C, nature of gas and process should be known. Nature of gas will give us C_V and process the value of x.*

Method 2. We can also find Q by finding ΔU and W by using the equation

$$Q = W + \Delta U$$

(ii) **Change in internal energy (ΔU)** There are two methods of finding ΔU.

Method 1. Change in internal energy of an ideal gas is given by :

$$\Delta U = nC_V \Delta T$$

Students are often confused that the result $\Delta U = nC_V \Delta T$ can be applied only in case of an isochoric process (as C_V is used in this expression). However, it is not so. It can be applied in any process, whether it is isobaric, isothermal, adiabatic or else. Because ΔU is a state function which depends only upon the initial and final states.

Note *In the above expression, value of C_V depends upon the nature of gas (mono, dia or polyatomic).*

Method 2. We can also find ΔU from the basic equation of first law of thermodynamics,

$$\Delta U = Q - W$$

(iii) **Work done (W)** This is the most important of the three.

Work Done During Volume Changes

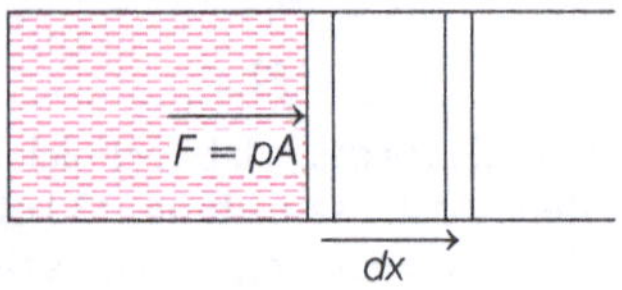

Figure shows a gas confined to a cylinder that has a movable piston at one end. If the gas expands against the piston, it exerts a force and does work on the piston. If the piston compresses the gas as it is moved inward, work is done on the gas. The work associated with such volume changes can be determined as follows.

Let the gas pressure on the piston face be p. Then, the force on the piston due to the gas is pA, where A is the area of the face.

When the piston is pushed outward an infinitesimal distance dx, the work done by the gas is

$$dW = Fdx = pA\,dx$$

which, since the change in volume of the gas is $dV = Adx$, becomes

$$\boxed{dW = pdV}$$

For a finite change in volume from V_i to V_f, this equation is then integrated between V_i to V_f to find the net work

$$\boxed{W = \int dW = \int_{V_i}^{V_f} pdV}$$

Now, there are five methods of finding work done by a gas.

Method 1. This is used when p-V equation is known to us. Suppose p as a function of V is known to us.

$$p = f(V)$$

then work done can be found by

$$W = \int_{V_i}^{V_f} f(V)\, dV$$

Method 2. The work done by a gas is also equal to the area under p-V graph. This is because,

$$W = \int_{V_i}^{V_f} pdV = \text{area under } p\text{-}V \text{ graph.}$$

Following different cases are possible :

Case 1 When volume is constant

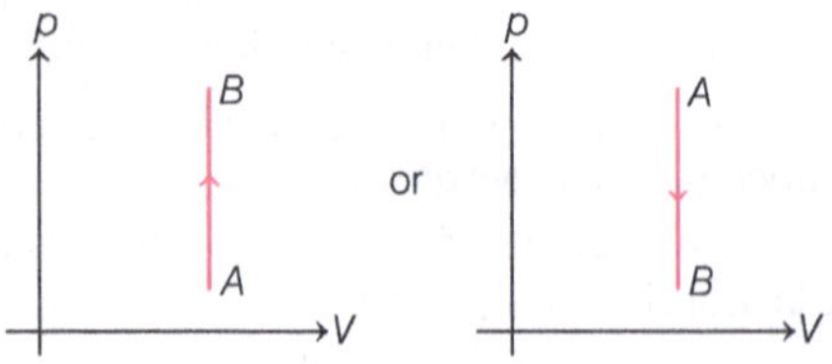

$$V = \text{constant}$$

$$\therefore \qquad W_{AB} = 0$$

Case 2 When volume is increasing

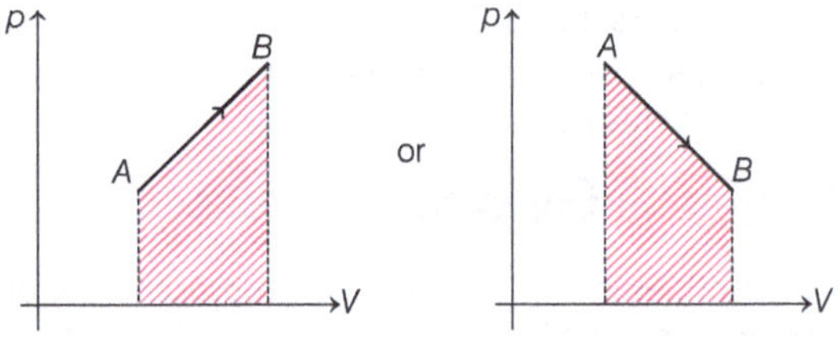

V is increasing

$$\therefore \qquad W_{AB} > 0$$

$$W_{AB} = \text{Shaded area}$$

Case 3 When volume is decreasing

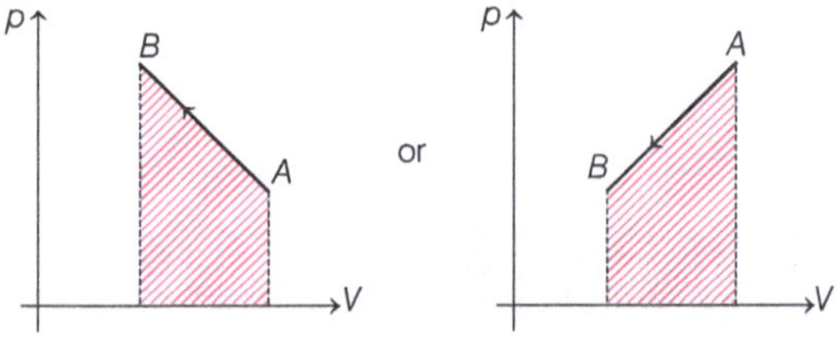

V is decreasing

$$\therefore \qquad W_{AB} < 0$$

$$W_{AB} = -\text{Shaded area}$$

Case 4 Cyclic process

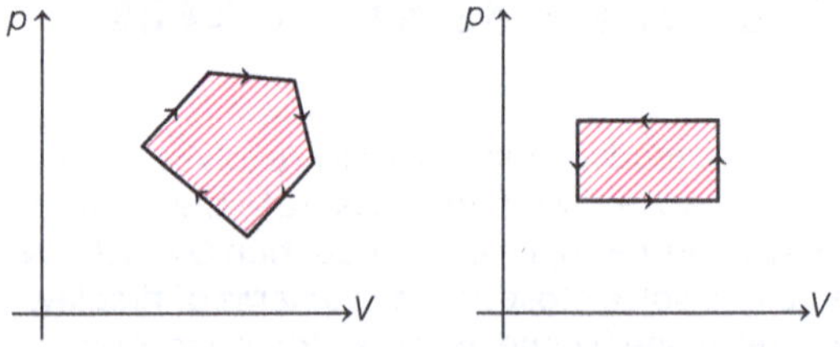

(a) (b)

$$W_{\text{clockwise cycle}} = +\text{Shaded area} \qquad \text{[in figure (a)]}$$

$$W_{\text{anticlockwise cycle}} = -\text{Shaded area} \qquad \text{[in figure (b)]}$$

Exercise : Prove that work done in a cyclic process is the area under the cycle in p-V diagram. If cycle is clockwise then W is positive if p is along y-axis.

Case 5 Incomplete cycle

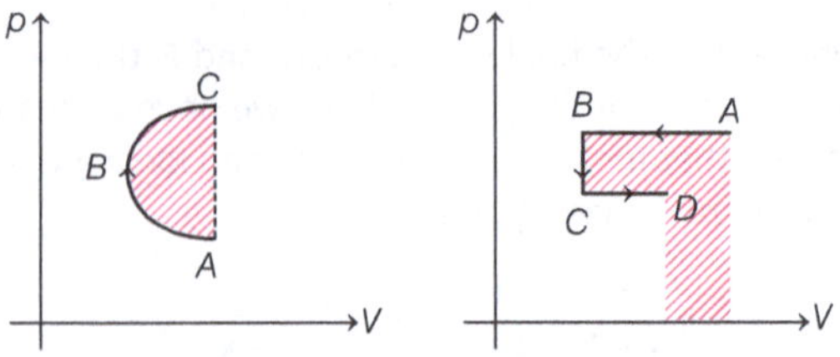

$$W_{ABC} = +\text{Shaded area}$$

$$W_{ABCD} = -\text{Shaded area}$$

Exercise : Prove the above results.

Method 3. Sometimes work done by the gas is also obtained by finding the forces against which work is done by the gas.

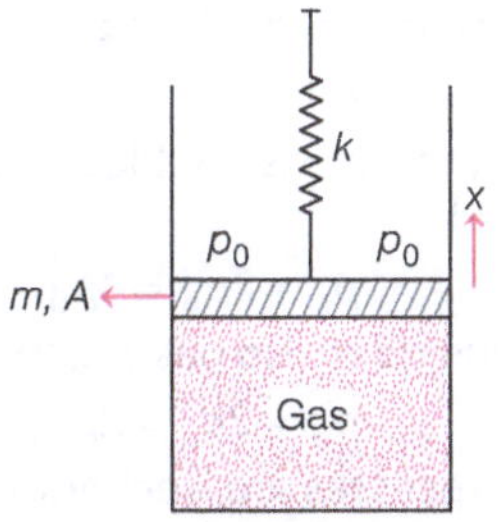

For example, in the figure shown, work is done by the gas against the following forces (when the piston is displaced upwards)

(i) Against gravity force mg. Since, mg is a constant force.

$\therefore \quad W_1 = \text{Force} \times \text{displacement} = mgx$

(ii) Against the force p_0A. This is also a constant force.

$\therefore \quad W_2 = \text{Force} \times \text{displacement} = p_0Ax$

But, $\quad Ax = \Delta V$

$\therefore \quad W_2 = p_0 \Delta V$

(iii) Against spring force kx. This is a variable force. Hence,

$$W_3 = \int_0^x (kx)\,dx = \frac{1}{2}kx^2$$

Note *While calculating W_3, we have assumed that initially spring is in its natural length.*

Method 4. In some cases, a process and limits of temperature (or temperature change) is given. In those cases, with the help of given process and the standard ideal gas equation $pV = nRT$, first convert pdV into $f(T)dT$ and then integrate this expression with the limits of temperature. Thus,

$$W = \int pdV = \int_{T_i}^{T_f} f(T)\,dT$$

Method 5. The last method of finding work done is from the fundamental equation of first law.

or $$W = Q - \Delta U$$

Now, let us take example of each method discussed above.

Example 1 **Method 1 of Q**

Temperature of two moles of a monoatomic gas is increased by 300 K in the process $p \propto V$.

(a) Find molar heat capacity of the gas in the given process.

(b) Find heat given to the gas in that.

Sol. (a) $p \propto V$

$$\Rightarrow \quad pV^{-1} = \text{constant}$$

If we compare with $pV^x = \text{constant}$, then

$$x = -1$$

Now,

$$C = C_V + \frac{R}{1-x}$$

$$C_V = \frac{3}{2}R \text{ for a monoatomic gas}$$

$$\therefore \quad C = \frac{3}{2}R + \frac{R}{1-(-1)} = 2R \qquad \textbf{Ans.}$$

(b) $Q = nC\Delta T$

Substituting the values, we get

$$Q = (2)(2R)(300)$$
$$= 1200R \qquad \textbf{Ans.}$$

Example 2 **Method 2 of Q**

In a given process work done on a gas is 40 J and increase in its internal energy is 10 J. Find heat given or taken to/from the gas in this process.

Sol. Given, $\Delta U = +10$ J

Work done on the gas is 40 J. Therefore, work done by the gas used in the equation, $Q = W + \Delta U$ will be -40 J. Now, putting the values in the equation,

$$Q = W + \Delta U$$

We have, $$Q = -40 + 10$$
$$= -30 \text{ J} \qquad \textbf{Ans.}$$

Here, negative sign indicates that heat is taken out from the gas.

Example 3 **Method 1 of ΔU**

Temperature of two moles of a monoatomic gas is increased by 600 K in a given process. Find change in internal energy of the gas.

Sol. Using the equation,

$$\Delta U = nC_V\Delta T \qquad \text{(for change in internal energy)}$$

$$C_V = \frac{3}{2}R \qquad \text{(for monoatomic gas)}$$

$$\therefore \quad \Delta U = (2)\left(\frac{3}{2}R\right)(600)$$
$$= 1800\,R \qquad \textbf{Ans.}$$

Example 4 **Method 2 of ΔU**

Work done by a gas in a given process is -20 J. Heat given to the gas is 60 J. Find change in internal energy of the gas.

Sol. $\Delta U = Q - W$

Substituting the values, we have

$$\Delta U = 60 - (-20) = 80 \text{ J} \qquad \textbf{Ans.}$$

ΔU is positive. Hence, internal energy of the gas is increasing.

Example 5 **Method 1 of W**

With the help of integration, make expressions of work done by a gas in

(a) Isobaric process (p = constant)

(b) Isothermal process (pV = constant)

(c) Adiabatic process (pV^γ = constant)

Sol. (a) **Isobaric process**

$$W = \int_{V_i}^{V_f} p\,dV = p\int_{V_i}^{V_f} dV \qquad \text{(as } p = \text{constant)}$$

$$= p[V]_{V_i}^{V_f} = p(V_f - V_i)$$

$$= p\Delta V \qquad \textbf{Ans.}$$

Note *Any process freely taking place in atmosphere is considered isobaric. For example, melting of ice, boiling of water etc. Here, the constant pressure is p_0. Therefore,*

$$W = p_0\Delta V = p_0(V_f - V_i)$$

(b) **Isothermal process**

$$W = \int_{V_i}^{V_f} p\,dV = \int_{V_i}^{V_f}\left(\frac{nRT}{V}\right)dV \qquad \left(\text{as } p = \frac{nRT}{V}\right)$$

$$= nRT\int_{V_i}^{V_f}\frac{dV}{V} \qquad \text{(as } T = \text{constant)}$$

$$= nRT\ln\left(\frac{V_f}{V_i}\right) = nRT\ln\left(\frac{p_i}{p_f}\right)$$

$$\left(\text{as } p_iV_i = p_fV_f, \text{ So, } \frac{V_f}{V_i} = \frac{p_i}{p_f}\right)$$

(c) **Adiabatic process**

$$pV^{\gamma} = \text{constant} = k \text{ (say)} = p_iV_i^{\gamma} = p_fV_f^{\gamma}$$

$$\text{Further, } p = \frac{k}{V^{\gamma}} = kV^{-\gamma}$$

$$W = \int_{V_i}^{V_f} p\,dV = \int_{V_i}^{V_f} kV^{-\gamma}dV = \left[\frac{kV^{-\gamma+1}}{-\gamma+1}\right]_{V_i}^{V_f}$$

$$= \frac{kV_f^{-\gamma+1} - kV_i^{-\gamma+1}}{-\gamma+1}$$

$$= \frac{p_fV_f^{\gamma}V_f^{-\gamma+1} - p_iV_i^{\gamma}V_i^{-\gamma+1}}{1-\gamma}$$

$$= \frac{p_fV_f - p_iV_i}{1-\gamma} = \frac{nRT_f - nRT_i}{1-\gamma}$$

$$= \frac{nR\Delta T}{1-\gamma}$$

Example 6 **Method 2 of W**

In the given p-V diagram, find

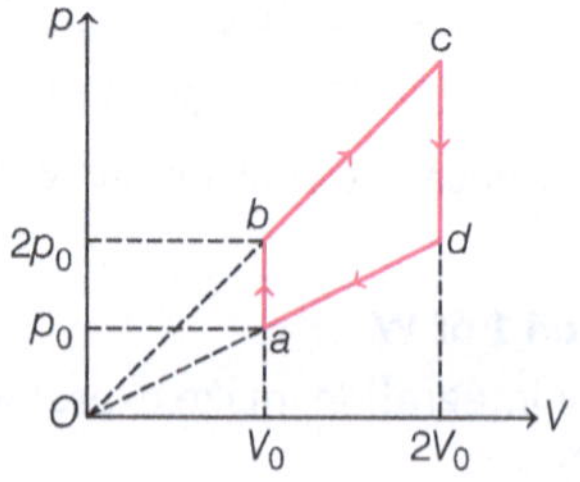

(a) pressures at c and d

(b) work done in different processes separately

(c) work done in complete cycle *abcd*.

Sol. (a) Line *bc* is passing through origin. Hence,

$$p \propto V$$

From b to c, volume is doubled. Hence, pressure is also doubled.

$$\therefore \qquad p_c = 2p_b = 4p_0 \qquad \textbf{Ans.}$$

Similarly, line *ad* is also passing through origin.

$$\therefore \qquad p_d = 2p_a = 2p_0 \qquad \textbf{Ans.}$$

(b) *ab* and *cd* processes are isochoric (V = constant).

Hence, $W_{ab} = W_{cd} = 0$

$$W_{bc} = \text{area under the line } bc$$
$$= \text{area of trapezium}$$
$$= \frac{1}{2}(p_b + p_c)(2V_0 - V_0)$$
$$= \frac{1}{2}(2p_0 + 4p_0)(V_0)$$
$$= 3\,p_0V_0 \qquad \textbf{Ans.}$$

Since, volume is increasing. Therefore, W_{bc} is positive.

$$W_{da} = -\text{area under the line } da$$
$$= -\text{area of trapezium}$$
$$= -\frac{1}{2}(p_a + p_d)(2V_0 - V_0)$$
$$= -\frac{1}{2}(p_0 + 2p_0)(V_0)$$
$$= -1.5\,p_0V_0 \qquad \textbf{Ans.}$$

Volume is decreasing. Therefore, work done is negative.

(d) Work done in complete cycle

$$W_{net} = W_{ab} + W_{bc} + W_{cd} + W_{da}$$
$$= 0 + 3p_0V_0 + 0 - 1.5p_0V_0$$
$$= 1.5p_0V_0 \qquad \textbf{Ans.}$$

Note *Total work done in a cyclic process is also equal to the area between the cycle. Since, cycle is clockwise. Hence, net work done is positive.*

Example 7 **Method 3 of W**

Mass of a piston shown in figure is m and area of cross-section is A. Initially spring is in its natural length. Find work done by the gas if piston is displaced x towards right.

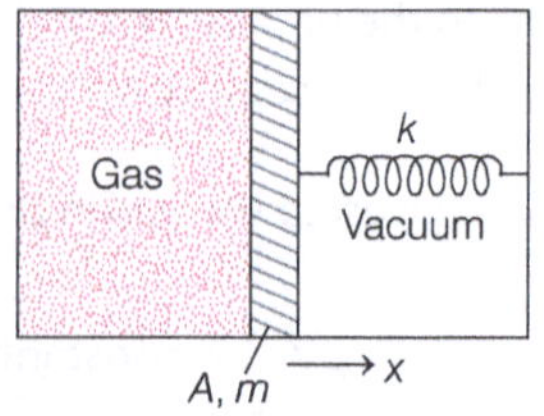

Sol. In the given condition, work is done by the gas only against spring force kx. This force is a variable force. Hence,

$$W = \int_0^x (kx)\,dx = \frac{1}{2}kx^2$$

Example 8 **Method 4 of W**

The temperature of n-moles of an ideal gas is increased from T_0 to $2T_0$ through a process $p = \frac{\alpha}{T}$. Find work done in this process.

Sol. $pV = nRT$ (ideal gas equation) ...(i)

and $p = \frac{\alpha}{T}$ ...(ii)

Dividing Eq. (i) by Eq. (ii), we get

$$V = \frac{nRT^2}{\alpha} \quad \text{or} \quad dV = \frac{2nRT}{\alpha} dT$$

$$\therefore \quad W = \int_{V_i}^{V_f} p\, dV = \int_{T_0}^{2T_0} \left(\frac{\alpha}{T}\right)\left(\frac{2nRT}{\alpha}\right) dT$$

$$= 2nR \int_{T_0}^{2T_0} dT = 2nRT_0 \quad \textbf{Ans.}$$

Example 9 **Method 5 of W**

Heat taken from a gas in a process is 80 J and increase in internal energy of the gas is 20 J. Find work done by the gas in the given process.

Sol. Heat is taken from the gas.

Therefore, Q is negative.

Or, $Q = -80$ J

Internal energy of the gas is increasing.

Therefore, ΔU is positive.

Or, $\Delta U = +20$ J

Using the first law equation,

$$Q = W + \Delta U \quad \text{or} \quad W = Q - \Delta U = -80 - 20$$

$$= -100 \text{ J} \quad \textbf{Ans.}$$

Here, negative sign indicates that volume of the gas is decreasing and work is done on the gas.

INTRODUCTORY Exercise 1

1. A gas in a cylinder is held at a constant pressure of 1.7×10^5 Pa and is cooled and compressed from 1.20 m^3 to 0.8 m^3. The internal energy of the gas decreases by 1.1×10^5 J.
   (a) Find the work done by the gas.
   (b) Find the magnitude of the heat flow into or out of the gas and state the direction of heat flow.
   (c) Does it matter whether or not the gas is ideal?
2. A thermodynamic system undergoes a cyclic process as shown in figure.

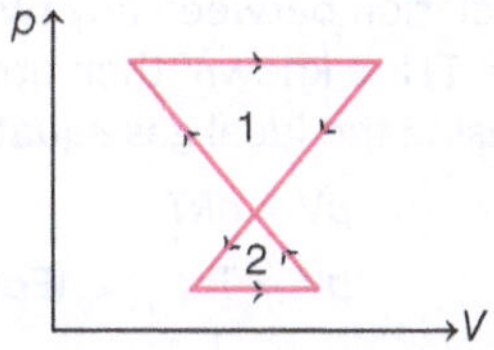

   (a) over one complete cycle, does the system do positive or negative work.
   (b) over one complete cycle, does heat flow into or out of the system.
   (c) In each of the loops 1 and 2, does heat flow into or out of the system.
3. How many moles of helium at temperature 300 K and 1.00 atm pressure are needed to make the internal energy of the gas 100 J?
4. Temperature of four moles of a monoatomic gas is increased by 300 K in isochoric process. Find W, Q and ΔU.
5. Find work done by the gas in the process AB shown in the following figures.

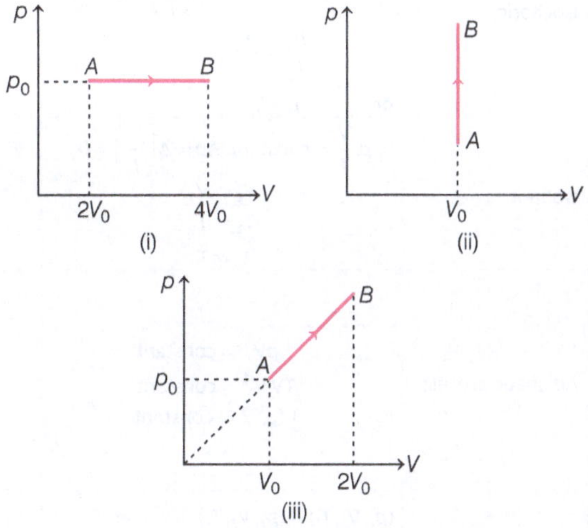

6. Temperature of two moles of an ideal gas is increased by 300 K in a process $V = \frac{a}{T}$, where a is positive constant. Find work done by the gas in the given process.
7. Pressure and volume of a gas changes from (p_0, V_0) to $\left(\frac{p_0}{4}, 2V_0\right)$ in a process pV^2 = constant. Find work done by the gas in the given process.

Answers

1. (a) -6.8×10^4 J (b) 1.78×10^5 J, out of gas (c) No
2. (a) Positive (b) Into the system (c) In loop 1, into the system; In loop 2, out of the system
3. 2.67×10^{-2} mol
4. $W = 0, Q = \Delta U = 1800\,R$
5. (i) $2\,p_0V_0$ (ii) zero (iii) $\frac{3}{2}\,p_0V_0$
6. $-600\,R$
7. $\frac{1}{2}\,p_0V_0$

See hints on page 305.

Different Thermodynamic Processes

Different thermodynamic processes and their important points are given below in tabular form.

Table 1.

S.No	Name of the process	Important points in the process	$Q = nC\Delta T = W + \Delta U$	$\Delta U = nC_V\Delta T$	W
1.	Isothermal	$T, pV, U =$ constant $\Delta T = \Delta(pV) = \Delta U = 0$ $p_1V_1 = p_2V_2$ or $p \propto \frac{1}{V}$	$Q = W$	0	$nRT \ln\left(\frac{V_f}{V_i}\right) = nRT \ln\left(\frac{p_i}{p_f}\right)$
2.	Isochoric	$V, p, \frac{p}{T} =$ constant $\Delta V = \Delta p = \Delta\left(\frac{p}{T}\right) = 0$ $\frac{p_1}{T_1} = \frac{p_2}{T_2}$ or $p \propto T$	$C = C_V$ $\therefore Q = nC_V\Delta T$	$nC_V\Delta T$	0
3.	Isobaric	$p, \frac{V}{T} =$ constant $\Delta p = \Delta\left(\frac{V}{T}\right) = 0$ $\frac{V_1}{T_1} = \frac{V_2}{T_2}$ or $V \propto T$	$C = C_p$ $\therefore Q = nC_p\Delta T$	$nC_V\Delta T$	$p\Delta V \to$ For any system $Q - \Delta U = n(C_p - C_V)\Delta T$ $= nR\Delta T \to$ for an ideal gas
4.	Adiabatic process	$pV^\gamma =$ constant $TV^{\gamma-1} =$ constant $T^\gamma p^{1-\gamma} =$ constant	0	$nC_V\Delta T$	$W = -\Delta U$ $\therefore W = -nC_V\Delta T$ $= -n\left(\frac{R}{\gamma-1}\right)(T_f - T_i)$ $= \frac{nRT_i - nRT_f}{\gamma - 1} = \frac{p_iV_i - p_fV_f}{\gamma - 1}$
5.	Cyclic process	$(p_i, V_i, T_i) = (p_f, V_f, T_f)$ Since $T_i = T_f$ $\Rightarrow U_i = U_f$ or $\Delta T = \Delta U = 0$	$Q_{net} = W_{net}$	0	W_{net} = area between cycle on p-V diagram
6.	Polytropic process $pV^x =$ constant	$C = \frac{R}{\gamma - 1} + \frac{R}{1 - x}$ $= C_V + \frac{R}{1-x}$	$nC\Delta T$	$nC_V\Delta T$	$Q - \Delta U = \frac{nR\Delta T}{1-x}$ $= \frac{nR(T_f - T_i)}{1-x}$ $= \frac{(p_iV_i - p_fV_f)}{x-1}$
7.	Free expansion in vacuum	$\Delta U = 0$ $\Rightarrow U, T$ and $pV =$ constant or $p \propto \frac{1}{V}$	0	0	0

Important Points in the Above Table

Isobaric process In isobaric process, neither of the three terms (Q, ΔU and W) is zero but they have a constant ratio which depends on nature of gas (like monoatomic or diatomic etc.)

$$Q : \Delta U : W = nC_p\Delta T : nC_V\Delta T : nR\Delta T = C_p : C_V : R$$

So, this ratio is $C_p : C_V : R$. For example, $C_p = \frac{5}{2}R$ and $C_V = \frac{3}{2}R$ for a monoatomic gas. Therefore, for a monoatomic gas this ratio is $\frac{5}{2}R : \frac{3}{2}R : R$ or $5 : 3 : 2$.

If Q is 50 J, then ΔU will be 30 J and W is 20 J.

Adiabatic process

(i) In a thermodynamic process, there are three variables p, V and T. If relation between any two (p-V, V-T or p-T) are known, then other relations can be obtained using the ideal gas equation

$$pV = nRT$$

or $pV \propto T$ (For given value of n)

or $p \propto \frac{T}{V}$

and $$V \propto \frac{T}{p}$$

For example, p-V equation : pV^{γ} = constant can be converted into p-T or V-T equation.

***p*-*T* equation** Replace V with $\frac{T}{p}$

$$\therefore \quad p\left(\frac{T}{p}\right)^{\gamma} = \text{constant}$$

or $$p^{1-\gamma}T^{\gamma} = \text{constant}$$

***V*-*T* equation** Replace p with $\frac{T}{V}$

$$\therefore \quad \left(\frac{T}{V}\right)V^{\gamma} = \text{constant}$$

or $$TV^{\gamma-1} = \text{constant}$$

(ii) An adiabatic process is defined as one with no heat transfer into or out of a system : $Q = 0$. We can prevent heat flow either by surrounding the system with thermally insulating material or by carrying out the process so **quickly** that there is not enough time for appreciable heat flow. From the first law, we find that for every adiabatic process,

$$W = -\Delta U \qquad (\text{as } Q = 0)$$

Therefore, if the work done by a gas is positive (i.e. volume of the gas is increasing), then ΔU will be negative. Hence, U and therefore T will decrease. The cooling of air can be experienced practically during bursting of a tyre. The process is so fast that it can be assumed as adiabatic. As the gas expands, its temperature decrease. So, it cools. On the other hand, the compression stroke in an internal combustion engine is an approximately adiabatic process. The temperature rises as the air fuel mixture in the cylinder is compressed.

Note *Contrary to adiabatic process which is very fast an isothermal process is very slow. Because the system needs sufficient time to interact with surroundings to keep its temperature constant.*

Cyclic process In a cyclic process, initial and final points are same.

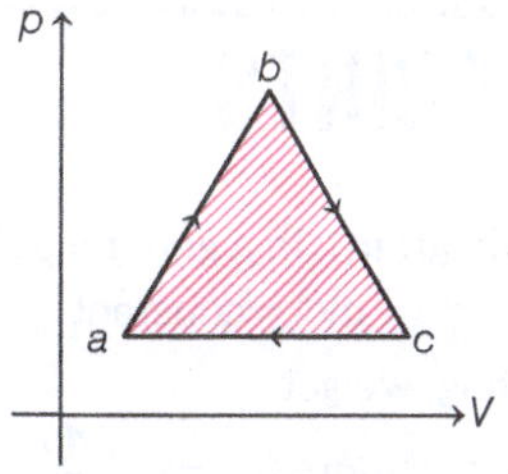

Therefore, $$(p_i, V_i, T_i) = (p_f, V_f, T_f)$$

Internal energy is a state function which only depends on temperature (in case of an ideal gas).

$$T_i = T_f \Rightarrow U_i = U_f$$

or $$\Delta U_{\text{net}} = 0$$

If there are three processes in a cycle abc, then

$$\Delta U_{ab} + \Delta U_{bc} + \Delta U_{ca} = 0$$

From first law of thermodynamics,

$$Q = W + \Delta U$$

If $\Delta U_{\text{net}} = 0$, then

$$Q_{\text{net}} = W_{\text{net}}$$

or $$Q_{ab} + Q_{bc} + Q_{ca} = W_{ab} + W_{bc} + W_{ca}$$

Further, W_{net} = area under p-Vdiagram. For example, W_{net} = + area of triangle 'abc' in the shown diagram. Cycle is clockwise. So, work done will be positive.

Free expansion in vacuum A gas in a closed adiabatic chamber is taken to vacuum and then chamber is opened. So, the gas expands. Since, there is no external force which opposes this expansion. So, work done by gas

$$W = 0$$

Further no heat is supplied or taken from the gas. Therefore, heat exchange is also zero. Or

$$Q = 0$$

From first law of thermodynamics, $Q = W + \Delta U$ change in internal energy is also zero. Or

$$\Delta U = 0 \quad \text{or} \quad U = \text{constant}$$

$$\Rightarrow \quad T \text{ or } pV \text{ is also constant}$$

or $$p \propto \frac{1}{V}$$

This behaviour is similar to an isothermal process. The only difference is : in this process all three terms Q, ΔU and W are zero. But in isothermal process, only ΔU is zero.

Important POINTS

- **Slope of p-V diagram** In a general polytropic process,

$$pV^x = \text{constant}$$

or differentiating, we get

$$p(xV^{x-1})\,dV + V^x(dp) = 0 \quad \Rightarrow \quad \frac{dp}{dV} = -x\frac{p}{V}$$

or slope of p-V graph $= -x\dfrac{p}{V}$

In isobaric process $p =$ constant

$\Rightarrow \quad pV^0 =$ constant

$\Rightarrow \quad x = 0$, therefore slope $= 0$

In isothermal process $pV =$ constant

$\Rightarrow \quad x = 1$, therefore slope $= -\dfrac{p}{V}$

In adiabatic process $pV^\gamma =$ constant

$\Rightarrow \quad x = \gamma$, therefore slope $= -\gamma\dfrac{p}{V}$

Thus, slope of an adiabatic graph is γ times slope of isothermal graph at that point.

Because $\gamma > 1$, the isothermal curve is not as steep as that for the adiabatic process.

Adiabatic and isothermal expansion

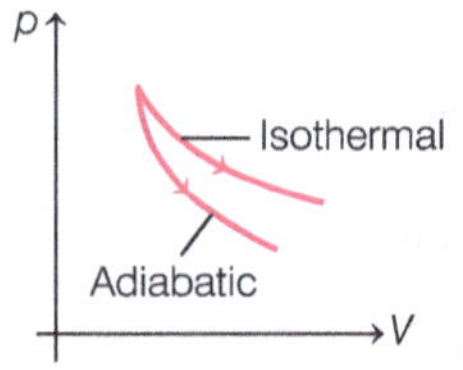

Adiabatic expansion of mono,dia and polyatomic gases.

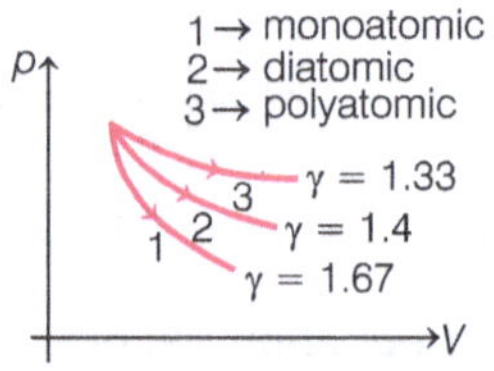

p-V diagram of different processes is shown in one graph as below.

Adiabatic and isothermal compression

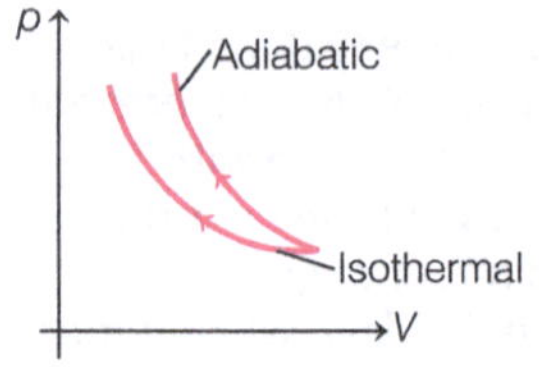

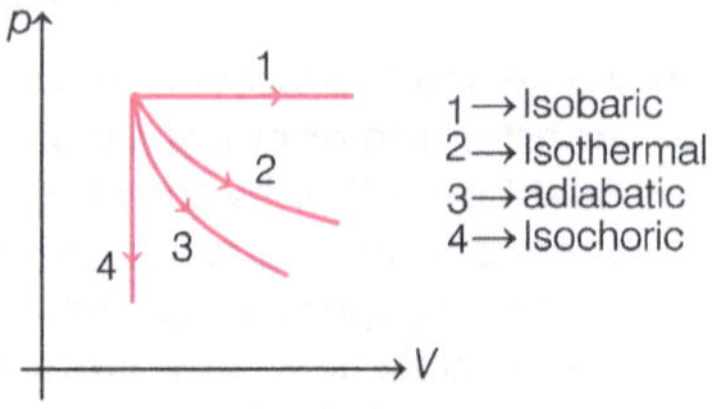

Example 10 p-V plots for two gases during adiabatic processes are shown in the figure. Plots 1 and 2 should correspond respectively to **(2001 JEE)**

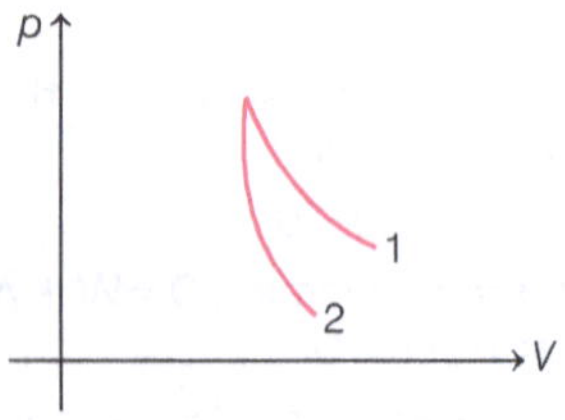

(a) He and O_2 (b) O_2 and He
(c) He and Ar (d) O_2 and N_2

Sol. In adiabatic process :

slope of p-V graph, $\dfrac{dp}{dV} = -\gamma\dfrac{p}{V}$

$$\text{slope} \propto \gamma \qquad \text{(with negative sign)}$$

From the given graph,

$$|\text{Slope}|_2 > |\text{Slope}|_1$$

$\therefore \quad \gamma_2 > \gamma_1$

Therefore, 1 should correspond to O_2 ($\gamma = 1.4$) and 2 should correspond to He ($\gamma = 1.67$).

Hence, the correct option is (b).

Example 11 Starting with the same initial conditions, an ideal gas expands from volume V_1 to V_2 in three different ways, the work done by the gas is W_1 if the process is purely isothermal, W_2 if purely isobaric and W_3 if purely adiabatic, then **(2000 JEE)**

(a) $W_2 > W_1 > W_3$ (b) $W_2 > W_3 > W_1$
(c) $W_1 > W_2 > W_3$ (d) $W_1 > W_3 > W_2$

Sol. The corresponding p-V graphs (also called indicator diagram) in three different processes will be as shown below.

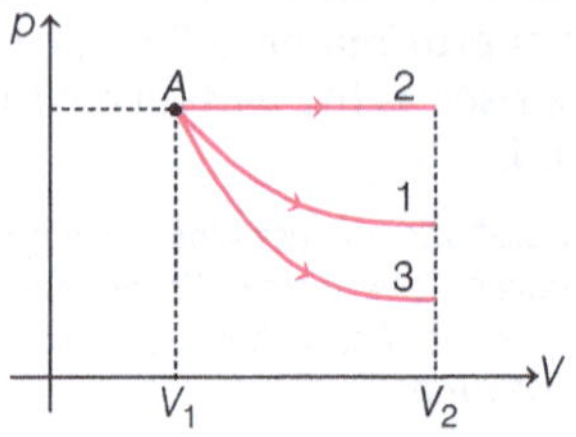

Area under the graph gives the work done by the gas.

$$(\text{Area})_2 > (\text{Area})_1 > (\text{Area})_3$$

$$\Rightarrow \quad W_2 > W_1 > W_3$$

Therefore, the correct option is (a).

Example 12 When an ideal diatomic gas is heated at constant pressure, the fraction of the heat energy supplied, which increases the internal energy of the gas, is **(1990 JEE)**

(a) $\dfrac{2}{5}$ (b) $\dfrac{3}{5}$

(c) $\dfrac{3}{7}$ (d) $\dfrac{5}{7}$

Sol. The desired fraction is

$$f = \frac{\Delta U}{\Delta Q} = \frac{nC_V \Delta T}{nC_p \Delta T} = \frac{C_V}{C_p} = \frac{1}{\gamma}$$

or $$f = \frac{5}{7} \qquad \left(\text{as } \gamma = \frac{7}{5}\right) \qquad \textbf{Ans.}$$

Therefore, the correct option is (d).

Example 13 What is the heat input needed to raise the temperature of 2 moles of helium gas from 0°C to 100°C

(a) at constant volume,

(b) at constant pressure?

(c) What is the work done by the gas in part (b)?

Give your answer in terms of R.

Sol. Helium is monoatomic gas. Therefore,

$$C_V = \frac{3R}{2} \quad \text{and} \quad C_p = \frac{5R}{2}$$

(a) At constant volume,

$$Q = nC_V \Delta T = (2)\left(\frac{3R}{2}\right)(100)$$
$$= 300R$$

(b) At constant pressure,

$$Q = nC_p \Delta T = (2)\left(\frac{5R}{2}\right)(100)$$
$$= 500R$$

(c) At constant pressure,

$$W = Q - \Delta U = nC_p \Delta T - nC_V \Delta T$$
$$= nR\Delta T = (2)(R)(100)$$
$$= 200R$$

Example 14 An ideal monoatomic gas at 300K expands adiabatically to twice its volume. What is the final temperature?

Sol. For an ideal monoatomic gas,

$$\gamma = \frac{5}{3}$$

In an adiabatic process,

$$TV^{\gamma - 1} = \text{constant}$$

$$\therefore \quad T_f V_f^{\gamma - 1} = T_i V_i^{\gamma - 1}$$

or $$T_f = T_i \left(\frac{V_i}{V_f}\right)^{\gamma - 1}$$

$$= (300)\left(\frac{1}{2}\right)^{\frac{5}{3} - 1} = 189\ \text{K}$$

Example 15 p-T graph of 2 moles of an ideal monoatomic gas $\left(C_V = \frac{3}{2}R \text{ and } C_p = \frac{5}{2}R\right)$ is as shown below. Find Q, W and ΔU for each of the four processes separately and then show that,

$$\Delta U_{\text{net}} = 0 \quad \text{and} \quad Q_{\text{net}} = W_{\text{net}}$$

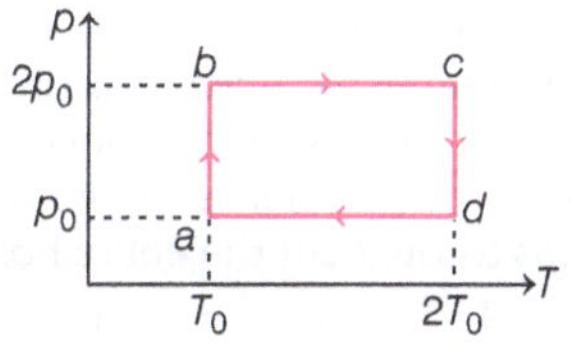

Sol.

Table 2

Process	Name of process	Q	ΔU	W
ab	Isothermal (as T = constant)	$Q = W = -2RT_0 \ln(2)$	0	$nRT \ln\left(\frac{p_i}{p_f}\right)$ $= 2RT_0 \ln\left(\frac{p_0}{2p_0}\right)$ $= -2RT_0 \ln(2)$
bc	Isobaric (as p = constant)	$Q = nC_p \Delta T$ $= 2\left(\frac{5}{2}R\right)(2T_0 - T_0)$ $= 5RT_0$	$\Delta U = nC_V \Delta T$ $= 2\left(\frac{3}{2}R\right)(T_0)$ $= 3RT_0$	$Q - \Delta U$ or $nR\Delta T$ $= 2RT_0$
cd	Isothermal (as T = constant)	$Q = W = 4RT_0 \ln(2)$	0	$nRT \ln\left(\frac{p_i}{p_f}\right)$ $= 2R(2T_0)\ln\left(\frac{2p_0}{p_0}\right)$ $= 4RT_0 \ln(2)$
da	Isobaric (as p = constant)	$Q = nC_p \Delta T$ $= 2\left(\frac{5}{2}R\right)(T_0 - 2T_0)$ $= -5RT_0$	$\Delta U = nC_V \Delta T$ $= 2\left(\frac{3}{2}R\right)(-T_0)$ $= -3RT_0$	$Q - \Delta U$ or $nR\Delta T$ $= -2RT_0$
	Net values	$2RT_0 \ln(2)$	0	$2RT_0 \ln(2)$

In the given table, we can see that

$$\Delta U_{\text{net}} = 0$$

and $$Q_{\text{net}} = W_{\text{net}}$$

INTRODUCTORY Exercise 2

1. One mole of an ideal monoatomic gas is initially at 300 K. Find the final temperature if 200 J of heat are added as follows :

   (a) at constant volume (b) at constant pressure.

2. An ideal gas expands while the pressure is kept constant. During this process, does heat flow into the gas or out of the gas? Justify your answer.

3. Consider the cyclic process depicted in figure. If Q is negative for the process BC and if ΔU is negative for the process CA, what are the signs of Q, W and ΔU that are associated with each process?

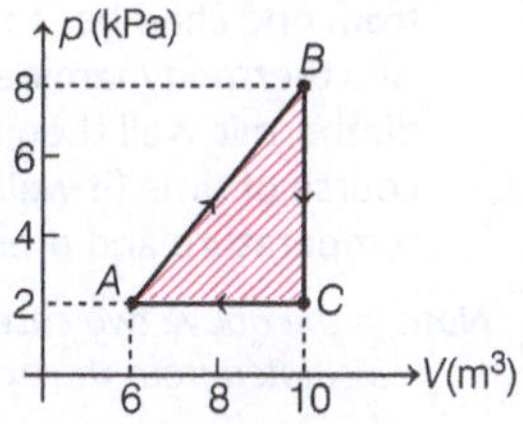

4. A well insulated box contains a partition dividing the box into two equal volumes as shown in figure. Initially, the left hand side contains an ideal monoatomic gas and the other half is a vacuum. The partition is suddenly removed so that the gas expands throughout the entire box.

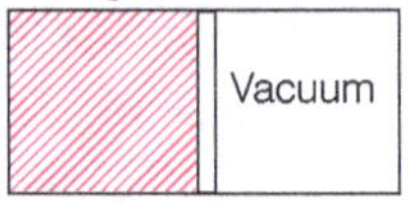

(a) Does the temperature of the gas change?

(b) Does the internal energy of the system change?

(c) Does the gas work?

5. Find the ratio of $\dfrac{\Delta Q}{\Delta U}$ and $\dfrac{\Delta Q}{\Delta W}$ in an isobaric process. The ratio of molar heat capacities $\dfrac{C_p}{C_V}=\gamma$.

6. A certain amount of an ideal gas passes from state A to B first by means of process 1, then by means of process 2. In which of the process is the amount of heat absorbed by the gas greater?

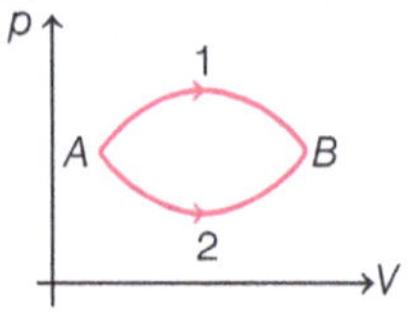

7. A sample of ideal gas is expanded to twice its original volume of $1.00\,\text{m}^3$ in a process for which $p=\alpha V^2$, with $\alpha = 5.00\ \text{atm/m}^6$, as shown in figure. How much work is done by the expanding gas?

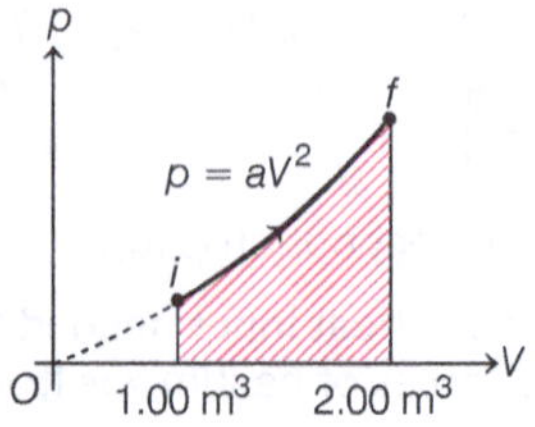

Answers

1. (a) 316 K (b) 309.6 K 2. Into gas

3.

Process	Q	W	ΔU
AB	+	+	+
BC	–	0	–
CA	–	–	–

4. (a) No (b) No (c) No

5. γ and $\dfrac{\gamma}{\gamma-1}$

6. $Q_1 > Q_2$ 7. 1.18 MJ

See hints on pages 305-306.

Important POINTS

1. **Adiabatic and Diathermic Wall**

Adiabatic wall An insulating wall (can be movable also) that does not allow flow of heat from one chamber to another is called an adiabatic wall. If two thermodynamic systems A and B are separated by an adiabatic wall then the thermodynamic state of A will be independent of the state of B and *vice-versa* if the wall is fixed otherwise if the wall is movable, only pressure will be same on both sides.

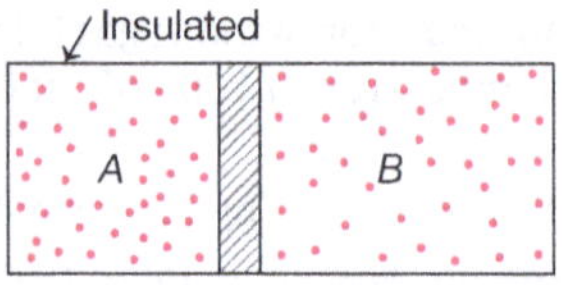

Diathermic wall A conducting wall that allows heat flow from one chamber to another is called a diathermic wall. If two thermodynamic systems A and B are separated by a diathermic wall then thermal equilibrium is attained in due course of time (if wall is fixed). If wall is movable, then temperature and pressure on both sides will become same.

Note *In the above two cases, thermodynamic systems A and B are insulated from the external surroundings.*

Adiabatic wall		Diathermic wall	
Fixed	**Movable**	**Fixed**	**Movable**
Unchanged	$(p_A)_f=(p_B)_f$	$(T_A)_f=(T_B)_f$	$(T_A)_f=(T_B)_f$ and $(p_A)_f=(p_B)_f$

2. **Quasi-Static Process** Quasi means almost or near to.

Quasi-static process means very nearly static process. Let us consider a system of gas contained in a cylinder. The gas is held by a moving piston. A weight w is placed over the piston. Due to the weight , the gas in cylinder is compressed. After the gas reaches equilibrium, the properties of gas are denoted by p_1, V_1 and T_1. The weight placed over the piston is balanced by upward force exerted by the gas. If the weight is suddenly removed, then there will be an unbalanced force between the system and the surroundings. The gas under pressure will expand and push the piston upwards. The properties at this state after reaching equilibrium are P_2, V_2 and T_2. But the intermediate states passed through, by the system are non-equilibrium states which cannot be described by thermodynamic coordinates. In this case, we only have initial and final states and do not have a path connecting them.

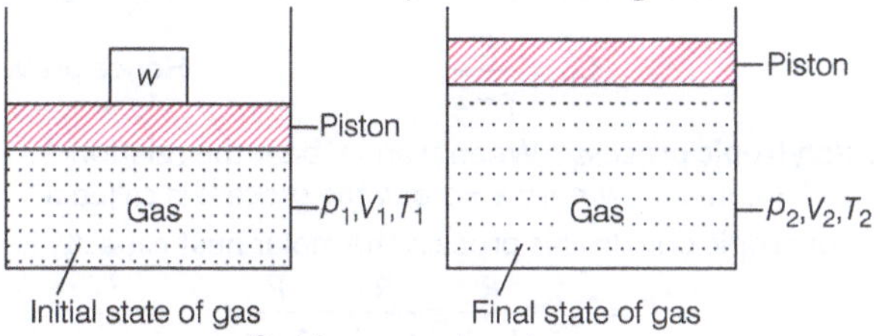

Sudden expansion of gas

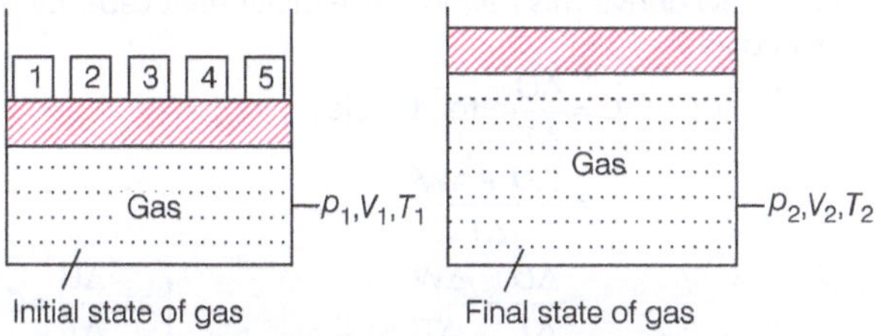

Quasi-static expansion of gas

Suppose, the weight is made of large numbers of small weights. And one by one each of these small weights are removed and allowed the system to reach an equilibrium state.

Then, we have intermediate equilibrium states and the path described by these states will not deviate much from the thermodynamic equilibrium state. Such a process, which is the locus of all the intermediate points passed by the system is known as **quasi-static process**. It means, this process is almost near to the thermodynamically equilibrium process. Infinite slowness is the characteristic feature of quasi-static process.

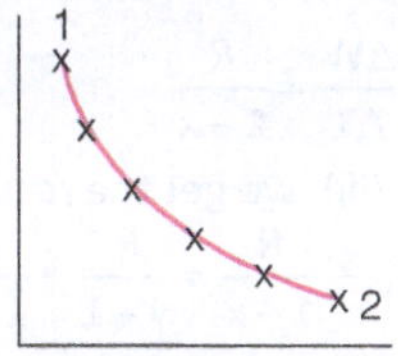

A quasi-static process

A quasi-static process is obviously a hypothetical concept. In practice, processes that are sufficiently slow and do not involve accelerated motion of the piston are reasonably approximation to an ideal quasi-static process. We shall from now onwards deal with quasi-static processes only, except when stated otherwise.

3. **Reversible and Irreversible Process**

Reversible process The process in which the system and surroundings can be restored to the initial state from the final state without producing any changes in the thermodynamic properties of the universe is called a reversible process.

In the figure below, let us suppose that the system has undergone a change from state *A* to state *B*. If the system can be restored from state *B* to state *A*, and there is no change in the universe, then the process is said to be a reversible process. The reversible process can be reversed completely and there is no trace left to show that the system had undergone thermodynamic change.

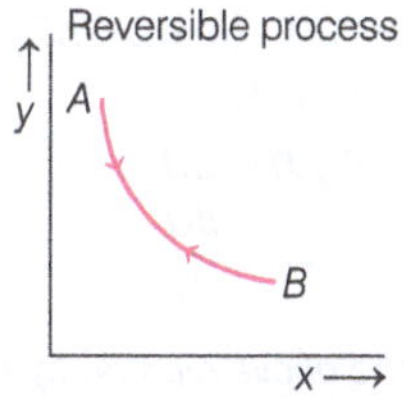

For the system to undergo reversible change, it should occur infinitely slowly or it should be quasi-static process. During reversible process, all the changes in state that occur in the system are in thermodynamic equilibrium with each other.

Thus, there are two important conditions for the reversible process to occur. Firstly, the process should occur very slowly and secondly all of the initial and final states of the system should be in equilibrium with each other.

For example, a quasi-static isothermal expansion of an ideal gas in a cylinder fitted with a frictionless movable piston is a reversible process.

In actual practice, the reversible process never occurs, thus it is an ideal or hypothetical process.

Irreversible process The process is said to be an irreversible process if it cannot return the system and the surroundings to their original conditions when the process is reversed. The irreversible process is not at equilibrium throughout the process. Several examples can be cited. For examples,

(i) When we are driving the car uphill, it consumes a lot of fuel and this fuel is not returned when we are driving down the hill.

(ii) The base of a vessel on an oven is hotter than its other parts. When the vessel is removed, heat is transferred from the base to the other parts, bringing the vessel to a uniform temperature (which in due course cools to the temperature of the surroundings). The process cannot be reversed; a part of the vessel will not get cooler spontaneously and warm up the base.

(iii) The free expansion of a gas is irreversible.

(iv) Cooking gas leaking from a gas cylinder in the kitchen diffuses to the entire room. The diffusion process will not spontaneously reverse and bring the gas back to the cylinder.

Many factors contribute in making any process irreversible. The most common of these are: friction, viscosity and other dissipative effects.

The irreversible process is also called the natural process because all the processes occurring in nature are irreversible processes.

4. $\boldsymbol{C_V = \frac{dU}{dT}}$ Let us derive the relation $C_V = \frac{dU}{dT}$, where

U = internal energy of 1 mole of the gas.

Consider 1 mole ($n = 1$) of an ideal monoatomic gas which undergoes an isochoric process (V = constant).

From the first law of thermodynamics.

$$dQ = dW + dU \qquad ...(i)$$

Here, $dW = 0$ as $V =$ constant

$$dQ = CdT = C_V dT \quad (\text{In } dQ = nC_V dT,\ n = 1 \text{ and } C = C_V)$$

Substituting in Eq. (i), we have

$$C_V dT = dU$$

or $$C_V = \frac{dU}{dT}$$ **Hence proved.**

Note *We have derived the above relation by taking an isochoric process. But it is true for all processes. This is because dU or ΔU is a state function which does not depend upon process.*

5. $C_p - C_V = R$ To prove this relation (also known as **Mayor's formula**) let us consider 1 mole of an ideal gas which undergoes an isobaric ($p =$ constant) process.

From first law of thermodynamics,

$$dQ = dW + dU \qquad ...(ii)$$

Here, $dQ = C_p dT$ (as $n = 1$ and $C = C_p$)

$dU = C_V dT$

and $$dW = pdV = p\left[d\left(\frac{RT}{p}\right)\right] \qquad \left(\text{as } V = \frac{RT}{P}\right)$$

$$= d\,(RT) \qquad (\text{as } P = \text{constant})$$

$$= RdT$$

Substituting these values in Eq. (ii), We have

$C_p dT = RdT + C_V dT$ or $C_p - C_V = R$ **Hence proved.**

Note *We have derived this relation for an isobaric process. But C_p and C_V are constant for a given gas. There difference is equal to a constant R. This constant we can find from any process and we have found by using an isobaric process.*

6. $C_V = \dfrac{R}{\gamma - 1}$

We have already derived,

$$C_p - C_V = R$$

Dividing this equation by C_V, we have

$$\frac{C_p}{C_V} - 1 = \frac{R}{C_V}$$

or $$\gamma - 1 = \frac{R}{C_V} \qquad \left(\text{as } \frac{C_P}{C_V} = \gamma\right)$$

$\therefore$ $$C_V = \frac{R}{\gamma - 1}$$ **Hence proved.**

7. **Polytropic process** When p and V bear the relation $pV^x =$ constant, where $x \neq 1$ or γ the process is called a polytropic one. In this process the molar heat capacity is,

$$C = C_V + \frac{R}{1-x} = \frac{R}{\gamma - 1} + \frac{R}{1-x}$$

Let us now derive this relation. The molar heat capacity is defined as

$$C = \frac{\Delta Q}{\Delta T} \quad \text{for 1 mole}$$

$$= \frac{\Delta U + \Delta W}{\Delta T}$$

$$= \frac{\Delta U}{\Delta T} + \frac{\Delta W}{\Delta T} \qquad \left(\text{as } \frac{\Delta U}{\Delta T} = C_V\right)$$

$\therefore$ $$C = C_V + \frac{\Delta W}{\Delta T} \qquad ...(iii)$$

Here, $$\Delta W = \int_{V_i}^{V_f} pdV = \int_{V_i}^{V_f} kV^{-x} dV = \left[\frac{kV^{-x+1}}{-x+1}\right]_{V_i}^{V_f}$$

$$= \frac{kV_f^{-x+1} - kV_i^{-x+1}}{-x+1}$$

$$= \frac{p_f V_f^x V_f^{-x+1} - p_i V_i^x V_i^{-x+1}}{1-x}$$

$$= \frac{p_f V_f - p_i V_i}{1-x} = \frac{RT_f - RT_i}{1-x} = \frac{R\Delta T}{1-x}$$

$\therefore$ $$\frac{\Delta W}{\Delta T} = \frac{R}{1-x}$$

Substituting in Eq. (iii), we get the result i.e.

$\therefore$ $$C = C_V + \frac{R}{1-x} = \frac{R}{\gamma - 1} + \frac{R}{1-x}$$

Typed Problems

Type 1. *Based on first law of thermodynamics applied to a general system.*

Concept

First law of thermodynamics is simply law of conservation of energy which can be applied to any system.

Ex. 1 Boiling water : Suppose 1.0 g of water vaporizes isobarically at atmospheric pressure (1.01×10^5 Pa). Its volume in the liquid state is $V_i = V_{\text{liquid}} = 1.0\ \text{cm}^3$ and its volume in vapour state is $V_f = V_{\text{vapour}} = 1671\ \text{cm}^3$. Find the work done in the expansion and the change in internal energy of the system. Ignore any mixing of the steam and the surrounding air. Take latent heat of vaporization $L_v = 2.26 \times 10^6$ J/kg..

Sol. Because the expansion takes place at constant pressure, the work done is

$$W = \int_{V_i}^{V_f} p_0 dV = p_0 \int_{V_i}^{V_f} dV$$

$$= p_0 (V_f - V_i)$$

$$= (1.01 \times 10^5)(1671 \times 10^{-6} - 1.0 \times 10^{-6})$$

$$= 169\ \text{J}$$ **Ans.**

$$Q = mL_v = (1.0 \times 10^{-3})(2.26 \times 10^6)$$

$$= 2260\ \text{J}$$ **Ans.**

Hence, from the first law, the change in internal energy

$$\Delta U = Q - W = 2260 - 169$$

$$= 2091\ \text{J}$$ **Ans.**

Note *The positive value of ΔU indicates that the internal energy of the system increases. We see that most $\left(\frac{2091\ J}{2260\ J} = 93\%\right)$ of the energy transferred to the liquid goes into increasing the internal energy of the system only $\frac{169\ J}{2260\ J} = 7\%$ is used by the system in doing work by the steam on the surrounding atmosphere.*

Ex. 2 A metal of mass 1 kg at constant atmospheric pressure and at initial temperature 20°C is given a heat of 20000 J. Find the following **(2005 JEE)**

(a) change in temperature,
(b) work done and
(c) change in internal energy.
(Given, specific heat = 400 J/kg-°C, coefficient of cubical expansion, $\gamma = 9 \times 10^{-5}$/°C, density $\rho = 9000\ kg/m^3$, atmospheric pressure $= 10^5\ N/m^2$)

Sol. (a) From $\Delta Q = ms\Delta T$

$$\Delta T = \frac{\Delta Q}{ms} = \frac{20000}{1 \times 400} = 50°C$$

(b) $\Delta V = V\gamma\Delta T = \left(\frac{1}{9000}\right)(9 \times 10^{-5})(50) = 5 \times 10^{-7}\ m^3$

$$\therefore \quad W = p_0 \cdot \Delta V = (10^5)(5 \times 10^{-7}) = 0.05\ J$$

(c) $\Delta U = \Delta Q - W = (20000 - 0.05)\ J$

$$= 19999.95\ J$$

Type 2. *To make p-V, V-T or p-T equation corresponding to a given process.*

Concept

Suppose we wish to make *p-V* equation for a given process then with the help of equation of first law of thermodynamics and $pV = nRT$, first make an equation of type

$$f(p)dp + f(V)dV = 0$$

Now, integrating this equation we will get the desired *p-V* equation.

Ex. 3 Make *p-V* equation for an adiabatic process.

Sol. In adiabatic process, $dQ = 0$

$$dU = -dW \qquad (n = 1)$$

or $\quad C_V dT = -pdV \qquad$ ...(i)

Also, for 1 mole of an ideal gas,

$$pV = RT$$

$\therefore \quad d(pV) = d(RT)$

or $\quad pdV + Vdp = RdT$

or $\quad dT = \frac{pdV + Vdp}{R} \qquad$ ...(ii)

$\frac{(i)}{(ii)}$ gives, $\quad C_V = \frac{-R(pdV)}{pdV + Vdp}$

$\Rightarrow \quad C_V Vdp + (C_V + R)pdV = 0$

or $\quad C_V Vdp + C_p pdV = 0$

Dividing this equation by *pV*, we are left with

$$C_V \frac{dp}{p} + C_p \frac{dV}{V} = 0$$

Dividing by C_V, we get

or $\quad \frac{dp}{p} + \gamma \frac{dV}{V} = 0$

or $\quad \int \frac{dp}{p} + \gamma \int \frac{dV}{V} = 0$

or $\quad \ln(p) + \gamma \ln(V) = \text{constant}$

or $\quad \ln(pV^\gamma) = \text{constant}$

We can write this in the form

$\Rightarrow \quad pV^\gamma = \text{constant}$

Miscellaneous Examples

Ex. 4 An ideal gas expands isothermally along *AB* and does 700 J of work.

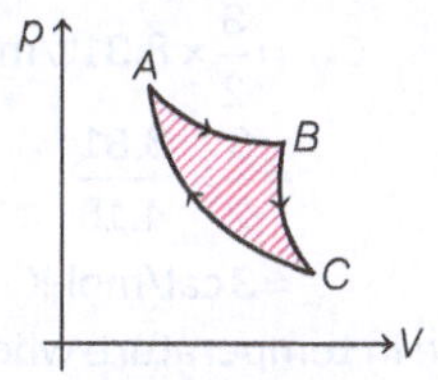

(a) How much heat does the gas exchange along *AB*?
(b) The gas then expands adiabatically along *BC* and does 400 J of work. When the gas returns to *A* along *CA*, it exhausts 100 J of heat to its surroundings. How much work is done on the gas along this path?

Sol. (a) *AB* is an isothermal process. Hence,

$$\Delta U_{AB} = 0$$

and $\quad Q_{AB} = W_{AB} = 700\ J \qquad$ **Ans.**

(b) *BC* is an adiabatic process. Hence,

$$Q_{BC} = 0 \Rightarrow W_{BC} = 400\ J$$

$\therefore \quad \Delta U_{BC} = -W_{BC} = -400\ J$

ABC is a cyclic process and internal energy is a state function. Therefore,

$$(\Delta U)_{\text{whole cycle}} = 0 = \Delta U_{AB} + \Delta U_{BC} + \Delta U_{CA}$$

and from first law of thermodynamics,

$$Q_{AB} + Q_{BC} + Q_{CA} = W_{AB} + W_{BC} + W_{CA}$$

Substituting the values,

$$700 + 0 - 100 = 700 + 400 + \Delta W_{CA}$$

$\therefore \quad \Delta W_{CA} = -500\ J \qquad$ **Ans.**

Negative sign implies that work is done on the gas. Table below shows different values in different processes.

Table 3

Process	Q(J)	W(J)	ΔU(J)
AB	700	700	0
BC	0	400	– 400
CA	–100	–500	400
For complete cycle	600	600	0

Note *Total work done is 600 J, which implies that area of the closed curve is also 600 J.*

Ex. 5 Find the molar specific heat of the process $p = \frac{a}{T}$ for a monoatomic gas, a being constant.

Sol. We know that

$$dQ = dU + dW$$

Specific heat, $$C = \frac{dQ}{dT} = \frac{dU}{dT} + \frac{dW}{dT} \quad \text{...(i)}$$

Since, $$dU = C_V dT \quad \text{...(ii)}$$

$$C = C_V + \frac{dW}{dT}$$

$$= C_V + \frac{pdV}{dT}$$

$$pV = RT$$

$\therefore$ For the given process, $$V = \frac{RT}{p} = \frac{RT^2}{a} \quad \left(\because p = \frac{a}{T}\right)$$

$$\frac{dV}{dT} = \frac{2RT}{a}$$

$$\therefore \quad C = C_V + p\left(\frac{2RT}{a}\right) \quad \left(\because \frac{T}{a} = \frac{1}{p}\right)$$

$$= C_V + 2R$$

$$= \frac{3}{2}R + 2R = \frac{7}{2}R$$

Note *C_V of a monoatomic gas is $\frac{3}{2}R$.*

Ex. 6 At 27°C two moles of an ideal monatomic gas occupy a volume V. The gas expands adiabatically to a volume $2V$. Calculate **(1996 JEE)**

(a) final temperature of the gas

(b) change in its internal energy and

(c) the work done by the gas during the process.

[$R = 8.31$ J/mol-K]

Sol. (a) In case of adiabatic change

$$TV^{\gamma - 1} = \text{constant}$$

$$\therefore \quad T_1 V_1^{\gamma - 1} = T_2 V_2^{\gamma - 1}$$

with $\gamma = \left(\frac{5}{3}\right)$

$$\Rightarrow \quad 300 \times V^{2/3} = T(2V)^{2/3}$$

or $$T = \frac{300}{(2)^{2/3}} = 189 \text{ K}$$

(b) As $\Delta U = nC_V \Delta T = n\left(\frac{3}{2}R\right)\Delta T$

So, $$\Delta U = 2 \times \left(\frac{3}{2}\right) \times 8.31\,(189 - 300)$$

$$= -2767.23 \text{ J}$$

Negative sign means internal energy will decrease.

(c) According to first law of thermodynamics

$$Q = \Delta U + \Delta W$$

And as for adiabatic change $Q = 0$,

$$\Delta W = -\Delta U = 2767.23 \text{ J}$$

Ex. 7 Two moles of a diatomic ideal gas is taken through pT = constant. Its temperature is increased from T to $2T$. Find the work done by the system?

Sol. pT = constant

$\therefore$ $$p(pV) = \text{constant} \quad (\text{as } T \propto pV)$$

or $$pV^{1/2} = \text{constant}$$

Comparing with $$pV^x = \text{constant}$$

We have, $$x = \frac{1}{2}$$

$$W = \frac{nR\Delta T}{1 - x} = \frac{2R(2T - T)}{1 - \frac{1}{2}}$$

$$= 4RT$$

Ex. 8 An ideal monatomic gas at temperature 27°C and pressure 10^6 N/m^2 occupies 10 L volume. 10,000 cal of heat is added to the system without changing the volume. Calculate the change in temperature of the gas. Given : $R = 8.31$ J/mol-K and $J = 4.18$ J/cal.

Sol. For n moles of gas, we have $pV = nRT$

Here, $p = 10^6 \text{ N/m}^2$, $V = 10 \text{ L} = 10^{-2} \text{ m}^3$ and $T = 27°\text{C} = 300 \text{ K}$

$$\therefore \quad n = \frac{pV}{RT} = \frac{10^6 \times 10^{-2}}{8.31 \times 300} = 4.0$$

For monatomic gas, $$C_V = \frac{3}{2}R$$

Thus, $$C_V = \frac{3}{2} \times 8.31 \text{ J/mol-K}$$

$$= \frac{3}{2} \times \frac{8.31}{4.18}$$

$$\approx 3 \text{ cal/mol-K}$$

Let ΔT be the rise in temperature when n moles of the gas is given Q cal of heat at constant volume. Then,

$$Q = nC_V \Delta T$$

or $$\Delta T = \frac{Q}{nC_V}$$

$$= \frac{10000 \text{ cal}}{4.0 \text{ mole} \times 3 \text{ cal/mol-K}}$$

$$= 833 \text{ K}$$

Ex. 9 One mole of a monoatomic ideal gas is taken through the cycle shown in figure.

$A \to B$ Adiabatic expansion
$B \to C$ Cooling at constant volume
$C \to D$ Adiabatic compression.
$D \to A$ Heating at constant volume

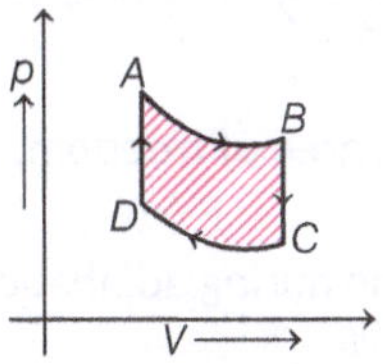

The pressure and temperature at A, B etc., are denoted by p_A, T_A; p_B, T_B etc. respectively.

Given, $T_A = 1000K$, $p_B = \left(\frac{2}{3}\right)p_A$ and $p_C = \left(\frac{1}{3}\right)p_A$.

Calculate

(a) the work done by the gas in the process $A \to B$

(b) the heat lost by the gas in the process $B \to C$

Given, $\left(\frac{2}{3}\right)^{0.4} = 0.85$ and $R = 8.31$ J/mol-K

Sol. (a) As for adiabatic change

$$T^\gamma p^{1-\gamma} = \text{constant}$$

$$\therefore \quad T_B^\gamma p_B^{1-\gamma} = T_A^\gamma p_A^{1-\gamma}$$

i.e $T_B = T_A\left(\frac{p_B}{p_A}\right)^{1-\frac{1}{\gamma}} = T_A\left(\frac{2}{3}\right)^{1-\frac{1}{\gamma}} = 1000\left(\frac{2}{3}\right)^{2/5} = 850\text{K}$

So, $W_{AB} = \frac{nR[T_F - T_I]}{[1-\gamma]} = \frac{nR[T_i - T_f]}{\gamma - 1}$ $\left(\text{as } \gamma = \frac{5}{3}\right)$

$$= \frac{1 \times 8.31\,[1000 - 850]}{\left[\left(\frac{5}{3}\right) - 1\right]}$$

i.e. $W_{AB} = 1869.75$ J

(b) For $B \to C$, $V =$ constant

$\Rightarrow \quad \Delta W = 0$

So, from first law of thermodynamics

$$\Delta Q = \Delta U + \Delta W = nC_V\Delta T + 0$$

or $\Delta Q = 1 \times \left(\frac{3}{2}R\right)(T_C - 850)$ $\left(\text{as } C_V = \frac{3}{2}R\right)$

Now, along path BC, V=constant; $p \propto T$

i.e. $\frac{p_C}{p_B} = \frac{T_C}{T_B}$

$$T_C = \frac{\left(\frac{1}{3}\right)p_A}{\left(\frac{2}{3}\right)p_A} \times T_B = \frac{T_B}{2} = \frac{850}{2} = 425\text{ K}$$

So, $\Delta Q = 1 \times \frac{3}{2} \times 8.31\,(425 - 850) = -5297.625$ J

[Negative heat means, heat is lost by the system]

Ex. 10 A gas undergoes a process such that $p \propto \frac{1}{T}$. If the molar heat capacity for this process is $C = 33.24$ J/mol-K, find the degree of freedom of the molecules of the gas.

Sol. In the process $pV^x =$ constant, molar heat capacity is given by

$$C = \frac{R}{\gamma - 1} + \frac{R}{1 - x}$$

The given process is $pT =$ constant

$\Rightarrow \quad p(pV) =$ constant

or $\quad pV^{\frac{1}{2}} =$ constant

or $\quad x = \frac{1}{2}$

$$\therefore \quad C = \frac{R}{\gamma - 1} + \frac{R}{1 - \frac{1}{2}} = \frac{R}{\gamma - 1} + 2R$$

Substituting the values,

$$33.24 = R\left(\frac{1}{\gamma - 1} + 2\right)$$

$$= 8.31\left(\frac{1}{\gamma - 1} + 2\right)$$

Solving this we get $\quad \gamma = 1.5$

Now, $\quad \gamma = 1 + \frac{2}{F}$

Degree of freedom, $F = \frac{2}{\gamma - 1} = \frac{2}{1.5 - 1} = 4$

Ex. 11 A gaseous mixture enclosed in a vessel consists of one gram mole of a gas A with $\gamma = \left(\frac{5}{3}\right)$ and some amount of gas B with $\gamma = \frac{7}{5}$ at a temperature T. The gases A and B do not react with each other and are assumed to be ideal. Find the number of gram moles of the gas B if γ for the gaseous mixture is $\left(\frac{19}{13}\right)$.

Sol. $\gamma_A = \frac{5}{3}$, so A is monoatomic.

$\gamma_B = \frac{7}{5}$, so B is diatomic.

$$\therefore \quad (C_V)_A = \frac{3}{2}R \text{ and } (C_V)_B = \frac{5}{2}R$$

$$(C_V)_{\text{mixture}} = \frac{R}{\gamma - 1} = \frac{R}{\frac{19}{13} - 1} = \frac{13}{6}R$$

From conservation of energy,

i.e $\quad \Delta U = \Delta U_A + \Delta U_B$

$$(n_A + n_B)(C_V)_{\text{mix}}\,\Delta T = [n_A(C_V)_A + n_B(C_V)_B]\,\Delta T$$

i.e. $$(C_V)_{mix} = \frac{n_A (C_V)_A + n_B (C_V)_B}{n_A + n_B}$$

We have $$\frac{13}{6}R = \frac{1 \times \frac{3}{2}R + n_B \frac{5}{2}R}{1 + n_B}$$

$$= \frac{(3 + 5n_B)R}{2(1 + n_B)}$$

or $$13 + 13n_B = 9 + 15n_B$$

i.e. $$n_B = 2$$ **Ans.**

Ex. 12 An ideal gas having initial pressure p, volume V and temperature T is allowed to expand adiabatically until its volume becomes 5.66 V, while its temperature falls to $T/2$. **(1990 JEE)**

(a) How many degrees of freedom do the gas molecules have?

(b) Obtain the work done by the gas during the expansion as a function of the initial pressure p and volume V.

Given that $(5.66)^{0.4} = 2$

Sol. (a) For adiabatic expansion,

$$TV^{\gamma - 1} = \text{constant}$$

i.e. $$TV^{\gamma - 1} = T'V'^{\gamma - 1}$$

$$= \frac{T}{2}(5.66V)^{\gamma - 1}$$

i.e. $$(5.66)^{\gamma - 1} = 2$$

$\therefore$ $$\gamma - 1 = 0.4$$

i.e. $$\gamma = 1.4$$

Using $\gamma = 1 + \frac{2}{F}$

We get degree of freedom,

$$F = 5$$ **Ans.**

(b) Work done during adiabatic process for one mole gas is

$$W = \frac{1}{1 - \gamma}[p'V' - pV]$$

From relation, $\frac{pV}{T} = \frac{p'V'}{T'}$

We get $$p' = \frac{T'}{T} \cdot \frac{pV}{V'} = \frac{1}{2} \times \frac{1}{5.66} p = \frac{p}{11.32}$$

$\therefore$ $$W = \frac{1}{1 - 1.4}\left[\frac{p}{11.32} \times \frac{V}{5.66} - pV\right]$$

$$= \frac{1}{0.4}\left[1 - \frac{1}{11.32 \times 5.66}\right] pV$$

$$= 2.461\, pV$$ **Ans.**

MODULE 2 Exercise

Assertion and Reason

See directions on page 14.

1. **Assertion :** In a thermodynamic process, initial volume of gas is equal to final volume of gas. Work done by the gas in this process should be zero.

   Reason : Work done by gas in isochoric process is zero.

2. **Assertion :** When ice melts, work is done by atmosphere on (ice + water) system.

   Reason : On melting of ice volume of (ice + water) system decreases.

3. **Assertion :** In the process pT = constant, if temperature of gas is increased, work done by the gas is positive.

   Reason : For the given process, $V \propto T$.

4. **Assertion :** If volume of a gas is increasing but temperature of the gas is decreasing, then heat given to the gas may be positive, negative or zero.

   Reason : Heat given to a gas is a state function. It is not path function.

Single Correct Option

5. In a process, the pressure of an ideal gas is proportional to square of the volume of the gas. If the temperature of the gas increases in this process, then work done by this gas

   (a) is positive
   (b) is negative
   (c) is zero
   (d) may be positive or negative

6. n moles of a gas are filled in a container at temperature T. If the gas is slowly and isothermally compressed to half its initial volume, the work done by the atmosphere on the gas is

   (a) $\frac{nRT}{2}$ (b) $-\frac{nRT}{2}$
   (c) $nRT \ln 2$ (d) $-nRT \ln 2$

7. A gas undergoes A to B through three different processes 1, 2 and 3 as shown in the figure. The heat supplied to the gas is Q_1, Q_2 and Q_3 respectively, then

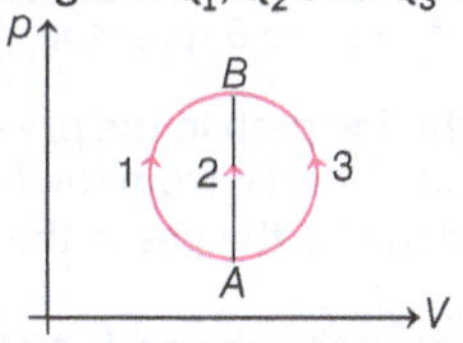

(a) $Q_1 = Q_2 = Q_3$ (b) $Q_1 < Q_2 < Q_3$
(c) $Q_1 > Q_2 > Q_3$ (d) $Q_1 = Q_3 > Q_2$

8. For an adiabatic compression the quantity pV
(a) increases (b) decreases
(c) remains constant (d) depends on γ

9. In a thermodynamic process, pressure of a fixed mass of a gas is changed in such a manner that the gas molecules gives out 20 J of heat and 10 J of work is done on the gas. If the initial internal energy of the gas was 40 J, then the final internal energy will be
(a) 30 J (b) 20 J
(c) 60 J (d) 40 J

10. Figure shows two processes a and b for a given sample of a gas. If $\Delta Q_1, \Delta Q_2$ are the amounts of heat absorbed by the system in the two cases and $\Delta U_1, \Delta U_2$ are changes in internal energies respectively, then

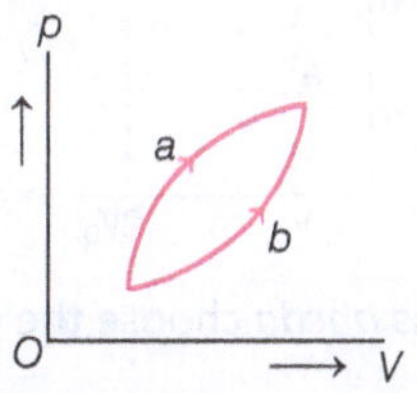

(a) $\Delta Q_1 = \Delta Q_2; \Delta U_1 = \Delta U_2$ (b) $\Delta Q_1 > \Delta Q_2; \Delta U_1 > \Delta U_2$
(c) $\Delta Q_1 < \Delta Q_2; \Delta U_1 < \Delta U_2$ (d) $\Delta Q_1 > \Delta Q_2; \Delta U_1 = \Delta U_2$

11. Air in a cylinder is suddenly compressed by a piston which is then maintained at the same position. As the time passes pressure of the gas
(a) increases
(b) decreases
(c) remains the same
(d) may increase or decrease depending on the nature of the gas

12. A cycle pump becomes hot near the nozzle after a few quick strokes even if they are smooth because
(a) the volume of air decreases
(b) the number of air molecules increases
(c) the compression is adiabatic
(d) collision between air particles increases

13. In an adiabatic change, the pressure p and temperature T of a diatomic gas are related by the relation $p \propto T^{\alpha}$, where α equals
(a) 1.67 (b) 0.4
(c) 0.6 (d) 3.5

14. A diatomic gas obeys the law pV^x = constant. For what value of x, it has negative molar specific heat ?
(a) $x > 1.4$ (b) $x < 1.4$
(c) $1 < x < 1.4$ (d) $0 < x < 1$

15. p-V diagram of a diatomic gas is a straight line passing through origin. The molar heat capacity of the gas in the process will be
(a) $4R$ (b) $2.5R$ (c) $3R$ (d) $\frac{4R}{3}$

16. Heat energy absorbed by a system in going through a cyclic process as shown in the figure [V in litres and p in kPa] is

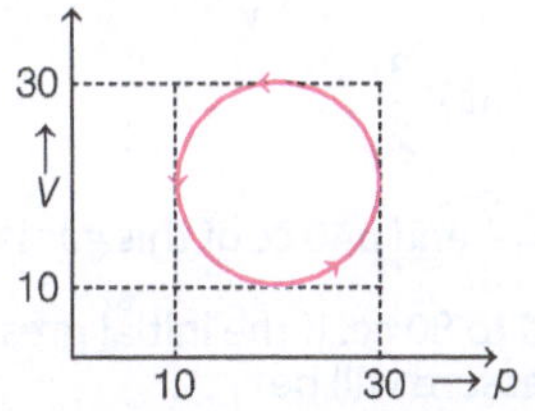

(a) $10^7 \pi J$ (b) $10^4 \pi J$ (c) $10^2 \pi J$ (d) $10^3 \pi J$

17. If W_{ABC} is the work done in process $A \to B \to C$ and W_{DEF} is work done in process $D \to E \to F$ as shown in adjacent figure, then

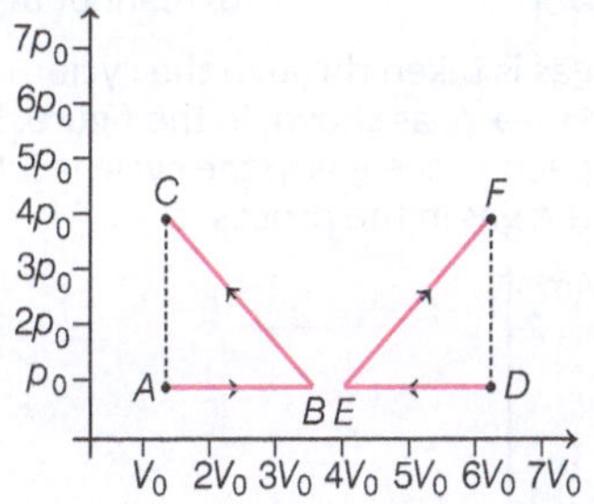

(a) $|W_{DEF}| > |W_{ABC}|$ (b) $|W_{DEF}| < |W_{ABC}|$
(c) $W_{DEF} = W_{ABC}$ (d) $W_{DEF} = -W_{ABC}$

18. If ΔQ and ΔW represent the heat supplied to the system and the work done on the system respectively, then the first law of thermodynamics can be written as
(a) $\Delta Q = \Delta U + \Delta W$ (b) $\Delta Q = \Delta U - \Delta W$
(c) $\Delta Q = \Delta W - \Delta U$ (d) $\Delta Q = -\Delta W - \Delta U$

19. Consider two processes on a system as shown in figure. The volumes in the initial states are the same in the two processes and the volumes in the final states are also the same. Let ΔW_1 and ΔW_2 be the work done by the system in the processes A and B respectively. Then :

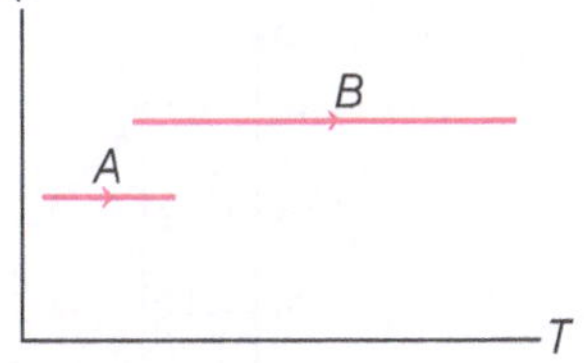

(a) $\Delta W_1 > \Delta W_2$ (b) $\Delta W_1 = \Delta W_2$
(c) $\Delta W_1 < \Delta W_2$ (d) None of these

20. An ideal gas of volume $1.5 \times 10^{-3}\ m^3$ and at pressure 1.0×10^5 Pa is supplied with 70 J of energy. The volume increases to $1.7 \times 10^{-3}\ m^3$, the pressure remaining constant. The internal energy of the gas is
(a) increased by 90 J (b) increased by 70 J
(c) increased by 50 J (d) decreased by 50 J

21. During an adiabatic process, the pressure of a gas is found to be proportional to the cube of its absolute temperature. The ratio $\frac{C_p}{C_V} = \gamma$ for the gas is
(a) 2 (b) $\frac{3}{2}$ (c) $\frac{5}{3}$ (d) $\frac{4}{3}$

22. For a gas $\gamma = \frac{5}{3}$ and 640 cc of this gas is suddenly compressed to 80 cc. If the initial pressure is p, then the final pressure will be
(a) $8p$ (b) $32p$ (c) $16p$ (d) $64p$

23. An ideal gas mixture filled inside a balloon expands according to the relation $pV^{2/3}$ = constant. The temperature inside the balloon is
(a) increasing (b) decreasing
(c) constant (d) Cannot be defined

24. An ideal gas is taken through the cycle $A \to B \to C \to A$, as shown in the figure. If the net heat supplied to the gas in the cycle is 5 J, the work done by the gas in the process $C \to A$ is **(2002 JEE)**

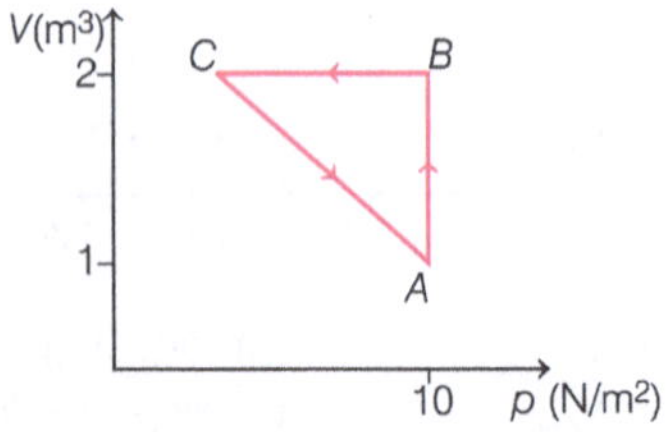

(a) −5 J (b) −10 J (c) −15 J (d) −20 J

25. An ideal diatomic gas is carried around a closed cycle *abca* in which *bc* is an isothermal process as shown in the figure. The gas absorbs 7000 J of heat as its temperature increases from 300 K to 1000 K in going from *a* to *b*. The quantity of heat rejected by the gas during the process *ca* is approximately

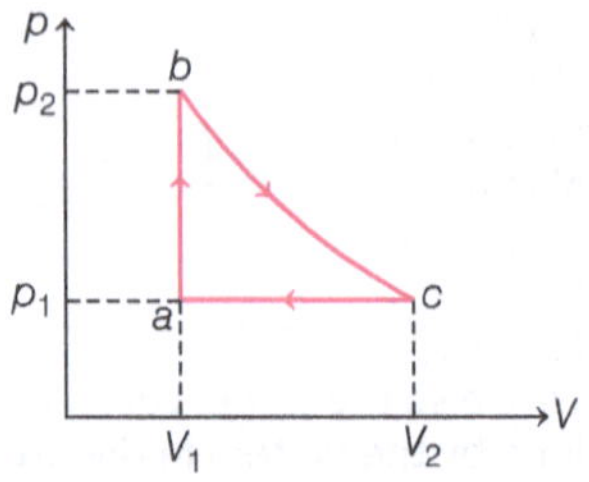

(a) 4200 J (b) 5000 J (c) 9000 J (d) 9800 J

Multiple Correct Options

26. An ideal gas is taken from the state A (pressure p, volume V) to the state B (pressure $\frac{p}{2}$, volume $2V$) along a straight line path in the p-V diagram. Select the correct statement(s) from the following.
(a) The work done by the gas in the process A to B is negative
(b) In the T-V diagram, the path AB becomes a part of a parabola
(c) In the p-T diagram, the path AB becomes a part of a hyperbola
(d) In going from A to B, the temperature T of the gas first increases to a maximum value and then decreases

27. In the process pV^2 = constant, if temperature of gas is increased, then
(a) change in internal energy of gas is positive
(b) work done by gas is positive
(c) heat is given to the gas
(d) heat is taken out from the gas

28. T-V diagram of two moles of a monoatomic gas is as shown in figure.

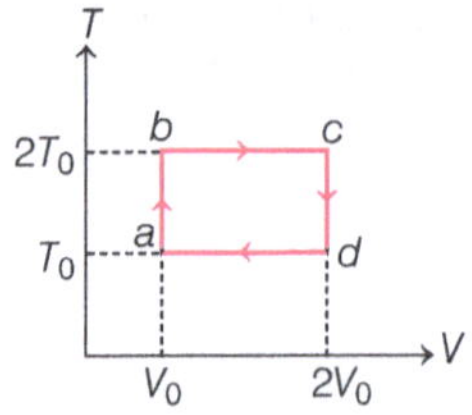

For the process *abcda* choose the correct options given below
(a) $\Delta U = 0$
(b) work done by gas > 0
(c) heat given to the gas is $4RT_0$
(d) heat given to the gas is $2RT_0$

Match the Columns

29. Temperature of 2 moles of a monatomic gas is increased from T to $2T$. Match the following two columns.

	Column I		Column II
(a)	Work done by gas in isobaric process	(p)	3RT
(b)	Change in internal energy in isobaric process	(q)	4RT
(c)	Work done by gas in adiabatic process	(r)	2RT
(d)	Change in internal energy in an adiabatic process	(s)	None of these

30. For V-T diagrams of two processes a - b and c - d as shown in the figure for same gas, match the following two columns.

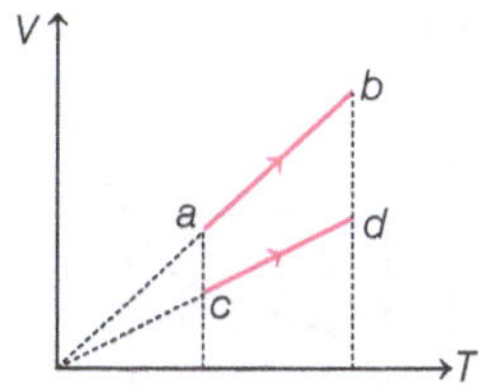

Column I		Column II	
(a)	Work done	(p)	is more in process *ab*
(b)	Change in internal energy	(q)	is more in process *cd*
(c)	Heat exchange	(r)	is same in both processes
(d)	Molar heat capacity	(s)	can't say anything

31. Temperature of a monatomic gas is increased by ΔT in the process p^2V = constant. Match the following two columns.

Column I		Column II	
(a)	Work done by gas	(p)	$2nR\Delta T$
(b)	Change in internal energy of gas	(q)	$5nR\Delta T$
(c)	Heat taken by the gas	(r)	$3nR\Delta T$
(d)	Work done on the gas	(s)	None of these

32. Match the following two columns.

Column I		Column II	
(a)	Isobaric expansion	(p)	$W > \Delta U$
(b)	Isochoric cooling	(q)	$W < \Delta U$
(c)	Adiabatic expansion	(r)	$Q = \Delta U$
(d)	Isothermal expansion	(s)	$Q < \Delta U$

Subjective Questions

33. Show how internal energy U varies with T in isochoric, isobaric and adiabatic process?

34. An ideal gas is carried through a thermodynamic cycle consisting of two isobaric and two isothermal processes as shown in figure. Show that the net work done in the entire cycle is given by the equation.

$$W_{net} = p_1 (V_2 - V_1) \ln \frac{p_2}{p_1}$$

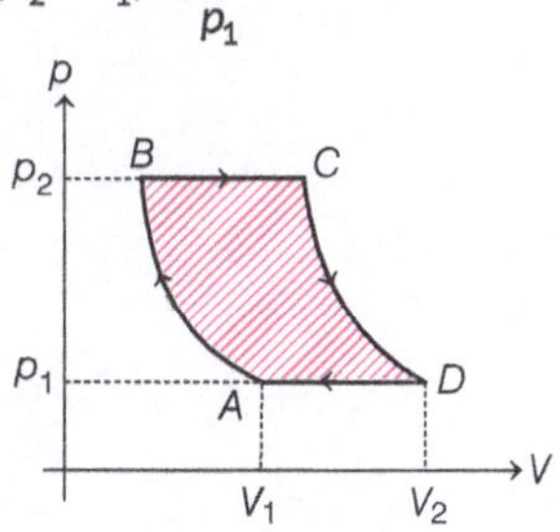

35. A gas undergoes the cycle shown in figure. The cycle is repeated 100 times per minute. Determine the power generated.

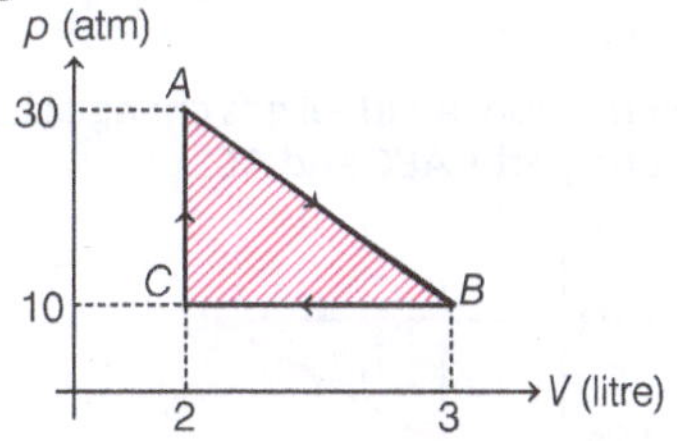

36. A closed vessel 10 L in volume contains a diatomic gas under a pressure of 10^5 N/m^2. What amount of heat should be imparted to the gas to increase the pressure in the vessel five times?

37. One mole of an ideal monatomic gas is taken round the cyclic process *ABCA* as shown in figure. Calculate **(1998 JEE)**

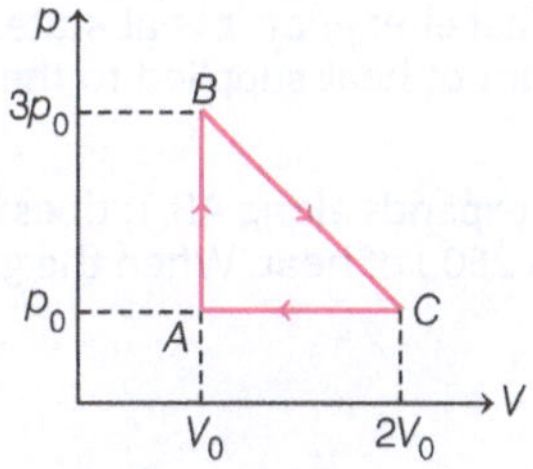

(a) the work done by the gas.

(b) the heat rejected by the gas in the path *CA* and heat absorbed in the path *AB*.

(c) the net heat absorbed by the gas in the path *BC*.

(d) the maximum temperature attained by the gas during the cycle.

38. A diatomic ideal gas is heated at constant volume until its pressure becomes three times. It is again heated at constant pressure until its volume is doubled. Find the molar heat capacity for the whole process.

39. *p-V* diagram of an ideal gas for a process *ABC* is as shown in the figure.

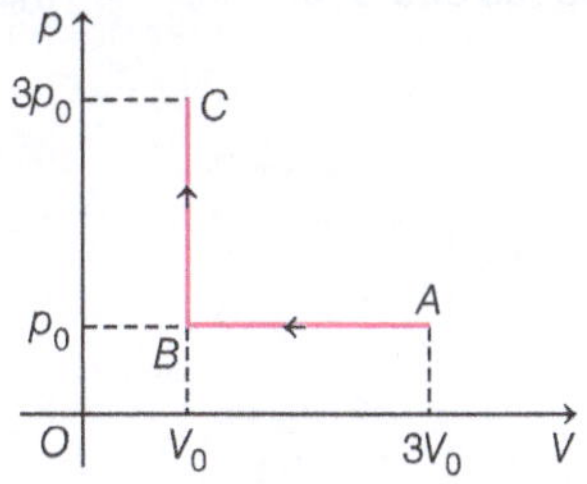

(a) Find total heat absorbed or released by the gas during the process *ABC*.

(b) Change in internal energy of the gas during the process *ABC*.
(c) Plot pressure *versus* density graph of the gas for the process *ABC*.

40. In the given graph, an ideal gas changes its state from *A* to *C* by two paths *ABC* and *AC*.

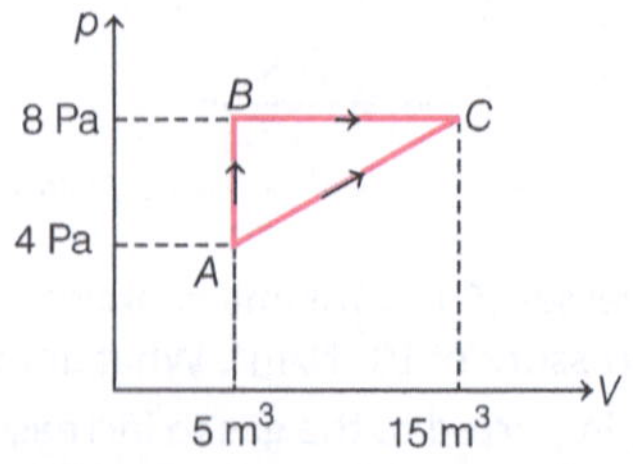

(a) Find the path along which work done is less.
(b) The internal energy of gas at *A* is 10 J and the amount of heat supplied in path *AC* is 200 J. Calculate the internal energy of gas at *C*.
(c) The internal energy of gas at state *B* is 20 J. Find the amount of heat supplied to the gas to go from *A* to *B*.

41. When a gas expands along *AB*, it does 500 J of work and absorbs 250 J of heat. When the gas expands along *AC*, it does 700 J of work and absorbs 300 J of heat.

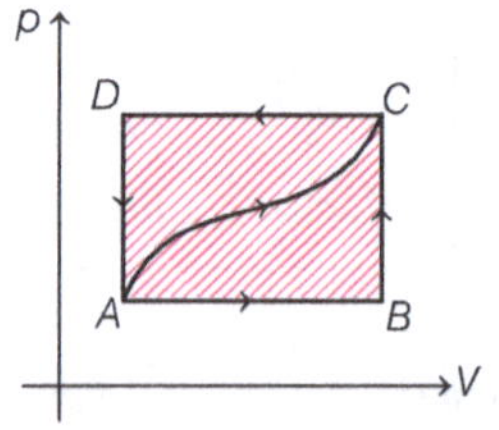

(a) How much heat does the gas exchange along *BC* ?
(b) When the gas makes the transition from *C* to *A* along *CDA*, 800 J of work are done on it from *C* to *D*. How much heat does it exchange along *CDA*?

42. One mole of an ideal monoatomic gas occupies a volume of $1.0 \times 10^{-2}\ m^3$ at a pressure of $2.0 \times 10^5\ N/m^2$.
(a) What is the temperature of the gas?
(b) The gas undergoes an adiabatic compression until its volume is decreased to $5.0 \times 10^{-3}\ m^3$. What is the new gas temperature?
(c) How much work is done on the gas during the compression?
(d) What is the change in the internal energy of the gas?

Answers

1. (d) **2.** (a) **3.** (c) **4.** (c) **5.** (a) **6.** (c) **7.** (c) **8.** (a) **9.** (a) **10.** (d)
11. (b) **12.** (c) **13.** (d) **14.** (c) **15.** (c) **16.** (c) **17.** (d) **18.** (b) **19.** (c) **20.** (c)
21. (b) **22.** (b) **23.** (a) **24.** (a) **25.** (d) **26.** (b, d) **27.** (a,c) **28.** (a, b)
29. (a) → r (b) → p (c) → s (d) → p **30.** (a) → s (b) → s (c) → s (d) → r **31.** (a) → p (b) → s (c) → s (d) → s
32. (a) → q (b) → p,r (c) → p (d) → p **33.** $\Delta U = \frac{nR\Delta T}{\gamma - 1}$ for all processes **35.** 1683 J/s **36.** 10^4 J
37. (a) p_0V_0 (b) $\frac{5}{2}p_0V_0$, $3p_0V_0$ (c) $\frac{p_0V_0}{2}$ (d) $\frac{25p_0V_0}{8R}$ **38.** $C = 3.1R$
39. (a) $Q_{ABC} = -2p_0V_0$ (b) $\Delta U_{ABC} = 0$ (c) See the hints **40.** (a) *AC* (b) 150 J (c) 10 J **41.** (a) –150 J (b) – 400 J
42. (a) 240.7 K (b) 383 K (c) 1770 J (d) 1770 J

See hints on pages 306-310.

MODULE 3

Heat Engine and Refrigerator

Heat Engine and its Efficiency

A heat engine is a device which converts heat energy into mechanical energy. In every heat engine, there are the following three components :

(i) Working substance (which is normally a gas in a cylinder)

(ii) Source (at temperature T_1)

(iii) Sink (at temperature T_2).

$T_2 < T_1$ and sink is normally atmosphere.

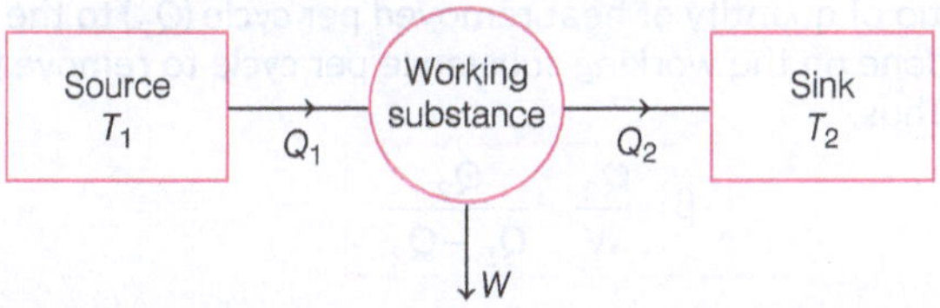

The working substance absorbs some heat (Q_1) from the source, converts a part of it into work (W) and the rest (Q_2) is rejected to the sink.

From conservation of energy,

$$Q_1 = W + Q_2$$

Now, the above work done is used by us for different purposes.

Working of any heat engine is just like the working of a shopkeeper. He takes some money from you. (Suppose he takes Rs. 100/- from you). So, you are the source. In lieu of this he provides some item to you (suppose he gives a colgate of worth Rs. 80/-). This is work done. The remaining Rs. 20/- is his profit which goes to his account and this is basically sink. Then, the efficiency of the shopkeeper is 80%. There can't be a shopkeeper whose efficiency is 100%.

Similarly, efficiency of a heat engine is defined as the ratio of net work done per cycle by the engine to the total amount of heat absorbed per cycle by the working substance from the source. It is denoted by η. Thus,

$$\eta = \frac{W}{Q_1} = \frac{Q_1 - Q_2}{Q_1} = 1 - \frac{Q_2}{Q_1}$$

Work is done by the working substance in a cyclic process. In the above expression of efficiency, W is net work done in the complete cycle which should be positive. So, cycle should be clockwise on p-V diagram. Q_1 is the total heat given to the working substance or the total positive heat. Q_2 is the total heat rejected by the working substance or it is the magnitude of total negative heat.

Thus, efficiency (η) of a cycle can also be defined as

$$\eta = \left(\frac{\text{Work done by the working substance (an ideal gas in our case) during a cycle}}{\text{Heat supplied to the gas during the cycle}} \right) \times 100$$

$$= \frac{W_{\text{Total}}}{|Q_{+\text{ve}}|} \times 100$$

$$= \frac{|Q_{+\text{ve}}| - |Q_{-\text{ve}}|}{|Q_{+\text{ve}}|} \times 100 = \left\{ 1 - \left| \frac{Q_{-\text{ve}}}{Q_{+\text{ve}}} \right| \right\} \times 100$$

$$\text{Thus, } \eta = \frac{W_{\text{Total}}}{|Q_{+\text{ve}}|} \times 100 = \left\{ 1 - \left| \frac{Q_{-\text{ve}}}{Q_{+\text{ve}}} \right| \right\} \times 100$$

Depending on the number of processes in a cycle, it may be called a two-stroke engine or four-stroke engine.

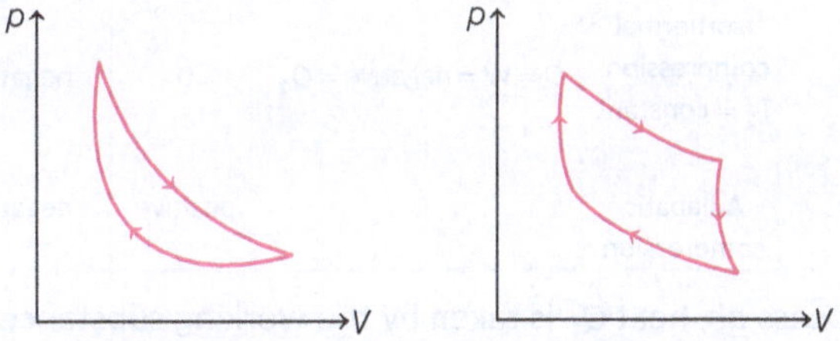

Two stroke-engine　　Four stroke-engine

Note *There cannot be a heat engine whose efficiency is 100%. It is always less than 100%. Thus,*

$$\eta \neq 100\%$$

or $W \neq Q_1$ *or* $W_{net} \neq Q_{+ve}$

or $Q_2 \neq 0$ *or* $|Q_{-ve}| \neq 0$

Efficiency of a Cycle

By the similar method discussed above, we can also find efficiency of a cycle provided net work done in the whole cycle comes out to be positive or it is clockwise cycle on p-V diagram. But always remember that, in a cyclic process,

$$\Delta U_{\text{net}} = 0$$

and $$Q_{\text{net}} = W_{\text{net}}$$

If there are four processes in the cycle, then

$$\Delta U_1 + \Delta U_2 + \Delta U_3 + \Delta U_4 = 0 \text{ and}$$
$$Q_1 + Q_2 + Q_3 + Q_4 = W_1 + W_2 + W_3 + W_4$$

Carnot Engine

Carnot cycle consists of the following four processes :

(i) Isothermal expansion (process *ab*)

(ii) Adiabatic expansion (process *bc*)

(iii) Isothermal compression (process *cd*) and

(iv) Adiabatic compression (process *da*)

The *p*-*V* diagram of the cycle is shown in the figure.

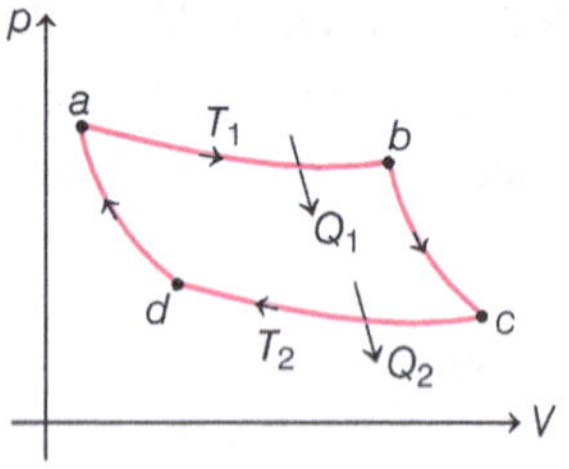

Table 1

Process	Name of the process	Q	ΔU	W
ab	Isothermal expansion T_1 = constant	$Q = W = \text{positive} = Q_1$	0	positive
bc	Adiabatic expansion	0	negative	positive
cd	Isothermal compression T_2 = constant	$Q = W = \text{negative} = Q_2$	0	negative
da	Adiabatic compression	0	positive	negative

In process *ab*, heat Q_1 is taken by the working substance at constant temperature T_1 and in process *cd* heat Q_2 is rejected from the working substance at constant temperature T_2. The net work done is area of graph *abcd*.

Note (i) *In the whole cycle only Q_1 is the positive heat and Q_2 the negative heat. Thus,*

$$Q_{+ve} = Q_1 \text{ and } |Q_{-ve}| = Q_2$$

$$\therefore \quad \eta = \left(1 - \frac{Q_2}{Q_1}\right) \times 100$$

Specially for Carnot cycle, $\frac{Q_2}{Q_1}$ also comes out to be $\frac{T_2}{T_1}$.

$$\therefore \quad \eta = \left(1 - \frac{T_2}{T_1}\right) \times 100$$

(ii) *Efficiency of Carnot engine is maximum (not 100%) for given temperatures T_1 and T_2. But still Carnot engine is not a practical engine because many ideal situations have been assumed while designing this engine which can not be obtained.*

Refrigerator

Refrigerator is an apparatus which takes heat from a cold body, work is done on it and the work done together with the heat absorbed is rejected to the source.

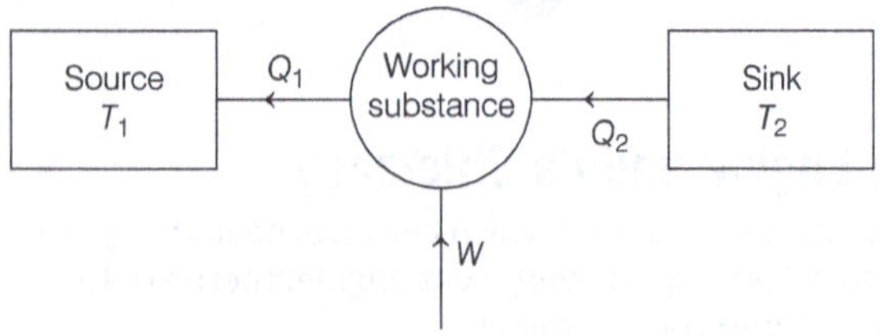

An ideal refrigerator can be regarded as Carnot ideal heat engine working in the reverse direction.

Coefficient of Performance

Coefficient of performance (β) of a refrigerator is defined as the ratio of quantity of heat removed per cycle (Q_2) to the work done on the working substance per cycle to remove this heat. Thus,

$$\beta = \frac{Q_2}{W} = \frac{Q_2}{Q_1 - Q_2}$$

We can also show that

$$\beta = \frac{T_2}{T_1 - T_2} = \frac{1 - \eta}{\eta}$$

Here, η is the efficiency of Carnot cycle.

Example 1 For a Carnot cycle (or engine) discussed as earlier prove that efficiency of cycle is given by

$$\eta = \left(1 - \frac{T_2}{T_1}\right)$$

Sol. Efficiency $= \dfrac{\text{net work done by gas}}{\text{heat absorbed by gas}}$

$$= \frac{|W_1| + |W_2| - |W_3| - |W_4|}{|Q_1|} \quad \text{...(i)}$$

Process *ab* On this isothermal expansion process, the constant temperature is T_1 so work done by the gas

$$W_1 = nRT_1 \ln\left(\frac{V_b}{V_a}\right) \quad \text{...(ii)}$$

Remember that $V_b > V_a$, so this quantity is positive, as expected. (In process 1, the gas does work by lifting something)

In isothermal process,

$$Q = W$$

$$\therefore \quad |Q_1| = |W_1| \quad \text{...(iii)}$$

Process *bc* On this adiabatic expansion process, the temperature and volume are related through

$$TV^{\gamma-1} = \text{constant}$$

$$\therefore \quad T_1 V_b^{\gamma-1} = T_2 V_c^{\gamma-1}$$

or $$\frac{T_1}{T_2} = \left(\frac{V_c}{V_b}\right)^{\gamma-1} \quad \text{...(iv)}$$

Work done by the gas in this adiabatic process is

$$W_2 = \frac{p_c V_c - p_b V_b}{1-\gamma} = \frac{nRT_c - nRT_b}{1-\gamma}$$

$$= \left(\frac{T_2 - T_1}{1-\gamma}\right) nR = \left(\frac{T_1 - T_2}{\gamma - 1}\right) nR \quad \text{...(v)}$$

Once again, as expected, this quantity is positive.

Process *cd* In the isothermal compression process, the work done by the gas is

$$W_3 = nRT_2 \ln \frac{V_d}{V_c} \quad \text{...(vi)}$$

Because $V_d < V_c$, the work done by the gas is negative. The work done on the gas is

$$|W_3| = -nRT_2 \ln \frac{V_d}{V_c} = nRT_2 \ln \frac{V_c}{V_d} \quad \text{...(vii)}$$

Furthermore, just as in process 1,

$$|Q_3| = |W_3| \quad \text{...(viii)}$$

Process *da* In the adiabatic compression process, the calculations are exactly the same as they were in process *bc* but of course with different variables. Therefore,

$$\frac{T_2}{T_1} = \left(\frac{V_a}{V_d}\right)^{\gamma-1} \quad \text{...(ix)}$$

and $$W_4 = \frac{nR}{\gamma - 1}(T_2 - T_1) \quad \text{...(x)}$$

As expected, this quantity is negative and

$$|W_4| = -W_4 = \frac{nR}{\gamma - 1}(T_1 - T_2) \quad \text{...(xi)}$$

We can now calculate the efficiency.

$$\text{Efficiency} = \frac{|W_1| + |W_2| - |W_3| - |W_4|}{|Q_1|}$$

$$= 1 + \frac{|W_2| - |W_3| - |W_4|}{|Q_1|} \quad (\text{as } |W_1| = |Q_1|)$$

But our calculations show that $|W_2| = |W_4|$.

$$\therefore \text{Efficiency} = 1 - \frac{|W_3|}{|Q_1|}$$

$$= 1 - \frac{nRT_2 \ln (V_c/V_d)}{nRT_1 \ln (V_b/V_a)} = 1 - \frac{T_2 \ln (V_c/V_d)}{T_1 \ln (V_b/V_a)} \quad \text{...(xii)}$$

We have seen that

$$\frac{T_1}{T_2} = \left(\frac{V_c}{V_b}\right)^{\gamma-1} = \left(\frac{V_d}{V_a}\right)^{\gamma-1}$$

or $$\frac{V_c}{V_b} = \frac{V_d}{V_a} \quad \text{or} \quad \frac{V_c}{V_d} = \frac{V_b}{V_a}$$

Substituting in Eq. (xii), we get

$$\text{Efficiency} = 1 - \frac{T_2}{T_1}$$

Example 2 An ideal gas is taken through a cyclic thermodynamic process through four steps. The amounts of heat involved in these steps are $Q_1 = 5960$ J, $Q_2 = -5585$ J, $Q_3 = -2980$ J and $Q_4 = 3645$ J respectively. The corresponding quantities of work involved are $W_1 = 2200$ J, $W_2 = -825$ J, $W_3 = -1100$ J and W_4 respectively. **(1994 JEE)**

(a) Find the value of W_4.

(b) What is the efficiency of the cycle?

Sol. (a) In a cyclic process, $\Delta U = 0$

Therefore, $Q_{net} = W_{net}$

or $Q_1 + Q_2 + Q_3 + Q_4 = W_1 + W_2 + W_3 + W_4$

Hence, $W_4 = (Q_1 + Q_2 + Q_3 + Q_4) - (W_1 + W_2 + W_3)$

$= \{(5960 - 5585 - 2980 + 3645) - (2200 - 825 - 1100)\}$

or $W_4 = 765$ J **Ans.**

(b) Efficiency,

$$\eta = \frac{\text{Total work done in the cycle}}{\text{Heat absorbed (positive heat) by the gas during the cycle}} \times 100$$

$$= \left(\frac{W_1 + W_2 + W_3 + W_4}{Q_1 + Q_4}\right) \times 100$$

$$= \left\{\frac{(2200 - 825 - 1100 + 765)}{5960 + 3645}\right\} \times 100$$

$$= \frac{1040}{9605} \times 100$$

$\eta = 10.82\%$ **Ans.**

Example 3 The density versus pressure graph of one mole of an ideal monatomic gas undergoing a cyclic process is shown in figure. The molecular mass of the gas is M.

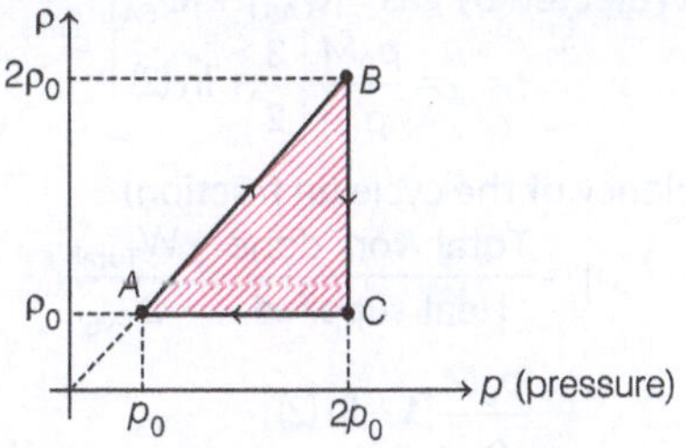

(a) Find the work done in each process.

(b) Find heat rejected by gas in one complete cycle.

(c) Find the efficiency of the cycle.

Sol. (a) Given, $n = 1 \quad \therefore \quad m = M$

Process AB

$\rho \propto p$, i.e. It is an isothermal process (T = constant), because $\rho = \dfrac{pM}{RT}$.

$$\therefore \quad W_{AB} = RT_A \ln \left(\frac{p_A}{p_B}\right) = RT_A \ln \left(\frac{1}{2}\right)$$

$$= -\frac{p_0 M}{\rho_0} \ln (2)$$

$$\Delta U_{AB} = 0$$

and $$Q_{AB} = W_{AB} = -\frac{p_0 M}{\rho_0}\ln(2)$$

Process BC

is an isobaric process (p = constant)

$$W_{BC} = p_B(V_C - V_B)$$

$$= 2p_0\left(\frac{M}{\rho_C} - \frac{M}{\rho_B}\right) = 2p_0\left(\frac{M}{\rho_0} - \frac{M}{2\rho_0}\right) = \frac{p_0 M}{\rho_0}$$

$$\Delta U_{BC} = C_V \Delta T$$

$$= \left(\frac{3}{2}R\right)\left[\frac{2p_0 M}{\rho_0 R} - \frac{2p_0 M}{2\rho_0 R}\right] = \frac{3p_0 M}{2\rho_0}$$

$$Q_{BC} = W_{BC} + \Delta U_{BC} = \frac{5p_0 M}{2\rho_0}$$

Process CA

As ρ = constant

$\therefore$ V = constant

So, it is an isochoric process.

$$W_{CA} = 0$$

$$\Delta U_{CA} = C_V \Delta T$$

$$= \left(\frac{3}{2}R\right)(T_A - T_C)$$

$$= \left(\frac{3}{2}R\right)\left[\frac{p_0 M}{\rho_0 R} - \frac{2p_0 M}{\rho_0 R}\right]$$

$$= -\frac{3p_0 M}{2\rho_0}$$

$$Q_{CA} = \Delta U_{CA} = -\frac{3p_0 M}{2\rho_0}$$

(b) Heat rejected by gas $= |Q_{AB}| + |Q_{CA}|$

$$= \frac{p_0 M}{\rho_0}\left[\frac{3}{2} + \ln(2)\right]$$ **Ans.**

(c) Efficiency of the cycle (in fraction)

$$\eta = \frac{\text{Total work done}}{\text{Heat supplied}} = \frac{W_{\text{Total}}}{Q_{+ve}}$$

$$= \frac{\frac{p_0 M}{\rho_0}[1 - \ln(2)]}{\frac{5}{2}\left(\frac{p_0 M}{\rho_0}\right)}$$

$$= \frac{2}{5}[1 - \ln(2)]$$ **Ans.**

Example 4 Carnot engine takes one thousand kilo calories of heat from a reservoir at 827°C and exhausts it to a sink at 27°C. How, much work does it perform? What is the efficiency of the engine?

Sol. Given, $Q_1 = 10^6$ cal

$$T_1 = (827 + 273) = 1100 \text{ K}$$

and $$T_2 = (27 + 273) = 300 \text{ K}$$

as, $$\frac{Q_2}{Q_1} = \frac{T_2}{T_1} \Rightarrow Q_2 = \frac{T_2}{T_1}\cdot Q_1 = \left(\frac{300}{1100}\right)(10^6)$$

$$= 2.72 \times 10^5 \text{ cal}$$

$$W = Q_1 - Q_2 = 7.28 \times 10^5 \text{ cal}$$ **Ans.**

Efficiency of the cycle,

$$\eta = \left(1 - \frac{T_2}{T_1}\right) \times 100 \quad \text{or} \quad \eta = \left(1 - \frac{300}{1100}\right) \times 100$$

$$= 72.72\,\%$$ **Ans.**

Example 5 In a refrigerator, heat from inside at 277 K is transferred to a room at 300 K. How many joules of heat shall be delivered to the room for each joule of electrical energy consumed ideally?

Sol. Coefficient of performance of a refrigerator,

$$\beta = \frac{Q_2}{W} = \frac{T_2}{T_1 - T_2}$$

$$\therefore \quad Q_2 = W\frac{T_2}{T_1 - T_2}$$

But W = Energy consumed by the refrigerator = 1 J,

$$T_1 = 300 \text{ K}, T_2 = 277 \text{ K}$$

$$\therefore \quad Q_2 = 1 \times \frac{277}{300 - 277} = \frac{277}{23} = 12 \text{ J}$$

Heat rejected by the refrigerator,

$$Q_1 = W + Q_2 = 1 + 12$$

$$= 13 \text{ J}$$ **Ans.**

Example 6 Calculate the least amount of work that must be done to freeze one gram of water at 0°C by means of a refrigerator. Temperature of surroundings is 27°C. How much heat is passed on the surroundings in this process? Latent heat of fusion $L = 80$ cal/g.

Sol. $Q_2 = mL = 1 \times 80 = 80$ cal

$$T_2 = 0°\text{C} = 273 \text{ K}$$

and $$T_1 = 27°\text{C} = 300 \text{ K}$$

Least amount of work will be needed for carnot's type of cycle.

$$\frac{Q_2}{W} = \frac{T_2}{T_1 - T_2}$$

$$\therefore \quad W = \frac{Q_2(T_1 - T_2)}{T_2} = \frac{80\,(300 - 273)}{273}$$

$$= 7.91 \text{ cal}$$ **Ans.**

$$Q_1 = Q_2 + W = (80 + 7.91)$$

$$= 87.91 \text{ cal}$$ **Ans.**

INTRODUCTORY Exercise

1. Carnot engine takes 1000 K cal of heat from a reservoir at 827°C and exhausts it to a sink at 27°C. How much heat is rejected to the sink? What is the efficiency of the engine?
2. One of the most efficient engines ever developed operated between 2100 K and 700 K. Its actual efficiency is 40%. What percentage of its maximum possible efficiency is this?
3. In a heat engine, the temperature of the source and sink are 500 K and 375 K. If the engine consumes 25×10^5 J per cycle, find (a) the efficiency of the engine, (b) work done per cycle, and (c) heat rejected to the sink per cycle.
4. A Carnot engine takes 3×10^6 cal of heat from a reservoir at 627 °C and gives it to a sink at 27 °C. Find the work done by the engine.
5. The efficiency of a Carnot cycle is 1/6. If on reducing the temperature of the sink by 65 °C, the efficiency becomes 1/3, find the source and sink temperatures between which the cycle is working.
6. Refrigerator *A* works between −10 °C and 27 °C, while refrigerator *B* works between −27 °C and 17 °C, both removing heat equal to 2000 J from the freezer. Which of the two is the better refrigerator?
7. A refrigerator has to transfer an average of 263 J of heat per second from temperature −10 °C to 25 °C. Calculate the average power consumed, assuming no energy losses in the process.
8. *n* moles of a monoatomic gas are taken around in a cyclic process consisting of four processes along *ABCDA* as shown. All the lines on the *p-V* diagram have slope of magnitude p_0 / V_0. The pressure at *A* and *C* is p_0 and the volumes at *A* and *C* are $V_0/2$ and $3V_0/2$, respectively. Calculate the percentage efficiency of the cycle.

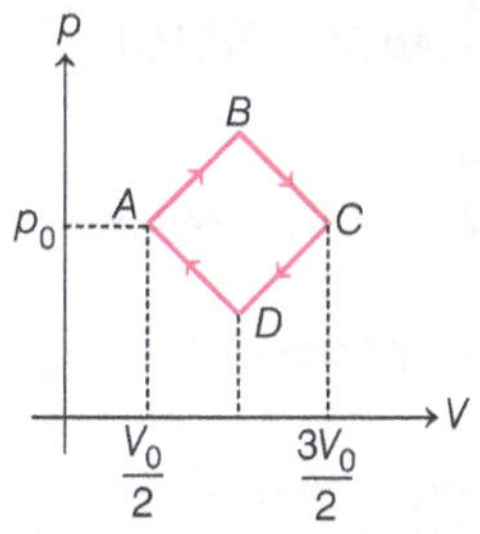

Answers

1. 2.72×10^5 cal, 72.72% 2. 60%
3. (a) 25% (b) 6.25×10^5 J (c) 18.75×10^5 J
4. 2×10^6 cal 5. 117°C and 52°C 6. Refrigerator *A*
7. 35 W 8. 18.18%

See hints on pages 310-312.

Typed Problems

Type 1. *To find values of all three terms of first law of thermodynamics from a p-V diagram provided nature of gas is given.*

Concept

Use the equation $nRT = pV$

Ex. 1 A cyclic process *abcd* is given for a monoatomic gas $\left(C_V = \frac{3}{2}R \text{ and } C_p = \frac{5}{2}R\right)$ as shown in figure. Find *Q*, *W* and ΔU in each of the four processes separately. Also find the efficiency of cycle.

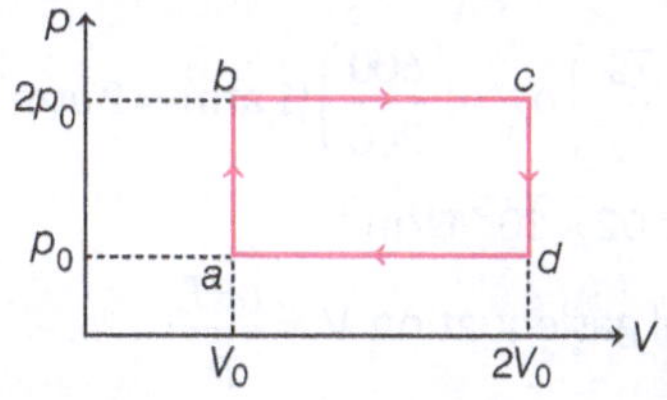

Sol. Process *ab*

$V = \text{constant}$ (∴ Isochoric process)

$W_{ab} = 0$

$\therefore \quad Q_{ab} = \Delta U_{ab} = nC_V \Delta T$

$$= n\left(\frac{3}{2}R\right)(T_b - T_a)$$
$$= \frac{3}{2}(nRT_b - nRT_a)$$
$$= \frac{3}{2}(p_bV_b - p_aV_a)$$
$$= \frac{3}{2}(2p_0V_0 - p_0V_0)$$
$$= 1.5\, p_0V_0$$

Process *bc*

$p = \text{constant}$ (∴ Isobaric process)

$$Q_{bc} = nC_p\Delta T$$
$$= n\left(\frac{5}{2}R\right)(T_c - T_b)$$
$$= \frac{5}{2}(nRT_c - nRT_b)$$
$$= \frac{5}{2}(p_cV_c - p_bV_b)$$
$$= \frac{5}{2}(4p_0V_0 - 2p_0V_0)$$
$$= 5p_0V_0$$

$$\Delta U_{bc} = nC_V \Delta T = n\left(\frac{3}{2}R\right)(T_c - T_b)$$
$$= \frac{3}{2}(nRT_c - nRT_b)$$
$$= \frac{3}{2}(p_cV_c - p_bV_b)$$
$$= \frac{3}{2}(4p_0V_0 - 2p_0V_0)$$
$$= 3p_0V_0$$
$$W_{bc} = Q_{bc} - \Delta U_{bc} = 2p_0V_0$$

Process *cd*

Again an isochoric process.

$\therefore \quad W_{cd} = 0$

$$Q_{cd} = \Delta U_{cd} = nC_V \Delta T = n\left(\frac{3}{2}R\right)(T_d - T_c)$$
$$= \frac{3}{2}(nRT_d - nRT_c)$$
$$= \frac{3}{2}(p_dV_d - p_cV_c)$$
$$= \frac{3}{2}(2p_0V_0 - 4p_0V_0)$$
$$= -3p_0V_0$$

Process *da*

This is an isobaric process.

$$\therefore \quad Q_{da} = nC_p \Delta T = n\left(\frac{5}{2}R\right)(T_a - T_d)$$
$$= \frac{5}{2}(nRT_a - nRT_d)$$
$$= \frac{5}{2}(p_aV_a - p_dV_d)$$
$$= \frac{5}{2}(p_0V_0 - 2p_0V_0)$$
$$= -2.5\, p_0V_0$$
$$\Delta U_{da} = nC_V \Delta T = n\left(\frac{3}{2}R\right)(T_a - T_d)$$
$$= \frac{3}{2}(nRT_a - nRT_d)$$
$$= \frac{3}{2}(p_aV_a - p_dV_d)$$
$$= \frac{3}{2}(p_0V_0 - 2p_0V_0)$$
$$= -1.5\, p_0V_0$$
$$W_{da} = Q_{da} - \Delta U_{da} = -p_0V_0$$

Efficiency of cycle

In the complete cycle,

$$W_{net} = W_{ab} + W_{bc} + W_{cd} + W_{da}$$
$$= 0 + 2p_0V_0 + 0 - p_0V_0$$
$$= p_0V_0$$

Note *This W_{net} is also equal to area under the cycle.*

$$\Sigma Q_{+ve} = Q_{ab} + Q_{bc}$$
$$= 1.5p_0V_0 + 5p_0V_0$$
$$= 6.5p_0V_0$$
$$\therefore \quad \eta = \frac{W_{net}}{\Sigma Q_{+ve}} \times 100$$
$$= \left(\frac{p_0V_0}{6.5p_0V_0}\right) \times 100$$
$$= 15.38\%$$

Miscellaneous Examples

Ex. 2 The *p-V* diagram of 0.2 mol of a diatomic ideal gas is shown in figure. Process *BC* is adiabatic. The value of γ for this gas is 1.4.

(a) Find the pressure and volume at points *A*, *B* and *C*.

(b) Calculate ΔQ, ΔW and ΔU for each of the three processes.

(c) Find the thermal efficiency of the cycle.

Take $1 \text{ atm} = 1.01 \times 10^5 \text{ N/m}^2$.

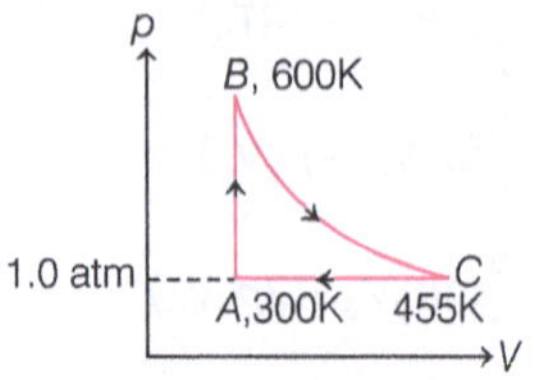

Sol. (a) $p_A = p_C = 1 \text{ atm} = 1.01 \times 10^5 \text{ N/m}^2$

Process *AB* is an isochoric process.

$$\therefore \quad p \propto T \quad \text{or} \quad \frac{p_B}{p_A} = \frac{T_B}{T_A}$$
$$\therefore \quad p_B = \left(\frac{T_B}{T_A}\right)p_A = \left(\frac{600}{300}\right)(1 \text{ atm}) = 2 \text{ atm}$$
$$= 2.02 \times 10^5 \text{ N/m}^2$$

From ideal gas equation $V = \frac{nRT}{p}$

$$\therefore \quad V_A = V_B = \frac{nRT_A}{p_A} = \frac{(0.2)(8.31)(300)}{(1.01 \times 10^5)}$$
$$\approx 5.0 \times 10^{-3} \text{ m}^3 = 5 \text{ L}$$

and $V_C = \dfrac{nRT_C}{p_C} = \dfrac{(0.2)(8.31)(455)}{(1.01\times 10^5)}$

$= 7.5\times 10^{-3}\ \text{m}^3 \approx 7.5\ \text{L}$

Table 2

State	p	V
A	1 atm	5 L
B	2 atm	5 L
C	1 atm	7.5 L

(b) **Process *AB*** is an isochoric process. Hence,

$\Delta W_{AB} = 0$

$\Delta Q_{AB} = \Delta U_{AB} = nC_V\Delta T = n\left(\dfrac{5}{2}R\right)(T_B - T_A)$

$= (0.2)\left(\dfrac{5}{2}\right)(8.31)(600-300)$

$\approx 1246\ \text{J}$

Process *BC* is an adiabatic process. Hence,

$\Delta Q_{BC} = 0$

$\therefore \quad \Delta W_{BC} = -\Delta U_{BC}$

$\Delta U_{BC} = nC_V\Delta T = nC_V\,(T_C - T_B)$

$= (0.2)\left(\dfrac{5}{2}R\right)(455-600)$

$= (0.2)\left(\dfrac{5}{2}\right)(8.31)(-145)\ \text{J}$

$\approx -602\ \text{J}$

$\therefore \quad \Delta W_{BC} = -\Delta U_{BC} = 602\ \text{J}$

Process *CA* is an isobaric process. Hence,

$\Delta Q_{CA} = nC_p\Delta T = n\left(\dfrac{7}{2}R\right)(T_A - T_C)$

$= (0.2)\left(\dfrac{7}{2}\right)(8.31)(300-455)$

$\approx -902\ \text{J}$

$\Delta U_{CA} = nC_V\Delta T$

$= \dfrac{\Delta Q_{CA}}{\gamma} \quad \left(\text{as } \gamma = \dfrac{C_p}{C_V}\right)$

$= -\dfrac{902}{1.4} \approx -644\ \text{J}$

$\therefore \quad W_{CA} = \Delta Q_{CA} - \Delta U_{CA}$

$= -258\ \text{J}$

Table 3

Process	ΔQ (in J)	ΔW (in J)	ΔU (in J)
AB	1246	0	1246
BC	0	602	– 602
CA	– 902	– 258	– 644
Total	344	344	0

(c) Efficiency of the cycle

$\eta = \dfrac{W_{\text{Total}}}{|Q_{+\text{ve}}|}\times 100$

$= \dfrac{344}{1246}\times 100 = 27.6\%$

MODULE 3 Exercise

Assertion and Reason

See directions on page 14.

1. **Assertion :** Efficiency of a heat engine can't be greater than efficiency of Carnot engine.

   Reason : Efficiency of any engine is never 100%.

Single Correct Option

2. A Carnot engine works between 600 K and 300 K. The efficiency of the engine is
   (a) 50% (b) 70%
   (c) 20% (d) 80%

3. The heat reservoir of an ideal Carnot engine is at 800 K and its sink is at 400 K. The amount of heat taken in one second to produce useful mechanical work at the rate of 750 J/s is
   (a) 2250 J (b) 1125 J (c) 1500 J (d) 750 J

4. Two Carnot engines *A* and *B* are operated in succession. The first one, *A* receives heat from a source at $T_1 = 800$ K and rejects to sinks at T_2 K. The second engine *B* receives heat rejected by the first engine and rejects to another sink at $T_3 = 300$ K. If the work outputs of two engines are equal, then the value of T_2 is
   (a) 100 K (b) 300 K (c) 550 K (d) 700 K

5. An engine operating between the boiling and freezing points of water will have
   A. efficiency more than 27%.
   B. efficiency less than the efficiency of a Carnot engine operating between the same two temperatures.
   C. efficiency equal to 27%.
   D. efficiency less than 27%.
   Choose the correct answer from the options given below **(2023 Main)**
   (a) B, C and D only (b) A and B only
   (c) B and C only (d) B and D only

6. Work done by a Carnot engine operating between temperatures 127°C and 27°C is 2 kJ. The amount of heat transferred to the engine by the reservoir is **(2023 Main)**
   (a) 2 kJ (b) 2.67 kJ
   (c) 8 kJ (d) 4 kJ

7. A Carnot engine with efficiency 50% takes heat from a source at 600 K. In order to increase the efficiency to 70%, keeping the temperature of sink same, the new temperature of the source will be **(2023 Main)**
   (a) 1000 K (b) 900 K
   (c) 360 K (d) 300 K

8. A Carnot engine operating between two reservoirs has efficiency 1/3. When the temperature of cold reservoir raised by x, its efficiency decreases to 1/6. The value of x, if the temperature of hot reservoir is 99°C, will be **(2023 Main)**
   (a) 62 K (b) 16.5 K
   (c) 33 K (d) 66 K

9. A Carnot engine has efficiency of 50%. If the temperature of sink is reduced by 40°C, its efficiency increases by 30%. The temperature of the source will be **(2022 Main)**
   (a) 166.7 K (b) 255.1 K
   (c) 266.7 K (d) 367.7 K

10. Let η_1 is the efficiency of an engine at $T_1 = 447°C$ and $T_2 = 147°C$ while η_2 is the efficiency at $T_1 = 947°C$ and $T_2 = 47°C$. The ratio $\frac{\eta_1}{\eta_2}$ will be **(2022 Main)**
    (a) 0.41 (b) 0.56 (c) 0.73 (d) 0.70

11. The efficiency of a Carnot's engine, working between steam point and ice point, will be **(2022 Main)**
    (a) 26.81% (b) 37.81%
    (c) 47.81% (d) 57.81%

12. A Carnot engine whose heat sinks at 27°C, has an efficiency of 25%. By how many degrees should the temperature of the source be changed to increase the efficiency by 100% of the original efficiency? **(2022 Main)**
    (a) Increase by 18°C (b) Increase by 200°C
    (c) Increase by 120°C (d) Increase by 73°C

13. A Carnot engine take 5000 kcal of heat from a reservoir at 727°C and gives heat to a sink, at 127°C. The work done by the engine is **(2022 Main)**
    (a) 3×10^6 J (b) Zero
    (c) 12.6×10^6 J (d) 8.4×10^6 J

Integer Type Questions

14. 300 cal. of heat is given to a heat engine and it rejects 225 cal. of heat. If source temperature is 227°C, then the temperature of sink will be .... °C. **(2022 Main)**

15. In a carnot engine, the temperature of reservoir is 527°C and that of sink is 200 K. If the work done by the engine when it transfers heat from reservoir to sink is 12000 kJ, the quantity of heat absorbed by the engine from reservoir is .... $\times 10^6$ J. **(2022 Main)**

16. A heat engine operates with the cold reservoir at temperature 324 K. The minimum temperature of the hot reservoir, if the heat engine takes 300 J heat from the hot reservoir and delivers 180 J heat to the cold reservoir per cycle, is .... K. **(2022 Main)**

Answers

1. (d)	**2.** (a)	**3.** (c)	**4.** (c)	**5.** (d)	**6.** (c)	**7.** (a)	**8.** (a)	**9.** (c)	**10.** (b)
11. (a)	**12.** (b)	**13.** (c)	**14.** (102)	**15.** (16)	**16.** (540)				

See hints on pages 312-313.

MODULE 4

Zeroth and Second Law of Thermodynamics

Zeroth Law of Thermodynamics

The zeroth law of thermodynamics states that if two system A and B are in thermal equilibrium with a third system C, then A and B are also in thermal equilibrium with each other. It is analogous to the transitive property in math (if $A = C$ and $B = C$, then $A = B$). Another way of stating the zeroth law is that every object has a certain temperature, and when two objects are in thermal equilibrium, their temperatures are equal. It is called the zeroth law because it came to light after the first and second laws of thermodynamics had already been established and named, but was considered more fundamental and thus was given a lower number zero.

Second Law of Thermodynamics

The first law of thermodynamics is the principle of conservation of energy. Common experience shows that there are many conceivable processes that are perfectly allowed by the first law and yet are never observed. For example, nobody has ever seen a heat transfer from a cold body to a hot body by itself. But such a thing would be possible if the principle of conservation of energy were the only restriction.

Thus, the second law of thermodynamics is a general principle which places constraints upon the direction of and the attainable efficiency of or coefficient of performance. It also imposes restrictions on entropy.

Second law of thermodynamics can be better understood by the following three statements

In Terms of Entropy

The entropy in loose terms, is a measure of the amount of disorder within a system.

The second law of thermodynamics in terms of entropy says that the entropy of an isolated natural system will always tend to stay the same or increase — in other words, the energy in the universe is gradually moving towards disorder.

Kelvin-Planck's Statement

Kelvin-Planck's statement is based on the fact that the efficiency of the heat engine cycle is never 100%. This means that in the heat engine cycle some heat is always rejected to the low temperature reservoir.

Clausius Statement

The natural tendency of the heat is to flow from high temperature reservoir to the low temperature reservoir.

The Clausius statement says that, to transfer the heat from low temperature to high temperature reservoir some external work should be done on the cycle. This statement has been the basis for the working for all refrigerators, heat pumps and air-conditioners. This work cannot be zero or coefficient of performance of a refrigerator cannot be infinite.

Unit Exercise (Cumulative)

Level 1

Assertion and Reason

See directions on page 14.

1. **Assertion :** A system of ideal gas is heated by constant power. If temperature *versus* time graph is a straight line, then the process must be isochoric.

   Reason : For isochoric process,

$$dQ = nC_V dT$$

$$\Rightarrow \quad \frac{dQ}{dt} = P = nC_V \frac{dT}{dt}$$

$$\Rightarrow \quad \frac{dT}{dt} = \frac{P}{nC_V} = \text{constant}$$

2. **Assertion :** There are two processes : Process 1 is pV = constant and process 2 is pV^2 = constant. In both the processes volume of gas is increased from V_1 to V_2. Initial coordinates (p_1, V_1) of the gas were same. Then, more work is done by the gas in process 1.

   Reason : In second process, pressure drops more rapidly with increase in volume.

3. **Assertion :** If dQ and dW represent the heat supplied to the system and the work done on the system respectively. Then according the equation of first law of thermodynamics can be written as $dQ = dU - dW$.

   Reason : First law of thermodynamics is based on the law of conservation of energy. **(2023 Main)**

Statement Type Question

4. Given below are two statements

   Statement I : If heat is added to a system, its temperature must increase.

   Statement II : If positive work is done by a system in a thermodynamic process, its volume must increase.

   In the light of the above statements, choose the correct answer from the options given below **(2023 Main)**

   (a) Statement I is true but Statement II is false
   (b) Statement I is false but Statement II is true
   (c) Both Statement I and Statement II are false
   (d) Both Statement I and Statement II are true

Single Correct Option

5. A gas is compressed adiabatically, which one of the following statement is **NOT** true? **(2023 Main)**

   (a) There is no heat supplied to the system.
   (b) The temperature of the gas increases.
   (c) There is no change in the internal energy.
   (d) The change in the internal energy is equal to the work done on the gas.

6. A source supplies heat to a system at the rate of 1000 W. If the system performs work at a rate of 200 W. The rate at which internal energy of the system increases is **(2023 Main)**

   (a) 600 W (b) 500 W (c) 800 W (d) 1200 W

7. A thermodynamic system is taken through cyclic process. The total work done in the process is **(2023 Main)**

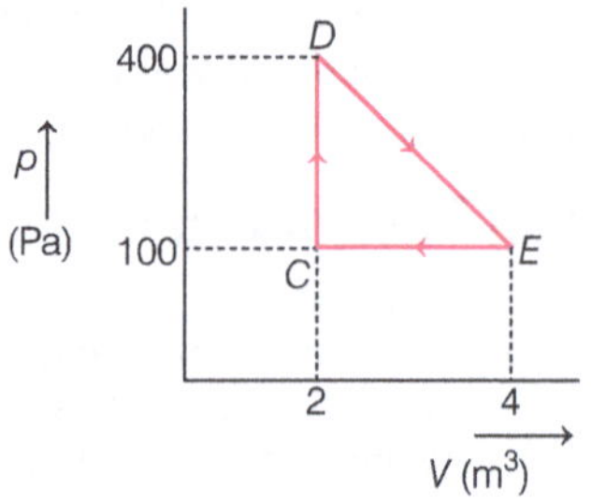

   (a) 200 (b) zero (c) 300 J (d) 100 J

8. 1 g of a liquid is converted to vapour at 3×10^5 Pa pressure. If 10% of the heat supplied is used for increasing the volume by 1600 cm^3 during this phase change, then the increase in internal energy is the process will be **(2023 Main)**

   (a) 4.32×10^8 J (b) 432000 J
   (c) 4320 J (d) 4800 J

9. Heat is given to an ideal gas in an isothermal process.

   A. Internal energy of the gas will decrease.
   B. Internal energy of the gas will increase.
   C. Internal energy of the gas will not change.
   D. The gas will do positive work.
   E. The gas will do negative work.

   Choose the correct answer from the options given below **(2023 Main)**

   (a) C and D only (b) A and E only
   (c) B and D only (d) C and E only

10. One mole of a sample of gas at temperature T is adiabatically expanded to double its volume. The work done by the gas in the process is $\left(\text{given}, \gamma = \frac{3}{2}\right)$ **(2023 Main)**

(a) $W = \frac{R}{T}[2-\sqrt{2}]$ (b) $W = \frac{T}{R}[\sqrt{2}-2]$

(c) $W = RT[\sqrt{2}-2]$ (d) $W = RT[2-\sqrt{2}]$

11. A cylinder of fixed capacity of 44.8 litres contains helium gas at standard temperature and pressure. The amount of heat needed to raise the temperature of gas in the cylinder by 20.0°C will be

(Given gas constant $R = 8.3\ \text{J K}^{-1}\ \text{mol}^{-1}$) **(2022 Main)**

(a) 249 J (b) 415 J (c) 498 J (d) 830 J

12. A sample of an ideal gas is taken through the cyclic process *ABCA* as shown in figure. It absorbs, 40 J of heat during the part *AB*, no heat during *BC* and rejects 60 J of heat during *CA*. A work of 50 J is done on the gas during the part *BC*. The internal energy of the gas at *A* is 1560 J. The work done by the gas during the part *CA* is **(2022 Main)**

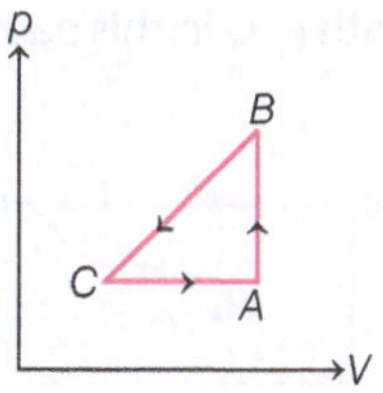

(a) 20 J (b) 30 J (c) – 30 J (d) – 60 J

13. A thermodynamic system is taken from an original state *D* to an intermediate state *E* by the linear process shown in the figure. Its volume is then reduced to the original volume from *E* to *F* by an isobaric process. The total work done by the gas from *D* to *E* to *F* will be **(2022 Main)**

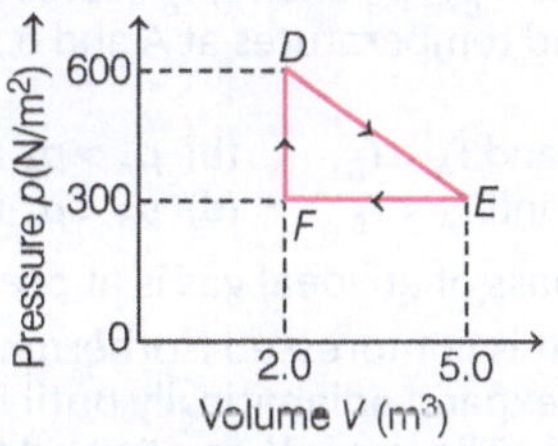

(a) –450 J (b) 450 J (c) 900 J (d) 1350 J

14. 7 mol of a certain monoatomic ideal gas undegoes a temperature increase of 40 K at constant pressure. The increase in the internal energy of the gas in this process is

(Given, $R = 8.3\ \text{J K}^{-1}\ \text{mol}^{-1}$) **(2022 Main)**

(a) 5810 J (b) 3486 J
(c) 11620 J (d) 6972 J

15. A sample of monoatomic gas is taken at initial pressure of 75 kPa. The volume of the gas is then compressed from 1200 cm^3 to 150 cm^3 adiabatically. In this process, the value of work done on the gas will be **(2022 Main)**

(a) 79 J (b) 405 J
(c) 4050 J (d) 9590 J

16. An ideal gas undergoes a four step cycle as shown in the *p*-*V* diagram below. During this cycle, heat is absorbed by the gas in **(2021 Adv.)**

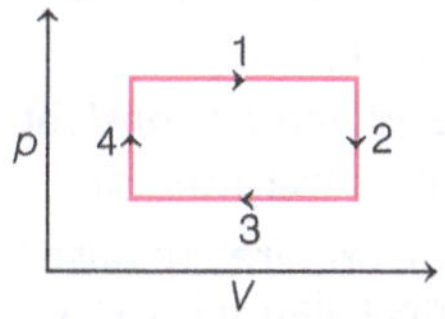

(a) steps 1 and 2 (b) steps 1 and 3
(c) steps 1 and 4 (d) steps 2 and 4

17. A diatomic gas, having $C_p = \frac{7}{2}R$ and $C_V = \frac{5}{2}R$, is heated at constant pressure. The ratio $dU : dQ : dW$ is **(2021 Main)**

(a) 5 : 7 : 2 (b) 3 : 5 : 2 (c) 3 : 7 : 2 (d) 5 : 7 : 3

18. A cylinder with fixed capacity of 67.2 L contains helium gas at STP. The amount of heat needed to raise the temperature of the gas by 20°C is

[Take, $R = 8.31\ \text{J mol}^{-1}\text{K}^{-1}$] **(2019 Main)**

(a) 700 J (b) 748 J (c) 374 J (d) 350 J

19. In a process, temperature and volume of one mole of an ideal gas monoatomic gas are varied according to the relation $VT = k$, where k is a constant. In this process, the temperature of the gas is increased by ΔT. The amount of heat absorbed by gas is (where, R is gas constant) **(2019 Main)**

(a) $\frac{1}{2}kR\Delta T$ (b) $\frac{2k}{3}\Delta T$ (c) $\frac{1}{2}R\Delta T$ (d) $\frac{3}{2}R\Delta T$

20. When heat Q is supplied to a diatomic gas of rigid molecules, at constant volume, its temperature increases by ΔT. The heat required to produce the same change in temperature, at a constant pressure is **(2019 Main)**

(a) $\frac{2}{3}Q$ (b) $\frac{5}{3}Q$ (c) $\frac{3}{2}Q$ (d) $\frac{7}{5}Q$

21. Two moles of an ideal monoatomic gas occupies a volume V at 27°C. The gas expands adiabatically to a volume $2V$. Calculate (i) the final temperature of the gas and (ii) change in its internal energy. **(2018 Main)**

(a) (i) 195 K (ii) 2.7 kJ (b) (i) 189 K (ii) 2.7 kJ
(c) (i) 195 K (ii) –2.7 kJ (d) (i) 189 K (ii) –2.7 kJ

22. Two moles of ideal helium gas are in a rubber balloon at 30°C. The balloon is fully expandable and can be assumed to require no energy in its expansion. The temperature of the gas in the balloon is slowly changed to 35°C. The amount of heat required in raising the temperature is nearly

(Take $R = 8.31$ J/mol-K) **(2012 JEE)**

(a) 62 J (b) 104 J (c) 124 J (d) 208 J

23. 5.6 L of helium gas at STP is adiabatically compressed to 0.7 L. Taking the initial temperature to be T_1, the work done in the process is **(2011 JEE)**

(a) $\frac{9}{8}RT_1$ (b) $\frac{3}{2}RT_1$ (c) $\frac{15}{8}RT_1$ (d) $\frac{9}{2}RT_1$

24. In a given process of an ideal gas, $dW = 0$ and $dQ < 0$. Then for the gas, **(2001 JEE)**
(a) the temperature will decrease
(b) the volume will increase
(c) the pressure will remain constant
(d) the temperature will increase

25. 70 cal of heat are required to raise the temperature of 2 moles of an ideal diatomic gas at constant pressure from 30°C to 35°C. The amount of heat required (in calorie) to raise the temperature of the same gas through the same range (30°C to 35°C) at constant volume is **(1985 JEE)**
(a) 30 (b) 50 (c) 70 (d) 90

26. A reversible engine has an efficiency of $\frac{1}{4}$. If the temperature of the sink is reduced by 58°C, its efficiency becomes double. Calculate the temperature of the sink **(2021, 2019 Main)**
(a) 174°C (b) 280°C (c) 180.4°C (d) 382°C

27. A refrigerator consumes an.average 35 W power to operate between temperature −10°C to 25°C. If there is no loss of energy then how much average heat per second does it transfer? **(2021 Main)**
(a) 263 J/s (b) 298 J/s (c) 350 J/s (d) 35 J/s

28. A Carnot's engine working between 400 K and 800 K has a work output of 1200 J per cycle, The amount of heat energy supplied to the engine from the source in each cycle is **(2021 Main)**
(a) 1800 J (b) 3200 J (c) 1600 J (d) 2400 J

29. Two identical containers joined by a small pipe initially contain the same gas at pressure p_0 and absolute temperature T_0. One container is now maintained at the same temperature while the other is heated to $2T_0$. The common pressure of the gases will be
(a) $\frac{3}{2}p_0$ (b) $\frac{4}{3}p_0$
(c) $\frac{5}{3}p_0$ (d) $2p_0$

30. One mole of helium is adiabatically expanded from its initial state (p_i, V_i, T_i) to its final state (p_f, V_f, T_f). The decrease in the internal energy associated with this expansion is equal to
(a) $C_V(T_i - T_f)$ (b) $C_p(T_i - T_f)$
(c) $\frac{1}{2}(C_p + C_V)(T_i - T_f)$ (d) $(C_p - C_V)(T_i - T_f)$

31. One mole of a perfect gas in a cylinder fitted with a piston has a pressure p, volume V and temperature 273 K. If the temperature is increased by 1 K keeping pressure constant, the increase in volume is
(a) $\frac{2V}{273}$ (b) $\frac{V}{91}$
(c) $\frac{V}{273}$ (d) V

32. The p-V diagram of a system undergoing thermodynamic transformation is shown in figure. The work done by the system in going from $A \rightarrow B \rightarrow C$ is 50 cal and 80 cal heat is given to the system. The change in internal energy between A and C is

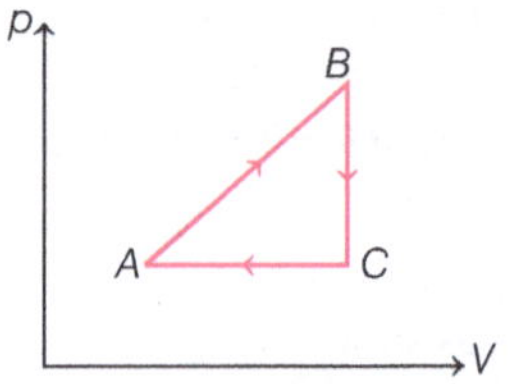

(a) −130 cal (b) −30 cal
(c) 130 cal (d) 30 cal

33. When a system is taken from state i to a state f along path iaf, $Q = 50$ J and $W = 20$ J. If $W = -13$ J for the curved return path fi, Q in this path is

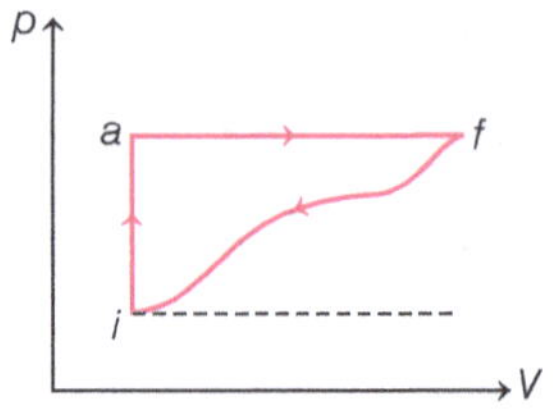

(a) 33 J (b) 23 J
(c) −7 J (d) −43 J

34. Two different ideal diatomic gases A and B are initially in the same state. A and B are then expanded to same final volume through adiabatic and isothermal process respectively. If p_A, p_B and T_A, T_B represent the final pressure and temperatures at A and B respectively, then
(a) $p_A < p_B$ and $T_A < T_B$ (b) $p_A > p_B$ and $T_A > T_B$
(c) $p_A > p_B$ and $T_A < T_B$ (d) $p_A < p_B$ and $T_A > T_B$

35. A certain mass of an ideal gas is at pressure p_1 and volume V_1. It is compressed isothermally and then allowed to expand adiabatically until its pressure returns to p_1. The gas is then allowed to expand to its original volume. Upon which of the following p-V graphs are these processes correctly shown?

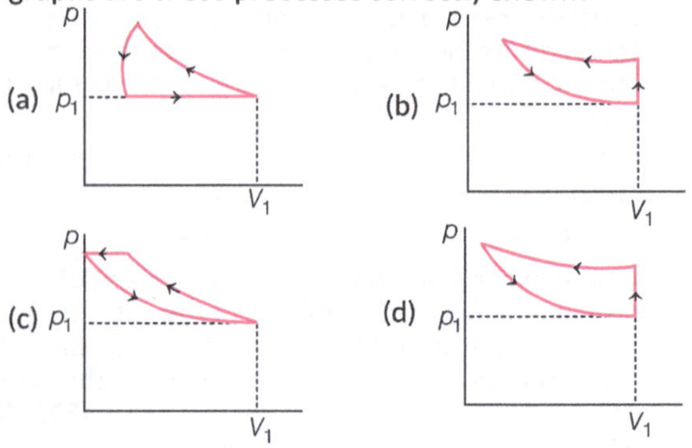

Match the Columns

36. Match List I with List II

	List I		List II
A.	Isothermal process	I.	Work done by the gas decreases internal energy
B.	Adiabatic process	II.	No change in internal energy
C.	Isochoric process	III.	The heat absorbed goes partly to increase internal energy and partly to do work
D.	Isobaric process	IV.	No work is done on or by the gas

Choose the correct answer from the options given below. **(2023 Main)**

(a) A-II, B-I, C-IV, D-III (b) A-II, B-I, C-III, D-IV
(c) A-I, B-II, C-IV, D-III (d) A-I, B-II, C-III, D-IV

Subjective Questions

37. A system is taken around the cycle shown in figure from state a to state b and then back to state a. The absolute value of the heat transfer during one cycle is 7200 J. (a) Does the system absorb or liberate heat when it goes around the cycle in the direction shown in the figure? (b) What is the work W done by the system in one cycle? (c) If the system goes around the cycle in a counter-clock wise direction, does it absorb or liberate heat in one cycle? What is the magnitude of the heat absorbed or liberated in one counter-clockwise cycle?

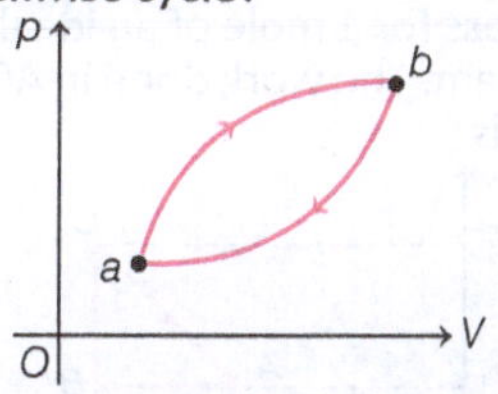

38. An ideal gas is enclosed in a cylinder with a movable piston on top. The piston has mass of 8000 g and an area of 5.00 cm^2 and is free to slide up and down, keeping the pressure of the gas constant. How much work is done as the temperature of 0.200 mol of the gas is raised from 200°C to 300°C?

39. Two moles of a certain gas at a temperature $T_0 = 300$ K were cooled isochorically so that the pressure of the gas got reduced 2 times. Then as a result of isobaric process, the gas is allowed to expand till its temperature got back to the initial value. Find the total amount of heat absorbed by gas in this process. **(Irodov 2.32)**

40. Five moles of an ideal monoatomic gas with an initial temperature of 127 °C expand and in the process absorb 1200 J of heat and do 2100 J of work. What is the final temperature of the gas?

41. Find the change in the internal energy of 2 kg of water as it is heated from 0°C to 4°C. The specific heat capacity of water is 4200 J/kg-K and its densities at 0°C and 4°C are 999.9 kg/m^3 and 1000 kg/m^3, respectively. Atmospheric pressure = 10^5 Pa.

42. Calculate the increase in the internal energy of 10 g of water when it is heated from 0°C to 100°C and converted into steam at 100 kPa. The density of steam = 0.6 kg/m^3. Specific heat capacity of water = 4200 J/kg-°C and the latent heat of vaporisation of water = 2.5×10^6 J/kg.

43. A bullet of mass 10 g travelling horizontally at 200 m/s strikes and embeds in a pendulum bob of mass 2.0 kg.
(a) How much mechanical energy is dissipated in the collision?
(b) Assuming that C_v for the bob plus bullet is 3 R, calculate the temperature increase of the system due to the collision. Take the molecular mass of the system to be 200 g/mol.

44. A gas in a cylinder is held at a constant pressure of 2.30×10^5 Pa and is cooled and compressed from 1.70 m^3 to 1.20 m^3. The internal energy of the gas decreases by 1.40×10^5 J. (a) Find the work done by the gas. (b) Find the absolute value $|Q|$ of the heat flow into or out of the gas and state the direction of the heat flow. (c) Does it matter whether or not the gas is ideal? Why or why not?

45. A 1.0 kg bar of copper is heated at atmospheric pressure (1.01×10^5 N/m^2). If its temperature increases from 20°C to 50°C, calculate the change in its internal energy. $\alpha = 7.0 \times 10^{-6}$/°C, $\rho = 8.92 \times 10^3$ kg/m^3 and $c = 387$ J/kg-°C.

46. Gaseous hydrogen contained initially under standard conditions in a sealed vessel of volume $V = 5.0$ L was cooled by $\Delta T = 55$ K. Find how much the internal energy of the gas will change and what amount of heat will be lost by the gas. **(Irodov 2.29)**

47. What amount of heat is to be transferred to nitrogen in the isobaric heating process for that gas to perform the work $W = 2.0$ J? **(Irodov 2.30)**

48. As a result of the isobaric heating by $\Delta T = 72$ K one mole of a certain ideal gas obtains an amount of heat $Q = 1.60$ kJ. Find the work performed by the gas, the increment of its internal energy, and the value of $\gamma = C_p/C_V$. **(Irodov 2.31)**

49. One mole of oxygen being initially at a temperature $T_0 = 290$ K is adiabatically compressed to increase its pressure $\eta = 10.0$ times. Find: **(Irodov 2.39)**
(a) the gas temperature after the compression
(b) the work that has been performed on the gas.

50. A certain mass of nitrogen was compressed $\eta = 5.0$ times (in terms of volume), first adiabatically, and then isothermally. In both cases the initial state of the gas was the same. Find the ratio of the respective works expended in each compression. **(Irodov 2.40)**

51. The volume of one mole of an ideal gas with the adiabatic exponent γ is varied according to the law $V = a/T$, where a is a constant. Find the amount of heat obtained by the gas in this process if the gas temperature is increased by ΔT. **(Irodov 2.43)**

52. Find the molar heat capacity of an ideal gas in a polytropic process $pV^n =$ constant, if the adiabatic exponent of the gas is equal to γ. At what values of the polytropic constant n will the heat capacity of the gas be negative? **(Irodov 2.45)**

53. In a certain polytropic process the volume of argon was increased $\alpha = 4.0$ times. Simultaneously, the pressure decreased $\beta = 8.0$ times. Find the molar heat capacity of argon in this process, assuming the gas to be ideal. **(Irodov 2.46)**

54. One mole of argon is expanded polytropically, the polytropic constant being $n = 1.50$. In the process, the gas temperature changes by $\Delta T = -26$ K. Find :
(a) the amount of heat obtained by the gas
(b) the work performed by the gas. **(Irodov 2.47)**

55. An ideal gas has an adiabatic exponent γ. In some process its molar heat capacity varies as $C = \alpha/T$, where α is a constant. Find the work performed by one mole of the gas during its heating from the temperature T_0 to the temperature η times higher. **(Irodov 2.56)**

56. A thermally insulated vessel with gaseous nitrogen at a temperature $t = 27°C$ moves with velocity $v = 100$ m/s. How much (in per cent) and in what way will the gas pressure change on a sudden stoppage of the vessel? **(Irodov 2.74)**

57. A gas consisting of rigid diatomic molecules is expanded adiabatically. How many times has the gas to be expanded to reduce the root mean square velocity of the molecules $\eta = 1.50$ times? **(Irodov 2.76)**

58. The mass $m = 15$ g of nitrogen is enclosed in a vessel at a temperature $T = 300$ K. What amount of heat has to be transferred to the gas to increase the root mean square velocity of its molecules $\eta = 2.0$ times? **(Irodov 2.77)**

59. A gas consisting of rigid diatomic molecules was initially under standard conditions. Then the gas was compressed adiabatically $\eta = 5.0$ times. Find the mean kinetic energy of a rotating molecule in the final state. **(Irodov 2.79)**

60. A heat engine employing a Carnot cycle with an efficiency of $\eta = 10\%$ is used as a refrigerating machine, the thermal reservoirs being the same. Find its refrigerating efficiency ε (coefficient of performance). **(Irodov 2.115)**

Integer Type Questions

61. At a certain temperature, the degrees of freedom per molecule for gas is 8. The gas performs 150 J of work when it expands under constant pressure. The amount of heat absorbed by the gas will be ...... J. **(2022 Main)**

62. A diatomic gas ($\gamma = 1.4$) does 400 J of work when it is expanded isobarically. The heat given to the gas in the process is .... J. **(2022 Main)**

63. A monoatomic gas performs a work of $\frac{Q}{4}$ where Q is the heat supplied to it. The molar heat capacity of the gas will be .... R during this transformation. Where R is the gas constant. **(2022 Main)**

64. A heat engine operates between a cold reservoir at temperature $T_2 = 400$ K and a hot reservoir at temperature T_1. It takes 300 J of heat from the hot reservoir and delivers 240 J of heat to the cold reservoir in a cycle. The minimum temperature of the hot reservoir has to be .... K. **(2021 Main)**

65. For an ideal heat engine, the temperature of the source is 127°C. In order to have 60% efficiency the temperature of the sink should be .... °C. (Round off to the nearest integer). **(2021 Main)**

Level 2

Single Correct Option

66. The equation of a state of a gas is given by $p(V - b) = nRT$. If 1 mole of a gas is isothermally expanded from volume V and $2V$, the work done during the process is
(a) $RT \ln\left|\frac{2V-b}{V-b}\right|$
(b) $RT \ln\left|\frac{V-b}{V}\right|$
(c) $RT \ln\left|\frac{V-b}{2V-b}\right|$
(d) $RT \ln\left|\frac{V}{V-b}\right|$

67. A cyclic process for 1 mole of an ideal gas is shown in the V-T diagram. The work done in AB, BC and CA respectively is

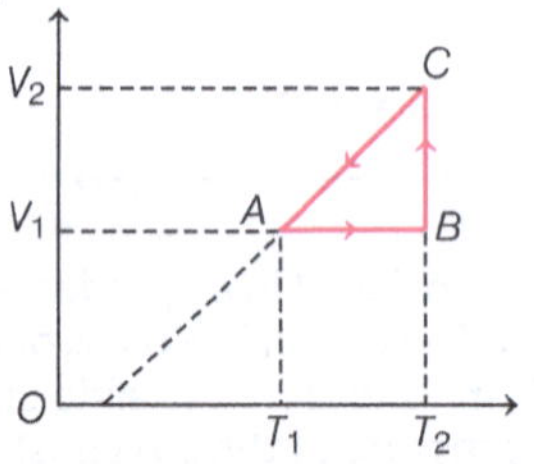

(a) $0, RT_2 \ln\left|\frac{V_2}{V_1}\right|, R(T_1 - T_2)$
(b) $R(T_1 - T_2), 0, RT_1 \ln\left|\frac{V_1}{V_2}\right|$
(c) $0, RT_1 \ln\left|\frac{V_1}{V_2}\right|, R(T_1 - T_2)$
(d) $0, RT_2 \ln\left|\frac{V_2}{V_1}\right|, R(T_2 - T_1)$

68. Ten moles of a diatomic perfect gas are allowed to expand at constant pressure. The initial volume and temperature are V_0 and T_0, respectively. If $\frac{7}{2} RT_0$ heat is transferred to the gas, then the final volume and temperature are
(a) $1.1 V_0, 1.1 T_0$
(b) $0.9 V_0, 0.9 T_0$
(c) $1.1 V_0, \frac{10}{11} T_0$
(d) $0.9 V_0, \frac{10}{9} T_0$

69. An ideal monoatomic gas is carried around the cycle *ABCDA* as shown in the figure. The efficiency of the gas cycle is

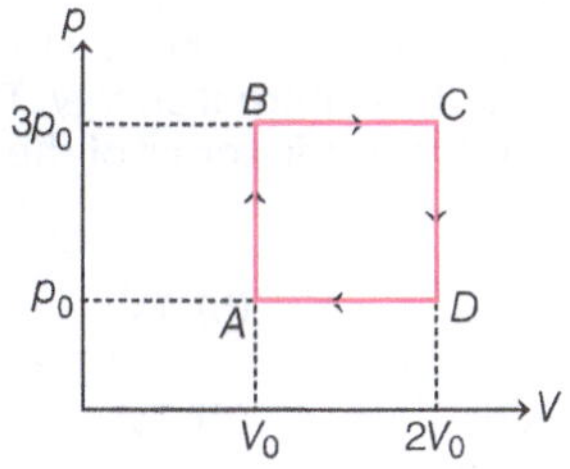

(a) $\frac{4}{21}$ (b) $\frac{2}{21}$ (c) $\frac{4}{31}$ (d) $\frac{2}{31}$

70. In the process shown in figure, the internal energy of an ideal gas decreases by $\frac{3p_0V_0}{2}$ in going from point *C* to *A*. Heat transfer along the process *CA* is

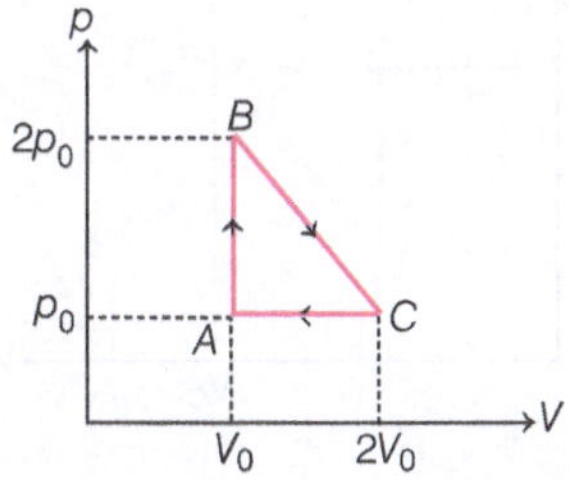

(a) $(-3\,p_0V_0)$
(b) $(-5\,p_0V_0/2)$
(c) $(-3\,p_0V_0/2)$
(d) zero

71. One mole of an ideal monoatomic gas at temperature T_0 expands slowly according to the law $\frac{p}{V}$ = constant. If the final temperature is $2T_0$, heat supplied to the gas is

(a) $2RT_0$ (b) $\frac{3}{2}RT_0$ (c) RT_0 (d) $\frac{1}{2}RT_0$

72. A mass of gas is first expanded isothermally and then compressed adiabatically to its original volume. What further simplest operation must be performed on the gas to restore it to its original state?

(a) An isobaric cooling to bring its temperature to initial value
(b) An isochoric cooling to bring its pressure to its initial value
(c) An isothermal process to take its pressure to its initial value
(d) An isochoric heating to bring its temperature to initial value

73. A monoatomic ideal gas, initially at temperature T_1, is enclosed in a cylinder fitted with a frictionless piston. The gas is allowed to expand adiabatically to a temperature T_2 by releasing the piston suddenly. If L_1 and L_2 are the lengths of gas column before and after expansion respectively, then $\frac{T_1}{T_2}$ is given by

(a) $\left(\frac{L_1}{L_2}\right)^{\frac{2}{3}}$ (b) $\frac{L_1}{L_2}$ (c) $\frac{L_2}{L_1}$ (d) $\left(\frac{L_2}{L_1}\right)^{\frac{2}{3}}$

74. One mole of an ideal gas is taken through a cyclic process. The minimum temperature during the cycle is 300 K. Then, net exchange of heat for complete cycle is

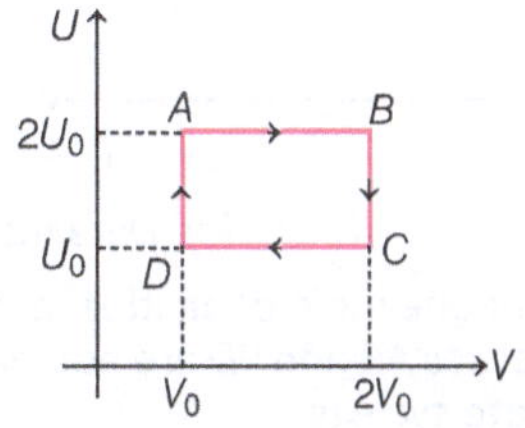

(a) $600\,R\ln 2$
(b) $300\,R\ln 2$
(c) $-300\,R\ln 2$
(d) $900\,R\ln 2$

75. Two moles of an ideal gas are undergone a cyclic process 1-2-3-1. If net heat exchange in the process is 300 J, the work done by the gas in the process 2-3 is

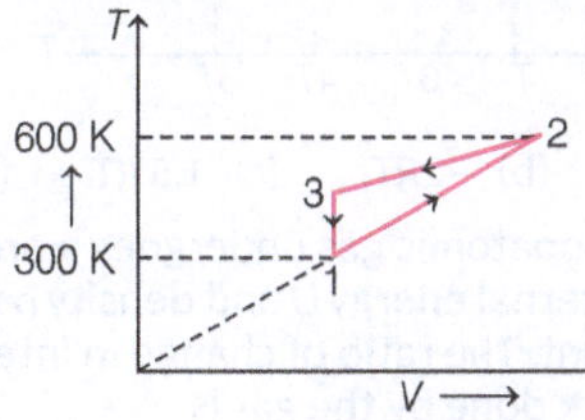

(a) −500 J
(b) −5000 J
(c) −3000 J
(d) None of these

76. Two cylinders fitted with pistons contain equal amount of an ideal diatomic gas at 300 K. The piston of *A* is free to move, while that of *B* is held fixed. The same amount of heat is given to the gas in each cylinder. If the rise in temperature of the gas in *A* is 30 K, then the rise in temperature of gas in *B* is **(1998 JEE)**

(a) 30 K
(b) 18 K
(c) 50 K
(d) 42 K

77. A gas follows a process TV^{n-1} = constant, where T = absolute temperature of the gas and V = volume of the gas. The bulk modulus of the gas in the process is given by

(a) $(n-1)p$
(b) $p/(n-1)$
(c) np
(d) p/n

78. 600 J of heat is added to a monoatomic gas in a process in which the gas performs a work of 150 J. The molar heat capacity for the process is

(a) $3R$
(b) $4R$
(c) $2R$
(d) $6R$

79. The internal energy of a gas is given by $U = 2pV$. It expands from V_0 to $2V_0$ against a constant pressure p_0. The heat absorbed by the gas in the process is

(a) $2p_0V_0$
(b) $4p_0V_0$
(c) $3p_0V_0$
(d) p_0V_0

80. The figure shows two paths for the change of state of a gas from A to B. The ratio of molar heat capacities in path 1 and path 2 is

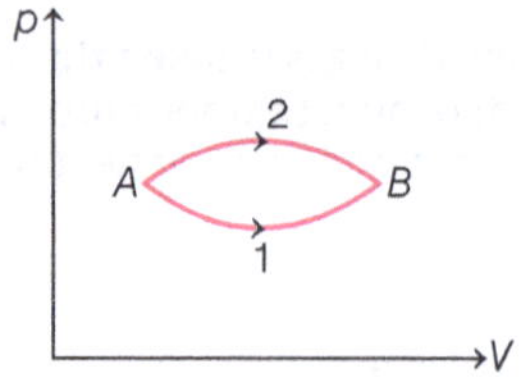

(a) < 1 (b) > 1
(c) 1 (d) Data insufficient

81. p-T diagram of one mole of an ideal monatomic gas is shown. Processes AB and CD are adiabatic. Work done in the complete cycle is

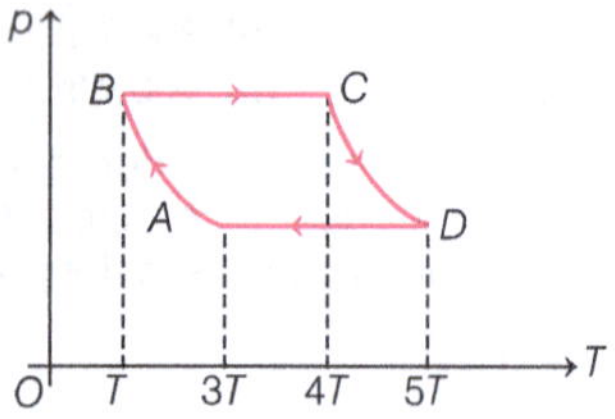

(a) 2.5 RT (b) $-2RT$ (c) 1.5 RT (d) $-3.5\,RT$

82. An ideal monoatomic gas undergoes a process in which its internal energy U and density ρ vary as $U\rho =$ constant. The ratio of change in internal energy and the work done by the gas is

(a) $\frac{3}{2}$ (b) $\frac{2}{3}$ (c) $\frac{1}{3}$ (d) $\frac{3}{5}$

83. The given figure shows the variation of force applied by ideal gas on a piston which undergoes a process during which piston position changes from 0.1 to 0.4 m. If the internal energy of the system at the end of the process is 2.5 J higher, then the heat absorbed during the process is

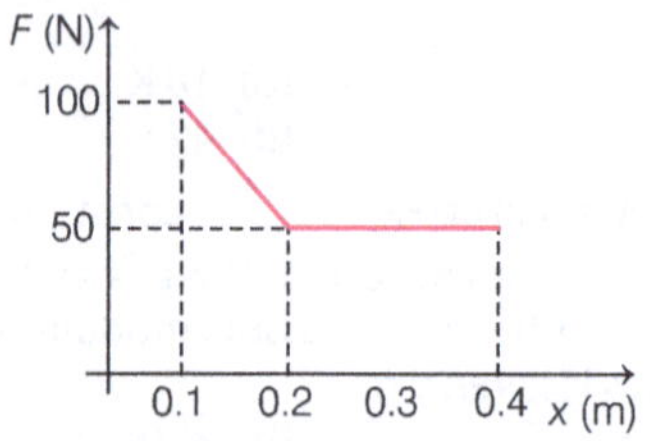

(a) 15 J (b) 17.5 J (c) 20 J (d) 22.5 J

84. A gas can expand through two processes : (i) isobaric, (ii) $\frac{p}{V} =$ constant. Assuming that the initial pressure and volume are same in both processes and the final volume which is two times the initial volume is also same in both processes, which of the following is true?

(a) Work done by gas in process (i) is greater than the work done by the gas in process (ii)
(b) Work done by gas in process (i) is smaller than the work done by the gas in process (ii)
(c) Final pressure is greater in process (i)
(d) Final temperature is greater in process (i)

85. An ideal gas of adiabatic exponent γ is expanded so that the amount of heat transferred to the gas is equal to the decrease of its internal energy. Then, the equation of the process in terms of the variables T and V is

(a) $TV^{\frac{(\gamma-1)}{2}} = C$ (b) $TV^{\frac{(\gamma-2)}{2}} = C$
(c) $TV^{\frac{(\gamma-1)}{4}} = C$ (d) $TV^{\frac{(\gamma-2)}{4}} = C$

86. A thermodynamical process is shown in the figure with $p_A = 3 \times p_{atm}, V_A = 2 \times 10^{-4}\ m^3, p_B = 8 \times p_{atm}$, $V_C = 5 \times 10^{-4}\ m^3$. In the process AB and BC, 600 J and 200 J heat are added to the system. Find the change in internal energy of the system in the process CA. $[1\ p_{atm} = 10^5\ N/m^2]$

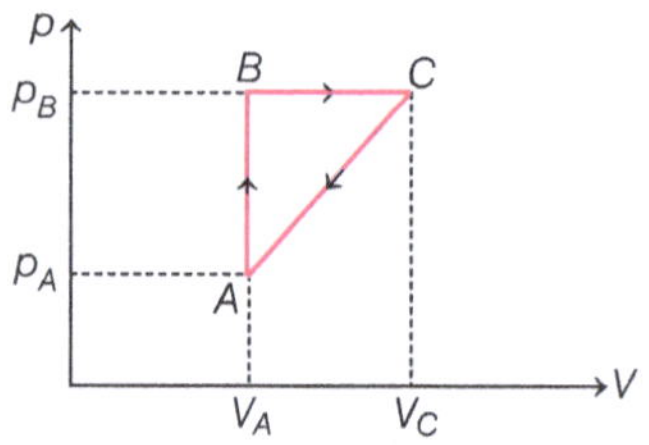

(a) 560 J (b) – 560 J
(c) – 240 J (d) 240 J

87. A gas takes part in two processes in which it is heated from the same initial state 1 to the same final temperature. The processes are shown on the p-V diagram by the straight lines 1-3 and 1-2. 2 and 3 are the points on the same isothermal curve. Q_1 and Q_2 are the heat transfer along the two processes. Then,

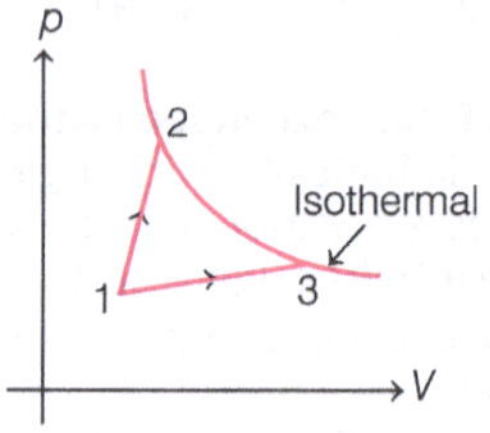

(a) $Q_1 = Q_2$ (b) $Q_1 < Q_2$
(c) $Q_1 > Q_2$ (d) Insufficient data

88. A closed system receives 200 kJ of heat at constant volume. It then rejects 100 kJ of heat while it has 50 kJ of work done on it at constant pressure. If an adiabatic process can be found which will restore the system to its initial state, the work done by the system during this process is

(a) 100 kJ
(b) 50 kJ
(c) 150 kJ
(d) 200 kJ

89. 100 moles of an ideal monatomic gas undergoes the thermodynamic process as shown in the figure

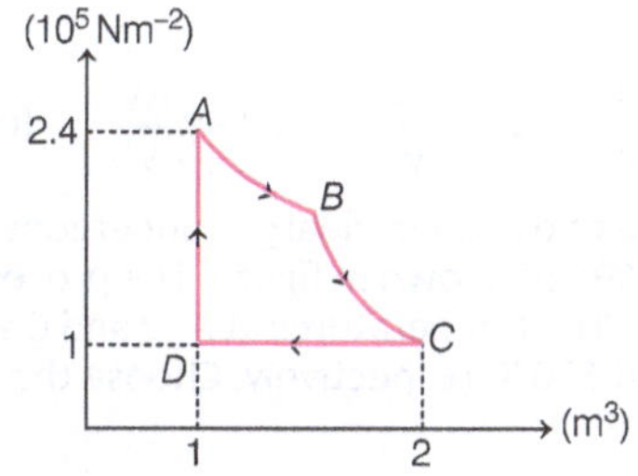

$A \rightarrow B$: isothermal expansion
$B \rightarrow C$: adiabatic expansion
$C \rightarrow D$: isobaric compression
$D \rightarrow A$: isochoric process

The heat transfer along the process AB is 9×10^4 J.The net work done by the gas during the cycle is (Take $R = 8$ JK^{-1} mol^{-1})

(a) -0.5×10^4 J (b) $+0.5 \times 10^4$ J
(c) -5×10^4 J (d) $+5 \times 10^4$ J

90. Two moles of an ideal monoatomic gas are expanded according to the equation pT = constant from its initial state (p_0, V_0) to the final state due to which its pressure becomes half of the initial pressure. The change in internal energy is

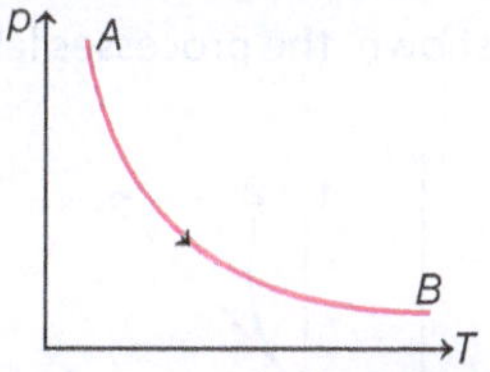

(a) $\frac{3p_0V_0}{4}$ (b) $\frac{3p_0V_0}{2}$
(c) $\frac{9p_0V_0}{2}$ (d) $\frac{5p_0V_0}{2}$

91. The state of an ideal gas is changed through an isothermal process at temperature T_0 as shown in figure. The work done by the gas in going from state B to C is double the work done by gas in going from state A to B. If the pressure in the state B is $\frac{p_0}{2}$, then the pressure of the gas in state C is

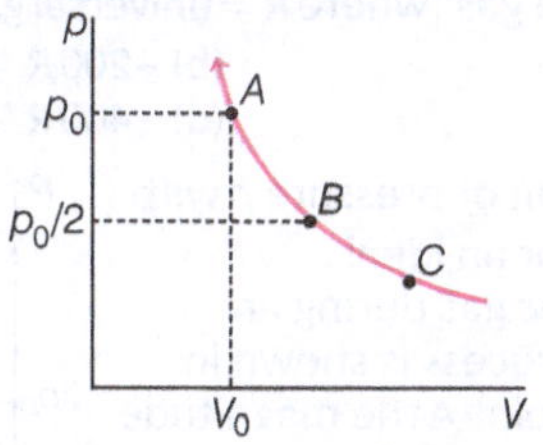

(a) $\frac{p_0}{3}$ (b) $\frac{p_0}{4}$
(c) $\frac{p_0}{6}$ (d) $\frac{p_0}{8}$

92. An ideal monoatomic gas is taken through a process $dQ = 2dU$. The molar heat capacity for the process is (where dQ is heat supplied and dU is a change in internal energy)

(a) 2.4 R (b) 3R (c) R (d) 2R

93. Pressure *versus* density graph of an ideal gas is shown in figure.

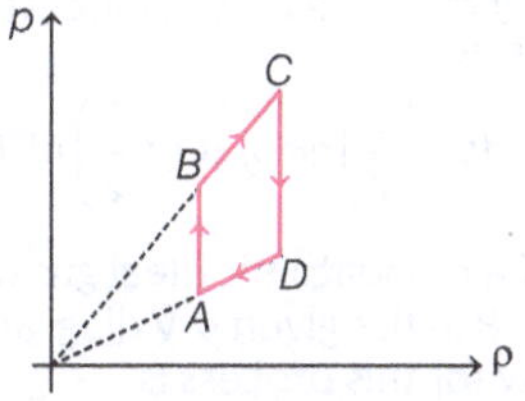

(a) during the process AB work done by the gas is positive
(b) during the process AB work done by the gas is negative
(c) during the process BC internal energy of the gas is increasing
(d) None of the above

94. An ideal gas expands isothermally from a volume V_1 to V_2 and then compressed to original volume V_1 adiabatically. Initial pressure is p_1 and final pressure is p_3. The total work done is W. Then, **(2004 Main)**

(a) $p_3 > p_1, W > 0$ (b) $p_3 < p_1, W < 0$
(c) $p_3 > p_1, W < 0$ (d) $p_3 = p_1, W = 0$

95. Corresponding to the process shown in figure, what is the heat given to the gas in the process $ABCA$?

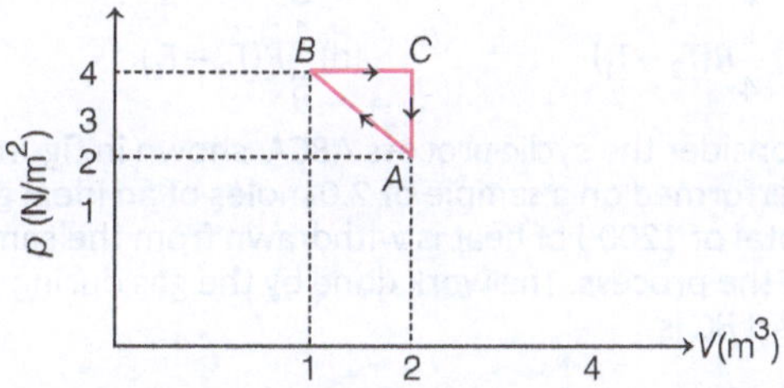

(a) 1 J (b) $\frac{3}{2}$ J (c) $\frac{1}{2}$ J (d) zero

96. A closed system undergoes a change of state by process $1 \rightarrow 2$ for which $Q_{12} = 10$ J and $W_{12} = -3$ J. The system is now returned to its initial state by a different path $2 \rightarrow 1$ for which Q_{21} is -5 J. The work done by the gas in the process $2 \rightarrow 1$ is

(a) 8 J (b) zero
(c) -2 J (d) +5 J

97. An ideal monoatomic gas undergoes the process AB as shown in the figure. If the heat supplied and the work done in the process are ΔQ and ΔW respectively. The ratio $\Delta Q : \Delta W$ is

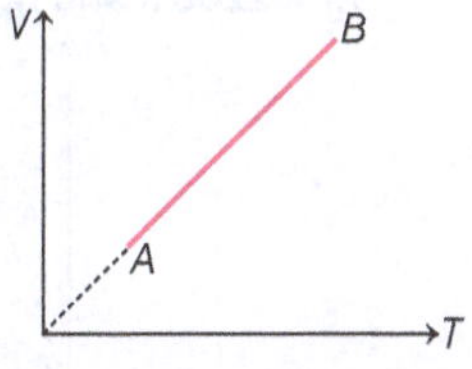

(a) 2.50 (b) 1.67
(c) 1.25 (d) 0.40

98. One mole of a gas expands with temperature T such that its volume, $V = kT^2$, where k is a constant. If the temperature of the gas changes by 60°C, then the work done by the gas is

(a) $120R$ (b) $R\ln 60$ (c) $kR\ln 60$ (d) $60kR$

99. n moles of an ideal gas undergo a process in which the temperature changes with volume as $T = KV^2$. The work done by the gas as the temperature changes from T_0 to $4T_0$ is

(a) $3nRT_0$ (b) $\left(\frac{5}{2}\right)nRT_0$ (c) $\left(\frac{3}{2}\right)nRT_0$ (d) zero

100. One mole of a monoatomic ideal gas undergoes the process $A \to B$ in the given p-V diagram. The molar heat capacity for this process is

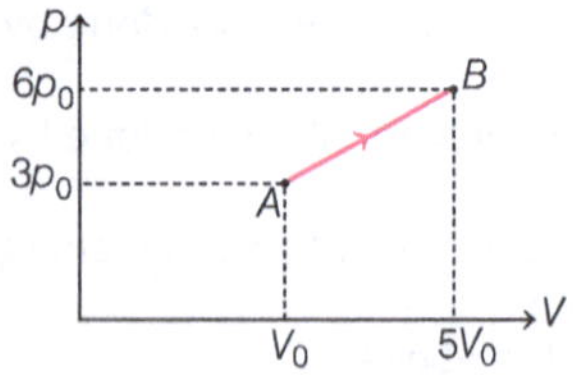

(a) $\frac{3R}{2}$ (b) $\frac{13R}{6}$ (c) $\frac{5R}{2}$ (d) $2R$

101. One mole of an ideal gas at temperature T_1 expands according to the law $\frac{p}{V^2} = a$ (constant). The work done by the gas till temperature of gas becomes T_2 is

(a) $\frac{1}{2}R(T_2 - T_1)$ (b) $\frac{1}{3}R(T_2 - T_1)$

(c) $\frac{1}{4}R(T_2 - T_1)$ (d) $\frac{1}{5}R(T_2 - T_1)$

102. Consider the cyclic process $ABCA$, shown in figure is performed on a sample of 2.0 moles of an ideal gas. A total of 1200 J of heat is withdrawn from the sample in the process. The work done by the gas during the part BC is

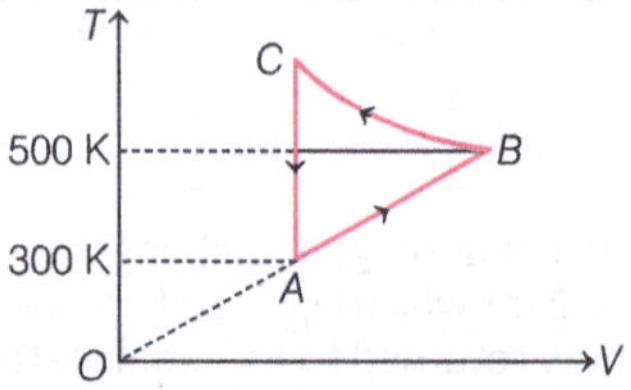

(a) −2520 J (b) −3250 J (c) −4520 J (d) −5520 J

103. Six moles of an ideal gas perform a cycle shown in figure. The temperatures are $T_A = 600$ K, $T_B = 800$ K, $T_C = 2200$ K and $T_D = 1200$ K, the work done per cycle is

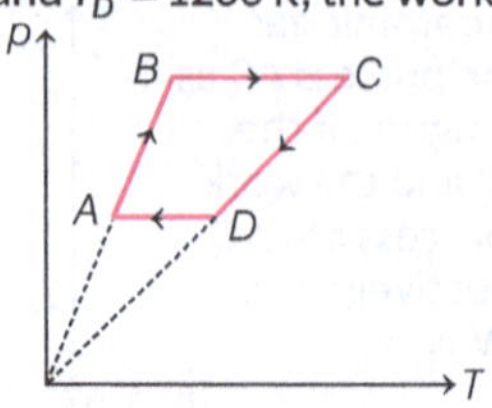

(a) 20 kJ (b) 30 kJ (c) 40 kJ (d) 60 kJ

104. For an adiabatic expansion of a perfect gas, the value of $\frac{\Delta p}{p}$ is equal to

(a) $-\gamma^{\frac{1}{2}}\frac{\Delta V}{V}$ (b) $-\frac{\Delta V}{V}$ (c) $-\gamma\frac{\Delta V}{V}$ (d) $-\gamma^2\frac{\Delta V}{V}$

105. One mole of diatomic ideal gas undergoes a cyclic process ABC as shown in figure. The process BC is adiabatic. The temperatures at A, B and C are 400 K, 800 K and 600 K, respectively. Choose the correct statement. **(2014 Main)**

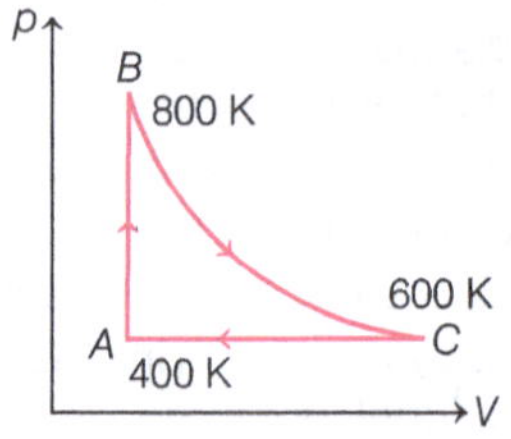

(a) The change in internal energy in whole cyclic process is 250 R

(b) The change in internal energy in the process CA is 700 R

(c) The change in internal energy in the process AB is −350 R

(d) The change in internal energy in the process BC is −500 R

106. In the figure shown, the processes labelled 1, 2, 3 and 4 are

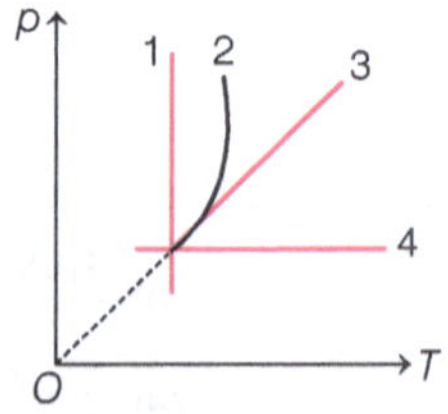

(a) isothermal, adiabatic, isobaric, isochoric

(b) isothermal, adiabatic, isochoric, isobaric

(c) adiabatic, isothermal, isobaric, isochoric

(d) adiabatic, isobaric, isothermal, isochoric

107. In a thermodynamic process two moles of a monotomic ideal gas obeys $p \propto V^{-2}$. If temperature of the gas increases from 300 K to 400 K, then find work done by the gas (where R = universal gas constant)

(a) 200 R (b) −200 R

(c) −100 R (d) −400 R

108. The variation of pressure p with volume V for an ideal monoatomic gas during an adiabatic process is shown in figure. At point A the magnitude of rate of change of pressure with volume V is

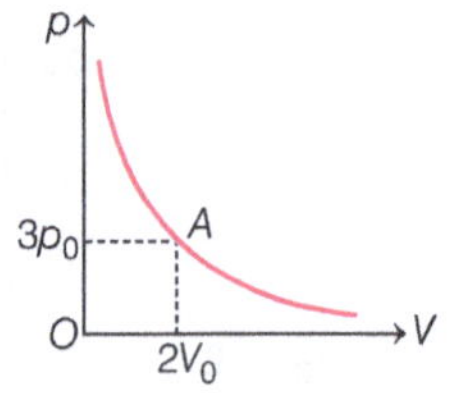

(a) $\frac{3p_0}{5V_0}$ (b) $\frac{5p_0}{3V_0}$ (c) $\frac{3p_0}{2V_0}$ (d) $\frac{5p_0}{2V_0}$

Multiple Correct Options

109. Density (ρ) *versus* internal energy (U) graph of a gas is as shown in figure. Choose the correct options.

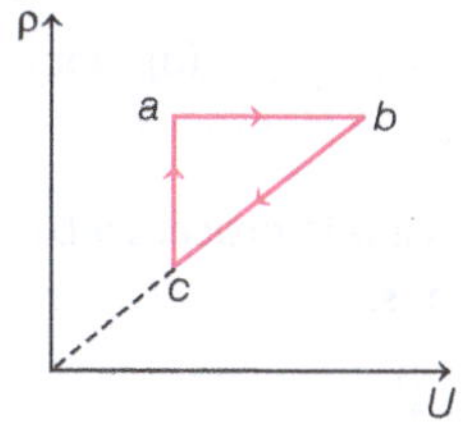

(a) $Q_{bc} = 0$ (b) $W_{bc} = 0$ (c) $W_{ca} < 0$ (d) $Q_{ab} > 0$

Here, W is work done by gas and Q is heat given to the gas.

110. Temperature of a monatomic gas is increased from T_0 to $2T_0$ in three different processes : isochoric, isobaric and adiabatic. Heat given to the gas in these three processes are Q_1, Q_2 and Q_3 respectively. Then, choose the correct option.

(a) $Q_1 > Q_3$ (b) $Q_2 > Q_1$ (c) $Q_2 > Q_3$ (d) $Q_3 = 0$

111. A cyclic process 1-2-3-4-1 is depicted on V-T diagram. The p-T and p-V diagrams for this cyclic process are given below. Select the correct choices (more than one options is/are correct)

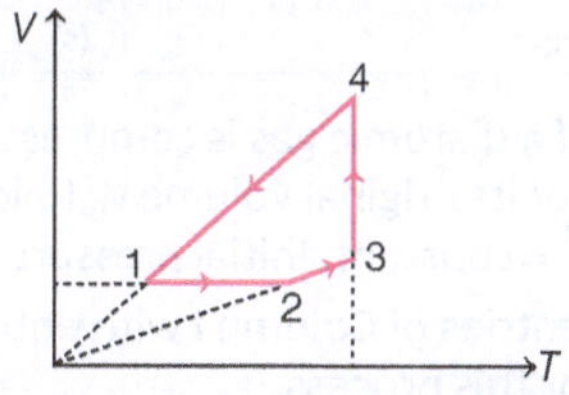

(a)
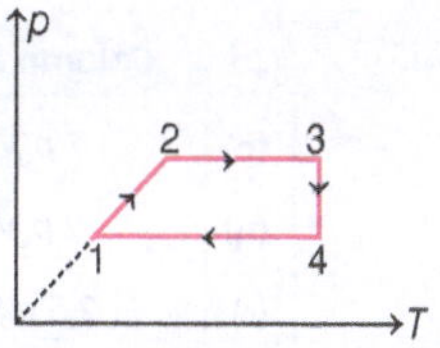

(b)
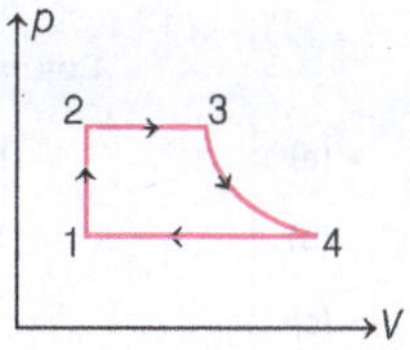

(c)
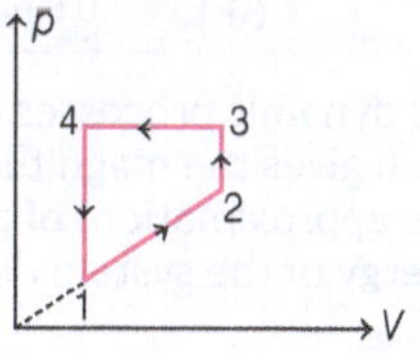

(d) None of these

112. An ideal diatomic gas undergoes a process such that, $p \propto V$. At the end of process, rms speed of gas molecules is found double of its inital value. Initially gas is at pressure p_1 and have volume V_1. Choose the correct options.

(a) Molar specific heat for the process is $\frac{5}{2}R$

(b) Molar specific heat for the process is $3R$

(c) Heat added to the gas during the process is $9\,p_1V_1$

(d) Heat added to the gas during the process is $\frac{15}{2}p_1V_1$

113. In the given p-V diagram, a monoatomic gas $\left(\gamma = \frac{5}{3}\right)$ is first compressed adiabatically from state A to state B. Then, it expands isothermally from state B to state C. [Given, $\left(\frac{1}{3}\right)^{0.6} \simeq 0.5$, $\ln 2 \simeq 0.7$]. **(2022 Adv.)**

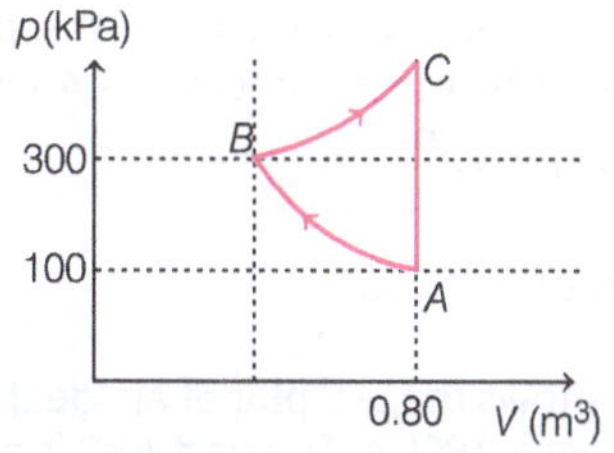

Which of the following statement(s) is(are) correct?

(a) The magnitude of the total work done in the process $A \to B \to C$ is 144 kJ.

(b) The magnitude of the work done in the process $B \to C$ is 84 kJ.

(c) The magnitude of the work done in the process $A \to B$ is 60 kJ.

(d) The magnitude of the work done in the process $C \to A$ is zero.

114. An ideal monoatomic gas is confined in a horizontal cylinder by a spring loaded piston (as shown in the figure). Initially the gas is at temperature T_1, pressure p_1 and volume V_1 and the spring is in its relaxed state. The gas is then heated very slowly to temperature T_2, pressure p_2 and volume V_2. During this process the piston moves out by a distance x. **(2015 Adv.)**

Ignoring the friction between the piston and the cylinder, the correct statements is/are

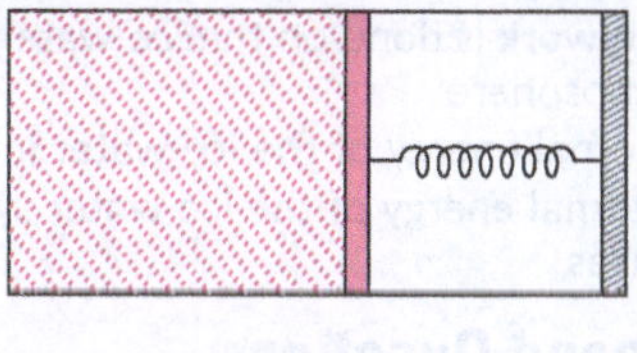

(a) If $V_2 = 2V_1$ and $T_2 = 3T_1$, then the energy stored in the spring is $\frac{1}{4}p_1V_1$

(b) If $V_2 = 2V_1$ and $T_2 = 3T_1$, then the change in internal energy is $3p_1V_1$

(c) If $V_2 = 3V_1$ and $T_2 = 4T_1$, then the work done by the gas is $\frac{7}{3}p_1V_1$

(d) If $V_2 = 3V_1$ and $T_2 = 4T_1$, then the heat supplied to the gas is $\frac{17}{6}p_1V_1$

115. One mole of an ideal gas in initial state A undergoes a cyclic process $ABCA$, as shown in the figure. Its pressure at A is p_0. Choose the correct option(s) from the following. **(2010 JEE)**

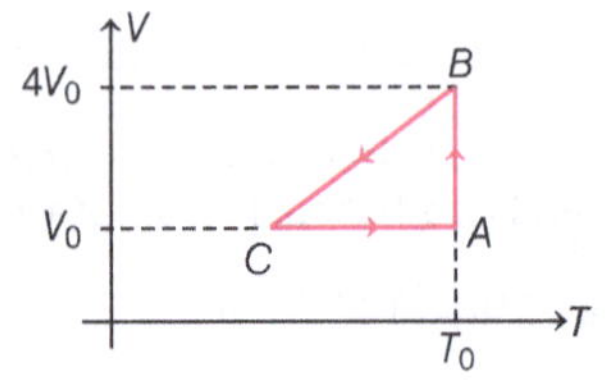

(a) Internal energies at A and B are the same
(b) Work done by the gas in process AB is $p_0V_0 \ln 4$
(c) Pressure at C is $\frac{p_0}{4}$
(d) Temperature at C is $\frac{T_0}{4}$

116. The figure shows the p-V plot of an ideal gas taken through a cycle $ABCDA$. The part ABC is a semi-circle and CDA is half of an ellipse. Then, **(2009 JEE)**

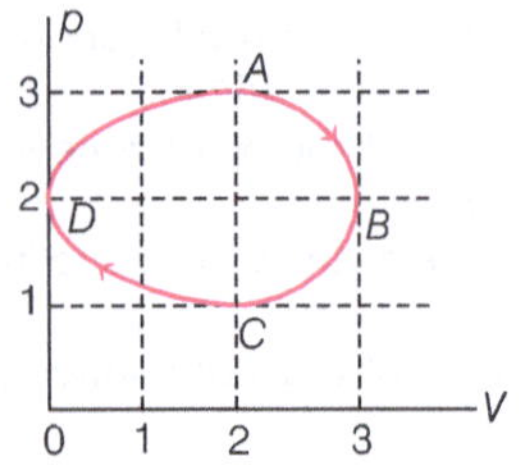

(a) the process during the path $A \to B$ is isothermal
(b) heat flows out of the gas during the path $B \to C \to D$
(c) work done during the path $A \to B \to C$ is zero
(d) positive work is done by the gas in the cycle $ABCDA$

117. During the melting of a slab of ice at 273 K at atmospheric pressure, **(1998 JEE)**
(a) positive work is done by the ice-water system on the atmosphere
(b) positive work is done on the ice-water system by the atmosphere
(c) the internal energy of the ice-water increases
(d) the internal energy of the ice-water system decreases

Passage Based Questions

Passage (Q. No. 118-119)

One mole of a monatomic ideal gas is taken along the cycle ABCA as shown in the diagram.

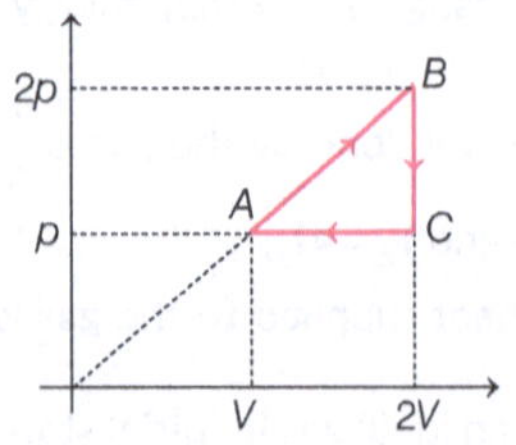

118. The net heat absorbed by the gas in the given cycle is
(a) pV (b) $\frac{pV}{2}$ (c) $2pV$ (d) $4pV$

119. The ratio of specific heat in the process CA to the specific heat in the process BC is
(a) 2 (b) $\frac{5}{3}$
(c) 4 (d) None of these

Match the Columns

120. Heat taken by a gas in process a-b is $6p_0V_0$. Match the following columns.

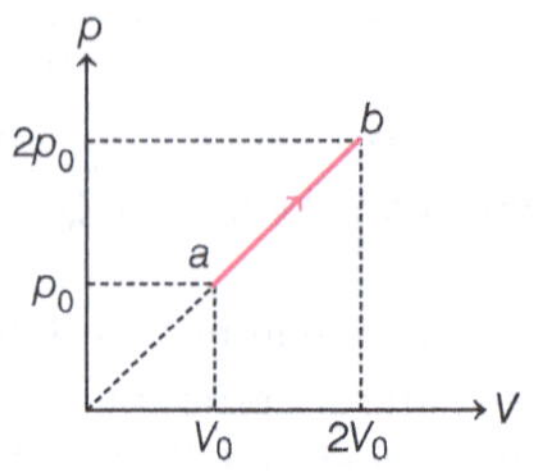

	Column I		Column II
(a)	W_{ab}	(p)	$2p_0V_0$
(b)	ΔU_{ab}	(q)	$4p_0V_0$
(c)	Molar heat capacity in given process	(r)	$2R$
(d)	C_V of gas	(s)	None of these

121. One mole of a diatomic gas is compressed to one-fourth of its original volume V_0 following a process VT^2 = constant. Initial pressure of gas is p_0. Match the entries of Column I with entries of Column II for this process.

	Column I		Column II
(a)	$\lvert Q \rvert$	(p)	$7\, p_0V_0$
(b)	$\lvert \Delta U \rvert$	(q)	$2\, p_0V_0$
(c)	$\lvert W \rvert$	(r)	$2.5\, p_0V_0$
(d)	$\lvert (\Delta p) V_0 \rvert$	(s)	$0.5\, p_0V_0$

122. Column-I describes thermodynamic processes in four different systems. Column-II gives the magnitudes (either exactly or as a close approximation) of possible changes in the internal energy of the system due to the process.

	Column-I		Column-II
I.	10^{-3} kg of water at 100°C is converted to steam at the same temperature, at a pressure of 10^5 Pa. The volume of the system changes from 10^{-6} m^3 to 10^{-3} m^3 in this process. Latent heat of water = 2250 kJ/kg.	P.	2 kJ
II.	0.2 moles of a rigid diatomic ideal gas with volume V at temperature 500 K undergoes an isobaric expansion to volume $3V$. Assume $R = 8.0$ J mol^{-1} K^{-1}.	Q.	7 kJ

	Column-I		Column-II
III.	One mole of a monoatomic ideal gas is compressed adiabatically from volume $V = \frac{1}{3}\,m^3$ and pressure 2 kPa to volume $V/8$.	R.	4 kJ
IV.	Three moles of a diatomic ideal gas whose molecules can vibrate, is given 9 kJ of heat and undergoes isobaric expansion.	S.	5 kJ
		T.	3 kJ

Which one of the following options is correct? **(2022 Adv.)**

	I	II	III	IV		I	II	III	IV
(a)	T	R	S	Q	(b)	S	P	T	P
(c)	P	R	T	Q	(d)	Q	R	S	T

Directions (Q.Nos. 123-125)

Match the information given in the three columns of the following table.

	Column 1		Column 2		Column 3
(I)	$W_{1\to2} = \frac{1}{\gamma-1}(p_2V_2 - p_1V_1)$	(i)	Isothermal	(P)	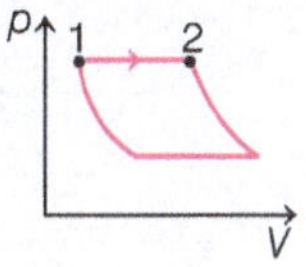
(II)	$W_{1\to2} = -pV_2 + pV_1$	(ii)	Isochoric	(Q)	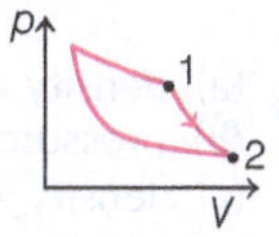
(III)	$W_{1\to2} = 0$	(iii)	Isobaric	(R)	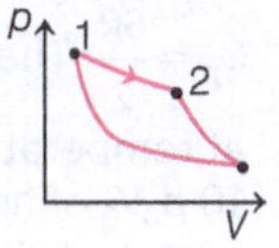
(IV)	$W_{1\to2} = -nRT \ln\left(\frac{V_2}{V_1}\right)$	(iv)	Adiabatic	(S)	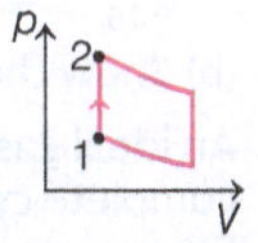

An ideal gas is undergoing a cyclic thermodynamic process in different ways as shown in the corresponding *p*-*V* diagrams in column 3 of the table. Consider only the path from state 1 to state 2. *W* denotes the corresponding work done on the system. The equations and plots in the table have standards notations and used in thermodynamic processes. Here γ is the ratio of heat capacities at constant pressure and constant volume. The number of moles in the gas is *n*. **(2017 Adv.)**

123. Which one of the following options correctly represents a thermodynamic process that is used as a correction in the determination of the speed of sound in an ideal gas?

(a) (IV) (ii) (R) (b) (I) (ii) (Q)
(c) (I), (iv) (Q) (d) (III) (iv) (R)

124. Which of the following options is the only correct representation of a process in which $\Delta U = \Delta Q - p\Delta V$?

(a) (II) (iii) (S) (b) (II) (iii) (P)
(c) (III) (iii) (P) (d) (II) (iv) (R)

125. Which one of the following options is the correct combination?

(a) (II) (iv) (P) (b) (III) (ii) (S)
(c) (II) (iv) (R) (d) (IV) (ii) (S)

126. One mole of a monoatomic ideal gas is taken along two cyclic processes $E \to F \to G \to E$ and $E \to F \to H \to E$ as shown in the *p*-*V* diagram. **(2013 Adv.)**

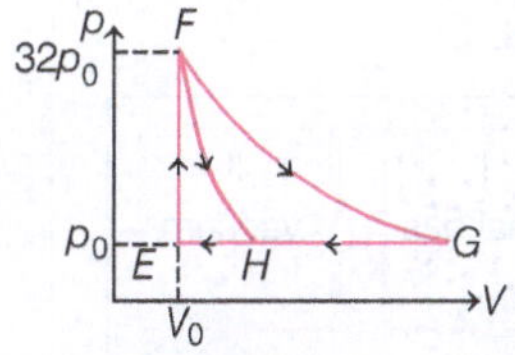

The processes involved are purely isochoric, isobaric, isothermal or adiabatic.

Match the paths in List I with the magnitudes of the work done in List II and select the correct answer using the codes given below the lists.

	List I		List II
P.	$G \to E$	1.	$160\,p_0V_0 \ln 2$
Q.	$G \to H$	2.	$36\,p_0V_0$
R.	$F \to H$	3.	$24\,p_0V_0$
S.	$F \to G$	4.	$31\,p_0V_0$

Codes

	P	Q	R	S		P	Q	R	S
(a)	4	3	2	1	(b)	4	3	1	2
(c)	3	1	2	4	(d)	1	3	2	4

127. One mole of a monoatomic ideal gas is taken through a cycle *ABCDA* as shown in the *p*-*V* diagram. **Column II** gives the characteristics involved in the cycle. Match them with each of the processes given in **Column I**. **(2011 JEE)**

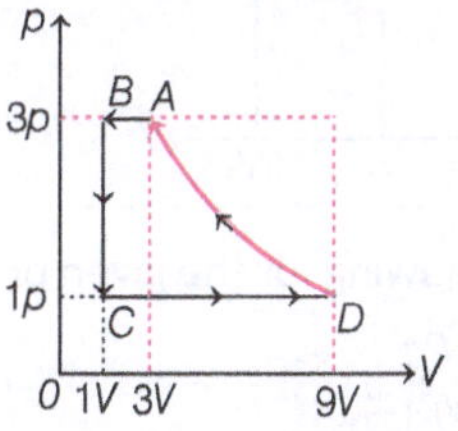

	Column I		Column II
(a)	Process $A \to B$	(p)	Internal energy decreases
(b)	Process $B \to C$	(q)	Internal energy increases
(c)	Process $C \to D$	(r)	Heat is lost

	Column I		Column II
(d)	Process $D \rightarrow A$	(s)	Heat is gained
		(t)	Work is done on the gas

128. **Column I** contains a list of processes involving expansion of an ideal gas. Match this with **Column II** describing the thermodynamic change during this process. **(2008 JEE)**

	Column I		Column II
(a)	An insulated container has two chambers separated by a valve. Chamber I contains an ideal gas and the Chamber II has vacuum. The valve is opened. 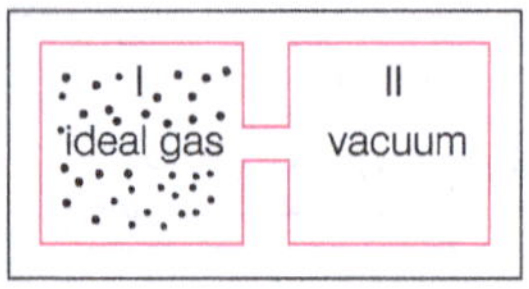	(p)	The temperature of the gas decreases
(b)	An ideal monoatomic gas expands to twice its original volume such that its pressure $p \propto \frac{1}{V^2}$, where V is the volume of the gas.	(q)	The temperature of the gas increases or remains constant
(c)	An ideal monoatomic gas expands to twice its original volume such that its pressure $p \propto \frac{1}{V^{4/3}}$, where V is its volume.	(r)	The gas loses heat
(d)	An ideal monoatomic gas expands such that its pressure p and volume V follows the behaviour shown in the graph. 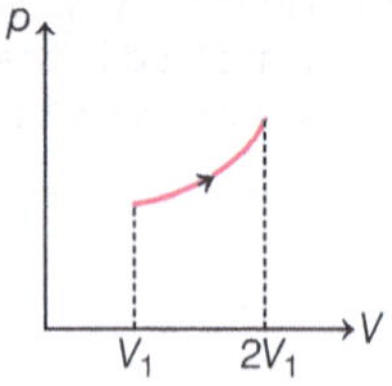	(s)	The gas gains heat

129. Match the following for the given process. **(2006 JEE)**

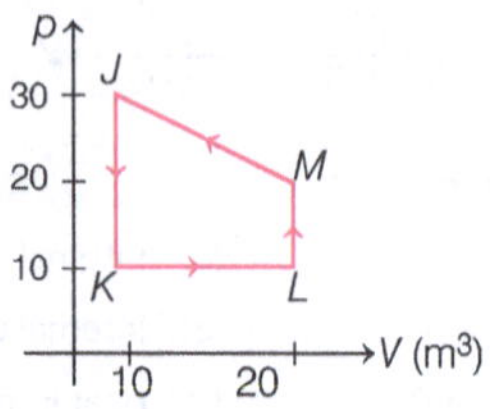

	Column I		Column II
(a)	Process $J \rightarrow K$	(p)	$Q > 0$
(b)	Process $K \rightarrow L$	(q)	$W < 0$
(c)	Process $L \rightarrow M$	(r)	$W > 0$
(d)	Process $M \rightarrow J$	(s)	$Q < 0$

Subjective Questions

130. Three moles of an ideal gas being initially at a temperature $T_i = 273$ K were isothermally expanded 5 times its initial volume and then isochorically heated so that the pressure in the final state becomes equal to that in the initial state. The total heat supplied in the process is 80 kJ. Find $\gamma \left(= \frac{C_p}{C_V} \right)$ of the gas.

(Irodov 2.37)

131. Pressure *versus* temperature (p-T) graph of n moles of an ideal gas is shown in figure. Plot the corresponding:

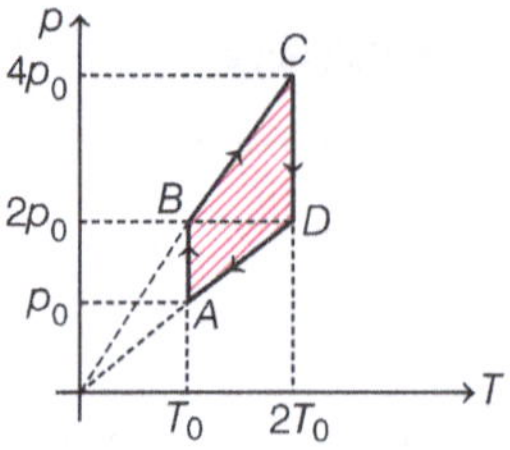

(a) density *versus* volume (ρ-V) graph,
(b) pressure *versus* volume (p-V) graph and
(c) density *versus* pressure (ρ-p) graph.

132. An ideal gas has a specific heat at constant pressure $C_p = \frac{5R}{2}$. The gas is kept in a closed vessel of volume V_0 at temperature T_0 and pressure p_0. An amount of $10\, p_0V_0$ of heat is supplied to the gas.
(a) Calculate the final pressure and temperature of the gas.
(b) Show the process on p-V diagram.

133. An ideal gas goes through the cycle abc. For the complete cycle 800 J of heat flows out of the gas. Process ab is at constant pressure and process bc is at constant volume. In process c-a, $p \propto V$. States a and b have temperatures $T_a = 200$ K and $T_b = 300$ K.
(a) Sketch the p-V diagram for the cycle. (b) What is the work done by the gas for the process ca?

134. A cylinder of ideal gas is closed by an 8 kg movable piston of area 60 cm^2. The atmospheric pressure is 100 kPa. When the gas is heated from 30 °C to 100 °C, the piston rises 20 cm. The piston is then fastened in the place and the gas is cooled back to 30 °C. If ΔQ_1 is the heat added to the gas during heating and ΔQ_2 is the heat lost during cooling, find the difference.

135. Three moles of an ideal gas $\left(C_p = \frac{7}{2} R \right)$ at pressure p_0 and temperature T_0 is isothermally expanded to twice its initial volume. It is then compressed at a constant pressure to its original volume. **(1991 JEE)**

(a) Sketch p-V and p-T diagram for complete process.

(b) Calculate net work done by the gas.

(c) Calculate net heat supplied to the gas during complete process.

(Write your answer in terms of gas constant $= R$)

136. Two moles of a gas ($\gamma = 5/3$) are initially at temperature 27°C and occupy a volume of 20 litres. The gas is first expanded at constant pressure until the volume is doubled. Then, it is subjected to an adiabatic change until the temperature returns to its initial value.

(a) Sketch the process on a p-V diagram.

(b) What are final volume and pressure of the gas?

(c) What is the work done by the gas?

137. An ideal monoatomic gas is confined by a spring loaded massless piston of cross-section $8.0 \times 10^{-3} \text{m}^2$. Initially, the gas is at 300 K and occupies a volume of $2.4 \times 10^{-3} \text{m}^3$ and the spring is in its relaxed state. The gas is heated by an electric heater until the piston moves out slowly without friction by 0.1 m. Calculate

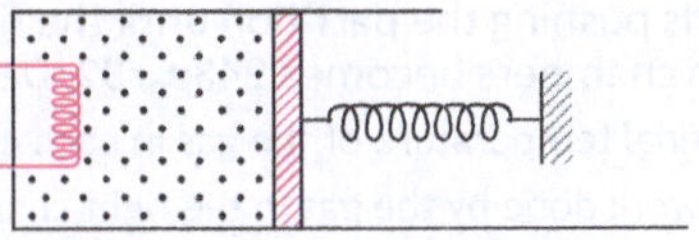

(a) the final temperature of the gas and

(b) the heat supplied by the heater.

The force constant of the spring is 8000 N/m, atmospheric pressure is $1.0 \times 10^5 \text{N/m}^2$. The cylinder and the piston are thermally insulated.

138. An ideal diatomic gas $\left(\gamma = \frac{7}{5}\right)$ undergoes a process in which its internal energy relates to the volume as $U = \alpha\sqrt{V}$, where α is a constant.

(a) Find the work performed by the gas to increase its internal energy by 100 J.

(b) Find the molar specific heat of the gas.

139. For an ideal gas the molar heat capacity varies as $C = C_V + 3aT^2$. Find the equation of the process in the variables (T, V) where a is a constant.

140. One mole of an ideal monatomic gas undergoes the process $p = \alpha T^{1/2}$, where α is a constant.

(a) Find the work done by the gas if its temperature increases by 50 K.

(b) Also, find the molar specific heat of the gas.

141. One mole of a gas is put under a weightless piston of a vertical cylinder at temperature T. The space over the piston opens into atmosphere. Initially, piston was in equilibrium. How much work should be performed by some external force to increase isothermally the volume under the piston to twice the volume? (Neglect friction of piston).

142. An ideal monatomic gas undergoes a process where its pressure is inversely proportional to its temperature.

(a) Calculate the molar specific heat for the process.

(b) Find the work done by two moles of gas if the temperature changes from T_1 to T_2.

143. Two moles of a monatomic ideal gas undergo a cyclic process $ABCDA$ as shown in adjacent figure. BCD is a semicircle. Find the efficiency of the cycle.

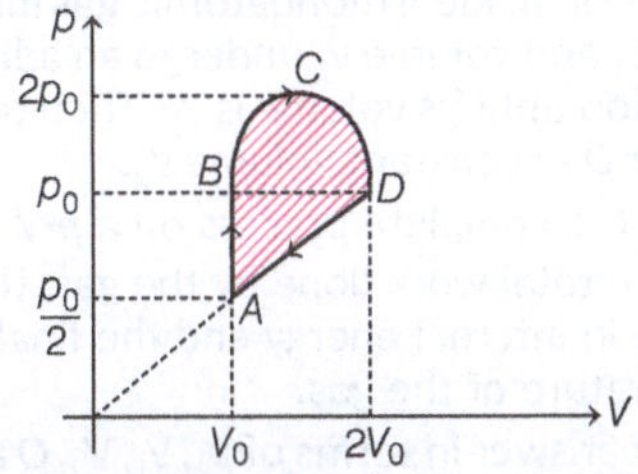

144. Pressure p, volume V and temperature T for a certain gas are related by

$$p = \frac{\alpha T - \beta T^2}{V}$$

where, α and β are constants. Find the work done by the gas if the temperature changes from T_1 to T_2 while the pressure remains the constant.

145. A monoatomic ideal gas of two moles is taken through a cyclic process starting from A as shown in the figure. The volume ratio are $\frac{V_B}{V_A} = 2$ and $\frac{V_D}{V_A} = 4$. If the temperature T_A at A is 27°C.

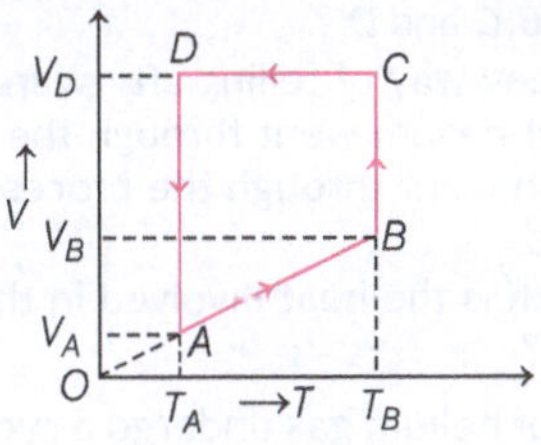

Calculate **(2001 JEE)**

(a) the temperature of the gas at point B,

(b) heat absorbed or released by the gas in each process,

(c) the total work done by the gas during the complete cycle.

Express your answer in terms of the gas constant R.

146. Two moles of an ideal monoatomic gas is taken through a cycle $ABCA$ as shown in the p-T diagram. During the process AB, pressure and temperature of the gas vary such that pT = constant. If $T_1 = 300$ K, calculate **(2000 JEE)**

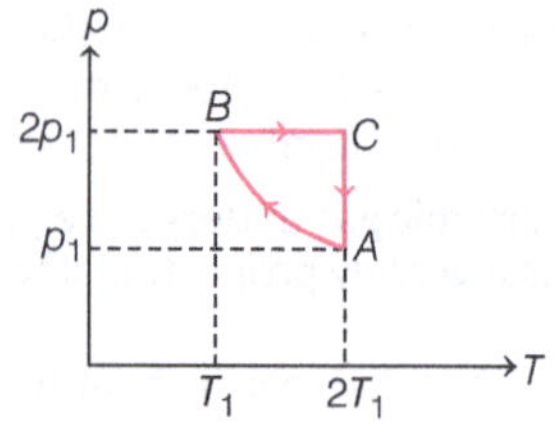

(a) the work done on the gas in the process AB and

(b) the heat absorbed or released by the gas in each of the processes.

Give answers in terms of the gas constant R.

147. Two moles of an ideal monoatomic gas initially at pressure p_1 and volume V_1 undergo an adiabatic compression until its volume is V_2. Then the gas is given heat Q at constant volume V_2. **(1999 JEE)**

(a) Sketch the complete process on a p-V diagram.

(b) Find the total work done by the gas, the total change in internal energy and the final temperature of the gas.

(Give your answer in terms of p_1, V_1, V_2, Q and R).

148. A sample of 2 kg monoatomic helium (assumed ideal) is taken through the process ABC and another sample of 2 kg of the same gas is taken through the process ADC (see fig). Given molecular mass of helium = 4. **(1997 JEE)**

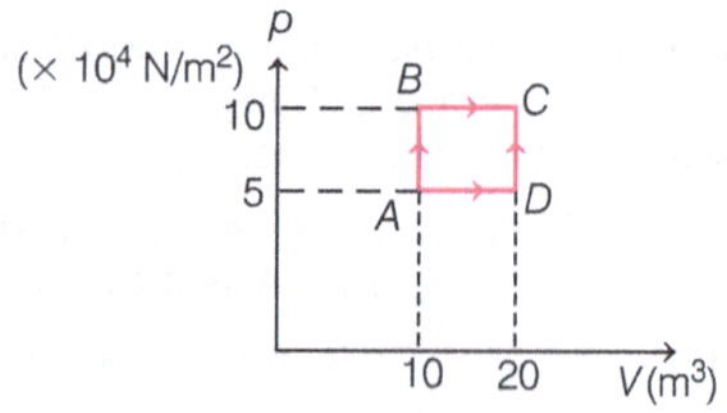

(a) What is the temperature of helium in each of the states A, B, C and D ?

(b) Is there any way of telling afterwards which sample of helium went through the process ABC and which went through the process ADC? Write Yes or No.

(c) How much is the heat involved in the process ABC and ADC?

149. Two moles of helium gas undergo a cyclic process as shown in figure. Assuming the gas to be ideal, calculate the following quantities in this process. **(1992 JEE)**

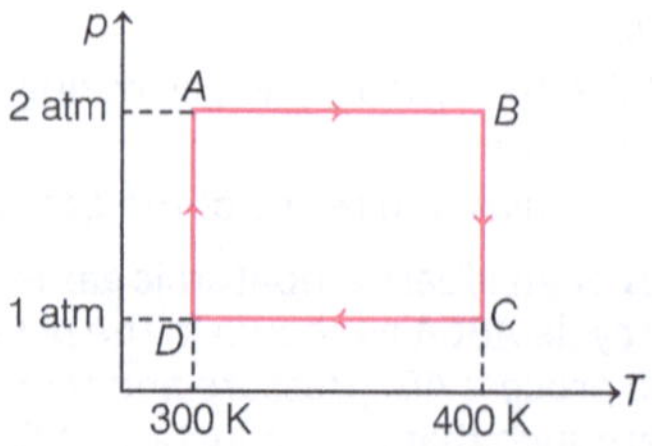

(a) The net change in the heat energy.

(b) The net work done.

(c) The net change in internal energy.

150. An ideal gas has a specific heat at constant pressure $C_p = \frac{5R}{2}$. The gas is kept in a closed vessel of volume $0.0083\,m^3$, at a temperature of 300 K and a pressure of $1.6 \times 10^6\,N/m^2$. An amount of 2.49×10^4 J of heat energy is supplied to the gas. Calculate the final temperature and pressure of the gas. **(1987 JEE)**

151. The rectangular box shown in figure has a partition which can slide without friction along the length of the box.

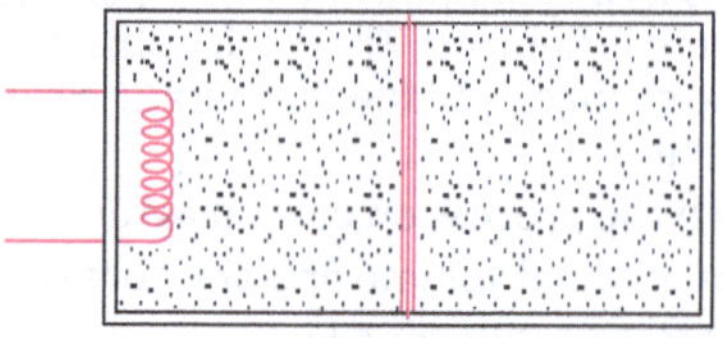

Initially each of the two chambers of the box has one mole of a monoatomic ideal gas ($\gamma = 5/3$) at a pressure p_0, volume V_0 and temperature T_0. The chamber on the left is slowly heated by an electric heater. The walls of the box and the partition are thermally insulated. Heat loss through the lead wires of the heater is negligible. The gas in the left chamber expands pushing the partition until the final pressure in both chambers becomes $243p_0/32$. Determine

(a) the final temperature of the gas in each chamber and

(b) the work done by the gas in the right chamber. **(1984 JEE)**

152. Calculate the work done when one mole of a perfect gas is compressed adiabatically. The initial pressure and volume of the gas are $10^5\,N/m^2$ and 6L respectively. The final volume of the gas is 2L. Molar specific heat of the gas at constant volume is $3R/2$. **(1982 JEE)**

153. One mole of a diatomic ideal gas ($\gamma = 1.4$) is taken through a cyclic process starting from point A. The process $A \to B$ is an adiabatic compression. $B \to C$ is isobaric expansion, $C \to D$ an adiabatic expansion and $D \to A$ is isochoric.

The volume ratio are $V_A/V_B = 16$ and $V_C/V_B = 2$ and the temperature at A is $T_A = 300\,K$. Calculate the temperature of the gas at the points B and D and find the efficiency of the cycle. **(1997 JEE)**

154. Two thermally insulated vessels 1 and 2 are filled with air and connected by a short tube equipped with a valve. The volumes of the vessels, the pressures and temperatures of air in them are known (V_1, p_1, T_1 and V_2, p_2, T_2). Find the air temperature and pressure established after the opening of the valve. **(Irodov 2.28)**

155. One mole of a certain ideal gas is contained under a weightless piston of a vertical cylinder at a temperature T. The space over the piston opens into the atmosphere. What work has to be performed in order to increase isothermally the gas volume under the piston n times by slowly raising the piston? The friction of the piston against the cylinder walls is negligibly small. **(Irodov 2.35)**

156. A piston can freely move inside a horizontal cylinder closed from both ends. Initially, the piston separates the inside space of the cylinder into two equal parts each of volume V_0, in which an ideal gas is contained under the same pressure p_0 and at the same temperature. What work has to be performed in order to increase isothermally the volume of one part of gas η times compared to that of the other by slowly moving the piston? **(Irodov 2.36)**

157. A heat-conducting piston can freely move inside a closed thermally insulated cylinder with an ideal gas. In equilibrium the piston divides the cylinder into two equal parts, the gas temperature being equal to T_0. The piston is slowly displaced. Find the gas temperature as a function of the ratio η of the volumes of the greater and smaller sections. The adiabatic exponent of the gas is equal to γ. **(Irodov 2.41)**

158. Demonstrate that the process in which the work performed by an ideal gas is proportional to the corresponding increment of its internal energy is described by the equation pV^n = constant, where n is a constant. **(Irodov 2.44)**

159. An ideal gas whose adiabatic exponent equals γ is expanded according to the law $p = \alpha V$, where α is a constant. The initial volume of the gas is equal to V_0. As a result of expansion the volume increases η times. Find: **(Irodov 2.48)**

(a) the increment of the internal energy of the gas

(b) the work performed by the gas

(c) the molar heat capacity of the gas in the process.

160. An ideal gas whose adiabatic exponent equals γ is expanded so that the amount of heat transferred to the gas is equal to the decrease of its internal energy. Find:

(a) the molar heat capacity of the gas in this process

(b) the equation of the process in the variables T, V

(c) the work performed by one mole of the gas when its volume increases η times if the initial temperature of the gas is T_0. **(Irodov 2.49)**

161. One mole of an ideal gas whose adiabatic exponent equals γ undergoes a process in which the gas pressure relates to the temperature as $p = \alpha T^a$, where α and a are constants. Find:

(a) the work performed by the gas if its temperature gets an increment ΔT **(Irodov 2.50)**

(b) the molar heat capacity of the gas in this process. At what value of α will the heat capacity be negative?

162. An ideal gas with the adiabatic exponent γ undergoes a process in which its internal energy relates to the volume as $U = \alpha V^a$, where a and α are constants. Find:

(a) the work performed by the gas and the amount of heat to be transferred to this gas to increase its internal energy by ΔU **(Irodov 2.51)**

(b) the molar heat capacity of the gas in this process.

163. An ideal gas has a molar heat capacity C_V at constant volume. Find the molar heat capacity of this gas as a function of its volume V, if the gas undergoes the following process:

(a) $T = T_0 e^{\alpha V}$

(b) $p = p_0 e^{\alpha V}$,

where T_0, p_0 and α are constants. **(Irodov 2.52)**

164. One mole of an ideal gas whose adiabatic exponent equals γ undergoes a process $p = p_0 + \alpha/V$, where p_0 and α are positive constants. Find:

(a) heat capacity of the gas as a function of its volume

(b) the internal energy increment of the gas, the work performed by it, and the amount of heat transferred to the gas, if its volume increased from V_1 to V_2. **(Irodov 2.53)**

165. One mole of an ideal gas with heat capacity at constant pressure C_p undergoes the process $T = T_0 + \alpha V$, where T_0 and α are constants. Find:

(a) heat capacity of the gas as a function of its volume

(b) the amount of heat transferred to the gas, if its volume increased from V_1 to V_2. **(Irodov 2.54)**

166. For the case of an ideal gas find the equation of the process (in the variables T, V) in which the molar heat capacity varies as:

(a) $C = C_V + \alpha T$

(b) $C = C_V + \beta V$

(c) $C = C_V + ap$,

where α, β and a are constants. **(Irodov 2.55)**

167. Hydrogen is used in a Carnot cycle as a working substance. Find the efficiency of the cycle, if as a result of an adiabatic expansion

(a) the gas volume increases $n = 2.0$ times

(b) the pressure decreases $n = 2.0$ times. **(Irodov 2.114)**

168. An ideal gas goes through a cycle consisting of alternate isothermal and adiabatic curves. The isothermal processes proceed at the temperatures T_1, T_2 and T_3. Find the efficiency of such a cycle, if in each isothermal expansion the gas volume increases in the same proportion. **(Irodov 2.116)**

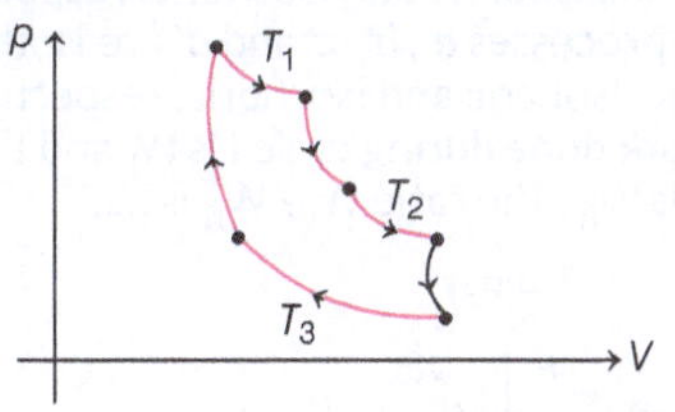

169. Find the efficiency of a cycle consisting of two isochoric and two adiabatic lines, if the volume of the ideal gas changes $n = 10$ times within the cycle. The working substance is nitrogen. **(Irodov 2.117)**

170. Find the efficiency of a cycle consisting of two isobaric and two adiabatic lines, if the pressure changes n

times within the cycle. The working substance is an ideal gas whose adiabatic exponent is equal to γ. **(Irodov 2.118)**

171. An ideal gas whose adiabatic exponent equals γ goes through a cycle consisting of two isochoric and two isobaric lines. Find the efficiency of such a cycle, if the absolute temperature of the gas rises n times both in the isochoric heating and in the isobaric expansion. **(Irodov 2.119)**

172. An ideal gas goes through a cycle consisting of
(a) isochoric, adiabatic, and isothermal lines
(b) isobaric, adiabatic, and isothermal lines, with the isothermal process proceeding at the minimum temperature of the whole cycle. Find the efficiency of each cycle if the absolute temperature varies n-fold within the cycle. **(Irodov 2.120)**

173. The conditions are the same as in the foregoing problem with the exception that the isothermal process proceeds at the maximum temperature of the whole cycle. **(Irodov 2.121)**

174. In a cylinder filled up with ideal gas and closed from both ends there is a piston of mass m and cross-sectional area S. In equilibrium the piston divides the cylinder into two equal parts, each with volume V_0. The gas pressure is p_0. The piston was slightly displaced from the equilibrium position and released. Find its oscillation angular frequency, assuming the processes in the gas to be adiabatic and the friction negligible. **(Irodov 4.62)**

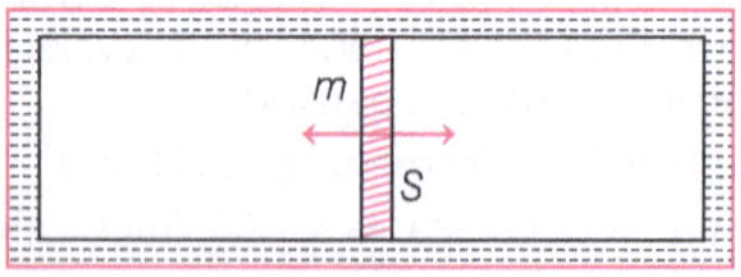

Integer Type Questions

175. One mole of an ideal gas undergoes two different cyclic processes I and II, as shown in the p-V diagrams below. In cycle I, processes a, b, c and d are isobaric, isothermal, isobaric and isochoric, respectively. In cycle II, processes a', b', c' and d' are isothermal, isochoric, isobaric and isochoric, respectively. The total work done during cycle I is W_{I} and that during cycle II is W_{II}. The ratio $W_{\text{I}} / W_{\text{II}}$ is ...... **(2023 Adv.)**

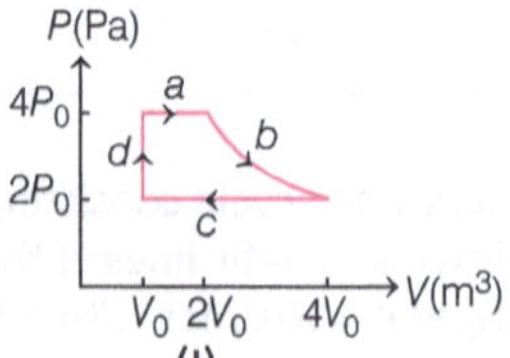

(I)

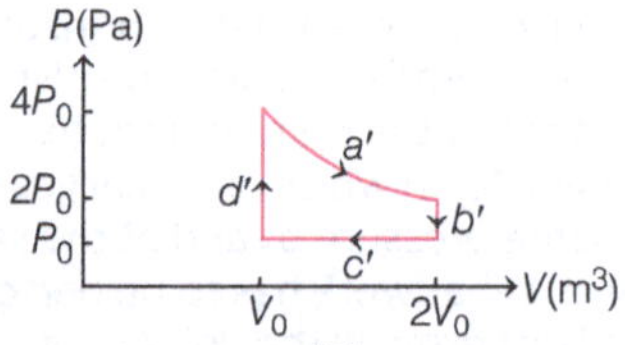

(II)

176. A closed container contains a homogeneous mixture of two moles of an ideal monoatomic gas ($\gamma = 5/3$) and one mole of an ideal diatomic gas ($\gamma = 7/5$). Here, γ is the ratio of the specific heats at constant pressure and constant volume of an ideal gas. The gas mixture does a work of 66J when heated at constant pressure. The change in its internal energy is .... joule. **(2023 Adv.)**

177. The volume V of a given mass of monoatomic gas changes with temperature T according to the relation $V = KT^{\frac{2}{3}}$. The work done when temperature changes by 90 K will be xR. The value of x is ....
[R = universal gas constant] **(2021 Main)**

178. The temperature of 3.00 mol of an ideal diatomic gas is increased by 40.0°C without changing the pressure of the gas. The molecules in the gas rotate but do not oscillate. If the ratio of change in internal energy of the gas to the amount of work done by the gas is $\frac{x}{10}$. Then the value of x (round off to the nearest integer) is ....
(Given, $R = 8.31\ \text{J mol}^{-1}\ \text{K}^{-1}$) . **(2021 Main)**

179. One mole of a monoatomic ideal gas undergoes an adiabatic expansion in which its volume becomes eight times its initial value. If the initial temperature of the gas is 100 K and the universal gas constant $R = 8.0\ \text{J mol}^{-1}\text{K}^{-1}$, the decrease in its internal energy in joule, is .... **(2018 Adv.)**

180. A thermodynamic system is taken from an initial state i with internal energy $U_i = 100$ J to the final state f along two different paths iaf and ibf, as schematically shown in the figure. The work done by the system along the paths af, ib and bf are $W_{af} = 200$ J, $W_{ib} = 50$ J and $W_{bf} = 100$ J, respectively. The heat supplied to the system along the path iaf, ib and bf are Q_{iaf}, Q_{ib} and Q_{bf}, respectively. If the internal energy of the system in the state b is $U_b = 200$ J and $Q_{iaf} = 500$ J, the ratio Q_{bf} / Q_{ib} is **(2014 Adv.)**

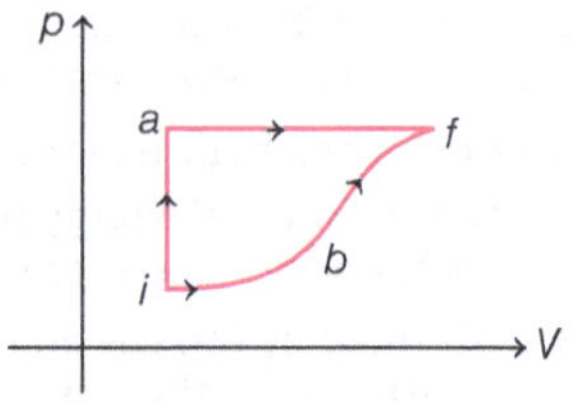

Answers

Level 1

1. (d) **2.** (b) **3.** (a) **4.** (b) **5.** (c) **6.** (c) **7.** (c) **8.** (c) **9.** (a) **10.** (c)
11. (c) **12.** (b) **13.** (b) **14.** (b) **15.** (b) **16.** (c) **17.** (a) **18.** (b) **19.** (c) **20.** (d)
21. (d) **22.** (d) **23.** (a) **24.** (a) **25.** (b) **26.** (a) **27.** (a) **28.** (d) **29.** (b) **30.** (a)
31. (c) **32.** (d) **33.** (d) **34.** (a) **35.** (a) **36.** (a) **37.** (a) Absorbs (b) 7200 J (c) Liberates, 7200 J
38. 166.2 J **39.** 2493 J **40.** 113°C **41.** 33600 J **42.** 27530 J **43.** (a) 199 J (b) 0.80°C
44. (a) -1.15×10^5 J (b) 2.55×10^5 J, out of gas (c) No **45.** 11609.99287 J **46.** $\Delta U = -0.25$ kJ, $Q_{\text{Lost}} = 0.25$ kJ
47. $Q = 7$ J **48.** $\gamma = 1.6$, $\Delta U \approx 1.0$ kJ, $W = 0.6$ kJ **49.** (a) $T_2 = 559$ K (b) $W_{\text{on gas}} = 5.6$ kJ **50.** $\frac{W_1}{W_2} = 1.4$
51. $Q = \frac{(2-\gamma)R\Delta T}{\gamma - 1}$ **52.** $C = \frac{(n-\gamma)R}{(n-1)(\gamma-1)}$, $C < 0$ for $1 < n < \gamma$ **53.** $C \approx -4.2$ J/mol-K **54.** (a) $Q \approx 0.11$ kJ (b) $W = 0.43$ kJ
55. $W = a \ln \eta - \frac{RT_0(\eta - 1)}{\gamma - 1}$ **56.** 2.2% **57.** $V_f = 7.6\, V_i$ **58.** $Q \approx 10$ kJ **59.** $\approx 0.7 \times 10^{-20}$ J
60. $\varepsilon = 9$ **61.** (750) **62.** (1400) **63.** (2) **64.** (500) **65.** (–113)

Level 2

66. (a) **67.** (a) **68.** (a) **69.** (a) **70.** (b) **71.** (a) **72.** (b) **73.** (d) **74.** (b) **75.** (d)
76. (d) **77.** (c) **78.** (c) **79.** (c) **80.** (a) **81.** (a) **82.** (a) **83.** (c) **84.** (b) **85.** (a)
86. (b) **87.** (c) **88.** (c) **89.** (d) **90.** (b) **91.** (d) **92.** (b) **93.** (d) **94.** (c) **95.** (a)
96. (a) **97.** (a) **98.** (a) **99.** (c) **100.** (b) **101.** (b) **102.** (c) **103.** (c) **104.** (c) **105.** (d)
106. (b) **107.** (b) **108.** (d) **109.** (c, d) **110.** (a, b, c, d) **111.** (a, b) **112.** (b, c)
113. (b, c, d) **114.** (a, b, c) **115.** (a, b) **116.** (b, d) **117.** (b, c) **118.** (b) **119.** (b)
120. (a) → s, (b) → s, (c) → r, (d) → s **121.** (a) → s, (b) → r, (c) → q, (d) → p **122.** (c)
123. (c) **124.** (b) **125.** (b) **126.** (a) **127.** (a) → p,r,t (b) → p,r (c) → q, s, (d) → r, t
128. (a) → q, (b) → p, r, (c) → p, s (d) → q, s **129.** (a) → s, (b) → r, (c) → p, (d) → q **130.** 1.4
131.

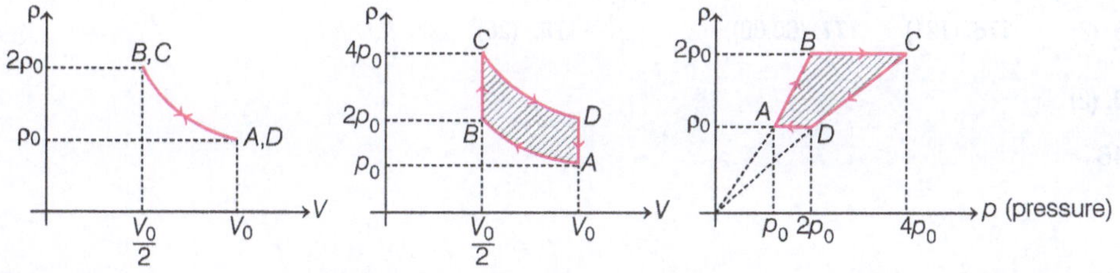

132. (a) $\frac{23}{3} p_0, \frac{23}{3} T_0$ **133.** (b) – 4000 J **134.** 136 J **135.** (b) $3RT_0 \ln(2) - \frac{3}{2} RT_0$ (c) $3RT_0 \ln(2) - \frac{21}{4} RT_0$
136. (b) 113.1 L, 0.44×10^5 N/m^2 (c) 12479 J **137.** (a) 800 K (b) 720 J **138.** (a) 80 J (b) $\frac{9R}{2}$
139. $Ve^{-\left(\frac{3a}{2R}\right)T^2} = \text{constant}$ **140.** (a) 207.75 J (b) $2R$ **141.** $RT(1 - \ln 2)$
142. (a) $\frac{7R}{2}$ (b) $4R(T_2 - T_1)$ **143.** 25.8% **144.** $\alpha(T_2 - T_1) - \beta(T_2^2 - T_1^2)$
145. (a) 600 K (b) $Q_{AB} = 1500\,R$, $Q_{BC} = 831.6\,R$, $Q_{CD} = -900\,R$, $Q_{DA} = -831.6\,R$ (c) $600\,R$
146. (a) $-1200\,R$ (b) $-2100\,R, 1500\,R, 831.6\,R$
147. (b) (i) $-\frac{3}{2} p_1 V_1 \left[\left(\frac{V_1}{V_2}\right)^{2/3} - 1\right]$ (ii) $\frac{3}{2} p_1 V_1 \left[\left(\frac{V_1}{V_2}\right)^{2/3} - 1\right] + Q$ (iii) $\frac{Q}{3R} + \frac{p_1 V_1}{2R} \left(\frac{V_1}{V_2}\right)^{2/3}$
148. (a) 240.68 K (b) No (c) 3.25×10^6 J, 2.75×10^6 J **149.** (a) 1152 J (b) 1152 J (c) 0
150. $T_f = 675$ K, $p_2 = 3.6 \times 10^6$ N/m^2 **151.** (a) $12.94\, T_0, 2.25 T_0$ (b) $-1.875\, RT_0$

152. –972 J **153.** 909 K, 791.4 K, 61.4% **154.** $T = \dfrac{T_1 T_2(p_1 V_1 + p_2 V_2)}{(p_1 V_1 T_2 + p_2 V_2 T_1)}$, $p = \dfrac{p_1 V_1 + p_2 V_2}{V_1 + V_2}$

155. $W_{ext} = RT(n - 1 - \ln n)$ **156.** $W_{ext} = p_0 V_0 \ln \dfrac{(\eta + 1)^2}{4\eta}$ **157.** $T_f = T_0 \left[\left\{ \dfrac{(\eta + 1)^2}{4\eta} \right\}^{\frac{\gamma - 1}{2}} \right]$

159. (a) $\Delta U = \left(\dfrac{\eta^2 - 1}{\gamma - 1} \right) \alpha V_0^2$ (b) $W = \dfrac{\alpha V_0^2}{2} (\eta^2 - 1)$ (c) $C = \dfrac{(\gamma + 1)R}{2(\gamma - 1)}$

160. (a) $C = -\dfrac{R}{(\gamma - 1)}$ (b) $TV^{\frac{\gamma - 1}{2}} = \text{constant}$ (c) $W = \dfrac{2RT_0}{\gamma - 1} \left(1 - \eta^{\frac{1 - \gamma}{2}} \right)$

161. (a) $W = (1 - a)R\Delta T$ (b) $C = \dfrac{R}{\gamma - 1} + R(1 - a)$, $C < 0$ for $a > \dfrac{\gamma}{\gamma - 1}$

162. (a) $Q = \left(1 + \dfrac{\gamma - 1}{a} \right) \Delta U$, $W = \dfrac{(\gamma - 1)\Delta U}{a}$ (b) $C = \dfrac{R}{\gamma - 1} + \dfrac{R}{a}$

163. (a) $C = C_V + \dfrac{R}{\alpha V}$ (b) $C = C_V + \dfrac{R}{1 + \alpha V}$

164. (a) $C = \dfrac{\gamma R}{\gamma - 1} + \dfrac{\alpha R}{p_0 V}$ (b) $\Delta U = \dfrac{p_0(V_2 - V_1)}{\gamma - 1}$, $W = p_0(V_2 - V_1) + \alpha \ln(V_2 / V_1)$, $Q = \dfrac{\gamma\, p_0(V_2 - V_1)}{\gamma - 1} + \alpha \ln\left(\dfrac{V_2}{V_1} \right)$

165. (a) $C = C_p + \dfrac{RT_0}{\alpha V}$ (b) $Q = \alpha C_p (V_2 - V_1) + RT_0 \ln\left(\dfrac{V_2}{V_1} \right)$

166. (a) $Ve^{-\frac{\alpha T}{R}} = \text{constant}$ (b) $Te^{\frac{R}{\beta V}} = \text{constant}$ (c) $V - aT = \text{constant}$ **167.** (a) $\eta = 0.25$ (b) $\eta = 0.18$

168. $\eta = 1 - \dfrac{2T_3}{T_1 + T_2}$ **169.** $\eta \approx 60\%$ **170.** $\eta = 1 - (n)^{\frac{1}{\gamma} - 1}$ **171.** $\eta = 1 - \left(\dfrac{n + \gamma}{1 + n\gamma} \right)$

172. (a) $\eta = 1 - \dfrac{\ln(n)}{n - 1}$ (b) $\eta = 1 - \dfrac{\ln(n)}{n - 1}$ **173.** (a) $\eta = 1 - \dfrac{(n - 1)}{n \ln(n)}$ (b) $\eta = 1 - \dfrac{(n - 1)}{n \ln(n)}$

174. $\omega = S \sqrt{\dfrac{2p_0\gamma}{mV_0}}$ **175.** (2) **176.** (121) **177.** (60.00) **178.** (25)

179. (900) **180.** (2)

See hints on pages 313-346.

Hints & SOLUTIONS

Module 1.

Introductory Exercise

1. ΔU will be same along all paths. Then, we can apply $Q = W + \Delta U$ for all.

2. $\Delta U = Q - W$

$$= 254 - (-73) = 327 \text{ J}$$

Module 2.

Introductory Exercise 1

1. (a) Work done by gas under constant pressure is

$$W = p(V_f - V_i)$$
$$= (1.7 \times 10^5)(0.8 - 1.2)$$
$$= -6.8 \times 10^4 \text{ J}$$

(b) $$Q = W + \Delta U$$
$$= -6.8 \times 10^4 - 1.1 \times 10^5$$

or $|Q| = 1.78 \times 10^5$ J

As Q is negative. So, net heat flow is out of the gas.

2. (a) $W_1 = +$ve, as cycle is clockwise

$W_2 = -$ve, as cycle is anti-clockwise

Since, $|W_1| > |W_2|$

$\therefore$ Net work done by the system is positive.

(b) In cyclic process, $Q_{net} = W_{net}$

Since, W_{net} is positive. So, Q_{net} is also positive. So, heat flows into the system.

(c) $W_1 = Q_1 = +$ ve , so into the system.

$W_2 = Q_2 = -$ve , so out of the system.

3. Helium is monoatomic. So, degree of freedom $f = 3$.

$$U = \frac{nf}{2}RT = \frac{3n}{2}RT$$

or $$n = \frac{2U}{3RT} = \frac{2 \times 100}{3 \times 8.31 \times 300}$$

$$= 2.67 \times 10^{-2} \text{ mol}$$ **Ans.**

4. In isochoric process,

$$W = 0$$

$$Q = \Delta U = nC_V \Delta T = 4\left(\frac{3}{2}R\right)(300)$$

$$= 1800 R$$

5. $W =$ Area under p-V diagram

Further $p \propto V$ along AB in figure (iii).

Therefore, $p_B = 2p_A = 2p_0$

6. $VT =$ constant

or $\quad V(pV) =$ constant $\quad$ (as $T \propto pV$)

$\therefore \quad pV^2 =$ constant

Comparing with $pV^x =$ constant, we have

$$x = 2$$

$$W = \frac{nR\Delta T}{1-x} \quad \text{(Table 1.)}$$

$$= \frac{(2)(R)(300)}{1-2} = -600 R$$

7. $pV^2 =$ constant

$\therefore$ Comparing with $pV^x =$ constant

We have, $\quad x = 2$

$$W = \frac{p_f V_f - p_i V_i}{1-x}$$

Substituting the values, we get

$$W = \frac{1}{2} p_0 V_0$$

Introductory Exercise 2

1. (a) $Q = nC_V \Delta T$

$$200 = (1)\left(\frac{3}{2}R\right)(T_f - 300)$$

or $\quad 200 = 1.5 \times 8.31(T_f - 300)$

Solving, we get

$$T_f = 316 \text{ K}$$

(b) $Q = nC_p \Delta T$

$$200 = (1)\left(\frac{5}{2}R\right)(T_f - 300)$$

or $\quad 200 = 2.5 \times 8.31\,(T_f - 300)$

Solving, we get

$$T_f = 309.6 \text{ K}$$

2. $p =$ constant

$\therefore \quad T \propto V$

As the gas expands V increases. So, T also increases. Hence, ΔT is positive. Therefore, in the expression,

$$Q = nC_p \Delta T$$

Q is positive.

3. **AB**

V is increasing, so $W = +$ ve . Product of pV and therefore T and therefore U is increasing.

So, ΔU is also + ve.

$$Q = W + \Delta U$$

$\therefore$ Q is also positive.

BC $\quad V =$ constant

$\therefore \quad W = 0$

$\therefore \quad Q = \Delta U = -$ve

CA $\quad V$ is decreasing.

$\therefore \quad W = -\text{ve}$

ΔU is also negative.

$\therefore \quad Q = W + \Delta U$ is also negative.

4. $Q = 0$ as the box is insulated.

$W_{gas} = 0$ as on the right hand side there is vacuum.

$$\therefore \quad \Delta U = Q - W = 0$$

$\therefore$ ΔT is also zero,

as $\quad U \propto T$

5. In an isobaric process $p =$ constant.

Therefore, $C = C_p$.

Now, $$\frac{\Delta Q}{\Delta U} = \frac{nC_p \Delta T}{nC_V \Delta T} = \frac{C_p}{C_V} = \gamma$$

and $$\frac{\Delta Q}{\Delta W} = \frac{\Delta Q}{\Delta Q - \Delta U}$$

$$= \frac{nC_p \Delta T}{nC_p \Delta T - nC_V \Delta T}$$

$$= \frac{C_p}{C_p - C_V} = \frac{C_p/C_V}{C_p/C_V - 1}$$

$$= \frac{\gamma}{\gamma - 1}$$

6. $Q_1 = W_1 + \Delta U_1$

and $\quad Q_2 = W_2 + \Delta U_2$

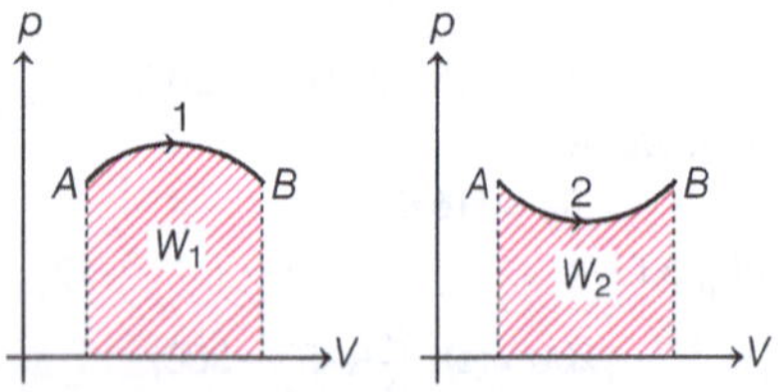

U is a state function. Hence, ΔU depends only on the initial and final positions. Therefore,

$$\Delta U_1 = \Delta U_2$$

But, $\quad W_1 > W_2$

as the area under 1 is greater than area under 2.

Hence,

$$Q_1 > Q_2$$

7. $W = \int_{V_i}^{V_f} p\,dV = \int_1^2 (\alpha V^2)\,dV$

$$= \int_1^2 (5 \times 1.01 \times 10^5) V^2 dV$$

Solving, we get

$$W = 1.18 \times 10^6 \text{ J}$$
$$= 1.18 \text{ MJ}$$

Exercise

1.

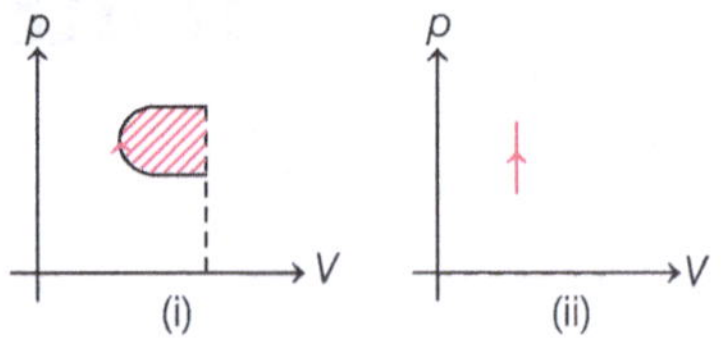

In both figures, $V_i = V_f$

but $W_1 =$ Hatched area

$$W_2 = 0$$

3. $pT =$ constant

$\therefore \quad \left(\frac{T}{V}\right) T = \text{constant} \quad \text{or} \quad V \propto T^2$

If temperature is increased, then volume will also increase. So, work done is positive.

4. Volume is increasing. Therefore, W is positive. Therefore, ΔU is negative.

Now, $\quad Q = W + \Delta U$

Therefore, Q may be positive, negative or zero.

Further, heat given to gas is path function.

5. $p \propto V^2$

$\therefore \quad \frac{T}{V} \propto V^2$

or $\quad T \propto V^3$

$\Rightarrow \quad V \propto T^{1/3}$

T is increasing. So, V will also increase. Hence, work done will be positive.

6. $W_{gas} = nRT \ln\left(\frac{V_f}{V_i}\right) = nRT \ln\left(\frac{1}{2}\right)$

$$= -nRT \ln 2$$

$\therefore$ Work done on the gas $= +\,nRT \ln 2$

7. ΔU is same.

$$Q = W + \Delta U$$
$$W_1 = +\text{ve}, W_2 = 0$$

and $\quad W_3 = -\text{ve}$

8. In adiabatic compression temperature increases. Hence, pV increases, as $T \propto pV$

9. $\quad \Delta Q = -20 \text{ J}, \Delta W = -10 \text{ J}, U_i = 40 \text{ J}$

$$\Delta Q = \Delta U + \Delta W = U_f - U_i + \Delta W$$
$$-20 = U_f - 40 - 10$$

$\Rightarrow \quad U_f = 30 \text{ J}$

10. $W_1 > W_2$ as area under graph-a is more. Hence,

$$\Delta Q_1 > \Delta Q_2, \text{ as}$$
$$\Delta Q = W + \Delta U$$
and $$\Delta U_1 = \Delta U_2$$

11. $p = \dfrac{nRT}{V}$

where, V = constant, but temperature will decrease with time. So, p will decrease.

12. In adiabatic compression, internal energy of gas increases. So, temperature increases.

13. $pT^{\frac{\gamma}{1-\gamma}} = \text{constant}$

or $$p \propto T^{\frac{\gamma}{\gamma-1}}$$

$\therefore$ $$\alpha = \frac{\gamma}{\gamma-1} = \frac{1.4}{1.4-1} = 3.5$$

14. $C = C_V + \dfrac{R}{1-x}$

$$= \frac{5}{2}R + \frac{R}{1-x} = \frac{5}{2}R - \frac{R}{x-1}$$

C is negative, if

$$x - 1 < \frac{2}{5}$$

$\therefore$ $$x < 1.4$$

If x lies between 1 and 1.4, then also C is negative.

15. p-V diagram of the gas is a straight line passing through origin. Hence $p \propto V$ or pV^{-1} = constant

Molar heat capacity in the process pV^x = constant is

$$C = \frac{R}{\gamma-1} + \frac{R}{1-x}$$

Here $\gamma = 1.4$ (For diatomic gas)

$\Rightarrow$ $$C = \frac{R}{1.4-1} + \frac{R}{1+1}$$

$\Rightarrow$ $$C = 3R$$

16. $Q_{net} = W_{net}$ = area under the graph

$$= \pi\,(\text{Radius})(\text{Radius})$$
$$= \pi(10 \times 10^3\ \text{Pa})(10 \times 10^{-3}\ \text{m}^3)$$
$$= 10^2 \pi\ \text{J}$$

17. Area is same, signs are opposite.

18. $\Delta Q = \Delta U + \Delta W$

$\because$ Heat is supplied to the system so $\Delta Q \rightarrow$ Positive and work is done on the system so

$$\Delta W \rightarrow \text{Negative}$$

Hence, $$+\Delta Q = \Delta U - \Delta W$$

19. $\Delta W_1 = p_A \Delta V, \Delta W_2 = p_B \Delta V$

$$p_B > p_A \Rightarrow \Delta W_2 > \Delta W_1$$

20. Work done by gas, $W = p(V_f - V_i)$

$$= 1.0 \times 10^5 (1.7 \times 10^{-3} - 1.5 \times 10^{-3})$$
$$= 20\ \text{J}$$
$$\Delta U = Q - W = 70 - 20 = 50\ \text{J}$$

21. $p \propto T^3$

In adiabatic process, $p^{1-\gamma}T^{\gamma}$ = constant

or $$p \propto T^{\frac{\gamma}{\gamma-1}}$$

i.e. $$\frac{\gamma}{\gamma-1} = 3$$

Solving this equation, we get $\gamma = \dfrac{3}{2}$

22. First processes are adiabatic. Hence,

$$p_1V_1^{\gamma} = p_2V_2^{\gamma}$$

$\therefore$ $$p_2 = p_1\left(\frac{V_1}{V_2}\right)^{\gamma} = p\left(\frac{640}{80}\right)^{5/3}$$
$$= p(8)^{5/3} = 32p$$

23. $pV^{2/3}$ = constant

$\therefore$ $$\left(\frac{T}{V}\right) \cdot V^{2/3} = \text{constant}$$

or $$TV^{-1/3} = \text{constant}$$

or $$T \propto V^{1/3}$$

with increase in V, temperature T will also increase.

24. For cyclic process,

Total work done $= W_{AB} + W_{BC} + W_{CA}$

$$\Delta W_{AB} = p\,\Delta V = 10(2-1) = 10\ \text{J}$$

and $$\Delta W_{BC} = 0 \quad (\text{as } V = \text{constant})$$

From first law of thermodynamics,

$$\Delta Q = \Delta U + \Delta W$$
$$\Delta U = 0 \text{ (Process } ABCA \text{ is cyclic)}$$

$\Rightarrow$ $$\Delta Q = \Delta W_{AB} + \Delta W_{BC} + \Delta W_{CA}$$

$\Rightarrow$ $$5 - 10 + 0 + \Delta W_{CA}$$

$\Rightarrow$ $$\Delta W_{CA} = -5\ \text{J}$$

25. **For path *ab*** $(\Delta U)_{ab} = 7000$ J

By using $$\Delta U = nC_V\,\Delta T$$

$$7000 = n \times \frac{5}{2}R \times 700$$

$\Rightarrow$ $$n = 0.48$$

For path *ca*

$$(\Delta Q)_{ca} = (\Delta U)_{ca} + (\Delta W)_{ca} \quad \text{...(i)}$$

$\because$ $$(\Delta U)_{ab} + (\Delta U)_{bc} + (\Delta U)_{ca} = 0$$

$\therefore$ $$7000 + 0 + (\Delta U)_{ca} = 0$$

$\Rightarrow$ $$(\Delta U)_{ca} = -7000\ \text{J} \quad \text{...(ii)}$$

Also, $$(\Delta W)_{ca} = p_1(V_1 - V_2) = nR(T_1 - T_2)$$
$$= 0.48 \times 8.31 \times (300 - 1000) = -2792.16\ \text{J} \quad \text{...(iii)}$$

By solving Eqs. (i), (ii) and (iii)

$$(\Delta Q)_{ca} = -7000 - 2792.16$$
$$= -9792.16 \text{ J}$$
$$\approx -9800 \text{ J}$$

26.

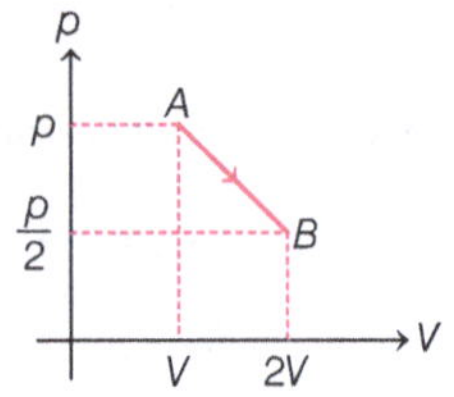

Since the process AB is an expansion process, work done by the gas is positive.

Equation of the given process AB is

$$p' = p - \frac{p}{2V}(V' - V) \quad \text{...(i)}$$

Equation of state is $p'V' = nRT'$ ...(ii)

Combining Eqs. (i) and (ii),

$$nRT' = \frac{3p}{2}V' - \frac{p}{2V}V'^2 \quad \text{...(iii)}$$

and
$$nRT' = 3Vp' - \frac{2V}{p}p'^2 \quad \text{...(iv)}$$

Eqs. (iii) and (iv) represent parabola. So option (b) is right and option (c) is wrong.

Also points A and B in the p - V diagram lie on isothermal process. Deviation of the straight AB is maximum at its mid-point.

Hence option (d) is correct.

27. Temperature is increased. So, internal energy will also increase.

$\therefore$ $\Delta U = +\text{ ve}$

Further, $pV^2 = \text{constant}$

$\therefore$ $\left(\frac{T}{V}\right)V^2 = \text{constant}$ or $V \propto \frac{1}{T}$

Temperature is increased. So, volume will decrease and work done will be negative.

In the process $pV^x = \text{constant}$, molar heat capacity is given by

$$C = C_V + \frac{R}{1-x}$$

Here, $x = 2$

$\therefore$ $C = C_V - R$

C_V of any gas is greater than R.

So, C is positive. Hence, from the equation,

$$Q = nC\Delta T$$

Q is positive if T is increased.

or ΔT is positive.

28. ***ab*** $W = 0$ (as $V = \text{constant}$)

$$Q_1 = \Delta U_1 = nC_V\Delta T$$
$$= (2)\left(\frac{3}{2}R\right)(2T_0 - T_0) = 3RT_0$$

bc $\Delta U = 0$ (as $T = \text{constant}$)

$\therefore$ $Q_2 = W_2 = nRT\ln\left(\frac{V_f}{V_i}\right)$

$$= (2)(R)(2T_0)\ln(2)$$
$$= 4RT_0\ln(2)$$

cd $W = 0$

$$Q_3 = \Delta U_3 = nC_V\Delta T$$
$$= (2)\left(\frac{3}{2}R\right)(T_0 - 2T_0)$$
$$= -3RT_0$$

da $\Delta U = 0$

$$Q_4 = W_4 = nRT\ln\left(\frac{V_f}{V_i}\right)$$
$$= (2)(R)(T_0)\ln\left(\frac{1}{2}\right)$$
$$= -2RT_0\ln(2)$$

Now in complete cycle,

$$\Delta U_{net} = 0$$
$$Q_{net} = W_{net} = 2RT_0\ln(2) = +\text{ ve}$$

29. (a) $W = nR\Delta T$

$$= (2)(R)(T) = 2RT$$

(b) $\Delta U = nC_V\Delta T = (2)\left(\frac{3}{2}R\right)(T) = 3RT$

(c) $W = -\Delta U = -3RT$

(d) $\Delta U = 3RT$ (in all processes)

30. For both processes,

$p = \text{constant}$ (as $V \propto T$)

$\therefore$ $C = C_p$ for same gases.

For W, ΔU and Q we will require number of moles also.

31. $p^2V = \text{constant}$ or $pV^{1/2} = \text{constant}$

Comparing with $pV^x = \text{constant}$, we get

$$x = \frac{1}{2}$$

$\therefore$ Molar heat capacity,

$$C = C_V + \frac{R}{1-x}$$
$$= \left(\frac{3}{2}R\right) + 2R = 3.5\,R$$

$$Q = nC\Delta T = n(3.5R)(\Delta T)$$
$$= 3.5\,nR\Delta T$$
$$\Delta U = nC_V\Delta T$$
$$= n\left(\frac{3}{2}R\right)\Delta T$$
$$= 1.5\,nR\Delta T$$

$\therefore$ W by the gas $= Q - \Delta U = 2nR\Delta T$ and work done on the gas $= -2nR\Delta T$

32. (a) $Q = nC_p\Delta T$

$$\Delta U = nC_V\Delta T$$

$$W = Q - \Delta U = nR\Delta T$$
$$W < \Delta U \text{ as } C_V > R$$

(b) $W = 0$

$$\Delta U = -\text{ve}$$
$$\therefore \quad Q = \Delta U = -\text{ve}$$

(c) $Q = 0$

$$W = +\text{ve} \quad \text{(as } V \text{ is increasing)}$$
$$\therefore \quad \Delta U = -W = -\text{ve}$$

(d) $\Delta T = 0 \Rightarrow \Delta U = 0$

and $\quad Q = W = nRT \ln\left(\frac{V_f}{V_i}\right) = +\text{ve}$

33. For all process,

$$\Delta U = nC_V \Delta T = \frac{nR\Delta T}{\gamma - 1} \quad \left(\text{as } C_V = \frac{R}{\gamma - 1}\right)$$

34. Along the process CD apply,

pV = constant and find V_C

Similarly along path AB, again apply,

pV = constant and find V_B.

Now, $\quad W_{net} = W_{AB} + W_{BC} + W_{CD} + W_{DA}$

$$= nRT_A \ln\left(\frac{V_B}{V_A}\right) + p_B(V_C - V_B)$$
$$+ nRT_C \ln\left(\frac{V_D}{V_C}\right) + p_D(V_A - V_D)$$

Further, $\quad nRT_A = p_A V_A$

and $\quad nRT_C = p_C V_C$

35. Work done per cycle = area under the cycle

$$= \frac{1}{2}(3-2)(10^{-3})(30-10)(1.01 \times 10^5)$$
$$= 1010 \text{ J}$$

Total work done per second

$$= 1010 \times \frac{100}{60} = 1683 \text{ J/s}$$

36. V = constant

From $\quad pV = nRT$,

$$V\Delta p = nR(\Delta T)$$
$$Q = nC_V \Delta T$$
$$= n\left(\frac{5}{2}R\right)\Delta T = \frac{5}{2}(V\Delta p)$$
$$= \frac{5}{2} \times (10 \times 10^{-3})(4 \times 10^5)$$
$$= 10^4 \text{ J}$$

Ans.

37. (a) $W = +$ (Area of the cycle)

$$= +\frac{1}{2}(2V_0 - V_0)(3p_0 - p_0)$$
$$= p_0 V_0$$

(b) $Q_{CA} = nC_p \Delta T$

$$= n\left(\frac{5}{2}R\right)(T_A - T_C)$$
$$= \frac{5}{2}(p_A V_A - p_C V_C)$$
$$= \frac{5}{2}(p_0 V_0 - 2p_0 V_0) = -\frac{5}{2}p_0 V_0$$

$$Q_{AB} = nC_V \Delta T$$
$$= n\left(\frac{3}{2}R\right)(T_B - T_A)$$
$$= \frac{3}{2}(p_B V_B - p_A V_A)$$
$$= 3p_0 V_0$$

(c) $W_{BC} = +$ (Area under the graph)

$$= 2p_0 V_0$$
$$\Delta U_{BC} = nC_V \Delta T$$
$$= n\left(\frac{3}{2}R\right)(T_C - T_B)$$
$$= \frac{3}{2}(p_C V_C - p_B V_B) = -\frac{3}{2}p_0 V_0$$
$$\therefore \quad Q_{BC} = W_{BC} + \Delta U_{BC} = \frac{p_0 V_0}{2}$$

(d) p-V equation along path BC is

$$p = -\left(\frac{2p_0}{V_0}\right)V + 5p_0$$

or $\quad pV = -\left(\frac{2p_0}{V_0}\right)V^2 + 5p_0 V$

or $\quad RT = -\left(\frac{2p_0}{V_0}\right)V^2 + 5p_0 V$

$$\therefore \quad T = \frac{1}{R}\left[5p_0 V - \frac{2p_0}{V_0} \cdot V^2\right] \quad \text{...(i)}$$

For T to be maximum,

$$\frac{dT}{dV} = 0$$
$$\therefore \quad 5p_0 - \frac{4p_0}{V_0}V = 0$$
$$\therefore \quad V = \frac{5}{4}V_0$$

So at this volume, temperature is maximum. Substituting this value of V in Eq. (i), we get

$$T_{max} = \frac{25p_0 V_0}{8R}$$

38. First process

$$V = \text{constant}$$
$$\therefore \quad p \propto T$$

Pressure becomes three times.

Therefore, temperature also becomes three times.

$$(T_f = 3T_i)$$

Second process

$$p = \text{constant}$$
$$\therefore \quad V \propto T$$

Volume is doubled. So, temperature also becomes two times. ($T_f' = 6T_i$)

Now, $C = \frac{Q}{n\Delta T} = \frac{Q_1 + Q_2}{n\Delta T}$

$= \frac{nC_V \Delta T_1 + nC_p \Delta T_2}{n\Delta T}$

$= \frac{\left(\frac{5}{2}R\right)(3T_i - T_i) + \left(\frac{7}{2}R\right)(6T_i - 3T_i)}{(6T_i - T_i)}$

$= 3.1R$

39. (a) and (b) $(pV)_A = (pV)_C = 3p_0V_0$

$\therefore \quad T_A = T_C$ or $\Delta T = 0$

$\therefore \quad \Delta U_{ABC} = 0$

$Q_{ABC} = W_{ABC} =$ Area under the graph

$= -2p_0V_0$ **Ans.**

i.e. Heat is released during the process.

(c) **Process AB**

ρ-p graph will be a straight line parallel to ρ-axis because pressure is constant. Further, V is decreasing. Therefore, ρ will increase.

Process BC

$V =$ constant

$\Rightarrow \quad \rho =$ constant

Therefore, ρ-p graph is a straight line parallel to p-axis.

ρ-p graph is as shown below.

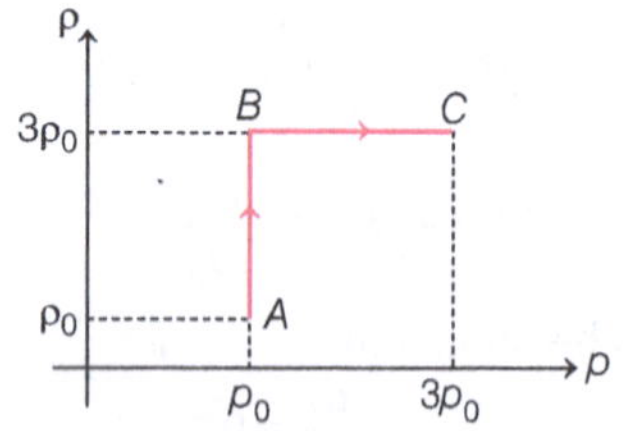

40. (a) W_{AC} is less than W_{ABC} as area under graph is less.

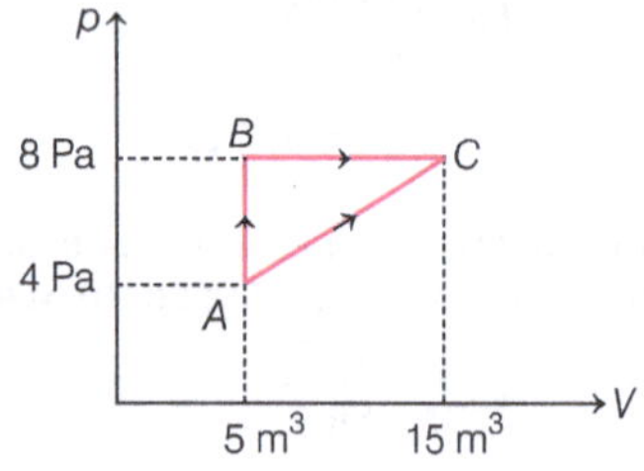

(b) For process A to C,

$Q = 200$ J

Work done,

$W_{AC} =$ area under AC

$= \frac{1}{2}(8+4) \times 10 = 60$ J

From first law of thermodynamics,

$\Delta U = Q - W_{AC}$

$U_C - U_A = 200 - 60$

$\therefore \quad U_C = U_A + 140$

$= 10 + 140 = 150$ J **Ans.**

(c) From A to B,

$U_B = 20$ J

$\therefore \quad \Delta U = Q - W_{AB}$

$U_B - U_A = Q - 0$

$20 - 10 = Q$

$\therefore \quad Q = 10$ J **Ans.**

41. (a) $U_C - U_A$ along two paths should be same.

$\therefore \quad (Q_{AB} + Q_{BC}) - (W_{AB} + W_{BC}) = Q_{AC} - W_{AC}$

$\therefore \quad (250 + Q_{BC}) - (500 + 0) = 300 - 700$

Solving, we get

$Q_{BC} = -150$ J

(b) $Q_{CDA} = (W_{CD} + W_{DA}) + (U_A - U_C)$

$= (-800 + 0) - (U_C - U_A)$

$= -800 - (300 - 700)$

$= -400$ J

42. (a) $T = \frac{pV}{nR}$

$= \frac{(2 \times 10^5)(1.0 \times 10^{-2})}{(1)(8.31)}$

$= 240.7$ K

(b) In adiabatic process,

$TV^{\gamma - 1} =$ constant

$\therefore \quad T_fV_f^{\gamma-1} = T_iV_i^{\gamma-1}$

$\therefore \quad T_f = T_i\left(\frac{V_i}{V_f}\right)^{\gamma-1}$

$= (240.7)\left[\frac{1.0 \times 10^{-2}}{5.0 \times 10^{-3}}\right]^{(5/3)-1}$

≈ 383 K

(c) Work done on the gas $= \Delta U$

$= nC_V\Delta T = (1)\left(\frac{3}{2}R\right)(T_f - T_i)$

$= 1.5 \times 8.31(383 - 240.7)$

≈ 1770 J

(d) $\Delta U \approx 1770$ J

Module 3.

Introductory Exercise

1. Given, $Q_1 = 10^6$ cal

$T_1 = (827 + 273) = 1100$ K

and $T_2 = (27 + 273) = 300$ K

As, $\frac{Q_2}{Q_1} = \frac{T_2}{T_1}$ (in Carnot engine)

$\therefore \quad Q_2 = \frac{T_2}{T_1} \cdot Q_1 = \left(\frac{300}{1100}\right)(10^6)$

$= 2.72 \times 10^5$ cal.

Efficiency of the cycle,

$$\eta = \left(1 - \frac{T_2}{T_1}\right) \times 100$$

or $$\eta = \left(1 - \frac{300}{1100}\right) \times 100$$

$$= 72.72\%$$

2. $T_1 = 2100\,K, T_2 = 700\,K, \eta_{actual} = 40\%$

Maximum possible efficiency of Carnot engine is

$$\eta_{max} = 1 - \frac{T_2}{T_1} = 1 - \frac{700}{2100}$$

$$= 0.666 = 66.6\%$$

Actual efficiency as the percentage of the maximum possible efficiency is

$$\frac{\eta_{actual}}{\eta_{max}} \times 100 = \frac{40}{66.6} \times 100$$

$$= 60\%$$

3. (a) $\eta = 1 - \frac{T_2}{T_1} = 1 - \frac{375}{500} = 0.25 = 25\%$

(b) $W = \eta Q_1 = 0.25 \times 25 \times 10^5$

$$= 6.25 \times 10^5\ J$$

(c) $Q_2 = Q_1 - W = (25 - 6.25) \times 10^5$

$$= 18.75 \times 10^5\ J$$

4. $T_1 = 627 + 273 = 900\,K$

$T_2 = 27 + 273 = 300\,K$

$Q_1 = 3 \times 10^6$ cal

$$\eta = \left(1 - \frac{T_2}{T_1}\right) = \left(1 - \frac{Q_2}{Q_1}\right)$$

$\therefore$ $$\frac{Q_2}{Q_1} = \frac{T_2}{T_1}$$

$\Rightarrow$ $$Q_2 = \frac{T_2}{T_1} \times Q_1$$

$$= \frac{300 \times 3 \times 10^6}{900} - 10^6\ \text{cal}$$

Work done by the engine,

$$W = Q_1 - Q_2 = 3 \times 10^6 - 10^6\ \text{cal}$$

$$= 2 \times 10^6\ \text{cal}$$

5. $\eta_1 = 1 - \frac{T_2}{T_1}$ or $\frac{1}{6} = 1 - \frac{T_2}{T_1}$ ...(i)

In the second case, the temperature of the sink is reduced by 65°C. Hence,

$$\eta_2 = 1 - \frac{T_2 - 65}{T_1}$$

or $$\frac{1}{3} = 1 - \frac{T_2 - 65}{T_1}$$ ...(ii)

Solving Eqs. (i) and (ii), we get

$$T_1 = 390\,K = 117°C,$$

$$T_2 = 325\,K$$

$$= 52°C$$

6. Coefficient of performance is given by

$$\beta = \frac{T_2}{T_1 - T_2}$$

$$\beta_A = \frac{(-10 + 273)}{(27 + 273) - (-10 + 273)}$$

$$= 7.1$$

$$\beta_B = \frac{(-27 + 273)}{(17 + 273) - (-27 + 273)} = 5.6$$

$$\beta_A > \beta_B$$

Therefore, refrigerator *A* is better.

7. Here, $T_1 = 25 + 273 = 298\,K$

$T_2 = -10 + 273 = 263\,K$

$Q_2 = 263$ J/s

Coefficient of performance is given by

$$\beta = \frac{Q_2}{Q_1 - Q_2} = \frac{T_2}{T_1 - T_2}$$

$\therefore$ $$\frac{Q_1}{Q_2} = \frac{T_1}{T_2}$$

$\Rightarrow$ $$Q_1 = \frac{T_1}{T_2} \times Q_2 = \frac{298}{263} \times 263$$

$$= 298\ Js^{-1}$$

Average power consumed

$$= 298 - 263 = 35\ J\,s^{-1}$$

$$= 35\ W$$

8. $\eta = \frac{W_{net}}{\Sigma Q_{+ve}} \times 100$

W_{net} = Area under the cycle

$$= \frac{p_0 V_0}{2}$$

$$\Sigma Q_{+ve} = Q_{ABC}$$

$$= W_{ABC} + \Delta U_{ABC}$$

$$= (\text{Area under } ABC) + nC_V\,\Delta T$$

$$= \left(\frac{5}{4} p_0 V_0\right) + n\left(\frac{3}{2}R\right)(T_C - T_A)$$

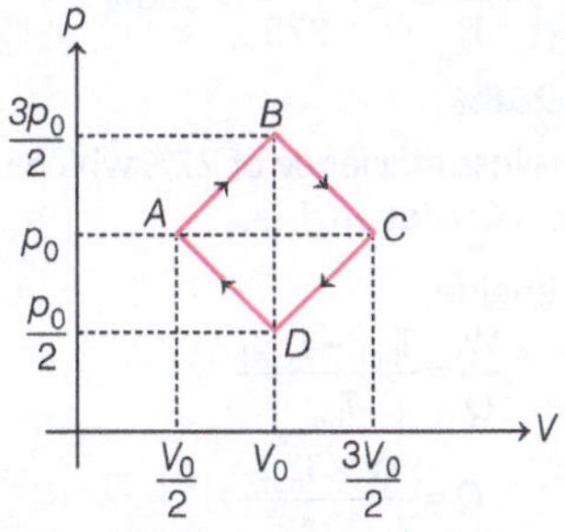

$$= \frac{5}{4} p_0 V_0 + \frac{3}{2}(p_C V_C - p_A V_A)$$

$$= \frac{5}{4} p_0 V_0 + \frac{3}{2}\left(\frac{3p_0V_0}{2} - \frac{p_0V_0}{2}\right)$$

$$= \frac{11}{4} p_0 V_0$$

$$\therefore \quad \eta = \frac{(p_0V_0/2)}{(11p_0V_0/4)} \times 100$$

$$= 18.18\,\%$$

Exercise

1. For given temperatures T_1 and T_2 efficiency of a heat engine can't be greater than efficiency of Carnot engine.

2. $\eta = \left(1 - \frac{T_2}{T_1}\right) \times 100$

$$T_2 = 300\,\text{K}$$

and $T_1 = 600\,\text{K}$

$\therefore \quad \eta = 50\%$

3. $\frac{W}{Q} = 1 - \frac{T_2}{T_1} = 1 - \frac{400}{800} = 0.5$

or $\quad Q = \frac{W}{0.5} = \frac{750}{0.5} = 1500\,\text{J}$

4. $\eta_A = \frac{T_1 - T_2}{T_1} = \frac{W_A}{Q_1}$

$\Rightarrow \quad \eta_B = \frac{T_2 - T_3}{T_2} = \frac{W_B}{Q_2}$

$\therefore \quad \frac{Q_1}{Q_2} = \frac{T_1}{T_2} \times \frac{T_2 - T_3}{T_1 - T_2} = \frac{T_1}{T_2}$

$\therefore \quad W_A = W_B$

$\therefore \quad T_2 = \frac{T_1 + T_3}{2}$

$$= \frac{800 + 300}{2} = 550\,\text{K}$$

5. Given, temperature of reservoir (boiling point of water),

$$T_1 = 100°\,\text{C} = 373\,\text{K}$$

Temperature of sink (freezing point of water),

$$T_2 = 0°\text{C} = 273\,\text{K}$$

Efficiency of heat engine,

$$\eta = 1 - \frac{T_2}{T_1} = \left(1 - \frac{273}{373}\right) \times 100\%$$

$$= 26.8\%$$

Hence, it has less efficiency of 27% which is less than the efficiency of a Carnot engine.

6. In a Carnot engine,

$$\frac{W}{Q} = \frac{T_{hot} - T_{cold}}{T_{hot}}$$

$$\Rightarrow \quad Q = \frac{W \times T_{hot}}{T_{hot} - T_{cold}}$$

$$= \frac{2 \times (127 + 273)}{(127 + 273) - (27 + 273)}$$

$$= \frac{2 \times 400}{100} = 8\,\text{kJ}$$

7. Efficiency of Carnot engine,

$$\eta = 1 - \frac{T_2}{T_1} \quad \text{...(i)}$$

where, T_2 = temperature of sink

T_1 = temperature of source.

In first case, $\eta = 50\% = \frac{1}{2}$

$$T_1 = 600\,\text{K}$$

From Eq. (i), we get

$$\frac{1}{2} = 1 - \frac{T_2}{600}$$

$$\Rightarrow \quad \frac{T_2}{600} = 1 - \frac{1}{2} = \frac{1}{2}$$

$$\Rightarrow \quad T_2 = \frac{600}{2} = 300\,\text{K}$$

In second case, $\eta = 70\% = 0.7$

$$T_2' = T_2 = 300\,\text{K}, T_1' = ?$$

From Eq. (i), $\eta' = 1 - \frac{T_2'}{T_1'}$

$$\Rightarrow \quad 0.7 = 1 - \frac{300}{T_1'}$$

$$\Rightarrow \quad \frac{300}{T_1'} = 1 - 0.7 = 0.3$$

$$\Rightarrow \quad T_1' = 1000\,\text{K}$$

8. The efficiency of a Carnot engine is given as,

$$\eta = 1 - \frac{T_2}{T_1}$$

where, T_2 = absolute temperature of sink

T_1 = absolute temperature of reservoir.

In case (i), $\quad \frac{1}{3} = 1 - \frac{T}{273 + 99}$

$$\frac{T}{372} = \frac{2}{3}$$

or $\quad T = 248\,\text{K}$

In case (ii), $\frac{1}{6} = 1 - \frac{T + x}{273 + 99}$

$$\Rightarrow \quad \frac{T + x}{372} = \frac{5}{6}$$

$$\Rightarrow \quad \frac{248 + x}{372} = \frac{5}{6}$$

$$\Rightarrow \quad 248 + x = 5 \times 62 = 310$$

$$\Rightarrow \quad x = 62\,\text{K}$$

9. For a Carnot engine, efficiency is given by

$$\eta = 1 - \frac{T_{sink}}{T_{source}}$$

Given $\eta = 50\%$

$$\therefore \quad \frac{1}{2} = 1 - \frac{T_{sink}}{T_{source}}$$

When η increases 30%, then

$$\frac{1}{2}(1.3)=1-\left(\frac{T_{sink}-40}{T_{source}}\right)$$

$$\Rightarrow \quad \frac{1}{2}(1.3)=\frac{1}{2}+\frac{40}{T_{source}}$$

$$\therefore \quad T_{source}=266.7\text{ K}$$

10. Efficiency of heat engine is given as $\eta=1-\frac{T_1}{T_2}$

For $T_1=447°C$ and $T_2=147°C$

$$\eta_1=1-\frac{147+273}{447+273}=1-\frac{420}{720}$$

$$\Rightarrow \quad \eta_1=\frac{300}{720}$$

For $T_1=947°C$ and $T_2=47°C$

$$\eta_2=1-\frac{47+273}{947+273}=1=\frac{320}{1220}$$

$$\Rightarrow \quad \eta_2=\frac{900}{1220}$$

$$\text{So,} \quad \frac{\eta_1}{\eta_2}=\frac{300}{720}\times\frac{1220}{900}=\frac{122}{72\times 3}$$

$$\Rightarrow \quad \frac{\eta_1}{\eta_2}=0.56$$

11. We have

$$\eta=1-\frac{T_{sink}}{T_{source}}=1-\frac{273}{373}$$

$$=\frac{100}{373}=0.2681$$

So, % $\eta=26.81\%$

12. According to question,

Initially, $\eta=0.25$

$$1-\frac{T_{sink}}{T_{source}}=0.25 \Rightarrow 0.75=\frac{T_{sink}}{T_{source}}$$

$$\Rightarrow \quad T_{source}=400\text{ K}$$

Finally, $\eta=0.25+100\%$ of $0.25\ \eta=0.5$

$$\Rightarrow \quad 1-\frac{T_{sink}}{T'_{source}}=0.5 \Rightarrow 0.5=\frac{300}{T'_{source}}$$

$$\Rightarrow \quad T'_{source}=600\text{ K}$$

$$\therefore \quad \Delta T=(600-400)\text{ K}$$

$$=200\text{ K}=200°C$$

13. We know that, $\eta=\frac{W}{Q_{absorbed}}$

$$\Rightarrow \quad W=\eta Q_{absorbed}$$

$$=\left(1-\frac{T_{sink}}{T_{source}}\right)Q_{absorbed}$$

$$=\left(1-\frac{400}{1000}\right)5000\text{ kcal}$$

$$=\frac{6}{10}\times 5000\text{ kcal}=3000\text{ kcal}$$

$$=12.6\times 10^6\text{ J}$$

14. We know that efficiency,

$$\eta=1-\frac{T_2}{T_1}=1-\frac{Q_2}{Q_1}$$

$$\Rightarrow \quad T_2=\frac{Q_2}{Q_1}\times T_1$$

$$=\frac{225}{300}\times 500=375\text{ K}$$

$$=102°C$$

15. Efficiency of a Carnot engine is

$$\eta=1-\frac{T_{sink}}{T_{source}}=1-\frac{200}{800}=\frac{3}{4}$$

$$\text{Also,} \quad \eta=\frac{W}{Q_{abs}} \Rightarrow Q_{abs}=\frac{W}{\eta}=\frac{12000\text{ kJ}}{\frac{3}{4}}$$

$$=16000\text{ kJ}=16\times 10^6\text{ J}$$

16. Efficiency,

$$\eta=1-\frac{Q_{sink}}{Q_{source}}=1-\frac{T_{sink}}{T_{source}}$$

$$\Rightarrow \quad \frac{Q_{sink}}{Q_{source}}=\frac{T_{sink}}{T_{source}}$$

$$\Rightarrow \quad T_{source}=T_{sink}\times\frac{Q_{source}}{Q_{sink}}$$

$$=324\times\frac{300}{180}=540\text{ K}$$

Unit Exercise (Cumulative)

Level 1

1. For isobaric process also T-t graph under given condition may be a straight line. Replace C_V by C_p.

2. Area under p-V graph in process-1 will be more.

3. When a system is given heat dQ and the work done on system is dW, then

$$dQ+dW=dU$$

or

$$dQ=dU-dW$$

4. When heat is added to a system isothermally its temperature remains constant. So, Statement I is incorrect.

$$W=p(V_f-V_i)$$

As $V_f>V_i$, so work done is positive.

Hence, Statement II is correct.

5. Since, the given process is adiabatic, hence $\Delta Q=0$.

From first law of thermodynamics, we get

$$\Delta Q=\Delta U+\Delta W$$

$$\Rightarrow \quad \Delta U=-\Delta W$$

The process is adiabatic compression, therefore volume decreases. Hence,

$$\Delta W=-\text{ve}$$

$\Rightarrow \quad \Delta U = +\text{ve}$

Thus, internal energy of the system increases positively with change in temperature as gas is compressed adiabatically.

Hence, option (c) is not true.

6. From the first law of thermodynamics,

$$dQ = dU + dW$$

Also, we can write this as,

$$\frac{dQ}{dt} = \frac{dU}{dt} + \frac{dW}{dt}$$

$$1000 = \frac{dU}{dt} + 200$$

$$\frac{dU}{dt} = 800 \text{ W}$$

7. Work done in the cyclic process,

$$W = \text{area of closed curve}$$

$$= \text{Area of } \Delta DCE$$

$$= \frac{1}{2} \times CE \times CD = \frac{1}{2} \times (4-2) \times (400-100)$$

$$= 300 \text{ J}$$

8. Total energy used in doing work

$$= p\Delta V$$

$$= 3 \times 10^5 \times 1600 \times 10^{-6}$$

$$= 480 \text{ J}$$

If only 10% energy = 480 J, is used in doing work.

Then, total energy = 4800 J

Therefore, the rest 90% of the remaining energy is used in increasing internal energy.

So, increase in internal energy = 90% of 4800 J

$$= \frac{90}{100} \times 4800 \text{ J}$$

$$= 4320 \text{ J}$$

9. In an isothermal process,

$$\Delta T = 0, \text{ so } \Delta U = 0$$

By using first law of thermodynamics,

$$\Delta Q = \Delta U + \Delta W \quad \text{...(i)}$$

So, in isothermal process,

$$\Delta Q = \Delta W \quad \text{...(ii)}$$

Now, when $\Delta Q = +\text{ve}$ (Heat is added to system)

Then, $\Delta W = +\text{ve}$ [from Eq. (ii)]

So, both C and D are correct.

10. For adiabatic process,

$$TV^{\gamma-1} = \text{constant} \quad \text{or} \quad T_2 = T_1\left(\frac{V_1}{V_2}\right)^{\gamma-1}$$

Given that, $V_2 = 2V_1$ and $\gamma = \frac{3}{2}$

$$T_2 = T\left(\frac{V_1}{2V_1}\right)^{\frac{3}{2}-1} = T\left(\frac{1}{2}\right)^{\frac{1}{2}}$$

$$\Rightarrow \quad T_2 = \frac{T}{\sqrt{2}}$$

Work done in adiabatic process,

$$W = -\Delta U = -nC_V\Delta T$$

$$= -n\left(\frac{R}{\gamma-1}\right)(T_f - T_i)$$

$$= \frac{R}{\frac{3}{2}-1}\left(T - \frac{T}{\sqrt{2}}\right)$$

$$= RT(2-\sqrt{2}) = \frac{R}{\gamma-1}[T_2 - T_1]$$

$$= \frac{R}{\frac{3}{2}-1}\left[\frac{T}{\sqrt{2}} - T\right] = 2R\left[\frac{T-\sqrt{2}T}{\sqrt{2}}\right]$$

$$= \sqrt{2}R[1-\sqrt{2}]T$$

$$\Rightarrow \quad W = RT[\sqrt{2}-2]$$

11. Number of moles of gas,

$$n = \frac{44.8}{22.4} = 2$$

Heat supplied, $\Delta Q = nC_V\, \Delta T$ at constant volume

$$= 2 \cdot \frac{3}{2}R \times 20 = 60R$$

$$= 60 \times 8.3 = 498 \text{ J}$$

12. In a complete cycle, change in internal energy is zero.

Therefore, $\Delta Q = \Delta W$ $[\because \Delta U_{cycle} = 0]$

$$\Rightarrow \quad 40 + 0 - 60 = 0 - 50 + W_{CA}$$

$$\Rightarrow \quad -20 = -50 + W_{CA}$$

$$\Rightarrow \quad W_{CA} = 30 \text{ J}$$

13. Work down by the gas

$$= \text{Area under the curve}$$

i.e. $W_{DE} = \frac{1}{2}(600+300)3 \text{ J} = 1350 \text{ J}$

Similarly, $W_{EF} = -300 \times 3$

$$= -900 \text{ J}$$

The total work done by the gas,

$$W_{DEF} = 1350 \text{ J} - 900 \text{ J}$$

$$= 450 \text{ J}$$

14. Given, $\Delta T = 40$ K

Number of moles, $n = 7$

$$R = 8.3 \text{ J K}^{-1} \text{ mol}^{-1}$$

For monoatomic gas, $C_V = \frac{3}{2}R$

The increase in the internal energy of the gas will be,

$$\Delta U = nC_V\Delta T = n\frac{3}{2}R\Delta T$$

$$= 7 \times \frac{3}{2} \times 8.3 \times 40$$

$$\Rightarrow \quad \Delta U = 3486 \text{ J}$$

15. Work done in adiabatic process is given by

$$W = \frac{p_2V_2 - p_1V_1}{1-x}$$

Here, $x = \gamma$

For adiabatic process,

$$p_2V_2^{\gamma} = p_1V_1^{\gamma}$$

$$p_2 = p_1\left(\frac{V_1}{V_2}\right)^{\gamma} = 75\left(\frac{1200}{150}\right)^{\frac{5}{3}} = 75(8)^{\frac{5}{3}}$$

$$= 75 \times 32 = 2400 \text{ kPa}$$

So, $$W = \frac{p_2V_2 - p_1V_1}{1-\gamma}$$

$$= \left(\frac{2400 \times 150 - 75 \times 1200}{1 - \frac{5}{3}}\right) \times 10^{-3}$$

$$= 405000 \times 10^{-3} = 405 \text{ J}$$

16. From p-V diagram,

Process 1

$p =$ constant, volume (V) increases and temperature (T) also increases.

Work down, $W = \int p\,dV =$ positive,

$$\Delta U = \frac{f}{2} nR\Delta T = \text{positive}$$

Therefore, heat is absorbed by the gas

(From first law of thermodynamics)

Process 2

Volume $V =$ constant, pressure (p) decreases.

$\therefore$ Temperature (T) decreases.

$\because$ $p \propto T$

$\therefore$ $W = \int p dV = 0$

ΔT is negative and $\Delta U = \frac{f}{2} nR\Delta T$

$\therefore$ ΔU is negative.

$$\Delta Q = \Delta U + W \text{ (Negative)}$$

$\therefore$ Heat is rejected by the gas.

Process 3

$p =$ constant, volume (V) decreases.

$\therefore$ Temperature (T) also decreases.

$$W = p\Delta V = \text{negative}$$

$$\Delta U = \frac{f}{2} nR\Delta T = \text{negative}$$

$\therefore$ $\Delta Q = W + \Delta U =$ negative

$\therefore$ Heat is rejected by the gas.

Process 4

$V =$ constant, pressure (p) increases.

$\therefore$ $W = \int p\,dV = 0$

$pV = nRT \Rightarrow$ Temperature increases

$\therefore$ $\Delta U = \frac{f}{2} nR\Delta T$ is positive

$\therefore$ $\Delta Q = \Delta U + W =$ Positive

Therefore, heat is absorbed by the gas.

17. At constant pressure, $dU = nC_V dT = n\frac{5}{2}RdT$

$$dQ = nC_p dT = n\left(\frac{7R}{2}\right)dT \text{ and } dW = nRdT$$

$$\Rightarrow dU : dQ : dW = \frac{5}{2} : \frac{7}{2} : 1$$

$$= 5 : 7 : 2$$

18. Given, capacity of cylinder is, 67.2 L and $\Delta T = 20°\text{C}$

At STP, volume $= 22.4$ L

$\therefore$ Number of moles $= \frac{67.2}{22.4} = 3$

Now, change in heat is given as

$$\Delta Q = nC_V\Delta T$$

Substituting the given values, we get

$$\Delta Q = 3 \times \frac{3R}{2} \times 20 \qquad \left(\because \text{ For He gas, } C_V = \frac{3}{2}R\right)$$

$$= 90R \text{ J}$$

Given, $R = 8.31 \text{ J mol}^{-1}\text{K}^{-1}$

$\therefore$ $\Delta Q = 90 \times 8.31$

$$= 747.9 \text{ J} = 748 \text{ J}$$

19. $VT =$ constant

$\Rightarrow$ $pV^2 =$ constant (as $T \propto pV$)

Comparing with $pV^x =$ constant, we get $x = 2$. Therefore, molar heat capacity,

$$C = C_V + \frac{R}{1-x} = \frac{3}{2}R + \frac{R}{1-2} = \frac{R}{2}$$

Now, $Q = nC\Delta T = 1(R/2)(\Delta T) = \frac{R\Delta T}{2}$

20. Given, heat supplied at constant volume is Q.

$\therefore$ $Q = nC_V\Delta T$

For same change in temperature, if heat supplied at constant pressure is Q, then

$$Q' = nC_p\Delta T$$

So, we have

$$\frac{Q'}{Q} = \frac{nC_p\Delta T}{nC_V\Delta T}$$

$$\Rightarrow \frac{Q'}{Q} = \frac{C_p}{C_V}$$

$$\Rightarrow Q' = Q\gamma \qquad \left[\because \gamma = \frac{C_p}{C_V}\right]$$

As given gas is diatomic,

so $\gamma = 7/5$

$\therefore$ $Q' = \frac{7}{5}Q$

21. For adiabatic process,

$$T_1V_1^{\gamma-1} = T_2V_2^{\gamma-1} \qquad \left(\because \gamma = \frac{5}{3}\right)$$

$$\Rightarrow \quad 300(V)^{\frac{2}{3}} = T_2(2V)^{\frac{2}{3}}$$

$$\Rightarrow \quad T_2 = \frac{300}{2^{\frac{2}{3}}} \approx 189\text{ K}$$

$$\Delta U = \frac{f}{2}nR\Delta T = \left(\frac{3}{2}\right)(2)\left(\frac{25}{3}\right)(189-300)$$

$$= -2.7\text{ kJ}$$

22. The process may be assumed to be isobaric.

$$\therefore \quad \Delta Q = nC_p\Delta T = 2 \times \frac{5}{2}R \times 5$$

$$= 5 \times 8.31 \times 5$$

$$= 207.75\text{ J} \approx 208\text{ J}$$

23. At STP, 22.4 L of any gas is 1 mole.

$$\therefore \quad 5.6\text{ L} = \frac{5.6}{22.4} = \frac{1}{4}\text{ moles} = n$$

In adiabatic process, $TV^{\gamma-1} = \text{constant}$

$$\therefore \quad T_2V_2^{\gamma-1} = T_1V_1^{\gamma-1}$$

$$\text{or} \quad T_2 = T_1\left(\frac{V_1}{V_2}\right)^{\gamma-1}$$

$$\gamma = \frac{C_p}{C_V} = \frac{5}{3}$$

For monoatomic He gas,

$$T_2 = T_1\left(\frac{5.6}{0.7}\right)^{\frac{5}{3}-1} = 4T_1$$

Further in adiabatic process, $Q = 0$

$$\therefore \quad W + \Delta U = 0$$

$$\text{or} \quad W = -\Delta U$$

$$= -nC_V\Delta T$$

$$= -n\left(\frac{R}{\gamma-1}\right)(T_2 - T_1)$$

$$= -\frac{1}{4}\left(\frac{R}{\frac{5}{3}-1}\right)(4T_1 - T_1)$$

$$= -\frac{9}{8}RT_1$$

$\therefore$ Work done $= \frac{9}{8}RT_1$

24. From first law of thermodynamics,

$$dQ = dU + dW$$

$$dQ = dU, \text{ if } dW = 0$$

Since, $dQ < 0$

Therefore, $dU < 0$

or $U_{final} < U_{initial}$

or temperature will decrease.

25. $Q_1 = nC_p\,\Delta T,\ Q_2 = nC_V\,\Delta T$

$$\because \quad \frac{Q_2}{Q_1} = \frac{C_V}{C_p} = \frac{1}{\gamma}$$

$$\text{or} \quad Q_2 = \frac{Q_1}{\gamma} = \frac{70}{1.4} = 50\text{ cal}$$

26. Efficiency of heat engine is given as

$$\eta = 1 - \frac{T_1}{T} \Rightarrow \frac{1}{4} = 1 - \frac{T_1}{T} \quad [T_1 = \text{sink temperature}]$$

$$\Rightarrow \quad 4T_1 = 3T \quad \text{or} \quad T_1 = \frac{3}{4}T \quad \text{... (i)}$$

$$\Rightarrow \quad \frac{1}{2} = 1 - \frac{T_1 - 58}{T} \quad \text{... (ii)}$$

From Eqs. (i) and (ii), we get

$$\frac{3}{4} = \frac{58}{T} + \frac{1}{2}$$

$$\Rightarrow \quad \frac{1}{4} = \frac{58}{T}$$

$$\Rightarrow \quad T = 232$$

$$\therefore \quad T_1 = \frac{3}{4}T = 174°\text{C}$$

27. Coefficient of performance

$$= \frac{\theta_2}{W} = \frac{T_{sink}}{T_{source} - T_{sink}}$$

$$\Rightarrow \quad \frac{\frac{d\theta_2}{dt}}{\frac{dW}{dt}} = \frac{263}{298-263} = \frac{263}{35}$$

$$\Rightarrow \quad \frac{d\theta_2}{dt} = \frac{263}{35} \times \frac{dW}{dt} = \frac{263}{35} \times 35$$

$$\Rightarrow \quad \frac{d\theta_2}{dt} = 263\text{ J/s}$$

28. $\frac{W}{Q} = \left(1 - \frac{T_1}{T_2}\right) \Rightarrow \frac{1200}{Q} = \left(1 - \frac{400}{800}\right)$

$\therefore$ Amount of heat energy supplied to the engine from the source, $Q = 2400$ J.

29. $(n_1 + n_2)_i = (n_1 + n_2)_f$

$$\text{or} \quad \frac{p_0V}{RT_0} + \frac{p_0V}{RT_0} = \frac{pV}{RT_0} + \frac{pV}{2RT_0}$$

$$\text{or} \quad \frac{2p_0V}{RT_0} = \frac{3pV}{2RT_0}$$

$$\therefore \quad p = \frac{4}{3}p_0$$

30. $\Delta U = C_V\,\Delta T = C_V(T_f - T_i) = -C_V(T_i - T_f)$

$$\Rightarrow \quad |\Delta U| = C_V(T_i - T_f)$$

31. For isobaric process, $\frac{V_2}{V_1} = \frac{T_2}{T_1}$

$$\Rightarrow \quad V_2 = V \times \frac{274}{273}$$

$$\text{Increase} = \frac{274V}{273} - V = \frac{V}{273}$$

32. $\Delta U = \Delta Q - \Delta W = 80 - 50 = 30\text{ cal}$

33. ΔU remains same for both paths.

For path *iaf* $\Delta U = \Delta Q - \Delta W$

$= 50 - 20 = 30$ J

For path *fi* $\Delta U = -30$ J and $\Delta W = -13$ J

$\Rightarrow \quad \Delta Q = -30 - 13 = -43$ J

34. In adiabatic process, pressure will be less. Further temperature is the product of p and V. Hence, $p_A < p_B$ and $T_A < T_B$.

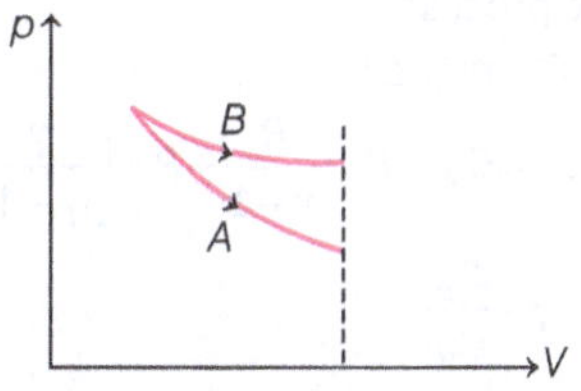

35. p-V graph in isothermal process is rectangular hyperbola and $p \propto \frac{1}{V}$. In isothermal compression, volume will decrease and pressure will increase. In adiabatic expansion, volume will increase and pressure will decrease. Further, in isobaric process pressure remains constant.

36. A $\to$ II, For an isothermal process, the temperature remains constant. So, the change in internal energy is zero.

B $\to$ I, In adiabatic process, no heat transfer takes place. Hence, by first law of thermodynamics, work done by the gas is equal to decrease in internal energy.

C $\to$ IV, In isochoric process, change in volume is zero.

i.e., $\Delta V = 0$

Hence, work done,

$$W = p \cdot \Delta V = p \times 0 = 0$$

Thus, in isochoric process, no work is done on or by the gas.

D $\to$ III, In isobaric process, when heat is supplied, a part of it goes in the expansion of gas and remaining part is used to increase the temperature of the gas which is turn increase in the internal energy.

37. (a) In a cyclic process,

$$Q_{net} = W_{net}$$

cyclic is clockwise. Hence, work done is positive. So, Q_{net} is also positive.

(b) $W_{net} = Q_{net} = 7200$ J

(c) In counter-clockwise direction,

$$W_{net} = Q_{net} = -\text{ve}$$

$$|Q_{net}| = 7200 \text{ J}$$

38. $pV = nRT$

$\therefore \quad p\Delta V = nR\Delta T$

Work done under constant pressure is

$$W = p\Delta V = nR\Delta T$$
$$= (0.2)(8.31)(100)$$
$$= 166.2 \text{ J}$$

39. First Process

$V =$ constant

$\therefore \quad T \propto p$

Pressure becomes half. So, temperature also becomes half.

$$Q_1 = n_1 C_V \Delta T = 2C_V(150 - 300)$$
$$= -300\, C_V$$

Second Process

$p =$ constant

$$Q_2 = nC_p \Delta T$$
$$= 2C_p(300 - 150) = 300\, C_p$$
$$Q = Q_1 + Q_2$$
$$= 300(C_p - C_V) = 300\, R$$
$$= 300 \times 8.31 = 2493 \text{ J}$$

40. $\Delta U = Q - W = nC_V\, \Delta T = n\left(\frac{3}{2}R\right)(T_f - T_i)$

$\therefore \quad 1200 - 2100 = 5\left(\frac{3}{2} \times 8.31\right)(T_f - 400)$

$\therefore \quad T_f = 385$ K

$\approx 113\,°\text{C}$

41. $V_i = \frac{m}{\rho_i} = \frac{2}{999.9} = 2.0002 \times 10^{-3}\ \text{m}^3$

$$V_f = \frac{m}{\rho_f} = \frac{2}{1000} = 2 \times 10^{-3}\text{m}^3$$

$$\Delta U = Q - W$$
$$= ms\, \Delta\theta - p_a \Delta V$$
$$= (2)(4200)(4) - (10)^5(-0.0002 \times 10^{-3})$$
$$\approx 33600 \text{ J}$$

42. $V_i = \frac{m}{\rho_i} = \frac{0.01}{1000} = 10^{-5}\,\text{m}^3$

$$V_f = \frac{m}{\rho_f} = \frac{0.01}{0.6} = 0.0167\ \text{m}^3$$

$$\Delta U = Q - W$$
$$- ms\Delta\theta + mL - p_0 \Delta V$$
$$= (0.01 \times 4200 \times 100) + (0.01)(2.5 \times 10^6)$$
$$- 10^5(0.0167 - 10^{-5})$$
$$\approx 27530 \text{ J}$$

43. (a) From conservation of linear momentum,

$$0.01 \times 200 = (2 + 0.01)\, v$$

$\therefore \quad v \approx 1$ m/s

Mechanical energy dissipated in collision

$$= K_i - K_f$$
$$= \frac{1}{2} \times (0.01)(200)^2 - \frac{1}{2}(2.01)(1)^2$$
$$\approx 199 \text{ J}$$

(b) $n = \frac{m}{M} = \frac{2000 + 10}{200} = 10.05$

Using, $\quad Q = nC_V\, \Delta T$

$\therefore \quad \Delta T = \dfrac{Q}{nC_V} = \dfrac{199}{10.05 \times 3 \times 8.31}$

$= 0.80°C$

44. (a) $W = p\Delta V = (2.30 \times 10^5)(1.2 - 1.7)$

$= -1.15 \times 10^5$ J

(b) $Q = W + \Delta U$

$= (-1.15 \times 10^5) + (-1.40 \times 10^5)$

$= -2.55 \times 10^5$ J

(c) No, as first law of thermodynamics is an energy equation, which can be applied for any system.

45. $V = \dfrac{m}{\rho} = \dfrac{1.0}{8.92 \times 10^3} = 1.12 \times 10^{-4} \text{m}^3$

$\gamma = 3\alpha = 2.1 \times 10^{-5}$ per °C

$\Delta V = V\gamma\,\Delta\theta$

$= (1.12 \times 10^{-4})(2.1 \times 10^{-5})(30)$

$= 7.056 \times 10^{-8} \text{m}^3$

$W = p\Delta V$

$= (1.01 \times 10^5)(7.056 \times 10^{-8})$

$= 7.13 \times 10^{-3}$ J

$Q = mc\,\Delta\theta$

$= (1)(387)(30) = 11610$ J

$\Delta U = Q - W$

$= 11609.99287$ J

46. Vessel is sealed. Therefore volume is constant or process is isochoric. Therefore,

$W = 0$

$\Delta U = nC_V\,\Delta T$

Here, $n = \dfrac{5}{22.4}$ and C_V for diatomic hydrogen $= \dfrac{5}{2}R$

$\therefore \quad \Delta U = \left(\dfrac{5}{22.4}\right)\left(\dfrac{5}{2}R\right)(\Delta T)$

$= \dfrac{5}{22.4} \times \dfrac{5}{2} \times 8.314 \times (-55)$

or $\quad \Delta U = -255$ J

or $\quad \Delta U = -0.25$ kJ

From first law of thermodynamics,

$Q = W + \Delta U$

or $\quad Q = \Delta U = -0.25$ kJ $\quad$ (as $W = 0$)

Therefore, heat lost by the gas is 0.25 kJ.

$Q_{\text{Lost}} = 0.25$ kJ

47. In isobaric process, $Q = nC_p\,\Delta T$ $\quad$ ...(i)

and work done by the gas,

$W = nR\Delta T$ $\quad$ ...(ii)

Dividing Eq. (i) by Eq. (ii), we get

$\dfrac{Q}{W} = \dfrac{C_p}{R}$ $\quad$ ...(iii)

Nitrogen is a diatomic gas. So taking

$C_p = \dfrac{7}{2}R$

Substituting in Eq. (iii), we get

$\dfrac{Q}{W} = \dfrac{7}{2}$

or $\quad Q = \dfrac{7}{2}W = \dfrac{7}{2}(2\text{J})$

$\therefore \quad Q = 7$ J

48. In isobaric process,

$Q = nC_p\,\Delta T$ $\quad$ ...(i)

For $n = 1, C_p = C_V + R = \dfrac{R}{\gamma - 1} + R = \left(\dfrac{\gamma}{\gamma - 1}\right)R$

where, $\quad \gamma = \dfrac{C_p}{C_V}$

With these substitutions, Eq. (i) becomes,

$Q = \left(\dfrac{\gamma}{\gamma - 1}\right)R\Delta T$

$\therefore \quad 1600 = \left(\dfrac{\gamma}{\gamma - 1}\right)(8.314)(72)$

Solving this equation, we get

$\gamma = 1.6$

$\Delta U = nC_V\Delta T$

$= (1)\left(\dfrac{R}{\gamma - 1}\right)(\Delta T)$

$= \dfrac{(1)(8.314)(72)}{1.6 - 1} = 997$ J

or $\quad \Delta U \approx 1.0$ kJ

From the equation of first law of thermodynamics,

$W = Q - \Delta U = (1.6 - 1.0)$ kJ

or $\quad W = 0.6$ kJ

49. (a) p - T graph in adiabatic process is given by,

$T^{\gamma}\,p^{1-\gamma} = \text{constant}$

For oxygen, $\gamma = \dfrac{7}{5}$

$\therefore \quad T^{7/5}\,p^{-2/5} = \text{constant}$

or $\quad p \propto T^{3.5}$

$\Rightarrow \quad \dfrac{T_2}{T_1} = \left(\dfrac{p_2}{p_1}\right)^{\frac{1}{3.5}}$

or $\quad T_2 = \left(\dfrac{p_2}{p_1}\right)^{\frac{1}{3.5}} T_1 = (10)^{\frac{1}{3.5}} \times 290$

$= 559$ K

$\therefore \quad T_2 = 559$ K

(b) In adiabatic process,

$Q = 0$

$\therefore \quad W = -\Delta U = -nC_V\Delta T$

$$= -n\left(\frac{R}{\gamma-1}\right)\Delta T$$

For oxygen, $\gamma = 1.4$. Putting these values in above equation, we get

$$W = -\frac{(1)(8.314)(559-290)}{1.4-1.0}$$
$$= -5591\text{ J}$$
$$\approx -5.6\text{ kJ}$$

This is work done by the gas. So, work done on the gas will be 5.6 kJ.

$\therefore \quad W_{\text{on gas}} = 5.6\text{ kJ}$

50. In adiabatic process,

$$p_i V_i^\gamma = p_f V_f^\gamma$$

Given $V_f = \frac{V_i}{5}$

$\therefore \quad p_f = (5)^\gamma p_i$

Work done is given by

$$W_1 = \frac{p_i V_i - p_f V_f}{\gamma - 1} = \frac{p_i V_i - (5)^\gamma p_i \frac{V_i}{5}}{\gamma-1}$$
$$= \frac{p_i V_i (1-5^{\gamma-1})}{\gamma-1} = \frac{nRT_i(1-5^{\gamma-1})}{\gamma-1}$$
$$= -\frac{nRT_i(5^{\gamma-1}-1)}{\gamma-1}$$

In isothermal process,

$$W_2 = nRT_i \ln\left(\frac{V_f}{V_i}\right) = nRT_i \ln\left(\frac{1}{5}\right)$$
$$= -nRT_i \ln 5$$

$$\therefore \quad \frac{W_1}{W_2} = \frac{(5^{\gamma-1}-1)}{(\gamma-1)\ln 5}$$

Putting $\gamma = 1.4$ for ideal diatomic nitrogen gas, we get

$$\frac{W_1}{W_2} = 1.4$$

51. $V = \frac{a}{T} \Rightarrow VT - \text{constant}$

$$\Rightarrow \quad V\left(\frac{pV}{nR}\right) = \text{constant}$$

or $\quad pV^2 = \text{constant}$

Molar heat capacity in the process $pV^x = \text{constant}$ is given by,

$$C = C_V + \frac{R}{1-x} \qquad \text{...(i)}$$

Here, $x = 2$ and $C_V = \frac{R}{\gamma-1}$

$$\therefore \quad C = \frac{R}{\gamma-1} + \frac{R}{1-2} = \left(\frac{2-\gamma}{\gamma-1}\right)R$$

Now, $\quad Q = nC\Delta T \qquad (n = 1)$

Substituting the values, we get

$$Q = \frac{(2-\gamma)R\Delta T}{\gamma-1}$$

52. Molar heat capacity in the polytropic process $pV^n = \text{constant}$ is given by

$$C = C_V + \frac{R}{1-n}$$

or $$C = \frac{R}{\gamma-1} + \frac{R}{1-n}$$
$$= \frac{R}{\gamma-1} - \frac{R}{n-1}$$

or $$C = \frac{(n-\gamma)R}{(n-1)(\gamma-1)}$$

C will be negative if

$$n - 1 > 0$$

or $\quad n > 1$

and $\quad n - 1 < \gamma - 1$

$$n < \gamma$$

$\Rightarrow \quad 1 < n < \gamma$

53. Argon is monoatomic. So its γ is $\frac{5}{3}$.

Let the process is,

$$pV^n = \text{constant}$$

or $$p_i V_i^n = \left(\frac{p_i}{8}\right)(4V_i)^n = p_i V_i^n \left(\frac{4^n}{8}\right)$$

Solving this equation, we get

$$n = \frac{3}{2}$$

In the polytropic process, molar heat capacity is given by

$$C = \frac{(n-\gamma)R}{(n-1)(\gamma-1)}$$

or $$C = \frac{\left(\frac{3}{2}-\frac{5}{3}\right)}{\left(\frac{3}{2}-1\right)\left(\frac{5}{3}-1\right)}R$$
$$= -\frac{R}{2} = -\frac{8.314}{2}$$

or $\quad C \approx -4.2\text{ J/mol-K}$

54. Argon is monoatomic. So, $\gamma = \frac{5}{3}$ and $n = 1.5$ or $\frac{3}{2}$.

So, from the result of previous question we can see that,

$$C = -4.2\text{ J/mol-K}$$

(a) $Q = fC\Delta T \qquad (f = \text{number of moles})$

$$= (1)(-4.2)(-26) = 109.2\text{ J}$$

or $\quad Q \approx 0.11\text{ kJ}$

(b) $\Delta U = fC_V\Delta T$

$$= (1)\left(\frac{3}{2}R\right)(-26)$$
$$= \frac{3}{2} \times 8.314(-26)$$

$$= -324\text{ J} \approx -0.32\text{ kJ}$$

Now, $W = Q - \Delta U$

$$= 0.11 - (-0.32)$$

$$= 0.43\text{ kJ}$$

Thus, $W = 0.43$ kJ

55. $\Delta U = nC_V \Delta T$

$$= (1)\left(\frac{R}{\gamma - 1}\right)(\eta T_0 - T_0)$$

$$= \frac{RT_0(\eta - 1)}{\gamma - 1}$$

$$Q = \int_{T_0}^{\eta T_0} nCdT = \int_{T_0}^{\eta T_0} (1)\left(\frac{a}{T}\right) dT$$

$$= a \ln \eta$$

$\therefore$ $W = Q - \Delta U$

or $W = a\ln \eta - \dfrac{RT_0(\eta - 1)}{\gamma - 1}$

56. Volume is constant. Therefore,

$$p \propto T$$

or, percentage change in p is also the percentage change in T.

When vessel is stopped, kinetic energy of gas molecules converts into its internal energy.

(For N_2, $C_V = \frac{5}{2}R$ and $M = 28$ g/mol $= 28 \times 10^{-3}$ kg/mol)

$\therefore$ $\frac{1}{2}mv^2 = \Delta U = nC_V \Delta T = \frac{m}{M}\left(\frac{5}{2}R\right)\Delta T$

or $\Delta T = \dfrac{Mv^2}{5R}$

$\therefore$ % increase in p (or T)

$$= \frac{\Delta T}{T_i} \times 100 = \frac{100\, Mv^2}{5RT_i}$$

$$= \frac{(100)(28 \times 10^{-3})(100)^2}{5 \times 8.314 \times 300}$$

$$= 2.2\,\%$$

57. $v_{rms} = \sqrt{\dfrac{3RT}{M}}$

or $v_{rms} \propto \sqrt{T}$

or $T \propto v_{rms}^2$

v_{rms} has reduced to 1.5 times.

Therefore, $T_f = \dfrac{T_i}{(rms)^2}$

For diatomic gas, $\gamma = \frac{7}{5} \Rightarrow \gamma - 1 = \frac{2}{5}$

and $TV^{\gamma - 1} = \text{constant}$

or $T_f V_f^{2/5} = T_i V_i^{2/5}$

$\therefore$ $V_f = \left(\dfrac{T_i}{T_f}\right)^{5/2} V_i$

$$= (1.5)^5\, V_i$$

Thus, $V_f = 7.6\, V_i$

58. $v_{rms} \propto \sqrt{T}$

To increase v_{rms} to two times, T has to be increased to four times.

$\therefore$ $\Delta T = 4T_i - T_i = 3T_i = 900\text{ K}$

$$n = \frac{m}{M} = \frac{15}{28}$$

C_V for diatomic N_2 is $\frac{5}{2}R$, vessel is closed. So, process is isochoric.

$\therefore$ $Q = nC\Delta T$ $\quad (C = C_V)$

$$= nC_V\, \Delta T$$

$\therefore$ $Q = \dfrac{15}{28}\left(\dfrac{5}{2}R\right)(\Delta T)$

$$= \frac{15}{28} \times \frac{5}{2} \times 8.314 \times 900$$

$$= 10021\text{ J or } Q \approx 10\text{ kJ}$$

59. For diatomic gas, $\gamma = \frac{7}{5}$

or $\gamma - 1 = \frac{2}{5}$

In adiabatic process,

$$TV^{\gamma - 1} = \text{constant}$$

or $T_f V_f^{2/5} = T_i V_i^{2/5}$

$\Rightarrow$ $T_f = \left(\dfrac{V_i}{V_f}\right)^{2/5} T_i$

$$= \left(\frac{V_i}{V_i/5}\right)^{2/5} (273)$$

$$T_f = (5)^{2/5}\,(273)$$

Rotational degree of freedom of a diatomic molecule is 2. Therefore from law of equipartition of energy, rotational kinetic energy in final state:

$$= 2\left(\frac{1}{2}kT_f\right) = kT_f$$

$$= (1.38 \times 10^{-23})(5)^{2/5}(273)$$

$$\approx 0.7 \times 10^{-20}\text{ J}$$

60. Coefficient of performance of a refrigerator,

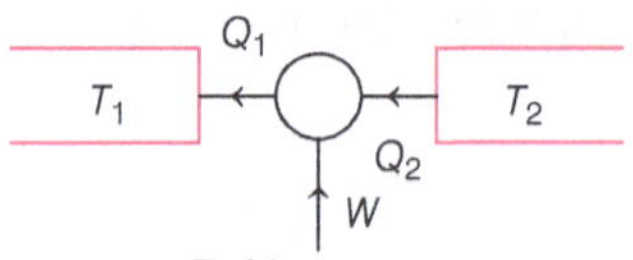

Refrigerator

$$\varepsilon = \frac{Q_2}{W} = \frac{Q_2}{Q_1 - Q_2}$$

and efficiency of Carnot's engine is given by

$$\eta = \frac{W}{Q_1} = \frac{Q_1 - Q_2}{Q_1}$$

From these two equations, we get

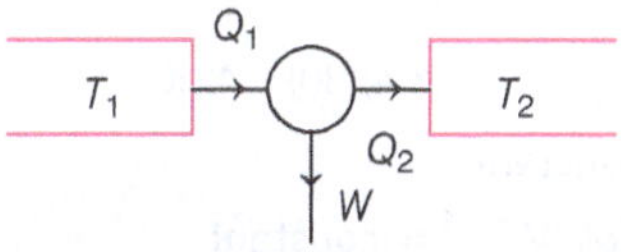

Heat engine

$$\varepsilon = \frac{1-\eta}{\eta} = \frac{1-0.1}{0.1} = 9$$

$\therefore \quad \varepsilon = 9$

61. Work done under constant pressure is given by

$$W = nR\,\Delta T = 150\text{ J} \qquad [\because p\Delta V = nR\Delta T]$$

From first law of thermodynamics,

$$Q = \Delta U + W = \frac{f}{2} nR\,\Delta T + nR\,\Delta T$$

$$\Rightarrow \quad Q = \left(\frac{f}{2}+1\right) nR\Delta T$$

$$= \left(\frac{8}{2}+1\right) 150 = 750\text{ J}$$

62. Work done is given by,

$$W = p\Delta V$$

$$\Rightarrow \quad 400 = p\Delta V$$

$$\Rightarrow \quad 400 = nR\Delta T \qquad \text{(At constant pressure)}$$

$$= n\frac{R\gamma}{\gamma-1}\Delta T = 400 \times \frac{\gamma}{\gamma-1}$$

$$= 400 \times \frac{1.4}{0.4} = 1400\text{ J}$$

63. From first law of thermodynamics, $\Delta U = \Delta Q + \Delta W$

$$\Delta U = \Delta Q - \Delta W = Q - Q/4 = 3Q/4$$

Now, $\Delta U = \frac{3}{2} nR\Delta T \qquad \left(\because \Delta U = \frac{f}{2} nR\Delta T\right)$

$$\Rightarrow \quad \frac{3Q}{4} = \frac{3}{2} Rn\Delta T$$

$$\Rightarrow \quad n\Delta T = \frac{Q}{2R}$$

As, $Q = nC\Delta T$

$$\Rightarrow \quad Q = \frac{Q}{2R} \times C$$

$$\Rightarrow \quad C = 2R$$

64. Given, heat taken, $Q_1 = 300$ J

Heat delivered, $Q_2 = 240$ J

Work done by heat engine,

$$W = Q_1 - Q_2 = 300 - 240 = 60\text{ J}$$

$$\text{Efficiency } \eta = \frac{W}{Q_{in}} = \frac{60}{300} = 1 - \frac{T_2}{T_1}$$

$$\Rightarrow \quad \frac{1}{5} = 1 - \frac{400}{T_1}$$

$$\Rightarrow \quad \frac{400}{T_1} = \frac{4}{5} \Rightarrow T_1 = 500\text{ K}$$

65. We know that, efficiency,

$$\eta = 1 - \frac{T_{Sink}}{T_{Source}}$$

$$0.6 = 1 - \frac{T_{Sink}}{400} \qquad [\because T_{Source} = 127 + 273 = 400\text{ K}]$$

$$400 - T_{Sink} = 240$$

$$\Rightarrow \quad T_{Sink} = 160\text{ K}$$

$$\therefore \quad T_{Sink} = 160 - 273$$

$$= -113°\text{C}$$

Level 2

66. $W = \int_V^{2V} p\,dV$

$$= \int_V^{2V} \left(\frac{nRT}{V-b}\right) dV = nRT \ln\left(\frac{2V-b}{V-b}\right)$$

Put $n = 1$,

$$\therefore \quad W = RT \ln\left(\frac{2V-b}{V-b}\right)$$

67. **For AB** $\quad V = \text{constant}$

$\therefore \quad W = 0$

For BC $\quad W = nRT_2 \ln\left(\frac{V_f}{V_i}\right)$

$$= RT_2 \ln\left(\frac{V_2}{V_1}\right)$$

For CA $\quad V \propto T$

$\therefore \quad p = \text{constant}$

$$W = nR\Delta T$$

$$= R(T_1 - T_2)$$

68. $\because \quad Q = nC_p\Delta T$

$$\frac{7}{2}RT_0 = (10)\left(\frac{7}{2}R\right)(T_f - T_0)$$

$$T_f = 1.1\,T_0$$

If $p = \text{constant}$, then $V \propto T$

If temperature becomes 1.1 times, then volume will also become 1.1 times.

69. W_{net} = area under the cycle

$$= 2p_0V_0$$

$$Q_{+ve} = Q_{ABC} = W_{ABC} + \Delta U_{ABC}$$

$$= \text{area under the graph } + nC_V\,\Delta T$$

$$= (3p_0V_0) + n\left(\frac{3}{2}R\right)(T_C - T_A)$$

$$= (3p_0V_0) + \frac{3}{2}(p_CV_C - p_AV_A)$$

$$= 10.5\,p_0V_0$$

$$\eta = \frac{W_{net}}{Q_{+ve}} = \frac{4}{21}$$

70. $Q = W + \Delta U$

$$= \text{area under the graph} + \Delta U$$

$$= -p_0V_0 - \frac{3p_0V_0}{2}$$
$$= -\frac{5}{2}p_0V_0$$

71. $pV^{-1} = \text{constant}$

In the process, $pV^x = \text{constant}$

$$C = C_V + \frac{R}{1-x}$$

Here, $C = \frac{3}{2}R + \frac{R}{1+1} = 2R$

$$Q = nC\Delta T = (1)(2R)(2T_0 - T_0)$$
$$= 2RT_0$$

72.

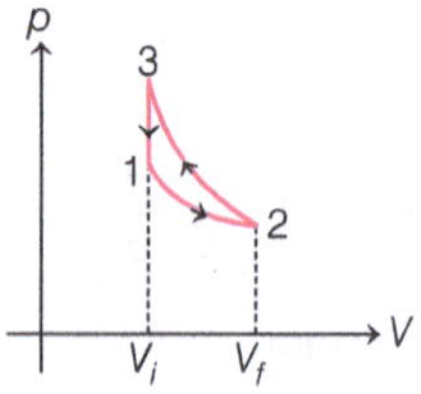

In process 3 - 1

$$V = \text{constant}$$
$$\therefore \quad T \propto p$$

If p is decreasing, then T will also decrease.

73. $TV^{\gamma-1} = \text{constant}$

$$\therefore \quad \frac{T_1}{T_2} = \left(\frac{V_2}{V_1}\right)^{\gamma-1} = \left(\frac{L_2}{L_1}\right)^{5/3-1} = \left(\frac{L_2}{L_1}\right)^{2/3}$$

74. $T \propto U$

$$T_C = T_D = T_0 = 300\,\text{K}$$
$$T_A = T_B = 2T_0 = 600\,\text{K}$$
$$Q_{net} = Q_{AB} + Q_{BC} + Q_{CD} + Q_{DA}$$
$$= nRT_A \ln\left(\frac{V_f}{V_i}\right) + nC_V(T_C - T_B) + nRT_C \ln\left(\frac{V_f}{V_i}\right) + nC_V(T_A - T_D)$$
$$= (1)(R)(600)\ln(2) + (1)(C_V)(-300) + (1)(R)(300)\ln\left(\frac{1}{2}\right) + (1)(C_V)(300)$$
$$= 300\,R\ln 2$$

75. **1-2** $T \propto V$

$$\therefore \quad p = \text{constant}$$
$$Q_{net} = W_{net} = W_{12} + W_{23} + W_{31}$$
$$\therefore \quad W_{23} = Q_{net} - W_{12} \qquad (\text{as } W_{31} = 0)$$
$$= -300 - nR\Delta T$$
$$= -300 - 2 \times 8.31 \times 300$$
$$= -5286\,\text{J}$$

76. $Q_A = Q_B$

$$nC_p\Delta T_A = nC_V\Delta T_B$$
$$\therefore \quad \Delta T_B = \frac{C_p}{C_V}\cdot\Delta T_A = \gamma\Delta T_A$$
$$= (1.4)(30) = 42\,\text{K}$$

77. $TV^{n-1} = \text{constant}$

$$\therefore \quad (pV)V^{n-1} = \text{constant} \qquad (\text{as } T \propto pV)$$
$$\therefore \quad pV^n = \text{constant}$$

Bulk modulus in the process $pV^\gamma = \text{constant}$ is γp. Hence, in the given process Bulk modulus is np.

78. $\Delta U = Q - W = 450\,\text{J} = nC_V\Delta T$

$$= n\left(\frac{3}{2}R\right)\Delta T$$
$$\therefore \quad n\,\Delta T = \left(\frac{300}{R}\right)$$

Now, $C = \frac{Q}{n\,\Delta T} = \frac{600}{300/R} = 2R$

79. $W = p\Delta V = p_0(2V_0 - V_0) = p_0V_0$

$$\Delta U = U_f - U_i$$
$$= 2p_0(2V_0) - 2p_0V_0$$
$$= 2p_0V_0$$
$$\therefore \quad Q = W + \Delta U = 3p_0V_0$$

80. $C = \frac{Q}{n\,\Delta T}$

or $\quad C \propto Q$

ΔU is same. But $W_1 < W_2$ as area under p-V graph is less.

Hence, $\quad Q_1 < Q_2$

or $\quad C_1 < C_2$

$\therefore \quad \frac{C_1}{C_2} < 1$

81. $Q_{net} = W_{net}$

$$Q_{AB} = Q_{CD} = 0$$
$$Q_{BC} = nC_p\Delta T = (1)\left(\frac{5}{2}R\right)(4T - T)$$
$$= 7.5\,RT$$
$$Q_{DA} = nC_p\Delta T$$
$$= (1)\left(\frac{5}{2}R\right)(3T - 5T)$$
$$= -5RT$$
$$\therefore \quad W_{net} = Q_{net} = 7.5\,RT - 5RT$$
$$= 2.5RT$$

82. $U\rho = \text{constant}$

$$\therefore \quad T\left(\frac{1}{V}\right) = \text{constant}$$

or $\quad T \propto V$

$\therefore \quad p = \text{constant}$

$$\frac{\Delta U}{W} = \frac{\Delta U}{Q - \Delta U}$$

$$= \frac{nC_V\,\Delta T}{nC_p\Delta T - nC_V\Delta T}$$

$$= \frac{1}{\gamma - 1} = \frac{1}{\frac{5}{3} - 1} = \frac{3}{2}$$

83. $W =$ Area under F-x graph

$$= 17.5\ \text{J}$$

Now, $Q = W + \Delta U$

$$= 20\ \text{J}$$

84. In second process, $p \propto V$ i.e. p-V graph is straight line passing through origin.

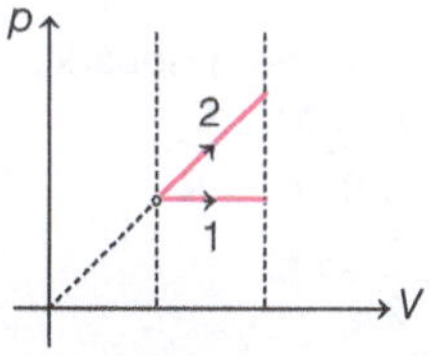

Area under graph-2 is more.

$\therefore$ $W_2 > W_1$

Further, $T \propto pV$

$(pV)_2 > (pV)_1$

$\therefore$ $T_2 > T_1$

85. $dQ = -dU$

or $dU + dW = -dU$

or $2dU + dW = 0$

$\therefore$ $2\,[nC_V dT] + pdV = 0$

or $2\left[n\left(\frac{R}{\gamma - 1}\right)dT\right] + pdV = 0$

or $\frac{2nRdT}{\gamma 1} + \left(\frac{nRT}{V}\right)dV = 0$

or $\left(\frac{2}{\gamma - 1}\right)\frac{dT}{T} + \frac{dV}{V} = 0$

Integrating we get,

$$\left(\frac{2}{\gamma - 1}\right)\ln(T) + \ln(V) = \ln(C)$$

Solving we get

$$TV^{\frac{\gamma - 1}{2}} = \text{constant}$$

86. In a cyclic process,

$$Q_{\text{net}} = W_{\text{net}}$$

$\therefore$ $Q_{AB} + Q_{BC} + Q_{CA} =$ area under the graph

$\therefore$ $600 + 200 + Q_{CA} = \frac{1}{2}(3 \times 10^{-4})(5 \times 10^5)$

$$= 75\ \text{J}$$

$\therefore$ $Q_{CA} = -725\ \text{J} = W_{CA} + \Delta U_{CA}$

$= -725 = (-\text{Area under the graph}) + \Delta U_{CA}$

$= -\left(\frac{1}{2} \times 11 \times 10^5\right)(3 \times 10^{-4}) + \Delta U_{CA}$

Solving we get,

$$\Delta U_{CA} = -560\ \text{J}$$

87. $T_2 = T_3$ (lying on same isotherm)

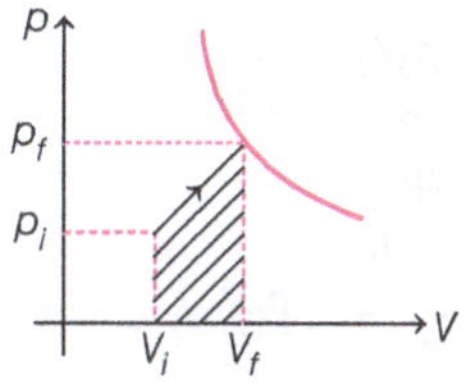

$\therefore$ $\Delta U_1 = \Delta U_2$

$W =$ Hatched area

$$= \frac{1}{2}(p_i + p_f)(V_f - V_i)$$

$$= \frac{1}{2}(p_i V_f - p_i V_i + p_f V_f - p_f V_i)$$

Now, $p_i V_i$ and $p_f V_f$ are same for both processes. Further p_i and V_i, area also same for both processes. For $1 \to 3$ V_f is more and p_f is less. Hence, W will be more.

Now, $Q = W + \Delta U \Rightarrow W_{13} > W_{12}$

$\therefore$ $Q_{13} > Q_{12}$ (as ΔU is same)

88. $\Delta U_{\text{net}} = 0$

$\therefore$ $\Delta U_1 + \Delta U_2 + \Delta U_3 = 0$

$\therefore$ $Q_1 + (Q_2 - W_2) + \Delta U_3 = 0$

$(200\ \text{kJ}) + (-100 + 50)\ \text{kJ} + \Delta U_3 = 0$

$\therefore$ $\Delta U_3 = -150\ \text{kJ}$

In adiabatic process,

$$W = -\Delta U$$

$\therefore$ $W_3 = -\Delta U_3 = 150\ \text{kJ}$

89. $Q_{BC} = 0$

$$Q_{CD} = nC_p\Delta T$$

$$= n\left(\frac{5}{2}R\right)(T_D - T_C)$$

$$= \frac{5}{2}(p_D V_D - p_C V_C)$$

$$= \frac{5}{2}(10^5 - 2 \times 10^5)$$

$$= -25 \times 10^4\ \text{J}$$

$$Q_{DA} = nC_V\,\Delta T$$

$$= n\left(\frac{3}{2}R\right)(T_A - T_D)$$

$$= \frac{3}{2}(p_A V_A - p_D V_D)$$

$$= \frac{3}{2}(2.4 \times 10^5 - 10^5)$$

$$= 21 \times 10^4\ \text{J}$$

Now, $W_{\text{net}} = Q_{\text{net}}$

$$= (9 - 25 + 21) \times 10^4\ \text{J}$$

$$= 5 \times 10^4\ \text{J}$$

90. Pressure becomes half. So, temperature is doubled. $\left(\text{as } T \propto \frac{1}{p}\right)$

$$\Delta U = nC_V \, \Delta T$$

$$T_i = \frac{p_0 V_0}{nR}$$

$$T_f = \frac{2p_0 V_0}{nR}$$

$$\therefore \quad \Delta T = T_f - T_i = \frac{p_0 V_0}{nR}$$

$$\therefore \quad \Delta U = n\left(\frac{3}{2}R\right)\left(\frac{p_0 V_0}{nR}\right) = \frac{3p_0 V_0}{2}$$

91. $W = nRT_0 \ln\left(\frac{p_i}{p_f}\right) \Rightarrow W_{BC} = 2W_{AB}$

$$\therefore \quad nRT_0 \ln\left(\frac{p_C}{p_0/2}\right) = 2nRT_0 \ln\left(\frac{p_0/2}{p_0}\right)$$

Solving this equation, we get

$$p_C = \frac{p_0}{8}$$

92. $dQ = 2 \cdot dU$ (given)

$$\therefore \quad nC \cdot dT = 2(nC_V \, dT)$$

or $C = 2C_V = 2 \times \frac{3}{2}R = 3R$

93. In process AB, density is constant. Hence, volume is constant. Therefore, work done will be zero.

In process BC $p \propto \rho$ but $\rho \propto \frac{1}{V}$

$$\therefore \quad p \propto \frac{1}{V}$$

Or the process is isothermal. Hence, internal energy is constant.

94. Slope of adiabatic process at a given state (p, V, T) is more than the slope of isothermal process. The corresponding p-V graph for the two processes is as shown in figure.

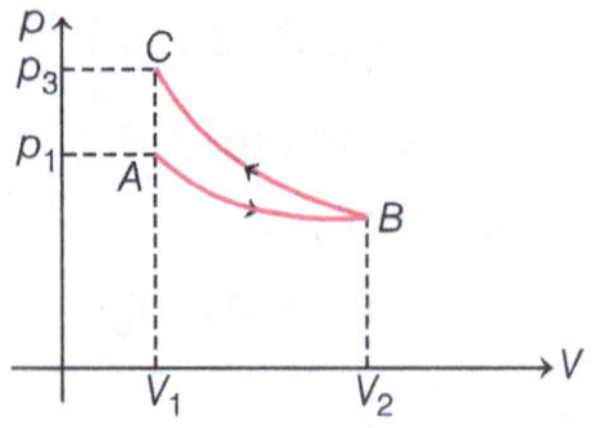

In the graph, AB is isothermal and BC is adiabatic.

W_{AB} = positive (as volume is increasing)

and W_{BC} = negative (as volume is decreasing) plus, $|W_{BC}| > |W_{AB}|$, as area under p-V graph gives the work done.

Hence, $W_{AB} + W_{BC} = W < 0$

From the graph itself, it is clear that $p_3 > p_1$.

Note *At point B, magnitude of slope of adiabatic (process BC) is greater than the slope of isothermal (process AB).*

95. Cycle is clockwise. Hence, heat will be given to the gas, as work done will be positive.

$$Q = W = \text{area of cycle}$$
$$= 1 \text{ J}$$

96. In a cyclic process $\Delta U = 0$

$$\therefore \quad Q_{\text{total}} = W_{\text{total}}$$

or $10 - 5 = -3 + W_{21}$

or $W_{21} = 8 \text{ J}$

97. V-T graph is a straight line passing through origin. Or $V \propto T$.

Hence, the given process is isobaric.

$$\frac{\Delta Q}{\Delta W} = \frac{nC_p \, \Delta T}{nR\Delta T} = \frac{C_p}{R}$$
$$= \frac{5}{2} = 2.5$$

98. $V = kT^2 \Rightarrow 2kT \cdot dT = dV$

and $p = \frac{RT}{V} = \frac{RT}{kT^2} = \frac{R}{kT}$

or $p \, dV = 2R \, dT$

$$W = \int p \, dV = 2R \int dT$$
$$= 2R(60) = 120R$$

99. $T = kV^2$

$$\therefore \quad dT = (2kV) \cdot dV$$

or $dV = \frac{dT}{2kV}$ and $p = \frac{nRT}{V}$

$$p \, dV = \frac{nRT}{2kV^2} \cdot dT = \frac{nRT}{2(T)} \cdot dT = \frac{nR}{2} \cdot dT$$

$$W = \int p \, dV = \int_{T_0}^{4T_0} \frac{nR}{2} \cdot dT = \frac{3}{2} nRT_0$$

100. $W_{A \to B}$ = Area under p-V diagram $= 18 p_0 V_0$

$$\Delta U_{A \to B} = nC_V \Delta T$$
$$= (1)\left(\frac{3}{2}R\right)\left(\frac{30p_0V_0}{R} - \frac{3p_0V_0}{R}\right) = \frac{81}{2} p_0V_0$$

$$\therefore Q_{A \to B} = W_{A \to B} + \Delta U_{A \to B} = \frac{117}{2} p_0 V_0$$

Molar heat capacity, $C = \frac{Q}{n\Delta T}$

$$= \frac{\frac{117}{2} p_0 V_0}{\left(\frac{30p_0V_0}{R}\right) - \left(\frac{3p_0V_0}{R}\right)}$$
$$= \frac{13}{6} R$$

101. pV^{-2} = constant

Comparing with pV^x = constant, we have

$$x = -2$$

$$W = \frac{nR\Delta T}{1-x} = \frac{(1)(R)(T_2 - T_1)}{1-(-2)}$$
$$= \frac{1}{3}R(T_2 - T_1)$$

102. $n = 2, \Delta Q_{cyclic} = -1200\text{ J}$

AB : isobaric process

$$\Delta W_{AB} = nR\Delta T = nR(T_B - T_A)$$
$$= 2 \times 8.3(500 - 300) = 3320\text{ J}$$

CA : isochoric process

$$\Delta W_{CA} = 0$$
$$\Delta W_{cyclic} = \Delta W_{AB} + \Delta W_{BC} + \Delta W_{CA} = \Delta Q_{cyclic}$$
$$3320 + \Delta W_{BC} + 0 = -1200$$
$$\Delta W_{BC} = -4520\text{ J}$$

103. $n = 6$

AB : isochoric process, $\Delta W_{AB} = 0$

BC : isobaric process,

$$\Delta W_{BC} = nR\Delta T = nR(T_C - T_B)$$
$$= 6R(2200 - 800)$$
$$= 8400\,R$$

CD : isochoric process, $\Delta W_{CD} = 0$

DA : isobaric process,

$$\Delta W_{DA} = nR\Delta T = nR(T_A - T_D)$$
$$= 6R(600 - 1200)$$
$$= -3600\,R$$
$$\Delta W_{cyclic} = \Delta W_{AB} + \Delta W_{BC} + \Delta W_{CD} + \Delta W_{DA}$$
$$= 8400R - 3600R = 4800R$$
$$= 4800 \times 8.3$$
$$= 39840\text{ J} \approx 40\text{ kJ}$$

104. $pV^{\gamma} = \text{constant}$

$$p\gamma V^{\gamma - 1}dV + V^{\gamma}dp = 0$$
$$\frac{dp}{dV} = -\frac{\gamma p}{V}$$
$$\frac{\Delta p}{\Delta V} = -\frac{\gamma p}{V}$$
$$\frac{\Delta p}{p} = -\gamma\frac{\Delta V}{V}$$

105. According to first law of thermodynamics, we get

(i) Change in internal energy from A to B, i.e.

$$\Delta U_{AB} = nC_V(T_B - T_A)$$
$$= 1 \times \frac{5R}{2}(800 - 400)$$
$$= 1000\,R$$

(ii) Change in internal energy from B to C, i.e.

$$\Delta U_{BC} = nC_V(T_C - T_B)$$
$$= 1 \times \frac{5R}{2}(600 - 800)$$
$$= -500\,R$$

(iii) $\Delta U_{isothermal} = 0$

(iv) Change in internal energy from C to A, i.e.

$$\Delta U_{CA} = nC_V(T_A - T_C)$$
$$= 1 \times \frac{5R}{2}(400 - 600)$$
$$= -500\,R$$

106. In isothermal process, $T = \text{constant}$

In isochoric process, $V = \text{constant}$, $p \propto T$. Therefore p-T graph is a straight line passing through origin.

In isobaric process, $p = \text{constant}$. Therefore, p-T graph is a straight line parallel to T-axis.

107. $pV^2 = \text{constant}$ (as $p \propto V^{-2}$)

Comparing with $pV^x = \text{constant}$, we have

$$x = 2 \Rightarrow W = \frac{nR\Delta T}{1-x}$$

Substituting the values, we have

$$W = \frac{(2)(R)(400 - 300)}{1-2} = -200R$$

108. In adiabatic process,

$$\frac{dp}{dV} = -\gamma\frac{p}{V}$$

For monoatomic gas, $\gamma = \frac{5}{3}$

Hence, $$\frac{dp}{dV} = -\frac{5}{3}\left(\frac{3p_0}{2V_0}\right) = -\frac{5}{2}\frac{p_0}{V_0}$$

or $$\left|\frac{dp}{dV}\right| = \frac{5}{2}\frac{p_0}{V_0}$$

109. ***ab*** $\rho = \text{constant}$

$\therefore$ $V = \text{constant}$

$\therefore$ $W = 0$

$Q = \Delta U$

ΔU is positive, as U is increasing.

Hence, Q is also positive.

bc $\rho \propto U$

$\therefore$ $\frac{1}{V} \propto T$

ρ is decreasing, so V is increasing. Hence, work done is positive.

Further, $\frac{1}{V} \propto T$ ($T \propto pV$)

$\therefore$ $pV^2 = \text{constant}$

In the process, $pV^x = \text{constant}$

Molar heat capacity is given by

$$C = C_V + \frac{R}{1-x}$$

Here, $x = 2$

$\therefore$ $C = C_V - R$

For any of the gas, $C_V \neq R$.

$\therefore$ $C \neq 0$

$\therefore \quad Q = nC\Delta T \neq 0$ as $\Delta U \neq 0$ and $\Delta T \neq 0$

ca

ρ is increasing. Hence, V is decreasing. So, work done is negative.

110. $Q_1 = nC_V \Delta T$

$$Q_2 = nC_p \Delta T$$
$$Q_3 = 0$$
$$C_p > C_V$$
$$\therefore \quad Q_2 > Q_1 > Q_3$$

111. **1-2** $V =$ constant

$$\therefore \quad p \propto T$$

T is increasing. So, p will also increase.

2-3 $\quad V \propto T$

$\therefore \quad p =$ constant.

V and T both are increasing.

Process 4-1 is reverse of 2-3.

112. $p \propto V \Rightarrow pV^{-1} =$ constant, process is polytropic with $x = -1$ and $C =$ specific heat for the process

$$= \frac{R}{\gamma - 1} + \frac{R}{1 - x}$$
$$= C_V + \frac{R}{1 - x}$$
$$= \frac{5}{2}R + \frac{R}{2} = 3R$$

$$\Delta Q = nC\Delta T$$
$$= nC(T_f - T_i)$$
$$= nC(4T_i - T_i)$$
$$= 3nCT_i$$
$$= 9nRT_i = 9p_1V_1$$

As, $v_{rms} \propto \sqrt{T}$, rms speed is doubled.

$\therefore$Temperature becomes four times.

113. For adiabatic process ($A \rightarrow B$),

$$p_A V_A^\gamma = p_B V_B^\gamma$$
$$10^5 \times (0.8)^{5/3} = 3 \times 10^5 (V_B)^{5/3}$$
$$\Rightarrow \quad V_B = 0.8 \times \left(\frac{1}{3}\right)^{0.6} = 0.4$$

Work done in process $A \rightarrow B$,

$$W_{AB} = \frac{p_A V_A - p_B V_B}{\gamma - 1}$$
$$\Rightarrow \quad W_{AB} = \frac{10^5 \times 0.8 - 3 \times 10^5 \times 0.4}{\frac{5}{3} - 1}$$
$$\Rightarrow \quad W_{AB} = -60 \text{ kJ}$$
$$\Rightarrow \quad |W_{AB}| = 60 \text{ kJ}$$

Work done in process $B \rightarrow C$ (isothermal process),

$$W_{BC} = nRT \ln \frac{V_C}{V_B}$$
$$= p_B V_B \ln \frac{V_C}{V_B}$$
$$\Rightarrow \quad W_{BC} = 3 \times 10^5 \times 0.4 \ln \frac{0.8}{0.4}$$
$$\Rightarrow \quad W_{BC} = 84 \text{ kJ}$$

Work done in process $C \rightarrow A$,

$$W_{CA} = p\Delta V = 0 \qquad (\because \Delta V = 0)$$

So, total work done in the process $A \rightarrow B \rightarrow C$,

$$W_{ABC} = W_{AB} + W_{BC} + W_{CA}$$
$$= -60 + 84 + 0$$
$$\Rightarrow \quad W_{ABC} = 24 \text{ kJ}$$

So, correct options are (b, c, d).

114. ***Note*** *This question can be solved if right hand side chamber is assumed to be open, so that its pressure remains constant.*

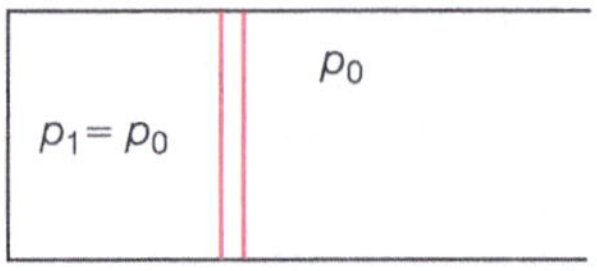

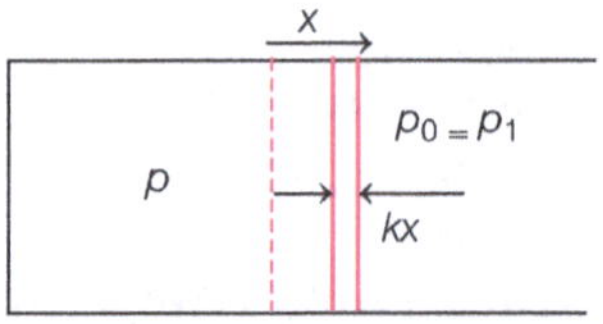

(a) $pV = nRT \Rightarrow \quad p \propto \dfrac{T}{V}$

Temperature is made three times and volume is doubled

$$\Rightarrow \quad p_2 = \frac{3}{2} p_1$$

Further

$$x = \frac{\Delta V}{A} = \frac{V_2 - V_1}{A} = \frac{2V_1 - V_1}{A} = \frac{V_1}{A}$$
$$p_2 = \frac{3p_1}{2} = p_1 + \frac{kx}{A}$$
$$\Rightarrow \quad kx = \frac{p_1 A}{2}$$

Energy of spring,

$$\frac{1}{2}kx^2 = \frac{p_1 A}{4} x = \frac{p_1 V_1}{4}$$

(b) $\Delta U = nc_v \Delta T = n\left(\frac{3}{2}R\right)\Delta T$

$$= \frac{3}{2}(p_2 V_2 - p_1 V_1)$$
$$= \frac{3}{2}\left[\left(\frac{3}{2}p_1\right)(2V_1) - p_1 V_1\right] = 3p_1 V_1$$

(c) $p_2 = \dfrac{4p_1}{3}$

$$\Rightarrow \quad p_2 = \frac{4}{3}p_1 = p_1 + \frac{kx}{A}$$

$$\Rightarrow \quad kx = \frac{p_1 A}{3} \Rightarrow x = \frac{\Delta V}{A} = \frac{2V_1}{A}$$

$$W_{gas} = (p_0\,\Delta V + W_{spring})$$

$$= (p_1 Ax + \frac{1}{2}kx \cdot x)$$

$$= +\left(p_1 A \cdot \frac{2V_1}{A} + \frac{1}{2} \cdot \frac{p_1 A}{3} \cdot \frac{2V_1}{A}\right)$$

$$= 2p_1V_1 + \frac{p_1V_1}{3} = \frac{7p_1V_1}{3}$$

(d) $\Delta Q = W + \Delta U$

$$= \frac{7p_1V_1}{3} + \frac{3}{2}(p_2V_2 - p_1V_1)$$

$$= \frac{7p_1V_1}{3} + \frac{3}{2}\left(\frac{4}{3}p_1 \cdot 3V_1 - p_1V_1\right)$$

$$= \frac{7p_1V_1}{3} + \frac{9}{2}p_1\,V_1 = \frac{41p_1V_1}{6}$$

115. Given, $T_A = T_B$

$\therefore \quad U_A = U_B$

$$W_{AB} = (1)(R)T_0 \ln\left(\frac{V_f}{V_i}\right)$$

$$= RT_0 \ln\left(\frac{4V_0}{V_0}\right)$$

$$= p_0V_0 \ln(4)$$

Information regarding p and T at C cannot be obtained from the given graph. Unless it is mentioned that line BC passes through origin or not.

Hence, the correct options are (a) and (b).

116. (a) p-V graph is not rectangular hyperbola. Therefore, process A-B is not isothermal.

(b) In process BCD, product of pV (therefore temperature and internal energy) is decreasing. Further, volume is decreasing. Hence, work done is also negative. Hence, Q will be negative or heat will flow out of the gas.

(c) W_{ABC} = positive

(d) For clockwise cycle on p-V diagram with p on Y-axis, net work done is positive.

117. There is a decrease in volume during melting of an ice slab at 273 K. Therefore, negative work is done by ice-water system on the atmosphere or positive work is done on the ice-water system by the atmosphere. Hence, option (b) is correct. Secondly, heat is absorbed during melting (i.e. Q is positive) and as we have seen, work done by ice-water system is negative (W is negative). Therefore, from first law of thermodynamics

$$\Delta U = Q - W$$

change in internal energy of ice-water system, ΔU will be positive or internal energy will increase.

118. $Q_{net} = W_{net}$ = area under the cycle $= \frac{pV}{2}$

119. $\frac{C_p}{C_V} = \gamma = \frac{5}{3}$

120. (a) W_{ab} = area under p-V graph

$$= \frac{3p_0V_0}{2} = 1.5\,p_0V_0$$

(b) $\Delta U_{ab} = Q_{ab} - W_{ab}$

$$= 6p_0V_0 - \frac{3p_0V_0}{2} = 4.5\,p_0V_0$$

(c) $C = \frac{Q}{n\Delta T} = \frac{W + \Delta U}{n\Delta T}$

$$= \frac{6p_0V_0}{n\left(\frac{p_bV_b}{nR} - \frac{p_aV_a}{nR}\right)} = 2R$$

(d) $C_V = \frac{\Delta U}{n\Delta T} = \frac{4.5\,p_0V_0}{n\left(\frac{p_bV_b}{nR} - \frac{p_aV_a}{nR}\right)}$

$$= 1.5R$$

121. VT^2 = constant $\qquad \left(T = \frac{pV}{nR} \propto pV\right)$

$\therefore \quad V(pV)^2$ = constant or $pV^{3/2}$ = constant

Comparing with pV^x = constant, we have

$$\Delta U = nC_V\Delta T, W = \frac{nR\Delta T}{1-x}$$

and $\qquad Q = W + \Delta U$

For diatomic gas,

$$C_V = \frac{5}{2}R$$

$$\Delta T = \frac{\Delta(pV)}{nR}$$

$$pV^{3/2} = \text{constant}$$

$$\therefore \quad p \propto \frac{1}{V^{3/2}}$$

Volume is made $\frac{1}{4}$ th, therefore pressure will become 8-times. Using all these equations we can find different quantities.

$$T_i = \frac{p_0V_0}{nR}, T_f = \frac{(8p_0)\left(\frac{V_0}{4}\right)}{nR} = \frac{2p_0V_0}{nR}$$

$$\therefore \quad \Delta T = \frac{p_0V_0}{nR}$$

$$\Delta U = nC_V\Delta T = n\left(\frac{5}{2}R\right)\left(\frac{p_0V_0}{nR}\right) = 2.5\,p_0V_0$$

$$W = \frac{nR\Delta T}{1-x} = \frac{nR\left(\frac{p_0V_0}{nR}\right)}{1-\frac{3}{2}} = -2p_0V_0$$

$$Q = W + \Delta U = 0.5\,p_0V_0$$

$$(\Delta p)V_0 = (8p_0 - p_0)V_0 = 7p_0V_0$$

122. (I) $U = mL - p\Delta V$

$$= 10^{-3} \times 2250 \times 10^3 - 10^2 \times (10^{-3} - 10^{-6})$$
$$= 2.25 \times 10^3 - 0.1 \times 10^3$$
$$= 2.15 \times 10^3 \text{ J} = 2.15 \text{ kJ}$$

(I) → (P)

(II) $C_V = \frac{5R}{2}$ (rigid diatomic)

For isobaric expansion,

$$V \propto T$$
$$\Rightarrow \quad \frac{V_1}{V_2} = \frac{T_1}{T_2}$$
$$\Rightarrow \quad \frac{V}{3V} = \frac{500}{T_2}$$
$$\Rightarrow \quad T_2 = 1500 \text{ K}$$
$$\Delta U = nC_V\Delta T = 0.2 \times \frac{5 \times 8}{2} \times (1500 - 500) \text{ J}$$
$$= 4 \text{ kJ}$$

(II) → (R)

(III) Adiabatic expansion $\left(\gamma = \frac{5}{3}\right)$

$$p_1 \cdot V_1^\gamma = p_2 V_2^\gamma$$
$$\Rightarrow \quad (2\text{kPa}) \times V_0^{\frac{5}{3}} = p_2 \times \left(\frac{V_0}{8}\right)^{\frac{5}{3}}$$
$$p_2 = 64 \text{ kPa}$$
$$\Delta U = nC_V\Delta T$$
$$= \frac{3nR\Delta T}{2} = \frac{3}{2}(p_2V_2 - p_1V_1)$$
$$= \frac{3}{2} \times \left(64 \times \frac{1}{3 \times 8} - 2 \times \frac{1}{3}\right)$$
$$= \frac{3}{2} \times \left(\frac{8}{3} - \frac{2}{3}\right) = 3 \text{ kJ}$$

(III) → (T)

(IV) For isobaric expansion,

$$\Delta U = nC_V\Delta T = \frac{7}{2} nR\Delta T$$
$$\Delta Q = nC_p\Delta T = \frac{9}{2} nR\Delta T$$
$$\frac{\Delta U}{\Delta Q} = \frac{7}{9}$$
$$\Rightarrow \quad \Delta U = \frac{7}{9}\Delta Q = 7 \text{ kJ}$$

(IV) → Q

123. $v_{\text{sound}} = \sqrt{\frac{\gamma RT}{M}}$. As the sound wave propagates, the air in a chamber undergoes compression and rarefaction very fastly, hence it is an adiabatic process. So, curves are steeper than isothermal.

$$\left(\frac{dp}{dV}\right)_{\text{Adi}} = -\gamma\left(\frac{p}{V}\right) \quad \ldots\text{(i)}$$

$$\left(\frac{dp}{dV}\right)_{\text{Iso}} = -\left(\frac{p}{V}\right) \quad \ldots\text{(ii)}$$

Graph Q satisfies Eq. (i).

124. $\Delta U = \Delta Q - p\Delta V$

$$\Delta U + p\Delta V = \Delta Q$$

As $\Delta U \neq 0, W \neq 0, \Delta Q \neq 0$. The process represents isobaric process

$$W_{\text{gas}} = -p(\Delta V)$$
$$= -p(V_2 - V_1) = -pV_2 + pV_1$$

Graph P satisfies isobaric process.

125. Work done in isochoric process is zero.

$$W_{12} = 0 \text{ as } \Delta V = 0$$

Graph S represents isochoric process.

126.

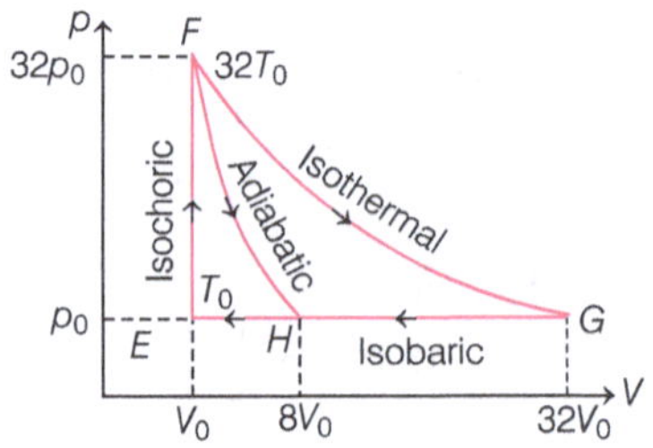

In F - G process:

$$T = \text{constant}$$
$$V \propto \frac{1}{p} \quad \Rightarrow \quad p_G = \frac{p_F}{32}$$
$$\therefore \quad V_G = 32 V_F$$
$$= 32V_0$$

In $F \to G$, work done in isothermal process is

$$nRT \ln\left(\frac{V_f}{V_i}\right) = 32\, p_0V_0 \ln\left(\frac{32\, V_0}{V_0}\right)$$
$$= 32\, p_0V_0 \ln 2^5 = 160 p_0\, V_0 \ln 2$$

In $G \to E, \Delta W = p_0\Delta V$

$$= p_0(31\, V_0) = 31\, p_0V_0$$

In $G \to H$, work done is less than $31\, p_0V_0$ i.e. $24\, p_0V_0$

In $F \to H$, $p_FV_F^\gamma = p_HV_H^\gamma$

$$\Rightarrow \quad V_H = \left(\frac{p_F}{p_H}\right)^{\frac{1}{\gamma}} V_F = (32)^{\frac{1}{5/3}}(V_0) = 8V_0$$

Now, $W = \frac{p_iV_i - p_fV_f}{\gamma - 1} = \frac{32p_0V_0 - 8p_0V_0}{\frac{5}{3} - 1} = 36\, p_0V_0$

127. Internal energy $\propto T \propto pV$

This is because $U = \frac{nf}{2}RT = \frac{f}{2}(pV)$

Here, n = number of moles, f = degree of freedom.

∴ If the product pV increases, then internal energy will increase and if product decreases, the internal energy will decrease.

Further, work is done on the gas, if volume of gas decreases. For heat exchange, $Q = W + \Delta U$

Work done is area under p-V graph. If volume increases, work done by gas is positive and if volume decreases, work done by gas is negative. Further, ΔU is positive, if product of pV is increasing and ΔU is negative if product of pV is decreasing.

If heat is taken by the gas, then Q is positive and if heat is lost by the gas, Q is negative. Keeping the above points in mind the answer to this question is as under.

(a) → (p, r, t) ; (b) → (p, r); (c) → (q, s) ; (d) → (r, t)

128. (a) In case of free expansion under adiabatic conditions, Q, W and $\Delta U = 0$.

∴ Internal energy and temperature will remain constant.

(b) $p \propto \frac{1}{V^2}$

$$\Rightarrow \quad pV^2 = \text{constant} \quad \text{... (i)}$$

$$\text{or} \quad \left(\frac{nRT}{V}\right).V^2 = \text{constant}$$

$$\therefore \quad T \propto \frac{1}{V} \quad \text{...(ii)}$$

If volume is doubled, temperature will decrease as per Eq. (ii).

Further, molar heat capacity in process pV^x = constant is

$$C = C_V + \frac{R}{1-x}$$

From Eq. (i), $x = 2$

$$\therefore \quad C = \frac{3}{2}R + \frac{R}{1-2} = +\frac{R}{2}$$

Since, molar heat capacity is positive, according to $Q = nC\Delta T$, Q will be negative if ΔT is negative. Or gas loses heat if temperature is decreasing.

(c) $p \propto \frac{1}{V^{4/3}}$, $pV^{4/3} = \text{constant}$

$$\therefore \quad \left(\frac{nRT}{V}\right)V^{4/3} = \text{constant}$$

$$\therefore \quad T \propto \frac{1}{V^{1/3}}$$

Further, with increase in volume temperature will decrease.

Here, $x = \frac{4}{3} \Rightarrow C = \frac{3}{2}R + \frac{R}{1-4/3}$

$$= -1.5R$$

As molar heat capacity is negative, Q will be positive if ΔT is negative. Or gas gains heat with decrease in temperature.

(d) $T \propto pV$

In expansion from V_1 to $2V_1$, product of pV is increasing. Therefore, temperature will increase. Or, $\Delta U = +\text{ve}$. Further, in expansion work done is also positive.

Hence, $Q = W + \Delta U = +\text{ve}$

or gas gains heat.

The correct match is

A → q, B → p, r, C → p, s, D → q, s

129. **In process $J \to K$** V is constant whereas p is decreasing. Therefore, T should also decrease.

$$\therefore \quad W = 0, \Delta U = -\text{ve and } Q < 0$$

(a) → s

In process $K \to L$ p is constant while V is increasing. Therefore, temperature should also increase.

$$\therefore \quad W > 0, \Delta U > 0$$

and $\quad Q > 0$

(b) → r

In process $L \to M$ This is inverse of process $J \to K$.

$$\therefore \quad W = 0, \Delta U > 0 \text{ and } Q > 0$$

(c) → p

In process $M \to J$

V is decreasing. Therefore, $W < 0$

$$(pV)_J < (pV)_M$$

$$\therefore \quad T_J < T_M \quad \text{or} \quad \Delta U < 0$$

Therefore, $Q < 0$.

(d) → q

130. First process

$$T = \text{constant} \quad \therefore \quad p \propto \frac{1}{V}$$

V is made 5 times. Therefore, p will become $\frac{1}{5}$th.

Second process

$$V = \text{constant} \Rightarrow T \propto p$$

Pressure again becomes five times. So, temperature will also become 5 times.

$$Q_1 + Q_2 = 80 \times 10^3$$

$$\therefore \quad nRT \ln\left(\frac{V_f}{V_i}\right) + nC_V \,\Delta T = 80 \times 10^3$$

$$\therefore (3)(8.31)(273)\ln(5) + (3)\left(\frac{8.31}{\gamma - 1}\right)(5 \times 273 - 273) = 80 \times 10^3$$

Solving we get, $\gamma = 1.4$

131. **Process A-B** is an isothermal process

i.e. $\quad T = \text{constant}$

Hence, $\quad p \propto \frac{1}{V}$

or p-V graph will be a rectangular hyperbola with increasing p and decreasing V.

$\rho \propto \frac{1}{V}$. Hence, ρ-V graph is also a rectangular hyperbola with decreasing V and hence increasing ρ.

$$\rho \propto p \quad \left[\rho = \frac{pM}{RT}\right]$$

Hence, ρ-p graph will be a straight line passing through origin, with increasing ρ and p.

Process B-C is an isochoric process, because p-T graph is a straight line passing through origin i.e. $V =$ constant

Hence, p-V graph will be a straight line parallel to p-axis with increasing p.

Since, $V =$ constant hence ρ will also be constant. Hence ρ-V graph will be a dot.

ρ-p graph will be a straight line parallel to p-axis with increasing p, because

$$\rho = \text{constant}$$

Process *C-D* is inverse of A-B and D-A is inverse of B-C.

Different values of p, V, T and ρ in tabular form are shown below

	p	V	T	ρ
A	p_0	V_0	T_0	ρ_0
B	$2p_0$	$\frac{V_0}{2}$	T_0	$2\rho_0$
C	$4p_0$	$\frac{V_0}{2}$	$2T_0$	$2\rho_0$
D	$2p_0$	V_0	$2T_0$	ρ_0

Here, $V_0 = nR\left(\frac{T_0}{p_0}\right)$ and $\rho_0 = \frac{p_0 M}{RT_0}$

The corresponding graphs are as follows

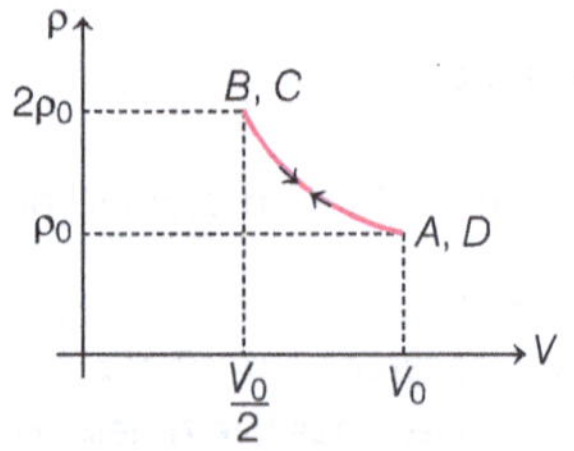

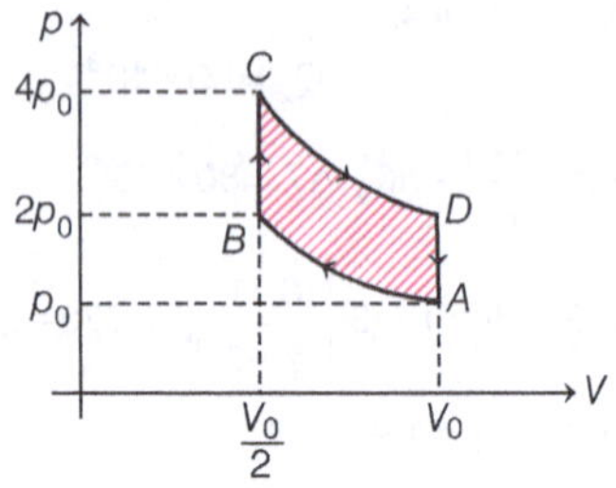

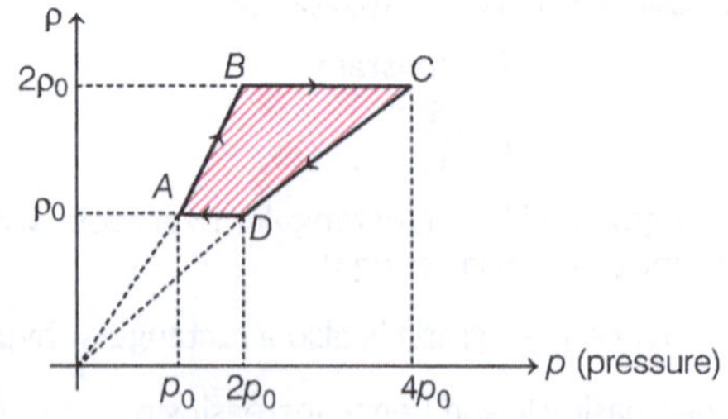

132. (a) First law of thermodynamics for the given process from state 1 to state 2

$$Q_{12} - W_{12} = U_2 - U_1$$

Here, $Q_{12} = +10 p_0 V_0$ joule

$W_{12} = 0$ (Volume remains constant)

$$U_2 - U_1 = nC_V (T_2 - T_1)$$

$$nC_V (T_2 - T_1) = 10\, p_0 V_0$$

For an ideal gas,

$$p_0 V_0 = nRT_0$$

and $\quad C_p - C_V = R$

$\therefore \quad C_V = C_p - R$

$$= \frac{5R}{2} - R = \frac{3R}{2}$$

$\therefore \quad n\left(\frac{3R}{2}\right)(T_2 - T_0) = 10\, nRT_0$

$$T_2 = \frac{23}{3} T_0$$

As $p \propto T$ for constant volume

$$p_2 = \frac{23}{3} p_0$$

(b)

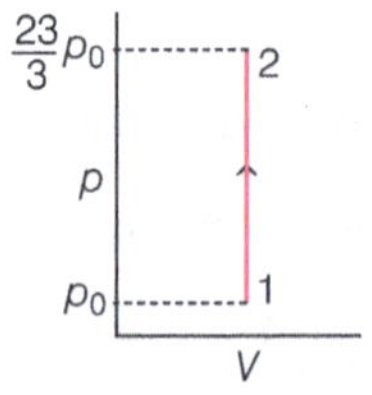

133.

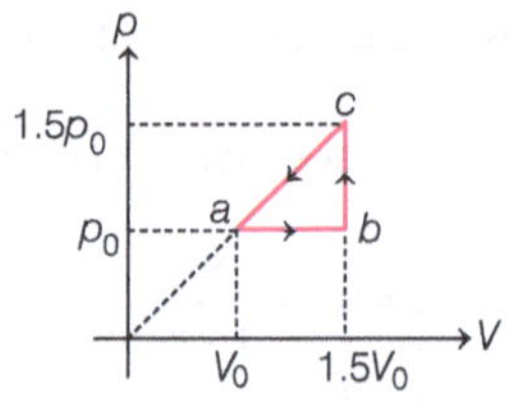

$W_{net} = Q_{net}$ in a cycle.

Since, Q_{net} is negative (flows out of the gas). Hence, W_{net} should also be negative. Or, cycle should be anti-clockwise as shown in figure.

From *a* to *b*

$$p = \text{constant}$$

$\therefore \quad V \propto T$

T has become 1.5 times. Therefore, V will also become 1.5 times.

From *c* to *a*

$$p \propto V$$

V has become $\frac{1}{1.5}$ times. Therefore,

p will also become $\frac{1}{1.5}$ times.

In a cycle

$$|Q_{net}| = |W_{net}| = \text{Area of cycle}$$

$\therefore \quad 800 = \frac{1}{2}(0.5 p_0)(0.5 V_0)$

$\therefore \quad p_0 V_0 = 6400 \text{ J}$

$$W_{ca} = -\text{Area under the graph}$$

$$= -\frac{1}{2}(2.5 p_0)(0.5 V_0)$$

$$= -0.625\, p_0 V_0$$

$$= -0.625 \times 6400 = -4000 \text{ J}$$

134. First process is isobaric.

$\therefore \quad \Delta Q_1 = nC_V \Delta T + p\Delta V$

Second process is isochoric.

$\therefore \quad \Delta Q_2 = nC_V \Delta T$

$$\Delta Q_1 - \Delta Q_2 = p\Delta V = \left[p_0 + \frac{mg}{A}\right][Ax]$$

$$= (p_0 A + mg)x$$

$$= [10^5 \times 60 \times 10^{-4} + 8 \times 10](0.2)$$

$$= 136 \text{ J}$$ **Ans.**

135. (a)

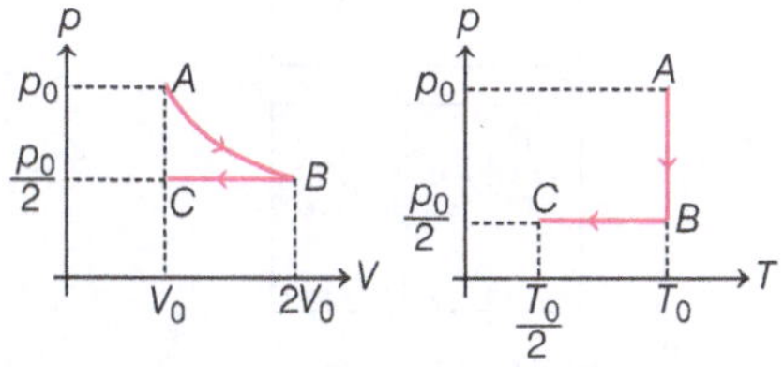

(b) For the process AB,

$$\frac{p_0 V_0}{T_0} = \frac{p_B(2V_0)}{T_0}$$

$$\therefore \quad p_B = \frac{p_0}{2}$$

$$\Delta U = 0$$

$$Q = W + \Delta U$$

$$= nRT \ln \frac{V_B}{V_A}$$

$$= 3RT_0 \ln 2$$

For the process BC,

$$\frac{2V_0}{T_0} = \frac{V_0}{T_C}$$

$$\therefore \quad T_C = \frac{T_0}{2}$$

$$W = nR\Delta T = 3R\left(\frac{T_0}{2} - T_0\right) = -\frac{3}{2}RT_0$$

$$Q = nC_p \Delta T = -\frac{21}{4}RT_0$$

$$\therefore \quad W_{\text{Total}} = 3RT_0 \ln(2) - \frac{3}{2}RT_0$$

(c) $Q_{\text{Total}} = 3RT_0 \ln(2) - \frac{21}{4}RT_0$

136. (a)

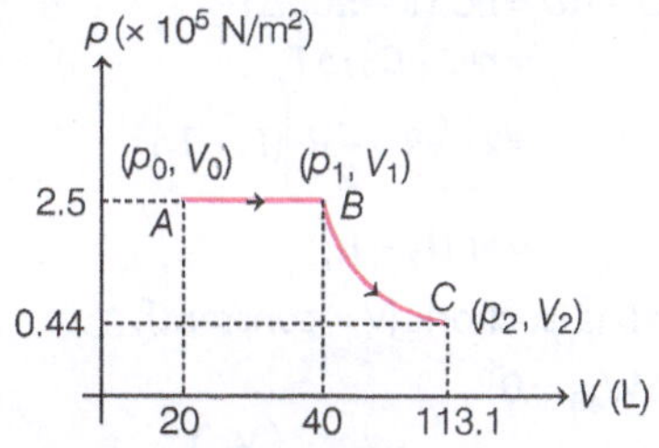

(b) $p_0 = \frac{nRT_0}{V_0} = \frac{2 \times 8.31 \times 300}{20 \times 10^{-3}}$

$$= 2.5 \times 10^5 \text{ N/m}^2$$

$$p_1 = p_0 = 2.5 \times 10^5 \text{ N/m}^2$$

$$V_1 = 2V = 40 \times 10^{-3} \text{ m}^3$$

Process AB : $\quad V \propto T$

$\therefore \quad T_1 = 2T_0 = 600 \text{ K}$

Process BC

Using $T_1 V_1^{\gamma - 1} = T_2 V_2^{\gamma - 1}$, we get

$$V_2 = 2\sqrt{2}V_1 = 113.1 \times 10^{-3} \text{ m}^3$$

$$= 113.1 \text{ L}$$

and $\quad p_2 = \frac{nRT_2}{V_2} = \frac{(2)(8.31)(300)}{113.1 \times 10^{-3}}$

$$= 0.44 \times 10^5 \text{ N/m}^2$$

(c) $W_{\text{Total}} = W_1 + W_2$

$$= p_0(V_1 - V_0) + \frac{nR}{\gamma - 1}(T_1 - T_2)$$

Substituting the values, we get

$$W_{\text{Total}} = 12479 \text{ J}$$

137. (a) $\frac{p_1 V_1}{T_1} = \frac{p_2 V_2}{T_2}$

$$T_2 = \left(\frac{p_2 V_2 T_1}{p_1 V_1}\right) \quad \text{...(i)}$$

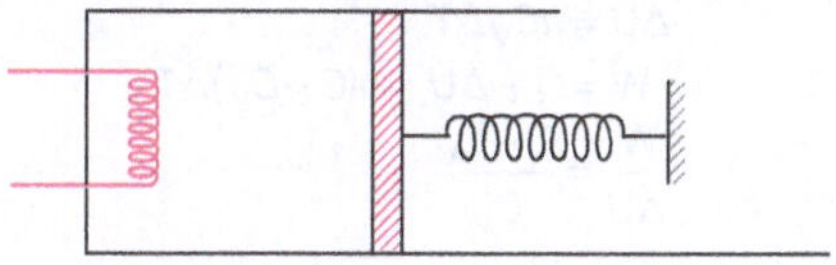

Here, $\quad p_1 = 1.0 \times 10^5 \text{ N/m}^2$

$$V_1 = 2.4 \times 10^{-3} \text{ m}^3$$

$$T_1 = 300 \text{ K}$$

$$p_2 = p_1 + \frac{kx}{A}$$

$$= 1.0 \times 10^5 + \frac{8000 \times 0.1}{8 \times 10^{-3}}$$

$$= 2.0 \times 10^5 \text{ N/m}^2$$

$$V_2 = V_1 + Ax$$

$$= 2.4 \times 10^{-3} + 8 \times 10^{-3} \times 0.1$$

$$= 3.2 \times 10^{-3} \text{ m}^3$$

Substituting in Eq. (i), we get

$$T_2 = 800 \text{ K}$$

(b) Heat supplied by the heater,

$$Q = W + \Delta U$$

Here, $\Delta U = nC_V \Delta T$

$$= \left(\frac{p_1 V_1}{RT_1}\right)\left(\frac{3}{2}R\right)(800 - 300)$$

$$= \frac{(1.0 \times 10^5)(2.4 \times 10^{-3})(1.5)(500)}{(300)}$$

$$= 600 \text{ J}$$

$$W = \frac{1}{2}kx^2 + p_1\Delta V$$
$$= \frac{1}{2}\times(8000)(0.1)^2 + (1.0\times10^5)(0.1)(8\times10^{-3})$$
$$= (40 + 80)\text{ J} = 120\text{ J}$$
$\therefore$ $Q = 600 + 120 = 720$ J

138. $U \propto \sqrt{V}$

As $U \propto T$

$\therefore$ $T \propto V^{1/2}$

or $TV^{-1/2} = \text{constant}$

or $pV^{1/2} = \text{constant}$

Comparing with $pV^x = \text{constant}$, we have

$$x = \frac{1}{2}$$

$\therefore$ Molar specific heat

$$C = \frac{R}{\gamma - 1} + \frac{R}{1 - x}$$
$$= \frac{R}{7/5 - 1} + \frac{R}{1 - 1/2} \qquad (\gamma = 7/5)$$
$$= \frac{5}{2}R + 2R = \frac{9R}{2}$$
$$Q = nC\Delta T$$
$$\Delta U = nC_V\Delta T$$
$\therefore$ $W = Q - \Delta U = n(C - C_V)\Delta T$
$$\frac{W}{\Delta U} = \frac{C - C_V}{C_V}$$
$\therefore$ $W = \left(\frac{C - C_V}{C_V}\right)\Delta U$
$$= \left(\frac{9/2 - 5/2}{5/2}\right)(100) = 80\text{ J}$$

139. $dQ = dU + dW$

$$CdT = C_V\,dT + pdV$$
$$(C_V + 3aT^2)\,dT = C_V\,dT + pdV$$
$\therefore$ $3aT^2\,dT = pdV = \left(\frac{RT}{V}\right)dV$

$\therefore$ $\left(\frac{3a}{R}\right)TdT = \frac{dV}{V}$

On integrating, we get

$$\left(\frac{3aT^2}{2R}\right) = \ln V - \ln C$$
$$V = Ce^{\frac{3aT^2}{2R}} \quad \text{or} \quad Ve^{-\frac{3aT^2}{2R}} = \text{constant}$$

140. (a) $p = \alpha T^{1/2}$

or $pT^{-1/2} = \text{constant}$

$$p^{1/2}V^{-1/2} = \text{constant}$$
$$pV^{-1} = \text{constant}$$
$\therefore$ $x = -1$

$$\Delta W = \left(\frac{R}{1 - x}\right)(\Delta T)$$
$$= \left(\frac{8.31}{2}\right)(50)$$
$$= 207.75\text{ J}$$

(b) $C = C_V + \frac{R}{1 - x} = \frac{3}{2}R + \frac{R}{2} = 2R$

141.

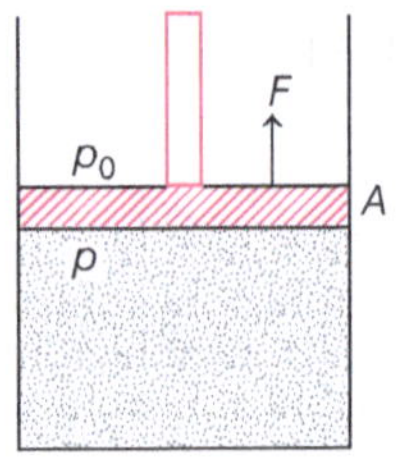

$$F + pA = p_0A$$
$$F = (p_0 - p)A$$
$$W = \int_V^{2V}(p_0 - p)A\,dx$$
$$= \int_V^{2V}p_0\,dV - \int_V^{2V}pdV$$
$$= p_0V - \int_V^{2V}RT\left(\frac{dV}{V}\right)$$
$$= p_0V - RT\ln(2)$$
$$= RT - RT\ln(2)$$
$$= RT(1 - \ln 2)$$

142. (a) $p \propto \frac{1}{T}$ or $pT = \text{constant}$

$\therefore$ $p(pV)) = \text{constant}$

or $pV^{1/2} = \text{constant}$

In the process, $pV^x = \text{constant}$

Molar heat capacity is

$$C = C_V + \frac{R}{1 - x}$$
or $C = \frac{3}{2}R + \frac{R}{1 - \frac{1}{2}}$
$$= \frac{3}{2}R + 2R = \frac{7}{2}R$$

(b) $W = Q - \Delta U = nC\Delta T - nC_V\Delta T$
$$= n(C - C_V)\Delta T$$
$$= 2\left[\frac{7}{2}R - \frac{3}{2}R\right](T_2 - T_1)$$
$$= 4R(T_2 - T_1)$$

143. Process AB is isochoric ($V = \text{constant}$).

Hence, $\Delta W_{AB} = 0$

$$\Delta W_{BCD} = p_0V_0 + \frac{\pi}{2}(p_0)\left(\frac{V_0}{2}\right)$$
$$= \left(\frac{\pi}{4} + 1\right)p_0V_0$$

$$\Delta W_{DA} = -\frac{1}{2}\left(\frac{p_0}{2} + p_0\right)(2V_0 - V_0)$$

$$= -\frac{3}{4}p_0V_0$$

$$\Delta U_{AB} = nC_V\Delta T = (2)\left(\frac{3}{2}R\right)(T_B - T_A) \qquad \left(n = 2, C_V = \frac{3}{2}R\right)$$

$$= 3R\left(\frac{p_0V_0}{2R} - \frac{p_0V_0}{4R}\right)$$

$$= \frac{3}{4}p_0V_0 = \Delta Q_{AB} \qquad \left(T = \frac{pV}{nR}\right)$$

$$\Delta U_{BCD} = nC_V\Delta T = (2)\left(\frac{3}{2}R\right)(T_D - T_B)$$

$$= (3R)\left(\frac{2p_0V_0}{2R} - \frac{p_0V_0}{2R}\right) = \frac{3}{2}p_0V_0$$

Hence, $\Delta Q_{BCD} = \Delta U_{BCD} + \Delta W_{BCD}$

$$= \left(\frac{\pi}{4} + \frac{5}{2}\right)p_0V_0$$

$$\Delta U_{DA} = nC_V\Delta T$$

$$= (2)\left(\frac{3}{2}R\right)(T_A - T_D)$$

$$= (3R)\left(\frac{p_0V_0}{4R} - \frac{2p_0V_0}{2R}\right)$$

$$= -\frac{9}{4}p_0V_0$$

$$\therefore \quad \Delta Q_{DA} = \Delta U_{DA} + \Delta W_{DA}$$

$$= -\frac{9}{4}p_0V_0 - \frac{3}{4}p_0V_0$$

$$= -3p_0V_0$$

Net work done is,

$$W_{net} = \left(\frac{\pi}{4} + 1 - \frac{3}{4}\right)p_0V_0$$

$$= 1.04\,p_0V_0$$

and heat absorbed is

$$Q_{ab} = \Delta Q_{+ve}$$

$$= \left(\frac{3}{4} + \frac{\pi}{4} + \frac{5}{2}\right)p_0V_0 = 4.03\,p_0V_0$$

Hence, efficiency of the cycle is

$$\eta = \frac{W_{net}}{Q_{ab}} \times 100$$

$$= \frac{1.04\,p_0V_0}{4.03\,p_0V_0} \times 100$$

$$= 25.8\%$$

144. $p = \dfrac{\alpha T - \beta T^2}{V}$ $\qquad (p = \text{constant})$

Hence, $\quad V = \dfrac{\alpha T - \beta T^2}{p}$

or $\quad dV = \left(\dfrac{\alpha - 2\beta T}{p}\right)dT$

$$W = \int p\,dV = \int_{T_1}^{T_2} p\left(\frac{\alpha - 2\beta T}{p}\right)dT$$

or $\quad W = [\alpha T - \beta T^2]_{T_1}^{T_2}$

$$= \alpha(T_2 - T_1) - \beta(T_2^2 - T_1^2)$$

145. Given,

Number of moles, $n = 2$

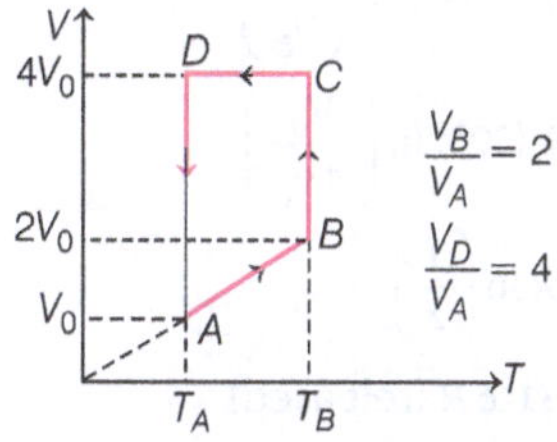

$\dfrac{V_B}{V_A} = 2$ and $\dfrac{V_D}{V_A} = 4$

$$C_V = \frac{3}{2}R$$

and $\quad C_p = \dfrac{5}{2}R \qquad$ (monoatomic)

$$T_A = 27°C = 300\,K$$

Let $\quad V_A = V_0$, then $V_B = 2V_0$

and $\quad V_D = V_C = 4V_0$

(a) **Process $A \to B$**

$$V \propto T \Rightarrow \frac{T_B}{T_A} = \frac{V_B}{V_A}$$

$$\therefore \quad T_B = T_A\left(\frac{V_B}{V_A}\right) = (300)(2) = 600\,K$$

$$\therefore \quad T_B = 600\,K$$

(b) **Process $A \to B$**

$$V \propto T \Rightarrow p = \text{constant}$$

$$\therefore \quad Q_{AB} = nC_p dT = nC_p(T_B - T_A)$$

$$= (2)\left(\frac{5}{2}R\right)(600 - 300)$$

$$Q_{AB} = 1500R \qquad \text{(absorbed)}$$

Process $B \to C$

$$T = \text{constant}$$

$$\therefore \quad \Delta U = 0$$

$$\therefore \quad Q_{BC} = W_{BC} = nRT_B \ln\left(\frac{V_C}{V_B}\right)$$

$$= (2)(R)(600)\ln\left(\frac{4V_0}{2V_0}\right)$$

$$= (1200R)\ln(2)$$

$$= (1200R)(0.693)$$

or $Q_{BC} \approx 831.6\,R$ (absorbed)

Process $C \to D$

$$V = \text{constant}$$

$$\therefore Q_{CD} = nC_V\,dT$$

$$= nC_V(T_D - T_C)$$

$$= n\left(\frac{3}{2}R\right)(T_A - T_B)$$

($T_D = T_A$ and $T_C = T_B$)

$$= (2)\left(\frac{3}{2}R\right)(300 - 600)$$

$$Q_{CD} = -900\,R \text{ (released)}$$

Process $D \to A$

$$T = \text{constant} \Rightarrow \Delta U = 0$$

$$\therefore Q_{DA} = W_{DA} = nRT_D \ln\left(\frac{V_A}{V_D}\right)$$

$$= (2)(R)(300)\ln\left(\frac{V_0}{4V_0}\right)$$

$$= 600 R \ln\left(\frac{1}{4}\right)$$

$$Q_{DA} \approx -831.6\,R \text{ (released)}$$

(c) **In the complete cycle**

$$\Delta U = 0$$

Therefore, from conservation of energy

$$W_{net} = Q_{AB} + Q_{BC} + Q_{CD} + Q_{DA}$$

$$W_{net} = 1500R + 831.6R - 900R - 831.6R$$

$$= 600\,R$$

146. (a) Number of moles,

$$n = 2,\ T_1 = 300\text{ K}$$

During the process $A \to B$

$$pT = \text{constant}$$

or $$p^2V = \text{constant} = K \text{ (say)}$$

$$\therefore \quad p = \frac{\sqrt{K}}{\sqrt{V}}$$

$$\therefore \quad W_{A \to B} = \int_{V_A}^{V_B} p.dV$$

$$= \int_{V_A}^{V_B} \frac{\sqrt{K}}{\sqrt{V}} dV$$

$$= 2\sqrt{K}[\sqrt{V_B} - \sqrt{V_A}]$$

$$= 2[\sqrt{KV_B} - \sqrt{KV_A}]$$

$$= 2[\sqrt{(p_B^2V_B)V_B} - \sqrt{(p_A^2V_A)V_A}]$$

$$= 2[p_BV_B - p_AV_A]$$

$$= 2[nRT_B - nRT_A]$$

$$= 2\,nR\,[T_1 - 2T_1]$$

$$= (2)(2)(R)[300 - 600]$$

$$= -1200\,R$$

$\therefore$ Work done on the gas in the process AB is $1200\,R$.

(b) **Heat absorbed/released in different processes.**

Since, the gas is monoatomic.

Therefore, $C_V = \frac{3}{2}R$

and $$C_p = \frac{5}{2}R$$

and $$\gamma = \frac{5}{3}$$

Process $A \to B$

$$\Delta U = nC_V\Delta T$$

$$= (2)\left(\frac{3}{2}R\right)(T_B - T_A)$$

$$= (2)\left(\frac{3}{2}R\right)(300 - 600)$$

$$= -900\,R$$

$$\therefore \quad Q_{A \to B} = W_{A \to B} + \Delta U$$

$$= (-1200R) - (900R)$$

$$Q_{A \to B} = -2100R \quad \text{(released)}$$

Process $B \to C$

Process is isobaric.

$$\therefore Q_{B \to C} = nC_p\Delta T = (2)\left(\frac{5}{2}R\right)(T_C - T_B)$$

$$= 2\left(\frac{5}{2}R\right)(2T_1 - T_1) = (5R)(600 - 300)$$

$$Q_{B \to C} = 1500\,R \text{ (absorbed)}$$

Process $C \to A$

Process is isothermal.

$$\therefore \quad \Delta U = 0$$

and $$Q_{C \to A} = W_{C \to A} = nRT_C \ln\left(\frac{p_C}{p_A}\right)$$

$$= nR(2T_1)\ln\left(\frac{2p_1}{p_1}\right) = (2)(R)(600)\ln(2)$$

$$Q_{C \to A} = 831.6\,R \quad \text{(absorbed)}$$

Alternate Solution

(a)

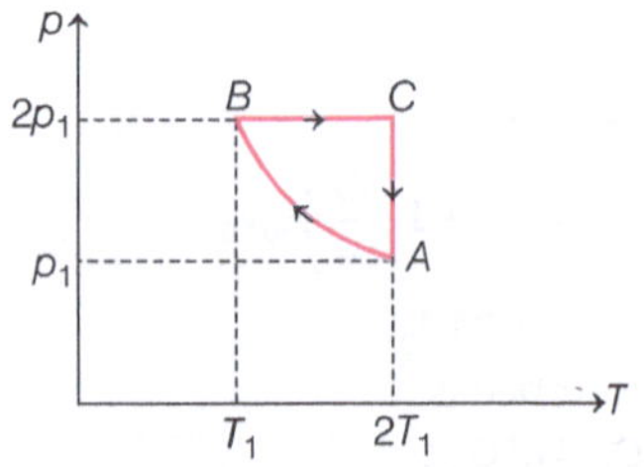

$$pV = nRT$$

$$\therefore \quad pdV + Vdp = nRdT$$

or $$pdV + \frac{(nRT)}{p}\cdot dp = nRdT \quad \text{... (i)}$$

From the given condition

$$pT = \text{constant}$$

$$pdT + Tdp = 0 \quad \text{... (ii)}$$

From Eqs. (i) and (ii), we get

$$pdV = 2nRdT$$

$$\therefore \quad W_{A \to B} = \int pdV = 2nR\int_{T_A}^{T_B} dT = 2nR(T_B - T_A)$$

$$= 2nR(T_1 - 2T_1) = (2)(2)(R)(300 - 600)$$

or $$W_{A \to B} = -1200\,R$$

(b) In the process $pV^x = \text{constant}$

Molar heat capacity, $C = \frac{R}{\gamma - 1} + \frac{R}{1-x}$

Here the process is $p^2V = \text{constant}$

or $pV^{1/2} = \text{constant}$

i.e. $x = \frac{1}{2}$

$\therefore \quad C = \frac{R}{\frac{5}{3} - 1} + \frac{R}{1 - \frac{1}{2}}$

$\therefore \quad C = 3.5\,R$

$\therefore \quad Q_{A \to B} = nC\Delta T = (2)(3.5\,R)(300 - 600)$

or $Q_{A \to B} = -2100\,R$

147. (a) The p-V diagram for the complete process will be as shown below :

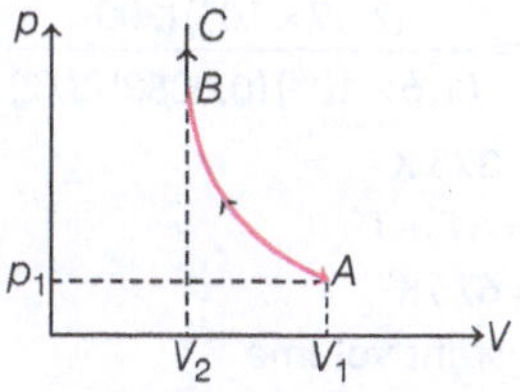

Process $A \to B$ is adiabatic compression and Process $B \to C$ is isochoric.

(b) **(i) Total work done by the gas**

Process $A \to B$

$$W_{AB} = \frac{p_A V_A - p_B V_B}{\gamma - 1}$$

$$W_{\text{adiabatic}} = \frac{p_i V_i - p_f V_f}{\gamma - 1}$$

$$= \frac{p_1 V_1 - p_2 V_2}{\frac{5}{3} - 1}$$

$\gamma = 5/3$ for monoatomic gas

$$= \frac{p_1 V_1 - p_1 \left(\frac{V_1}{V_2}\right)^{\gamma} V_2}{2/3} \quad \left[\begin{array}{c} p_1 V_1^{\gamma} = p_2 V_2^{\gamma} \\ \therefore\ p_2 = p_1 \left(\frac{V_1}{V_2}\right)^{\gamma} \end{array}\right]$$

$$= \frac{3}{2} p_1 V_1 \left[1 - \left(\frac{V_1}{V_2}\right)^{\gamma - 1}\right]$$

$$= -\frac{3}{2} p_1 V_1 \left[\left(\frac{V_1}{V_2}\right)^{5/3 - 1} - 1\right]$$

$$= -\frac{3}{2} p_1 V_1 \left[\left(\frac{V_1}{V_2}\right)^{2/3} - 1\right]$$

Process $B \to C$

$W_{BC} = 0 \qquad (V = \text{constant})$

$\therefore \quad W_{\text{Total}} = W_{AB} + W_{BC}$

$$= -\frac{3}{2} p_1 V_1 \left[\left(\frac{V_1}{V_2}\right)^{2/3} - 1\right]$$

(ii) Total change in internal energy

Process $A \to B$

$Q_{AB} = 0 \qquad$ (Process is adiabatic)

$\therefore \quad \Delta U_{AB} = -W_{AB}$

$$= \frac{3}{2} p_1 V_1 \left[\left(\frac{V_1}{V_2}\right)^{2/3} - 1\right]$$

Process $B \to C$ $W_{BC} = 0$

$\therefore \quad \Delta U_{BC} = Q_{BC} = Q \qquad$ (Given)

$\therefore \quad \Delta U_{\text{Total}} = \Delta U_{AB} + \Delta U_{BC}$

$$= \frac{3}{2} p_1 V_1 \left[\left(\frac{V_1}{V_2}\right)^{2/3} - 1\right] + Q$$

(iii) Final temperature of the gas

$$\Delta U_{\text{Total}} = nC_V \Delta T = 2\left(\frac{R}{\gamma - 1}\right)(T_C - T_A)$$

$$\therefore \quad \frac{3}{2} p_1 V_1 \left[\left(\frac{V_1}{V_2}\right)^{2/3} - 1\right] + Q$$

$$= \frac{2R}{5/3 - 1}\left(T_C - \frac{p_A V_A}{2R}\right)$$

$$\text{or} \quad \frac{3}{2} p_1 V_1 \left[\left(\frac{V_1}{V_2}\right)^{2/3} - 1\right] + Q$$

$$= 3R\left(T_C - \frac{p_1 V_1}{2R}\right)$$

$$\therefore \quad T_C = \frac{Q}{3R} + \frac{p_1 V_1}{2R}\left(\frac{V_1}{V_2}\right)^{2/3} = T_{\text{final}}$$

148. Number of gram moles of He,

$$n = \frac{m}{M} = \frac{2 \times 10^3}{4} = 500$$

(a) $V_A = 10\,\text{m}^3$, $p_A = 5 \times 10^4\ \text{N/m}^2$

$$\therefore \quad T_A = \frac{p_A V_A}{nR} = \frac{(10)(5 \times 10^4)}{(500)(8.31)}\,\text{K}$$

or $T_A = 120.34\ \text{K}$

Similarly, $V_B = 10\,\text{m}^3$, $p_B = 10 \times 10^4\ \text{N/m}^2$

$$\therefore \quad T_B = \frac{(10)(10 \times 10^4)}{(500)(8.31)}\,\text{K}$$

$\therefore \quad T_B = 240.68\ \text{K}$

$V_C = 20\ \text{m}^3$, $p_C = 10 \times 10^4\ \text{N/m}^2$

$$\therefore \quad T_C = \frac{(20)(10 \times 10^4)}{(500)(8.31)}\,\text{K}$$

$T_C = 481.36\ \text{K}$

and $V_D = 20\text{m}^3$, $p_D = 5 \times 10^4\ \text{N/m}^2$

$\therefore \quad V_D = \frac{(20)(5\times 10^4)}{(500)(8.31)} K$

$T_D = 240.68$ K

(b) No, it is not possible to tell afterwards which sample went through the process *ABC* or *ADC*. But during the process if we note down the work done in both the processes, then the process which require more work goes through process *ABC*.

(c) In the process *ABC*,

$$\Delta U = nC_V \, \Delta T = n\left(\frac{3}{2}R\right)(T_C - T_A)$$

$$= (500)\left(\frac{3}{2}\right)(8.31)(481.36 - 120.34) \text{ J}$$

$$\Delta U = 2.25 \times 10^6 \text{ J}$$

and W = Area under *BC*

$$= (20-10)(10)\times 10^4 \text{ J} = 10^6 \text{ J}$$

$$\therefore Q_{ABC} = \Delta U + W = (2.25\times 10^6 + 10^6) \text{ J}$$

$$Q_{ABC} = 3.25 \times 10^6 \text{ J}$$

In the process *ADC* ΔU will be same (because it depends on initial and final temperatures only)

W = Area under *AD*

$$= (20-10)(5\times 10^4) \text{ J} = 0.5\times 10^6 \text{ J}$$

$$Q_{ADC} = \Delta U + W = (2.25\times 10^6 + 0.5\times 10^6) \text{ J}$$

$$Q_{ADC} = 2.75 \times 10^6 \text{ J}$$

149. Given number of moles $n = 2$

Process *AB* and *CD* are isobaric.

Hence, $Q_{AB} = -Q_{CD}$

[Because $(\Delta T)_{AB} = +100$ K whereas $(\Delta T)_{CD} = -100$ K

and $Q_{\text{isobaric}} = nC_p\Delta T$]

or $Q_{AB} + Q_{CD} = 0$

Process *BC* is isothermal ($\Delta U = 0$)

$$\therefore Q_{BC} = W_{BC} = nRT_B \ln\left(\frac{p_B}{p_C}\right) = (2)(8.31)(400)\ln\left(\frac{2}{1}\right)$$

$$Q_{BC} = 4608 \text{ J}$$

Similarly, process *DA* is also isothermal hence,

$$Q_{DA} = W_{DA} = nRT_D \ln\left(\frac{p_D}{p_A}\right) = (2)(8.31)(300)\ln\left(\frac{1}{2}\right)$$

$$Q_{BC} = -3456 \text{ J}$$

(a) Net heat exchange in the process

$$Q = Q_{AB} + Q_{BC} + Q_{CD} + Q_{DA}$$

$$= (4608 - 3456) \text{ J}$$

$$Q = 1152 \text{ J}$$

(b) From first law of thermodynamics, $\Delta U = 0$ (in complete cycle) $Q_{\text{net}} = W_{\text{net}}$

Hence, $W = Q = 1152$ J

(c) Since, $T_i = T_f$, therefore net change in internal energy, $\Delta U = 0$.

150. Vessel is closed. Therefore,

$$W = 0 \quad \text{or} \quad Q = \Delta U = nC_V \, \Delta T$$

$$\Delta T = \frac{Q}{nC_V} = \frac{\Delta Q}{\left(\frac{pV}{RT}\right)(C_p - R)} = \frac{(Q)(RT)}{pV(C_p - R)}$$

Substituting the values, we have

$$\Delta T = \frac{(2.49\times 10^4)(300)}{(1.6\times 10^6)(0.0083)(3/2)} = 375 \text{ K}$$

$$\therefore \quad T_f = \Delta T + T = 675 \text{ K}$$

Further at constant volume

$$\frac{p_2}{p_1} = \frac{T_2}{T_1} \Rightarrow p_2 = \frac{T_2}{T_1} p_1 = \left(\frac{675}{300}\right)(1.6\times 10^6) = 3.6\times 10^6 \text{ N/m}^2$$

151. (a) Applying $\frac{pV}{T}$ = constant for both the chambers.

$$\frac{p_0V_0}{T_0} = \frac{pV_1}{T_1} = \frac{pV_2}{T_2} \qquad \left(\text{Here, } p = \frac{243p_0}{32}\right)$$

$$\therefore \quad V_1 = \frac{32}{243}\left(\frac{T_1}{T_0}\right)V_0$$

and $$V_2 = \left(\frac{32}{243}\right)\left(\frac{T_2}{T_0}\right)V_0$$

Further, $V_1 + V_2 = 2V_0$

or $$\left(\frac{16}{243}\right)(T_1 + T_2) = T_0$$

or $$T_1 + T_2 = \frac{243}{16}T_0 \qquad \text{...(i)}$$

Applying the *p*-*T* equation of adiabatic process to the right chamber,

$$\left(\frac{T_0}{T_2}\right)^{5/3} = \left(\frac{243p_0}{32p_0}\right)^{1-5/3}$$

Solving this equation, we get

$$T_2 = 2.25\,T_0$$

From Eq. (i), $T_1 = 12.94\,T_0$

(b) Work done by the gas in right chamber ($\Delta Q = 0$, adiabatic process)

$$\Delta W = -\Delta U = nC_V(T_i - T_f)$$
$$= (1)\left(\frac{3}{2}R\right)(T_0 - 2.25T_0)$$
$$= -1.875\,RT_0$$

152. In adiabatic process

$$p_i V_i^\gamma = p_f V_f^\gamma$$
$$p_f = \left(\frac{V_i}{V_f}\right)^\gamma p_i \quad \text{...(i)}$$

Further, $C_V = \frac{3R}{2}$

$\therefore$ $C_p = C_V + R = \frac{5R}{2}$

or $\gamma = \frac{C_p}{C_V} = \frac{5}{3}$

$\therefore$ $p_f = \left(\frac{6}{2}\right)^{5/3}(10)^5$

$$= 6.24 \times 10^5\ \text{N/m}^2$$

Now, work done in adiabatic process is given by

$$W = \frac{p_i V_i - p_f V_f}{\gamma - 1}$$
$$= \frac{10^5 \times 6 \times 10^{-3} - 6.24 \times 10^5 \times 2 \times 10^{-3}}{\left(\frac{5}{3}\right) - 1}$$
$$= -972\ \text{J}$$

153. The corresponding p-V diagram is as shown in figure

Given $T_A = 300\,\text{K}$, $n = 1$, $\gamma = 1.4$, $V_A/V_B = 16$

and $V_C/V_B = 2$

Let $V_B = V_0$ and $p_B = p_0$

Then, $V_C = 2V_0$ and $V_A = 16V_0$

Temperature at B

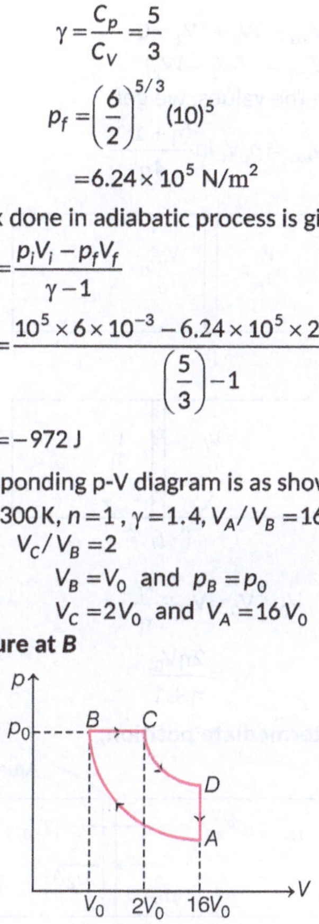

Process *A-B* is adiabatic.

Hence, $T_A V_A^{\gamma-1} = T_B V_B^{\gamma-1}$

or $T_B = T_A\left(\frac{V_A}{V_B}\right)^{\gamma-1}$

$$= (300)(16)^{1.4-1}$$
$$T_B = 909\,\text{K}$$

Temperature at D

$B \to C$ is an isobaric process. (p = constant)

$\therefore$ $T \propto V, V_C = 2V_B$

$\therefore$ $T_C = 2T_B = (2)(909)\,\text{K}$

$$T_C = 1818\,\text{K}$$

Now, the process $C \to D$ is adiabatic.

Therefore,

$$T_D = T_C\left(\frac{V_C}{V_D}\right)^{\gamma-1} = (1818)\left(\frac{2}{16}\right)^{1.4-1}$$
$$T_D = 791.4\ \text{K}$$

Efficiency of cycle

Efficiency of cycle (in percentage) is defined as

$$\eta = \frac{\text{Net work done in the cycle}}{\text{Heat absorbed in the cycle}} \times 100$$

or $\eta = \frac{W_{\text{Total}}}{Q_{+\text{ve}}} \times 100$

$$= \frac{Q_{+\text{ve}} - Q_{-\text{ve}}}{Q_{+\text{ve}}} \times 100$$
$$= \left(1 - \frac{Q_1}{Q_2}\right) \times 100 \quad \text{...(i)}$$

where, Q_1 = negative heat in the cycle (heat released)

and Q_2 = positive heat in the cycle (heat absorbed)

In the cycle

$Q_{AB} = Q_{CD} = 0$ (Adiabatic process)

$$Q_{DA} = nC_V\,\Delta T = (1)\left(\frac{5}{2}R\right)(T_A - T_D)$$

($C_V = \frac{5}{2}R$ for a diatomic gas)

$$= \frac{5}{2} \times 8.31(300 - 791.4)\ \text{J}$$

or $Q_{DA} = -10208.8\ \text{J}$

and $Q_{BC} = nC_p\Delta T$

$$= (1)\left(\frac{7}{2}R\right)(T_C - T_B)$$

($C_p = \frac{7}{2}R$ for a diatomic gas)

$$= \left(\frac{7}{2}\right)(8.31)(1818 - 909)\ \text{J}$$

or $Q_{BC} = 26438.3\ \text{J}$

Therefore, substituting $Q_1 = 10208.8\ \text{J}$ and $Q_2 = 26438.3\ \text{J}$ in Eq. (i), we get

$\therefore$ $\eta = \left\{1 - \frac{10208.8}{26438.3}\right\} \times 100$

or $\eta = 61.4\ \%$

154. Let final temperature is T and the pressure is p.

$$(n_1 + n_2)_i = (n_1 + n_2)_f$$

$\Rightarrow$ $\frac{p_1V_1}{RT_1} + \frac{p_2V_2}{RT_2} = \frac{p(V_1 + V_2)}{RT}$

$\therefore$ $\frac{p_1V_1}{T_1} + \frac{p_2V_2}{T_2} = \frac{p(V_1 + V_2)}{T}$ ...(i)

Vessels are thermally insulated. So,

$$\Delta U_1 + \Delta U_2 = 0$$

Here $\Delta U = nC_V \Delta T = \left(\frac{pV}{RT}\right) C_V \Delta T$

$$\therefore \quad \frac{p_1V_1}{RT_1} C_V (T - T_1) + \frac{p_2V_2}{RT_2} C_V (T - T_2) = 0$$

or
$$\frac{p_1V_1(T - T_1)}{T_1} + \frac{p_2V_2(T - T_2)}{T_2} = 0 \qquad \text{...(ii)}$$

We have two equations p and T.

Solving these two equations, we get

$$T = T_1T_2 \left(\frac{p_1V_1 + p_2V_2}{p_1V_1T_2 + p_2V_2T_1}\right)$$

and
$$p = \frac{p_1V_1 + p_2V_2}{V_1 + V_2}$$

155. In isothermal process, work done by the gas is given by, (for 1 mole)

$$W_1 = RT \ln \frac{V_f}{V_i}$$

Here, $\frac{V_f}{V_i} = n$

$$\therefore \quad W_1 = RT \ln (n) \qquad \text{...(i)}$$

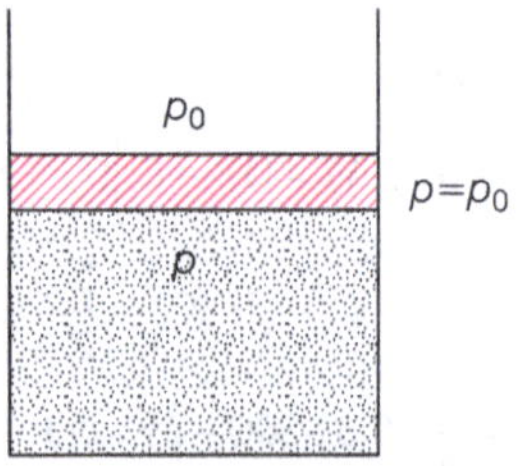

Now negative work is done on the gas by the atmosphere ($p_{gas} = p_0 = p$, say). Because force due to atmospheric pressure is opposite to displacement of piston. This work is done under isobaric process.

Hence,
$$W_2 = -p\Delta V = -p(nV - V) = -pV(n-1) = -RT(n-1)$$

Let, net work done by external forces is W_{ext}. Then using work-energy theorem,

$$W_1 + W_2 + W_{ext} = \Delta KE = 0$$

$$\therefore \quad W_{ext} = -(W_1 + W_2)$$

Substituting the values of W_1 and W_2, we get

$$W_{ext} = RT\,(n - 1 - \ln n)$$

Note *To move the piston slowly some external work will have to be done. Some external force will have to be applied to keep the piston moving slowly.*

156.

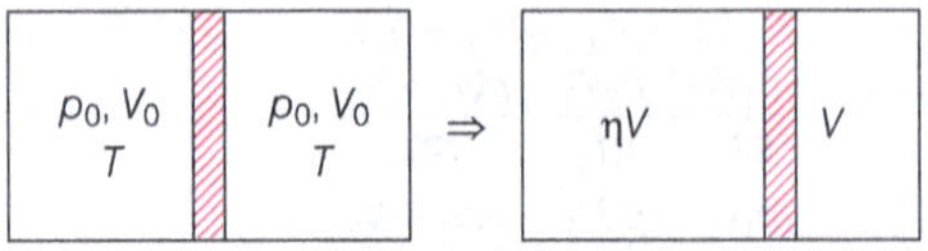

$$\eta V + V = 2V_0$$

$$\therefore \quad \frac{V}{V_0} = \frac{2}{\eta + 1}$$

Work is done under isothermal conditions. Work done by left hand side of the gas,

$$W_1 = nRT \ln \frac{V_f}{V_i} \qquad (nRT = p_0V_0)$$

$$= p_0V_0 \ln \frac{\eta V}{V_0} = p_0V_0 \ln \left(\frac{2\eta}{\eta + 1}\right)$$

Similarly, work done by right hand side of the gas,

$$W_2 = nRT \ln \frac{V_f}{V_i} = nRT \ln \left(\frac{V}{V_0}\right)$$

$$= p_0V_0 \ln \left(\frac{2}{\eta + 1}\right)$$

Proceeding in the same way as was done in previous question,

$$W_{ext} + W_1 + W_2 = 0 \qquad (\text{as } \Delta KE = 0)$$

$$\therefore \quad W_{ext} = -(W_1 + W_2)$$

Substituting the values, we get

$$W_{ext} = p_0V_0 \ln \frac{(\eta + 1)^2}{4\eta}$$

157.

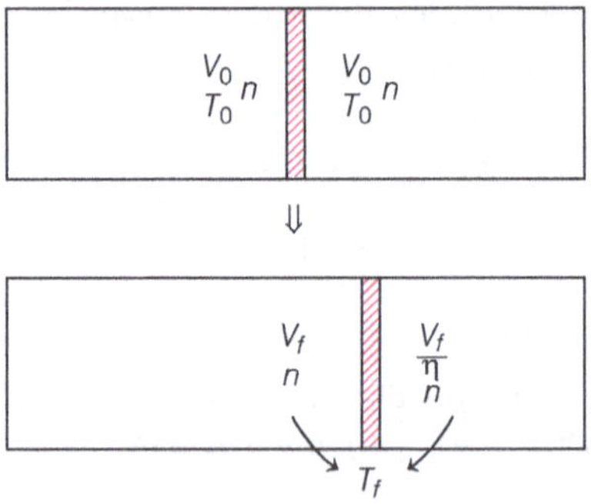

$$V_0 + V_0 = V_f + \frac{V_f}{\eta}$$

$$\Rightarrow \quad V_f = \frac{2\eta V_0}{\eta + 1} \qquad \text{...(i)}$$

At some intermediate position,

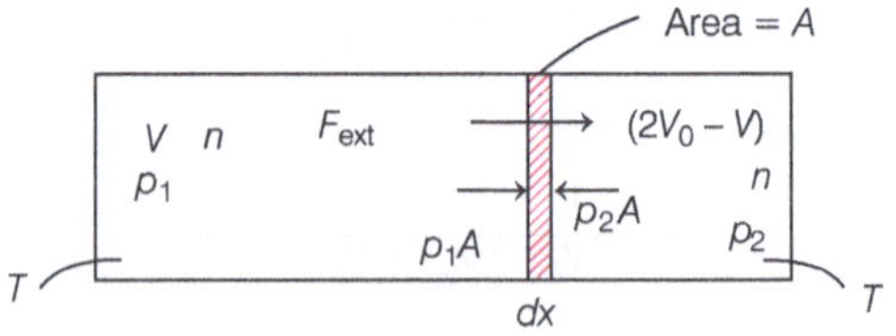

$$F_{ext} = (p_2 - p_1)A$$

$$dW_{ext} = F_{ext}\,dx = (p_2 - p_1)\,A dx = (p_2 - p_1)\,dV$$

$$dW_{ext} = \left[\frac{nRT}{2V_0 - V} - \frac{nRT}{V}\right] dV \qquad \text{...(ii)}$$

System is isolated. Therefore $dQ = 0$.

Or,
$$dW_{ext} = dU_{Total} = dU_{RHS} + dU_{LHS} = 2nC_V dT$$

$$dW_{ext} = 2n\left(\frac{R}{\gamma - 1}\right) dT \qquad \text{...(iii)}$$

Equating Eqs. (ii) and (iii), we get

$$nRT\left[\frac{1}{2V_0-V}-\frac{1}{V}\right]dV=\frac{2nRdT}{\gamma-1}$$

$$\therefore \quad \int_{T_0}^{T_f}\frac{dT}{T}=\frac{\gamma-1}{2}\int_{V_0}^{V_f}\left[\frac{1}{2V_0-V}-\frac{1}{V}\right]dV$$

Solving this integration with V_f given by Eq. (i), we get

$$T_f=T_0\left[\left\{\frac{(\eta+1)^2}{4\eta}\right\}^{\frac{\gamma-1}{2}}\right]$$

158. $dW=dU$

$$\Rightarrow \quad pdV=nC_VdT=n\left(\frac{R}{\gamma-1}\right)dT \quad ...(i)$$

Further, $\quad pV=nRT$

$\therefore \quad pdV+Vdp=nRdT$

Substituting this value of $nRdT$ in Eq. (i), we have

$$(\gamma-1)\,pdV=(pdV)+Vdp$$

$$\Rightarrow \quad (\gamma-2)\,pdV=Vdp$$

Dividing this equation by pV, we get

$$(\gamma-2)\frac{dV}{V}=\frac{dp}{p}$$

Integrating, we get

$$C+\ln V^{\gamma-2}=\ln p$$

or $\quad \ln pV^{2-\gamma}=C$

or $\quad pV^{2-\gamma}=e^C=\text{constant}$

or $\quad pV^n=\text{constant}$

where, $n=2-\gamma=\text{constant}$ **Hence proved.**

159. (c) $p=\alpha V$ or $p\propto V$

$$\Rightarrow \quad pV^{-1}=\text{constant}$$

$$n=-1$$

$\therefore$ Molar heat capacity

$$C=\frac{(n-\gamma)R}{(n-1)(\gamma-1)}$$

$$C=\frac{(\gamma+1)R}{2(\gamma-1)}$$

$$p=\alpha V$$

$$\frac{fRT}{V}=\alpha V$$

(Here f = number of moles)

$$T=\frac{\alpha V^2}{fR}$$

$$T_i=\frac{\alpha V_0^2}{fR}$$

$$T_f=\frac{\alpha(\eta^2V_0^2)}{fR}$$

$$\therefore \quad \Delta T=T_f-T_i=\frac{(\eta^2-1)\alpha V_0^2}{fR}$$

(a) $\Delta U=fC_V\Delta T$

$$=f\left(\frac{R}{\gamma-1}\right)\frac{(\eta^2-1)\,\alpha\, V_0^2}{fR}$$

or $\quad \Delta U=\left(\frac{\eta^2-1}{\gamma-1}\right)\alpha V_0^2$

(b) $Q=fC\Delta T$

$$=f\left[\frac{\gamma+1}{2(\gamma-1)}\right]R\left[\frac{(\eta^2-1)\,\alpha\, V_0^2}{fR}\right]$$

$$=\frac{(\gamma+1)(\eta^2-1)}{2(\gamma-1)}\alpha V_0^2$$

$$W=Q-\Delta U$$

Substituting the values of Q and ΔU, we get

$$W=\frac{\alpha V_0^2}{2}(\eta^2-1)$$

160. (a) $dQ=-dU$ (Given)

$\therefore \quad nCdT=-nC_VdT$

or $\quad C=-C_V$

or $\quad C=-\dfrac{R}{(\gamma-1)}$

(b) $dQ=dU+dW=-dU$

$$\therefore \quad 2dU+dW=0 \quad ...(i)$$

$$\therefore \quad 2nC_V\,dT+pdV=0$$

$$\Rightarrow \quad 2n\left(\frac{R}{\gamma-1}\right)dT+pdV=0$$

$$\Rightarrow \quad \frac{2nRdT}{\gamma-1}+\frac{nRT}{V}\cdot dV=0 \quad \left(p=\frac{nRT}{V}\right)$$

Dividing this equation by nRT, we have

$$\frac{2}{\gamma-1}\frac{dT}{T}+\frac{dV}{V}=0$$

Integrating, we get

$$\frac{2}{\gamma-1}\ln T+\ln V=C$$

or $\quad \ln\left[T^{\frac{2}{\gamma-1}}V\right]=C$

or $\quad T^{\frac{2}{\gamma-1}}V=e^C=\text{constant}$

or, we can also write

$$TV^{\frac{\gamma-1}{2}}=\text{constant}$$

(c) $TV^{\frac{\gamma-1}{2}}=\text{constant}$

$$\therefore \quad T_fV_f^{\frac{\gamma-1}{2}}=T_iV_i^{\frac{\gamma-1}{2}}$$

$$\Rightarrow \quad T_f=\left(\frac{V_i}{V_f}\right)^{\frac{\gamma-1}{2}}T_i$$

$$=\left(\frac{1}{\eta}\right)^{\frac{\gamma-1}{2}}T_0=\eta^{\frac{1-\gamma}{2}}T_0$$

Now from Eq. (i), we have

$$W = -2\,\Delta U$$
$$= -2\,nC_V\Delta T$$
$$= -2(1)\left(\frac{R}{\gamma-1}\right)(T_f - T_i)$$
$$= \frac{2R}{\gamma-1}(T_i - T_f)$$
$$= \frac{2R}{\gamma-1}\left[T_0 - \eta^{\frac{1-\gamma}{2}}T_0\right]$$

Thus, $W = \frac{2RT_0}{\gamma-1}\left(1-\eta^{\frac{1-\gamma}{2}}\right)$

161. (a) $p = \alpha T^a$

$\Rightarrow \quad pT^{-a} = \text{constant}$

or $\quad p\left(\frac{pV}{nR}\right)^{-a} = \text{constant}$

$\Rightarrow \quad p^{1-a}V^{-a} = \text{constant}$

or $\quad pV^{\frac{-a}{1-a}} = \text{constant}$

or $\quad pV^{\frac{a}{a-1}} = \text{constant}$

Comparing with $pV^n = \text{constant}$, we have

$$n = \frac{a}{a-1}$$

In the process $pV^n = \text{constant}$.

Molar heat capacity is given by,

$$C = C_V + \frac{R}{1-n} \qquad \text{...(i)}$$

Now, $W = Q - \Delta U$

$$= nC\Delta T - nC_V\Delta T$$
$$= n(C - C_V)\,\Delta T$$

From Eq. (i), $C - C_V = \frac{R}{1-n}$

$\therefore \quad W = \frac{nR\Delta T}{1-n}$

Substituting the values, we get

$$W = \frac{(1)(R)\,\Delta T}{1-\left(\frac{a}{a-1}\right)} = \frac{R\,(a-1)\Delta T}{-1}$$

or $\quad W = (1-a)\,R\Delta T$

(b) From Eq. (i),

$$C = C_V + \frac{R}{1-n} = \frac{R}{\gamma-1} + \frac{R}{1-n}$$
$$= \frac{R}{\gamma-1} + \frac{R}{1-\frac{a}{a-1}}$$

or $\quad C = \frac{R}{\gamma-1} + R(1-a)$

From the above express, we can see that C will be negative if

$$a - 1 > \frac{1}{\gamma-1}$$

or $\quad a > 1 + \frac{1}{\gamma-1}$

or $\quad a > \frac{\gamma}{\gamma-1}$

162. (a) $\Delta U = nC_V\Delta T = n\left(\frac{R}{\gamma-1}\right)\Delta T$

$\Rightarrow \quad nR\Delta T = (\gamma-1)\,\Delta U$

$$Q = nC\Delta T$$
$$= n\left[\frac{R}{\gamma-1} + \frac{R}{a}\right]\Delta T$$

Substituting $nR\Delta T = (\gamma-1)\,\Delta U$, we get

$$Q = \left(1 + \frac{\gamma-1}{a}\right)\Delta U$$
$$W = Q - \Delta U$$
$$= nC\Delta T - nC_V\Delta T$$
$$= n(C - C_V)\,\Delta T$$
$$= n\left[\frac{R}{\gamma-1} + \frac{R}{a} - \frac{R}{\gamma-1}\right]\Delta T$$
$$= \frac{nR\Delta T}{a}$$

Substituting $nR\Delta T = (\gamma-1)\,\Delta U$, we have

$$W = \frac{(\gamma-1)\,\Delta U}{a}$$

(b) Internal energy of an ideal gas is given by,

$$U = \frac{nf}{2}RT$$

Here n = number of moles and

f = degree of freedom

Putting $nRT = pV$, we have

$$U = \frac{f}{2}pV = \alpha V^a \qquad \text{(Given)}$$

$\Rightarrow \quad pV^{1-a} = \text{constant}$

Comparing with $pV^n = \text{constant}$, we have

$$n = 1-a \quad \text{or} \quad 1-n = a$$

$\therefore$ Molar heat capacity,

$$C = C_V + \frac{R}{1-n} = \frac{R}{\gamma-1} + \frac{R}{a}$$

or $\quad C = \frac{R}{\gamma-1} + \frac{R}{a}$

163. (a) $C = \frac{dQ}{ndT} = \frac{dU + dW}{ndT}$

$$= \frac{nC_VdT + pdV}{ndT}$$
$$C = C_V + \frac{pdV}{ndT} \qquad \text{...(i)}$$

Now let us find $\frac{pdV}{ndT}$.

$$p = \frac{nRT}{V} = \frac{nRT_0e^{\alpha V}}{V} \quad \text{...(ii)}$$

$$T = T_0e^{\alpha V}$$

$$\therefore \quad \frac{dT}{dV} = T_0\alpha e^{\alpha V}$$

or $$\frac{dV}{dT} = \frac{1}{T_0\alpha e^{\alpha V}} \quad \text{...(iii)}$$

From Eqs. (ii) and (iii), we get

$$\frac{pdV}{ndT} = \frac{R}{\alpha V}$$

Substituting in Eq. (i), we get

$$C = C_V + \frac{R}{\alpha V}$$

(b) $p = p_0\, e^{\alpha V}$ ...(iv)

$$T = \frac{pV}{nR} = \left(\frac{p_0e^{\alpha V}}{nR}\right)V$$

$$\frac{dT}{dV} = \frac{p_0\alpha e^{\alpha V}}{nR}(1 + \alpha V)$$

or $$\frac{dV}{dT} = \frac{nR}{p_0\alpha e^{\alpha V}(1 + \alpha V)} \quad \text{...(v)}$$

From Eqs. (iv) and (v), we get

$$\frac{pdV}{ndT} = \frac{R}{1 + \alpha V}$$

Substituting in Eq. (i), we get

$$C = C_V + \frac{R}{1 + \alpha V}$$

164. (a) We will use the result of previous Q.No-164.

$$p = p_0 + \frac{\alpha}{V}$$

$$T = \frac{pV}{nR} = \frac{p_0V + \alpha}{nR}$$

$$\frac{dT}{dV} = \frac{p_0}{nR} \text{ or } \frac{dV}{dT} = \frac{nR}{p_0}$$

$$\therefore \quad \frac{pdV}{ndT} = \left(p_0 + \frac{\alpha}{V}\right)\left(\frac{R}{p_0}\right) = R\left[1 + \frac{\alpha}{Vp_0}\right]$$

Using Eq. (i) of Q-164, we have

$$C = C_V + \frac{pdV}{ndT}$$

or $$C = \frac{R}{\gamma - 1} + R\left[1 + \frac{\alpha}{Vp_0}\right]$$

or $$C = \frac{\gamma R}{\gamma - 1} + \frac{\alpha R}{p_0V}$$

(b) $T = \frac{p_0V + \alpha}{nR}$

At volume V_1, temperature,

$$T_1 = \frac{p_0V_1 + \alpha}{nR}$$

At volume V_2, temperature,

$$T_2 = \frac{p_0V_2 + \alpha}{nR}$$

So, $\Delta T = T_2 - T_1 = \frac{p_0(V_2 - V_1)}{nR}$

$$n = 1$$

ΔU

$$\Delta U = nC_V\Delta T = n\left(\frac{R}{\gamma - 1}\right)\left[\frac{p_0(V_2 - V_1)}{nR}\right]$$

$$\Delta U = \frac{p_0\,(V_2 - V_1)}{\gamma - 1}$$

W $$W = \int_{V_1}^{V_2} pdV = \int_{V_1}^{V_2}\left(p_0 + \frac{\alpha}{V}\right)dV$$

or $$W = p_0(V_2 - V_1) + \alpha\ln\left(\frac{V_2}{V_1}\right)$$

Q $$Q = W + \Delta U$$

$$\therefore \quad Q = \frac{\gamma p_0(V_2 - V_1)}{\gamma - 1} + \alpha\ln\left(\frac{V_2}{V_1}\right)$$

165. (a) ***Note*** In the given process molar heat capacity C is asked. Using the result of Eq. (i) used in Q-164,

$$C = C_V + p\frac{dV}{ndT} \quad \text{...(i)}$$

Here, $T = T_0 + \alpha V$

$$p = \frac{nRT}{V} = nR\left(\alpha + \frac{T_0}{V}\right)$$

$$\frac{dT}{dV} = \alpha$$

or $$\frac{dV}{dT} = \frac{1}{\alpha} \quad \text{...(ii)}$$

$$\therefore \quad \frac{pdV}{ndT} = R\left(1 + \frac{T_0}{\alpha V}\right)$$

Substituting in Eq. (i), we have

$$C = C_V + R\left(1 + \frac{T_0}{\alpha V}\right)$$

But $C_V + R = p$

$$\therefore \quad C = C_p + \frac{RT_0}{\alpha V}$$

(b) From Eq. (ii), we have

$$dT = \alpha dV$$

$$dQ = nCdT = (1)\left[C_p + \frac{RT_0}{\alpha V}\right](\alpha dV)$$

$$= \left[\alpha C_pdV + RT_0\frac{dV}{V}\right]$$

$$\therefore \quad Q = \int_{V_1}^{V_2} dQ = \int_{V_1}^{V_2}\left(\alpha C_pdV + RT_0\frac{dV}{V}\right)$$

or $$Q = \alpha\, C_p(V_2 - V_1) + RT_0\ln\left(\frac{V_2}{V_1}\right)$$

166. (a) $dQ = nCdT = dU + dW$

or $\quad n(C_V + \alpha T)dT = nC_V dT + pdV$

or $\quad n\alpha TdT = pdV = \dfrac{nRT}{V}dV$

or $\quad \alpha dT = R\dfrac{dV}{V}$

Integrating, we get

$$\alpha T = R\ln V + \ln C$$

$\Rightarrow \quad \dfrac{\alpha T}{R} = \ln V + \dfrac{1}{R}\ln C$

$\Rightarrow \quad \ln VC^{\frac{1}{R}} = \dfrac{\alpha T}{R}$

$\therefore \quad VC^{\frac{1}{R}} = e^{\frac{\alpha T}{R}}$

or $\quad Ve^{-\frac{\alpha T}{R}} = \dfrac{1}{C^{1/R}} = \text{constant}$

or $\quad Ve^{-\frac{\alpha T}{R}} = \text{constant}$

(b) $dQ = nCdT = dU + dW$

$\therefore \quad n(C_V + \beta V)\, dT = nC_V dT + pdV$

or $\quad n\beta VdT = pdV = \dfrac{nRT}{V}dV$

or $\quad \dfrac{dT}{T} = \dfrac{R}{\beta}\cdot\dfrac{dV}{V^2}$

Integrating, we get

$\ln C + \ln T = -\dfrac{R}{\beta V}$

or $\quad \ln CT = -\dfrac{R}{\beta V}$

$\therefore \quad CT = e^{-\frac{R}{\beta V}}$

or $\quad Te^{\frac{R}{\beta V}} = \dfrac{1}{C} = \text{constant}$

Thus, $\quad Te^{\frac{R}{\beta V}} = \text{constant}$

(c) $dQ = nCdT = dU + dW$

$\Rightarrow \quad n\,(C_V + ap)\, dT = nC_V dT + pdV$

or $\quad napdT = pdV$

or $\quad nadT = dV$

Integrating, we get

$$naT = V + C$$

For 1 mole we can write $n = 1$

$$V - aT = \text{constant}$$

167. (a)

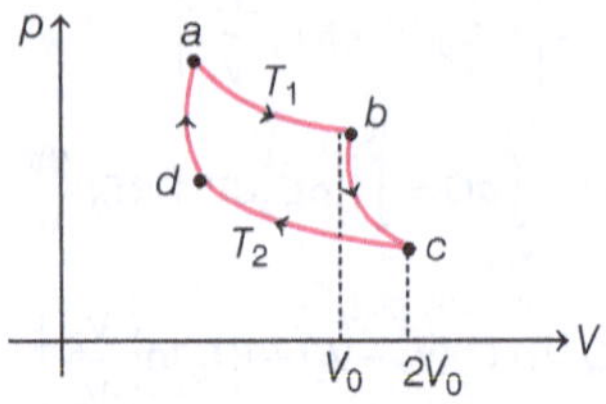

In adiabatic process *bc*

$$T_b V_b^{\gamma-1} = T_c V_c^{\gamma-1} \qquad (TV^{\gamma-1} = \text{constant})$$

For diatomic hydrogen gas,

$$\gamma = \frac{7}{5}$$

or $\quad \gamma - 1 = \dfrac{2}{5}$

$\therefore \quad T_1 V_0^{2/5} = T_2 (2V_0)^{2/5}$

or $\quad \dfrac{T_2}{T_1} = (2)^{-2/5}$

$$\eta = 1 - \frac{T_2}{T_1} = 1 - (2)^{-2/5}$$

or $\quad \eta = 0.25$

(b)

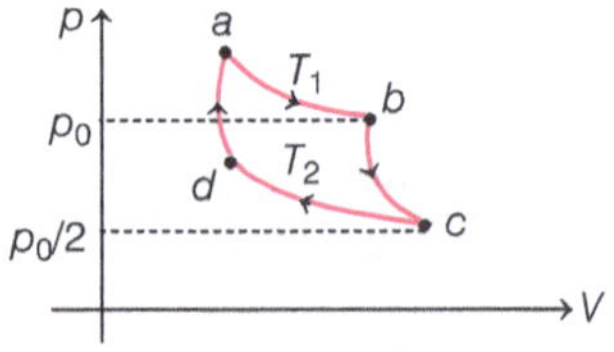

In adiabatic process *bc*

$$T_b^{\gamma} p_b^{1-\gamma} = T_c^{\gamma} p_c^{1-\gamma} \qquad (T^{\gamma} p^{1-\gamma} = \text{constant})$$

or $\quad T_1^{7/5} p_0^{-2/5} = T_2^{7/5} (p_0/2)^{-2/5}$

Solving this equation, we get

$$\frac{T_2}{T_1} = 0.82$$

$\therefore \quad \eta = 1 - \dfrac{T_2}{T_1}$

or $\quad \eta = 0.18$

168.

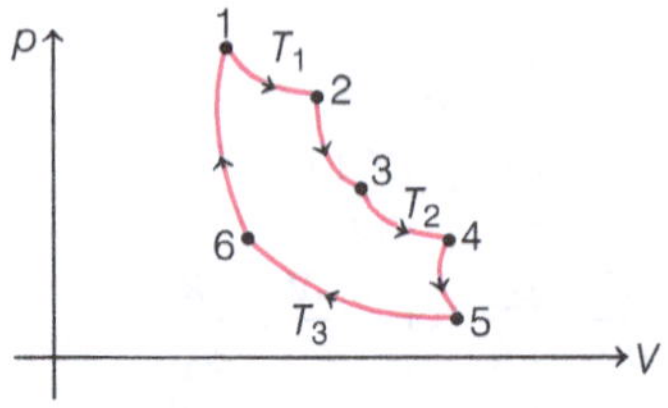

According to the question,

$$\frac{V_2}{V_1} = \frac{V_4}{V_3} = \alpha \text{ (say)}$$

Positive heat (or heat taken by the gas)

$$Q_1 = Q_{12} + Q_{34} \qquad \text{(both isothermal processes)}$$

$$= nRT_1 \ln\left(\frac{V_2}{V_1}\right) + nRT_2 \ln\left(\frac{V_4}{V_3}\right)$$

$$= nR(T_1 + T_2)\ln(\alpha) \qquad \text{...(i)}$$

In adiabatic processes $2 \to 3, 4 \to 5$ and $6 \to 1$,

$$T_1 V_2^{\gamma-1} = T_2 V_3^{\gamma-1}$$

$\Rightarrow \quad V_3 = \left(\dfrac{T_1}{T_2}\right)^{\frac{1}{\gamma-1}} V_2 \qquad \text{...(ii)}$

Similarly, $$V_5 = \left(\frac{T_2}{T_3}\right)^{\frac{1}{\gamma-1}} V_4 \qquad \text{...(iii)}$$

and $$V_6 = \left(\frac{T_1}{T_3}\right)^{\frac{1}{\gamma-1}} V_1 \qquad \text{...(iv)}$$

From Eqs. (iii) and (iv), we get

$$\frac{V_6}{V_5} = \left(\frac{T_1}{T_2}\right)^{\frac{1}{\gamma-1}} \left(\frac{V_1}{V_4}\right)$$

Substituting the value of $\left(\frac{T_1}{T_2}\right)^{\frac{1}{\gamma-1}}$ from Eq. (ii), we have

$$\frac{V_6}{V_5} = \left(\frac{V_3}{V_2}\right)\left(\frac{V_1}{V_4}\right) = \alpha^{-2}$$

Now heat rejected by the gas in the process $5 \to 6$,

$$Q_2 = |Q_{56}| = \left| nRT_3 \ln \frac{V_6}{V_5} \right|$$

$$= 2nRT_3 \ln(\alpha)$$

Now efficiency,

$$\eta = 1 - \frac{Q_2}{Q_1} = 1 - \frac{2nRT_3 \ln(\alpha)}{nR(T_1 + T_2)\ln(\alpha)}$$

or $$\eta = 1 - \frac{2T_3}{T_1 + T_2}$$

169.

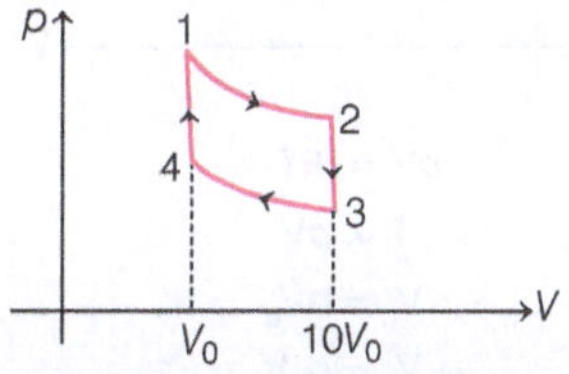

Heat taken by the gas in the process $4 \to 1$,

$$Q_1 = Q_{41} = nC_V \Delta T_{41} = nC_V (T_1 - T_4) \qquad \text{...(i)}$$

Heat rejected by the gas in process $2 \to 3$,

$$Q_2 = |Q_{23}| = |nC_V \Delta T_{23}| = nC_V (T_2 - T_3) \qquad \text{...(ii)}$$

Now efficiency,

$$\eta = 1 - \frac{Q_2}{Q_1} = 1 - \frac{(T_2 - T_3)}{(T_1 - T_4)} \qquad \text{...(iii)}$$

γ for diatomic nitrogen is $\frac{7}{5}$. Hence $\gamma - 1 = \frac{2}{5}$.

In adiabatic process $1 \to 2$,

$$T_1 V_0^{2/5} = T_2 (10V_0)^{2/5} \qquad (TV^{\gamma-1} = \text{constant})$$

or $$T_1 = (10)^{2/5} T_2 \qquad \text{...(iv)}$$

Similarly, $$T_4 = (10)^{2/5} T_3 \qquad \text{...(v)}$$

On dividing Eq. (iv) by Eq. (v), we get

$$\frac{T_1}{T_4} = \frac{T_2}{T_3}$$

$$\Rightarrow \quad T_2 = \left(\frac{T_1}{T_4}\right) T_3$$

Substituting value of T_2 in Eq. (iii), we get

$$\eta = 1 - \frac{T_3\left(\frac{T_1}{T_4} - 1\right)}{T_1 - T_4} = 1 - \frac{T_3}{T_4}$$

and $\frac{T_3}{T_4}$ from Eq. (v) is $(10)^{-2/5}$.

$$\therefore \quad \eta = 1 - (10)^{-2/5} = 0.602$$

$$\therefore \quad \eta \approx 60\%$$

170.

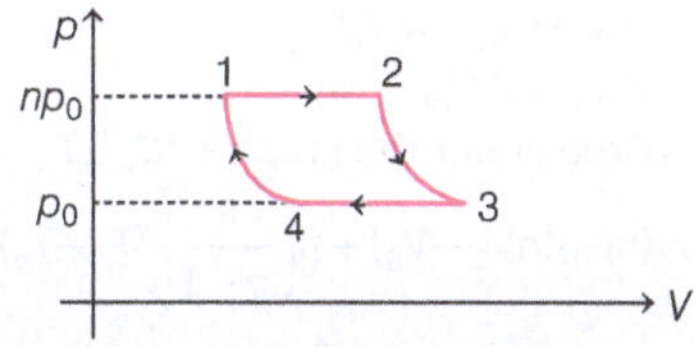

Heat taken by the gas in process $1 \to 2$,

$$Q_1 = Q_{12} = nC_p \Delta T_{12} = nC_p (T_2 - T_1) \qquad \text{...(i)}$$

Now heat rejected by the gas in process $3 \to 4$,

$$Q_2 = |Q_{34}| = |nC_p \Delta T_{34}| = nC_p (T_3 - T_4) \qquad \text{...(ii)}$$

Now efficiency,

$$\eta = 1 - \frac{Q_2}{Q_1} = 1 - \left(\frac{T_3 - T_4}{T_2 - T_1}\right) \qquad \text{...(iii)}$$

In adiabatic process $2 \to 3$,

$$T_2 p_2^{(1-\gamma)/\gamma} = T_3 p_3^{(1-\gamma)/\gamma}$$

as $$(Tp)^{(1-\gamma)/\gamma} = \text{constant}$$

or $$T_2 = (n)^{(\gamma-1)/\gamma} T_3 \qquad \text{...(iv)}$$

Similarly, $T_1 = (n)^{(\gamma-1)/\gamma} T_4 \qquad \text{...(v)}$

From Eqs. (iv) and (v), we get

$$\frac{T_2}{T_1} = \frac{T_3}{T_4} \Rightarrow T_3 = \left(\frac{T_2}{T_1}\right) T_4$$

Substituting in Eq. (iii), we get

$$\eta = 1 - \left[\frac{T_4\left(\frac{T_2}{T_1} - 1\right)}{T_2 - T_1}\right] = 1 - \frac{T_4}{T_1}$$

From Eq. (v), we get

$$\frac{T_4}{T_1} = (n)^{\frac{1}{\gamma} - 1}$$

$$\therefore \quad \eta = 1 - (n)^{\frac{1}{\gamma} - 1}$$

171. $pV = fRT$ $\qquad$ (f = number of moles)

$$\Rightarrow \quad T \propto pV$$

Temperature rises to n - times means, product of p and V should become n - times. So, p - V graph should be as below:

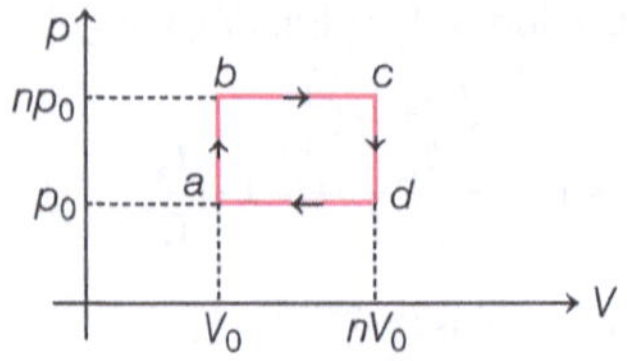

$$W_{net} = \text{Area under the graph}$$
$$= (np_0 - p_0)(nV_0 - V_0)$$
$$= (n-1)^2 p_0 V_0$$
$$\Sigma Q_{+ve} = Q_{ab} + Q_{bc} = Q_{abc}$$
$$= W_{abc} + \Delta U_{abc}$$
$$= \text{Area under the graph} + fC_V \Delta T$$
$$= (np_0)(nV_0 - V_0) + f\left(\frac{R}{\gamma-1}\right)(T_c - T_a)$$
$$= n(n-1)p_0V_0 + \frac{1}{\gamma-1}(p_cV_c - p_aV_a) \quad [fRT = pV]$$
$$= n(n-1)\,p_0V_0 + \frac{1}{\gamma-1}(n^2p_0V_0 - p_0V_0)$$
$$= (n^2 - n)\,p_0V_0 + \frac{(n^2-1)}{\gamma-1}\,p_0V_0$$

Now efficiency,

$$\eta = \frac{W_{net}}{\Sigma Q_{+ve}}$$

Substituting the values, we get

$$\eta = 1 - \left(\frac{n+\gamma}{1+n\gamma}\right)$$

172. (a) $ab \rightarrow$ isochoric

$bc \rightarrow$ adiabatic

$ca \rightarrow$ isothermal

$$pV = fRT$$
$$\Rightarrow \quad T \propto pV$$

f = number of moles

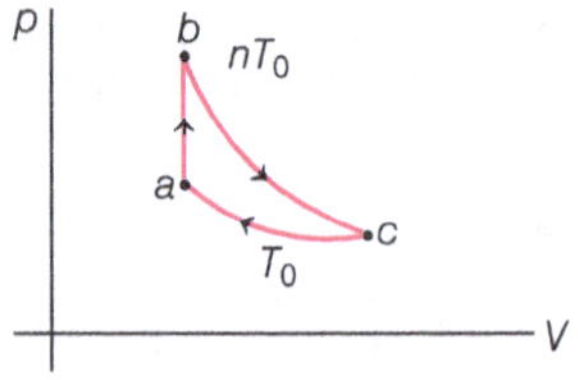

For the given cycle,

$$p_b = np_a \quad \text{...(i)}$$
$$p_aV_a = p_cV_c \quad \text{...(ii)}$$
$$np_aV_a^\gamma = p_cV_c^\gamma \quad \text{...(iii)}$$

Positive heat taken by the gas in process ab,

$$Q_1 = Q_{ab} = fC_V\Delta T = f\left(\frac{R}{\gamma-1}\right)(nT_0 - T_0) = \frac{fRT_0}{\gamma-1}(n-1)$$

Negative heat rejected by the gas in process ca,

$$Q_2 = |Q_{ca}| = fRT_0 \ln\frac{V_c}{V_a} \quad \text{...(iv)}$$

On dividing Eq. (iii) by Eq. (ii), we get

$$V_c^{\gamma-1} = nV_a^{\gamma-1}$$
$$\therefore \quad \frac{V_c}{V_a} = n^{\frac{1}{\gamma-1}}$$

Substituting in Eq. (iv), we get

$$Q_2 = fRT_0 \ln(n)^{\frac{1}{\gamma-1}}$$

Now efficiency,

$$\eta = 1 - \frac{Q_2}{Q_1}$$

Substituting the values of Q_1 and Q_2, we get

$$\eta = 1 - \frac{\ln(n)}{n-1}$$

(b) $ab \rightarrow$ isobaric

$bc \rightarrow$ adiabatic

$ca \rightarrow$ isothermal

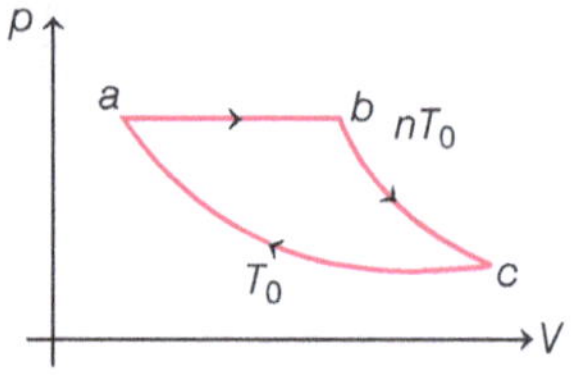

$$pV = fRT$$
$$\Rightarrow \quad T \propto pV$$
$$V_b = nV_a$$
$$p_aV_a = p_cV_c \quad \text{...(v)}$$
$$p_a(nV_a)^\gamma = p_cV_c^\gamma \quad \text{...(vi)}$$

From Eqs. (v) and (vi), we have

$$\frac{V_c}{V_a} = n^{\frac{\gamma}{\gamma-1}} \quad \text{...(vii)}$$

Positive heat given to the gas in the process ab,

$$Q_1 = fC_p\Delta T = f\left(\frac{\gamma R}{\gamma-1}\right)(n-1)T_0$$

Negative heat rejected by the gas in the process ca,

$$Q_2 = |Q_{ca}| = fRT_0 \ln\left(\frac{V_c}{V_a}\right)$$

Substituting value of $\frac{V_c}{V_a}$ from Eq. (vii), we have

$$Q_2 = fRT_0 \ln n^{\frac{\gamma}{\gamma-1}} = \left(\frac{\gamma}{\gamma-1}\right) fRT_0 \ln(n)$$

Now efficiency,

$$\eta = 1 - \frac{Q_2}{Q_1}$$

Substituting the values of Q_1 and Q_2, we get

$$\eta = 1 - \frac{\ln(n)}{n-1}$$

173. (a) $ab \to$ isothermal

$bc \to$ isochoric

$ca \to$ adiabatic

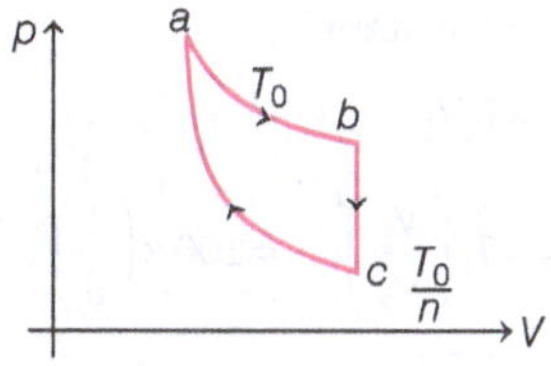

$$p_b V_b = p_a V_a$$

and $$p_c = \frac{p_b}{n}$$

$$p_c V_b^\gamma = p_a V_a^\gamma$$

Putting $p_c = \frac{p_b}{n}$, we get

$$p_b V_b^\gamma = n p_a V_a^\gamma$$

From above equations, we get

or $$\frac{V_b}{V_a} = n^{\frac{1}{\gamma-1}}$$

Now, $Q_1 = Q_{+ve} = Q_{ab} = fRT_0 \ln\frac{V_b}{V_a} = fRT_0 \ln(n)^{\frac{1}{\gamma-1}}$

(f = degree of freedom)

or $$Q_1 = \frac{fRT_0}{\gamma-1}\ln(n)$$

Q_2 = negative heat $= |Q_{bc}| = |fC_V\Delta T|$

$$= f\left(\frac{R}{\gamma-1}\right)T_0\left(1-\frac{1}{n}\right)$$

Efficiency of cycle, $\eta = 1 - \frac{Q_2}{Q_1}$

Substituting the values of Q_1 and Q_2, we get

$$\eta = 1 - \frac{(n-1)}{n\ln(n)}$$

(b) $ab \to$ isothermal

$bc \to$ isobaric

$ca \to$ adiabatic

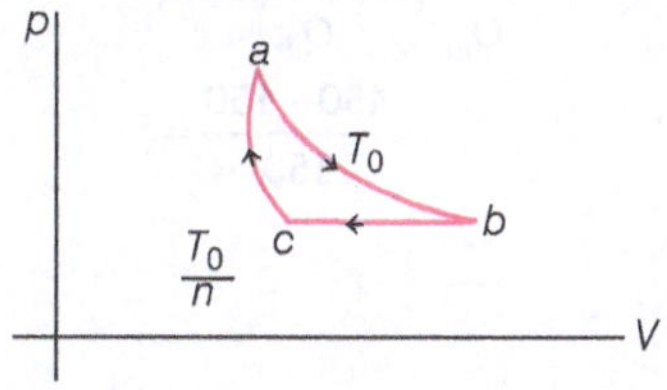

$$T \propto pV$$

$\therefore$ $V_c = \frac{V_b}{n}$ and $p_a V_a = p_b V_b$

$$p_a V_a^\gamma = p_b V_c^\gamma = p_b (n^{-\gamma})(V_b)^\gamma$$

From above equations, we get

$$\Rightarrow \quad \frac{V_b}{V_a} = n^{\frac{\gamma}{\gamma-1}}$$

$$Q_1 = Q_{ab} = fRT_0 \ln\frac{V_b}{V_a} = \left(\frac{\gamma}{\gamma-1}\right)fRT_0\ln(n)$$

$$Q_2 = |Q_{bc}| = |fC_p\Delta T|$$

$$= f\left(\frac{\gamma R}{\gamma-1}\right)T_0\left(1-\frac{1}{n}\right)$$

Now efficiency of cycle,

$$\eta = 1 - \frac{Q_2}{Q_1}$$

Substituting the values of Q_1 and Q_2, we get

$$\eta = 1 - \frac{(n-1)}{n\ln(n)}$$

174. In adiabatic process,

$$\frac{dp}{dV} = -\gamma\left(\frac{p}{V}\right)$$

$$\therefore \quad dp = -\gamma\left(\frac{p}{V}\right)dV$$

or $$\Delta p = -\gamma\left(\frac{p}{V}\right)\Delta V$$

When displaced a small distance x towards right, change in volume on both sides will be,

$$\Delta V = S \cdot x$$

Now pressure of left side will decrease by Δp and on right side will increase by Δp. So, net difference in pressure on two sides will be,

$$\Delta p_{net} = 2\Delta p$$

$\therefore$ Restoring force,

$$F = (\Delta p)_{net} S = -\left[2\gamma\left(\frac{p}{V}\right)Sx\right]S$$

Here, $p = p_0$ and $V = V_0$

$$\therefore \quad F = -\left(\frac{2\gamma p_0 S^2}{V_0}\right)x$$

This is of type $F = -Kx$, so motion is simple harmonic with $K = \frac{2\gamma p_0 S^2}{V_0}$.

Angular frequency is given by,

$$\omega = \sqrt{\frac{K}{m}}$$

$$\therefore \quad \omega = S\sqrt{\frac{2p_0\gamma}{mV_0}}$$

175. (2) $W_l = W_a + W_b + W_c + W_d$

$$= 4p_0(2V_0 - V_0) + (4p_0)(2V_0)\ln\frac{4V_0}{2V_0} + 2p_0(V_0 - 4V_0) + 0$$

$$= 8p_0V_0\ln 2 - 2p_0V_0$$

$$W_{II} = W'_a + W'_b + W'_c + W'_d$$
$$= 4p_0V_0 \ln\left(\frac{2V_0}{V_0}\right) + 0 + p_0(V_0 - 2V_0) + 0$$
$$= 4p_0V_0 \ln 2 - p_0V_0$$
$$\frac{W_I}{W_{II}} = \frac{2}{1} = 2$$

176. We know that for isobaric process, work done,

$$W = (n_1 + n_2)R\Delta T$$
$$\Rightarrow \quad 66 = (2+1)R\Delta T$$
$$\Rightarrow \quad 66 = 3R\Delta T$$
$$\Rightarrow \quad R\Delta T = 22 \quad \text{...(i)}$$

Change in internal energy,

$$\Delta U = \frac{f_1}{2}n_1R\Delta T + \frac{f_2}{2}n_2R\Delta T$$
$$= \frac{R\Delta T}{2}[f_1n_1 + f_2n_2]$$
$$= \frac{22}{2}[f_1n_1 + f_2n_2] \quad \text{[from Eq. (i)]}$$
$$\Rightarrow \quad \Delta U = 11\,[f_1n_1 + f_2n_2] \quad \text{...(ii)}$$

Now, $f_1 = \dfrac{2}{\gamma_1 - 1} = \dfrac{2}{\left(\frac{5}{3} - 1\right)} = 3$

and $f_2 = \dfrac{2}{\gamma_2 - 1} = \dfrac{2}{\left(\frac{7}{5} - 1\right)} = 5$

Now, putting the values of n_1, n_2, f_1 and f_2 in Eq. (ii), we get

$$\Delta U = 11\,(3 \times 2 + 5 \times 1)$$
$$= 121\text{ J}$$

177. Given, $V = KT^{2/3}$

$$TV^{-2/3} = \text{constant}$$

Comparing it with $TV^{m-1} = \text{constant}$, we get

$$m = -\frac{1}{2}$$

So, $W = \dfrac{nR\Delta T}{1-m} = \dfrac{1R \times 90}{1 - \left(-\frac{1}{2}\right)} = 60R$

$$\therefore \quad x = 60$$

178. In isobaric process, pressure remains constant.

$\therefore$ Change in internal energy,

$$\Delta U = nC_V\,\Delta T = \frac{5nR\Delta T}{2}$$

Work done, $W = nR\Delta T$

$$\therefore \quad \frac{\Delta U}{W} = \frac{5nR\Delta T}{2nR\Delta T} = \frac{5}{2} = \frac{x}{10}$$
$$\Rightarrow \quad x = 25$$

179. Given, $n = 1, \gamma = 5/3$

T-V equation in adiabatic process is

$$TV^{\gamma-1} = \text{constant}$$
$$\therefore \quad T_1V_1^{\gamma-1} = T_2V_2^{\gamma-1}$$
$$\Rightarrow \quad T_2 = T_1\left(\frac{V_1}{V_2}\right)^{\gamma-1} = 100 \times \left(\frac{1}{8}\right)^{\frac{2}{3}}$$
$$\Rightarrow \quad T_2 = 25\text{ K}$$

$C_V = \dfrac{3}{2}R$ for monoatomic gas

$$\therefore \quad \Delta U = nC_V\Delta T = n \times \left(\frac{3R}{2}\right)(T_2 - T_1)$$
$$= 1 \times \frac{3}{2} \times 8 \times (25 - 100)$$
$$= -900\text{ J}$$

$\therefore$ Decrease in internal energy $= 900$ J

180.

$$W_{ibf} = W_{ib} + W_{bf}$$
$$= 50\text{ J} + 100\text{ J} = 150\text{ J}$$
$$W_{iaf} = W_{ia} + W_{af}$$
$$= 0 + 200\text{ J} = 200\text{ J}$$
$$Q_{iaf} = 500\text{ J}$$

So $\quad \Delta U_{iaf} = Q_{iaf} - W_{iaf}$

$$= 500\text{ J} - 200\text{ J}$$
$$= 300\text{ J} = U_f - U_i$$

So, $\quad U_f = \Delta U_{iaf} + U_i$

$$= 300\text{ J} + 100\text{ J} = 400\text{ J}$$
$$\Delta U_{ib} = U_b - U_i$$
$$= 200\text{ J} - 100\text{ J} = 100\text{ J}$$
$$Q_{ib} = \Delta U_{ib} + W_{ib}$$
$$= 100\text{ J} + 50\text{ J} = 150\text{ J}$$
$$Q_{ibf} = \Delta U_{ibf} + W_{ibf} = \Delta U_{iaf} + W_{ibf}$$
$$= 300\text{ J} + 150\text{ J} = 450\text{ J}$$

So, the required ratio

$$\frac{Q_{bf}}{Q_{ib}} = \frac{Q_{ibf} - Q_{ib}}{Q_{ib}}$$
$$= \frac{450 - 150}{150} = 2$$

UNIT-22

CALORIMETRY AND HEAT TRANSFER

Learning Modules

1. Calorimetry
2. Heat Transfer

MODULE 1

Calorimetry

Heat transfer between two substances, due to a temperature difference (may be in same or different states) comes under the topic calorimetry. Let us discuss this topic pointwise.

Specific Heat (c)

The amount of heat required to raise the temperature of unit mass of a substance by 1 °C (or 1 K) is called its specific heat. Thus,

$$c = \frac{Q}{m\Delta\theta} \quad \text{or} \quad \frac{Q}{m\Delta T} \qquad \ldots\text{(i)}$$

The SI unit of specific heat is J/kg-K. Because heat is so frequently measured in calories, the unit cal/g-°C is also used quite often.

Heat Required to Change The Temperature

From Eq. (i), we can write

$$Q = mc\Delta\theta \quad \text{or} \quad mc\Delta T \qquad \ldots\text{(ii)}$$

Thus Eq. (ii) is used when temperature of a substance changes without change in state.

Note (i) *In general c is a function of temperature. But normally variation in c is small. So, it is assumed to be constant for wide range of temperature. For example*

"Specific heat of water is 1 cal/g-°C between 14.5 °C to 15.5 °C". This implies that 1 cal of heat will be required to raise the temperature of 1 g of water from 14.5 °C to 15.5 °C. From 15.5 °C to 16.5 °C, a different amount of heat (≠ 1 cal) will be required. But normally this variation is very small. So, it is assumed constant (= 1 cal/g-°C) from `0 °C to 100 °C.

(ii) *If c is given a function of temperature, then Eq. (ii) cannot be applied directly for calculation of Q. Rather integration will be used. Thus,*

$$Q = m\int_{T_i}^{T_f} c\,dT \quad \text{or} \quad m\int_{\theta_i}^{\theta_f} c\,d\theta \qquad \ldots\text{(iii)}$$

In the above expression, c is a function of T(or θ).

(iii) *The specific heat of water is much larger than that of most other substances. Consequently, for the same amount of added heat, the temperature change of a given mass of water is generally less than that for the same mass of another substance. For this reason a large body of water moderates the climate of nearby land. In the winter, the water cools off more slowly than the surrounding land and tends to warm the land. In the summer, the opposite effect occurs as the water heats up more slowly than the land.*

(iv) *Specific heat is also represented by s or S. So, in different problems we have taken all notations for it.*

(v) ***Heat capacity***

$$C = mc \quad \text{or} \quad ms$$

is defined as the heat required to raise the temperature of whole mass of a substance by 1°C or 1K.

$$\therefore \quad C = \frac{Q}{\Delta\theta} \quad \text{or} \quad \frac{Q}{\Delta T}$$

$$\therefore \quad Q = C\Delta T \quad \text{or} \quad C\Delta\theta$$

Latent Heat (L)

The amount of heat required to change the state (or phase) of unit mass of a substance at constant temperature is called latent heat L. Thus,

$$L = \frac{Q}{m} \qquad \ldots\text{(iv)}$$

For a solid-liquid transition, the latent heat is known as the **latent heat of fusion (L_f)** and for the liquid-gas transition, it is known as the **latent heat of vaporization (L_v).**

For water at 1 atmosphere, latent heat of fusion is 80.0 cal/g. This simply means 80.0 cal of heat are required to melt 1.0 g of water or 80.0 cal heat is liberated when 1.0 g of water freezes at 0°C. Similarly, latent heat of vaporization for water at 1 atmosphere is 539 cal/g.

Heat Required to Change the State (or Phase) at Constant Temperature

From Eq. (iv), we can see that

$$Q = mL \qquad \ldots\text{(v)}$$

So, this is the heat required to change the state (or phase) at constant temperature.

Important POINTS

- In some problems, two or more than two substances at different temperatures are mixed. Heat is given by the hot bodies and taken by the cold bodies. Finally, all substances reach to a common equilibrium temperature.
- All such problems can be solved by a single equation,

  Heat given by hot bodies = Heat taken by cold bodies

  But note that, on both sides of this equation, we have to take the positive signs.

  To make them positive, always write

  $$\Delta\theta = \theta_{Higher} - \theta_{Lower}$$

  in the equation $Q = mc\Delta\theta$ when there is a change of temperature without change in state.
- **Water equivalent of a container** Normally, a liquid is heated in a container. So, some heat is wasted in heating the container also. Suppose water equivalent of a container is 10 g, then it implies that heat required to increase the temperature of this container is equal to the heat required to increase the temperature of 10 g of water.

Example 1 How much heat is required to convert 8.0 g of ice at −15°C to steam at 100°C? (Given, $c_{ice} = 0.53$ cal/g-°C, $L_f = 80$ cal/g and $L_v = 539$ cal/g, and $c_{water} = 1$ cal/g-°C)

Sol.

Ice		Ice		Water		Water		Steam
−15°C	$\xrightarrow{Q_1}$	0°C	$\xrightarrow{Q_2}$	0°C	$\xrightarrow{Q_3}$	100°C	$\xrightarrow{Q_4}$	100°C

$$Q_1 = mc_{ice}(T_f - T_i)$$
$$= (8.0)(0.53)[0-(-15)] = 63.6 \text{ cal}$$
$$Q_2 = mL_f = (8)(80) = 640 \text{ cal}$$
$$Q_3 = mc_{water}(T_f - T_i)$$
$$= (8.0)(1.0)[100-0] = 800 \text{ cal}$$
$$Q_4 = mL_v = (8.0)(539) = 4312 \text{ cal}$$

∴ Net heat required, $Q = Q_1 + Q_2 + Q_3 + Q_4$

$= 5815.6$ cal **Ans.**

Example 2 In the above problem if heat is supplied at a constant rate of $q = 10$ cal/min, then plot temperature versus time graph.

Sol.

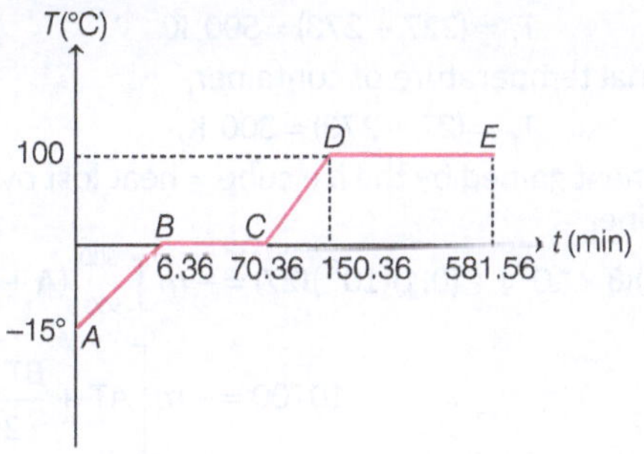

From A to B

(i) Temperature of ice will increase from −15°C to 0°C.

(ii) $t_{AB} = \dfrac{\text{Total heat required}}{\text{Heat supplied per minute}} = \dfrac{Q_1}{q} = \dfrac{63.6}{10}$

$= 6.36$ min

(iii) Between A and B we will get only ice.

From B to C

(i) Temperature of (ice + water) mixture will remain constant at 0 °C.

(ii) $t_{BC} = \dfrac{Q_2}{q} = \dfrac{640}{10} = 64$ min

∴ $t_{Total} = t_{AB} + t_{BC} = 70.36$ min

(iii) Between B and C we will get both ice and water.

From C to D

(i) Temperature of water increases from 0 °C to 100 °C

(ii) $t_{CD} = \dfrac{Q_3}{q} = \dfrac{800}{10} = 80$ min

∴ $t_{Total} = t_{AB} + t_{BC} + t_{CD} = 150.36$ min

(iii) Between C and D we will get only water.

From D to E

(i) Temperature of (water + steam) mixture will remain constant at 100 °C.

(ii) $t_{DE} = \dfrac{Q_4}{q} = \dfrac{4312}{10} = 431.2$ min

∴ $t_{Total} = t_{AB} + t_{BC} + t_{CD} + t_{DE}$

$= 581.56$ min

(iii) Between D and A we will get both water and steam.

The corresponding graph is as shown in above figure.

Exercise AB and CD correspond to temperature change without change in state. BC and DE correspond to state change without change in temperature.

In the given condition, prove that AB and CD are straight lines and slope of these lines is inversely proportional to specific heat in that state. Further, prove that lengths of lines BC and DE are proportional to latent heat.

Example 3 10 g of water at 70°C is mixed with 5 g of water at 30°C. Find the temperature of the mixture in equilibrium. Specific heat of water is 1 cal/g-°C.

Sol. Let t°C be the temperature of the mixture. From energy conservation,

Heat given by 10 g of water = Heat taken by 5 g of water

or $m_1 c_{water} |\Delta t_1| = m_2 c_{water} |\Delta t_2|$

∴ $(10)(1)(70 - t) = 5(1)(t - 30)$

Solving this equation, we get

$t = 56.67$°C **Ans.**

Example 4 The temperature of equal masses of three different liquids A, B and C are 12°C, 19°C and 28°C respectively. The equilibrium temperature when A and B are mixed is 16°C and when B and C are mixed it is 23°C. What should be the temperature when A and C are mixed?

Sol. Let m be the mass of each liquid and s_A, s_B, s_C specific heats of liquids A, B and C respectively. When A and B are mixed. The final temperature is 16°C.

∴ Heat gained by A = Heat lost by B

i.e. $$ms_A(16-12)=ms_B\,(19-16)$$

i.e. $$s_B=\frac{4}{3}s_A \qquad \text{...(i)}$$

When B and C are mixed.

Heat gained by B = Heat lost by C

i.e. $$ms_B(23-19)=ms_C\,(28-23)$$

i.e. $$s_C=\frac{4}{5}s_B \qquad \text{...(ii)}$$

From Eqs. (i) and (ii), $$s_C=\frac{4}{5}\times\frac{4}{3}s_A=\frac{16}{15}s_A$$

∴ $$\frac{s_C}{s_A}=\frac{16}{15}$$

When A and C are mixed, let the final temperature be θ

Heat gained by A = Heat lost by C

∴ $$ms_A(\theta-12)=ms_C(28-\theta)$$

i.e. $$\theta-12=\frac{s_C}{s_A}(28-\theta)=\frac{16}{15}(28-\theta)$$

By solving, we get

$$\theta=\frac{628}{31}=20.26\,°\text{C}$$ **Ans.**

Example 5 In a container of negligible mass 30 g of steam at 100°C is added to 200 g of water that has a temperature of 40°C. If no heat is lost to the surroundings, what is the final temperature of the system? Also find masses of water and steam in equilibrium. Take $L_v = 539$ cal/g and $c_{water}=1$ cal/ g-°C.

Sol. Let Q be the heat required to convert 200 g of water at 40°C into 100°C, then

$$Q=mc\Delta T=(200)\,(1.0)\,(100-40)=12000\ \text{cal}$$

Now, suppose m_0 mass of steam converts into water to liberate this much amount of heat, then

$$m_0=\frac{Q}{L}=\frac{12000}{539}=22.26\ \text{g}$$

Since, it is less than 30 g, the temperature of the mixture is 100°C. **Ans.**

Mass of steam in the mixture

$$=30-22.26=7.74\ \text{g}$$ **Ans.**

and mass of water in the mixture

$$=200+22.26=222.26\ \text{g}$$ **Ans.**

Example 6 In an insulated vessel, 0.05 kg steam at 373 K and 0.45 kg of ice at 253 K are mixed. Find the final temperature of the mixture (in kelvin).

Given, $L_{fusion}=80$ cal/g $=336$ J/g

$L_{vaporization}=540$ cal/g $=2268$ J/g

$s_{ice}=2100$ J/kg-K $=0.5$ cal/g-K

and $s_{water}=4200$ J/kg-K $=1$ cal/g-K **(2006 JEE)**

Sol. $$0.05\text{ kg steam at }373\text{ K}\xrightarrow{Q_1}0.05\text{ kg water at }373\text{ K}$$

$$0.05\text{ kg water at }373\text{ K}\xrightarrow{Q_2}0.05\text{ kg water at }273\text{ K}$$

$$0.45\text{ kg ice at }253\text{ K}\xrightarrow{Q_3}0.45\text{ kg ice at }273\text{ K}$$

$$0.45\text{ kg ice at }273\text{ K}\xrightarrow{Q_4}0.45\text{ kg water at }273\text{ K}$$

$$Q_1=(50)\,(540)=27{,}000\text{ cal}=27\text{ k cal}$$

$$Q_2=(50)\,(1)\,(100)=5000\text{ cal}=5\text{ k cal}$$

$$Q_3=(450)\,(0.5)\,(20)=4500\text{ cal}=4.5\text{ k cal}$$

$$Q_4=(450)\,(80)=36000\text{ cal}=36\text{ k cal}$$

Now, since $Q_1+Q_2>Q_3$ but $Q_1+Q_2<Q_3+Q_4$. So, ice will come to 273 K from 253 K, but whole ice will not melt. Therefore, temperature of the mixture is 273 K.

Example 7 An ice cube of mass 0.1 kg at 0°C is placed in an isolated container which is at 227°C. The specific heats of the container varies with temperature T according to the empirical relation $s=A+BT$, where $A=100$ cal/kg-K and $B=2\times10^{-2}$ cal/kg-K^2. If the final temperature of the container is 27°C, determine the mass of the container. (Latent heat of fusion for water $=8\times10^4$ cal/kg, specific heat of water $=10^3$ cal/kg-K). **(2001 JEE)**

Sol. Let m be the mass of the container.

Initial temperature of container,

$$T_i=(227+273)=500\ \text{K}$$

and final temperature of container,

$$T_f=(27+273)=300\ \text{K}$$

Now, heat gained by the ice cube = heat lost by the container

$$\therefore\ (0.1)(8\times10^4)+(0.1)(10^3)(27)=-m\int_{500}^{300}(A+BT)\,dT$$

or $$10700=-m\left[AT+\frac{BT^2}{2}\right]_{500}^{300}$$

After substituting the values of A and B and the proper limits, we get

$$m=0.495\text{ kg}$$ **Ans.**

Note *After putting negative sign on right hand side, its value comes out to be positive.*

Example 8 5 g of water at 30°C and 5 g of ice at −20°C are mixed together in a calorimeter. Find the final temperature of mixture. Water equivalent of calorimeter is negligible, specific heat of ice = 0.5 cal/g-°C and latent heat of ice = 80 cal/g.

Sol. In this case heat is given by water and taken by the ice

Heat available with water to cool from 30°C to 0°C

$$= ms\Delta\theta = 5 \times 1 \times 30$$
$$= 150 \text{ cal}$$

Heat required by 5 g ice to increase its temperature upto 0°C

$$ms\Delta\theta = 5 \times 0.5 \times 20 = 50 \text{ cal}$$

Out of 150 cal heat available, 50 cal is used for increasing temperature of ice from $-20°C$ to $0°C$. The remaining heat 100 cal is used for melting the ice.

If mass of ice melted is m g, then

$$m \times 80 = 100 \Rightarrow m = 1.25 \text{ g}$$

Thus, 1.25 g ice out of 5 g melts and mixture of ice and water is at 0°C.

Example 9 A bullet of mass 10 g moving with a speed of 20 m/s hits an ice block of mass 990 g kept on a frictionless floor and gets stuck in it. How much ice will melt if 50% of the lost kinetic energy goes to ice? (Temperature of ice block = 0°C).

Sol. Velocity of bullet + ice block,

$$V = \frac{(10 \text{ g}) \times (20 \text{ m/s})}{1000 \text{ g}} = 0.2 \text{ m/s} \qquad (P_i = P_f)$$

$$\text{Loss of KE} = \frac{1}{2}mv^2 - \frac{1}{2}(m+M)V^2$$

$$= \frac{1}{2}[0.01 \times (20)^2 - 1 \times (0.2)^2]$$

$$= \frac{1}{2}[4 - 0.04] = 1.98 \text{ J}$$

$\therefore$ Heat received by ice block

$$= \frac{1.98}{4.18 \times 2} \text{ cal} \approx 0.24 \text{ cal}$$

$$\therefore \text{Mass of ice melted} = \frac{Q}{L} = \frac{(0.24 \text{ cal})}{(80 \text{ cal/g})}$$

$$= 0.003 \text{ g}$$ **Ans.**

Example 10 At 1 atmospheric pressure, 1.000 g of water having a volume of 1.000 cm³ becomes 1.091 cm³ of ice on freezing. The heat of fusion of water at 1 atmosphere is 80.0 cal/g. What is the change in internal energy during the process?

Sol. Heat given out during freezing,

$$Q = -mL = -1 \times 80 = -80 \text{ cal}$$

External work done $W = P(V_{ice} - V_{water})$

$$= 1.013 \times 10^5 \times (1.091 - 1.000) \times 10^{-6}$$
$$= 9.22 \times 10^{-3} \text{ J}$$
$$= \frac{9.22 \times 10^{-3}}{4.18} \text{ cal}$$
$$= 0.0022 \text{ cal}$$

$\therefore$ Change in internal energy,

$$\Delta U = Q - W = -80 - 0.0022$$
$$= -80.0022 \text{ cal}$$ **Ans.**

MODULE 1 Exercise

Take $c_{ice} = 0.53$ cal/g-°C, $c_{water} = 1.0$ cal/g-°C, $(L_f)_{water} = 80$ cal/g and $(L_v)_{water} = 540$ cal/g unless given in the question.

Single Correct Option

1. Which of the substances A, B and C has the lowest heat capacity if heat is supplied to all of them at equal rates. The temperatures *versus* time graph is shown

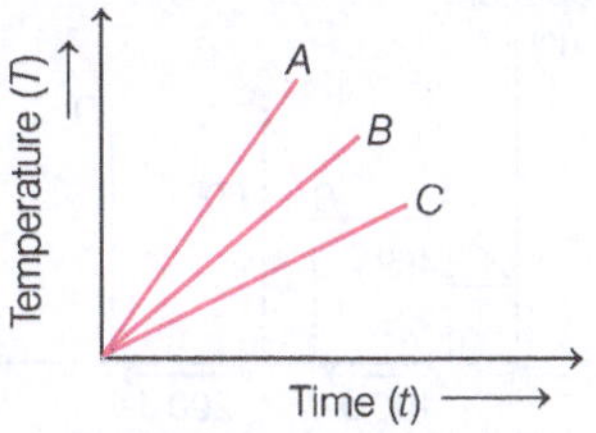

(a) A (b) B
(c) C
(d) All have equal heat capacity

2. A substance of mass m requires a power input of P to remain in the molten state at its melting point. When the power is turned off, the sample completely solidifies in time t. What is the latent heat of fusion of the substance?

(a) $\frac{Pm}{t}$ (b) $\frac{Pt}{m}$ (c) $\frac{m}{Pt}$ (d) $\frac{t}{Pm}$

3. A ball of mass 1 kg is dropped on a floor from a height of 2.0 m. After the collision, it rises up to a height of 1.5 m. Assume that 40% of the mechanical energy lost goes as thermal energy into the ball. The rise in the temperature of the ball is (Heat capacity of the ball is 800 J/K)

(a) 10^{-3} °C (b) 1.5×10^{-3} °C
(c) 2×10^{-3} °C (d) 2.5×10^{-3} °C

4. Two liquids are at temperatures 20°C and 40°C. When same mass of both of them is mixed, the temperature of the mixture is 32°C. What is the ratio of their specific heats?

(a) 1/3 (b) 2/5
(c) 3/2 (d) 2/3

5. The specific heat of a metal at low temperatures varies according to $S = aT^3$, where a is a constant and T is absolute temperature. The heat energy needed to raise unit mass of the metal from temperature $T = 1$ K to $T = 2$ K is

(a) $3a$ (b) $\frac{15a}{4}$
(c) $\frac{2a}{3}$ (d) $\frac{13a}{4}$

6. 1 g of ice at 0°C is mixed with 1 g of steam at 100°C. After thermal equilibrium is achieved, the temperature of the mixture is

(a) 100°C (b) 55°C
(c) 75°C (d) 0°C

7. Two substances A and B of equal mass m are heated at uniform rate of 6 cal s^{-1} under similar conditions. A graph between temperature and time is shown in figure. Ratio of heat absorbed $\frac{H_A}{H_B}$ by them for complete fusion is

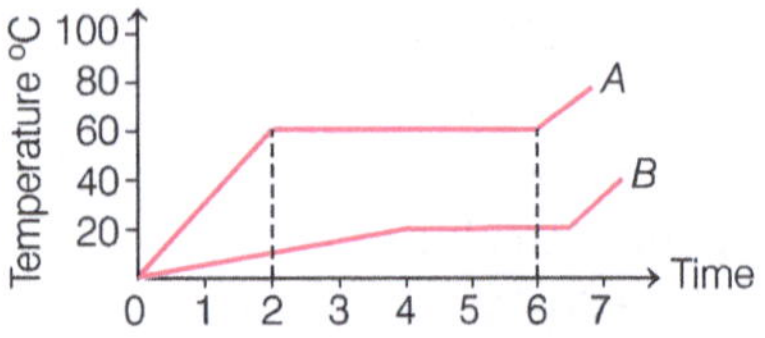

(a) $\frac{9}{4}$ (b) $\frac{4}{9}$
(c) $\frac{8}{5}$ (d) $\frac{5}{8}$

8. An iron ball of mass 0.2 kg is heated to 100°C and put into a block of ice at 0°C. 25 g of ice melts. If the latent heat of fusion of ice is 80 cal/g, then the specific heat of iron in cal/g°C is

(a) 1 (b) 0.1
(c) 0.8 (d) 0.08

9. A metal block is made from a mixture of 2.4 kg of aluminium 1.6 kg of brass and 0.8 kg of copper. The amount of heat required to raise the temperature of this block from 20° C to 80°C is (specific heats of aluminium, brass and copper are 0.216, 0.0917 and 0.0931 cal/kg°C, respectively)

(a) 96.2 cal
(b) 44.4 cal
(c) 86.2 cal
(d) 62.8 cal

10. Figure shows the temperature variation when heat is added continuously to a specimen of ice (10 g) at −40°C at constant rate. (Specific heat of ice is 0.53 cal/g°C and $L_{ice} = 80$ cal/g, $L_{water} = 540$ cal/g)

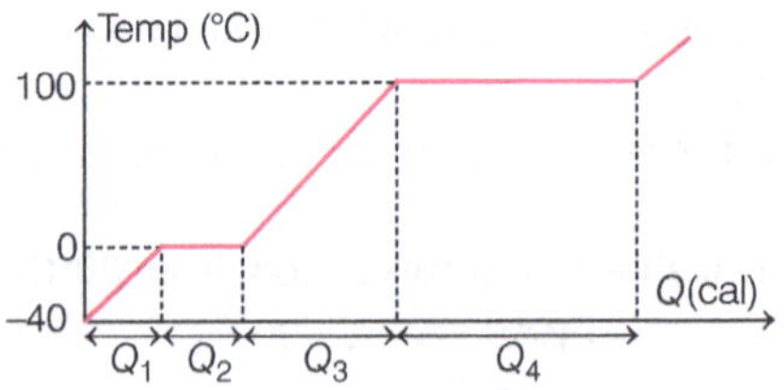

	Column I		Column II
A	Value of Q_1 (in cal)	P	800
B	Value of Q_2 (in cal)	Q	1000
C	Value of Q_3 (in cal)	R	5400
D	Value of Q_4 (in cal)	S	212

(a) A → S; B → P; C → R; D → Q
(b) A → P; B → S; C → Q; D → R
(c) A → P; B → S; C → R; D → Q
(d) A → S; B → P; C → Q; D → R

11. A block of ice of mass $M = 10$ kg is moved back and forth over the flat horizontal surface of a large block of ice. Both blocks are at 0°C and the force that produces the back-and-forth motion acts only horizontally. The coefficient of friction between the two surfaces is 0.060. If $m = 15.2$ g of water is produced, the total distance travelled by the upper block relative to the lower is ($L_{ice} = 3.34 \times 10^5$ J/kg)

(a) 432 m (b) 863 m
(c) 368 m (d) 216 m

Multiple Correct Options

12. Two liquids of specific heat ratio 1 : 2 are at temperatures 2 θ and θ

(a) if equal amounts of them are mixed, then temperature of mixture is 1.5 θ
(b) if equal amounts of them are mixed, then temperature of mixture is $\frac{4}{3}\theta$
(c) for their equal amounts, the ratio of heat capacities is 1 : 1
(d) for their equal amounts, the ratio of their heat capacities is 1 : 2

13. The temperature change *versus* heat supplied curve is given for 1 kg of a solid block. Then, which of the following statements is/are correct?

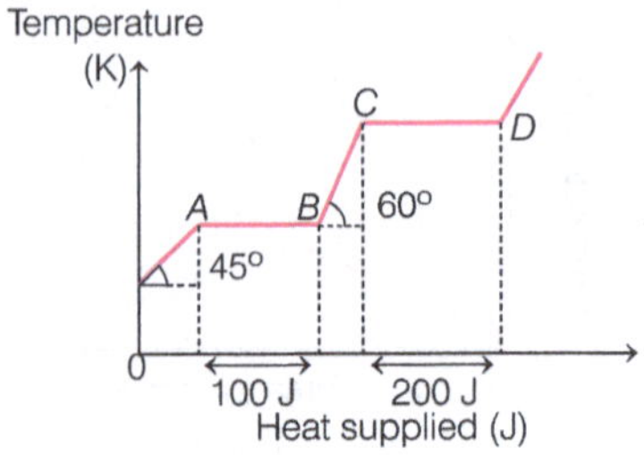

(a) Specific heat capacity of the solid is 1 J/kg-K
(b) Specific heat capacity of liquid phase is $\sqrt{3}$ J/kg-K
(c) Latent heat of vaporization is 100 J/kg
(d) Latent heat of vaporization is 200 J/kg

14. Equal masses of three different liquids *A*, *B* and *C* are taken at 10°C, 15°C and 20°C respectively. The steady state temperature when *A* and *B* are mixed, is 13°C and when *B* and *C* are mixed, is 16°C. Which of the following statements is/are correct ?
(a) Ratio of specific heats of *A* and *B* is 2/3
(b) Ratio of specific heats of *A* and *C* is $\frac{8}{3}$
(c) When *A* and *C* are mixed, temperature of mixture is $\left(\frac{140}{11}\right)$°C
(d) When all of three *A*, *B* and *C* are mixed, temperature of mixture is 15°C

Match the Columns

15. Heat is supplied to a substance in solid state at a constant rate. Its temperature varies with time as shown in figure. Match the following two columns.

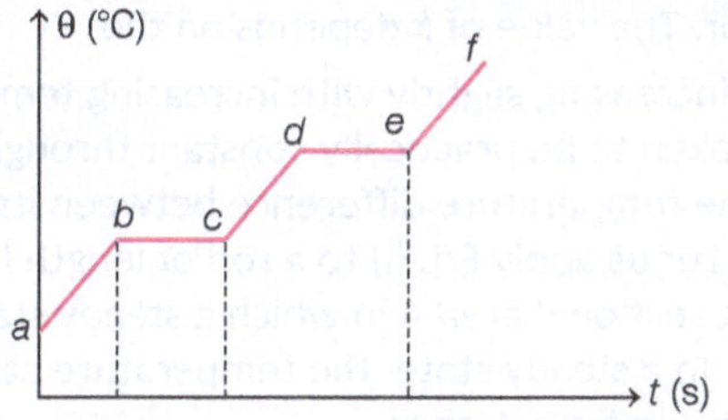

	Column I		Column II
(a)	Slope of line *ab*	(p)	*de*
(b)	Length of line *bc*	(q)	*cd*
(c)	Solid + liquid state	(r)	directly proportional to mass
(d)	Only liquid state	(s)	None of these

16. Three liquids *A*, *B* and *C* having same specific heats have masses *m*, 2*m* and 3*m*. Their temperatures are, θ, 2θ and 3θ respectively. For temperature of mixture, match the following two columns.

	Column I		Column II
(a)	When *A* and *B* are mixed	(p)	$\frac{5}{2}\theta$
(b)	When *A* and *C* are mixed	(q)	$\frac{5}{3}\theta$
(c)	When *B* and *C* are mixed	(r)	$\frac{7}{3}\theta$
(d)	When *A*, *B* and *C* all are mixed	(s)	$\frac{13}{5}\theta$

Subjective Questions

17. 10 g ice at 0°C is converted into steam at 100°C. Find total heat required.

18. Three liquids *A*, *B* and *C* of specific heats 1 cal/g -°C, 0.5 cal/g -°C and 0.25 cal/g -°C are at temperatures 20 °C, 40 °C and 60 °C respectively. Find temperature in equilibrium if they are mixed together. Their masses are equal.

19. Equal masses of ice (at 0°C) and water are in contact. Find the temperature of water needed to just melt the complete ice.

20. 15 g ice at 0°C is mixed with 10 g water at 40°C. Find the temperature of mixture. Also, find mass of water and ice in the mixture.

21. Three liquids *P*, *Q* and *R* are given. When 4 kg of *P* at 60 °C and 1 kg of *R* at 50 °C are mixed, equilibrium temperature becomes 55 °C. A mixture of 1 kg of *P* at 60 °C and 1 kg of *Q* at 50 °C shows an equilibrium temperature of 55 °C.
What will be the equilibrium temperature when 1 kg of *Q* at 60 °C is mixed with 1 kg of *R* at 50 °C?

22. A lead bullet penetrates into a solid object and melts. Assuming that 50% of its kinetic energy was used to heat it, calculate the initial speed of the bullet. The initial temperature of the bullet is 27°C and its melting point is 327 °C. Latent heat of fusion of lead $= 2.5 \times 10^4$ J/kg and specific heat capacity of lead = 125 J/kg-K. **(2022 Main)**

23. A nuclear power plant generates 500 MW of waste heat that must be carried away by water pumped from a lake. If the water temperature is to rise by 10°C, what is the required flow rate in kg/s?

Answers

1. (a) **2.** (b) **3.** (d) **4.** (d) **5.** (b) **6.** (a) **7.** (c) **8.** (b) **9.** (b) **10.** (d)
11. (b) **12.** (b, d) **13.** (a, d) **14.** (a, b, c) **15.** a → s; b → r; c → s; d → q **16.** a → q; b → p; c → s; d → r
17. 7200 cal **18.** 31.43°C **19.** 80°C **20.** 0°C, $m_w = 15$ g, $m_i = 10$ g **21.** 52°C **22.** 500 m/s
23. 1.2×10^4 kg/s

See hints on pages 383-384.

MODULE 2

Heat Transfer

Heat can be transferred from one place to the other by any of three possible ways : **conduction, convection** and **radiation.** In the first two processes, a medium is necessary for the heat transfer. Radiation, however, does no have this restriction. This is also the fastest mode of heat transfer, in which heat is transferred from one place to the other in the form of electromagnetic radiation.

Conduction

Figure shows a rod whose ends are in thermal contact with a hot reservoir at temperature T_1 and a cold reservoir at temperature T_2. The sides of the rod are covered with insulating medium, so the transport of heat is along the rod, not through the sides. The molecules at the hot reservoir have greater vibrational energy. This energy is transferred by collisions to the atoms at the end face of the rod. These atoms in turn transfer energy to their neighbours further along the rod. Such transfer of heat through a substance in which heat is transported without direct mass transport is called conduction.

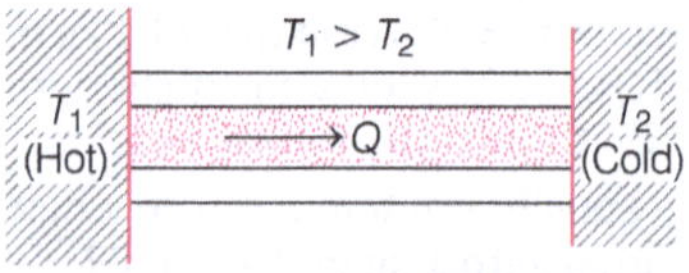

Most metals use another, more effective mechanism to conduct heat. The free electrons, which move throughout the metal can rapidly carry energy from the hotter to cooler regions, so metals are generally good conductors of heat. The presence of 'free' electrons also causes most metals to be good electrical conductors. A metal rod at 5°C feels colder than a piece of wood at 5°C because heat can flow more easily from your hand into the metal.

Heat transfer occurs only between regions that are at different temperatures, and the rate of heat flow is $\frac{dQ}{dt}$. This rate is also called the **heat current**, denoted by H. Experiments show that the heat current is proportional to the cross-section area A of the rod and to the temperature gradient $\frac{dT}{dx}$, which is the rate of change of temperature with distance along the bar. In general,

$$H = \frac{dQ}{dt} = -KA\frac{dT}{dx} \quad \text{...(i)}$$

The negative sign is used to make $\frac{dQ}{dt}$ a positive quantity since $\frac{dT}{dx}$ is negative. The constant K, called the **thermal conductivity** is a measure of the ability of a material to conduct heat.

A substance with a large thermal conductivity k is a good heat conductor. The value of k depends on the temperature, increasing slightly with increasing temperature, but K can be taken to be practically constant throughout a substance if the temperature difference between its ends is not too great. Let us apply Eq. (i) to a rod of length l and constant cross-sectional area A in which a steady state has been reached. In a steady state, the temperature at each point is constant in time. Hence,

$$-\frac{dT}{dx} = T_1 - T_2$$

Therefore, the heat ΔQ transferred in time Δt is

$$\Delta Q = KA\left(\frac{T_1 - T_2}{l}\right)\Delta t \quad \text{...(ii)}$$

Thermal Resistance (*R*)

Eq. (ii) in differential form can be written as

$$\frac{dQ}{dt} = H = \frac{\Delta T}{l/KA} = \frac{\Delta T}{R} \quad \text{...(iii)}$$

Here, ΔT = temperature difference (TD) and

$R = \frac{l}{KA}$ = thermal resistance of the rod.

Important POINTS

- Consider a section *ab* of a rod as shown in figure. Suppose Q_1 heat enters into the section at '*a*' and Q_2 leaves at '*b*', then $Q_2 < Q_1$. Part of the energy $Q_1 - Q_2$ is utilized in raising the
- temperature of section *ab* and the remaining is lost to atmosphere through *ab*. If heat is continuously supplied from the left end of the rod, a stage comes when temperature of the section becomes constant. In that case, $Q_1 = Q_2$ if rod is insulated from the surroundings (or loss through *ab* is zero). This is called the **steady state** condition. Thus, in steady state temperature of different sections of the rod becomes constant (but not same).

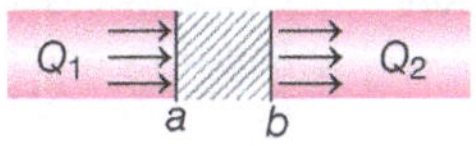

Hence, in the figure :

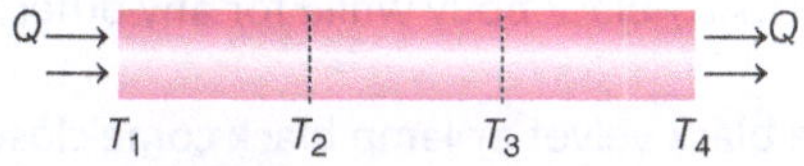

Insulated rod in steady state

$T_1 =$ constant, $T_2 =$ constant etc.

and $T_1 > T_2 > T_3 > T_4$

Now, a natural question arises, why the temperature of whole rod not becomes equal when heat is being continuously supplied? The answer is : there must be a temperature difference in the rod for the heat flow, same as we require a potential difference across a resistance for the current flow through it.

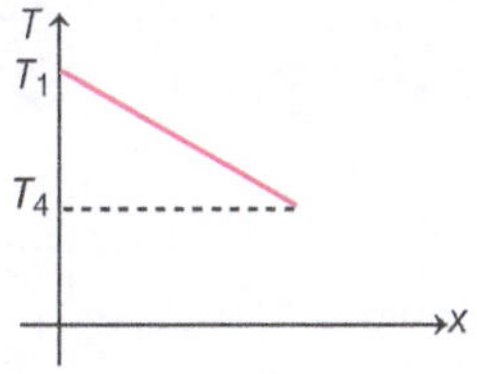

In steady state, the temperature varies linearly with distance along the rod if it is insulated.

- Comparing equation number (iii), i.e. heat current

$$H = \frac{dQ}{dt} = \frac{\Delta T}{R} \quad \left(\text{where, } R = \frac{l}{KA}\right)$$

with the equation, of current flow through a resistance,

$$I = \frac{dq}{dt} = \frac{\Delta V}{R} \quad \left(\text{where, } R = \frac{l}{\sigma A}\right)$$

We find the following similarities in heat flow through a rod and current flow through a resistance.

Table 1

S.No	Heat flow through a conducting rod	Current flow through a resistance
1.	Conducting rod	Electrical resistance
2.	Heat flows	Charge flows
3.	TD is required	PD is required
4.	Heat current $H = \frac{dQ}{dt}$ = rate of heat flow	Electric current $I = \frac{dq}{dt}$ = rate of charge flow
5.	$H = \frac{\Delta T}{R} = \frac{TD}{R}$	$I = \frac{\Delta V}{R} = \frac{PD}{R}$
6.	$R = \frac{l}{KA}$	$R = \frac{l}{\sigma A}$
7.	K = thermal conductivity	σ = electrical conductivity

Here TD = temperature difference and
PD = potential difference.

From the above table it is evident that flow of heat through rods in series and parallel is analogous to the flow of current through resistance in series and parallel. This analogy is of great importance in solving complicated problems of heat conduction.

Convection

Although conduction does occur in liquids and gases also, heat is transported in these media mostly by convection. In this process, the actual motion of the material is responsible for the heat transfer.

You probably have warmed your hands by holding them over an open flame. In this situation, the air directly above the flame is heated and expands. As a result, the density of this air decreases and then air rises. When the movement results from differences in density, as with air around fire, it is referred to as **natural convection.**

Air flow at a beach is an example of natural convection. If it were not for convection currents, it would be very difficult to boil water. As water is heated in a kettle, the heated water expands and rises to the top because its density is lowered. At the same time, the denser, cool water at the surface sinks to the bottom of the kettle and is heated. When the heated substance is forced to move by a fan or pump, the process is called **forced convection.** Heating a room by a radiator is an example of forced convection.

Radiation

The third means of energy transfer is radiation which does not require a medium. The best known example of this process is the radiation from sun.

All objects radiate energy continuously in the form of electromagnetic waves. Now, let us define few terms before studying the other topics.

Radiant Energy

All bodies radiate energy in the form of electromagnetic waves by virtue of their temperature. This energy is called the radiant energy.

Absorptive Power 'a'

"It is defined as the ratio of the radiant energy absorbed by it in a given time to the total radiant energy incident on it in the same interval of time."

$$a = \frac{\text{energy absorbed}}{\text{energy incident}}$$

$$a \leq 1$$

Further, a is unitless and dimensionless.

A perfectly black body absorbs all radiations incident on it, the absorptive power of a perfectly black body is maximum and unity.

Alternate definition

Absorptive power can also be defined as energy absorbed by that body divided by energy absorbed by perfectly black body under identical conditions.

Spectral Absorptive Power 'a_λ'

The absorptive power 'a' refers to radiations of all wavelengths (or the total energy) while the spectral absorptive power is the ratio of radiant energy absorbed by a surface to the radiant energy incident on it for a particular wavelength λ in the range from λ to $\lambda + d\lambda$. It may have different values for different wavelengths for a given surface. Let us take an example, suppose $a = 0.6$, $a_\lambda = 0.4$ for 1000 Å and $a_\lambda = 0.7$ for 2000 Å for a given surface. Then, it means that this surface will absorb only 60% of the total radiant energy incident on it. Similarly, it absorbs 40% of the energy incident on it corresponding to 1000 Å and 70% corresponding to 2000 Å.

Emissive Power 'e'

(Do not confuse it with the emissivity e which is different from it, although both have the same symbol e).

"For a given surface it is defined as the radiant energy emitted per second per unit area of the surface." It has the units of W/m^2 or J/s-m^2.

For a black body

$$e = \sigma T^4$$

Spectral Emissive Power 'e_λ'

"It is emissive power for a particular wavelength λ from range λ to $d\lambda$." Thus,

$$e = \int_0^\infty e_\lambda d\lambda$$

Stefan's Law

The rate at which an object radiates energy is proportional to the fourth power of its absolute temperature. This is known as the **Stefan's law** and is expressed in equation form as

$$P = \sigma A e T^4$$

Here, P is the power in watts (J/s) radiated by the object, A is the surface area in m^2, e is unitless and a fraction between 0 and 1 called the **emissivity** of the object and σ is a universal constant called **Stefan's constant**, which has the value

$$\sigma = 5.67 \times 10^{-8} \text{ W/m}^2\text{-K}^4$$

Note *(i) Emissivity e is also sometimes denoted by e_r.*

(ii) Emissivity and emissive power both are represented by e. But they are different. So, do not confuse between them.

Perfectly Black Body

A body that absorbs all the radiation incident upon it and has an emissivity equal to 1 is called a perfectly black body. A black body is also an ideal radiator. It implies that if a black body and an identical another body are kept at the same temperature, then the black body will radiate maximum power as is obvious from equation $P = eA\sigma T^4$ also. Because $e = 1$ for a perfectly black body while for any other body $e < 1$.

Materials like black velvet or lamp black come close to being ideal black bodies, but the best practical realization of an ideal black body is a small hole leading into a cavity, as this absorbs 98% of the radiation incident on them.

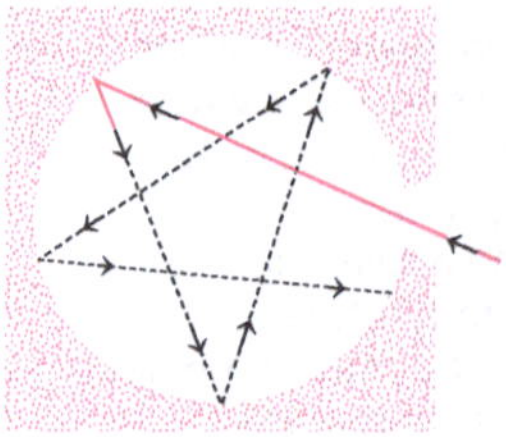

Cavity approximating an ideal black body. Radiation entering the cavity has little chance of leaving before it is completely absorbed.

Note *(i) Energy radiated by a body per unit area per unit time is called emissive power and given by*

$$e = e_r \sigma T^4 \qquad (e_r = \text{emissivity})$$

It has the units of W/m^2 or $J/s\text{-}m^2$.

Energy radiated per unit time is called power and it is given by

$$P = e_r \sigma T^4 A$$

It has the unit J/s or watt.

Total energy radiated by the body in time t is

$$E = e_r \sigma T^4 A t$$

(ii) Absorptive power (a), spectral absorptive power (a_λ) and emissivity (e_r) are the constants which are temperature independent. But emissive power (e) and spectral emissive power (e_λ) are temperature dependent. As,

$$e = e_r \sigma T^4 \Rightarrow e \propto T^4$$

(iii) $e = \int_0^\infty e_\lambda d\lambda = e_r \sigma T^4$ *but*

$$a \neq \int_0^\infty a_\lambda d\lambda$$

Kirchhoff's Law

"According to this law the ratio of emissive power to absorptive power is same for all surfaces at the same temperature."

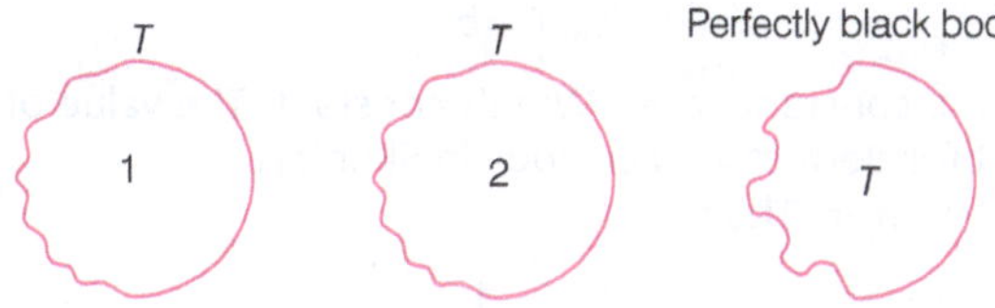

Hence, $$\frac{e_1}{a_1} = \frac{e_2}{a_2} = \left(\frac{e}{a}\right)_{\text{perfectly black body}}$$

but $$(a)_{\text{black body}} = 1$$

and $$(e)_{\text{black body}} = E \quad \text{(say)}$$

Then, $$\boxed{\left(\frac{e}{a}\right)_{\text{for any surface}} = \text{constant} = E}$$

Similarly, for a particular wavelength λ,

$$\boxed{\left(\frac{e_\lambda}{a_\lambda}\right)_{\text{for any body}} = E_\lambda}$$

Here, E = emissive power of black body at temperature T

$= \sigma T^4$

From the above expression, we can see that

$$\boxed{e_\lambda \propto a_\lambda}$$

i.e. good absorbers for a particular wavelength are also good emitters of the same wavelength.

Note *According to Kirchhoff's law, at a given temperature, the ratio $\frac{e}{a}$ is constant for all bodies and this constant is equal to e of perfectly black body at that temperature. Similarly, the ratio $\frac{e_\lambda}{a_\lambda}$ is constant for all bodies at given temperature and value of this constant is e_λ of perfectly black body at that temperature.*

At different temperatures value of this constant will be different.

Cooling by Radiation

Consider a hot body at temperature T placed in an environment at a lower temperature T_0. The body emits more radiation than it absorbs and cools down while the surroundings absorb radiation from the body and warm up. The body is losing energy by emitting radiations at a rate

$$P_1 = eA\sigma T^4$$

and is receiving energy by absorbing radiations at a rate

$$P_2 = aA\sigma T_0^4$$

Here, 'a' is a pure number between 0 and 1 indicating the relative ability of the surface to absorb radiation from its surroundings. Note that this 'a' is different from the absorptive power 'a'. In thermal equilibrium, both the body and the surroundings have the same temperature (say T_c) and,

$$P_1 = P_2 \quad \text{or} \quad eA\sigma T_c^4 = aA\sigma T_c^4 \quad \text{or} \quad e = a$$

Thus, when $T > T_0$, the net rate of heat transfer from the body to the surroundings is

$$\frac{dQ}{dt} = eA\sigma(T^4 - T_0^4) \quad \text{or} \quad mc\left(-\frac{dT}{dt}\right) = eA\sigma(T^4 - T_0^4)$$

Rate of cooling

$$\boxed{\left(-\frac{dT}{dt}\right) = \frac{eA\sigma}{mc}(T^4 - T_0^4) \quad \text{or} \quad -\frac{dT}{dt} \propto (T^4 - T_0^4)}$$

Newton's Law of Cooling

According to this law, if the temperature T of the body is not very different from that of the surroundings T_0, then rate of cooling $-\frac{dT}{dt}$ is proportional to the temperature difference between them. To prove it, let us assume that

$$T = T_0 + \Delta T$$

So that $$T^4 = (T_0 + \Delta T)^4 = T_0^4\left(1 + \frac{\Delta T}{T_0}\right)^4$$

$$\approx T_0^4\left(1 + \frac{4\Delta T}{T_0}\right) \quad \text{(from binomial expansion)}$$

$$\therefore \quad (T^4 - T_0^4) = 4T_0^3(\Delta T)$$

or $$(T^4 - T_0^4) \propto \Delta T \quad (\text{as } T_0 = \text{constant})$$

Now, we have already shown that rate of cooling

$$\left(-\frac{dT}{dt}\right) \propto (T^4 - T_0^4)$$

and here we have shown that

$$(T^4 - T_0^4) \propto \Delta T$$

if the temperature difference is small.

Thus, rate of cooling

$$\boxed{-\frac{dT}{dt} \propto \Delta T} \quad \text{or} \quad \boxed{-\frac{d\theta}{dt} \propto \Delta\theta}$$

as $$dT = d\theta \quad \text{or} \quad \Delta T = \Delta\theta$$

Variation of Temperature of a Body According to Newton's Law

Suppose a body has a temperature θ_i at time $t = 0$. It is placed in an atmosphere whose temperature is θ_0. We are interested in finding the temperature of the body at time t. Assuming Newton's law of cooling to hold good or by assuming that the temperature difference is small. As per this law,

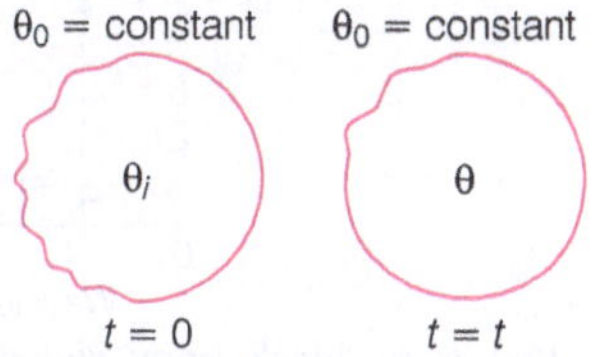

Rate of cooling $\propto$ temperature difference

Using the equations derived earlier we can write,

$$\left(-\frac{d\theta}{dt}\right)=\left(\frac{eA\sigma}{mc}\right)(4\theta_0^3)(\theta-\theta_0)$$

or $$\left(-\frac{d\theta}{dt}\right)=\alpha(\theta-\theta_0)$$

Here, $$\alpha=\left(\frac{4eA\sigma\theta_0^3}{mc}\right) \quad \text{(is a constant)}$$

$\therefore$ $$\int_{\theta_i}^{\theta}\frac{d\theta}{\theta-\theta_0}=-\alpha\int_0^t dt$$

$\therefore$ $$\boxed{\theta=\theta_0+(\theta_i-\theta_0)\,e^{-\alpha t}}$$

From this expression we see that $\theta=\theta_i$ at $t=0$ and $\theta=\theta_0$ at $t=\infty$, i.e. temperature of the body decreases exponentially with time from θ_i to θ_0 $(<\theta_i)$. The temperature *versus* time graph is as shown in figure.

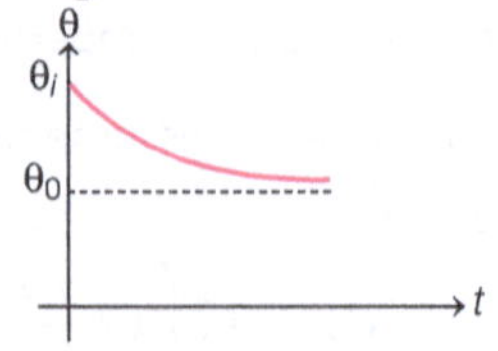

Note *If the body cools by radiation from θ_1 to θ_2 in time t, then taking the approximation*

$$\left(-\frac{d\theta}{dt}\right)=\frac{\theta_1-\theta_2}{t} \quad \textit{and} \quad \theta=\theta_{av}=\left(\frac{\theta_1+\theta_2}{2}\right)$$

The equation $\left(-\frac{d\theta}{dt}\right)=\alpha(\theta-\theta_0)$ *becomes*

$$\boxed{\frac{\theta_1-\theta_2}{t}=\alpha\left(\frac{\theta_1+\theta_2}{2}-\theta_0\right)}$$

This form of the law helps in solving numerical problems related to ***Newton's law of cooling****.*

Wien's Displacement Law

At ordinary temperatures (below about 600°C) the thermal radiation emitted by a body is not visible, most of it is concentrated in wavelengths much longer than those of visible light.

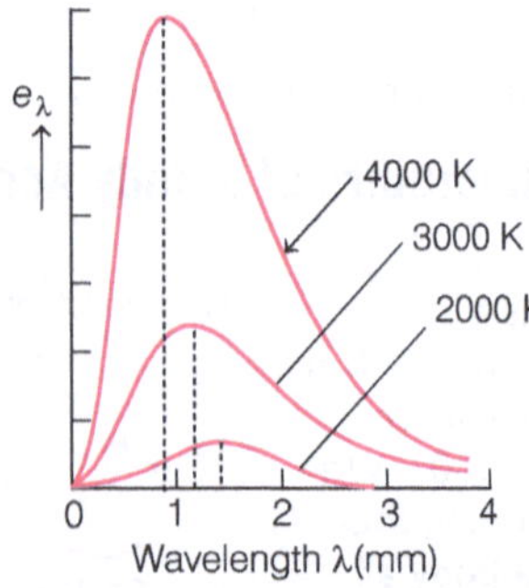

Power of black body radiation *versus* wavelength at three temperatures. Note that the amount of radiation emitted (the area under a curve) increase with increasing temperature.

Figure shows how the energy of a black body radiation varies with temperature and wavelength. As the temperature of the black body increases, two distinct behaviors are observed. The first effect is that the peak of the distribution shifts to shorter wavelengths. This shift is found to obey the following relationship called **Wien's displacement law.**

$$\boxed{\lambda_m T=b}$$

Here, b is a constant called Wien's constant. The value of this constant for perfectly black body in SI unit is 2.898×10^{-3} m-K. Thus,

$$\boxed{\lambda_m\propto\frac{1}{T}}$$

Here, λ_m is the wavelength corresponding to the maximum spectral emissive power e_λ.

The second effect is that the total amount of energy the black body emits per unit area per unit time $(=\sigma T^4)$ increases with fourth power of absolute temperature T. This is also known as the emissive power.

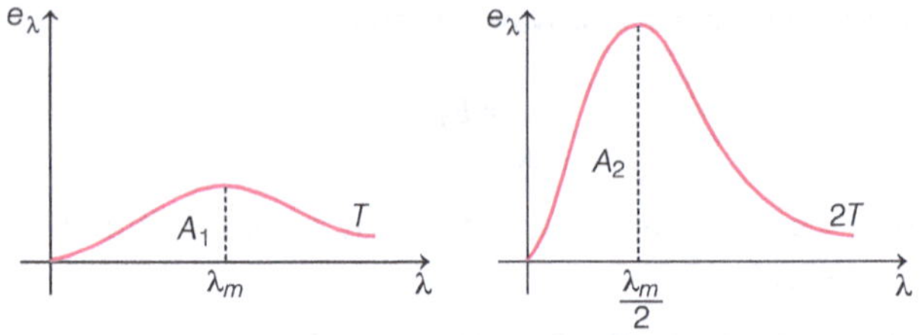

We know

$$e=\int_0^\infty e_\lambda d\lambda=\text{Area under } e_\lambda\text{-}\lambda \text{ graph}=\sigma T^4$$

or $\boxed{\text{Area}\propto T^4}$ $\Rightarrow$ $A_2=(2)^4A_1=16A_1$

Thus, if the temperature of the black body is made two fold, λ_m remains half (from Wien's law) while the area becomes 16 times.

Example 1 In which of the following process, convection does not take place primarily? **(2005 JEE)**

(a) Sea and land breeze
(b) Boiling of water
(c) Warming of glass of bulb due to filament
(d) Heating air around a furnace

Sol. (c) Glass of bulb heats due to filament by the process radiation.

Example 2 A copper rod 2 m long has a circular cross-section of radius 1 cm. One end is kept at 100°C and the other at 0°C. The surface is insulated so that negligible heat is lost through the surface. In steady state, find

(a) the thermal resistance of the bar
(b) the thermal current H
(c) the temperature gradient $\frac{dT}{dx}$ and
(d) the temperature at a distance 25 cm from the hot end.

Thermal conductivity of copper is 401 W/m-K.

Sol. (a) Thermal resistance, $R = \frac{l}{KA} = \frac{l}{K(\pi r^2)}$

or $R = \frac{(2)}{(401)(\pi)(10^{-2})^2}$

$= 15.9 \text{ K/W}$ **Ans.**

(b) Thermal current, $H = \frac{\Delta T}{R} = \frac{\Delta\theta}{R} = \frac{100}{15.9}$

or $H = 6.3 \text{ W}$ **Ans.**

(c) Temperature gradient

$= \frac{0-100}{2} = -50 \text{ K/m}$

$= -50°\text{C/m}$ **Ans.**

(d) Let θ be the temperature at 25 cm from the hot end, then

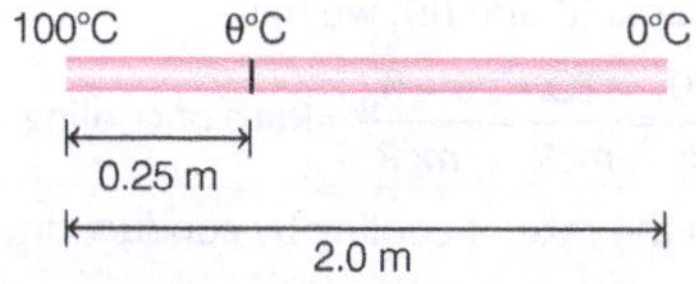

$(\theta - 100) = \text{(temperature gradient)} \times \text{(distance)}$

or $\theta - 100 = (-50)(0.25)$

or $\theta = 87.5°\text{C}$ **Ans.**

Example 3 Three rods made of the same material and having the same cross-section have been joined as shown in the figure. Each rod is of the same length. The left and right ends are kept at 0°C and 90°C, respectively. The temperature of junction of the three rods will be **(2001 JEE)**

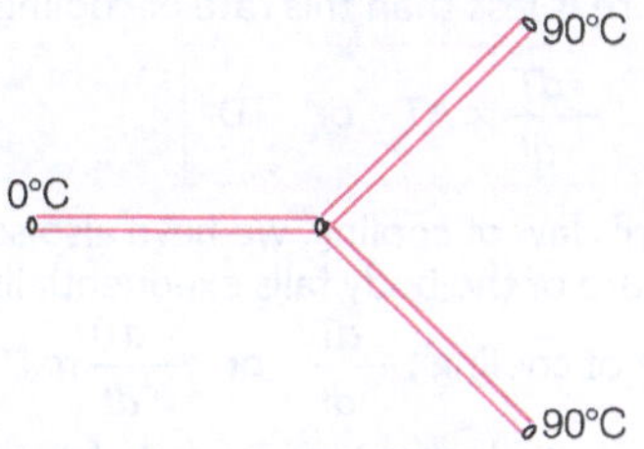

(a) 45 °C (b) 60 °C
(c) 30 °C (d) 20 °C

Sol. (b) Let θ be the temperature of the junction (say B). Thermal resistance of all the three rods is equal. Rate of heat flow through AB + Rate of heat flow through CB = Rate of heat flow through BD

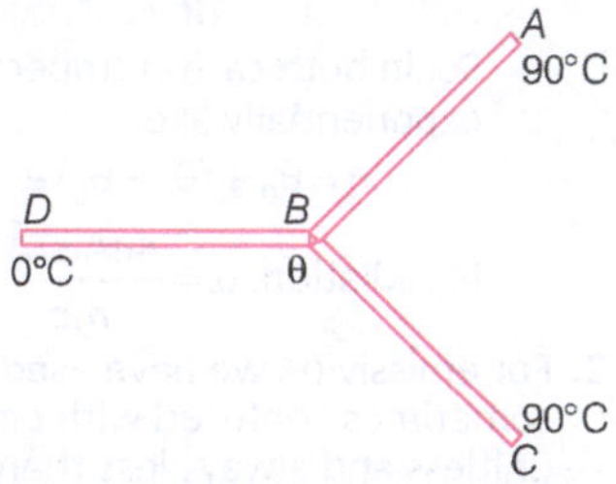

Rate of heat flow,

$H = \frac{\text{Temperature difference (TD)}}{\text{Thermal resistance }(R)}$

$\therefore \frac{90° - \theta}{R} + \frac{90° - \theta}{R} = \frac{\theta - 0}{R}$

Solving this equation, we get $\theta = 60°\text{C}$

∴ The correct option is (b).

Example 4 Figure shows a copper rod joined to a steel rod. The rods have equal length and equal cross- sectional area. The free end of the copper rod is kept at 0°C and that of the steel rod is kept at 100°C. Find the temperature θ at the junction of the rods. Conductivity of copper
= 390 W/m-°C and that of steel = 46 W/m-°C.

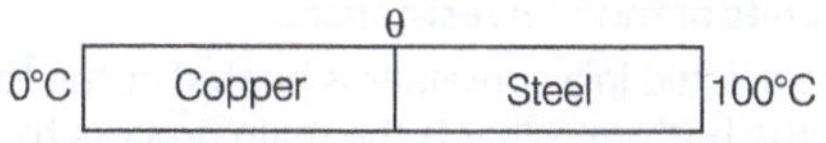

Sol. $H_{steel} = H_{copper}$ (two rods are in series)

$\therefore \frac{(TD)_S}{(l/KA)_S} = \frac{(TD)_C}{(l/KA)_C}$

or $K_S (TD)_S = K_C (TD)_C$

or $46(100 - \theta) = 390(\theta - 0)$

Solving we get, $\theta = 10.6°\text{C}$ **Ans.**

Note *In the above problem heat flows from right to left or from higher temperature to lower temperature.*

Example 5 A spherical black body with a radius of 12 cm radiates 450 W power at 500 K. If the radius were halved and the temperature doubled, the power radiated in watt would be **(1997 JEE)**

(a) 225 (b) 450 (c) 900 (d) 1800

Sol. (d) Power radiated $= e_r \sigma T^4 A$

$\Rightarrow$ Power radiated $\propto$ (surface area) $(T)^4$

The radius is halved, hence, surface area will become $\frac{1}{4}$ times. Temperature is doubled, therefore, T^4 becomes 16 times.

New power $= (450)\left(\frac{1}{4}\right)(16)$

$= 1800 \text{ W}.$

∴ The correct option is (d).

Example 6 A body cools in 10 minutes from 60°C to 40°C. What will be its temperature after next 10 minutes? The temperature of the surroundings is 10°C.

Sol. According to Newton's law of cooling,

$$\left(\frac{\theta_1 - \theta_2}{t}\right) = \alpha\left[\left(\frac{\theta_1 + \theta_2}{2}\right) - \theta_0\right]$$

For the given conditions, $\frac{60-40}{10} = \alpha\left[\frac{60+40}{2} - 10\right]$ ...(i)

Let θ be the temperature after next 10 minutes. Then,

$\frac{40-\theta}{10} = \alpha\left[\frac{40+\theta}{2} - 10\right]$ ...(ii)

Solving Eqs. (i) and (ii), we get

$\theta = 28°\text{C}$ **Ans.**

INTRODUCTORY Exercise

1. A rod is heated at one end as shown in figure. In steady state, temperature of different sections becomes constant but not same. Why so?

2. Show that the SI units of thermal conductivity are W/m-K.
3. Find SI units of thermal resistance.
4. Suppose a liquid in a container is heated at the top rather than at the bottom. What is the main process by which the rest of the liquid becomes hot?
5. Three rods each of same length and cross-section are joined in series. The thermal conductivity of the materials are K, $2K$ and $3K$ respectively. If one end is kept at 200°C and the other at 100°C, what would be the temperature of the junctions in the steady state? Assume that no heat is lost due to radiation from the sides of the rods.

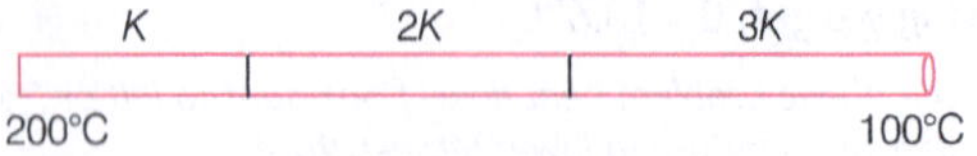

6. A rod CD of thermal resistance 5.0 K/W is joined at the middle of an identical rod AB as shown in figure. The ends A, B and D are maintained at 100°C and 25°C respectively. Find the heat current in CD.

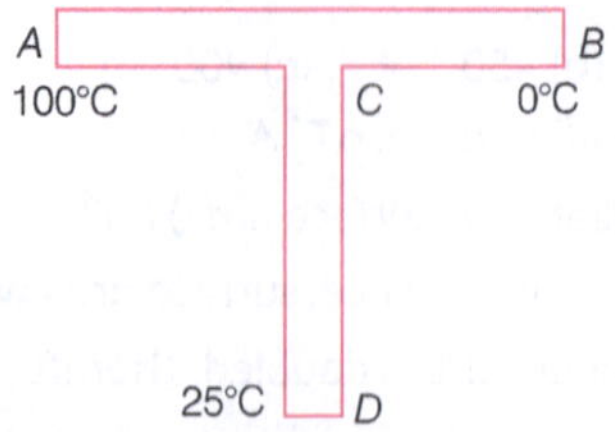

7. A liquid takes 5 minutes to cool from 80 °C to 50 °C. How much time will it take to cool from 60 °C to 30°C? The temperature of surroundings is 20 °C.

Answers

1. For heat flow to take place, there must be a temperature difference along the rod.

3. KW^{-1} 4. Conduction

5. 145.5°C, 118.2°C 6. 4 W 7. 9 min

See hints on pages 384-385.

Summary

1. Cooling by conduction or radiation

(i) By conduction

A body P of mass m and specific heat c is connected to a large body Q (of specific heat infinite) through a rod of length l, thermal conductivity K and area of cross-section A. Temperature of Q is $\theta_0 (< \theta_i)$. This temperature will remain constant as its specific heat is very high.

Heat will flow from P to Q through the rod. If we neglect the loss of heat due to radiation then due to this heat transfer, temperature of P will decrease but temperature of Q will remain almost constant.

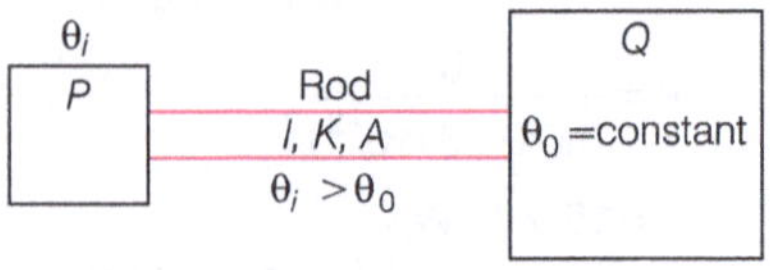

At time t, suppose temperature of P becomes θ then due to temperature difference heat transfer through the rod.

$$\frac{dQ}{dt} = H = \frac{\text{TD}}{R} = \frac{\theta - \theta_0}{R} \qquad \ldots\text{(i)}$$

Here, $R = \frac{l}{KA}$

Now, if we apply equation of calorimetry in P, then

$$Q = mc(-\Delta\theta) \quad \text{or} \quad \frac{dQ}{dt} = mc\left(\frac{-d\theta}{dt}\right) \qquad \ldots\text{(ii)}$$

Equating Eqs. (i) and (ii), we have

$$\boxed{-\frac{d\theta}{dt} = \frac{\text{TD}}{mcR} = \frac{\theta - \theta_0}{mcR} = \text{Rate of cooling}} \qquad \ldots\text{(iii)}$$

So, this is the rate of cooling by conduction.

$$\text{or} \qquad \boxed{-\frac{d\theta}{dt} \propto \text{TD}} \qquad \ldots\text{(iv)}$$

(ii) By radiation We have already derived the expression of rate of cooling in radiation,

$$\boxed{-\frac{dT}{dt} = \frac{eA\sigma}{mc}(T^4 - T_0^4) \quad \text{or} \quad -\frac{dT}{dt} \propto (T^4 - T_0^4)} \qquad \ldots\text{(v)}$$

Further in Newton's law of cooling, we have also seen that, if temperature difference between body and atmosphere is less than this rate of cooling,

$$\boxed{-\frac{dT}{dt} \propto \Delta T \quad \text{or} \quad \text{TD}} \qquad \ldots\text{(vi)}$$

In Newton's law of cooling, we have also seen that temperature of the body falls exponentially, if

$$\text{rate of cooling} : -\frac{dT}{dt} \quad \text{or} \quad -\frac{d\theta}{dt} \propto \text{TD}$$

In Eq. (iv) of conduction and Eq. (vi) of radiation (special case when TD is small)

$$-\frac{dT}{dt} \quad \text{or} \quad -\frac{d\theta}{dt} \propto \text{TD}$$

So, in both cases temperature of the body will fall exponentially like,

$$\theta = \theta_0 + (\theta_i - \theta_0)\, e^{-\alpha t} \quad \text{or} \quad T = T_0 + (T_i - T_0)\, e^{-\alpha t}$$

In radiation, $\alpha = \frac{4eA\sigma T_0^3}{mc}$ and in conduction $\alpha = \frac{1}{mcR}$

2. For emissivity, we have used the term e or e_r. This is sometimes confused with emissive power e. Emissivity is unitless and always less than or equal to one. But emissive power has the units J/s-m^2 or watt/m^2.

3. Solar constant The solar energy reaching in unit area at outer edge of the earth's atmosphere exposed perpendicularly to the rays of the sun at the average distance between the sun and earth is known as the solar constant.

$$\boxed{\text{solar constant} = 1.4\ \text{kW/m}^2}$$

Typed Problems

Type 1. *Based on calculation of thermal resistance.*

Concept

(i) A thermal resistance of a conducting rod is calculated/required between two points or two surfaces (say *a* and *b*). The formula of thermal resistance is

$$R = \frac{l}{KA}$$

Here, *l* is that dimension of conductor which is parallel to *a* and *b* and *A* is that cross-sectional area which is perpendicular to *a* and *b*.

(ii) From *a* to *b* if *A* is uniform at every point then direct formula $R = \frac{l}{KA}$ can be applied otherwise we will have to use integration.

Ex. 1 Thermal conductivity of the conductor shown in figure is K. Find thermal resistance between points *a* and *b*.

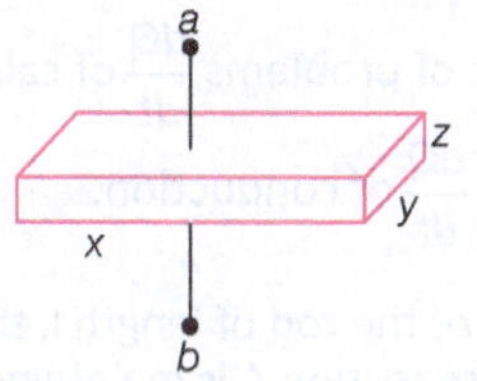

Sol. From *a* to *b* area of cross-section perpendicular to *ab* is uniform ($A = xy$) and length along *ab* is *z*. Therefore, using the formula

$$R = \frac{l}{KA}, \text{ we have}$$

$$R = \frac{z}{Kxy}$$ **Ans.**

Ex. 2 Thermal conductivity of inner core of radius *r* is *K* and of the outer one of radius 2*r* is 2*K*. Find equivalent value of thermal conductivity between its two ends.

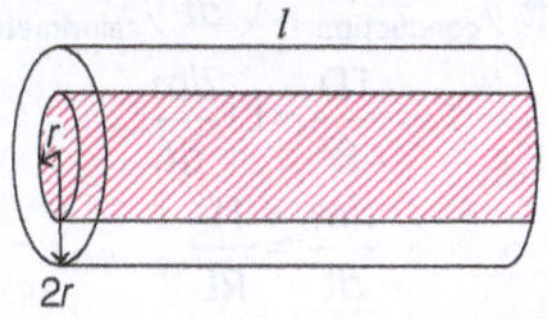

Sol. The meaning of equivalent value of thermal conductivity means, if a single material of K_e is used with same dimensions then value of thermal resistance should remain unchanged.

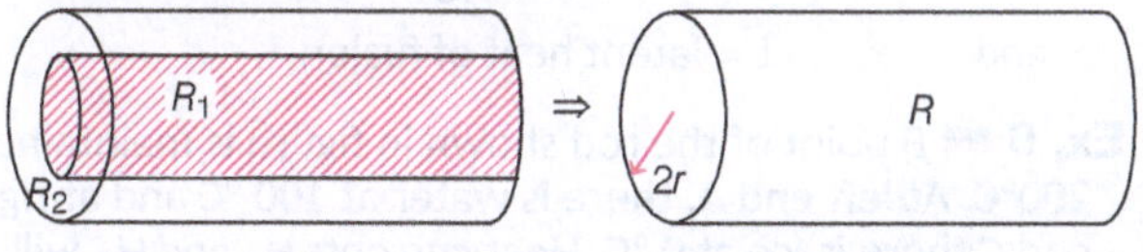

Between two ends R_1 and R_2 are in parallel. Hence,

$$\frac{1}{R_1} + \frac{1}{R_2} = \frac{1}{R} \quad \text{...(i)}$$

R is given by $\frac{l}{KA}$. Therefore, $\frac{1}{R}$ will be given by $\frac{KA}{l}$. Using this in Eq. (i), we have

$$\frac{K(\pi r^2)}{l} + \frac{2K[(\pi)(2r)^2 - \pi r^2]}{l} = \frac{K_e(\pi)(2r)^2}{l}$$

Solving this equation, we get

$$K_e = \frac{7}{4}K$$ **Ans.**

Ex. 3 A spherical body of radius '*b*' has a concentric cavity of radius '*a*' as shown. Thermal conductivity of the material is K. Find thermal resistance between inner surface P and outer surface Q.

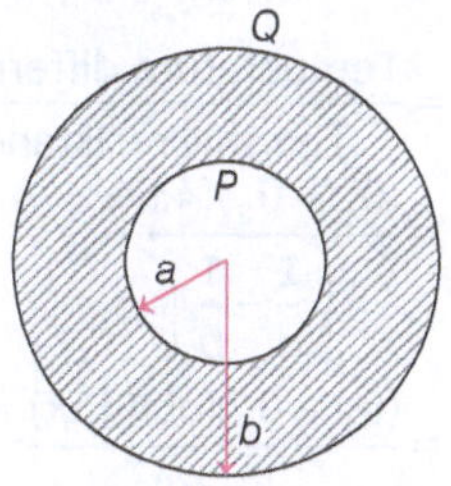

Sol. As we move from P to Q surface perpendicular to PQ is spherical and its size keeps on increasing (just like different layers of a spherical onion). So, first we will calculate thermal resistance of one layer at a distance *r* from centre and thickness *dr* by using the formula $R = \frac{l}{KA}$.

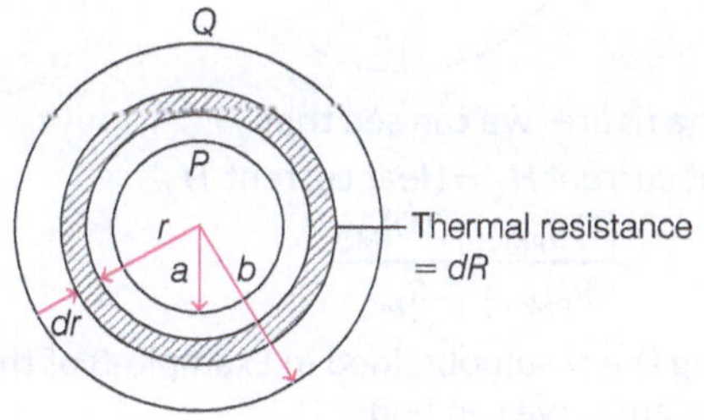

In this formula, dimension of the layer along PQ is *dr* and the surface area perpendicular to PQ is $4\pi r^2$.

$$\therefore \quad dR = \frac{dr}{K(4\pi r^2)}$$

Now, if we integrate *dR* from $r = a$ to $r = b$, we will get the total thermal resistance between P and Q. Thus,

$$R = \int_a^b dR = \int_a^b \frac{dr}{K(4\pi r^2)}$$

Solving this expression, we get

$$R = \frac{1}{4\pi K}\left(\frac{1}{a} - \frac{1}{b}\right) \qquad \textbf{Ans.}$$

Ex. 4 In the above example, if temperature of inner surface P is kept constant at θ_1 and of the outer surface Q at $\theta_2 (< \theta_1)$. Then,

Find

(a) rate of heat flow or heat current from inner surface to outer surface.

(b) temperature θ at a distance $r (a < r < b)$ from centre.

Sol. (a)

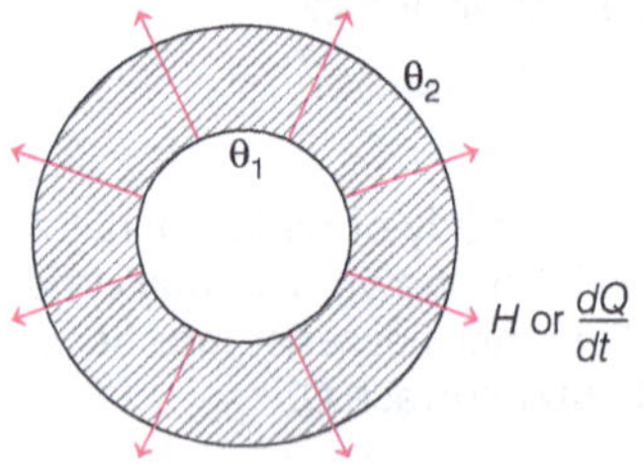

$$H \text{ or } \frac{dQ}{dt} = \frac{\text{Temperature difference}}{\text{Thermal resistance}}$$

$$= \frac{(\theta_1 - \theta_2)(4\pi K)}{\left(\frac{1}{a} - \frac{1}{b}\right)}$$

$$= \frac{(\theta_1 - \theta_2)(ab)(4\pi K)}{(b - a)} \qquad \textbf{Ans.}$$

(b)

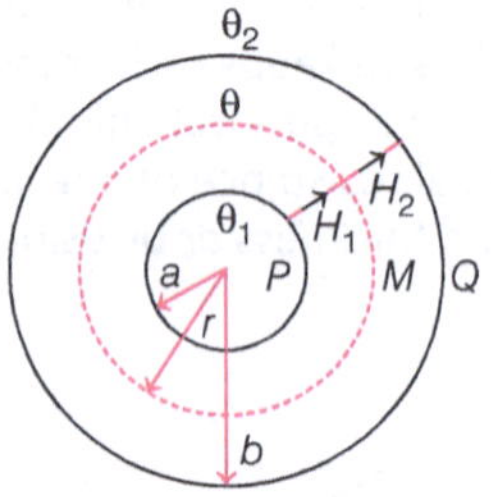

In the figure, we can see that

Heat current H_1 = Heat current H_2

$$\therefore \quad \frac{(TD)_{PM}}{R_{PM}} = \frac{(TD)_{MQ}}{R_{MQ}} \qquad \ldots\text{(i)}$$

Using the result obtained in Example-3 of thermal resistance, we can find

$$R_{PM} = \frac{1}{4\pi K}\left(\frac{1}{a} - \frac{1}{r}\right)$$

and

$$R_{MQ} = \frac{1}{4\pi K}\left(\frac{1}{r} - \frac{1}{b}\right)$$

Substituting the values in Eq. (i), we have

$$\frac{\theta_1 - \theta}{\frac{1}{4\pi K}\left(\frac{1}{a} - \frac{1}{r}\right)} = \frac{\theta - \theta_2}{\frac{1}{4\pi K}\left(\frac{1}{r} - \frac{1}{b}\right)}$$

Solving this equation we can find θ.

Type 2. *Mixed problems of calorimetry and conduction.*

Concept

(i) In calorimetry, we have two equations,

$Q = mc\Delta\theta$ (when temperature changes without change in state)

and $Q = mL$ (when state changes without change in temperature)

The above two equations in differential form can be written as

$$\frac{dQ}{dt} = mc\left(\pm\frac{d\theta}{dt}\right) \text{ or } L\left(\frac{dm}{dt}\right) \qquad \ldots\text{(i)}$$

In the above equation $\frac{dm}{dt}$ is the rate of conversion of mass from one state to another state.

(ii) In conduction, we have the equation,

$$\frac{dQ}{dt} \text{ or } H = \frac{TD}{R} \qquad \ldots\text{(ii)}$$

where,

$$R = \frac{l}{KA}$$

In these types of problems $\frac{dQ}{dt}$ of calorimetry is equated with $\frac{dQ}{dt}$ of conduction.

Ex. 5 One end of the rod of length l, thermal conductivity K and area of cross-section A is maintained at a constant temperature of 100 °C. At the other end large quantity of ice is kept at 0 °C. Due to temperature difference, heat flows from left end to right end of the rod. Due to this heat ice will start melting. Neglecting the radiation losses find the expression of rate of melting of ice.

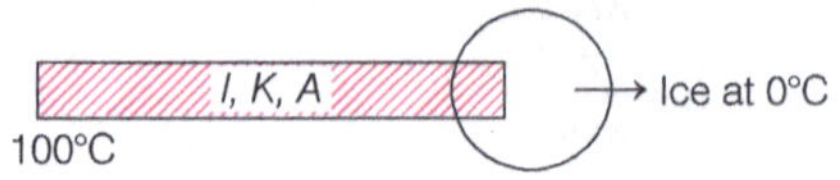

Sol. Putting,

$$\left(\frac{dQ}{dt}\right)_{\text{conduction}} = \left(\frac{dQ}{dt}\right)_{\text{calorimetry}}$$

$$\therefore \quad \frac{TD}{R} = L \cdot \frac{dm}{dt}$$

$$\Rightarrow \quad \frac{dm}{dt} = \frac{TD}{RL} \qquad \textbf{Ans.}$$

So, this is the desired expression of $\frac{dm}{dt}$.

In the above expression,

$$TD = 100°C, R = \frac{l}{KA}$$

and L = latent heat of fusion

Ex. 6 B point of the rod shown in figure is maintained at 200°C. At left end A, there is water at 100 °C and at right end C there is ice at 0 °C. Heat currents H_1 and H_2 will flow on both sides. Due to H_1, water will convert into steam and due to H_2 ice will be melted. If latent heat of vaporization is 540 cal/g and latent heat of fusion is 80 cal/g then neglecting the radiation losses find $\frac{l_1}{l_2}$ so that rate of melting of ice is two times the rate of conversion of water into steam.

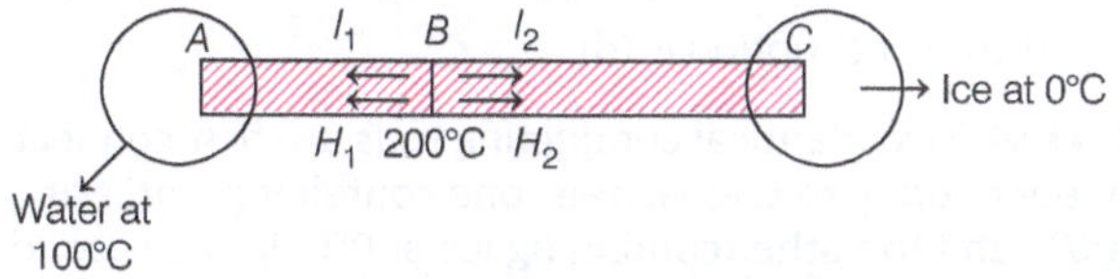

Sol. Using the relation of $\frac{dm}{dt}$ derived in above example,

$$\frac{dm}{dt}=\frac{\text{TD}}{RL}=\frac{(\text{TD})KA}{lL} \qquad \left(\text{as } R=\frac{l}{KA}\right)$$

Given that, $$\left(\frac{dm}{dt}\right)_{\text{RHS}}=2\left(\frac{dm}{dt}\right)_{\text{LHS}}$$

or $$\left[\frac{(\text{TD})KA}{lL}\right]_{\text{RHS}}=2\left[\frac{(\text{TD})KA}{lL}\right]_{\text{LHS}}$$

K and A are same on both sides. Hence,

$$\left(\frac{\text{TD}}{lL}\right)_{\text{RHS}}=2\left(\frac{\text{TD}}{lL}\right)_{\text{LHS}}$$

Substituting the proper values, we have

$$\frac{200}{l_2\times 80}=2\left[\frac{100}{l_1\times 540}\right]$$

$$\therefore \qquad \frac{l_1}{l_2}=\frac{80}{540}=\frac{4}{27} \qquad \textbf{Ans.}$$

Type 3. *Mixed problems of Stefan's law and Wien's displacement law.*

Concept

Stefan's law

Energy radiated per unit area and per unit time = emissive power $=e_r\sigma T^4$

Energy radiated per unit time = power $=e_r\sigma T^4 A$

Total energy radiated in time $t=e_r\sigma T^4 At$

Above all three terms $\propto T^4$

Wien's displacement law

$$\lambda_m\propto\frac{1}{T}$$

From Wien's law normally we find the ratio of temperatures of two bodies and then this ratio is used in Stefan's law.

Ex. 7 Three discs, A, B and C having radii 2m, 4m and 6m respectively are coated with carbon black on their outer surfaces. The wavelengths corresponding to maximum intensity are 300 nm, 400 nm and 500 nm, respectively. The power radiated by them are Q_A, Q_B and Q_C respectively **(2004 JEE)**

(a) Q_A is maximum (b) Q_B is maximum

(c) Q_C is maximum (d) $Q_A=Q_B=Q_C$

Sol. (b) $Q\propto AT^4$ and $\lambda_m T=$ constant.

Hence, $$Q\propto\frac{A}{(\lambda_m)^4}$$

or $$Q\propto\frac{r^2}{(\lambda_m)^4}$$

$$Q_A:Q_B:Q_C=\frac{(2)^2}{(3)^4}:\frac{(4)^2}{(4)^4}:\frac{(6)^2}{(5)^4}=\frac{4}{81}:\frac{1}{16}:\frac{36}{625}$$
$$=0.05:0.0625:0.0576$$

i.e. Q_B is maximum.

Type 4. *Problems of cooling either by conduction or radiation.*

Concept

We have seen that if a body cools by conduction, then

$$\text{rate of cooling, } -\frac{d\theta}{dt}=\frac{\text{TD}}{mcR} \qquad \text{...(i)}$$

Here, $mc=C=$ heat capacity of the body

This C is the heat required to raise the temperature of whole body by 1 °C or 1K and R is the thermal resistance of conducting rod. So, Eq. (i) can also be written as

$$-\frac{d\theta}{dt}=\frac{\text{TD}}{CR}$$

If the body cools by radiation, then

$$\text{rate of cooling or } -\frac{dT}{dt}=\frac{eA\sigma}{mc}(T^4-T_0^4) \qquad \text{...(ii)}$$

For small temperature difference, Newton's law of cooling can be applied and

$$-\frac{dT}{dt}\propto\text{TD} \qquad \text{...(iii)}$$

Further, if rate of cooling $\propto$ TD as Eqs. (i) or (iii), temperature of the body falls exponentially.

Ex. 8 Two spheres, one solid and the other hollow are kept in atmosphere at same temperature. They are made of same material and their radii are also same. Which sphere will cool at a faster rate initially?

Sol. In the equation,

$$-\frac{dT}{dt}=\frac{eA\sigma}{mc}(T^4-T_0^4)$$

Only mass is different. Therefore,

$$-\frac{dT}{dt}\propto\frac{1}{m}$$

Mass of hollow sphere is less. So, hollow sphere will cool at a faster rate initially.

Ex. 9 The ratio of specific heats of two spheres is 2 : 3, radii 1 : 2, emissivity 3 : 1 and density 1 : 1. Initially, they are kept at same temperatures in atmosphere. Which sphere will cool at a faster rate initially.

Sol. In the equation,

$$-\frac{dT}{dt} = \frac{eA\sigma}{mc}(T^4 - T_0^4)$$

A = surface area = $4\pi R^2$

m = Volume × density = $\frac{4}{3}\pi R^3 \rho$

Substituting in the above equation, we have

$$-\frac{dT}{dt} = \frac{3e\sigma}{R\rho c}(T^4 - T_0^4) \quad \text{or} \quad -\frac{dT}{dt} \propto \frac{e}{R\rho c}$$

Now, $\left(\frac{e}{R\rho c}\right)_{\text{sphere-1}} = \frac{3}{1 \times 1 \times 2} = \frac{3}{2}$

and $\left(\frac{e}{R\rho c}\right)_{\text{sphere-2}} = \frac{1}{2 \times 1 \times 3} = \frac{1}{6}$

$\left(\frac{e}{R\rho c}\right)$ for sphere-1 is more.

So, first sphere will cool at faster rate initially.

Ex 10 Two metallic spheres S_1 and S_2 are made of the same material and have got identical surface finish. The mass of S_1 is thrice that of S_2. Both the spheres are heated to the same high temperature and placed in the same room having lower temperature but are thermally insulated from each other. The ratio of the initial rate of cooling of S_1 to that of S_2 is **(1995 JEE)**

(a) $\frac{1}{3}$ (b) $\frac{1}{\sqrt{3}}$ (c) $\frac{\sqrt{3}}{1}$ (d) $\left(\frac{1}{3}\right)^{1/3}$

Sol. (d) $-\frac{dT}{dt} = \frac{eA\sigma}{mc}(T^4 - T_0^4)$

$$m_1 = 3m_2$$

$\therefore$ $R_1 = (3)^{\frac{1}{3}} R_2$

$$\left(-\frac{dT}{dt}\right) \propto \frac{A}{m} \propto \frac{R^2}{R^3} \propto \frac{1}{R}$$

$\therefore$ $\frac{(-dT/dt)_1}{(-dT/dt)_2} = \frac{R_2}{R_1} = \left(\frac{1}{3}\right)^{\frac{1}{3}}$

$\therefore$ The correct option is (d).

Ex. 11 Two identical conducting rods are first connected independently to two vessels, one containing water at 100°C and the other containing ice at 0°C. In the second case, the rods are joined end to end and connected to the same vessels. Let q_1 and q_2 gram per second be the rate of melting of ice in the two cases respectively. The ratio $\frac{q_1}{q_2}$ is **(2004 JEE)**

(a) $\frac{1}{2}$ (b) $\frac{2}{1}$ (c) $\frac{4}{1}$ (d) $\frac{1}{4}$

Sol. (c) $\frac{dQ}{dt} = L\left(\frac{dm}{dt}\right)$

or $\frac{\text{Temperature difference}}{\text{Thermal resistance}} = L\left(\frac{dm}{dt}\right)$

or $\frac{dm}{dt} \propto \frac{1}{\text{Thermal resistance}} \Rightarrow q \propto \frac{1}{R}$

In the first case rods are in parallel and thermal resistance is $\frac{R}{2}$ while in second case rods are in series and thermal resistance is $2R$.

$$\frac{q_1}{q_2} = \frac{R_2}{R_1} = \frac{2R}{R/2} = \frac{4}{1}$$

Miscellaneous Examples

Ex. 12 Two metal cubes with 3 cm-edges of copper and aluminium are arranged as shown in figure. Find

(a) the total thermal current from one reservoir to the other

(b) the ratio of the thermal current carried by the copper cube to that carried by the aluminium cube.

Thermal conductivity of copper is 401 W/m-K and that of aluminium is 237 W/m-K.

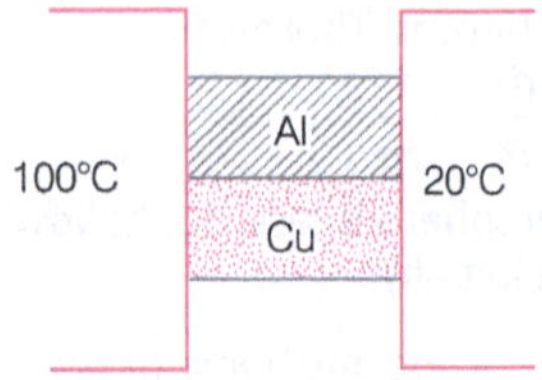

Sol. (a) Thermal resistance of aluminium cube, $R_1 = \frac{l}{KA}$

or $R_1 = \frac{(3.0 \times 10^{-2})}{(237)(3.0 \times 10^{-2})^2} = 0.14$ K/W

and thermal resistance of copper cube, $R_2 = \frac{l}{KA}$

or $R_2 = \frac{(3.0 \times 10^{-2})}{(401)(3.0 \times 10^{-2})^2} = 0.08$ K/W

As these two resistance are in parallel, their equivalent resistance will be

$$R = \frac{R_1 R_2}{R_1 + R_2}$$

$$= \frac{(0.14)(0.08)}{(0.14) + (0.08)} = 0.05 \text{ K/W}$$

$\therefore$ Thermal current, $H = \frac{\text{Temperature difference}}{\text{Thermal resistance}}$

$$= \frac{(100-20)}{0.05} = 1.6 \times 10^3 \text{ W} \quad \textbf{Ans.}$$

(b) In parallel thermal current distributes in the inverse ratio of resistance. Hence,

$$\frac{H_{Cu}}{H_{Al}} = \frac{R_{Al}}{R_{Cu}} = \frac{R_1}{R_2}$$

$$= \frac{0.14}{0.08} = 1.75 \quad \textbf{Ans.}$$

Ex. 13 One end of a copper rod of length 1 m and area of cross-section $4.0 \times 10^{-4} \text{m}^2$ is maintained at 100°C. At the other end of the rod ice is kept at 0°C. Neglecting the loss of heat from the surroundings, find the mass of ice melted in 1 h. Given, $K_{Cu} = 401$ W/m - K and $L_f = 3.35 \times 10^5$ J/kg.

Sol. Thermal resistance of the rod,

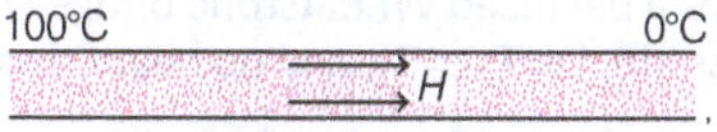

$$R = \frac{l}{KA}$$

$$= \frac{1.0}{(401)(4 \times 10^{-4})}$$

$$= 6.23 \text{ K/W}$$

$$\therefore \text{Heat current, } H = \frac{\text{Temperature difference}}{\text{Thermal resistance}}$$

$$= \frac{(100-0)}{6.23} = 16 \text{ W}$$

Heat transferred in 1 h,

$$Q = Ht \qquad \left(\because H = \frac{Q}{t}\right)$$

$$= (16)(3600) = 57600 \text{ J}$$

Now, let m mass of ice melts in 1 h, then

$$m = \frac{Q}{L} \qquad (Q = mL)$$

$$= \frac{57600}{3.35 \times 10^5}$$

$$= 0.172 \text{ kg}$$

$$= 172 \text{ g}$$

Ex. 14 Two bodies A and B have thermal emissivities of 0.01 and 0.81 respectively. The outer surface areas of the two bodies are same. The two bodies emit total radiant power at the same rate. The wavelength λ_B corresponding to maximum spectral radiancy from B is shifted from the wavelength corresponding to maximum spectral radiancy in the radiation from A by 1.0 μm. If the temperature of A is 5802 K, calculate (a) the temperature of B, (b) wavelength λ_B.

Sol. (a) $P_A = P_B$

$$\therefore \quad e_A \sigma A_A T_A^4 = e_B \sigma A_B T_B^4$$

$$\therefore \quad T_B = \left(\frac{e_A}{e_B}\right)^{1/4} T_A \qquad (\text{as } A_A = A_B)$$

Substituting the values,

$$T_B = \left(\frac{0.01}{0.81}\right)^{1/4} (5802) = 1934 \text{ K} \quad \textbf{Ans.}$$

(b) According to Wien's displacement law,

$$\lambda_A T_A = \lambda_B T_B$$

$$\therefore \quad \lambda_B = \left(\frac{T_A}{T_B}\right)\lambda_A = \left(\frac{5802}{1934}\right)\lambda_A$$

or $\quad \lambda_B = 3\lambda_A$

Also, $\quad \lambda_B - \lambda_A = 1 \,\mu\text{m}$

or $\quad \lambda_B - \left(\frac{1}{3}\right)\lambda_B = 1 \,\mu\text{m}$

or $\quad \lambda_B = 1.5 \,\mu\text{m} \quad$ **Ans.**

Ex. 15 Two plates each of area A, thickness L_1 and L_2 thermal conductivities K_1 and K_2 respectively are joined to form a single plate of thickness $(L_1 + L_2)$. If the temperatures of the free surfaces are T_1 and T_2. Calculate

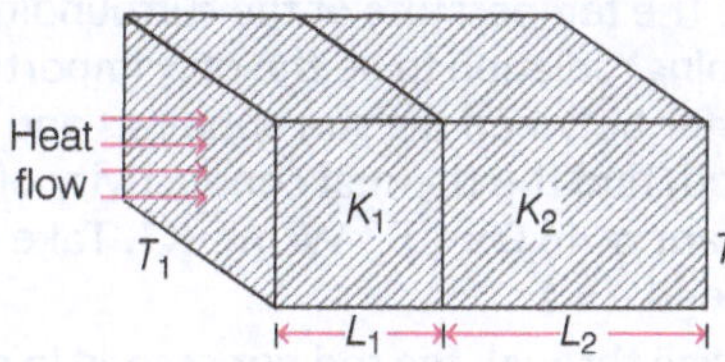

(a) rate of flow of heat

(b) temperature of interface and

(c) equivalent thermal conductivity.

Sol. (a) Let the thermal resistance of the two plates are R_1 and R_2 respectively. Plates are in series.

$$R_S = R_1 + R_2 = \frac{L_1}{AK_1} + \frac{L_2}{AK_2}$$

as $\quad R = \frac{L}{KA}$

and so $\quad H = \frac{dQ}{dt} = \frac{\Delta T}{R}$

$$= \frac{(T_1 - T_2)}{(R_1 + R_2)} = \frac{A(T_1 - T_2)}{\left[\frac{L_1}{K_1} + \frac{L_2}{K_2}\right]} \quad \textbf{Ans.}$$

(b) If T is the common temperature of interface, then as in series rate of flow of heat remains same, i.e.

$$H = H_1$$

$$\therefore \quad \frac{T_1 - T_2}{R_1 + R_2} = \frac{T_1 - T}{R_1}$$

i.e. $\quad T = \frac{T_1 R_2 + T_2 R_1}{(R_1 + R_2)}$

or $$T=\frac{\left[T_1\frac{L_2}{K_2}+T_2\frac{L_1}{K_1}\right]}{\left[\frac{L_1}{K_1}+\frac{L_2}{K_2}\right]} \qquad \left(\text{as } R=\frac{L}{KA}\right)$$

(c) If K is the equivalent conductivity of composite slab, i.e. slab of thickness L_1+L_2 and cross-sectional area A, then as in series

$$R_S=R_1+R_2$$

or $$\frac{(L_1+L_2)}{AK_{eq}}=R_1+R_2$$

i.e. $$K_{eq}=\frac{L_1+L_2}{A(R_1+R_2)}$$

$$=\frac{L_1+L_2}{\left[\frac{L_1}{K_1}+\frac{L_2}{K_2}\right]} \qquad \left(\text{as } R=\frac{L}{KA}\right)$$

Ex. 16 One end of a rod of length 20 cm is inserted in a furnace at 800 K. The sides of the rod are covered with an insulating material and the other end emits radiation like a black body. The temperature of this end is 750 K in the steady state. The temperature of the surrounding air is 300 K. Assuming radiation to be the only important mode of energy transfer between the surroundings and the open end of the rod, find the thermal conductivity of the rod. Stefan constant $\sigma=6.0\times10^{-8}$ W/m^2-K^4. Take emissivity of the open end $e=1$

Sol. Heat flowing through the rod per second in steady state,

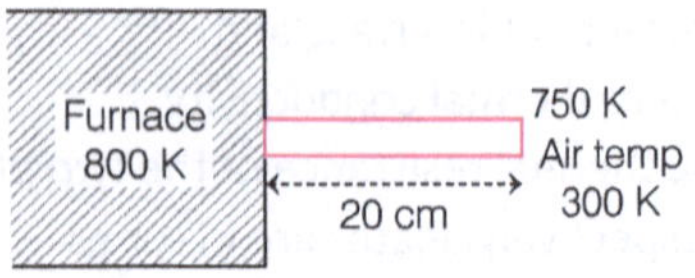

$$\frac{dQ}{dt}=\frac{KA\Delta T}{L} \qquad \text{...(i)}$$

Heat radiated from the open end of the rod per second in steady state,

$$\frac{dQ}{dt}=A\sigma(T^4-T_0^4) \qquad \text{...(ii)}$$

From Eqs. (i) and (ii),

$$\frac{K\Delta T}{L}=\sigma(T^4-T_0^4)$$

$$\frac{K\times50}{0.2}=6.0\times10^{-8}[(7.5)^4-(3)^4]\times10^8$$

or $$K=74\text{ W/m-K}$$ **Ans.**

Ex. 17 Three rods of material x and three rods of material y are connected as shown in figure. All the rods are of identical length and cross-sectional area. If the end A is maintained at 60°C and the junction E at 10°C, calculate temperature of junctions B, C and D. The thermal conductivity of x is 0.92 cal/cm-s°C and that of y is 0.46 cal/cm-s°C.

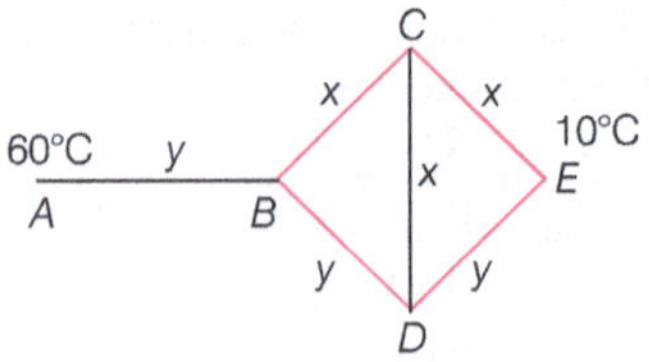

Sol. Thermal resistance, $R=\frac{l}{KA}$

$\therefore$ $$\frac{R_x}{R_y}=\frac{K_y}{K_x} \qquad (\text{as } l_x=l_y \text{ and } A_x=A_y)$$

$$=\frac{0.46}{0.92}=\frac{1}{2}$$

So, if $R_x=R$ then $R_y=2R$

CEDB forms a balanced Wheatstone bridge (You will learn this in class XII), i.e. $T_C=T_D$ and no heat flows through *CD*.

$\therefore$ $$\frac{1}{R_{BE}}=\frac{1}{R+R}+\frac{1}{2R+2R}$$

or $$R_{BE}=\frac{4}{3}R$$

The total resistance between A and E will be

$$R_{AE}=R_{AB}+R_{BE}$$
$$=2R+\frac{4}{3}R=\frac{10}{3}R$$

$\therefore$ Heat current between A and E is

$$H=\frac{(\Delta T)_{AE}}{R_{AE}}=\frac{(60-10)}{(10/3)R}=\frac{15}{R}$$

Now, if T_B is the temperature at B,

$$H_{AB}=\frac{(\Delta T)_{AB}}{R_{AB}}$$

or $$\frac{15}{R}=\frac{60-T_B}{2R}$$

or $$T_B=30°\text{C}$$ **Ans.**

Further, $$H_{AB}=H_{BC}+H_{BD}$$

or $$\frac{15}{R}=\frac{30-T_C}{R}+\frac{30-T_D}{2R} \qquad [T_C=T_D=T\text{ (say)}]$$

or $$15=(30-T)+\frac{(30-T)}{2}$$

Solving this, we get

$$T=20°\text{C}$$

or $$T_C=T_D=20°\text{C}$$ **Ans.**

Ex. 18 A hollow sphere of glass whose external and internal radii are 11 cm and 9 cm respectively is completely filled with ice at 0°C and placed in a bath of boiling water. How long will it take for the ice to melt completely? Given that density of ice $=0.9$ g/cm^3, latent heat of fusion of ice $=80$ cal/g and thermal conductivity of glass $=0.002$ cal/cm-s°C.

Sol. In steady state, rate of heat flow

$$\frac{dQ}{dt} = H = \frac{4\pi K r_1 r_2 \Delta T}{r_2 - r_1}$$

Note *The above result is derived in example 4, part (a).*

Substituting the values,

$$\frac{dQ}{dt} = \frac{(4)(\pi)(0.002)(11)(9)(100-0)}{(11-9)}$$

or $$\frac{dQ}{dt} = 124.4 \text{ cal/s}$$

This rate should be equal to, $L\frac{dm}{dt}$

$$\therefore \quad \left(\frac{dm}{dt}\right) = \frac{dQ/dt}{L}$$

$$= \frac{124.4}{80} = 1.555 \text{ g/s}$$

Total mass of ice, $m = \rho_{\text{ice}}\left(\frac{4}{3}\pi r_1^3\right)$

$$= (0.9)\left(\frac{4}{3}\right)(\pi)(9)^3$$

$$= 2747 \text{ g}$$

$\therefore$ Time taken for the ice to melt completely

$$t = \frac{m}{(dm/dt)}$$

$$= \frac{2747}{1.555} \approx 1766 \text{ s}$$ **Ans.**

Ex. 19 A steam cylindrical pipe of radius 5 cm carries steam at 100°C. The pipe is covered by a jacket of insulating material 2 cm thick having a thermal conductivity 0.07 W/m-K. If the temperature at the outer wall of the pipe jacket is 20°C, how much heat is lost through the jacket per metre length in an hour?

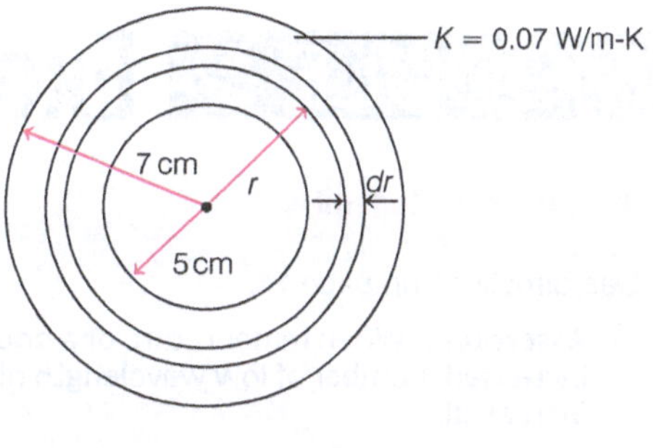

Sol. Thermal resistance per metre length of an element at distance r of thickness dr is

$$dR = \frac{dr}{K(2\pi r)} \qquad \left(R = \frac{l}{KA}\right)$$

$$\therefore \quad \text{Total resistance } R = \int_{r_1 = 5\text{ cm}}^{r_2 = 7\text{ cm}} dR$$

$$= \frac{1}{2\pi K}\int_{5.0\times10^{-2}\text{ m}}^{7.0\times10^{-2}\text{ m}} \frac{dr}{r}$$

$$= \frac{1}{2\pi K}\ln\left(\frac{7}{5}\right)$$

$$= \frac{1}{(2\pi)(0.07)}\ln(1.4)$$

$$= 0.765 \text{ K/W}$$

$$\text{Heat current, } H = \frac{\text{Temperature difference}}{\text{Thermal resistance}}$$

$$= \frac{(100-20)}{0.765} = 104.6 \text{ W}$$

$$\therefore \quad \text{Heat lost in one hour} = \text{Heat current} \times \text{time}$$

$$= (1.4.6)(3600) \text{ J}$$

$$= 3.76 \times 10^5 \text{ J}$$ **Ans.**

MODULE 2 Exercise

Assertion and Reason

See directions on page 14.

1. **Assertion :** When temperature of a body is increased, number of low wavelength photons get increased.

   Reason : According to Wien's displacement law $\lambda_m \propto \frac{1}{T}$.

2. **Assertion :** A normal body can radiate energy more than a perfectly black body.

   Reason : A perfectly black body is always black in colour.

3. **Assertion :** Good conductors of electricity are also good conductors of heat due to large number of free electrons.

   Reason : It is easy to conduct heat from free electrons.

4. **Assertion :** Heat is supplied at constant rate from one end of a conducting rod. In steady state, temperature of all points of the rod becomes uniform.

   Reason : In steady state, temperature of rod does not increase.

5. **Assertion :** Two conducting rods of same material and same lengths are joined end to end as shown in figure. Heat current H is flowing through them as shown. Temperature difference across rod-1 is more than the temperature difference across rod-2.

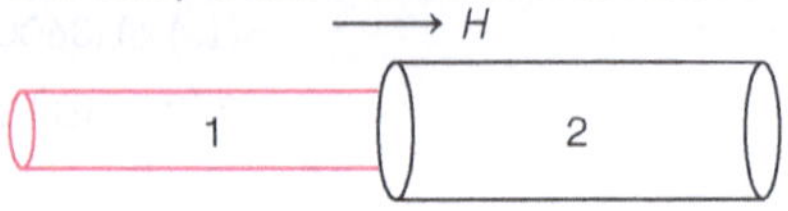

   Reason : Thermal resistance of rod-1 is less compared to rod-2.

6. **Assertion :** Evaporation of water is fast on the surface of moon as compared to earth.

   Reason : On the surface of moon temperature is less than the temperature on the surface of earth.

Single Correct Option

7. On heating one end of a rod, the temperature of whole rod will be uniform when

   (a) $K = 1$ (b) $K = 0$ (c) $K = 100$ (d) $K = \infty$

8. The ratio of the emissive power to the absorptive power of all substances for a particular wavelength is the same at given temperature. The ratio is known as
   (a) the emissive power of a perfectly black body
   (b) the absorptive power of perfectly black body
   (c) the Stefan's constant
   (d) the Wien's constant

9. Two metal spheres have radii r and $2r$ and they emit thermal radiation with maximum intensities at wavelengths λ and 2λ, respectively. The respective ratio of the radiant energy emitted by them per second will be

   (a) 4 : 1 (b) 1 : 4 (c) 16 : 1 (d) 8 : 1

10. Two thin blankets keep more hotness than one blanket of thickness equal to these two. The reason is
    (a) their surface area increases
    (b) a layer of air is formed between these two blankets which is bad conductor of heat
    (c) these have more wool
    (d) they absorb more heat from outside

11. Ice formed over lakes
    (a) has very high thermal conductivity and helps in further ice formation
    (b) has very low conductivity and retards further formation of ice
    (c) permits quick convection and retards further formation of ice
    (d) is very good radiator

12. Mud houses are cool in summers and warm in winters because
    (a) mud has low specific heat
    (b) mud is good conductor of heat
    (c) mud is bad conductor of heat
    (d) mud has high specific heat

13. Air is bad conductor of heat, still vacuum is preferred between the walls of the thermoflask because
    (a) it is difficult to fill the air between the walls of thermo flask
    (b) due to more pressure of air, the flask can crack
    (c) by convection, heat can flow through air
    (d) None of the above

14. In MKS system, Stefan's constant is denoted by σ. In CGS system multiplying factor of σ will be

    (a) 1 (b) 10^3
    (c) 10^5 (d) 10^2

15. An ideal black body at room temperature is thrown into a furnace. It is observed that **(2002 JEE)**
    (a) initially, it is the darkest body and at later brightest
    (b) it is the darkest body at all times
    (c) it cannot be distinguished at all times
    (d) initially, it is the darkest body and later cannot be distinguished

16. A sphere, a cube and a thin circular plate are heated to the same temperature. All are made of the same material and have the equal masses. If t_1, t_2 and t_3 are the respective time taken by the sphere, cube and

the circular plate in cooling down to a common temperature, then

(a) $t_1 > t_2 > t_3$ (b) $t_1 < t_2 < t_3$ (c) $t_2 > t_1 > t_3$ (d) $t_1 = t_2 = t_3$

17. If e_λ and a_λ be the spectral emissive power and aborptive power of a body at a given temperature, then according to Kirchhoff's law, which is true? (E_λ = emissive power of perfectly black body at that temperature)

(a) $e_\lambda = a_\lambda = E_\lambda$ (b) $e_\lambda E_\lambda = a_\lambda$
(c) $e_\lambda = a_\lambda E_\lambda$ (d) $e_\lambda a_\lambda E_\lambda = \text{constant}$

18. A substance cools from 75°C to 70°C in T_1 minute, from 70°C to 65°C in T_2 minute and from 65°C to 60°C in T_3 minute, then

(a) $T_1 = T_2 = T_3$ (b) $T_1 < T_2 < T_3$
(c) $T_1 > T_2 > T_3$ (d) $T_1 < T_2 > T_3$

19. The spectrum of a black body at two temperatures 27°C and 327°C is shown in the figure. Let A_1 and A_2 be the areas under the two curves respectively. The value of $\frac{A_2}{A_1}$ is

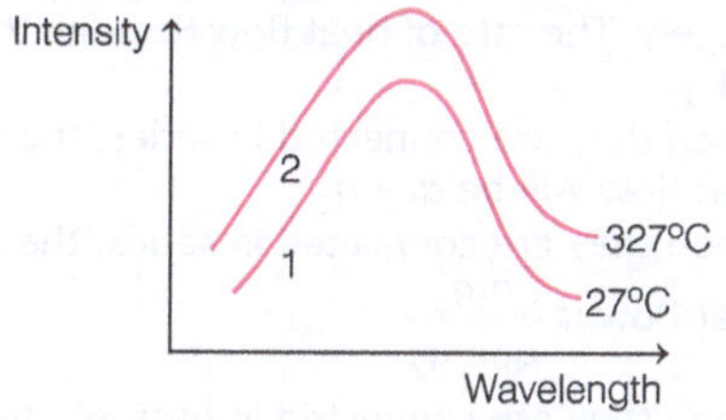

(a) 1 : 16 (b) 4 : 1 (c) 2 : 1 (d) 16 : 1

20. Two rods of copper and brass ($K_C > K_B$) of same length and area of cross-section are joined as shown. End A is kept at 100°C and end B at 0°C. The temperature at the junction

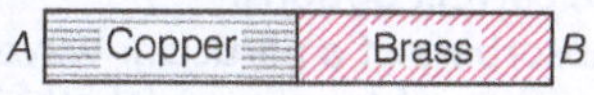

(a) will be more than 50°C
(b) will be less than 50°C
(c) will be 50°C
(d) may be more or less than 50°C

21. Two rods (one semi-circular and the other straight) of same material and of same cross-sectional area are joined as shown in the figure. The points A and B are maintained at different temperatures. The ratio of the heat transferred through a cross-section of a semi-circular rod to the heat transferred through a cross-section of the straight rod in a given time is

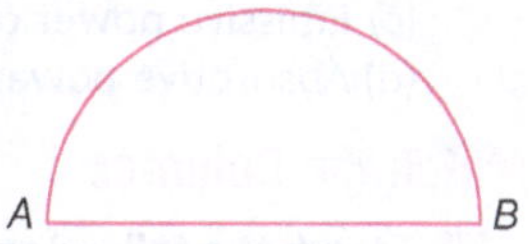

(a) $2 : \pi$ (b) 1 : 2 (c) $\pi : 2$ (d) 3 : 2

22. For an enclosure maintained at 2000 K, the maximum radiation occurs at wavelength λ_m. If the temperature is raised to 3000 K, the peak will shift to

(a) $0.5\,\lambda_m$ (b) λ_m (c) $\frac{2}{3}\lambda_m$ (d) $\frac{3}{2}\lambda_m$

23. The intensity of radiation emitted by the sun has its maximum value at a wavelength of 510 nm and that emitted by the North star has the maximum value at 350 nm. If these stars behave like black bodies, then the ratio of the surface temperatures of the sun and the north star is **(1997 JEE)**

(a) 1.46 (b) 0.69 (c) 1.21 (d) 0.83

24. Two ends of rods of length L and radius R of the same material are kept at the same temperature. Which of the following rods conducts the maximum heat?

(a) $L = 50$ cm, $R = 1$ cm (b) $L = 100$ cm, $R = 2$ cm
(c) $L = 25$ cm, $R = 0.5$ cm (d) $L = 75$ cm, $R = 1.5$ cm

25. A wall has two layers A and B each made of different materials. The layer A is 10 cm thick and B is 20 cm thick. The thermal conductivity of A is thrice that of B. Under thermal equilibrium, temperature difference across the wall is 35°C. The difference of temperature across the layer A is

(a) 30°C (b) 14°C (c) 8.75°C (d) 5°C

26. The end of two rods of different materials with their thermal conductivities, area of cross-section and lengths all in the ratio 1 : 2 are maintained at the same temperature difference. If the rate of flow of heat in the first rod is 4 cal/s. Then, in the second rod rate of heat flow in cal/s will be

(a) 1 (b) 2 (c) 8 (d) 16

27. Two spherical black bodies of radii r_1 and r_2 and with surface temperatures T_1 and T_2 respectively radiate the same power. Then, $\frac{r_1}{r_2}$ must be equal to

(a) $\left(\frac{T_1}{T_2}\right)^2$ (b) $\left(\frac{T_2}{T_1}\right)^2$ (c) $\left(\frac{T_1}{T_2}\right)^4$ (d) $\left(\frac{T_2}{T_1}\right)^4$

28. Equal temperature differences exist between the ends of two metallic rods 1 and 2 of equal lengths. Their thermal conductivities are K_1 and K_2 and area of cross-section are A_1 and A_2, respectively. The condition of equal rates of heat transfer is

(a) $K_1A_2 = K_2A_1$ (b) $K_1A_1 = K_2A_2$
(c) $K_1A_1^2 = K_2A_2^2$ (d) $K_1^2A_2 = K_2^2A_1$

29. Three rods of same dimensions are arranged as shown in figure. They have thermal conductivities K_1, K_2 and K_3. The points P and Q are maintained at different temperatures. For the heat flow at the same rate along PRQ and PQ which of the following option is correct?

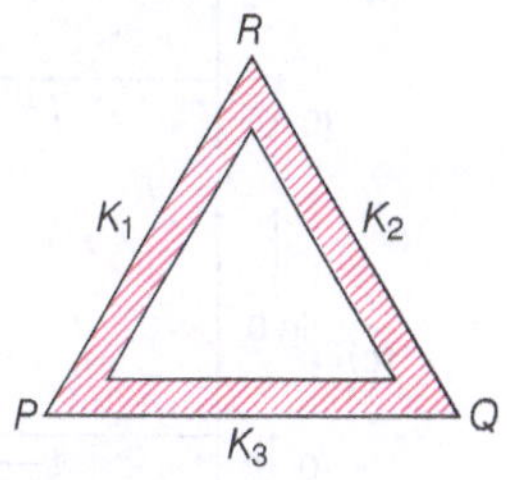

(a) $K_3 = \frac{1}{2}(K_1 + K_2)$ (b) $K_3 = K_1 + K_2$
(c) $K_3 = \frac{K_1K_2}{K_1 + K_2}$ (d) $K_3 = 2(K_1 + K_2)$

30. Five rods of same dimensions are arranged as shown in figure. They have thermal conductivities K_1, K_2, K_3, K_4 and K_5. When points A and B are maintained at different temperatures, no heat flows through the central rod if

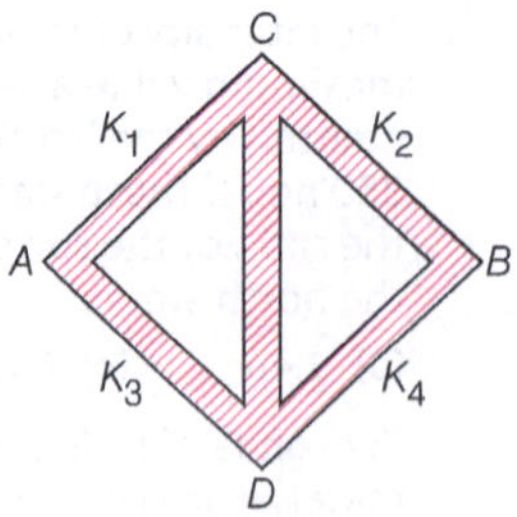

(a) $K_1 = K_4$ and $K_2 = K_3$
(b) $K_1K_4 = K_2K_3$
(c) $K_1K_2 = K_3K_4$
(d) None of these

31. Two similar rods are joined as shown in figure. Then, temperature of junction is (assume no heat loss through lateral surface of rod and temperatures at the ends are shown in steady state)

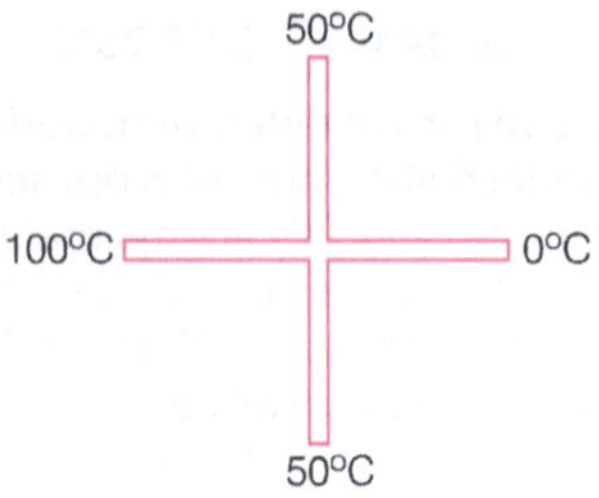

(a) 50°C (b) 75°C (c) 66.6°C (d) 33.3°C

32. A body coated black at 600 K and surrounded by atmosphere at 300 K has cooling rate r_0. The same body at 900 K, surrounded by the same atmosphere, will have cooling rate equal to

(a) $\frac{16}{3}r_0$ (b) $\frac{8}{16}r_0$ (c) $16r_0$ (d) $4r_0$

33. Instantaneous temperature difference between cooling body and the surroundings obeying Newton's law of cooling is θ. Which of the following represents the variation of $\ln\theta$ with time t?

(a)
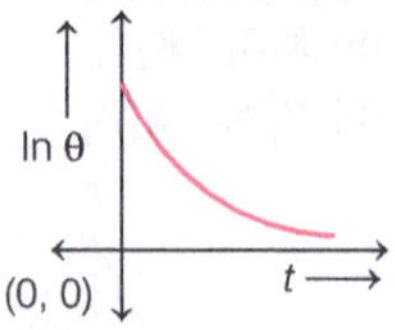

(b)
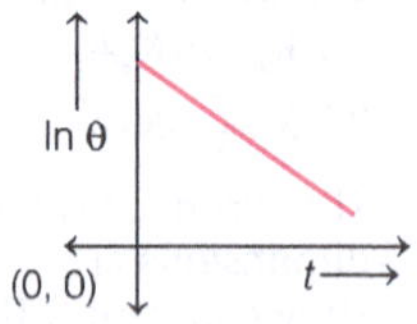

(c)
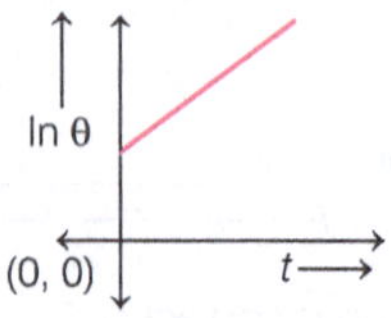

(d)
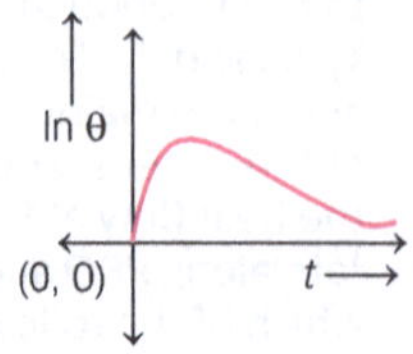

Multiple Correct Options

34. A solid sphere and a hollow sphere of the same material and of equal radii are heated to the same temperature

(a) both will emit equal amount of radiation per unit time in the beginning
(b) both will absorb equal amount of radiation per second from the surroundings in the beginning
(c) the initial rate of cooling will be the same for both the spheres
(d) the two spheres will have equal temperatures at any instant

35. Three identical conducting rods are connected as shown in figure. Given that $\theta_a = 40°C$, $\theta_c = 30°C$ and $\theta_d = 20°C$. Choose the correct options.

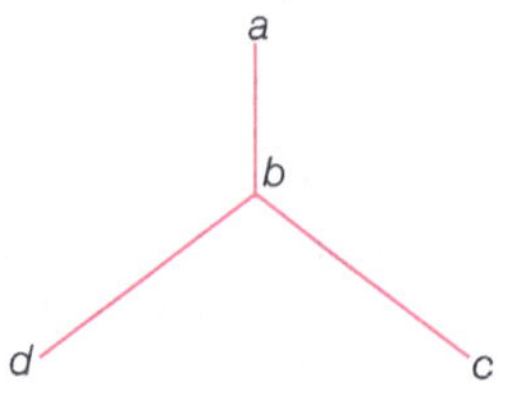

(a) temperature of junction b is 15°C
(b) temperature of junction b is 30°C
(c) heat will flow from c to b
(d) heat will flow from b to d

36. Two conducting rods are connected between two points at constant but different temperatures separately. The rate of heat flow through them is q_1 and q_2.

(a) When they are connected in series, the net rate of heat flow will be $q_1 + q_2$
(b) When they are connected in series, the net rate of heat flow is $\frac{q_1q_2}{q_1 + q_2}$
(c) When they are connected in parallel, the net rate of heat flow is $q_1 + q_2$
(d) When they are connected in parallel, the net rate of heat flow is $\frac{q_1q_2}{q_1 + q_2}$

37. Choose the correct options.

(a) Good absorbers of a particular wavelength are good emitters of same wavelength. This statement was given by Kirchhoff
(b) At low temperature of a body the rate of cooling is directly proportional to temperature of the body. This statement was given by Newton
(c) Emissive power of a perfectly black body is 1
(d) Absorptive power of a perfectly black body is 1

Match the Columns

38. Match the following two columns.

	Column I		Column II
(a)	Stefan's constant	(p)	$[L\theta]$
(b)	Wien's constant	(q)	$[ML^2T^{-3}\theta^{-2}]$
(c)	Emissive power	(r)	$[MT^{-3}]$
(d)	Thermal resistance	(s)	None of these

39. Six identical conducting rods are connected as shown in figure. In steady state temperature of point a is fixed at 100°C and temperature of e at –80°C. Match the following two columns.

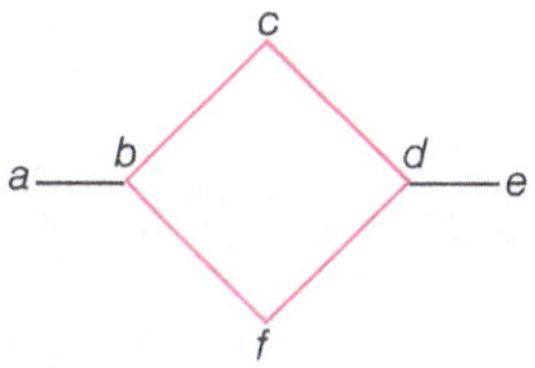

	Column I		Column II
(a)	Temperature of *b*	(p)	10°C
(b)	Temperature of *c*	(q)	40°C
(c)	Temperature of *f*	(r)	−20°C
(d)	Temperature of *d*	(s)	None of these

40. Match the following two columns.

	Column I		Column II
(a)	Specific heat	(p)	watt
(b)	Heat capacity	(q)	J/kg-°C
(c)	Heat current	(r)	J/s
(d)	Latent heat	(s)	None of these

Subjective Questions

41. A copper sphere is suspended in an evacuated chamber maintained at 300 K. The sphere is maintained at a constant temperature of 500 K by heating it electrically. A total of 210 W of electric power is needed to do it. When the surface of the copper sphere is completely blackened, 700 W is needed to maintain the same temperature of the sphere. Calculate the emissivity of copper.

42. The emissivity of tungsten is 0.4. A tungsten sphere with a radius of 4.0 cm is suspended within a large evacuated enclosure whose walls are at 300 K. What power input is required to maintain the sphere at a temperature of 3000 K, if heat conduction along supports is neglected? Take, $\sigma = 5.67 \times 10^{-8}$ Wm^2-K^4.

43. A pot with a steel bottom 1.2 cm thick rests on a hot stove. The area of the bottom of the pot is 0.150 m^2. The water inside the pot is at 100°C and 0.440 kg are evaporated every 5.0 minute. Find the temperature of the lower surface of the pot, which is in contact with the stove. (Take $L_v = 2.256 \times 10^6$ J/kg and $k_{steel} = 50.2$ W/m-K)

44. A carpenter builds an outer house wall with a layer of wood 2.0 cm thick on the outside and a layer of an insulation 3.5 cm thick as the inside wall surface. The wood has $K = 0.08$ W/m-K and the insulation has $K = 0.01$ W/m - K. The interior surface temperature is 19 °C and the exterior surface temperature is −10°C.

(a) What is the temperature at the plane where the wood meets the insulation?

(b) What is the rate of heat flow per square metre through this wall?

45. A closely thermally insulated vessel contains 100 g of water at 0°C. If the air from this vessel is rapidly pumped out, intensive evaporation will produce cooling and as a result of this, water freeze. How much ice will be formed by this method? If latent heat of fusion is 80 cal/g and of evaporation 560 cal/g.
[**Hint** If *m* gram ice is formed, $mL_f = (100 - m) L_v$]

46. The ends of a copper rod of length 1 m and area of cross-section 1 cm^2 are maintained at 0 °C and 100°C. At the centre of the rod there is a source of heat of power 25 W. Calculate the temperature gradient in the two halves of the rod in steady state. Thermal conductivity of copper is 400 Wm^{-1}K^{-1}.

47. A certain amount of ice is supplied heat at a constant rate for 7 minutes. For the first one minute the temperature rises uniformly with time. Then, it remains constant for the next 4 minutes and again the temperature rises at uniform rate for the last two minutes. Calculate the final temperature at the end of seven minutes.
(Given, $L_f = 336 \times 10^3$ J/kg and specific heat of water = 4200 J/kg-K)

Answers

1. (a) **2.** (c) **3.** (a) **4.** (d) **5.** (c) **6.** (b) **7.** (d) **8.** (a) **9.** (a) **10.** (b)
11. (b) **12.** (c) **13.** (c) **14.** (b) **15.** (a) **16.** (a) **17.** (c) **18.** (b) **19.** (d) **20.** (a)
21. (a) **22.** (c) **23.** (b) **24.** (b) **25.** (d) **26.** (c) **27.** (b) **28.** (b) **29.** (c) **30.** (b)
31. (a) **32.** (a) **33.** (b) **34.** (a, b) **35.** (b, d) **36.** (b, c) **37.** (a, d) **38.** a → s; b → p; c → r; d → s
39. a → q; b → p; c → p; d → r **40.** a → q; b → s; c → p; r; d → s **41.** 0.3 **42.** 3.7×10^4 W **43.** 105°C
44. (a) − 8.1°C (b) 7.7 W/m^2 **45.** 87.5 g **46.** 424° C/m, 212° C/m **47.** 40°C

See hints on pages 385-388.

Unit Exercise (Cumulative)

Level 1

Fill in the Blanks

1. Earth receives 1400 W/m^2 of solar power. If all the solar energy falling on a lens of area 0.2 m^2 is focussed onto a block of ice of mass 280 g, at 0°C the time taken to melt the ice will be ...minutes. (Latent heat of fusion of ice $= 3.3 \times 10^5$ J/kg) **(1997 JEE)**

2. A point source of heat of power *P* is placed at the centre of a spherical shell of mean radius *R*. The material of the shell has thermal conductivity *K*. If the temperature difference between the outer and inner surface of the shell is not to exceed *T*, the thickness of the shell should not be less than .... **(1991 JEE)**

3. A solid copper sphere (density ρ and specific heat *c*) of radius *r* at an initial temperature 200 K is suspended inside a chamber whose walls are at almost 0 K. The time required for the temperature of the sphere to drop to 100 K is ...... **(1991 JEE)**

4. The earth receives at its surface radiation from the sun at the rate of 1400 Wm^{-2}. The distance of the centre of the sun from the surface of the earth is 1.5×10^{11} m and the radius of the sun is 7×10^8 m. Treating the sun as a black body, it follows from the above data that its surface temperature is ...... K. **(1989 JEE)**

True/False

5. Two spheres of the same material have radii 1 m and 4 m, temperature 4000 K and 2000 K respectively. The energy radiated per second by the first sphere is greater than that by the second. **(1988 JEE)**

Single Correct Option

6. Heat energy of 184 kJ is given to ice of mass 600 g at $-12°C$. Specific heat of ice is 2222.3 J $kg^{-1°}C^{-1}$ and latent heat of ice is 336 kJ kg^{-1}. **(2023 Main)**

   A. Final temperature of system will be 0°C.
   B. Final temperature of the system will be greater than 0°C.
   C. The final system will have a mixture of ice and water in the ratio of 5 : 1.
   D. The final system will have a mixture of ice and water in the ratio of 1: 5.
   E. The final system will have water only.

   Choose the correct answer from the options given below

   (a) A and C Only (b) A and D Only
   (c) B and D Only (d) A and E Only

7. A copper block of mass 5.0 kg is heated to a temperature of 500°C and is placed on a large ice block. What is the maximum amount of ice that can melt? [Specific heat of copper : 0.39 J g^{-1} °C^{-1} and latent heat of fusion of water : 335 J g^{-1}] **(2022 Main)**

   (a) 1.5 kg (b) 5.8 kg (c) 2.9 kg (d) 3.8 kg

8. A 100 g of iron nail is hit by a 1.5 kg hammer striking at a velocity of 60 ms^{-1} .What will be the rise in the temperature of the nail if one fourth of energy of the hammer goes into heating the nail?
   [Specific heat capacity of iron = 0.42 Jg^{-1}°C^{-1}] **(2022 Main)**

   (a) 675°C (b) 1600°C (c) 16.07°C (d) 6.75°C

9. The height of victoria falls is 63 m. What is the difference in temperature of water at the top and at the bottom of fall?
   [Given 1 cal = 4.2 J and specific heat of water = 1 cal g^{-1}°C^{-1}] **(2021 Main)**

   (a) 0.147°C (b) 14.76°C (c) 1.476°C (d) 0.014°C

10. The temperature of equal masses of three different liquids *x*, *y* and *z* are 10°C, 20°C and 30°C respectively. The temperature of mixture when *x* is mixed with *y* is 16°C and that when *y* is mixed with *z* is 26°C. The temperature of mixture when *x* and *z* are mixed will be **(2021 Main)**

    (a) 28.32°C (b) 25.62°C
    (c) 23.84°C (d) 20.28°C

11. Two different metal bodies *A* and *B* of equal mass are heated at a uniform rate under similar conditions. The variation of temperature of the bodies is graphically represented as shown in the figure. The ratio of specific heat capacities is **(2021 Main)**

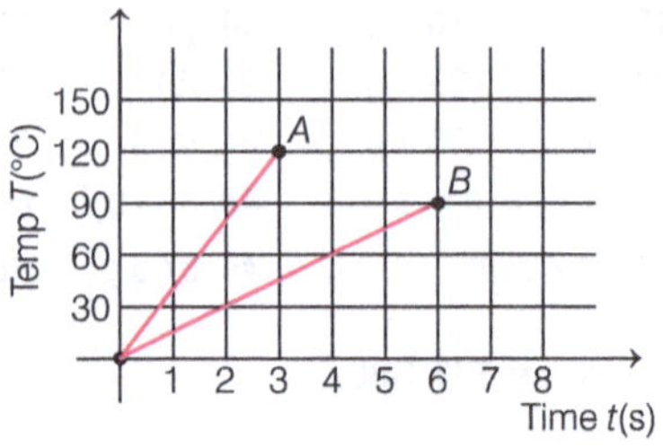

(a) $\frac{8}{3}$ (b) $\frac{3}{8}$ (c) $\frac{3}{4}$ (d) $\frac{4}{3}$

12. A massless spring ($k = 800$ N/m), attached with a mass (500 g) is completely immersed in 1 kg of water. The spring is stretched by 2 cm and released, so that it starts vibrating. What would be the order of magnitude of the change in the temperature of water when the vibrations stop completely? (Assume that the water container and spring receive negligible heat and specific heat of mass = 400 J/kg K, specific heat of water = 4184 J/kg K) **(2019 Main)**

(a) 10^{-4} K (b) 10^{-3} K (c) 10^{-1} K (d) 10^{-5} K

13. M_1 gram of ice at $-10°C$ (specific heat $= 0.5$ cal $g^{-1}°C^{-1}$) is added to M_2 gram of water at 50°C. Finally no ice is left and the water is at 0°C. The value of latent heat of ice, in cal g^{-1} is **(2019 Main)**

(a) $\frac{50M_2}{M_1} - 5$ (b) $\frac{50M_1}{M_2} - 50$

(c) $\frac{50M_2}{M_1}$ (d) $\frac{5M_2}{M_1} - 5$

14. A thermally insulated vessel contains 150 g of water at 0°C. Then, the air from the vessel is pumped out adiabatically. A fraction of water turns into ice and the rest evaporates at 0°C itself. The mass of evaporated water will be closest to

(Latent heat of vaporisation of water $= 2.10 \times 10^6$ J kg^{-1} and latent heat of fusion of water $= 3.36 \times 10^5$ J kg^{-1}) **(2019 Main)**

(a) 150 g (b) 20 g (c) 130 g (d) 35g

15. When 100 g of a liquid A at 100°C is added to 50 g of a liquid B at temperature 75°C, the temperature of the mixture becomes 90°C. The temperature of the mixture, if 100 g of liquid A at 100°C is added to 50 g of liquid B at 50°C will be **(2019 Main)**

(a) 60°C (b) 80°C (c) 70°C (d) 85°C

16. A metal ball of mass 0.1 kg is heated upto 500°C and dropped into a vessel of heat capacity 800 JK^{-1} and containing 0.5 kg water. The initial temperature of water and vessel is 30°C. What is the approximate percentage increment in the temperature of the water? [Take, specific heat capacities of water and metal are respectively 4200 $Jkg^{-1}K^{-1}$ and 400 $Jkg^{-1}K^{-1}$] **(2019 Main)**

(a) 25% (b) 15% (c) 30% (d) 20%

17. Ice at $-20°C$ is added to 50 g of water at 40°C. When the temperature of the mixture reaches 0°C, it is found that 20 g of ice is still unmelted. The amount of ice added to the water was close to (Take, specific heat of water = 4.2 J/g/°C specific heat of ice = 2.1 J/g/°C and heat of fusion of water at 0°C = 334 J/g) **(2019 Main)**

(a) 40 g (b) 50 g (c) 60 g (d) 100 g

18. An unknown metal of mass 192 g heated to a temperature of 100°C was immersed into a brass calorimeter of mass 128 g containing 240 g of water at a temperature of 8.4°C. Calculate the specific heat of the unknown metal, if water temperature stabilises at 21.5°C. (Specific heat of brass is 394 J kg^{-1} K^{-1}) **(2019 Main)**

(a) 916 J kg^{-1} K^{-1} (b) 654 J kg^{-1} K^{-1}
(c) 1232 J kg^{-1} K^{-1} (d) 458 J kg^{-1} K^{-1}

19. A copper ball of mass 100 g is at a temperature T. It is dropped in a copper calorimeter of mass 100 g, filled with 170 g of water at room temperature. Subsequently, the temperature of the system is found to be 75°C. T is (Given, room temperature = 30°C, specific heat of copper = 0.1 cal/g°C) **(2017 Main)**

(a) 885°C (b) 1250°C (c) 825°C (d) 800°C

20. Calorie is defined as the amount of heat required to raise temperature of 1 g of water by 1°C and it is defined under which of the following conditions? **(2005 JEE)**

(a) From 14.5°C to 15.5°C at 760 mm of Hg
(b) From 98.5°C to 99.5°C at 760 mm of Hg
(c) From 13.5°C to 14.5°C at 76 mm of Hg
(d) From 3.5°C to 4.5°C at 76 mm of Hg

21. Water of volume 2 L in a container is heated with a coil of 1 kW at 27°C. The lid of the container is open and energy dissipates at a rate of 160 J/s. In how much time temperature will rise from 27°C to 77°C? [Specific heat of water is 4.2 kJ/kg] **(2005 JEE)**

(a) 8 min 20s (b) 6 min 2s (c) 7 min (d) 14 min

22. 2 kg of ice at $-20°C$ is mixed with 5 kg of water at 20°C in an insulating vessel having a negligible heat capacity. Calculate the final mass of water remaining in the container. It is given that the specific heats of water and ice are 1 kcal/kg /°C and 0.5 kcal/kg /°C while the latent heat of fusion of ice is 80 kcal/kg **(2003 JEE)**

(a) 7 kg (b) 6 kg (c) 4 kg (d) 2 kg

23. Steam at 100°C is passed into 1.1 kg of water contained in a calorimeter of water equivalent 0.02 kg at 15°C till the temperature of the calorimeter and its contents rises to 80°C. The mass of the steam condensed in kg is **(1986 JEE)**

(a) 0.130 (b) 0.065 (c) 0.260 (d) 0.135

24. If K_1 and K_2 are the thermal conductivities, L_1 and L_2 are the lengths and A_1 and A_2 are the cross-sectional areas of steel and copper rods respectively, such that $K_2 / K_1 = 9$, $A_1 / A_2 = 2$, $L_1/L_2 = 2$. Then, for the arrangement as shown in the figure, the value of temperature T of the steel-copper junction in the steady state will be **(2022 Main)**

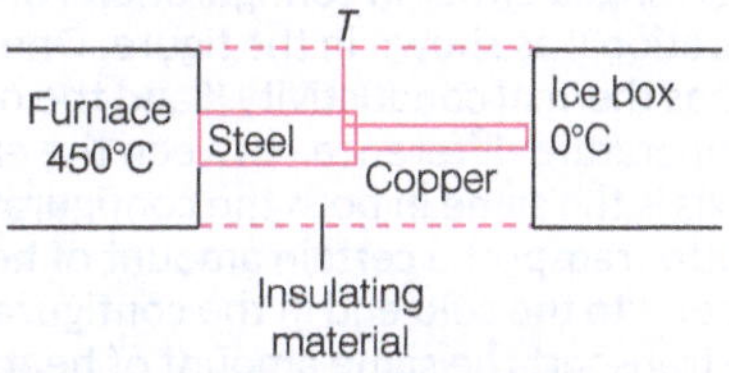

(a) 18°C (b) 14°C (c) 45°C (d) 150°C

25. Two materials having coefficients of thermal conductivity $3K$ and K and thickness d and $3d$ respectively, are joined to form a slab as shown in the figure. The temperatures of the outer surfaces are θ_2 and θ_1 respectively, ($\theta_2 > \theta_1$). The temperature at the interface is **(2019 Main)**

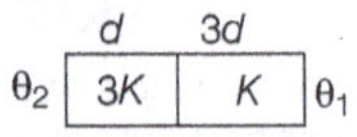

(a) $\frac{\theta_2+\theta_1}{2}$ (b) $\frac{\theta_1}{3}+\frac{2\theta_2}{3}$
(c) $\frac{\theta_1}{6}+\frac{5\theta_2}{6}$ (d) $\frac{\theta_1}{10}+\frac{9\theta_2}{10}$

26. Temperature difference of 120°C is maintained between two ends of a uniform rod AB of length $2L$. Another bent rod PQ, of same cross-section as AB and length $\frac{3L}{2}$ is connected across AB (see figure). In steady state, temperature difference between P and Q will be close to **(2019 Main)**

(a) 45°C (b) 35°C (c) 75°C (d) 60°C

27. A heat source at $T_1 = 10^3$ K is connected to another heat reservoir at $T_2 = 10^2$ K by a copper slab which is 1 m thick. Given that the thermal conductivity of copper is 0.1 $WK^{-1}m^{-1}$, the energy flux through it in the steady state is **(2019 Main)**

(a) 90 Wm^{-2} (b) 65 Wm^{-2}
(c) 120 Wm^{-2} (d) 200 Wm^{-2}

28. Three rods of copper, brass and steel are welded together to form a Y-shaped structure. Area of cross-section of each rod is 4 cm^2. End of copper rod is maintained at 100°C whereas ends of brass and steel are kept at 0°C. Lengths of the copper, brass and steel rods are 46, 13 and 12 cm respectively. The rods are thermally insulated from surroundings except at ends. Thermal conductivities of copper, brass and steel are 0.92, 0.26 and 0.12 in CGS units, respectively. Rate of heat flow through copper rod is **(2014 Main)**

(a) 1.2 cal/s
(b) 2.4 cal/s
(c) 4.8 cal/s
(d) 6.0 cal/s

29. Two rectangular blocks, having indentical dimensions, can be arranged either in configuration I or in configuration II as shown in the figure. One of the blocks has thermal conductivity K and the other $2K$. The temperature difference between the ends along the X-axis is the same in both the configurations. It takes 9 s to transport a certain amount of heat from the hot end to the cold end in the configuration I. The time to transport the same amount of heat in the configuration II is **(2013 Adv.)**

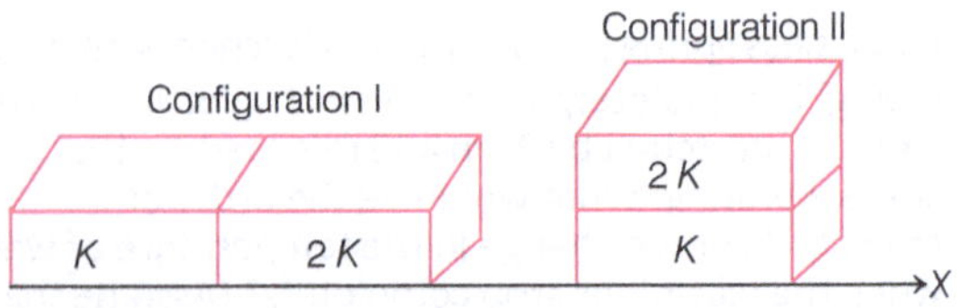

(a) 2.0 s (b) 3.0 s (c) 4.5 s (d) 6.0 s

30. A body cools in 7 minutes from 60°C to 40°C. The temperature of the surrounding is 10°C. The temperature of the body after the next 7 minutes will be **(2023 Main)**

(a) 32°C (b) 30°C (c) 34°C (d) 28°C

31. A body cools from 80°C to 60°C in 5 minutes. The temperature of the surrounding is 20°C. The time it takes to cool from 60°C to 40°C is **(2023 Main)**

(a) 450 s (b) 420 s (c) 500 s (d) $\frac{25}{3}$ s

32. If a piece of metal is heated to temperature θ and then allowed to cool in a room which is at temperature θ_0. The graph between the temperature T of the metal and time t will be closed to **(2013 Main)**

(a) 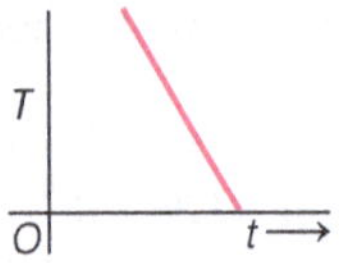

(b) 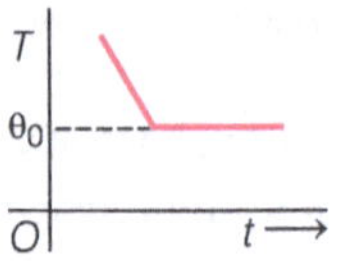

(c) 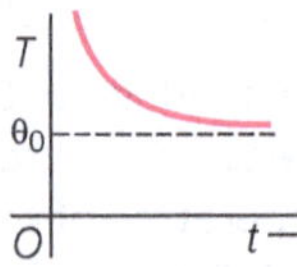

(d) 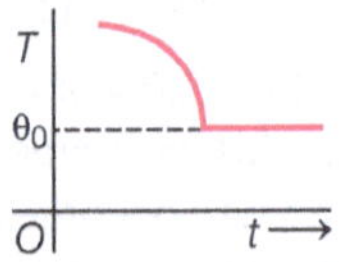

33. Three very large plates of same area are kept parallel and close to each other. They are considered as ideal black surfaces and have very high thermal conductivity. The first and third plates are maintained at temperatures $2T$ and $3T$ respectively. The temperature of the middle (i.e. second) plate under steady state condition is **(2012 JEE)**

(a) $\left(\frac{65}{2}\right)^{\frac{1}{4}} T$ (b) $\left(\frac{97}{4}\right)^{\frac{1}{4}} T$
(c) $\left(\frac{97}{2}\right)^{\frac{1}{4}} T$ (d) $(97)^{\frac{1}{4}} T$

34. A black body of temperature T is inside a chamber of temperature T_0. Now the closed chamber is slightly opened to sun such that temperature of black body (T) and chamber (T_0) remains constant **(2006 JEE)**

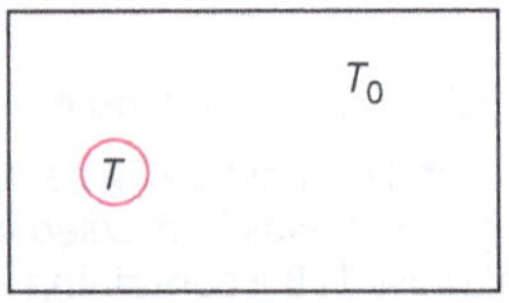

(a) black body will absorb more radiation
(b) black body will absorb less radiation
(c) black body emit more energy
(d) black body emit energy equal to energy absorbed by it

Subjective Questions

35. A 5 m long cylindrical steel wire with radius 2×10^{-3} m is suspended vertically from a rigid support and carries a bob of mass 100 kg at the other end. If the bob gets snapped, calculate the change in temperature of the wire ignoring losses. (For the steel wire : Young's modulus $= 2.1 \times 10^{11}$ Pa; Density $= 7860$ kg/m^3; Specific heat $= 420$ J/kg-K). **(2001 JEE)**

36. A double-pane window used for insulating a room thermally from outside consists of two glass sheets each of area 1 m^2 and thickness 0.01 m separated by a 0.05 m thick stagnant air space. In the steady state, the room glass interface and the glass-outdoor interface are at constant temperatures of 27°C and 0°C respectively. Calculate the rate of heat flow through the window pane. Also, find the temperatures of other interfaces. Given, thermal conductivities of glass and air as 0.8 and 0.08 $Wm^{-1}K^{-1}$ respectively. **(1997 JEE)**

37. A room is maintained at 20°C by a heater of resistance 20 Ω connected to 200 V mains. The temperature is uniform throughout the room and the heat is transmitted through a glass window of area 1 m^2 and thickness 0.2 cm. Calculate the temperature outside. Thermal conductivity of glass is 0.2 cal $m^{-1} s^{-1} (°C)^{-1}$ and mechanical equivalent of heat is 4.2 J cal^{-1}. **(1978 JEE)**

Integer Type Questions

38. A block of ice of mass 120 g at temperature 0°C is put in 300 g of water at 25°C. The x g of ice melts as the temperature of the water reaches 0°C. The value of x is [Use : Specific heat capacity of water = 4200 J kg^{-1} K^{-1}, Latent heat of ice $= 3.5 \times 10^{-5}$ Jkg^{-1}] **(2022 Main)**

39. A geyser heats water flowing at a rate of 2.0 kg per minute from 30°C to 70°C. If geyser operates on a gas burner, the rate of combustion of fuel will be ______ g min^{-1} [Heat of combustion $= 8 \times 10^3$ Jg^{-1} Specific heat of water = 4.2 Jg^{-1} °C^{-1}] **(2022 Main)**

40. A piece of ice (heat capacity = 2100 Jkg^{-1} °C^{-1} and latent heat $= 3.36 \times 10^5$ J kg^{-1}) of mass m gram is at −5°C at atmospheric pressure. It is given 420 J of heat so that the ice starts melting. Finally when the ice-water mixture is in equilibrium, it is found that 1 g of ice has melted. Assuming there is no other heat exchange in the process, the value of m is **(2010 JEE)**

41. Two plates A and B have thermal conductivities 84 Wm^{-1}K^{-1} and 126 Wm^{-1}K^{-1} respectively. They have same surface area and same thickness. They are placed in contact along their surfaces. If the temperatures of the outer surfaces of A and B are kept at 100°C and 0°C respectively, then the temperature of the surface of contact in steady state is .... °C. **(2023 Main)**

42. As per the given figure, two plates A and B of thermal conductivity K and $2K$ are joined together to form a compound plate. The thickness of plates are 4.0 cm and 2.5 cm, respectively and the area of cross-section is 120 cm^2 for each plate. The equivalent thermal conductivity of the compound plate is $\left(1 + \frac{5}{\alpha}\right)K$, then the value of α will be .... **(2022 Main)**

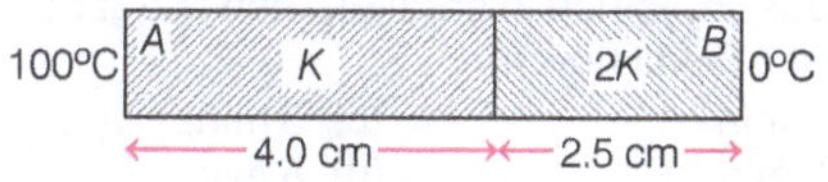

43. A metal rod AB of length $10x$ has its one end A in ice at 0°C and the other end B in water at 100°C. If a point P on the rod is maintained at 400°C, then it is found that equal amounts of water and ice evaporate and melt per unit time. The latent heat of evaporation of water is 540 calg^{-1} and latent heat of melting of ice is 80 calg^{-1}. If the point P is at a distance of λx from the ice end A, find the value of λ. (Neglect any heat loss to the surrounding.) **(2009 JEE)**

44. Two spherical stars A and B emit black body radiation. The radius of A is 400 times that of B and A emits 10^4 times the power emitted from B. The ratio $\left(\frac{\lambda_A}{\lambda_B}\right)$ of their wavelengths λ_A and λ_B at which the peaks occur in their respective radiation curves is **(2015 Adv.)**

45. Two spherical bodies A (radius 6 cm) and B (radius 18 cm) are at temperatures T_1 and T_2, respectively. The maximum intensity in the emission spectrum of A is at 500 nm and in that of B is at 1500 nm. Considering them to be black bodies, what will be the ratio of the rate of total energy radiated by A to that of B? **(2010 JEE)**

Level 2

Single Correct Option

46. A cylindrical rod with one end in a steam chamber and the other end in ice results in melting of 0.1 g of ice per second. If the rod is replaced by another with half the length and double the radius of the first and if the thermal conductivity of material of second rod is 1/4 that of first, the rate at which ice melts in g/s will be
(a) 0.4 (b) 0.05 (c) 0.2 (d) 0.1

47. Two sheets of thickness d and $3d$, are touching each other. The temperature just outside the thinner sheet is T_1 and on the side of the thicker sheet is T_3. The interface temperature is T_2. T_1, T_2 and T_3 are in arithmetic progression. The ratio of thermal conductivity of thinner sheet to thicker sheet is
(a) 1 : 3 (b) 3 : 1 (c) 2 : 3 (d) 3 : 9

48. A long rod has one end at 0°C and other end at a high temperature. The coefficient of thermal conductivity varies with distance from the low temperature end as $K = K_0(1 + ax)$, where $K_0 = 10^2$ SI unit and $a = 1\ m^{-1}$. At what distance from the first end the temperature will be 100°C ? The area of cross-section is 1 cm^2 and rate of heat conduction is 1 W.

(a) 2.7 m (b) 1.7 m
(c) 3 m (d) 1.5 m

49. Two rods are of same material and having same length and area. If heat ΔQ flows through them for 12 min when they are joined side by side. If now both the rods are joined in parallel, then the same amount of heat ΔQ will flow in

(a) 24 min (b) 3 min
(c) 12 min (d) 6 min

50. Three rods of identical cross-sectional area and made from the same metal form the sides of an isosceles triangle ABC right angled at B as shown in the figure. The points A and B are maintained at temperatures T and $\sqrt{2}\,T$ respectively in the steady state. Assuming that only heat conduction takes place, temperature of point C will be **(1995 JEE)**

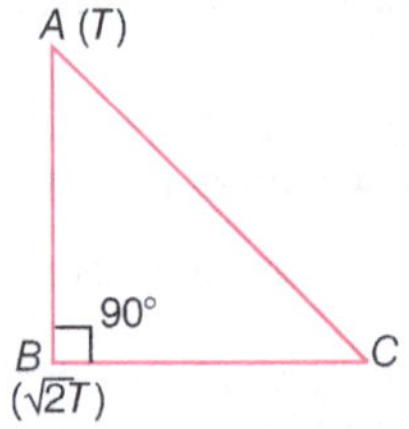

(a) $\frac{T}{\sqrt{2}-1}$ (b) $\frac{T}{\sqrt{2}+1}$
(c) $\frac{3T}{\sqrt{2}+1}$ (d) $\frac{T}{\sqrt{3}(\sqrt{2}-1)}$

51. The temperature of the two outer surfaces of a composite slab consisting of two materials having coefficients of thermal conductivity K and $2K$ and thickness x and $4x$ respectively are T_2 and $T_1 (T_2 > T_1)$. The rate of heat transfer through the slab in steady state is $\frac{AK(T_2 - T_1)}{x} f$. where, f is equal to

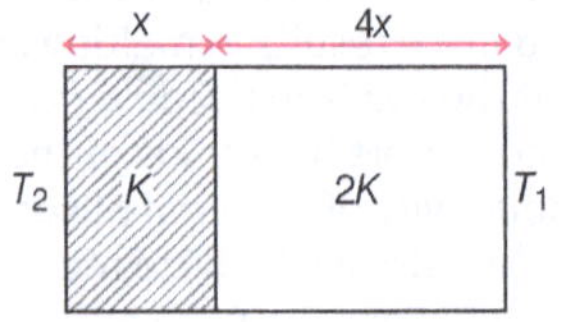

(a) 1 (b) 1/2
(c) 2/3 (d) 1/3

52. Water is being boiled in a flat bottomed kettle placed on a stove. The area of the bottom is 300 cm^2 and the thickness is 2 mm. If the amount of steam produced is 1 g min^{-1}, then the difference of the temperature between the inner and the outer surfaces of the bottom is (thermal conductivity of the material of the kettle = 0.5 cal. $cm^{-1}\,°C^{-1}\,s^{-1}$ and latent heat of the steam is equal to 540 cal g^{-1})

(a) 12°C (b) 1.2°C
(c) 0.2°C (d) 0.012°C

53. Three conducting rods of same material and cross-section are shown in figure. Temperatures of A, D and C are maintained at 20°C, 90°C and 0°C. The ratio of lengths BD and BC, if there is no heat flow in AB is

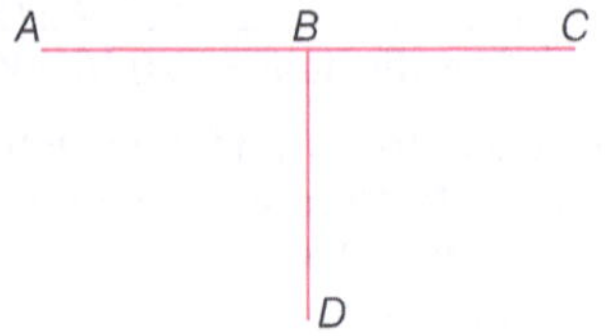

(a) $\frac{2}{7}$ (b) $\frac{7}{2}$
(c) $\frac{9}{2}$ (d) $\frac{2}{9}$

54. Two rods with the same dimensions have thermal conductivities in the ratio 1 : 2. They are arranged between heat reservoirs with the same temperature difference, in two different configurations, A and B. The rates of heat flow in A and B are I_A and I_B respectively. The ratio $\frac{I_A}{I_B}$ is equal to

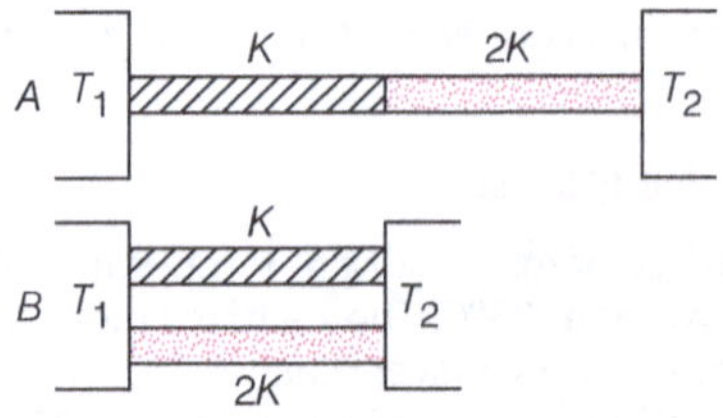

(a) 1 : 2 (b) 1 : 3
(c) 2 : 5 (d) 2 : 9

55. Two identical conducting rods AB and CD are connected to a circular conducting ring at two diametrically opposite points B and C. The radius of the ring is equal to the length of rods AB and CD. The area of cross-section, and thermal conductivity of the rod and ring are equal. Points A and D are maintained at temperatures of 100°C and 0°C. Temperature of point C will be

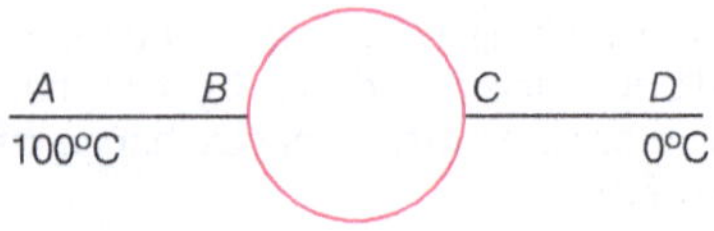

(a) 62°C (b) 37°C
(c) 28°C (d) 45°C

56. Rate of heat flow through a cylindrical rod is H_1. Temperatures of ends of rod are T_1 and T_2. If all the dimensions of rod become double, temperature difference remains same and rate of heat flow becomes H_2. Then,

(a) $H_2 = 2H_1$ (b) $H_2 = H_1$

(c) $H_2 = \frac{H_1}{4}$ (d) $H_2 = 4H_1$

57. A ring consisting of two parts *ADB* and *ACB* of same conductivity *K* carries an amount of heat *H*. The *ADB* part is now replaced with another metal keeping the temperatures T_1 and T_2 constant. The heat carried increases to 2*H*. What should be the conductivity of the new *ADB* part? Given $\frac{ACB}{ADB} = 3$.

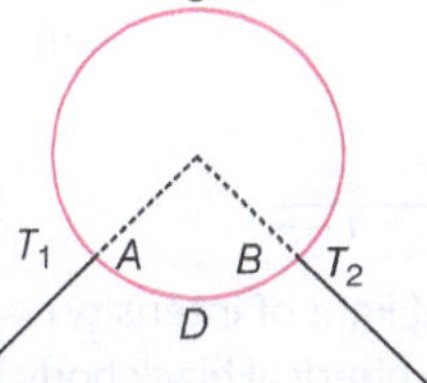

(a) $\frac{7}{3}K$ (b) $2K$ (c) $\frac{5}{2}K$ (d) $3K$

58. *A* and *B* are two points on a uniform metal ring whose centre is *C*. The angle $ACB = \theta$. *A* and *B* are maintained at two different constant temperatures. When $\theta = 180°$, the rate of total heat flow from *A* to *B* is 1.2 W. When $\theta = 90°$, this rate will be

(a) 0.6 W (b) 0.9 W (c) 1.6 W (d) 1.8 W

59. Consider the situation as shown in figure. The amount of heat flowing per second through a cross-section of the bent part, if the total heat taken out per second from the end at 100°C is 130 J.

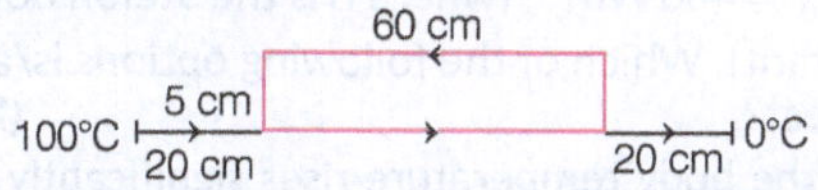

(a) 50 J (b) 60 J (c) 70 J (d) 80 J

60. A black body is at a temperature of 2880 K. The energy of radiation emitted by this body with wavelength between 499 nm and 500 nm is U_1, between 999 nm and 1000 nm is U_2 and between 1499 nm and 1500 nm is U_3. The Wien constant, $b = 2.88 \times 10^6$ nm-K. Then, **(1998 JEE)**

(a) $U_1 = 0$ (b) $U_3 = 0$ (c) $U_1 > U_2$ (d) $U_2 > U_1$

61. A spherical black body of radius *r* radiates power *P* and its rate of cooling is *R*. Then

(i) $P \propto r$ (ii) $P \propto r^2$ (iii) $R \propto r^2$ (iv) $R \propto \frac{1}{r}$

(a) (i), (ii) (b) (ii), (iii)

(c) (i), (iv) (d) (ii), (iv)

62. Two bodies *A* and *B* of equal masses, area and emissivity cooling according to Newton's law from same temperature are represented by the graph. If θ is the instantaneous temperature of the body and θ_0 is the temperature of surroundings, then relationship between their specific heats is

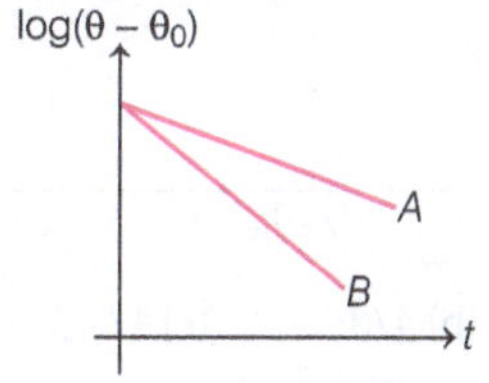

(a) $S_A = S_B$ (b) $S_A > S_B$

(c) $S_A < S_B$ (d) data insufficient

63. A solid cylinder of length *L* and radius *r* is heated up to same temperature as that of a cube of edge length *a*. If both have same material as well as volume and allowed to cool under similar conditions, then ratio of amount of radiations radiated per second will be (Neglect radiation emitted from flat surfaces of the cylinder)

(a) $\frac{a}{3r}$ (b) $\frac{2a}{rL}$ (c) $\frac{a^2}{rL}$ (d) $\frac{\pi a^2}{2rL}$

64. The figure shows the face and interface temperature of a composite slab containing of four layers of two materials having identical thickness. Under steady state condition, find the value of temperature θ. Where, *K* is thermal conductivity.

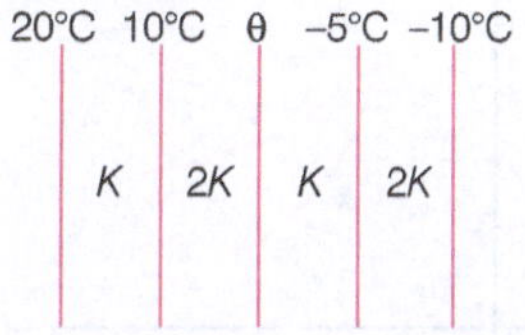

(a) 5°C (b) 10°C (c) −15°C (d) 15°C

65. In the square frame of side *l* of identical metallic rods, the corners *A* and *C* are maintained at temperatures T_1 and T_2 respectively. The rate of heat flow from *A* to *C* is *H*. If *A* and *D* are instead maintained at T_1 and T_2 respectively, find the total rate of heat flow.

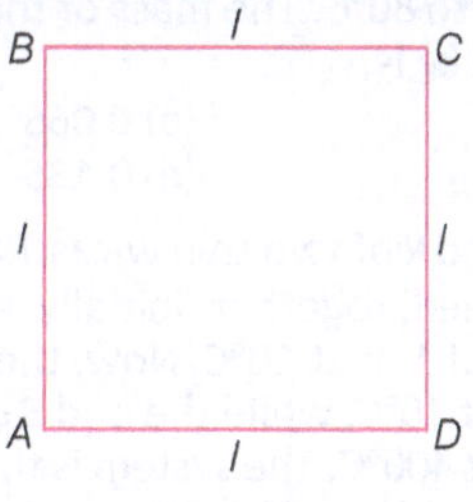

(a) (4/3)*H* (b) (3/4)*H* (c) *H* (d) (5/3)*H*

66. The spectral emissive power E_λ for a body at temperature T_1 is plotted against the wavelength and area under the curve is found to be *A*. At a different temperature T_2, the area is found to be 9 A. Then, λ_1/λ_2 is equal to

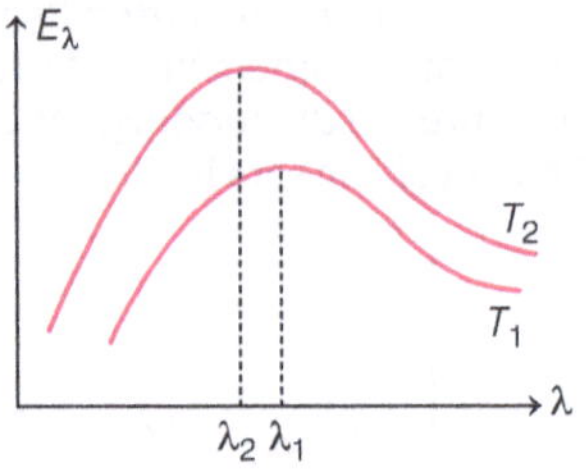

(a) 3 (b) 1/3 (c) $1/\sqrt{3}$ (d) $\sqrt{3}$

67. Three identical rods A, B and C are placed end to end. A temperature difference is maintained between the free ends of A and C. The thermal conductivity of B is thrice that of C and half of that of A. The effective thermal conductivity of the system will be (K_A is the thermal conductivity of rod A)

(a) $\frac{1}{3}K_A$ (b) $3K_A$
(c) $2K_A$ (d) $\frac{2}{3}K_A$

68. The graph shown in the diagram represents the variation of temperature (T) of the bodies x and y having same surface area with time (t) due to the emission of radiation. Find the correct relation between the emissivity and absorptivity power of the two bodies **(2003 JEE)**

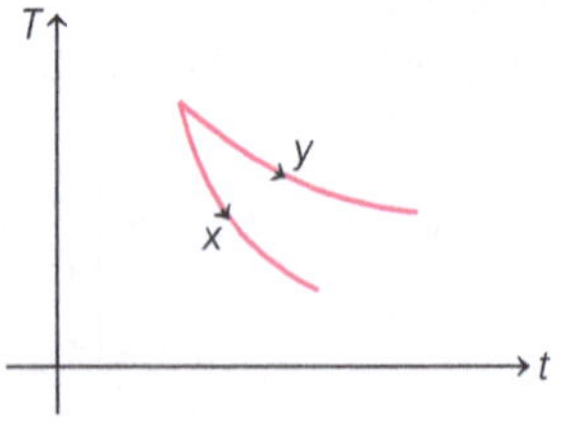

(a) $E_x > E_y$ and $a_x < a_y$ (b) $E_x < E_y$ and $a_x > a_y$
(c) $E_x > E_y$ and $a_x > a_y$ (d) $E_x < E_y$ and $a_x < a_y$

69. Steam at 100°C is passed into 1.1 kg of water contained in a calorimeter of water equivalent 0.02 kg at 15°C till the temperature of the calorimeter and its content rises to 80°C. The mass of the steam condensed in kg is

(a) 0.130 (b) 0.065
(c) 0.260 (d) 0.135

70. The ends Q and R of two thin wires, PQ and RS, are soldered (joined) together. Initially, each of the wire has a length of 1 m at 10°C. Now, the end P is maintained at 10°C, while the end S is heated and maintained at 400°C. The system is thermally insulated from its surroundings. If the thermal conductivity of wire PQ is twice that of the wire RS and the coefficient of linear thermal expansion of PQ is $1.2 \times 10^{-5}\ K^{-1}$, the change in length of the wire PQ is **(2016 Adv.)**

(a) 0.78 mm (b) 0.90 mm
(c) 1.56 mm (d) 2.34 mm

71. Two identical beakers A and B contain equal volumes of two different liquids at 60°C each and left to cool down. Liquid in A has density of $8 \times 10^2\ kg/m^3$ and specific heat of 2000 J $kg^{-1}K^{-1}$ while liquid in B has density of $10^3\ kg\ m^{-3}$ and specific heat of 4000 J $kg^{-1}K^{-1}$. Which of the following best describes their temperature *versus* time graph schematically? (Assume the emissivity of both the beakers to be the same) **(2019 Main)**

(a)
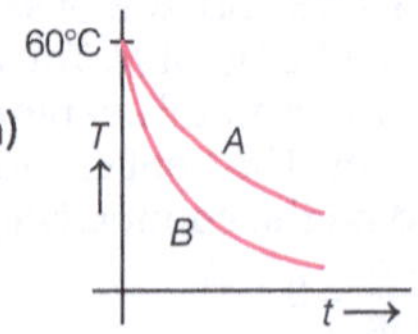

(b)
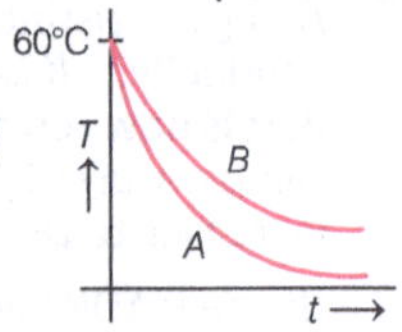

(c)
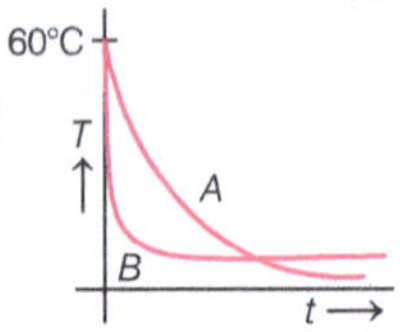

(d)
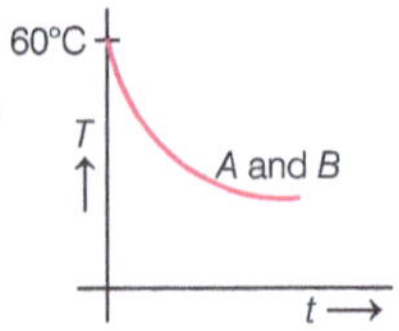

72. Parallel rays of light of intensity $I = 912\ Wm^{-2}$ are incident on a spherical black body kept in surroundings of temperature 300 K. Take Stefan constant $\sigma = 5.7 \times 10^{-8}\ Wm^{-2}K^{-4}$ and assume that the energy exchange with the surroundings is only through radiation. The final steady state temperature of the black body is close to **(2014 Main)**

(a) 330 K (b) 660 K
(c) 990 K (d) 1550 K

Multiple Correct Options

73. A human body has a surface area of approximately $1\ m^2$. The normal body temperature is 10 K above the surrounding room temperature T_0. Take the room temperature to be $T_0 = 300$ K. For $T_0 = 300$ K, the value of $\sigma T_0^4 = 460\ Wm^{-2}$ (where σ is the Stefan Boltzmann constant). Which of the following options is/are correct? **(2017 Adv.)**

(a) If the body temperature rises significantly, then the peak in the spectrum of electromagnetic radiation emitted by the body would shift to longer wavelengths
(b) If the surrounding temperature reduces by a small amount $\Delta T_0 << T_0$, then to maintain the same body temperature the same (living) human being needs to radiate $\Delta W = 4\sigma T_0^3 \Delta T_0$ more energy per unit time
(c) The amount of energy radiated by the body in 1s is close to 60 J
(d) Reducing the exposed surface area of the body (e.g. by curling up) allows humans to maintain the same body temperature while reducing the energy lost by radiation

74. The rate of flow of heat through 12 identical conductors made of same material is as shown in the figure. Then, which of the following is correct?

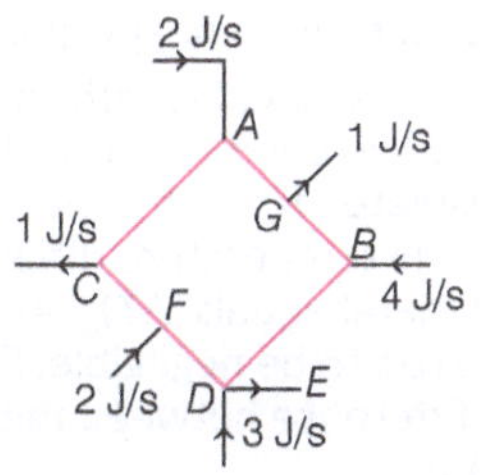

(a) The rate of flow of heat through rod DE is 9 J/s
(b) Junctions C and F are at the same temperature
(c) Junctions A and G are at the same temperature
(d) The rate of flow of heat through CF is 5 J/s

75. A composite block is made of slabs A, B, C, D and E of different thermal conductivities (given in terms of a constant K) and sizes (given in terms of length, L) as shown in the figure. All slabs are of same width. Heat Q flows only from left to right through the blocks. Then, in steady state

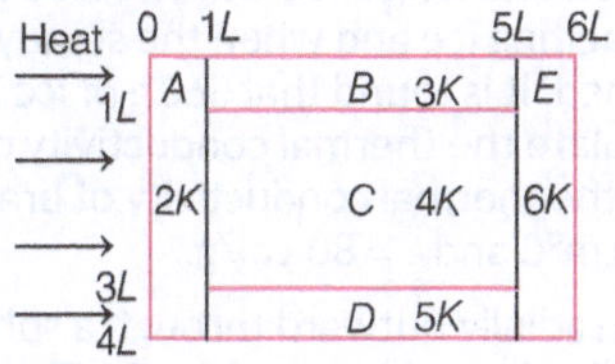

(a) heat flow through A and E slabs are same
(b) heat flow through slab E is maximum
(c) temperature difference across slab E is smallest
(d) heat flow through C = heat flow through B + heat flow through D

Note *Thickness of block A is $(1L - 0) = L = L_x$. Length of block A is $(4L - 0) = 4L = L_y$. Similarly for B, $L_x = (5L - L) = 4L$ and $L_y = (1L - 0) = L$ and so on.*

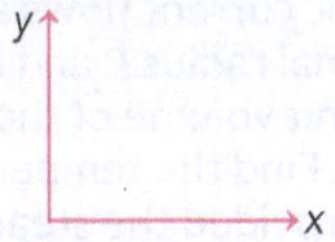

76. Two bodies A and B have thermal emissivities of 0.01 and 0.81 respectively. The outer surface areas of the two bodies are the same. The two bodies emit total radiant power at the same rate. The wavelength λ_B corresponding to maximum spectral radiancy in the radiation from B shifted from the wavelength corresponding to maximum spectral radiancy in the radiation from A, by 1.00 μm. If the temperature of A is 5802 K, then **(1999 JEE)**

(a) the temperature of B is 1934 K
(b) $\lambda_B = 1.5\,\mu$m
(c) the temperature of B is 11604 K
(d) the temperature of B is 2901 K

Passage Based Questions

Passage (Q. No. 77 to 79)

In an experiment of study of Newton's law of cooling, a ball of metal is heated from inside a heater of 20 W in a room maintained at constant temperature of 20°C.
Following observations are made.
i. Mass of the ball is 1 kg.
ii. Rate of increase of temperature decreases with rise of temperature.
iii. Temperature of ball becomes 50°C after some time and then remains constant.
iv. Specific heat of metal is 500 $Jkg^{-1}°C^{-1}$.
Corresponding to above observations, answer the following questions.

77. Rate of loss of heat, when ball is at 50°C is
(a) 10 W (b) 15 W
(c) 20 W (d) 25 W

78. Assuming Newton's law of cooling holds for the ball, rate of loss of heat, when the ball is at 30°C is
(a) $\frac{10}{3}$ W (b) $\frac{20}{3}$ W (c) $\frac{30}{3}$ W (d) $\frac{40}{3}$ W

79. In 5 min temperature of ball rises from 20°C to 30°C. Total energy lost from the ball in this time interval is
(a) 250 J (b) 500 J
(c) 750 J (d) 1000 J

Subjective Questions

80. A layer of ice of thickness y is on the surface of a lake. The air is at a constant temperature $-\theta$°C and the ice water interface is at 0°C. Show that the rate at which the thickness increases is given by

$$\frac{dy}{dt} = \frac{K\theta}{L\rho y}$$

where, K is the thermal conductivity of the ice, L the latent heat of fusion and ρ is the density of the ice.

81. A hot body placed in air is cooled according to Newton's law of cooling, the rate of decrease of temperature being k times the temperature difference from the surroundings. Starting from $t = 0$, find the time in which the body will lose half the maximum temperature it can lose.

82. Three rods of copper, brass and steel are welded together to form a Y-shaped structure. The cross-sectional area of each rod is 4cm^2. The end of copper rod is maintained at 100°C and the ends of the brass and steel rods at 80°C and 60°C respectively. Assume that there is no loss of heat from the surfaces of the rods. The lengths of rods are : copper 46 cm, brass 13 cm and steel 12 cm.

(a) What is the temperature of the junction point?

(b) What is the heat current in the copper rod?

K(copper) = 0.92, K(steel) = 0.12 and
K(brass) = 0.26 cal/ cm-s °C

83. Ice at 0°C is added to 200 g of water initially at 70°C in a vacuum flask. When 50 g of ice has been added and has all melted the temperature of the flask and contents is 40°C. When a further 80 g of ice has been added and has all melted the temperature of the whole becomes 10°C. Find the latent heat of fusion of ice.

84. A copper cube of mass 200 g slides down a rough inclined plane of inclination 37° at a constant speed. Assuming that the loss in mechanical energy goes into the copper block as thermal energy. Find the increase in temperature of the block as it slides down through 60 cm. Specific heat capacity of copper is equal to 420 J/kg-K. (Take, $g = 10\ m/s^2$)

85. A cylindrical block of length 0.4 m and area of cross-section $0.04\ m^2$ is placed coaxially on a thin metal disc of mass 0.4 kg and of the same cross-section. The upper face of the cylinder is maintained at a constant temperature of 400 K and the initial temperature of the disc is 300 K. If the thermal conductivity of the material of the cylinder is 10 watt/m-K and the specific heat of the material of the disc is 600 J/kg-K, how long will it take for the temperature of the disc to increase to 350 K? Assume for purpose of calculation the thermal conductivity of the disc to be very high and the system to be thermally insulated except for the upper face of the cylinder. **(1992 JEE)**

86. A metallic cylindrical vessel whose inner and outer radii are r_1 and r_2 is filled with ice at 0°C. The mass of the ice in the cylinder is m. Circular portions of the cylinder is sealed with completely adiabatic walls. The vessel is kept in air. Temperature of the air is 50°C. How long will it take for the ice to melt completely? Thermal conductivity of the cylinder is K and its length is l. Latent heat of fusion is L.

87. An electric heater is placed inside a room of total wall area $137\ m^2$ to maintain the temperature inside at 20 °C. The outside temperature is −10 °C. The walls are made of three composite materials. The inner most layer is made of wood of thickness 2.5 cm, the middle layer is of cement of thickness 1 cm and the exterior layer is of brick of thickness 2.5 cm. Find the power of electric heater assuming that there is no heat losses through the floor and ceiling. The thermal conductivities of wood, cement and brick are 0.125 W/m-°C, 1.5 W/m-°C and 1.0 W/m-°C, respectively. **(1986 JEE)**

88. A 2 m long wire of resistance 4Ω and diameter 0.64 mm is coated with plastic insulation of thickness 0.66 mm. A current of 5 A flows through the wire. Find the temperature difference across the insulation in the steady state. Thermal conductivity of plastic is 0.16×10^{-2} cal/s cm-°C.

89. Two chunks of metal with heat capacities C_1 and C_2 are interconnected by a rod of length l and cross-sectional area A and fairly low conductivity K. The whole system is thermally insulated from the environment. At a moment $t = 0$, the temperature difference between two chunks of metal equals $(\Delta T)_0$. Assuming the heat capacity of the rod to be negligible, find the temperature difference between the chunks as a function of time. **(Irodov 2.250)**

90. A rod of length l with thermally insulated lateral surface consists of material whose heat conductivity coefficient varies with temperature as $k = a/T$, where a is a constant. The ends of the rod are kept at temperatures T_1 and T_2. Find the function $T(x)$, where x is the distance from the end whose temperature is T_1. **(Irodov 2.249)**

91. One end of a uniform brass rod 20 cm long and $10\ cm^2$ cross-sectional area is kept at 100 °C. The other end is in perfect thermal contact with another rod of identical cross-section and length 10 cm. The free end of this rod is kept in melting ice and when the steady state has been reached, it is found that 360 g of ice melts per hour. Calculate the thermal conductivity of the rod, given that the thermal conductivity of brass is 0.25 cal/s cm°C and L = 80 cal/g.

92. Heat flows radially outward through a spherical shell of outside radius R_2 and inner radius R_1. The temperature of inner surface of shell is θ_1 and that of outer is θ_2. At what radial distance from centre of shell the temperature is just half way between θ_1 and θ_2?

93. Find the temperature distribution in the space between two coaxial cylinders of radii R_1 and R_2 filled with a uniform heat conducting substance if the temperatures of the cylinders are constant and are equal to T_1 and T_2 respectively. **(Irodov 2.254)**

94. A constant electric current flows along a uniform wire with cross-sectional radius R and heat conductivity coefficient K. A unit volume of the wire generates a thermal power P. Find the temperature distribution across the wire provided the steady-state temperature at the wire surface is equal to T_0. **(Irodov 2.256)**

95. The thermal power of density P is generated uniformly inside a uniform sphere of radius R and heat conductivity coefficient K. Find the temperature distribution in the sphere provided the steady-state temperature at its surface is equal to T_0. **(Irodov 2.257)**

96. The spectral composition of solar radiation is much the same as that of a black body whose maximum emission corresponds to the wavelength 0.48 μm.

(a) Find the mass lost by the Sun every second due to radiation.

(b) Evaluate the time interval during which the mass of the Sun diminishes by 1 per cent. **(Irodov 5.249)**

97. A copper ball of diameter $d = 1.2$ cm was placed in an evacuated vessel whose walls are kept at the absolute zero temperature. The initial temperature of the ball is $T_0 = 300$ K. Assuming the surface of the ball to be absolutely black, find how soon its temperature decreases $\eta = 2.0$ times. **(Irodov 5.251)**

98. One end of a rod of length L and cross-sectional area A is kept in a furnace of temperature T_1. The other end of the rod is kept at a temperature T_2. The thermal conductivity of the material of the rod is K and emissivity of the rod is e.

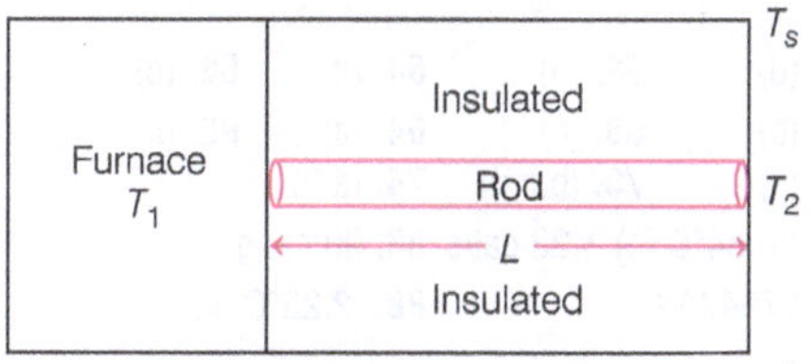

It is given that $T_2 = T_s + \Delta T$, where $\Delta T << T_s$, T_s being the temperature of the surroundings. If $\Delta T \propto (T_1 - T_s)$, find the proportionality constant. Consider that heat is lost only by radiation at the end where the temperature of the rod is T_2. **(2004 JEE)**

99. The top of an insulated cylindrical container is covered by a disc having emissivity 0.6 and conductivity 0.167 W/Km and thickness 1 cm. The temperature is maintained by circulating oil as shown. **(2003 JEE)**
(a) Find the radiation loss to the surroundings in W/m^2 if temperature of the upper surface of disc is 127°C and temperature of surroundings is 27°C.
(b) Also find the temperature of the circulating oil. Neglect the heat loss due to convection.
(Given, $\sigma = \frac{17}{3} \times 10^{-8}$ $Wm^{-2}K^{-4}$)

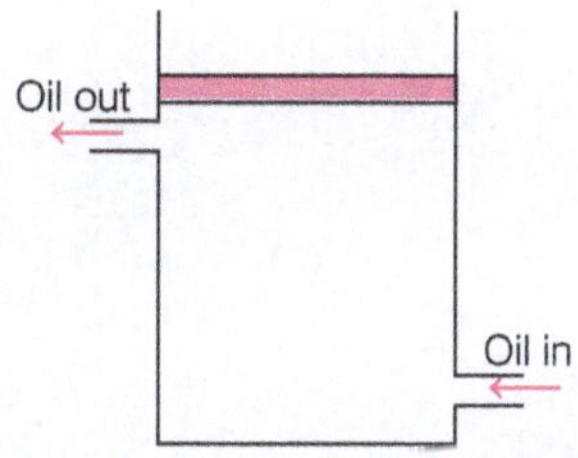

100. A solid body X of heat capacity C is kept in an atmosphere whose temperature is $T_A = 300$ K. At time $t = 0$, the temperature of X is $T_0 = 400$ K. It cools according to Newton's law of cooling. At time t_1 its temperature is found to be 350 K.
At this time (t_1) the body X is connected to a large body Y at atmospheric temperature T_A through a conducting rod of length L, cross-sectional area A and thermal conductivity K. The heat capacity of Y is so large that any variation in its temperature may be neglected. The cross-sectional area A of the connecting rod is small compared to the surface area of X. Find the temperature of X at time $t = 3t_1$. **(1998 JEE)**

Integer Type or Numerical Value Based Questions

101. A hollow sphere of inner radius r_0 and outer radius $2r_0$ is made of a uniform material of constant thermal conductivity K. The temperature within the ball is maintained at $2T_0$ and outside temperature of the ball is T_0. If temperature at distance $\frac{3r_0}{2}$ from centre is $\frac{pT_0}{3}$, then find the value of p.

102. In an experment to verify Newton's law of cooling, a graph is plotted between the temperature difference (ΔT) of the water and surroundings and time as shown in figure. The initial temperature of water is taken as 80°C. The value of t_2 as mentioned in the graph will be .... min. **(2022 Main)**

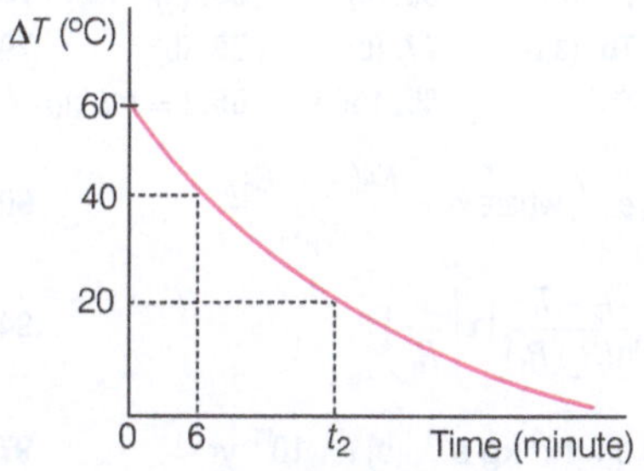

103. A small object is placed at the centre of a large evacuated hollow spherical container. Assume that, the container is maintained at 0 K. At time $t = 0$, the temperature of the object is 200 K. The temperature of the object becomes 100 K at $t = t_1$ and 50 K at $t = t_2$. Assume the object and the container to be ideal black bodies. The heat capacity of the object does not depend on temperature.
The ratio (t_2/t_1) is .... **(2021 Adv.)**

104. A container with 1 kg of water in it is kept in sunlight, which causes the water to get warmer than the surroundings. The average energy per unit time per unit area received due to the sunlight is 700 Wm^{-2} and it is absorbed by the water over an effective area of 0.05 m^2.
Assuming that the heat loss from the water to the surroundings is governed by Newton's law of cooling, the difference (in °C) in the temperature of water and the surroundings after a long time will be ....
(Ignore effect of the container and take constant for Newton's law of cooling = 0.001 s^{-1}, Heat capacity of water = 4200 $Jkg^{-1}K^{-1}$) **(2020 Adv.)**

105. A metal is heated in a furnace where a sensor is kept above the metal surface to read the power radiated (P) by the metal. The sensor has a scale that displays $\log_2(P/P_0)$, where P_0 is a constant. When the metal surface is at a temperature of 487°C, the sensor shows a value 1. Assume that the emissivity of the metallic surface remains constant. What is the value displayed by the sensor when the temperature of the metal surface is raised to 2767°C? **(2016 Adv.)**

Answers

Level 1

1. (5.5) **2.** $\frac{4\pi KTR^2}{P}$ **3.** ($1.71\,\rho rc$)s **4.** 5803 **5.** False **6.** (b) **7.** (c) **8.** (c) **9.** (a) **10.** (c)

11. (b) **12.** (d) **13.** (a) **14.** (b) **15.** (b) **16.** (d) **17.** (a) **18.** (a) **19.** (a) **20.** (a)

21. (a) **22.** (b) **23.** (a) **24.** (c) **25.** (d) **26.** (a) **27.** (a) **28.** (c) **29.** (a) **30.** (d)

31. (c) **32.** (c) **33.** (c) **34.** (d) **35.** 4.568×10^{-3} °C **36.** 41.6 W; 26.48°C, 0.52°C

37. 15.24°C **38.** (90) **39.** (42) **40.** (8) **41.** (40) **42.** (21) **43.** (9) **44.** (2) **45.** (9)

Level 2

46. (c) **47.** (a) **48.** (b) **49.** (b) **50.** (c) **51.** (d) **52.** (d) **53.** (b) **54.** (d) **55.** (c)

56. (a) **57.** (a) **58.** (c) **59.** (b) **60.** (d) **61.** (d) **62.** (b) **63.** (a) **64.** (a) **65.** (a)

66. (d) **67.** (a) **68.** (c) **69.** (a) **70.** (a) **71.** (b) **72.** (a) **73.** (b,c,d) **74.** (a,b)

75. (a,c,d) **76.** (a,b) **77.** (c) **78.** (b) **79.** (d) **81.** $\ln(2)/K$ **82.** (a) 84°C (b) 1.28 cal/s **83.** 90 cal/g

84. 8.6×10^{-3}°C **85.** 166 s **86.** $t = mL\ln(r_2/r_1)/100\pi Kl$ **87.** 17647 W **88.** 2.23°C

89. $T = \Delta T_0 e^{-\alpha t}$, where $\alpha = \frac{KA(C_1 + C_2)}{lC_1C_2}$ **90.** $T = T_1\left(\frac{T_2}{T_1}\right)^{x/l}$ **91.** 0.222 cal/cm-s-°C **92.** $\frac{2R_1R_2}{R_1 + R_2}$

93. $T = T_1 + \frac{T_2 - T_1}{\ln(R_2/R_1)}\ln\left(\frac{r}{R_1}\right)$ **94.** $T = T_0 + \frac{P}{4K}(R^2 - r^2)$ **95.** $T = T_0 + \frac{P}{6K}(R^2 - r^2)$

96.(a) $\frac{dm}{dt} = 5 \times 10^9$ kg s^{-1} (b) $t \approx 10^{11}$ yr **97.** $t \approx 3$ h **98.** $\left(\frac{K}{4e\sigma LT_s^3 + K}\right)$

99. (a) 595 W/m^2 (b) 162.6°C **100.** $\left(300 + 12.5e^{\frac{-2KAt_1}{CL}}\right)$ Kelvin **101.** (4) **102.** (16) **103.** (9)

104. (8.33) **105.** (9)

See hints on pages 388-405.

Hints & SOLUTIONS

Module 1.

1. Substances having more heat capacity take longer time to get heated to a higher temperature and longer time to get cooled.

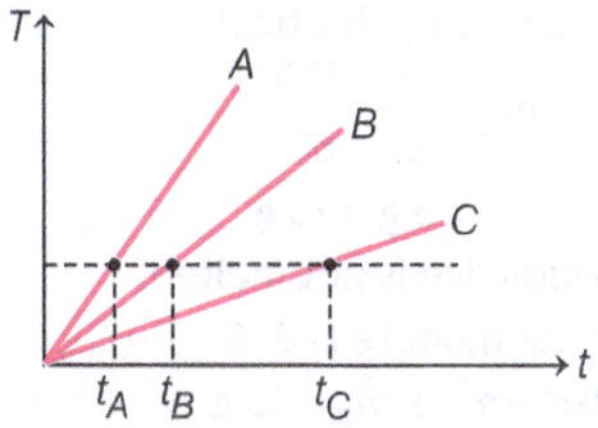

If we draw a line parallel to the time axis, then it cuts the given graphs at three different points. Corresponding points on the time axis shows that

$$t_C > t_B > t_A \;\Rightarrow\; C_C > C_B > C_A$$

2. Heat lost in t s = mL or heat lost per sec $= \frac{mL}{t}$. This must be the heat supplied for keeping the substance in molten state per sec.

$$\therefore \quad \frac{mL}{t} = P \quad \text{or} \quad L = \frac{Pt}{m}$$

3. Loss in potential energy $\times \frac{40}{100}$ = Heat produced

$$mg(2-1.5)\times 0.4 = ms\Delta\theta$$
$$1\times 10\times 0.5\times 0.4 = 800\,\Delta\theta$$
$$\Delta\theta = 0.0025°\text{C}$$
$$= 2.5\times 10^{-3}\,°\text{C}$$

4. $Q_1 = Q_2$

$$\therefore \quad ms_1(32-20) = ms_2(40-32)$$
$$\therefore \quad \frac{s_1}{s_2} = \frac{8}{12} = \frac{2}{3}$$

5. $Q = \int dQ = \int_1^2 ms\,dT$

$$= \int_1^2 (1)(aT^3)\,dT = \frac{15a}{4}$$

6. Heat taken by 1 g ice in transformation from ice at 0°C to water at 100°C is

$$Q = mL + ms\Delta\theta$$
$$= (1)(80) + (1)(1)(100)$$
$$= 180 \text{ cal}$$

Mass of steam condensed to give this much heat is

$$m = \frac{Q}{L} = \frac{180}{540} = \frac{1}{3}\text{ g}$$

This is less than 1g or total mass of steam. Therefore, whole steam is not condensed and mixture temperature is 100 °C.

7. From given curve,

Melting point for $A = 60°$C

and melting point for $B = 20°$C

Time taken by A for fusion $= (6-2) = 4$ min

Time taken by B for fusion $= (6.5-4) = 2.5$ min

Then, $$\frac{H_A}{H_B} = \frac{6\times 4\times 60}{6\times 2.5\times 60} = \frac{8}{5}$$

8. Heat taken = Heat given

or $$Ms\Delta\theta = mL$$
$$\therefore \quad (200)(s)(100) = 25\times 80$$
$$\therefore \quad s = 0.1 \text{ cal/g°C}$$

9. $Q = m_1 s_1\Delta\theta + m_2 s_2\Delta\theta + m_3 s_3\Delta\theta$

$$= (2.4\times 0.216 + 1.6\times 0.0917 + 0.8\times 0.0931)(60)$$
$$= 44.376 \text{ cal} \approx 44.44 \text{ cal}$$

10. $$Q_1 = mS_i\Delta\theta = 10\times 0.53\times 40 = 212 \text{ cal}$$
$$Q_2 = mL_i = 10\times 80 = 800 \text{ cal}$$
$$Q_3 = mS_w\Delta\theta = 10\times 1\times 100 = 1000 \text{ cal}$$
$$Q_4 = mL_w = 10\times 540 = 5400 \text{ cal}$$

11. $\mu Mgd = mL$

$$\therefore \quad d = \frac{mL}{\mu Mg}$$
$$= \frac{(15.2\times 10^{-3})(3.34\times 10^5)}{0.060\times 10\times 9.8} = 863.4 \text{ m}$$

12. $ms(2\theta - \theta') = m(2s)(\theta' - \theta)$

Solving this equation, we get

$$\theta' = \frac{4}{3}\theta$$

Further, heat capacity

$$C = ms \quad \text{or} \quad C \propto s \qquad \text{(as } m \text{ is same)}$$
$$\therefore \quad \frac{C_1}{C_2} = \frac{s_1}{s_2} = \frac{1}{2}$$

13. $dQ = msdT$

$$m = 1 \text{ kg}$$
$$\therefore \quad s = \frac{dQ}{dT} = \text{Slope of } Q\text{-}T \text{ graph}$$
$$S_{\text{solid}} = \tan 45° = 1 \text{ J/kg-K}$$
$$S_{\text{liquid}} = \tan 30° = \frac{1}{\sqrt{3}} \text{ J/kg-K}$$

Latent heat of vaporisation

= heat required to melt complete 1 kg

= 200 J/kg

14. When A and B are mixed,

$$ms_A(13-10) = ms_B(15-13)$$

$$3s_A = 2s_B \Rightarrow \frac{s_A}{s_B} = \frac{2}{3}$$

When B and C are mixed, $s_B \times 1 = s_C \times 4$

$$\Rightarrow \frac{s_B}{s_C} = 4 \Rightarrow \frac{3}{2}\frac{s_A}{s_C} = 4 \Rightarrow \frac{s_A}{s_C} = \frac{8}{3}$$

When A and C are mixed,

$$s_A(\theta - 10) = s_B(20 - \theta) \Rightarrow \theta = \frac{140}{11}\,°C$$

15. (a) $\frac{dQ}{dt} = ms\frac{d\theta}{dt}$

$$\therefore \left(\frac{d\theta}{dt}\right) = \frac{dQ/dt}{ms}$$

$\therefore$ Slope of θ-t graph $\propto \frac{1}{m}$

(b) $Q_{Total} = mL$

or $\left(\frac{dQ}{dt}\right)(\text{time}) = mL$

or time $\propto m$ or length of line $bc \propto m$

(d) ab : only solid state

bc : solid + liquid state

cd : only liquid state

de : liquid + gaseous state

ef : only gaseous state.

16. (a) $m(s)(\theta' - \theta) = 2m(s)(2\theta - \theta')$

Solving we get,

$$\theta' = \frac{5}{3}\theta$$

(b) $ms(\theta' - \theta) = 3m(s)(3\theta - \theta')$

Solving we get,

$$\theta' = \frac{5}{2}\theta$$

(c) $2m(s)(\theta' - 2\theta) = 3m(s)(3\theta - \theta')$

Solving we get,

$$\theta' = \frac{13}{5}\theta$$

(d) $ms(\theta' - \theta) + 2ms(\theta' - 2\theta) + 3ms(\theta' - 3\theta) = 0$

Solving, we get

$$\theta' = \frac{7}{3}\theta$$

17. $Q = mL_f + ms_w\Delta\theta + mL_f$

$$= m(L_f + s_w\Delta\theta + L_f)$$
$$= 10[80 + 1 \times 100 + 540]$$
$$= 7200 \text{ cal}$$

18. Let $\theta\,(>60°)$ is the mixture temperature in equilibrium.

Heat given = Heat taken

$$0 = m(1)(\theta - 20) + m(0.5)(\theta - 40) + m(0.25)(\theta - 60)$$

Solving the equation, we get

$$\theta = 31.43°C$$

19. $mL = ms(\theta - 0°)$

$$\therefore \theta = \frac{L}{s} = \frac{80}{1} = 80°C$$

20. Heat liberated by 10 g water (at 40°C) when it converts into water at 0°C

$$Q = m_1 s\Delta\theta$$
$$= 10 \times 1 \times 40$$
$$= 400 \text{ cal}$$

Mass of ice melted by this heat,

$$m_2 = \frac{Q}{L} = \frac{400}{80}$$
$$= 5\text{ g} < 15\text{ g}$$

Therefore, whole ice is not melted.

Temperature of mixture is 0°C.

Mass of water $= m_1 + m_2 = 15$ g

Mass of ice $= 15 - m_2 = 10$ g

21. $(4)(s_P)(60 - 55) = (1)(s_R)(55 - 50)$ ...(i)

$(1)(s_Q)(55 - 50) = (1)(s_P)(60 - 55)$ ...(ii)

$(1)(s_R)(\theta - 50) = (1)(s_Q)(60 - \theta)$ ...(iii)

Multiplying all three equations, we get

$$4(5)(5)(\theta - 50) = (5)(5)(60 - \theta)$$

Solving this equation, we get

$$\theta = 52°C$$

22. $\frac{1}{2}\left(\frac{1}{2}mv^2\right) = ms\Delta\theta + mL$

$$\therefore v = 2\sqrt{s\Delta\theta + L}$$
$$= 2\sqrt{(125)(327 - 27) + 2.5 \times 10^4}$$
$$= 500 \text{ m/s}$$

23. $P = \left(\frac{dm}{dt}\right)s \cdot \Delta\theta$

$$\therefore \frac{dm}{dt} = \frac{P}{s\Delta\theta} = \frac{500 \times 10^6}{(4200) \times 10}$$
$$= 11904 \text{ kg/s}$$
$$= 1.2 \times 10^4 \text{ kg/s}$$

Module 2

Introductory Exercise

2. $Q = \frac{KA(\theta_1 - \theta_2)t}{l}$

$$\therefore K = \frac{Ql}{A(\theta_1 - \theta_2)t} = \frac{\text{J-m}}{\text{m}^2\text{K-s}}$$
$$= \frac{\text{W}}{\text{m-K}} \quad (\text{as J/s} = \text{W})$$

3. $R = \frac{l}{kA} = \frac{\text{m}}{(\text{W/m-K})\text{m}^2} = \frac{\text{K}}{\text{W}} = \text{KW}^{-1}$

Here k is thermal conductivity.

4. In convection, liquid is heated from the bottom.

5. 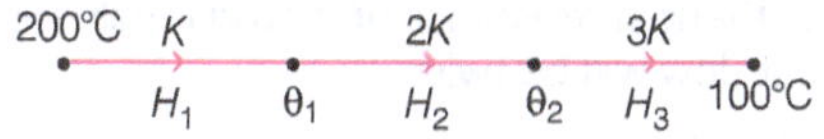

$$H_1 = H_2 = H_3$$

$$\therefore \quad \frac{200 - \theta_1}{(l/KA)} = \frac{\theta_1 - \theta_2}{(l/2KA)} = \frac{\theta_2 - 100}{(l/3KA)}$$

Solving these equations, we get

$$\theta_1 = 145.5°C$$

and $$\theta_2 = 118.2°C$$

6. 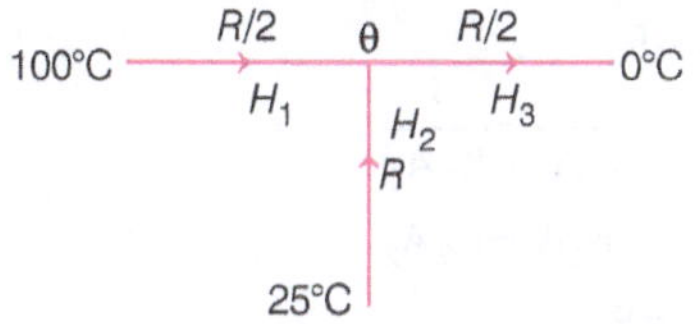

$$H_1 + H_2 = H_3$$

$$\frac{100 - \theta}{(R/2)} + \frac{25 - \theta}{R} = \frac{\theta - 0°}{R/2}$$

Solving, we get $\theta = 45°C$

$$H_{CD} = \frac{TD}{R} = \frac{45°C - 25°C}{5}$$

$$= 4W$$

7. Let us start with the assumption that

$$\left|\frac{\Delta\theta}{\Delta}\right| \propto \text{Temperature difference}$$

$$\therefore \quad \left(\frac{80-50}{5}\right) = \alpha\left[\frac{80+50}{2} - 20\right]$$

and $$\left(\frac{60-30}{t}\right) = \alpha\left[\frac{60+30}{2} - 20\right]$$

Solving these two equations, we get

$$t = 9 \text{ min}$$

Exercise

2. If temperature of a normal body is more than a perfectly black body, it can radiate more energy.

4. In steady state, temperature of different sections (perpendicular to the direction of heat flow) becomes constant but not same.

5. $R = \frac{l}{KA}$ or $R \propto \frac{1}{A}$

$\therefore \quad R_1 > R_2$

Further, $TD = H \times R$

Here TD = temperature difference

or $\quad TD \propto R$

$\therefore \quad (TD)_1 > (TD)_2$

6. In the absence of atmosphere on moon, evaporation is fast.

7. $\frac{dQ}{dt} = -KA\frac{d\theta}{dx}$; when $K = \infty, \frac{d\theta}{dx} = 0$

i.e. θ is independent of x, i.e. constant or uniform.

8. According to Kirchhoff's law,

$$\left(\frac{e_\lambda}{a_\lambda}\right)_{\text{any body}} = \left(\frac{e_\lambda}{a_\lambda}\right)_{\text{Perfectly black body}}$$

But $a_\lambda = 1$, for perfectly black body. Hence, $\frac{e_\lambda}{a_\lambda}$ for any body is equal to e_λ for perfectly black.

9. $T \propto \frac{1}{\lambda_m}$

$$\Rightarrow \quad \frac{T_1}{T_2} = \frac{(\lambda_m)_2}{(\lambda_m)_1} = \frac{2\lambda}{\lambda} = 2$$

Energy radiated per second (or power)

$$P = e_r \sigma T^4 A = e_r \sigma T^4 (4\pi R^2)$$

$$\therefore \quad P \propto T^4 R^2$$

$$\frac{P_1}{P_2} = \left(\frac{T_1}{T_2}\right)^4 \left(\frac{R_1}{R_2}\right)^2 = (2)^4 \left(\frac{r}{2r}\right)^2 = 4:1$$

12. Mud is bad conductor of heat. So, it prevents the flow of heat between surroundings and inside.

13. No flow of heat by convection takes place in vacuum.

14. In MKS system, unit of σ is $\frac{J}{m^2 \times s \times K^4}$

$$\Rightarrow \quad \frac{J}{m^2 \times s \times K^4} = \frac{10^7 \text{ erg}}{10^4 \text{ cm}^2 \times s \times K^4}$$

$$= 10^3 \frac{\text{erg}}{\text{cm}^2 \times s \times K^4}$$

15. Initially, it will absorb heat and then it will radiate.

16. A body having maximum surface area will cool at fastest rate.

17. According to Kirchhoff's law, the ratio of emissive power to absorptive power is same for all bodies. Which is equal to the emissive power of a perfectly black body, i.e.

$$\left(\frac{e_\lambda}{a_\lambda}\right)_{\text{body}} = (E_\lambda)_{\text{Black body}}$$

$$\Rightarrow \quad e_\lambda = a_\lambda E_\lambda$$

18. At higher temperature radiation is more. So, cooling is fast.

19. Area $\propto$ Total energy radiated $\propto T^4$

$$T_1 = 300 \text{ K and } T_2 = 600 \text{ K}$$

Temperature has doubled. Therefore, area will become 16 times.

20. $K_C > K_B \Rightarrow \quad R_C < R_B$

Temperature difference across copper

$$= HR_C = (TD)_C$$

and temperature difference across brass

$$= HR_B = (TD)_B$$

Heat current H will be same in both, as they are in series.

Since, $R_C < R_B$

$\therefore$ $(TD)_C < (TD)_B$

Or temperature of junction is more than 50°C.

21.

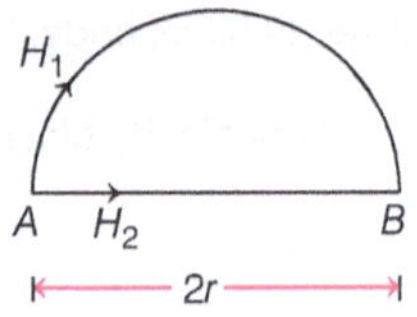

$$R_{circular} = R_1 \propto \pi r$$
$$R_{straight} = R_2 \propto 2r$$
$$\theta_A - \theta_B = H_1R_1 = H_2R_2$$
$$\frac{H_1}{H_2} = \frac{R_2}{R_1} = \frac{2r}{\pi r} = \frac{2}{\pi}$$

22. $\lambda_m \propto \frac{1}{T}$

$\therefore$ $$\frac{(\lambda_m)_2}{(\lambda_m)_1} = \frac{T_1}{T_2} = \frac{2000}{3000} = \frac{2}{3}$$

$\therefore$ $$(\lambda_m)_2 = \frac{2}{3}(\lambda_m)_1$$

23. $\lambda_m \propto \frac{1}{T}$

$\therefore$ $$\frac{(\lambda_m)_1}{(\lambda_m)_2} = \frac{T_2}{T_1} \quad \text{or} \quad \frac{T_1}{T_2} = \frac{(\lambda_m)_2}{(\lambda_m)_1}$$
$$= \frac{350}{510} = 0.69$$

24. Thermal resistance $= \frac{l}{KA} = \frac{l}{K(\pi R^2)} \propto \frac{l}{R^2}$

The rod for which $\frac{l}{R^2}$ is minimum will conduct maximum heat.

25. $H_A = H_{Total}$

$\therefore$ $$\frac{(TD)_A}{R_A} = \frac{TD}{R_A + R_B}$$

$\therefore$ $$(TD)_A = \left(\frac{R_A}{R_A + R_B}\right)TD$$
$$= \left(\frac{1}{1 + R_B/R_A}\right)TD \quad \text{...(i)}$$
$$\frac{R_B}{R_A} = \left(\frac{l_B}{l_A}\right)\left(\frac{K_AA}{K_BA}\right) = \left(\frac{20}{10}\right)(3) = 6$$

Substituting in Eq. (i), we get

$$(TD)_A = \left(\frac{1}{1+6}\right) \times 35 = 5°C$$

26. $R = \frac{l}{KA}$

$$\frac{R_2}{R_1} = \left(\frac{l_2}{l_1}\right)\left(\frac{K_1}{K_2} \cdot \frac{A_1}{A_2}\right) = (2)\left(\frac{1}{2}\right)\left(\frac{1}{2}\right) = \frac{1}{2}$$

Therefore, thermal resistance of 2nd rod is half. Hence, rate of heat flow will be twice.

27. $4\pi r_1^2 T_1^4 = 4\pi r_2^2 T_2^4$

$\therefore$ $$\frac{r_1}{r_2} = \frac{T_2^2}{T_1^2}$$

28. $H_1 = H_2$

$\therefore$ $$\left(\frac{TD}{R}\right)_1 = \left(\frac{TD}{R}\right)_2 \quad \text{(TD = Temperature difference)}$$

or $R_1 = R_2$

$\therefore$ $$\frac{l}{K_1A_1} = \frac{l}{K_2A_2}$$

or $K_1A_1 = K_2A_2$

29. $R_{PR} + R_{RQ} = R_{PQ}$

$\therefore$ $$\frac{l}{K_1A} + \frac{l}{K_2A} = \frac{l}{K_3A}$$

or $$K_3 = \frac{K_1K_2}{K_1 + K_2}$$

30. For no current flow between C and D,

$$\left(\frac{Q}{t}\right)_{AC} = \left(\frac{Q}{t}\right)_{CB}$$
$$\Rightarrow \frac{K_1A(\theta_A - \theta_C)}{l} = \frac{K_2A(\theta_C - \theta_B)}{l}$$
$$\Rightarrow \frac{\theta_A - \theta_C}{\theta_C - \theta_B} = \frac{K_2}{K_1} \quad \text{...(i)}$$

Also, $$\left(\frac{Q}{t}\right)_{AD} = \left(\frac{Q}{t}\right)_{DB}$$
$$\Rightarrow \frac{K_3A(\theta_A - \theta_D)}{l} = \frac{K_4A(\theta_D - \theta_B)}{l}$$
$$\Rightarrow \frac{\theta_A - \theta_D}{\theta_D - \theta_B} = \frac{K_4}{K_3} \quad \text{...(ii)}$$

It is given that $\theta_C = \theta_D$, hence from Eqs. (i) and (ii), we get $$\frac{K_2}{K_1} = \frac{K_4}{K_3}$$
$$\Rightarrow K_1K_4 = K_2K_3$$

31. Let θ be the temperature of junction.

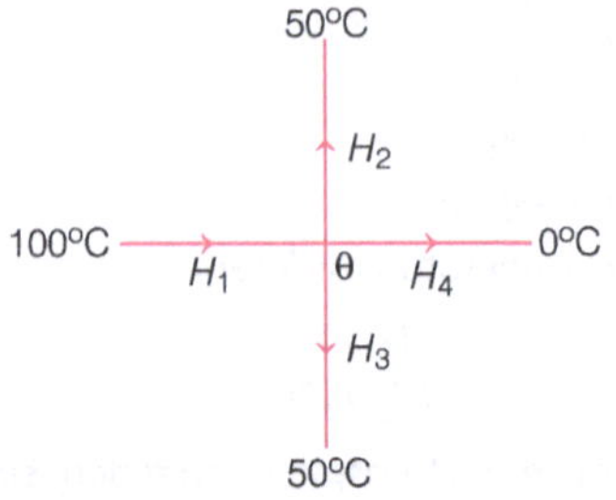

H_1, H_2, H_3 and H_4 be the heat currents. Then,

$$H_1 = H_2 + H_3 + H_4$$

or $$\frac{100 - \theta}{R} = \frac{\theta - 50}{R} + \frac{\theta - 50}{R} + \frac{\theta - 0}{R}$$

($R =$ Thermal resistance of each part of two rods)
Solving these two equations, we get

$$\theta = 50°C$$

32. Cooling rate $\propto T^4 - T_0^4$

$$r = \left\{\frac{(900)^4 - (300)^4}{(600)^4 - (300)^4}\right\} r_0$$

$$= \frac{16}{3} r_0$$

33. From Newton's law of cooling,

$$\ln\left(\frac{T_1 - T_0}{T_2 - T_0}\right) = kt$$

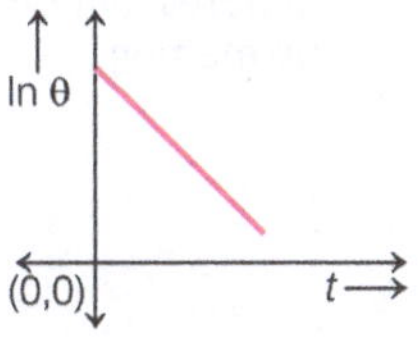

Let θ_i be the initial temperature of body and θ_s be the temperature of the surroundings. Suppose θ is the instantaneous temperature difference between the body and surroundings.

Then, $\ln\left(\frac{\theta_i - \theta_s}{\theta}\right) = kt$

$\Rightarrow \quad \ln(\theta_i - \theta_s) - \ln\theta = kt$

$\Rightarrow \quad \ln\theta = -kt + \ln(\theta_i - \theta_0)$

Comparing to $y = mx + C$, option (b) is correct.

34. Total radiation per second is given by

$$P = e_r \sigma T^4 A$$

Here, $e_r : \sigma : T$ and A all are same.
Hence, P will be same.
Same is the case with absorption per second.

Now, $\quad P = ms\left(-\frac{dT}{dt}\right)$

or Rate of cooling $\left(-\frac{dT}{dt}\right) = \frac{P}{ms} \propto \frac{1}{m}$

Mass of hollow sphere is less. So, its initial rate of cooling will be more.

35. $$H_1 = H_2 + H_3$$

$\therefore \quad \frac{40 - \theta}{R} = \frac{\theta - 20}{R} + \frac{\theta - 30}{R}$

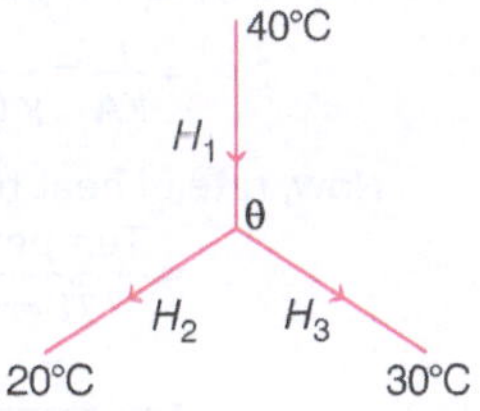

where, $R =$ thermal resistance of each rod
Solving this equation, we get

$$\theta = 30°C$$

Heat flows from higher temperature to lower temperature.

36. $q_1 = \frac{TD}{R_1}$

$\therefore \quad R_1 = \frac{TD}{q_1}$

Similarly, $R_2 = \frac{TD}{q_2}$

In series,

$$q_s = \frac{TD}{R_1 + R_2} = \frac{TD}{\frac{TD}{q_1} + \frac{TD}{q_2}} = \frac{q_1 q_2}{q_1 + q_2}$$

In parallel, $\quad q_p = \frac{TD}{R_{net}} = TD\left(\frac{1}{R_{net}}\right)$

$$= TD\left(\frac{1}{R_1} + \frac{1}{R_2}\right)$$

$$= TD\left(\frac{q_1}{TD} + \frac{q_2}{TD}\right) = q_1 + q_2$$

37. If temperature difference is small, the rate of cooling is proportional to TD.

38. (a) $E = \sigma T^4 =$ energy radiated per unit surface area per unit time by a black body

$\therefore \quad \sigma = \left[\frac{E}{T^4}\right] = \left[\frac{ML^2T^{-2}}{L^2T\theta^4}\right] = [MT^{-3}\theta^{-4}]$

(b) $b = \lambda_m T$

$\therefore \quad [b] = [L\theta]$

(c) Emissive power is energy radiated per unit time per unit surface area.

$\therefore \quad [E] = \left[\frac{ML^2T^{-2}}{L^2T}\right] = [MT^{-3}]$

(d) $H = \frac{dQ}{dt} = \frac{TD}{R}$

$\therefore \quad R = \frac{TD}{(dQ/dt)} = \frac{\theta}{[ML^2T^{-2}/T]}$

$$= [M^{-1}L^{-2}T^3\theta]$$

39. If $R =$ thermal resistance of one rod

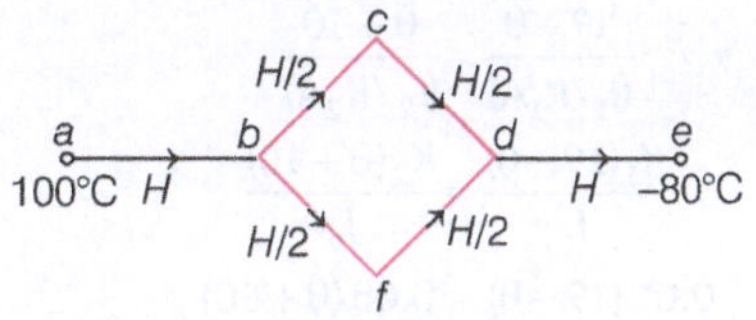

Then, $\quad R_{net} = 3R$

$\therefore \quad H = \frac{100 - (-80)}{3R} = \frac{60}{R}$

(a) ***ab*** $\quad H = \frac{60}{R} = \frac{100 - \theta_b}{R}$

$\therefore \quad \theta_b = 40°C$

(b) ***bc*** $\quad \frac{H}{2} = \frac{30}{R} = \frac{40 - \theta_c}{R}$

$\therefore \quad \theta_c = 10°C$

(c) Same as above

(d) ***de***

$$H = \frac{60}{R} = \frac{\theta_d - (-80)}{R}$$

$\therefore \quad \theta_d = -20°C$

40. Unit of heat capacity is J/°C.
Unit of latent heat is J/kg.

41. Net power $= e_r \sigma (T^4 - T_0^4) A$

In first case,

$$210 = e_r \sigma [(500)^4 - (300)^4] A \quad \text{...(i)}$$

In second case,

$$700 = \sigma [(500)^4 - (300)^4] A \quad \text{...(ii)}$$

Dividing Eq. (i) by Eq. (ii), we get

$$e_r = \frac{210}{700} = 0.3$$

42. $P = e_r \sigma A (T^4 - T_0^4)$

$$= (0.4)(5.67 \times 10^{-8})(4\pi)(4 \times 10^{-2})^2 [(3000)^4 - (300)^4]$$

$$= 3.7 \times 10^4 \text{ W}$$

43. $L\left(\frac{dm}{dt}\right) = \frac{dQ}{dt} = H = \frac{\text{TD}}{R} = \frac{\theta - 100}{(l/KA)}$

$$\therefore \quad \theta = 100 + \left(\frac{Ll}{KA}\right)\left(\frac{dm}{dt}\right)$$

$$= 100 + \left(\frac{2.256 \times 10^6 \times 1.2 \times 10^{-2}}{50.2 \times 0.15}\right)\left(\frac{0.44}{60 \times 5}\right)$$

$$= 105°\text{C}$$

44. (a) $H_1 = H_2$

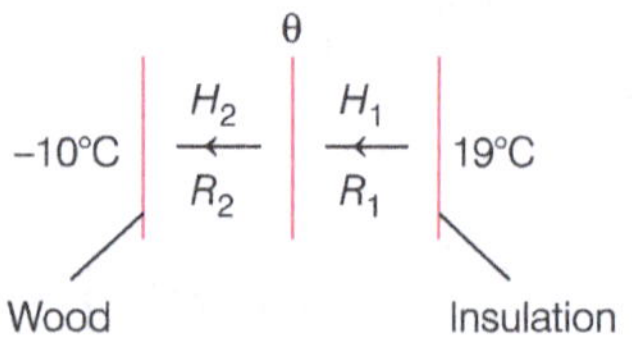

$$\therefore \quad \frac{19 - \theta}{R_1} = \frac{\theta + 10}{R} \qquad \left(H = \frac{\text{TD}}{R}\right)$$

or

$$\frac{19 - \theta}{(l_1 / K_1 A)} = \frac{\theta + 10}{(l_2 / K_2 A)}$$

$$\therefore \quad \frac{K_1 (19 - \theta)}{l_1} = \frac{K_2 (\theta + 10)}{l_2}$$

$$\therefore \quad \frac{0.01(19 - \theta)}{3.5} = \frac{0.08(\theta + 10)}{2.0}$$

Solving, we get

$$\theta = -8.1°\text{C}$$

(b) $H = H_1 = \frac{19 - \theta}{(l_1 / K_1 A)} = \frac{K_1 A (19 - \theta)}{l_1}$

$$= \frac{(0.01)(19 + 8.1)(1)}{3.5 \times 10^{-2}}$$

$$= 7.7 \text{ W/m}^2$$

45. Hint is already given in the question.

46.

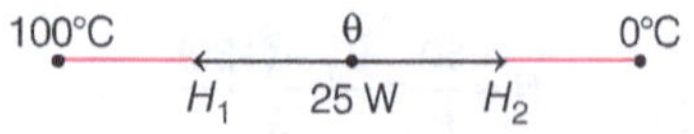

$$H_1 + H_2 = 25$$

$$\therefore \quad \frac{\theta - 100}{0.5/(400 \times 10^{-4})} + \frac{\theta - 0}{0.5/(400 \times 10^{-4})} = 25$$

Solving this equation, we get

$$\theta \approx 206°\text{C}$$

Now, temperature gradient on

$$\text{LHS} = \frac{\theta - 100}{0.5} = 212°\text{C/m}$$

and on

$$\text{RHS} = \frac{\theta - 0}{0.5} = 424°\text{C/m}$$

47. Let heat is supplied at a constant rate of $(\alpha) \frac{\text{J}}{\text{min}}$. In 4 minutes, (when temperature remains constant) ice will be melting.

$$\therefore \quad mL = (4)\,\alpha$$

$$\therefore \quad \frac{\alpha}{m} = \frac{L}{4} = \frac{336 \times 10^3}{4}$$

$$= 84 \times 10^3 \text{ J/min-kg}$$

Now in last two minutes,

$$Q = ms\Delta\theta$$

$$\therefore \quad (\alpha)(2) = (m)(4200)(\theta - 0°\text{C})$$

Substituting the value of $\frac{\alpha}{m}$, we get

$$\theta = 40°\text{C}$$

Unit Exercise (Cumulative)

Level 1

1. Heat required to melt the block

$$= (0.28 \text{ kg})(3.3 \times 10^5 \text{ J/kg})$$

$$= 9.24 \times 10^4 \text{ J}$$

Heat received per second

$$= (1400 \text{ J/m}^2)(0.2 \text{ m}^2) = 280 \text{ J}$$

$\therefore$ Time taken (in minutes)

$$= \frac{9.24 \times 10^4}{280 \times 60} = 5.5$$

2. Thermal resistance

$$= \frac{l}{KA} = \frac{t}{K(4\pi R^2)} \qquad (t = \text{thickness})$$

Now, rate of heat transfer

$$= \frac{\text{Temperature difference}}{\text{Thermal resistance}}$$

$$= \frac{T}{t / 4\pi K R^2} = \frac{4\pi K T R^2}{t}$$

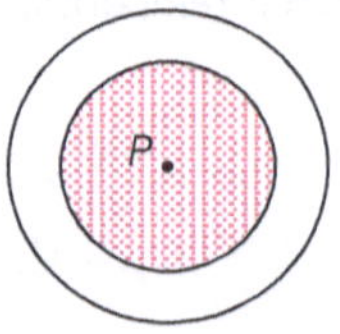

Equating this rate with the power of the source.

$$\therefore \quad P = \frac{4\pi K T R^2}{t} \quad \text{or} \quad t = \frac{4\pi K T R^2}{P}$$

or thickness t should not exceed

$$\frac{4\pi KTR^2}{P}$$

3. Area of sphere, $A = 4\pi r^2$

Mass of sphere, $m = \left(\frac{4}{3}\pi \rho r^3\right)$

Now, energy radiated per second

$$= (\sigma A T^4)$$

$$\therefore \quad mc\left(-\frac{dT}{dt}\right) = \sigma A T^4$$

or $$\int_0^t dt = \left(\frac{-mc}{\sigma A}\right)\int_{200}^{100} T^{-4} dT$$

or $$t = \frac{mc}{3\sigma A}\left[\frac{1}{(100)^3} - \frac{1}{(200)^3}\right]$$

$$= \frac{7mc}{3 \times 8\,\sigma A} \times 10^{-6}$$

$$= \frac{7mc \times 10^{-6}}{24\,\sigma A}$$

Substituting the values,

$$t = \frac{\left(7 \times \frac{4}{3}\pi \rho r^3\right)(c) \times 10^{-6}}{3 \times 8 \times 5.67 \times 10^{-8} \times 4\pi r^2}$$

$$= (1.71\ \rho r c)\ \text{s}$$

4. Given, $\dfrac{(\sigma T^4)(4\pi R^2)}{(4\pi r^2)} = 1400$

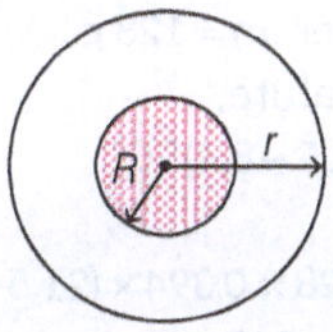

$$\therefore \quad T = \left(\frac{1400 \times r^2}{\sigma R^2}\right)^{1/4} = \left[\frac{1400 \times (1.5 \times 10^{11})^2}{(5.67 \times 10^{-8}) \times (7 \times 10^8)^2}\right]^{1/4}$$

$$= 5803\ \text{K}$$

5. Energy radiated per second is directly proportional to area and to the fourth power of temperature.

i.e. $$E \propto AT^4$$

$$\Rightarrow \quad E \propto (R^2)T^4$$

$$\Rightarrow \quad \frac{E_1}{E_2} = \left(\frac{1}{4}\right)^2\left(\frac{4000}{2000}\right)^4 = 1$$

or $$E_1 = E_2$$

6.

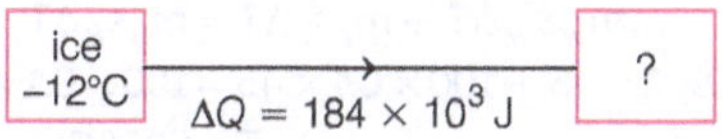

First ice absorbs heat and it's temperature rises to 0°C.

Now using, $\Delta Q = mc\Delta T$

We have,

$$\Delta Q = (600 \times 10^{-3})(2222.3)(12)$$

$$= 16000.56\ \text{J}$$

$$\approx 16\ \text{kJ}$$

Now, ice at 0°C starts melting. Let m kg of ice melts due to remaining heat.

Heat available $= (184 - 16)$ kJ

$= 168$ kJ

Now using

$$\Delta Q = mL, \text{ we have}$$

$$168 = m(336)$$

$$\Rightarrow \quad m = 0.5\ \text{kg} = 500\ \text{g}$$

As out of 600 g of ice, 500 g is converted into water, final mixture contains 100 g ice and 500 g water.

7. According to calorimetry, heat lost by Cu block = Heat gain by ice

$$\Rightarrow \quad m_{cu} \cdot s_{cu}(T_{500} - T_0) = m_{ice} L_f$$

$$\Rightarrow \quad m_{ice} = \frac{m_{cu} \cdot s_{cu}(T_{500} - T_0)}{L_f}$$

$$= \frac{5 \times 390 \times 500}{335 \times 10^3} = 2.9\ \text{kg}$$

8. Given, mass of iron nail, $m = 100$ g

$= 0.1$ kg

Mass of hammer, $M = 1.5$ kg

Velocity of hammer, $v = 60\ \text{ms}^{-1}$

According to question, $\frac{1}{4} \times$ KE of hammer $= ms\Delta T$

$$\Rightarrow \quad \frac{1}{4} \times 1.5 \times (60)^2 \times \frac{1}{2} = 0.1 \times 0.42 \times 10^3 \times \Delta T$$

$$= 16.07°\text{C}$$

9. Given, height of waterfall, $h = 63$ m. The potential energy of water will convert into kinetic energy while falling down and when this moving water will strike the bottom of the fall, it will change into heat energy, which will raise its temperature.

Therefore, $mg(\Delta h) = ms\Delta T$

$$\Rightarrow \quad g(\Delta h) = s\Delta T$$

$$9.8 \times 63 = 4.2 \times 10^3 \times \Delta T$$

$$\Rightarrow \quad \Delta T = 0.147°\text{C}$$

10. Given, temperature of liquid (x)

$$T_1 = 10°\text{C}$$

Temperature of liquid (y) $T_2 = 20°\text{C}$

Temperature of liquid (z) $T_3 = 30°\text{C}$

Let masses of liquid x, y and z be $m_1, m_2, m_3 = m$

When x and y are mixed, $T_{f_1} = 16°\text{C}$

$$\Rightarrow m_1 s_1 T_1 + m_2 s_2 T_2 = (m_1 s_1 + m_2 s_2)T_{f_1}$$

$$\Rightarrow s_1 \times 10 + s_2 \times 20 = (s_1 + s_2) \times 16$$

$$\Rightarrow \quad s_1 = \frac{2}{3}s_2 \quad \text{...(i)}$$

When y and z are mixed, $T_{f_2} = 26°C$

$$\Rightarrow \quad m_2s_2T_2 + m_3s_3T_3 = (m_3s_3 + m_2s_2)T_{f_2}$$

$$\Rightarrow \quad s_2 \times 20 + s_3 \times 30 = (s_2 + s_3) \times 26$$

$$\Rightarrow \quad s_3 = \frac{3}{2}s_2 \quad \text{...(ii)}$$

where x and z are mixed.

$$m_1s_1T_1 + m_3s_3T_3 = (s_1m_1 + m_3s_3)T_f$$

$$\Rightarrow \quad \frac{2}{3}s_2 \times 10 + \frac{3}{2} \times 30 = \left(\frac{2}{3}s_2 + \frac{3}{2}s_2\right)T_f$$

$$\Rightarrow \quad T_f = 23.84°C$$

11. As the heat is supplied at same rate to both bodies.

Therefore, $\left(\frac{\Delta Q}{\Delta t}\right)_A = \left(\frac{\Delta Q}{\Delta t}\right)_B$

$$\Rightarrow \quad ms_A\left(\frac{\Delta T}{\Delta t}\right)_A = ms_B\left(\frac{\Delta T}{\Delta t}\right)_B$$

$$\Rightarrow \quad \frac{s_A}{s_B} = \frac{\left(\frac{\Delta T}{\Delta t}\right)_B}{\left(\frac{\Delta T}{\Delta t}\right)_A}$$

$$= \frac{\frac{90}{6}}{\frac{120}{3}} = \frac{15}{40} = \frac{3}{8}$$

12. $\frac{1}{2}kx^2 = (m_1s_1 + m_2s_2)\Delta T$

Substituting values given in question, we have

$$\frac{1}{2} \times 800 \times (2 \times 10^{-2})^2 = \left[\left(\frac{500}{1000}\right) \times 400 + 1 \times 4184\right]\Delta T$$

$$\Rightarrow \Delta T = 3.65 \times 10^{-5}\,K$$

13. $M_1(0.5)(10) + M_1L = M_2(1)(50)$

$$\Rightarrow \quad L = 50\frac{M_2}{M_1} - 5$$

14. Let x grams of water is evaporated.

Heat lost by freezing water (that turns into ice) = Heat gained by evaporated water

$$m_1L_1 = m_2L_2$$

$$\Rightarrow (150 - x) \times 10^{-3} \times 3.36 \times 10^5 = x \times 10^{-3} \times 2.10 \times 10^6$$

$$\therefore \quad x \approx 20\text{ g}$$

15. $m_As_A\Delta T_A = m_Bs_B\Delta T_B$

$$\Rightarrow \quad 100 \times s_A(100 - 90) = 50 \times s_B(90 - 75)$$

or $\quad 4s_A = 3s_B \quad$ ...(i)

Similarly, in second case,

$$100 \times s_A(100 - T) = 50 \times s_B(T - 50)$$

Substituting $\frac{s_A}{s_B} = \frac{3}{4}$, we get

or $\quad T = 80°C$

16. $0.1 \times 400(500 - T)$

$$= 0.5 \times 4200(T - 30) + 800(T - 30)$$

$$T = 36.39\text{ K}$$

So, percentage increment in temperature of water

$$\% = \frac{36.39 - 30}{30} \times 100 \approx 20\%$$

17. Let amount of ice be 'x' g.

According to the principle of calorimetry,

heat lost by water = heat gained by ice

$$ms_{water}\Delta T = xs_{ice}\Delta T + (x - 20)L$$

$$\Rightarrow \quad 50 \times 4.2 \times 40 = x \times 2.1 \times 20 + (x - 20) \times 334$$

$$\Rightarrow \quad 50 \times 4.2 \times 40 = 20x \times 2.1 + 334x - 6680$$

$$\Rightarrow \quad x \simeq 40\text{ g}$$

18. Let specific heat of unknown metal be s and heat lost by this metal be ΔQ.

$$\Delta Q = ms\Delta T \quad \text{...(i)}$$

For unknown metal,

$$m = 192\text{ g}$$

and $\quad \Delta T = (100 - 21.5)°C$

$\therefore \quad \Delta Q' = 192(100 - 21.5) \times s \quad$ ...(ii)

Now, this heat is gained by the calorimeter and water inside it.

So, for brass specific heat,

$$s = 394\text{ J kg}^{-1}\text{K}^{-1} \quad \text{(given)}$$

$$= 0.394\text{ Jg}^{-1}\text{K}^{-1}$$

Mass of calorimeter, $m = 128$ g

Change in temperature,

$$\Delta T = (21.5 - 8.4)°C$$

Therefore,

$$\Delta Q_1 = 128 \times 0.394 \times (21.5 - 8.4) \quad \text{...(iii)}$$

Mass of water, $m = 240$ g

Specific heat of water,

$$s = 4.18\text{ J g}^{-1}\text{K}^{-1}$$

Change in temperature,

$$\Delta T = (21.5 - 8.4)°C$$

Heat gained by water,

$$\Delta Q_2 = 240 \times 4.18 \times (21.5 - 8.4) \quad \text{...(iv)}$$

$$\Delta Q' = \Delta Q_1 + \Delta Q_2$$

Putting the values of ΔQ_1 and ΔQ_2

we get $\quad s = 916\text{ J kg}^{-1}\text{K}^{-1}$

19. Heat gained (water + calorimeter) = Heat lost by copper ball

$$\Rightarrow \quad m_ws_w\Delta T + m_cs_c\Delta T = m_Bs_B\Delta T$$

$$\Rightarrow \quad 170 \times 1 \times 45 + 100 \times 0.1 \times 45 = 100 \times 0.1 \times (T - 75)$$

$$\Rightarrow \quad T = 885°C$$

20. 1 calorie is the heat required to raise the temperature of 1 g of water from 14.50°C to 15.5°C at 760 mm of Hg. Hence, correct option is (a).

21. Energy gained by water (in 1 s)

$= \text{energy supplied} - \text{energy lost} = 1000\text{ J} - 160\text{ J} = 840\text{ J}$

Total heat required to raise the temperature of water from 27°C to 77°C is $ms\Delta\theta$.

Hence, the required time

$$t = \frac{ms\Delta T}{\text{rate by which energy is gained by water}}$$

$$= \frac{(2)(4.2 \times 10^3)(50)}{840}$$

$$= 500\text{ s} = 8\text{ min } 20\text{ s}$$

22. Heat released by 5 kg of water when its temperature falls from 20°C to 0°C is,

$$Q_1 = ms\Delta T = (5)(10^3)(20-0)$$

$$= 10^5\text{ cal}$$

When 2 kg ice at – 20°C comes to a temperature of 0°C, it takes an energy

$$Q_2 = ms\Delta T = (2)(500)(20)$$

$$= 0.2 \times 10^5\text{ cal}$$

The remaining heat $Q = Q_1 - Q_2 = 0.8 \times 10^5$ cal will melt a mass m of the ice, where

$$m = \frac{Q}{L} = \frac{0.8 \times 10^5}{80 \times 10^3} = 1\text{ kg}$$

So, the temperature of the mixture will be 0°C, mass of water in it is $5+1=6$ kg and mass of ice is $2-1=1$ kg.

23. Heat required

$$Q_1 = (1.1 + 0.02) \times 10^3 \times 1 \times (80-15)$$

$$= 72800\text{ cal}$$

Heat given to m (in kg) steam is condensed :

$$Q_2 = (m \times 540 \times 10^3) + m \times 1 \times 10^3 \times (100-80)$$

Equating $Q_1 = Q_2$, we get

$$m = 0.130\text{ kg}$$

24. Given, for steel and copper rods,

$$\frac{K_2}{K_1} = 9, \frac{A_1}{A_2} = 2, \frac{L_1}{L_2} = 2$$

From the diagram given in question, for steel rod

$$\frac{dQ}{dt} = K_1 A_1 \frac{(450-T)}{L_1} \quad \text{...(i)}$$

and for copper rod

$$\frac{dQ}{dt} = K_2 A_2 \frac{(T-0)}{L_2} \quad \text{...(ii)}$$

Dividing Eq. (i) by Eq. (ii), we get

$$1 = \frac{K_1}{K_2}\frac{A_1}{A_2}\left(\frac{450-T}{T}\right)\frac{L_2}{L_1}$$

$$\Rightarrow \quad \frac{450-T}{T} = \frac{K_2}{K_1} \cdot \frac{A_2}{A_1} \cdot \frac{L_1}{L_2}$$

$$\Rightarrow \quad \frac{450}{T} - 1 = 9 \times \frac{1}{2} \times 2 \Rightarrow \frac{450}{T} = 9 + 1$$

$$\Rightarrow \quad T = \frac{450}{10} = 45°\text{C}$$

25. Let interface temperature in steady state conduction be θ, then assuming no heat loss through sides;

$$\begin{pmatrix}\text{Rate of heat}\\ \text{flow through}\\ \text{first slab}\end{pmatrix} = \begin{pmatrix}\text{Rate of heat}\\ \text{flow through}\\ \text{second slab}\end{pmatrix}$$

$$\Rightarrow \quad \frac{(3K)A(\theta_2 - \theta)}{d} = \frac{KA(\theta - \theta_1)}{3d}$$

$$\Rightarrow \quad 9(\theta_2 - \theta) = \theta - \theta_1$$

$$\Rightarrow \quad 9\theta_2 + \theta_1 = 10\theta$$

$$\Rightarrow \quad \theta = \frac{9}{10}\theta_2 + \frac{1}{10}\theta_1$$

26. According to the given question, the given figure with its length for each section is given as below.

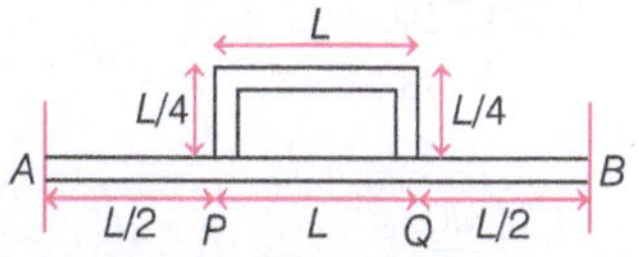

The above figure considering that every section has the same thermal conductivity, then in terms of thermal resistance is shown in the figure below,

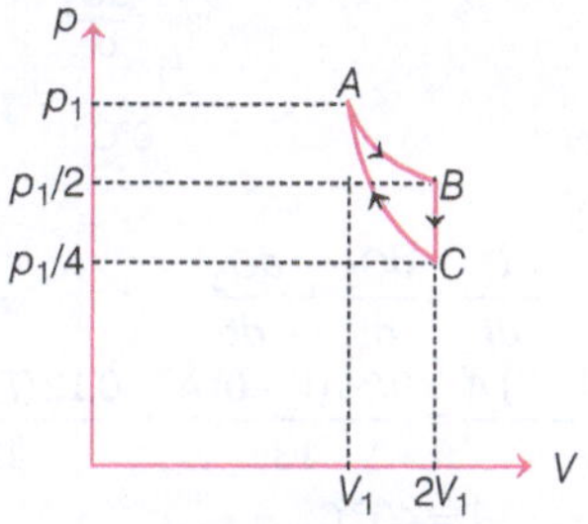

Net resistance of the section $PQRS$ is

$$= \frac{R \times \frac{3R}{2}}{\frac{5R}{2}} = \frac{3R}{5} \quad \text{...(i)}$$

Total resistance of the net network, R_{net}

$$= \frac{R}{2} + \frac{R}{2} + \frac{3R}{5} = \frac{8R}{5}$$

$\therefore$ Thermal current,

$$I = \frac{\Delta T_{AB}}{R_{net}}$$

$$I = \frac{120-0}{\left(\frac{8R}{5}\right)} = \frac{120 \times 5}{8R}$$

Thus, the net temperature difference between point P and Q is

$$T_P - T_Q = I \times \frac{3R}{5} \quad \text{[using Eq. (i)]}$$

$$= \frac{120 \times 5}{8R} \times \frac{3R}{5}$$

$$= 45°\text{C}$$

27. Given, $k = 0.1\ WK^{-1}m^{-1}, l = 1\,m$

$$T_1 = 1000\,K \text{ and } T_2 = 100\,K$$

Energy flux is the rate of heat flow per unit area through the rod,

$$\frac{\Delta Q}{\Delta t} = \frac{kA(T_1 - T_2)}{l}$$

$$\frac{1}{A}\cdot\frac{\Delta Q}{\Delta t} = \frac{k(T_1 - T_2)}{l}$$

$\therefore$ $$\text{Energy flux} = \frac{0.1(1000-100)}{1}$$

$$= 90\ Wm^{-2}$$

28. $\frac{dQ}{dt}$ = heat current

$$= \frac{KA(T_1 - T_2)}{x}$$

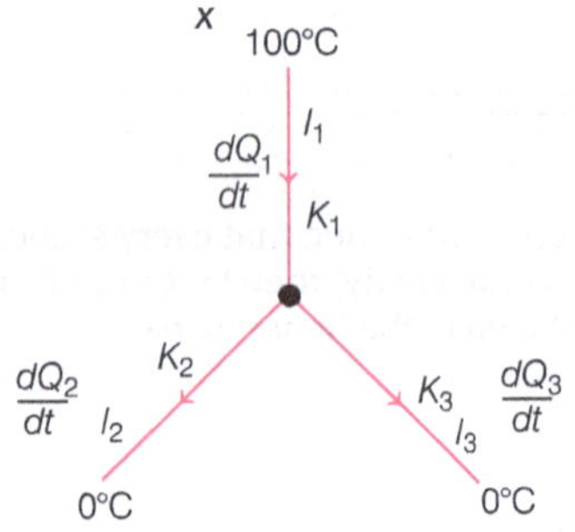

In the figure,

$$\frac{dQ_1}{dt} = \frac{dQ_2}{dt} + \frac{dQ_3}{dt}$$

$$\frac{0.92\,(100-T)\,A}{46} = \frac{0.26\,(T-0)\,A}{13} + \frac{0.12\,(T-0)\,A}{12}$$

$\Rightarrow$ $$T = 40°\,C$$

$\therefore$ $$\frac{dQ_1}{dt} = \frac{0.92\times 4\,(100-40)}{46}$$

$$= 4.8\ cal/s$$

29. We know that in series

$$R_I = R_1 + R_2$$

$$= \left(\frac{l}{KA}\right) + \left(\frac{l}{2KA}\right) = \frac{3}{2}\left(\frac{l}{KA}\right)$$

For parallel

$$\frac{1}{R_{II}} = \frac{1}{R_1} + \frac{1}{R_2} = \frac{KA}{l} + \frac{2KA}{l}$$

or $$R_{II} = \frac{l}{3KA} = \frac{R_I}{4.5}$$

Since thermal resistance R_{II} is 4.5 times less than thermal resistance R_I.

$\therefore$ $$t_{II} = \frac{t_I}{4.5} = \frac{9}{4.5}\,s$$

$$= 2\,s$$

30. Using Newton's law of cooling,

$$\frac{T_i - T_f}{t} = k\left(\frac{T_i + T_f}{2} - T_s\right)$$

Case I $$\frac{60-40}{7} = k\left[\frac{60+40}{2} - 10\right]$$

$\Rightarrow$ $$\frac{20}{7} = k[40] \quad \text{...(i)}$$

Case II $$\frac{40-T}{7} = k\left(\frac{40+T}{2} - 10\right)$$

$$\frac{40-T}{7} = k\left[\frac{20+T}{2}\right] \quad \text{...(ii)}$$

Dividing Eq. (ii) by Eq. (i), we get

$$\frac{40-T}{20} = \frac{20+T}{40\times 2}$$

$$160 - 4T = 20 + T$$

$$5T = 140$$

$$T = 28°C$$

31. Given, initial temperature,

$$T_i = 80°C$$

Final temperature, $T_f = 60°C$

Time taken, $t = 5\,min$

According to question,

$$\frac{80-60}{5} = k(70-20) \quad \text{... (i)}$$

and $$\frac{60-40}{t} = k(50-20) \quad \text{... (ii)}$$

Dividing Eq. (i) by Eq. (ii), we get

$$\frac{4t}{20} = \frac{50}{30}$$

$\Rightarrow$ $$t = \frac{25}{3}\,min$$

$$= 500\ s$$

32. We know that $\frac{-dT}{dt} \propto (T - T_0)$.

So option (c) is correct.

As temperature will start decreasing time increases and come to T_0 after some time elapsed.

33. Let temperature of middle plate in steady state is T_0.

$$Q_1 = Q_2$$

$$Q = \text{ net rate of heat flow}$$

$$\therefore\ \sigma A(3T)^4 - \sigma A T_0^4 = \sigma A T_0^4 - \sigma A(2T)^4$$

Solving this equation, we get

$$T_0 = \left(\frac{97}{2}\right)^{1/4} T$$

34. Since, the temperature of black body is constant.

$\therefore$ Total heat absorbed = total heat radiated.

35. Given,

Length of the wire, $l = 5\,m$

Radius of the wire, $r = 2\times 10^{-3}\,m$

Density of wire, $\rho = 7860\,kg/m^3$

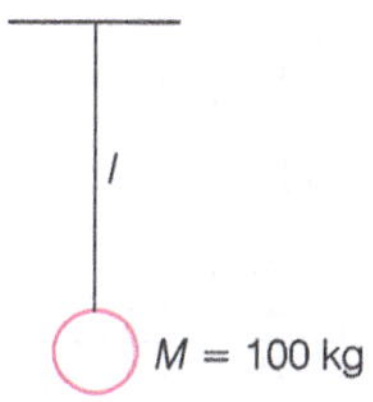

Young's modulus,

$$Y = 2.1 \times 10^{11}\ N/m^2$$

and specific heat, $s = 420$ J/kg-K

Mass of wire, m = (density) (volume)

$$= (\rho)(\pi r^2 l)$$
$$= (7860)(\pi)(2 \times 10^{-3})^2(5)\ kg$$
$$= 0.494\ kg$$

Elastic potential energy stored in the wire,

$$U = \frac{1}{2}\text{(stress) (strain) (volume)}$$
$$\left[\because \frac{\text{Energy}}{\text{Volume}} = \frac{1}{2} \times \text{stress} \times \text{strain}\right]$$

or $$U = \frac{1}{2}\left(\frac{Mg}{\pi r^2}\right)\left(\frac{\Delta l}{l}\right)(\pi r^2 l)$$
$$= \frac{1}{2}(Mg) \cdot \Delta l$$
$$= \frac{1}{2}(Mg)\frac{(Mgl)}{(\pi r^2)Y} \qquad \left(\because \Delta l = \frac{Fl}{AY}\right)$$
$$= \frac{1}{2}\frac{M^2 g^2 l}{\pi r^2 Y}$$

Substituting the values, we have

$$U = \frac{1}{2}\frac{(100)^2(10)^2(5)}{(3.14)(2 \times 10^{-3})^2(2.1 \times 10^{11})}\ J$$
$$= 0.9478\ J$$

When the bob gets snapped, this energy is utilised in raising the temperature of the wire.

So, $$U = ms\,\Delta\theta$$

$\therefore$ $$\Delta\theta = \frac{U}{ms} = \frac{0.9478}{0.494(420)}\ °C \text{ or } K$$
$$\Delta\theta = 4.568 \times 10^{-3}\ °C$$

36. Let θ_1 and θ_2 be the temperatures of the two interfaces as shown in figure.

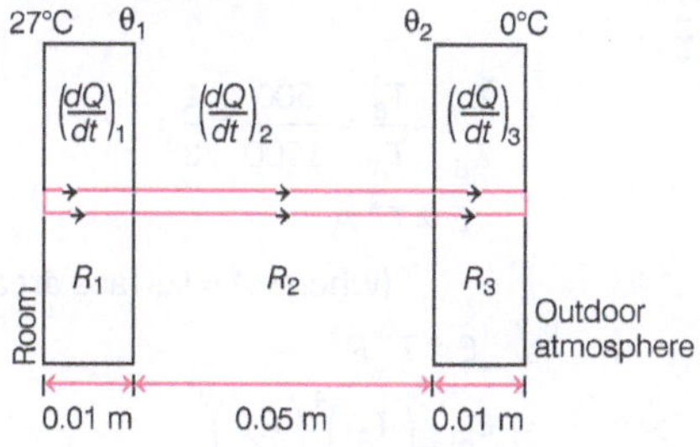

Thermal resistance, $R = \frac{l}{KA}$

$\therefore$ $$R_1 = R_3 = \frac{(0.01)}{(0.8)(1)}$$
$$= 0.0125\ K/W \text{ or } °C/W$$

and $$R_2 = \frac{(0.05)}{(0.08)(1)} = 0.625\ °C/W$$

Now, the rate of heat flow $\left(\frac{dQ}{dt}\right)$ will be equal from all the three sections and since rate of heat flow is given by

$$\frac{dQ}{dt} = \frac{\text{Temperature difference}}{\text{Thermal resistance}}$$

and $$\left(\frac{dQ}{dt}\right)_1 = \left(\frac{dQ}{dt}\right)_2 = \left(\frac{dQ}{dt}\right)_3$$

Therefore,

$$\frac{27 - \theta_1}{0.0125} = \frac{\theta_1 - \theta_2}{0.625} = \frac{\theta_2 - 0}{0.0125}$$

Solving this equation, we get

$$\theta_1 = 26.48\ °C$$

and $$\theta_2 = 0.52\ °C$$

and $$\frac{dQ}{dt} = \frac{27 - \theta_1}{0.0125}$$

$\Rightarrow$ $$\frac{dQ}{dt} = \frac{(27 - 26.48)}{0.0125} = 41.6\ W$$

37. Power produced by heater

= rate of heat flow through window

$\therefore$ $$\frac{V^2}{R} = \frac{\text{Temperature difference}}{\text{Thermal resistance}}$$
$$= \frac{20 - \theta}{(l/KA)}$$

$\Rightarrow$ $$\theta = 20 - \frac{V^2 l}{KAR}$$

Substituting the values, we have

$$\theta = 20 - \frac{(200)^2(0.2 \times 10^{-2})}{(0.2 \times 4.2)(1)(20)}$$
$$= 15.24°C$$

38. Energy released by water

$$= ms\Delta T$$
$$= 0.3 \times 25 \times 4200$$
$$= 31500\ J$$

Let m kg ice melts by releasing energy

$$= mL$$

$$m \times 3.5 \times 10^5 = 31500 \qquad [\because \text{Heat lost} = \text{Heat absorbed}]$$

$\Rightarrow$ $$m = \frac{31500 \times 10^{-5}}{3.5}$$
$$= 9000 \times 10^{-5}$$
$$m = 0.09\ kg = 90\ g$$

$\Rightarrow$ $$x = 90$$

39. Heat absorbed by water per min

$$=2\times 4200\times 40=336000\text{ J}$$

Heat produced by combustion

$$=8\times 10^3\text{ J}$$

So, 336000 J of heat is produced by 1 g

$$=\frac{1}{8\times 10^3}\times 336000\text{ g}$$

So, rate of combustion = 42 g/min.

40. Language of question is slightly wrong. As heat capacity and specific heat are two different physical quantities. Unit of heat capacity is J-kg^{-1} not J-kg^{-1}-$°C^{-1}$. The heat capacity given in the question is really the specific heat. Now applying the heat exchange equation.

$$420=(m\times 10^{-3})(2100)(5)+(1\times 10^{-3})(3.36\times 10^5)$$

Solving this equation, we get

$$m=8\text{ g}$$

∴ The correct answer is 8.

41.

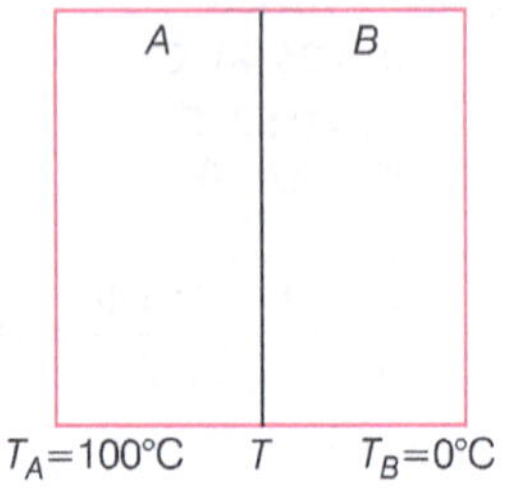

Let the temperature of contact surface is T, then

$$\frac{K_A A(T_A-T)}{L}=\frac{K_B A(T-T_B)}{L}$$

$$\Rightarrow \quad 84(100-T)=126(T-0)$$

$$\Rightarrow \quad 8400-84T=126T$$

$$\Rightarrow \quad 8400=210T$$

$$\Rightarrow \quad T=\frac{8400}{210}=40°\text{ C}$$

42.

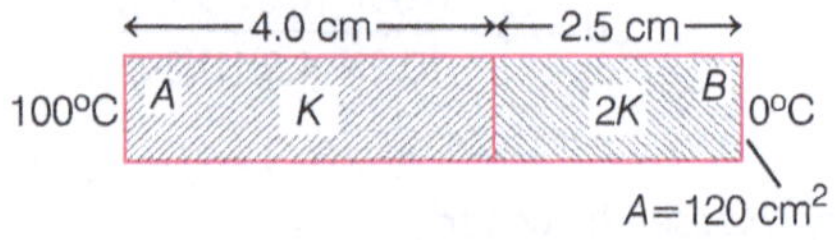

For series combination,

$$R_{series}=R_1+R_2+\ldots$$

$$\Rightarrow \quad \frac{l_1+l_2+\ldots}{K_{eq}A}=\frac{l_1}{K_1A}+\frac{l_2}{K_2A}+\ldots$$

⇒ For two slabs of same area, we have

$$\frac{l_1+l_2}{K_{eq}}=\frac{l_1}{K_1}+\frac{l_2}{K_2}$$

Here, $l_1=4$ cm, $K_1=K, l_2=2.5$ cm and $K_2=2K$

So, $$\frac{4+2.5}{K_{eq}}=\frac{4}{K}+\frac{2.5}{2K}$$

or $$K_{eq}=\frac{13K}{10.5}=\frac{26}{21}K=\left(1+\frac{5}{21}\right)K$$

$$=\left(1+\frac{5}{\alpha}\right)K \quad \text{(given)}$$

$$\alpha=21$$

43.

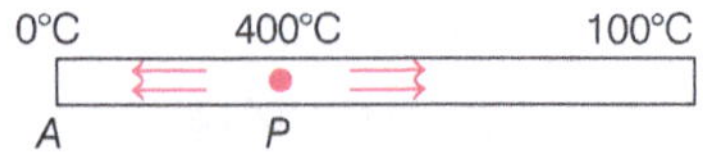

Heat will flow both sides from point P.

$$\Rightarrow \left(\frac{dQ}{dt}\right)_{calorimetry}=\left(\frac{dQ}{dt}\right)_{conduction}$$

$$L_1\frac{dm_1}{dt}=\left(\frac{\text{Temperature difference}}{\text{Thermal resistance}}\right)_1$$

$$=\frac{400}{(\lambda x)/kA} \quad \ldots\text{(i)}$$

Similarly,

$$L_1\frac{dm_2}{dt}=\frac{400-100}{(100-\lambda)x/kA} \quad \ldots\text{(ii)}$$

In above two equations,

$$\frac{dm_1}{dt}=\frac{dm_2}{dt} \quad \text{(given)}$$

$$L_1=80\text{ cal}g^{-1}$$

and $$L_2=540\text{ cal}g^{-1}$$

Solving these two equations, we get

$$\lambda=9$$

44. Power,

$$P=(\sigma T^4A)=\sigma T^4(4\pi R^2)$$

or $$P\propto T^4R^2 \quad \ldots\text{(i)}$$

According to Wien's displacement law,

$$\lambda\propto\frac{1}{T}$$

(λ is the wavelength at which peak occurs)

∴ Eq. (i) will become,

$$P\propto\frac{R^2}{\lambda^4}\text{ or }\lambda\propto\left[\frac{R^2}{P}\right]^{1/4}$$

$$\Rightarrow \quad \frac{\lambda_A}{\lambda_B}=\left[\frac{R_A}{R_B}\right]^{1/2}\left[\frac{P_B}{P_A}\right]^{1/4}$$

$$=[400]^{1/2}\left[\frac{1}{10^4}\right]^{1/4}=2$$

45. $\lambda_m\propto\frac{1}{T}$

$$\therefore \quad \frac{\lambda_A}{\lambda_B}=\frac{T_B}{T_A}=\frac{500}{1500}=\frac{1}{3}$$

$$E\propto T^4A$$

(where, A = surface area $=4\pi R^2$)

$$\therefore \quad E\propto T^4R^2$$

$$\frac{E_A}{E_B}=\left(\frac{T_A}{T_B}\right)^4\left(\frac{R_A}{R_B}\right)^2$$

$$=(3)^4\left(\frac{6}{18}\right)^2=9$$

$\therefore$ Answer is 9.

Level 2

46. $R=\frac{l}{KA}$

l is halved, A is four times and K is $\frac{1}{4}$ times.

$\therefore$ R will become half. Hence, heat current will become two times. Therefore, rate of melting of ice will also become two times or 0.2 g/s.

47.

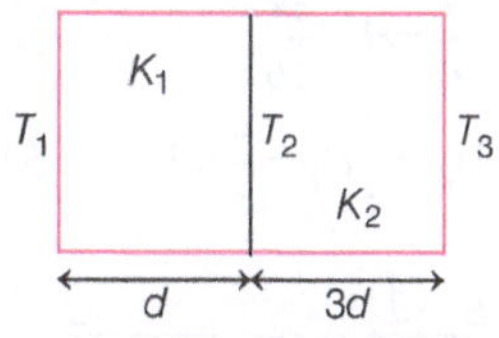

$$H_1=H_2$$

$$\therefore \quad \frac{T_1-T_2}{(d/K_1A)}=\frac{T_2-T_3}{(3d/K_2A)}$$

$$\therefore \quad \frac{K_1}{K_2}=\left(\frac{T_2-T_3}{T_1-T_2}\right)\cdot\frac{1}{3}$$

But T_1, T_2 and T_3 are in AP

$$\therefore \quad T_2-T_3=T_1-T_2$$

$$\therefore \quad \frac{K_1}{K_2}=\frac{1}{3}$$

48. $H=\frac{\text{TD}}{R}$

$$\therefore \quad R=\frac{\text{TD}}{H}=\frac{100-0}{1}$$

$$=100\,\text{kW}^{-1}$$

Now, $$R=\int_0^x dR=\int_0^x \frac{dx}{K_0(1+ax)A}$$

or $$100=\int_0^x \frac{dx}{10^2(1+x)(10^{-4})}$$

Solving this equation, we get

$$x=1.7\text{ m}$$

49. Let R = thermal resistance of each rod.

In first case, $R_{net}=R+R=2R$ (in series)

In second case, $R_{net}=\frac{R}{2}$ (in parallel)

In second case thermal resistance has become $\frac{1}{4}$th. So, heat current will become 4 times. So time taken to flow same amount of heat will be reduced to $\frac{1}{4}$th.

50.

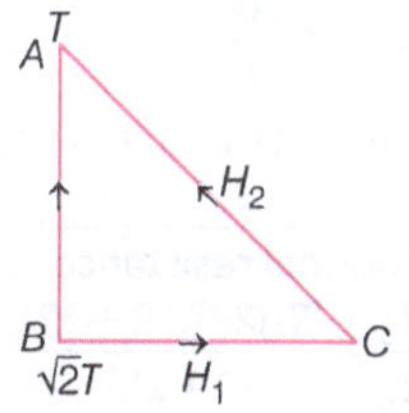

$$H_1=H_2$$

$$\therefore \quad \frac{\sqrt{2}T-T_C}{(l/KA)}=\frac{T_C-T}{(\sqrt{2}l/KA)}$$

Solving, we get

$$T_C=\frac{3T}{\sqrt{2}+1}$$

51. $R_{net}=R_1+R_2=\left(\frac{X}{KA}\right)+\frac{4X}{2KA}=\frac{3X}{KA}$

Now, $$H=\frac{dQ}{dt}=\frac{\text{TD}}{R_{net}}$$

$$=\frac{(T_2-T_1)}{(3X/KA)}=\left[\frac{KA(T_2-T_1)}{x}\right]\left(\frac{1}{3}\right)$$

$$\therefore \quad f=\frac{1}{3}$$

52. $\frac{d\theta}{dt}=L\cdot\frac{dm}{dt}=\text{Heat transfer from bottom}=\frac{\text{TD}}{(l/KA)}$

Here, TD = desired temperature difference

$$\therefore \quad \text{TD}=\frac{L\cdot l\cdot\frac{dm}{dt}}{KA}$$

$$=\frac{(540)(2\times10^{-1})\left(\frac{1}{60}\right)}{0.5\times300}$$

$$=0.012\,°\text{C}$$

53. There will be no heat flow through AB, if temperature of B is also 20°C and heat current in DB is equal to heat current in BC.

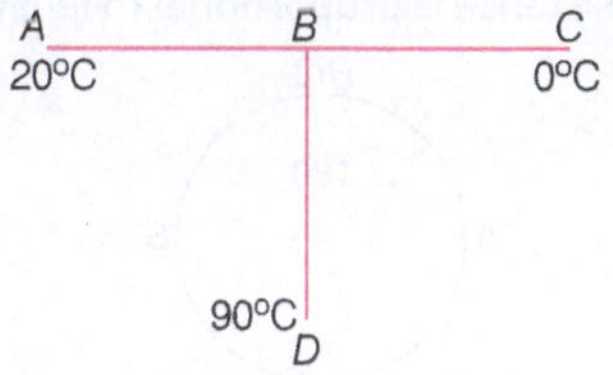

$$\therefore \quad H_{DB}=H_{BC} \qquad (\because H=\text{TD}/R)$$

or $$\frac{70}{(l_{BD}/KA)}=\frac{20}{(l_{BC}/KA)}$$

or $$\frac{l_{BD}}{l_{BC}}=\frac{7}{2}$$

54. Rate of heat flow, $H \propto \frac{TD}{R}$

$\therefore$ TD = temperature difference is same.

$$\therefore \quad H \propto \frac{1}{\text{Thermal resistance}}$$

$$\frac{H_A}{H_B} = \frac{R_B}{R_A} = \frac{(R)(2R)/R+2R}{(R+2R)}$$

$$= \frac{2}{9}$$

55. $R_{AB} = R_{CD} = R$ (say)

Resistance of semicircle $= \pi R$ as $R \propto l$

$$R_{BC} = \frac{\pi R}{2} \qquad \text{(in parallel)}$$

Heat current, $H = \dfrac{100-0}{R+R+\frac{\pi}{2}\cdot R}$

Now, $\theta_C - 0° = HR$

Substituting value of H, we get

$$\theta_C = 28°C$$

56. $H = \frac{Q}{t} = \frac{KA(\theta_1 - \theta_2)}{l}$

or $\quad H \propto \frac{A}{l}$ or $H_2 = 2H_1$

57. Heat carried increases to 2 times. Therefore, net thermal resistance will remain half.

$$\therefore \quad R' = \frac{R}{2}$$

$$\frac{R'_1 R'_2}{R'_1 + R'_2} = \frac{R_1 R_2}{2(R_1 + R_2)}$$

or $$\frac{(3l/KA)(l/K'A)}{(3l/KA)+(l/K'A)} = \frac{(3l/KA)(l/KA)}{2\left\{\frac{3l}{KA}+\frac{l}{KA}\right\}}$$

Solving this, we get $K' = \frac{7}{3}K$

58. Thermal resistance is proportional to length,

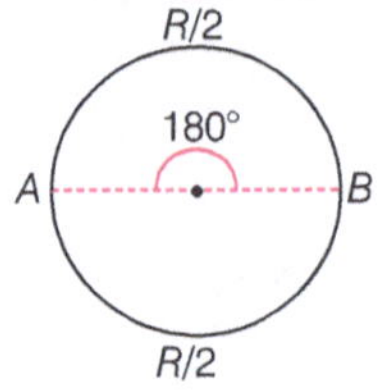

$$R_{eq} = \frac{R}{4}$$

$$\theta_A - \theta_B = H_1 R_{eq} = H_1 \frac{R}{4} \qquad \text{...(i)}$$

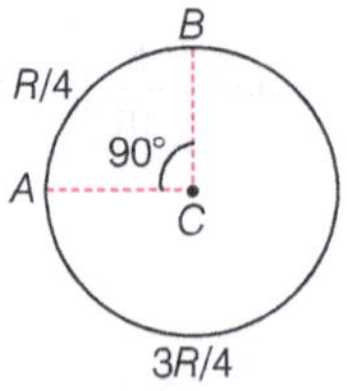

$$R_{eq} = \frac{\frac{R}{4}\cdot\frac{3R}{4}}{\frac{R}{4}+\frac{3R}{4}} = \frac{3R}{16}$$

$$\theta_A - \theta_B = H_2 \cdot \frac{3R}{16} \qquad \text{...(ii)}$$

$$H_1 \cdot \frac{R}{4} = H_2 \cdot \frac{3R}{16}$$

$$H_2 = \frac{4}{3}H_1 = \frac{4}{3} \times 1.2 = 1.6 \text{ W}$$

59.

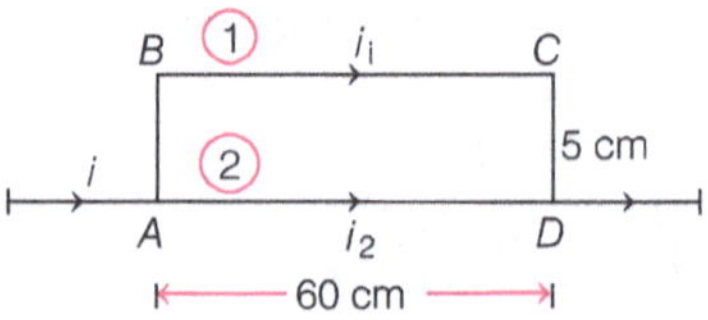

Length, $AD = 60$ cm

Length of bent part $= 5 + 60 + 5 = 70$ cm

Resistance $\propto$ Length

$$R_1 = 70R, R_2 = 60R$$

$$H_1 = \frac{R_2}{R_1 + R_2}H$$

$$= \frac{60R}{70R + 60R} \times 130 = 60 \text{ J}$$

60. Wien's displacement law is

$$\lambda_m T = b \qquad (b = \text{Wien's constant})$$

$$\therefore \quad \lambda_m = \frac{b}{T} = \frac{2.88 \times 10^6 \text{ nm-K}}{2880\text{K}}$$

$$\therefore \quad \lambda = 1000 \text{ nm}$$

Energy distribution with wavelength will be as follows

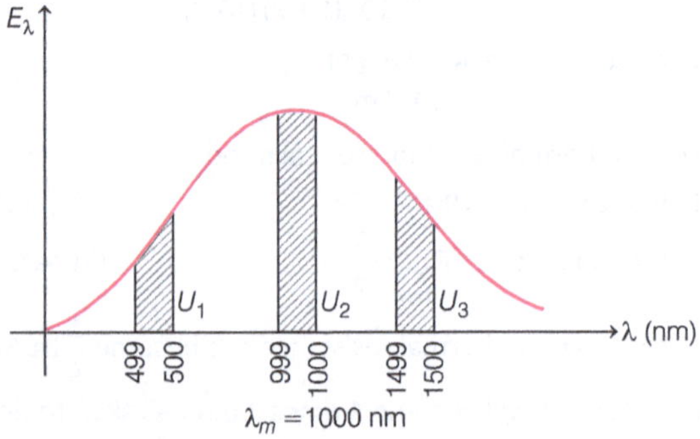

From the graph, it is clear that

$U_2 > U_1$ (In fact U_2 is maximum)

61. $P = e\sigma A(T^4 - T_0^4) = e\sigma \cdot 4\pi r^2 (T^4 - T_0^4)$

$$P \propto r^2$$

$$-ms\frac{dT}{dt} = e\sigma A(T^4 - T_0^4)$$

$$-\frac{dT}{dt} = \frac{e\sigma A(T^4 - T_0^4)}{ms} = \frac{e\sigma 4\pi r^2 (T^4 - T_0^4)}{\rho \cdot \frac{4}{3}\pi r^3 s}$$

Rate of cooling, $-\frac{dT}{dt} \propto \frac{1}{r}$

62. Temperature of B is falling at a faster rate. Hence, its specific heat should be less.

63. Energy radiated per second,

$$P = e_r \sigma T^4 A$$

or $P \propto A$

$$\therefore \quad \frac{P_1}{P_2} = \frac{A_1}{A_2} = \frac{2\pi r L}{6a^2} = \frac{\pi r L}{3a^2} \quad \ldots(i)$$

Their volumes are equal,

$$\pi r^2 L = a^3$$

$$\therefore \quad L = \frac{a^3}{\pi r^2}$$

Substituting in Eq. (i), we have,

$$\frac{P_1}{P_2} = \frac{(\pi r)\left(\frac{a^3}{\pi r^2}\right)}{3a^2} = \frac{a}{3r}$$

64. Temperature difference across similar slabs will be same.

$$\therefore \quad 20 - 10 = \theta - (-5)$$

$$\therefore \quad \theta = 5°C$$

65. Let thermal resistance of each rod is R. In the first case, net resistance between A and C is :

$$R_1 = R$$

In the second case, net resistance between A and D is,

$$R_2 = \frac{(3R)(R)}{3R + R} = \frac{3}{4}R$$

Since, net resistance has become $\frac{3}{4}$ times. Temperature difference is same. Therefore, rate of heat flow will be $\frac{4}{3}$ times. As,

$$H = \frac{TD}{R_{net}} \quad \text{or} \quad H \propto \frac{1}{R_{net}}$$

66. Area $\propto T^4$

Area has become 9 times. Hence,

$$\frac{T_2}{T_1} = (9)^{\frac{1}{4}}$$

From Wien's displacement law,

$$\lambda \propto \frac{1}{T}$$

$$\therefore \quad \frac{\lambda_1}{\lambda_2} = \frac{T_2}{T_1} = (9)^{\frac{1}{4}} = \sqrt{3}$$

67. Given, $K_B = K_A/2$ and $K_B = 3K_C$

$$\therefore \quad K_C = K_A/6$$

Rods are in series, so

$$\frac{L}{K} = \frac{l_1}{K_A} + \frac{l_2}{K_B} + \frac{l_3}{K_C} \quad [\because l = l_1 = l_2 = l_3]$$

$$\frac{3l}{K} = \frac{l}{K_A} + \frac{l}{K_A/2} + \frac{l}{K_A/6}$$

or $\frac{3l}{K} = \frac{9l}{K_A}$ or $K = \frac{K_A}{3}$

68. Rate of cooling $\left(-\frac{dT}{dt}\right) \propto$ emissivity (e)

From the graph,

$$\left(-\frac{dT}{dt}\right)_x > \left(-\frac{dT}{dt}\right)_y$$

$$\therefore \quad E_x > E_y$$

Further emissivity (E) = absorptive power (a)
(good absorbers are good emitters also)

$$a_x > a_y$$

69. Heat required,

$$Q_1 = (1.1 + 0.02) \times 10^3 \times 1 \times (80 - 15)$$
$$= 72800 \text{ cal}$$

Heat given if m kg steam is condensed :

$$Q_2 = (m \times 540 \times 10^3) + m \times 1 \times 10^3 \times (100 - 80)$$

Equating $Q_1 = Q_2$, we get

$$m = 0.130 \text{ kg}$$

70.

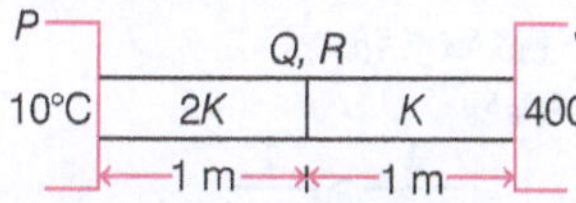

Rate of heat flow from Q to P

$$\frac{dQ}{dt} = \frac{2KA(T - 10)}{1}$$

Rate of heat flow from S to Q

$$\frac{dQ}{dt} = \frac{KA(400 - T)}{1}$$

At steady state, rate of heat flow is same.

$$\therefore \quad \frac{2KA(T - 10)}{1} = KA(400 - T)$$

or $2T - 20 = 400 - T$ or $3T = 420$

$$\therefore \quad T = 140\ °C$$

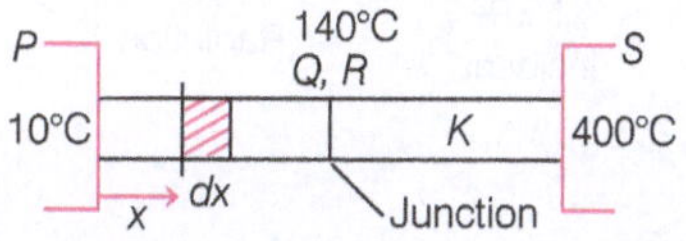

Temperature of junction is 140° C.
Temperature at a distance x from end P is

$$T_x = (130x + 10)\,°C$$

Change in length dx is suppose dy.

Then, $dy = \alpha dx\,(T_x - 10)$

$$\int_0^{\Delta y} dy = \int_0^1 \alpha dx\,(130x + 10 - 10)$$

$$\Delta y = \left[\frac{\alpha x^2}{2} \times 130\right]_0^1$$

$\Rightarrow$ $\Delta y = 1.2 \times 10^{-5} \times 65$

$\Rightarrow$ $\Delta y = 78.0 \times 10^{-5}\,\text{m}$

$= 0.78\,\text{mm}$

71. From Newton's law of cooling, we have rate of cooling,

$$\frac{dQ}{dt} = \frac{h}{ms}(T - T_0)$$

We know, $m = V \cdot \rho$

So, we have

$$\frac{dQ}{dt} = \frac{h}{ms}(T - T_0) = \frac{h(T - T_0)}{V \cdot \rho s}$$

Since, h, $(T - T_0)$ and V are constant for both beaker.

$\therefore$ $\dfrac{dQ}{dt} \propto \dfrac{1}{\rho s}$

We have given that

$\rho_A = 8 \times 10^2\,\text{kgm}^{-3}$,

$\rho_B = 10^3\,\text{kgm}^{-3}$,

$s_A = 2000\,\text{J kg}^{-1}\,\text{K}^{-1}$ and

$s_B = 4000\,\text{J kg}^{-1}\,\text{K}^{-1}$,

$\rho_A s_A = 16 \times 10^5$

and $\rho_B s_B = 4 \times 10^6$

So, $\rho_A < \rho_B,\ s_A < s_B$

and $\rho_A s_A < \rho_B s_B$

$\Rightarrow$ $\dfrac{1}{\rho_A s_A} > \dfrac{1}{\rho_B s_B}$

$\Rightarrow$ $\dfrac{dQ_A}{dt} > \dfrac{dQ_B}{dt}$

So, for container B, rate of cooling is smaller than the container A. Hence, graph of B lies above the graph of A and it is not a straight line (slope of A is greater than B).

72. In steady state,

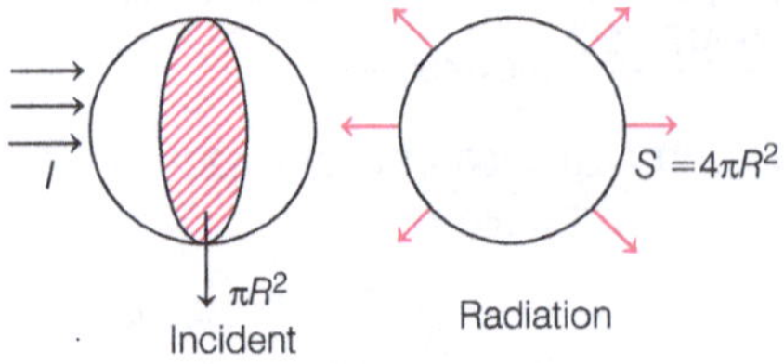

Energy incident per second = Energy radiated per second

$\therefore$ $I(\pi R^2) = \sigma(T^4 - T_0^4)\,4\pi R^2$

$\Rightarrow$ $I = 4\sigma(T^4 - T_0^4)$

$\Rightarrow$ $T^4 - T_0^4 = 40 \times 10^8$

$\Rightarrow$ $T^4 - 81 \times 10^8 = 40 \times 10^8$

$\Rightarrow$ $T^4 = 121 \times 10^8$

$\Rightarrow$ $T \approx 330\,\text{K}$

73. Assumption $e = 1$ [black body radiation]

$$P = \sigma A(T^4 - T_0^4)$$

(c) $P_{rad} = \sigma A T^4 = \sigma \cdot 1 \cdot (T_0 + 10)^4$

$= \sigma \cdot T_0^4 \left(1 + \dfrac{10}{T_0}\right)^4$ [$T_0 = 300\,\text{K}$ (given)]

$= \sigma \cdot (300)^4 \cdot \left(1 + \dfrac{40}{300}\right)$

$\approx 460 \times \dfrac{17}{15} \approx 520\,\text{J}$

$P_{net} = 520 - 460 \approx 60\,\text{W}$

$\Rightarrow$ Energy radiated in 1 s = 60 J

(b) $P = \sigma A(T^4 - T_0^4)$

$dP = \sigma A(0 - 4T_0^3 \cdot dT)$

and $dT = -\Delta T$

$\Rightarrow$ $dP = 4\sigma A T_0^3 \Delta T$

(d) If surface area decreases, then energy radiation also decreases.

74. No heat is flowing through C and F. Therefore, they are at same temperature.

75. Thermal resistance, $R = \dfrac{l}{KA}$

$\therefore$ $R_A = \dfrac{L}{(2K)(4Lw)}$

(Here, w = width perpendicular to paper)

$= \dfrac{1}{8Kw}$

$R_B = \dfrac{4L}{3K\,(Lw)} = \dfrac{4}{3Kw}$

$R_C = \dfrac{4L}{(4K)(2Lw)} = \dfrac{1}{2Kw}$

$R_D = \dfrac{4L}{(5K)(Lw)} = \dfrac{4}{5Kw}$

$R_E = \dfrac{L}{(6K)(Lw)} = \dfrac{1}{6Kw}$

$R_A : R_B : R_C : R_D : R_E = 15 : 160 : 60 : 96 : 12$

So, let us write, $R_A = 15\,R$, $R_B = 160\,R$ etc. and draw a simple electrical circuit as shown in figure

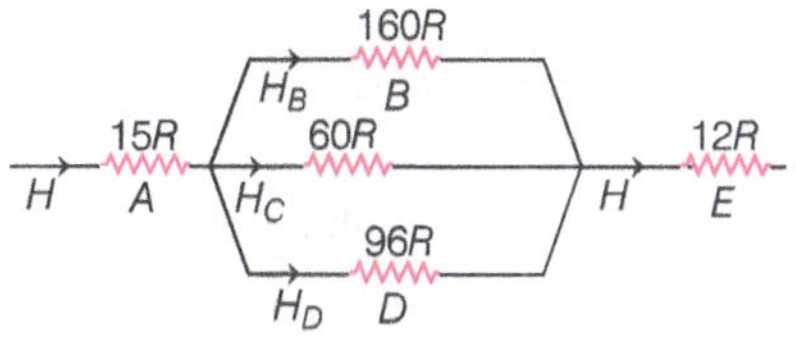

H = Heat current = Rate of heat flow

$$H_A = H_E = H \quad \text{(let)}$$

$\therefore$ Option (a) is correct.

In parallel, current distributes in inverse ratio of resistance.

$$\therefore H_B : H_C : H_D = \frac{1}{R_B} : \frac{1}{R_C} : \frac{1}{R_D}$$
$$= \frac{1}{160} : \frac{1}{60} : \frac{1}{96}$$
$$= 9 : 24 : 15$$

$$\therefore \quad H_B = \left(\frac{9}{9+24+15}\right) H = \frac{3}{16} H$$

$$H_C = \left(\frac{24}{9+24+15}\right) H = \frac{1}{2} H$$

and $$H_D = \left(\frac{15}{9+24+15}\right) H = \frac{5}{16} H$$

$$H_C = H_B + H_D$$

$\therefore$ Option (d) is correct.

Temperature difference (let us call it T)

= (Heat current) $\times$ (Thermal resistance)

$$T_A = H_A R_A = (H)(15R) = 15\,HR$$

$$T_B = H_B R_B = \left(\frac{3}{16} H\right)(160\,R) = 30\,HR$$

$$T_C = H_C R_C = \left(\frac{1}{2} H\right)(60\,R) = 30\,HR$$

$$T_D = H_D R_D = \left(\frac{5}{16} H\right)(96\,R) = 30\,HR$$

$$T_E = H_E R_E = (H)(12\,R) = 12\,HR$$

Here, T_E is minimum. Therefore, option (c) is also correct.

76. Power radiated and surface area is same for both A and B.

Therefore, $e_A \sigma T_A^4 A = e_B \sigma T_B^4 A$

$$\therefore \quad \frac{T_A}{T_B} = \left(\frac{e_B}{e_A}\right)^{1/4} = \left(\frac{0.81}{0.01}\right)^{1/4} = 3$$

$$\therefore \quad T_B = \frac{T_A}{3} = \frac{5802}{3}$$

$$\Rightarrow \quad T_B = 1934 \text{ K}$$

According to Wien's displacement law,

$$\lambda_m T = \text{constant}$$

$$\therefore \quad \lambda_A T_A = \lambda_B T_B$$

or $$\lambda_A = \lambda_B \left(\frac{T_B}{T_A}\right) = \frac{\lambda_B}{3}$$

Given, $$\lambda_B - \lambda_A = 1\,\mu\text{m}$$

$$\Rightarrow \quad \lambda_B - \frac{\lambda_B}{3} = 1\,\mu\text{m}$$

or $$\frac{2}{3}\lambda_B = 1\,\mu\text{m}$$

$$\Rightarrow \quad \lambda_B = 1.5\,\mu\text{m}$$

Note *$\lambda_m T = b$ = Wien constant value of this constant for perfectly black body is 2.89×10^{-3} m-K. For other bodies this constant will have some different value. In the opinion of author option (b) has been framed by assuming b to be constant for all bodies. If we take b different for different bodies. Option (b) is incorrect.*

77. At 50°C, temperature of ball is constant.

So, rate of heat generation = Rate of heat loss

$\therefore$ Heat loss rate is 20 W.

78. At 30°C, rate of heat loss will be

$$\frac{dQ}{dt} = \frac{20}{3}\frac{\text{J}}{\text{s}} = \frac{20}{3}\text{W}$$

79. In 5 min = 5 × 60 s, heat generated

$$= P \times t = 20\,\text{W} \times 5 \times 60\,\text{s} = 6000\,\text{J}$$

Heat absorbed by metal $= ms\,\Delta T = 1 \times (500) \times 10 = 5000$ J

So, heat lost by ball = 6000 − 5000 = 1000 J

80.

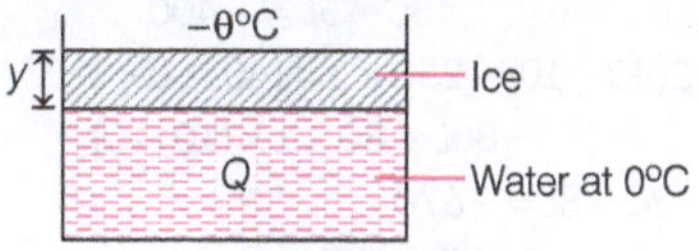

$$\frac{dQ}{dt} = L \cdot \frac{dm}{dt}$$

$$\frac{\text{TD}}{(y/KA)} = L\frac{d}{dt}[Ay\rho] \qquad (\text{TD} = \theta)$$

or $$\frac{dy}{dt} = \frac{K\theta}{L\rho y}$$

81. Let T_0 be the temperature of surrounding and T be the temperature of hot body at some instant. Then,

$$-\frac{dT}{dt} = K(T - T_0)$$

or $$\int_{T_m}^{T} \frac{dT}{T - T_0} = -K\int_0^t dT \qquad (T_m = \text{temperature at } t = 0)$$

Solving this equation, we get

$$T = T_0 + (T_m - T_0)e^{-Kt} \qquad \text{...(i)}$$

Maximum temperature it can lose is $(T_m - T_0)$

From Eq. (i),

$$T - T_0 = (T_m - T_0)e^{-Kt}$$

Given that $$T - T_0 = \frac{T_m - T_0}{2}$$
$$= (T_m - T_0)e^{-Kt}$$

Solving this equation, we get

$$t = \frac{\ln(2)}{K}$$

82. (a) Let θ be the temperature of junction. Then,

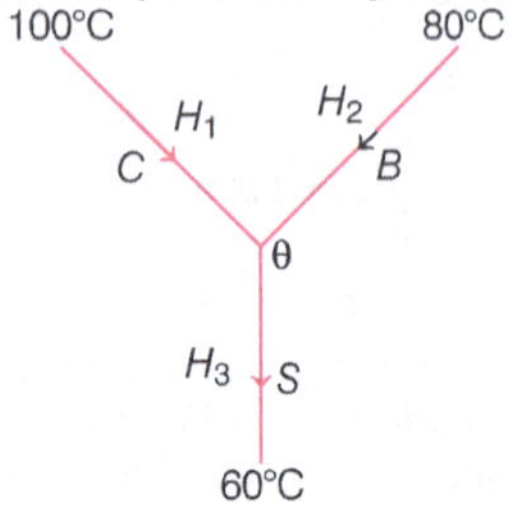

$$H_1 + H_2 = H_3$$

$$\therefore \quad \frac{100-\theta}{(46/0.92A)} + \frac{80-\theta}{(13/0.26A)} = \frac{\theta-60}{(12/0.12A)}$$

Solving this equation, we have

$$\theta = 84°C$$

(b) Heat current in copper rod,

$$H_1 = \frac{100-\theta}{(46/0.92 \times 4)}$$
$$= 1.28 \text{ cal/s}$$

83. Let heat capacity of flask is C and latent heat of fusion of ice is L.

Then,

$$C(70-40) + 200 \times 1 \times (70-40) = 50L + 50 \times 1 \times (40-0)$$

or $\quad 3C - 5L = -400 \quad$ ...(i)

Further, $C(40-10) + 250 \times 1 \times (40-10)$
$$= 80L + 80 \times 1 \times (10-0)$$

or $\quad 3C - 8L = -670 \quad$ ...(ii)

Solving Eqs. (i) and (ii), we have

$$L = 90 \text{ cal/g}$$

84. $ms\Delta\theta$ = work done against friction

$= (\mu mg \cos\theta) d \quad$ (but $\mu mg \cos\theta = mg \sin\theta$)

$$\Delta\theta = \frac{(\mu g \cos\theta) d}{s} = \frac{(g \sin\theta) d}{s}$$

$$= \frac{(10)\left(\frac{3}{5}\right)(0.6)}{420}$$

$$= 8.57 \times 10^{-3} \text{ °C}$$

$$\approx 8.6 \times 10^{-3} \text{ °C}$$

85. Using $\quad \dfrac{dQ}{dt} = mc\dfrac{d\theta}{dt} = \dfrac{KA(\theta_1 - \theta_2)}{l}$

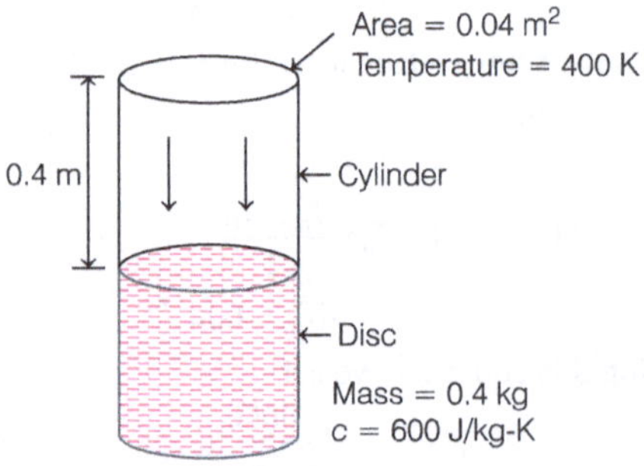

We have,

$$mc\left(\frac{d\theta}{dt}\right) = \frac{KA(400-\theta)}{0.4}$$

$$(0.4)(600)\frac{d\theta}{dt} = \frac{(10)(0.04)(400-\theta)}{0.4}$$

$$\therefore \quad \left(\frac{d\theta}{400-\theta}\right) = \frac{1}{240} dt$$

$$\therefore \quad \int_0^t dt = 240 \int_{300}^{350} \frac{d\theta}{400-\theta}$$

Solving this, we get

$$t \approx 166 \text{ s}$$ **Ans.**

86. Consider a differential cylinder

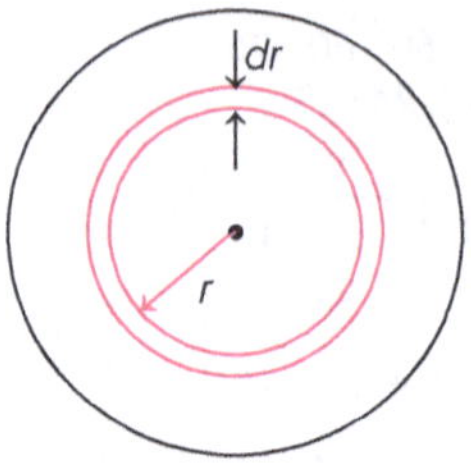

$$H = \frac{dQ}{dt} = KA\frac{d\theta}{dr} = (2\pi Krl)\frac{d\theta}{dr}$$

$$\therefore \quad \frac{H}{2\pi Kl}\int_{r_1}^{r_2}\frac{dr}{r} = \int_0^{50} d\theta$$

or $\quad \dfrac{H}{2\pi Kl} \ln\left(\dfrac{r_2}{r_1}\right) = 50$

$$\therefore \quad H = \frac{100\pi Kl}{\ln(r_2/r_1)}$$

Now, $\quad Ht = mL$

$$\therefore \quad t = \frac{mL}{H} = \frac{mL\ln(r_2/r_1)}{100\pi Kl}$$ **Ans.**

87. Three thermal resistances are in series. $\left(R = \dfrac{l}{KA}\right)$

$$\therefore \quad R = R_1 + R_2 + R_3$$

$$= \frac{2.5 \times 10^{-2}}{0.125 \times 137} + \frac{1.0 \times 10^{-2}}{1.5 \times 137} + \frac{2.5 \times 10^{-2}}{1.0 \times 137}$$

$$= 0.0017 \text{ °C-s/J}$$

Now, heat current $H = \dfrac{\text{Temperature difference}}{\text{Net thermal resistance}}$

$$= \frac{30}{0.0017} = 17647 \text{ W}$$

88. Thermal resistance of plastic coating $\left(R_t = \dfrac{l}{KA}\right)$

$$R_t = \frac{t}{K(\pi d)l} \quad (d = \text{diameter})$$

$$= \frac{0.66 \times 10^{-3}}{(0.16 \times 10^{-2} \times 4.18 \times 10^2)(\pi)(0.64 \times 10^{-3})(2)}$$

$$= 0.0223 \text{ °C-s/J}$$

Now, $i^2R_e = \frac{TD}{R_t}$

$\therefore \quad TD = i^2R_eR_t$

$= (5)^2(4)(0.0223)$

$= 2.23°C$

89. Let T_1 be the temperature of C_1 and T_2 the temperature of C_2 at some instant of time. Further let T be the temperature difference at that instant.

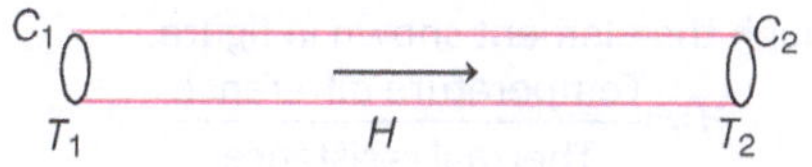

Then,

$$C_1\left(-\frac{dT_1}{dt}\right) = H = \frac{T}{l/KA} = \frac{KA}{l}(T) \qquad (\because T = T_1 - T_2)$$

and

$$C_2\left(+\frac{dT_2}{dt}\right) = H = \frac{T}{l/KA} = \frac{KA}{l}(T)$$

$$\therefore \quad -\frac{dT}{dt} = -\frac{dT_1}{dt} + \frac{dT_2}{dt}$$

$$\therefore \quad -\frac{dT_1}{dt} = \frac{KA}{lC_1}(T)$$

and

$$+\frac{dT_2}{dt} = \frac{KA}{lC_2}$$

Further,

$$-\frac{dT}{dt} = -\frac{dT_1}{dt} + \frac{dT_2}{dt}$$

$$= \frac{KA(C_1 + C_2)}{lC_1C_1}T$$

or

$$\int_{\Delta T_0}^{T} \frac{dT}{T} = -\frac{KA(C_1 + C_2)}{lC_1C_2}\int_0^t dt$$

Solving, we get $\quad T = \Delta T_0 e^{-\alpha t}$

where, $\quad \alpha = \frac{KA(C_1 + C_2)}{lC_1C_2}$

90.

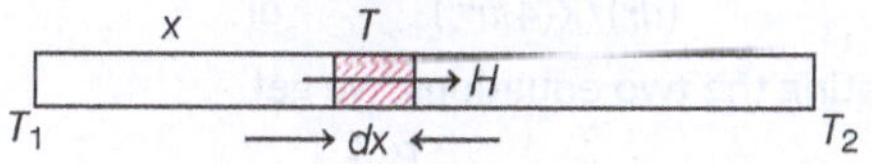

$$H = \frac{TD}{R} = \frac{(-dT)}{(dx)/KA}$$

$$= -\left(\frac{dT}{dx}\right)\left(\frac{a}{T}A\right) = \text{constant} \qquad \text{...(i)}$$

$$\therefore \quad \int_{T_1}^{T_2} -\frac{dT}{T} = \frac{H}{aA}\int_0^l dx$$

$$\ln\left(\frac{T_1}{T_2}\right) = \frac{Hl}{aA}$$

or

$$H = \frac{aA}{l}\ln(T_1/T_2)$$

Substituting in Eq. (i), we have

$$\frac{aA}{l}\ln\left(\frac{T_1}{T_2}\right) = -\left(\frac{dT}{dx}\right)\frac{aA}{T}$$

or

$$\int_{T_1}^{T} \frac{dT}{T} = -\frac{\ln\left(\frac{T_1}{T_2}\right)}{l}\int_0^x dx$$

$$\therefore \quad \ln\left(\frac{T}{T_1}\right) = -\frac{x}{l}\ln(T_1/T_2) = \ln\left(\frac{T_1}{T_2}\right)^{-\frac{x}{l}}$$

or

$$\frac{T}{T_1} = \left(\frac{T_1}{T_2}\right)^{-\frac{x}{l}}$$

or

$$T = T_1\left(\frac{T_1}{T_2}\right)^{-\frac{x}{l}} = T_1\left(\frac{T_2}{T_1}\right)^{\frac{x}{l}}$$

91. $L\left(\frac{dm}{dt}\right) = \frac{TD}{R_1 + R_2}$

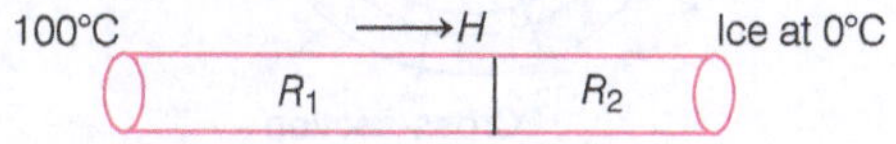

or

$$\frac{80 \times 360}{3600} = \frac{100}{\frac{20}{0.25 \times 10} + \frac{10}{K \times 10}}$$

Solving this equation, we get

$K = 0.222$ cal/cm-s-°C **Ans.**

92. $H = \frac{-d\theta}{dr/K(4\pi r^2)} = \left(-\frac{d\theta}{dr}\right)(4\pi K r^2) \qquad \text{...(i)}$

or

$$\int_{R_1}^{R_2} \frac{dr}{r^2} = -\frac{4\pi K}{H}\int_{\theta_1}^{\theta_2} d\theta$$

or

$$\frac{R_2 - R_1}{R_1R_2} = \frac{4\pi K}{H}(\theta_1 - \theta_2)$$

$$\therefore \quad H = \frac{4\pi K(R_1R_2)(\theta_1 - \theta_2)}{R_2 - R_1}$$

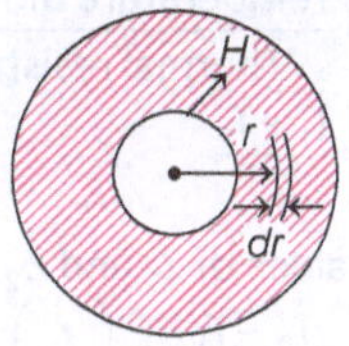

Substituting this value of H in Eq. (i), we have

$$\frac{R_1R_2}{R_2 - R_1}(\theta_1 - \theta_2) = -\frac{d\theta}{dr}(r^2)$$

$$\therefore \quad \int_{\theta_1}^{\left(\frac{\theta_1 + \theta_2}{2}\right)} d\theta = -\frac{R_1R_2}{R_2 - R_1}(\theta_1 - \theta_2)\int_{R_1}^{r} \frac{dr}{r^2}$$

or

$$\frac{\theta_1 + \theta_2}{2} - \theta_1 = \frac{R_1R_2}{R_2 - R_1}(\theta_1 - \theta_2)\left[\frac{1}{r} - \frac{1}{R_1}\right]$$

or $$\frac{\theta_1-\theta_2}{2}=\frac{R_1R_2}{R_2-R_1}(\theta_1-\theta_2)\left(\frac{1}{R_1}-\frac{1}{r}\right)$$

$$\frac{1}{R_1}-\frac{1}{r}=\frac{R_2-R_1}{2R_1R_2}$$

$$\frac{1}{r}=\frac{1}{R_1}-\frac{R_2-R_1}{2R_1R_2}=\frac{R_1+R_2}{2R_1R_2}$$

or $$r=\frac{2R_1R_2}{R_1+R_2}$$

93. Let $T_1 > T_2$ and thermal conductivity be K.

Let us suppose that length of cylinders (perpendicular to plane of paper) is l.

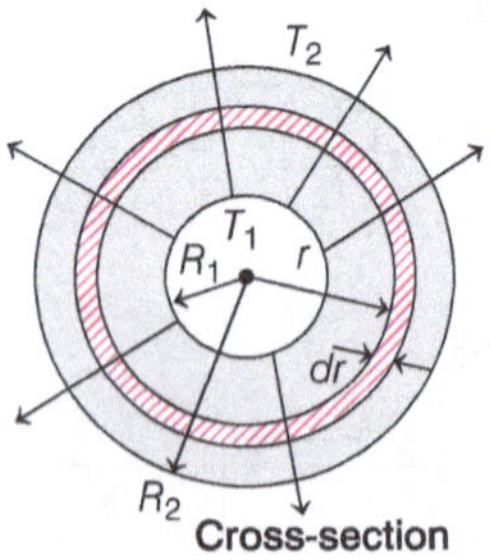

Cross-section

Thermal resistance of the elements shown in figure is,

$$dZ=\frac{dr}{K(2\pi rl)} \qquad \left(\because Z=\frac{l}{KA}\right)$$

From R_1 to R_2 thermal resistance is suppose Z_1 and from R_1 to r, thermal resistance is suppose Z_2. Then,

$$Z_1=\int_{R_1}^{R_2} dZ=\frac{1}{2\pi Kl}\int_{R_1}^{R_2}\frac{dr}{r}$$

$$=\frac{1}{2\pi Kl}\ln\left(\frac{R_2}{R_1}\right)$$

Similarly, $$Z_2=\frac{1}{2\pi Kl}\ln\left(\frac{r}{R_1}\right)$$

Now heat current from R_1 to r will be equal to heat current from R_1 to R_2.

$$\text{Heat current}=\frac{\text{Temperature difference}}{\text{Thermal resistance}}$$

$$\therefore \quad \frac{T_1-T}{Z_2}=\frac{T_1-T_2}{Z_1}$$

Substituting the values of Z_1 and Z_2, we get

$$T=T_1+\frac{T_2-T_1}{\ln(R_2/R_1)}\ln\left(\frac{r}{R_1}\right)$$

94. Let l = length of wire perpendicular to the plane.

$$\frac{dQ}{dt}=\text{Heat current from } r=0 \text{ to } r=r \text{ or } H$$

$$=(\text{Power per unit volume})\ (\text{Volume of wire})$$

$$=P(\pi r^2 l) \qquad \text{...(i)}$$

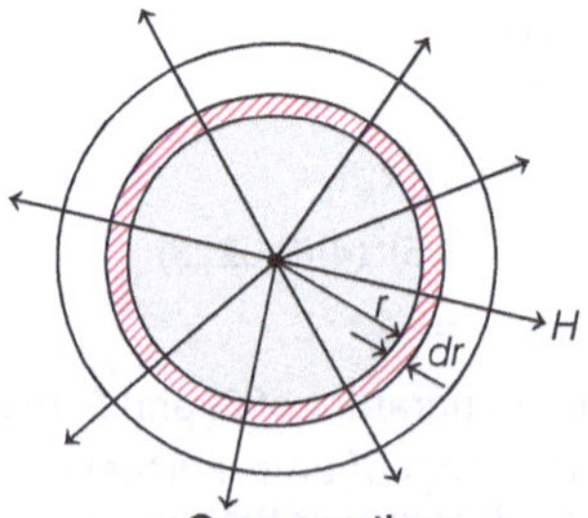

Cross-section

H through the element shown in figure,

$$H=\frac{\text{Temperature difference}}{\text{Thermal resistance}}$$

$$H=\frac{-dT}{(dr)/K(2\pi rl)} \qquad \text{...(ii)}$$

Here negative sign is used because temperature decreases with r and

$$\text{Thermal resistance}=\frac{l}{KA}$$

K = thermal conductivity and A is area perpendicular to the direction of H.

Equating Eqs. (i) and (ii), we get

$$P(\pi r^2 l)=-(2\pi rlK)\frac{dT}{dr}$$

$$\Rightarrow \quad \int_{T_0}^{T} dT=-\frac{P}{2K}\int_{R}^{r} r\,dr$$

Solving this integration, we get

$$T=T_0+\frac{P}{4K}(R^2-r^2)$$

95. Proceeding in the similar manner, Eq. (i) of Q-95, will become,

$$H=P\left(\frac{4}{3}\pi r^3\right) \qquad \text{...(i)}$$

and Eq. (ii) will becomes

$$H=\frac{-dT}{(dr)/K(4\pi r^2)}=-\frac{4\pi Kr^2 dT}{dr} \qquad \text{...(ii)}$$

Equating the two equations, we get

$$\int_{T_0}^{T} dT=-\frac{P}{3K}\int_{R}^{r} r\,dr$$

Solving, we get

$$T=T_0+\frac{P}{6K}(R^2-r^2)$$

96. (a) Temperature of Sun is suppose T. Then,

$$\lambda_m T=\text{Wien's constant}=b$$

$$\therefore \quad T=\frac{b}{\lambda_m}=\frac{2.89\times 10^{-3}}{0.48\times 10^{-6}}$$

$$=6021\text{ K}$$

Energy radiated per second (or power radiated),

$$P = (\sigma T^4)(A)$$

Here A = surface area $= 4\pi R^2$

where R = radius of Sun

$$\therefore \quad P = 4\pi\sigma T^4 R^2$$

Using $E = mc^2$,

we can find, mass lost per second,

$$(dm/dt) = \frac{(dE/dt)}{c^2} = \frac{P}{c^2} = \frac{4\pi\sigma T^4 R^2}{c^2}$$

Substituting the values, we get

$$\frac{dm}{dt} = 5 \times 10^9 \text{ kg s}^{-1}$$

(b) $t = \dfrac{\text{1\% of mass of Sun}}{\text{Mass lost per second}}$

Substituting the values, we get

$$t \approx 10^{11} \text{ yr}$$

97. Let us assume that heat capacity of vessel is large and its temperature remains constant at zero kelvin.

Heat lost per second by the copper ball (or dQ/dt),

$$\frac{dQ}{dt} = (\sigma T^4)(4\pi R^2) \quad \text{...(i)}$$

From this loss of heat, temperature of ball will decrease. So we can use,

heat lost per second, $\dfrac{dQ}{dt} = ms\left(-\dfrac{dT}{dt}\right)$ ...(ii)

Here m = mass of copper ball

$$= \left(\frac{4}{3}\pi R^3\right)\rho \quad (\rho = \text{density of copper})$$

and $\quad s$ = specific heat capacity

From Eqs. (i) and (ii), we get

$$\left(\frac{4}{3}\pi R^3 \rho s\right)\left(-\frac{dT}{dt}\right) = (\sigma T^4)(4\pi R^2)$$

$$\therefore \quad dt = -\frac{\rho s R}{3} \cdot \frac{dT}{T^4} \quad \left(R = \frac{d}{2}\right)$$

or

$$\int_0^t dt = -\frac{\rho s d}{6}\int_{T_i}^{T_i/2} \frac{dT}{T^4} \quad (T_i = 300 \text{ K})$$

Completing this integration with proper values, we get

$$t \approx 3 \text{ h}$$

98. Rate of heat conduction through rod = rate of the heat lost from right end of the rod.

$$\therefore \quad \frac{KA(T_1 - T_2)}{L} = eA\sigma(T_2^4 - T_s^4) \quad \text{...(i)}$$

Given that $T_2 = T_s + \Delta T$

$$\therefore \quad T_2^4 = (T_s + \Delta T)^4 = T_s^4\left(1 + \frac{\Delta T}{T_s}\right)^4$$

Using binomial expansion, we have

$$T_2^4 = T_s^4\left(1 + 4\frac{\Delta T}{T_s}\right) \quad (\text{as } \Delta T << T_s)$$

$$\therefore \quad T_2^4 - T_s^4 = 4(\Delta T)(T_s^3)$$

Substituting in Eq. (i), we have

$$\frac{K(T_1 - T_s - \Delta T)}{L} = 4e\sigma T_s^3 . \Delta T$$

or

$$\frac{K(T_1 - T_s)}{L} = \left(4e\sigma T_s^3 + \frac{K}{L}\right)\Delta T$$

$$\therefore \quad \Delta T = \frac{K(T_1 - T_s)}{(4e\sigma L T_s^3 + K)}$$

Comparing with the given relation, proportionality constant $= \dfrac{K}{4e\sigma L T_s^3 + K}$

99. (a) Rate of heat loss per unit area due to radiation

$$I = e\sigma(T^4 - T_0^4)$$

Here, $\quad T = 127 + 273 = 400 \text{ K}$

and $\quad T_0 = 27 + 273 = 300 \text{ K}$

$$\therefore \quad I = 0.6 \times \frac{17}{3} \times 10^{-8}[(400)^4 - (300)^4]$$

$$= 595 \text{ W/m}^2$$

(b) Let θ be the temperature of the oil.

Then, rate of heat flow through conduction = rate of heat loss due to radiation

$$\therefore \quad \frac{\text{Temperature difference}}{\text{Thermal resistance}} = (595)A$$

$$\frac{(\theta - 127)}{(l/KA)} = (595)A$$

Here, A = area of disc ; K = thermal conductivity

and $\quad l$ = thickness (or length) of disc

$$\therefore \quad (\theta - 127)\frac{K}{l} = 595$$

$$\therefore \quad \theta = 595\left(\frac{l}{K}\right) + 127$$

$$= \frac{595 \times 10^{-2}}{0.167} + 127$$

$$= 162.6\,°\text{C}$$

100. In the first part of the question ($t \le t_1$)

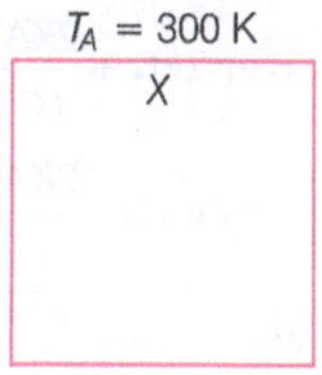

At $t = 0, T_X = T_0 = 400$ K

and at $t = t_1, T_X = T_1 = 350$K

Temperature of atmosphere,

$$T_A = 300\,\text{K} \qquad \text{(constant)}$$

This cools down according to Newton's law of cooling. Therefore, rate of cooling $\propto$ temperature difference.

$$\therefore \quad \left(-\frac{dT}{dt}\right) = k(T - T_A)$$

$$\Rightarrow \quad \frac{dT}{T - T_A} = -k\,dt$$

$$\Rightarrow \quad \int_{T_0}^{T_1} \frac{dT}{T - T_A} = -k\int_0^{t_1} dt$$

$$\Rightarrow \quad \ln\left(\frac{T_1 - T_A}{T_0 - T_A}\right) = -kt_1$$

$$\Rightarrow \quad kt_1 = -\ln\left(\frac{350 - 300}{400 - 300}\right)$$

$$\Rightarrow \quad kt_1 = \ln(2) \qquad \text{...(i)}$$

In the second part ($t > t_1$), body X cools by radiation (according to Newton's law) as well as by conduction.

In conduction,

$$\frac{dQ}{dt} = \frac{KA(T - T_A)}{L} = C\left(-\frac{dT}{dt}\right)$$

$$\therefore \quad \left(-\frac{dT}{dt}\right) = \frac{KA}{LC}(T - T_A)$$

where, C = heat capacity of body X

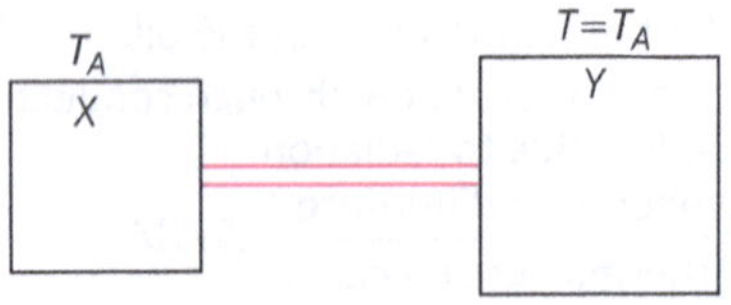

Therefore, net rate of cooling

= (cooling by radiation) + (cooling by conduction)

$$\therefore \quad \left(-\frac{dT}{dt}\right) = k(T - T_A) + \frac{KA}{CL}(T - T_A) \qquad \text{...(ii)}$$

$$\left(-\frac{dT}{dt}\right) = \left(k + \frac{KA}{CL}\right)(T - T_A) \qquad \text{... (iii)}$$

Let at $t = 3t_1$, temperature of X becomes T_2

Then from Eq. (iii)

$$\int_{T_1}^{T_2} \frac{dT}{T - T_A} = -\left(k + \frac{KA}{LC}\right)\int_{t_1}^{3t_1} dt$$

$$\ln\left(\frac{T_2 - T_A}{T_1 - T_A}\right) = -\left(k + \frac{KA}{LC}\right)(2t_1)$$

$$= -\left(2kt_1 + \frac{2KA}{LC}t_1\right)$$

$$\text{or} \quad \ln\left(\frac{T_2 - 300}{350 - 300}\right) = -2\ln(2) - \frac{2KAt_1}{LC};$$

$kt_1 = \ln(2)$ from Eq. (i).

This equation gives

$$T_2 = \left(300 + 12.5\,e^{\frac{-2KAt_1}{CL}}\right)\text{kelvin}$$

101. In steady state, thermal current

$$C_1 = \frac{dQ}{dt} = -K\,4\pi r^2\frac{dT}{dr}$$

$$\Rightarrow \quad \frac{dT}{dr} = \frac{-C_1}{4\pi K}\cdot\frac{1}{r^2}$$

$$\Rightarrow \quad dT = \frac{-C_1}{4\pi K}\cdot\frac{1}{r^2}\cdot dr$$

Integrating, we have

$$T = \frac{C_1}{4\pi Kr} + C_2$$

At $r = r_0$, $T = 2T_0$

and at $r = 2r_0$, $\quad T = T_0$

$$\Rightarrow \quad C_2 = 0$$

$$\text{and} \quad C_1 = 8\pi r_0 KT_0$$

$$\text{So,} \quad T = \frac{2r_0T_0}{r}$$

$$\therefore \quad T\left(r = \frac{3r_0}{2}\right) = \frac{4T_0}{3}$$

$$\therefore \quad p = 4$$

102. Using the given figure in the question, at $t = 6$ min, $T = 40$

$$\therefore \quad 40 = 60\,e^{-\lambda t}$$

$$\Rightarrow \quad \frac{40}{60} = e^{-\lambda\cdot 6}$$

$$\Rightarrow \quad \frac{2}{3} = e^{-3\lambda}$$

$$\Rightarrow \quad \ln\frac{3}{2} = 3\lambda \qquad \text{... (i)}$$

Similarly, at time $t_2, T = 20\,°\text{C}$

$$\therefore \quad 20 = 60e^{-\lambda t_2}$$

$$\frac{1}{3} = e^{-\lambda t_2}$$

$$\Rightarrow \quad \ln\frac{1}{3} = -\lambda t_2$$

$$\Rightarrow \quad t_2 = \frac{\ln 3}{\lambda} \qquad \text{... (ii)}$$

From Eqs. (i) and (ii), we get

$$t_2 = \frac{\ln 3}{\frac{1}{3}\ln 3/2}$$

$$= 3\left(\frac{\ln 3}{\ln 1.5}\right) \simeq 16.25\text{ min}$$

$$\simeq 16\text{ min}$$

103. Given, $T_s = 0\,\text{K}$

$$T_i = 200\,\text{K},\ e = 1$$

$$-ms\frac{dT}{dt} = \frac{dQ}{dt} = \sigma eAT^4$$

$$\Rightarrow \quad -\frac{dT}{dt} = \frac{\sigma A T^4}{ms}$$

$$\frac{\sigma A}{ms}\int_{t_i}^{t_f} dt = -\int_{T_i}^{T_f} \frac{dT}{T^4}$$

$$\frac{\sigma A}{ms}(t_f - t_i) = \frac{1}{3}\left(\frac{1}{T_f^3} - \frac{1}{T_i^3}\right)$$

$$\frac{\frac{\sigma A}{ms}(t_1 - 0) = \frac{1}{3}\left(\frac{1}{(100)^3} - \frac{1}{(200)^3}\right)}{\frac{\sigma A}{ms}(t_2 - 0) = \frac{1}{3}\left(\frac{1}{(50)^3} - \frac{1}{(200)^3}\right)}$$

$$\frac{t_1}{t_2} = \frac{\frac{(200)^3 - (100)^3}{(100)^3(200)^3}}{\frac{(200)^3 - (50)^3}{(50)^3(200)^3}}$$

$$\Rightarrow \quad \frac{t_2}{t_1} = \frac{9}{1}$$

104. $\frac{dQ}{dt} = e\sigma A(T^4 - T_0^4)$

For small temperature change,

$$\frac{dQ}{dt} = e\sigma A T^3 \Delta T \quad \ldots \text{(i)}$$

$$\frac{mcdT}{dt} = e\sigma A T^3 \Delta T$$

$$\frac{dT}{dt} = \frac{e\sigma A T^3}{mc}\Delta T$$

$\frac{e\sigma A T^3}{mc} \rightarrow$ constant for Newton's law of cooling

$$\frac{e\sigma A T^3}{mc} = 0.001$$

$$e\sigma A T^3 = mc \times 0.001$$

$$= 1 \times 4200 \times 0.001$$

$$e\sigma A T^3 = 4.2 \quad \ldots \text{(ii)}$$

$$\frac{dQ}{dt} = 700 \times 0.05 = 35 \text{ W} \quad \ldots \text{(iii)}$$

Putting the value of Eqs. (ii) and (iii) in Eq. (i), we get

$$35 = 4.2\,\Delta T$$

$$\Rightarrow \quad \frac{35}{4.2} = \Delta T$$

$$\Rightarrow \quad \Delta T = 8.33$$

105. $\log_2 \frac{P_1}{P_0} = 1$

Therefore, $\frac{P_1}{P_0} = 2$

According to Stefan's law,

$$P \propto T^4$$

$$\Rightarrow \quad \frac{P_2}{P_1} = \left(\frac{T_2}{T_1}\right)^4 = \left(\frac{2767 + 273}{487 + 273}\right)^4 = 4^4$$

$$\Rightarrow \quad \frac{P_2}{P_1} = \frac{P_2}{2P_0} = 4^4$$

$$\log_2 \frac{P_2}{P_0} = \log_2[2 \times 4^4]$$

$$= \log_2 2 + \log_2 4^4$$

$$= 1 + \log_2 2^8 = 9$$